Donated by
The Public Interest Institute
to The Heartland Institute
2016

Handbook of Campaign Spending

Handbook of Campaign Spending

Money in the 1992 Congressional Races

Dwight Morris

and

Murielle E. Gamache

Congressional Quarterly
Washington, D.C.

**For challenging us intellectually, for encouraging us to look beneath
what might at first appear obvious, for picking us up the thousands of times we fell,
we lovingly dedicate this book to Herbert Morris and Pauline Alice Masse Gamache.**

Copyright © 1994 Congressional Quarterly Inc.
1414 22nd Street, N.W., Washington, D.C. 20037

All rights reserved. No part of this book may be reproduced or
transmitted in any form or by any means, electronic or mechanical,
including photocopying, recording, or any information storage and
retrieval system, without permission in writing from the publisher.

Printed in the United States of America

Book design: Kaelin Chappell
Cover design: Ben Santora

Library of Congress Cataloging-in-Publication Data

Morris, Dwight, 1952-
    Handbook of campaign spending : money in the 1992
congressional races / Dwight Morris and Murielle E. Gamache.
      p.   cm.
    Includes index.
    ISBN 0-87187-997-2
    1. Campaign funds–United States–Handbooks, manuals, etc.
2. United States. Congress–Elections, 1992–Handbooks, manuals,
etc. I. Gamache, Murielle E., 1964- . II. Title.
JK1991.M78   1994
324.7'8'097309049–dc20   93-50217
                                         CIP

Contents

List of Tables vii
Preface ix
Acknowledgments xi
A Guide to the Tables xiii

PART I SPENDING MONEY: MYTH AND REALITY 1

1. 1992: The Year of Change? 3
2. What Campaign Money *Still* Buys: The Gold-Plated, Permanent Campaign Revisited 17
3. House Freshmen: Settling In 39
4. The Angry Electorate? Incumbents Fight to Survive 49
5. The "Year of the Woman": Sweeping Phenomenon or Political Cliché? 61
6. Independent and Coordinated Expenditures: A World of Unlimited Possibilities 73
7. Political Consultants: The Real Winners 83
8. Reform: The Broken Promise 97

PART II THE 1992 SENATE RACES 103

Alabama 105
Alaska 106
Arizona 107
Arkansas 108
California 109, 110
Colorado 111
Connecticut 112
Florida 113
Georgia 114
Hawaii 115
Idaho 116
Illinois 117
Indiana 118
Iowa 119
Kansas 120
Kentucky 121
Louisiana 122
Maryland 123
Missouri 124
Nevada 125
New Hampshire 126
New York 127
North Carolina 128
North Dakota 129, 130
Ohio 131
Oklahoma 132
Oregon 133
Pennsylvania 134, 135
South Carolina 136
South Dakota 137
Utah 138
Vermont 139
Washington 140
Wisconsin 141

PART III THE 1992 HOUSE RACES 143

Alabama 145
Alaska 152
Arizona 153
Arkansas 159
California 163
Colorado 215
Connecticut 221
Delaware 227
Florida 228
Georgia 251
Hawaii 262
Idaho 264
Illinois 266
Indiana 286
Iowa 296
Kansas 301
Kentucky 305
Louisiana 311
Maine 318
Maryland 320
Massachusetts 328
Michigan 338
Minnesota 354
Mississippi 362
Missouri 367
Montana 376
Nebraska 377
Nevada 380
New Hampshire 382
New Jersey 384
New Mexico 397
New York 400
North Carolina 431
North Dakota 443
Ohio 444
Oklahoma 463
Oregon 469
Pennsylvania 474
Rhode Island 495
South Carolina 497
South Dakota 503
Tennessee 504
Texas 513
Utah 543
Vermont 546
Virginia 547
Washington 558
West Virginia 567
Wisconsin 570
Wyoming 579

Index 581

List of Tables

1-1 What Campaign Money Buys in the 1992 Senate Races: Total Expenditures 6
1-2 What Campaign Money Buys in the 1992 Senate Races: Average Expenditures 7
1-3 What Campaign Money Buys in the 1992 Senate Races: Expenditures, by Percentage 8
1-4 What Campaign Money Buys in the 1992 House Races: Total Expenditures 10
1-5 What Campaign Money Buys in the 1992 House Races: Average Expenditures 11
1-6 What Campaign Money Buys in the 1992 House Races: Expenditures, by Percentage 12
1-7 Individuals in Violation of Federal Election Campaign Contribution Laws: 1992 Election Cycle 15

2-1 The Top Twenty-Five Spenders in the 1992 Congressional Races: Off-Year Spending 19
2-2 The Top Twenty-Five Spenders in the 1992 Congressional Races: Campaign Office Basics 19
2-3 The Top Twenty-Five Spenders in the 1992 Congressional Races: Salaries 22
2-4 The Top Fifteen Spenders in the 1992 House Races: Payrolls Without Taxes 23
2-5 The Top Fifteen Spenders in the 1992 Congressional Races: Congressional Staff Payroll 24
2-6 The Top Twenty-Five Spenders in the 1992 House Races: Legal Services 25
2-7 The Top Twenty-Five Spenders in the 1992 Congressional Races: Travel 26
2-8 The Top Fifteen Spenders in the 1992 Congressional Races: Campaign Cars 28
2-9 The Top Twenty-Five Spenders in the 1992 Congressional Races: Fund Raising 30
2-10 The Top Twenty-Five Spenders in the 1992 Congressional Races: Constituent Entertainment and Gifts 30
2-11 The Top Fifteen Spenders in the 1992 Congressional Races: Holiday Cards 32
2-12 The Top Fifteen Spenders in the 1992 Congressional Races: Restaurants/Meetings 34
2-13 The Top Twenty-Five Spenders in the 1992 Congressional Races: Donations 35
2-14 The Top Twenty-Five Spenders in the 1992 Congressional Races: Donations to Party Organizations 35
2-15 Donations by California Democrats to IMPAC 2000 37

3-1 What Campaign Money Buys in the 1992 House Races: Average Expenditures by 1990 Freshmen Versus More Entrenched Incumbents 41
3-2 What Campaign Money Buys in the 1992 House Races: Expenditures by 1990 Freshmen Versus More Entrenched Incumbents, by Percentage 42
3-3 What Campaign Money Buys in the 1992 House Races: Off-year Expenditures by 1990 Freshmen 43
3-4 What Campaign Money Buys in the 1992 and 1990 House Races: Expenditures by 1990 Freshmen 45
3-5 What Campaign Money Buys in the 1992 House Races: Total Expenditures by 1990 Freshmen 46

4-1 What Campaign Money Buys in the 1992 House Races: Average Expenditures by Nonincumbents 54
4-2 Background of Nonincumbent Candidates in the 1992 House Races 56
4-3 Background of Nonincumbent Winners in the 1992 House Races 56
4-4 Background of Nonincumbent Losers in the 1992 House Races 56
4-5 Average Receipts of Nonincumbents in 1992 House Races 57

4-6 What Campaign Money Buys in the 1992 House Races: Average Expenditures by Politicians, Operatives, and Novices 58

4-7 What Campaign Money Buys in the 1992 Senate Races: Expenditures by Nonincumbents 60

5-1 Background of Nonincumbent Female Candidates in the 1992 House Races 64

5-2 Background of Nonincumbent Female Winners in the 1992 House Races 64

5-3 Background of Nonincumbent Female Losers in the 1992 House Races 64

5-4 What Campaign Money Buys in the 1992 House Races: Average Expenditures by Open Seat Candidates 66

5-5 What Campaign Money Buys in the 1992 House Races: Average Expenditures by Challengers 67

5-6 What Campaign Money Buys in the 1992 Senate Races: Average Expenditures by Nonincumbents 68

5-7 What Campaign Money Buys in the 1992 House Races: Average Expenditures by Incumbents 71

5-8 What Campaign Money Buys in the 1992 House Races: Expenditures by Incumbents, by Percentage 72

6-1 What Campaign Money Buys in the 1992 Senate Races: Coordinated Expenditures by National Parties 77

6-2 What Campaign Money Buys in the 1992 Senate Races: Coordinated Expenditures of National Parties, by Percentage 77

6-3 What Campaign Money Buys in the 1992 House Races: Coordinated Expenditures by National Parties 78

6-4 What Campaign Money Buys in the 1992 House Races: Coordinated Expenditures of National Parties, by Percentage 78

6-5 The Top Fifteen Independent Expenditures in 1992 Congressional Elections, by Organization 79

6-6 The Top Ten Independent Campaigns Waged by the National Rifle Association 80

6-7 The Top Five Independent Campaigns Waged by Various Organizations 81

7-1 The Top Fifty Media Consultants in the 1992 Congressional Races 85

7-2 The Top Twenty-Five Direct-Mail Consultants in the 1992 Congressional Races 87

7-3 The Top Twenty-Five Event Consultants in the 1992 Congressional Races 87

7-4 The Top Twenty-Five Persuasion Mail Consultants in the 1992 Congressional Races 89

7-5 The Top Twenty-Five Pollsters in the 1992 Congressional Races 89

7-6 The Top Fifteen Campaign Management Consultants in the 1992 Congressional Races 91

7-7 The Top Fifteen General Strategy Consultants in the 1992 Congressional Races 91

7-8 The Top Fifteen Campaign Get-Out-the-Vote Consultants in the 1992 Congressional Races 91

7-9 The Top Fifty House Candidates' Spending on Consultants 93

7-10 The Top Fifty Senate Candidates' Spending on Consultants 95

8-1 The Top Fifteen Spenders in the 1992 Congressional Races: Unitemized Expenses 102

Preface

For years, journalists have struggled to explain the exploding cost of political campaigns but have been stymied by a lack of real information. Each year, thousands of pages of campaign expenditure data are filed with the Federal Election Commission (FEC), which microfiches the documents and places paper copies in filing cabinets for the curious public to peruse. However, unlike the information it routinely collects on political contributions, the FEC has never computerized the expenditure data, making any comprehensive analysis extremely difficult.

Lacking information and needing an explanation for the high cost of modern campaigns, journalists turned to the "experts," and a mythology was born. According to conventional wisdom, politicians used their campaign treasuries to pay for yard signs, buttons, bumper stickers, and various get-out-the-vote efforts. Most importantly, candidates were thought to be locked in a constant chase for campaign contributions in order to pay for increasingly expensive advertising, primarily on television. Until 1990, few bothered to question whether or not advertising was truly the villain of the campaign finance drama.

In the spring of 1990, the *Los Angeles Times* decided to test the campaign spending myths empirically, and the Washington bureau's special investigations unit was given the task of building a database that ultimately contained 437,753 separate expenditures reported to the FEC by congressional candidates who contested the November general elections. Analysis of that database punched gaping holes in the spending mythology, revealing that House candidates invested an average of only 22 percent of their campaign treasuries in advertising. The comparable figure for Senate candidates was a surprisingly low 33 percent.

What the investigations unit discovered gave rise to a series of articles by reporter Sara Fritz and Dwight Morris, editor for special investigations, that detailed questionable and improper expenditures by a host of congressional candidates. The 1990 database also served as the basis for the first edition of the *Handbook of Campaign Spending,* coauthored by Fritz and Morris.

Candidates in 1992 had to contend with redistricting, a supposed surge of anti-incumbent sentiment sweeping through the electorate, and the seemingly endless debate over campaign finance reform. Many observers believed there was a distinct possibility that campaigns would dramatically alter their spending habits, rendering moot many of the issues raised in the first edition of the *Handbook*. We decided to test that hypothesis.

Although the *Times* decided to limit its inquiry to California candidates in 1992, we felt the nationwide project was too important to drop. Moving the project into our basements and onto our home computers, we spent nearly two years coding and verifying the 1992 data.

We discovered that little had changed. While members of Congress continued to debate the subject of campaign finance reform, the questionable and improper spending practices uncovered in 1990 continued unabated in 1992. While spending on broadcast advertising increased significantly, so did spending on everything else. The result was only a modest shift in the allocation of funds. The forces that drove campaign spending in 1990 had been largely unaffected by either the electorate's mood or redistricting.

This second look at campaign spending is based on an analysis of 524,024 expenditures reported to the FEC by 933 candidates who sought congressional office in 1992. To ensure that our analysis was as complete and as accurate as possible, we contacted every campaign that spent at least $25,000 to clarify all ambiguous expenditures. In all but a few cases, candidates and their advisers were willing to cooperate.

Our analysis of House campaigns includes all expenditures during the two-year election cycle beginning January 1, 1991, and ending December 31, 1992. For Senate races, this book examines all campaign outlays during the six-year cycle beginning January 1, 1987, and ending December 31, 1992. No attempt was made to analyze the campaign expenditures of senators who were not up for reelection in 1992. In those instances where special elections were held during the cycle to fill House vacancies, the book includes data from the special election as well as the subsequent primary and general elections. In the case of Sen. Harris Wofford (D-Pa.), who was elected in 1991 to fill the vacancy created by the death of Sen. John Heinz, we have included only his special election spending. Wofford will be up for reelection in 1994.

It is important to note that very few of the spending practices outlined in this book are illegal. Rather, they are part of a continuously developing campaign system that has few strict rules. That, we believe, is the main problem.

Dwight Morris
Murielle E. Gamache
July 1994

Acknowledgments

This book could not have been written had it not been for the support of a small army of friends and colleagues who volunteered thousands of hours of their time. While most people were out having fun after work and on weekends, James Peterson, Charlotte Huff, and Michael Cheek gave generously of themselves to help us code and check data. Gary Feld spent nights and weekends chained to his computer, formatting and cranking out the tables that fed our analysis.

When we desperately needed help in entering data into our home computers, Jenifer Morris was there to make certain the work was done. Although unable to lend physical support, Monique Gamache Venne, Janine Gamache Triller, Daniel Charles Gamache, Jordan Morris, Herbert Morris, Minette Morris, and Gloria Morris provided much needed moral support.

For nearly one year, we committed virtually every free moment to this project, and we would like to thank Helen K. Duval for insisting that Murielle go out on an occasional Saturday night. Elizabeth Franzese, Kathleen Richards, and Melissa Michelsen were Helen's co-conspirators in keeping Murielle sane, and we are grateful to them as well. Thanks to Michael Casey Griffen for giving Murielle his enthusiastic backing and sympathetic ear. Deborah Hofmann and Gregory Henschel provided both moral support and periodic comic relief for Dwight.

We would also like to thank Deborah Hofmann of the *New York Times* for her work with Dwight in assembling campaign spending information during the heat of the 1982 campaign. While that study was more anecdotal than systematic, the ideas Dwight and Deborah generated during that hectic period laid the foundation for the massive spending project we began in 1990.

For their patience and understanding during the past year, we would like to give a special thanks to Jeanne Ferris and Kerry Kern, our editors in the Book Department at Congressional Quarterly. Although we sometimes cringed when the telephone rang, we knew their gentle prodding was matched by a tremendous belief in the value of the project.

We both owe a great deal to former political science professors who encouraged us to argue rather than sit quietly in class. Thanks to Dr. William K. Hall, whose love of politics was infectious and, without knowing it at the time, made Dwight realize that attending law school would be a mistake. Thanks to Dr. J. Barron Boyd for teaching Murielle many of the analytical skills necessary to do this book, even though she protested strenuously at the time.

Our work would have been far more difficult had it not been for Phil Ruiz, who set up our home computer systems and made certain they ran to perfection. Few people would have stayed in Dwight's basement until 9:00 on a Saturday night to troubleshoot a problem that was totally unrelated to his job.

We would also like to thank several of those who made the 1990 edition of this book possible. Thanks to Sara Fritz, who was responsible for developing the concept of this book and who coauthored the first edition. For their assistance in writing that first edition, we would also like to thank Richard S. Dunham, Eric Woodman, and Lisa Hoffman. A special thanks to Stephanie Grace for helping us create the original database.

A Guide to the Tables

The analysis of individual races that follows is based on an examination of all 524,024 separate expenditures reported to the Federal Election Commission (FEC) by 933 candidates who sought congressional office in 1992.

Copies of each campaign's financial reports were obtained from the FEC and entered into a database under 1 of 143 categories. To ensure that the categorization was accurate, we contacted officials of each campaign that spent $25,000 or more and asked for clarification of all vaguely reported expenditures. We also inquired about the work performed by every consultant employed by the campaign.

While most campaigns were cooperative, some were not. In cases where neither the candidate nor the campaign employees provided sufficient information, we contacted the consultants directly. In all, we conducted more than 800 interviews with candidates, campaign staff, and consultants.

In calculating expenditure totals, transfers between authorized committees, payments of debts from prior election cycles, contribution refunds, and loan repayments have been excluded in order to avoid double counting expenditures. All debts to vendors reported at the end of the 1992 cycle have been included.

The expenditures were subsequently assigned to one of eight major spending categories. Five categories were broken further into specific areas of spending. The following is a description of the categories and the types of items included in each.

OVERHEAD

Office furniture/supplies: Furniture and basic office supplies, telephone answering services, messenger and overnight delivery services, monthly cable television payments, newspaper and magazine subscriptions, clipping services, payments for file storage, small postage and photocopying charges, office moving expenses, and improvements or upkeep of the office (including office cleaning, garbage pickup, repairs, plumbers, and locksmiths).

Rent/utilities: Rent and utility payments for campaign offices. Purchases and leases of vehicles used as mobile offices, as well as their maintenance costs, are also included.

Salaries: Salary payments and employee benefits, including health insurance. In addition to payments specifically described as salary, this category includes regular payments to those people who performed routine office tasks, which were frequently misrepresented in campaign finance reports as "consulting." Whenever a housing allowance was part of a campaign employee's compensation package, it was considered to be salary.

Taxes: All federal and state taxes paid by the campaign, including payroll taxes and income taxes paid on the campaign's investments.

Bank/investment fees: Interest payments on outstanding loans, annual credit card fees, check charges, investment fees, and investment losses.

Lawyers/accountants: Fees paid for their services as well as any other expenses incurred by the campaign's lawyers and accountants. Five Senate and thirty-one House campaigns paid fines related to violations of federal or state election laws, and those fines have been included as part of legal fees.

Telephone: Purchases of telephone equipment (including cellular telephones and beepers), monthly payments for local and long-distance service, installation fees, repairs, and reimbursements to staff for telephone expenses.

Campaign automobile: All payments for the purchase or lease of a campaign vehicle (except mobile offices), maintenance, insurance, registration, licensing, and gasoline.

Computers/office equipment: All payments related to the purchase, lease, and repair of office equipment, such as computer equipment and software, typewriters, photocopiers, FAX machines, telephone answering machines, televisions, radios, and VCRs.

Travel: All general travel expenses, such as air fare and hotels, rental cars, taxies, daily parking, and entries such as "food for travel." Expenses for the national party conventions, including the costs of receptions and other entertainment, are also included.

Food/meetings: Meeting expenses (for example, steering committees, finance committees, state delegations) and other food costs not specifically related to fund raising, constituent entertainment, or travel.

FUND RAISING

Events: All costs related to fund-raising events, including invitations, postage, planning meetings, travel costs, room rental, food and catering costs, liquor, flowers, bartenders, follow-up thank-you cards, in-kind fund-raising expenses, general reimbursements to individuals for fund raising, tickets to sporting or theater events that served a fund-raising purpose, and fees paid to consultants who planned the events.

Direct mail: All costs related to fund-raising solicitations via the mail, including the purchase of mailing lists, computer charges, postage, printing, caging services, and consultant fees and expenses. Mailings that served a dual purpose, both to raise funds and inform voters, were included in this category.

Telemarketing: All expenses related to a telephone operation designed to raise money, including consultant fees, list purchases, and computer costs. Campaigns use the terms *telemarketing* and *phonebanking* loosely. Some items listed as telemarketing in campaign reports to the FEC were found to be inaccurately identified and were assigned to their proper category.

POLLING

All polling costs, including payments to consultants as well as in-kind contributions of polling results to the campaign.

ADVERTISING

Electronic media: All payments to consultants, separate purchases of broadcast time, and production costs associated with the development of radio and television advertising.

Other media: Campaign videos; payments for billboards; advertising in newspapers, journals, magazines, and publications targeted to religious groups, senior citizens, and other special constituencies; as well as program ads purchased from local charitable and booster organizations.

OTHER CAMPAIGN ACTIVITY

Persuasion mail/brochures: All costs associated with strictly promotional mailings and other campaign literature, including artwork, printing of brochures or other literature, postage, the purchase of mailing lists, as well as consultant fees and consultant expenses.

Actual campaigning: Filing fees and costs of petition drives, announcement parties, state party conventions, campaign rallies and parades, campaign training schools, opposition research, posters, signs, buttons, bumper stickers, speech writers and coaches, get-out-the-vote efforts, election day poll watchers, and all campaign promotional material (T-shirts, jackets, hats, embossed pencils, pens, nail files, pot holders, etc.). Fees and expenses billed by campaign management firms and general consultants for services unrelated to advertising, fund raising, and persuasion mail are also included.

Staff/volunteers: All food expenses for staff and volunteers, including phonebank and get-out-the-vote volunteers. These expenses included bottled water, soda machines, monthly coffee service, and food purchases that are specifically for the campaign office. Also included were expenditures for recruitment of volunteers, gifts for staff and volunteers, and staff retreats.

CONSTITUENT GIFTS/ENTERTAINMENT

Meals purchased for constituents, the costs of events that were designed purely for constituent entertainment (for example, a local dominos tournament), constituent gifts of all kinds, flowers, holiday greeting cards, awards and plaques, inaugural parties, and costs associated with the annual congressional art contest.

DONATIONS

To candidates (both in-state and out-of-state): Direct contributions to other candidates as well as the purchase price of fund-raiser tickets.

To civic organizations: Contributions to charitable organizations, such as the American Cancer Society, as well as local booster groups, such as the Chamber of Commerce and local high school athletic associations. Includes the cost of tickets to events sponsored by such groups.

To ideological groups: Contributions to ideological organizations, such as the NAACP, the National Organization for Women, and the Sierra Club.

To political parties: Contributions to national, state, and local party organizations, including tickets to party-sponsored fund-raising events.

UNITEMIZED EXPENSES

Candidates are not required to report expenditures of less than $200, and many do not list them on their FEC reports. This category also includes expenditures described in FEC reports merely as "petty cash," unitemized credit card purchases, and all reimbursements that were vaguely worded, such as "reimbursement," "political expenses," or "campaign expenses."

Part I

Spending Money
Myth and Reality

CHAPTER 1

1992
The Year of Change?

I am absolutely overjoyed that at least we now have something that illustrates the corruption of the entire system that people can understand and relate to. It is illustrative of what is wrong with the operation of the House of Representatives and its inability to address the real problems of real people.

Rep. Guy Vander Jagt, chairman of the National Republican Congressional Committee, commenting on the House bank scandal on Nightline, *March 12, 1992*

There is a ferocious tide against incumbents running across the country, and I could not swim strongly enough to offset it.

Vander Jagt, following his August 4, 1992 primary loss

Change. In some respects no word better symbolized the 1992 campaigns, as Rep. Guy Vander Jagt (R-Mich.) would undoubtedly attest. Democratic presidential nominee Bill Clinton vowed to reinvent government. Independent presidential aspirant H. Ross Perot promised to get "under the hood" of a gridlocked federal bureaucracy. An August 24 cover story in *U.S. News & World Report* proposed to tell readers "Why George Bush Can't Change."

Incumbency, it seemed, had become a dirty word. In September 1991 the House of Representatives was rocked by revelations that members had routinely written checks against their accounts at the House bank without having sufficient funds to cover them. On October 1, 1991 freshman Rep. Jim Nussle (R-Iowa) took the House floor to decry the leadership's decision not to make public the names of those who had overdrawn their accounts. Wearing a brown paper bag over his head, Nussle theatrically declared that it was "time to take the mask off this institution. It is time to expose the check-writing scandal that I like to call Rubbergate. It is time to bring some honor back to this institution." When, after six months of political wrangling, the names were finally made public, voters learned that Rep. Ronald V. Dellums (D-Calif.) had overdrawn his account 851 times over a thirty-nine-month period and ranked fifth on the overdraft list. At the other end of the spectrum, Rep. Jolene Unsoeld (D-Wash.) had overdrawn her account only once, and then by just thirty-eight cents.

Although no public funds were involved, the media jumped on the story, turning the overdrafts into "bounced checks." That nomenclature was quickly adopted by Vander Jagt and other Republicans who saw an opportunity to gain political advantage from their colleagues' misadventures. "There will be many, many members who will be taken out, lose their reelection because of their record of bounced checks," Vander Jagt told reporters. "I am absolutely overjoyed," he quickly added. Ultimately, challengers on both sides of the political aisle made these checks one of the central issues of the campaign, although the number of times a member had overdrawn his or her account frequently proved to be a poor predictor of the issue's impact.

The House bank scandal was one of several, both large and small. Federal prosecutors launched an investigation into allegations that Democratic Reps. Dan Rostenkowski (Ill.) and Joe Kolter (Pa.) had embezzled thousands of dollars through the House post office. A parallel investigation led to the conviction of six former employees of the House post office on drug and embezzlement charges. In addition, it was revealed that seven House members had abused their post office privileges by setting up special post office boxes to receive campaign donations.

In October 1991 it was revealed that many incumbents had failed to pay bills totaling more than $370,000 at the House restaurant, a report that proved grossly inaccurate. In October 1990 a *PrimeTime Live* hidden camera had caught members of Congress playing golf and frolicking on a beach in Barbados, all paid for by corporate lobbyists. House members were pilloried for the fact that they paid only $100 each year for the use of the House gymnasium. There were revelations that members of both chambers could have pictures framed for free, obtain free prescription drugs through the Office of Attending Physician, have their hair cut for under $5, park free at National and Dulles airports in suburban Washington, D.C., and have parking tickets fixed.

Scandals and "perkomania," as one challenger dubbed it, were not the only black marks on Congress's image. In 1991 Anita F. Hill, a professor of law at the University of Oklahoma, had come forth with allegations that she had been sexually harassed by Supreme Court nominee Clarence Thomas, her former supervisor at the Equal Employment Opportunity Commission. The Senate Judiciary Committee's nationally televised hearings into those allegations served for many as evidence that the institution was insensitive to women's concerns and produced several high-profile challengers to House and Senate campaigns.

Few women centered their campaigns entirely around Hill's treatment, but virtually all of the ninety-four women who challenged incumbents or contested open House or Senate seats in the general election ran "outsider" campaigns. State senator Patty Murray (D-Wash.) ran for the Senate as "the mom in tennis shoes." Community activist Claire Sargent (D-Ariz.) said it was time to "start electing senators with breasts; we've had boobs long enough." When Rep. Charles E. Bennett (D-Fla.) opted to retire, leaving Jacksonville City Council member Tillie Fowler (R-Fla.) without an incumbent to attack, she simply leveled her charges at the entire House. One of Fowler's ads scrolled across the screen the names of all congressional staffers who made more than $100,000.

As the negative news reports continued to mount, so too did voter anger. Frustrated voters forced term limit initiatives onto the ballot in fourteen states, including California, Florida, Michigan, Ohio, and House Speaker Thomas S. Foley's home state of Washington. Buffeted by a rising tide of anti-incumbent sentiment, fifty-two House members and seven senators chose to leave politics rather than seek reelection. Thirteen House members retired in order to make Senate or gubernatorial bids.

Among those voluntarily relinquishing their House seats was Rep. Bill Dickinson (R-Ala.), ranking member of the Armed Services Committee, who noted that Congress just was not "fun any more." Saying that he was "simply not ready to engage in character assassination and mud wrestling to win a campaign," six-term Rep. Bill Lowery (R-Calif.) stepped aside rather than wage a primary battle with fellow Republican Rep. Randy "Duke" Cunningham in California's District 51. Disillusioned with what he called "the money chase," forty-one-year-old Rep. Dennis E. Eckart (D-Ohio) walked away after six terms. Pointing to his growing frustration with "the scandals, the anti-incumbency, the term-limitation movement," Rep. William S. Broomfield (R-Mich.) decided to move on after thirty-six years in the House.

In announcing he would not seek a third term, Sen. Warren B. Rudman (R-N.H.) said he was "terribly frustrated" by Congress's failure to reduce the federal budget deficit and added that he felt Congress was incapable of "doing what has to be done while we still have time to do it." Hampered by negative publicity over his ties to the savings and loan industry and identified with a proposal to create a Senate bank modeled after the infamous House bank, Sen. Tim Wirth (D-Colo.) opted to retire after a single term. Among Wirth's reasons were the "continuous money chase," "the hysterical superficiality in the electronic media's focus on sensational themes," and "the stalemate to which economic mismanagement and partisan pettiness have reduced the work of our government."

Redistricting added to the woes of many House incumbents who opted to fight it out. In Georgia, which gained one seat following the census, the Democratic-dominated redistricting committee obliterated Republican Rep. Newt Gingrich's former district, parceling out his constituents to several other districts. Facing a totally new constituency, Gingrich survived the Republican primary in the redrawn District 6 by just 980 votes. In Illinois, which faced the loss of two House seats, a Republican-dominated plan set up Democratic primary battles between Reps. Glenn Poshard and Terry L. Bruce, William O. Lipinski and Marty Russo, and Dan Rostenkowski and Frank Annunzio. Annunzio opted to retire rather than fight; Bruce and Russo lost bitter contests. In California, which gained seven new seats, Democratic Rep. Anthony C. Beilenson found himself faced with a choice between waging an expensive primary battle with fellow Democratic Rep. Henry A. Waxman or waging an expensive general election campaign in a more heavily Republican district. He chose to avoid intraparty fratricide.

While the power of incumbency had historically discouraged spirited challenges in House campaigns, the surge of anti-incumbent sentiment brought forth scores of challengers in 1992. In 1990, 52 of the 405 House incumbents who sought reelection had won without facing either a primary or general election opponent. Only 8 of the 349 incumbents seeking reelection were so fortunate in 1992. Few challengers passed up the opportunity to portray themselves as agents of change.

More importantly, challengers seeking House seats in 1992 were able to spend $40,123 more on average than their 1990 counterparts to deliver that outsider message, an increase of 30 percent. Challengers involved in hotly contested races—those in which the winner received no more than 60 percent of the vote—spent $64,291 more than their 1990 counterparts, a 29 percent increase.

In some cases, the additional funding was a result of an ability to tap personal wealth. Businessman Michael Huffington poured about $3.5 million into the Republican primary in California's District 22, virtually all of it his own money. The continuous media blitz his money bought carried Huffington to a narrow upset victory over veteran Rep. Robert J. Lagomarsino, who spent $747,536. In the general election campaign, Huffington again dipped into his own bank account, putting together a $1.9 million effort to defeat Santa Barbara County Supervisor Gloria Ochoa, who spent $706,338. Huffington's total expenditures topped $5.4 million, making this the most expensive House campaign in history—more then doubling the previous record.

Although less dramatic, spending by Senate challengers increased from an average of $1,686,616 in 1990 to $1,922,001 in 1992, a modest 14 percent rise. Former San Francisco mayor Dianne Feinstein (D-Calif.) led all challengers, spending $8,041,099 to defeat Republican Sen. John Seymour. At the low end of the spending spectrum, independent candidate Jon Khachaturian (La.) spent only $94,920 on a token challenge to Democratic Sen. John B. Breaux, who spent $1.8 million.

Burdened by a litany of institutional negatives and faced by better funded challengers, many incumbents were forced to work considerably harder in 1992 than they had in 1990. In the 1990 election cycle, 127 of the 405 House members who managed to secure their party's nomination were involved in hotly contested primary or general election campaigns, including 15 incumbents who lost. The only House incumbent to lose a 1990 primary was Rep. Donald E. "Buz" Lukens (R-Ohio), who had been convicted on a misdemeanor charge stemming from his sexual encounter with a sixteen-year-old girl. Two years later,

150 of the 349 incumbents who won their party's nomination were involved in hotly contested races in the primary, the general election, or both, including 24 who were ousted on November 3. Another 19 House members never made it past the primary.

Twenty-eight incumbent senators were given the opportunity by their party to seek another term in 1992; of that total only nine received 61 percent of the vote or more in both their primary and general elections. Thirteen incumbents were held to 55 percent or less, including four who lost in the general election. In contrast, seventeen of the thirty-two senators who sought reelection in 1990 won easily, including three who ran unopposed and one whose only challenger was a supporter of fringe political activist Lyndon H. LaRouche, Jr. No senator who sought renomination failed to get it. Three incumbent senators opted to leave politics and one chose to run for governor. Only one incumbent senator was defeated.

Amidst this chaos, one might have anticipated that incumbents would feel the need to alter their approach to campaigning. One might have expected a significant change from 1990, when more than half the money invested in congressional elections was spent on items that had virtually nothing to do with pure election activity. Looking at the overall numbers, those expectations were only partially met.

Senate incumbents seeking reelection in 1992 spent slightly more on average than their 1990 counterparts. During the 1990 election cycle, senators spent a total of $131,242,807, an average of $4,101,338. Incumbents who contested the 1992 general election reported spending $116,177,549, an average of $4,149,198 (see Tables 1-1 and 1-2). This insignificant 1 percent increase resulted less from anti-incumbent fears than from the fact that three senators ran unopposed in 1990. The 1992 campaign also featured hotly contested races in California, New York, and Pennsylvania, all of which have expensive media markets and none of which had seats up for grabs during the previous election cycle.

Although the bottom line did not move for the average Senate incumbent, a cursory look at spending in various categories might lead one to conclude that priorities had shifted between 1990 and 1992. In fact, any shift in priorities was marginal, at most. Broadcast advertising expenditures, which represented 33 percent of spending by Senate incumbents in the 1990 election cycle, accounted for 40 percent of total outlays in 1992 (see Table 1-3). Again, this was more a reflection of the media markets represented in the two election cycles than a conscious change in behavior. As a percentage of total spending, outlays for overhead increased slightly, from 24 percent in 1990 to 25 percent in 1992. The percentage of total spending devoted to fund raising dropped significantly, from 31 percent in 1990 to 21 percent in 1992, but much of that difference is accounted for by the absence of Sen. Jesse Helms (R-N.C.) in the 1992 sample. In 1990 Helms led all incumbents in spending on direct-mail fund raising with outlays of $10,957,563. During the 1992 election cycle, combined spending on direct-mail solicitations by all twenty-eight incumbents totaled only $11,183,186.

On the other hand, average spending by House incumbents increased 46 percent from 1990 to 1992. During the 1990 election cycle, spending by incumbents totaled $156,545,183, an average of $390,387. Incumbents who contested the 1992 general election spent a total of $199,310,139, an average of $571,089 (see Tables 1-4 and 1-5).

The average House incumbent's investment in broadcast advertising nearly doubled, from $76,109 in 1990 to $141,791 in 1992. Average outlays for persuasion mail jumped from $37,825 to $70,198. Expenditures for yard signs, buttons, bumper stickers, rallies, get-out-the-vote-efforts, general strategic advice, and other items included under the rubric of "actual campaigning" climbed from $28,097 in 1990 to $42,196 in 1992.

Among those forced to alter their campaign style, at least temporarily, was Rep. Elton Gallegly (R-Calif.). Gallegly invested $434,418 in 1990 to defeat Democrat Richard D. Freiman, who spent just $18,018. In his solidly Republican district, only 15 percent of Gallegly's 1990 expenditures were devoted to direct appeals for votes.

Two significant problems confronted Gallegly in 1992. First, redistricting robbed him of almost three-quarters of his former constituency and handed him a new electorate in which registered Democrats slightly outnumbered Republicans. Perhaps more importantly, in a district where 30 percent of the population was Hispanic, Gallegly faced Democrat Anita Perez Ferguson, a Hispanic educational consultant who had taken 44 percent of the vote against Lagomarsino in 1990. As a result, Gallegly poured $851,701 into his 1992 campaign, and 53 percent of that total was invested in advertising, persuasion mail, and grass-roots campaigning.

Running unopposed in 1986, 1988, and 1990, Rep. Harold Rogers (R-Ky.) spent a combined total of $484,046. In 1991 his low-key, off-year campaign cost only $49,075. However, when redistricting transformed Rogers's safe Republican district into one in which 55 percent of the registered voters were Democrats, his days of relaxed campaigning quickly drew to a close. During the first six months of 1992, Rogers spent nearly $209,000—despite the fact that he was unopposed in the May primary. He then invested $627,624 over the final six months of the election cycle, more than half of which was spent in October, to defeat former state senator John Doug Hays.

For Rep. David E. Skaggs (D-Colo.) the problems were different, but the result was the same. In keeping with his 1990 pledge to hold down campaign spending, Skaggs spent only $68,315 to run his off-year campaign in 1991. With additional expenditures of roughly $140,000 through the first seven months of 1992, Skaggs looked as though he might contain his spending for the entire cycle to well under $400,000.

That was before Republican Bryan Day, a Southern Baptist minister with strong backing from both the evangelical Christian Coalition and the National Republican Congressional Committee, began hammering Skaggs over his fifty-seven overdrafts at the House bank. Skaggs spent more than $470,000 over the final months of the campaign, committing approximately $350,000 to the effort in October alone.

For the first time in his twenty-year congressional career, Rep. Ralph Regula (R-Ohio) ran a television commercial.

Table 1-1 What Campaign Money Buys in the 1992 Senate Races: Total Expenditures

Major Category	Incumbents in			Challengers in			Open Seats
	Total	Hot Races[a]	Contested Races[b]	Total	Hot Races[a]	Contested Races[b]	
Overhead							
Office furniture/supplies	$ 2,138,579	$ 1,655,100	$ 483,480	$ 959,838	$ 846,126	$ 113,711	$ 689,957
Rent/utilities	1,295,489	1,038,579	256,911	647,697	536,876	110,821	489,631
Salaries	9,062,286	6,968,809	2,093,478	6,124,369	5,446,217	678,152	5,182,451
Taxes	4,744,248	3,532,457	1,211,790	1,447,210	1,253,826	193,383	1,127,419
Bank/investment fees	140,733	114,660	26,074	48,842	46,627	2,214	56,936
Lawyers/accountants	1,520,892	1,150,329	370,563	378,807	372,002	6,805	260,456
Telephone	1,690,864	1,392,283	298,581	1,461,799	1,269,403	192,396	926,505
Campaign automobile	586,888	488,834	98,054	95,674	71,121	24,553	12,872
Computers/office equipment	1,483,906	1,117,387	366,519	817,681	749,928	67,753	450,141
Travel	5,647,008	4,111,695	1,535,313	1,711,246	1,561,675	149,571	1,332,866
Food/meetings	651,655	503,449	148,206	33,475	31,111	2,364	45,820
Total Overhead	**28,962,549**	**22,073,582**	**6,888,968**	**13,726,638**	**12,184,914**	**1,541,724**	**10,575,054**
Fund Raising							
Events	11,953,477	9,342,020	2,611,457	3,533,953	3,300,064	233,890	3,025,578
Direct mail	11,183,186	9,747,584	1,435,602	6,719,959	6,490,685	229,273	5,423,654
Telemarketing	690,252	339,944	350,308	715,069	696,805	18,265	475,225
Total Fund Raising	**23,826,914**	**19,429,548**	**4,397,366**	**10,968,982**	**10,487,554**	**481,428**	**8,924,458**
Polling	**3,452,440**	**2,644,700**	**807,739**	**1,426,095**	**1,253,330**	**172,765**	**1,114,642**
Advertising							
Electronic media	46,141,090	38,338,087	7,803,002	25,576,877	23,657,286	1,919,591	20,071,775
Other media	924,413	696,847	227,566	336,177	251,164	85,014	321,355
Total Advertising	**47,065,503**	**39,034,934**	**8,030,569**	**25,913,054**	**23,908,449**	**2,004,605**	**20,393,130**
Other Campaign Activity							
Persuasion mail/brochures	3,119,520	2,580,865	538,654	1,827,876	1,588,216	239,661	1,062,077
Actual campaigning	5,921,553	4,807,956	1,113,597	3,111,176	2,928,548	182,628	2,756,360
Staff/Volunteers	73,252	47,418	25,834	28,080	27,137	943	18,282
Total Other Campaign Activity	**9,114,325**	**7,436,239**	**1,678,086**	**4,967,132**	**4,543,901**	**423,231**	**3,836,719**
Constituent Gifts/Entertainment	**834,972**	**530,990**	**303,981**	**31,697**	**31,457**	**239**	**20,484**
Donations to							
Candidates from same state	100,941	37,758	63,183	3,986	3,986	0	4,988
Candidates from other states	170,643	74,581	96,062	1,026	1,026	0	2,000
Civic organizations	330,014	249,969	80,045	4,663	3,674	990	10,910
Ideological groups	70,820	39,087	31,733	5,849	5,579	270	2,712
Political parties	893,828	322,177	571,651	11,437	9,787	1,650	18,671
Total Donations	**1,566,247**	**723,573**	**842,674**	**26,961**	**24,052**	**2,910**	**39,280**
Unitemized Expenses	**1,354,599**	**1,011,801**	**342,797**	**599,478**	**453,917**	**145,561**	**331,569**
Total Expenditures	**$116,177,549**	**$92,885,368**	**$23,292,181**	**$57,660,036**	**$52,887,574**	**$4,772,463**	**$45,235,336**

Note: Totals are for the entire six-year cycle, including special elections.

[a] Races where incumbent garners 60 percent or less of the vote.
[b] Races where incumbent garners more than 60 percent of the vote.

Table 1-2 What Campaign Money Buys in the 1992 Senate Races: Average Expenditures

Major Category	Incumbents in			Challengers in			Open Seats
	Total	Hot Races[a]	Contested Races[b]	Total	Hot Races[a]	Contested Races[b]	
Overhead							
Office furniture/supplies	$ 76,378	$ 87,111	$ 53,720	$ 31,995	$ 40,292	$ 12,635	$ 43,122
Rent/utilities	46,267	54,662	28,546	21,590	25,566	12,313	30,602
Salaries	323,653	366,779	232,609	204,146	259,344	75,350	323,903
Taxes	169,437	185,919	134,643	48,240	59,706	21,487	70,464
Bank/investment fees	5,026	6,035	2,897	1,628	2,220	246	3,559
Lawyers/accountants	54,318	60,544	41,174	12,627	17,714	756	16,278
Telephone	60,388	73,278	33,176	48,727	60,448	21,377	57,907
Campaign automobile	20,960	25,728	10,895	3,189	3,387	2,728	805
Computers/office equipment	52,997	58,810	40,724	27,256	35,711	7,528	28,134
Travel	201,679	216,405	170,590	57,042	74,365	16,619	83,304
Food/meetings	23,273	26,497	16,467	1,116	1,481	263	2,864
Total Overhead	**1,034,377**	**1,161,767**	**765,441**	**457,555**	**580,234**	**171,303**	**660,941**
Fund Raising							
Events	426,910	491,685	290,162	117,798	157,146	25,988	189,099
Direct mail	399,399	513,031	159,511	223,999	309,080	25,475	338,978
Telemarketing	24,652	17,892	38,923	23,836	33,181	2,029	29,702
Total Fund Raising	**850,961**	**1,022,608**	**488,596**	**365,633**	**499,407**	**53,492**	**557,779**
Polling	**123,301**	**139,195**	**89,749**	**47,536**	**59,682**	**19,196**	**69,665**
Advertising							
Electronic media	1,647,896	2,017,794	867,000	852,563	1,126,537	213,288	1,254,486
Other media	33,015	36,676	25,285	11,206	11,960	9,446	20,085
Total Advertising	**1,680,911**	**2,054,470**	**892,285**	**863,768**	**1,138,498**	**222,734**	**1,274,571**
Other Campaign Activity							
Persuasion mail/brochures	111,411	135,835	59,850	60,929	75,629	26,629	66,380
Actual campaigning	211,484	253,050	123,733	103,706	139,455	20,292	172,272
Staff/Volunteers	2,616	2,496	2,870	936	1,292	105	1,143
Total Other Campaign Activity	**325,512**	**391,381**	**186,454**	**165,571**	**216,376**	**47,026**	**239,795**
Constituent Gifts/Entertainment	**29,820**	**27,947**	**33,776**	**1,057**	**1,498**	**27**	**1,280**
Donations to							
Candidates from same state	3,605	1,987	7,020	133	190	0	312
Candidates from other states	6,094	3,925	10,674	34	49	0	125
Civic organizations	11,786	13,156	8,894	155	175	110	682
Ideological groups	2,529	2,057	3,526	195	266	30	169
Political parties	31,922	16,957	63,517	381	466	183	1,167
Total Donations	**55,937**	**38,083**	**93,630**	**899**	**1,145**	**323**	**2,455**
Unitemized Expenses	**48,379**	**53,253**	**38,089**	**19,983**	**21,615**	**16,173**	**20,723**
Total Expenditures	**$4,149,198**	**$4,888,704**	**$2,588,020**	**$1,922,001**	**$2,518,456**	**$530,274**	**$2,827,209**

Note: Totals are for the entire six-year cycle, including special elections.
[a] Races where incumbent garners 60 percent or less of the vote.
[b] Races where incumbent garners more than 60 percent of the vote.

Table 1-3 What Campaign Money Buys in the 1992 Senate Races: Expenditures, by Percentage

Major Category	Incumbents in Total	Incumbents in Hot Races[a]	Incumbents in Contested Races[b]	Challengers in Total	Challengers in Hot Races[a]	Challengers in Contested Races[b]	Open Seats
Overhead							
Office furniture/supplies	1.84	1.78	2.08	1.66	1.60	2.38	1.53
Rent/utilities	1.12	1.12	1.10	1.12	1.02	2.32	1.08
Salaries	7.80	7.50	8.99	10.62	10.30	14.21	11.46
Taxes	4.08	3.80	5.20	2.51	2.37	4.05	2.49
Bank/investment fees	.12	.12	.11	.08	.09	.05	.13
Lawyers/accountants	1.31	1.24	1.59	.66	.70	.14	.58
Telephone	1.46	1.50	1.28	2.54	2.40	4.03	2.05
Campaign automobile	.51	.53	.42	.17	.13	.51	.03
Computers/office equipment	1.28	1.20	1.57	1.42	1.42	1.42	1.00
Travel	4.86	4.43	6.59	2.97	2.95	3.13	2.95
Food/meetings	.56	.54	.64	.06	.06	.05	.10
Total Overhead	**24.93**	**23.76**	**29.58**	**23.81**	**23.04**	**32.30**	**23.38**
Fund Raising							
Events	10.29	10.06	11.21	6.13	6.24	4.90	6.69
Direct mail	9.63	10.49	6.16	11.65	12.27	4.80	11.99
Telemarketing	.59	.37	1.50	1.24	1.32	.38	1.05
Total Fund Raising	**20.51**	**20.92**	**18.88**	**19.02**	**19.83**	**10.09**	**19.73**
Polling	**2.97**	**2.85**	**3.47**	**2.47**	**2.37**	**3.62**	**2.46**
Advertising							
Electronic media	39.72	41.27	33.50	44.36	44.73	40.22	44.37
Other media	.80	.75	.98	.58	.47	1.78	.71
Total Advertising	**40.51**	**42.02**	**34.48**	**44.94**	**45.21**	**42.00**	**45.08**
Other Campaign Activity							
Persuasion mail/brochures	2.69	2.78	2.31	3.17	3.00	5.02	2.35
Actual campaigning	5.10	5.18	4.78	5.40	5.54	3.83	6.09
Staff/Volunteers	.06	.05	.11	.05	.05	.02	.04
Total Other Campaign Activity	**7.85**	**8.01**	**7.20**	**8.61**	**8.59**	**8.87**	**8.48**
Constituent Gifts/ Entertainment	**.72**	**.57**	**1.31**	**.05**	**.06**	**.01**	**.05**
Donations to							
Candidates from same state	.09	.04	.27	.01	.01	0	.01
Candidates from other states	.15	.08	.41	0	0	0	0
Civic organizations	.28	.27	.34	.01	.01	.02	.02
Ideological groups	.06	.04	.14	.01	.01	.01	.01
Political parties	.77	.35	2.45	.02	.02	.03	.04
Total Donations	**1.35**	**.78**	**3.62**	**.05**	**.05**	**.06**	**.09**
Unitemized Expenses	**1.17**	**1.09**	**1.47**	**1.04**	**.86**	**3.05**	**.73**
Total Expenditures	**100.00**	**100.00**	**100.00**	**100.00**	**100.00**	**100.00**	**100.00**

Note: Totals are for the entire six-year cycle, including special elections.

[a] Races where incumbent garners 60 percent or less of the vote.
[b] Races where incumbent garners more than 60 percent of the vote.

Helped by rising anti-incumbent sentiment, underfunded college professor Warner D. Mendenhall had held Regula to 59 percent in 1990, and the incumbent worked hard to make certain their rematch would not be that close.

To reach voters in two counties added to his district, Regula invested about $25,000 to air one 30-second spot on Cleveland television stations. The ad, which dealt with his views on foreign trade and job creation, showed him on his farm, at a local steel mill, and at a trade school he helped establish. "It was an experiment," noted Regula in explaining his more aggressive campaign style. "This was the most expensive campaign I've ever been involved in."

As dramatic as these examples are, they suggest a far greater change in spending habits than actually occurred, even among House incumbents. Forty-nine percent of the money spent in the 1992 congressional elections went for purchases that had virtually nothing to do with appeals for votes: overhead, fund raising, constituent gifts and entertainment, donations, and unitemized expenditures (see Table 1-6). Of the $199,310,139 invested by House incumbents, 46 percent was spent by those whose reelection was never in doubt.

For example, Rep. John D. Dingell (D-Mich.) spent $1,085,395 to collect 65 percent of the vote against Republican Frank Beaumont, who spent just $5,402. Rep. Dennis Hastert (R-Ill.) spent $613,623 in winning 67 percent of the vote against Democrat Jonathan Abram Reich, who spent less than $5,000. Rep. Jack Fields (R-Texas) spent $744,065 and grabbed 77 percent of the vote against Democrat Charles E. Robinson, who invested less than $5,000. None of the three incumbents had primary opposition.

Dingell's 1992 campaign was truly a study in excess. First elected in 1955, Dingell had never received less than 63 percent of the vote. He had already turned back one underfunded challenge by Beaumont in 1990, and redistricting had done little to improve Beaumont's chances for their rematch in 1992. Nevertheless, Dingell's 1992 spending spree represented an 82 percent increase over the $596,591 he spent during the 1990 campaign.

Virtually every aspect of Dingell's effort reflected this massive increase. Overhead rose 97 percent, from $124,441 in 1990 to $244,744 in 1992.. His 1992 fund-raising costs of $161,127 represented an increase of 73 percent over the $92,890 he spent to fill his 1990 treasury. Expenditures on broadcast advertising more than doubled from $100,981 to $211,779. The only exception to the trend was Dingell's outlays for constituent entertainment and gifts, which declined from $57,921 to a still hefty $54,707.

Similarly, prior to 1992 Rep. Bill Thomas (R-Calif.) had seen his winning percentage drop as low as 60 percent only once in six reelection bids. Yet, in a district carried comfortably by George Bush, Thomas spent $610,997 to defeat Democrat Deborah A. Vollmer, who spent roughly 4 percent of that total. "You never know what the results are going to be until election day," remarked Catherine M. Abernathy, Thomas's administrative assistant.

In the Senate, electoral pressures clearly had nothing to do with Breaux's decision to invest $1,840,676 to beat back the challenge of the underfunded Khachaturian. Sen. Richard C. Shelby (D-Ala.) did not need to spend $2,638,104 to fend off the $146,556 challenge of Republican Richard Sellers. Rick Reed's (R-Hawaii) $482,953 campaign did not require Democratic Sen. Daniel K. Inouye's $3,503,564 response.

What then was driving these huge outlays? It most assuredly was not television advertising, which conventional wisdom has long blamed for the skyrocketing cost of campaigns. While the average amount invested by House incumbents in television and radio advertising nearly doubled between 1990 and 1992, those expenditures still represented only 25 percent of their total outlays. While some members felt the need to increase their broadcast budgets, others were able to cut them dramatically.

In 1990 Rep. Nancy L. Johnson (R-Conn.) had pumped $231,629 into television and radio commercials, despite the fact that her opponent could afford to spend just $1,961 on such advertising. Against an equally underfunded 1992 challenger, Eugene F. Slason, Johnson decided to forgo the three television commercials her campaigns generally run. That move sliced her broadcast advertising budget to the $72,569 it cost to produce and air three 60-second radio spots.

Fearing that the negative campaign tactics employed by Helms in his bitter Senate contest with Democrat Harvey B. Gantt would create a general anti-Republican backlash in 1990, Rep. Alex McMillan (R-N.C.) had paid Severin/Aviles Associates of New York $201,685 to create and place television commercials showcasing McMillan's work ethic. A secondary reason for the advertising push was redistricting. "We wanted to make a big push in 1990 to drive up the margin of victory," explained Frank H. Hill, McMillan's chief of staff. "We didn't want to give Democrats in the state legislature a reason to split up the district." The strategy apparently worked, since redistricting gave McMillan a more Republican constituency. With no such worries in 1992, McMillan opted to spend nothing on either television or radio commercials.

As in 1990, the $542,248,774 price tag attached to the 1992 campaigns was attributable in part to the fact that most members of Congress have created their own state-of-the-art, permanent political machines that operate 365 days each year, during off-years as well as election years. Between January 1, 1987 and December 31, 1991, incumbent senators seeking reelection in 1992 spent $30,128,255 to maintain their permanent campaign operations. During 1991, House incumbents spent $39,215,256 to keep their campaign engines humming.

Sen. Alfonse M. D'Amato (R-N.Y.) spent a staggering $3,753,302 to maintain his high-octane permanent campaign during the off-years. This outlay amounted to 32 percent of his total spending. Off-year overhead totaled $1,540,909, including after-tax salaries of $328,240. Fund-raising expenses during this period amounted to $1,352,607.

Direct-mail fund raising cost Sen. Bob Packwood (R-Ore.) $2,216,705 during the off-years, accounting for 69 percent of his total spending during that five-year period. Packwood's off-year expenses represented 40 percent of his total spending.

Still more impressive was the $937,542 Majority Leader Richard A. Gephardt (D-Mo.) invested in his "campaign" oper-

Table 1-4 What Campaign Money Buys in the 1992 House Races: Total Expenditures

Major Category	Incumbents in				Challengers in			Open Seats
	Total	Hot Races[a]	Contested Races[b]	Unopposed	Total	Hot Races[a]	Contested Races[b]	
Overhead								
Office furniture/supplies	$ 3,063,833	$ 1,567,795	$ 1,453,124	$ 42,914	$ 1,157,549	$ 817,953	$ 339,596	$ 972,210
Rent/utilities	3,210,015	1,698,212	1,458,080	53,724	1,107,949	744,741	363,208	968,932
Salaries	17,584,466	9,228,350	8,143,580	212,536	6,574,871	4,706,294	1,868,577	6,692,947
Taxes	5,726,173	2,794,972	2,840,847	90,354	1,021,178	796,484	224,694	1,009,987
Bank/investment fees	456,861	238,690	216,962	1,210	73,489	54,601	18,888	77,877
Lawyers/accountants	3,540,575	1,795,126	1,706,714	38,735	418,806	297,912	120,894	368,575
Telephone	2,987,569	1,647,308	1,280,893	59,369	1,497,218	1,047,122	450,096	1,208,963
Campaign automobile	1,103,064	609,773	444,267	49,024	85,959	55,449	30,510	91,266
Computers/office equipment	3,142,414	1,558,358	1,499,613	84,443	929,400	647,196	282,204	648,237
Travel	7,439,927	3,646,677	3,530,401	262,849	1,380,697	917,275	463,421	1,277,535
Food/meetings	1,250,157	484,878	654,326	110,953	90,338	65,490	24,849	72,742
Total Overhead	**49,505,056**	**25,270,139**	**23,228,807**	**1,006,110**	**14,337,454**	**10,150,517**	**4,186,937**	**13,389,272**
Fund Raising								
Events	22,917,783	10,600,198	11,917,392	400,193	3,287,026	2,480,155	806,872	3,626,302
Direct mail	7,429,739	4,206,801	3,187,778	35,160	1,852,774	1,372,676	480,099	1,356,013
Telemarketing	485,907	279,264	206,643	0	187,809	162,031	25,778	90,475
Total Fund Raising	**30,833,429**	**15,086,262**	**15,311,814**	**435,353**	**5,327,610**	**4,014,862**	**1,312,748**	**5,072,790**
Polling	**6,994,215**	**4,220,705**	**2,754,310**	**19,200**	**2,037,398**	**1,580,163**	**457,235**	**2,061,062**
Advertising								
Electronic media	49,484,954	31,232,428	18,230,545	21,981	20,457,833	16,902,381	3,555,452	18,249,374
Other media	5,236,282	2,374,824	2,840,220	21,238	1,929,805	1,365,950	563,854	1,587,920
Total Advertising	**54,721,236**	**33,607,252**	**21,070,764**	**43,219**	**22,387,638**	**18,268,332**	**4,119,306**	**19,837,294**
Other Campaign Activity								
Persuasion mail/brochures	24,499,213	14,784,542	9,666,302	48,369	10,139,985	7,562,416	2,577,569	13,604,775
Actual campaigning	14,726,433	7,776,335	6,695,385	254,713	6,190,367	4,397,739	1,792,628	6,255,507
Staff/Volunteers	527,244	283,559	237,442	6,243	52,577	36,932	15,646	88,246
Total Other Campaign Activity	**39,752,890**	**22,844,435**	**16,599,129**	**309,326**	**16,382,929**	**11,997,086**	**4,385,843**	**19,948,528**
Constituent Gifts/ Entertainment	**2,993,710**	**1,183,217**	**1,692,677**	**117,816**	**34,236**	**24,660**	**9,576**	**71,280**
Donations to								
Candidates from same state	1,816,962	372,727	1,278,550	165,685	17,123	10,597	6,525	28,692
Candidates from other states	1,356,449	311,972	1,007,476	37,001	2,385	2,360	25	5,850
Civic organizations	1,146,242	384,273	729,685	32,284	49,982	36,894	13,088	61,124
Ideological groups	534,750	222,122	309,112	3,515	10,630	5,013	5,617	17,501
Political parties	4,232,783	1,502,895	2,661,971	67,916	58,766	39,510	19,255	61,447
Total Donations	**9,087,185**	**2,793,989**	**5,986,795**	**306,402**	**138,885**	**94,375**	**44,511**	**174,613**
Unitemized Expenses	**5,422,418**	**2,497,737**	**2,746,014**	**178,667**	**1,414,758**	**920,600**	**494,158**	**1,249,966**
Total Expenditures	**$199,310,139**	**$107,503,735**	**$89,390,309**	**$2,416,095**	**$62,060,908**	**$47,050,594**	**$15,010,313**	**$61,804,805**

Note: Totals are for the entire two-year cycle, including special elections.

[a] Races where incumbent garners 60 percent or less of the vote.
[b] Races where incumbent garners more than 60 percent of the vote.

Table 1-5 What Campaign Money Buys in the 1992 House Races: Average Expenditures

Major Category	Incumbents in				Challengers in			Open Seats
	Total	Hot Races[a]	Contested Races[b]	Unopposed	Total	Hot Races[a]	Contested Races[b]	
Overhead								
Office furniture/supplies	$ 8,779	$ 10,452	$ 7,608	$ 5,364	$ 3,233	$ 5,018	$ 1,742	$ 6,396
Rent/utilities	9,198	11,321	7,634	6,715	3,095	4,569	1,863	6,375
Salaries	50,385	61,522	42,637	26,567	18,366	28,873	9,582	44,033
Taxes	16,407	18,633	14,874	11,294	2,852	4,886	1,152	6,645
Bank/investment fees	1,309	1,591	1,136	151	205	335	97	512
Lawyers/accountants	10,145	11,968	8,936	4,842	1,170	1,828	620	2,425
Telephone	8,560	10,982	6,706	7,421	4,182	6,424	2,308	7,954
Campaign automobile	3,161	4,065	2,326	6,128	240	340	156	600
Computers/office equipment	9,004	10,389	7,851	10,555	2,596	3,971	1,447	4,265
Travel	21,318	24,311	18,484	32,856	3,857	5,627	2,377	8,405
Food/meetings	3,582	3,233	3,426	13,869	252	402	127	479
Total Overhead	**141,848**	**168,468**	**121,617**	**125,764**	**40,049**	**62,273**	**21,471**	**88,087**
Fund Raising								
Events	65,667	70,668	62,395	50,024	9,182	15,216	4,138	23,857
Direct mail	21,289	28,045	16,690	4,395	5,175	8,421	2,462	8,921
Telemarketing	1,392	1,862	1,082	0	525	994	132	595
Total Fund Raising	**88,348**	**100,575**	**80,167**	**54,419**	**14,882**	**24,631**	**6,732**	**33,374**
Polling	**20,041**	**28,138**	**14,420**	**2,400**	**5,691**	**9,694**	**2,345**	**13,560**
Advertising								
Electronic media	141,791	208,216	95,448	2,748	57,145	103,696	18,233	120,062
Other media	15,004	15,832	14,870	2,655	5,391	8,380	2,892	10,447
Total Advertising	**156,794**	**224,048**	**110,318**	**5,402**	**62,535**	**112,076**	**21,125**	**130,509**
Other Campaign Activity								
Persuasion mail/brochures	70,198	98,564	50,609	6,046	28,324	46,395	13,218	89,505
Actual campaigning	42,196	51,842	35,054	31,839	17,292	26,980	9,193	41,155
Staff/Volunteers	1,511	1,890	1,243	780	147	227	80	581
Total Other Campaign Activity	**113,905**	**152,296**	**86,906**	**38,666**	**45,762**	**73,602**	**22,492**	**131,240**
Constituent Gifts/ Entertainment	**8,578**	**7,888**	**8,862**	**14,727**	**96**	**151**	**49**	**469**
Donations to								
Candidates from same state	5,206	2,485	6,694	20,711	48	65	33	189
Candidates from other states	3,887	2,080	5,275	4,625	7	14	0	38
Civic organizations	3,284	2,562	3,820	4,035	140	226	67	402
Ideological groups	1,532	1,481	1,618	439	30	31	29	115
Political parties	12,128	10,019	13,937	8,490	164	242	99	404
Total Donations	**26,038**	**18,627**	**31,344**	**38,300**	**388**	**579**	**228**	**1,149**
Unitemized Expenses	**15,537**	**16,652**	**14,377**	**22,333**	**3,952**	**5,648**	**2,534**	**8,223**
Total Expenditures	**$571,089**	**$716,692**	**$468,012**	**$302,012**	**$173,354**	**$288,654**	**$76,976**	**$406,611**

Note: Totals are for the entire two-year cycle, including special elections.
[a] Races where incumbent garners 60 percent or less of the vote.
[b] Races where incumbent garners more than 60 percent of the vote.

Table 1-6 What Campaign Money Buys in the 1992 House Races: Expenditures, by Percentage

Major Category	Incumbents in				Challengers in			Open Seats
	Total	Hot Races[a]	Contested Races[b]	Unopposed	Total	Hot Races[a]	Contested Races[b]	
Overhead								
Office furniture/supplies	1.54	1.46	1.63	1.78	1.87	1.74	2.26	1.57
Rent/utilities	1.61	1.58	1.63	2.22	1.79	1.58	2.42	1.57
Salaries	8.82	8.58	9.11	8.80	10.59	10.00	12.45	10.83
Taxes	2.87	2.60	3.18	3.74	1.65	1.69	1.50	1.63
Bank/investment fees	.23	.22	.24	.05	.12	.12	.13	.13
Lawyers/accountants	1.78	1.67	1.91	1.60	.67	.63	.81	.60
Telephone	1.50	1.53	1.43	2.46	2.41	2.23	3.00	1.96
Campaign automobile	.55	.57	.50	2.03	.14	.12	.20	.15
Computers/office equipment	1.58	1.45	1.68	3.50	1.50	1.38	1.88	1.05
Travel	3.73	3.39	3.95	10.88	2.22	1.95	3.09	2.07
Food/meetings	.63	.45	.73	4.59	.15	.14	.17	.12
Total Overhead	**24.84**	**23.51**	**25.99**	**41.64**	**23.10**	**21.57**	**27.89**	**21.66**
Fund Raising								
Events	11.50	9.86	13.33	16.56	5.30	5.27	5.38	5.87
Direct mail	3.73	3.91	3.57	1.46	2.99	2.92	3.20	2.19
Telemarketing	.24	.26	.23	0	.30	.34	.17	.15
Total Fund Raising	**15.47**	**14.03**	**17.13**	**18.02**	**8.58**	**8.53**	**8.75**	**8.21**
Polling	**3.51**	**3.93**	**3.08**	**.79**	**3.28**	**3.36**	**3.05**	**3.33**
Advertising								
Electronic media	24.83	29.05	20.39	.91	32.96	35.92	23.69	29.53
Other media	2.63	2.21	3.18	.88	3.11	2.90	3.76	2.57
Total Advertising	**27.46**	**31.26**	**23.57**	**1.79**	**36.07**	**38.83**	**27.44**	**32.10**
Other Campaign Activity								
Persuasion mail/brochures	12.29	13.75	10.81	2.00	16.34	16.07	17.17	22.01
Actual campaigning	7.39	7.23	7.49	10.54	9.97	9.35	11.94	10.12
Staff/Volunteers	.26	.26	.27	.26	.08	.08	.10	.14
Total Other Campaign Activity	**19.95**	**21.25**	**18.57**	**12.80**	**26.40**	**25.50**	**29.22**	**32.28**
Constituent Gifts/ Entertainment	**1.50**	**1.10**	**1.89**	**4.88**	**.06**	**.05**	**.06**	**.12**
Donations to								
Candidates from same state	.91	.35	1.43	6.86	.03	.02	.04	.05
Candidates from other states	.68	.29	1.13	1.53	.00	.01	.00	.01
Civic organizations	.58	.36	.82	1.34	.08	.08	.09	.10
Ideological groups	.27	.21	.35	.15	.02	.01	.04	.03
Political parties	2.12	1.40	2.98	2.81	.09	.08	.13	.10
Total Donations	**4.56**	**2.60**	**6.70**	**12.68**	**.22**	**.20**	**.30**	**.28**
Unitemized Expenses	**2.72**	**2.32**	**3.07**	**7.39**	**2.28**	**1.96**	**3.29**	**2.02**
Total Expenditures	**100.00**	**100.00**	**100.00**	**100.00**	**100.00**	**100.00**	**100.00**	**100.00**

Note: Totals are for the entire two-year cycle, including special elections.
[a] Races where incumbent garners 60 percent or less of the vote.
[b] Races where incumbent garners more than 60 percent of the vote.

ation during 1991. He spent $514,304 on overhead and $222,146 for fund-raising events and direct-mail solicitations. Throughout the election cycle he maintained a Washington, D.C., fund-raising office with a staff of eight, including Richard Sullivan, a national fund-raiser for the Democratic Senatorial Campaign Committee (DSCC) and Donald J. Foley, political director at the DSCC.

Entrenched incumbents were not the only ones pouring money into permanent campaigns. After garnering 67 percent of the vote to win an open seat in 1990, freshman Rep. Jim Ramstad immediately settled into the permanent campaign mode. Off-year expenses totaled $151,776, including monthly rent of $600 on his campaign headquarters. Campaign manager Tim Berkness was hired in May 1991, and Berkness added two part-time staffers four months later.

Ramstad began 1991 with debts of $122,580 and cash reserves of only $2,448. Twenty-four months later he had whittled his debts to $21,793 while increasing his cash-on-hand to $317,719. He raised $486,967 from individual contributors who gave at least $200, $270,772 from donors who gave less than $200, and $260,016 from political action committees (PACs). He accomplished this impressive feat by sinking 41 percent of his $599,672 campaign outlays into fund raising.

While both overhead and fund raising represented smaller proportions of the typical incumbent's budget during the election year itself, spending on these items was by no means insignificant. Senate incumbents spent $85,440,675 during 1992; $27,577,530 of that total, or 32 percent, was invested in overhead and fund raising. Of the $160,181,884 spent by House members in 1992, 33 percent was committed to overhead and raising money.

Even though we refer to it as "campaign overhead," many incumbents spent large sums of their campaign treasuries to enhance their personal lifestyles. During the six years leading up to his 1992 reelection, D'Amato spent $156,729 of his campaign funds to lease and maintain two Lincoln Towncars, one of which was leased for his use in Washington, D.C. Inouye used his campaign funds to finance 403 meals costing less than $200 each, including a $12.50 bill at the Szechuan Garden in Rockville, Md., and a $22.59 meal at the Wo Fat restaurant in Honolulu.

Together, members of the House and Senate simply gave away $10,653,432 of the money they collected for the 1992 campaigns. Although political party organizations were the chief beneficiaries of this philanthropic spirit, fellow members of Congress, local candidates, charities, local booster groups, and various ideological organizations benefited as well. In a year of turmoil, few incumbents felt they could afford to significantly reduce their political bridge-building efforts. Some significantly increased their giving.

The $66,186 Dellums donated from his treasury to other candidates, civic organizations, ideological groups, and Democratic party organizations represented a 39 percent increase over his 1990 donations. IMPAC 2000, a political action committee devoted to assisting Democrats in state redistricting battles, received $41,688. He donated $5,000 to the Democratic Congressional Campaign Committee. He spent $1,650 on tickets to a Congressional Black Caucus event, $1,315 on tickets to the Black Filmmakers Hall of Fame, and $1,000 on tickets to a dinner sponsored by the Black Women Organized for Educational Development.

Among the most important political bridges to maintain were those that tied incumbents to friendly, visiting constituents. House and Senate incumbents together spent $3,828,682 on constituent gifts and entertainment. Rep. John P. Murtha invested $45,395 of his treasury in constituent stroking. He spent $19,864 on gifts, including baubles from Lenox China and sweets from L&D candies. Tickets to various sporting events cost the campaign $8,513—$3,804 for season tickets to Pittsburgh Steelers football games, $1,176 for season tickets to Washington Redskins games, $1,804 for Pittsburgh Pirates tickets, $1,080 for University of Pittsburgh at Johnstown football tickets, and $649 for tickets to the Johnstown Chiefs, a minor league baseball club. He spent $6,896 on flowers for constituents, $5,300 on year-end holiday cards, and $4,822 on constituent meals and receptions.

Rep. Tom Bevill (D-Ala.) put $18,404 into his constituent stoking efforts during the 1992 election cycle—$2,724 more than in 1990. He spent $1,750 on cookbooks, $4,587 on constituent meals, $3,042 on calendars, $3,131 on year-end holiday cards, and $3,574 for glossy 8x10 photos, which he autographed for visitors. Each Christmas Bevill ran newspaper ads inviting people to drop by his home for coffee and cookies; the parties cost his campaign $1,574.

There were a few incumbents who had no reason to spend freely on their reelection bids and actually chose not to do so, proving it is possible to thrive politically without spending huge sums. As he had since his initial House race in 1953, Rep. William H. Natcher (D-Ky.) paid for his entire campaign—all $6,625 of it—from his own pocket. After refusing to take political contributions of any kind for thirty-nine years, Natcher had no reason to change.

Mirroring his past campaigns, Natcher ran no television commercials. He had no campaign office, no paid or unpaid campaign staff. As the second ranking Democrat and acting chair of the Appropriations Committee, he had no reason to curry favor with fellow House members by contributing to their campaigns.

Instead, Natcher's campaign was a throwback to the 1950s. His office was his Chevrolet Citation, which he drove through all twenty counties in the district. Campaign stops consisted of conversations in coffee shops and drug stores. He spent $6,580 to run fifty small preprimary ads in twenty-seven newspapers. Each ad simply advised readers that he was the incumbent and was seeking reelection. Items listed on his preprimary campaign financial statements as "miscellaneous and postage" amounted to $19.47. Natcher completely ignored his weak general election opponent, filing expenses of only $25.20 after May 27. When Natcher died in March 1994, it truly was an end of an era.

While not quite as frugal as Natcher, Rep. Andrew Jacobs, Jr. (D-Ind.) also has a decidedly different approach to campaigning. "I am willing to lose before I take PAC contributions," Jacobs remarked. "It's obscene that lobbyists are able to make campaign contributions."

Jacobs rarely raises or spends much on his campaigns, and his 1992 rematch with economics professor Janos Horvath proved to be no exception. Jacobs spent just $14,376 to dispatch Horvath, which was $294 less than Jacobs invested to beat him in 1990.

Jacobs raised his funds primarily from a list of 700 "friends" who had responded to past direct-mail solicitations. However, even then, Jacobs set strict limits. When, in September 1992, he realized that his campaign bank account had risen to more than $39,000, the nine-term incumbent mailed out a letter asking his supporters not to send more money. "It's fall and time for a solicitation, but this time we don't need any money, so thank you," Jacobs remembered writing.

Jacobs ran the same radio spots in 1992 that he has run for the past several elections. "Gregory Peck recorded several ads a few years ago that were suitably self-indulgent and said nothing negative about me," Jacobs noted. He added that his ads said nothing negative about Horvath because "I don't do that, and we can't afford it anyway."

With retirements setting a postwar record and redistricting creating twenty-four additional open House seats, open seat candidates accounted for 20 percent of the $542,248,774 spent in 1992. Candidates vying for seventy-seven open seats in the House spent a total of $61,804,805. The average expenditure of $406,611 was more than twice the average outlay reported by those who challenged incumbents. The sixteen candidates contesting eight open Senate seats spent a total of $45,235,336. Their $2,827,209 average exceeded that of Senate challengers by $905,208, or 47 percent (see Tables 1-1 and 1-2). This increased spending translated directly into closer races. The winner in sixty of the seventy-seven House open seat contests received 55 percent of the vote or less in the primary election, the general election, or both. Another seven open seat winners garnered no more than 60 percent at some point on their electoral journey to Washington. In ten cases, the winner cruised through the process with 61 percent or more. In six of the eight Senate open seat races the winner received 55 percent or less.

Yet, even in these hotly contested open seat races, the average House candidate spent just 30 percent of his or her budget on broadcast advertising. The comparable figure for Senate candidates was 44 percent—far less than the long-assumed standard of 50 to 75 percent.

Where did all the money come from to fund these campaigns? PACs contributed $173,939,292 to those candidates who survived the primary process and went on to contest the November general election. PACs donated $1,240,597 to Gephardt; $1,148,438 to Rep. Vic Fazio (D-Calif.); $962,937 to Rostenkowski; $934,613 to Rep. David E. Bonior (D-Mich.); $767,931 to Dingell; and $711,367 to Rep. Steny H. Hoyer (D-Md.). In all, 28 House incumbents collected more than $500,000 from PACs and 189 received between $200,000 and $499,999 over the two-year cycle. Twenty-four senators had PAC donations of at least $1 million, led by Sen. Arlen Specter (R-Pa.), who collected $2,017,041 over the six-year cycle.

To trace Rep. George E. Brown, Jr. (D-Calif.) to his position as chairman of the Committee on Science, Space and Technology, one need look no further than his fund-raisers. In early 1991 Brown held a $1,000-a-head event aimed at PACs representing aerospace companies; in July Lockheed's PAC spent $763 to stage a small reception on his behalf. In May 1992 Brown drew close to 100 contributors to a fund-raiser at Houston's Clear Lake Space Club. One month later he traveled to New York for a fund-raising breakfast thrown for him by the Loral Corporation. In all, PACs representing aerospace, science, and technology interests contributed $115,488 to Brown's reelection effort.

As chairman of the subcommittee on Health and the Environment, Waxman was able to tap PACs representing health care interests for $177,800. In all, 203 PACs contributed a total of $402,915 to Waxman's coffers, which amounted to 64 percent of his donations. Individual contributions of $200 or less accounted for only 6 percent of his total contributions.

Although PACs donated primarily to incumbents, twenty-five candidates who vied for open seats in the House and five House challengers proved they had already mastered the fund-raising game by collecting at least $200,000 from PACs. Among this group were open seat winners Maria Cantwell (D-Wash.), Michael N. Castle (R-Del.), and Karen L. Thurman (D-Fla.), as well as losing challengers Anita Perez Ferguson (D-Calif.), Gwen Margolis (D-Fla.), and Andy Fox (D-Va.). Rep. Rod Chandler (R-Wash.), who gave up his House seat in an unsuccessful bid to succeed retiring Republican Sen. Brock Adams, led all Senate challengers with PAC donations of $1,143,695.

Democratic state representative Cynthia A. McKinney raised $166,642 from PACs for her open seat contest in Georgia's newly created majority-black District 11; this represented 54 percent of her total contributions. The closer she came to victory, the easier it became to raise PAC money. In the primary, PACs accounted for only 11 percent of her contributions. While McKinney failed to secure the 50 percent necessary to avoid a runoff in the five-candidate primary, her opponent was the only white candidate in the race. With McKinney's victory virtually assured, PACs accounted for 61 percent of her donations preceding the runoff. That figure grew to 65 percent in the perfunctory general election campaign.

However, while PACs have been cursed as the source of fund-raising evil—special interest money—they accounted for just 32 percent of the $543,398,701 raised by congressional candidates who contested the November general elections. Fifty-five percent of the money raised by these candidates came from individual contributors.

In 1990 federal records showed that 62 people had violated the $25,000 annual limit on contributions to federal candidates and political committees set in 1974 by Congress. Replicating that study on 1992 contribution data yielded 110 violators, including Angelo Parisi, a chef who at one time owned restaurants in both New York and Huntington Beach, Calif. During 1991 and 1992, Parisi made federal contributions totaling $100,004, of

Table 1-7 Individuals in Violation of Federal Election Campaign Contribution Laws: 1992 Election Cycle

		City	1991	1992			City	1991	1992
1	Angelo Parisi	New Rochelle, N.Y.	$33,742	**$66,262**	56	Robert Gumbiner	Long Beach, Calif.	**$33,000**	$24,450
2	William C. Mow	Los Angeles	18,285	**65,350**	57	Eugene Dinsmore	Omaha, Neb.	11,356	**32,985**
3	D. Lloyd Wilson	Cozad, N.M.	6,815	**52,500**	58	William Lerach[a]	San Diego	3,000	**32,468**
4	David Packard	Los Altos, Calif.	4,805	**50,950**	59	Thomas F. Kranz	Los Angeles	18,500	**32,183**
5	John D. Murchinson	Dallas	1,000	**50,500**	60	Bruce C. Gottwald	Richmond, Va.	8,250	**31,500**
6	Edmund A. Stanley, Jr.	Oxford, Md.	19,250	**50,450**	61	Mary M. Ashmore	Boynton Beach, Fla.	14,850	**31,000**
7	Abe Pollin	Landover, Md.	3,500	**50,250**	62	Elinor Goodspeed[a]	Washington, D.C.	14,900	**30,700**
8	John A. Gabriel	Sante Fe Springs, Calif.	1,640	**49,840**	63	Candace Straight	Bloomfield, N.J.	18,500	**30,540**
9	Thomas A. Kershaw	Boston	19,000	**49,144**	64	Ray B. Auel	Sherwood, Ore.	17,000	**30,500**
10	Joseph W. Cotchett	Burlingame, Calif.	5,000	**48,000**	65	Ian Cumming	Salt Lake City	10,500	**30,302**
11	Richard B. Cray	Kansas City, Mo.	13,000	**47,750**	66	Michael Keiser[a]	Chicago	20,700	**30,250**
12	Charles Intriago	Miami	0	**47,500**	67	Elsie H. Hillman[a]	Pittsburgh	13,250	**30,150**
13	Charles White	San Diego	22,440	**46,641**	68	Stanley C. Gault	Wooster, Ohio	0	**30,100**
14	Grover Connell	Westfield, N.J.	2,000	**46,319**	69	Peter M. Flanigan	New York	18,250	**30,050**
15	William Hambrecht	San Francisco	21,000	**46,250**	70	William M. Keck II	Los Angeles	10,000	**30,000**
16	Ann Cox Chambers	Atlanta, GA	1,500	**44,750**	71	Mary M. Newman	Corona Del Mar, Calif.	14,750	**30,000**
17	Henry Salvatori	Los Angeles	13,410	**43,900**	72	Harriet Stimson Bullitt	Seattle	0	**29,750**
18	Don Henley	Beverly Hills	3,500	**43,850**	73	Irwin M. Rosenthal	New York	0	**29,750**
19	Edgar Uihlein	Northbrook, Ill.	17,000	**43,700**	74	Arthur B. Belfer	New York	24,430	**29,645**
20	Glenn E. Stinson	Naples, Fla.	17,000	**43,300**	75	Howard Gilman	New York	10,000	**29,500**
21	Peter C. Cook	Grand Rapids, Mich.	24,000	**43,110**	76	Lawrence Lewis Jr	Richmond, Va.	23,000	**29,475**
22	John P. Manning	Boston	21,000	**42,800**	77	Paul J. Meyer	Dallas	**29,300**	20,000
23	Herbert F. Collins	Boston	17,000	**42,000**	78	Thomas D. Barrow	Houston	22,000	**29,000**
24	Thomas Hansberger	Ft. Lauderdale, Fla.	24,000	**40,650**	79	James E. Davis	Jacksonville, Fla.	10,000	**29,000**
25	C. Thomas Clagett, Jr.	Washington, D.C.	18,250	**40,392**	80	Julian Klein	New York	13,700	**28,850**
26	Don Gray Angell, Jr.	Pompano Beach, Fla.	0	**40,000**	81	Gary David Goldberg	Los Angeles	2,750	**28,750**
27	Robert Coates	Dallas	0	**40,000**	82	Zora Charles	Beverly Hills	0	**28,500**
28	David Rosenberg	Exton, Pa.	20,000	**40,000**	83	Andrew Athens	Chicago	13,500	**28,475**
29	Laurence W. Levine	New York	1,297	**39,500**	84	Stanley Hirch[a]	Studio City, Calif.	23,500	**28,300**
30	Patricia Connell	Westfield, N.J.	2,000	**39,319**	85	Sheldon Silverston	New York	15,510	**28,245**
31	Chesley Pruet	El Dorado, Ark.	17,250	**39,200**	86	James A. Ortenzio	New York	10,000	**28,000**
32	Norman V. Kinsey[a]	Shreveport, La.	**28,000**	**38,750**	87	John N. Irwin, II	New York	**27,500**	24,000
33	Eugene Applebaum	Troy, Mich.	15,250	**38,000**	88	Joshua L. Mailman	New York	21,000	**27,500**
34	S. Daniel Abraham	New York	14,000	**38,000**	89	Clifford L. Michel	Gladstone, N.J.	**27,500**	14,750
35	Robert Day	New York	22,000	**38,000**	90	William W. Harris	Cambridge, Mass.	23,000	**27,250**
36	Stephen C. Swid	New York	0	**38,000**	91	George Argyros	Costa Mesa, Calif.	17,500	**27,000**
37	Bruce D. Benson	Denver	4,000	**37,625**	92	Thomas Klutznick	Chicago	1,000	**27,000**
38	Henry L. Hillman	Pittsburgh	7,000	**37,500**	93	John N. Palmer	Jackson, Miss.	13,000	**27,000**
39	Jonathan Tisch	New York	1,250	**36,750**	94	Andrew A. Kiss	Washington, D.C.	23,791	**26,956**
40	Phillip B. Rooney Sr.	Hinsdale, Ill.	10,000	**36,250**	95	Allan C. Greenberg	New York	1,000	**26,775**
41	John K. Funk	Houston	12,530	**35,660**	96	Cynthia Friedman	Washington, D.C.	14,750	**26,750**
42	Henry J. Smith	Dallas	10,500	**35,500**	97	Albert Abramson	Bethesda, Md.	16,000	**26,500**
43	W. Clement Stone	Lake Forest, Ill.	11,500	**35,500**	98	David S. Steiner	West Orange, N.J.	**26,500**	23,140
44	Charles J. Harrington	Wilmington, Del.	**35,430**	28,735	99	Karl M. Samuelian	Los Angeles	21,360	**26,500**
45	John F. Hotchkis	Los Angeles	16,000	**35,000**	100	Anita Hirsh	Studio City	6,500	**26,500**
46	Susan Quinn Keck	Los Angeles	10,000	**35,000**	101	H. Wayne Huizenga	Ft. Lauderdale, Fla.	15,000	**26,000**
47	Jerome S. Moss	Hollywood	10,000	**34,750**	102	Charles M. Pigott	Bellevue, Wash.	17,000	**26,000**
48	James Bronce Henderson	Detroit	22,797	**34,500**	103	Steven J. Ross	New York	**26,000**	13,500
49	Frederick A. Klingenstein	New York	18,000	**34,500**	104	Paul J. Elston	New York	4,500	**25,850**
50	Edward Lozick	Highland Heights, Ohio	17,000	**34,500**	105	Bernard Rapoport	Waco, Texas	**25,750**	24,211
51	Robert A. Daly	Los Angeles	5,500	**33,718**	106	Frederick W. Field	Beverly Hills	24,500	**25,500**
52	Robert J. Stein	Washington, D.C.	17,500	**33,605**	107	Sylvia Steiner	West Orange, N.J.	7,000	**25,500**
53	J. Weldon Granger	Houston	8,000	**33,575**	108	William W. Boeschstein	Toledo, Ohio	20,000	**25,250**
54	James A. Elkins Jr.	Houston	21,000	**33,250**	109	John H. Lindsey	Houston	16,000	**25,250**
55	James R. Houghton[a]	Corning, N.Y.	6,000	**33,150**	110	Peter L. Buttenwieser	Pittsburgh	19,000	**25,106**

Note: Totals in bold indicate contributors in excess of the $25,000 limit established in 1974 by Congress.
[a] Also exceeded the federal $25,000 contribution limit in 1990.

which $66,262 was credited to 1992. In all, seven people donated more than $50,000 during 1992, more than twice the legal limit. Twenty-one others gave at least $40,000 (see Table 1-7).

Reflecting the fact that the Federal Election Commission rarely acts to enforce the law, does so only when violations are brought to its attention, and rarely negotiates anything more than token fines, seven of those on the 1992 list were repeat offenders from 1990, including Corning executive James R. Houghton, the brother of Rep. Amo Houghton (R-N.Y.)

Some violators, including William C. Mow, chairman of Bugle Boy Jeans in Los Angeles, Calif., indicated they were unaware of the law. Julian Klein, a retired New Yorker, explained that he simply responded to requests from Republican campaigns without bothering to keep track of the total amount. "I just kept getting requests in the mail, and when I could I sent money" Klein noted. "I didn't know about any limit." In all, Klein wrote ninety-one checks totaling $28,850 during 1992.

Others blamed their violations on mistakes made by the campaigns. "I requested that those checks be credited to my wife, but the individual campaigns credited all of it to me," complained Michael L. Keiser, a repeat offender from 1990 and president of Recycled Paper Products of Chicago, Ill., the country's fourth-largest greeting card manufacturer. Unfortunately for Keiser, his wife was the only person who could request that contributions be credited to her, and she had to do so in writing at the time the contributions were made. Barring such notice, campaigns are required to credit the contribution to the person whose signature appeared on the check.

Some were simply unrepentant. "Let them come and get me," taunted Charles J. Harrington, a retired Du Pont executive. "I keep getting requests for donations, and I'm going to keep on donating."

Given that PACs can donate no more than $10,000 to any candidate, corporate executives who wish to help have increasingly taken to "bundling" checks from a number of their colleagues, frequently passing them on to candidates in a single envelope. Sen. Patrick J. Leahy (D-Vt.) passed through Beverly Hills on June 4, 1991 and left with $52,250 from movie studio executives and their spouses. Prominent among the attendees were executives from the Walt Disney Company and its various subsidiaries. At that one reception, Disney executives and their spouses gave Leahy forty-three checks totaling $31,750. The Disney PAC did not contribute to Leahy's 1992 campaign.

While the law firm of Skadden, Arps, Slate, Meagher and Flom did not contribute through its PAC to Democrat Robert Abrams's unsuccessful challenge to D'Amato, the firm's members gave individual contributions to Abrams totaling $36,700. Twenty-four checks totaling $9,500 were passed to Abrams on December 31, 1991.

In short, while news reports were filled with talk of change, candidates collected and spent their money much as they had before. Fueled by special-interest money that flowed from individuals and PACs alike, the cost of the 1992 elections was unnecessarily inflated by spending that went far beyond the business of directly appealing for votes. While Congress continues its seemingly endless debate over campaign finance reform, few on Capitol Hill have proposed changes in the way money is spent. Until that issue is addressed, the aggregate cost of campaigns will remain unnecessarily high.

CHAPTER 2

What Campaign Money *Still* Buys
The Gold-Plated, Permanent Campaign Revisited

> Maybe we can finally get away from having those of us who run for office have to manage large sums of money in order to run for office; in essence, run a small business on the side through a campaign committee in order to participate in the electoral process.
> *Sen. David L. Boren (D-Okla.), June 7, 1993, from remarks delivered during Senate floor debate on campaign finance reform*

> I maintain a campaign headquarters year-round, and I have done so since I first came to Congress.
> *Rep. James H. Quillen (R-Tenn.), first elected to the House in 1962*

To understand why the cost of modern campaigns rises with each election, one need look no further than the permanent campaign organization devised by Rep. Richard A. Gephardt (D-Mo.), the House majority leader. Gephardt had won 57 percent of the general election vote in 1990, marking the first time in eight House campaigns that his winning percentage had fallen below 60 percent. While pundits pointed to his $1,448,831 effort as evidence that an anti-incumbent groundswell was building, few noticed that only 40 percent of his massive treasury had been spent on direct appeals for votes. Fifty-three percent of his spending had been pumped into overhead and fund raising.

The 1992 campaign proved to be no different. Courtesy of a redistricting deal he struck with incumbents in neighboring districts prior to the 1990 election, Gephardt was assured of a more Democratic constituency in 1992. Although one of the deal's participants, Republican Rep. Jack Buechner, lost his 1990 reelection bid, Gephardt refused to cede back to Buechner's successor, Democratic Rep. Joan Kelly Horn, any of the Democratic voters he had been promised.

Yet, despite his strengthened position, Gephardt sank $937,542 into his permanent campaign during 1991. Gephardt's off-year spending amounted to more than five times what the typical challenger had to spend on his or her entire campaign. It was nearly three times what his Republican challenger, Malcolm L. Holekamp, spent during 1992. As impressive as those numbers are, they do not include the $112,313 Gephardt transferred from his House campaign treasury to the Gephardt for President Committee to repay debts accumulated during his unsuccessful 1988 presidential bid.

Gephardt began 1991 with $193,486 in his campaign bank account. One year later, he had increased his cash reserves to $1,055,609. He accomplished that astounding feat by pouring $190,584 into fund-raising events and $31,562 into direct-mail solicitations. Gephardt's fund-raising itinerary took him to the Regency Hotel in New York City; the Commerce Club in Atlanta, Ga.; the Sterling Hotel in Sacramento, Calif.; the Park Hyatt in San Francisco, Calif.; and the Decathlon Club in Santa Clara, Calif. He traveled to Houston, Texas; Minneapolis, Minn.; and New Orleans, La., where the law firm of Barham & Markle sponsored a reception. In Washington, D.C., the American Council of Life Insurance organized a reception, as did CAREPAC, the political action committee (PAC) established by Blue Cross and Blue Shield, and the Realtors Political Action Committee. In all, Gephardt collected $1,851,589 during 1991, including $727,309 from PACs.

To support his off-year fund-raising operation, Gephardt spent $10,976 to lease office space in Washington, D.C. The Washington operation employed seven people who drew after-tax salaries totaling $106,310. Telephone bills, parking fees, and office supplies totaled $3,314, $2,060 and $1,033, respectively.

Gephardt also maintained an off-year headquarters in St. Louis, where rent and utilities amounted to $24,200. His campaign manager, Joyce Aboussie, collected $44,392 during 1991, and eight other employees collected after-tax salaries totaling $61,100. Off-year telephone bills for the St. Louis office totaled $25,126. He paid $3,996 to Federal Express, bought $1,988 in office supplies from Bizmart Office Supplies in St. Louis, and spent $2,114 to have his photocopier repaired, $1,785 to have the office cleaned, and $1,863 for a telephone answering service.

Between his hectic fund-raising schedule and his work as House majority leader, Gephardt accumulated off-year campaign travel bills of $99,806, including a total of $21,407 paid to eighteen corporations for the use of their private jets. Among those corporations putting their aircraft at Gephardt's disposal were Federal Express of Memphis, Tenn.; the Perot Company of Dallas, Texas; Healthsouth Rehabilitation Corp. of Birmingham, Ala.; Syntex Communication of San Jose, Calif.; Ren Corp. of Nashville, Tenn.; and Hospital Investors Management of Englewood Cliffs, N.J.

Over the two-year election cycle, overhead and fund-raising expenses accounted for half of Gephardt's $3,065,439 campaign outlays. With a staff that never dropped below fifteen, Gephardt's permanent campaign was nothing less than a thriving small business dedicated to his reelection.

While Gephardt's was the Cadillac of permanent campaigns, it was by no means unique (see Table 2-1). Off-year expenses reported by the 349 House incumbents who contested the November general election totaled $39,128,255, or 20 percent of the money spent by these incumbents during the two-year election cycle. Rep. Robert K. Dornan (R-Calif.) spent $463,777 during 1991, including $403,929 on his nationwide direct-mail fund-raising effort. Minority Whip Newt Gingrich (R-Ga.) invested $461,636 in his off-year effort, including $169,514 in overhead and $139,273 in fund raising. Rep. Martin Frost (D-Texas) spent $406,199 in 1991, including $195,982 on overhead and $106,350 on fund raising. Rep. Ronald V. Dellums (D-Calif.) invested $385,644 to keep his permanent campaign operation humming, $186,018 of which was spent on direct-mail solicitations. Excluding four 1991 special election victors, 47 incumbents spent more during the off-year than the typical challenger spent on his or her entire campaign.

Similarly, the 28 senators who won renomination reported spending a total of $30,736,874 during the five-year period between January 1, 1987, and December 31, 1991, an average of $1,097,746. Overhead costs during this period amounted to $12,839,612, including $3,323,953 for after-tax salaries, $2,172,519 for payroll and income taxes, $2,634,013 for travel, and $1,008,747 for office furniture and supplies. Fund-raising outlays added $12,372,322, of which $6,176,246 was invested in events, $5,923,807 was spent on direct-mail solicitations, and $272,270 was put into telemarketing. Off-year expenses represented 26 percent of the money spent by Senate incumbents. Those with the largest off-year budgets were Alfonse M. D'Amato (R-N.Y.), $3,753,302; Bob Packwood (R-Ore.), $3,190,034; Arlen Specter (R-Pa.), 2,288,367; John Seymour (R-Calif.), $1,856,709; and Bob Kasten (R-Wis.), $1,687,704 (see Table 2-1).

This heavy investment in the "bricks and mortar" of politics continued into the election year. During 1992, House incumbents who won renomination reported spending $34,570,993 on office overhead and $19,049,546 on fund raising, which together accounted for 33 percent of their spending for the year. Senate incumbents spent $16,122,938 on overhead and $11,454,592 on fund raising, or 32 percent of their election-year outlays.

Put simply, in an age of entrepreneurial politics, the candidate's own organization has virtually replaced the local political party as the vehicle to electoral success. Whereas the local parties once supplied candidates with fund-raising assistance, office space, campaign literature and other campaign paraphernalia, and an army of eager volunteers who worked the phones and knocked on doors to turn out supporters on election day, candidates must now largely provide these things for themselves. Once elected, candidates have no reason to disband the campaign apparatus and every reason to maintain it. If anything, the real or imagined anti-incumbent fears that rippled through the 1992 elections served to increase many incumbents' investment in their permanent campaigns.

The 1992 versions of these modern political machines tended to have:

- *Well-appointed offices.* While some members opened additional offices as the election neared, most members have replaced the temporary storefront campaign headquarters with permanent offices to house their computers and other equipment. During the 1992 election cycle, rent and utilities payments reported by the 349 House members who contested the November general elections amounted to $3,210,015. Over the six-year Senate election cycle, the 28 incumbents who won renomination spent a total of $1,295,489 on rent and utilities.

- *Well-paid professional staffs.* During the 1992 election cycle, salaries, benefits, and payroll taxes represented 12 percent of the average House incumbent's budget, the same percentage as in 1990. In the Senate, the average outlay for these items climbed from 11 percent in 1990 to 12 percent in 1992. Many incumbent's leaned heavily on their congressional staffs to run their campaigns.

- *Lawyers and accountants.* Many members of Congress kept a lawyer, an accountant, or both on retainer. Incumbents with legal difficulties invariably used campaign funds to pay their legal bills, even when the matter had absolutely nothing to do with the election. During the 1992 cycle, House members paid $3,540,575 in legal and accounting fees; Senate incumbents spent $1,520,892.

- *Large travel budgets.* During 1991 and 1992, House incumbents reported spending a total of $7,439,927 on travel, an average of $21,318. In 1990 the average expenditure for travel among House incumbents was $16,247. Senate incumbents, all of whom traveled extensively to raise money, reported travel expenses totaling $5,647,008 during the six-year election cycle. The average outlay of $201,679 was $37,729 higher than the average travel expenses reported by senators who ran in 1990.

- *A year-round fund-raising operation.* Most members of Congress raise money continuously. The typical senator raised more than $14,000 a week during his or her six-year term, while the average House member raised more than $5,000 each week. That nonstop fund-raising effort had a high price tag: $54,660,343. The average House incumbent sank 15 percent of his or her budget into raising money; the comparable figure for senators was 21 percent.

- *Large entertainment budgets.* Most incumbents invested some of their campaign funds in constituent stroking. Some did nothing more than send year-end holiday cards, but many members also used campaign funds to purchase gifts, send flowers, and treat their supporters to lunch or dinner. On average, House incumbents spent $8,578 to stoke their constituents; the typical senator spent $29,820 over the six-year cycle. Comparable figures for House and Senate incumbents in 1990 were $6,741 and $30,038, respectively.

Table 2-1 The Top Twenty-Five Spenders in the 1992 Congressional Races: Off-Year Spending

	House		Senate	
Rank	Candidate	Expenditures	Candidate	Expenditures
1	Richard A. Gephardt, D-Mo.	$937,542	Dick Thornburgh,[a] R-Pa.	$4,261,596
2	John W. Olver,[a] D-Mass.	817,878	Alfonse M. D'Amato, R-N.Y.	3,753,302
3	Ed Pastor,[a] D-Ariz.	661,337	Harris Wofford,[a] D-Pa.	3,257,485
4	Sam Johnson,[a] R-Texas	500,880	Bob Packwood, R-Ore.	3,190,034
5	Robert K. Dornan, R-Calif.	463,777	Arlen Specter, R-Pa.	2,288,367
6	Newt Gingrich, R-Ga.	461,636	John Seymour, R-Calif.	1,856,709
7	Martin Frost, D-Texas	406,199	Bob Kasten, R-Wis.	1,687,704
8	Ronald V. Dellums, D-Calif.	385,644	Tom Daschle, D-S.D.	1,669,963
9	John P. Murtha, D-Pa.	377,282	Barbara Boxer,[a] D-Calif.	1,586,179
10	John D. Dingell, D-Mich.	364,960	Terry Sanford, D-N.C.	1,488,679
11	Joseph P. Kennedy II, D-Mass.	355,317	Dianne Feinstein,[a] D-Calif.	1,244,805
12	David E. Bonior, D-Mich.	339,097	Wyche Fowler, Jr., D-Ga.	1,218,666
13	Thomas W. Ewing,[a] R-Ill.	328,294	Barbara A. Mikulski, D-Md.	1,194,782
14	Robert T. Matsui, D-Calif.	320,895	Christopher S. Bond, R-Mo.	1,111,859
15	Helen Delich Bentley, R-Md.	308,352	Robert Abrams, D-N.Y.	1,036,036
16	Ron Marlenee, D-Mont.	307,797	Christopher J. Dodd, D-Conn.	977,286
17	Jerry F. Costello, D-Ill.	307,505	Bruce Herschensohn, R-Calif.	926,863
18	Tom McMillen, D-Md.	306,273	Daniel K. Inouye, D-Hawaii	886,842
19	Thomas J. Downey, D-N.Y.	282,725	Ernest F. Hollings, D-S.C.	881,100
20	Norman Y. Mineta, D-Calif.	280,393	John McCain, R-Ariz.	875,064
21	Les Aspin, D-Wis.	270,167	Daniel R. Coats, R-Ind.	816,501
22	Sam M. Gibbons, D-Fla.	262,265	Harry Reid, D-Nev.	716,617
23	Howard L. Berman, D-Calif.	258,958	Wendell H. Ford, D-Ky.	716,151
24	Charles B. Rangel, D-N.Y.	253,237	Bob Dole, R-Kan.	680,274
25	Bud Shuster, R-Pa.	252,110	John B. Breaux, D-La.	647,257

Note: Totals are for entire two-year House and six-year Senate cycles; both include special election expenditures.
[a] Nonincumbent or special election candidate.

Table 2-2 The Top Twenty-Five Spenders in the 1992 Congressional Races: Campaign Office Basics

	House		Senate	
Rank	Candidate	Expenditures	Candidate	Expenditures
1	Michael Huffington,[a] R-Calif.	$261,749	Alfonse M. D'Amato, R-N.Y.	$792,772
2	Richard A. Gephardt, D-Mo.	249,832	Carol Moseley-Braun,[a] D-Ill.	702,201
3	Newt Gingrich, R-Ga.	156,461	Barbara Boxer,[a] D-Calif.	636,649
4	Thomas J. Downey, D-N.Y.	131,366	Arlen Specter, R-Pa.	634,367
5	Tom McMillen, D-Md.	129,882	Dianne Feinstein,[a] D-Calif.	425,521
6	Martin Frost, D-Texas	122,378	Bob Kasten, R-Wis.	420,380
7	Sam Gejdenson, D-Conn.	118,315	Bruce Herschensohn,[a] R-Calif.	388,305
8	Joe Moakley, D-Mass.	110,174	Daniel K. Inouye, D-Hawaii	379,225
9	Helen Delich Bentley, R-Md.	109,902	Lynn Yeakel,[a] D-Pa.	360,622
10	Pete Geren, D-Texas	108,051	Christopher J. Dodd, D-Conn.	327,718
11	Elton Gallegly, R-Calif.	106,898	John Seymour, R-Calif.	311,292
12	Joseph P. Kennedy II, D-Mass.	105,607	Robert Abrams, D-N.Y.	310,722
13	Joe L. Barton, R-Texas	103,969	Tom Daschle, D-S.D.	302,616
14	Ron Marlenee, D-Mont.	98,876	Terry Sanford, D-N.C.	252,811
15	Richard H. Baker, R-La.	96,968	Ernest F. Hollings, D-S.C.	242,196
16	John P. Murtha, D-Pa.	95,480	John McCain, R-Ariz.	241,612
17	Steny H. Hoyer, D-Md.	88,523	Les AuCoin,[a] D-Ore.	239,103
18	Michael A. Andrews, D-Texas	88,184	Daniel R. Coats, R-Ind.	237,314
19	Bob Carr, D-Mich.	86,009	Robert F. Bennett, R-Utah	231,313
20	Jane Harman,[a] D-Calif.	85,918	Wyche Fowler, Jr., D-Ga.	228,748
21	Vic Fazio, D-Calif.	85,758	Christopher S. Bond, R-Mo.	221,875
22	Sam M. Gibbons, D-Fla.	85,729	Bob Graham, D-Fla.	179,948
23	Jack Fields, R-Texas	84,789	Russell D. Feingold,[a] D-Wis.	179,284
24	John W. Olver,[a] D-Mass.	81,709	Harris Wofford,[a] D-Pa.	170,600
25	Joseph J. DioGuardi,[a] R-N.Y.	79,547	Wendell H. Ford, D-Ky.	166,715

Note: Totals are for entire two-year House and six-year Senate cycles; both include special election expenditures.
[a] Nonincumbent or special election candidate.

- *Sizable donations.* To build political bridges with constituents and other politicians, House members donated $9,087,185 to other candidates, political party committees, ideological groups, and civic organizations during the 1992 election cycle. The 28 Senators seeking reelection in 1992 collectively gave away $1,566,247 of their campaign funds during their six-year cycle.
- *Political consultants.* To one degree or another, most candidates depended on consultants to mold their campaign. Some candidates simply turned over their day-to-day campaign operations to general consultants. Others used consultants for specific tasks—to help orchestrate the nonstop fund-raising activities, design persuasion mailers, or create an advertising campaign. During the 1992 election cycle, House candidates paid these braintrusts a total of $126,335,527; Senate candidates paid their consultants $121,258,601. In all, payments to consultants accounted for 46 percent of total spending.
- *Investments.* Members of Congress earned substantial income by investing their campaign cash reserves. D'Amato collected $575,115 in interest on his cash reserves over the six-year Senate cycle. Rep. David Dreier (R-Calif.) collected $245,083 in investment income on his $2 million campaign treasury; this accounted for 38 percent of his total receipts during 1991 and 1992. Dreier's investment income was more than ten times as much as his Democratic opponent, Al Wachtel, managed to scrape together for his token challenge. Rep. Dan Rostenkowski (D-Ill.) reported investment income of $212,723. However, in Rostenkowski's case, not all his investments proved to be money-makers. He reported investment expenses and losses with Prudential Securities totaling $60,314. He also paid Salomon Brothers $18,942 for what he termed "decreased bond value."

As in the 1990 election cycle, these permanent campaign organizations were built almost entirely without regard to the strength of real or anticipated political opposition. Of the $80,338,485 House incumbents spent on overhead and fund raising, 50 percent was spent by members whose reelection was never really in doubt. The 130 incumbents who received between 61 percent and 70 percent of the vote in both their primary and general elections spent an average of $511,838. The average expenditure reported by the 69 incumbents who received 71 percent of the vote or more was $366,194. On average, the 9 Senate incumbents who garnered more than 60 percent of the vote reported spending $2,588,020.

First elected in 1986, Rep. Mike Espy (D-Miss.) won reelection with 65 percent of the vote in 1988 and 84 percent in 1990. He had no Democratic primary opposition in 1992 and garnered 76 percent in the general election. Nevertheless, Espy spent $256,309 on his 1992 campaign. His off-year overhead expenses of $49,656 actually exceeded his election year outlays for overhead by $28,319. The $18,728 he spent to raise money in 1992 was $16,813 less than he invested in fund raising during 1991.

Rep. Dan Burton (R-Ind.) had received 63 percent of the vote or better in each of his five previous House races, and redistricting made his solidly Republican district even more Republican. Even so, Burton invested $399,952 in his 1992 reelection effort—nearly fifteen times as much as his Democrat challenger, Natalie M. Bruner, was able to spend. Burton spent $123,484 in 1991 alone to keep his permanent campaign operation running smoothly, including $73,298 on overhead and $24,809 on fund raising. He spent $11,743 in 1991 on meals apparently unrelated to his fund-raising efforts or constituent entertainment, which amounted to 44 percent of Bruner's entire campaign budget. Burton prevailed with 72 percent of the vote.

Rep. Tom Lantos (D-Calif.) ran the quintessential permanent campaign. Having received two-thirds of the vote or more in four successive contests and having been helped, if anything, by redistricting, Lantos spent $600,660 during the 1992 election cycle. In the off-year, Lantos spent $216,505 to keep his campaign machinery well oiled, including $73,025 on overhead and $112,934 on fund raising. His Republican opponent, realtor Jim Tomlin, spent a total of $5,555.

In a district where registered Republicans comprised 52 percent of the electorate and registered Democrats accounted for only slightly more than 30 percent, Republican Rep. John Kyl (Ariz.) outspent his Democratic challenger, Walter R. Mybeck, by one hundred to one. Needless to say, most of Kyl's efforts were directed at maintaining his political machine, not at defeating the underfunded Mybeck. In 1991 Kyl spent $104,785, including $60,219 on overhead, $29,321 on fund raising, and $3,989 on year-end holiday cards and constituent gifts. Over the two-year election cycle, such expenditures accounted for 65 percent of Kyl's spending.

Having garnered 70 percent of the vote in winning his fourth term in 1986 and facing a 1992 challenger who spent $331,513 to attract 31 percent of the votes, Sen. Bob Dole (R-Kan.) put $2,177,754 into his reelection effort. Off-year spending accounted for 31 percent of Dole's investment.

Kentucky's senior senator, Democrat Wendell H. Ford, had won 65 percent of the vote or more in his two previous reelection bids. His 1992 Republican opponent, David L. Williams, had just $353,805 to invest in the campaign. Nevertheless, Ford spent $2,283,638, in part because he invested $716,151 to keep his permanent campaign running during the off-years.

As these examples illustrate, the permanent, high-octane campaign was a bipartisan phenomenon. It could be found in every state. It has become a hallmark of modern politics. While the House ethics committee has ruled that campaign funds should not be used for any purpose that is not "exclusively and solely" for the benefit of the campaign, some members routinely treat their campaign treasuries as slush funds, paying for a host of purchases that fall well outside even a loose interpretation of that rule.

CAMPAIGN HEADQUARTERS

There is perhaps no greater misnomer in the political lexicon than "campaign headquarters." While candidates once opened their offices a few months before the election and closed them the day after the campaign ended, those days are long gone. Discouraged by House and Senate rules from using their taxpayer-funded congressional offices for purely political purposes and largely robbed of an effective local political party structure, most incumbents maintain a "political office," which is dedicated to a host of activities that further their political fortunes.

During the 1992 election cycle, House and Senate incumbents spent a total of $19,014,669 on their most basic political office expenses: $4,505,504 on rent and utilities, $5,204,412 on office furniture and supplies, $4,678,433 on telephone service, and $4,626,320 on computers and other office equipment. Over the two-year cycle, the typical House member reported spending $35,541 on such items; the comparable figure for senators was $236,030 over the six-year cycle. Thirty-five percent of this spending on political infrastructure, or $6,705,619, was spent during the off-years. During 1991, the average House incumbent spent $11,060 on such items. Between January 1, 1987, and December 31, 1991, these items cost the average senator seeking reelection $102,422.

Taken at face value, these numbers would suggest considerable change between the 1990 and 1992 election cycles. Compared with 1990, average reported spending in 1992 on infrastructure was up 22 percent among House incumbents and down 12 percent among Senate incumbents. However, when such payments are examined as a proportion of total spending, these shifts appear much less dramatic.

In the 1990 cycle, rent, utilities, office furniture, supplies, telephone service, computers, and other office equipment accounted for 7.47 percent of the typical House incumbent's budget; for 1992 the comparable figure was 6.23 percent. The average senator committed 6.57 percent of his or her budget to such items during the 1990 cycle; in 1992 the average was 5.70 percent. What had been considered a political necessity in 1990 remained a political necessity in 1992. This marginal decline in the proportion of the average budget devoted to these basic items was as much a function of the record number of retirements by entrenched incumbents as it was evidence of a fundamental change in politics.

D'Amato set the pace for Senate incumbents, with outlays of $792,772, including $217,716 for rent and utilities (see Table 2-2). Over the six-year cycle, his campaign paid $278,180 for office furniture and supplies and $118,648 for computer hardware, software, and other office equipment. Telephone service cost $178,228, including $52,253 for the use of cellular telephones and $3,963 for beepers. Sixty percent of these outlays were made between January 1, 1987, and December 31, 1991.

Other incumbent senators who invested heavily in their most basic campaign overhead were Specter, $634,367; Kasten, $420,380; Daniel K. Inouye (D-Hawaii), $379,225; Christopher J. Dodd (D-Conn.), $327,718; and Seymour, $311,292. The biggest off-year spenders on infrastructure were D'Amato, $472,634; Specter, $342,662; Kasten $215,507; Tom Daschle (D-S.D.), $191,616; Terry Sanford (D-N.C.), $122,767; and Daniel R. Coats (R-Ind.), $108,392.

In the House, those who invested most heavily in basic office overhead were Reps. Gephardt, $249,832; Gingrich, $156,461; Thomas J. Downey (D-N.Y.), $131,366; Tom McMillen (D-Md.), $129,882; Frost, $122,378; and Sam Gejdenson (D-Conn.), $118,315 (see Table 2-2). The heaviest off-year spenders were Gephardt, $95,509; Downey, $63,897; Gejdenson, $55,937; Helen Delich Bentley (D-Md.), $52,226; Joe L. Barton (R-Texas), $50,751; and Joseph P. Kennedy II (D-Mass.), $48,231.

In some cases, these outlays benefited members of Congress personally, as well as politically. During the 1992 election cycle, Rostenkowski's campaign paid $30,000 to rent space in a building he and his sisters owned. Rostenkowski's campaign had rented the space continuously since 1986, and during that time its monthly rent had risen from $500 to $1,250—a steeper rise than justified by market conditions, according to local real estate analysts. The campaign paid $1,642 for cable television service, which included several premium movie channels, for the office space. The space was connected by a hallway to Rostenkowski's home in an adjacent building and, according to local press reports, no cable service was provided to his residence.

Rostenkowski was not alone. The permanent campaign office of Rep. Lamar Smith (R-Texas) was located on the bottom floor of a condominium he owns. Smith charged his campaign monthly rent of $857 for the first thirteen months of the election cycle; in February 1992 he raised the rent to $926. The campaign also paid for upkeep on the property, including $314 to Orkin Pest Control, $221 for the repair of an air conditioning unit, $194 to repair an alarm system for the building, $169 for service on a heat pump, $50 for a furnace checkup, and $203 for unspecified office repairs.

Sen. Dale Bumpers (D-Ark.) used campaign funds to rent an apartment in Little Rock where he stayed whenever he traveled home to Arkansas. By the end of 1992, the apartment rent cost the campaign $530 a month.

CAMPAIGN STAFF

As Gephardt's permanent campaign illustrates, year-round campaign offices do not run themselves. During the 1992 election cycle, incumbents who contested the November general elections paid their full-time and part-time employees a total of $26,646,752, an 11 percent increase over 1990. Given the fact that many fewer incumbents sought reelection in 1992—349 in 1992 versus 405 in 1990—this increase is particularly astounding. Off-year payroll expenses amounted to $7,599,342.

In the Senate, Specter paid after-tax salaries and benefits totaling $994,312, of which $507,704 was paid out during the off-years. D'Amato's payroll reached $716,721 by the end of 1992, with off-year salaries totaling $328,240. Daschle's employees received $686,475 over the six-year cycle, $409,327 of which was collected in the off-years. Total and off-year payrolls for Sen. Ernest F. Hollings (D-S.C.) were $563,941 and $246,064, respectively (see Table 2-3).

Table 2-3 The Top Twenty-Five Spenders in the 1992 Congressional Races: Salaries

	House		Senate	
Rank	Candidate	Expenditures	Candidate	Expenditures
1	Michael Huffington,[a] R-Calif.	$424,215	Barbara Boxer,[a] D-Calif.	$1,165,444
2	Richard A. Gephardt, D-Mo.	413,335	Carol Moseley-Braun,[a] D-Ill.	1,038,949
3	Joe Moakley, D-Mass.	247,780	Arlen Specter, R-Pa.	994,312
4	Newt Gingrich, R-Ga.	229,477	Bruce Herschensohn,[a] R-Calif.	973,918
5	Helen Delich Bentley, R-Md.	218,190	Alfonse M. D'Amato, R-N.Y.	716,721
6	Jane Harman,[a] D-Calif.	205,990	Tom Daschle, D-S.D.	686,475
7	Sam M. Gibbons, D-Fla.	189,218	Dianne Feinstein,[a] D-Calif.	669,526
8	Thomas J. Downey, D-N.Y.	188,203	Lynn Yeakel,[a] D-Pa.	574,358
9	John W. Olver,[a] D-Mass.	167,419	Ernest F. Hollings, D-S.C.	563,941
10	John Bryant, D-Texas	163,639	Bob Kasten, R-Wis.	550,284
11	Dave Nagle, D-Iowa	162,436	Robert F. Bennett,[a] R-Utah	503,326
12	Gerry E. Studds, D-Mass.	162,371	Robert Abrams,[a] D-N.Y.	495,344
13	Martin Frost, D-Texas	154,438	John Seymour, R-Calif.	491,765
14	Pat Williams, D-Mont.	154,365	Christopher J. Dodd, D-Conn.	467,713
15	Jack Reed, D-R.I.	153,485	Terry Sanford, D-N.C.	453,870
16	Thomas J. Bliley, Jr., R-Va.	152,971	Les AuCoin,[a] D-Ore.	439,190
17	Les Aspin, D-Wis.	152,786	Paul Coverdell,[a] R-Ga.	419,091
18	Bill Green, R-N.Y.	152,322	Daniel R. Coats, R-Ind.	369,179
19	Ron Marlenee, D-Mont.	148,620	Rod Chandler,[a] R-Wash.	328,441
20	Frank Pallone, Jr., D-N.J.	146,855	Richard Williamson,[a] R-Ill.	322,458
21	Marjorie Margolies-Mezvinsky,[a] D-Pa.	140,261	Bob Packwood, R-Ore.	318,469
22	Dick Chrysler,[a] R-Mich.	135,889	Harris Wofford,[a] D-Pa.	309,474
23	Joan Milke Flores,[a] R-Calif.	135,173	John Glenn, D-Ohio	306,395
24	Jack Fields, R-Texas	134,718	Christopher S. Bond, R-Mo.	294,603
25	Sander M. Levin, D-Mich.	132,854	Don Nickles, R-Okla.	290,731

Note: Totals are for entire two-year House and six-year Senate cycles; both include special election expenditures.

[a] Nonincumbent or special election candidate.

Among House incumbents, Gephardt's $413,335 payroll was the largest by far. It was more than twice what he spent on salaries and benefits in 1990. Others who invested heavily in staff were Joe Moakley (D-Mass.), $247,780; Gingrich, $229,477; Bentley, $218,190; Rep. Sam M. Gibbons (D-Fla.), $189,218; Downey, $188,203; John Bryant (D-Texas), $163,639; Dave Nagle (D-Iowa), $162,436; and Gerry E. Studds (D-Mass.), $162,371 (see Table 2-3).

Incumbents were not the only ones building sizable campaign staffs. During her nonstop two-year Senate campaign to succeed retiring Sen. Alan Cranston, Rep. Barbara Boxer (D-Calif.) incurred the largest payroll of any Senate candidate—$1,165,444. While she was in the race for considerably less than two years, Carol Moseley-Braun ran up the second highest payroll among Senate candidates. A hefty 14 percent of Moseley-Braun's $1,038,949 payroll, or $144,550, was paid to her campaign manager, Z. Kgosie Matthews, who was also her fiancee at one point. Matthews made considerably more during his brief tenure than any other campaign manager.

California Republican Michael Huffington, who knocked off Rep. Robert J. Lagomarsino in the primary, led all House candidates by paying out $424,215 in salaries. More than fifty people drew payroll checks from Huffington's campaign during 1992. Democrat Jane Harman, who prevailed in one of California's fifteen open seat contests, ranked sixth among all House candidates, spending $205,990 on salary payments.

Many campaigns referred to members of their staff as "consultants," despite the fact that they worked regular hours under the supervision of the candidate or another senior staff member. By labeling their employees consultants, candidates avoided paying payroll taxes and other benefits. Ordinary entrepreneurs have been routinely called to task by the Internal Revenue Service for this practice, but since campaigns are rarely audited, few candidates have ever been fined or even questioned.

Nagle paid no taxes on his $162,436 payroll. Republican Joan Milke Flores, who was defeated by Harman in California's District 36, dispensed payroll checks totaling $135,173 without paying any taxes. Pennsylvania Republican Jon D. Fox, who lost to Democrat Marjorie Margolies-Mezvinsky, paid no taxes on his $127,510 payroll. Bob Filner (D-Calif.) paid no taxes, yet his payroll amounted to $124,414. In all, forty House candidates had payrolls in excess of $50,000 and opted not to pay taxes (see Table 2-4).

Although congressional staffers are forbidden from doing campaign work on government time, they are not prohibited from donating their own time to their boss's reelection efforts. Some members of Congress take full advantage of this caveat, leaning heavily on their congressional staffs to manage the day-to-day operations of their campaigns.

At $99,041, the payroll of Rep. Nancy L. Johnson (R-Conn.)

was not one of the fifty highest, but 89 percent of what she paid out in salaries went to members of her congressional staff. Rep. Bob Carr (D-Mich.) invested $128,968, or about 10 percent of his $1.3 million campaign, in salaries. Carr's congressional staff collected 66 percent, or $85,640, of those payments. Downey paid $84,631 of his $188,203 payroll to congressional staffers. Rep. Peter H. Kostmayer (D-Pa.) paid 63 percent of his $117,601 payroll to congressional staffers in his loss to Republican James C. Greenwood. In Maryland, McMillen, who lost to Republican Rep. Wayne T. Gilchrest, sank $119,391 of his $1,527,903 treasury into salaries, $63,761 of which went to congressional staffers. In all, eleven House incumbents paid members of their congressional staffs salaries totaling more than $50,000 (see Table 2-5).

Of the $80,776 Lantos paid out in campaign salaries, $29,500 went to fifteen members of his congressional staff. These payments included $20,500 in bonuses, which ranged from $500 to $5,000. Nine of the staffers receiving bonuses had not been paid by the campaign previously.

As in 1990, one of the more interesting examples of this double-dipping involved Rep. Bill McCollum (R-Fla.). Staff salaries accounted for a hefty 15 percent of McCollum's campaign budget, largely because he paid two of his congressional staffers a total of $56,815. McCollum's chief of staff, Vaughn S. Forrest, drew large, lump-sum payments from the 1992 campaign for "consulting," as he had in the 1990 campaign. Forrest received four campaign checks totaling $38,190 between April 16, 1991, and June 1, 1992. Forrest's last check from the McCollum campaign came just months before his request that he be allowed to remain on the congressional payroll while campaigning for the District 7 House race against John L. Mica, which he ultimately lost. "I am not a millionaire. Millionaires quit to run," Forrest told a local newspaper.

Over the six-year Senate election cycle, seventeen members of Daschle's staff received salary payments totaling $243,472 from the campaign, 80 percent of which went to three staffers. State director Richard P. Weiland collected $87,850 to augment his government salary. Staff assistant Rita Lewis and special assistant Peter Stavrianos received campaign salaries totaling $66,879 and $39,172 respectively. On December 21, 1992 the campaign issued checks ranging from $1,500 to $4,000 to fourteen Senate staffers for what appeared to be year-end bonuses (see Table 2-5).

Specter was also heavily dependent upon his congressional staff to keep his campaign on an even keel. Eighteen of his Senate staffers drew payroll checks totaling $237,075. Mark Meyer, a caseworker in Specter's Pittsburgh office, collected $64,362. Other staffers drawing sizable checks were staff assistant Tom Bowman, $42,393; legislative assistant Charles D. Brooks, $27,539; press secretary Daniel J. McKenna, $18,799; executive director Patrick L. Meehan, $18,255; executive director Steve Dunkle, $14,334; and legislative assistant Anne Pizzoli, $13,809.

Packwood paid eleven Senate employees a total of $163,058, with $87,428 of it going to Elaine Franklin, his chief of staff. Press and community liaison Matt Evans and staff

Table 2-4 The Top Fifteen Spenders in the 1992 House Races: Payrolls Without Taxes

Rank	Candidate	Expenditures
1	Dave Nagle, D-Iowa	$162,436
2	Joan Milke Flores,[a] R-Calif.	135,173
3	Jon D. Fox,[a] R-Pa.	127,510
4	Bob Filner,[a] D-Calif.	124,414
5	Bill Filante,[a] R-Calif.	122,312
6	Hamilton Fish, Jr., R-N.Y.	118,433
7	Peter Torkildsen,[a] R-Mass.	98,912
8	Jim McCrery, R-La.	98,227
9	Ken Calvert,[a] R-Calif.	97,308
10	Terry Everett,[a] R-Ala.	95,715
11	Cathey Steinberg,[a] D-Ga.	94,900
12	Lamar Smith, R-Texas	90,964
13	Jay C. Kim,[a] R-Calif.	82,012
14	Charles Wilson, D-Texas	81,284
15	John Linder,[a] R-Ga.	77,974

Note: Totals are for the entire two-year cycle.
[a] Nonincumbent or special election candidate.

assistant Laura Fetuuaho collected $27,182 and $16,790, respectively.

D'Amato paid special assistant Kieran Mahoney and public affairs director Zenia Mucha campaign salaries of $73,826 and $44,173, respectively. Susan LaBombard, the Washington, D.C., congressional office manager for Sen. Christopher S. Bond (R-Mo.), collected campaign payroll checks totaling $53,471.

In all, thirty Senate staffers collected campaign checks of $20,000 or more.

While some members are extremely careful to separate their official government business from the business of campaigning, others are not. The gray area that has been established between the two staff functions has opened the door to ethical abuses. Take, for example, the case of Rep. Carroll Hubbard, Jr. (D-Ky.), who lost to Tom Barlow in the Democratic primary.

In April 1994 Hubbard plead guilty to federal charges that he had misappropriated more than $50,000 in campaign funds and had ordered members of his congressional staff to work on his and his wife's 1992 House campaigns while on the government payroll. According to Hubbard's statement, his staff members arranged campaign schedules, solicited campaign contributions, and campaigned in Kentucky under assumed names, all at taxpayer expense.

Although it was fairly common practice for members of Congress to rely heavily on spouses or other family members to run their campaigns, some members took the opportunity to pay their relatives handsomely for their time. Most incumbents who opted to pay family members had done so in 1990, as well.

In his final campaign before joining the new Clinton administration as secretary of agriculture, Espy reached out to his brother Tom. Payments to his brother and to his brother's firm,

Table 2-5 The Top Fifteen Spenders in the 1992 Congressional Races: Congressional Staff Payroll

	House		Senate	
Rank	Candidate	Expenditures	Candidate	Expenditures
1	Nancy L. Johnson, R-Conn.	$87,823	Tom Daschle, D-S.D.	$243,472
2	Bob Carr, D-Mich.	85,640	Arlen Specter, R-Pa.	237,075
3	Thomas J. Downey, D-N.Y.	84,631	Bob Packwood, R-Ore.	163,058
4	Peter H. Kostmayer, D-Pa.	73,579	Harry Reid, D-Nev.	139,689
5	Tom McMillen, D-Md.	63,761	Kent Conrad, D-N.D.	134,130
6	David E. Bonior, D-Mich.	62,707	Alfonse M. D'Amato, R-N.Y.	129,089
7	Jim McCrery, R-La.	60,292	Rod Chandler, R-Wash.	110,825
8	Pat Williams, D-Mont.	59,154	Christopher S. Bond, R-Mo.	108,950
9	Steny H. Hoyer, D-Md.	59,099	Don Nickles, R-Okla.	98,488
10	Joe Moakley, D-Mass.	57,986	Terry Sanford, D-N.C.	92,759
11	Bill McCollum, R-Fla.	56,815	Barbara A. Mikulski, D-Md.	69,743
12	Michael A. Andrews, D-Texas	48,684	John McCain, R-Ariz.	65,511
13	Frank Pallone, Jr., D-N.J.	47,458	Wyche Fowler, Jr., D-Ga.	59,278
14	Bernard Sanders, I-Vt.	46,825	Ernest F. Hollings, D-S.C.	45,335
15	E. Clay Shaw, Jr., R-Fla.	44,802	Dale Bumpers, D-Ark.	40,992

Note: Totals are for entire two-year House and six-year Senate cycles; both include special election expenditures.

Reliance Consultants, amounted to $66,369, or 26 percent of Espy's total spending. Neither of the Espys returned calls to clarify precisely what services Tom Espy performed for the campaign, although in 1990 Reliance had collected $24,608 for fund raising and get-out-the-vote efforts.

Fund raising, in particular, proved to be a family affair. Rep. Gary A. Franks (R-Conn.) paid his wife Donna $23,890 for serving as his principal fund-raiser. Robin Dornan Griffin, Dornan's daughter and chief creative consultant on his direct-mail fund-raising program, received $55,353 for her efforts. Rep. Donald M. Payne (D-N.J.) paid his brother William $68,024 for serving as his campaign's fund-raising consultant. Rep. Jolene Unsoeld paid her daughter, Terres Unsoeld, $18,637 to stage events in Los Angeles.

Rep. Steve Gunderson (R-Wis.) paid his brother Matthew $26,400 for serving as his campaign manager. His sister, Naomi Bodway, served as the campaign's general consultant. Her firm, KaestnerBodway of Middleton, Wis., collected $31,585 for that advice, as well as for supplying yard signs, campaign buttons, and bumper stickers.

Rep. Esteban E. Torres (D-Calif.) again chose to leave the management of his permanent campaign to his daughter, Carmen Garcia. Payments to Garcia, who also coordinated fund-raising events, crafted the persuasion mail, and wrote the campaign's fund-raising solicitations, amounted to $66,990, or more than one-quarter of Torres's $256,596 budget for the two-year election cycle.

Others who put their relatives on the campaign payroll included Rep. Sander M. Levin (D-Mich.), who paid his son Matthew $13,426 for work on the campaign during the off-year. As in 1990, Lantos paid his daughter, Katrina Lantos-Swett, $22,600 for serving as his campaign treasurer. Rep. Ralph M. Hall (D-Texas) had only one permanent employee, his daughter-in-law, Jody Hall, who collected $39,644 in salary payments.

Legal Services

The 1992 election cycle produced its share of high-profile legal and ethical investigations involving members of Congress. While House and Senate rules allow members to establish separate committees to raise money to cover the legal bills incurred during such investigations, most members tap their campaign treasuries to cover at least part of the cost.

In the House, Rostenkowski found himself under federal scrutiny for possible misuse of both his campaign and congressional office accounts. During 1992 he spent $156,953 of his campaign treasury on his legal defense (see Table 2-6). The Washington, D.C., law firms of Brand & Lowell and Katten, Muchin, Zavis & Dombroff collected $71,892 and $10,132, respectively. Chicago attorney Thomas A. Jaconetty received $3,018. Rostenkowski also tapped his campaign for $71,911 to cover legal bills incurred by his administrative assistant, Virginia C. Fletcher, and one of his staff assistants, Mary Lesinski. In all, bills associated with his well-publicized legal problems accounted for 11 percent of Rostenkowski's campaign outlays.

The target of a federal investigation that led to his indictment on bribery charges in May 1992, Rep. Joseph M. McDade (R-Pa.) tapped his campaign treasury to cover $97,217 in legal fees associated with his defense. Two Washington, D.C., law firms, Brand & Lowell and McCamish, Martin & Loeffler, received $50,000 and $10,000, respectively. Sal Cognetti, Jr., of Scranton, Pa., collected $37,000.

Rep. Nicholas Mavroules (D-Mass.) was indicted by a federal grand jury in August 1992 on seventeen counts of racketeering, bribery, and income tax evasion. He spent $78,148 of his campaign treasury to defray the cost of his defense. Following his November loss to Republican Peter G. Torkildsen, Mavroules was convicted and sent to prison.

Heading into the 1992 campaign, Rep. Harold E. Ford (D-Tenn.) was facing a second trial on federal mail, bank, and tax fraud charges. Between January 1, 1987 and December 31, 1991, he had spent $393,976 from his campaign treasury to pay legal bills associated with his defense. At the beginning of 1992, he began paying for all such expenses out of a separate legal defense committee, which allowed him to reduce campaign outlays for his defense from $172,000 in 1990 to $51,413 in the 1992 cycle. On April 9, 1993 Ford was acquitted on all charges.

Under the cloud of a grand jury investigation that would ultimately lead to his indictment and conviction on federal bribery and racketeering charges, Rep. Albert G. Bustamante (D-Texas) diverted $46,380 of his campaign funds to his legal defense.

In the Senate, members set up separate legal defense committees, which have not been included as part of their campaign outlays. In August 1991 the Senate ethics committee dropped a two-year probe of D'Amato, who had been accused, among other things, of allowing his brother to use his Senate office facilities for personal business. Rather than tapping his campaign funds to repay more than $400,000 in legal bills, D'Amato established a "Legal Expense Trust Fund" in December 1991.

Criminal and ethical investigations were not the only reasons for incurring large legal bills. Once it became clear that Illinois would lose two House seats, Democratic Rep. Jerry F. Costello paid $84,000 to his attorney, Grey Chatham of Belleville, to make sure his interests in the redistricting process would be well taken care of.

State senator Gene Green (D-Texas) appeared to win his runoff election by a mere 180 votes, after finishing second to Houston City Council member Ben Reyes in the five-candidate Democratic primary. However, the results were overturned by a state district judge when it was discovered that several hundred people who had voted in the Republican primary illegally crossed over to vote in the Democratic runoff. That necessitated a third campaign, which Green won by 1,132 votes. Green's legal bills and court costs associated with the case amounted to $63,499 and $17,555, respectively.

Following the 1990 campaign, New Hampshire Democrat Joseph F. Keefe filed a nuisance complaint with the Federal Election Commission (FEC), charging that Republican Bill Zeliff had made an improper $150,000 loan to his campaign. Since the loan was made using proceeds from the sale of property Zeliff and his wife jointly owned, Keefe argued that half the loan was really an illegal campaign contribution made by Zeliff's wife. Zeliff paid the Washington, D.C., law firm Wiley, Rein & Fielding $40,250 from his 1992 campaign treasury for its work on the complaint.

Other candidates relied on their attorneys to make certain that campaign financial statements were filed correctly with the FEC. In all, House and Senate candidates paid their attorneys $2,646,921.

TRAVEL

Travel is a fact of life for members of Congress (see Table 2-7). Many House members return to their districts several times a month, if not every weekend. In addition to trips home,

Table 2-6 The Top Twenty-Five Spenders in the 1992 House Races: Legal Services

Rank	Candidate	Expenditures
1	Dan Rostenkowski, D-Ill.	$156,953
2	Joseph M. McDade, R-Pa.	97,217
3	Jerry F. Costello, D-Ill.	84,000
4	Nicholas Mavroules, D-Mass.	78,148
5	Michael Huffington,[a] R-Calif.	72,501
6	Gene Green,[a] D-Texas	63,499
7	Joe L. Barton, R-Texas	56,322
8	Martin Frost, D-Texas	56,290
9	Harold E. Ford, D-Tenn.	51,413
10	Nita M. Lowey, D-N.Y.	47,347
11	Albert G. Bustamante, D-Texas	46,380
12	Joe Moakley, D-Mass.	45,885
13	Bill Green, R-N.Y.	44,069
14	Gary A. Condit, D-Calif.	40,422
15	Bill Zeliff, R-N.H.	40,250
16	Tom Lantos, D-Calif.	39,898
17	Vic Fazio, D-Calif.	37,563
18	Robert T. Matsui, D-Calif.	35,168
19	Sonny Callahan, R-Ala.	35,000
20	John D. Dingell, D-Mich.	33,900
21	Cardiss Collins, D-Ill.	32,863
22	Sander M. Levin, D-Mich.	32,721
23	Peter Hoagland, D-Neb.	31,340
24	Eliot L. Engel, D-N.Y.	30,332
25	Mary Rose Oakar, D-Ohio	28,960

Note: Totals are for the entire two-year cycle.
[a] Nonincumbent or special election candidate.

Senators scour the country for money. With far more money than they need to campaign, many incumbents choose to travel in a style reserved only for the very wealthy. In the more than 7,000 campaign financial reports we examined, we found thousands of expenditures for chartered airplanes, expensive hotels, and fine restaurants. In many instances, the travel clearly had nothing to do with their campaigns.

Rep. Louis Stokes tapped his campaign treasury in January 1991 for $1,841 to pay the bill at the Washington Hilton and Towers for "candidate and family hotel accommodations." He spent $1,285 of his campaign funds to pay for him and his family to participate in "the New York Congressional Tour" in March 1991. The campaign picked up another $1,861 tab in September 1991 at the Washington Hilton and Towers for "candidate and family hotel accommodations." In April 1992 his campaign paid $351 for his family's hotel accommodations at Walt Disney World Resorts in Orlando, Fla., and $2,385 for "candidate's family air fare." He spent $2,343 of his treasury to take his family to New York for the Democratic National Convention in July 1992, and there was another $555 expense in October for his family's air fare and a $3,199 hotel bill at the Washington Hilton and Towers, where he and his family stayed during the Congressional Black Caucus's annual weekend bash. Stokes closed out the election cycle with December payments of $682 to cover "candidate and family hotel accommodations" at

Table 2-7 The Top Twenty-Five Spenders in the 1992 Congressional Races: Travel

	House		Senate	
Rank	Candidate	Expenditures	Candidate	Expenditures
1	Richard A. Gephardt, D-Mo.	$191,711	Bob Kasten, R-Wis.	$462,716
2	Ron Marlenee, D-Mont.	119,392	Daniel K. Inouye, D-Hawaii	442,292
3	Bud Shuster, R-Pa.	102,561	Carol Moseley-Braun,[a] D-Ill.	401,492
4	Bill Richardson, D-N.M.	96,788	Arlen Specter, R-Pa.	372,297
5	Jim Ross Lightfoot, R-Iowa	91,407	Bob Dole, R-Kan.	368,244
6	Albert G. Bustamante, D-Texas	89,884	Alfonse M. D'Amato, R-N.Y.	340,733
7	Don Sundquist, R-Tenn.	88,576	Ernest F. Hollings, D-S.C.	323,769
8	Thomas S. Foley, D-Wash.	82,659	John Seymour, R-Calif.	310,522
9	Don Young, R-Alaska	76,232	Christopher S. Bond, R-Mo.	270,041
10	Pat Williams, D-Mont.	74,306	Tom Daschle, D-S.D.	267,654
11	Martin Frost, D-Texas	73,541	Barbara Boxer,[a] D-Calif.	250,390
12	Michael A. Andrews, D-Texas	71,912	Richard C. Shelby, D-Ala.	237,154
13	Tom Ridge, R-Pa.	68,561	Harry Reid, D-Nev.	225,279
14	Bob McEwen, R-Ohio	68,268	Frank H. Murkowski, R-Alaska	211,085
15	Tom Bevill, D-Ala.	67,965	John B. Breaux, D-La.	179,242
16	Charles Wilson, D-Texas	66,709	Terry Sanford, D-N.C.	176,413
17	Newt Gingrich, R-Ga.	66,547	Dianne Feinstein,[a] D-Calif.	167,327
18	Dave McCurdy, D-Okla.	61,390	Lynn Yeakel,[a] D-Pa.	166,949
19	Joseph P. Kennedy II, D-Mass.	60,402	Dick Thornburgh,[a] R-Pa.	165,742
20	Barbara F. Vucanovich, R-Nev.	58,981	Bruce Herschensohn,[a] R-Calif.	157,510
21	John P. Murtha, D-Pa.	58,638	Christopher J. Dodd, D-Conn.	157,323
22	Tom McMillen, D-Md.	58,558	Wendell H. Ford, D-Ky.	157,284
23	Ronald V. Dellums, D-Calif.	58,416	Wyche Fowler, Jr., D-Ga.	153,601
24	Clark Kent Ervin,[a] R-Texas	58,088	Harris Wofford,[a] D-Pa.	129,946
25	Norm Dicks, D-Wash.	57,656	John McCain, R-Ariz.	126,023

Note: Totals are for entire two-year House and six-year Senate cycles; both include special election expenditures.

[a] Nonincumbent or special election candidate.

the Marriott Hotel in Cleveland and $4,270 for "candidate's family air fare."

Rep. Henry A. Waxman (D-Calif.) spent $47,294 on travel unrelated to his fund-raising efforts. He used $4,500 of his campaign funds to defray the costs of a trip he and his wife took to Jerusalem in March 1991, including $753 for lodging at the King David Hotel and $3,699 for air fare. While there, Waxman attended a conference of Jewish parliamentarians from around the world. He justified using his campaign funds to pay for the trip by saying that he met with constituents and monitored the airlift of Ethiopian Jews, an issue of importance to his West Hollywood constituency.

During the four-day 1992 Democratic National Convention in New York, Moseley-Braun spent $22,445, including a hefty $15,367 bill at the Le Parker Meridian Hotel. No other Senate candidate, Democrat or Republican, diverted as much of their campaign funds to cover convention expenses.

After the election but before she was sworn in, Moseley-Braun used $4,028 from her treasury to pay lodging expenses at the Four Seasons Hotel in Maui, Hawaii. When first queried about the trip, a spokeswoman for Moseley-Braun said the Hawaiian trip was envisioned as a fund-raising excursion, but when that did not work out as planned, Moseley-Braun did not seek compensation for an equal amount of personal expenses. After a story on the trip appeared in the *Los Angeles Times* in January 1994, the spokeswoman said that the money had been repaid to the campaign, referring us to the senator's mid-year 1993 report, which showed these "off-sets to loan" payments. However, the three "payments"—dated January 1, February 4, and March 11, 1993—amounted to $3,877, or $151 less than the hotel bill. No connection between the offsets and the hotel bill were specifically noted.

Hawaii was not a lucrative destination for anyone outside Hawaii who might have been looking for campaign contributions. Moseley-Braun collected only one Hawaiian contribution—a $1,075 donation from a Honolulu resident on November 2, 1992. Having paid four professional event planners a total of $68,498 for their fund-raising advice, Moseley-Braun would have been ill-advised to have considered a serious fund-raising trip to Hawaii.

Among all challengers, 433 House members, and 98 senators who do not call Hawaii home, including those who lost in primaries, only Rep. William Lehman (D-Fla.) appeared to have ventured to Hawaii for a major-donor event. On December 31, 1991, prior to his decision to retire, Lehman picked up $11,750 in contributions of $200 or more from Honolulu residents. While 37 other House and Senate candidates from the mainland collected at least one contribution of $200 or more from Hawaii, only Sen. Ford collected more than five such contributions. Maui, a vacationer's paradise, was not a fund-raising destination for any member of Congress from the mainland.

At the time Moseley-Braun tapped her treasury to cover her stay in Maui, her campaign was reporting debts of nearly $550,000, including $46,990 owed to campaign employees and contract workers.

This was not the first time Moseley-Braun had commingled her personal and campaign funds. In July 1992 she had "borrowed" $10,000 from her campaign to pay for a new home computer, fax machine, and cellular telephone. When queried by the local press, her campaign spokesman said she had tapped her treasury to cover these blatantly personal expenses because she was "a single mother with a fourteen-year-old son and a mother in a nursing home." The spokesman also noted that Moseley-Braun had made the purchases to help her "stay in touch with her family." Moseley-Braun's attorney, Lou Vitullo, said he would not comment on the $10,000 "loan." The FEC is currently auditing Moseley-Braun's campaign.

As the travel outlays by Stokes and Moseley-Braun illustrate, many candidates tapped their campaign treasuries to pay their expenses at the 1992 national conventions. In all, House candidates spent a total of $479,940 while attending their national party conventions; Senate candidates spent $131,613.

Among House candidates, Rep. Thomas S. Foley (D-Wash.) easily led the way, spending $29,206 of his campaign funds during the four-day 1992 Democratic National Convention in New York. His campaign paid an astounding $25,000 in expenses at the New York Hilton for Foley and his staff.

Before leaving for New York, Bustamante spent $7,123 of his campaign funds on a "pre-convention kickoff party" at the National Democratic Club. While in New York, he spent another $8,444, including $390 on tickets to *Miss Saigon*, $390 on tickets to the *Phantom of the Opera*, and $240 on tickets to *Les Miserables*. During their four-day stay in New York, Democratic Reps. Pelosi, Harold Ford, John Lewis (Ga.), and Dave McCurdy (Okla.) tapped their campaigns for $11,371, $10,328, $10,168, and $10,023, respectively. Among House candidates who used campaign money to pay for convention expenses, only four Republicans ranked in the top twenty-five. During their stay in Houston, Reps. Franks, Tom DeLay (Texas), Tom Ridge (Pa.), and Bud Shuster (Pa.) spent $8,989, $7,035, $5,579, and $4,855, respectively. Other Senate candidates who spent liberally from their campaign funds to cover convention expenses were incumbents Dodd, $21,706; Bumpers, $11,276; Dole, $10,496; and Glenn, $7,407.

While members are forbidden by law from soliciting campaign contributions or anything else of value from corporations, congressional leaders such as Gephardt were all too happy to accept the use of jets owned by companies that routinely lobby them. Indeed, flying aboard corporate jets amounted to nothing less than a thinly disguised corporate contribution, which has been illegal since 1907. In the 1992 election cycle, members were required to reimburse their corporate benefactors for no more than the equivalent of first-class commercial airfare, usually far less than the cost incurred by the corporation for supplying the plane, pilot, and fuel.

Over the two-year House election cycle, Gephardt reimbursed twenty-eight different corporations a total of $38,877— an amount that exceeds what 135 challengers spent on their entire campaigns. As the health care reform debate was heating up, Gephardt paid six corporations with interests in health care legislation a total of $16,669 for the use of their jets. None of the firms are headquartered in Gephardt's district.

Gephardt paid Ren Corp.-U.S.A. of Nashville, Tenn., which specializes in dialysis patient treatment, $4,940 for seven trips. For making its aircraft available on four occasions, Hospital Investors Management of Englewood Cliffs, N.J., received $2,770. Syntex of San Jose, Calif., and Pfizer Inc. of New York, both pharmaceutical manufacturers, collected single charter reimbursements of $3,782 and $880, respectively. Gephardt paid HealthSouth Rehabilitation Corp. of Birmingham, Ala., $1,985 for two flights. AFLAC, a health and life insurance company headquartered in Columbus, Ga., was reimbursed a total of $2,312 for two trips.

Throughout the six-year Senate election cycle, Dole also made frequent use of corporate jets. Among others, Dole paid reimbursements to Archer, Daniels, Midland for $52,834; ConAgra, $24,991; Torchmark Corp., $24,495; Federal Express, $14,635; Chambers Development Co., $10,725; and U.S. Tobacco, $7,383.

While politicians routinely object to the inference of a quid pro quo relationship between contributions and votes, the development of these special relationships creates the impression of a potential conflict of interest.

Candidates were not the only ones traveling. Field workers were routinely reimbursed for mileage and gasoline for their trips around the district. However, in D'Amato's case, even these clearly legitimate expenses took on the smell of excess. Over the six-year Senate election cycle, D'Amato spent $23,645 on limousine services, $16,002 of which was spent to ferry members of his staff around New York City. "There are parts of New York you don't want to be out hailing a yellow cab in," explained staffer Kieran Mahoney.

Campaign Cars

Just as corporations often provide their chief executive officers with luxury automobiles as a perquisite of employment, 110 members of Congress tapped their campaign treasuries for a total of $1,689,952 to pay for campaign cars (see Table 2-8). Although some would argue that such automobiles are a legitimate political expense when used to ferry members around their districts, it is debatable whether a Lincoln Continental or Cadillac is necessary. There is certainly some question as to whether members restrict their use of campaign cars to campaigning or use them regularly for personal errands. This is particularly true for those who purchase, license, repair, and fuel their "campaign cars" in the greater Washington, D.C., metropolitan area.

During the six years leading up to his reelection, D'Amato spent $156,729 to lease and maintain various automobiles, the

Table 2-8 The Top Fifteen Spenders in the 1992 Congressional Races: Campaign Cars

	House		Senate	
Rank	Candidate	Expenditures	Candidate	Expenditures
1	John P. Murtha, D-Pa.	$46,177	Alfonse M. D'Amato, R-N.Y.	$156,729
2	William D. Ford, D-Mich.	40,778	Christopher J. Dodd, D-Conn.	90,024
3	Charlie Rose, D-N.C.	31,201	Daniel K. Inouye, D-Hawaii	63,931
4	Gary L. Ackerman, D-N.Y.	31,131	John B. Breaux, D-La.	62,274
5	Glenn English, D-Okla.	30,796	Terry Sanford, D-N.C.	55,874
6	W. G. "Bill" Hefner, D-N.C.	30,373	Patrick J. Leahy, D-Vt.	52,531
7	Ron Marlenee, R-Mont.	28,507	Carol Moseley-Braun,[a] D-Ill.	33,920
8	John T. Myers, R-Ind.	28,250	Wyche Fowler, Jr., D-Ga.	23,597
9	Bob Stump, R-Ariz.	24,784	Arlen Specter, R-Pa.	23,421
10	Joseph D. Early, D-Mass.	24,214	Wendell H. Ford, D-Ky.	15,637
11	Thomas J. Downey, D-N.Y.	23,698	Frank H. Murkowski, R-Alaska	15,627
12	Richard Ray, D-Ga.	23,091	Charlene Haar,[a] R-S.D.	13,163
13	Don Sundquist, R-Tenn.	22,211	Steve Lewis,[a] D-Okla.	10,940
14	Floyd H. Flake, D-N.Y.	21,899	Russell D. Feingold,[a] D-Wis.	10,785
15	Robert E. "Bud" Cramer, D-Ala.	20,878	Mike DeWine,[a] R-Ohio	9,273

Note: Totals are for entire two-year House and six-year Senate cycles; both include special election expenditures.

[a] Nonincumbent or special election candidate.

most recent of which were a 1992 Lincoln Towncar, which was kept in New York, and a 1990 Lincoln Towncar, which was kept in Washington, D.C. The 1992 Lincoln cost the campaign $647 each month; the 1990 Lincoln used by D'Amato in Washington cost his campaign $927 each month. Repairs to his campaign cars totaled $20,315, including $10,022 paid to Dave Pyle's Lincoln Mercury in Annandale, Va. Insurance, registration, and licensing fees added $28,217. He spent $31,495 on gasoline over the six-year cycle. D'Amato's investment accounted for 27 percent of the $586,888 spent on campaign cars by the fifteen Senate incumbents who leased or purchased automobiles during the cycle.

Dodd spent $90,024 on his campaign car over the six-year cycle—$60,701 on lease payments; $10,682 to insure, register, and license it; $5,648 to repair it; and $12,993 to fill it with gas. Inouye spent $15,773 of his campaign treasury to purchase a van from Avis Rent-A-Car and $20,691 to lease an Acura. Insurance and registration fees added $22,132. Repairs and gasoline cost $5,335. Sen. John B. Breaux (D-La.) spent $62,274 to lease and maintain two campaign automobiles: a van for hauling campaign paraphernalia and a sedan driven by Breaux.

In the House, the leading spenders on campaign cars were John P. Murtha (D-Pa.), $46,177; William D. Ford (D-Mich.), $40,778; Charlie Rose (D-N.C.), $31,201; Gary L. Ackerman (D-N.Y.), $31,131; Glenn English (D-Okla.), $30,796; W. G. "Bill" Hefner (D-N.C.), $30,373: Ron Marlenee (R-Mont.), $28,507; and John T. Myers (R-Ind.), $28,250. In all, ninety-five House incumbents reported spending a total of $1,103,064 on their campaign cars.

Murtha's campaign leased a 1989 Ford Crown Victoria from Central Transportation in Edensburg, Pa., for the first seventeen months of the cycle. In May 1992 Murtha's campaign treasury paid $7,000 to buy out the lease. He began leasing a second car in September 1991 from Jim Dewar Olds Leasing in Johnstown, Pa. Total lease and purchase payments were $28,180. The campaign spent $8,103 to repair the cars, $5,886 to license and register them, and $4,008 to fuel them.

In February 1991 Ford's campaign made its last $411 payment on a car he used in Washington, D.C. That same month, his campaign made a $2,603 down payment on a new car from Dave Pyle's, the same Lincoln Mercury dealership frequented by D'Amato, and began making monthly loan payments of $732. The campaign also spent $16,416 on a new car in Michigan.

Rose had spent $8,288 of his 1990 campaign treasury to purchase a car, but apparently it proved insufficient. In June 1992 the campaign bought a $13,821 car from Fair Bluff Motors in Fair Bluff, N.C. Six months later, the campaign shelled out $10,594 to Valley Motors in Fayetteville, N.C., for another car. The $6,786 he spent to insure, maintain, and fuel the automobiles included a $272 bill at Precision Tune in Alexandria, Va.

Ackerman tapped his campaign funds for $14,608 to lease a Lincoln Towncar. Insurance and registration cost the campaign $10,224. Maintenance and gasoline added $3,205 and $3,094, respectively.

In October 1991 English spent $26,140 of his campaign treasury to purchase a new Buick. Together with registration and licensing fees, English's campaign car accounted for 40 percent of his off-year spending.

Hefner drove a Cadillac at campaign expense. Lease payments over the two-year cycle amounted to $23,643. Insurance, registration, and repairs to the car cost the campaign $3,483. Gasoline added $3,247.

Myers invested $19,635 of his campaign treasury in a new Chrysler LeBaron convertible. In addition to the registration and license fees for the LeBaron, the campaign also picked up the tab for insurance premiums and upkeep on three other cars—a 1970 white Impala convertible, a 1989 Plymouth Sundance, and a 1984 Chrysler.

Fund Raising

Permanent campaigns require a constant cash flow. The typical House incumbent invested $88,348 in his or her fund-raising operation, $33,959 of which was spent during 1991. The average Senate incumbent spent $850,961 to raise money, with an average of $441,869 being spent between January 1, 1987 and December 31, 1991. In all, the 377 House and Senate incumbents who contested the 1992 general election spent $54,660,343 to raise money, of which $24,156,205 was spent during years in which they did not face the voters.

Although one might assume that the goal is to collect as much money as possible while spending as little as possible to raise it, that is frequently not the case. Fund-raising activities often serve a broad range of political goals beyond the immediate campaign. In fact, many members of Congress organized their campaigns around their fund-raising operations. Some focused on direct mail because it freed them from the demands of PACs and "fat cats," who frequently expect access in return for their large contributions. Others used events of various types to regularly bring together their most ardent supporters and to engage more people in the political process.

As he had in 1990, Dornan spent far more than any other House candidate to raise money during the 1992 election cycle—$1,151,338 (see Table 2-9). This staggering total represented 74 percent of his spending, and with contributions totaling $1,407,922, Dornan collected only $1.22 for each dollar he invested.

Driving this inefficient fund-raising operation were his outlays for direct-mail solicitations, which amounted to $1,121,604, of which $403,929 was spent during 1991. Each month Dornan's consultants fired off a letter to approximately 7,500 regular contributors. Four to six times each year the campaign mailed prospecting letters in an effort to expand the donor base. Dornan paid Response Dynamics of Alexandria, Va., $967,650 for list rental, production, postage, and caging services. His daughter said the average contribution was only $11.50.

On the other side of the political spectrum, Rep. Bernard Sanders (I-Vt.), the only socialist in the House, also relied primarily on direct mail to fund his campaign. However, unlike Dornan, Sanders's direct-mail operation was handled entirely in-house. As a result, he got to keep far more of what he collected. Over the two-year election cycle, Sanders spent $119,596 on his direct-mail program and $5,023 on events, including $1,000 directed at raising money from PACs. Sanders's efforts to raise money from individual donors yielded $3.43 for each dollar invested. "Bernie has been associated with certain issues since he was mayor [of Burlington]—labor, education, and women's issues—and that's how people around the country have gotten to know him," noted Sanders's wife Jane. "We have one of the best mailing lists in the country, and we got at least one contribution from every state."

Many permanent campaigns were built around "congressional clubs," which confer special benefits to those who donate. Rep. Dennis Hastert (R-Ill.) treated his congressional club members to three or four events each year, as well as a trip to the nation's capital. The Hastert campaign spent $3,908 in 1991 on the Washington excursion, including $817 for part of the tab at the J. W. Marriott, $827 for dinner at Gadsby's Tavern in Alexandria, Va., and another $641 for food at the House restaurant. Expenses for the 1992 Washington briefing totaled $3,852, including $1,630 for lodging at the Mount Vernon Inn and $625 at the House restaurant. The congressional club members also received $2,887 in gifts.

Gunderson operated a two-tiered congressional club. For a $1,000 donation, supporters became members of his "Executive Club," which entitled them to a lapel pin; a special gift, such as a pen-and-pencil set; and invitations to all his major fund-raising events. Among these events was the annual "brat party," which was held in his parent's back yard and featured sausage, beer, and ice cream. A more formal reception featured Vice President Dan Quayle. The campaign also held seven more intimate dinners for congressional club members. For a $250 donation, Gunderson provided members with a reduced package of these same benefits.

As in past campaign's, the fund-raising operation of Rep. Dean A. Gallo (R-N.J.) was inefficient by design. While he held an annual high-yield reception for PACs in Washington, D.C., and staged both periodic dinners and an annual Christmas party for his $1,000 donors, many of Gallo's events were designed primarily to get more people involved in the campaign and to maintain contact with loyal supporters. One low-dollar event was an annual golf outing, which cost the campaign $11,863 in 1991 and $11,552 in 1992. Each year Gallo rented a luxury box at the Meadowlands Racetrack and invited supporters to join him for an evening of harness racing. The two catered events cost the campaign $18,261 and raised little more than they cost. An afternoon of professional football at Giants Stadium cost $1,802 in 1991 and $2,501 in 1992. He spent $3,651 on souvenir shirts and mugs, which he gave away at these events.

For some House candidates and virtually all Senate candidates, the fund-raising focus was more global, either by choice or by necessity. The 1992 campaigns of 248 successful congressional candidates, most of them incumbents, were financed primarily with PAC donations and contributions of $200 or more from individuals who lived beyond the borders of the states they sought to represent. In the House, thirty-eight incumbents and two open seat candidates relied on PACs and out-of-state contributors for at least 75 percent of their campaign funds. In the Senate, thirteen incumbents and five open seat candidates collected at least 50 percent of their cash from PACs and out-of-state donors.

Having been appointed in May 1991 to succeed Sen. John Heinz, a three-term Republican who had been killed in a plane crash, Democratic Sen. Harris Wofford was initially given little chance of winning the November 1991 special election against Republican Dick Thornburgh, a former two-term governor and U.S. attorney general. With just six months to prove the pundits wrong, Wofford launched a nationwide search for money. The campaign employed four professional fund-raisers, who

Table 2-9 The Top Twenty-Five Spenders in the 1992 Congressional Races: Fund Raising

	House		Senate	
Rank	Candidate	Expenditures	Candidate	Expenditures
1	Robert K. Dornan, R-Calif.	$1,151,338	Bob Packwood, R-Ore.	$3,189,922
2	Randy "Duke" Cunningham, R-Calif.	435,252	Barbara Boxer,[a] D-Calif.	2,938,393
3	Richard A. Gephardt, D-Mo.	433,500	Dianne Feinstein,[a] D-Calif.	2,727,505
4	Gerry E. Studds, D-Mass.	338,709	John Seymour, R-Calif.	2,726,687
5	Ronald V. Dellums, D-Calif.	325,649	Bruce Herschensohn,[a] R-Calif.	2,712,734
6	Frank Riggs, R-Calif.	323,986	Carol Moseley-Braun,[a] D-Ill.	2,340,023
7	Newt Gingrich, R-Ga.	317,409	Alfonse M. D'Amato, R-N.Y.	2,268,931
8	Steny H. Hoyer, D-Md.	275,483	Arlen Specter, R-Pa.	1,855,639
9	Les Aspin, D-Wis.	265,828	John McCain, R-Ariz.	1,476,090
10	Dean A. Gallo, R-N.J.	247,603	Barbara A. Mikulski, D-Md.	1,403,752
11	Dick Zimmer, R-N.J.	246,516	Terry Sanford, D-N.C.	1,135,533
12	Ron Marlenee, R-Mont.	246,018	Bob Kasten, R-Wis.	1,069,644
13	Tom Lantos, D-Calif.	245,960	Robert Abrams,[a] D-N.Y.	1,045,544
14	Jim Ramstad, R-Minn.	245,583	Christopher S. Bond, R-Mo.	971,604
15	Joseph P. Kennedy II, D-Mass.	239,646	Dick Thornburgh,[a] R-Pa.	935,866
16	Tom McMillen, D-Md.	231,757	Wyche Fowler, Jr., D-Ga.	935,194
17	Dave McCurdy, D-Okla.	231,613	John Glenn, D-Ohio	753,173
18	Sam Johnson,[a] R-Texas	226,796	Daniel R. Coats, R-Ind.	725,587
19	Joseph D. Early, D-Mass.	221,066	Tom Daschle, D-S.D.	673,775
20	James P. Moran, Jr., D-Va.	215,148	Richard Williamson,[a] R-Ill.	651,735
21	Vic Fazio, D-Calif.	210,731	Lynn Yeakel,[a] D-Pa.	651,726
22	Sander M. Levin, D-Mich.	208,992	Charles E. Grassley, R-Iowa	629,171
23	Martin Frost, D-Texas	205,691	Lauch Faircloth,[a] R-N.C.	556,161
24	Pat Williams, D-Mont.	194,607	Christopher J. Dodd, D-Conn.	502,485
25	H. L. "Bill" Richardson, R-Calif.	193,037	Daniel K. Inouye, D-Hawaii	471,769

Note: Totals are for entire two-year House and six-year Senate cycles; both include special election expenditures.
[a] Nonincumbent or special election candidate.

Table 2-10 The Top Twenty-Five Spenders in the 1992 Congressional Races: Constituent Entertainment and Gifts

	House		Senate	
Rank	Candidate	Expenditures	Candidate	Expenditures
1	Charles Wilson, D-Texas	$86,226	Christopher S. Bond, R-Mo.	$92,083
2	John D. Dingell, D-Mich.	54,707	Bob Graham, D-Fla.	86,965
3	Cardiss Collins, D-Ill.	50,201	Christopher J. Dodd, D-Conn.	81,730
4	Ike Skelton, D-Mo.	46,989	Alfonse M. D'Amato, R-N.Y.	53,446
5	Don Sundquist, R-Tenn.	46,871	Arlen Specter, R-Pa.	50,770
6	John P. Murtha, D-Pa.	45,395	Wendell H. Ford, D-Ky.	50,364
7	Norman Y. Mineta, D-Calif.	44,575	Bob Dole, R-Kan.	49,765
8	Thomas J. Manton, D-N.Y.	42,911	Wyche Fowler, Jr., D-Ga.	40,089
9	Barbara-Rose Collins, D-Mich.	40,772	Harry Reid, D-Nev.	37,047
10	Solomon P. Ortiz, D-Texas	39,104	Patrick J. Leahy, D-Vt.	36,711
11	Robert T. Matsui, D-Calif.	35,673	Ernest F. Hollings, D-S.C.	29,932
12	Jerry Huckaby, D-La.	34,382	Tom Daschle, D-S.D.	27,402
13	Don Young, R-Alaska	34,296	Bob Kasten, R-Wis.	25,768
14	Kweisi Mfume, D-Md.	34,231	Kent Conrad, D-N.D.	25,310
15	Joseph D. Early, D-Mass.	31,963	Frank H. Murkowski, R-Alaska	24,745
16	Edolphus Towns, D-N.Y.	30,738	Dianne Feinstein,[a] D-Calif.	24,520
17	Leon E. Panetta, D-Calif.	30,390	John B. Breaux, D-La.	20,184
18	Sherwood Boehlert, R-N.Y.	30,146	Barbara A. Mikulski, D-Md.	19,246
19	Michael Bilirakis, R-Fla.	29,123	Don Nickles, R-Okla.	18,241
20	James H. Quillen, R-Tenn.	28,032	John McCain, R-Ariz.	14,875
21	Robert H. Michel, R-Ill.	26,643	John Seymour, R-Calif.	13,792
22	Toby Roth, R-Wis.	24,697	Terry Sanford, D-N.C.	12,662
23	Duncan Hunter, R-Calif.	24,649	Wayne Owens,[a] D-Utah	9,882
24	Mary Rose Oakar, D-Ohio	23,493	Dale Bumpers, D-Ark.	7,932
25	Tim Valentine, D-N.C.	23,424	Daniel R. Coats, R-Ind.	6,839

Note: Totals are for entire two-year House and six-year Senate cycles; both include special election expenditures.
[a] Nonincumbent or special election candidate.

together were paid $86,744, which accounted for 70 percent of Wofford's event costs.

Only 5 percent of Wofford's total spending was invested in fund-raising events and direct mail, but a substantial proportion of his overhead was directly related to raising money. After his appointment he immediately opened a Washington fund-raising office that employed twenty people throughout much of the six-month campaign. Rent for the office cost $17,000. The campaign also employed fourteen people across the country to raise money, including four in Massachusetts, two in New York, and others in California, Connecticut, New Jersey, North Carolina, South Carolina, Texas, Virginia, and West Virginia. These efforts enabled Wofford to raise more than $3.3 million, 61 percent of which came from PACs and out-of-state donors who gave $200 or more.

Sen. Charles E. Grassley (R-Iowa) collected 56 percent of his $2,456,091 in nonparty contributions from PACs and large out-of-state contributors. Campaign manager Bob Hauss said Grassley made a concerted effort to raise his national profile by holding events aimed at pro-Israel supporters in Illinois, Florida, and California.

McCurdy spent considerable time and money exploring a possible presidential bid, at on point devoting a month to visiting swing districts around the country. Although he opted not to enter the race, McCurdy continued to travel extensively for Democratic presidential nominee Bill Clinton. As long as he was making the trips, McCurdy decided he should expand his own fund-raising network. He paid Tim Phillips of Washington, D.C., $48,053 to serve as a one-man advance team. Phillips planned the travel, set up meetings with like-minded supporters, and introduced McCurdy to people that his chief of staff, Stephen K. Patterson, described as "potential contributors and people who could help us down the road." In addition to Phillips, McCurdy hired three professional fund-raisers to help fill his coffers. They collected a total of $115,852 for their work. Together, Phillips and these three firms helped raise $270,250 from PACs and $115,950 from out-of-state donors who gave $200 or more. Large donations from in-state residents amounted to $93,700. McCurdy raised no more than 28 percent of his contributions from individual donors in Oklahoma.

Upon hearing that Democratic Rep. Byron L. Dorgan (D-N.D.) would be seeking the open Senate seat created by the temporary retirement of fellow Democrat Kent Conrad, state insurance commissioner Earl Pomeroy announced plans to seek Dorgan's House seat. Having served as president of the National Association of Insurance Commissioners, Pomeroy knew who to ask for the money he needed.

Pomeroy traveled to Washington, D.C., where the Independent Insurance Agents of America's PAC, INSUR PAC, spent $1,238 to sponsor a fund-raiser on his behalf. During the six-month campaign, PACs representing MetLife, Continental Insurance, the Principal Group, the American International Group, and the Alliance of American Insurers also sponsored in-kind fund-raising events for Pomeroy. These six insurance PACs together picked up $9,112 of Pomeroy's event costs, which represented 35 percent of his total event expenses.

Less than one month after opening his Bismarck headquarters, Pomeroy opened a Washington, D.C., fund-raising office to make certain that a steady stream of PAC dollars continued to flow into the campaign. Rent of the Washington office and payments to the staff who ran it amounted to $29,071. With PACs accounting for 69 percent of his total receipts, the office proved well worth the expense. Pomeroy raised $61,904 from individuals who gave at least $200, but only $7,077 was collected from North Dakotans. Donors from twenty-three states anted up $54,827, with at least $15,900 coming from insurance company executives. At most, Pomeroy raised 15 percent of his money in-state.

CONSTITUENT STROKING

In the absence of a strong political party structure, members of Congress must build and maintain a network of contacts and supporters who can be called upon at a moment's notice to help fend off any strong electoral challenge that may arise. For most members, that network is established over time through the expenditure of thousands of dollars on year-end holiday cards, gifts, and entertainment. During the 1992 election cycle, members of Congress spent $3,828,682 on constituent stroking, including $1,482,174 on cards; $863,084 on parties, including inaugural festivities; $527,329 on meals with constituents; $456,081 on gifts; $233,939 on flowers; $106,078 on calendars; $71,718 on awards and commemorative plaques; $70,683 on sports and theater tickets; and $17,596 on the congressional art contest.

As in 1990, Rep. Charles Wilson (D-Texas) led all House incumbents in expenditures on constituent entertainment and gifts (see Table 2-10). His annual dominoes tournament, which drew about 400 people in 1986, swelled to approximately 1,600 constituents in both 1991 and 1992. These two events cost a total of $54,681, including $37,323 for the dominoes, $2,967 to engrave them with "Vote for Charles Wilson," $1,135 for trophies, and $9,166 for fried chicken and biscuits. Wilson also spent $21,948 on constituent meals and other entertainment, $7,484 on various gifts, and $2,113 on flowers.

Rep. Kweisi Mfume (D-Md.) spent $10,798 to host a free open house for district residents in the spring of 1991 and 1992. He rented tents, tables, and chairs and set them up in a parking lot near his main congressional office in Baltimore. The campaign hired magicians and supplied face painting and balloons for the children. Adults received a picture of Mfume. Attendees were fed by local caterers and entertained by musicians from Morgan State University.

Mfume's campaign hosted an annual year-end holiday reception at the Walters Art Gallery in Baltimore, where local elected officials and other invited guests celebrated the season. No one paid to attend the affairs, which together cost $7,566. He spent $6,286 of his treasury on holiday cards. Plaques given in recognition of various constituent achievements cost the campaign $1,155. He spent $1,364 on lunches with visiting constituents, primarily at the House restaurant. Assorted gifts added $4,883.

Table 2-11 The Top Fifteen Spenders in the 1992 Congressional Races: Holiday Cards

	House		Senate	
Rank	Candidate	Expenditures	Candidate	Expenditures
1	John D. Dingell, D-Mich.	$34,730	Christopher S. Bond, R-Mo.	$89,540
2	Norman Y. Mineta, D-Calif.	22,592	Wyche Fowler, Jr., D-Ga.	34,438
3	Toby Roth, R-Wis.	21,572	Arlen Specter, R-Pa.	31,359
4	Harold Rogers, R-Ky.	19,793	Christopher J. Dodd, D-Conn.	30,998
5	Don Sundquist, R-Tenn.	19,110	Alfonse M. D'Amato, R-N.Y.	27,219
6	Robert H. Michel, R-Ill.	17,799	Patrick J. Leahy, D-Vt.	21,530
7	Patricia Schroeder, D-Colo.	16,573	Bob Kasten, R-Wis.	16,475
8	George Miller, D-Calif.	16,435	Kent Conrad, D-N.D.	13,391
9	Bob McEwen, R-Ohio	16,319	Bob Graham, D-Fla.	10,993
10	Bill Archer, R-Texas	16,152	Ernest F. Hollings, D-S.C.	9,936
11	Robert T. Matsui, D-Calif.	14,264	Frank H. Murkowski, R-Alaska	7,925
12	Benjamin A. Gilman, R-N.Y.	13,609	Daniel R. Coats, R-Ind.	4,455
13	Tom Lantos, D-Calif.	12,822	John B. Breaux, D-La.	3,944
14	Leon E. Panetta, D-Calif.	12,387	John McCain, R-Ariz.	3,500
15	Paul E. Kanjorski, D-Pa.	11,771	Harry Reid, D-Nev.	3,185

Note: Totals are for entire two-year House and six-year Senate cycles; both include special election expenditures.

As in past years, Mfume used campaign funds to frame the winning entry in the district's congressional art contest. In 1991 the campaign also gave cash awards of $500 to the winner, $200 to the runner-up, and $100 to the third-place entrant. A catered party to celebrate the winners cost the campaign $200. Mfume increased the prizes in 1992 for finishing second and third to $300 and $200, respectively. The party to toast the winners cost $180.

Rep. John D. Dingell (D-Mich.), elected to his nineteenth term in 1992, spent $34,730 of his campaign treasury to send year-end holiday cards (see Table 2-11). Constituent gifts cost his campaign $8,127, including $3,680 for calendars from the Capitol Historical Society. He spent $7,881 on flowers and $3,968 on meals and other entertainment.

Rep. Cardiss Collins (D-Ill.) invested $50,201 of her treasury in constituent gifts and entertainment, a 68 percent increase over 1990. Her annual picnic for senior citizens cost $3,750 in 1991 and $11,336 in 1992; half the difference in cost was accounted for by a $3,870 expenditures for aprons she passed out in 1992. She spent a total of $25,634 on four bingo events, and a brunch for local ministers cost the campaign $3,869. Collins spent $1,810 on Easter cards and $2,554 on year-end holiday cards.

Rep. Ike Skelton (D-Mo.) tapped his campaign treasury for $24,600 to pay for constituent meals, including $3,683 for meals at the House dining room and $2,228 for seven dinners at Maison Blanche near the White House. He reported spending $5,371 on dinners with constituents at restaurants near his home in McLean, Va., including a $1,414 Turkish feast at Kazan Restaurant. Various constituent gifts cost the campaign $11,939, including $1,272 for congressional club cookbooks, $350 for Christmas ornaments from the White House Historical Society, and $327 for edibles from Burger's Smokehouse in California, Mo. Holiday greeting cards and various parties cost the campaign $4,221 and $6,229, respectively.

Expenditures on "meals for supporters" by Rep. Solomon P. Ortiz (D-Texas) totaled $18,601 over the course of the 1992 election cycle. Ortiz paid $7,033 for such meals at restaurants in Washington, D.C., including a $612 dinner at Mr. K's and a $153 dinner at Le Rivage. Back home, he spent $7,406 to dine with constituents, including a $14 repast at Whataburger and a $15 meal at a local Denny's restaurant. He also billed the campaign for $1,028 for dinners with constituents in Matamoros, Mexico, as well as $2,372 in constituent meals consumed at unspecified locations. "He tries to see constituents outside the office," press secretary Cathy A. Travis explained. "There are too many distractions in the office—phone calls, staff people wanting to see him. It's better if they leave."

Ortiz's annual Christmas party for constituents and volunteers cost his campaign $9,530. Year-end holiday cards added $4,686. His treasury was tapped for $1,000 to help pay for the funeral of a constituent killed in Operation Desert Storm. Continental Airlines was paid $2,500 to ferry the Robstown, Texas, High School band to and from Washington. Flowers and other gifts cost $1,506 and $1,281 was invested in the congressional art contest for high school students.

Rep. William Ford increased his expenditures for constituent stroking from $5,771 in 1990 to $13,461 in 1992. He spent $1,364 on trees, which were donated to local schools on Arbor Day. He sent poinsettias to volunteers and local elected officials each Christmas, at a total cost of $2,562. Annual Christmas parties catered by the Culinary Arts Department at the William D. Ford Vocational Tech Center cost a total of $3,192. Year-end holiday cards cost the campaign $4,388.

Some members liked to reward supporters with tickets to athletic events. Rep. James H. Quillen (R-Tenn.) spent $10,801 of his campaign treasury to purchase tickets to various sporting events, including $1,800 for Super Bowl tickets, $1,814 for tickets to the Kentucky Derby, $5,395 for tickets to University of Tennessee football games, and $1,792 for Washington Redskins tickets. Quillen said he preferred to give the tickets to lucky supporters, rather than attend. "I haven't been to a Redskins game in twenty-five years," Quillen explained. "The last time I went, it was a night game and I fell asleep."

Myers tapped his campaign treasury in both 1991 and 1992 to pay for sixteen season tickets to Indianapolis Colts football games and four season tickets to Purdue University football games. Unlike Quillen, Myers and his wife personally used the tickets to entertain constituents, campaign volunteers, and county party chairs. Total cost: $10,153.

Among Senate incumbents, Bond topped the list for constituent stroking, spending $92,083 over the six-year cycle, $89,540 of which was spent on year-end holiday cards. Others who spent liberally on their constituents included Bob Graham (D-Fla.), $86,965; Dodd, $81,730; D'Amato, $53,446; Specter, $50,770; and Ford, $50,364 (see Table 2-10).

Over the course of the six-year cycle, Graham spent $58,722 on various constituent events and $10,993 on holiday cards. The campaign paid $4,633 for tickets to sporting events, including $3,905 for tickets to the 1991 Super Bowl in Tampa. Press secretary Ken Klein said the tickets were passed out to the senator's friends. Graham also used $4,156 in campaign money to buy gifts, including boxes of pecans and "Florida Ties," which were given at Christmas to fellow senators and employees of the congressional barbershop and shoeshine stand.

Each year Graham gathered together his long-time friends and supporters for a weekend of golf, tennis, and political seminars. According to Klein, these weekends were not a pitch for money but, rather, were a way to stay in touch. The 150 to 200 guests paid their own transportation and hotel expenses, as well as any golf and tennis fees, but the campaign paid for some of the meals and entertainment. For instance, in 1991 the campaign paid $12,989 for food at the Senate restaurant and $5,500 to hire the Capitol Steps, who entertained Graham's guests with political satire and song.

Dodd invested $33,536 in constituent meals, regularly hosting receptions in the Senate restaurant for groups such as the Connecticut Senior Intern Program. The program sponsored an annual week-long trip to Washington for one hundred high school seniors from across the state. A similar reception for members of the Peace Corps cost the Dodd campaign $1,088. He spent $30,998 on year-end holiday cards, $5,225 on flowers for constituents, and $3,111 on miscellaneous gifts. To celebrate his victory and that of the Democratic presidential ticket, Dodd spent $8,861 of his campaign treasury on inaugural festivities.

Whatever the method, the extravagant gifts and entertainment have the same intent—to build a strong base of support from which to run, either for reelection or for higher office. Few but the richest challengers can compete in such a system.

OTHER MEALS AND ENTERTAINMENT

Members of Congress routinely spent campaign funds for meals and entertainment that had absolutely nothing to do with campaigning. Once again, D'Amato had the dubious distinction of spending significantly more than any of his Senate colleagues (see Table 2-12). Over the six-year Senate election cycle, he spent $163,098 on meals and entertainment that had no apparent connection to his constituent entertainment or fund-raising activities. This spending averaged $523 for each of the 312 weeks in the cycle. D'Amato spent $35,252 of his campaign treasury at Gandel's Gourmet, a delicatessen on Capitol Hill. The campaign also spent thousands of dollars at the Senate restaurant for meals that were not campaign related, including a $4,439 harvest day celebration of New York agriculture products, to which senators and their staffs were invited.

Inouye spent $106,894 on meals that had no apparent connection to fund raising or constituent entertainment. For example, Inouye reported PAC and individual contributions totaling only $4,100 for 1989, but he billed the campaign $1,250 that year for one meal at Germaine's restaurant in Washington, D.C. Inouye also reported "campaign meals" totaling $545 at the Borobudur Intercontinental Hotel in Jakarta, Indonesia, and $349 at the Sherwood in Taipei, Taiwan. Over the six-year cycle, the campaign paid $26,120 for 403 meals that cost less than $200—183 in Hawaii, 168 in Washington, D.C., 46 near his Maryland home, and 6 in Virginia. Total cost to the campaign: $26,120.

As in 1990, no one in the House could compete with Shuster when it came to dining out on the campaign. Over the two-year cycle, Shuster spent $70,913 on meals that were unrelated to fund raising, including $25,163 in unitemized credit card bills. He spent $11,355 of his treasury on meals in Washington, D.C., including $7,218 for seventeen meals at Tortilla Coast and $428 for two meals at the Willard Hotel. Across the river in suburban Virginia, Shuster spent $17,308 on meals, including $8,054 for twenty-four meals from Sutton Place Gourmet in Alexandria and $1,288 for ten meals at the Ritz Carlton Hotel in Arlington. To satisfy his sweet tooth, Shuster spent $1,731 at Alexandria Pastry.

While the heart of Shuster's Pennsylvania district was a two-hour drive from Washington, $5,543 of his Washington, D.C, and Virginia meal expenses were listed as "food for volunteers." His Washington volunteers ate $2,462 worth of food from Tortilla Coast, $513 in chicken from Popeye's, and $845 in food from Peking Duck Gourmet. One "happy hour" visit to the Crowbar cost the campaign $226. Shuster billed the campaign for $11,848 in itemized meals in his home state, and none of these meals were listed as "meals for volunteers."

Between January 1, 1991 and December 31, 1992, Rostenkowski charged his campaign $28,734 for seventy-four meals—an average of $388 each time he dined out at campaign expense. His favorite haunt when the campaign was picking up the tab was Gibson's in Chicago, where he dined twelve times at a total cost of $5,943. Seven meals at Morton's in Chicago cost the campaign $3,304. Four meals at the Big Foot Country Club in Fontana, Wis., and a dinner at Lake Benedict Manor in Genoa City, Wis.—both of which are near his summer vacation home—cost the campaign $1,839 and $1,465, respectively.

Rep. Jerry Lewis (R-Calif.) paid out nearly $26,000 from his campaign coffers for meals that were unrelated to his fund-

Table 2-12 The Top Fifteen Spenders in the 1992 Congressional Races: Restaurants/Meetings

	House		Senate	
Rank	Candidate	Expenditures	Candidate	Expenditures
1	Bud Shuster, R-Pa.	$70,913	Alfonse M. D'Amato, R-N.Y.	$163,098
2	Dan Rostenkowski, D-Ill.	28,734	Daniel K. Inouye, D-Hawaii	106,894
3	Jerry Lewis, R-Calif.	25,840	Christopher J. Dodd, D-Conn.	36,210
4	Dan Burton, R-Ind.	24,154	Christopher S. Bond, R-Mo.	33,564
5	John D. Dingell, D-Mich.	23,666	Frank H. Murkowski, R-Alaska	28,963
6	Kweisi Mfume, D-Md.	22,181	Bob Graham, D-Fla.	26,222
7	John P. Murtha, D-Pa.	19,281	Barbara A. Mikulski, D-Md.	26,161
8	Robert T. Matsui, D-Calif.	16,519	John B. Breaux, D-La.	25,198
9	Edolphus Towns, D-N.Y.	15,336	Ernest F. Hollings, D-S.C.	22,170
10	Barbara B. Kennelly, D-Conn.	15,189	Arlen Specter, R-Pa.	21,831
11	Albert G. Bustamante, D-Texas	14,686	Terry Sanford, D-N.C.	21,696
12	Michael Huffington,[a] R-Calif.	14,539	Patrick J. Leahy, D-Vt.	17,258
13	Charles Wilson, D-Texas	14,293	Harry Reid, D-Nev.	16,936
14	Dale E. Kildee, D-Mich.	13,208	Tom Daschle, D-S.D.	14,264
15	Joseph D. Early, D-Mass.	13,133	Wyche Fowler, Jr., D-Ga.	12,773

Note: Totals are for entire two-year House and six-year Senate cycles; both include special election expenditures.

[a] Nonincumbent or special election candidate.

raising activities, many at posh restaurants on Capitol Hill. During the first six months of 1991, contributions to Lewis's campaign totaled only $4,810. During that same period, meals at the Monocle amounted to $2,072, meals at La Brasserie came to $1,214, and a single dinner at Le Mistral cost the campaign $1,097. Bills at Gandel's delicatessen totaled $405. Press secretary David M. LesStrang could not provide details on any specific meal, but said they were for both business and constituent entertainment.

Rep. Douglas Applegate (D-Ohio) consumed 171 meals at campaign expense, or an average of one meal every four days for the entire two-year cycle. He spent $2,094 on 83 meals in Ohio. Forty-five meals in Washington, D.C., and its suburbs cost the campaign $1,785. He spent $466 at restaurants in Pennsylvania, including a $6.98 meal at a Red Lobster in Pittsburgh. Meals in West Virginia cost the campaign $617. According to James R. Hart, Applegate's administrative assistant, most of these meals were in connection with speaking engagements when Applegate "can't use his official House account."

In all, members of Congress spent $1,901,812 on meals, an average of $3,582 for House members and $23,273 for Senate incumbents.

DONATIONS

Rep. Waxman had far more money than he needed to defeat his opponent, so he simply gave away $338,803 of his treasury, which accounted for 47 percent of his "campaign" spending for the 1992 cycle. This modern-day Robin Hood took from rich PACs and gave to poor candidates and party organizations. As chairman of the subcommittee on Health and Environment, Waxman was able to tap PACs representing health care interests for $177,800. In all, 203 PACs donated $402,915 to Waxman's campaign coffers, which amounted to 64 percent of his contributions.

Waxman bestowed $67,688 on IMPAC 2000, the PAC established to assist Democrats in redistricting. He gave $55,000 to the Democratic Congressional Campaign Committee, $40,000 to the United Democratic Fund of Minnesota, $20,000 to the Democratic Senatorial Campaign Committee, and $5,000 to the California Democratic party.

State senator Herschel Rosenthal received a $50,000 check from Waxman's campaign just four days before Rosenthal lost his primary contest to California state representative Tom Hayden. California state representative Terry B. Friedman received $10,000 for his race. Six House colleagues with whom he shared committee assignments each collected $2,000; another six received $1,000 donations. His donations to other candidates totaled $123,500.

Waxman's reasons for sharing his wealth with other candidates were simple. "First of all, they vote for or fight for the issues I care about," he noted. "Secondly, when you help somebody you develop a good working relationship with them."

Waxman was by no means alone (see Table 2-13). Representing one of the safest Democratic seats in the country, Rep. Howard L. Berman devoted only 15 percent of the $720,810 he spent in 1992 to direct appeals for votes. He gave $353,428, or 49 percent of his total campaign outlays, to other candidates, party organizations, and civic groups. He donated $90,001 to Rosenthal's state senate campaign. Other Californians benefiting from Berman's largess included state representatives Friedman and Dave Elder, who received $25,000 and $22,000, respectively. State representative Teresa Hughes picked up $12,000 for her successful state senate bid. To assist Democratic redistricting efforts, Berman donated $65,688 to IMPAC 2000. He gave $11,500 to the Democratic Congressional Campaign Committee and $1,500 to the Democratic National Com-

Table 2-13 The Top Twenty-Five Spenders in the 1992 Congressional Races: Donations

	House		*Senate*	
Rank	Candidate	Expenditures	Candidate	Expenditures
1	Howard L. Berman, D-Calif.	$353,428	Tom Daschle, D-S.D.	$263,721
2	Henry A. Waxman, D-Calif.	338,803	Daniel K. Inouye, D-Hawaii	189,707
3	Charles B. Rangel, D-N.Y.	197,018	Kent Conrad, D-N.D.	178,888
4	Robert T. Matsui, D-Calif.	185,092	Bob Dole, R-Kan.	95,570
5	Nancy Pelosi, D-Calif.	173,308	Patrick J. Leahy, D-Vt.	94,270
6	David E. Bonior, D-Mich.	150,979	Barbara A. Mikulski, D-Md.	76,119
7	Jerry Lewis, R-Calif.	128,564	John McCain, R-Ariz.	75,909
8	Vic Fazio, D-Calif.	120,754	Wendell H. Ford, D-Ky.	75,295
9	Edolphus Towns, D-N.Y.	117,158	Alfonse M. D'Amato, R-N.Y.	74,024
10	Joe L. Barton, R-Texas	115,939	John B. Breaux, D-La.	59,711
11	George Miller, D-Calif.	109,229	Bob Graham, D-Fla.	58,222
12	Paul E. Gillmor, R-Ohio	95,285	Christopher J. Dodd, D-Conn.	54,219
13	Norman Y. Mineta, D-Calif.	94,435	Richard C. Shelby, D-Ala.	48,352
14	John D. Dingell, D-Mich.	94,099	Harry Reid, D-Nev.	45,879
15	Thomas M. Foglietta, D-Pa.	91,605	Don Nickles, R-Okla.	30,502
16	James L. Oberstar, D-Minn.	86,541	Frank H. Murkowski, R-Alaska	23,203
17	Julian C. Dixon, D-Calif.	85,437	Bob Packwood, R-Ore.	21,450
18	Bill Richardson, D-N.M.	84,523	Wyche Fowler, Jr., D-Ga.	16,315
19	Dick Armey, R-Texas	83,451	Dale Bumpers, D-Ark.	15,832
20	Thomas J. Manton, D-N.Y.	82,860	Ernest F. Hollings, D-S.C.	15,020
21	Charles E. Schumer, D-N.Y.	82,304	Terry Sanford, D-N.C.	12,046
22	John P. Murtha, D-Pa.	80,782	Charles E. Grassley, R-Iowa	11,946
23	Michael R. McNulty, D-N.Y.	80,291	Robert F. Bennett, R-Utah	11,403
24	Jim McDermott, D-Wash.	79,580	Arlen Specter, R-Pa.	10,352
25	Tom Lantos, D-Calif.	78,952	Byron L. Dorgan,[a] D-N.D.	7,015

Note: Totals are for entire two-year House and six-year Senate cycles; both include special election expenditures.
[a] Nonincumbent or special election candidate.

Table 2-14 The Top Twenty-Five Spenders in the 1992 Congressional Races: Donations to Party Organizations

	House		*Senate*	
Rank	Candidate	Expenditures	Candidate	Expenditures
1	Henry A. Waxman, D-Calif.	$189,903	Tom Daschle, D-S.D.	$221,382
2	Robert T. Matsui, D-Calif.	93,983	Kent Conrad, D-N.D.	149,079
3	Vic Fazio, D-Calif.	92,075	Patrick J. Leahy, D-Vt.	85,171
4	Howard L. Berman, D-Calif.	88,688	John McCain, R-Ariz.	57,051
5	Nancy Pelosi, D-Calif.	85,338	Wendell H. Ford, D-Ky.	55,550
6	Bruce F. Vento, D-Minn.	73,400	Bob Dole, R-Kan.	52,995
7	James L. Oberstar, D-Minn.	68,322	Richard C. Shelby, D-Ala.	40,055
8	Joe L. Barton, R-Texas	65,773	Christopher J. Dodd, D-Conn.	37,135
9	Norman Y. Mineta, D-Calif.	63,831	Barbara A. Mikulski, D-Md.	36,274
10	Edolphus Towns, D-N.Y.	59,390	Harry Reid, D-Nev.	32,399
11	Julian C. Dixon, D-Calif.	49,167	Bob Graham, D-Fla.	32,000
12	Thomas S. Foley, D-Wash.	48,865	Alfonse M. D'Amato, R-N.Y.	21,874
13	Ronald V. Dellums, D-Calif.	48,589	John B. Breaux, D-La.	18,669
14	Don Edwards, D-Calif.	47,538	Dale Bumpers, D-Ark.	13,690
15	George Miller, D-Calif.	45,289	Ernest F. Hollings, D-S.C.	10,195
16	Leon E. Panetta, D-Calif.	39,941	Arlen Specter, R-Pa.	8,225
17	Richard H. Lehman, D-Calif.	39,550	Robert F. Bennett,[a] R-Utah	5,642
18	Michael G. Oxley, R-Ohio	39,404	Byron L. Dorgan,[a] D-N.D.	5,500
19	Robert S. Walker, R-Pa.	39,245	Daniel K. Inouye, D-Hawaii	4,868
20	Calvin Dooley, D-Calif.	38,688	Frank H. Murkowski, R-Alaska	3,366
21	Jack Brooks, D-Texas	38,400	John Glenn, D-Ohio	3,250
22	John D. Dingell, D-Mich.	36,901	Les AuCoin,[a] D-Ore.	2,850
23	Thomas J. Manton, D-N.Y.	36,861	Terry Sanford, D-N.C.	2,739
24	David Dreier, R-Calif.	35,500	Wyche Fowler, Jr., D-Ga.	2,500
25	Anthony C. Beilenson, D-Calif.	35,000	Charles E. Grassley, R-Iowa	2,336

Note: Totals are for entire two-year House and six-year Senate cycles; both include special election expenditures.
[a] Nonincumbent or special election candidate.

mittee. Sixty-one House and Senate candidates received donations ranging from $250 to $2,000.

For many members of Congress, donations to other candidates, political organizations, and civic groups serve as a cornerstone of political success. During the 1992 cycle, House and Senate incumbents gave away $10,653,432. The typical House member gave away $26,038, only $454 less on average than they donated in 1990. On average, Senate incumbents gave away $55,937, or $4,071 less than their 1990 counterparts.

Those involved in leadership battles invariably use their campaign treasuries to build bridges to other members whose votes they need or to demonstrate to their peers that they possess the proper party spirit. For example, Rep. Dick Armey (R-Texas) spent $277,198 more on his 1992 campaign than he had in 1990, but his underfunded opponent had nothing to do with it. The 1992 contest Armey worried most about was his successful fight to wrest the chairmanship of the Republican Conference away from Rep. Jerry Lewis.

To win that fight, Armey liberally distributed his campaign funds to a host of fellow Republicans. He made $1,000 donations to twenty-three candidates, $950 contributions to thirty-four candidates, and $500 donations to fourteen others. Most of his $1,000 gifts went to incumbents in hotly contested races, such as Gingrich, Gilchrest, Frank Riggs of California, Marlenee, and Iowans Jim Nussle and Jim Ross Lightfoot. His largest donation, $1,450, went to Michael D. Crapo of Idaho, who won the District 2 seat vacated by Richard Stallings. He donated $900 to Texan David Hobbs, who lost to Rep. Pete Geren.

Armey also sent "issue mailers" valued at $25 each to 159 challengers and open seat contestants. These unsolicited mailings dispensed helpful hints on how to successfully campaign against their Democratic opponents. Armey spent $816 on travel related to campaign appearances he made on behalf of four Republican challengers.

Lewis countered Armey's monetary onslaught by giving $110,864 to Republican House and Senate candidates. He also spent a total of $3,519 to attend campaign "schools" in Fair Oaks, Va., and Los Angeles, lending his expertise to Republican hopefuls from around the country. Unfortunately for Lewis, many of those he backed were not around to vote for him in December 1992, when he lost the leadership battle to Armey. Lewis donated $40,500 to challengers and open seat candidates who lost their House bids; he also gave $5,000 to House incumbents who lost.

As the list of donations dispensed by Berman and Waxman suggests, national, state, and local party organizations depended at least as much upon incumbents as incumbents depended upon them. Over the two-year election cycle, House incumbents who won renomination donated $4,232,783 to party coffers. Those contributing most heavily were Waxman, $189,903; Robert T. Matsui (D-Calif.), $93,983; Vic Fazio (D-Calif.), $92,075; Berman, $88,688; Nancy Pelosi (D-Calif.), $85,338; Bruce F. Vento (D-Minn.), $73,400; James L. Oberstar (D-Minn.), $68,322; and Joe L. Barton (R-Texas), $65,773 (see Table 2-14).

California Democrats dominated the list primarily because of their large donations to IMPAC 2000, which totaled $683,040. In addition to collecting $67,688 from Waxman and $65,688 from Berman, the redistricting PAC received $66,688 from Matsui, $47,168 from Julian C. Dixon, and $41,688 each from Pelosi, Dellums, Don Edwards, and Norman Y. Minetta (see Table 2-15).

Senate incumbents who gave freely to party organizations included Daschle, $221,382; Kent Conrad (D-N.D.), $149,079; Patrick J. Leahy (D-Vt.), $85,171; John McCain (R-Ariz.), $57,051; Ford, $55,550; Dole, $52,995; and Richard C. Shelby (D-Ala.), $40,055. Together, the twenty-eight incumbents who contested the November general election gave $893,828 to help various party organizations (see Table 2-14).

Elected in 1986 with only 52 percent of the vote, Daschle had anticipated a strong challenge in 1992, so he never stopped running. Between January 1, 1987 and December 31, 1991, he invested nearly $1.7 million in his permanent campaign, including $988,002 for staff, travel, and other overhead; $368,504 for fund raising; $42,128 for polling; $20,402 for constituent gifts and entertainment; and $125,632 for advertising. However, once Daschle realized that no strong challenge was coming, he began to give his campaign funds away. Between October 15 and October 30, 1992, Daschle's campaign contributed $210,000 to the South Dakota Democratic party for its efforts on behalf of state and local candidates.

Freshman Sen. Kent Conrad announced on April 2, 1992 that he would not seek a second term, citing his 1986 campaign pledge to serve only six years if the federal budget and trade deficits had not been brought under control. Five months later, Conrad reversed course and announced he would seek the Senate seat left vacant by the death of Sen. Quentin Burdick. In the interim, Conrad had dispatched a letter to those who had already contributed to his general election fund asking them whether they wanted their money refunded or donated to the North Dakota Democratic party. As a result of that letter, Conrad funneled $52,336 to the state party during his brief retirement. This accounted for 35 percent of his total party donations.

While most members of Congress used donations to build political influence within their own parties, Rep. David E. Bonior (D-Mich.) spent $94,319 of his campaign treasury on television advertising in support of a proposed ballot initiative that would have mandated a $500 property tax cut for middle income homeowners. The initiative was sponsored by the Michigan Homeowners Tax Break Committee, which Bonior cochaired.

As a way to foster goodwill in their communities, House and Senate incumbents dipped into their campaign funds for $1,476,256 to satisfy an almost continuous stream of requests from charities and booster organizations. Rep. Jim McDermott (D-Wash.), one of two physicians in the House, spent $3,696 of his campaign treasury to print materials for the international AIDS conference held in June 1992. He spent $4,000 of his campaign funds to help defray the costs of an AIDS cartoon exhibit displayed at that same convention. Most of his other charitable contributions were more modest, such as his $35 gift to Girls Inc. of Puget Sound and his $30 donation to the Union Gospel Mission.

Table 2-15 Donations by California Democrats to IMPAC 2000

Representative	Donation
Henry A. Waxman	$ 67,688
Robert T. Matsui	66,688
Howard L. Berman	65,688
Julian C. Dixon	47,168
Ronald V. Dellums	41,688
Don Edwards	41,688
Norman Y. Mineta	41,688
Nancy Pelosi	41,688
Calvin Dooley	38,188
Anthony C. Beilenson	35,000
Richard H. Lehman	35,000
Vic Fazio	34,000
Leon E. Panetta	29,000
Matthew G. Martinez	23,000
George Miller	22,688
George E. Brown, Jr.	19,180
Esteban E. Torres	13,000
Gary Condit	12,500
Pete Stark	7,000
Maxine Waters	500
Total	**$683,040**

Over his six-year election cycle, Inouye donated $171,686 of his campaign treasury to various charities and booster groups. In April 1988 he gave $150,000 to the Hawaii Education Foundation, an organization he founded that provides college scholarships to Hawaiian high school students.

Some members gave for much more personal reasons. Looking only at his campaign financial statements, it would be difficult to tell whether Lantos represented California or New Hampshire. While he contributed $16,296 to candidates and party organizations in California, he donated $33,500 to candidates and party organizations in New Hampshire. He gave $12,500 to the New Hampshire Democratic party. He contributed to three of New Hampshire's gubernatorial candidates—$5,000 each to Ned Helms, Norman E. D'Amours, and the eventual nominee, Deborah Arnesen. He even contributed to both Democratic candidates for mayor of Nashua. Not coincidentally, Lantos's son-in-law, Rep. Dick Swett, represents New Hampshire's District 2, which includes Nashua.

In Ohio, Republican Rep. Paul E. Gillmor essentially used his campaign as an auxiliary fund for his wife Karen, who waged a successful campaign for the state senate. Gillmor's campaign donated $72,000 to his wife's campaign, including a $22,000 loan he later forgave. He spent $13,198 of his treasury on postage, which he then gave to his wife's campaign as an in-kind contribution.

In 1988 Rep. Pete Stark (D-Calif.) made an interest-free loan of $88,645 from his campaign funds to his son Jeff, who used it to make an unsuccessful bid for Alameda county supervisor. In 1992 that loan was forgiven, although it was not included in his contributions for the 1992 election cycle, since he had "spent" the money four years earlier.

SEEKING HIGHER OFFICE

Rep. Arthur Ravenel, Jr. (R-S.C.) was seeking a fourth term in 1992, but he was already running for governor in 1994. Having spent just $3,522 on fund raising during his virtually uncontested 1990 campaign, Ravenel sank $22,088 into a single event in March 1992. The dinner, held to coincide with Ravenel's sixty-fifth birthday, netted roughly $50,000. "We made a bigger effort for the birthday party in 1992 because we knew we were running for governor," noted Sharon H. Chellis, Ravenel's administrative assistant. Such fund-raising efforts and the lack of strong opposition allowed Ravenel to increase his cash reserves from $284,458 to $430,586. On December 28, 1992, less than two months after winning reelection, Ravenel transferred those reserves into his gubernatorial campaign account.

Ravenel was not alone. Like entrepreneurs everywhere, many members of Congress are eager to expand their horizons. In 1991 and 1992 thirteen House members decided to relinquish their seats to seek Senate seats or wage gubernatorial campaigns. Many others used their 1992 campaign treasuries to explore the possibilities open to them in 1994.

Rep. Don Sundquist (R-Tenn.) spent $995,922 during the 1992 election cycle—more than twice what he spent on his 1990 reelection effort. That massively increased spending was partly the result of a redistricting plan that increased Democratic strength in his district. It also reflected the fact that Sundquist's 1990 Democratic opponent had put less than $5,000 into his token challenge, while his 1992 Democratic challenger, retired minister David R. Davis, had $93,582 to spend. However, much of the increased spending related more to Sundquist's plans to run for governor in 1994 than to his 1992 reelection effort.

Sundquist began airing his television and radio commercials in July, despite being unopposed in the August 8 primary. During July and August he spent $17,090 for air time on Memphis television stations, $18,319 for radio spots, and $3,252 for time on local cable television outlets. With an eye toward the 1994 gubernatorial campaign, he also spent $27,914 to buy time on Nashville television, which reached only a small portion of his constituents but allowed him to reach large numbers of voters crucial to any statewide bid. Testimonial ads featuring former senator Howard Baker and former governor Lamar Alexander focused on Sundquist's integrity and his commitment to Tennessee, not simply the parochial interests of his district.

In 1991 Rep. Matsui transferred $437,448 from his House committee to the Matsui for Senate Committee, which he intended to use to run for the seat vacated by Democratic Sen. Alan Cranston. At the end of 1991, Matsui abruptly withdrew from the crowded field, opting to remain in his safe House seat.

Seriously considering a 1994 gubernatorial bid, Rep. Bob Clement (D-Tenn.) asked his media adviser, Morgan/Fletcher

& Co. of Nashville, to develop a two-minute biographical television commercial. The spot highlighted the Clement family's political history, pointing to his father's three terms as governor and his aunt's service in the state senate. Morgan/Fletcher produced several hundred copies of an eight-minute video, which were given to key supporters.

Fortunately for Rep. John Conyers, Jr. (D-Mich.), the contest for mayor of Detroit takes place every four years during the off-year for congressional candidates. Having unsuccessfully challenged Mayor Coleman A. Young in the 1989 Democratic primary, Conyers transferred $92,660 of his excess 1992 funds into a mayoral campaign fund he established for another unsuccessful bid in 1993.

Facing only token challenges or having the ability to raise far more than they needed for their campaigns, some members used their 1992 war chests to pay off campaign debts accumulated during previous, unsuccessful campaigns for higher office. Over the six-year Senate election cycle, Dole transferred more than $1.3 million from his campaign treasury to repay debts from his 1988 presidential bid and still found nearly $2.2 million to spend on his Senate campaign. His opponent managed to scrape together less than $332,000 for her token challenge.

Between 1987 and 1992, Sen. John Glenn (D-Ohio) used $958,945 from his Senate campaign account to repay debts from his failed 1984 presidential campaign. The fact that he did not use more of his treasury for that purpose fueled a blistering television ad campaign by his Republican opponent, Lt. Gov. Mike DeWine. "He's got a condo in Vail, a million-dollar home, and a fifty-three foot yacht. But John Glenn still owes $3 million." In a takeoff on the Energizer bunny commercials, the ad ended with a toy astronaut breaking through the on-screen graphics, pounding on a drum with the Glenn campaign logo on it. "John Glenn. He keeps owing, and owing, and owing," intoned the voice-over.

Over the two-year House cycle, Gephardt spent $244,999 of his treasury to pay off debts accumulated during his short-lived 1988 presidential campaign. Rep. W. J. "Billy" Tauzin (D-La.) spent a much more modest $15,922 to repay the last of his debts from a failed gubernatorial bid in 1987. Tauzin had previously tapped his 1990 House campaign for $275,600 to reduce that debt.

In short, while the cost of political campaigns is rising rapidly, that cost is only partially related to the increased cost of things most people think of as campaigning—appealing to constituents for votes. Modern campaign funds are, in fact, political funds that provide many of the same services that local party organizations once supplied. For some members of Congress, their campaign treasuries are little more than private slush funds that enable them to live a lifestyle not afforded by their congressional paycheck.

Chapter 3

House Freshmen
Settling In

We believe if you're going to have real reform, you must push from the bottom up. Once you're here three or four terms, you have a vested interest in the way things are run.
                                      1990 Freshman Rep. John A. Boehner (R-Ohio)

Members have 730 days to get reelected.
                                      1990 Freshman Rep. Mike Kopetski (D-Ore.)

Freshman Rep. Scott L. Klug (R-Wis.) had beaten long odds to win his seat in 1990, upsetting fifteen-term Democratic incumbent Robert W. Kastenmeier. A well-known television reporter and news anchor in Madison, Klug had entered the race with one big advantage—60 percent of the voters already knew his name. However, like most challengers, Klug had struggled to overcome one big disadvantage—a shortage of money. While Kastenmeier had pumped $184,753 into advertising, Klug had spent $184,315 on his entire campaign, $64,041 of which was invested in advertising. Klug emerged with a 6-point victory by convincing voters that Kastenmeier was an entrenched incumbent who had been in Congress too long.

Once in office, Klug quickly embraced the monetary advantages of incumbency. During the 1992 election cycle he spent $153,815 to raise money—more than five times what he spent on fund raising in 1990. As a challenger, Klug had raised only $32,800 from political action committees (PACs). During the 1992 cycle, his change in status allowed him to tap that same PAC community for $226,266. Incumbency opened the spigot on large individual donations, as well. With events such as a Mother's Day reception featuring First Lady Barbara Bush that grossed $100,000 and his Team '92 congressional club, Klug raised $300,096 from individuals who gave at least $200—$236,999 more than he had raised from such donors in 1990. A $48,699 investment in direct-mail solicitations helped push his receipts from smaller donors to $311,971, a $243,282 increase over 1990.

During the off-year, Klug spent $106,294 to keep his permanent campaign operation running smoothly. While he closed his campaign office, he still managed to spend $38,673 on overhead and $57,762 on fund raising. When Democratic activist Ada Deer spent $443,644 to challenge Klug in 1992, his new-found fund-raising prowess allowed him to counter with an additional $717,738 election-year splurge—nearly four times as much as he had invested in the 1990 effort.

While Deer invested $176,951 in advertising, Klug poured $321,406 into his ad campaign. Strapped for cash in 1990, Klug had spent $62,584 on a series of ten-second commercials, but in 1992 he pumped $261,689 into producing and airing both fifteen-second and standard thirty-second spots. His tight budget in 1990 had allowed for only $1,457 in other advertising, but in 1992 he had sufficient resources to invest $26,435 in billboards and $32,103 in newspaper advertising.

In 1990 Klug had been unable to afford persuasion mailings, but in 1992 he spent $86,069 on brochures and persuasion mail that targeted farmers, veterans, and undecided voters. A four-page tabloid-style brochure was dropped on doorsteps throughout the district, and volunteers swept through the district with door-hangers on the campaign's final weekend. Unable to afford a phonebank operation in 1990, Klug paid Payco Teleservices of Herndon, Va., $45,119 for such services in 1992. As Brandon R. Scholz, Klug's chief of staff, put it, "You have a level of comfort with more money."

That level of comfort was perhaps best illustrated by the campaign's final weekend. "We knew one of the local newspapers was going to profile the race on the Sunday before the election," recalled Scholz. "So we hired a helicopter to fly us around the district to eight prearranged rallies on the Saturday before the election. We took a reporter and a photographer with us, and the next morning they ran aerial photos of 200 people waiting for Scott, of him in the helicopter, and of him on a wooden box addressing the crowd. They ran a file photo of Ada Deer. That's what having money enabled us to do."

On election day, Klug steamrolled Deer, collecting 63 percent of the vote.

If anything, Klug's experience was somewhat unusual because he prevailed in 1990 with relatively limited resources. While most challengers struggled mightily to raise money, most successful challengers had no such problems. The forty-two freshmen who contested the 1992 general elections had spent a total of $23,837,306 on their 1990 bids, an average of $567,555.

That was $177,168 more than the typical incumbent spent that year and even $10,410 higher than the average outlay reported by incumbents involved in hotly contested races.

The principal difference between these successful outsiders and well-heeled incumbents in 1990 was resource allocation. Challengers and open seat candidates elected in 1990 invested 59 percent of their money in direct appeals to voters, while the typical incumbent invested only 40 percent of his or her budget in communicating with the electorate. However, by 1992 this spending difference had virtually disappeared.

Just two years removed from their initial campaigns, the freshman class pumped a total of $22,474,819 into their reelection bids, an average of $535,115. Their investment in direct appeals for votes dropped from 59 in 1990 to 49 percent in 1992. Conversely, concerned over redistricting and anti-incumbent sentiment, those elected prior to 1990 allocated a larger percentage of their 1992 budgets to direct appeals for votes. On average, these longer-term incumbents reported spending $572,555, and 47 percent of that was spent on direct appeals for votes—a 7-point increase (see Tables 3-1 and 3-2).

Although many had run outsider campaigns, most members of the 1990 freshman class quickly adopted the permanent campaign mode in preparing for their reelection. Led by Rep. Jack Reed (D-R.I.), who spent $213,068, and by Randy "Duke" Cunningham (R-Calif.), who spent $167,664, the forty-two freshmen who won renomination spent a total of $3,770,056 during the off-year to lay the groundwork for their reelection bids, an average of $89,763. The typical freshman sank $32,577 into overhead and $38,413 into fund raising, which together accounted for 79 percent of their off-year spending (see Table 3-3). Twenty of these newly elected members opted to maintain permanent campaign offices throughout their first term.

The heavy investment in campaign infrastructure continued into 1992. Of the $18,704,763 spent by freshmen during 1992, 36 percent was devoted to overhead and fund raising. The comparable figure for those elected prior to 1990 was 33 percent.

While they reported spending an average of $32,440 less on their first reelection bids than they had invested in winning their seats, the typical freshman reduced his or her investment in advertising by $55,090. Outlays for persuasion mail and other grass-roots appeals for votes dropped an average of $19,282. On the other hand, average fund-raising expenses more than doubled from $54,347 to $111,761. As challengers in 1990, these forty-two candidates had given away an average of only $2,159. Running as incumbents in 1992, these same candidates donated an average of $10,336. While constituent entertainment had been an unaffordable luxury in 1990, by 1992 the typical freshman found enough room in his or her budget to spend $4,817 on constituent stroking (see Table 3-4).

To pay for their nonstop campaigns, the new freshmen quickly adopted the fund-raising style of their Capitol Hill brethren. As successful challengers and open seat candidates in 1990, the forty-two freshmen had raised a very respectable $7,994,740 from PACs. During the 1992 election cycle, their PAC receipts jumped 45 percent, to $11,568,763.

Rep. Calvin Dooley (D-Calif.) discovered that PACs were suddenly looking for him and were willing to give him more money than he was looking for. Tickets to his 1991 Washington, D.C., PAC events were $350; by 1992 PACs were encouraging Dooley to raise his prices to $500. "PACs were telling us that they were willing to give us that much, so we said great," explained chief of staff Lisa Quigley. Dooley held three PAC events during the two-year cycle, helping to push his PAC donations to $242,583, a 42 percent increase over 1990.

With cash reserves of only $9,233 at the beginning of 1991 and 1990 campaign debts of $79,406, Rep. Collin C. Peterson (D-Minn.) put considerable emphasis on his off-year fund-raising efforts. During 1991, 55 percent of the $53,942 spent to maintain his permanent campaign was invested in raising money. Those efforts yielded contributions totaling $197,677, including PAC donations of $154,985. By January 1992, Peterson had eliminated his debts and increased his cash-on-hand to $100,431. Over the two-year cycle, he raised $321,507 from PACs, an increase of $135,909 over 1990. In all, contributions from PACs accounted for 70 percent of his total contributions for the 1992 cycle.

Following his 1990 triumph, Rep. Bill Zeliff (R-N.H.) had told us he would actively work to increase contributions from PACs to help repay both the $263,000 he had loaned the campaign and the $112,000 in bank loans the campaign had been forced to take out. He made good on that promise, more than doubling his PAC contributions, from $130,601 in 1990 to $325,915 in 1992.

As a group, freshmen raised 6 percent less in the 1992 election cycle than they had in 1990 from individuals who gave at least $200. Given his debt load, Zeliff could not afford to be one of those who scaled back his fund-raising efforts in any way. During the 1992 cycle, Zeliff raised $309,837 in large individual donations, a 41 percent increase over 1990. He raised $86,599 from out-of-state contributors who gave $200 or more—twice what he raised from such donors in 1990. Zeliff was so pleased with the results of his increased fund-raising efforts that he threw his major donors a thank-you party after the election. The party, held at his Christmas tree farm in Jackson, N.H., cost $6,439.

Arguably, freshmen might be expected to run permanent campaigns because of their potentially tenuous electoral positions. Few could blame these new members for doing everything possible to hold onto their seats, having just spent considerable energy and money to win them. That certainly was the case with Frank Riggs (R-Calif.).

Riggs had pulled off one of the biggest upsets of 1990 by defeating Democratic Rep. Douglas H. Bosco by 3,314 votes, despite being outspent by $175,732. Riggs owed his victory, at least in part, to the candidacy of Darlene G. Comingore, a Peace and Freedom party candidate who garnered 15 percent of the vote. Having won the seat while only capturing 43 percent of the vote, Riggs could not afford to stop running.

Riggs's initial victory had cost $262,809. During 1991 alone, he spent $149,448 to keep his campaign running smoothly. Although he decided not to maintain a permanent campaign headquarters, he spent $43,332 on overhead, including $21,942 on

Table 3-1 What Campaign Money Buys in the 1992 House Races: Average Expenditures by 1990 Freshmen Versus More Entrenched Incumbents

Major Category	Representatives Elected in 1990			Representatives Elected Before 1990			Unopposed Seats
	Total	Hot Races[a]	Contested Races[b]	Total	Hot Races[a]	Contested Races[b]	
Overhead							
Office furniture/supplies	$ 8,501	$ 10,177	$ 7,245	$ 8,741	$ 10,487	$ 7,540	$ 5,364
Rent/utilities	7,533	9,391	6,140	9,357	11,637	7,703	6,715
Salaries	45,000	47,094	43,430	50,650	63,172	42,028	26,567
Taxes	9,999	11,789	8,656	17,395	19,659	15,920	11,294
Bank/investment fees	3,392	4,380	2,651	1,037	1,230	928	151
Lawyers/accountants	9,889	10,055	9,764	10,145	12,301	8,717	4,842
Telephone	9,350	11,086	8,047	8,353	10,887	6,418	7,421
Campaign automobile	1,353	972	1,639	3,449	4,555	2,454	6,128
Computers/office equipment	8,077	8,940	7,430	9,141	10,587	7,942	10,555
Travel	15,497	19,155	12,753	22,016	25,085	19,090	32,856
Food/meetings	1,276	1,568	1,056	3,903	3,417	3,800	13,869
Total Overhead	**119,867**	**134,608**	**108,812**	**144,188**	**173,018**	**122,541**	**125,764**
Fund Raising							
Events	79,766	80,921	78,899	63,394	69,057	59,615	50,024
Direct mail	30,625	45,063	19,797	20,010	26,286	15,861	4,395
Telemarketing	1,370	7	2,393	1,385	2,086	904	0
Total Fund Raising	**111,761**	**125,990**	**101,089**	**84,789**	**97,429**	**76,380**	**54,419**
Polling	**16,567**	**17,869**	**15,590**	**20,241**	**29,177**	**14,121**	**2,400**
Advertising							
Electronic media	156,814	193,364	129,401	138,884	210,152	89,766	2,748
Other media	10,528	9,087	11,609	15,787	16,997	15,478	2,655
Total Advertising	**167,342**	**202,451**	**141,010**	**154,671**	**227,149**	**105,244**	**5,402**
Other Campaign Activity							
Persuasion mail/brochures	56,013	63,592	50,328	71,282	103,048	49,610	6,046
Actual campaigning	35,592	37,200	34,387	42,050	52,981	33,998	31,839
Staff/Volunteers	886	708	1,019	1,525	2,069	1,135	780
Total Other Campaign Activity	**92,491**	**101,500**	**85,734**	**114,857**	**158,098**	**84,744**	**38,666**
Constituent Gifts/ Entertainment	**4,817**	**2,311**	**6,697**	**9,135**	**8,680**	**9,220**	**14,727**
Donations to							
Candidates from same state	1,619	1,136	1,981	5,752	2,673	7,435	20,711
Candidates from other states	1,980	456	3,123	4,186	2,301	5,638	4,625
Civic organizations	1,348	649	1,872	3,578	2,831	4,140	4,035
Ideological groups	718	424	939	1,657	1,632	1,734	439
Political parties	4,672	2,469	6,324	13,350	11,289	15,196	8,490
Total Donations	**10,336**	**5,134**	**14,238**	**28,522**	**20,726**	**34,144**	**38,300**
Unitemized Expenses	**11,933**	**10,849**	**12,746**	**16,152**	**17,674**	**14,662**	**22,333**
Total Expenditures	**$535,115**	**$600,712**	**$485,917**	**$572,555**	**$731,951**	**$461,055**	**$302,012**

Note: Totals are for the entire two-year cycle.

[a] Races where incumbent garners 60 percent or less of the vote.
[b] Races where incumbent garners more than 60 percent of the vote.

Table 3-2 What Campaign Money Buys in the 1992 House Races: Expenditures by 1990 Freshmen Versus More Entrenched Incumbents, by Percentage

Major Category	Representatives Elected in 1990			Representatives Elected Before 1990			Unopposed Seats
	Total	Hot Races[a]	Contested Races[b]	Total	Hot Races[a]	Contested Races[b]	
Overhead							
Office furniture/supplies	1.59	1.69	1.49	1.53	1.43	1.64	1.78
Rent/utilities	1.41	1.56	1.26	1.63	1.59	1.67	2.22
Salaries	8.41	7.84	8.94	8.85	8.63	9.12	8.80
Taxes	1.87	1.96	1.78	3.04	2.69	3.45	3.74
Bank/investment fees	.63	.73	.55	.18	.17	.20	.05
Lawyers/accountants	1.85	1.67	2.01	1.77	1.68	1.89	1.60
Telephone	1.75	1.85	1.66	1.46	1.49	1.39	2.46
Campaign automobile	.25	.16	.34	.60	.62	.53	2.03
Computers/office equipment	1.51	1.49	1.53	1.60	1.45	1.72	3.50
Travel	2.90	3.19	2.62	3.85	3.43	4.14	10.88
Food/meetings	.24	.26	.22	.68	.47	.82	4.59
Total Overhead	**22.40**	**22.41**	**22.39**	**25.18**	**23.64**	**26.58**	**41.64**
Fund Raising							
Events	14.91	13.47	16.24	11.07	9.43	12.93	16.56
Direct mail	5.72	7.50	4.07	3.49	3.59	3.44	1.46
Telemarketing	.26	0	.49	.24	.29	.20	0
Total Fund Raising	**20.89**	**20.97**	**20.80**	**14.81**	**13.31**	**16.57**	**18.02**
Polling	**3.10**	**2.97**	**3.21**	**3.54**	**3.99**	**3.06**	**.79**
Advertising							
Electronic media	29.30	32.19	26.63	24.26	28.71	19.47	.91
Other media	1.97	1.51	2.39	2.76	2.32	3.36	.88
Total Advertising	**31.27**	**33.70**	**29.02**	**27.01**	**31.03**	**22.83**	**1.79**
Other Campaign Activity							
Persuasion mail/brochures	10.47	10.59	10.36	12.45	14.08	10.76	2.00
Actual campaigning	6.65	6.19	7.08	7.34	7.24	7.37	10.54
Staff/Volunteers	.17	.12	.21	.27	.28	.25	.26
Total Other Campaign Activity	**17.28**	**16.90**	**17.64**	**20.06**	**21.60**	**18.38**	**12.80**
Constituent Gifts/ Entertainment	**.90**	**.38**	**1.38**	**1.60**	**1.19**	**2.00**	**4.88**
Donations to							
Candidates from same state	.30	.19	.41	1.00	.37	1.61	6.86
Candidates from other states	.37	.08	.64	.73	.31	1.22	1.53
Civic organizations	.25	.11	.39	.62	.39	.90	1.34
Ideological groups	.13	.07	.19	.29	.22	.38	.15
Political parties	.87	.41	1.30	2.33	1.54	3.30	2.81
Total Donations	**1.93**	**.85**	**2.93**	**4.98**	**2.83**	**7.41**	**12.68**
Unitemized Expenses	**2.23**	**1.81**	**2.62**	**2.82**	**2.41**	**3.18**	**7.39**
Total Expenditures	**100.00**	**100.00**	**100.00**	**100.00**	**100.00**	**100.00**	**100.00**

Note: Totals are for the entire two-year cycle.
[a]Races where incumbent garners 60 percent or less of the vote.
[b]Races where incumbent garners more than 60 percent of the vote.

legal and accounting fees. For his initial campaign, Riggs had invested $23,553 in fund raising; during 1991 he spent $85,581 to raise money.

Ultimately, Riggs spent $668,438 on his unsuccessful attempt to hold onto his seat—well over twice what he spent to win it in the first place. Unfortunately for him, 48 percent of his money was invested in raising money, and another 19 percent was put into overhead. Only about 26 percent of his treasury was invested in direct appeals for votes. Without a strong third-party candidate to dilute Democratic strength in the district, he lost by 6,410 votes.

Rep. Gary A. Franks (R-Conn.), the first black Republican elected to the House since 1934, also had good reason to worry. Franks had spent $621,499 during his successful 1990 campaign and had emerged with 52 percent of the general election votes. After a shaky first term in which he was plagued by high staff turnover, sued by a savings and loan for defaulting on loans totaling $471,000, and sued by his 1990 campaign manager for back wages, it looked like Franks would need a minor miracle to win a second term.

Franks never closed his campaign office following the 1990 election, and rent and utilities on that space amounted to $4,315 during 1991. Off-year salaries and taxes added $26,397 and $7,316, respectively, helping to push his overhead for the year to $61,112. With fund-raising costs of $60,225 and miscellaneous expenses of $13,279, Franks's total investment in his off-year campaign totaled $134,616, or 23 percent of the $589,991 he spent during the two-year election cycle.

Even with this substantial preliminary effort, Franks would have probably lost the 1992 election to Democrat James J. Lawlor had it not been for Lynn H. Taborsak, who ran as an independent following her defeat in a bitter Democratic primary. With Taborsak attracting 23 percent and Lawlor 31 percent of the general election votes, Franks slipped through with a 44 percent plurality.

Reapportionment cost Iowa one of its five House seats, and freshman Republican Rep. Jim Nussle found himself locked in a battle for political survival against Democratic Rep. Dave Nagle. To prepare for that 1992 fight, Nussle invested $117,665 in his off-year campaign, including $43,672 in overhead and $56,115 in fund raising. With the help of a $737,077 election-year push, Nussle emerged with a razor-thin 2,966-vote victory.

However, not all freshmen were faced with such difficult circumstances in their first reelection contests. Nine of the freshman class received 70 percent of the vote or better in both the primary and general elections, and fifteen collected at least 60 percent of the vote at each stage of the reelection process. Nineteen of these twenty-four easy winners were already so safely ensconced that they drew no primary opposition.

Most of these lopsided races were financially uncompetitive, as well. Rep. David L. Hobson (R-Ohio) spent $266,760 in garnering 71 percent of the votes in his contest with Democrat Clifford S. Heskett, a retired teacher who spent less than $5,000. Rep. Bill Brewster (D-Okla.) invested $351,147 in his initial reelection bid and collected 75 percent of the vote against

Table 3-3 What Campaign Money Buys in the 1992 House Races: Off-year Expenditures by 1990 Freshmen

Major Category	Total	Average	Percent
Overhead			
Office furniture/supplies	$ 96,813	$ 2,305	2.57
Rent/utilities	90,494	2,155	2.40
Salaries	378,163	9,004	10.03
Taxes	96,089	2,288	2.55
Bank/investment fees	95,689	2,278	2.54
Lawyers/accountants	159,091	3,788	4.22
Telephone	104,584	2,490	2.77
Campaign automobile	23,522	560	.62
Computers/office equipment	116,975	2,785	3.10
Travel	190,860	4,544	5.06
Food/meetings	15,954	380	.42
Total Overhead	**1,368,234**	**32,577**	**36.29**
Fund Raising			
Events	1,266,912	30,165	33.60
Direct mail	323,310	7,698	8.58
Telemarketing	23,104	550	.61
Total Fund Raising	**1,613,326**	**38,413**	**42.79**
Polling	**40,685**	**969**	**1.08**
Advertising			
Electronic media	63,463	1,511	1.68
Other media	28,628	682	.76
Total Advertising	**92,091**	**2,193**	**2.44**
Other Campaign Activity			
Persuasion mail/brochures	69,496	1,655	1.84
Actual campaigning	185,364	4,413	4.92
Staff/Volunteers	4,748	113	.13
Total Other Campaign Activity	**259,608**	**6,181**	**6.89**
Constituent Gifts/ Entertainment	**114,699**	**2,731**	**3.04**
Donations to			
Candidates from same state	12,489	297	.33
Candidates from other states	5,385	128	.14
Civic organizations	22,340	532	.59
Ideological groups	8,592	205	.23
Political parties	85,033	2,025	2.26
Total Donations	**133,839**	**3,187**	**3.55**
Unitemized Expenses	**147,572**	**3,514**	**3.91**
Total Expenditures	**$3,770,056**	**$89,763**	**100.00**

Note: Totals are for the entire two-year cycle.

Republican Robert W. Stokes, a teaching assistant who scraped together $5,723 for the race. Rep. Jim Ramstad (R-Minn.) spent $599,672 in collecting 64 percent of the general election vote; his opponent, Democrat Paul Mandell, spent $18,166. None of these three freshmen faced primary opposition.

In all, freshmen who won reelection with 60 percent of the vote or more spent $11,661,997 on their 1992 bids, while their opponents spent only $3,576,109. Excluding the $1,441,694 spent by Republican Linda Bean (Maine), who unsuccessfully challenged Democratic Rep. Thomas H. Andrews, challengers in these lopsided races spent only $2,134,415. Although their reelections were never really in doubt, spending by the twenty-four freshmen in these contests accounted for 52 percent of the money spent by members of the 1990 freshman class (see Table 3-5).

Rep. Bill Barrett (R-Neb.) had few worries in his first reelection campaign, even though he had won his 1990 open seat contest by only 4,373 votes. Barrett's predecessor, Republican Virginia Smith, had held the seat from 1974 until her retirement in 1990. President George Bush had carried the district by a two-to-one margin in 1988. Bush ultimately carried District 3 by 23 points in 1992, with independent presidential candidate Ross Perot finishing second. Barrett's 1992 Democratic opponent, farmer Lowell Fisher, had little money and no prior political experience. On election day, Barrett captured 72 percent of the votes.

Reflecting his easy path to reelection, Barrett spent $242,768 less on his 1992 campaign than he had in 1990, a decrease of 39 percent. He spent $85,276 less on advertising and $82,064 less on other direct appeals for votes. Barrett had invested $34,041 in polls during the 1990 campaign; with the 1992 race never in doubt, he spent just $9,700 on polls. Overhead expenses dropped from $165,640 in 1990 to $81,919 in 1992.

Yet, at a time when Barrett was slashing his spending on many aspects of his campaign operation, he significantly increased his investment in fund raising. Having emerged from the 1990 campaign with debts of $70,000 and campaign cash reserves of only $19,982, raising money became a top priority. During 1991, fund-raising expenses accounted for 57 percent of the $67,768 he spent to keep his permanent campaign running smoothly. These efforts reaped individual contributions totaling $81,598 and PAC donations of $74,775. He began 1992 with no debts and cash reserves of $27,847.

Over the two-year cycle, Barrett spent $97,821 to raise money—a $45,225 increase over 1990. As a percentage of total spending, his fund-raising costs jumped from 9 percent in 1990 to 26 percent in 1992. While direct appeals for votes accounted for 56 percent of his 1990 outlays, such spending accounted for 48 percent of his total spending in 1992.

Similarly, Rep. Chet Edwards (D-Texas) had spent more than $730,000 in 1990 to defeat Republican Hugh D. Shine, who had invested nearly $859,000 in the bitterly contested battle for the open seat created by the retirement of Democratic Rep. Marvin Leath. Challenged in 1992 by a Republican opponent who spent just $17,000, Edwards coasted to victory with 67 percent of the vote, spending "only" $357,418.

Edwards chose to follow the lead of the more experienced incumbents and kept a campaign office open during the off-year. He invested $149,106 in his off-year campaign, spending $61,348 on overhead, $32,685 on staff salaries, $5,876 on telephone service, $4,734 on supplies, $3,213 on rent and utilities, and $3,200 on office equipment. Edwards also invested $57,764 in fund raising in 1991. A birthday celebration in Waco featured Democratic Gov. Ann Richards and attracted approximately 2,500 supporters who paid $10 each to dine on barbecue, Mexican food, and a huge chocolate cake. With costs totaling $22,825, the event barely broke even. Edwards also held one major off-year event aimed at PACs that brought in $168,660 of the $258,792 he raised in 1991.

Even though he had virtually no opposition in 1992, Edwards pumped another $208,312 into his election-year campaign effort. Not surprisingly, only 37 percent of that 1992 spending was put into direct appeals for votes; 42 percent was invested in overhead and fund raising.

Rep. Dick Swett was thought to be a marked man from the moment he upset Republican Rep. Chuck Douglas in 1990, thereby becoming the first Democrat elected to represent New Hampshire's District 2 since 1912. But he soon discovered that incumbency had its distinct advantages. Determined not to be a one-term aberration, Swett spent $319,578 more to defend his seat than he spent to win it. However, much of that 69 percent increase in spending was the result of a dramatic shift in his approach to raising money, not a matter of investing more in direct appeals for votes.

In 1990 fund raising consumed less than 1 percent of Swett's $465,540 treasury, a remarkable feat made possible by his wife's political connections. Katrina Lantos-Swett, the daughter of Rep. Tom Lantos (D-Calif.), had long served as a fund-raiser for her father, and she simply tapped into a network of donors across the country to fill her husband's treasury. The campaign augmented her efforts by holding in-home receptions that cost a total of only $3,463.

For the 1992 campaign, Swett followed his father-in-law's example and turned to Robert H. Bassin Associates of Washington, D.C., for help with PAC fund raising. Over the two-year election cycle, Swett paid Bassin $53,884 for coordinating PAC receptions that helped raise $403,900—more than twice the $186,000 he raised from PACs in 1990.

Fund-raising trips to New York, Atlanta, and Hillsborough, Calif., helped raise $317,968 from individual out-of-state donors who gave at least $200, which accounted for 85 percent of his large donations. To tap small donors, Swett initially turned to Intelligent Software Systems of San Carlos, Calif., a direct-mail consultant used by his father-in-law. As the need for money intensified, Swett also brought in A. B. Data of Milwaukee, Wis. Together, these firms helped push Swett's small contributions to $71,360. Intelligent Software and A. B. Data received $11,571 and $11,629, respectively. In all, Swett spent $155,326 to raise money for the 1992 campaign, an increase of $151,863 over 1990.

Swett's investment in overhead rose 38 percent, from $133,501 in the 1990 cycle to $184,252 in 1992. Having violated the state's voluntary spending limit for the 1990 general election campaign, Swett agreed to pay a $19,209 fine to the state of New Hampshire. He opted not to agree to abide by those voluntary limits in 1992. Payments to his lawyers amounted to $16,705.

In contrast, Swett's spending on direct appeals for votes rose

Table 3-4 What Campaign Money Buys 1992 and 1990 House Races: Expenditures by 1990 Freshmen

Major Category	1992 Cycle			1990 Cycle		
	Total	Average	Percent	Total	Average	Percent
Overhead						
Office furniture/supplies	$ 357,062	$ 8,501	1.59	$ 546,380	$ 13,009	2.29
Rent/utilities	316,393	7,533	1.41	331,056	7,882	1.39
Salaries	1,890,018	45,000	8.41	2,956,835	70,401	12.40
Taxes	419,943	9,999	1.87	488,736	11,637	2.05
Bank/investment fees	142,472	3,392	.63	23,292	555	.10
Lawyers/accountants	415,327	9,889	1.85	132,421	3,153	.56
Telephone	392,681	9,350	1.75	688,049	16,382	2.89
Campaign automobile	56,843	1,353	.25	92,631	2,205	.39
Computers/office equipment	339,251	8,077	1.51	318,120	7,574	1.33
Travel	650,856	15,497	2.90	474,128	11,289	1.99
Food/meetings	53,571	1,276	.24	37,910	903	.16
Total Overhead	**5,034,417**	**119,867**	**22.40**	**6,089,559**	**144,990**	**25.55**
Fund Raising						
Events	3,350,158	79,766	14.91	1,477,005	35,167	6.20
Direct mail	1,286,249	30,625	5.72	683,583	16,276	2.87
Telemarketing	57,557	1,370	.26	121,989	2,905	.51
Total Fund Raising	**4,693,964**	**111,761**	**20.89**	**2,282,577**	**54,348**	**9.58**
Polling	**695,813**	**16,567**	**3.10**	**847,039**	**20,168**	**3.55**
Advertising						
Electronic media	6,586,179	156,814	29.30	8,710,734	207,398	36.54
Other media	442,194	10,528	1.97	631,398	15,033	2.65
Total Advertising	**7,028,373**	**167,342**	**31.27**	**9,342,132**	**222,432**	**39.19**
Other Campaign Activity						
Persuasion mail/brochures	2,352,526	56,013	10.47	2,990,681	71,207	12.55
Actual campaigning	1,494,882	35,592	6.65	1,681,440	40,034	7.05
Staff/Volunteers	37,214	886	.17	22,365	532	.09
Total Other Campaign Activity	**3,884,622**	**92,491**	**17.28**	**4,694,486**	**111,773**	**19.69**
Constituent Gifts/Entertainment	**202,328**	**4,817**	**.90**	**11,449**	**273**	**.05**
Donations to						
Candidates from same state	67,994	1,619	.30	18,961	451	.08
Candidates from other states	83,142	1,980	.37	16,750	399	.07
Civic organizations	56,613	1,348	.25	21,190	505	.09
Ideological groups	30,157	718	.13	5,756	137	.02
Political parties	196,215	4,672	.87	28,029	667	.12
Total Donations	**434,121**	**10,336**	**1.93**	**90,687**	**2,159**	**.38**
Unitemized Expenses	**501,180**	**11,933**	**2.23**	**479,377**	**11,414**	**2.01**
Total Expenditures	**$22,474,819**	**$535,115**	**100.00**	**$23,837,306**	**$567,555**	**100.00**

Note: Totals are for the entire two-year cycle.

by only 18 percent, from $312,881 in 1990 to $370,316 in 1992. As a percentage of his total spending, Swett's investment in appeals for votes dropped from 67 percent to 47 percent.

Many in the 1990 freshman class quickly realized the importance of constituent stroking. Over the two-year cycle, freshmen who won renomination spent a total of $202,328 on constituent gifts and entertainment.

Rep. Barbara-Rose Collins (D-Mich.) spent $226,735 on her initial reelection effort, but eighteen cents of every dollar went for constituent entertainment and gifts. She invested $25,064 of her campaign funds to celebrate her 1991 inauguration, including $13,364 for a preinaugural prayer breakfast, $3,561 to transport supporters to Washington, and $7,603 for food and room rental at the Hyatt Regency Hotel near Capitol Hill. At the end of the election cycle, the campaign spent $4,500 for tickets to the presidential inaugural ball. Flowers and telegrams to express sympa-

Table 3-5 What Campaign Money Buys in the 1992 House Races: Total Expenditures by 1990 Freshmen

Major Category	Boiling Races[a]	Hot Races[b]	Warm Races[c]	Ice Cold Races[d]
Overhead				
Office furniture/supplies	$ 99,991	$ 83,195	$ 126,270	$ 47,607
Rent/utilities	93,520	75,521	105,140	42,211
Salaries	370,146	477,551	710,541	331,779
Taxes	102,076	110,128	133,865	73,874
Bank/investment fees	71,336	7,506	30,658	32,971
Lawyers/accountants	151,849	29,142	157,690	76,646
Telephone	117,637	81,905	144,980	48,160
Campaign automobile	317	17,179	20,878	18,469
Computers/office equipment	74,904	86,023	109,506	68,818
Travel	168,853	175,942	198,369	107,692
Food/meetings	12,859	15,360	16,896	8,456
Total Overhead	**1,263,489**	**1,159,452**	**1,754,793**	**856,683**
Fund Raising				
Events	940,927	515,648	1,337,180	556,403
Direct mail	596,628	214,504	404,307	70,810
Telemarketing	119	0	46,282	11,156
Total Fund Raising	**1,537,674**	**730,152**	**1,787,769**	**638,369**
Polling	**207,874**	**113,771**	**310,209**	**63,959**
Advertising				
Electronic media	1,977,238	1,503,319	2,528,538	577,083
Other media	102,075	61,493	173,254	105,373
Total Advertising	**2,079,313**	**1,564,812**	**2,701,792**	**682,456**
Other Campaign Activity				
Persuasion mail/brochures	906,049	238,599	1,010,640	197,237
Actual campaigning	424,638	244,962	594,231	231,051
Staff/Volunteers	2,386	10,361	17,959	6,508
Total Other Campaign Activity	**1,333,073**	**493,923**	**1,622,830**	**434,796**
Constituent Gifts/Entertainment	**15,930**	**25,663**	**109,181**	**51,553**
Donations to				
Candidates from same state	11,745	8,708	16,603	30,938
Candidates from other states	5,700	2,500	22,647	52,296
Civic organizations	3,313	8,376	21,414	23,509
Ideological groups	4,992	2,633	10,232	12,300
Political parties	30,315	14,132	98,890	52,878
Total Donations	**56,065**	**36,349**	**169,786**	**171,921**
Unitemized Expenses	**152,341**	**42,941**	**143,684**	**162,214**
Total Expenditures	**$6,645,760**	**$4,167,063**	**$8,600,045**	**$3,061,952**

Note: Totals are for the entire two-year cycle.
[a] Those races decided by 10 percentage points or less.
[b] Those races decided by 11-20 percentage points.
[c] Those races decided by 21-40 percentage points.
[d] Those races decided by 41 or more percentage points.

thy over a constituent's death or to celebrate a new constituent's birth cost the campaign $1,222. The campaign spent $5,463 on constituent meals, $2,875 on receptions for senior citizens and other groups, $1,433 on "oval pen stands" and other gifts, and $215 on commemorative plaques. In all, these constituent stroking efforts accounted for $40,772 of Collins's spending.

Trailing far behind Collins in such expenditures was Rep. Neil Abercrombie (D-Hawaii), who invested $14,946 in constituent gifts and entertainment. Abercrombie spent $9,325 on year-end holiday cards, $3,339 on constituent meals and entertainment, $1,234 on various gifts and commemorative awards, and $1,048 on flowers.

Rep. Dick Zimmer (R-N.J.) spent $10,793 on year-end holiday cards and $1,892 to celebrate his inauguration in 1991. Together, these two expenses accounted for 91 percent of the money he invested in constituent stroking.

Zimmer's inaugural party was nothing compared to the celebration hosted by Rep. Rosa DeLauro (D-Conn.). DeLauro paid the New Haven Bus Service $2,950 to ferry supporters to Washington to witness the swearing-in ceremony. A reception for her supporters at America, a restaurant near Capitol Hill, cost the campaign $5,734 and a second reception at a Hyatt hotel near the Capitol added $1,553. The $10,237 tab for her inaugural festivities accounted for 90 percent of her investment in constituent stroking.

Each year, Hobson and fellow Ohio Republican Rep. Paul E. Gillmor invited fifty people from each of their districts to attend what Joyce McGarry, Hobson's press secretary, described as "leadership and government workshops." In 1991 Hobson's campaign spent $595 to sponsor one attendee; $195 for gifts from Rothschild Berry Farm in Urbana, Ohio, to commemorate the event; and $1,222 for a reception. In 1992 conference sponsorship expenses climbed to $1,050, while the cost of the reception rose to $2,534. Hobson also sent out Christmas postcards that cost $3,476 over the two-year cycle. In all, Hobson spent $10,484 on constituent gifts and entertainment—something that had consumed only $64 of his 1990 budget.

Brewster had invested just $89 in constituent entertainment during the 1990 campaign. During the 1992 election cycle, he invested $8,368 in constituent stroking. He spent $1,810 on year-end holiday cards, $1,293 on meals at the House restaurant, $880 on commemorative certificates, $700 on various Christmas gifts, $409 on U.S. flags, $360 on congressional cookbooks, and $202 on calendars purchased from the Oklahoma Democratic party. Tickets to the presidential inaugural festivities cost the campaign $2,370.

Rep. James P. Moran, Jr. (D-Va.) had poured $952,253 into his 1990 battle with Rep. Stan Parris, and only $94 of that massive budget had been put into constituent gifts and entertainment. By 1992, Moran's position had been significantly improved by redistricting, and although Republican Kyle E. McSlarrow put up a strong fight, Moran's new incumbency status prompted him to divert $9,385 of his $902,140 budget to constituent stroking. He invested $3,750 in year-end holiday cards. His inaugural celebration cost $3,530—$1,600 for dinner at the Gas Light restaurant in Alexandria, Va., and $1,930 for a reception at the Radisson Plaza Hotel in Alexandria. He spent $1,402 on constituent events, including a $133 payment for "nursing homes refreshments." Gifts and flowers added $519 and $184, respectively.

While the typical freshman donated $10,336 of his or her own treasury to other candidates, political party organizations, and various causes, some gave away considerably more. The political donations of Rep. John A. Boehner (R-Ohio) amounted to $53,309, or 13 percent of his total spending. Concerned about redistricting, he gave $10,000 to the Ohio Republican Senate Committee; this pushed his donations to party organizations to $13,606. He gave $25,162 to Republican candidates from other states, including $1,000 each to Minority Whip Newt Gingrich (Ga.), Rick Santorum (Pa.), Riggs, Nussle, Charles H. Taylor (N.C.), and John T. Doolittle (Calif.). His donations to such candidates also included campaign packets valued at nearly $17,000. "We did a lot of outreach to Republicans around the country, sending them background information on issues and how to use them in the campaign," noted Barry Jackson, Boehner's chief of staff. Boehner also dipped into his treasury for $9,411 to make donations to other Ohio Republicans vying for various offices. He gave $4,491 to charitable and booster organizations and $640 to ideological groups.

As a challenger in 1990, Dooley had needed every penny he could lay his hands on to defeat Rep. Chip Pashayan. As a result, he donated just $646 to Democratic party organizations, $284 to civic groups, and $75 to other California candidates. However, once elected, Dooley found room in his budget for contributions totaling $46,043, which accounted for 9 percent of his total spending during the 1992 cycle. To protect his own interests and those of fellow California Democrats, Dooley gave $38,188 to IMPAC 2000, the political action committee established to help Democrats with redistricting.

Hobson's donations increased five-fold, from $5,910 in 1990 to $30,368 in 1992. He gave $10,005 to various Republican party organizations, including $8,500 to the Ohio Republican Senate Committee. He gave $7,263 to fellow Ohio Republicans, including $1,000 each to Reps. Bob McEwen and Ralph Regula and $1,100 to his predecessor in District 7, Lt. Gov. Mike DeWine, who decided to challenge Democratic Sen. John Glenn. Hobson donated $6,135 to candidates in other states, including $2,000 to Gingrich and $500 each to Santorum, Riggs, Wayne T. Gilchrest (Md.), Doolittle, Wayne Allard (Colo.), Nussle, and Zeliff. He spent $4,110 on livestock purchased at fairs and 4-H Club events, which accounted for 71 percent of his contributions to charitable and booster organizations. His ideological donations amounted to $1,200.

In 1990 Brewster donated just $890 to charities and Democratic party organizations. Two years later he gave away $22,465. Fellow Democrats Beryl Anthony, Jr. (Ark.), Thomas J. Downey (N.Y.), James A. Barcia (Mich.), Andy Fox (Va.), Laurie Williams (Okla.), and Sam Gejdenson (Conn.) each received checks for $1,000. Eight others received checks for $500.

While $19,858 in donations did not put Rep. William J. Jefferson (D-La.) in the same league with several of his freshman colleagues, those donations amounted to more than twice what he invested in advertising. The chief beneficiary of Jefferson's altruism was the NAACP, which received four contributions totaling $1,250. The Alumni Association of Southern University, Jefferson's alma mater, received a $500 check from his campaign, as did Rev. James Landrum. Young Democrats of America received two checks totaling $650. Jefferson gave $250 to the Close-Up Foundation, $340 to the Veterans of Foreign Wars, $400 to the Greater St. Matthew Chapel Baptist Church, $202 to the Louisiana Association of the Deaf, and $300 to the Anti-Defamation League of B'nai Brith. He also bought a $218 videocassette recorder for the Flint-Goodrich Hospital in New Orleans. He gave none of his campaign treasury away in 1990.

Following the example of many longtime incumbents, the 1990 freshman class wasted little time in taking advantage of some of the institutionalized perquisites of continuously seeking office. For instance, while Rep. Robert E. "Bud" Cramer (D-Ala.) briefly closed his campaign office, when it reopened in July 1991 his new landlord was the Cramer Corp., a company owned by his uncle. Travel was booked through Cramer Travel, his parent's travel agency. For his 1990 race, Cramer spent just $810 on his campaign car; once elected his campaign began paying $794 a month to lease a new 1991 Ford Explorer. Over the two-year cycle, Cramer spent $20,878 to lease, license, and insure his campaign car; this amounted to 7 percent of his total campaign spending.

During the 1990 campaign, Brewster invested $7,054 in short-term auto leases. Less than six months after taking office, he began making $391 monthly lease payments to Ford Credit. Over the course of the 1992 election cycle, those payments totaled $10,436. The campaign spent $1,375 on automobile repairs, $1,107 to insure and register the car, and $2,654 on gasoline.

Moran paid his daughter Mary Elise $13,500 for running his campaign office. Moran's brother Brian received a $5,000 payment for his campaign efforts, while Moran's son James Edward collected $2,000.

One-third of Collins's $15,790 travel budget was spent in New York during the four-day Democratic National Convention. After investing more than $7,000 of her 1990 campaign funds in clothes and image consulting, she spent more than $1,800 to finish off her wardrobe in early 1991.

Jefferson spent $24,960 on travel; $5,895 of that total was incurred during his stay in New York for the Democratic National Convention, including $2,610 for a party at the New York Hilton.

Rep. Maxine Waters (D-Calif.) tapped her campaign treasury for $5,661 to pay for the annual Congressional Black Caucus weekend in September 1991. Bills at the Hyatt Regency and the Washington Hilton and Towers were $3,249 and $494, respectively. Limousine service added $528; tickets to the evening gala cost $1,390.

Zeliff tapped his campaign treasury to pay the Washington law firm of Wiley, Rein & Fielding $40,250 for their help in disposing of a nuisance complaint filed with the Federal Election Commission by his 1990 opponent, Democrat Joseph F. Keefe. Keefe charged that a $150,000 loan Zeliff had made to his campaign was improper. Since the loan was made using proceeds from the sale of property Zeliff and his wife jointly owned, Keefe argued that half the loan was really an illegal campaign contribution made by Zeliff's wife. Three accounting firms charged Zeliff's campaign a total of $32,191.

Doolittle, who spent much of the election cycle calling for change and decrying the sorry state of politics as usual, spent $9,206 of his treasury to move his personal belongings from California to Washington.

Although most members of the freshman class of 1992 ran on a platform of change, there was strong evidence even before they were sworn in that the supposedly reform-minded new members had already begun the process of settling in.

State senator Frank Tejeda (D-Texas) was prepared to fight hard to win the state's newly created Hispanic-majority District 28. He opened his campaign office in September 1991 and raised more than $100,000 by the end of the year. However, no other Democrat or Republican bothered to enter the race. His only opposition in November came from libertarian David C. Slatter, who spent just $1,402. Yet, while he was the only freshman elected to a new district who did not face major-party opposition, Tejeda spent $351,961. Only 21 percent of that total was invested in direct appeals for votes.

Tejeda poured 44 percent of his budget into overhead. Monthly rent on his San Antonio office was $850. Salary payments to the eight people who worked on the primary campaign and to the five people who worked on the fall campaign totaled $72,631. Health insurance premiums for campaign manager Frances Ruiz amounted to $1,140. Tejeda spent $10,389 to lease, fuel, and maintain a 1989 Jeep Cherokee.

As a veteran politician, Tejeda knew well the political importance of well-placed charitable contributions. He donated $10,091 to charitable and booster organizations, including $1,664 to sponsor the Southside Junior Cardinals, $1,197 to the St. James Catholic Church, and $200 to McCollum Band Boosters. Tejeda also realized the importance of constituent stroking, spending $2,461 on Christmas cards, $1,532 on Easter cards, and $933 on flowers, gifts, and entertainment.

Tejeda was by no means alone in using his campaign funds for items that had little to do with direct appeals for votes. To celebrate his victory, state senator Robert Menendez (D-N.J.) spent $8,300 of his campaign funds on a luncheon at the J. W. Marriott in Washington, D.C., where approximately 1,000 supporters watched on big-screen televisions as he took the oath of office. While payroll accounted for 15 percent of Human Affairs Commissioner James E. Clyburn's (D-S.C.) $397,090 budget, and his campaign director and press secretary collected "salary" payments for months, he paid no payroll taxes. Attorney and former state senator Melvin Watt (D-N.C.) paid his son Brian $15,398 for serving as campaign manager. State representative Cynthia A. McKinney (D-Ga.) paid her mother a $2,500 bonus for serving as the campaign's scheduler. Real estate developer Ken Calvert (R-Calif.) tapped his campaign treasury for $2,514 to help pay for moving his belongings to Washington. Compton Mayor Walter R. Tucker III (D-Calif.) spent $1,100 of his treasury to move his car to Washington.

By far the clearest indication that reform was not on the minds of every member of the 1992 freshman class was the case of Diamond Bar, Calif., mayor and businessman Jay C. Kim (R-Calif.). In July 1993 the *Los Angeles Times* reported that records provided to the paper showed that Kim had illegally funneled money from his company, JayKim Engineers, to pay many of his 1992 campaign expenses—in violation of federal law. According to the *Times,* Kim used more than $400,000 of corporate money to pay for airline tickets, telephone service, office space, staff, and office supplies. Following these reports, the Federal Bureau of Investigation launched an inquiry into Kim's campaign funding practices.

Chapter 4

The Angry Electorate?
Incumbents Fight to Survive

All politics is local.
Former House Speaker Thomas P. O'Neill

On November 21, 1991, Fenn & King Communications of Washington, D.C., which created and placed broadcast advertising for twenty Democratic House incumbents in 1990, sent its clients and prospective clients on Capitol Hill a memorandum warning that "a year ago many incumbent members of Congress, Democrat and Republican, dodged a freight train of anti-incumbent feeling." Among other things, the five-page memo warned that "the anti-status quo, anti-incumbent sentiment in the country is growing, not waning" and cautioned that "relatively obscure challengers can beat incumbents in this climate." While Fenn & King's warning was a bit overstated, Rep. Beverly B. Byron (D-Md.) would have done well to heed their advice.

In seven previous House campaigns, Byron had never received less than 65 percent of the general election vote, and in five of those seven races she had collected 70 percent or more. While furniture salesman Anthony Patrick Puca had taken 36 percent of the Democratic primary votes in 1990, there was little evidence to suggest that Byron was in serious trouble heading into 1992.

Byron's opponent in the March 3 Democratic primary, state representative Thomas H. Hattery, had challenged her in 1980 and come away with only 12 percent of the vote. While most observers expected him to do considerably better this time, few gave him much chance of pulling off an upset.

However, Hattery came out swinging with a heavily negative, anti-incumbent campaign. His persuasion mailers attacked Byron for her 1989 vote in favor of the congressional pay raise; for taking numerous taxpayer-funded junkets, including one to Barbados; and for joining the rest of Congress "in letting the S&L profiteers run wild." Over the final two weeks of the campaign, Hattery aired a companion television commercial that pilloried Byron's junkets in a parody of *Life Styles of the Rich and Famous*. In all, Hattery committed nearly $230,000 to his long-shot primary bid.

For her part, Byron initially seemed unconcerned. She ran no ads directly refuting Hattery's charges. While she spent more than $116,000 during the off-year to maintain her permanent campaign operation, including monthly payments of $2,533 to her one full-time employee, Byron failed to capitalize on the advantage that such an organization is supposed to provide. She spent only $5,000 on polling and may never have seen what was coming. She invested $43,749 in persuasion mail, $4,472 in newspaper ads, $3,700 in phonebanking, $675 in signs, and $440 in bumper stickers. She paid Fenn & King $12,500, and over the final week put $10,235 into airing radio spots that attacked Hattery as "Taxing Tom." As it turned out, her $134,647 preprimary push did not reflect the gravity of her situation.

Hattery carried all six counties in the district and won with 56 percent of the vote. While only one incumbent had failed to win renomination in 1990, Hattery's anti-incumbent message carried him to a stunning upset victory in the first congressional primary of 1992, although he would later lose in the general election. It was only the beginning.

Rep. Bill Alexander (D-Ark.) had grown accustomed to stiff primary challenges. In the summer of 1985, Alexander had arranged for a military jet to take a "congressional delegation" on a fact-finding trip to Brazil. When it was revealed that he was the plane's only passenger and that the trip had cost taxpayers $50,000, Alexander found himself faced with the first of what would become strong, biennial anti-incumbent challenges from within his own party.

In 1992 Alexander came up against Blanche Lambert, a thirty-one-year-old former aide to Alexander, who began her bid to unseat him with virtually no money. She could not afford both preprimary polling and broadcast advertising, so she opted to forego the polls. She paid Strother-Duffy-Strother of Washington, D.C., $2,153 to create her preprimary commercials and Media Strategies of Falls Church, Va., $58,000 to buy air time. Her entire preprimary effort cost approximately $80,000.

Alexander spent $172,007 to keep his permanent campaign running during the off-year, and when Lambert took up the challenge, the fourteen-term incumbent pumped another $170,000 into his primary campaign. However, in a year when "change" was the operative campaign buzzword, Alexander's 487 overdrafts at the House bank proved to be more than voters could forgive.

Ten days before the primary, Lambert unveiled a television commercial that focused on Alexander's initial denial that he had any overdrafts. The spot opened with five seconds of footage showing Alexander's denial; his image was encased in a "Looney Tunes" cartoon box labeled "Bill Toons." Following the denial, a game show buzzer sounded, the Looney Tunes music started, and the words "Alexander had actually bounced 487 checks" appeared on the screen. Alexander received only 39 percent of the primary votes, losing twenty-three of the district's twenty-five counties.

As head of the National Republican Congressional Committee (NRCC), Rep. Guy Vander Jagt (R-Mich.) toured the country throughout the late spring and early summer of 1992 arguing that voters were disgusted with the way Washington worked and about to retire dozens of House members involuntarily. When Peter Hoekstra, a furniture executive with no prior political experience, knocked him out in the August 4 primary, Vander Jagt discovered just how right he had been.

Like many challengers, Hoekstra struggled to raise money. He found forty supporters who were each willing to write letters to one hundred acquaintances asking for donations, but that brought in no more than $15,000. He borrowed $24,300 from a local bank just to keep the campaign sputtering along.

On that budget, Hoekstra could only dream about television advertising. He spent $7,471 to print his campaign literature. Yard signs and posters cost $3,057. He spent $4,371 to send out one mailing to 15,000 past Republican primary voters and several more tightly targeted mailings. Arguing that Vander Jagt was a career politician who was too busy raising money for the national Republican party to stay in touch with his constituents, Hoekstra bicycled thirty miles through the heart of the district, stopping regularly to talk with voters. Whenever he appeared in a parade, his mode of transportation was a 1966 Nash Rambler, made the year Vander Jagt first went to Washington. The sign on the car read, "Isn't it time for a change?"

That message of change echoed throughout each of the three radio spots Hoekstra aired over the primary campaign's final week. One ad hammered Vander Jagt for his reliance on political action committee (PAC) money and pointed out that the fourteen-term incumbent also collected large sums from individual donors who did not live in Michigan. Another spot focused on Vander Jagt's junket to Barbados, which was entirely paid for by lobbyists and unflatteringly profiled on *PrimeTime Live*. "Who does Guy Vander Jagt represent?" the ads asked. Hoekstra's budget for air time was $7,539.

Redistricting had significantly altered Vander Jagt's constituency. The two most populous counties in the new District 2 were entirely new to him, opening the door for Hoekstra's outsider message. Vander Jagt made matters worse for himself. After publicly rejoicing on several occasions about the power of the House banking scandal to bring down long-time House members, he came to the defense of fellow Michigan Republican Robert W. Davis, whose 878 overdrafts at the bank earned him the dubious distinction of being named one of its twenty-two worst abusers. Davis opted to retire rather than try to explain his overdrafts to an angry electorate, but Vander Jagt was stuck with his decision to speak out on Davis's behalf. While that move was undoubtedly the appropriate response for the head of the NRCC, it was not the best message for Vander Jagt the candidate.

Realizing he was in trouble, Vander Jagt spent $60,130 on an eleventh-hour media blitz. Having railed for months against tax-and-spend Democrats, his advertising campaign focused on his ability to deliver pork-barrel projects to the district. It was a hard sell, and he fell 4,369 votes short. In the end, Vander Jagt carried every county that had been part of his old District 9 but lost both of the two newly acquired counties. Discussing his loss the next day, Vander Jagt quietly told reporters, "I don't think it had anything to do with partisanship. There is a much more transcendent feeling out there. And that's just anti-incumbent, throw the bums out, throw the rascals out, all of them, we don't care if they're Republican or Democrat, is the mood at this moment."

Reading Vander Jagt's words or any of the 3,394 stories containing the phrases "anti-incumbent" or "anti-incumbency" that appeared in major daily newspapers and magazines during 1992, one could not have been blamed for assuming that the electorate—every electorate in every jurisdiction—was angry. The question seemed not whether incumbents would lose in droves, but just how bad the carnage would eventually become. As media consultant John Franzen put it, "In one way or another, anti-incumbency was something everyone had to deal with."

Adding to the sense that anti-incumbent sentiment was running rampant were the campaigns of numerous open seat candidates, who repeatedly slammed Congress and politicians in general, since they had no specific incumbent to attack. A mailer touting state senator Karen English's (D-Ariz.) candidacy showed an overweight man sitting in a lawn chair, smoking a cigar. The tagline read: "Washington's been sitting down on the job again."

In Alabama, Republican newspaper executive Terry Everett's campaign slogan was "Send a message, not a politician." Throughout the general election campaign, Everett juxtaposed his political inexperience with the political resume of state treasurer George C. Wallace, Jr., son of the former governor and presidential candidate. "He focused on his status as an outsider, a nonpolitical type, and he frequently attacked Wallace as a person raised by his father to be another politician," recalled Mike Lewis, Everett's press secretary.

To foster his outsider image, businessman and former state representative John Linder (R-Ga.) aired one television commercial showing him helping a group of children clean up a broken piggy bank they had dropped. Proclaiming that the federal government had "broken the bank," the voice-over noted that Linder would "help pick up the pieces."

State senator Bill Baker (R-Calif.) spent $421,707 on campaign literature and advocacy mailers, including one touting his votes against "every legislative pay raise in the state assembly," his record as a champion of "the angry taxpayer," and his displeasure over "the bounced checks, the staggering federal deficit, and the special privileges for members of Congress."

Ironically, the power of the anti-incumbent message was best illustrated by several of the nine incumbent-versus-incumbent match-ups set up by redistricting—match-ups that guaranteed there would be at least nine incumbent losers. The victory of freshman Rep. Jim Nussle (R-Iowa) over three-term Democratic Rep. Dave Nagle showed all too clearly the power of outsider politics. While Nagle campaigned on his ability to deliver federal projects to the district, Nussle positioned himself as a congressional reformer and attacked Nagle as a career politician.

Six weeks before the November general election, Nussle began airing television commercials slamming Nagle for his four overdrafts at the House bank and for initially denying that he had any overdrafts. The most damaging of these spots showed Nagle saying "public opinion be damned" on the House floor, a statement he made in arguing against the release of the House banking records on the grounds that it would violate members' constitutional rights. While Nagle pointed to the projects he had delivered to the district as proof that he was looking out for his constituents' interests, Nussle blasted those same projects as wasteful, pork-barrel spending.

While Nagle paid Fenn & King $288,072 for creating and placing his broadcast advertising, for much of the campaign he ignored the firm's advice to attack Nussle. With early polls showing him ahead by 14 points, Nagle opted to take the high road and stick with his pro-incumbency pitch. One such ad showed Nagle standing near the Mississippi River discussing the need to build and maintain locks and dams. "There are some who say this is pork-barrel spending," Nagle noted. Kneeling next to an oinking pig, he concluded, "This is a river. This is pork. If you're going to represent Iowa in Congress, you'd better know the difference." This humorous message was no match for Nussle's negative bombardment, and while Nagle began counterattacking over the campaign's final two weeks, his efforts proved to be too little, too late.

In Illinois, redistricting pitted two-term Democratic Rep. Glenn Poshard against four-term Democratic Rep. Terry L. Bruce, and Bruce seemed to hold most of the cards. Their redrawn district contained more of Bruce's old constituents. In January 1992 Bruce had campaign cash reserves of $699,486; Poshard began 1992 with just $17,272 in his campaign bank account. Bruce's massive treasury allowed him to commit more than $740,000 to his three-month preprimary effort; Poshard spent only about $150,000 in the first three months of 1992. However, Poshard emerged with 62 percent of the votes, in part because he was successful at turning his financial weakness into a campaign issue. "We were the underdog, fighting the good fight. We were able to set up the contrast between our opponent's reliance on PAC contributions and our refusal to accept them," noted David D. Stricklin, Poshard's press secretary.

Rather than fight the good fight, sixty-five House members opted to retire instead of seeking another term. In addition to Davis, six-term Rep. Vin Weber (R-Minn.) chose not to face voters with his 125 House bank overdrafts. Rep. Chalmers P. Wiley (R-Ohio), with 515 overdrafts, and Carl C. Perkins (D-Ky.), with 514 overdrafts, also decided not to try and explain their problem to voters. Having announced his retirement to seek a Senate seat, Rep. Robert J. Mrazek (D-N.Y.) found his Senate bid derailed by his 920 overdrafts. However, while the press tended to view all retirements as a sign of running from voter anger, members retired for a variety of reasons.

Reps. Robin Tallon (D-S.C.) and Claude Harris (D-Ala.) decided to retire when redistricting reconfigured their districts to create new majority-black constituencies. Republican Rep. George F. Allen, who won a 1991 special election in Virginia's District 7, joined Reps. Frank Annunzio (D-Ill.), Bernard J. Dwyer (D-N.J.), Frank Horton (R-N.Y.), James H. Scheuer (D-N.Y.), and Bill Lowery (R-Calif.), all of whom found retirement preferable to facing fellow incumbents in match-ups created by redistricting. Allen successfully ran for governor in 1993, which may have helped make his decision to retire easier.

Rep. Lawrence J. Smith (D-Fla.) agreed to a $5,000 fine for spending some of his 1990 campaign funds for personal use, including the repayment of a gambling debt. After retiring, Smith spent three months in jail over the incident. In 1990 a former aide to Rep. Gus Yatron (D-Pa.) had accused the twelve-term incumbent of requiring salary kickbacks. Although the aide was ultimately indicted for embezzling campaign money, Yatron decided that his 57 percent victory in 1990 was a precursor of things to come and retired in 1992.

Thanks to a provision in the 1989 ethics and pay law, long-time incumbents who retired before December 31, 1992 were entitled to convert their excess campaign funds to personal use; after that date they lost their right to take the money. Seven members chose to exercise that option, including Reps. Larry J. Hopkins (R-Ky.), Bob Traxler (D-Mich.), and Carroll Hubbard, Jr. (D-Ky.), who pocketed $665,000, $296,000, and $216,000, respectively. At least eight other House members retired and transferred their excess treasuries into charitable trusts. Reps. Norman F. Lent (R-N.Y.) and Robert A. Roe (D-N.J.) personally control their trusts, which each contained more than $500,000 in 1992. Roe informed the Federal Election Commission that "in the event that I shall become disabled as determined by a certified physician, the trust property is to be used for my benefit. I have retained the power to amend or revoke the Foundation during my lifetime, or by providing for such amendment or revocation in my Will."

In addition to Mrazek, thirteen House members retired to seek Senate seats or wage gubernatorial campaigns. Although Reps. Barbara Boxer (D-Calif.), Ben Nighthorse Campbell (D-Colo.), and Byron L. Dorgan (D-N.D.) won Senate seats and Democratic Rep. Thomas R. Carper became governor of Delaware, much was made of the fact that the other nine lost along the way.

While virtually all the challengers portrayed themselves as fresh outsiders and their protagonists as elitist, morally bankrupt insiders, that message played very differently from district to district. Although 43 House incumbents fell in either the primary or general elections, 325 incumbents were returned for another term—88 percent of those who sought reelection. Many of those who lost, including the nine incumbents who were defeated by fellow incumbents, owed their defeats to a host of problems that were by no means limited to their incumbency.

Even when it did not create incumbent-versus-incumbent match-ups, the redistricting process caused problems for many of those who lost. One obvious example is Rep. Richard Ray (D-Ga.), who lost two-thirds of his former constituents through redistricting.

Despite the ultimate success of Hoekstra's anti-incumbent message, Vander Jagt carried every county that had been part of his old district.

While Charles Hatcher (D-Ga.) was undoubtedly hurt by his 819 House bank overdrafts, his 6-point loss to Sanford D. Bishop, Jr., in the Democratic primary had more to do with the fact that his district changed from one in which 62 percent of electorate was white to one in which only 42 percent was white. Bishop is black; Hatcher is white.

Rep. Ben Erdreich (D-Ala.) lost to former state Republican party chairman Spencer Bachus primarily because redistricting changed Erdreich's constituency from one that had provided George Bush with 57 percent of the vote in 1988 to one that had given Bush 77 percent in 1988.

Rep. Bill Green (R-N.Y.) carried the Manhattan precincts he had represented for fourteen years, but failed to win reelection because he lost by two to one in the Brooklyn and Queens precincts added by redistricting.

Freshman Joan Kelly Horn (D-Mo.), who defeated Rep. Jack Buechner by fifty-four votes in 1990, fell victim to a redistricting deal struck prior to the 1990 election by Buechner and Democrats Richard A. Gephardt and William L. Clay that ceded Democrats from Horn's district to Gephardt and Clay.

Rep. Stephen J. Solarz (D-N.Y.) chose to run in a newly created majority-Hispanic district after his district was obliterated by redistricting. His $3,158,822 million budget brought him within 1,869 votes of victory in the primary.

Rep. Gus Savage (D-Ill.) had defeated fellow Democrat Mel Reynolds twice but could not overcome the effects of redistricting, which replaced many of his southside Chicago constituents with suburban voters less attuned to Savage's vitriolic message and more attuned to Reynold's views.

Redistricting was only one of the problems plaguing incumbents who lost. Some self-destructed; others were overwhelmed.

Rep. Joe Kolter (D-Pa.) fell to third in the Democratic primary following publication of excerpts from an audiotape of one of his campaign strategy sessions. His own worst enemy, Kolter referred to himself during the meeting as a "political whore" and bragged about how he intended to manipulate the electorate.

Albert G. Bustamante (D-Texas) had thirty overdrafts at the House bank, had voted for the congressional pay raise, frequently took congressional junkets, and had just built a new home valued at more than $600,000 in a district where the median value of homes was $75,000. While most incumbents were fighting to keep their old districts intact, Bustamante had voluntarily accepted twenty-one new counties in the redistricting process, giving most of his old constituents to fellow Democratic Rep. Henry B. Gonzalez. However, Bustamante's biggest problem was a federal grand jury investigation that would ultimately lead to his indictment and conviction on federal bribery and racketeering charges. While it would normally be considered an upset when a Democratic incumbent from a heavily Democratic district outspent his Republican challenger by more than $250,000 and still lost, in Bustamante's case, it was no upset.

Freshman Reps. John W. Cox, Jr. (D-Ill.) and Frank Riggs (R-Calif.) were defeated for reelection, but the real surprise was that either one had been elected in the first place. In Cox's case, his brief two-year tenure provided him with the distinction of being the only Democrat to represent his northwestern Illinois district during the twentieth century. Riggs had upset Rep. Douglas H. Bosco in 1990 with a strong outsider campaign, but he owed his victory less to his outsider message than to a third-party candidate who collected 15 percent of the vote. When no third-party candidate surfaced in 1992, Riggs took 45 percent of the vote and still lost.

Rep. Robert J. Lagomarsino's $747,536 budget was no match for the $3.5 million businessman Michael Huffington pumped into his campaign. Although Lagomarsino had collected at least 61 percent of the vote in every election between 1976 and 1986, his electoral position had weakened significantly since that time. In 1988 he had been slightly outspent by Democratic state senator Gary K. Hart and eked out a 3,933-vote victory. In 1990 he had faced Democrat Anita Perez Ferguson, who held him to 55 percent. Put into the same district with fellow Republican Rep. Elton Gallegly following redistricting, Lagomarsino agreed to move further north to meet Huffington, giving Gallegly an easy path to the general election.

In fact, despite all the press reports trumpeting the anti-incumbent mood of the electorate, less than half of the incumbents who lost could be said to have been defeated solely on the strength of an anti-incumbent message. Most incumbents who won did so despite the fact that their challengers sought to tap into the supposed anti-incumbent vein. For a sizable number of incumbents who had overdrafts, had voted for the congressional pay raise, and availed themselves of numerous perquisites of office, the issues never became a problem.

Rep. Henry A. Waxman (D-Calif.) had 434 overdrafts and had voted for the pay raise, but to his liberal westside Los Angeles constituents, neither of those issues mattered. Waxman won the primary with 84 percent of the vote and the general election with 61 percent. While that winning percentage was his lowest ever, the drop did not occur in the face of an all-out effort by Waxman to woo voters. Of the $717,698 he spent on his campaign, $338,803 was simply given away to other candidates, Democratic party organizations, and various causes. Only 23 percent of his gigantic budget was invested in direct appeals for votes.

In Ohio, Democratic Rep. Louis Stokes had 551 overdrafts yet drew no primary opposition and won the general election with 69 percent of the vote. He spent only 20 percent of his

$339,188 budget on advertising, persuasion mail, and other grass-roots appeals. Donations and constituent stroking accounted for 23 percent of his budget.

Although Rep. Edolphus Towns (D-N.Y.) had 408 overdrafts and was named one of the House bank's twenty-two worst abusers for the period between September 1988 and October 1991, he cruised to victory with 62 percent of the primary vote and 96 percent of the general election vote. In his overwhelmingly Democratic district, local Republicans did not bother to contest the race. Towns spent $713,723 on his reelection bid, with 36 percent going to direct appeals for votes. He spent $30,738 on constituent stroking, gave away $117,158, invested $174,150 in overhead, and put $113,315 into fund raising.

Rep. Harold E. Ford (D-Tenn.) had 388 overdrafts, had voted for the congressional pay raise, and was facing his second trial on federal charges of conspiring to commit mail, bank, and tax fraud. Nevertheless, he garnered 65 percent of the votes in the four-candidate Democratic primary and won the five-candidate general election with 58 percent. His closest competitor, Republican Charles L. Black, took 28 percent. Overhead consumed 66 percent of Ford's outlays, driven by the $51,413 he paid his legal defense team.

Rep. William L. Clay (D-Mo.) had 328 overdrafts and was named one of the House bank's twenty-two worst abusers. He prevailed in both the primary and general elections with 68 percent of the vote, while devoting 51 percent of his budget to overhead and donations to other candidates, causes, and Democratic party organizations.

With 44 overdrafts, Republican Rep. Dennis Hastert (Ill.) nearly doubled his spending from $312,568 in 1990 to $613,623 in 1992, despite running unopposed in the primary and winning 67 percent of the vote in the general election. However, only 26 percent of his outlays were funneled into direct appeals for votes.

Ultimately, many of those incumbents who felt the need to campaign aggressively to defend themselves against outsider challenges had little difficulty in dispatching their opponents.

Rep. Bill Thomas (R-Calif.) took no chances that his 119 overdrafts at the House bank would prove his undoing. Thomas increased his spending from $496,850 in 1990 to $610,997. He sank $99,439 into advertising, $121,245 into campaign literature and persuasion mail, and $169,632 into other forms of grass-roots voter communication and actual campaigning. He won the Republican primary with 66 percent of the vote and prevailed in the general election with 65 percent, a 5-point increase over his 1990 winning percentage. It did not hurt that his Democratic challenger, Deborah A. Vollmer, had just $23,279 to spend.

Rep. Barbara B. Kennelly (D-Conn.) had spent $404,040 in 1990 to dispatch a Republican challenger who spent only $12,649. With votes in favor of both the congressional pay raise and the 1990 budget agreement that included several tax increases, as well as 60 overdrafts at the House bank, Kennelly bumped her spending up 42 percent to $572,602 in 1992. With no primary opposition and faced in the November general election by Republican Philip L. Steele, who spent just $7,053, Kennelly poured $226,886 into radio and television advertising. She spent $29,152 to put "Kennelly for Congress" signs on one hundred buses and invested $8,420 in newspaper ads, $8,043 in program and journal ads, and $43,970 in campaign literature and persuasion mail. She won with 67 percent of the vote.

Bowing to their fears of an anti-incumbent backlash, some incumbents chose to portray themselves as outsiders. With considerable resources at their disposal, many of those who tried this unlikely ploy were quite successful.

Three-term Rep. Jimmy Hayes (D-La.) spent virtually all of the $83,609 he invested in television, radio, and newspaper advertising during the two weeks leading up to the October 3 open primary. He ran ads promising that he would refuse future congressional pay raises and would not participate in the congressional retirement system.

In the primary, three-term Rep. Wally Herger (R-Calif.) ran television and radio commercials pointing out that he had no overdrafts at the House bank and had, in fact, voted to close the bank; voted against the congressional pay raise; voted against tax increases; and voted for a constitutional amendment requiring a balanced federal budget. Brad Zerbe, Herger's campaign management consultant, said the campaign also sent an "I'm not one of them" mailer to between 80,000 and 90,000 Republican households. His 65 percent vote tally was his largest ever.

Eight-term Rep. Anthony C. Beilenson (D-Calif.) succeeded in turning the tables on Republican state representative Tom McClintock with a $368,049 persuasion mail campaign that trumpeted Beilenson as "an independent leader for change." One mailing pointed out that McClintock had accepted $928,000 from PACs during his tenure in the state legislature while Beilenson refused PAC money.

New Jersey Democratic Rep. Frank Pallone, Jr., campaigned in a 1974 Ford Maverick to underscore the fact that he had frequently voted against the Democratic House leadership on issues such as the pay raise. He developed a "Declaration of Independence," which cited examples of his breaks from party ranks. His campaign slogan, "Our best hope—their worst nightmare," sought to portray that same outsider image, which he delivered with a $186,528 investment in advertising and a $258,583 investment in persuasion mail and campaign literature.

In the first of his three television spots, five-term Rep. Norman Sisisky (D-Va.) told his viewers that "the greatest satisfaction to me is helping people, whether it's finding a Social Security check that's lost, or getting someone in a veterans hospital, or just breaking down the bureaucratic mess that we have in Washington." To put as much distance as possible between himself and his House colleagues, Sisisky noted, "I didn't come to Congress for free banking or for $10 haircuts or anything else that they got. I came here to do a job for people." In all, Sisisky invested $279,759 in producing and airing his radio and television commercials.

While some of their colleagues were running from incumbency, other successful incumbents chose to embrace its power. "In the year of the anti-incumbent, we ran against the grain," remarked Robert L. Mitchell, district administrator for six-term Rep. Harold Rogers (R-Ky.). "Rogers likes to work on

Table 4-1 What Campaign Money Buys in the 1992 House Races: Average Expenditures by Nonincumbents

Major Category	Challengers		Open Seats	
	Winner	Loser	Winner	Loser
Overhead				
Office furniture/supplies	$ 6,724	$ 2,582	$ 7,649	$ 5,110
Rent/utilities	7,469	2,453	7,520	5,199
Salaries	41,918	14,798	52,352	35,491
Taxes	6,033	2,119	7,415	5,853
Bank/investment fees	611	165	589	434
Lawyers/accountants	3,443	659	3,215	1,613
Telephone	9,893	3,517	9,359	6,511
Campaign automobile	1,046	162	653	547
Computers/office equipment	4,964	2,220	4,539	3,983
Travel	8,429	3,270	10,193	6,569
Food/meetings	446	189	633	320
Total Overhead	**90,975**	**32,133**	**104,117**	**71,630**
Fund Raising				
Events	32,648	6,771	30,509	17,028
Direct mail	10,322	4,685	10,810	6,982
Telemarketing	1,618	419	169	1,033
Total Fund Raising	**44,588**	**11,874**	**41,487**	**25,044**
Polling	**14,364**	**4,362**	**16,747**	**10,288**
Advertising				
Electronic media	146,894	41,560	153,186	86,054
Other media	10,537	4,656	12,394	8,447
Total Advertising	**157,431**	**46,216**	**165,580**	**94,502**
Other Campaign Activity				
Persuasion mail/brochures	67,859	20,553	108,541	69,962
Actual campaigning	44,737	12,795	50,005	32,068
Staff/Volunteers	516	107	785	371
Total Other Campaign Activity	**113,112**	**33,456**	**159,331**	**102,401**
Constituent Gifts/Entertainment	**820**	**25**	**909**	**17**
Donations to				
Candidates from same state	103	43	325	49
Candidates from other states	31	4	69	7
Civic organizations	328	104	615	183
Ideological groups	71	26	190	38
Political parties	398	139	489	317
Total Donations	**932**	**315**	**1,689**	**594**
Unitemized Expenses	**6,853**	**3,607**	**8,493**	**7,946**
Total Expenditures	**$429,075**	**$131,987**	**$498,353**	**$312,421**

Note: Total for winning challengers does not include expenditures of $5,434,569 by Michael Huffington, R-Calif.

projects, and he gets things done for the district, so we ran on that." In all, Rogers pumped $383,153 into his pro-incumbency ad campaign.

Similarly, Rep. John M. Spratt, Jr. (D-S.C.), a former bank vice president, paid Geddings Communications of Alexandria, Va., $184,631 to create and place five television and five radio commercials that never mentioned his forty-six House bank overdrafts or his Republican opponent, William T. Horne. Instead, Spratt's ads touted his record of constituent service, his successful efforts to keep Shaw Air Force Base off the base closure list, his work to help protect the state's textile industry, and his efforts on the Armed Services Committee to monitor nuclear waste disposal at the Savannah River nuclear material production plant.

Rep. Tim Johnson (D-S.D.) invested $111,969 in television and radio commercials that trumpeted his work on the Agriculture Committee and his delivery of a federal pipeline project that would bring water to homes and ranches in western South Dakota. Several of his commercials featured constituent testimonials.

After twenty years in the House, Rep. Carlos J. Moorhead (R-Calif.) also felt it would be counterproductive to run against the institution. Instead, he invested $90,333 in ads that recited his accomplishments in office and concluded with Moorhead discussing his plans for the future. He spent $148,623 on brochures and six advocacy mailings that featured testimonials from constituents Moorhead had helped.

Representing a district that is heavily dependent on military spending, Rep. Earl Hutto (D-Fla.) focused many of his ads on his senior position on the Armed Services Committee and on the economic advantages that flowed from that position. Hutto spent $66,376 to air his commercials—about nine times as much as his Republican opponent, Terry Ketchel, spent on broadcast advertising.

In short, while the candidates' messages were undoubtedly important, there was no one message that guaranteed success. Protected by redistricting, unaffected for various reasons by their overdrafts and pay-raise votes, many incumbents had no problems. As former House Speaker Thomas P. O'Neill so eloquently put it, "All politics is local."

For weakened incumbents who survived, as well as successful challengers and open seat candidates, the primary determinant of success was money. Average spending by incumbents in hotly contested races was $716,692—more than twice the $288,654 spent by their challengers. However, excluding Huffington, whose $5,434,569 budget adds more than $150,000 to the average, the typical successful challenger spent $429,075. Average spending by challengers who won their party's nomination but lost the general election was $131,987. This considerable spending advantage allowed successful challengers to spend an average of $111,215 more than unsuccessful challengers on advertising, $47,306 more on persuasion mail, and $31,942 more on phonebanks, yard signs, bumper stickers, and other grass-roots voter contact (see Table 4-1).

On average, winners in open seat contests spent $498,353, or 60 percent more than the $312,421 spent by the typical loser in such races. With their substantially larger budgets, open seat winners were able to spend 78 percent more than losers on broadcast advertising, 55 percent more on persuasion mail, and 56 percent more on grass-roots appeals for votes.

Successful challengers and open seat candidates had the ability to raise money for one simple reason: connections. In a year symbolized by "change" and marked by a deluge of "outsider" rhetoric, those who succeeded in making it to Washington were anything but outsiders.

Of the 510 candidates who contested the November general elections and challenged House incumbents or sought open seats, 50 percent had never held public office or a political party position; 35 percent were either currently in public office or had previously held public office; and 16 percent were political operatives who had either served in government, held a senior position in a local or state political party, or had unsuccessfully sought public office in the past (see Table 4-2). However, among the 110 challengers and open seat candidates who were successful, only 13 percent were "novices," while 74 percent were "politicians," and 14 percent were "operatives" (see Table 4-3). Of the 177 state and local politicians who made bids for House seats, 81 emerged victorious. Only 14 of the 254 novices were as fortunate.

One reason for the success of state and local politicians was the fact that they were considerably less willing to take on incumbents, even in a year when that was supposedly a much less difficult task. While 217 of the 254 novices, or 85 percent, took on incumbents, only 83 of the 177 politicians, or 47 percent, were so foolhardy. Challenging an incumbent meant almost certain defeat, although politicians were a bit more successful: 207 of the 217 novices who challenged incumbents, or 95 percent, lost; 67 of the 83 politicians who took on incumbents, or 81 percent, met the same fate (see Table 4-4). Among the 94 politicians who sought open seats, 65, or 69 percent, won. That success rate would have been higher still had there not be an number of politician-versus-politician match-ups.

Clearly, another major reason for their success was the ability of state and local politicians to channel their already proven fund-raising ability into a new challenge. Those who had the most successful fund-raising organizations also had the greatest success at the ballot box. The 177 state and local politicians who challenged incumbents or sought open House seats reported raising an average of $385,197, including PAC donations of $108,300 (see Table 4-5). Among those who were successful, average receipts amounted to $476,220—$167,824 more than the amount raised by their unsuccessful counterparts. By comparison, the 79 party operatives raised an average of $308,579, of which $62,802 came from PACs; the 15 party operatives who were successful collected an average of $524,744, including PAC donations of $117,413. Excluding Huffington, the successful novices raised $450,877, compared with average receipts of $86,196 for those who lost.

Additional resources translated directly into higher advertising and persuasion mail budgets. The typical successful politician spent $469,033 on his or her campaign, while those who were unsuccessful invested an average of $310,380. Those who prevailed in November invested 57 percent of this $158,653 differential in additional broadcast advertising and advocacy mailers (see Table 4-6).

In the race to succeed retiring Rep. William E. Dannemeyer (R-Calif.), who opted to make an unsuccessful bid for the Senate, Republican state senator Ed Royce got an eight-month jump on his Democratic opponent, Fullerton City Council member Molly McClanahan. Royce announced his decision to run on August 11, 1991; he made his initial payment to fund-raising consultant Ann Hyde Co. of Glendale, Calif., nine days later. Over the next four months, Royce held three fund-raising events. These three receptions, including one featuring House Minority Whip Newt Gingrich (R-Ga.), raised a total of $164,066 from PACs and individual contributors. By the time McClanahan announced her candidacy on March 25, 1992, Royce had raised more than $180,000 and had cash reserves of

Table 4-2 Background of Nonincumbent Candidates in the 1992 House Races

	Politicians[a]		Operatives[b]		Novices[c]		
	Number	Percent	Number	Percent	Number	Percent	Total
Challengers	83	23	58	16	217	61	358
Open Seats	94	62	21	14	37	24	152
Total	177	35	79	16	254	50	510

Note: Percentages may not add to 100 percent due to rounding.
[a]Currently in public office or previously held public office.
[b]Served in government, held a senior position in a local or state political party, or unsuccessfully sought public office in the past.
[c]Never held public office or a political party position.

Table 4-3 Background of Nonincumbent Winners in the 1992 House Races

	Politicians[a]		Operatives[b]		Novices[c]		
	Number	Percent	Number	Percent	Number	Percent	Total
Challengers	16	49	7	21	10	30	33
Open Seats	65	84	8	10	4	5	77
Total	81	74	15	14	14	13	110

Note: Percentages may not add to 100 percent due to rounding.
[a]Currently in public office or previously held public office.
[b]Served in government, held a senior position in a local or state political party, or unsuccessfully sought public office in the past.
[c]Never held public office or a political party position.

Table 4-4 Background of Nonincumbent Losers in the 1992 House Races

	Politicians[a]		Operatives[b]		Novices[c]		
	Number	Percent	Number	Percent	Number	Percent	Total
Challengers	67	21	51	16	207	64	325
Open Seats	29	39	13	17	33	44	75
Total	96	24	64	16	240	60	400

Note: Percentages may not add to 100 percent due to rounding.
[a]Currently in public office or previously held public office.
[b]Served in government, held a senior position in a local or state political party, or unsuccessfully sought public office in the past.
[c]Never held public office or a political party position.

more than $100,000. The gap never closed, with Royce ultimately spending $639,833 to McClanahan's $90,114. Royce pulled down 57 percent of the general election votes to McClanahan's 38 percent.

Tillie Fowler (R-Fla.), a Jacksonville City Council member, had decided to challenge Democratic Rep. Charles E. Bennett long before his surprise announcement that he would not seek a twenty-third term. While she had officially announced her candidacy just one week prior to Bennett's abrupt withdrawal, Fowler had been working her local contacts for months to assemble a high-profile finance committee. By the time former Democratic state legislator and judge Mattox Hair decided to run, Fowler had already lined up the support of twenty-two people who had helped Hair raise money for a 1984 state senate campaign. Fowler had eighty people who each agreed to raise between $5,000 and $10,000. Those commitments allowed her to spend $522,363 to Hair's $421,098, a $101,265 differential. Fowler outspent Hair by $74,107 on advertising, and on November 3 she collected 57 percent of the votes.

Republican state senator James C. Greenwood put his fundraising machinery into overdrive, raising $721,654 for his successful challenge to seven-term Democratic Rep. Peter H. Kostmayer. Starting with an original direct-mail list of roughly 500 donors to his previous state campaigns, Greenwood expanded his base to more than 2,400 contributors by the end of the campaign. That new base yielded direct-mail contributions of more than $120,000, helping to push his small donations to $149,071. Originally hoping to raise $50,000 from PACs,

Greenwood's fund-raising advisers targeted 400 PACs as likely contributors; PACs ultimately donated $179,742. Greenwood raised $378,694 from individual contributors who gave at least $200, $33,680 of which came from out-of-state. Although he was outspent by $505,637, Greenwood's substantial budget allowed him to sink $299,486 into advertising and $168,016 into persuasion mail. Greenwood emerged with a 6-point victory.

The political operatives who won House seats spent an average of $512,974, while the sixty-four who lost spent an average of $310,380. With their larger budgets, the winners spent an average of $48,095 more on advertising and $45,852 more on persuasion mail (see Table 4-6).

Roosevelt University professor Mel Reynolds had tried in both 1988 and 1990 to oust Democratic Rep. Gus Savage, and his permanent campaign was well established by the time redistricting robbed Savage of part of his base of support. During his two unsuccessful bids, Reynolds had built up an impressive fund-raising base that allowed him to spend $88,548 during the off-year and commit another $389,997 to defeating Savage during the first three months of 1992. That investment included $107,623 paid to Fenn & King for developing and placing two preprimary radio commercials.

Attorney Steve Buyer (R-Ind.) had served as Indiana deputy attorney general from 1987 through 1988 and as vice chairman for the White County Republican party from 1988 through 1990. Although he had never held public office, he had the contacts that enabled him to raise $201,400 from individual contributors and $135,834 from PACs. Outspent by $204,359, Buyer funneled 40 percent of his resources into radio and television commercials. With a $34,626 infusion from his own bank account, he managed to spend $15,546 more than Democratic Rep. Jim Jontz on such ads.

While 254 novices battled for House seats in November, only 14 were elected. Among those who won, there were few Horatio Alger stories.

Huffington spent $5,191,728 of his own money, and his $5,434,569 budget was more than twice as much as any previous House candidate had ever spent.

Everett funded his outsider campaign with $931,291 of his own money, which accounted for 88 percent of his total receipts.

Martin R. Hoke's (R-Ohio) victory over Democratic Rep. Mary Rose Oakar cost $698,460. To help fuel that effort, Hoke tapped his own bank account for $265,000.

A television reporter for fourteen years, Ron Klink (D-Pa.) raised a total of $264,293 to fund his primary victory over Rep. Joe Kolter and his general election win over Republican Gordon R. Johnston. Twenty-one percent of Klink's receipts, $55,006, came from his own bank account.

Businessman Jay Dickey (R-Ark.) personally supplied 32 percent of the $412,465 his campaign took in.

Businessman Dan Miller (R-Fla.) loaned his campaign $122,500, which represented 27 percent of his total receipts.

Whether or not they depended largely on personal wealth to finance their campaigns, the politically successful novices had no trouble raising the necessary money to communicate their messages. Excluding Huffington, the remaining thirteen novices who were elected spent an average of $458,381, including $171,890 on radio and television advertising.

Those novices who lost—a group that included students, teachers, ministers, a typesetter, a homemaker, a geologist, a computer operator, and a hospital technician—spent an average of $85,121. Fifty-six of these less well-heeled challengers spent less than $5,000.

The power of money was also evident in those races where challengers might have won had they had the money to communicate with voters. For example, Republican Rick Hardy, a political science professor at the University of Missouri, came within 5,883 votes of denying Rep. Harold L. Volkmer (D-Mo.) a ninth term, despite being outspent by more than three to one.

While Volkmer's $511,554 treasury allowed him to spend $226,418 on advertising and $50,130 on campaign literature and advocacy mailings, Hardy's more modest $147,139 budget allowed him to spend only $31,984 on advertising and $2,034 on leaflets. "It was a suicide mission," recalled Hardy.

Nevertheless, Hardy nearly pulled off the upset with a strong outsider campaign fueled by more than 500 former students who volunteered to knock on doors. Without the money to advertise, Hardy held press conferences, hoping that the free media would carry his anti-incumbent message. Over the final two weeks of the campaign, when it became clear that the race had tightened, the National Republican Congressional Committee invested $40,000 in additional television and radio air time for Hardy, but it was too little, too late.

Similarly, Edward W. Munster (R-Conn.) garnered 49 percent of the votes in his bid to unseat Democratic Rep. Sam

Table 4-5 Average Receipts of Nonincumbents in 1992 House Races

Background	PAC Contributions	Individual Contributions	Total Receipts
Politicians[a]			
Winners	$151,907	$252,041	$476,220
Losers	71,507	184,588	308,396
Total	108,300	215,456	385,197
Operatives[b]			
Winners	117,413	291,680	524,744
Losers	50,003	130,793	257,915
Total	62,802	161,341	308,579
Novices[c]			
Winners	63,255	247,960	450,877
Losers	12,231	42,783	86,196
Total	15,044	54,092	106,297

Note: Total for winning novices does not include receipts of $5,443,247 by Michael Huffington, R-Calif.
[a] Currently in public office or previously held public office.
[b] Served in government, held a senior position in a local or state political party, or unsuccessfully sought public office in the past.
[c] Never held public office or a political party position.

Table 4-6 What Campaign Money Buys in the 1992 House Races: Average Expenditures by Politicians, Operatives, and Novices

Major Category	Politicians[a]			Operatives[b]			Novices[c]		
	Total	Winner	Loser	Total	Winner	Loser	Total	Winner	Loser
Overhead									
Office furniture/supplies	$ 6,087	$ 7,122	$ 5,214	$ 5,582	$ 7,722	$ 5,080	$ 2,000	$ 7,960	$ 1,652
Rent/utilities	5,935	7,018	5,022	5,629	10,546	4,477	2,008	6,528	1,744
Salaries	41,340	47,840	35,855	29,379	51,843	24,114	12,620	51,413	10,357
Taxes	6,432	6,909	6,029	3,533	3,913	3,444	1,867	10,407	1,369
Bank/investment fees	373	499	267	413	566	377	207	1,139	152
Lawyers/accountants	2,603	3,612	1,751	1,306	2,391	1,052	508	2,092	416
Telephone	8,401	9,433	7,531	6,765	9,537	6,115	2,547	9,295	2,154
Campaign automobile	685	843	552	557	995	454	47	34	48
Computers/office equipment	4,424	4,343	4,492	3,678	5,403	3,274	1,792	5,398	1,581
Travel	8,056	9,999	6,416	6,915	7,977	6,666	2,511	8,929	2,137
Food/meetings	535	589	489	280	486	232	125	568	99
Total Overhead	**84,870**	**98,208**	**73,617**	**64,037**	**101,379**	**55,285**	**26,231**	**103,762**	**21,709**
Fund Raising									
Events	25,308	33,117	18,720	13,557	24,721	10,940	5,201	24,331	4,085
Direct mail	11,018	10,114	11,781	7,246	9,056	6,822	2,701	14,824	1,994
Telemarketing	800	242	1,271	543	1,019	432	369	2,133	266
Total Fund Raising	**37,127**	**43,474**	**31,771**	**21,346**	**34,796**	**18,193**	**8,271**	**41,288**	**6,345**
Polling	**13,437**	**16,078**	**11,209**	**10,119**	**18,425**	**8,172**	**2,995**	**12,178**	**2,459**
Advertising									
Electronic media	117,079	141,505	96,470	97,751	175,169	79,606	31,541	171,890	23,354
Other media	8,630	10,289	7,229	10,144	15,388	8,916	4,369	16,235	3,676
Total Advertising	**125,709**	**151,794**	**103,699**	**107,896**	**190,557**	**88,522**	**35,910**	**188,125**	**27,031**
Other Campaign Activity									
Persuasion mail/brochures	76,303	101,172	55,320	62,123	114,095	49,942	15,916	44,484	14,250
Actual campaigning	36,156	46,951	27,048	29,311	47,570	25,032	12,324	54,670	9,854
Staff/Volunteers	455	720	230	422	827	328	102	443	82
Total Other Campaign Activity	**112,914**	**148,843**	**82,599**	**91,857**	**162,493**	**75,301**	**28,342**	**99,596**	**24,185**
Constituent Gifts/Entertainment	**479**	**1,009**	**32**	**98**	**387**	**30**	**51**	**623**	**18**
Donations to									
Candidates from same state	210	337	102	46	35	48	20	37	19
Candidates from other states	42	78	11	8	0	9	1	0	1
Civic organizations	420	635	239	177	206	170	67	239	57
Ideological groups	106	176	48	57	103	46	19	79	16
Political parties	411	491	343	196	143	208	123	609	94
Total Donations	**1,189**	**1,717**	**743**	**483**	**488**	**482**	**230**	**964**	**187**
Unitemized Expenses	**7,259**	**7,910**	**6,710**	**5,389**	**4,450**	**5,609**	**3,665**	**11,845**	**3,187**
Total Expenditures	**$382,984**	**469,033**	**$310,380**	**$301,224**	**$512,974**	**$251,595**	**$105,694**	**$458,381**	**$85,121**

Note: Total for winning novices does not include expenditures of $5,434,569 by Michael Huffington, R-Calif.
[a] Currently in public office or previously held public office.
[b] Served in government, held a senior position in a local or state political party, or unsuccessfully sought public office in the past.
[c] Never held public office or a political party position.

Gejdenson, despite pitting his $142,719 budget against the six-term incumbent's $898,562 treasury. Outspent by more than ten to one on broadcast advertising, Munster invested much of his $36,423 broadcast advertising budget in cable ads slamming Gejdenson for his fifty-one overdrafts at the House bank and his vote in favor of the congressional pay raise. At $3 apiece, Munster was able to air his ads thousands of times on CNN and ESPN. "If you don't request a specific time-slot and just saturate the channel, you are virtually guaranteed some prime-time slots," noted Munster. Had he had anything close to Gejdenson's $392,253 broadcast advertising budget, Munster might well have closed the 3,875-vote gap.

Forty-six successful candidates—ten incumbents, eighteen challengers, and eighteen open-seat candidates—managed to buck the system, spending less than the people they defeated.

Peter T. King (R-N.Y.) emerged victorious, despite being outspent by $897,950 in his open seat contest with Democrat Steve A. Orlins.

Rep. Wayne T. Gilchrest (R-Md.) spent $861,872 less than Democratic Rep. Tom McMillen in an incumbent-versus-incumbent match-up created by redistricting.

Outspent by $808,927, Rick A. Lazio (R-N.Y.) still managed to oust nine-term Rep. Thomas J. Downey, who had 151 overdrafts at the House bank.

In all, thirty-four winners were outspent by at least $100,000, including ten who were outspent by more than $500,000. However, that did not in most cases mean that the victors had limited resources. Only four of the forty-six spent less than $200,000. Thirteen spent more than $500,000, including incumbents Bob Carr (D-Mich.) and Pat Williams (D-Mont.), who spent $1,107,973 and $1,190,716, respectively. While Delaware Gov. Michael N. Castle was outspent by $309,689, his $708,671 budget was more than sufficient to communicate with voters who already knew him well. The same was true for freshman Rep. Thomas H. Andrews (D-Maine), who spent $861,564 to combat Republican Linda Bean's $1,469,959 challenge.

In Senate races, where effective communication with a statewide electorate required a substantial investment in television advertising, money also proved to be a powerful gatekeeper. On average, the twenty-eight incumbents who won renomination spent $4,149,198 on their campaigns. The average challenger spent $1,922,001. In twelve of these twenty-eight races, the challenger spent less than $500,000 and was little more than a name on the ballot.

Excluding his investment in maintaining his off-year campaign operation, Sen. John B. Breaux (D-La.) outspent Republican Jon Khachaturian $1,193,418 to $94,920.

While Sen. Richard C. Shelby (D-Ala.) was putting $1,212,935 into television and radio advertising, Republican Richard Sellers spent just $146,556 on his entire campaign.

Sen. John McCain (R-Ariz.) spent $875,064 to keep his campaign engine running smoothly during the off-years—nearly three times the $301,362 Democrat Claire Sargent spent trying to unseat him.

Over the six-year election cycle, Sen. Tom Daschle (D-S.D.) spent $1,010,233 on campaign salaries and taxes, $397,387 of which was spent during 1992. Daschle's Republican opponent, Charlene Haar, managed to scrape together $406,547 for her token effort.

These four races and eight similar financial mismatches helped ensure that there would not be massive turnover in the Senate as a result of anti-incumbent sentiment.

Even in those cases where challengers were well funded, their treasuries were generally dwarfed by the resources available to the incumbent in the race.

In Missouri, Democratic challenger Geri Rothman-Serot spent $1,114,580 in her unsuccessful bid to unseat Republican Sen. Christopher S. Bond. After spending $1,111,859 to maintain his permanent campaign during the off-years, Bond was able to respond to Rothman-Serot's challenge with a $3,770,172 burst in 1992.

Indiana Democrat Joseph H. Hogsett spent $1,544,475 on his challenge to Sen. Daniel R. Coats. Coats invested $816,501 in his campaign during 1991 and pumped $2,967,657 into his reelection effort in 1992.

Rep. Les AuCoin (D-Ore.) spent $2,641,756 trying to unseat Republican Sen. Bob Packwood. However, that was $548,278 less than Packwood spent during the off-years. In 1992 Packwood poured another $4,768,629 into the defense of his seat.

In New York, State Attorney General Robert Abrams spent a total of $6,374,304 to secure the Democratic nomination and challenge Republican Sen. Alphonse M. D'Amato. D'Amato's fund-raising ability allowed him to invest $3,753,302 in maintaining his permanent campaign and still spend $8,065,930 on his election-year push.

The successful challengers had campaign treasuries that looked more like a typical incumbent's. Former San Francisco mayor Dianne Feinstein spent $8,041,099 to defeat Republican Sen. John Seymour. While many challengers struggled to raise $500,000, Feinstein poured $3,277,559 into producing and airing her broadcast ads, and that sizable investment was augmented by a $1,235,000 infusion from the Democratic Senatorial Campaign Committee.

Cook County Recorder of Deeds Carol Moseley-Braun had only about $580,000 to invest in her long-shot bid to oust Sen. Alan J. Dixon in the Illinois Democratic primary, but she had plenty of help. Over the final six weeks of the primary campaign fellow Democratic challenger Albert F. Hofeld spent between $200,000 and $300,000 a week on television commercials blasting Dixon's record. Dixon, in turn, pounded Hofeld with a barrage of television commercials that virtually ignored Moseley-Braun, who slipped through to a 3-point win over Dixon. Once the nomination was hers, Moseley-Braun raised more than $6 million for her general election contest with Chicago attorney Richard Williamson, who spent $2,468,282.

In North Carolina, Lauch Faircloth and Sen. Terry Sanford were old political allies. However, when Faircloth opted in 1991 to become a Republican and challenge Sanford for his seat, Faircloth quickly gained a new friend and powerful ally: Sen. Jesse Helms (R-N.C.).

Carter Wren, a longtime aide to Helms, devised Faircloth's media strategy. Hanover Communications of Raleigh, N.C.—a key player in Helms's past campaigns under its old name, Campaign Management—produced and placed Faircloth's commercials. So great was the overlap between Helms's and Faircloth's campaign organizations that it even confused those responsible for filling out the campaign financial statements filed with the Federal Election Commission. One page of a Faircloth expense statement filed in July 1992 read: Helms for Senate Committee. Faircloth hired Helms's direct-mail fundraiser and during 1992 raised enough to outspend Sanford $2,904,061 to $2,295,449.

In all, the thirteen challengers and open seat candidates

Table 4-7 What Campaign Money Buys in the 1992 Senate Races: Expenditures by Nonincumbents

Major Category	Winners			Losers		
	Total	Average	Percent	Total	Average	Percent
Overhead						
Office furniture/supplies	$ 727,785	$ 55,983	1.53	$ 922,010	$ 27,940	1.66
Rent/utilities	504,687	38,822	1.06	632,641	19,171	1.14
Salaries	5,269,885	405,376	11.11	6,036,935	182,937	10.89
Taxes	954,435	73,418	2.01	1,620,194	49,097	2.92
Bank/investment fees	79,430	6,110	.17	26,348	798	.05
Lawyers/accountants	366,776	28,214	.77	272,487	8,257	.49
Telephone	1,068,357	82,181	2.25	1,319,947	39,998	2.38
Campaign automobile	55,191	4,245	.12	53,355	1,617	.10
Computers/office equipment	623,018	47,924	1.31	644,804	19,540	1.16
Travel	1,419,502	109,192	2.99	1,624,610	49,231	2.93
Food/meetings	39,185	3,014	.08	40,110	1,215	.07
Total Overhead	**11,108,250**	**854,481**	**23.41**	**13,193,442**	**399,801**	**23.80**
Fund Raising						
Events	3,461,174	266,244	7.29	3,098,358	93,890	5.59
Direct mail	6,095,890	468,915	12.85	6,047,722	183,264	10.91
Telemarketing	698,378	53,721	1.47	491,917	14,907	.89
Total Fund Raising	**10,255,442**	**788,880**	**21.61**	**9,637,997**	**292,061**	**17.38**
Polling	**1,176,772**	**90,521**	**2.48**	**1,363,965**	**41,332**	**2.46**
Advertising						
Electronic media	20,408,864	1,569,913	43.01	25,239,788	764,842	45.52
Other media	270,347	20,796	.57	387,185	11,733	.70
Total Advertising	**20,679,211**	**1,590,709**	**43.58**	**25,626,973**	**776,575**	**46.22**
Other Campaign Activity						
Persuasion mail/brochures	1,040,340	80,026	2.19	1,849,613	56,049	3.34
Actual campaigning	2,711,355	208,566	5.71	3,156,181	95,642	5.69
Staff/Volunteers	30,458	2,343	.06	15,904	482	.03
Total Other Campaign Activity	**3,782,153**	**290,935**	**7.97**	**5,021,698**	**152,173**	**9.06**
Constituent Gifts/ Entertainment	**40,158**	**3,089**	**.08**	**12,023**	**364**	**.02**
Donations to						
Candidates from same state	1,266	97	0	7,708	234	.01
Candidates from other states	3,000	231	.01	26	1	0
Civic organizations	8,519	655	.02	7,054	214	.01
Ideological groups	2,500	192	.01	6,061	184	.01
Political parties	14,404	1,108	.03	15,704	476	.03
Total Donations	**29,689**	**2,284**	**.06**	**36,553**	**1,108**	**.07**
Unitemized Expenses	**377,889**	**29,068**	**.80**	**553,158**	**16,762**	**1.00**
Total Expenditures	**$47,449,564**	**$3,649,966**	**100.00**	**$55,445,809**	**$1,680,176**	**100.00**

elected to the Senate in 1992 reported spending $47,449,564, an average of $3,649,966. The thirty-three losing challengers and open seat candidates spent a total of $55,445,809, an average of $1,680,176 (see Table 4-7).

More than anything else, this explains why twenty-four of the twenty-eight incumbents who won renomination were reelected on November 3. While the negative images associated with incumbency were of concern to virtually every senator, in the vast majority of cases those images melted under the heat generated by an average spending advantage of $1,969,790.

CHAPTER 5

The "Year of the Woman"
Sweeping Phenomenon or Political Cliché?

Our spending decisions, particularly on TV, were directly influenced by the fact that our opponent was a woman.
Wes Gullett, campaign manager for Sen. John McCain (R-Ariz.)

We were running against a man, but we never used the idea of the Year of the Woman in any of our ads or speeches. We never said, "It's time for a change and a woman is the best person to make that change."
Mary E. Fetsch, press secretary for Elizabeth Furse (D-Ore.)

On the eve of the 1960 elections, sixteen women held seats in the House of Representatives; in 1980 that number still stood at sixteen. In 1990, fueled by the rise in the number of women elected to state and local offices, sixty-eight women had sought House seats. Only twenty-eight of those 1990 hopefuls had come away victorious, including twenty-four incumbents (but excluding Eleanor Holmes Norton, Washington, D.C.'s nonvoting delegate). In thirty years, despite all the societal changes that had increased opportunities for women in other fields, women's representation in the House had grown from 4 percent to 6 percent. Over that same time span, the number of women in the Senate rose from one to two.

Then, virtually overnight, the logjam seemed to break. On November 3, 1992, voters in 101 congressional districts across the country were given the opportunity to cast their ballots for a woman who had won either the Republican or Democratic nomination. In five of those districts, both major party candidates were women. In addition, women finished second in Louisiana's open primaries against Republican Rep. Robert L. Livingston in District 1 and Democratic Rep. William J. Jefferson in District 2, but since both Livingston and Jefferson emerged with more than 50 percent of the vote, they were exempted under state election law from having to run in the November general election. In Massachusetts, Republicans chose not to challenge Rep. Joseph P. Kennedy II, and his only opposition came from independent Alice Harriett Nakash. Charles E. Schumer (D-N.Y.) escaped a Republican challenge, but drew limited opposition from Conservative party nominee Alice E. Gaffney. Women contested eleven of the thirty-six Senate seats up for grabs in November.

Given these numbers, it was little wonder that the primary contests that yielded this record field of female candidates also spawned in major newspapers and magazines more than 3,000 stories that contained the phrase "Year of the Woman." However, like "change" and "anti-incumbency," the phrase took on a life of its own. News reports placed emphasis on the body count, implying a cohesion among these women that simply did not exist.

Emblematic of this analysis was an Associated Press story on the fund-raising success enjoyed by Cook County Recorder of Deeds Carol Moseley-Braun (D-Ill.) and several other women seeking Senate seats. Assessing the Year of the Woman, the article noted that "the reason for the number of female candidates is the same rationale given for fund-raising success: the Senate Judiciary Committee's treatment of Anita Hill and her charges of sexual harassment against Supreme Court Justice Clarence Thomas."

Hill provided the cause celebre if not the impetus for several high-profile campaigns. Moseley-Braun noted in one of her fund-raising letters that "the hearings on the Clarence Thomas nomination gave us all a rude awakening. Of the 100 members of the United States Senate, the most important legislative body in the country, 98 are men.... A few days after the vote, I announced my candidacy for the United States Senate." A fifteen-minute video shown at in-home fund-raisers hit the issue several times.

Lynn Yeakel (D-Pa.), the founder and president of a Philadelphia-based organization that raises money for various women's groups, came within 3 points of upsetting Republican incumbent Arlen Specter in their Senate race. In one of her two television commercials shown before the Democratic primary, she took aim at Specter, who had taken the lead in attacking Hill's credibility. Opening with a brief segment of Specter's questioning of Hill, the ad quickly cut to a still photograph of Specter, as Yeakel asked, "Did this make you as angry as it made me? I'm Lynn Yeakel and it's time we do something about the mess in Washington."

DIVERSITY, NOT UNIFORMITY

While most of the press coverage focused on high-profile Senate races such as Moseley-Braun's and Yeakel's, female candidates, like their male counterparts, were scattered from one end of the liberal-conservative spectrum to the other. Their reasons for running, as well as the messages they delivered, went well beyond the controversy surrounding Hill's treatment by the Senate.

Lynn Woolsey (D-Calif.), who won the House seat vacated by Democratic Rep. Barbara Boxer, promised in an introductory mailer that she would "fight to protect a woman's right for reproductive choice, for passage of the ERA, for gay and lesbian rights." The cover of one of her brochures featured two pictures—one showing six members of the Senate Judiciary Committee, the other showing Hill being sworn in as a witness at that committee's hearings into her allegations against Thomas. Black lettering on a red background proclaimed: "Anita Hill made a lot of people realize we need more women like Lynn Woolsey in Congress." Another brochure focused on education, issues affecting the elderly, job creation, and, to pay for it all, her promise to fight for at least a 50 percent reduction in the defense budget.

Fellow California Democrat Patricia Garamendi, who lost an open seat contest to Republican Richard W. Pombo, found common ground with Woolsey on a host of issues, including abortion rights and health care, but her position on defense cuts was considerably more cautious. In one mailer she promised to support "sensible cuts in the defense budget while implementing conversion and adjustment programs to prevent economic disaster in communities impacted by those cuts." That same mailer touted Garamendi's commitment to "strong crime-fighting programs," an issue never discussed in Woolsey's mailings. None of Garamendi's advocacy mailers mentioned Hill.

Narrowly reelected in 1992, Rep. Barbara F. Vucanovich (R-Nev.) opposed abortion. An article in *McCall* magazine had dubbed her one of the top ten congressional enemies of women's issues. Asked by a reporter why she had chosen not to join the Congressional Caucus on Women's Issues, Vucanovich replied, "I can't see spending money on a caucus to have Pat Schroeder out there representing me."

Douglas T. Gray, administrative assistant to Democratic state senator Pat Danner, who defeated Republican Rep. Tom Coleman in Missouri, noted that Danner had not used gender as an issue in her campaign."She even wanted to be called 'Congressman' at first," Gray added. "She did not want to be a woman in the Congress; she just wanted to be a member."

Republican Donna Peterson, who unsuccessfully challenged Rep. Charles Wilson (D-Texas), certainly was among the most conservative of the 121 women who sought House or Senate seats. Noting that she was "a conservative Texan with a strong background of service to America," one of Peterson's brochures pointed out that she was "the first woman from Southeast Texas to graduate from the United States Military Academy at West Point." Among the positions outlined in the brochure was her dedication "to traditional moral values," stating that she opposed "minority status for homosexuals and federal funding for abortions" and favored "school prayer and Pledge of Allegiance."

In addition to largely ignoring the diversity of opinion among those women running, press reports also ignored that fact that the Year of the Woman was not happening everywhere. While it was presented as a national phenomenon, half of the women contesting House seats on November 3 came from just six states—California, Florida, New York, Ohio, Texas, and Wisconsin. In sixteen states, including Pennsylvania, only one woman was successful in winning either the Republican or Democratic nomination for a House seat. In five of those sixteen states, the lone woman was an incumbent. In fifteen states, including Massachusetts, no women captured a major party's nomination for a House seat.

Even when they successfully navigated their party's primary, women frequently had a more difficult time doing so than their male counterparts. Twenty-five of the eighty-four women who challenged House incumbents or sought open seats, or 30 percent, fought their way through crowded fields in which they received less than 50 percent of the votes. The comparable percentage for nonincumbent men was 23 percent.

Judy Jarvis (R-Calif.) captured 21 percent of the primary votes against nine men. Woolsey won the nomination with just 26 percent of the vote in a nine-candidate field. Ellen E. Wedum (D-Ind.) prevailed with 27 percent in a four-candidate contest. Nydia M. Velazquez (D-N.Y.) collected 33 percent of the primary votes against Rep. Stephen J. Solarz and four others. In six other races with similar results, the women who captured the most votes were still required by state election laws to win primary runoffs after failing to garner at least 50 percent of the primary votes.

In the Senate, four of the ten women who sought to challenge incumbents or contest open seats failed to receive the support of 50 percent of their party's primary voters. In Missouri, Geri Rothman-Serot grabbed 36 percent in the fourteen-candidate Democratic primary free-for-all to pick a challenger to Republican Sen. Christopher S. Bond. Moseley-Braun took 38 percent of the Democratic primary vote in upsetting Sen. Alan J. Dixon. Yeakel and Boxer each collected 44 percent.

The so-called Year of the Woman was also much more of a Democratic party phenomenon than a broad-based political phenomenon. Of the eighty-four women who provided the major opposition for House incumbents or sought open House seats, fifty-four were Democrats, twenty-eight were Republicans, and two were independents. Former South Dakota Republican party leader Charlene Haar was the only Republican among the ten women who sought open Senate seats or challenged incumbents, prompting Susan Brankin Hirschmann, executive director of the conservative Eagle Forum political action committee (PAC), to remark to one reporter, "What the media really means by 'The Year of the Woman' is 'The Year of the Radical Democratic Pro-Abortion Woman.' "

Dolly Madison McKenna (R-Texas), who unsuccessfully challenged Democratic Rep. Michael A. Andrews, said the Year of the Woman helped her campaign by instantly giving her more credibility and by providing her with national publicity that she would not have received otherwise. Peterson had precisely the opposite reaction. "I was constantly having to defend myself in this conservative district that I am not some radical, liberal feminist," she recalled.

On election day, forty-seven women were elected to the

House, including twenty-three incumbents (but excluding Norton), raising women's representation in the House to an all-time high of 11 percent. The net gain by women of nineteen seats was the direct result of the decisions by sixty-five incumbents to retire from politics or seek other offices. Only one of the open House seats was previously occupied by a woman. Mirroring the pattern for nonincumbent victors in general, those women who joined the 1992 freshman class tended to be open seat contestants. While forty-nine women challenged incumbents, only four emerged victorious. Among the thirty-five women who contested open seats, twenty won. This 57 percent batting average was 8 points higher than the success rate for men in open seat contests.

In the Year of the Woman, the four victories by women challengers represented an 8 percent success rate, which was essentially the same as the 9 percent success rate recorded by men who challenged incumbents—29 of 309. Further belying the gender hype, none of the women who successfully challenged House incumbents won primarily because of anger over Hill's treatment or their opponent's position on abortion and other issues on which women might be expected to have the edge.

Blanche Lambert (D-Ark.) upset her former boss, Rep. Bill Alexander, in the Democratic primary largely as a result of his 487 overdrafts at the House bank. Danner's campaign was built on an anti-incumbent message that included attacks on Coleman's vote in favor of the congressional pay raise, his penchant for taxpayer-funded travel, and his heavy use of the congressional franking privilege. Velazquez narrowly ousted Solarz in the New York Democratic primary because redistricting had dismantled his predominantly Jewish district in Brooklyn, and he had chosen to seek refuge in a district gerrymandered to elect a Hispanic. While her campaign slogan was "there are too many millionaires and not enough women" in Congress, former city council member Carolyn B. Maloney (D-N.Y.) owed her victory over liberal, pro-choice Republican Bill Green to redistricting, which added heavily Democratic precincts in Brooklyn and Queens to Green's wealthy Manhattan constituency. Green carried the Manhattan precincts he had represented for fourteen years, but lost by a two-to-one margin in the newly acquired precincts.

As these four victorious women were ending the House careers of men, four men were replacing female members for many of the same reasons. In Maryland, Democratic state representative Thomas H. Hattery rode a negative, anti-incumbent campaign to a Democratic primary victory over Rep. Beverly B. Byron. Hattery then lost the general election to Republican Roscoe G. Bartlett, who tarred Hattery with the negatives of incumbency. Rep. Joan Kelly Horn (D-Mo.) had won her seat by just 54 votes in 1990, and when redistricting added Republicans to her constituency, she fell to Republican James M. Talent by 8,865 votes. Attorney and businessman Martin R. Hoke (R-Ohio) ended the sixteen-year House career of Rep. Mary Rose Oakar largely because of her status as one of the House bank's twenty-two worst abusers and the political fallout over erroneous reports in the *Cleveland Plain Dealer* that she had placed ghost employees on the House post office staff. Three-term Rep. Liz J. Patterson (D-S.C.) was ousted by the anti-incumbent onslaught of attorney Bob Inglis. "Our strategy was to run against Congress, not Patterson," recalled Jeff Parker, Inglis's campaign manager. "We said, 'Here are some things you don't like about Congress, but guess what, Patterson shares some of those same characteristics.'"

In the Senate, the number of women jumped from two to six (a seventh, Kay Bailey Hutchison, R-Texas, won a June 1993 special election to fill the seat vacated by Democratic Sen. Lloyd Bentson). Two of the four newly elected members—Moseley-Braun and former San Francisco mayor Dianne Feinstein (D-Calif.)—upset incumbents, although Feinstein's opponent, Sen. John Seymour, had been appointed to the seat in 1991 by Gov. Pete Wilson, who had resigned the seat in order to make his successful gubernatorial bid. State senator Patty Murray (D-Wash.) and Boxer took open seats.

Once again, the single biggest key to success for those who sought to become House or Senate incumbents was incumbency in some other office. Thirty-eight of the eighty-four women who sought open House seats or challenged House incumbents had held neither public office nor a political party post; thirty currently held or had recently held public office; and sixteen had some prior political experience (see Table 5-1). However, of the twenty-four women who won House seats for the first time in 1992, nineteen were "politicians," including five state senators, a former state senator, five state representatives, and three city council members. Three of the successful women were "operatives," and only two were "novices" (see Table 5-2). None of the twenty-eight novices who challenged incumbents won (see Table 5-3).

Six of the ten women who sought open Senate seats or challenged incumbents were politicians—Boxer, Feinstein, Moseley-Braun, Murray, state senator Jean Lloyd-Jones (D-Iowa), and city council member Rothman-Serot. All four of the newly elected senators came from this group. Although voters were supposedly anxious to throw incumbents out of office, in reality most voters simply traded one set of career politicians for another.

As was the case with nonincumbents in general, women with political experience proved to be more successful on election day in large part because they were more successful fundraisers. In the House, the thirty-five women who contested open seats spent a total of $17,426,029, an average of $497,887. The twenty winners—sixteen of whom were politicians—spent $12,729,474, or $636,474 on average. These twenty women spent $186,584 more on average than the men who won open seats.

In contrast, the fifteen losers in these open seat contests—only three of whom were politicians—spent a total of $4,696,555, an average of $313,104. If the $1,701,907 spent by the three politicians who lost is removed from the equation, the typical loser's outlays amounted to $249,554 (see Table 5-4).

Having headed the Washington state Republican party for eleven years, Jennifer Dunn was adept at raising money. When Republican Rep. Rod Chandler decided to leave Congress to

Table 5-1 Background of Nonincumbent Female Candidates in the 1992 House Races

	Politicians[a]		Operatives[b]		Novices[c]		
	Number	Percent	Number	Percent	Number	Percent	Total
Challengers	11	37	10	63	28	74	49
Open Seats	19	63	6	38	10	26	35
Total	30	36	16	19	38	45	84

Note: Percentages may not add to 100 percent due to rounding.
[a] Currently in public office or previously held public office.
[b] Served in government, held a senior position in a local or state political party, or unsuccessfully sought public office in the past.
[c] Never held public office or a political party position.

Table 5-2 Background of Nonincumbent Female Winners in the 1992 House Races

	Politicians[a]		Operatives[b]		Novices[c]		
	Number	Percent	Number	Percent	Number	Percent	Total
Challengers	3	16	1	33	0	0	4
Open Seats	16	84	2	67	2	100	20
Total	19	79	3	13	2	8	24

Note: Percentages may not add to 100 percent due to rounding.
[a] Currently in public office or previously held public office.
[b] Served in government, held a senior position in a local or state political party, or unsuccessfully sought public office in the past.
[c] Never held public office or a political party position.

Table 5-3 Background of Nonincumbent Female Losers in the 1992 House Races

	Politicians[a]		Operatives[b]		Novices[c]		
	Number	Percent	Number	Percent	Number	Percent	Total
Challengers	8	73	9	69	28	78	45
Open Seats	3	27	4	31	8	22	15
Total	11	18	13	22	36	60	60

Note: Percentages may not add to 100 percent due to rounding.
[a] Currently in public office or previously held public office.
[b] Served in government, held a senior position in a local or state political party, or unsuccessfully sought public office in the past.
[c] Never held public office or a political party position.

wage an unsuccessful Senate campaign, Dunn decided it was time to turn that fund-raising prowess to her own advantage. "We raised most of our money by Jennifer Dunn personally asking for it," recalled campaign manager John Myers. With the help of friends and volunteers, Dunn worked her way through the 5,000 names in her personal files, raising $492,444 from individual donors and $168,373 from PACs. Helped by a $25,000 infusion from her own bank account, Dunn was able to outspend businessman George O. Tamblyn by $287,578.

State senator Eddie Bernice Johnson (D-Texas) had one substantial advantage in the contest for the state's newly created District 30: she chaired the state senate's congressional redistricting committee and had a major role in drawing the district's boundaries to her liking. Once that battle was won, Johnson had no trouble collecting $114,176 from PACs and $149,761 from individual contributors. Her Republican opponent spent only $4,707, and Johnson coasted to victory with 72 percent of the vote.

San Diego Port Commissioner Lynn Schenk (D-Calif.) had extensive experience in state Democratic politics and fund raising—experience that undoubtedly spelled the difference in her match-up with Republican Judy Jarvis, a registered nurse who, like Schenk, took a pro-choice stance on abortion. Schenk raised $653,104 from individual contributors and $300,129 from PACs; comparable figures for Jarvis were $87,799 and $149,993, respectively. Schenk's fund-raising prowess allowed her to spend $1,122,504, including $470,292 on broadcast advertising and $243,352 on campaign literature and persuasion mailers. Jarvis spent just $40,973 on her broadcast advertising campaign and $160,345 on advocacy mailings and handouts.

San Mateo County Supervisor Anna G. Eshoo (D-Calif.) had spent $1.1 million on an unsuccessful challenge to Republican Rep. Tom Campbell in 1988, and when Campbell announced his decision to seek the open Senate seat created by the retirement of Democratic Sen. Alan Cranston, Eshoo simply turned on the fund-raising spigot. Among those Eshoo turned to for help was Gloria Steinem, who was the featured guest at an afternoon fund-raiser in April 1992. Billed in the invitation as a "Tea for Two Terrific Women" and sponsored by Palo Alto City Council member Liz Kniss, the event drew 200 supporters who each paid $100 to witness an informal conversation between Eshoo and Steinem. All of the attendees left with a signed copy of Steinem's book, *Revolution from Within*. The campaign asked Steinem back in June for a sit-down luncheon attended by more than a dozen supporters who each paid $500. Dozens of events such as these helped Eshoo raise $610,938 from individual contributors and $296,322 from PACs. She ultimately spent $957,101 on her campaign, outspending her Republican opponent, fellow San Mateo County Supervisor Tom Huening, by $282,070. She invested $196,994 of that spending advantage in persuasion mail and coasted to an 18-point win.

Having served on the staff of former California Sen. John V. Tunney and as a White House aide in the Carter administration, attorney and businesswoman Jane Harman (D-Calif.) had the political connections to raise $598,176 from individual contributors and $199,208 from PACs. Married to the founder of Harman International Industries, a manufacturer of high fidelity audio equipment with assets of more than $350 million, Harman also had the personal wealth to augment her fund-raising efforts whenever necessary. In winning the seven-candidate Democratic primary and her general election contest with Los Angeles City Council member Joan Milke Flores, Harman tapped her personal bank account for a total of $823,000. The ability to write personal checks whenever her campaign required them allowed Harman to invest $630,998 in television and radio advertising. While Flores spent $905,455 and matched Harman dollar-for-dollar on persuasion mail and grass-roots appeals for votes, she had nothing left for broadcast advertising in the pricey Los Angeles market. Harman emerged with a 6-point win.

While only four women succeeded in defeating incumbents in the 1992 House races, those who did spent an average of $406,006—almost twice as much as the average expenditure of $208,508 by the forty-five challengers who lost (Table 5-5). While these winners did not outspend their male counterparts, once Michael Huffington's (R-Calif.) $5,434,569 outlays are removed from the equation, spending by successful female challengers was only 6 percent less than the average spending reported by successful male challengers.

Lambert, the only political operative to vanquish an incumbent, immediately began to reap the benefits of her primary victory over Alexander. Facing a Republican opponent with only $28,372 to spend in an overwhelmingly Democratic district, Lambert was virtually assured of victory in the November general election. Able to spend only about $80,000 in the months leading up to the May 26 primary, she discovered there were suddenly many people anxious to help her after her primary win. Over the final six months of 1992, she raised $310,404, including $159,950 from PACs. Flush with cash, she spent about $246,000 while collecting 70 percent of the vote against her underfunded Republican opponent.

Although Coleman outspent Danner $548,902 to $413,246, $60,017 of his spending advantage was invested in maintaining his off-year campaign operation. By pouring 61 percent of her treasury into broadcast advertising and 18 percent of her funds into other direct appeals for votes, Danner was able to come within $19,475 of Coleman's outlays for communicating with voters. Her ability to tap PACs for $183,992 and individual contributors for $149,538 flowed directly from her service in the state senate and the fact that her chief fund-raiser—her son Steve—was also a state senator.

Unsuccessful challengers were not nearly so well-heeled. While the forty-five losers spent an average of $208,508, eighteen of these women spent less than $25,000, including six challengers who spent less than $5,000. Deborah A. Vollmer (D-Calif.) scraped together $23,279 for her challenge to Republican Rep. Bill Thomas. Thomas countered by spending $610,997, a 23 percent increase over his 1990 outlays, and cruised to victory with 65 percent of the vote. Republican businesswoman Martha A. "Mickey" Strickland spent $20,119 on her challenge to Democratic Rep. Tom Bevill, who invested $514,418 in his reelection bid and emerged with 69 percent of the vote. The $15,152 budget of homemaker Lisa A. Donaldson (D-Mich.) was no match for Republican Rep. Dave Camp's $401,290 response.

In the Senate, the limited number of races and the even smaller number of female candidates make detailed comparisons between winners and losers and between women and men problematic, at best. The dramatic differences in the resources required to run a statewide race in Kansas and California further complicate the comparisons. Nevertheless, led by Boxer's $10,445,695 open seat effort, the four successful women who challenged incumbents or contested open seats spent an average of $6,696,062 (see Table 5-6). Feinstein spent $8,041,099 to defeat Seymour. Moseley-Braun's campaign cost $6,957,821. All three raised millions of dollars more than their male opponents. Of the four winners, only Murray was outspent by her male opponent, but her $1,339,632 budget was still sufficient to get her message out.

Among the six women who lost Senate bids, the average outlay was $1,296,156. However, when you exclude Yeakel's $5,213,198 challenge to Specter, the women whose Senate bids fell short spent an average of only $512,747. While Claire Sargent (D-Ariz.) had a positive message that echoed Moseley-Braun's, Boxer's, Feinstein's, and Murray's on issues such as abortion and health care, she had only $301,362 with which to deliver it. Her opponent, Republican Sen. John McCain, spent $3,740,479.

Lloyd-Jones refused PAC money, which cut her off from

Table 5-4 What Campaign Money Buys in the 1992 House Races: Average Expenditures by Open Seat Candidates

	Female Candidates			Male Candidates		
Major Category	Total	Winner	Loser	Total	Winner	Loser
Overhead						
Office furniture/supplies	$ 7,824	$ 10,334	$ 4,477	$ 5,969	$ 6,707	$ 5,268
Rent/utilities	7,127	10,318	2,874	6,149	6,538	5,780
Salaries	60,772	78,465	37,181	39,025	43,189	35,069
Taxes	6,838	9,856	2,813	6,587	6,559	6,614
Bank/investment fees	410	377	455	543	663	428
Lawyers/accountants	3,375	3,020	3,849	2,141	3,284	1,054
Telephone	8,946	11,595	5,414	7,657	8,575	6,785
Campaign automobile	239	418	0	709	735	684
Computers/office equipment	5,357	6,300	4,101	3,938	3,922	3,953
Travel	8,841	13,138	3,112	8,274	9,160	7,433
Food/meetings	499	735	185	472	597	354
Total Overhead	**110,229**	**144,555**	**64,461**	**81,464**	**89,928**	**73,423**
Fund Raising						
Events	28,139	37,453	15,721	22,576	28,072	17,355
Direct mail	12,251	17,894	4,727	7,925	8,324	7,546
Telemarketing	276	472	14	691	62	1,288
Total Fund Raising	**40,666**	**55,819**	**20,462**	**31,192**	**36,459**	**26,189**
Polling	**17,946**	**23,975**	**9,906**	**12,248**	**14,210**	**10,383**
Advertising						
Electronic media	153,753	206,129	83,919	109,983	134,609	86,588
Other media	7,107	7,240	6,929	11,446	14,203	8,827
Total Advertising	**160,860**	**213,369**	**90,848**	**121,429**	**148,812**	**95,415**
Other Campaign Activity						
Persuasion mail/brochures	106,191	121,525	85,745	84,514	103,985	66,016
Actual campaigning	48,561	60,177	33,072	38,939	46,436	31,817
Staff/Volunteers	460	633	228	617	838	406
Total	**155,211**	**182,336**	**119,045**	**124,070**	**151,259**	**98,240**
Constituent Gifts/Entertainment	**276**	**481**	**2**	**527**	**1,059**	**21**
Donations to						
Candidates from same state	340	592	3	144	231	61
Candidates from other states	14	25	0	46	85	8
Civic organizations	299	486	49	433	661	217
Ideological groups	134	226	11	109	177	45
Political parties	473	794	45	384	382	385
Total Donations	**1,260**	**2,123**	**109**	**1,116**	**1,536**	**716**
Unitemized Expenses	**11,439**	**13,815**	**8,272**	**7,261**	**6,626**	**7,865**
Total Expenditures	**$497,887**	**$636,474**	**$313,104**	**$379,306**	**$449,890**	**$312,251**

labor support, and she raised only $191,758 from individual contributors. With a $175,057 infusion from her own bank account, she managed to spend $409,737 on her challenge to Sen. Charles E. Grassley (R-Iowa). Grassley took $1,077,564 from PACs and raised $1,378,527 from individual contributors, which allowed him to counter Lloyd-Jones's anemic effort with a $2,429,899 campaign that included $641,465 in broadcast advertising.

Their substantial cash advantage over unsuccessful female challengers did not mean that all male incumbents could afford to entirely ignore the gender issue, although some clearly did. While Sargent had few resources, her campaign was built around the hope that she could pry Republican women away from McCain. McCain invested much of his money to make certain that did not happen.

McCain invested $92,065 in polls which showed him that, among other things, his support among pro-choice Republican women was soft. To shore up that support, McCain's media

Table 5-5 What Campaign Money Buys in the 1992 House Races: Average Expenditures by Challengers

Major Category	Female Candidates			Male Candidates		
	Total	Winner	Loser	Total	Winner	Loser
Overhead						
Office furniture/supplies	$ 3,928	$ 3,176	$ 3,994	$ 2,798	$ 7,231	$ 2,354
Rent/utilities	2,515	3,892	2,393	2,964	7,980	2,463
Salaries	21,589	38,599	20,077	16,535	42,392	13,949
Taxes	2,415	0	2,630	2,478	6,895	2,037
Bank/investment fees	135	433	108	217	637	175
Lawyers/accountants	2,632	9,605	2,013	634	2,563	441
Telephone	4,842	9,167	4,457	3,968	9,996	3,365
Campaign automobile	254	0	277	239	1,195	143
Computers/office equipment	2,379	1,644	2,444	2,480	5,438	2,184
Travel	5,090	8,582	4,780	3,516	8,407	3,027
Food/meetings	111	179	105	228	484	203
Total Overhead	**45,891**	**75,277**	**43,279**	**36,058**	**93,217**	**30,342**
Fund Raising						
Events	12,741	25,068	11,645	8,510	33,731	5,987
Direct mail	7,627	505	8,260	4,802	11,724	4,110
Telemarketing	408	429	406	545	1,788	420
Total Fund Raising	**20,775**	**26,002**	**20,311**	**13,857**	**47,244**	**10,518**
Polling	**8,909**	**16,636**	**8,222**	**4,678**	**14,039**	**3,742**
Advertising						
Electronic media	84,702	124,113	81,198	45,640	150,149	35,189
Other media	5,116	6,704	4,975	5,194	11,084	4,605
Total Advertising	**89,817**	**130,816**	**86,173**	**50,834**	**161,233**	**39,794**
Other Campaign Activity						
Persuasion mail/brochures	32,647	91,736	27,394	23,544	64,448	19,454
Actual campaigning	21,851	60,097	18,452	14,673	42,542	11,886
Staff/Volunteers	232	774	183	130	479	95
Total Other Campaign Activity	**54,729**	**152,607**	**46,029**	**38,347**	**107,470**	**31,435**
Constituent Gifts/Entertainment	**112**	**807**	**50**	**93**	**822**	**20**
Donations to						
Candidates from same state	70	525	29	45	43	45
Candidates from other states	5	0	5	7	36	4
Civic organizations	93	145	89	129	354	106
Ideological groups	51	0	56	26	81	21
Political parties	176	319	163	160	409	135
Total Donations	**394**	**989**	**341**	**367**	**924**	**311**
Unitemized Expenses	**4,002**	**2,873**	**4,103**	**3,881**	**7,421**	**3,527**
Total Expenditures	**$224,630**	**$406,006**	**$208,508**	**$148,115**	**$432,371**	**$119,690**

Note: Total for winning male candidates does not include expenditures of $5,434,569 by Michael Huffington, R-Calif.

advisers, Smith & Harroff of Alexandria, Va., developed a series of commercials highlighting McCain's positions on issues relating to the environment, health care, and senior citizens. "The message we tried to get out was that even though McCain is pro-life, he's a good guy, and that there are other issues besides abortion to consider," recalled Wes Gullett, McCain's campaign manager.

Given the nature of Yeakel's early attacks over his treatment of Hill, Specter could not afford to sit back and hope the gender issue would fizzle. Instead, he developed a host of appeals targeted at mending his severely damaged image with women voters. In July he began airing commercials that touted his record of support for increased funding of breast cancer research. Later, he rolled out a sixty-second commercial featuring Teresa Heinz, the widow of the late Republican senator John Heinz, asking voters not to judge Specter by his tough questioning of Hill. Hundreds of copies of a video touting Specter's record on abortion rights and other issues deemed important to

Table 5-6 What Campaign Money Buys in the 1992 Senate Races: Average Expenditures by Nonincumbents

Major Category	Female Candidates			Male Candidates		
	Total	Winner	Loser	Total	Winner	Loser
Overhead						
Office furniture/supplies	57,892	111,527	22,135	29,747	31,298	29,230
Rent/utilities	40,059	80,390	13,172	20,465	20,348	20,504
Salaries	395,924	759,877	153,289	204,099	247,820	189,526
Taxes	80,108	133,243	44,684	49,265	46,829	50,077
Bank/investment fees	5,600	13,519	320	1,383	2,817	905
Lawyers/accountants	24,318	58,465	1,554	11,002	14,768	9,747
Telephone	92,382	170,331	40,415	40,680	43,004	39,906
Campaign automobile	5,255	9,848	2,194	1,555	1,756	1,489
Computers/office equipment	55,086	103,710	22,670	19,916	23,131	18,844
Travel	109,086	212,256	40,306	54,257	63,387	51,214
Food/meetings	1,586	3,692	183	1,762	2,713	1,445
Total Overhead	**867,295**	**1,656,856**	**340,921**	**434,132**	**497,869**	**412,886**
Fund Raising						
Events	274,004	631,497	35,676	106,097	103,909	106,826
Direct mail	561,780	1,245,984	105,645	181,272	123,550	200,513
Telemarketing	70,849	170,508	4,409	13,384	1,816	17,239
Total Fund Raising	**906,633**	**2,047,989**	**145,730**	**300,753**	**229,276**	**324,579**
Polling	**54,588**	**108,686**	**18,523**	**55,413**	**82,448**	**46,401**
Advertising						
Electronic media	1,383,283	2,404,458	702,499	883,773	1,199,003	778,696
Other media	13,003	18,837	9,113	14,653	21,666	12,315
Total Advertising	**1,396,286**	**2,423,296**	**711,613**	**898,426**	**1,220,670**	**791,011**
Other Campaign Activity						
Persuasion mail/brochures	66,990	112,439	36,691	61,668	65,621	60,351
Actual campaigning	134,205	288,447	31,377	125,708	173,063	109,923
Staff/Volunteers	2,235	5,135	301	667	1,102	522
Total Other Campaign Activity	**203,429**	**406,020**	**68,369**	**188,043**	**239,786**	**170,796**
Constituent Gifts/Entertainment	**2,749**	**6,872**	**0**	**686**	**1,408**	**445**
Donations to						
Candidates from same state	82	37	112	226	124	261
Candidates from other states	0	0	0	84	333	1
Civic organizations	337	381	307	339	777	193
Ideological groups	236	381	139	172	108	194
Political parties	275	196	327	760	1,513	509
Total Donations	**930**	**996**	**885**	**1,582**	**2,856**	**1,157**
Unitemized Expenses	**24,208**	**45,347**	**10,115**	**19,138**	**21,834**	**18,240**
Total Expenditures	**3,456,118**	**6,696,062**	**1,296,156**	**1,898,172**	**2,296,146**	**1,765,514**

women were passed out to women who had been organized under the name "Women for Specter," who in turn showed the video to other women at coffees and various in-home gatherings. To drive up Yeakel's negatives, one of Specter's ads slammed her for failing to pay $17,000 in back taxes until the day before she announced her candidacy.

Remarkably, after seizing on Specter's treatment of Hill as the rallying cry for her primary campaign, Yeakel all but abandoned the issue once she had the nomination. Of the nearly two dozen commercials that aired heavily from late September until election day, only one even mentioned Hill, and it ran only over the final week of the campaign.

While Rep. David Price (D-N.C.) was not overly concerned by Republican Lavinia "Vicky" Goudie's $13,188 challenge, he was still careful to run television commercials touting his pro-choice stance on abortion to guard against any drop in his support among women. Price won with 65 percent of the vote.

A number of men who prevailed in open seat contests had to

deal with the gender issue at some point in the process, and in several cases it did not require a well-funded female opponent to sensitize them to the problem. In California, Democrat Bob Filner was concerned as much with Libertarian Barbara Hutchinson as he was with Republican Tony Valencia. Afraid that Hutchinson might run just well enough to give Valencia the victory in the solidly Democratic District 50, Filner devoted one of his two television commercials to attacking what he described as her "strange" beliefs.

Sanford D. Bishop, Jr. (D-Ga.), who ousted Rep. Charles Hatcher in the Democratic primary and faced Republican Jim Dudley in the general election, spent $1,000 for advice on women's issues. "In the 'Year of the Woman,' I wanted to make sure I had all my bases covered," Bishop explained.

Arguing that she was the true agent of change in the Year of the Woman, Binghamton Mayor Juanita M. Crabb (D-N.Y.) was considered the early favorite to win the Democratic nomination in the race to succeed retiring Rep. Matthew F. McHugh. However, state representative Maurice D. Hinchey successfully blunted that argument with television ads listing endorsements from female legislators and a radio spot featuring actress Mary Tyler Moore. Hinchey took 54 percent of the primary votes.

Fund Raising: Women Helping Women

One area in which the Senate Judiciary Committee's treatment of Anita Hill had a powerful impact was fund raising. Throughout 1992, but particularly in the primary campaigns, female candidates depended heavily on the financial support of other women, many of whom had been energized to contribute by what they saw during Thomas's confirmation hearings. EMILY's List, a PAC dedicated to raising money for pro-choice Democratic women, directly donated $365,318 to House and Senate candidates in 1992. More importantly, through its fund-raising direct-mail program, the organization collected approximately $6 million in earmarked contributions from its members, bundled them, and passed them on to fifty-five female candidates. WISH List, a PAC dedicated to assisting pro-choice Republican women, directly contributed $73,109 to 19 candidates, including 6 incumbents. The Women's Campaign Fund donated a total of $390,399 to 71 Democratic candidates, a total of $112,668 to 24 Republicans, and $10,000 to Lynn H. Taborsak in Connecticut, who waged an independent campaign to oust Republican Rep. Gary A. Franks following her Democratic primary loss to James J. Lawlor. The National Organization for Women's PAC donated $322,385 to 102 candidates, virtually all of them women. The National Women's Political Caucus Victory Fund and the National Women's Political Caucus Campaign Support Committee, two connected PACs, donated $136,220 and $69,800, respectively, to a total of 75 women.

Contributions from women's groups and individual donations from women were particularly crucial to Boxer's success in her primary battle with Rep. Mel Levine and Lt. Gov. Leo T. McCarthy. Prior to the primary, Boxer received $197,369 in individual contributions from 1,676 members of EMILY's List. Through the Hollywood Women's Political Committee she attracted donations from actresses Joanne Woodward, Marlo Thomas, Marsha Mason, and Katherine Hepburn, among others. Singer Bonnie Raitt performed at a Beverly Hills event that raised $70,000 for the campaign.

Having never raised more than $500,000 for her House races and beginning with a donor list of roughly 7,000, Boxer poured nearly $1.2 million into a preprimary direct-mail fund-raising effort that churned out more than 1.5 million letters. Capitalizing on the fall-out from Hill's testimony, most of the mail contained a pro-feminist pitch. By the end of the primary campaign, Boxer's extensive direct-mail program had helped her raise well over $4 million, roughly two-thirds of which came from women. Her donor list had grown to more than 54,000.

Yeakel also looked to other women to supply the early seed money for her Senate contest. "When we were first hired by the campaign, I told them they couldn't raise money through direct mail," recalled David H. Gold, president of Gold Communications in Austin, Texas. "Yeakel was at 1 percent in the polls, and I even made a bet that the direct mail wouldn't work. It was a bet I didn't mind losing."

One of the preprimary appeals Gold put together for Yeakel was a four-page mailing that featured a picture of Specter on the envelope. Inside, the message dovetailed with the campaign's television commercial, asking recipients if Specter's treatment of Hill had made them angry and inviting them to send money if the answer was yes. Like Boxer, approximately two-thirds of Yeakel's preprimary money came from women.

In the House, women's groups directly donated a total of $49,006 to Elaine Baxter (D-Iowa), $49,005 to Elizabeth Furse (D-Ore.), $47,151 to Eshoo, $46,155 to Karen Shepherd (D-Utah), $43,073 to Garamendi, $40,132 to Harman, $40,112 to Anita Perez Ferguson (D-Calif.), and $30,000 or more to seven other candidates.

However, while women's groups extended a helping hand to numerous candidates, they could not be expected to support all the women running. There simply was not enough money to allow for that kind of generosity. Thirty-three of the eight-four female challengers and open seat candidates in House races received no direct contributions from any of the women's PACs. While they comprised 20 percent of the female challengers and open seat candidates, Californians received 34 percent of the money donated by women's PACs.

Most of the money went to the experienced politicians, rather than political operatives or novices. Collectively, Boxer, Feinstein, Moseley-Braun, Murray, and Rothman-Serot received $293,672 in direct contributions from PACs representing women's organizations. Yeakel and Sargent, the two novices who received direct contributions from these PACs, collected $52,068 and $12,720, respectively. The only other Senate candidate to receive direct financial assistance, Democratic activist Gloria O'Dell, collected just $6,000 for her token challenge to Sen. Bob Dole (R-Kan.). Lloyd-Jones and Haar received no assistance from women's PACs in their uphill battles against male incumbents.

In the House, twenty-six of the thirty female challengers and open seat candidates who had held elective office received direct contributions totaling $642,585 from PACs representing women's groups. Nine of the sixteen operatives received such help, collecting a total of $208,331. The only Democrat not to receive any assistance was Ada E. Deer (Wis.), who refused all PAC funds. Seventeen of the thirty-eight novices received some money from women's organizations, but these contributions totaled just $176,942.

Much of this financial help was provided prior to the primary. Once candidates had secured their party's nomination, the traditional money sources kicked in immediately for those considered likely to succeed. Following her primary victory, Boxer's contributor profile shifted so dramatically that by election day men accounted for 60 percent of her donations of $200 or more. While Yeakel's experience was not as dramatic, she also saw a substantial shift. "We started out targeting women, but we quickly discovered that many men on our lists were just as enthusiastic as women about supporting a female candidate," noted Yeakel's direct-mail fund-raiser.

WOMEN INCUMBENTS

Among the 110 women seeking House seats in the general election were 26 incumbents. While they were routinely added to the body count to enhance the Year of the Woman hype, female incumbents faced a very different political reality than the women seeking to join them in the House. With the possible exception of the four members of the 1990 freshman class, these women had all of the problems and benefits of incumbency. As a result, their campaigns looked remarkably like those of their male counterparts, both in terms of how much they spent and how they spent it (see Table 5-7).

On average, female incumbents reported spending $564,024 on their campaigns, only 1 percent less than their male counterparts. In hotly contested races, female incumbents reported spending an average of $688,631, or only 4 percent less than the average spending reported by the 139 men facing similarly difficult reelection bids. Average spending by incumbents in less competitive races showed women outspending men by $5,029, a 1 percent advantage.

Overall, the 26 women who sought reelection reported committing 29 percent of their budgets to advertising; the comparable figure for male incumbents was 27 percent. On average, both male and female incumbents invested 20 percent of their budgets in advocacy mailings, leaflets, yard signs, buttons, bumper stickers, phonebanks, rallies, and other grass-roots campaign expenses. Spending on overhead and fund raising was virtually identical, as well. While women tended to invest slightly more than men in constituent stroking, the difference was essentially meaningless (see Table 5-8).

At the operational level, women and men faced the same redistricting problems and the same anti-incumbent sentiments. The solutions were gender neutral, as well.

Vucanovich and Rep. James Bilbray (D-Nev.) had worked out a mutually beneficial redistricting deal that ceded Republicans in Bilbray's district to Vucanovich and moved more Democratic areas from Vucanovich's old district into Bilbray's District 1. Yet despite that deal, Vucanovich drew just 48 percent of the general election votes, escaping with a 5-point victory in a five-candidate field.

Reno Mayor Pete Sferrazza pumped 92 percent of his $198,391 budget into advertising and advocacy mailings that hammered Vucanovich for her acceptance of PAC money, her vote in favor of the congressional pay raise, and her anti-abortion stance. Vucanovich responded by spending $315,455 more on her 1992 campaign than she had in 1990. She increased her outlays for broadcast advertising from $48,052 in 1990 to $216,415 in 1992. Her investment in persuasion mail jumped from $4,389 to $38,368.

Given that her opponent was also a politician with a record, Vucanovich worked hard to tar him with the anti-incumbent stain. When Sferrazza attacked her for supporting the congressional pay raise, Vucanovich struck back with an ad attacking him for supporting a pay raise for Reno government employees during his tenure as mayor. Portraying him as a career politician, Vucanovich slammed Sferrazza for missing numerous mayoral commission meetings and for presiding over a 60 percent increase in city government spending. Leaping on the "change" bandwagon, the five-term incumbent also touted her support for congressional reforms.

Pounded by Monroe County legislator William P. Polito for accepting $1.5 million from PACs during her six years in Congress and accused of being just another tax-and-spend liberal, Rep. Louise M. Slaughter took the opposite approach from Vucanovich. To defend her seat, Slaughter depended on the free media to critique the accuracy of Polito's charges. She invested most of her $305,376 broadcast advertising budget in pro-incumbency television spots, including one testimonial that described how Slaughter had helped restore electricity to a constituent's home following an ice storm.

Had it not been for her $387,004 spending advantage, nine-term Rep. Marilyn Lloyd (D-Tenn.) would probably not have pulled out her 2,930-vote victory over Republican Zach Wamp. Wamp put $78,370 into advertising and $45,138 into advocacy mailings that included calls for voters to "Wamp Congress" and attacks on Lloyd's 1989 vote in favor of the congressional pay raise.

Lloyd opened her reelection bid with positive television commercials showing her visiting with school children and senior citizens, but as the race grew progressively tighter, her advertising campaign grew progressively nastier. One of her commercials dredged up Wamp's "criminal" past, which included writing two bad checks for a total of $20 when he was in college. While her mailers initially pointed to federal projects she had helped bring to the district, they mirrored the negative television spots by campaign's end. In all, she spent $266,123 on broadcast advertising and $50,261 on leaflets and persuasion mailers.

While the task for most female challengers and open seat candidates was to demonstrate leadership and decisiveness, Rep. Jolene Unsoeld had somewhat the opposite problem. Hav-

Table 5-7 What Campaign Money Buys in the 1992 House Races: Average Expenditures by Incumbents

Major Category	Female Candidates			Male Candidates		
	Total	*Winner*	*Loser*	*Total*	*Winner*	*Loser*
Overhead						
Office furniture/supplies	$ 8,540	$ 8,455	$ 9,197	$ 8,798	$ 8,642	$ 11,038
Rent/utilities	10,890	10,739	12,046	9,062	8,787	13,009
Salaries	54,089	54,059	54,314	50,087	48,005	80,026
Taxes	20,045	20,783	14,387	16,115	15,929	18,784
Bank/investment fees	511	381	1,511	1,373	1,413	804
Lawyers/accountants	9,404	9,341	9,887	10,205	9,691	17,597
Telephone	8,010	7,991	8,159	8,605	8,239	13,865
Campaign automobile	575	650	0	3,369	3,083	7,474
Computers/office equipment	8,881	8,333	13,086	9,014	8,875	11,017
Travel	14,694	15,202	10,806	21,851	21,196	31,272
Food/meetings	2,906	3,126	1,215	3,637	3,692	2,835
Total Overhead	**138,545**	**139,059**	**134,608**	**142,114**	**137,552**	**207,721**
Fund Raising						
Events	59,773	59,988	58,120	66,141	64,718	86,607
Direct mail	19,646	21,131	8,261	21,421	21,261	23,722
Telemarketing	99	112	0	1,496	1,573	389
Total Fund Raising	**79,518**	**81,231**	**66,382**	**89,059**	**87,553**	**110,718**
Polling	**20,632**	**19,505**	**29,273**	**19,993**	**18,687**	**38,771**
Advertising						
Electronic media	147,825	127,130	306,481	141,305	130,631	294,810
Other media	18,467	18,753	16,279	14,725	14,691	15,213
Total Advertising	**166,292**	**145,883**	**322,760**	**156,030**	**145,322**	**310,023**
Other Campaign Activity						
Persuasion mail/brochures	76,809	70,687	123,748	69,666	66,131	120,502
Actual campaigning	37,360	35,373	52,591	42,585	41,352	60,325
Staff/Volunteers	670	553	1,567	1,578	1,601	1,255
Total Other Campaign Activity	**114,839**	**106,612**	**177,906**	**113,830**	**109,084**	**182,082**
Constituent Gifts/Entertainment	**10,278**	**10,313**	**10,010**	**8,441**	**8,487**	**7,786**
Donations to						
Candidates from same state	3,372	3,714	750	5,354	5,620	1,522
Candidates from other states	3,314	3,660	667	3,933	4,111	1,364
Civic organizations	3,513	3,730	1,848	3,266	3,236	3,693
Ideological groups	1,613	1,707	895	1,526	1,572	863
Political parties	9,716	10,548	3,342	12,322	12,800	5,459
Total Donations	**21,529**	**23,359**	**7,502**	**26,401**	**27,339**	**12,902**
Unitemized Expenses	**12,392**	**8,587**	**41,564**	**15,790**	**15,571**	**18,947**
Total Expenditures	**$564,024**	**$534,549**	**$790,005**	**$571,658**	**$549,595**	**$888,950**

Note: Totals are for the entire two-year cycle.

ing established a reputation for toughness, the anti-incumbent mood of the electorate prompted her to project a softer image in some of her advertising. One spot developed by Fenn & King Communications of Washington, D.C., consisted largely of home movies of a younger Unsoeld hiking in the mountains and playing with her small children. "We decided we needed to soften her image a bit," explained Peter Fenn.

Freshman Rep. Maxine Waters (D-Calif.) had no difficulties with her initial reelection campaign. In an overwhelmingly Democratic district, facing a Republican opponent who had just $6,919 to spend on his challenge, Waters invested only 26 percent of her $207,957 budget in direct appeals for votes. Virtually all of the $35,682 she spent on advocacy mailings was spent prior to the Democratic primary.

Instead of worrying about her campaign, Waters was free to allocate her funds to other activities. In January 1991 she invited between 100 and 200 supporters to Washington to witness and celebrate her swearing in. While guests paid for their own

Table 5-8 What Campaign Money Buys in the 1992 House Races: Expenditures by Incumbents, by Percentage

Major Category	Female Candidates			Male Candidates		
	Total	Winner	Loser	Total	Winner	Loser
Overhead						
Office furniture/supplies	1.51	1.58	1.16	1.54	1.57	1.24
Rent/utilities	1.93	2.01	1.52	1.59	1.60	1.46
Salaries	9.59	10.11	6.88	8.76	8.73	9.00
Taxes	3.55	3.89	1.82	2.82	2.90	2.11
Bank/investment fees	.09	.07	.19	.24	.26	.09
Lawyers/accountants	1.67	1.75	1.25	1.79	1.76	1.98
Telephone	1.42	1.49	1.03	1.51	1.50	1.56
Campaign automobile	.10	.12	0	.59	.56	.84
Computers/office equipment	1.57	1.56	1.66	1.58	1.61	1.24
Travel	2.61	2.84	1.37	3.82	3.86	3.52
Food/meetings	.52	.58	.15	.64	.67	.32
Total Overhead	**24.56**	**26.01**	**17.04**	**24.86**	**25.03**	**23.37**
Fund Raising						
Events	10.60	11.22	7.36	11.57	11.78	9.74
Direct mail	3.48	3.95	1.05	3.75	3.87	2.67
Telemarketing	.02	.02	0	.26	.29	.04
Total Fund Raising	**14.10**	**15.20**	**8.40**	**15.58**	**15.93**	**12.45**
Polling	**3.66**	**3.65**	**3.71**	**3.50**	**3.40**	**4.36**
Advertising						
Electronic media	26.21	23.78	38.79	24.72	23.77	33.16
Other media	3.27	3.51	2.06	2.58	2.67	1.71
Total Advertising	**29.48**	**27.29**	**40.86**	**27.29**	**26.44**	**34.88**
Other Campaign Activity						
Persuasion mail/brochures	13.62	13.22	15.66	12.19	12.03	13.56
Actual campaigning	6.62	6.62	6.66	7.45	7.52	6.79
Staff/Volunteers	.12	.10	.20	.28	.29	.14
Total Other Campaign Activity	**20.36**	**19.94**	**22.52**	**19.91**	**19.85**	**20.48**
Constituent Gifts/Entertainment	**1.82**	**1.93**	**1.27**	**1.48**	**1.54**	**.88**
Donations to						
Candidates from same state	.60	.69	.09	.94	1.02	.17
Candidates from other states	.59	.68	.08	.69	.75	.15
Civic organizations	.62	.70	.23	.57	.59	.42
Ideological groups	.29	.32	.11	.27	.29	.10
Political parties	1.72	1.97	.42	2.16	2.33	.61
Total Donations	**3.82**	**4.37**	**.95**	**4.62**	**4.97**	**1.45**
Unitemized Expenses	**2.20**	**1.61**	**5.26**	**2.76**	**2.83**	**2.13**
Total Expenditures	**100.00**	**100.00**	**100.00**	**100.00**	**100.00**	**100.00**

Note: Totals are for the entire two-year cycle.

transportation and lodging, Waters tapped her campaign treasury to pay for the party. A reception at the Washington Court Hotel cost the campaign $3,820, and other miscellaneous expenses added $550. Waters also tapped her campaign funds to cover $5,661 in expenses incurred during the annual Black Caucus Weekend in September 1991. The campaign picked up the tab for $4,346 in transportation and lodging expenses connected with her stay in New York during the 1992 Democratic National Convention.

While Donald McDonough, general strategist for state representative Maria Cantwell (D-Wash.), was absolutely correct when he noted that "women candidates symbolized change" in 1992, the politics of victory looked the same, regardless of gender.

CHAPTER 6

Independent and Coordinated Expenditures
A World of Unlimited Possibilities

This is not a contest between two men. This is a battle between me and the special interests I have been opposing.

Rep. Mike Synar (D-Okla.), commenting on his 1992 campaign

During his fourteen-year House career, Rep. Mike Synar (D-Okla.) had succeeded in alienating a number of moneyed interests. As one of the leading advocates of raising fees paid by ranchers who graze their cattle on public lands, Synar had angered ranchers throughout the West. Tobacco companies had taken umbrage at his strong support for a total ban on all advertising and promotion of tobacco products. Health insurance companies had been alienated by his position on mandatory universal coverage. An advocate of a strong national energy policy, Synar had frequently irritated the oil lobby. His support of a seven-day waiting period on handgun purchases and a ban on the sale of combat assault weapons had enraged the National Rifle Association (NRA). In 1992 it was payback time, and in the solidly Democratic District 2, the battleground was the Democratic primary.

Synar's primary opponent was Muskogee District Attorney Drew Edmondson, son of the late Rep. Ed Edmondson, who had represented District 2 from 1953 to 1973, and the nephew of a former governor and senator. Sensing a golden opportunity to rid themselves of a longtime foe, political action committees (PACs) representing tobacco, health insurance, petroleum, and ranching interests pumped more than $150,000 into Edmondson's campaign coffers. The NRA's PAC kicked in $9,900. Edmondson received individual contributions from ranchers totaling more than $100,000. Together these interests donated more than 30 percent of the $836,742 Edmondson spent on his challenge.

However, that sizable boost proved to be just the first installment of anti-Synar money that came pouring into the district. Taking full advantage of a 1976 Supreme Court ruling that affirmed the right of individuals and organizations to spend unlimited sums in support of or in opposition to candidates—as long as there is no communication between the organization and the candidates it supports or opposes—the NRA invested $226,088 in an independent campaign—$141,275 in opposition to Synar and $84,813 in support of Edmondson.

The NRA spent $127,561 on anti-Synar radio and television commercials, attacking him in one television spot for voting "with liberals like Ted Kennedy and Barney Frank over 90 percent of the time." One radio ad, a parody of the game show *Jeopardy,* began with a mock contestant saying, "I'll take 'No Home on the Range' for $400." The game show host then read, "He owns a beautiful home in Washington, D.C., but doesn't even have a trailer in Oklahoma," and asked the contestant for the question that the statement answered. "Who is Mike Synar?" came the instant response.

Full-page newspaper ads costing the NRA a total of $43,479 criticized Synar as "the only congressman from Oklahoma who voted to take away your guns," attacked his votes against constitutional amendments to balance the federal budget and ban flag-burning, and cautioned voters that "if Synar wins, hunters lose." The NRA opened an office in the district and spent $14,007 on travel for the staff who orchestrated the anti-Synar campaign. A series of letters sent to NRA members attacking Synar and endorsing Edmondson cost $13,887. Additional funds were invested in bumper stickers and a phonebanking operation that placed calls to the roughly 10,000 NRA members in the district.

Synar also had supporters willing to invest in independent campaigns on his behalf, although they were token efforts compared with the massive display put on by the NRA. The Small Business Coalition spent $10,364 on Synar's behalf, while independent campaigns launched by Teamsters Local 523, the AFL-CIO, and the National Committee to Preserve Social Security and Medicare cost $5,000, $4,679, and $2,187, respectively.

Coupled with his own spending, the NRA's sizable investment in the race helped carry Edmondson to a second-place finish in the four-candidate primary on August 25 and to within 6,578 of unseating Synar in the September 15 runoff. In effect, the NRA's cash infusion increased Edmondson's budget by 27 percent, allowing him to outspend Synar and his supporters by nearly $220,000 during the first nine months of 1992.

Similarly, in the race for the Senate seat vacated by Pete Wilson (R-Calif.), who successfully ran for governor, records filed with the Federal Election Commission (FEC) show that former San Francisco mayor Dianne Feinstein (D-Calif.) outspent Republican Senate appointee John Seymour by $1,166,863—$8,041,099 to $6,874,236. Feinstein's campaign reported spending $3,277,559 on television and radio advertising, or $1,371,408 more than Seymour spent on his commercials. Those numbers do not begin to tell the story of their confrontation.

The National Republican Senatorial Committee (NRSC) paid $2,449,955 to Target Enterprises of Hollywood, Calif., the firm responsible for placing Seymour's commercials, to buy additional air time. The California Association of Realtors and the National Association of Realtors (NAR) spent a total of $267,050 on Seymour's behalf, primarily for advocacy mailings, newspaper advertising inserts, and phonebanks. The conservative English Language PAC invested $49,718, and ten other organizations spent a total of $12,362 on independent campaigns, either in support of Seymour or in opposition to Feinstein. Together, the party coordinated expenditures and the independent campaigns that benefited Seymour amounted to $2,779,085, effectively increasing his budget by 40 percent.

Feinstein had her share of outside support, as well. The Democratic Senatorial Campaign Committee (DSCC) dedicated $1,313,826 of its coordinated campaign to Feinstein, including eight payments totaling $1,235,000 to her media adviser, Morris & Carrick of New York. The DSCC's coordinated expenditures also included $30,000 for postage, $29,000 for a pro-choice voter guide, and $12,500 for demographic research. The balance of its outlays went for opposition research, travel, fund raising, and subscriptions to political journals. The Democratic State Central Committee of California spent $175,976 in support of Feinstein's candidacy, including three payments totaling $50,000 to Morris & Carrick; three payments totaling $74,501 to Gold Communications Co. of Austin, Texas, for persuasion mailers; and two payments amounting to $30,453 for postage. The Democratic National Committee (DNC) picked up $15,920 of her polling costs with Greenberg-Lake of Washington, D.C. Feinstein also had the benefit of $44,767 in independent support from a dozen organizations, including the AFL-CIO and the National Abortion Rights Action League (NARAL). In all, the party coordinated expenditures and the independent campaigns on Feinstein's behalf totaled $1,550,489, essentially increasing her budget by 19 percent.

When all the party money and independent expenditures were added to their own campaign expenditures, Seymour and his supporters had narrowly outspent Feinstein and her supporters $9,653,321 to $9,591,588. What looked like a contest in which the two protagonists spent a total of $14,915,335 was actually a $19,244,909 battle. Feinstein won that fight 54 percent to 38 percent on election day.

In the race to succeed retiring Sen. Tim Wirth (D-Colo.), records filed with the FEC show former Republican state senator Terry Considine outspending Democratic Rep. Ben Nighthorse Campbell by nearly $500,000. To make matters worse, while Considine skated through the Republican primary without opposition, Campbell was forced to spend more than $400,000 to prevail in a three-candidate Democratic primary that included former governor Richard D. Lamm and the party's 1990 Senate nominee, Josie Heath. In the general election, Considine outspent Campbell by $274,836 on broadcast advertising and by $129,657 on persuasion mail.

As in virtually every closely contested Senate race, the party coordinated expenditures for Campbell and Considine were nearly identical. Together, the DSCC and the DNC paid out $245,156 in support of Campbell, including $82,400 to Joe Slade White & Co. of New York for creating broadcast ads; $89,990 to Shafto & Barton of Houston, Texas, for placing the ads; and $59,314 to Mellman & Lazarus of Washington, D.C., for polling. The NRSC countered with $275,427 in expenditures for Considine, $275,082 of which went to his media adviser, Barnhart Advertising of Denver.

However, Considine's vocal opposition to abortion rights drew the attention of NARAL, which targeted him for defeat. In the final month of the campaign, NARAL invested $149,986 to elect Campbell, including payments totaling $65,420 to Greer, Margolis, Mitchell & Associates of Washington, D.C., for television buys during the final week and a $40,825 payment to Great Lakes Communication of Milwaukee, Wis., for phonebanking. Campbell emerged with a 9-point victory in the general election.

Although most of the 435 House races and 37 Senate races did not involve the level of outside financial assistance channeled into the Synar-Edmondson, Feinstein-Seymour, and Campbell-Considine races, dozens of contests were similarly targeted. Coordinated campaign expenditures by national Democratic and Republican committees totaled $39,092,810—$16,484,017 by the NRSC; $11,283,934 by the DSCC; $5,181,932 by the National Republican Congressional Committee (NRCC); $4,179,032 by the Democratic Congressional Campaign Committee (DCCC); $1,139,809 by the DNC; and $824,086 by the Republican National Committee (RNC). Independent campaigns added another $10,000,025.

PARTY COORDINATED EXPENDITURES

The level of national party coordinated expenditures is established by federal election law, and in 1992 such expenditures were limited to $27,620 for each House race, except in the six states with only one congressional district, where the limit was doubled to $55,240. The national party committee limits for Senate races are based on state voting age population and ranged in 1992 from a low of $55,240 to a maximum of $1,227,322. State parties were allowed to contribute an equal amount or transfer their spending quotas to the national party committees, effectively doubling the national committee's spending limits.

Sixty-eight Senate candidates received some support from their national party committee. In thirty-nine cases, the state parties transferred their entire spending limit to the national parties, which in turn provided essentially the maximum possible support to the candidate. Among the candidates in this group were former television commentator Bruce Herschensohn (R-Calif.), $2,454,644; Seymour, $2,449,955; Sen. Alfonse M. D'Amato (R-N.Y.), $1,512,543; Robert Abrams (D-N.Y.), $1,508,835; and Sen. Arlen Specter (R-Pa.), $1,008,903.

In eleven additional cases, the national party committees spent their maximum allotment and picked up at least a portion of the state parties' spending limit, as well. National Democratic party committees spent their allotted $1,227,322 on behalf of Rep. Barbara Boxer (D-Calif.), who successfully battled Herschensohn for the vacant seat created by the retirement of Democratic Sen. Alan Cranston, and picked up $403,680 of the California Democratic party's limit. The state party spent only $132,914 of its remaining $823,642 allotment. The DSCC and the DNC combined to spend $1,329,746 on behalf of Feinstein, including $102,424 of the state party's allotment. As with Boxer, the California Democrats did not come close to spending the balance of its $1.2 million spending limit for Feinstein. Other Senate candidates receiving more than the national party maximum but less than the combined national and state allotment were Lynn Yeakel (D-Pa.), $842,275; Sen. John Glenn (D-Ohio), $622,896; Cook County Recorder of Deeds Carol Moseley-Braun (D-Ill.), $478,329; Sen. Christopher S. Bond (R-Mo.), $379,904; and state senator Patty Murray (D-Wash.), $379,614.

None of the five women who won Senate seats received the maximum combined national-state party limit. FEC records show that Yeakel received $164,780 less than the maximum, despite being involved in one of the more high-profile Senate races in the country.

In two cases—Sens. Kent Conrad (D-N.D.) and Tom Daschle (D-S.D.)—the national party committees spent their limit but picked up none of the state party's allotment. In fifteen cases the national party committees did not bother to spend the maximum, since it was clear the races were essentially uncontested. For example, the DSCC spent only $42,643 of the $100,647 it was allowed to spend in support of Gloria O'Dell (Kan.), who challenged Sen. Bob Dole. The DSCC invested only $35,756 of the $114,292 it was allowed to spend in support of Claire Sargent's challenge to Sen. John McCain (R-Ariz.). Democratic Sens. Bob Graham (Fla.) and Dale Bumpers (Ark.) did not need the DSCC's money, taking only $656 and $156, respectively.

One Senate race where party money clearly made a difference was in Georgia. Democratic Sen. Wyche Fowler, Jr., received a 49 percent plurality of the 2,251,576 votes cast in the November 3 general election. However, Georgia's state election law requires a candidate to garner a 50 percent or greater majority in the election or face a runoff. Having fallen just short, Fowler was forced into a runoff with Republican Paul Coverdell, who had collected 48 percent.

Immediately following the general election, the NRSC requested that the FEC issue an advisory opinion on whether the runoff should constitute a new election, thus providing the state and national parties with an opportunity to spend another $535,607 on each candidate's behalf. On its face, the request was clearly contrary to a 1983 FEC ruling that declared that a runoff was a continuation of the general election, not a new election. The decision was of particular interest to the Republicans, since they had exhausted their limit in the general election. The Democrats had stopped $200,000 short of the limit, anticipating that a runoff would occur.

When the FEC failed to rule on its request, the NRSC decided to spend nearly $450,000 during the three weeks leading up to the runoff. The Democrats spent only the remaining $200,000 of their general election limit, assuming that they could not spend more. In an election that drew only 1,253,991 voters to the polls—997,585 fewer than had voted in the general election—Coverdell won by 16,237 votes. The DSCC filed a complaint with the FEC asking that the NRSC be fined for its actions, since the FEC has no power to overturn election results.

In March 1993, after Coverdell had been sworn in, the FEC ruled in a similar case that a runoff to fill the Senate seat vacated by Lloyd Bentsen (D-Texas) constituted a continuation of the special election. In this case, the NRSC supported applying a single spending limit to the party committees. Nevertheless, one month later the FEC split 3-3 along party lines, and the DSCC's complaint against the NRSC for overspending on behalf of Coverdell was dropped.

In the House, 589 of the 859 candidates who contested the November general elections benefited from at least some coordinated expenditures by their party's national committees. At the low end, the NRCC spent $32 in support of John M. Shimkus, who challenged Democratic Rep. Richard J. Durbin in Illinois' District 20. At the high end, 159 House candidates received the maximum $27,620 in national party coordinated assistance. While the state party committees shifted their full coordinated limit to the federal party committees in only 17 cases, thereby providing those candidates with the $55,240 combined maximum, the national parties spent at least $40,000 on behalf of 102 candidates.

National party committees were not nearly as careful to balance spending in contested House races, since even the maximum allotment placed severe limits on their ability to have an impact on races where the average incumbent spent $571,089 and the average open seat candidate invested $406,611. For example, open seat candidate Judy Jarvis (R-Calif.) received the full $55,240 national-state allotment from the NRCC; her Democratic counterpart, Lynn Schenk, received only $7,265 in coordinated support from the DCCC. However, since Schenk's campaign was able to outspend Jarvis by $745,514, the difference in the level of coordinated party support provided Jarvis with only a marginal boost, at best. Schenk received 51 percent of the vote to Jarvis's 43 percent in the marginally Republican District 49.

In Georgia's District 1, the DCCC spent $54,239 in support of school principal Barbara Christmas, including $40,925 for "media services," $7,500 for polling, and $5,000 for opposition research. The NRCC spent $25,000 to augment state representative Jack Kingston's advertising buys. With Kingston spending $273,922 on advertising and Christmas investing only $164,014 in her ads, the $15,925 net gain in advertising supplied by the DCCC was undoubtedly small consolation to Christmas. Including the party money, Kingston still outspent Christmas on advertising by $93,983. He collected 58 percent of the votes.

The coordinated expenditures did yield more advertising. The NRSC invested 91 percent of its $16,484,017 in broadcast advertising; the DSCC spent 85 percent of its $11,283,934 on such ads (see Tables 6-1 and 6-2). Given the nature of House races, less of the DCCC's and NRCC's coordinated assistance was invested in broadcast ads—77 percent and 32 percent, respectively—and more was spent on persuasion mail, particularly on the Republican side (see Tables 6-3 and 6-4).

In several instances, Republican candidates relied on the NRCC to provide their entire advocacy mailing effort. In Maine, Rep. Olympia J. Snowe did not invest any of her campaign's resources in mailers; instead, the NRCC's in-house team designed her mail and spent $44,360 on printing and postage. In other cases, the party's assistance amounted to matching funds. Republican Douglas Carl (Mich.), who unsuccessfully challenged Rep. David E. Bonior, spent $36,119 on his own persuasion mail effort; the NRCC kicked in $45,667 for printing, postage, and mailing lists. However, the boost Carl received from the NRCC was no match for Bonior's $556,380 spending advantage on television and radio advertising.

While the DCCC's and NRCC's coordinated spending frequently failed to have much impact on the final outcome of the campaign, in some cases the assistance clearly helped tighten the race. Bill Townsend (R-Pa.), who challenged Democratic Rep. Austin J. Murphy, was outspent by more than six to one. Townsend spent just $4,692 of his $50,280 budget on persuasion mail. Townsend came within 3,307 votes of pulling off the upset, in large part because the NRCC spent $39,391 on his mailers.

In the case of the DNC, its coordinated assistance in House races appeared to be little more than poorly disguised expenditures on behalf of presidential nominee Bill Clinton. FEC records show that the DNC invested $908,866 in House campaigns across the country, all of which was spent on polls (see Table 6-3). In contrast, the DCCC spent $404,596 on polls, roughly 10 percent of its budget. The RNC spent just $11,940, or 1 percent of its $824,086 investment in House campaigns, on polls. While polling is an important part of any campaign, many of the DNC's polls were conducted in districts where the outcome of the House race was never in doubt but where the attitudes of voters concerning the presidential race was of great interest.

In California, a state considered a must win if Democratic presidential nominee Bill Clinton was to be elected, the DNC paid Greenberg-Lake of Washington, D.C., $73,878 to conduct polls in fourteen House districts represented by Democrats: fifteen-term Rep. Don Edwards; eleven-term Rep. Ronald V. Dellums; ten-term Rep. Pete Stark; nine-term Rep. George Miller; nine-term Rep. Henry A. Waxman; eight-term Rep. Leon E. Panetta; seven-term Rep. Julian C. Dixon; seven-term Rep. Robert T. Matsui; six-term Rep. Tom Lantos; five-term Rep. Howard L. Berman; five-term Rep. Esteban E. Torres; two-term Rep. Nancy Pelosi; Rep. Gary A. Condit, a 1989 special election winner; and freshman Rep. Maxine Waters. None of these incumbents had a difficult race. All won with 60 percent of the vote or more. Four won with 83 percent of the vote or better, and three others received between 70 and 80 percent. Only three of the candidates spent any of their own resources on polls of their constituents, and the $5,277 the DNC spent in each district could not have produced results that would have been of more than marginal interest to any of the incumbents. However, collectively these results would have been of considerable interest to the Clinton camp. Perhaps not coincidentally, Greenberg-Lake was also Clinton's pollster.

In Ohio, another key battleground in the presidential contest, the DNC paid $12,026 each for polls in districts represented by Democrats Marcy Kaptur, Louis Stokes, James A. Traficant, Jr., and Douglas Applegate. None of the four candidates was ever in danger: Kaptur garnered 74 percent of the general election vote, Stokes grabbed 69 percent, Traficant collected a whopping 84 percent, and Applegate received 68 percent. Greenberg-Lake split the polling duties with Mellman & Lazarus of Washington, D.C., in each of the four districts. Clinton's advisers thought the state sufficiently crucial to the election that the Clintons and Gores visited the state forty-five times during the fall campaign.

The DNC spent $16,039 on polls in each of four Michigan districts, only one of which produced a race in which the Democratic incumbent failed to get at least 65 percent of the vote. In Pennsylvania, yet another key state in the Clinton strategy to reach 270 electoral votes, Greenberg-Lake conducted polls in six districts for $7,393 each. Among the five incumbents who "benefited" from this effort, none received less than 65 percent of the vote. The DNC thought challenger Bill Sturges's $59,027 challenge to Republican Rep. George Gekas warranted sending in Greenberg-Lake, despite the fact that Gekas ultimately collected 70 percent of the vote.

In all, Greenberg-Lake received $410,872 from the DNC for its work on House campaigns. That represented 45 percent of the DNC's investment in polling for House races.

Without question, the best example of how much more the DNC's polls meant to the presidential campaign than to the House members who received them was the case of Rep. William H. Natcher (D-Ky.). Elected in a 1953 special election, Natcher had run unopposed in seven of his twenty House campaigns. In those twenty campaigns, he had received less than 60 percent of the vote only three times. Throughout his entire House career, he had never accepted a campaign contribution. He funded his campaigns, which rarely exceeded $7,000, from his own pocket. His 1992 opponent was a college student, who Natcher completely ignored. Nevertheless, the DNC paid Lauer, Lalley & Associates of Washington, D.C., $17,633 for a poll of Natcher's constituents, who again showed their strong support by giving him 61 percent of the vote.

In contrast, when the DCCC felt polling assistance was called for, it generally paid the candidate's own pollster rather

Table 6-1 What Campaign Money Buys in the 1992 Senate Races: Coordinated Expenditures by National Parties

	From the Democratic party			From the Republican party		
Major Category	Total	DSCC	DNC	Total	NRSC	RNC
Overhead						
Office furniture/supplies	$ 15,000	$ 15,000	$ 0	$ 679	$ 679	$ 0
Rent/utilities	11,475	11,475	0	0	0	0
Salaries	35,538	35,538	0	0	0	0
Lawyers/accountants	21,247	21,247	0	0	0	0
Campaign automobile	0	0	0	25,963	25,963	0
Computers/office equipment	5,350	5,350	0	0	0	0
Travel	25,008	25,008	0	23,910	23,910	0
Total Overhead	**113,618**	**113,618**	**0**	**50,552**	**50,552**	**0**
Fund Raising						
Events	45,547	45,547	0	393	393	0
Direct mail	45,136	45,136	0	0	0	0
Total Fund Raising	**90,682**	**90,682**	**0**	**393**	**393**	**0**
Polling	**730,426**	**611,075**	**119,351**	**54,225**	**54,225**	**0**
Advertising						
Electronic media	9,684,431	9,608,431	76,000	14,960,225	14,960,225	0
Other media	2,249	2,249	0	28,722	28,722	0
Total Advertising	**9,686,680**	**9,610,680**	**76,000**	**14,988,947**	**14,988,947**	**0**
Other Campaign Activity						
Persuasion mail/brochures	389,690	389,690	0	1,109,714	1,109,714	0
Actual campaigning	503,781	468,190	35,592	280,187	280,187	0
Total Other Campaign Activity	**893,471**	**857,879**	**35,592**	**1,389,900**	**1,389,900**	**0**
Total Expenditures	**$11,514,876**	**$11,283,934**	**$230,943**	**$16,484,017**	**$16,484,017**	**$ 0**

Table 6-2 What Campaign Money Buys in the 1992 Senate Races: Coordinated Expenditures of National Parties, by Percentage

	From the Democratic party			From the Republican party		
Major Category	Total	DSCC	DNC	Total	NRSC	RNC
Overhead						
Office furniture/supplies	.13	.13	0	0	0	0
Rent/utilities	.10	.10	0	0	0	0
Salaries	.31	.31	0	0	0	0
Lawyers/accountants	.18	.19	0	0	0	0
Campaign automobile	0	0	0	.16	.16	0
Computers/office equipment	.05	.05	0	0	0	0
Travel	.22	.22	0	.15	.15	0
Total Overhead	**.99**	**1.01**	**0**	**.31**	**.31**	**0**
Fund Raising						
Events	.40	.40	0	0	0	0
Direct mail	.39	.40	0	0	0	0
Total Fund Raising	**.79**	**.80**	**0**	**0**	**0**	**0**
Polling	**6.34**	**5.42**	**51.68**	**.33**	**.33**	**0**
Advertising						
Electronic media	84.10	85.15	32.91	90.76	90.76	0
Other media	.02	.02	0	.17	.17	0
Total Advertising	**84.12**	**85.17**	**32.91**	**90.93**	**90.93**	**0**
Other Campaign Activity						
Persuasion mail/brochures	3.38	3.45	0	6.73	6.73	0
Actual campaigning	4.38	4.15	15.41	1.70	1.70	0
Total Other Campaign Activity	**7.76**	**7.60**	**15.41**	**8.43**	**8.43**	**0**
Total Expenditures	**100.00**	**100.00**	**100.00**	**100.00**	**100.00**	**0**

Table 6-3 What Campaign Money Buys in the 1992 House Races: Coordinated Expenditures by Party National Parties

	From the Democratic party			From the Republican party		
Major Category	Total	DSCC	DNC	Total	NRSC	RNC
Overhead						
Office furniture/supplies	$ 500	$ 500	$ 0	$ 0	$ 0	$ 0
Salaries	106,356	106,356	0	0	0	0
Lawyers/accountants	5,506	5,506	0	0	0	0
Travel	27,566	27,566	0	0	0	0
Food/meetings	0	0	0	5,540	5,540	0
Total Overhead	**139,928**	**139,928**	**0**	**5,540**	**5,540**	**0**
Fund Raising						
Events	3,472	3,472	0	2,700	2,700	0
Telemarketing	1,326	1,326	0	0	0	0
Total Fund Raising	**4,799**	**4,799**	**0**	**2,700**	**2,700**	**0**
Polling	**1,313,462**	**404,596**	**908,866**	**376,606**	**364,666**	**11,940**
Advertising						
Electronic media	3,201,151	3,201,151	0	2,281,348	1,667,912	613,436
Other media	0	0	0	16,797	16,797	0
Total Advertising	**3,201,151**	**3,201,151**	**0**	**2,298,145**	**1,684,709**	**613,436**
Other Campaign Activity						
Persuasion mail/brochures	275,069	275,069	0	3,202,417	3,066,764	135,654
Actual campaigning	153,489	153,489	0	120,610	57,554	63,056
Total Other Campaign Activity	**428,559**	**428,559**	**0**	**3,323,027**	**3,124,318**	**198,709**
Total Expenditures	**$5,087,898**	**$4,179,032**	**$908,866**	**$6,006,018**	**$5,181,932**	**$824,086**

Table 6-4 What Campaign Money Buys in the 1992 House Races: Coordinated Expenditures of National Parties, by Percentage

	From the Democratic party			From the Republican party		
Major Category	Total	DSCC	DNC	Total	NRSC	RNC
Overhead						
Office furniture/supplies	.01	.01	0	0	0	0
Salaries	2.09	2.54	0	0	0	0
Lawyers/accountants	.11	.13	0	0	0	0
Travel	.54	.66	0	0	0	0
Food/meetings	0	0	0	.09	.11	0
Total Overhead	**2.75**	**3.35**	**0**	**.09**	**.11**	**0**
Fund Raising						
Events	.07	.08	0	.04	.05	0
Telemarketing	.03	.03	0	0	0	0
Total Fund Raising	**.09**	**.11**	**0**	**.04**	**.05**	**0**
Polling	**25.82**	**9.68**	**100.00**	**6.27**	**7.04**	**1.45**
Advertising						
Electronic media	62.92	76.60	0	37.98	32.19	74.44
Other media	0	0	0	.28	.32	0
Total Advertising	**62.92**	**76.60**	**0**	**38.26**	**32.51**	**74.44**
Other Campaign Activity						
Persuasion mail/brochures	5.41	6.58	0	53.32	59.18	16.46
Actual campaigning	3.02	3.67	0	2.01	1.11	7.65
Total Other Campaign Activity	**8.42**	**10.25**	**0**	**55.33**	**60.29**	**24.11**
Total Expenditures	**100.00**	**100.00**	**100.00**	**100.00**	**100.00**	**100.00**

Table 6-5 The Top Fifteen Independent Expenditures in 1992 Congressional Elections, by Organization

Rank	Organization	For	Against	Total
1	National Rifle Association	$2,529,241	$492,474	$3,021,715
2	National Association of Realtors	1,536,067	0	1,536,067
3	American Medical Association	1,024,210	0	1,024,210
4	National Right to Life Committee	797,896	10,415	808,311
5	AFL-CIO	741,579	1,636	743,215
6	National Abortion Rights Action League	477,055	242,506	719,561
7	Clean Up Congress	155,807	13,626	169,433
8	California Teachers Association	153,114	0	153,114
9	Public Citizen	0	150,193	150,193
10	California Association of Realtors	143,992	0	143,992
11	Auto Dealers & Drivers for Free Trade	125,539	0	125,539
12	Handgun Control	123,373	700	124,073
13	Pennsylvania AFL-CIO	123,259	0	123,259
14	Minnesota Concerned Citizens for Life	92,129	15,135	107,264
15	National Council of Senior Citizens	83,869	11,408	95,277

Note: Figures include "independent expenditures" and "communication costs," as reported by the organizations to the Federal Election Commission.

than sending in one of its own. Challenger Paul McHale (D-Pa.), who knocked off Republican Rep. Don Ritter, received $8,750 in coordinated polling assistance from the DCCC. The payment went to McHale's pollster, Cooper & Secrest Associates of Alexandria, Va.

INDEPENDENT EXPENDITURES

While the money involved was substantially less than the aggregate invested by the various national Republican and Democratic party committees, independent expenditures topped $10 million in the 1992 election cycle. This money was concentrated in a relatively small number of races where those interested in influencing the outcome felt they had the best chance of success. The NRA invested $3,021,715 in independent campaigns (see Table 6-5), but spent $1,272,884 of that total in just ten races. The National Association of Realtors, which ranked a distant second among organizations putting money into independent campaigns, dedicated $852,926 of its $1,536,067 investment to five races. While the American Medical Association (AMA) spent $1,024,210 on its independent efforts, $868,042 of that total, or 85 percent, was spent in support of five candidates.

In addition to its efforts to defeat Synar, the NRA pumped $172,011 into an independent campaign in support of Specter (see Table 6-6), most of which was invested in mailings. Prior to the Republican primary, the NRA spent $81,219 to send letters to its members urging them to vote for Specter. In the fall campaign against Yeakel, the NRA spent another $84,558 on mailings to its members.

In a newly drawn District 29, which was designed to maximize the chances of electing a new Hispanic member from Texas, Gene Green, who is white, emerged with the Democratic nomination after three rounds of bitter campaigning against Houston City Council member Ben Reyes. Green succeeded by sinking $124,441 into commercials and $298,572 into preprimary mailings reminding voters that Reyes had declared personal bankruptcy, had been delinquent in paying his property taxes, had been arrested for driving under the influence of alcohol, and had been placed on probation after pleading no contest to misdemeanor charges of theft and violating campaign finance laws.

The NRA spent $157,926 on an independent campaign on Green's behalf, including $41,411 for radio commercials and $11,647 for a phonebanking operation. While there was supposedly no coordination between Green's campaign and the NRA effort, letters mailed to voters by the NRA echoed Green's messages. One letter called attention to a district attorney's investigation into alleged ties between Reyes and a local drug ring. After dispatching Reyes, Green easily won the November election.

Herschensohn benefited from a $130,316 NRA campaign, all of which was spent on mailings to its California members.

Arkansas Secretary of State W. J. "Bill" McCuen ousted Rep. Beryl Anthony, Jr., in a June 9 primary runoff that McCuen's media adviser, Jim Duffy of Washington, D.C.-based Strother-Duffy-Strother, described as a "media war." Yet, while Duffy produced four television spots, including ads attacking Anthony's vote for a congressional pay raise and his 109 overdrafts at the House bank, this effort to defeat Anthony was significantly enhanced when the NRA dedicated $128,239 of its resources to oust the seven-term incumbent. Radio and newspaper ads condemning Anthony for supporting the Brady Bill cost the NRA $116,549.

The NRA sponsored a radio spot similar to the *Jeopardy* game show parody used to attack Synar, in which the mock contestant began, "I'll take 'Two-Faced Politicians' for $1,000."

Table 6-6 The Top Ten Independent Campaigns Waged by the National Rifle Association

Race	Expenditures	For or against	Total
1. Oklahoma District 2			$226,088
Mike Synar (D)	$141,275	against	
Drew Edmondson (D)	84,813	for	
2. Pennsylvania Senate			172,011
Arlen Specter (R)	172,011	for	
3. Texas District 29			157,926
Gene Green (D)	156,698	for	
Ben Reyes (D)	1,228	against	
4. California Senate			130,316
Bruce Herschensohn (R)	130,316	for	
5. Arkansas District 4			128,239
Beryl Anthony, Jr. (D)	86,412	against	
W. J. "Bill" McCuen (D)	41,827	for	
6. Pennsylvania Senate			101,938
Harris Wofford (D)	71,115	against	
Dick Thornburgh (R)	30,823	for	
7. Wisconsin Senate			99,942
Bob Kasten (R)	99,942	for	
8. Missouri District 6			94,502
Tom Coleman (R)	61,209	against	
Patsy Danner (D)	33,293	for	
9. Georgia Senate			87,081
Paul Coverdell (R)	87,081	for	
10. North Carolina Senate			74,241
Lauch Faircloth (R)	74,241	for	

Note: Figures include "independent expenditures" and "communication costs" as reported by the National Rifle Association to the Federal Election Commission.

Following the *Jeopardy* format, the game show host then provided the answer to a question: "He tells folks in Arkansas that he's a hunter, but voted for a nationwide ban on dozens of commonly used hunting rifles." "Uh, who is Beryl Anthony?" shot back the contestant.

The single most expensive independent campaign of the 1992 elections was the $329,289 effort mounted by the NAR in support of Rep. Les AuCoin (D-Ore.), who fell short in his challenge to Republican Sen. Bob Packwood (see Table 6-7). Terris & Jaye of San Francisco, Calif., received $200,000 for producing advocacy mailers. Fenn & King Communications of Washington, D.C., collected $87,745 for creating and placing broadcast ads. Target Inc. of Washington, D.C., received $38,584 for polling. National Telecommunications Services of Washington, D.C., collected $2,960 for phonebanking.

In another losing battle, the NAR spent $169,950 in support of Republican Rep. Rod Chandler, who lost an open Senate seat contest to state senator Patty Murray in Washington. John Maddox & Associates of Alexandria, Va., collected $150,000 for creating and placing television commercials. American Viewpoint, also of Alexandria, received the remaining $19,950 for polling.

The only winner among the top five candidates targeted by the NAR was Rep. E. Clay Shaw, Jr. (R-Fla.), who won a seventh term by defeating Democratic state senator Gwen Margolis in what proved to be Shaw's costliest race ever. Shaw spent $1,136,419 to Margolis's $932,420. The NAR weighed in with a $125,208 effort on behalf of Shaw, including a $97,508 payment to Public Opinion Strategies of Alexandria, Va., for advocacy mailers, $17,700 to the same firm for polling, and $10,000 to John Maddox for additional polls.

In preparation for what it assumed would be a contentious fight over health care reform, the AMA weighed in heavily in an attempt to affect the outcome of several races. The organization spent $255,085 in support of Rep. Vic Fazio (D-Calif.): $195,885 for television commercials produced and placed by Fenn & King; $43,000 for radio spots, also produced and placed by Fenn & King; and $16,200 for polling with Mellman & Lazarus.

The AMA spent $227,809 in support of Packwood, including $121,404 paid to National Media of Alexandria, Va., for producing and placing broadcast ads. James R. Foster & Associates of Carrollton, Texas, received $92,405 from the AMA to produce pro-Packwood mailings. To refine the messages delivered by those ads and mailings, the AMA paid Tarrance & Associates of Alexandria, Va., $14,000 for polling.

The AMA spent $184,910 to help put state representative Scott McInnis (R-Colo.) over the top in his open seat contest with Lt. Gov. Mike Callihan, $102,800 of which was poured into a television campaign designed by Sandler-Innocenzi of Washington, D.C. The AMA also paid John Maddox $43,690 for persuasion mail and $22,920 for phonebanking, while Public Opinion Strategies collected $15,500 for polling. The AMA's sizable investment equaled 43 percent of what McInnis spent on his own campaign.

Rep. Michael A. Andrews (D-Texas) also received a considerable push from the AMA, which spent $15,600 on polls conducted by Mellman & Lazarus and paid Fenn & King $103,385 to produce and place radio commercials on his behalf. The ads never mentioned health care, but instead trumpeted Andrews's support for a middle-class income tax cut, his support for troop reductions in Europe, and his record as a crime fighter.

Rounding out their top five targeted races, the AMA backed freshman Rep. Gary A. Franks (R-Conn.) in his contest with Democrat James J. Lawlor and state representative Lynn H. Taborsak, who ran as an independent following her loss in the Democratic primary. The AMA spent $81,256 on Franks's behalf, including payments of $10,500 to American Viewpoint for polling, $39,009 for radio spots, and $31,747 for targeted mailings.

The National Right to Life Committee focused considerable effort on the presidential campaign, spending $801,573 on an independent campaign in support of George Bush. While it spent some money in 208 House and Senate races, the organization spent no more than $27,644 in support of any one candidate.

The AFL-CIO was the fifth most active organization among those waging independent campaigns, although for the most part its efforts were on par with those of the National Right to Life Committee. Primarily, these campaigns consisted of phonebanking and mailings directed to its members. The one notable exception was the special election contest between appointed Sen. Harris Wofford (D-Pa.) and former U.S. attorney general and Pennsylvania governor Dick Thornburgh. The union spent $155,583 in support of Wofford, most of which went for advocacy mailings to its members.

Seventy-nine percent of the money invested by NARAL in its independent campaigns was funneled into five races, including $148,426 to support Democratic state senator Russell D. Feingold in his successful bid to topple Wisconsin Sen. Bob Kasten. NARAL spent $85,000 on radio and television commercials and $43,000 on phonebanking to back Feingold.

As these examples suggest, many races that fostered one major independent campaign also drew other organizations into the fray. The NAR's $329,289 campaign on behalf of AuCoin was largely offset by the $227,809 effort by the AMA on behalf of Packwood. The American Auto Dealers and Drivers and the NRA also threw their support behind Packwood, with independent campaigns totaling $65,539 and $43,106, respectively. The Feingold-Kasten race spawned fifteen independent campaigns.

Although federal law requires those waging independent efforts to report their spending to the FEC, the law would appear to have several gaping loopholes.

Rep. Dan Glickman (D-Kan.) had to fight off four independent efforts against him, including a $68,983 campaign by the NRA. However, the cost of the biggest independent campaign against him will never be known. Following his vote in favor of imposing federal regulations on the cable television industry, Multimedia Cablevision of Wichita began airing editorials denouncing Glickman and urging viewers to vote for his Republican opponent, state senator Eric R. Yost. The editorials aired more than 100 times a day on as many as ten cable stations, including CNN. Because Multimedia Cablevision called the spots editorials, the firm did not have to report the cost of this campaign to the FEC. Glickman paid $10,790 in legal fees to Perkins Coie of Washington, D.C., for their work in reaching an agreement with Multimedia Cablevision, which ultimately allowed him to run 600 free spots over the campaign's final week.

Similarly, televangelist Pat Robertson's Christian Coalition distributed more than 40 million "nonpartisan" voter guides. The leaflets, distributed in all fifty states, told voters which candidates opposed abortion, homosexual rights, higher taxes, gun control, and congressional term limits. Because its voter guides are supposedly nonpartisan, the Christian Coalition was not required to report any of the costs associated with the 40 million fliers.

Table 6-7 The Top Five Independent Campaigns Waged by Various Organizations

Organization	Race	Expenditures	For or against
National Association of Realtors			
1. Les AuCoin (D-Ore.)	Senate	$329,289	for
2. Rod Chandler (R-Wash.)	Senate	169,950	for
3. E. Clay Shaw, Jr. (R-Fla.)	House	130,629	for
4. John Seymour (R-Calif.)	Senate	123,058	for
5. Beryl Anthony, Jr. (D-Ark.)	House	100,000	for
American Medical Association			
1. Vic Fazio (D-Calif.)	House	255,085	for
2. Bob Packwood (R-Ore.)	Senate	227,809	for
3. Scott McInnis (R-Colo.)	House	184,910	for
4. Michael A. Andrews (D-Texas)	House	118,985	for
5. Gary A. Franks (R-Conn.)	House	81,256	for
National Right to Life Committee			
1. Mike DeWine (R-Ohio)	Senate	27,644	for
2. Don Davis (R-N.C.)	House	27,419	for
3. Morrison J. Hosley, Jr. (R-N.Y.)	House	24,564	for
4. Richard Ray (D-Ga.)	House	23,141	for
5. Bruce Herschensohn	Senate	19,982	for
AFL-CIO			
1. Harris Wofford (D-Pa.)	Senate	155,583	for
2. Wyche Fowler, Jr. (D-Ga.)	Senate	40,801	for
3. Les AuCoin (D-Ore.)	Senate	21,260	for
4. Ben Nighthorse Campbell (D-Colo.)	Senate	17,614	for
5. John S. Devens (D-Alaska)	House	14,967	for
National Abortion Rights Action League			
1. Russell D. Feingold (D-Wis.)	Senate	148,426	for
2. Steven D. Pierce (R-Mass.)	House	144,091	against
3. Ben Nighthorse Campbell (D-Colo.)	Senate	137,487	for
4. Pat Williams (D-Mont.)	House	77,885	for
5. Judith M. Ryan (R-Calif.)	House	59,827	for

Note: Figures include "independent expenditures" and "communication costs," as reported by the organizations to the Federal Election Commission.

If efforts to place voluntary spending limits on candidates are eventually pushed through Congress, it will almost certainly produce an explosion of independent campaigns. Having already declared such spending a protected form of free speech, it is unlikely that the Supreme Court would uphold any congressional action designed to stop them.

CHAPTER 7

Political Consultants
The Real Winners

Mike was a first-time candidate, and most of the people around him hadn't been involved in congressional campaigns before. We made sure we had the help we needed when we needed it.
John Hoehne, chief of staff for Rep. Michael D. Crapo (R-Idaho)

My husband has always done campaigns the old-fashioned way, all with volunteers."
Becky Browder, wife of Rep. Glen Browder (D-Ala.) and treasurer of his campaign

By mid-October 1992, former Mendocino County supervisor Dan Hamburg (D-Calif.) knew his bid to oust freshman Rep. Frank Riggs was in trouble. Hamburg also knew that with just three weeks left in the campaign, he was rapidly running out of time. Convinced that the race could be won but that his current strategy would fail, he dropped his chief consultants, Directions By King & Associates and Hopcraft Communications, both of Sacramento, Calif. "We needed more punch," recalled Meg O'Donnell, Hamburg's campaign finance director.

With the blessing of the Democratic Congressional Campaign Committee (DCCC), which dispatched a staffer to serve as his campaign manager during the final push, Hamburg brought in the Campaign Group of Philadelphia, Pa., to refocus his radio and television commercials and Campaign Performance Group of San Francisco, Calif., to develop advocacy mailers. In turn, Campaign Performance brought in Terris & Jaye, also of San Francisco, to help with both the conceptualization and production of the mailings.

"Hamburg had run the typical California campaign, making mail the main focus," recalled Richard M. Schlackman, president of Campaign Performance. "I spent the whole weekend in a hotel room going over poll results, and they had the right message. It just wasn't being communicated effectively. We did mail in the southern part of the district where TV was too expensive, but in the northern areas we bought television. Cable buys were $12 a point in Humbolt [County], so we bought lots of CNN. We'd have been crazy not to buy that time."

On election day, Hamburg carried Humbolt and Mendocino counties in the north and District 1's portion of Solano County in the south by sufficiently wide margins to offset losses in the district's other four counties. His margin of victory: 6,410 votes.

Although the circumstances are rarely this dramatic, Hamburg's experience reflects the professionalization of modern politics, a process in which candidates turn themselves over to a cadre of highly skilled advisers who develop campaign strategy, mold and project the candidate's image, make certain people show up to vote on election day, and find the money to pay for it all.

Well before any ballots were cast on November 3, congressional candidates across the country had seen to it that political consultants would emerge from the 1992 campaigns as huge financial winners. When all the bills were finally totaled, $248,515,641—or 46 percent of the $542,248,774 spent by the 933 House and Senate candidates who contested the general election—had been funneled through media consultants, fundraisers, persuasion mail specialists, pollsters, general and campaign management consultants, and get-out-the-vote specialists.

While the percentage of total spending accounted for by payments to consultants was virtually identical to the 45 percent recorded in 1990, the amount of money involved was substantially greater. Fueled by incumbents' concerns over the mood of the electorate, the greater number of challengers with sufficient resources to make races competitive, and the record number of open seat contests, consultant billings in congressional campaigns jumped more than $60 million between 1990 and 1992, a 32 percent rise.

In addition to the nearly $249 million shelled out by House and Senate candidates, party coordinated campaigns generated another $32,268,249 in consultant fees. We did not have the resources required to collect and code the additional millions paid to consultants by state party organizations or those waging independent campaigns on behalf of congressional candidates.

MEDIA CONSULTANTS

The biggest winners in this bonanza were the media consultants, who fashioned and projected the images that spelled the difference between winning and losing in many competitive races. During the 1992 election cycle, these "kingmakers" billed congressional campaign committees a total of

$165,589,508—a 42 percent increase over 1990. The national party committees kicked in another $27,212,742.

As in 1990, Squier/Eskew/Knapp/Ochs Communications of Washington, D.C., led the way, billing fourteen campaigns a total of $11,273,185 (see Table 7-1). The firm billed Sen. Christopher J. Dodd (D-Conn.), $1,831,630; Sen. Bob Graham (D-Fla.), $1,743,642; Sen. Richard C. Shelby (D-Ala.), $1,211,492; Sen. Terry Sanford (D-N.C.), $1,037,228; and Sen. Dale Bumpers (D-Ark.), $931,181. In addition, Squier/Eskew handled the media chores for two unsuccessful Senate candidates seeking open seats and one unsuccessful challenger, billing Rep. Les AuCoin (D-Ore.), $1,131,196; Rep. Richard Stallings (D-Idaho), $375,952; and challenger Joseph H. Hogsett (D-Ind.), $1,229,031. The firm's leading clients in the House were Rep. Vic Fazio (D-Calif.), $669,827; and 1991 special election victor John W. Olver (D-Mass.), $573,556.

When the additional $1,195,674 in coordinated expenditures coming in from national Democratic party committees are all factored in, Squier/Eskew's 1992 billings amounted to $12,468,859, a 52 percent increase over 1990. Including party coordinated expenditures, the firm's eight Senate clients accounted for 85 percent of those revenues.

Greer, Margolis, Mitchell & Associates of Washington, D.C., landed six Senate and two House campaigns in 1992, and its billings jumped from $2,388,526 in 1990 to $11,096,778. Ranked twelfth in terms of total billings in 1990, this 365 percent increase moved Greer, Margolis into second place in 1992. Their work on the Senate campaign of Rep. Barbara Boxer (D-Calif.) accounted for nearly half of the firm's receipts, with Boxer paying $4,299,960 and the Democratic Senatorial Campaign Committee (DSCC) adding $1,217,000. Sen. Wyche Fowler, Jr. (D-Ga.) paid Greer, Margolis $2,579,820 in his loosing bid for a second term, and the DSCC added $510,000. Sens. Wendell H. Ford (D-Ky.), Kent Conrad (D-N.D.), and Patrick J. Leahy (D-Vt.) paid Greer, Margolis $947,393, $337,842, and $210,035, respectively. The firm's most lucrative House account belonged to Rosa DeLauro (D-Conn.), who contributed $394,496 to Greer, Margolis's receipts.

National Media of Alexandria, Va., collected more than twice as much from its House and Senate clients in 1992 as they had in 1990, but that growth did no more than maintain its third-place ranking. National Media worked on eighteen campaigns, including six Senate races. Lt. Gov. Mike DeWine (R-Ohio) paid them $1,595,353 during his unsuccessful bid to oust Sen. John Glenn. Sen. Don Nickles (R-Okla.) paid the firm $1,216,607. Former attorney general and Pennsylvania governor Dick Thornburgh pumped $1,976,126 through the firm during his unsuccessful 1991 special election contest with Sen. Harris Wofford, who had been appointed to the seat following the death of Sen. John Heinz. Although Sen. Bob Dole (R-Kan.) did not have much of a race, his advertising campaign generated $481,168 worth of business for the firm. Unsuccessful challengers Brook Johnson (R-Conn.) and Steve Sydness (R-N.D.) paid the firm $1,207,012 and $110,970, respectively. National Media's two most profitable House races involved Reps. E. Clay Shaw, Jr. (R-Fla.) and Jim Bunning (R-Ky.), who paid $543,424 and $438,137, respectively. The firm collected another $1,418,228 in national party coordinated expenses, including $892,000 for DeWine's campaign and $279,182 for Johnson's.

Multi Media Services Corp. of Alexandria, Va., owed its fourth-place ranking largely to Sen. Alfonse M. D'Amato (R-N.Y.), who paid the time-buyer $4,982,589. With the National Republican Senatorial Committee (NRSC) spending $1,507,718 on D'Amato's behalf, that one campaign accounted for 70 percent of Multi Media's $9,270,463 total billings. The unsuccessful campaign of Richard Williamson (R-Ill.) against Carol Moseley-Braun generated revenues of $1,673,251, including $944,052 in party coordinated expenditures.

Another media buyer, Target Enterprises of Hollywood, Calif., earned most of its money from two Senate campaigns. Target collected $2,665,048 from Bruce Herschensohn (R-Calif.) and another $2,454,644 from the NRSC. Payments of $1,338,360 by Sen. John Seymour (R-Calif.) were augmented by a $2,449,955 infusion from the NRSC.

FUND-RAISERS

Whether they relied primarily on political action committees (PACs) or on individual donors to fund their campaigns, whether they raised their money primarily through events or by mail, most candidates hired at least one fund-raising consultant to help fill their 1992 campaign coffers. Of the $84,954,183 congressional candidates spent on fund-raising events, direct-mail solicitations, and telemarketing, $29,336,066 was paid to professional fund-raisers. This represented a drop of about $8.7 million between 1990 and 1992, a 23 percent decrease explained largely by a reduction in spending on direct-mail consultants. In 1992 only three direct-mail fund-raisers had billings of at least $1 million; in 1990 eight firms had topped the $1 million mark and two had exceeded $2 million.

This marked dropoff in direct-mail expenses was largely due to the absence of Sen. Jesse Helms (R-N.C.) from the 1992 candidate roster. In 1990 Helms paid five direct-mail consultants a total of $4.6 million, including $1,334,275 to Bruce W. Eberle & Associates of Vienna, Va.; $1,246,726 to Computer Operations of Raliegh, N.C.; and $1,039,027 to Jefferson Marketing, also of Raleigh.

Without the campaigns of Democratic Sens. Tom Harkin (Iowa), Paul Simon (Ill.), and John Kerry (Mass.), who together spent $2,979,082, Coyle, McConnell & O'Brien of Washington, D.C., dropped from first to ninth on the list.

While Response Dynamics of Vienna, Va., saw its billings drop from $1,872,116 in 1990 to $1,763,935 in 1992, the company emerged as the top direct-mail fund-raiser, having leapfrogged from third place (see Table 7-2). The firm charged Rep. Robert K. Dornan (R-Calif.) $967,651 for list rental, production, postage, and processing returns. Dornan's payments accounted for 55 percent of the money paid to Response Dynamics by House and Senate candidates in 1992. Among the company's other major clients were Sens. Seymour and John

Table 7-1 The Top Fifty Media Consultants in the 1992 Congressional Races

			Payments from		
Rank	Company	Location	Candidate	National Party	Total
1	Squier/Eskew/Knapp/Ochs Communications	Washington, D.C.	$11,273,185	$1,195,674	$12,468,859
2	Greer, Margolis, Mitchell & Associates	Washington, D.C.	9,237,278	1,859,500	11,096,778
3	National Media	Alexandria, Va.	8,532,931	1,418,228	9,951,160
4	Multi Media Services Corp.	Alexandria, Va.	6,687,370	2,583,093	9,270,463
5	Target Enterprises	Hollywood, Fla.	4,195,056	4,904,599	9,099,655
6	Campaign Group	Philadelphia, Pa.	7,466,215	731,775	8,197,990
7	The Media Company	Washington, D.C.	6,133,757	966,000	7,099,757
8	Fenn & King Communications	Washington, D.C.	5,776,706	22,637	5,799,343
9	The Garth Group	New York, N.Y.	4,643,143	980,540	5,623,683
10	Morris & Carrick	New York, N.Y.	3,840,981	1,235,000	5,075,981
11	Sipple Strategic Communications	Washington, D.C.	5,043,919	0	5,043,919
12	Doak, Shrum & Associates	Washington, D.C.	2,430,061	923,000	3,353,061
13	Smith & Harroff	Alexandria, Va.	3,042,748	106,393	3,149,141
14	Pro Media	Needham, Mass.	3,079,210	0	3,079,210
15	Shafto & Barton	Houston, Texas	2,600,951	114,990	2,715,941
16	The Media Team	Alexandria, Va.	1,629,252	931,099	2,560,351
17	Shorr Associates	Philadelphia, Pa.	2,459,103	0	2,459,103
18	Hanover Communications	Raleigh, N.C.	1,790,218	560,928	2,351,146
19	Media Strategies & Research	Washington, D.C.	2,304,695	44,000	2,348,695
20	Geto & De Milly	New York, N.Y.	2,262,199	0	2,262,199
21	Jan Crawford Communications	Paris, Va.	769,219	1,370,000	2,139,219
22	Trippi, McMahon & Squier	Alexandria, Va.	2,092,307	25,000	2,117,307
23	The Perkins Group	Indianapolis, Ind.	1,637,987	452,415	2,090,402
24	Austin-Sheinkopf	New York, N.Y.	1,733,875	243,000	1,976,875
25	Media Solutions	Atlanta, Ga.	1,121,400	796,083	1,917,483
26	Twede-Evans Political	Salt Lake City, Utah	1,753,198	141,523	1,894,721
27	Profit Marketing & Communications	New Berlin, Wis.	1,498,586	290,919	1,789,506
28	Sandler-Innocenzi	Washington, D.C.	1,586,806	106,324	1,693,130
29	Axelrod & Associates	Chicago, Ill.	1,564,693	40,000	1,604,693
30	Struble-Totten Communications	Washington, D.C.	1,427,447	65,596	1,493,044
31	Eichenbaum, Henke & Associates	Milwaukee, Wis.	1,112,500	303,500	1,416,000
32	Mike Murphy Media	Washington, D.C.	1,186,083	107,000	1,293,083
33	Nordlinger Associates	Washington, D.C.	1,260,625	20,000	1,280,625
34	Joe Slade White & Co.	New York, N.Y.	1,134,869	142,795	1,277,664
35	Barnhart Advertising	Denver, Colo.	965,175	275,082	1,240,257
36	The Robert Goodman Agency	Baltimore, Md.	1,185,141	15,750	1,200,891
37	Media Plus	Seattle, Wash.	751,074	407,838	1,158,911
38	Mentzer Media Service	Baltimore, Md.	1,051,095	97,145	1,148,240
39	Schreurs & Associates	Waterloo, Iowa	836,838	304,072	1,140,910
40	Starr, Seigle & McCombs	Honolulu, Hawaii	1,115,551	0	1,115,551
41	Russo, Marsh & Associates	Sacramento, Calif.	1,110,591	0	1,110,591
42	Specialized Media Services	Charlotte, N.C.	1,089,540	0	1,089,540
43	Marketing Resource Group	Lansing, Mich.	942,819	50,972	993,791
44	Western International Media	Los Angeles, Calif.	980,970	10,000	990,970
45	Paul Kinney Productions	Sacramento, Calif.	654,112	333,000	987,112
46	Kranzler Kingsley Communications Corp.	Bismark, N.D.	881,797	25,000	906,797
47	Edmonds Powell Media	Washington, D.C.	777,635	89,669	867,304
48	Cottington & Marti	Edina, Minn.	735,261	108,322	843,582
49	John Franzen Multimedia	Washington, D.C.	826,447	0	826,447
50	Edward Mitchell Communications	Wilkes-Barre, Pa.	817,685	5,500	823,185

McCain (R-Ariz.), who were billed $310,340 and $295,837, respectively.

Karl Rove & Co. of Austin, Texas, jumped from fourth in 1990 to second in 1992, despite the fact that its earnings dropped by $555,635. Rove's major clients included Thornburgh, $336,725; Sen. Bob Kasten (R-Wis.), $330,388; and Sen. Christopher S. Bond (R-Mo.), $279,479. Terry Considine (R-Colo.), who lost an open Senate seat contest to Rep. Ben Nighthorse Campbell, paid Rove $160,515.

On the strength of the $562,599 paid by former San Francisco mayor Dianne Feinstein's (D-Calif.) Senate campaign and the $400,586 paid by Lynn Yeakel's (D-Pa.) Senate campaign, Gold Communications Co. of Austin, Texas, saw its total revenues rise from $327,830 in 1990 to $1,146,223 in 1992, a 250 percent increase. Feinstein and Yeakel accounted for 84 percent of Gold's earnings.

Robbed of the large direct-mail operations run by 1990 candidates Sens. Simon (D-Ill.), J. Bennett Johnston (D-La.), and Carl Levin (D-Mich.), A. B. Data of Milwaukee, Wis., took in $1,416,097 less in 1992 than it had two years earlier. A. B. Data's best client in 1992, Senate hopeful Robert Abrams (D-N.Y.), paid the company $359,814. Sen. Glenn and Rep. Les Aspin (D-Wis.) spent $303,813 and $101,493, respectively.

Pamela D. Needham of Washington, D.C., topped the list of 359 fund-raising event planners who worked for congressional candidates (see Table 7-3), collecting 91 percent of the $495,337 she earned in the 1992 cycle from one campaign. Sen. Barbara A. Mikulski (D-Md.) paid Needham $452,167 over the six-year cycle to coordinate her fund-raising receptions.

Scott Gale, president of Fundraising Management Group in Washington, D.C., took the opposite approach, collecting a total of $432,577 from eleven campaigns. Gale billed Abrams $95,536; Shelby, $75,203; Senate challenger Tony Smith (D-Alaska), $68,954; and Wofford, $36,247. Democratic Reps. Greg Laughlin, Martin Frost, and Pete Geren, all Texans, paid Fundraising Management $46,345, $42,913, and $15,973, respectively.

Robert H. Bassin Associates of Washington, D.C., raised money for four Democratic Senate candidates, collecting $70,191 from Glenn, $33,147 from Hogsett, $32,952 from Campbell, and just $4,785 from Conrad. Among his fifteen clients seeking House seats, Olver rung up bills totaling $55,544. Rep. Dick Swett (D-N.H.) was not far behind, paying $53,884. Robert E. Andrews (D-N.J.) spent $37,839. Swett's father-in-law, Tom Lantos (D-Calif.), paid Bassin $30,573.

Fraioli/Jost of Washington, D.C., pulled in $402,316 by working on twenty-six House and Senate campaigns, earning as little as $1,160 from Rep. Gary L. Ackerman (D-N.Y.) to as much as $73,290 from Rep. Richard H. Lehman (D-Calif.). In addition to Lehman, the firm's most lucrative contracts were Stallings, $67,271; Rep. Pat Williams (D-Mont.), $36,282; and Rep. Richard J. Durbin (D-Ill.), $29,521.

While John L. Plaxco & Associates of Los Angeles, Calif., worked for three candidates, Feinstein accounted for 92 percent of the company's billings—$365,220. Plaxco also received $15,603 from House Majority Leader Richard A. Gephardt (D-Mo.) and $14,316 from Lehman.

None of the top five fund-raising event planners in 1992 had been among the top five in 1990.

Outlays for telemarketing dropped from $5,115,550 in 1990 to $2,644,737 in 1992, a 48 percent decline that was largely explained by the absence of Senate candidates who relied heavily on this tool during the 1990 election cycle. In the 1990 cycle, Simon alone had spent $706,298 with his telemarketers.

Although forty-three firms provided telemarketing services to congressional candidates during the 1992 cycle, five firms received 66 percent of the $2,416,207 paid to professional telemarketers.

Most campaigns avoided telemarketing because of its high costs and increasing public dissatisfaction with telephone sales pitches. Gordon & Schwenkmeyer of El Segundo, Calif., topped the list of telemarketers, billing its clients a total of $596,164. However, 92 percent of those earnings came from two campaigns: Feinstein paid $317,292 and Moseley-Braun paid $233,966. The firm's next biggest client was Rep. Bill Richardson (D-N.M.), who paid them $33,796 for telemarketing and another $31,098 for their help on his fund-raising direct-mail program.

Meyer Associates of St. Cloud, Minn., received a total of $424,247 from ten campaigns, $229,963 of which was paid by Sen. Tom Daschle (D-S.D.). AuCoin, who lost his bid to unseat Sen. Bob Packwood, spent $56,507. Reps. Pete Stark (D-Calif.), Lane Evans (D-Ill.), and Tim Johnson (D-S.D.) paid Meyer $43,858, $24,504, and $18,462, respectively.

Rounding out the top five telemarketing consultants were Optima Direct of Washington, D.C., which billed its clients a total of $280,571; Product Development of Costa Mesa, Calif., which collected 99 percent of its $143,028 from Herschensohn; and Synhorst & Schraad of Russell, Kan., which collected a total of $139,651 for its work on twelve campaigns, including $50,743 for its efforts on behalf of Sen. Charles E. Grassley (R-Iowa).

Persuasion Mail Specialists

Persuasion mail remained an integral part of virtually every 1992 campaign, particularly in House races, where television frequently proved not to be an economical means of communicating with voters. In Los Angeles, New York, Chicago, and other major media markets, most candidates relied almost exclusively on advocacy mailers to communicate their messages. The consultants who designed those mailings received $17,457,860 from candidates and another $1,740,549 from the national party committees. In all, eleven persuasion mail consultants collected more than $500,000.

As in 1990, Campaign Performance was the biggest player by far (see Table 7-4). While the firm had only one Senate candidate among its clients, it worked to one degree or another for forty Democratic House candidates. Some simply paid Campaign Performance a retainer to guarantee access to its

Table 7-2 The Top Twenty-Five Direct-Mail Consultants in the 1992 Congressional Races

			Payments from		
Rank	Company	Location	Candidate	National Party	Total
1	Response Dynamics	Vienna, Va.	$1,763,935	$ 0	$1,763,935
2	Karl Rove & Co.	Austin, Texas	1,201,658	0	1,201,658
3	Gold Communications Co.	Austin, Texas	1,146,223	0	1,146,223
4	A.B. Data	Milwaukee, Wis.	844,558	0	844,558
5	Craver Matthews Smith & Co.	Falls Church, Va.	761,284	18,435	779,719
6	MWM	Washington, D.C.	600,913	0	600,913
7	Tim Macy & Associates	Sacramento, Calif.	523,914	0	523,914
8	Malchow & Co.	Washington, D.C.	479,047	0	479,047
9	Coyle, McConnell & O'Brien	Washington, D.C.	422,686	0	422,686
10	The Lukens Co.	Arlington, Va.	418,837	0	418,837
11	Polly A. Agee	Arlington, Va.	244,646	0	244,646
12	Mal Warwick & Associates	Berkeley, Calif.	230,730	0	230,730
13	Jim Wise Associates	Alexandria, Va.	218,575	0	218,575
14	Direct Mail Systems	St. Petersburg, Fla.	199,056	0	199,056
15	The Madison Group	Bellevue, Wash.	173,819	0	173,819
16	Lungren & Co.	Sacramento, Calif.	171,410	0	171,410
17	Odell, Roper & Associates	Golden, Colo.	150,146	0	150,146
18	Bennett & Associates	Raleigh, N.C.	131,623	0	131,623
19	Betsy Crone	Washington, D.C.	126,796	0	126,796
20	Losser & Associates	Washington, D.C.	119,472	0	119,472
21	Campaign Services Group	Austin, Texas	113,181	0	113,181
22	Winning Direction	San Francisco, Calif.	103,318	0	103,318
23	Fundamentals	Rock River, Ohio	76,474	0	76,474
24	James R. Foster & Associates	Carrollton, Texas	71,921	0	71,921
25	Marketing Associates	Charlotte, N.C.	70,797	0	70,797

Table 7-3 The Top Twenty-Five Event Consultants in the 1992 Congressional Races

			Payments from		
Rank	Company	Location	Candidate	National Party	Total
1	Pamela D. Needham	Washington, D.C.	$495,337	$ 0	$495,337
2	Fundraising Management Group	Washington, D.C.	432,577	0	432,577
3	Robert H. Bassin Associates	Washington, D.C.	429,676	0	429,676
4	Fraioli/Jost	Washington, D.C.	402,316	0	402,316
5	John L. Plaxco & Associates	Los Angeles, Calif.	395,138	0	395,138
6	Steven H. Gordon & Associates	St. Paul, Minn.	371,753	0	371,753
7	Springer Associates	Falls Church, Va.	371,616	0	371,616
8	Dan Morgan & Associates	Arlington, Va.	357,487	0	357,487
9	Erickson & Co.	Washington, D.C.	357,434	0	357,434
10	Paula Levine	Washington, D.C.	318,156	0	318,156
11	Creative Campaign Consultant	Washington, D.C.	310,366	2,700	313,066
12	Ziebart Associates	Washington, D.C.	241,115	0	241,115
13	Shelby/Blaskeg	Washington, D.C.	222,394	0	222,394
14	Maxwell & Associates	Alexandria, Va.	211,104	0	211,104
15	Joyce Valdez & Associates	Los Angeles, Calif.	208,897	0	208,897
16	PAC-COM	New York, N.Y.	201,772	0	201,772
17	Mary Pat Bonner	Springfield, Va.	198,763	0	198,763
18	Jim Wise Associates	Alexandria, Va.	183,578	0	183,578
19	Carey Hagglund	Sausalito, Calif.	180,854	0	180,854
20	Conroy & Co.	Washington, D.C.	158,906	0	158,906
21	Barbara Klein Associates	Washington, D.C.	157,409	0	157,409
22	Barbara Silby & Associates	Potomac, Md.	151,741	0	151,741
23	Kimberly A. Scott	Washington, D.C.	145,584	0	145,584
24	Hammelman Associates	Arlington, Va.	145,400	0	145,400
25	CT Associates	Seattle, Wash.	117,810	23,250	141,060

expertise in the event a race developed, but most put Schlackman and his colleagues to work. For its efforts, Campaign Performance collected $2,693,376 from its clients and $40,847 from national Democratic party committees—more than doubling its 1990 receipts. The company billed three clients more than $200,000: California Reps. Fazio and George E. Brown, Jr., and unsuccessful open seat candidate Steve A. Orlins (D-N.Y.). Democratic Reps. Robert Andrews, Norman Y. Mineta (Calif.), and Tom McMillen (Md.) each paid the firm more than $100,000, as did Thomas H. Hattery (D-Md.), who defeated Rep. Beverly B. Byron in the primary before losing in the general election to Roscoe G. Bartlett. Another eleven campaigns paid Campaign Performance between $50,000 and $100,000.

Although its billings were nearly $1.9 million less than Campaign Performance's, Karl Rove collected $691,547 more from its clients in 1992 than it had in 1990. Payments from national Republican party committees jumped from $52,534 in 1990 to $479,833 in 1992. While Bond paid them $79,934, the NRSC picked up the tab for mailers costing $226,888. Although Sens. Nickles and Kasten paid the firm nothing for work on advocacy mailings, the party paid Rove $141,276 to produce mailings for Nickles and $111,670 to create mailers for Kasten. In the House, Reps. Joe L. Barton, Lamar Smith, and Jack Fields, all Texas Republicans, paid Rove $127,088, 58,219, and $56,955, respectively.

McNally, Temple & Associates in Sacramento, Calif., worked on five House campaigns, the most lucrative of which was the $291,019 effort of Michael Huffington (R-Calif.). Bill Baker (R-Calif.), who won an open seat contest with Democrat Wendell H. Williams, paid the firm $277,629.

The November Group of Washington, D.C., worked on thirteen House campaigns and one Senate campaign. Sen. Ernest F. Hollings (D-S.C.) paid the firm $31,550 and the DSCC spent another $40,800 on his behalf. Democratic Reps. Thomas J. Downey (N.Y.) and Gerry E. Studds (Mass.) paid the company $181,570 and $138,608, respectively. The party picked up another $10,000 in expenses for Studds. Gwen Margolis (D-Fla.), who lost to Republican Clay Shaw, paid $50,746.

Direct Mail Systems of St. Petersburg, Fla., created voter persuasion mail for nine House campaigns. Shaw paid them $157,508, and Rep. Michael Bilirakis (R-Fla.) anted up $114,519. Dan Miller (R-Fla.) and John L. Mica (R-Fla.), who both won open seats, spent $109,337 and $73,405, respectively.

POLLSTERS

In a year marked by tighter races, it should come as no surprise that candidates paid their polling consultants a total of $16,627,764—32 percent more than pollsters collected from House and Senate campaigns during the 1990 election cycle. These payments were augmented by checks totaling $2,474,719 from the national party committees.

Greenberg-Lake of Washington, D.C., collected a total of $1,770,613 from congressional candidates, the DSCC, the DCCC, and the Democratic National Committee (DNC), a 23 percent increase over 1990. Even without the huge sums the firm collected for working on Bill Clinton's presidential campaign, these payments were enough to vault the firm to the top of the polling list (see Table 7-5). While twenty-five candidates paid Greenberg-Lake directly, the party committees together paid the firm for its involvement in sixty-one campaigns, including forty-nine that did not tap their own treasuries to pay for the polls. The firm's two biggest Senate clients, Dodd and Boxer, paid $176,173 and $151,774, respectively. The DSCC kicked in an additional $24,860 for Dodd, and the DNC picked up $16,735 of Boxer's polling costs. Among House candidates, the company's top clients were Democratic Reps. David E. Bonior (Mich.), Downey, and Bob Carr (Mich.), who paid $135,691, $109,873, and $104,907, respectively. Of the three, only Carr had an additional $3,775 picked up by the party.

Cooper & Secrest Associates of Alexandria, Va., the leading pollster of the 1990 cycle, worked on thirty-seven House campaigns and two Senate campaigns. While the firm's billings increased by a modest 2 percent over 1990, that was not enough to hold on to its top ranking. On the Senate side, Cooper & Secrest collected $295,288 from Fowler and $51,507 from Stallings. McMillen and Studds were the firm's best House clients, paying $98,101 and $64,234, respectively. Another twelve candidates, only two of whom were nonincumbents, paid Cooper & Secrest between $30,000 and $50,000.

As in 1990, Garin-Hart ranked third on the revenue list, collecting $1,061,152 from twenty-six campaigns and another $340,368 in Democratic party coordinated expenditures. Sens. Conrad, Hollings, Graham, and Leahy paid Garin-Hart $114,250, $74,717, and $51,500, respectively. The firm received $90,500 from AuCoin and $37,377 from Feinstein. Topping the list of clients involved in House open seat contests were Jane Harman (D-Calif.) at $76,445 and Orlins at $52,035. Due to tight races or redistricting, Democratic Reps. Michael A. Andrews (Texas), Peter Hoagland (Neb.), Fazio, and Richard J. Durbin (Ill.) each paid between $43,000 and $53,000 for Garin-Hart's services. Rep. John D. Dingell (D-Mich.), who was neither affected by redistricting nor seriously challenged, paid the firm $45,000.

Mellman & Lazarus of Washington, D.C., provided polling services to twenty-one campaigns. Boxer topped the company's client list with direct payments of $107,860 and coordinated payments by the DSCC of $163,207. Glenn paid the firm $221,993 and received a DNC stipend of $5,740. Six other Senate campaigns tapped the firm's expertise. Among House candidates using Mellman & Lazarus, Gephardt's $78,821 outlay led the pack. Rep. Gerry Sikorski (D-Minn.), who had 697 overdrafts, was not far behind with direct payments of $73,802 and a $5,000 infusion from the DCCC.

The top pollster used by Republican candidates, Arthur J. Finkelstein & Associates of New York, collected $1,109,708. Although Finkelstein provided polling for fifteen campaigns, four Senate campaigns accounted for 77 percent of his firm's billings. Finkelstein served as both D'Amato's pollster and general campaign strategist, collecting $356,194 for his polling ser-

Table 7-4 The Top Twenty-Five Persuasion Mail Consultants in the 1992 Congressional Races

			Payments from		
Rank	Company	Location	Candidate	National Party	Total
1	Campaign Performance Group	San Francisco, Calif.	$2,693,376	$ 40,847	$2,734,224
2	Karl Rove & Co.	Austin, Texas	370,111	479,833	849,944
3	McNally, Temple & Associates	Sacramento, Calif.	720,990	25,888	746,878
4	The November Group	Washington, D.C.	553,000	53,561	606,561
5	Direct Mail Systems	St. Petersburg, Fla.	563,922	33,480	597,402
6	Welch Communications	Arlington, Va.	492,753	101,959	594,712
7	Gold Communications Co.	Austin, Texas	593,872	0	593,872
8	Bates & Associates	Washington, D.C.	576,392	0	576,392
9	Russo, Marsh & Associates	Sacramento, Calif.	499,127	60,692	559,819
10	Roger Lee & Carol Beddo Associates	San Jose, Calif.	509,858	0	509,858
11	James R. Foster & Associates	Carrollton, Texas	456,771	47,500	504,271
12	Ambrosino & Muir	San Francisco, Calif.	436,106	0	436,106
13	Precision Marketing	Easton, Pa.	393,826	0	393,826
14	David J. Murray & Associates	Princeton, N.J.	302,340	53,540	355,880
15	Brabender Cox	Pittsburgh, Pa.	270,548	55,472	326,020
16	Brown Inc.	Santa Fe, N.M.	308,567	14,805	323,372
17	Campaign Strategies	San Antonio, Texas	288,547	0	288,547
18	Kevin B. Tynan & Associates	Chicago, Ill.	159,517	112,235	271,752
19	Marketing Resource Group	Lansing, Mich.	255,756	6,501	262,257
20	Clinton Reilly Campaigns	San Francisco, Calif.	241,524	0	241,524
21	Bay Communications	Edgewater, Md.	215,553	0	215,553
22	Blaemire Communications	Reston, Va.	194,015	9,110	203,124
23	The Madison Group	Bellevue, Wash.	148,395	31,726	180,121
24	John Grotta Company	Arlington, Va.	123,402	37,734	161,135
25	Pavlik & Associates	Fort Worth, Texas	158,061	0	158,061

Table 7-5 The Top Twenty-Five Pollsters in the 1992 Congressional Races

			Payments from		
Rank	Company	Location	Candidate	National Party	Total
1	Greenberg-Lake	Washington, D.C.	$1,255,391	$515,222	$1,770,613
2	Cooper & Secrest Associates	Alexandria, Va.	1,421,428	91,650	1,513,078
3	Garin-Hart	Washington, D.C.	1,061,152	340,368	1,401,520
4	Mellman & Lazarus	Washington, D.C.	1,038,464	286,438	1,324,902
5	Arthur J. Finkelstein & Associates	New York, N.Y.	1,099,269	10,439	1,109,708
6	Tarrance & Associates	Alexandria, Va.	861,495	28,900	890,395
7	Public Opinion Strategies	Alexandria, Va.	775,096	43,382	818,478
8	Hickman-Brown Research	Washington, D.C.	644,928	69,000	713,928
9	Penn & Schoen Associates	New York, N.Y.	475,268	84,800	560,068
10	American Viewpoint	Alexandria, Va.	533,185	7,000	540,185
11	Moore Information	Portland, Ore.	504,882	3,500	508,382
12	Hill Research Consultants	Woodlands, Texas	385,629	0	385,629
13	Fairbank, Bregman & Maullin	San Francisco, Calif.	351,872	32,500	384,372
14	Bennett & Petts	Washington, D.C.	210,610	164,834	375,444
15	Lauer, Lalley & Associates	Washington, D.C.	237,150	134,860	372,010
16	Frederick/Schneiders	Washington, D.C.	325,878	36,800	362,678
17	Market Strategies	Southfield, Mich.	274,771	29,500	304,271
18	Kitchens, Powell & Kitchens	Orlando, Fla.	292,250	10,000	302,250
19	Bill Johnson Survey Research	Mt. Vernon, N.Y.	247,200	0	247,200
20	Fabrizio, McLaughlin & Associates	Alexandria, Va.	229,576	13,500	243,076
21	Western Wats Center	Provo, Utah	43,718	196,415	240,133
22	Feldman Group	Washington, D.C.	78,586	146,619	225,205
23	Arnold Steinberg & Associates	Calabasas, Calif.	205,425	0	205,425
24	KRC Research	New York, N.Y.	190,106	0	190,106
25	Thomas Kielhorn & Associates	Oklahoma City, Okla.	186,250	0	186,250

vices alone. Lauch Faircloth (R-N.C.), who defeated Democratic Sen. Terry Sanford, paid Finkelstein $280,226. Polls conducted for Williamson and Nickles brought the firm $128,437 and $86,450, respectively. Former Rep. Joseph J. DioGuardi (R-N.Y.), who lost a rematch with Democratic Rep. Nita Lowey, paid Finkelstein $57,229.

GENERAL AND CAMPAIGN MANAGEMENT CONSULTANTS

With the increased specialization in the political consulting industry, some candidates have begun hiring consultants to coordinate the activities of their various consultants.

Geto & De Milly of New York was paid $444,082 to handle the day-to-day operations of the Abrams Senate campaign (see Table 7-6). While other firms created the campaign's ads, produced the commercials, and bought much of the air time, Geto & De Milly also collected $2,262,199 for consulting on the media campaign and purchasing time. Abrams paid an additional $11,250 to rent space in the firm's Manhattan office.

Kam Kuwata's firm, Kuwata Communications of Santa Monica, Calif., received $261,419 for managing Feinstein's successful special election campaign against Seymour to fill the remaining two years of former Sen. Pete Wilson's term. After the election, Feinstein named Kuwata director of her Los Angeles congressional office. In early 1994 he changed hats again, leaving the congressional staff to begin managing Feinstein's 1994 campaign for a full six-year term.

Seymour also had a campaign management consultant, Richard H. McBride of RHM in Round Rock, Texas. RHM collected $200,538 for coordinating the day-to-day campaign activities, including those undertaken by the other thirty-one consultants Seymour employed.

Rep. Robert H. Michel (R-Ill.) ran his 1992 campaign as he had every campaign since 1986, when his campaign manager, MaryAlice Erickson, created her own management firm. That firm, Campaigns & Elections of Peoria, Ill., collected $188,433 for running Michel's permanent campaign throughout the 1992 cycle. Erickson managed a small direct-mail fund-raising operation, arranged fund-raising events, published and mailed out a newsletter, sent out Michel's year-end holiday cards, sent congratulations to recent high school graduates, and coordinated the activities of his fund-raising, polling, and public relations consultants.

Some candidates opted not to turn their entire operations over to a single firm, but leaned heavily on general consultants for strategic advice. In some cases, those planning the general campaign strategy and orchestrating the activities of other consultants were also acting in some other campaign capacity.

In addition to his polling fees, Finkelstein was also paid to mold the strategy on four campaigns. D'Amato paid $265,295 for this service (see Table 7-7). In the House, Sam Johnson (R-Texas) paid $38,486 for Finkelstein's input to his 1991 special election. Stephen A. Sohn (R-Mass.) paid Finkelstein $34,500 for general advice on his losing effort against Rep. Edward J. Markey. Rep. Duncan Hunter (R-Calif.) paid Finkelstein a $2,000 retainer.

Campaign Design Group of Washington, D.C., collected $105,103 from Boxer and $39,686 from the DSCC for work on Boxer's behalf. State senator Patty Murray (D-Wash.) paid the firm $75,536. Lynn Woolsey (D-Calif.) paid Campaign Design $2,076 for their input on her open seat campaign.

Spencer-Roberts & Associates of Irvine, Calif., received $193,740 for providing general strategic advice to Seymour and $18,757 for its work on the successful House campaign of real estate executive Ken Calvert (R-Calif.). Eddie Mahe, Jr. & Associates of Washington, D.C., provided general consulting services to three House and two Senate campaigns. His two biggest clients, DeWine and Sen. Frank H. Murkowski (R-Alaska), paid $109,475 and $60,802, respectively.

While Maxwell & Associates of Alexandria, Va., usually handled fund raising for campaigns, the firm consulted with three campaigns on their overall strategies. Grassley paid $129,004 for that service. The firm received $21,577 from Jim Ross Lightfoot (R-Iowa) and $14,498 from John J. Rhodes III (R-Ariz.).

GET-OUT-THE-VOTE SPECIALISTS

In the largely bygone days of machine politics, candidates depended on block and precinct captains in their party organizations to make certain that supporters made their way to the polls on election day. In the age of entrepreneurial politics, most candidates have taken on that task for themselves. While most run in-house phonebanking operations, many candidates have begun to contract out that labor-intensive process to consultants. In all, candidates contesting the 1992 elections paid such consultants $5,351,046. Coordinated payments by the national party committees added $400,497.

The Tyson Organization of Fort Worth, Texas, received $567,098 for its phonebanking efforts on behalf of seven candidates (see Table 7-8). Senators Shelby and Fowler paid Tyson $191,996 and $31,114, respectively. The company billed Democratic Reps. Frost, $101,045; Geren, $84,565; Mike Synar (Okla.), $81,340; Bart Gordon (Tenn.), $58,757; and Bob Clement (Tenn.), $18,280.

Campaign Telecommunications of New York received $441,077 from ten campaigns for phonebanking, including $225,047 paid by Brook Johnson. Other Republicans who made use of the firm's services included Rep. Newt Gingrich (Ga.), $45,096; Nickles, $43,847; Rep. Richard H. Baker (La.), $34,533; and Dornan, $21,790. Although Bond did not hire them directly, the NRSC paid for $81,307 worth of telephone calls made on his behalf.

Telemark in Wilsonville, Ore., had a client list with a distinctly bipartisan flavor, an unusual phenomenon in the consulting business. Packwood's phonebanking payments totaled $223,000 and accounted for 45 percent of the firm's receipts. Another Republican client was Thornburgh, who paid the firm $76,545. Among the firm's nine House clients were Democrats

Table 7-6 The Top Fifteen Campaign Management Consultants in the 1992 Congressional Races

			Payments from		
Rank	Company	Location	Candidate	National Party	Total
1	Geto & De Milly	New York, N.Y.	$444,082	$ 0	$444,082
2	Kuwata Communications	Santa Monica, Calif.	261,419	0	261,419
3	RHM	Round Rock, Texas	200,538	0	200,538
4	Campaigns & Elections	Peoria, Ill.	188,433	0	188,433
5	Carville & Begala	Alexandria, Va.	156,657	0	156,657
6	Political Advertising Consultants	San Antonio, Texas	114,628	0	114,628
7	Hopcraft Communications	Sacramento, Calif.	96,205	0	96,205
8	Political Consulting & Management	St. George Island, Fla.	95,763	0	95,763
9	MBM Consulting	Richmond, Va.	91,631	0	91,631
10	Curt Stainer & Associates	Columbus, Ohio	87,977	0	87,977
11	Western Pacific Research	Bakersfield, Calif.	83,933	0	83,933
12	Attention!	Naperville, Ill.	79,842	0	79,842
13	Washington Political Group	Montgomery, Ala.	74,439	0	74,439
14	Hunt, Marmillion & Associates	Los Angeles, Calif.	69,866	0	69,866
15	Cutting Edge Communications	San Antonio, Texas	65,058	0	65,058

Table 7-7 The Top Fifteen General Strategy Consultants in the 1992 Congressional Races

			Payments from		
Rank	Company	Location	Candidate	National Party	Total
1	Arthur J. Finkelstein & Associates	New York, N.Y.	$340,281	$ 0	$340,281
2	Campaign Design Group	Washington, D.C.	182,715	39,686	222,401
3	Spencer-Roberts & Associates	Irvine, Calif.	212,498	0	212,498
4	Eddie Mahe, Jr. & Associates	Washington, D.C.	192,136	0	192,136
5	Maxwell & Associates	Alexandria, Va.	165,079	5,000	170,079
6	Joseph Gaylord & Co.	Washington, D.C.	146,999	0	146,999
7	Tony Payton & Associates	Arlington, Va.	139,331	0	139,331
8	Carlyle Gregory Co.	Falls Church, Va.	120,841	0	120,841
9	Richard Morris	West Redding, Conn.	110,333	0	110,333
10	Ridder/Braden	Denver, Colo.	101,333	6,841	108,174
11	Randy Hinaman	Alexandria, Va.	100,154	0	100,154
12	The Brier Group	Harrisburg, Pa.	93,043	0	93,043
13	Fabrizio, McLaughlin & Associates	Alexandria, Va.	88,441	0	88,441
14	Huckaby, Rodriguez	Sacramento, Calif.	85,746	0	85,746
15	Doyce Boesch	Washington, D.C.	85,380	0	85,380

Table 7-8 The Top Fifteen Campaign Get-Out-the-Vote Consultants in the 1992 Congressional Races

			Payments from		
Rank	Company	Location	Candidate	National Party	Total
1	The Tyson Organization	Fort Worth, Texas	$567,098	$ 0	$567,098
2	Campaign Telecommunications	New York, N.Y.	441,077	94,807	535,884
3	Telemark	Wilsonville, Ore.	492,459	0	492,459
4	Payco American Corp.	Brookfield, Wis.	330,736	9,953	340,689
5	Timbes & Yeager	Mobile, Ala.	293,693	0	293,693
6	Optima Direct	Washington, D.C.	105,741	187,483	293,224
7	Campaign Tele-Resources	Omaha, Neb.	262,966	0	262,966
8	Mason Lundberg & Associates	Orange, Calif.	248,760	0	248,760
9	Cherry Communications	Gainesville, Fla.	158,047	5,000	163,047
10	Gordon & Schwenkmeyer	El Segundo, Calif.	111,157	2,500	113,657
11	Campaign Strategies	San Antonio, Texas	106,268	0	106,268
12	Parker Group	Birmingham, Ala.	101,071	0	101,071
13	Telemark America	London, Ky.	63,333	34,077	97,410
14	Matrixx Marketing	Ogden, Utah	88,494	0	88,494
15	Precision Marketing	Easton, Pa.	86,954	0	86,954

Olver and Bob Filner (D-Calif.), who paid $43,977 and $32,229, respectively.

Payco American Corp. of Brookfield, Wis., collected $340,689 for its phonebanking efforts on behalf of a dozen Republican candidates, including Robert F. Bennett (Utah), who won an open Senate seat.

Shelby was Timbes & Yeager's sole phonebanking client, but the Mobile, Ala., firm collected $293,693 for helping to place 250,000 calls on his behalf prior to the primary.

HOUSE CANDIDATES AND CONSULTANTS: A HOST OF APPROACHES

During the 1992 cycle, Huffington led all House candidates in spending on consultants, pumping $3,054,032 of his record-breaking $5,434,569 campaign through his advisers (see Table 7-9). He paid Ringe Media of Purcellville, Va., $546,197 for creating his broadcast advertising. Crest Films of New York collected $280,501 for production work. Specialized Media Services of Charlotte, N.C., billed Huffington $1,089,540 to cover the cost of air time and the firm's advertising placement fees. Target Enterprises collected $151,648 for purchasing additional air time.

To drive his advertising campaign and monitor the mood of the electorate, Huffington employed a bevy of research firms. Hill Research Consultants of Woodlands, Texas, received $186,742 for polling and demographic research. Benchmark Research Group of Sacramento, Calif., collected $31,230 for polling and research. Huffington paid Moore Information of Portland, Ore., and Market Strategies of Southfield, Mich., $23,090 and $19,399, respectively, for still more polls and strategic advice. Competitive Edge Research of San Diego, Calif., billed the campaign $10,196 for providing opposition research.

Huffington paid McNally, Temple $321,012 for producing advocacy mailers and working to turn out the vote. The Michael D. Meyers Co. of Kirkland, Wash., received $10,550 for consultations on the persuasion mailers. Mason Lundberg & Associates of Orange, Calif., collected $235,404 for phonebanking, and Sandy Bodner Consulting of Marina Del Rey, Calif., received $22,282 for coordinating public relations efforts. For providing general strategic advice, consulting on the advocacy mailers, and buying air time, Huckaby Rodriguez of Sacramento received $126,241. With the exception of the $3,065,439 Gephardt spent on his reelection effort, Huffington's massive payments to his consultants amounted to more than any other House candidate spent on his or her entire campaign.

Gephardt placed a distant second to Huffington in spending on consultants, paying eleven advisers a total of $1,342,737. Doak, Shrum & Associates of Washington, D.C., received $97,632 for creating his television and radio commercials. The Media Company, also of Washington, collected $703,217 for placing the spots.

Unlike Huffington, who simply wrote personal checks whenever his campaign needed money, Gephardt had to raise the money he needed. In addition to a permanent fund-raising staff of eight who worked out of his Washington, D.C., campaign office, Gephardt paid three event planners a total of $27,792 for organizing events in Washington, Los Angeles, and New York. Malchow & Co. of Washington, D.C., and Gold Communications received $27,081 and $17,230, respectively, for their direct-mail fund-raising efforts.

Gephardt paid Gold Communications and The November Group $140,099 and $16,946, respectively, for creating advocacy mailers. Two was also the magic number for pollsters, with KRC Research of New York collecting $128,924 and Mellman & Lazarus receiving $78,821. Telephone Contact of St. Louis, Mo., collected $104,996 for phonebanking and mailing out follow-up materials to potential supporters.

Other House candidates who funneled at least $1 million through their consultants were Dick Chrysler (R-Mich.), $1,294,249; Dornan, $1,142,072; and Fazio, $1,090,711. Forty-six House candidates spent more than $500,000 through their consultants.

Spurred on by fears over redistricting or their constituents' anti-incumbent leanings, a sizable number of House incumbents dramatically increased their reliance on expert advice. Rep. William J. Hughes (D-N.J.) had not found it necessary to hire a media consultant in any of his previous nine campaigns, preferring instead to develop his ads in-house. For his 1990 reelection effort, Hughes had simply recycled spots from his 1988 campaign. "For eighteen years he ran a mom-and-pop operation," noted administrative assistant Mark H. Brown. However, faced with a well-funded Republican challenger and concerned with the widespread anger over tax increases pushed through by Democratic Gov. James J. Florio, Hughes paid the Campaign Group of Philadelphia, Pa., $210,030 for creating and placing four television commercials in 1992.

In addition to handing Rep. Richard J. Durbin (D-Ill.) a host of new constituents and a well-funded Republican challenger, redistricting placed him in a new media market. "Seventy percent of our district is now in the St. Louis market, and that means it's four times as expensive to advertise as before," lamented district staff director Michael E. Daly. While Durbin had not hired a media consultant in 1990 and had spent just $10,690 on broadcast ads, his new political reality forced him to invest $378,052 in such ads during 1992. Shorr Associates of Philadelphia, Pa., collected $340,265 for designing and placing ten television and radio commercials. Durbin spent nothing on persuasion mail in 1990, but in 1992 he invested $150,907 in brochures and advocacy mailers, $83,509 of which went to Campaign Performance. Durbin spent nothing on polls in 1990, but to help formulate his message and strategy in 1992 he invested $43,500 in surveys conducted by Garin-Hart. Fraioli/Jost received $29,521 for coordinating Durbin's Washington events—$10,621 more than he spent on fund-raising consultants in 1990. In all, Durbin increased his expenditures on consultants by $477,895—twenty-six times his 1990 outlay.

Redistricting drastically altered the campaign style of Rep. George "Buddy" Darden (D-Ga.) for his rematch with Republican Al Beverly. In the new District 7, Republicans pulled from Gingrich's old district had replaced those from Cobb County,

Table 7-9 The Top Fifty House Candidates' Spending on Consultants

Rank	Candidate	Candidate	National Party	Total
1	Michael Huffington,[a] R-Calif.	$3,054,032	$ 0	$3,054,032
2	Richard A. Gephardt, D-Mo.	1,342,737	137	1,342,875
3	Dick Chrysler,[a] R-Mich.	1,294,249	6,501	1,300,750
4	Robert K. Dornan, R-Calif.	1,142,072	0	1,142,072
5	Vic Fazio, D-Calif.	1,090,711	275	1,090,986
6	Gerry E. Studds, D-Mass.	892,042	15,137	907,180
7	John W. Olver,[a] D-Mass.	867,821	5,137	872,958
8	Jane Harman,[a] D-Calif.	865,330	0	865,330
9	E. Clay Shaw, Jr., R-Fla.	804,750	0	804,750
10	Linda Bean,[a] R-Maine	789,905	0	789,905
11	Michael A. Andrews, D-Texas	787,570	137	787,708
12	Bob Carr, D-Mich.	764,377	3,912	768,289
13	Lynn Schenk,[a] D-Calif.	767,675	0	767,675
14	Steny H. Hoyer, D-Md.	762,836	137	762,973
15	Terry Everett,[a] R-Ala.	749,890	0	749,890
16	Martin T. Meehan,[a] D-Mass.	727,531	10,000	737,531
17	Newt Gingrich, R-Ga.	683,437	44,880	728,317
18	Steve A. Orlins,[a] D-N.Y.	724,571	0	724,571
19	Thomas J. Downey, D-N.Y.	722,893	137	723,031
20	Peter H. Kostmayer, D-Pa.	698,460	20,137	718,598
21	Ben Erdreich, D-Ala.	697,212	10,137	707,350
22	Mike Synar, D-Okla.	700,758	137	700,896
23	Gerry Sikorski, D-Minn.	688,224	10,137	698,362
24	David E. Bonior, D-Mich.	694,254	137	694,391
25	Herbert C. Klein,[a] D-N.J.	682,903	0	682,903
26	Tom McMillen, D-Md.	656,478	17,637	674,115
27	Martin Frost, D-Texas	663,530	137	663,668
28	Charles Wilson, D-Texas	635,617	17,137	652,754
29	Ron Marlenee, R-Mont.	626,384	25,024	651,408
30	Les Aspin, D-Wis.	644,099	5,137	649,237
31	Richard Ray, D-Ga.	614,697	15,274	629,971
32	Pat Williams, D-Mont.	607,065	22,448	629,513
33	Dan Glickman, D-Kan.	610,101	5,137	615,239
34	Don Ritter, R-Pa.	613,053	0	613,053
35	Sander M. Levin, D-Mich.	590,148	16,176	606,324
36	Robert E. Andrews, D-N.J.	579,277	9,216	588,494
37	Jim Bacchus, D-Fla.	565,273	137	565,411
38	Jim Bunning, R-Ky.	545,633	17,804	563,437
39	Rosa DeLauro, D-Conn.	556,969	5,137	562,107
40	Dan Rostenkowski, D-Ill.	546,451	11,873	558,324
41	Richard H. Lehman, D-Calif.	525,411	25,137	550,548
42	Bob Filner,[a] D-Calif.	546,316	0	546,316
43	Jerry Huckaby, D-La.	518,919	20,537	539,456
44	Mark Neumann,[a] R-Wis.	537,903	0	537,903
45	Harold Rogers, R-Ky.	503,583	34,077	537,660
46	Jim Nussle, R-Iowa	470,133	54,975	525,108
47	Leslie L. Byrne,[a] D-Va.	506,975	15,000	521,975
48	Richard J. Durbin, D-Ill.	496,795	11,873	508,669
49	James C. Greenwood,[a] R-Pa.	465,904	35,771	501,675
50	Mary Rose Oakar, D-Ohio	498,882	137	499,020

[a] Nonincumbent or special election candidate.

who had become accustomed to voting for Darden. As a result, he drastically increased his communication budget for the 1992 race; along with that went a similar increase in his consultant budget. In 1990 Darden had paid the FMR Group of Washington, D.C., $9,425 to create his broadcast ads. For producing and placing his commercials in 1992, McKinnon Media of Austin, Texas, collected $143,850. Advocacy mailings had been produced in-house for the 1990 campaign, but in 1992 Darden paid Gold Communications $29,250. Kitchens, Powell & Kitchens of Orlando, Fla., received $18,100 for conducting the 1992 campaign's polls; no polls were done in 1990.

Pennsylvania's redistricting plan dealt Republican Rep. Robert S. Walker a constituency that was 50 percent new to him, and that translated into a $30,626 increase over 1990 in expenditures for advertising and persuasion mail. Faced with a 1990 opponent who spent less than $5,000, Walker had chosen not to hire a media consultant. Redistricting, not the $10,488 spent by his 1992 challenger, led Walker to hire Brabender Cox of Pittsburgh, Pa. The firm designed and placed Walker's broadcast and newspaper advertising and handled his advocacy mailings, for a fee of $58,226. Walker paid Maxwell & Associates $3,498, and, in turn, the event planners helped him collect about one-third more from political action committees than he had in 1990, when he hired no fund-raising consultants.

Not everyone spent more on consultants in 1992. For example, Rep. Tim Johnson (D-S.D.) faced a 1992 challenger who had $60,992 less to spend than his 1990 opponent, so Johnson cut his spending by $89,123. Johnson slashed his spending on broadcast advertising from $204,852 in 1990 to $111,969 in 1992 by almost entirely cutting out consultants. While Struble-Totten Communications of Washington, D.C., had collected $20,000 for creating his 1990 broadcast ads, his 1992 spots were created in-house and produced at the DCCC's Harriman Communications Center. The Media Group of Columbus, Ohio, and Struble-Totten received $1,078 and $877, respectively, for miscellaneous production costs. Johnson's campaign placed its ads directly rather than turn that chore over to a consultant, thereby reducing expenditures on air time to $107,675 from $150,000. "It was a matter of cost effectiveness," explained John Y. Deveraux, Johnson's deputy chief of staff. "In a highly competitive race where you want to be sure each ad is correctly placed to get the most for your money, we would hire a consultant."

In 1990 Rep. H. James Saxton (R-N.J.) spent $454,178, or 62 percent of his budget, on consultants. The Media Team of Alexandria, Va., and Ailes Communications of New York designed and produced Saxton's broadcast media, receiving $42,179 and $5,000, respectively. Farrell Media of New York bought most of the air time for $295,274. Advanced Communications in Richmond, Va., handled phonebanking for $35,049. Pollster Tarrance & Associates of Houston, Texas, collected $21,250. Public Sector in Florence, N.J., collected $4,000 for providing general strategic advice. To help him raise money through the mail, Saxton paid Direct Mail Specialists of Ocean Springs, Miss., $48,626. Gurney Sloan of Washington, D.C., received $2,800 for planning fund-raising events.

Facing a 1992 opponent whose budget was roughly one-seventh of his 1990 challenger's, Saxton sliced his spending on consultants to just $66,128—a 587 percent reduction. The Media Team was called on once again, but this time they received just $23,735 for consulting and design work. National Media of Alexandria, Va., collected only $5,057 to place the ads. Tarrance conducted the campaign's polls, but their cost was reduced to $9,950. Direct Mail Specialists and Sloan helped with fund raising, receiving $21,034 and $3,150, respectively.

While some House candidates invested their resources with nationally known consultants, others turned to former staff members who had left government service to form their own consulting firms. Rep. Greg Laughlin (D-Texas) funneled more than one-third of the $449,063 he spent on his 1992 campaign through Maverick Communications of Austin, Texas, a firm founded in 1989 by Laughlin's former congressional district director, Ken Bryan. Bryan collected $153,225 for creating and placing Laughlin's radio and television commercials, designing and placing newspaper advertising, managing a large phonebanking operation, conducting polls, and handling direct-mail fund-raising solicitations. Included in Bryan's remuneration was a postelection "winner's bonus" of $25,000.

The largest single expense listed by Rep. Thomas M. Foglietta (D-Pa.) under "actual campaigning" was a $20,000 lump-sum payment for "consulting" to Bob Barnett, his former chief-of-staff, on December 29, 1992. Barnett also received a $10,000 contribution from Foglietta in December 1991 for his unsuccessful bid for a seat on the Philadelphia City Council.

Mark Fierro, press secretary for Rep. James Bilbray (D-Nev.) until April 1992, collected $14,000 from his former boss's campaign for helping to create five television and three radio commercials. Fierro, like Barnett and Bryan, worked for no other congressional candidates during the 1992 election cycle.

However, all three are undoubtedly hoping to follow in the footsteps of Dolly Angle, former administrative assistant for Frost. Angle gave up her government job in 1991 to found Dolly Angle & Associates of Arlington, Texas, a fund-raising firm that earned $11,110 from Frost, $31,112 from Rep. Gene Green (D-Texas), and $50,242 from Rep. Chet Edwards (D-Texas) during the 1992 cycle.

Some members allowed their employees to launch consulting businesses while still on the government payroll. Freshman Rep. John T. Doolittle (R-Calif.) paid $48,774, or 67 percent of his fund-raising event costs, to Event Planners of Roseville, Calif. The firm is owned by Doolittle's congressional staff director, David G. Lopez, and Lopez's wife, although Lopez said he had no formal connection to the 1992 campaign.

Rep. James L. Oberstar (D-Minn.) paid Jim Berard Media Services of Washington, D.C., $77,058 to place broadcast ads, $11,030 to place newspaper ads, and $2,664 for coordinating press access to Oberstar during the 1992 Democratic National Convention. James A. Berard was also Oberstar's congressional communications director.

Some House members decided they could do very well without consultants. Rep. C. W. Bill Young (R-Fla.) increased his spending from $194,043 in 1990 to $458,366 in 1992. His spending on advertising and advocacy mailings rose by $307,397, but

Table 7-10 The Top Fifty Senate Candidates' Spending on Consultants

Rank	Candidate	Candidate	National Party	Total
1	Alfonse M. D'Amato, R-N.Y.	$6,762,965	$1,512,543	$8,275,508
2	Barbara Boxer,[a] D-Calif.	5,962,551	1,506,570	7,469,121
3	Dianne Feinstein,[a] D-Calif.	5,638,512	1,250,920	6,889,432
4	Arlen Specter, R-Pa.	5,700,962	980,540	6,681,502
5	Bruce Herschensohn,[a] R-Calif.	3,973,523	2,454,644	6,428,167
6	John Seymour, R-Calif.	3,896,617	2,449,955	6,346,572
7	Robert Abrams,[a] D-N.Y.	4,760,288	1,500,316	6,260,603
8	Lynn Yeakel,[a] D-Pa.	3,455,023	811,371	4,266,394
9	Wyche Fowler, Jr., D-Ga.	3,591,642	513,431	4,105,073
10	Dick Thornburgh,[a] R-Pa.	3,112,805	950,999	4,063,804
11	Bob Packwood, R-Ore.	3,739,763	29,000	3,768,763
12	John Glenn, D-Ohio	2,974,030	622,240	3,596,270
13	Bob Kasten, R-Wis.	3,101,893	402,589	3,504,483
14	Christopher S. Bond, R-Mo.	3,140,117	337,695	3,477,812
15	Harris Wofford,[a] D-Pa.	2,392,471	948,000	3,340,471
16	Mike DeWine,[a] R-Ohio	2,358,127	892,000	3,250,127
17	Daniel R. Coats, R-Ind.	2,482,915	452,415	2,935,330
18	Lauch Faircloth,[a] R-N.C.	2,234,583	560,928	2,795,510
19	Paul Coverdell,[a] R-Ga.	1,529,979	984,487	2,514,466
20	Carol Moseley-Braun,[a] D-Ill.	2,007,207	404,323	2,411,529
21	Christopher J. Dodd, D-Conn.	2,213,242	163,340	2,376,582
22	Terry Sanford, D-N.C.	1,787,468	532,000	2,319,468
23	Ernest F. Hollings, D-S.C.	2,150,614	111,396	2,262,011
24	Robert F. Bennett,[a] R-Utah	2,065,242	124,621	2,189,863
25	Don Nickles, R-Okla.	1,960,370	179,010	2,139,380
26	Richard Williamson,[a] R-Ill.	1,130,894	944,052	2,074,945
27	Rod Chandler,[a] R-Wash.	1,629,146	407,838	2,036,983
28	Richard C. Shelby, D-Ala.	1,879,184	85,282	1,964,466
29	Bob Graham, D-Fla.	1,931,007	0	1,931,007
30	Barbara A. Mikulski, D-Md.	1,912,394	10,714	1,923,108
31	John McCain, R-Ariz.	1,731,636	173,104	1,904,740
32	Brook Johnson,[a] R-Conn.	1,541,924	279,182	1,821,106
33	Les AuCoin,[a] D-Ore.	1,484,550	235,208	1,719,757
34	Terry Considine,[a] R-Colo.	1,359,597	275,082	1,634,678
35	Harry Reid, D-Nev.	1,513,837	108,805	1,622,642
36	Russell Feingold,[a] D-Wis.	1,188,623	336,910	1,525,533
37	Joseph H. Hogsett,[a] D-Ind.	1,294,454	194,800	1,489,254
38	Tom Daschle, D-S.D.	1,327,189	0	1,327,189
39	Ben Nighthorse Campbell,[a] D-Colo.	1,062,318	243,545	1,305,862
40	Daniel K. Inouye, D-Hawaii	1,243,202	0	1,243,202
41	Wendell H. Ford, D-Ky.	1,201,067	0	1,201,067
42	Geri Rothman-Serot,[a] D-Mo.	880,369	293,908	1,174,277
43	Kent Conrad, D-N.D.	1,112,509	55,812	1,168,321
44	Charles E. Grassley, R-Iowa	916,280	227,093	1,143,373
45	Patty Murray,[a] D-Wash.	751,596	373,730	1,125,326
46	Dale Bumpers, D-Ark.	1,111,170	0	1,111,170
47	Dirk Kempthorn,[a] R-Idaho	896,385	109,535	1,005,919
48	Frank H. Murkowski, R-Alaska	873,792	110,480	984,272
49	John B. Breaux, D-La.	925,749	8,872	934,621
50	Wayne Owens,[a] D-Utah	782,344	110,000	892,344

[a] Nonincumbent or special election candidate.

none of that increased spending went to consultants. Young personally wrote all his voter contact mail, television and radio commercials, and newspaper ad copy. The campaign bought the air time and placed the newspaper ads directly, leaving only the production to be done by others. As administrative assistant Douglas M. Gregory put it, Young believes that "after being in politics for thirty-two years, if he doesn't know what his constituents want, then how will some consultant know."

Rep. Earl Hutto (D-Fla.) felt the same way. While he looked to Frederick/Schneiders of Washington, D.C., for polling, Hutto, a former sportscaster and advertising agency executive, preferred to write and produce all his ads. "It saves money, and with the small amount I raise, I try to guard my funds," noted Hutto in explaining the paucity of outside advisers.

Outspent by nearly five to one in his primary contest with Rep. Terry L. Bruce (D-Ill.), Rep. Glenn Poshard maximized his $150,000 budget by creating his own commercials. "He's his own campaign manager, strategist, and creative designer," noted press secretary David D. Stricklin. Poshard emerged with 62 percent of the primary vote.

In an effort to reach younger, newly registered voters, Walter R. Tucker III (D-Calif.) wrote and produced his own campaign song with a decidedly upbeat tempo. "He's very artsy," said administrative assistant Marcus S. Mason. In addition to giving away cassette tapes of the tune, Tucker edited it into a sixty-second commercial that aired on two rhythm and blues stations. Tucker also developed what Mason described as "a more traditional commercial" that ran on CNN and Black Entertainment Television.

In 1989 Rep. Craig Washington (D-Texas) had spent more than $600,000 to win a special election, and he swore he would never let his spending reach that level again. "This job isn't worth $600,000," he proclaimed. In that spirit, Washington continued his practice of using consultants sparingly in 1992. Campaign Strategies of Houston, his only paid consultant, received $13,424 for designing a small persuasion mail effort. "I decide my own methods, come up with my own slogans," he explained. "I want to get me across, not some image of me."

SENATE CAMPAIGNS: CONSULTANTS BY THE DOZENS

Virtually every Senate campaign was a consultant's dream come true, but the battle between D'Amato and Abrams proved to be the most lucrative of all. D'Amato pumped $6,762,965 through his consultants, which accounted for 57 percent of his total spending. The NRSC added $1,512,543 (see Table 7-10). Russo, Marsh & Associates of Sacramento, Calif., billed D'Amato $754,230 for creating his broadcast ads. Multi Media Services collected $4,982,589 from D'Amato and $1,507,718 from the NRSC for placing the ads. D'Amato paid Finkelstein $621,489 for polling and general strategic advice; the NRSC paid Finkelstein $4,825. For their organizational efforts, James E. Murphy of Gaithersburg, Md., and Serphin Maltese of New York received $24,884 and $23,000, respectively. Bernstein & Associates of Arlington, Va., handled opposition research for $30,275. To pay for his campaign, D'Amato relied heavily on Barbara Klein Associates of Washington, D.C., who collected $61,243 for helping him raise $1,361,231 from PACs. MWM of Washington, D.C., received $257,775 for direct-mail fund raising. He paid Anne Hyde Co. of Glendale, Calif., $2,500 for coordinating a fund-raising reception in Los Angeles and American Telecom of Horsham, Pa., $4,980 for telemarketing.

Abrams paid fifteen consultants a total of $4,760,287, which represented 75 percent of his total outlays. The DSCC augmented those payments with checks totaling $1,500,316.

To win his caustic Democratic primary battle with 1984 vice presidential nominee Geraldine A. Ferraro, New York City Comptroller Elizabeth Holtzman, and black activist Al Sharpton, and wage an equally acrid general election campaign against D'Amato, Abrams invested 54 percent of his $6,374,304 budget in television and radio advertising. Struble-Totten Communications of Washington, D.C., collected $411,384 from Abrams and $55,000 from the DSCC for creating and producing broadcast ads. Jan Crawford Communications of Paris, Va., received $748,786 from Abrams and $1,370,000 from the DSCC for buying air time. Abrams paid Geto & De Milly $2,717,531, including $2,262,199 for creative input to the ad campaign and additional purchases of air time. Media Strategy Associates of New York billed Abrams $6,000.

Abrams sank $667,674 into his direct-mail fund-raising efforts, including payments of $359,814 to A. B. Data, $54,032 to Penn & Schoen Associates of New York, and $13,704 to Craver, Matthews, Smith & Co. of Falls Church, Va. For coordinating fund-raising receptions, Fundraising Management and Pamela Lippe of New York received $95,536 and $99,543, respectively. Telemarketers Great Lakes Communications of Milwaukee and Meyer Associates were paid $28,431 and $3,457, respectively.

In addition to orchestrating Abrams's first direct-mail fund-raising solicitations, Penn & Schoen collected $171,000 from Abrams and $45,000 from the DSCC for polling. Jeff Gillienkirk of New York provided opposition research for $20,261, and the DSCC paid the Research Group of Chicago, Ill., $30,316 for additional opposition research. Speech writer Michael Sheehan of Washington, D.C., and general campaign consultant Anita Burson of New York collected $13,252 and $17,557, respectively.

Together, the Abrams and D'Amato campaigns generated consultant billings of $14,536,111. As astounding as that total was, it was not all that much greater than the $13,897,288 spent by Boxer and Herschensohn.

For their work on her successful Senate bid, forty consultants billed Boxer's campaign, the DSCC and the DNC a total of $7,469,121. Seventeen consultants billed Herschensohn $3,973,523, while the NRSC kicked in $2,454,644 for additional media buys. In all, forty-three Senate candidates spent at least $1 million through consultants, including twenty-two who paid their advisers more than $2 million. When coordinated expenditures by the national party committees are included, forty-seven candidates generated billings in excess of $1 million, including twenty-seven whose consultants billed at least $2 million.

CHAPTER 8

Reform
The Broken Promise

In the 1992 election, the American public made a bold statement about gridlock and change in Washington. What the public got with this package does not meet the true test of reform.
*Rep. Mike Synar (D-Okla.), May 7, 1993, commenting on
President Clinton's campaign finance reform proposals*

Mr. Chairman, our charter was to provide real campaign reform, not a sham, not campaign deform, not a mockery, not an incumbent protection plan, not an embarrassment.
*Rep. Robert L. Livingston (R-La.), Nov. 22, 1993, during
House floor debate on the campaign finance reform bill*

In May 1992 President George Bush vetoed legislation that would have established, among other things, voluntary spending limits of $600,000 in House races and limits in Senate campaigns ranging from $950,000 to $8.9 million, depending on state population. Adherence to these limits would have entitled House candidates to a number of benefits, including the ability to tap public funds for as much as $200,000 in matching funds for contributions of less than $200. Among the rewards accorded to Senate candidates for agreeing to the limits were taxpayer-funded vouchers for up to 20 percent of their spending limit to purchase television air time.

Democratic presidential hopeful Bill Clinton's reaction to that veto was sure and swift. "Well, I think his actions speak louder than his words.... I hope they will take his veto, write another bill, make it even tougher, and send it right back to him." Candidate Clinton promised throughout the fall campaign to place campaign finance reform high on his agenda. Following his election, Clinton included such reform language in his legislative agenda for his first one hundred days in office, a document he dubbed "Putting People First."

Democratic congressional leaders seemed to agree. Appearing on the November 29 edition of *This Week with David Brinkley,* Senate Majority Leader George J. Mitchell (D-Maine) said, "I hope we're going to pass a [campaign finance reform] bill—we passed a good, strong, fair bill last year. It was unfortunately vetoed by President Bush. We're going to come back early this year, because I think we have to change the process, and ... restore public confidence." Despite Republican objections over public financing provisions, Democratic control of the House, Senate, and White House seemed to assure that reforms would be quickly forthcoming.

Eighteen months later, the House and Senate had succeeded in passing significantly different campaign finance reform bills but had not managed to name conferees to work out the differences. One major stumbling block to compromise was political action committee (PAC) contributions, which the Senate sought to ban and the House agreed grudgingly to restrict to $200,000.

Realizing that the proposed ban would probably not survive a constitutional test, the Senate stipulated that if the ban was struck down, PACs would be limited to contributing $1,000 per election cycle; individual campaigns would be barred from collecting PAC money in excess of 20 percent of the spending limit. Many in the House sought to leave the current $10,000 maximum PAC contribution in place.

The reason for this fundamental disagreement was simple. While the typical victorious Senate candidate in 1992 depended on PACs for only 27 percent of his or her receipts, 180 victors in House races collected 50 percent or more of their money from PACs. Nearly half—216 of the 435 elected on November 3—collected more than $200,000 from PACs, or one-third of the proposed House spending limit. Cutting their PAC receipts to $200,000 would be painful enough, but slicing them to $120,000 to conform with the Senate's 20 percent cap was more than most House members seemed willing to do.

On paper, if this impass over PAC contributions could be resolved, the two bills seem to provide the possibility for real reform, although in reality they provide little more than cosmetic changes. Take for example the notion—implied by some, explicitly stated by others—that one goal of reform is to "level the playing field" for incumbents and challengers. For obvious reasons, few incumbents are likely to look with favor upon that concept, just as most view term limits as an unnecessary check on the wisdom of the electorate.

The current House bill provides both incumbents and challengers with up to $200,000 in matching funds, delivered in the form of taxpayer-funded communication vouchers that could be used to pay for television or radio air time or for printing and postage. However, the bill declares that access to the vouchers does not kick in until a candidate has raised at least $60,000 in small contributions, including the first $200 of each larger contribution. The threshhold was explicitly intended to discourage challengers. As Rep. Sam Gejdenson (D-Conn.)—Democratic point-man on campaign finance reform in the House—explained to his House colleagues during the November 22, 1993, floor debate on the reform package, "The threshhold, estimated to around $66,000 in 1996, is high enough so that we are not arbitrarily creating viable challengers where there would be none." In 1992 at least 311 challengers did not raise enough to gain access to the full $200,000 in matching funds. There was no incumbent who would have had difficulty raising enough to collect the maximum had they chosen to do so, particularly if they had been weaned off PAC funds.

GETTING AROUND THE LIMITS

While most members of Congress say they want "reform," the definitions of that term differ so vastly that any meaningful reform is unlikely. One thing is clear, if the conference committee produced anything closely resembling the House version of the reform package, it would be spending reform in name only.

For instance, while the $600,000 spending limit has been widely touted, it is, in reality, more of a floor than a cap. If a candidate wins the primary by 20 points or less—a still very comfortable 60-to-40 percent spread in a two-way race and a virtual certainty in a multicandidate primary—that candidate's spending limit is automatically raised by $200,000. Then, if a runoff is required, the cap is raised by another $200,000. If the current House bill had been in effect during the 1992 campaign, and if all 859 House candidates had agreed to abide by the limit, only 159 would have had to change *anything* about their campaign spending.

The current House bill further excludes from the spending limit the costs of legal services and taxes, as well as an exemption of up to 10 percent of the cycle limit for overhead, fundraising, and accounting costs. Once the exemption for legal fees and taxes is taken into account, the number of candidates who would have had to alter their campaigns in 1992 drops to 150. Applying the 10 percent exemption for accounting and fundraising costs brings down to 121 the number of House candidates affected by the legislation. Of that number, 93 were incumbents, 11 were challengers, and 17 were open seat candidates. Ninety-five of the 121 emerged victorious, which means that at most only 22 percent of those elected would have had to change their spending patterns in any way.

The equation is further complicated by the implicit but erroneous assumption that all candidates would agree to the limits. Under the House bill, the spending limit would be lifted and federal matching funds retained if candidates who had chosen to comply with the limits found themselves faced with opponents who rejected the limits. In the Senate version, candidates not complying with the limits would be subject to a stiff tax on campaign receipts.

Would Republican Linda Bean (Maine) have agreed not to spend $1,228,962 of her own money—85 percent of her total expenditures—in her attempt to oust Democratic Rep. Thomas H. Andrews? Most assuredly not. The current House bill calls for federal matching funds in the form of communication vouchers to kick in only after a candidate raises at least $60,000 in contributions of $200 or less, including the first $200 of each larger contribution. Since Bean raised only $60,066 from small contributors, and $123,304 from donors who gave her $200 or more, the total value of her communication vouchers would have been well under $200,000. Given that she invested $921,195 on broadcast ads and persuasion mailers alone, spending less in order to get $200,000 worth of vouchers would not have made much sense.

If Bean had opted not to abide by the voluntary limits, the $782,034 Andrews spent to defend his seat would have been, and should have been, permissible under the House bill. However, because Andrews raised more than $200,000 from small contributors, he would have been eligible for the full $200,000 cash infusion from federal taxpayers, who in effect would have helped protect an incumbent from possible upset by a well-funded challenger.

Would Dick Chrysler (R-Mich.) have opted not to dip into his personal bank account for $1,585,108 of the $1,762,128 he spent on his bid to unseat Democratic Rep. Bob Carr? Without the ability to self-finance an $849,340 broadcast advertising campaign and a $384,838 advocacy mail effort, Chrysler probably would not have come within 2 points of retiring Carr. Had Chrysler decided not to abide by the limits, taxpayers would have subsidized Carr's $1,353,305 campaign with another $200,000 in communication vouchers, which would have substantially reduced the $499,886 spending advantage on broadcast advertising and persuasion mail enjoyed by Chrysler.

It is highly unlikely that Michael Huffington (R-Calif.) would have agreed not to spend the $3.5 million he invested in upsetting Rep. Robert J. Lagomarsino in the primary or the $1.9 million he spent to dispatch Democrat Gloria Ochoa in the general election. If not, then the $706,338 Ochoa spent trying to win the seat would have been perfectly legal, and she would have received the $200,000 federal matching funds to further help her balance the spending mismatch. Again, had the current House bill been law in 1992, the taxpayers—people who lived throughout the country and did not have a stake in the outcome or who opposed Ochoa's candidacy—would have found themselves paying part of the bill.

Rep. Mike Synar (D-Okla.) would have been granted the additional $200,000 spending quota by virtue of his 43-to-38 percent primary victory over Drew Edmondson. Since Oklahoma election law requires primary winners who do not receive a majority of the votes to face a runoff with the second-place finisher, Synar's limit would have then been boosted by another $200,000 for the runoff. When the National Rifle Association weighed in with its $226,088 independent campaign, Synar would have been allowed under the current House bill to spend a comparable amount in excess of his normal spending limit, effectively raising his spending limit to $1,226,088. Synar would not have had to make any adjustments to his $1,185,676 campaign in order to come in under the limits.

At most, in a year marked by the greatest House turnover in fifty years, less than one-quarter of all House members would have been affected by the proposed spending limits. Instead of trimming spending substantially, the taxpayer-funded communications vouchers—which the Congressional Budget Office estimated would cost $90 million the first year—would free up campaign funds to pay for a host of other items only tangentially related to campaigning.

Rep. George Miller (D-Calif.) spent $657,215 on his 1992 reelection effort, $206,713 of which was spent on advertising and persuasion mail. After the various exemptions are taken into account, Miller's spending was just below the $600,000 threshhold. Miller would have had to trim his PAC contributions by nearly $62,000, which presumably would have necessitated additional fund-raising expenditures in order to meet the matching funds requirement. Dave Scholl, his Republican opponent, managed to raise just $61,888 in individual contributions and lacked the requisite amount of small contributions to qualify for matching funds. Had Miller opted to take the matching grant he could easily have qualified for, the taxpayer in essence would have picked up the tab for his $109,229 in contributions to other candidates, party organizations, and various causes. The $200,000 public grant would also have covered his $17,037 constituent entertainment costs and much of the $115,184 he spent on overhead.

Similarly, Jerry F. Costello (D-Ill.) spent $603,886 during the 1992 cycle, leaving him well under the limit after the fund-raising and tax exemptions are factored in. He collected only $145,175 from PACs, requiring no change in behavior. His individual contributions qualified him for the federal matching funds, which he did not need. Whether or not it was considered part of the exempt expenses, Costello's $84,000 payment to his lawyer to ensure that his interests were well served during the redistricting fight effectively would have been covered by taxpayers, as would the $42,961 he simply gave away.

By subsidizing Rep. Pete Stark (D-Calif.) in his reelection effort, the taxpayer essentially would have been picking up the tab for the Cadillac Seville he drove at campaign expense. Taxpayers would have been given the chance to pay the $30,390 constituent entertainment tab Rep. Leon E. Panetta (D-Calif.) racked up, and pay for his stay at the Maui Prince Hotel in Maui, Hawaii, where he attended a conference that he did not feel the taxpayers should pay for out of his congressional office account. As the examples in Chapter 2 illustrate, the list of excesses potentially billed, at least in part, to the taxpayer through this system is virtually endless.

The Senate bill includes a new federal tax on campaign receipts equal to the highest corporate tax rate, 36 percent. Those agreeing to abide by the limit established for their state would be exempted from the tax; those opting not to abide by the limit would pay it, in effect paying at least a portion of the cost of providing communication vouchers. Exemptions from the limits include legal and accounting fees, taxes, and travel between the candidate's home state and Washington, D.C. Exempted travel would include trips taken by spouses and children.

Had the Senate version of the bill been in effect in 1992, twenty-seven candidates would have either had to trim their spending or opt not to abide by the spending limits. Sen. Alfonse M. D'Amato would have had to slash his spending in the nonexempt categories by $4,392,335 to bring his spending below New York's $6,720,498 limit. Had he decided to live within the limits, D'Amato might have had a much more difficult time justifying the $156,729 he spent on campaign cars and the $163,098 he spent on meals, including $35,252 at Gandel's Gourmet in Washington, D.C. Living within the limit would have put his campaign spending on par with that of New York Attorney General Robert Abrams, D'Amato's Democratic opponent.

The Senate limits would have effected both candidates in only five states. In Pennsylvania, Republican Sen. Arlen Specter would have had to decrease his outlays by $4,587,902 to meet Pennsylvania's $4,828,388 limit, while Democrat Lynn Yeakel would have been able to get by with a modest $109,227 reduction. Had Specter decided to adhere to those limits, in all likelihood the seat would have gone to Yeakel. Rep. Les AuCoin (D-Ore.) would have needed to cut his spending against Sen. Bob Packwood by less than $400,000 after all the exemptions were taken into account, including the independent campaign adjustment. In order to meet Oregon's $2,004,000 spending cap, Packwood would have needed to slash his outlays by more than $5 million. Paul Coverdell (R-Ga.) would have needed to drop his spending by less than $60,000; Democratic Sen. Wyche Fowler, Jr., would have needed to reduce his spending by $2.1 million to come in under Georgia's $3,069,043 limit. Both Sen. Terry Sanford (D-N.C.) and Republican Lauch Faircloth could have made adjustments of less than $200,000 and met the North Carolina's $3,164,650 cap. Sen. Christopher J. Dodd (D-Conn.) would have had to cut his budget by roughly half in order to comply with the state's $2,004,000 limit. Dodd's Republican opponent, Brook Johnson, would have had to slice about $380,000 from his outlays.

Had the limits been in effect for 1992, Rep. Barbara Boxer (D-Calif.) would have had to figure out a way to slice nearly $1.7 million from the $9,947,007 in nonexempt spending she put into her open Senate seat contest. While she might have still prevailed against Republican Bruce Herschensohn, it would have been a decidedly different campaign.

Nevertheless, while twenty-seven Senate candidates would have been affected, forty-seven would not have been. Among those who would not have needed to change anything about their campaign style were Sen. Bob Dole (R-Kan.), who could have asked taxpayers indirectly to help pay his $265,827 tab for chartered airplanes or his $49,765 bill for constituent entertainment.

While both the Senate and the House bills intend to restrict the flow of PAC money, both bills would also have at least one unintended consequence. Campaigns would be forced by the economics of fund raising to significantly reduce or abandon direct mail and telemarketing, which would reduce the number of small contributions flowing into campaigns.

By eliminating direct mail and telemarketing from his fund-raising mix, Packwood could have saved $2,871,538 over his six-year election cycle. While some of that cost would have been shifted to standard fund-raising receptions, which generally yield a far greater return on investment, that one decision would have gotten him more than half way to the $5 million reduction he would have needed to bring him under Oregon's spending limit. However, that move would have also radically changed his donor profile. Packwood would not have collected anything close to the $3,728,299 he received from contributors who gave less than $200.

Locked in a tight open Senate seat contest, Boxer could not have afforded to slash her $4.3 million broadcast advertising budget. However, she could have brought herself under California's 1992 cap by eliminating her $2,003,533 direct-mail effort and shifting a portion of the savings into additional high-donor receptions. If that had been required, Boxer never would have been able to collect the millions of dollars she raised in small contributions from women all across the country who were excited to help elect another female senator. Without that outreach to other women, Boxer might very well have lost her primary contest with Rep. Mel Levine, who raised millions from large donors. Of the $10,431,140 Boxer raised for her campaign, $4,453,685 came from supporters who gave less than $200.

Rep. Robert K. Dornan raised $1,188,786 from small donors, only $143,158 from contributors who gave $200 or more, and just $75,978 from PACs. He could afford to do what most reformers say they want—restrict the flow of special interest money into his campaign—because he operated a $1,121,604 direct-mail fund-raising program that reached out to small contributors who share his philosophy. Had the spending limits been in effect and had he chosen to abide by them, Dornan would have been allowed to spend $800,000 by virtue of his 20-point victory in the primary, but his $1,552,281 budget would have left him $752,281 over the limit. Dornan gave away only $1,000; he spent $3,432 on constituent entertainment, $39,920 on overhead, $310,566 on direct appeal for votes, and had $46,024 in unitemized expenses. Reducing all those outlays to zero would have still left him $351,339 over the limit. He could not possibly have brought himself under the spending cap without gutting the direct-mail program he built to raise his small donations.

Ironically, the reform packages as currently written would have the effect of pushing congressional candidates into the arms of the very people who were considered the root of political evil in the 1970s—"fat cat" individual contributors.

OUR PROPOSALS

If the bills currently winding their way through the legislative process are seriously flawed, and we strongly believe they are, what are the alternatives? We believe that the path to finding those alternatives begins with the realization that the proposals currently under discussion evolve from the false premise that television advertising rates are responsible for the rising cost of campaigning. In fact, even in a year when incumbents were supposedly running scared, when there was a record number of open seat contests, and when challengers had considerably more money to spend, television and radio advertising accounted for 27 percent of all spending in House races and 42 percent of spending in Senate contests. House incumbents allocated only 25 percent of their spending to broadcast advertising; Senate incumbents invested 40 percent of their money in such ads.

The reform attempts also evolve from the misconception promulgated by many reformers that public financing will *automatically* lead to less costly campaigns. However, our research found that incumbents spent $3,828,682 on constituent entertainment; $1,689,952 on campaign automobiles, many of them Cadillacs and Lincolns driven in Washington, D.C., not the incumbent's state or district; and $1,901,812 on meals that apparently had nothing to do with fund raising or constituent entertainment, many consumed at fancy restaurants in Washington, D.C., or in other countries. While incumbents spent a total of $95,626,044 on broadcast advertising, they also invested $78,467,605 in overhead, $54,660,343 in fund raising, and gave away $10,653,432. Most candidates would have been able to meet the loose spending limits without altering their behavior in any way and, in fact, would have been able to effectively tap the taxpayer for as much as one-third of their spending.

No reform that allows candidates to spend campaign money on luxury automobiles and other items that do little more than enhance their personal lifestyles can be called reform. Campaign spending should be limited to campaigns. If members of Congress are serious about campaign finance reform, then Rep. William L. Clay (D-Mo.) should not be able to tap his campaign to pay the $799 monthly lease and repair bills on a car he drives in Washington, D.C. He should be forbidden from using campaign money to buy season tickets to Washington Redskins games or pay for travel to New Jersey for meetings with the Board of Benedict College and with the United Negro College Fund. He most certainly should not be allowed to use campaign funds to pay for his $310 dues at the Robin Hood Swim Club in Silver Spring, Md. If he wants to attend the Congressional Black Caucus Weekend retreats, his campaign should not pick up the tab, nor should it pay for expenses incurred on trips to Jamaica, N.Y., for meetings of the Clay Scholarship Board and for a reception for former Rep. William H. Gray III.

If Congress is serious about reducing the cost of campaigns, as opposed to the cost of politics, then Rep. Barbara-Rose Collins (D-Mich.) should not be able to spend nearly $9,000 over two election cycles on clothes and image consultations. D'Amato should not be able to tap his campaign treasury for $156,729 to lease and maintain two luxury automobiles, one of which is used by the senator in Washington, D.C., not in New York. Nor should D'Amato be able to spend campaign funds to cover a $4,439 harvest day celebration of New York agricultural products to which senators and their staffs are invited. Rep. Henry A. Waxman (D-Calif.) should never again be permitted to spend $4,500 of his campaign treasury to help defray the cost of a trip that he and his wife take to Israel or any other foreign destination.

Under anything that would pass for real reform, Rep. Louis Stokes (D-Ohio) would not be allowed to spend $4,111 on a reception at the House restaurant for attendees of the National

Baptist Convention, nor would he be allowed to tap his campaign treasury to cover the cost of his family's accommodations at Walt Disney World Resorts, as he did in April 1992, or to cover the $3,199 bill at the Washington Hilton and Towers, where he and his family stayed during a Congressional Black Caucus annual weekend bash. Sen. Bob Graham (D-Fla.) would not be able to spend $3,905 of his campaign funds on Super Bowl tickets given to his friends, nor would he be allowed to spend $4,156 on gifts, including boxes of pecans and "Florida ties" handed out to fellow senators and employees of the congressional barbershop and shoe-shine stand. Challenger Allan L. Keyes (R-Md.) would not be permitted to pay himself an $8,500 monthly salary from campaign funds should he decide to run again, a practice that brought him a $49,614 income during his challenge to Democratic Sen. Barbara A. Mikulski. Real reform would forbid the lavish, lifestyle enhancing expenditures of Senate hopeful Carol Moseley-Braun, who dropped $22,445 of her campaign funds during the four-day Democratic National Convention in New York. True reform would provide for a careful review of D'Amato's $35,252 tab at Gandel's Gourmet and the 220 meals of $200 or less consumed by Sen. Daniel K. Inouye (D-Hawaii) in the Washington, D.C., metropolitan area.

Real reform would ban contributions such as the $85,198 Rep. Paul E. Gillmor (R-Ohio) funneled from his own campaign treasury into that of his wife Karen, who waged a successful campaign for the state senate. It would prohibit Inouye from tapping his campaign treasury for a $150,000 donation to the Hawaii Education Foundation, an organization he founded to provide scholarships to Hawaiian high school students. While it may be a worthy cause, Inouye's foundation has nothing to do with campaigning. The $94,319 television campaign spearheaded by Rep. David E. Bonior (D-Mich.) on behalf of a proposed ballot initiative to give middle income homeowners a $500 property tax cut also had nothing to do with the 1992 campaign. The initiative was sponsored by the Michigan Homeowners Tax Break Committee, which Bonior cochaired.

When members find themselves in need of a lawyer to defend them against ethical and criminal charges, they should not be able to tap their funds to pay for legal counsel. Such expenses certainly should not be included in the list of exemptions from any spending limits that are imposed. Eliminating these expenditures would do far more to reduce the cost of campaigns than any of the spending limits currently under discussion.

No reform will be useful unless the Federal Election Commission (FEC) is given the power to act. Its current six-member structure, which mandates that the commission have three Republican and three Democratic members, was from the beginning an invitation to failure. While Congress seems unlikely to create an agency that truly has watchdog authority over campaign practices, that is ultimately the only path to true reform.

Rather than cutting the FEC's budget, as both President Clinton and members of Congress have proposed, the agency's budget should be increased. As our examination of the FEC's record of enforcing the $25,000 spending limit demonstrates, no election law is worth anything if it is not enforced. At present, the FEC's budget does not allow them to pursue all the cases that we have routinely brought to their attention over the past four years.

Along with that increased budget, Congress should also give the FEC authority to conduct random audits of campaigns. The FEC should invest some of that larger budget in additional staff auditors. Following the 1992 campaign, FEC staff analysts identified forty-six campaigns that deserved an audit according to the agency's formula developed to score accounting problems. Citing insufficient staff, the FEC launched audits of only eight campaigns with the most egregious problems, including Moseley-Braun's.

Random audits might have discouraged some campaigns from spending money in questionable ways. A random audit of the 1989 and 1990 campaign books of Sen. Charles S. Robb (D-Va.) most certainly would have raised questions about purposefully misleading entries made by David K. McCloud, Robb's then-chief of staff.

In May 1992 McCloud plead guilty to authorizing the use of campaign funds to purchase an illegal audiotape of a conversation between Virginia Gov. Douglas Wilder and a supporter. The $2,375 bill from the law firm of Hofheimer, Nusbaum, McPhaul, and Samuels was originally rejected by the campaign because McCloud "could not pay the bill as submitted." The law firm then folded the charge into a $4,790 bill for "research services." McCloud also admitted to recording as fund-raising costs a $500 payment that was actually used to pay the travel expenses of an aide who went to Boston to meet with a woman who claimed she had had an affair with Robb while he was governor.

Random audits would also have uncovered that Rep. Carroll Hubbard, Jr. (D-Ky.) diverted $50,000 in campaign funds to personal use. This began in 1990 when he ordered his staffers not to report to the FEC campaign payments to him totaling $5,500. Such diversions were carried on throughout much of the 1992 cycle. He used the money to pay his home heating bills, school tuition for his daughter, credit card bills, and his ex-wife's cable television bills, among other things. He used his campaign assets as collateral to obtain a $15,000 personal loan, another violation of federal law. Hubbard routinely demanded that congressional staffers campaign for him and his current wife—who also sought a House seat in Kentucky—while on the government payroll. Hubbard's foibles accidentally came to light as a result of the investigation into the House banking scandal. In April 1994 Hubbard plead guilty to federal charges of conspiring to defraud the FEC, stealing government property, and obstructing justice.

The FEC should more carefully scrutinize those who routinely fail to itemize thousands of dollars in expenses (see Table 8-1). While it is possible that the campaign of Rep. Mary Rose Oakar (D-Ohio) spent $121,630 in two years on items that cost less than $200, the fact that this represented 10 percent of her total spending should raise questions. Rep. John P. Murtha (D-Pa.) should not have been permitted to list only the vendors on an $8,139 Visa bill without stating what he bought from each vendor or how much each item cost.

Table 8-1 The Top Fifteen Spenders in the 1992 Congressional Races: Unitemized Expenses

	House		Senate	
Rank	Candidate	Expenditures	Candidate	Expenditures
1	Mary Rose Oakar, D-Ohio	$121,630	Don Nickles, R-Okla.	$174,341
2	John D. Dingell, D-Mich.	107,792	Arlen Specter, R-Pa.	174,114
3	Ronald V. Dellums, D-Calif.	95,740	Charles E. Grassley, R-Iowa	119,203
4	Austin J. Murphy, D-Pa.	94,801	Tom Daschle, D-S.D.	102,447
5	Bud Shuster, R-Pa.	92,127	Bob Kasten, R-Wis.	99,948
6	William D. Ford, D-Mich.	91,875	Harry Reid, D-Nev.	92,586
7	Alan B. Mollohan, D-W.Va.	72,566	Barbara Boxer,[a] D-Calif.	79,570
8	Charles B. Rangel, D-N.Y.	70,686	Bob Packwood, R-Ore.	70,970
9	Harold Rogers, R-Ky.	68,397	Wyche Fowler, Jr., D-Ga.	68,846
10	Lynn Woolsey,[a] D-Calif.	64,455	Alfonse D'Amato, R-N.Y.	64,203
11	Bart Gordon, D-Tenn.	64,252	Carol Moseley-Braun,[a] D-Ill.	56,160
12	Jerry Huckaby, D-La.	63,170	Christopher S. Bond, R-Mo.	55,110
13	Mike Synar, D-Okla.	61,256	Steve Lewis,[a] D-Okla.	49,623
14	Joseph M. McDade, R-Pa.	59,468	Russell Feingold,[a] D-Wis.	47,728
15	Newt Gingrich, R-Ga.	58,682	John McCain, R-Ariz.	47,576

Note: Totals are for entire two-year House and six-year Senate cycles; both include special election expenditures.

[a] Nonincumbent or special election candidate.

Roughly 10 percent of the spending reported by Rep. John D. Dingell (D-Mich.) was either completely unitemized or so vaguely described that it was impossible to tell how the money was spent. Dingell chose not to itemize $67,801 in expenditures of less than $200. Reimbursements to individuals for "campaign expenses" amounted to $27,991, including $17,593 paid to Dingell. Payments for "petty cash" totaled $12,000. Entries such as "campaign materials" or "campaign expenses" or "reimbursement" fail to provide any information that conforms with the spirit of the existing law and should be banned from the candidates' reporting lexicon.

Reform is possible, and in a system increasing characterized by voter cynicism, it is absolutely crucial that *meaningful* reforms be instituted. If, as Synar put it, "the American public made a bold statement about gridlock and change in Washington" in 1992, then artful dodges in the name of reform will only serve to deepen the public's distrust of politicians and the government they represent.

Part II
The 1992 Senate Races

ALABAMA

Sen. Richard C. Shelby (D)

1992 Election Results

Richard C. Shelby (D) 1,022,698 (65%)
Richard Sellers (R) 522,015 (33%)

During the off-years, Sen. Richard C. Shelby's campaign was extremely low key, with no campaign office and no staff. Between Jan. 1, 1987 and Dec. 31, 1991 Shelby spent $403,512, two-thirds of which went for travel and fund raising.

However, when Chris McNair, a popular black commissioner from Jefferson County, announced he would challenge Shelby for the Democratic nomination, the incumbent quickly revved up his campaign engine. Within weeks, Shelby had hired campaign manager Palmer Hamilton and launched a multi-pronged voter contact effort.

Hamilton said the campaign telephoned 250,000 households to identify Shelby's supporters. Those that indicated they definitely would support Shelby, a group Hamilton estimated at between 40,000 and 50,000, received a postcard reminding them to vote. Supporters were also asked to post a yard sign. Hamilton said the campaign received 15,000 sign requests in three weeks through the phonebank operation alone. Days before the primary, the phonebank operation made one final round of calls to supporters.

Shelby paid five consultants a total of $458,698 for their work on this massive preprimary get-out-the-vote effort. The Tyson Organization of Dallas, Texas, received $191,196; Barbara Bryant of Gadsden, $22,500; John Teague & Associates of Montgomery, $10,000; and Booker & Booker of Birmingham, $3,000. Timbes & Yeager of Mobile received $275,000, roughly 84 percent of which was for phonebanking, according to partner Bill Yeager.

Shelby's advertising expenditures were heavily loaded into the primary campaign. For designing and placing the campaign's preprimary television ads, Squier/Eskew/Knapp/Ochs Communications of Washington, D.C., collected $779,275. According to Yeager, the remaining 16 percent of the $275,000 paid to his firm during the primary was invested in radio and newspaper ads.

Shelby captured 62 percent of the 480,976 Democratic primary votes. McNair, who spent only $103,398 on his entire campaign, received 28 percent. The general election campaign against Republican Richard Sellers was relatively uneventful. Media consultant Squier/Eskew was paid $432,217 by Shelby and another $83,000 by the Democratic Senatorial Campaign Committee, or about two-thirds of the amount the firm collected during the primary. The Tyson Organization, Barbara Bryant, and Timbes & Yeager collected only $800, $5,000, and $18,693, respectively, for the general election, in contrast to their extensive work during the primary campaign.

Shelby also donated $30,000 to the Alabama Democratic party for "party building and voter education."

Campaign Expenditures	Shelby Amount Spent	Shelby % of Total	Sellers Amount Spent	Sellers % of Total
Overhead				
Office furniture/supplies	$ 17,562	.67	$ 25,056	17.10
Rent/utilities	0		2,852	1.95
Salaries	71,924	2.73	1,195	.82
Taxes	84,918	3.22	0	
Bank/investment fees	5,142	.19	0	
Lawyers/accountants	0		0	
Telephone	2,888	.11	4,609	3.14
Campaign automobile	0		0	
Computers/office equipment	12,860	.49	175	.12
Travel	237,154	8.99	8,063	5.50
Food/meetings	500	.02	0	
Subtotal	**432,948**	**16.41**	**41,950**	**28.62**
Fund Raising				
Events	185,954	7.05	0	
Direct mail	6,646	.25	76,762	52.38
Telemarketing	0		0	
Subtotal	**192,600**	**7.30**	**76,762**	**52.38**
Polling	**66,300**	**2.51**	**0**	
Advertising				
Electronic media	1,212,935	45.98	14,339	9.78
Other media	25,205	.96	0	
Subtotal	**1,238,140**	**46.93**	**14,339**	**9.78**
Other Campaign Activity				
Persuasion mail/brochures	34,086	1.29	0	
Actual campaigning	621,698	23.57	2,590	1.77
Staff/volunteers	0		0	
Subtotal	**655,784**	**24.86**	**2,590**	**1.77**
Constituent Gifts/ Entertainment	**98**	**.00**	**0**	
Donations to				
Candidates from same state	2,650	.10	0	
Candidates from other states	0		0	
Civic organizations	242	.01	0	
Ideological groups	5,405	.20	0	
Political parties	40,055	1.52	0	
Subtotal	**48,352**	**1.83**	**0**	
Unitemized Expenses	**3,881**	**.15**	**10,915**	**7.45**
Total Campaign Expenses	**$ 2,638,104**		**$ 146,556**	
PAC Contributions	**$ 1,694,944**		**$ 0**	
Individual Contributions	1,724,740		28,680	
Total Receipts*	3,778,582		149,603	

Includes PAC and individual contributions as well as interest earned, party contributions, etc.

ALASKA

Sen. Frank H. Murkowski (R)

1992 Election Results

Frank H. Murkowski (R)	127,163	(53%)
Tony Smith (D)	92,065	(38%)
Mary E. Jordan † (I)	20,019	(8%)

Sen. Frank H. Murkowski knew he was in for a fight. In 1986, despite spending $1.5 million against an opponent who spent slightly more than $400,000, Murkowski had won reelection with only 54 percent of the vote. He was widely viewed as one of the most vulnerable incumbents in 1992.

Murkowski wasted no time, launching his television advertising campaign against attorney Tony Smith even before Smith had secured the Democratic nomination. According to Murkowski's campaign spokesman, Charles A. Kleeschulte, the campaign had produced forty-seven commercials by November. However, Kleeschulte added that "mercifully" only forty-three of the ads were ever aired.

While television and radio were the most effective ways to advertise in the so-called rail belt between Anchorage and Fairbanks, Murkowski also invested nearly $85,000 in newspaper ads. "Alaska's not like other states," noted Kleeschulte. "There are ten towns that have no commercial TV or radio stations, so you have to do newspapers in those areas."

The campaign did not spend much money on brochures and persuasion mail because "Alaskan's don't like mass mailings," Kleeschulte said. The campaign limited its persuasion mail to two tightly targeted pieces, one mailed to Alaskan natives and another sent to owners of small businesses.

To make certain the campaign got on track, Murkowski paid Eddie Mahe, Jr. & Associates of Washington, D.C., $60,802 for strategic advice. To ensure the campaign stayed on track, William McConkey, a general consultant from Tallahassee, Fla., was paid $87,506 to serve as the day-to-day campaign manager and to provide the creative force behind most of the television ads. Dittman Research Corp. of Anchorage conducted the campaign's polls.

In addition to McConkey, three consultants from Anchorage shared in the advertising largess. Pendleton Productions collected $222,073 for production services and for purchasing air time. Kirschbaum Corporate Marketing collected $240,085 from Murkowski's campaign and another $110,480 from the National Republican Senatorial Committee to purchase broadcast time. Jack Frost Productions was paid $107,831 for production and placement of the campaign's newspaper and radio ads.

Murkowski ranked fifteenth among incumbents for his spending on constituent gifts and entertainment. The campaign spent $7,158 on constituent meals, mostly for breakfasts at the Senate restaurant. Another $6,638 was spent on gifts, including $3,711 for cookbooks. Year-end holiday cards cost $7,925.

The campaign also paid for gifts and annual Christmas parties for his Washington Senate staffers. Total cost: $7,631.

Campaign Expenditures	Murkowski Amount Spent	Murkowski % of Total	Smith Amount Spent	Smith % of Total
Overhead				
Office furniture/supplies	$ 41,606	2.23	$ 12,506	1.30
Rent/utilities	31,076	1.67	31,282	3.24
Salaries	75,470	4.04	123,679	12.82
Taxes	14,109	.76	40,404	4.19
Bank/investment fees	2,720	.15	217	.02
Lawyers/accountants	38,575	2.07	6,805	.71
Telephone	23,227	1.24	28,445	2.95
Campaign automobile	15,627	.84	0	
Computers/office equipment	12,445	.67	12,992	1.35
Travel	211,085	11.31	55,222	5.72
Food/meetings	28,963	1.55	204	.02
Subtotal	**494,902**	**26.52**	**311,755**	**32.31**
Fund Raising				
Events	295,855	15.85	84,006	8.71
Direct mail	62,769	3.36	5,798	.60
Telemarketing	0		0	
Subtotal	**358,624**	**19.22**	**89,804**	**9.31**
Polling	**55,400**	**2.97**	**75,730**	**7.85**
Advertising				
Electronic media	566,192	30.34	316,169	32.77
Other media	84,735	4.54	12,019	1.25
Subtotal	**650,927**	**34.88**	**328,188**	**34.01**
Other Campaign Activity				
Persuasion mail/brochures	45,614	2.44	94,169	9.76
Actual campaigning	187,540	10.05	26,830	2.78
Staff/volunteers	7,631	.41	0	
Subtotal	**240,786**	**12.90**	**120,998**	**12.54**
Constituent Gifts/ Entertainment	**24,745**	**1.33**	**62**	**.01**
Donations to				
Candidates from same state	3,700	.20	0	
Candidates from other states	9,500	.51	0	
Civic organizations	4,717	.25	0	
Ideological groups	1,920	.10	0	
Political parties	3,366	.18	150	.02
Subtotal	**23,203**	**1.24**	**150**	**.02**
Unitemized Expenses	**17,631**	**.94**	**38,156**	**3.95**
Total Campaign Expenses	**$ 1,866,217**		**$ 964,843**	
PAC Contributions	**$ 778,841**		**$ 246,996**	
Individual Contributions	**898,884**		**587,837**	
Total Receipts*	**1,872,991**		**913,975**	

*Includes PAC and individual contributions as well as interest earned, party contributions, etc.

†No expenditures or receipts on file. Candidates raising or spending less than $5,000 are not required to file reports with the Federal Election Commission.

ARIZONA

Sen. John McCain (R)

1992 Election Results

John McCain (R)	771,395	(56%)
Claire Sargent (D)	436,321	(32%)
Evan Mecham (I)	145,361	(11%)

Facing Democrat Claire Sargent, who declared that "it's time we start electing some senators with breasts; we've had boobs long enough," Sen. John McCain discovered firsthand what the Year of the Woman was all about. "Our spending decisions, particularly on TV, were directly influenced by the fact that our opponent was a woman," said Wes Gullett, McCain's campaign manager.

Armed with polling data indicating that McCain's support was relatively weak among pro-choice Republican women, Smith & Harroff of Alexandria, Va., developed a series of television commercials designed to strengthen his standing among that group. They produced ads on the environment, health care, senior citizens, as well as a conservative economic spot. "The message we tried to get out was that even though McCain is pro-life, he's a good guy, and that there were other issues besides abortion to consider," said Gullett.

McCain spent nearly 40 percent of his funds to raise money; the average incumbent invested just under 21 percent. Only three incumbents spent more than McCain's $875,769 on direct mail. The $600,321 he spent on fund-raising events placed him seventh among incumbents.

McCain's largest fund-raiser, a tribute to former Arizona senator Barry Goldwater, turned out to be as much a Republican celebration as a fund-raiser. The event, which featured President George Bush, Labor Secretary Lynn Martin, and Housing and Urban Development Secretary Jack Kemp, drew more than 1,500 people to the Phoenix Civic Center. Yet, while political action committees paid $5,000 a table and individual contributors anted up between $250 and $1,000 each, Gullett said the high cost of staging the evening meant a lower payoff than he had hoped for.

The campaign paid PM Consulting Corp. of Washington, D.C., $14,270 to produce a video tribute to Goldwater. Rental and set-up of the civic center cost the campaign $41,000, catering cost $53,000, and the invitations and programs ran another $12,000. Since President Bush was already in the state for another purpose, his travel cost the campaign only $5,800. Total cost of the fund-raiser: more than $126,000.

About $1,723,000 of McCain's spending was funneled through consultants, including $1,061,984 paid to Smith & Harroff for developing and placing the campaign's eight television and four radio commercials, consultation on the campaign's persuasion mail campaign, and general strategic advice. Response Dynamics of Vienna, Va., received $295,837 for its work on direct-mail fund raising.

Outspent by more than twelve to one, Sargent was simply overwhelmed.

	McCain		Sargent	
Campaign Expenditures	Amount Spent	% of Total	Amount Spent	% of Total
Overhead				
Office furniture/supplies	$ 71,138	1.90	$ 12,826	4.26
Rent/utilities	59,171	1.58	13,698	4.55
Salaries	193,023	5.16	65,078	21.59
Taxes	73,237	1.96	947	.31
Bank/investment fees	2,307	.06	233	.08
Lawyers/accountants	80,094	2.15	3,722	1.23
Telephone	39,026	1.04	16,289	5.41
Campaign automobile	0		0	
Computers/office equipment	72,278	1.93	4,437	1.47
Travel	126,023	3.37	5,174	1.72
Food/meetings	7,401	.20	0	
Subtotal	723,698	19.35	122,404	40.62
Fund Raising				
Events	600,321	16.05	8,465	2.81
Direct mail	875,769	23.41	534	.18
Telemarketing	0		0	
Subtotal	1,476,090	39.46	8,999	2.99
Polling	92,065	2.46	0	
Advertising				
Electronic media	980,103	26.20	62,765	20.83
Other media	12,024	.32	22,493	7.46
Subtotal	992,127	26.52	85,258	28.29
Other Campaign Activity				
Persuasion mail/brochures	154,037	4.12	42,564	14.12
Actual campaigning	161,463	4.32	27,755	9.21
Staff/volunteers	2,638	.07	102	.03
Subtotal	318,138	8.51	70,422	23.37
Constituent Gifts/ Entertainment	14,875	.40	0	
Donations to				
Candidates from same state	1,000	.03	0	
Candidates from other states	1,000	.03	0	
Civic organizations	11,608	.31	0	
Ideological groups	5,250	.14	0	
Political parties	57,051	1.53	0	
Subtotal	75,909	2.03	0	
Unitemized Expenses	47,576	1.27	14,279	4.74
Total Campaign Expenses	$ 3,740,479		$ 301,362	
PAC Contributions	$ 1,276,444		$ 40,770	
Individual Contributions	2,011,847		152,473	
Total Receipts*	3,623,397		288,413	

*Includes PAC and individual contributions as well as interest earned, party contributions, etc.

The 1992 Senate Races 107

ARKANSAS

Sen. Dale Bumpers (D)

1992 Election Results

Dale Bumpers (D)	553,635	(60%)
Mike Huckabee (R)	366,373	(40%)

From the outset, Sen. Dale Bumpers was the clear favorite, having garnered roughly 60 percent of the votes in his two previous reelection bids. On July 1, 1992, having spent $350,000 on the primary campaign, Bumpers had nearly $750,000 in the bank. His Republican opponent, Mike Huckabee, was a little-known Baptist minister with no political experience and a campaign treasury that totaled less than $16,000 on July 1.

Yet despite having to combat an incumbent who began the general election campaign with a cash advantage of nearly forty-seven to one, Huckabee refused to go quietly.

Huckabee paid his media consultants, Combs & Heathcott of Little Rock, $37,498 to produce a series of television ads attacking Bumpers for, among other things, his support of "pornographic art" funded by the National Endowment for the Arts, his vote for a congressional pay raise, and his opposition to a balanced budget amendment. Combs & Heathcott then collected $81,000 from the campaign and another $191,154 from the National Republican Senatorial Committee to buy air time in late September and October.

The Huckabee campaign never gathered momentum, however. News reports revealed that Huckabee's wife had been drawing a salary of $2,000 a month from the campaign for her services as assistant treasurer and that the campaign had paid $20,000 to a company Huckabee formed to produce his campaign ads. These expenditures, although ruled legal by the Federal Election Commission, provided Bumpers with ample whistle-stop ammunition.

Nevertheless, in a year when conventional wisdom had anti-incumbent sentiment running rampant, Bumpers left nothing to chance. Harrison & Goldberg of Cambridge, Mass., was paid $70,030 to conduct opinion polls for the campaign, and Attitude Research Corp. of St. Louis, Mo., received another $1,500 for their polling advice.

Bumpers paid media heavyweights Squier/Eskew/Knapp/Ochs Communications of Washington, D.C., $931,180 for consulting, production services, and purchasing radio and television air time. Combined expenditures on broadcast and print media accounted for 50 percent of Bumpers's spending during the six-year election cycle and 57 percent of his spending in 1992.

Bumpers's permanent campaign operation cost $247,103 through the first five years of the election cycle, accounting for 12 percent of his total spending over the six-year period. One notable expense was the rent paid for an apartment where Bumpers stayed whenever he was in Little Rock. By the end of 1992, the apartment rent cost the campaign $530 a month.

	Bumpers		Huckabee	
Campaign Expenditures	Amount Spent	% of Total	Amount Spent	% of Total
Overhead				
Office furniture/supplies	$ 55,626	2.78	$ 18,268	2.01
Rent/utilities	45,308	2.26	10,017	1.10
Salaries	137,497	6.87	108,234	11.89
Taxes	81,637	4.08	5,406	.59
Bank/investment fees	1,145	.06	154	.02
Lawyers/accountants	3,546	.18	0	
Telephone	31,573	1.58	35,379	3.89
Campaign automobile	0		0	
Computers/office equipment	26,698	1.33	17,682	1.94
Travel	97,050	4.85	89,521	9.83
Food/meetings	2,620	.13	50	.01
Subtotal	**482,700**	**24.11**	**284,712**	**31.27**
Fund Raising				
Events	157,179	7.85	131,917	14.49
Direct mail	10,265	.51	74,614	8.19
Telemarketing	0		0	
Subtotal	**167,444**	**8.36**	**206,531**	**22.68**
Polling	**71,530**	**3.57**	**6,950**	**.76**
Advertising				
Electronic media	948,174	47.36	165,933	18.22
Other media	50,728	2.53	9,838	1.08
Subtotal	**998,901**	**49.90**	**175,771**	**19.30**
Other Campaign Activity				
Persuasion mail/brochures	75,466	3.77	65,860	7.23
Actual campaigning	135,269	6.76	129,008	14.17
Staff/volunteers	5,686	.28	1,000	.11
Subtotal	**216,421**	**10.81**	**195,868**	**21.51**
Constituent Gifts/ Entertainment	7,932	.40	0	
Donations to				
Candidates from same state	0		0	
Candidates from other states	0		0	
Civic organizations	1,250	.06	0	
Ideological groups	893	.04	0	
Political parties	13,690	.68	287	.03
Subtotal	**15,833**	**.79**	**287**	**.03**
Unitemized Expenses	41,117	2.05	40,401	4.44
Total Campaign Expenses	$ 2,001,877		$ 910,521	
PAC Contributions	$ 723,585		$ 13,119	
Individual Contributions	1,220,383		866,176	
Total Receipts*	2,063,717		905,215	

*Includes PAC and individual contributions as well as interest earned, party contributions, etc.

CALIFORNIA

Sen. Barbara Boxer (D)

1992 Election Results

Barbara Boxer (D)	5,173,467	(48%)
Bruce Herschensohn (R)	4,644,182	(43%)

With combined spending of more than $18.2 million and coordinated party expenditures totaling more than $4 million, Rep. Barbara Boxer and former television commentator Bruce Herschensohn waged the most expensive Senate campaign of 1992. It was a consultant's dream come true.

Boxer paid thirty-five consultants a total of $5,960,597. The Democratic Senatorial Campaign Committee (DSCC) and the Democratic National Committee paid ten consultants $1,506,570 for work on her behalf. Herschensohn used seventeen consultants, who collected $3,973,523 directly from his treasury and another $2,454,644 from the National Republican Senatorial Committee (NRSC).

The big winners in this consultant slugfest were the media advisers. Greer, Margolis, Mitchell & Associates of Washington, D.C., were paid $4,299,960 by Boxer and another $1,217,000 by the DSCC for consulting fees, production of commercials, and purchasing air time. Herschensohn's Hollywood-based media guru, Bienstock Enterprises, and its subsidiary, Target Enterprises, received $2,665,047 from his campaign and $2,454,644 from the NRSC. Including the party coordinated expenditures, broadcast advertising accounted for 46 percent of Boxer's and 52 percent of Herschensohn's total campaign costs.

To help raise more than $10 million, Boxer relied heavily on direct mail, particularly in the primary. By the end of the cycle, Boxer had spent more than $2 million on direct-mail fund raising, a sum topped only by Sen. Bob Packwood (R-Ore.). According to campaign manager Rose Kapolczynski, the direct-mail program expanded so rapidly that the campaign twice outgrew its database vendors. For its early direct-mail work, Jim Wise Associates of Alexandria, Va., was paid $24,856. Craver Matthews Smith & Co. of Falls Church, Va., and its subsidiary, Production Solutions, received $744,060 from the campaign and another $18,435 from the DSCC for performing the bulk of the work on the massive direct-mail program.

Nineteen different consultants concentrated on Boxer's fund-raising events, including hundreds of in-kind, in-home events. National Telecommunications Services of Washington, D.C., received $66,000 for telemarketing work, and Services for Organizational Renewal of San Rafael collected $19,020 for implementing an unusual program to encourage donors to charge their contributions on credit cards.

According to Kapolczynski, by the end of the cycle the campaign had more than 82,400 donors, with about 80 percent from within California. However, despite all the energy devoted to raising money, Kapolczynski said the campaign raised "much less money" than they had originally anticipated.

	Boxer		Herschensohn	
Campaign Expenditures	Amount Spent	% of Total	Amount Spent	% of Total
Overhead				
Office furniture/supplies	$ 158,354	1.52	$ 122,030	1.57
Rent/utilities	144,118	1.38	67,226	.86
Salaries	1,165,444	11.16	973,918	12.49
Taxes	349,145	3.34	42,221	.54
Bank/investment fees	29,283	.28	1,554	.02
Lawyers/accountants	24,347	.23	91,206	1.17
Telephone	272,346	2.61	124,023	1.59
Campaign automobile	3,585	.03	2,372	.03
Computers/office equipment	61,830	.59	75,026	.96
Travel	250,390	2.40	157,510	2.02
Food/meetings	5,317	.05	5,016	.06
Subtotal	**2,464,161**	**23.59**	**1,662,101**	**21.32**
Fund Raising				
Events	845,314	8.09	608,006	7.80
Direct mail	2,003,533	19.18	1,958,218	25.12
Telemarketing	89,546	.86	146,510	1.88
Subtotal	**2,938,393**	**28.13**	**2,712,734**	**34.80**
Polling	**262,133**	**2.51**	**86,275**	**1.11**
Advertising				
Electronic media	4,319,233	41.35	2,894,179	37.12
Other media	445	.00	4,198	.05
Subtotal	**4,319,678**	**41.35**	**2,898,378**	**37.18**
Other Campaign Activity				
Persuasion mail/brochures	82,426	.79	207,398	2.66
Actual campaigning	291,381	2.79	183,699	2.36
Staff/volunteers	3,584	.03	2,135	.03
Subtotal	**377,390**	**3.61**	**393,232**	**5.04**
Constituent Gifts/ Entertainment	**1,361**	**.01**	**0**	
Donations to				
Candidates from same state	150	.00	0	
Candidates from other states	0		0	
Civic organizations	1,200	.01	0	
Ideological groups	975	.01	465	.01
Political parties	683	.01	1,775	.02
Subtotal	**3,008**	**.03**	**2,240**	**.03**
Unitemized Expenses	**79,570**	**.76**	**41,367**	**.53**
Total Campaign Expenses	**$10,445,695**		**$ 7,796,326**	
PAC Contributions	$ 908,655		$ 627,158	
Individual Contributions	8,787,664		6,812,904	
Total Receipts*	10,431,140		7,915,259	

*Includes PAC and individual contributions as well as interest earned, party contributions, etc.

CALIFORNIA

Sen. Dianne Feinstein (D)

1992 Election Results

Dianne Feinstein (D)	5,853,651	(54%)
John Seymour (R)	4,093,501	(38%)

Former San Francisco mayor Dianne Feinstein's 1990 bid for governor had provided her with a strong fund-raising base. In this race for the seat vacated by Pete Wilson she outspent Sen. John Seymour, Wilson's interim replacement, by nearly $1.2 million. Her edge in advertising was nearly $1.4 million.

Fortunately for Seymour, he had plenty of friends interested in saving his seat. The National Republican Senatorial Committee spent more than $2.4 million on a coordinated television advertising campaign. The California Association of Realtors and the National Association of Realtors spent a total of $267,050 on his behalf, mostly for persuasion mail, advertising inserts, and phonebanks. The conservative English Language Political Action Committee invested $49,718 and ten other organizations spent a total of $12,362 in the effort to defeat Feinstein.

To help balance the financial equation, national Democratic party committees countered with a $1,329,746 coordinated advertising campaign. The Democratic State Central Committee of California added $175,976 for media and persuasion mail. Feinstein received nearly $45,000 in independent support from a dozen organizations, including the National Abortion Rights Action League and the AFL-CIO.

When these outside expenditures were added to the campaign expenditures, Seymour's campaign had outspent Feinstein's $9,653,321 to $9,591,588.

To fill her treasury, Feinstein relied on twenty fund-raising consultants, including sixteen that concentrated on events. Coyle, McConnell & O'Brien of Washington, D.C., was paid $342,575 for direct-mail fund-raising services throughout 1991 and early 1992. Gold Communications Co. of Austin, Texas, picked up the direct-mail contract in March 1992 and collected $562,599 during the campaign's final nine months. Gordon & Schwenkmeyer of El Segundo handled the campaign's telemarketing.

While most of Feinstein's 80,000 contributors came from direct-mail and telemarketing small-donor programs, campaign manager Kam Kuwata noted that most of the money was raised through major events that featured such Democratic luminaries as Sens. Lloyd Bentsen of Texas, George J. Mitchell of Maine, Bill Bradley of New Jersey, John D. Rockefeller IV of West Virginia, Joseph R. Biden, Jr., of Delaware, and Joseph I. Lieberman of Connecticut.

In March 1992 Feinstein retained New York-based media consultant Morris & Carrick, and over the next nine months they collected a total of $4,505,981 from her campaign and the Democratic Senatorial Campaign Committee to design, produce, and buy her broadcast advertising and to provide strategic advice.

	Feinstein		Seymour	
Campaign Expenditures	Amount Spent	% of Total	Amount Spent	% of Total
Overhead				
Office furniture/supplies	$ 145,416	1.81	$ 72,741	1.06
Rent/utilities	79,612	.99	60,042	.87
Salaries	669,526	8.33	491,765	7.15
Taxes	55,200	.69	158,782	2.31
Bank/investment fees	7,666	.10	6,952	.10
Lawyers/accountants	73,821	.92	70,712	1.03
Telephone	138,243	1.72	129,063	1.88
Campaign automobile	1,885	.02	0	
Computers/office equipment	62,250	.77	49,446	.72
Travel	167,327	2.08	310,522	4.52
Food/meetings	5,931	.07	8,567	.12
Subtotal	**1,406,877**	**17.50**	**1,358,592**	**19.76**
Fund Raising				
Events	1,175,356	14.62	1,452,036	21.12
Direct mail	1,234,857	15.36	1,274,651	18.54
Telemarketing	317,292	3.95	0	
Subtotal	**2,727,505**	**33.92**	**2,726,687**	**39.67**
Polling	**47,377**	**.59**	**165,065**	**2.40**
Advertising				
Electronic media	3,277,559	40.76	1,906,151	27.73
Other media	4,195	.05	7,565	.11
Subtotal	**3,281,754**	**40.81**	**1,913,716**	**27.84**
Other Campaign Activity				
Persuasion mail/brochures	81,431	1.01	50,000	.73
Actual campaigning	441,209	5.49	626,613	9.12
Staff/volunteers	4,408	.05	1,465	.02
Subtotal	**527,048**	**6.55**	**678,078**	**9.86**
Constituent Gifts/ Entertainment	**24,520**	**.30**	**13,792**	**.20**
Donations to				
Candidates from same state	0		0	
Candidates from other states	0		0	
Civic organizations	0		825	.01
Ideological groups	0		0	
Political parties	0		600	.01
Subtotal	**0**		**1,425**	**.02**
Unitemized Expenses	**26,019**	**.32**	**16,881**	**.25**
Total Campaign Expenses	**$ 8,041,099**		**$ 6,874,236**	
PAC Contributions	$ 941,048		$ 1,388,708	
Individual Contributions	6,740,790		5,359,710	
Total Receipts*	8,114,867		6,908,617	

*Includes PAC and individual contributions as well as interest earned, party contributions, etc.

COLORADO

Sen. Ben Nighthorse Campbell (D)

1992 Election Results   Ben Nighthorse Campbell (D)   803,725   (52%)
                          Terry Considine (R)   662,893   (43%)

Ben Nighthorse Campbell was ready when first-term Sen. Tim Wirth announced he would not seek reelection in 1992. Campbell had spent $40,000 of his 1990 House campaign fund to explore a potential Senate bid but opted to remain in the House. Within days of Wirth's withdrawal, Campbell was off and running.

To win the Democratic nomination, Campbell first had to overcome former governor Richard D. Lamm and the party's 1990 Senate nominee, Josie Heath. That process cost Campbell well over $400,000.

After agreeing not to run negative campaign ads, the three Democrats wasted little time in breaking that pledge. Heath struck first with a sixty-second ad painting Campbell as an invisible candidate who was weak on the environment, gun control, and children's issues. In a thinly veiled slap at Campbell, one Lamm ad denounced politicians who accept contributions from political action committees (PACs). A Campbell ad returned fire directly, criticizing Lamm for serving on the board of directors of American Water Development, a company that sought to pump water from beneath rural Colorado and sell it to cities both in Colorado and California.

Campbell emerged with 46 percent of the primary votes. Lamm finished second with 36 percent.

In the general election Campbell faced Terry Considine, a former state senator who was unopposed in the Republican primary. Considine pumped more than $800,000 of his own money into the campaign, and his unobstructed path into the general election allowed him to significantly outspend Campbell over the final two months of the campaign.

Campbell poured half his total spending into advertising designed and produced by New York-based Joe Slade White. On the positive side, White developed a two-minute video that opened with scenes of Campbell's life and proclaimed, "Real life. Real work. Real leadership. Ben Nighthorse Campbell for Colorado's U.S. senator. The time is now." On a less "warm and fuzzy" note, Campbell ads questioned Considine's dealings with the failed Silverado Savings and Loan, accusing Considine of sticking taxpayers with $25 million in bad loans.

White collected $94,246 from Campbell's campaign and another $82,400 from the Democratic Senatorial Campaign Committee (DSCC) for his efforts. Shafto & Barton of Houston placed Campbell's ads, collecting $749,924 from the campaign and another $89,990 from the DSCC.

The National Abortion Rights Action League provided $150,000 in independent expenditures in support of Campbell, mostly for advertising and phonebanking. The National Association of Realtors PAC spent $98,953 on his behalf.

Campaign Expenditures	Campbell Amount Spent	Campbell % of Total	Considine Amount Spent	Considine % of Total
Overhead				
Office furniture/supplies	$ 17,013	.99	$ 37,271	1.69
Rent/utilities	14,962	.87	21,619	.98
Salaries	208,531	12.09	192,584	8.71
Taxes	62,452	3.62	58,624	2.65
Bank/investment fees	278	.02	1,223	.06
Lawyers/accountants	0		5,200	.24
Telephone	30,328	1.76	35,647	1.61
Campaign automobile	0		0	
Computers/office equipment	20,527	1.19	15,489	.70
Travel	65,748	3.81	62,942	2.85
Food/meetings	2,063	.12	6,322	.29
Subtotal	**421,901**	**24.46**	**436,923**	**19.76**
Fund Raising				
Events	135,912	7.88	71,514	3.23
Direct mail	20,221	1.17	168,634	7.63
Telemarketing	422	.02	1,470	.07
Subtotal	**156,555**	**9.08**	**241,618**	**10.93**
Polling	**39,526**	**2.29**	**64,024**	**2.90**
Advertising				
Electronic media	848,153	49.18	1,122,989	50.79
Other media	11,466	.66	10,117	.46
Subtotal	**859,619**	**49.85**	**1,133,106**	**51.25**
Other Campaign Activity				
Persuasion mail/brochures	60,619	3.52	190,276	8.61
Actual campaigning	141,387	8.20	137,173	6.20
Staff/volunteers	409	.02	283	.01
Subtotal	**202,415**	**11.74**	**327,732**	**14.82**
Constituent Gifts/ Entertainment	**5,366**	**.31**	**10**	**.00**
Donations to				
Candidates from same state	0		40	.00
Candidates from other states	0		0	
Civic organizations	148	.01	1,197	.05
Ideological groups	0		0	
Political parties	709	.04	730	.03
Subtotal	**857**	**.05**	**1,967**	**.09**
Unitemized Expenses	**38,286**	**2.22**	**5,561**	**.25**
Total Campaign Expenses	**$ 1,724,525**		**$ 2,210,941**	
PAC Contributions	**$ 741,686**		**$ 428,319**	
Individual Contributions	**830,642**		**1,351,195**	
Total Receipts*	**1,594,544**		**2,704,514**	

*Includes PAC and individual contributions as well as interest earned, party contributions, etc.

CONNECTICUT

Sen. Christopher J. Dodd (D)

1992 Election Results

Christopher J. Dodd (D)   882,569   (59%)
Brook Johnson (R)   572,036   (38%)

When Sen. Christopher J. Dodd needed to raise money, his supporters were handed the best seats in the house—or the theater, to be more precise. Over the six-year election cycle, Dodd's campaign shelled out $20,493 for theater tickets, an investment that yielded huge returns.

In the spring of 1988 Dodd's campaign spent $6,730 to rent the National Theater in Washington, D.C., for a private showing of *Cats*. According to administrative assistant Doug Sosnik, several hundred supporters paid $500 each to attend the musical and a reception following the show. The evening's take was approximately $100,000.

Tickets for a similar event held at New Haven's Long Wharf Theater in 1992 set the campaign back $3,200, but again the payoff was well worth the modest investment, raising close to $50,000.

While Senate incumbents invested an average of 21 percent of their resources in fund raising, high-yield events such as these helped Dodd hold his fund-raising costs to roughly 11 percent of total spending.

In most respects, Dodd ran a typical Senate incumbent's campaign. While his overall expenditures were 8 percent greater than the typical incumbent's, his allocations for advertising, brochures and persuasion mail, "actual campaigning," polling, and donations were on or near the average.

Like most Senate candidates, Dodd depended heavily on consultants. Malchow & Co. of Washington, D.C., received $31,080 for coordinating direct-mail fund-raising efforts. Marye Wagner of Clinton, Conn., and Susan Pollack of Los Angeles, Calif., were paid $41,484 and $5,565, respectively, for their work on fund-raising events. Squier/Eskew/Knapp/Ochs Communications of Washington, D.C., collected $1,831,630 from Dodd and $95,570 from the Democratic Senatorial Campaign Committee (DSCC) for designing and placing broadcast advertising. Pollsters Greenberg-Lake of Washington, D.C., received $176,173 from Dodd and $24,860 from the DSCC.

The one area in which Dodd clearly exceeded the average for Senate incumbents was overhead. Only Sen. Alfonse M. D'Amato (R-N.Y.) spent more than the $90,024 Dodd paid to lease and maintain his campaign car. The $89,444 Dodd spent on lawyers and accountants was more than all but five incumbents; only three incumbents spent more on office furniture and supplies; and only two incumbents—D'Amato and Sen. Daniel K. Inouye (D-Hawaii)—spent more on meals and entertainment that were apparently unrelated to the campaign's fund-raising efforts.

Republican challenger Brook Johnson personally contributed $1.9 million to his campaign. He invested more than $1.2 million with National Media of Alexandria, Va., for broadcast advertising.

Campaign Expenditures	Dodd Amount Spent	Dodd % of Total	Johnson Amount Spent	Johnson % of Total
Overhead				
Office furniture/supplies	$ 106,538	2.38	$ 15,702	.65
Rent/utilities	49,770	1.11	7,779	.32
Salaries	467,713	10.45	193,603	8.01
Taxes	224,648	5.02	22,916	.95
Bank/investment fees	398	.01	866	.04
Lawyers/accountants	94,444	2.11	6,609	.27
Telephone	108,920	2.43	44,759	1.85
Campaign automobile	90,024	2.01	5,405	.22
Computers/office equipment	62,491	1.40	19,012	.79
Travel	157,323	3.52	11,074	.46
Food/meetings	36,210	.81	188	.01
Subtotal	**1,398,477**	**31.25**	**327,912**	**13.57**
Fund Raising				
Events	334,525	7.47	9,336	.39
Direct mail	167,960	3.75	45,983	1.90
Telemarketing	0		0	
Subtotal	**502,485**	**11.23**	**55,319**	**2.29**
Polling	**176,173**	**3.94**	**46,595**	**1.93**
Advertising				
Electronic media	1,834,236	40.98	1,207,390	49.96
Other media	8,576	.19	5,270	.22
Subtotal	**1,842,813**	**41.18**	**1,212,659**	**50.18**
Other Campaign Activity				
Persuasion mail/brochures	129,049	2.88	376,096	15.56
Actual campaigning	261,800	5.85	368,064	15.23
Staff/volunteers	11,853	.26	0	
Subtotal	**402,702**	**9.00**	**744,160**	**30.79**
Constituent Gifts/Entertainment	**81,730**	**1.83**	**0**	
Donations to				
Candidates from same state	8,975	.20	1,715	.07
Candidates from other states	6,500	.15	26	.00
Civic organizations	1,249	.03	150	.01
Ideological groups	360	.01	100	.00
Political parties	37,135	.83	150	.01
Subtotal	**54,219**	**1.21**	**2,141**	**.09**
Unitemized Expenses	**16,831**	**.38**	**27,711**	**1.15**
Total Campaign Expenses	**$ 4,475,429**		**$ 2,416,499**	
PAC Contributions	$ 1,544,084		$ 0	
Individual Contributions	2,589,276		430,063	
Total Receipts*	4,342,880		2,399,715	

*Includes PAC and individual contributions as well as interest earned, party contributions, etc.

FLORIDA

Sen. Bob Graham (D)

1992 Election Results

Bob Graham (D)	3,244,299	(65%)
Bill Grant (R)	1,715,156	(35%)

In the wake of Hurricane Andrew, which devastated south Florida in August 1992, Sen. Bob Graham pledged not to hold additional campaign fund-raisers. Instead, Graham announced he would donate the proceeds from his two remaining events to the relief fund We Will Rebuild.

The decision was an easy one to make. At the time, Graham's campaign had cash reserves of $2.2 million. His Republican opponent, former Democratic Rep. Bill Grant, had $1,000 in his campaign treasury. Grant's negatives included 106 overdrafts at the House bank, and his switch to the Republican party had not won him many friends.

Nevertheless, while Graham invested just $582,311 to maintain his permanent campaign during the five off-years, he spent more than $2.6 million during 1992. Sixty-eight percent of the money Graham spent in 1992 was poured into advertising.

For designing, producing, and placing the ads, Squier/Eskew/Knapp/Ochs Communications of Washington, D.C., collected $1,743,642. Creative Marketing & Advertising of Miami collected $30,260 to buy time on Spanish-language radio stations.

While most of Graham's other expenses were below the average for Senate incumbents, only Sen. Christopher S. Bond (R-Mo.) spent more on constituent gifts and entertainment. Over the course of the six-year cycle, Graham spent $58,722 on various constituent events and $10,993 on holiday cards. The campaign paid $4,633 for tickets to various sporting events, including $3,905 for tickets to the 1991 Super Bowl in Tampa. Press secretary Ken Klein said the tickets were passed out to the senator's friends. Graham also used $4,156 in campaign money to buy gifts, including boxes of pecans and "Florida ties," which were given at Christmas to fellow senators and employees of the congressional barbershop and shoeshine stand.

Among the more expensive constituent events was Graham's annual weekend gathering with long-time friends and supporters. According to Klein, these weekends, which split time between political seminars and recreation, were not a pitch for money. Rather, Klein said the meetings were nothing more than a way to stay in touch.

While the 150 to 200 weekend guests paid their own transportation and hotel expenses, as well as any golf and tennis fees, the campaign paid for some of the meals and entertainment. In 1991 the campaign paid $12,989 for food at the Senate restaurant and $5,500 to hire the Capitol Steps, who entertained Graham's guests with political satire and song.

Grant's campaign never got off the ground. Overhead took 58 percent of his $308,145 budget. Grant spent nothing on broadcast advertising.

Campaign Expenditures	Graham Amount Spent	Graham % of Total	Grant Amount Spent	Grant % of Total
Overhead				
Office furniture/supplies	$ 73,250	2.28	$ 11,070	3.59
Rent/utilities	27,777	.86	28,917	9.38
Salaries	285,400	8.88	25,895	8.40
Taxes	162,613	5.06	8,013	2.60
Bank/investment fees	2,512	.08	0	
Lawyers/accountants	4,238	.13	6,755	2.19
Telephone	23,581	.73	34,488	11.19
Campaign automobile	0		0	
Computers/office equipment	55,340	1.72	3,512	1.14
Travel	81,215	2.53	58,733	19.06
Food/meetings	26,222	.82	0	
Subtotal	**742,147**	**23.09**	**177,383**	**57.56**
Fund Raising				
Events	336,691	10.48	10,411	3.38
Direct mail	71,548	2.23	22,313	7.24
Telemarketing	0		0	
Subtotal	**408,239**	**12.70**	**32,724**	**10.62**
Polling	**53,834**	**1.67**	**0**	
Advertising				
Electronic media	1,774,148	55.20	0	
Other media	4,600	.14	1,068	.35
Subtotal	**1,778,748**	**55.34**	**1,068**	**.35**
Other Campaign Activity				
Persuasion mail/brochures	7,265	.23	5,154	1.67
Actual campaigning	71,891	2.24	83,452	27.08
Staff/volunteers	1,891	.06	0	
Subtotal	**81,048**	**2.52**	**88,607**	**28.75**
Constituent Gifts/ Entertainment	**86,965**	**2.71**	**0**	
Donations to				
Candidates from same state	0		0	
Candidates from other states	2,000	.06	0	
Civic organizations	24,222	.75	0	
Ideological groups	0		0	
Political parties	32,000	1.00	0	
Subtotal	**58,222**	**1.81**	**0**	
Unitemized Expenses	**4,782**	**.15**	**8,363**	**2.71**
Total Campaign Expenses	**$ 3,213,985**		**$ 308,145**	
PAC Contributions	$ 1,247,448		$ 19,050	
Individual Contributions	2,191,829		192,316	
Total Receipts*	3,696,833		248,228	

*Includes PAC and individual contributions as well as interest earned, party contributions, etc.

GEORGIA

Sen. Paul Coverdell (R)

1992 Election Results

Paul Coverdell (R)	635,114	(51%)
Wyche Fowler (D)	618,877	(49%)

To defeat Sen. Wyche Fowler, former Peace Corps director Paul Coverdell had to survive four elections in less than four months: the July Republican primary, an August primary runoff, the November general election, and a general election runoff. In the process, Coverdell spent $1.2 million more than the average Senate challenger, investing heavily in broadcast advertising and persuasion mail.

Coverdell's biggest weapon was an unrelenting barrage of television and radio ads developed by his team of Atlanta-based consultants, including pollster Whit Ayers, ad copywriter Ralph Chandler, and media buyer Pat Sibley of Media Solutions.

The ads attacked Fowler for his opposition to the Persian Gulf War; his support for defense cuts, which Coverdell argued cost Georgia thousands of jobs; his votes for tax increases and congressional pay raises; and even his involvement in the House bank scandal, despite Fowler's insistence that he had never written bad checks during his tenure in the House.

However, according to campaign manager Eric Tannenblatt, the campaign's best ads were the "Margie" spots, which featured a grandmotherly woman sitting on her front porch singing a jingle she had written for Coverdell. While Tannenblatt called the ads "rather annoying," he added that Coverdell's name recognition shot up 17 percentage points after the ads began running. In all, the campaign developed a dozen TV ads and a similar number of radio spots.

According to Tannenblatt, the campaign mailed roughly 30,000 pieces of literature during the primary and primary runoff, 200,000 pieces during the general election campaign, and 1 million pieces during the general election runoff. Only six Senate candidates spent more on their persuasion mail efforts.

To make certain his supporters showed up on election days, Coverdell invested $73,999 in his own get-out-the-vote efforts, including a phone bank that generated nearly 1 million calls during the general election runoff, according to Tannenblatt. The campaign also spent $90,450 on the state party's coordinated get-out-the-vote program.

The Coverdell campaign received help from a number of interest groups that saw an opportunity to knock off Fowler. The National Rifle Association spent more than $87,000 on phone banks and mail. National Right to Life and Minnesota Citizens Concerned for Life spent nearly $24,000 on his behalf.

The biggest boost came from the National Republican Senatorial Committee, which gave $796,083 for advertising, $146,404 for the get-out-the-vote effort, and another $42,000 for persuasion mail.

Fowler spent $1,218,666 to maintain his permanent campaign operation during the off-years, which consumed half his spending edge.

	Coverdell		Fowler	
Campaign Expenditures	Amount Spent	% of Total	Amount Spent	% of Total
Overhead				
Office furniture/supplies	$ 41,681	1.32	$ 78,983	1.45
Rent/utilities	18,990	.60	24,627	.45
Salaries	419,091	13.25	280,458	5.16
Taxes	631	.02	151,480	2.78
Bank/investment fees	883	.03	21,325	.39
Lawyers/accountants	243	.01	0	
Telephone	63,227	2.00	75,663	1.39
Campaign automobile	0		23,597	.43
Computers/office equipment	27,484	.87	49,475	.91
Travel	71,339	2.26	153,601	2.82
Food/meetings	2,222	.07	12,773	.23
Subtotal	**645,791**	**20.42**	**871,982**	**16.03**
Fund Raising				
Events	156,008	4.93	613,608	11.28
Direct mail	260,639	8.24	291,167	5.35
Telemarketing	0		30,418	.56
Subtotal	**416,647**	**13.17**	**935,194**	**17.19**
Polling	**61,198**	**1.94**	**304,288**	**5.59**
Advertising				
Electronic media	1,409,789	44.58	2,665,558	49.00
Other media	45,958	1.45	49,735	.91
Subtotal	**1,455,748**	**46.03**	**2,715,293**	**49.92**
Other Campaign Activity				
Persuasion mail/brochures	226,833	7.17	146,849	2.70
Actual campaigning	319,068	10.09	334,567	6.15
Staff/volunteers	412	.01	6,152	.11
Subtotal	**546,313**	**17.27**	**487,568**	**8.96**
Constituent Gifts/ Entertainment	**1,113**	**.04**	**40,089**	**.74**
Donations to				
Candidates from same state	200	.01	1,990	.04
Candidates from other states	1,000	.03	1,000	.02
Civic organizations	200	.01	3,975	.07
Ideological groups	0		6,850	.13
Political parties	1,380	.04	2,500	.05
Subtotal	**2,780**	**.09**	**16,315**	**.30**
Unitemized Expenses	**32,962**	**1.04**	**68,846**	**1.27**
Total Campaign Expenses	**$ 3,162,552**		**$ 5,439,573**	
PAC Contributions	$ 585,557		$ 2,050,362	
Individual Contributions	2,553,470		3,233,885	
Total Receipts*	3,281,002		5,583,791	

*Includes PAC and individual contributions as well as interest earned, party contributions, etc.

HAWAII

Sen. Daniel K. Inouye (D)

1992 Election Results

Daniel K. Inouye (D)	208,266	(57%)
Rick Reed (R)	97,928	(27%)
Linda B. Martin † (I)	49,921	(14%)

Sen. Daniel K. Inouye spent $850,452 more on overhead than challenger Rick Reed spent on his entire campaign.

Inouye's campaign spent $106,894 on restaurant meals that had no connection to his fund-raising activities. For example, political action committee and individual contributions totaling only $4,100 were reported during 1989, but one meal at Germaine's restaurant in Washington, D.C., that year cost the campaign $1,250. Inouye also reported "campaign meals" totaling $545 at the Borobudur Intercontinental Hotel in Jakarta, Indonesia, and $349 at the Sherwood in Taipei, Taiwan.

Over the six-year cycle, the campaign paid for 403 meals that cost less than $200—183 in Hawaii, 168 in Washington, D.C., 46 in Maryland, and 6 in Virginia. Total cost to the campaign: $26,120. These included a $12.50 meal at Szechuan Garden in Rockville, Md., a $58.97 meal at Mikado Food in Washington, D.C., and a $22.59 meal at Wo Fat Restaurant in Honolulu.

The campaign also covered a $259 bill at the Hotel New Otani in Singapore and a $94 bill at the Hotel Damman Oberoi in Saudi Arabia. Even though the senator maintains a condominium on the island of Oahu, the campaign picked up the tab for hotel bills in Honolulu totaling $24,354.

Inouye used $3,694 of his campaign funds to pay for "office supplies" at Baraka Art & Frame in Washington, D.C. The Tropical Lagoon Aquarium in Silver Spring, Md., received a $649 check for "office supplies and expenses." Lighting Designers in Rockville, Md., collected $223 for "office supplies."

Only two senators spent more on accountants than Inouye, and even then payments from the campaign did not cover all the bills; the Democratic Senatorial Campaign Committee paid another $12,000. Only two Senators spent more to lease and maintain their campaign cars.

Inouye was also extremely generous with his campaign funds. In April 1988 Inouye donated $150,000 from his campaign treasury to the Hawaii Education Foundation, an organization he founded that provides college scholarships to Hawaiian high school students.

Once the campaign started in earnest, Inouye had more than enough resources to best the underfunded Reed. Starr, Seigle & McCombs of Honolulu collected $1,115,551 for producing and placing Inouye's broadcast ads, including a thirty-minute documentary. The company also received $26,109 for work on the campaign's newspaper ads.

While Inouye emerged with 57 percent of the vote, the opposition vote was split between Reed with 27 percent, Green party nominee Linda B. Martin with 14 percent, and Libertarian Richard O. Rowland with 2 percent.

Campaign Expenditures	Inouye Amount Spent	Inouye % of Total	Reed Amount Spent	Reed % of Total
Overhead				
Office furniture/supplies	$ 155,203	4.43	$ 21,877	4.53
Rent/utilities	88,744	2.53	34,860	7.22
Salaries	79,253	2.26	71,222	14.75
Taxes	83,482	2.38	0	
Bank/investment fees	5,797	.17	162	.03
Lawyers/accountants	172,530	4.92	0	
Telephone	54,386	1.55	17,180	3.56
Campaign automobile	63,931	1.82	450	.09
Computers/office equipment	80,892	2.31	6,599	1.37
Travel	442,292	12.62	10,584	2.19
Food/meetings	106,894	3.05	308	.06
Subtotal	**1,333,405**	**38.06**	**163,242**	**33.80**
Fund Raising				
Events	471,769	13.47	32,946	6.82
Direct mail	0		21,993	4.55
Telemarketing	0		0	
Subtotal	**471,769**	**13.47**	**54,939**	**11.38**
Polling	**37,781**	**1.08**	**6,813**	**1.41**
Advertising				
Electronic media	1,120,267	31.98	160,418	33.22
Other media	41,541	1.19	54,670	11.32
Subtotal	**1,161,808**	**33.16**	**215,088**	**44.54**
Other Campaign Activity				
Persuasion mail/brochures	211,371	6.03	21,564	4.47
Actual campaigning	76,969	2.20	14,535	3.01
Staff/volunteers	5,123	.15	567	.12
Subtotal	**293,462**	**8.38**	**36,666**	**7.59**
Constituent Gifts/Entertainment	**5,195**	**.15**	**118**	**.02**
Donations to				
Candidates from same state	1,699	.05	0	
Candidates from other states	6,000	.17	0	
Civic organizations	171,686	4.90	453	.09
Ideological groups	5,455	.16	0	
Political parties	4,868	.14	0	
Subtotal	**189,707**	**5.41**	**453**	**.09**
Unitemized Expenses	**10,436**	**.30**	**5,635**	**1.17**
Total Campaign Expenses	**$ 3,503,564**		**$ 482,953**	
PAC Contributions	**$ 852,465**		**$ 500**	
Individual Contributions	**1,873,466**		**334,681**	
Total Receipts*	**2,929,237**		**457,052**	

* Includes PAC and individual contributions as well as interest earned, party contributions, etc.

† No expenditures or receipts on file. Candidates raising or spending less than $5,000 are not required to file reports with the Federal Election Commission.

IDAHO

Sen. Dirk Kempthorne (R)

1992 Election Results

Dirk Kempthorne (R)	270,468	(57%)
Richard Stallings (D)	208,036	(43%)

Contributions of $200 or more are rare in Idaho, guaranteeing that the state's Senate races are always among the country's least expensive. Despite the fact that Boise Mayor Dirk Kempthorne and Rep. Richard Stallings were battling over an open seat, their combined expenditures ranked a modest eighth for total spending among the thirty-seven Senate races.

To fill his campaign coffers, Kempthorne relied heavily on out-of-state contributors and political action committees (PACs), which together accounted for 53 percent of his total receipts. To attract the attention of PAC managers, Mike Murphy Media of Washington, D.C., put together a six-minute video on Kempthorne that was sent to Washington PACs. Steven H. Gordon & Associates of St. Paul, Minn., was paid $31,682 for coordinating out-of-state events.

In-state events tended to be small-dollar affairs organized by Kempthorne's staff. Sit-down meals were avoided unless they were sponsored by a supporter who was willing to absorb part of the cost. "We shy away from meals in restaurants because that means someone else is getting the money instead of the candidate," explained campaign manager Phil Reberger.

More typical was the birthday party thrown for Kempthorne in October 1991. Nearly 700 people paid $10 to eat donuts and bob for apples. In August 1992 the campaign decided to cool off with a whitewater rafting event. According to Reberger, about ninety supporters paid $100 each to raft down the Salmon River and eat dinner with Kempthorne at journey's end. The campaign paid Epley's Idaho Outdoor Adventures $2,250 to organize the day; another $1,417 was spent on food.

For Stallings, it was much the same story. In-state events were generally held in supporters' homes, parks, or senior citizens centers, with ticket prices ranging from $25 to $500. His largest out-of-state event, held at the Washington home of Pamela Harriman, raised roughly $100,000.

In their ad campaigns, both candidates tried to paint the other as an entrenched incumbent. Democrat Stallings, a four-term member of the House, attacked his Republican opponent for raising taxes in Boise and for accepting a pay raise while mayor. Kempthorne ran one ad that featured him acting as a tour guide of the Capitol, pointing out supposed excesses. Another Kempthorne spot attacked Stallings for having eight overdrafts at the House bank.

In the end, the race probably came down to the fact that Kempthorne spent considerably less than Stallings on campaign overhead and polling and nearly twice as much as Stallings on advertising and other campaign activity.

	Kempthorne		Stallings	
Campaign Expenditures	Amount Spent	% of Total	Amount Spent	% of Total
Overhead				
Office furniture/supplies	$ 17,698	1.19	$ 39,243	3.17
Rent/utilities	10,753	.72	14,703	1.19
Salaries	153,417	10.28	245,561	19.87
Taxes	60,221	4.03	26,753	2.16
Bank/investment fees	205	.01	410	.03
Lawyers/accountants	3,367	.23	902	.07
Telephone	21,156	1.42	35,823	2.90
Campaign automobile	0		0	
Computers/office equipment	8,884	.60	17,952	1.45
Travel	66,545	4.46	82,280	6.66
Food/meetings	4,881	.33	315	.03
Subtotal	**347,128**	**23.26**	**463,942**	**37.53**
Fund Raising				
Events	89,771	6.01	114,403	9.26
Direct mail	111,796	7.49	66,740	5.40
Telemarketing	0		1,500	.12
Subtotal	**201,567**	**13.50**	**182,643**	**14.78**
Polling	**35,803**	**2.40**	**87,507**	**7.08**
Advertising				
Electronic media	713,243	47.79	376,946	30.50
Other media	32,423	2.17	16,682	1.35
Subtotal	**745,666**	**49.96**	**393,628**	**31.85**
Other Campaign Activity				
Persuasion mail/brochures	0		9,709	.79
Actual campaigning	157,039	10.52	80,340	6.50
Staff/volunteers	50	.00	0	
Subtotal	**157,089**	**10.52**	**90,048**	**7.29**
Constituent Gifts/ Entertainment	16	.00	0	
Donations to				
Candidates from same state	0		0	
Candidates from other states	1,000	.07	0	
Civic organizations	25	.00	0	
Ideological groups	0		0	
Political parties	150	.01	0	
Subtotal	**1,175**	**.08**	**0**	
Unitemized Expenses	4,109	.28	18,259	1.48
Total Campaign Expenses	**$ 1,492,553**		**$ 1,236,027**	
PAC Contributions	$ 599,151		$ 605,068	
Individual Contributions	701,312		580,837	
Total Receipts*	1,351,127		1,224,232	

*Includes PAC and individual contributions as well as interest earned, party contributions, etc.

ILLINOIS

Sen. Carol Moseley-Braun (D)

1992 Election Results

Carol Moseley-Braun (D)   2,631,229   (53%)
Richard Williamson (R)   2,126,833   (43%)

Six weeks before the Democratic primary, a poll conducted for the *Chicago Tribune* showed Cook County Recorder of Deeds Carol Moseley-Braun trailing Sen. Alan J. Dixon by a margin of nearly two to one. At the time, Moseley-Braun's treasury contained slightly more than $50,000; Dixon's cash reserves totaled nearly $2 million.

However, Moseley-Braun had a secret weapon: fellow Democratic challenger Albert F. Hofeld. With a net worth of roughly $17 million, Hofeld spent between $200,000 and $300,000 a week on a blizzard of television commercials blasting Dixon's record. Dixon, in turn, focused his negative advertising on Hofeld, leaving Mosely-Braun virtually ignored. Moseley-Braun's stunning primary victory cost her campaign little more than $580,000.

Almost over night Moseley-Braun became a national figure, gaining access to funding that had eluded her throughout the primary. By the end of 1992, only six Senate candidates had outspent her.

Moseley-Braun's best source of funds proved to be her direct-mail and telemarketing small-donor programs, which together accounted for 56 percent of her total receipts. Telemarketers Gordon & Schwenkmeyer of El Segundo, Calif., and Clec Canvas Network of Washington, D.C., were paid $233,966 and $16,017, respectively. Losser & Associates of Washington, D.C., collected $117,972 for its efforts as principal direct-mail consultant.

The search for wealthier donors took Moseley-Braun to Beverly Hills, Boston, Dallas, New York, and San Francisco, and the trips paid off handsomely. Out-of-state contributions accounted for $849,800, or 44 percent, of her $1,932,594 in large donations.

While the bulk of Moseley-Braun's preprimary money was invested in polling and advertising, there was a substantial expansion of her office staff after the primary. Only then-Rep. Barbara Boxer spent more than the $1,038,949 Moseley-Braun invested in staff salaries. A hefty 14 percent of that total, or $144,550, was paid to Moseley-Braun's campaign manager and former fiancee, Z. Kgosie Matthews.

The $401,492 Moseley-Braun spent on travel that was not clearly tied to fund-raising activities exceeded the travel expenditures of all but two Senate candidates, incumbents Bob Kasten (R-Wis.) and Daniel K. Inouye (D-Hawaii). During the four-day 1992 Democratic National Convention in New York, she spent $22,445, including a lodging bill of $15,367 at Le Parker Meridian Hotel.

Despite a $944,052 infusion from the National Republican Senatorial Committee for broadcast advertising, Williamson's treasury could not compete.

Campaign Expenditures	Moseley-Braun Amount Spent	% of Total	Williamson Amount Spent	% of Total
Overhead				
Office furniture/supplies	$ 122,951	1.77	$ 33,613	1.36
Rent/utilities	87,380	1.26	14,626	.59
Salaries	1,038,949	14.93	322,458	13.06
Taxes	71,403	1.03	138,076	5.59
Bank/investment fees	16,004	.23	0	
Lawyers/accountants	135,692	1.95	25,822	1.05
Telephone	207,351	2.98	56,844	2.30
Campaign automobile	33,920	.49	0	
Computers/office equipment	284,519	4.09	42,534	1.72
Travel	401,492	5.77	93,979	3.81
Food/meetings	3,114	.04	0	
Subtotal	**2,402,775**	**34.53**	**727,952**	**29.49**
Fund Raising				
Events	453,122	6.51	223,292	9.05
Direct mail	1,621,707	23.31	428,443	17.36
Telemarketing	265,194	3.81	0	
Subtotal	**2,340,023**	**33.63**	**651,735**	**26.40**
Polling	**75,694**	**1.09**	**128,437**	**5.20**
Advertising				
Electronic media	1,427,110	20.51	877,552	35.55
Other media	67,737	.97	10,020	.41
Subtotal	**1,494,847**	**21.48**	**887,572**	**35.96**
Other Campaign Activity				
Persuasion mail/brochures	259,496	3.73	0	
Actual campaigning	314,380	4.52	27,112	1.10
Staff/volunteers	12,482	.18	0	
Subtotal	**586,357**	**8.43**	**27,112**	**1.10**
Constituent Gifts/ Entertainment	**991**	**.01**	**0**	
Donations to				
Candidates from same state	0		0	
Candidates from other states	0		0	
Civic organizations	325	.00	0	
Ideological groups	550	.01	0	
Political parties	100	.00	0	
Subtotal	**975**	**.01**	**0**	
Unitemized Expenses	56,160	.81	45,474	1.84
Total Campaign Expenses	**$ 6,957,821**		**$ 2,468,282**	
PAC Contributions	$ 716,567		$ 472,839	
Individual Contributions	5,739,218		1,825,246	
Total Receipts*	6,770,711		2,320,713	

*Includes PAC and individual contributions as well as interest earned, party contributions, etc.

INDIANA

Sen. Daniel R. Coats (R)

1992 Election Results

Daniel R. Coats (R)	1,267,972	(57%)
Joseph H. Hogsett (D)	900,148	(41%)

Following his special election victory in 1990, Sen. Daniel R. Coats never stopped running. His campaign office remained open throughout 1991. Rent and utilities cost $19,257. Office equipment and supplies amounted to $69,304. Staff salaries totaled $124,274. Fund raising ate up $335,401. Polling and strategic advice cost $64,132. In all, Coats's 1991 spending totaled $816,501, or 22 percent of his total outlays.

According to campaign manager Brose McVey, this nonstop campaign had both pluses and minuses. On the plus side, McVey noted that the senator had received four years of steady media attention, which helped raise Coats's name recognition. On the downside, McVey was quick to say that the process was "testing on supporters from a financial aspect." Apparently, it was not too testing.

Coats's 1992 fund raising was considerably more efficient than it had been in 1990 when his telemarketing and direct-mail fund-raising efforts included considerable prospecting. As a result, the campaign spent $1,038,574 to raise $3,624,220 from political action committees and individual contributors, figures that translate into $3.49 raised for every $1 spent. While the campaign did two rounds of telemarketing prospecting in 1992, McVey said the bulk of the fund raising used lists of past contributors. The result was $3,348,628 in contributions from expenditures of $725,587, or $4.62 raised for every $1 spent. As a percentage of total spending, Coats's fund-raising costs dropped from 28 percent in 1990 to 19 percent in 1992.

Coats sunk that $300,000 savings, as well as smaller savings realized in other areas of the campaign, into advertising, increasing his media expenditures by nearly $566,000 over 1990 levels. He released ads attacking his opponent, Democrat Joseph H. Hogsett, for breaking a promise to complete his term as Indiana's secretary of state and for using that office "as one big perk." In a spot that showed Coats sitting on the porch with his family, Hogsett was slammed for opposing term limits because "he says he has no life outside of politics," a line many viewed as a dig at Hogsett's bachelor status.

For developing Coats's ads, Stuart Stevens of New York was paid $125,376. The Perkins Group of Indianapolis collected $1,583,443 from the campaign and another $452,415 from the National Republican Senatorial Committee to cover their fees and the purchase of air time.

Hogsett hit back with his own $1.2 million ad campaign, attacking Coats for, among other things, supporting the North American Free Trade Agreement. The Democratic Senatorial Campaign Committee added only $170,000 to Hogsett's advertising effort.

	Coats		Hogsett	
Campaign Expenditures	Amount Spent	% of Total	Amount Spent	% of Total
Overhead				
Office furniture/supplies	$ 65,188	1.72	$ 11,384	.74
Rent/utilities	46,256	1.22	450	.03
Salaries	369,179	9.76	80,624	5.22
Taxes	174,862	4.62	25,359	1.64
Bank/investment fees	137	.00	467	.03
Lawyers/accountants	33,319	.88	0	
Telephone	62,333	1.65	8,054	.52
Campaign automobile	0		1,962	.13
Computers/office equipment	63,537	1.68	1,052	.07
Travel	121,954	3.22	32,391	2.10
Food/meetings	4,934	.13	1,330	.09
Subtotal	**941,700**	**24.89**	**163,072**	**10.56**
Fund Raising				
Events	291,337	7.70	87,105	5.64
Direct mail	373,848	9.88	34,058	2.21
Telemarketing	60,403	1.60	0	
Subtotal	**725,587**	**19.17**	**121,162**	**7.84**
Polling	**120,317**	**3.18**	**18,000**	**1.17**
Advertising				
Electronic media	1,912,322	50.53	1,229,031	79.58
Other media	3,124	.08	0	
Subtotal	**1,915,445**	**50.62**	**1,229,031**	**79.58**
Other Campaign Activity				
Persuasion mail/brochures	27,360	.72	0	
Actual campaigning	34,411	.91	3,739	.24
Staff/volunteers	153	.00	1,262	.08
Subtotal	**61,924**	**1.64**	**5,001**	**.32**
Constituent Gifts/ Entertainment	**6,839**	**.18**	**0**	
Donations to				
Candidates from same state	2,000	.05	0	
Candidates from other states	3,000	.08	0	
Civic organizations	450	.01	0	
Ideological groups	0		0	
Political parties	1,425	.04	0	
Subtotal	**6,875**	**.18**	**0**	
Unitemized Expenses	**5,471**	**.14**	**8,208**	**.53**
Total Campaign Expenses	**$ 3,784,158**		**$ 1,544,475**	
PAC Contributions	**$ 1,135,005**		**$ 439,042**	
Individual Contributions	**2,213,623**		**1,093,652**	
Total Receipts*	**3,642,012**		**1,621,467**	

*Includes PAC and individual contributions as well as interest earned, party contributions, etc.

IOWA

Sen. Charles E. Grassley (R)

1992 Election Results

Charles E. Grassley (R)	899,761	(70%)
Jean Lloyd-Jones (D)	351,561	(27%)

Sen. Charles E. Grassley had little to fear from state senator Jean Lloyd-Jones, who managed to raise only slightly more than half as much as Grassley spent on overhead.

With polls consistently showing him leading by margins of better than two to one, Grassley waited until the middle of October to unveil his advertising campaign. The campaign's positive ads reinforced two central themes: "Every county, every year," touting Grassley's annual visits to each of Iowa's ninety-nine counties, and "Fiercely Independent, like Iowa." Grassley's lone attack ad hit Lloyd-Jones for missing 621 votes while a member of the state senate.

New York-based media consultant Stuart Stevens received $60,583 for designing five television commercials and a similar number of radio spots. Grassley paid Cine Vision Films Co. of Cohassel, Mass., $107,771 to produce the ads. Schreurs & Associates of Waterloo collected $472,439 from Grassley and another $227,093 from the National Republican Senatorial Committee for ad placement.

While Grassley spent more than $400,000 on salaries and taxes and nearly $108,000 on accountants, the campaign spent only $20,789 on brochures and persuasion mail. Less than $23,000 was invested in posters, yard signs, bumper stickers, and other campaign material.

To keep an eye on the electorate, Grassley employed three pollsters. Tarrance & Associates of Alexandria, Va., was paid $20,225; Bruce D. Merrill of Tempe, Ariz., received $16,500; and Budget Marketing of Des Moines received $24,217.

To fund his campaign, Grassley depended heavily on political action committees and out-of-state contributors; these receipts accounted for 56 percent of his nonparty contributions. Campaign manager Bob Hauss said Grassley made a concerted effort to raise his national profile by holding events aimed at pro-Israel supporters in Illinois, Florida, and California.

Hauss noted that in-state events were primarily small gatherings held in Republican loyalists' homes. Former president Gerald Ford and Vice President Dan Quayle each put in appearances for Grassley, helping to raise a total of nearly $80,000.

Grassley also invested heavily in attracting small donors, sponsoring a number of events with ticket prices as low as $25. According to Hauss, the campaign's direct-mail efforts yielded another 20,000 donors. Synhorst & Schraad of Russell, Kan., collected $50,743 for telemarketing.

Lloyd-Jones demonstrated virtually no ability to raise money. She refused political action committee donations, which cut her off from labor support, and she raised only $191,758 from individuals who attended numerous small coffees.

Campaign Expenditures	Grassley Amount Spent	Grassley % of Total	Lloyd-Jones Amount Spent	Lloyd-Jones % of Total
Overhead				
Office furniture/supplies	$ 32,453	1.34	$ 11,061	2.70
Rent/utilities	19,581	.81	11,775	2.87
Salaries	273,287	11.25	115,766	28.25
Taxes	132,582	5.46	43,526	10.62
Bank/investment fees	1,173	.05	0	
Lawyers/accountants	107,930	4.44	0	
Telephone	49,751	2.05	22,923	5.59
Campaign automobile	0		0	
Computers/office equipment	48,636	2.00	5,397	1.32
Travel	96,802	3.98	25,056	6.12
Food/meetings	5,216	.21	0	
Subtotal	**767,410**	**31.58**	**235,504**	**57.48**
Fund Raising				
Events	175,992	7.24	12,566	3.07
Direct mail	398,182	16.39	10,649	2.60
Telemarketing	54,996	2.26	0	
Subtotal	**629,171**	**25.89**	**23,215**	**5.67**
Polling	**60,942**	**2.51**	**7,012**	**1.71**
Advertising				
Electronic media	641,465	26.40	96,951	23.66
Other media	702	.03	315	.08
Subtotal	**642,168**	**26.43**	**97,266**	**23.74**
Other Campaign Activity				
Persuasion mail/brochures	20,789	.86	20,163	4.92
Actual campaigning	177,851	7.32	6,558	1.60
Staff/volunteers	420	.02	0	
Subtotal	**199,059**	**8.19**	**26,721**	**6.52**
Constituent Gifts/Entertainment	**0**		**0**	
Donations to				
Candidates from same state	3,000	.12	0	
Candidates from other states	4,955	.20	0	
Civic organizations	655	.03	0	
Ideological groups	1,000	.04	0	
Political parties	2,336	.10	0	
Subtotal	**11,946**	**.49**	**0**	
Unitemized Expenses	**119,203**	**4.91**	**20,018**	**4.89**
Total Campaign Expenses	**$ 2,429,899**		**$ 409,737**	
PAC Contributions	**$ 1,077,564**		**$ 0**	
Individual Contributions	**1,378,527**		**191,758**	
Total Receipts*	**2,833,083**		**415,829**	

*Includes PAC and individual contributions as well as interest earned, party contributions, etc.

KANSAS

Sen. Bob Dole (R)

1992 Election Results

Bob Dole (R)	706,246	(63%)
Gloria O'Dell (D)	349,525	(31%)

In her longshot bid to unseat Sen. Bob Dole, Gloria O'Dell's campaign slogan was "Gloria versus Goliath." As it turned out, the slogan grossly overestimated O'Dell's chances for success. While O'Dell managed to scrape together less than $332,000 for the race, Dole transferred more than $1.3 million from his Senate campaign account to repay debts from his 1988 presidential bid and still found nearly $2.2 million to spend on the Senate campaign.

Dole spent 45 percent of his funds on overhead, nearly twice as much as he invested in advertising. One of every six dollars was spent on travel, including $265,827 for chartered airplanes. Many of these flights were to ferry him to fund-raisers and rallies for other Republican candidates.

Throughout the six-year cycle, Dole made frequent use of jets owned by American corporations with interest in legislation that comes before the Senate. For the use of these airplanes, Dole's campaign paid Archer, Daniels, Midland $52,834; ConAgra, $24,991; Torchmark Corp., $24,495; Federal Express, $14,635; Chambers Development Co., $10,725; and U.S. Tobacco, $7,383.

Befitting his status as a safe incumbent, Dole spent less on staff salaries than forty-one of the seventy-four Senate candidates, including twenty-three incumbents. However, only six Senate campaigns paid more in taxes. Dole's campaign paid $148,400 for taxes on its interest income.

Other overhead expenses included a $3,515 dinner for the "Soviet Delegation" on Dec. 19, 1989; a $937 "office expense" at Glenmar Draperies in Dunkirk, Md., in September 1990; a $3,997 payment for lodging at the Kahala Hilton in Honolulu, Hawaii; and a $37 payment to a hotel in La Paz, Bolivia.

The campaign also paid $49,765 for various constituent gifts and entertainment, including $18,423 for copies of *Unlimited Partners*, a book coauthored by Dole and his wife, Elizabeth. Press secretary Walt Riker said the books were given to people who wanted to know more about Dole's background. Dole spent $12,044 to throw an inaugural party and another $11,772 on constituent meals. Among his other constituent expenses was a $165 payment for an "ice carving for Gov. Finney's Easter egg roll."

Dole donated $95,570 of his campaign funds to other candidates and Republican party organizations and causes. These donations alone amounted to 29 percent of the money O'Dell was able to spend on her entire campaign. In September 1992 Dole contributed $15,000 to the Kansas Republican party state account and $10,000 to its federal account. He donated $3,500 to Sarah's Circle "in lieu of refund of S&L contributions" and $1,000 to the Durenberger Legal Defense Fund.

	Dole		O'Dell	
Campaign Expenditures	Amount Spent	% of Total	Amount Spent	% of Total
Overhead				
Office furniture/supplies	$ 71,279	3.27	$ 8,412	2.54
Rent/utilities	34,470	1.58	8,196	2.47
Salaries	175,909	8.08	39,369	11.88
Taxes	234,995	10.79	8,195	2.47
Bank/investment fees	4,002	.18	676	.20
Lawyers/accountants	22,212	1.02	0	
Telephone	35,580	1.63	18,287	5.52
Campaign automobile	3,857	.18	0	
Computers/office equipment	12,817	.59	8,608	2.60
Travel	368,244	16.91	5,245	1.58
Food/meetings	12,656	.58	109	.03
Subtotal	**976,021**	**44.82**	**97,097**	**29.29**
Fund Raising				
Events	102,223	4.69	6,177	1.86
Direct mail	20,266	.93	11,219	3.38
Telemarketing	9,808	.45	13,591	4.10
Subtotal	**132,297**	**6.07**	**30,987**	**9.35**
Polling	**114,516**	**5.26**	**0**	
Advertising				
Electronic media	489,011	22.45	183,002	55.20
Other media	25,100	1.15	1,326	.40
Subtotal	**514,111**	**23.61**	**184,328**	**55.60**
Other Campaign Activity				
Persuasion mail/brochures	178,128	8.18	5,689	1.72
Actual campaigning	104,943	4.82	6,224	1.88
Staff/volunteers	2,462	.11	142	.04
Subtotal	**285,533**	**13.11**	**12,055**	**3.64**
Constituent Gifts/ Entertainment	**49,765**	**2.29**	**0**	
Donations to				
Candidates from same state	9,500	.44	0	
Candidates from other states	10,000	.46	0	
Civic organizations	20,925	.96	0	
Ideological groups	2,150	.10	0	
Political parties	52,995	2.43	0	
Subtotal	**95,570**	**4.39**	**0**	
Unitemized Expenses	**9,941**	**.46**	**7,046**	**2.13**
Total Campaign Expenses	**$ 2,177,754**		**$ 331,513**	
PAC Contributions	**$ 1,600,855**		**$ 40,150**	
Individual Contributions	1,053,217		151,591	
Total Receipts*	3,143,115		246,056	

*Includes PAC and individual contributions as well as interest earned, party contributions, etc.

KENTUCKY

Sen. Wendell H. Ford (D)

1992 Election Results

Wendell H. Ford (D)	836,888	(63%)
David L. Williams (R)	476,604	(36%)

Sen. Wendell H. Ford's third reelection campaign proceeded very much like his first two. There was no real contest.

Nearly one-third of Ford's total expenditures, $716,151, was spent during the off-years, including $331,264 for office overhead, $137,876 for fund raising, and $45,858 for constituent entertainment and gifts. In September 1991 Ford celebrated his sixty-seventh birthday in fine style with a combination campaign kickoff/birthday party. Commemorative shirts cost the campaign $1,070. Birthday balloons added $676, and $4,250 was spent to videotape the festivities. None of the party-goers paid to attend.

Ford also invested $45,562 in off-year polling, much of which seemed to have more to do with his position in the party hierarchy than with his reelection bid. Ford paid Hickman-Brown Research of Washington, D.C., $18,000 to conduct a "poll concerning federal issues." The Preston Group of Lexington collected $7,562 for "national and international questionnaires."

As majority whip and chairman of the Rules and Administration Committee, Ford was a consummate Washington insider, clearly not the best thing to be in 1992. With that in mind, Ford's 1992 spending was dominated by advertising. Greer, Margolis, Mitchell & Associates of Washington, D.C., designed, produced, and placed ads to distance Ford from his Washington colleagues. One ad credited the eighteen-year incumbent with killing a 1988 proposal to establish a Senate version of the infamous House bank. "About five years ago a bunch of senators came to me and wanted to have a bank similar to the one they had in the House where they bounced all those checks. And I said no way. We're not going to have a bank on our side. If it ain't good for Kentucky, it ain't good for Wendell Ford."

Ford had little trouble filling his campaign treasury. He tapped political action committees (PACs) for more than $1.3 million, or 62 percent of his total contributions. His position as the third ranking Democrat on both the Commerce, Science and Transportation Committee and the Energy and Natural Resources Committee proved particularly useful. Ford took in $182,550 from PACs representing oil, coal, and other energy interests; he received $146,645 from PACs representing airlines and other transportation companies. Telecommunications PACs anted up another $59,000.

Ford's Republican opponent, state senator David L. Williams, had no such luck. The National Republican Senatorial Committee (NRSC) promised to invest the legal maximum of $304,000 if Williams could match it through his own efforts. He could not, and the NRSC spent only $1,000 on travel.

Campaign Expenditures	Ford Amount Spent	Ford % of Total	Williams Amount Spent	Williams % of Total
Overhead				
Office furniture/supplies	$ 46,733	2.05	$ 11,943	3.38
Rent/utilities	29,324	1.28	2,263	.64
Salaries	215,423	9.43	74,163	20.96
Taxes	135,027	5.91	17,125	4.84
Bank/investment fees	789	.03	173	.05
Lawyers/accountants	25,378	1.11	0	
Telephone	46,780	2.05	18,213	5.15
Campaign automobile	15,637	.68	0	
Computers/office equipment	43,878	1.92	10,417	2.94
Travel	157,284	6.89	8,628	2.44
Food/meetings	4,789	.21	311	.09
Subtotal	**721,042**	**31.57**	**143,236**	**40.48**
Fund Raising				
Events	226,200	9.91	23,475	6.63
Direct mail	8,246	.36	58,348	16.49
Telemarketing	0		1,810	.51
Subtotal	**234,446**	**10.27**	**83,632**	**23.64**
Polling	**80,562**	**3.53**	**8,500**	**2.40**
Advertising				
Electronic media	947,502	41.49	94,244	26.64
Other media	17,951	.79	688	.19
Subtotal	**965,453**	**42.28**	**94,931**	**26.83**
Other Campaign Activity				
Persuasion mail/brochures	46,069	2.02	0	
Actual campaigning	101,520	4.45	4,288	1.21
Staff/volunteers	4,030	.18	190	.05
Subtotal	**151,619**	**6.64**	**4,478**	**1.27**
Constituent Gifts/Entertainment	50,364	2.21	60	.02
Donations to				
Candidates from same state	4,505	.20	0	
Candidates from other states	9,819	.43	0	
Civic organizations	4,021	.18	0	
Ideological groups	1,400	.06	0	
Political parties	55,550	2.43	170	.05
Subtotal	**75,295**	**3.30**	**170**	**.05**
Unitemized Expenses	4,857	.21	18,798	5.31
Total Campaign Expenses	**$ 2,283,638**		**$ 353,805**	
PAC Contributions	$ 1,343,378		$ 19,940	
Individual Contributions	812,463		287,016	
Total Receipts*	2,406,052		345,291	

*Includes PAC and individual contributions as well as interest earned, party contributions, etc.

LOUISIANA

Sen. John B. Breaux (D)

1992 Election Results

John B. Breaux (D)	616,021	(73%)
Jon Khachaturian (I)	74,785	(9%)
Lyle Stockstill (R)	69,986	(8%)

Sen. John B. Breaux overwhelmed four challengers in Louisiana's open primary, outspending his closest rival, Jon Khachaturian, by more than nineteen to one. The $62,274 Breaux spent to lease and maintain his two campaign automobiles was $8,676 less than Khachaturian spent on advertising. Breaux's $179,242 travel budget was nearly twice as much as Khachaturian spent on his entire campaign.

Under Louisiana's open primary system, Breaux did not have to run in the November general election by virtue of his majority victory in the primary.

Faced with outstanding debts of $115,200 from his 1986 campaign, Breaux's first order of business had been fund raising. His debt retirement was made considerably easier when $48,400 in loans were converted to contributions during the first half of 1987. By the end of 1991, Breaux's treasury had swelled to more than $1.8 million.

To help fill his campaign coffers, Breaux employed four consultants. Event planners Pat Adams & Associates and Noel Gould, both of Washington, D.C., collected $28,719 and $54,719, respectively. Breaux paid a third event consultant, Assets Consulting Services of Falls Church, Va., $45,919. Together they helped pull in $1,697,455 from political action committees (PACs) and another $1,076,298 from individual contributors who gave at least $200.

Forest Industries PAC and the American Trucking Association sponsored in-kind events for Breaux in 1987. At that time he sat on the Subcommittee on Environmental Protection and the Subcommittee on Surface Transportation. The Interstate Natural Gas Association hosted an in-kind event in 1991. Breaux's campaign also reimbursed the American Sugar Cane League $6,619 for reception expenses.

Breaux's single biggest event of the cycle was held in February 1991 in conjunction with Mardi Gras and the Krewe of Endymion Ball. Between 400 and 500 supporters paid $1,000 each to gain entrance to a roped-off area inside the Superdome where they viewed floats from the Mardi Gras parade. The campaign's expenses for the event included $10,000 for tickets to the masquerade ball that followed the reception, $12,550 for lodging at the Intercontinental Hotel, and $2,829 for limousine service.

Breaux's small-donor program accounting for only 14 percent of his total receipts. Forty-six Senate candidates spent more than Breaux on direct-mail fund raising. Gold Communications Co. of Austin, Texas, was paid $29,727 to run the direct-mail operation.

Breaux invested a total of $657,699 with Kaplan Advertising of Lafayette. Kaplan collected $603,677 for work on the campaign's broadcast advertising, $50,000 for newspaper ads, and $4,022 for brokering the purchase of bumper stickers.

	Breaux		Khachaturian	
Campaign Expenditures	Amount Spent	% of Total	Amount Spent	% of Total
Overhead				
Office furniture/supplies	$ 38,598	2.10	$ 0	
Rent/utilities	4,320	.23	850	.90
Salaries	29,584	1.61	1,600	1.69
Taxes	11,401	.62	0	
Bank/investment fees	3,471	.19	0	
Lawyers/accountants	12,500	.68	0	
Telephone	11,153	.61	0	
Campaign automobile	62,274	3.38	0	
Computers/office equipment	15,010	.82	0	
Travel	179,242	9.74	0	
Food/meetings	25,198	1.37	0	
Subtotal	**392,751**	**21.34**	**2,450**	**2.58**
Fund Raising				
Events	379,676	20.63	0	
Direct mail	41,024	2.23	0	
Telemarketing	394	.02	0	
Subtotal	**421,094**	**22.88**	**0**	
Polling	**29,951**	**1.63**	**0**	
Advertising				
Electronic media	619,645	33.66	69,950	73.69
Other media	60,959	3.31	1,000	1.05
Subtotal	**680,604**	**36.98**	**70,950**	**74.75**
Other Campaign Activity				
Persuasion mail/brochures	0		5,965	6.28
Actual campaigning	193,329	10.50	15,545	16.38
Staff/volunteers	7,657	.42	0	
Subtotal	**200,986**	**10.92**	**21,509**	**22.66**
Constituent Gifts/ Entertainment	**20,184**	**1.10**	**0**	
Donations to				
Candidates from same state	9,950	.54	0	
Candidates from other states	15,000	.81	0	
Civic organizations	10,862	.59	0	
Ideological groups	5,230	.28	0	
Political parties	18,669	1.01	0	
Subtotal	**59,711**	**3.24**	**0**	
Unitemized Expenses	**35,393**	**1.92**	**11**	**.01**
Total Campaign Expenses	**$ 1,840,676**		**$ 94,920**	
PAC Contributions	$ 1,697,455		$ 0	
Individual Contributions	1,558,290		4,920	
Total Receipts*	3,481,494		94,920	

*Includes PAC and individual contributions as well as interest earned, party contributions, etc.

MARYLAND

Sen. Barbara A. Mikulski (D)

1992 Election Results

Barbara A. Mikulski (D) 1,307,610 (71%)
Alan L. Keyes (R) 533,688 (29%)

In announcing his decision to challenge Sen. Barbara A. Mikulski, Republican Alan L. Keyes said he would need $3 million to wage an effective campaign. It is unlikely that even $3 million would have made a difference.

Keyes began his Senate bid with a public relations disaster. Having resigned from a $150,000-a-year job as director of Citizens Against Government Waste in order to run for the Senate, Keyes began paying himself an $8,500-a-month salary from campaign funds. Against the advice of his own state party chair, Keyes ultimately collected $49,614 from his campaign.

On the eve of the Republican National Convention, Keyes angrily charged party leaders with ignoring his candidacy because he was black, stopping just short of labeling them racists. Keyes received the maximum direct contribution of $17,500 from the party before his remarks; after the comment the party provided no coordinated financial help.

With Keyes self-destructing, Mikulski could afford to relax somewhat. While she spent nearly $3.6 million on her reelection effort, Mikulski had spent $1.2 million of that total during the off-years, including $841,702 on fund raising.

Over the six-year cycle, Mikulski outspent all but three incumbents on fund-raising events. Unlike many of her colleagues who employed a dozen or more event planners, Mikulski depended almost exclusively on Pamela D. Needham of Washington, D.C., who collected $452,167 in fees and expenses. Mikulski's only other event planners, Lucie Lehmann of Columbia, Md., and Unger/Thomas of Los Angeles, were paid $24,097 and $5,016, respectively.

Many of Mikulski's events were anything but stuffy, black-tie affairs. The campaign spent $4,080 to purchase a block of 250 tickets to a Don Henley concert and resold them for $60 to $100 apiece. After the concert Henley attended a reception for Mikulski and signed autographs for the crowd. A block of 1,000 seats to a Baltimore Orioles baseball game cost the campaign $7,825 and ballpark food added another $6,962, but the admission price of $100 resulted in a tidy profit. She also held a fishing trip on the Chesapeake Bay and an event at the Babe Ruth Museum in Baltimore. As campaign spokeswoman Maggie McIntosh put it, "We're real jocks here. We like to make our events fun."

Mikulski employed eight other Washington-based consultants, including Betsy Crone, who collected $126,796 for orchestrating the direct-mail fund-raising effort; Paul Bennett, who made $30,875 for writing the fund-raising solicitations; pollster Hickman-Brown Research, who was paid $127,000; and Doak, Shrum & Associates, which collected $1,052,952 for designing and placing ads.

Campaign Expenditures	Mikulski Amount Spent	Mikulski % of Total	Keyes Amount Spent	Keyes % of Total
Overhead				
Office furniture/supplies	$ 46,860	1.30	$ 33,866	2.84
Rent/utilities	16,800	.47	31,736	2.66
Salaries	164,582	4.58	170,161	14.26
Taxes	96,782	2.69	86,449	7.24
Bank/investment fees	1,385	.04	492	.04
Lawyers/accountants	138,650	3.86	200	.01
Telephone	33,691	.94	25,170	2.11
Campaign automobile	0		0	
Computers/office equipment	43,220	1.20	13,148	1.10
Travel	70,485	1.96	16,597	1.39
Food/meetings	26,161	.73	0	
Subtotal	**638,615**	**17.77**	**377,820**	**31.65**
Fund Raising				
Events	721,307	20.07	19,726	1.65
Direct mail	648,805	18.05	350,101	29.33
Telemarketing	33,639	.94	0	
Subtotal	**1,403,752**	**39.05**	**369,827**	**30.98**
Polling	**127,000**	**3.53**	**52,535**	**4.40**
Advertising				
Electronic media	1,065,799	29.65	252,720	21.17
Other media	21,591	.60	25,937	2.17
Subtotal	**1,087,390**	**30.25**	**278,657**	**23.35**
Other Campaign Activity				
Persuasion mail/brochures	32,180	.90	18,233	1.53
Actual campaigning	205,415	5.71	87,669	7.34
Staff/volunteers	1,366	.04	0	
Subtotal	**238,961**	**6.65**	**105,902**	**8.87**
Constituent Gifts/ Entertainment	**19,246**	**.54**	**0**	
Donations to				
Candidates from same state	8,343	.23	0	
Candidates from other states	5,356	.15	0	
Civic organizations	6,877	.19	0	
Ideological groups	19,269	.54	400	.03
Political parties	36,275	1.01	0	
Subtotal	**76,119**	**2.12**	**400**	**.03**
Unitemized Expenses	**3,399**	**.09**	**8,503**	**.71**
Total Campaign Expenses	**$ 3,594,481**		**$ 1,193,644**	
PAC Contributions	**$ 1,072,697**		**$ 31,150**	
Individual Contributions	2,432,470		1,123,811	
Total Receipts*	3,789,523		1,185,385	

*Includes PAC and individual contributions as well as interest earned, party contributions, etc.

MISSOURI

Sen. Christopher S. Bond (R)

1992 Election Results

Christopher S. Bond (R)	1,221,901	(52%)
Geri Rothman-Serot (D)	1,057,967	(45%)

Sen. Christopher S. Bond looked vulnerable. A former two-term governor, Bond narrowly won his first Senate race in 1986, despite outspending his opponent by nearly $1 million. An independent poll conducted in June 1992 found only 51 percent of Missouri's electorate inclined to give Bond a second term.

Bond was ready to meet the challenge, however, having invested more than $1.1 million during the off-years to maintain his campaign operation. Between Jan. 1, 1987 and Dec. 31, 1991 Bond spent $585,519 on fund raising alone, and he began 1992 with cash reserves of more than $1.5 million.

To shore up his support, Bond spent considerable resources on early and frequent direct voter contact. According to campaign manager David T. Ayres, Bond visited all of Missouri's 114 counties during the first five years of the election cycle and revisited 75 percent of them during the final four months of the campaign. Charter flights associated with this frequent intrastate travel totaled $152,738.

Bond poured 65 percent of his election-year spending into advertising. Beginning in August, newspaper and radio ads announced each of Bond's precinct walking tours. Generic radio commercials focused on agriculture, highways, and jobs. Tightly targeted spots featured local residents endorsing Bond and describing what he had done to help their communities. A flood of television commercials began Labor Day weekend and continued unabated throughout the campaign's final two months.

Five consultants had a hand in Bond's media push. Sipple Strategic Consultants of Washington, D.C., received $2,292,431 for designing, producing, and placing broadcast ads. Noble & Associates of Springfield collected $147,881 for buying time. Group 53 of Kansas City received $21,224 for production and air time. Emprise Designs of St. Louis and P.A.C.E. of Blue Springs collected $16,500 and $6,000, respectively, for newspaper and radio ads.

Ayres said the campaign mailed "hundreds of thousands" of voter persuasion pieces between Labor Day and Nov. 4, including 50,000 copies of an advocacy letter to voters who had been identified as undecided. More than 200,000 pieces of literature were distributed door to door. In all, nearly $333,000 was invested in Bond's brochures and persuasion mail effort, including more than $227,000 spent by the National Republican Senatorial Committee.

With the help of $262,500 in coordinated advertising expenditures by the Democratic Senatorial Campaign Committee, challenger Geri Rothman-Serot countered with her own million-dollar ad campaign, but she fell short in her attempt to unseat the "vulnerable" incumbent.

Campaign Expenditures	Bond Amount Spent	Bond % of Total	Rothman-Serot Amount Spent	Rothman-Serot % of Total
Overhead				
Office furniture/supplies	$ 76,442	1.57	$ 11,999	1.08
Rent/utilities	35,990	.74	9,168	.82
Salaries	294,603	6.03	70,852	6.36
Taxes	162,961	3.34	22,349	2.01
Bank/investment fees	4,476	.09	185	.02
Lawyers/accountants	43,880	.90	0	
Telephone	62,278	1.28	27,000	2.42
Campaign automobile	7,649	.16	0	
Computers/office equipment	47,165	.97	1,444	.13
Travel	270,041	5.53	29,503	2.65
Food/meetings	33,564	.69	0	
Subtotal	**1,039,047**	**21.28**	**172,500**	**15.48**
Fund Raising				
Events	561,074	11.49	42,849	3.84
Direct mail	410,530	8.41	32,060	2.88
Telemarketing	0		10,000	.90
Subtotal	**971,604**	**19.90**	**84,909**	**7.62**
Polling	**42,926**	**.88**	**76,647**	**6.88**
Advertising				
Electronic media	2,485,035	50.90	751,828	67.45
Other media	44,494	.91	1,496	.13
Subtotal	**2,529,529**	**51.81**	**753,324**	**67.59**
Other Campaign Activity				
Persuasion mail/brochures	105,790	2.17	7,198	.65
Actual campaigning	43,091	.88	12,683	1.14
Staff/volunteers	57	.00	0	
Subtotal	**148,937**	**3.05**	**19,881**	**1.78**
Constituent Gifts/ Entertainment	**92,083**	**1.89**	**0**	
Donations to				
Candidates from same state	0		0	
Candidates from other states	0		0	
Civic organizations	2,375	.05	0	
Ideological groups	420	.01	0	
Political parties	0		0	
Subtotal	**2,795**	**.06**	**0**	
Unitemized Expenses	55,110	1.13	7,318	.66
Total Campaign Expenses	**$ 4,882,031**		**$ 1,114,580**	
PAC Contributions	$ 1,721,235		$ 306,860	
Individual Contributions	3,047,044		493,613	
Total Receipts*	5,087,184		1,156,647	

*Includes PAC and individual contributions as well as interest earned, party contributions, etc.

NEVADA

Sen. Harry Reid (D)

1992 Election Results

Harry Reid (D)	253,150	(51%)
Demar Dahl (R)	199,413	(40%)

Sen. Harry Reid proved to be an extremely efficient fund-raiser. While Senate incumbents allocated an average of 21 percent of their funds to raising money, Reid spent just 7 percent of his budget on fund raising.

Reid accomplished this feat by shunning the direct-mail approach and embracing high-dollar, high-yield events. A $1,000-a-plate dinner featuring then-Sen. Lloyd Bentsen (D-Texas) raised roughly $300,000. A dinner with Senate Majority Leader George Mitchell raised another $100,000, as did a Washington, D.C., political action committee event.

Television advertising consumed a smaller than average portion of Reid's budget. While the average incumbent spent $1,644,887 on broadcast ads, Reid spent only $956,079. "Nevada is a very efficient market to reach with TV," noted campaign strategist and persuasion mail consultant Chris Brown.

Brown added that since Nevada has historically had one of the lowest levels of voter registration in the country, targeted persuasion mail is one of the most cost effective ways to reach registered voters. Brown said the campaign targeted five groups with their mailings: veterans, women, senior citizens, registered independents, and newly registered voters. Reid spent $423,642 on persuasion mail, more than any other Senate candidate.

Reid's expenditure of $48,502 on newspaper ads ranked ninth among Senate candidates. The ads served as regional appeals to small towns and rural areas.

Brown collected $358,111 from Reid's treasury and another $14,805 from the Democratic Senatorial Campaign Committee (DSCC) for designing and placing the newspaper ads, producing signs and other campaign handouts, and serving as the campaign's general strategist and persuasion mail consultant.

Reid hired Michael Kaye & Associates of Los Angeles and Ross McCanse & Associates of Studio City, Calif., to design and produce his broadcast ads and paid them $135,000 and $68,893, respectively. The DSCC paid McCanse another $71,000. Reid paid $751,526 to Western International Media Corp. of Los Angeles for purchasing air time.

Not all of Reid's expenses were directly related to his campaign. Virginia-based Jan English Interiors collected $5,165 from Reid's campaign to supply "decorating materials" for his Senate office. Constituent entertainment and gifts totaled $37,047, including expenditures of $24,478 for constituent meals and $3,185 for holiday cards. Gifts ranging from clocks to framed pictures cost the campaign $7,843.

Republican rancher Demar Dahl spent less on his campaign than all but ten Senate challengers but received 40 percent of the vote.

Campaign Expenditures	Reid Amount Spent	Reid % of Total	Dahl Amount Spent	Dahl % of Total
Overhead				
Office furniture/supplies	$ 45,373	1.48	$ 28,208	6.22
Rent/utilities	33,464	1.09	10,309	2.27
Salaries	246,582	8.05	91,467	20.18
Taxes	94,327	3.08	24,272	5.35
Bank/investment fees	1,233	.04	298	.07
Lawyers/accountants	720	.02	11,647	2.57
Telephone	39,630	1.29	20,400	4.50
Campaign automobile	0		0	
Computers/office equipment	38,681	1.26	6,934	1.53
Travel	225,279	7.35	41,567	9.17
Food/meetings	16,936	.55	120	.03
Subtotal	**742,223**	**24.23**	**235,223**	**51.89**
Fund Raising				
Events	221,454	7.23	27,184	6.00
Direct mail	0		10,729	2.37
Telemarketing	0		0	
Subtotal	**221,454**	**7.23**	**37,913**	**8.36**
Polling	**182,419**	**5.96**	**15,500**	**3.42**
Advertising				
Electronic media	956,079	31.21	111,190	24.53
Other media	49,387	1.61	8,267	1.82
Subtotal	**1,005,466**	**32.82**	**119,457**	**26.35**
Other Campaign Activity				
Persuasion mail/brochures	423,642	13.83	9,282	2.05
Actual campaigning	311,128	10.16	19,628	4.33
Staff/volunteers	1,371	.04	147	.03
Subtotal	**736,142**	**24.03**	**29,057**	**6.41**
Constituent Gifts/ Entertainment	37,047	1.21	75	.02
Donations to				
Candidates from same state	0		1,000	.22
Candidates from other states	2,250	.07	0	
Civic organizations	8,700	.28	150	.03
Ideological groups	2,529	.08	110	.02
Political parties	32,399	1.06	580	.13
Subtotal	**45,879**	**1.50**	**1,840**	**.41**
Unitemized Expenses	92,586	3.02	14,265	3.15
Total Campaign Expenses	$ 3,063,215		$ 453,330	
PAC Contributions	$ 1,105,739		$ 0	
Individual Contributions	1,928,964		353,736	
Total Receipts*	3,371,146		510,297	

*Includes PAC and individual contributions as well as interest earned, party contributions, etc.

NEW HAMPSHIRE

Sen. Judd Gregg (R)

1992 Election Results

Judd Gregg (R)   249,591   (48%)
John Rauh (D)   234,982   (45%)

When two-term governor Judd Gregg and businessman John Rauh agreed to abide by the state's voluntary $500,000 spending limit in both the primary and general election campaigns, they virtually guaranteed that theirs would be one of the least expensive Senate races of 1992. In the end, this open seat contest cost less than all but the North Dakota and Vermont races.

Gregg, who had served four terms in Congress prior to running for governor, barely avoided a Republican primary runoff, getting 50.4 percent of the votes in a four-way race. His chief primary opponent, building contractor Harold Eckman, opted not to abide by the voluntary spending cap and spent $878,732, much of it to buy time on Boston television stations that reach the state. Gregg responded with three television ads of his own, spending $338,762 on his primary effort.

Having squeaked through the Sept. 8 primary, Gregg came out swinging in the two-month general election campaign. "When John Rauh was head of Clopay Corp., earnings went down, profits went down, and hundreds lost their jobs, including John Rauh. John Rauh: Bad for business, Bad for New Hampshire," intoned one television commercial.

Two of Gregg's television ads used excerpts from an endorsement by retiring Republican Sen. Warren B. Rudman to inflict the damage. In one, Rudman criticized Rauh's proposal to halve defense spending in five years. In the other, Rudman called Rauh's willingness to slowly reduce the budget deficit "preposterous."

O'Neil, Griffin & Associates of Manchester, N.H., collected $382,557 from Gregg's treasury and another $110,480 from the National Republican Senatorial Committee to produce several radio spots and to design and place television ads. Gregg paid $159,615 to the Granite Group of Bedford, N.C., to place the radio spots and newspaper ads.

During the first eight months of 1992, campaign press secretary Martha Austin said Gregg marched in more than 200 parades. He spent $3,136 on "Judd Gregg for Senate" souvenir headfeathers, which he handed out to children along the parade routes.

Gregg invested just 6 percent of his funds to raise money. Political action committees and contributors who donated at least $200 accounted for 80 percent of his receipts.

One of the few areas in which Rauh outspent Gregg was persuasion mail. Working from a list of 40,000 registered Democrats and with the help of 400 volunteers, Rauh did four mailings before the primary. Two additional mailings were done before the general election, including one to 23,000 pro-choice Republican women.

Campaign Expenditures	Gregg Amount Spent	Gregg % of Total	Rauh Amount Spent	Rauh % of Total
Overhead				
Office furniture/supplies	$ 6,265	.72	$ 23,530	2.87
Rent/utilities	5,637	.65	9,286	1.13
Salaries	102,074	11.74	151,784	18.52
Taxes	20,416	2.35	0	
Bank/investment fees	444	.05	946	.12
Lawyers/accountants	20,675	2.38	270	.03
Telephone	7,012	.81	29,326	3.58
Campaign automobile	0		0	
Computers/office equipment	2,606	.30	22,360	2.73
Travel	21,924	2.52	9,203	1.12
Food/meetings	1,262	.15	328	.04
Subtotal	188,315	21.67	247,033	30.14
Fund Raising				
Events	38,700	4.45	22,640	2.76
Direct mail	11,400	1.31	90,074	10.99
Telemarketing	0		0	
Subtotal	50,100	5.76	112,713	13.75
Polling	0		4,197	.51
Advertising				
Electronic media	530,568	61.05	343,016	41.85
Other media	12,063	1.39	23,672	2.89
Subtotal	542,631	62.44	366,688	44.73
Other Campaign Activity				
Persuasion mail/brochures	24,620	2.83	39,064	4.77
Actual campaigning	41,978	4.83	44,886	5.48
Staff/volunteers	1,715	.20	244	.03
Subtotal	68,314	7.86	84,194	10.27
Constituent Gifts/ Entertainment	2,315	.27	164	.02
Donations to				
Candidates from same state	0		0	
Candidates from other states	1,000	.12	0	
Civic organizations	250	.03	175	.02
Ideological groups	0		35	.00
Political parties	0		270	.03
Subtotal	1,250	.14	480	.06
Unitemized Expenses	16,187	1.86	4,251	.52
Total Campaign Expenses	$ 869,112		$ 819,720	
PAC Contributions	$ 367,605		$ 0	
Individual Contributions	576,126		391,129	
Total Receipts*	990,836		1,109,500	

* Includes PAC and individual contributions as well as interest earned, party contributions, etc.

NEW YORK

Sen. Alfonse M. D'Amato (R)

1992 Election Results

Alfonse M. D'Amato (R)	3,166,994	(49%)
Robert Abrams (D)	3,086,200	(48%)

While not the most expensive overall Senate race in 1992, Sen. Alfonse M. D'Amato and New York Attorney General Robert Abrams waged the most expensive media campaign of 1992. Together, D'Amato and Abrams invested more than $9.3 million on advertising, and that figure ballooned to nearly $12.3 million once the party coordinated expenditures were included.

The dust had barely settled on Abrams's victory in the acrid Democratic primary against 1984 vice presidential nominee Geraldine A. Ferraro, New York City Comptroller Elizabeth Holtzman, and black activist Al Sharpton when D'Amato began pouring money into the airwaves—roughly $1 million a week for three weeks following the September primary.

First there were radio and television endorsements by Housing and Urban Development Secretary Jack Kemp and former New York City mayor Edward Koch, a Democrat. The positive endorsements were followed almost immediately by ads that attacked Abrams for his negative campaign tactics during the primary. These ads, which referred to Abrams as "mudslide Bob Abrams," accused him of running a fund-raising shakedown operation. Other ads accused Abrams of cheating on his taxes and of being "hopelessly liberal."

Russo Marsh & Associates of Sacramento, Calif., was paid $754,230 for work on the D'Amato advertising campaign. Multi Media Services Corp. of Alexandria, Va., collected $4,982,589 directly from the campaign and another $1,507,718 from the National Republican Senatorial Committee to pay for air time.

Abrams quickly counterattacked. In late September he unveiled a series of ads charging, among other things, that D'Amato's record was filled with "Scandal after scandal. Housing grants to his friends. Contracts for his contributors, and backroom deals for his brother."

Yet as expensive and negative as the media campaign was, not all of D'Amato's spending was nearly this serious. During the six-year election cycle, D'Amato spent $156,729 to lease and maintain various automobiles, the most recent of which were a 1992 Lincoln Town Car, which was kept in New York, and a 1990 Lincoln Town Car, which was kept in Washington, D.C. The 1992 Lincoln cost the campaign $647 each month; the 1990 Lincoln cost the campaign $927 each month.

Over the cycle, D'Amato's campaign paid bills totaling $35,252 to Gandel's Gourmet, a delicatessen on Capitol Hill. The campaign also spent thousands of dollars at the Senate restaurants for meals that were not campaign related, including a $4,439 harvest day celebration of New York agricultural products to which senators and their staffs were invited.

	D'Amato		Abrams	
Campaign Expenditures	Amount Spent	% of Total	Amount Spent	% of Total
Overhead				
Office furniture/supplies	$ 278,180	2.35	$ 71,499	1.12
Rent/utilities	217,716	1.84	68,910	1.08
Salaries	716,721	6.06	495,344	7.77
Taxes	516,764	4.37	223,976	3.51
Bank/investment fees	1,481	.01	8,359	.13
Lawyers/accountants	19,268	.16	12,070	.19
Telephone	178,228	1.51	135,792	2.13
Campaign automobile	156,729	1.33	0	
Computers/office equipment	118,648	1.00	34,521	.54
Travel	340,733	2.88	115,698	1.82
Food/meetings	163,098	1.38	5,846	.09
Subtotal	**2,707,567**	**22.91**	**1,172,015**	**18.39**
Fund Raising				
Events	1,434,735	12.14	345,982	5.43
Direct mail	829,215	7.02	667,674	10.47
Telemarketing	4,980	.04	31,888	.50
Subtotal	**2,268,931**	**19.20**	**1,045,544**	**16.40**
Polling	**356,194**	**3.01**	**171,000**	**2.68**
Advertising				
Electronic media	5,743,496	48.59	3,437,731	53.93
Other media	133,316	1.13	7,041	.11
Subtotal	**5,876,812**	**49.72**	**3,444,773**	**54.04**
Other Campaign Activity				
Persuasion mail/brochures	0		4,683	.07
Actual campaigning	415,141	3.51	512,061	8.03
Staff/volunteers	2,913	.02	3,083	.05
Subtotal	**418,054**	**3.54**	**519,827**	**8.16**
Constituent Gifts/ Entertainment	53,446	.45	551	.01
Donations to				
Candidates from same state	3,900	.03	0	
Candidates from other states	5,000	.04	0	
Civic organizations	37,750	.32	1,020	.02
Ideological groups	5,500	.05	2,570	.04
Political parties	21,874	.19	2,225	.03
Subtotal	**74,024**	**.63**	**5,815**	**.09**
Unitemized Expenses	**64,203**	**.54**	**14,779**	**.23**
Total Campaign Expenses	**$11,819,232**		**$ 6,374,304**	
PAC Contributions	$ 1,361,231		$ 590,769	
Individual Contributions	8,636,824		6,091,942	
Total Receipts*	11,239,373		6,975,365	

*Includes PAC and individual contributions as well as interest earned, party contributions, etc.

NORTH CAROLINA

Sen. Lauch Faircloth (R)

1992 Election Results

Lauch Faircloth (R)	1,297,892	(50%)
Terry Sanford (D)	1,194,015	(46%)

Lauch Faircloth and Sen. Terry Sanford were old political allies. However, when Faircloth decided in 1991 to become a Republican and seek Sanford's Senate seat, he quickly made a powerful new friend, Sen. Jesse Helms (R-N.C.).

Faircloth won a bruising primary with the backing of Helms's National Congressional Club. Carter Wren, a longtime Helms aide and the founder of the Congressional Club, helped plan Faircloth's media strategy. Hanover Communications of Raleigh had responsibility for implementing Faircloth's broadcast advertising; under their old name, Campaign Management, this same firm had been a Helms stalwart. So great was the overlap that it must have been confusing even to those responsible for filling out the Faircloth campaign's financial reports. On page 14 of their July 15, 1992 report to the Federal Election Commission, the heading read "Helms for Senate Committee" rather than "Lauch Faircloth for Senate Committee."

According to Wren, the theme running through the campaign's television commercials and persuasion mail was "change." They were hard-hitting, charging Sanford with favoring "more foreign giveaways and more welfare giveaways," as Wren put it. To paint Sanford as too liberal, one ad pointed to Sanford's vote "for Ted Kennedy's billion dollar tunnel," part of a 1987 highway bill. What the ad failed to say was that Helms also voted for the bill, which passed 96-2.

For work on the ad campaign, Hanover Communications collected $1,740,818 from Faircloth's treasury and $560,928 from the National Republican Senatorial Committee. Faircloth paid Arthur J. Finkelstein & Associates of New York and its subsidiary, Diversified Research, a total of $280,226 for polling and strategic advice. Fabrizio, McLaughlin, & Associates of Alexandria, Va., the campaign's general consultant, collected $78,441.

Like Helms, Faircloth hired PEM Management of Raleigh as his principal direct-mail fund-raiser, paying them $42,356. Unlike Helms, Faircloth depended only marginally on his small-donor program. While Faircloth loaned his campaign $768,500, contributions of less than $200 totaled just $661,293, or 22 percent of total receipts. Donations of $200 or more added another $1,144,743 to his coffers. Political action committee money accounted for a modest $365,783, or just 12 percent of total receipts.

While Sanford's total campaign outlays exceeded Faircloth's by more than 404,000, he spent $810,219 less on his advertising. Nearly $1.5 million of his spending was invested in maintaining his off-year campaign operation. When coordinated expenditures by the national party organizations were included, Sanford was actually outspent in 1992 by $637,441.

	Faircloth		Sanford	
Campaign Expenditures	Amount Spent	% of Total	Amount Spent	% of Total
Overhead				
Office furniture/supplies	$ 46,744	1.38	$ 76,128	2.01
Rent/utilities	29,561	.87	44,593	1.18
Salaries	180,562	5.34	453,870	11.99
Taxes	74,399	2.20	167,916	4.44
Bank/investment fees	2,821	.08	47,893	1.27
Lawyers/accountants	0		186,154	4.92
Telephone	16,992	.50	79,590	2.10
Campaign automobile	0		55,874	1.48
Computers/office equipment	1,498	.04	52,500	1.39
Travel	54,214	1.60	176,413	4.66
Food/meetings	4,587	.14	21,696	.57
Subtotal	**411,377**	**12.17**	**1,362,627**	**36.01**
Fund Raising				
Events	97,170	2.87	703,113	18.58
Direct mail	458,990	13.58	432,419	11.43
Telemarketing	0		0	
Subtotal	**556,161**	**16.46**	**1,135,533**	**30.01**
Polling	**294,726**	**8.72**	**104,595**	**2.76**
Advertising				
Electronic media	1,879,181	55.60	1,056,618	27.92
Other media	604	.02	12,949	.34
Subtotal	**1,879,785**	**55.62**	**1,069,566**	**28.26**
Other Campaign Activity				
Persuasion mail/brochures	129,750	3.84	11,533	.30
Actual campaigning	100,898	2.99	68,314	1.81
Staff/volunteers	35	.00	5,275	.14
Subtotal	**230,683**	**6.83**	**85,122**	**2.25**
Constituent Gifts/ Entertainment	3,637	.11	12,662	.33
Donations to				
Candidates from same state	0		1,080	.03
Candidates from other states	0		3,500	.09
Civic organizations	0		3,918	.10
Ideological groups	250	.01	810	.02
Political parties	100	.00	2,739	.07
Subtotal	**350**	**.01**	**12,046**	**.32**
Unitemized Expenses	3,134	.09	1,977	.05
Total Campaign Expenses	**$ 3,379,853**		**$ 3,784,128**	
PAC Contributions	$ 365,783		$ 1,696,404	
Individual Contributions	1,806,036		2,786,915	
Total Receipts*	2,961,865		4,704,353	

*Includes PAC and individual contributions as well as interest earned, party contributions, etc.

NORTH DAKOTA

Sen. Byron L. Dorgan (D)

1992 Election Results

Byron L. Dorgan (D)	179,347	(59%)
Steve Sydness (R)	118,162	(39%)

Having served twelve years as North Dakota's only House member, Rep. Byron L. Dorgan was more than ready to move up to the Senate. On April 6, 1992, just four days after fellow North Dakota Democrat Kent Conrad announced he would not seek a second Senate term, Dorgan formally announced his plans to run for the seat against an old foe, Fargo City Commissioner Steve Sydness.

Dorgan had soundly defeated Sydness in 1988 to win a fifth House term, and four years later little had changed. "The issues were virtually the same," noted 1992 campaign manager Robert Valeau. "Sydness had left North Dakota, worked as a consultant to Henry Kissinger and several Wall Street firms, and came back to run for office. [Dorgan] has lived in North Dakota all his life. It was Wall Street versus the agrarian Midwest."

To defeat the underfunded Sydness, Dorgan felt it necessary to spend nearly two and one-half times as much as he spent to win his 1990 House race, at least in part because of ninety-eight overdrafts on his account at the House bank. Dorgan's advertising budget went from $203,839 in 1990 to $580,360 in 1992, including $555,360 from his own treasury and another $25,000 from the Democratic Senatorial Campaign Committee (DSCC). According to Valeau, "early poll figures showed that Byron had dropped a bit because of the House banking issue, so our opposition saw the race as more winnable."

With the exception of Valeau, who previously worked for Conrad, Dorgan assembled the same basic team of advisers that had carried him through the 1990 House campaign. Struble-Totten Communications of Washington, D.C., designed Dorgan's radio and television spots, collecting $107,230 for their efforts. The Media Group of Columbus, Ohio, received $67,697 for ad production. Kranzler Kingsley Communications of Bismark collected $377,106 from the campaign and $25,000 from the DSCC to buy air time. Garin-Hart of Washington, D.C., was paid $34,500 by the campaign and another $24,815 by the Democratic National Committee for polling and strategic advice.

Perhaps the biggest difference between Dorgan's 1990 House and 1992 Senate campaigns was overhead, which grew from 13 percent of total expenditures during the 1990 election cycle to 27 percent in 1992. Staff salaries ballooned from $23,448 during the 1990 campaign to $142,121 during 1992.

Befitting his higher profile race, Dorgan paid the state party $75,844 for phonebanking and coordinated get-out-the-vote efforts—more than five times as much as he spent on this in 1990.

	Dorgan		Sydness	
Campaign Expenditures	Amount Spent	% of Total	Amount Spent	% of Total
Overhead				
Office furniture/supplies	$ 25,599	2.17	$ 8,898	1.79
Rent/utilities	7,296	.62	5,280	1.06
Salaries	142,121	12.05	75,445	15.21
Taxes	55,725	4.72	21,624	4.36
Bank/investment fees	15	.00	0	
Lawyers/accountants	309	.03	0	
Telephone	23,187	1.97	12,627	2.54
Campaign automobile	4,942	.42	0	
Computers/office equipment	13,720	1.16	8,894	1.79
Travel	38,868	3.30	28,286	5.70
Food/meetings	1,810	.15	1,881	.38
Subtotal	**313,593**	**26.59**	**162,935**	**32.84**
Fund Raising				
Events	30,999	2.63	12,125	2.44
Direct mail	39,312	3.33	39,962	8.05
Telemarketing	0		0	
Subtotal	**70,311**	**5.96**	**52,087**	**10.50**
Polling	**34,500**	**2.92**	**13,215**	**2.66**
Advertising				
Electronic media	555,360	47.08	208,613	42.05
Other media	0		16,750	3.38
Subtotal	**555,360**	**47.08**	**225,363**	**45.42**
Other Campaign Activity				
Persuasion mail/brochures	44,368	3.76	0	
Actual campaigning	124,566	10.56	31,902	6.43
Staff/volunteers	990	.08	0	
Subtotal	**169,923**	**14.41**	**31,902**	**6.43**
Constituent Gifts/ Entertainment	**0**		**0**	
Donations to				
Candidates from same state	515	.04	0	
Candidates from other states	0		0	
Civic organizations	1,000	.08	0	
Ideological groups	0		0	
Political parties	5,500	.47	0	
Subtotal	**7,015**	**.59**	**0**	
Unitemized Expenses	**28,833**	**2.44**	**10,664**	**2.15**
Total Campaign Expenses	**$ 1,179,536**		**$ 496,165**	
PAC Contributions	$ 785,943		$ 154,553	
Individual Contributions	212,942		309,791	
Total Receipts*	1,054,618		507,163	

*Includes PAC and individual contributions as well as interest earned, party contributions, etc.

NORTH DAKOTA

Sen. Kent Conrad (D)

1992 Election Results

Kent Conrad (D)	103,246	(63%)
Jack Dalrymple (R)	55,194	(34%)

On April 2, 1992, freshman Sen. Kent Conrad announced he would not seek a second term, citing his 1986 campaign pledge to serve only one term if the nation's exploding budget and trade deficits had not been brought under control. However, five months later, Conrad reversed course and announced his intention to seek the Senate seat left vacant by the death of Sen. Quentin Burdick.

In the interim, press secretary Laurie L. Boeder said Conrad had dispatched a letter to those who had already contributed to his general election fund asking them whether they wanted their money refunded or donated to the state Democratic party. Conrad refunded $308,051 and contributed another $52,336 to the state party's coffers during his brief "retirement." Even so, on Sept. 21, 1992, Conrad entered the special election campaign against state representative Jack Dalrymple with nearly $600,000 in the bank.

To replenish his treasury, Conrad depended almost exclusively on political action committees (PACs) and out-of-state contributors. Between Sept. 21 and Dec. 31 Conrad collected $699,745, including $554,550 from PACs and another $70,000 from 111 out-of-state donors who contributed $200 or more. During that same period Conrad received checks of $200 or more from only 24 North Dakotans, who donated a total of $9,454. Interest on the campaign's cash balance and small contributions amounted to $48,241. As Boeder put it, "North Dakota only has 640,000 people and most of those with money aren't Democrats."

Over the course of the abbreviated special election campaign, Conrad sank nearly $1 million, or 62 percent of his 1992 spending, into advertising and persuasion mail. Greer, Margolis, Mitchell & Associates of Washington, D.C., collected $337,842, and Kranzler, Kingsley Communications of Bismark received another $504,691 for work on the campaign's broadcast ads. Kranzler, Kingsley garnered another $27,553 for designing and placing newspaper ads.

Conrad paid BBA of Washington, D.C., $89,420 for work on the campaign's persuasion mail and $23,585 to operate a phone bank. Garin-Hart of Washington, D.C., collected $114,250 for polling, including $39,750 for polls conducted prior to Conrad's initial decision not to seek reelection.

Dalrymple collected less than $224,000 in individual and PAC contributions and managed to funnel only about $194,000 of his campaign treasury into advertising. Even with $110,480 in coordinated media expenditures by the National Republican Senatorial Committee, Dalrymple's campaign was overwhelmed by Conrad's $2.1 million effort.

	Conrad		Dalrymple	
Campaign Expenditures	Amount Spent	% of Total	Amount Spent	% of Total
Overhead				
Office furniture/supplies	$ 53,818	2.53	$ 3,315	1.20
Rent/utilities	21,009	.99	700	.25
Salaries	187,349	8.81	3,718	1.34
Taxes	100,523	4.73	1,377	.50
Bank/investment fees	1,975	.09	0	
Lawyers/accountants	13,180	.62	0	
Telephone	21,027	.99	6,923	2.50
Campaign automobile	0		0	
Computers/office equipment	37,784	1.78	405	.15
Travel	103,961	4.89	1,624	.59
Food/meetings	4,738	.22	0	
Subtotal	**545,363**	**25.66**	**18,062**	**6.52**
Fund Raising				
Events	119,241	5.61	4,416	1.59
Direct mail	6,344	.30	0	
Telemarketing	10,383	.49	0	
Subtotal	**135,969**	**6.40**	**4,416**	**1.59**
Polling	**114,250**	**5.37**	**14,960**	**5.40**
Advertising				
Electronic media	843,654	39.69	192,003	69.29
Other media	29,009	1.36	1,954	.71
Subtotal	**872,662**	**41.05**	**193,957**	**69.99**
Other Campaign Activity				
Persuasion mail/brochures	167,060	7.86	26,195	9.45
Actual campaigning	41,093	1.93	15,740	5.68
Staff/volunteers	0		0	
Subtotal	**208,153**	**9.79**	**41,935**	**15.13**
Constituent Gifts/ Entertainment	**25,310**	**1.19**	**0**	
Donations to				
Candidates from same state	16,243	.76	0	
Candidates from other states	8,181	.38	0	
Civic organizations	5,384	.25	0	
Ideological groups	0		0	
Political parties	149,079	7.01	0	
Subtotal	**178,888**	**8.42**	**0**	
Unitemized Expenses	**45,145**	**2.12**	**3,776**	**1.36**
Total Campaign Expenses	**$ 2,125,740**		**$ 277,106**	
PAC Contributions	**$ 1,708,368**		**$ 28,400**	
Individual Contributions	**575,575**		**194,786**	
Total Receipts*	**2,524,425**		**300,843**	

*Includes PAC and individual contributions as well as interest earned, party contributions, etc.

OHIO

Sen. John Glenn (D)

1992 Election Results

John Glenn (D)	2,444,419	(51%)
Mike DeWine (R)	2,028,300	(42%)
Martha Kathryn Grevatt † (I)	321,237	(7%)

In a race dominated by television advertising, Lt. Gov. Mike DeWine pounded Sen. John Glenn early, often, and hard for his involvement with former Lincoln Savings and Loan Association owner Charles H. Keating, Jr., and for his failure to repay more than $3 million in campaign debts from his 1984 presidential bid.

The Media Team of Alexandria, Va., produced for DeWine a series of ads designed to remind voters that, even though Glenn had been cleared by the Senate Ethics Committee of any wrongdoing, Keating had donated more than $200,000 to the National Council on Public Policy, a political action committee set up by Glenn. In one 30-second ad, a photo of the smiling Glenn was shown next to a police mug shot of Keating.

Another particularly hard-hitting spot began with a recitation of Glenn's assets and ended with a pointed slap at Glenn's failure to repay his past campaign debts. "He's got a condo in Vail, a million-dollar home, and a fifty-three-foot yacht. But John Glenn still owes $3 million." In a takeoff on the Energizer bunny commercials, the ad ended with a toy astronaut breaking through the screen graphics, pounding on a drum with the Glenn campaign logo on it. "John Glenn. He just keeps owing, and owing, and owing," intoned the announcer.

The Media Team collected $238,601 for designing and producing DeWine's ad campaign. National Media of Alexandria, Va., collected $1,595,353 from DeWine's campaign and another $892,000 from the National Republican Senatorial Committee for purchasing air time.

On the stump, Glenn attacked DeWine's ads, particularly the Energizer bunny spinoff, as "the big lie technique" and "gutter TV politicking." While it was true that Glenn continued to carry a debt from his presidential campaign, DeWine's ads ignored the fact that between 1987 and 1992 Glenn's Senate campaign had transferred a total of $958,945 to his presidential campaign committee to pay off some of the debt.

Glenn also responded to DeWine's attacks with a $2.8 million ad campaign of his own, including nearly $2.2 million from his own campaign treasury and another $616,500 from the Democratic Senatorial Campaign Committee.

Glenn paid Doak, Shrum & Associates of Washington, D.C., $151,766 to develop his ad campaign, which criticized DeWine for accepting honoraria and corporate-sponsored junkets during his eight years as a member of Congress, "bouncing" $13,000 in checks at the infamous House bank, opposing the North American Free Trade Agreement, and opposing abortion rights.

Campaign Expenditures	Glenn Amount Spent	Glenn % of Total	DeWine Amount Spent	DeWine % of Total
Overhead				
Office furniture/supplies	$ 31,446	.79	$ 30,491	.98
Rent/utilities	47,786	1.20	4,565	.15
Salaries	306,395	7.68	152,974	4.93
Taxes	130,864	3.28	64,543	2.08
Bank/investment fees	1,157	.03	1,950	.06
Lawyers/accountants	17,579	.44	13,164	.42
Telephone	46,882	1.17	80,881	2.61
Campaign automobile	4,839	.12	9,273	.30
Computers/office equipment	29,160	.73	15,576	.50
Travel	62,908	1.58	50,094	1.62
Food/meetings	316	.01	1,818	.06
Subtotal	**679,333**	**17.02**	**425,330**	**13.71**
Fund Raising				
Events	360,087	9.02	144,222	4.65
Direct mail	393,086	9.85	298,314	9.62
Telemarketing	0		0	
Subtotal	**753,173**	**18.87**	**442,536**	**14.27**
Polling	**221,993**	**5.56**	**88,682**	**2.86**
Advertising				
Electronic media	2,184,842	54.74	1,843,675	59.45
Other media	3,377	.08	375	.01
Subtotal	**2,188,219**	**54.83**	**1,844,050**	**59.46**
Other Campaign Activity				
Persuasion mail/brochures	45,524	1.14	46,456	1.50
Actual campaigning	71,462	1.79	220,861	7.12
Staff/volunteers	0		0	
Subtotal	**116,986**	**2.93**	**267,318**	**8.62**
Constituent Gifts/ Entertainment	771	.02	500	.02
Donations to				
Candidates from same state	1,800	.05	0	
Candidates from other states	0		0	
Civic organizations	300	.01	0	
Ideological groups	250	.01	0	
Political parties	3,250	.08	0	
Subtotal	**5,600**	**.14**	**0**	
Unitemized Expenses	24,901	.62	33,005	1.06
Total Campaign Expenses	**$ 3,990,976**		**$ 3,101,421**	
PAC Contributions	$ 1,261,221		$ 587,975	
Individual Contributions	2,071,560		2,232,224	
Total Receipts*	4,245,138		3,057,054	

*Includes PAC and individual contributions as well as interest earned, party contributions, etc.

† No expenditures or receipts on file. Candidates raising or spending less than $5,000 are not required to file reports with the Federal Election Commission.

OKLAHOMA

Sen. Don Nickles (R)

1992 Election Results

Don Nickles (R)	757,876	(59%)
Steve Lewis (D)	494,350	(38%)

On June 30, 1992, Sen. Don Nickles's campaign treasury contained $2.2 million, while former state house speaker Steve Lewis had cash reserves of $224,408. The gap never closed.

Nickles sank much of that funding advantage into broadcast ads, outspending Lewis on advertising by a margin of nearly three to one. The Media Team of Alexandria, Va., received $350,094 for designing and producing the campaign's television commercials; National Media of Alexandria, Va., collected $1,216,607 to place the ads.

Throughout the campaign, Nickles blasted Lewis for being a tax-and-spend liberal, fashioning one ad around the Beatles' song "Tax Man." A second ad featured a picture of Lewis sitting in a pickup truck with the tagline: "The tax man is coming to get you."

In a year when unemployment and job creation took center stage in the presidential race, the Nickles camp developed one television ad that combined those themes with the soft-on-defense charge. The ad claimed that Lewis proposed cutting defense spending by $150 billion a year, thereby dramatically increasing the state's unemployment rate.

Lewis's initial response to Nickles's defense spending claims summed up the race. While Nickles hit Lewis on television, Lewis responded with a radio ad accusing Nickles of lying.

Nickles invested $111,448 in newspaper advertising, outspending all Senate candidates except Sen. Alfonse M. D'Amato (R-N.Y.). Campaign staffer Grant Todd noted that while newspapers were used to complement the broadcast advertising, the campaign could target its newspaper ads in specific counties that had been helped by Nickles in some way.

Campaign Telecommunications of New York co-ordinated the campaign's phonebanking efforts, which Todd said were largely handled in-house. Nickles also paid $30,000 to the state party's get-out-the-vote program.

Much of Nickles's persuasion mail costs were picked up by the National Republican Senatorial Committee (NRSC). Nickles paid the John Grotta Co. of Arlington, Va., $27,300, and the NRSC added $37,734. In addition, the NRSC paid Karl Rove & Co. of Austin, Texas, $141,276. In all, the NRSC spent $255,118 on its coordinated persuasion mail effort for Nickles.

On the lighter side, Nickles spent $9,821 on wooden nickels, which have been a trademark of his campaigns since 1980. The campaign logo is stamped on one side of the nickel; the other side says,"Don't send your dollars to Washington—send Nickles." Todd said the campaign has handed out hundreds of thousands of these wooden nickels over the years.

	Nickles		Lewis	
Campaign Expenditures	Amount Spent	% of Total	Amount Spent	% of Total
Overhead				
Office furniture/supplies	$ 42,832	1.23	$ 34,335	2.37
Rent/utilities	37,674	1.08	15,762	1.09
Salaries	290,731	8.35	194,324	13.39
Taxes	191,826	5.51	76,174	5.25
Bank/investment fees	0		707	.05
Lawyers/accountants	1,475	.04	0	
Telephone	40,687	1.17	64,276	4.43
Campaign automobile	0		10,940	.75
Computers/office equipment	43,339	1.24	16,671	1.15
Travel	87,072	2.50	33,301	2.29
Food/meetings	8,026	.23	1,269	.09
Subtotal	743,663	21.35	447,760	30.86
Fund Raising				
Events	172,683	4.96	66,022	4.55
Direct mail	198,981	5.71	53,870	3.71
Telemarketing	0		0	
Subtotal	371,664	10.67	119,893	8.26
Polling	88,513	2.54	59,750	4.12
Advertising				
Electronic media	1,567,931	45.01	650,396	44.82
Other media	139,555	4.01	10,815	.75
Subtotal	1,707,485	49.02	661,212	45.57
Other Campaign Activity				
Persuasion mail/brochures	54,612	1.57	49,217	3.39
Actual campaigning	293,394	8.42	61,923	4.27
Staff/volunteers	1,008	.03	0	
Subtotal	349,013	10.02	111,140	7.66
Constituent Gifts/ Entertainment	18,241	.52	0	
Donations to				
Candidates from same state	5,500	.16	0	
Candidates from other states	23,250	.67	0	
Civic organizations	1,752	.05	462	.03
Ideological groups	0		210	.01
Political parties	0		990	.07
Subtotal	30,502	.88	1,662	.11
Unitemized Expenses	174,341	5.00	49,623	3.42
Total Campaign Expenses	$ 3,483,423		$ 1,451,040	
PAC Contributions	$ 1,191,903		$ 274,668	
Individual Contributions	2,056,827		1,142,474	
Total Receipts*	3,686,883		1,456,533	

*Includes PAC and individual contributions as well as interest earned, party contributions, etc.

OREGON

Sen. Bob Packwood (R)

1992 Election Results

Bob Packwood (R)	717,455	(52%)
Les AuCoin (D)	639,851	(47%)

Although Sen. Bob Packwood outspent Rep. Les AuCoin by a margin of more than three to one, much of that spending was channeled into things that had little or nothing to do with influencing voters.

Packwood invested $3,190,034 to maintain his permanent campaign operation during the off-years, or 40 percent of his total spending on the race. Packwood's direct-mail fund-raising effort cost more than $2.2 million between Jan. 1, 1987 and Dec. 31, 1991. His office expenses during that same period totaled another $523,129, including $156,612 in staff salaries.

Packwood's direct-mail fund-raising campaign involved four copywriters, six sources for mailing lists, three firms to maintain the lists, fourteen mail houses, and a firm to process the returns. Over the six-year cycle, Polly A. Agee of Arlington, Va., was paid $244,646 for coordinating this massive effort. The total cost was $2,777,829, making it the most expensive direct-mail fund-raising campaign of the 1992 cycle.

With nearly half his money going to fund raising, off-year overhead expenses, and contributions to other candidates and party organizations, Packwood invested only 35 percent of his funds in advertising. Still, that amounted to more than $2.8 million.

Packwood began hitting AuCoin even before he won the Democratic nomination. He purchased $42,000 of air time before the May primary to attack AuCoin for supporting the congressional pay raise and for having eighty-three overdrafts at the House bank. Packwood continued to hammer away at these themes throughout the general election.

In a year supposedly marked by anti-incumbent sentiment, Packwood's media adviser, Sipple Strategic Communications of Washington, D.C., developed ads designed to turn his incumbency into an advantage. "Tough times demand a tough leader. Senator Bob Packwood," was the tagline of one ad. Sipple collected $2,751,488 for consulting fees, production costs, and the purchase of air time.

Packwood benefited from heavy independent expenditures by the American Medical Association Political Action Committee, which invested $227,808 in television advertising, voter surveys, and persuasion mailings. Independent expenditures by the Auto Dealers and Drivers for Free Trade totaled $65,539.

Possessing far fewer resources and emerging from a very costly primary, AuCoin also benefited considerably from independent expenditures made on his behalf. The National Association of Realtors PAC spent $329,289 for persuasion mail, broadcast advertising, voter surveys, and phone banks.

	Packwood		AuCoin	
Campaign Expenditures	Amount Spent	% of Total	Amount Spent	% of Total
Overhead				
Office furniture/supplies	$ 59,511	.75	$ 46,507	1.76
Rent/utilities	12,328	.15	51,625	1.95
Salaries	318,469	4.00	439,190	16.62
Taxes	240,484	3.02	156,367	5.92
Bank/investment fees	4,950	.06	2,956	.11
Lawyers/accountants	221,825	2.79	26,132	.99
Telephone	16,092	.20	74,260	2.81
Campaign automobile	0		6,545	.25
Computers/office equipment	45,764	.58	66,711	2.53
Travel	93,259	1.17	74,808	2.83
Food/meetings	8,978	.11	4,662	.18
Subtotal	**1,021,659**	**12.84**	**949,763**	**35.95**
Fund Raising				
Events	318,384	4.00	90,258	3.42
Direct mail	2,777,829	34.90	77,830	2.95
Telemarketing	93,709	1.18	56,507	2.14
Subtotal	**3,189,922**	**40.08**	**224,596**	**8.50**
Polling	**163,098**	**2.05**	**90,500**	**3.43**
Advertising				
Electronic media	2,751,900	34.58	1,195,088	45.24
Other media	64,630	.81	7,415	.28
Subtotal	**2,816,530**	**35.39**	**1,202,503**	**45.52**
Other Campaign Activity				
Persuasion mail/brochures	367,691	4.62	56,119	2.12
Actual campaigning	304,180	3.82	73,659	2.79
Staff/volunteers	152	.00	600	.02
Subtotal	**672,023**	**8.44**	**130,378**	**4.94**
Constituent Gifts/ Entertainment	**3,011**	**.04**	**42**	**.00**
Donations to				
Candidates from same state	4,000	.05	0	
Candidates from other states	14,500	.18	0	
Civic organizations	950	.01	0	
Ideological groups	2,000	.03	550	.02
Political parties	0		2,850	.11
Subtotal	**21,450**	**.27**	**3,400**	**.13**
Unitemized Expenses	**70,970**	**.89**	**40,574**	**1.54**
Total Campaign Expenses	**$ 7,958,662**		**$ 2,641,756**	
PAC Contributions	$ 1,275,358		$ 775,502	
Individual Contributions	6,241,298		1,440,913	
Total Receipts*	8,228,212		2,301,155	

*Includes PAC and individual contributions as well as interest earned, party contributions, etc.

PENNSYLVANIA

Sen. Arlen Specter (R)

1992 Election Results

Arlen Specter (R)	2,358,125	(49%)
Lynn Yeakel (D)	2,224,966	(46%)
John F. Perry III (I)	219,319	(5%)

Sen. Arlen Specter and the National Republican Senatorial Committee (NRSC) were able to spend $1.9 million more than women's activist Lynn Yeakel and the Democratic Senatorial Campaign Committee on advertising in this tight contest.

In late July Specter began running five issue-oriented ads, including two in the expensive Philadelphia market—one dealing with breast cancer, the other touting his record on protecting jobs. In a year when incumbency was considered a liability, many of Specter's television and radio spots sought to make it an asset, with testimonials from ordinary citizens on how his office had helped solve their problems.

According to campaign manager Patrick L. Meehan, one of Specter's most effective sixty-second spots featured Teresa Heinz, widow of the late senator John Heinz, asking voters not to judge Specter solely by his acerbic questioning of Anita Hill during the confirmation hearings for Supreme Court Justice Clarence Thomas. In obtaining the Democratic nomination, Yeakel had made much of Specter's treatment of Hill.

There was plenty of negative advertising. Specter ads hit Yeakel for her failure to pay $17,000 in back taxes until the day before she announced her candidacy and for her opposition to the death penalty. Perhaps his toughest attack featured three news clips of Yeakel gaffes. In one, Yeakel was shown charging that Specter was waffling on the issues. When asked by a reporter for examples, she could not name any.

The Garth Group of New York collected $4,643,143 from Specter and $980,540 from the NRSC for designing, producing, and placing the campaign's television and radio commercials.

To reach out to Republican women, the campaign also distributed hundreds of copies of a video designed to communicate a positive message on Specter's record on women's issues. Chris Mottola of Philadelphia was paid $8,167 for producing the video, which was shown at coffees held throughout the state.

Specter paid Precision Marketing of Easton $366,954 to orchestrate the persuasion mail and phonebanking efforts. One of the more controversial mailings targeted Jewish voters and suggested that Yeakel was backed by an anti-Israel network opposed to Specter because of his support for Israel.

Lacking Specter's resources, Yeakel waited until Sept. 22 to begin her television counterattack. Her most controversial ad referred to Specter as the most obnoxious man in the Senate, an assessment that was dubbed "objectionable" by a League of Women Voters-sponsored panel set up to monitor the campaign's advertising. Only in late October did Yeakel's advertising return to the initial catalyst for her campaign—Anita Hill.

Campaign Expenditures	Specter Amount Spent	Specter % of Total	Yeakel Amount Spent	Yeakel % of Total
Overhead				
Office furniture/supplies	$ 199,378	1.96	$ 78,250	1.50
Rent/utilities	134,049	1.32	31,058	.60
Salaries	994,312	9.80	574,358	11.02
Taxes	491,610	4.84	186,508	3.58
Bank/investment fees	3,155	.03	544	.01
Lawyers/accountants	54,607	.54	5,600	.11
Telephone	184,275	1.82	141,843	2.72
Campaign automobile	23,421	.23	0	
Computers/office equipment	116,665	1.15	109,471	2.10
Travel	372,297	3.67	166,949	3.20
Food/meetings	21,831	.22	824	.02
Subtotal	**2,595,600**	**25.58**	**1,295,405**	**24.85**
Fund Raising				
Events	753,945	7.43	139,716	2.68
Direct mail	1,012,179	9.97	512,010	9.82
Telemarketing	89,514	.88	0	
Subtotal	**1,855,639**	**18.28**	**651,726**	**12.50**
Polling	**217,963**	**2.15**	**27,481**	**.53**
Advertising				
Electronic media	4,643,733	45.76	2,963,993	56.86
Other media	45,631	.45	26,824	.51
Subtotal	**4,689,364**	**46.21**	**2,990,817**	**57.37**
Other Campaign Activity				
Persuasion mail/brochures	325,925	3.21	127,832	2.45
Actual campaigning	227,067	2.24	104,055	2.00
Staff/volunteers	1,863	.02	1,518	.03
Subtotal	**554,855**	**5.47**	**233,404**	**4.48**
Constituent Gifts/ Entertainment	50,770	.50	0	
Donations to				
Candidates from same state	1,147	.01	670	.01
Candidates from other states	0		0	
Civic organizations	980	.01	1,769	.03
Ideological groups	0		774	.01
Political parties	8,225	.08	1,625	.03
Subtotal	**10,352**	**.10**	**4,838**	**.09**
Unitemized Expenses	**174,114**	**1.72**	**9,528**	**.18**
Total Campaign Expenses	**$10,148,656**		**$ 5,213,198**	
PAC Contributions	$ 2,017,041		$ 371,721	
Individual Contributions	7,883,195		4,206,257	
Total Receipts*	10,451,746		5,020,867	

*Includes PAC and individual contributions as well as interest earned, party contributions, etc.

PENNSYLVANIA

Sen. Harris Wofford (D)

1992 Election Results

Harris Wofford (D)   1,860,760   (55%)
Dick Thornburgh (R)   1,521,986   (45%)

Appointed in May 1991 to succeed Sen. John Heinz, a three-term Republican who had been killed in a plane crash, Sen. Harris Wofford was initially given little chance of winning the November special election. Republican Dick Thornburgh, a former two-term governor and U.S. attorney general, was clearly the man to beat.

With just six months to prove the pundits wrong, Wofford launched a nationwide search for money. The campaign employed four professional fund-raisers: Cynthia Friedman Associates and the Fundraising Management Group, both of Washington, D.C.; New York-based PAC-COM; and the Brier Group of Harrisburg. Together, these firms were paid $86,744, which accounted for 70 percent of Wofford's event costs.

While only 5 percent of his total spending was invested in fund-raising events and direct mail, a substantial proportion of Wofford's overhead was directly related to raising money. Wofford immediately opened a Washington fund-raising office that employed twenty people throughout much of the six-month campaign. Rent for the office cost $17,000. The campaign also employed fourteen people across the country to raise money, including four in Massachusetts, two in New York, and others in California, Connecticut, New Jersey, North Carolina, South Carolina, Texas, Virginia, and West Virginia.

These efforts enabled Wofford to raise more than $3.3 million, 61 percent of which came from large, out-of-state donors and political action committees. Wofford raised 25 percent of his funds from Pennsylvanians who could afford $200 or more. Contributions of less than $200 accounted for only 13 percent of his receipts.

In June Wofford retained Carville & Begala of Washington, D.C., as his campaign management consultants and the $156,657 Wofford paid them was perhaps his wisest investment. James Carville's campaign strategy mixed positive messages on the need for national health care with pointed attacks on Thornburgh's tenure at the Justice Department and his record as governor. Wofford ads bashed Congress and hit Thornburgh for being a career politician.

With Thornburgh delaying his departure from the Justice Department until late summer, Wofford waited until September to make his first $364,000 media buy. The Media Co. of Washington, D.C., received $1,797,642 over the next two months. . Shafto & Barton of Houston, Texas, collected $54,644 for last-minute radio buys. Media consultants Doak, Shrum & Associates of Washington, D.C., collected $146,899 from the campaign and another $900,000 from the Democratic Senatorial Campaign Committee and the Democratic National Committee.

Campaign Expenditures	Wofford Amount Spent	Wofford % of Total	Thornburgh Amount Spent	Thornburgh % of Total
Overhead				
Office furniture/supplies	$ 33,593	1.03	$ 20,185	.47
Rent/utilities	39,159	1.20	39,006	.92
Salaries	309,474	9.50	222,275	5.22
Taxes	75,257	2.31	91,648	2.15
Bank/investment fees	2,207	.07	378	.01
Lawyers/accountants	54,923	1.69	5,109	.12
Telephone	60,337	1.85	43,372	1.02
Campaign automobile	0		0	
Computers/office equipment	37,511	1.15	53,798	1.26
Travel	129,946	3.99	165,742	3.89
Food/meetings	960	.03	2,000	.05
Subtotal	**743,367**	**22.82**	**643,513**	**15.10**
Fund Raising				
Events	123,098	3.78	280,613	6.58
Direct mail	24,057	.74	434,489	10.20
Telemarketing	0		220,763	5.18
Subtotal	**147,155**	**4.52**	**935,866**	**21.96**
Polling	**83,600**	**2.57**	**49,543**	**1.16**
Advertising				
Electronic media	2,011,660	61.76	2,247,072	52.73
Other media	5,281	.16	25,817	.61
Subtotal	**2,016,941**	**61.92**	**2,272,890**	**53.33**
Other Campaign Activity				
Persuasion mail/brochures	24,368	.75	0	
Actual campaigning	235,690	7.24	355,821	8.35
Staff/volunteers	162	.00	0	
Subtotal	**260,220**	**7.99**	**355,821**	**8.35**
Constituent Gifts/ Entertainment	**0**		**0**	
Donations to				
Candidates from same state	0		0	
Candidates from other states	0		0	
Civic organizations	0		0	
Ideological groups	0		0	
Political parties	0		0	
Subtotal	**0**		**0**	
Unitemized Expenses	**6,202**	**.19**	**3,964**	**.09**
Total Campaign Expenses	**$ 3,257,485**		**$ 4,261,596**	
PAC Contributions	$ 956,416		$ 866,367	
Individual Contributions	2,339,911		2,944,213	
Total Receipts*	3,334,768		3,881,889	

*Includes PAC and individual contributions as well as interest earned, party contributions, etc.

SOUTH CAROLINA

Sen. Ernest F. Hollings (D)

1992 Election Results

Ernest F. Hollings (D)   591,030   (50%)
Thomas F. Hartnett (R)   554,175   (47%)

The casual observer could not be blamed for thinking former president Ronald Reagan had endorsed Sen. Ernest F. Hollings in his bid for a fifth term. Among the twenty-two television commercials produced for Hollings by Struble-Totten Communications of Washington, D.C., was one showing Reagan praising the Gramm-Rudman-Hollings deficit reduction act, proclaiming: "From now on, when the public hears the names Gramm, Rudman, or Hollings, they'll think deficit reduction."

Reagan was not amused. After calling on Hollings to pull the ad, which Hollings refused to do, Reagan signed on to do one television and one radio ad endorsing former representative Thomas F. Hartnett.

The balance of Hollings's $2.1 million advertising blitz was driven by the dual need to paint the incumbent as a Senate leader who produced for South Carolina while trashing the Washington establishment. Interspersed were ads touting Hollings's achievements on behalf of the textile industry; his efforts to help a leukemia victim obtain a bone marrow transplant; and his work on behalf of Windward Farms, a residential treatment home for abused children that was damaged by Hurricane Hugo. "If those boys up in Washington cared half as much about your checkbook as they do their own, we could get this country moving again," intoned Hollings in one such ad.

For their design and production work, Struble-Totten received $135,782 from the campaign and another $10,596 from the Democratic Senatorial Campaign Committee (DSCC). The Media Group of Columbus, Ohio, received $74,375 for ad production; Pro Media of Needham, Mass., collected $1,809,020 from the campaign to purchase air time.

While Hollings initially planned no persuasion mailings, campaign spokesman Andy Brack said that decision was reversed by Hartnett's own 800,000 piece mailing. The November Group of Washington, D.C., collected $31,550 from Hollings's campaign and another $40,800 from the DSCC for their work on three persuasion pieces.

To fund his campaign, Hollings depended almost entirely on political action committees and out-of-state contributors, which together accounted for 77 percent of his total contributions. "He made friends all over the country when he was considering a run for the presidency," noted Brack, in a reference to Hollings's unsuccessful bid for the 1984 Democratic nomination.

Despite statements by Senate minority leader Bob Dole (R-Kan.) that this race provided the best chance for a Republican upset, the National Republican Senatorial Committee spent only $289,679 on Hartnett's behalf.

Campaign Expenditures	Hollings Amount Spent	Hollings % of Total	Hartnett Amount Spent	Hartnett % of Total
Overhead				
Office furniture/supplies	$ 97,703	2.39	$ 9,250	1.05
Rent/utilities	17,906	.44	15,620	1.77
Salaries	563,941	13.77	101,306	11.47
Taxes	148,248	3.62	16,464	1.86
Bank/investment fees	2,227	.05	1,026	.12
Lawyers/accountants	77,397	1.89	42,000	4.76
Telephone	70,254	1.72	31,187	3.53
Campaign automobile	3,777	.09	0	
Computers/office equipment	56,333	1.38	8,899	1.01
Travel	323,769	7.90	39,609	4.49
Food/meetings	22,170	.54	0	
Subtotal	**1,383,725**	**33.78**	**265,360**	**30.05**
Fund Raising				
Events	334,910	8.18	67,676	7.66
Direct mail	0		103,865	11.76
Telemarketing	0		0	
Subtotal	**334,910**	**8.18**	**171,541**	**19.42**
Polling	**74,717**	**1.82**	**0**	
Advertising				
Electronic media	2,047,532	49.99	337,933	38.27
Other media	4,692	.11	1,710	.19
Subtotal	**2,052,223**	**50.10**	**339,643**	**38.46**
Other Campaign Activity				
Persuasion mail/brochures	106,766	2.61	82,276	9.32
Actual campaigning	60,119	1.47	19,352	2.19
Staff/volunteers	576	.01	0	
Subtotal	**167,461**	**4.09**	**101,628**	**11.51**
Constituent Gifts/Entertainment	**29,932**	**.73**	**0**	
Donations to				
Candidates from same state	250	.01	0	
Candidates from other states	1,000	.02	0	
Civic organizations	1,250	.03	0	
Ideological groups	2,325	.06	0	
Political parties	10,195	.25	350	.04
Subtotal	**15,020**	**.37**	**350**	**.04**
Unitemized Expenses	**38,046**	**.93**	**4,590**	**.52**
Total Campaign Expenses	**$ 4,096,034**		**$ 883,111**	
PAC Contributions	$ 1,620,274		$ 153,311	
Individual Contributions	2,151,479		685,808	
Total Receipts*	4,016,311		907,376	

*Includes PAC and individual contributions as well as interest earned, party contributions, etc.

SOUTH DAKOTA

Sen. Tom Daschle (D)

1992 Election Results

Tom Daschle (D)	217,095	(65%)
Charlene Haar (R)	108,733	(33%)

Following his narrow victory in 1986, Sen. Tom Daschle expected a serious Republican challenge in 1992, so he never stopped running. Between Jan. 1, 1987 and Dec. 31, 1991 Daschle invested nearly $1.7 million in his permanent campaign, including $988,002 for staff, travel, and other overhead; $42,128 for polling; $20,402 for constituent gifts and entertainment; and $125,632 for advertising.

With debts of more than $148,000 at the beginning of 1987, Daschle sank $368,504 into his off-year fund-raising efforts. Events were held at the National Theater in Washington, D.C., and the Regency Club in Los Angeles, and an in-kind event was thrown by Citibank in New York, to name a few. The campaign sold T-shirts, sweatshirts, caps, and other promotional material emblazoned with the Daschle campaign logo.

Meyer Associates of St. Cloud, Minn., was paid nearly $172,000 for telemarketing during the first five years of the election cycle, and it paid off handsomely. Daschle took in more than $1 million, nearly $496,000 of it from political action committees (PACs), between Jan. 1, 1987 and Dec. 31, 1990. In 1991 he raised nearly $1.6 million, more than $858,000 of it from PACs.

By early 1990 Daschle's campaign had already hit the airwaves, and over the next twenty-two months sixteen television commercials were run, according to press secretary Steven Kinsella. Struble-Totten Communications of Washington, D.C., collected $77,667 from the campaign for designing the ads. The Media Group of Columbus, Ohio, received $85,679 for ad production; Pro Media of Needham, Mass., and Craft & Associates of Sioux Falls collected $520,462 and $68,898, respectively, to place the ads.

The expected strong challenge never materialized. Instead, Daschle found himself facing Charlene Haar, a former schoolteacher and state party chair who dispensed recipes at campaign stops. Nevertheless, while Haar raised only $317,145 from PACs and individual contributors, Daschle spent more than $2 million in 1992.

Once Daschle realized he had no race, the campaign began giving money away by the bushel. Between Oct. 15 and Oct. 30 Daschle's campaign contributed $210,000 to the South Dakota Democratic party for its efforts on behalf of state and local candidates.

Over the six-year cycle, seventeen members of Daschle's Senate staff received salary payments totaling $243,472 from the campaign, 80 percent of which went to three staffers. On Dec. 21, 1992 the campaign issued checks ranging from $1,500 to $4,000 to fourteen Senate staffers for what appeared to be end-of-year bonuses.

	Daschle		Haar	
Campaign Expenditures	Amount Spent	% of Total	Amount Spent	% of Total
Overhead				
Office furniture/supplies	$ 78,883	2.10	$ 10,262	2.52
Rent/utilities	72,554	1.93	5,134	1.26
Salaries	686,475	18.26	54,310	13.36
Taxes	323,758	8.61	6,582	1.62
Bank/investment fees	8,048	.21	280	.07
Lawyers/accountants	7,901	.21	0	
Telephone	53,791	1.43	16,149	3.97
Campaign automobile	0		13,163	3.24
Computers/office equipment	97,388	2.59	6,663	1.64
Travel	267,654	7.12	9,910	2.44
Food/meetings	14,264	.38	163	.04
Subtotal	**1,610,716**	**42.84**	**122,617**	**30.16**
Fund Raising				
Events	254,271	6.76	4,281	1.05
Direct mail	178,417	4.75	67,396	16.58
Telemarketing	241,088	6.41	2,865	.70
Subtotal	**673,775**	**17.92**	**74,541**	**18.34**
Polling	**171,284**	**4.56**	**0**	
Advertising				
Electronic media	771,345	20.52	156,458	38.48
Other media	67,160	1.79	2,227	.55
Subtotal	**838,505**	**22.30**	**158,685**	**39.03**
Other Campaign Activity				
Persuasion mail/brochures	41,549	1.11	16,698	4.11
Actual campaigning	30,015	.80	30,987	7.62
Staff/volunteers	377	.01	44	.01
Subtotal	**71,941**	**1.91**	**47,729**	**11.74**
Constituent Gifts/Entertainment	**27,402**	**.73**	**0**	
Donations to				
Candidates from same state	7,942	.21	0	
Candidates from other states	31,250	.83	0	
Civic organizations	2,382	.06	75	.02
Ideological groups	765	.02	60	.01
Political parties	221,382	5.89	340	.08
Subtotal	**263,721**	**7.01**	**475**	**.12**
Unitemized Expenses	**102,447**	**2.72**	**2,500**	**.62**
Total Campaign Expenses	**$ 3,759,792**		**$ 406,547**	
PAC Contributions	**$ 1,848,680**		**$ 71,491**	
Individual Contributions	**2,042,101**		**245,654**	
Total Receipts*	**4,122,119**		**479,045**	

*Includes PAC and individual contributions as well as interest earned, party contributions, etc.

UTAH

Sen. Robert F. Bennett (R)

1992 Election Results

Robert F. Bennett (R)	420,069	(55%)
Wayne Owens (D)	301,228	(40%)

The Republican primary between Robert F. Bennett and Joe Cannon proved to be the real race to succeed Sen. Jake Garn. It was a contest of multimillionaire industrialists.

Cannon, who emerged from the party's state convention as the early favorite, spent $5.2 million on his primary bid, including nearly $4 million of his own money. He outspent Bennett on advertising by roughly three to one, and yet Bennett emerged with the narrow victory.

As the son of a four-term Republican Senator, Bennett clearly had the advantages inherent in positive name recognition. However, his most powerful weapon turned out to be his media consultant, Evan Twede of Salt Lake City.

For the primary, Twede produced eleven television ads that were widely credited with jump-starting Bennett's come-from-behind victory. Twede's "in-your-face" ads painted Bennett as a determined political outsider by featuring close-ups of the candidate talking directly to the camera. "The reason I'm not using a narrator is because I want this to be between you and me," intoned Bennett in one ad. "I'm fifty-eight years old, and my kids are grown and gone—most of the time. When I look at my grandkids and then look at Washington, I get scared."

To combat Rep. Wayne Owens in the general election, Twede developed ads for Bennett that mixed attacks on the incumbent for his eighty-seven overdrafts at the House bank with issue-oriented commercials calling for term-limits and a line-item veto. For his work, Twede received $1,740,460, including $124,621 from the National Republican Senatorial Committee.

To reach areas outside the Salt Lake City television market, Bennett spent $67,834 on newspaper ads and $15,000 on billboards.

Bennett's office payroll was larger than all but ten Senate candidates, with four full-time employees in Ogden, three in Provo, and twenty in Salt Lake City. However, the $16,285 Bennett paid in payroll taxes was less than all but ten candidates.

The campaign's chief pollster, Dittman Research Corp. of Anchorage, Alaska, received $92,676. Kagel Research Associates of Salt Lake City collected $9,600 to conduct focus groups, which fed the advertising campaign. Dan Jones & Associates of Salt Lake City was paid another $14,312.

Owens never could compete monetarily, as he lacked Bennett's ability to put nearly $3 million of his own money into the campaign. This translated into an advertising gap of more than $1 million. Owen's television budget of $650,571 was just 70 percent of Bennett's overhead expenses.

	Bennett		Owens	
Campaign Expenditures	Amount Spent	% of Total	Amount Spent	% of Total
Overhead				
Office furniture/supplies	$ 51,834	1.47	$ 50,252	2.63
Rent/utilities	39,964	1.14	29,630	1.55
Salaries	503,326	14.30	242,468	12.71
Taxes	16,285	.46	87,954	4.61
Bank/investment fees	16,854	.48	1,056	.06
Lawyers/accountants	44,873	1.27	8,183	.43
Telephone	71,836	2.04	50,393	2.64
Campaign automobile	0		1,900	.10
Computers/office equipment	67,679	1.92	19,454	1.02
Travel	92,958	2.64	34,487	1.81
Food/meetings	6,568	.19	5,371	.28
Subtotal	**912,178**	**25.91**	**531,149**	**27.84**
Fund Raising				
Events	200,221	5.69	176,153	9.23
Direct mail	6,338	.18	87,629	4.59
Telemarketing	0		5,014	.26
Subtotal	**206,558**	**5.87**	**268,796**	**14.09**
Polling	**146,088**	**4.15**	**81,887**	**4.29**
Advertising				
Electronic media	1,704,117	48.41	650,571	34.10
Other media	94,473	2.68	74,052	3.88
Subtotal	**1,798,591**	**51.09**	**724,623**	**37.98**
Other Campaign Activity				
Persuasion mail/brochures	41,588	1.18	66,714	3.50
Actual campaigning	380,529	10.81	179,682	9.42
Staff/volunteers	4,057	.12	4,270	.22
Subtotal	**426,174**	**12.11**	**250,666**	**13.14**
Constituent Gifts/ Entertainment	**223**	**.01**	**9,882**	**.52**
Donations to				
Candidates from same state	0		3,999	.21
Candidates from other states	0		0	
Civic organizations	5,311	.15	80	.00
Ideological groups	450	.01	210	.01
Political parties	5,642	.16	1,722	.09
Subtotal	**11,403**	**.32**	**6,011**	**.32**
Unitemized Expenses	**19,059**	**.54**	**35,019**	**1.84**
Total Campaign Expenses	**$ 3,520,274**		**$ 1,908,032**	
PAC Contributions	$ 342,310		$ 601,937	
Individual Contributions	268,867		1,317,194	
Total Receipts*	3,524,942		1,934,683	

*Includes PAC and individual contributions as well as interest earned, party contributions, etc.

VERMONT

Sen. Patrick J. Leahy (D)

1992 Election Results

Patrick J. Leahy (D)	154,762	(54%)
James H. Douglas (R)	123,854	(43%)

In May 1992 Sen. Patrick J. Leahy challenged prospective Republican opponents John L. Gropper and James H. Douglas to join him in adopting a $440,000 voluntary spending limit for the general election campaign.

Under Leahy's plan, both sides would refrain from all broadcast advertising and instead submit to six one-hour television debates. Leahy's proposal also called for a complete rejection of political action committee (PAC) donations. To show that his heart was in the right place, Leahy called a halt to his PAC fund-raising efforts and put the proceeds from his off-year PAC events in escrow.

As it turned out, the $440,000 limit was far beyond what Douglas could raise. The $424,643 Leahy spent to maintain his permanent campaign during the off-years was more than twice what Douglas could raise for his entire campaign. As a result, the race was the least expensive Senate contest of 1992.

With only token opposition, Leahy was free to spend his money on a host of things that had little or nothing to do with his reelection. For example, only five incumbents spent more than the $52,531 Leahy paid to lease and maintain his campaign cars. For in-state campaigning he had a Chevy van. He kept an Oldsmobile, which was leased from Stohlman Oldsmobile in Alexandria, Va., for his own use.

Holiday cards cost the campaign $21,530. An inauguration party cost $5,852. Various other constituent gifts and entertainment added $9,329 to the tab. Leahy donated $48,000 from his campaign treasury to the Democratic Senatorial Campaign Committee (DSCC), another $30,000 to the Vermont Democratic Committee, $8,349 to other candidates, and $3,250 to the Presidential Inaugural Committee.

According to assistant campaign manager John Norris, the campaign was part of a coordinated Democratic effort involving the presidential ticket, as well as candidates for governor and lieutenant governor, so some of the persuasion mail was not specifically directed at reelecting Leahy.

However, Leahy did not entirely ignore his own reelection needs. He paid Greer, Margolis, Mitchell & Associates of Washington, D.C., $210,036 for designing, producing, and placing the campaign's broadcast ads. Garin-Hart of Washington, D.C., collected $51,500 from Leahy to conduct polls.

In a strange twist, while Leahy contributed money to the DSCC, the DSCC, in turn, paid Greer, Margolis $32,500 for their efforts on Leahy's behalf. The DSCC also paid Phone Ventures of Cambridge, Mass., $23,521 to turn out the vote for Leahy. Pollster Garin-Hart collected another $11,750 from the Democratic National Committee.

Campaign Expenditures	Leahy Amount Spent	Leahy % of Total	Douglas Amount Spent	Douglas % of Total
Overhead				
Office furniture/supplies	$ 32,649	2.91	$ 10,091	5.16
Rent/utilities	17,398	1.55	3,198	1.63
Salaries	142,090	12.66	33,568	17.16
Taxes	83,981	7.48	14,470	7.40
Bank/investment fees	1,061	.09	78	.04
Lawyers/accountants	24,370	2.17	0	
Telephone	25,202	2.24	13,680	6.99
Campaign automobile	52,531	4.68	0	
Computers/office equipment	34,624	3.08	800	.41
Travel	51,389	4.58	5,877	3.00
Food/meetings	17,258	1.54	355	.18
Subtotal	**482,553**	**42.98**	**82,117**	**41.97**
Fund Raising				
Events	36,850	3.28	6,963	3.56
Direct mail	22,369	1.99	0	
Telemarketing	0		0	
Subtotal	**59,220**	**5.27**	**6,963**	**3.56**
Polling	**51,500**	**4.59**	**5,420**	**2.77**
Advertising				
Electronic media	236,948	21.11	85,585	43.75
Other media	14,716	1.31	125	.06
Subtotal	**251,664**	**22.42**	**85,710**	**43.81**
Other Campaign Activity				
Persuasion mail/brochures	115,077	10.25	10,512	5.37
Actual campaigning	27,011	2.41	4,889	2.50
Staff/volunteers	123	.01	0	
Subtotal	**142,212**	**12.67**	**15,401**	**7.87**
Constituent Gifts/ Entertainment	**36,711**	**3.27**	**28**	**.01**
Donations to				
Candidates from same state	1,767	.16	0	
Candidates from other states	6,581	.59	0	
Civic organizations	711	.06	0	
Ideological groups	40	.00	0	
Political parties	85,171	7.59	0	
Subtotal	**94,270**	**8.40**	**0**	
Unitemized Expenses	**4,566**	**.41**	**0**	
Total Campaign Expenses	**$ 1,122,694**		**$ 195,639**	
PAC Contributions	$ 373,215		$ 0	
Individual Contributions	571,090		168,635	
Total Receipts*	1,144,189		196,635	

*Includes PAC and individual contributions as well as interest earned, party contributions, etc.

WASHINGTON

Sen. Patty Murray (D)

1992 Election Results

Patty Murray (D)	1,197,973	(54%)
Rod Chandler (R)	1,020,829	(46%)

For state senator Patty Murray, the campaign to capture the seat being vacated by Democrat Brock Adams began on a high note. In the political year of the woman, a television commercial narrated by Ed Asner recounted her inspiration for entering politics: a state legislator telling Murray she could never make a difference because "you're just a mom in tennis shoes."

This "mom" proved to be a quick study. After watching Rep. Rod Chandler virtually wipe out her double-digit lead in the polls with a barrage of negative advertising, Murray's own ad team went to work.

First, Murray supporters asked Chandler to pose for a picture shaking hands at an appearance, never bothering to tell him who they were. A cartoonish bag of money was then superimposed on Chandler's outstretched hand to create the backdrop for Murray's own attack ad. "Rod Chandler was paid eight hundred grand and passed only one bill in ten years."

Paul Kinney Productions of Sacramento, Calif., received $592,442 from Murray and $333,000 from the Democratic Senatorial Campaign Committee to design and place the campaign's broadcast ads.

Financially strapped, Murray's campaign chose not to invest in persuasion mail for the general election, opting instead to have precinct walkers distribute campaign literature.

Trailing Chandler in the money race by two to one, Murray was forced to make fund raising a high priority throughout the campaign, and no gathering was too small. A reception featuring Ellen Malcolm of the feminist political action committee EMILY's List drew approximately one hundred supporters, a breakfast attracted seventy-five, and a luncheon brought another sixty. In each case the initial ticket price was $35, and an additional pitch for money was made during the events. Small donors accounted for the largest share of Murray's receipts, 36 percent.

To attract larger checks, House Speaker Thomas S. Foley (D-Wash.) and Sen. John D. Rockefeller IV (D-W.Va.) lent their support to events with ticket prices ranging from $100 to $500. Those contributing at least $200 to the Murray effort accounted for 30 percent of her total receipts.

Chandler's tremendous monetary advantage allowed him to mount a three-pronged television, radio, and mail campaign in early October. Chris Mottola of Philadelphia, Pa., received $182,703 for designing Chandler's commercials. Media Plus of Seattle collected $751,074 from Chandler and another $407,838 from the National Republican Senatorial Committee to buy time. The Madison Group of Bellevue received $367,576 from the Chandler campaign, $133,218 of which was spent on persuasion mail.

Campaign Expenditures	Murray Amount Spent	Murray % of Total	Chandler Amount Spent	Chandler % of Total
Overhead				
Office furniture/supplies	$ 19,385	1.45	$ 58,805	2.20
Rent/utilities	10,450	.78	30,542	1.14
Salaries	165,587	12.36	328,441	12.27
Taxes	57,223	4.27	101,872	3.80
Bank/investment fees	1,124	.08	958	.04
Lawyers/accountants	0		1,092	.04
Telephone	63,384	4.73	45,706	1.71
Campaign automobile	0		0	
Computers/office equipment	6,241	.47	18,171	.68
Travel	29,813	2.23	96,297	3.60
Food/meetings	405	.03	1,318	.05
Subtotal	**353,612**	**26.40**	**683,202**	**25.51**
Fund Raising				
Events	52,197	3.90	223,913	8.36
Direct mail	123,838	9.24	237,412	8.87
Telemarketing	10,000	.75	0	
Subtotal	**186,036**	**13.89**	**461,325**	**17.23**
Polling	**49,540**	**3.70**	**76,806**	**2.87**
Advertising				
Electronic media	593,932	44.34	940,058	35.11
Other media	2,973	.22	3,005	.11
Subtotal	**596,905**	**44.56**	**943,064**	**35.22**
Other Campaign Activity				
Persuasion mail/brochures	26,403	1.97	244,525	9.13
Actual campaigning	106,817	7.97	263,472	9.84
Staff/volunteers	65	.00	318	.01
Subtotal	**133,285**	**9.95**	**508,314**	**18.98**
Constituent Gifts/ Entertainment	**616**	**.05**	**532**	**.02**
Donations to				
Candidates from same state	0		284	.01
Candidates from other states	0		0	
Civic organizations	0		1,524	.06
Ideological groups	0		577	.02
Political parties	0		1,490	.06
Subtotal	**0**		**3,875**	**.14**
Unitemized Expenses	**19,638**	**1.47**	**600**	**.02**
Total Campaign Expenses	**$ 1,339,632**		**$ 2,677,718**	
PAC Contributions	$ 439,766		$ 1,143,695	
Individual Contributions	994,383		1,234,791	
Total Receipts*	1,496,204		2,592,759	

*Includes PAC and individual contributions as well as interest earned, party contributions, etc.

WISCONSIN

Sen. Russell D. Feingold (D)

1992 Election Results

Russell D. Feingold (D) 1,290,662 (53%)
Bob Kasten (R) 1,129,599 (46%)

State senator Russell D. Feingold might never have won the Democratic primary were it not for his opponents' negative campaigning.

Political pundits and pollsters saw the primary as a race between Rep. Jim Moody and millionaire Joseph W. Checota. Two weeks before the Sept. 8 primary, a poll by the *Milwaukee Journal* showed Feingold attracting just 10 percent of likely voters.

However, Moody and Checota spent a total of more than $5 million, much of it on negative advertising aimed at each other. Feingold invested a far more modest $500,000, about half of which was spent on five amusing and off-beat ads. In one, Feingold held a fake tabloid newspaper with the headline "Elvis Supports Feingold" and joked that his record was so clean that opponents would have to make something up to use against him. In another, Feingold led voters on a tour of his home, at one point pausing at an open closet to say, "Look, no skeletons."

When the votes were counted, Feingold had 70 percent; Moody and Checota each had 14 percent.

In the general election, Feingold once again faced an opponent with far greater resources, Sen. Bob Kasten. The two-term incumbent wasted no time in going on the offensive with a $2 million ad campaign designed to paint Feingold as a liberal who would saddle small businesses and middle-class families with large tax increases.

Lacking Kasten's resources, Feingold's campaign decided to hold back on its media, running virtually no ads for the first two weeks and spending only one-quarter as much as Kasten for the next four weeks.

"The toughest decision we made was to hold our fire," noted campaign director Bob Decheine. "The key thing for us was not busting our budget in responding to Kasten. Our ads were so good, they were able to penetrate through the clutter."

For designing, producing, and placing eighteen television spots, Eichenbaum, Henke & Associates of Milwaukee collected $1,112,500 from Feingold's campaign and another $303,500 from the Democratic Senatorial Campaign Committee.

For conducting polls and providing strategic advice, Garin-Hart of Washington, D.C., collected $14,268 from the campaign and another $33,410 from the Democratic National Committee. Feingold also paid Wisconsin Research of Madison $32,320 for polling.

Feingold benefited from a $148,426 independent campaign waged by the National Abortion Rights Action League, which provided nearly $85,000 for radio and television ads and more than $43,000 for phonebanking.

Kasten paid nineteen consultants a total of $3,101,894 in his losing effort to retain his seat.

Campaign Expenditures	Feingold Amount Spent	Feingold % of Total	Kasten Amount Spent	Kasten % of Total
Overhead				
Office furniture/supplies	$ 41,250	1.98	$ 92,478	1.52
Rent/utilities	16,806	.81	65,757	1.08
Salaries	211,783	10.18	550,284	9.05
Taxes	56,079	2.70	270,431	4.45
Bank/investment fees	1,645	.08	3,823	.06
Lawyers/accountants	8,525	.41	48,410	.80
Telephone	92,957	4.47	145,314	2.39
Campaign automobile	10,785	.52	6,361	.10
Computers/office equipment	28,271	1.36	116,831	1.92
Travel	29,011	1.40	462,716	7.61
Food/meetings	63	.00	9,678	.16
Subtotal	**497,175**	**23.91**	**1,772,082**	**29.15**
Fund Raising				
Events	63,307	3.04	338,056	5.56
Direct mail	179,201	8.62	670,668	11.03
Telemarketing	15,924	.77	60,920	1.00
Subtotal	**258,432**	**12.43**	**1,069,644**	**17.60**
Polling	**46,588**	**2.24**	**107,263**	**1.76**
Advertising				
Electronic media	1,126,895	54.19	2,084,228	34.29
Other media	4,791	.23	9,099	.15
Subtotal	**1,131,686**	**54.42**	**2,093,327**	**34.44**
Other Campaign Activity				
Persuasion mail/brochures	38,441	1.85	196,091	3.23
Actual campaigning	56,413	2.71	710,764	11.69
Staff/volunteers	2,088	.10	1,009	.02
Subtotal	**96,942**	**4.66**	**907,864**	**14.93**
Constituent Gifts/ Entertainment	**0**		**25,768**	**.42**
Donations to				
Candidates from same state	401	.02	0	
Candidates from other states	0		1,000	.02
Civic organizations	60	.00	0	
Ideological groups	275	.01	1,000	.02
Political parties	140	.01	1,000	.02
Subtotal	**876**	**.04**	**3,000**	**.05**
Unitemized Expenses	**47,728**	**2.30**	**99,948**	**1.64**
Total Campaign Expenses	**$ 2,079,428**		**$ 6,078,896**	
PAC Contributions	$ 467,463		$ 1,425,073	
Individual Contributions	1,562,810		4,202,379	
Total Receipts*	2,094,575		5,973,353	

*Includes PAC and individual contributions as well as interest earned, party contributions, etc.

Part III

The 1992 House Races

District 1 — ALABAMA

Rep. Sonny Callahan (R)

1992 Election Results

Sonny Callahan (R)	128,874	(60%)
William A. Brewer (D)	78,742	(37%)

Rep. Sonny Callahan's biggest problem in 1992 was redistricting, not his eventual Democratic challenger, William A. Brewer. After the Alabama legislature's redistricting plan sought to virtually eliminate Callahan's district, he filed suit in federal court. Callahan prevailed but only after incurring about $160,000 in legal fees, according to chief of staff Jo R. Bonner. "People will ask why the campaign spent so much money on a no-name opponent," said Bonner. "Well, most of the money was spent on the redistricting lawsuit."

While Bonner's assessment proved to be a bit hyperbolic, the campaign did pay $35,000 in legal fees to Hamilton, Butler and Riddick of Mobile. Callahan also established a separate committee to help pay off the legal bills.

During 1991 Callahan invested $98,967 to maintain his permanent campaign operation, more than one-third of which was spent to raise money. His off-year expenses alone totaled more than seven times the amount spent by Brewer on his entire campaign. During 1992 Callahan outspent Brewer by more than twenty to one.

Callahan hired Public Opinion Strategies of Alexandria, Va., paying them $15,650 for two surveys of potential voters. "We were looking to see how the issues in southern Alabama compared to the entire nation," noted Bonner. "We were concerned about the polls showing George Bush trailing, and we wanted to see if that was true in our district."

With no opponent in 1990, Callahan limited his combined advertising and persuasion mail expenses to just over $18,000. With only token opposition in 1992, Callahan increased that total to $70,187. Timbes & Yeager of Mobile collected $38,815 to design and place broadcast ads; the firm also received $31,353 for its work on the persuasion mail effort.

The $78,823 Callahan spent to raise money during the 1992 election cycle was just $529 more than he spent on fund raising during the 1990 campaign. However, the yield was much better, with total 1992 receipts exceeding 1990 receipts by $57,407. Political action committees accounted for 60 percent of Callahan's 1992 contributions; individual donations of $200 or more accounted for another 33 percent. Small donations of less than $200 totaled just $24,235, or 7 percent of total contributions.

Callahan invested $5,126 of his campaign funds on a "media appreciation dinner," including payments to Timbes & Yeager totaling $3,515 for coordinating the affair. Another $425 was spent on tickets to a dinner sponsored by the Society of Professional Journalists.

Campaign Expenditures	Callahan Amount Spent	Callahan % of Total	Brewer Amount Spent	Brewer % of Total
Overhead				
Office furniture/supplies	$ 8,628	2.29	$ 556	4.15
Rent/utilities	7,666	2.03	0	
Salaries	11,303	3.00	207	1.54
Taxes	6,017	1.60	0	
Bank/investment fees	1,424	.38	243	1.81
Lawyers/accountants	41,494	11.01	1,075	8.01
Telephone	3,297	.87	19	.14
Campaign automobile	0		0	
Computers/office equipment	176	.05	196	1.46
Travel	17,889	4.75	0	
Food/meetings	7,082	1.88	0	
Subtotal	**104,976**	**27.86**	**2,297**	**17.12**
Fund Raising				
Events	63,572	16.87	0	
Direct mail	15,251	4.05	0	
Telemarketing	0		0	
Subtotal	**78,823**	**20.92**	**0**	
Polling	**15,650**	**4.15**	**0**	
Advertising				
Electronic media	38,834	10.31	5,210	38.84
Other media	0		2,350	17.52
Subtotal	**38,834**	**10.31**	**7,560**	**56.36**
Other Campaign Activity				
Persuasion mail/brochures	31,353	8.32	294	2.19
Actual campaigning	97,777	25.95	3,229	24.07
Staff/volunteers	0		0	
Subtotal	**129,130**	**34.27**	**3,524**	**26.26**
Constituent Gifts/Entertainment	**1,975**	**.52**	**0**	
Donations to				
Candidates from same state	500	.13	0	
Candidates from other states	2,500	.66	0	
Civic organizations	425	.11	0	
Ideological groups	0		0	
Political parties	500	.13	0	
Subtotal	**3,925**	**1.04**	**0**	
Unitemized Expenses	**3,502**	**.93**	**35**	**.26**
Total Campaign Expenses	**$ 376,815**		**$ 13,416**	
PAC Contributions	**$ 214,808**		**$ 0**	
Individual Contributions	**141,185**		**1,520**	
Total Receipts*	**376,087**		**13,500**	

*Includes PAC and individual contributions as well as interest earned, party contributions, etc.

ALABAMA   District 2

Rep. Terry Everett (R)

1992 Election Results

Terry Everett (R)	112,906 (49%)
George C. Wallace, Jr. (D)	109,335 (48%)

When Republican Rep. Bill Dickinson announced he would not seek reelection after more than twenty years in Congress, his 1990 Democratic opponent, Faye Baggiano, was already off and running. However, within two hours of Dickinson's withdrawal, state treasurer George C. Wallace, Jr., son of the former governor and presidential candidate, jumped into the race. After a bitter primary failed to produce a winner, Wallace knocked out Baggiano in a runoff.

On the Republican side, the nomination went to newspaper executive Terry Everett, who surprised highly favored state senator Larry Dixon by promoting a simple theme: "Send a message, not a politician." Everett spent $600,000 on his primary campaign, most of it his own money.

In the general election, press secretary Mike Lewis said Everett continued to hammer away with his one theme. "He focused on his status as an outsider, a nonpolitical type, and he frequently attacked Wallace as a person raised by his father simply to be another politician."

Everett also continued to send that message with his own money. While he spent $1,049,799, Everett raised only $109,635 from individual contributors and received no money from political action committees. Donations of less than $200 accounted for only $16,878, or 2 percent of his total receipts.

In addition to the $494,250 he paid for production and placement of his television and radio commercials, Everett spent $79,000 on billboards and $34,342 on newspaper ads. Journal ads and other advertising expenses added another $388.

To deliver his outsider message in both the primary and general election campaigns, Everett hired four Alabama consultants. Washington Political Group of Montgomery collected $603,195 to provide strategic advice, conduct polls, produce radio and television commercials, buy air time, purchase billboard ads, and handle the campaign's persuasion mail effort. McCullogh Advertising of Birmingham was paid $39,987 for ad production. Barry, Huey, Bullock & Cook Advertising of Birmingham collected another $64,369 to purchase air time. Everett paid New South Research of Birmingham $42,338 for managing the campaign's phonebanking effort.

To help with fund raising, Wallace hired consultants Mike Flint of Washinton, D.C., and JHM & Associates of Montgomery, paying them $47,967 and $7,000, respectively. Wallace's Washington-based campaign manager and media consultant Joseph Cowart developed six television spots, including two that featured Wallace's accomplishments as state treasurer. "Obviously, we missed something somewhere along the line," Cowart noted.

Campaign Expenditures	Everett Amount Spent	Everett % of Total	Wallace Amount Spent	Wallace % of Total
Overhead				
Office furniture/supplies	$ 8,967	.85	$ 17,484	2.60
Rent/utilities	24,780	2.36	10,768	1.60
Salaries	95,715	9.12	38,783	5.78
Taxes	0		3,166	.47
Bank/investment fees	10,694	1.02	643	.10
Lawyers/accountants	10,125	.96	500	.07
Telephone	29,490	2.81	23,011	3.43
Campaign automobile	0		0	
Computers/office equipment	2,527	.24	8,160	1.22
Travel	7,521	.72	13,400	2.00
Food/meetings	0		491	.07
Subtotal	**189,819**	**18.08**	**116,407**	**17.34**
Fund Raising				
Events	0		68,053	10.14
Direct mail	0		0	
Telemarketing	0		0	
Subtotal	**0**		**68,053**	**10.14**
Polling	**5,650**	**.54**	**41,840**	**6.23**
Advertising				
Electronic media	494,250	47.08	338,518	50.43
Other media	113,730	10.83	4,090	.61
Subtotal	**607,979**	**57.91**	**342,609**	**51.04**
Other Campaign Activity				
Persuasion mail/brochures	79,545	7.58	3,989	.59
Actual campaigning	136,371	12.99	82,253	12.25
Staff/volunteers	0		0	
Subtotal	**215,916**	**20.57**	**86,243**	**12.85**
Constituent Gifts/ Entertainment	**103**	**.01**	**588**	**.09**
Donations to				
Candidates from same state	0		0	
Candidates from other states	0		0	
Civic organizations	310	.03	0	
Ideological groups	0		0	
Political parties	5,000	.48	2,325	.35
Subtotal	**5,310**	**.51**	**2,325**	**.35**
Unitemized Expenses	**25,022**	**2.38**	**13,201**	**1.97**
Total Campaign Expenses	**$ 1,049,799**		**$ 671,265**	
PAC Contributions	$ 0		$ 247,409	
Individual Contributions	109,635		355,387	
Total Receipts*	1,070,472		639,142	

*Includes PAC and individual contributions as well as interest earned, party contributions, etc.

District 3 — ALABAMA

Rep. Glen Browder (D)

1992 Election Results

Glen Browder (D)	119,175	(60%)
Don Sledge (R)	73,800	(37%)

This rematch between Rep. Glen Browder and Republican Don Sledge went slightly better for the underfunded challenger, but that was small consolation. In 1990 Sledge spent $22,994 and captured 26 percent of the vote; in 1992 he garnered 37 percent of the vote with an investment of $21,562.

Browder operated a very inexpensive campaign, with no paid staff. A single payment of $1,000 for office rent was made to the Calhoun County Democratic Committee on Oct. 1, 1992. Telephone bills for the entire campaign amounted to $1,015. His wife Becky served as campaign treasurer. "My husband has always done campaigns the old-fashioned way, all with volunteers," she noted.

While many incumbents billed their campaigns for thousands of dollars in travel, hotel bills, and meal expenses incurred during the national party conventions, Browder spent $836 from his campaign on convention-related expenses. Only $378 in meals unrelated to fund raising were billed to his campaign.

His advertising was also extremely low tech. Browder spent $7,107 on newspaper ads, which was more than three times the amount he spent on broadcast advertising. Production costs for his television and radio commercials totaled $100; another $612 was spent to air the television commercials.

For his newspaper ads, Browder compiled news reports and favorable editorials from the local press. Some dealt with the 1992 campaign, others with previous campaigns, his years in the state legislature, and his tenure as Alabama secretary of state. Browder's ads simply showed a newspaper's masthead and an excerpt from the chosen article. "It was kind of like what movie promoters do in their ads when they summarize the reviews—the must-see candidate of the year," said Becky Browder.

Browder reproduced the newspaper ads and sent them out as his persuasion mail. The campaign also mailed a short biographical piece to newly registered voters. The entire persuasion mail effort cost $9,148.

Fund-raiser Christine Koerner of Alexandria, Va., who received $3,000 for organizing the campaign's Washington, D.C., events, was Browder's only campaign consultant. Browder collected $105,550 from political action committees, or 48 percent of his total contributions.

Other than his Washington events, Browder held no fund-raisers outside of Alabama. While he collected $60,913 from donors who gave at least $200, only $1,100 of that total was collected from out-of-state contributors.

Browder's lone direct-mail fund-raising solicitation was an in-kind contribution from the Democratic Congressional Campaign Committee. Donations of $200 or less totaled $49,534.

Campaign Expenditures	Browder Amount Spent	Browder % of Total	Sledge Amount Spent	Sledge % of Total
Overhead				
Office furniture/supplies	$ 6,291	5.78	$ 1,310	6.07
Rent/utilities	1,000	.92	0	
Salaries	0		0	
Taxes	2,600	2.39	0	
Bank/investment fees	0		10	.05
Lawyers/accountants	0		0	
Telephone	1,015	.93	0	
Campaign automobile	0		0	
Computers/office equipment	919	.84	0	
Travel	15,614	14.35	5,325	24.70
Food/meetings	378	.35	0	
Subtotal	**27,817**	**25.56**	**6,645**	**30.82**
Fund Raising				
Events	13,551	12.45	0	
Direct mail	300	.28	0	
Telemarketing	0		0	
Subtotal	**13,851**	**12.73**	**0**	
Polling	0		0	
Advertising				
Electronic media	2,206	2.03	7,187	33.33
Other media	7,107	6.53	441	2.04
Subtotal	**9,313**	**8.56**	**7,627**	**35.37**
Other Campaign Activity				
Persuasion mail/brochures	9,148	8.41	1,508	6.99
Actual campaigning	8,670	7.97	5,347	24.80
Staff/volunteers	50	.05	0	
Subtotal	**17,868**	**16.42**	**6,855**	**31.79**
Constituent Gifts/ Entertainment	0		0	
Donations to				
Candidates from same state	2,500	2.30	0	
Candidates from other states	1,250	1.15	0	
Civic organizations	500	.46	0	
Ideological groups	0		0	
Political parties	26,040	23.93	0	
Subtotal	**30,290**	**27.84**	**0**	
Unitemized Expenses	9,681	8.90	434	2.02
Total Campaign Expenses	**$ 108,819**		**$ 21,562**	
PAC Contributions	$ 105,550		$ 0	
Individual Contributions	110,447		11,629	
Total Receipts*	231,325		22,390	

*Includes PAC and individual contributions as well as interest earned, party contributions, etc.

ALABAMA District 4

Rep. Tom Bevill (D)

1992 Election Results
Tom Bevill (D) — 157,907 (69%)
Martha "Mickey" Strickland (R) — 66,934 (29%)

Had he chosen to retire at the end of 1992, Rep. Tom Bevill would have been allowed by House rules to pocket more than $560,000 in contributions left over from past campaigns. All he had to do was pay the income taxes. Instead, Bevill chose to spend $514,418 to defeat businesswoman Martha "Mickey" Strickland, who could muster only $20,119 for the race.

Running unopposed in 1990, Bevill had spent just $11,132 on advertising. However, faced with redistricting and a general sense that voters were not favorably disposed toward incumbents, Bevill took no chances in 1992. Fenn & King Communications of Washington, D.C., was paid $201,882 to produce and place the campaign's broadcast ads, which focused on job creation; Bevill's opposition to foreign aid; the need for better, more affordable health care; and his pledge to help make higher education more affordable. Nordlinger Associates of Washington, D.C., collected $3,932 for media production.

According to press secretary Olivia L. Barton, Bevill sent letters to registered voters in the newly acquired portions of his district letting them know he was "glad to be in their district." The campaign also spent $4,000 on sample ballots.

Garin-Hart of Washington, D.C., received $32,500 for polling; the Sinsheimer Group of Durham, N.C., provided opposition research for $5,374. In 1990 Bevill spent nothing on research.

Constituent gifts and entertainment, which had cost his campaign $15,680 in the 1990 election cycle, totaled $18,404 for the 1992 cycle. Expenditures included $1,750 for cookbooks, $4,587 for constituent meals, $3,042 for calendars, $3,131 for holiday cards, and $3,574 for glossy 8x10 autographed photographs of Bevill. Each Christmas, Bevill ran newspaper ads inviting people to drop by his home for coffee and cookies; the parties cost $1,574.

Bevill continued to share his campaign largess, increasing donations from his campaign treasury by 25 percent over 1990 levels. He contributed $10,000 to the University of Alabama Law School Foundation; $13,000 to the Democratic Congressional Campaign Committee; $7,800 to the Alabama Democratic party; $3,000 to the Alabama Democratic Leadership Council; and $1,000 to IMPAC 2000, the Democratic reapportionment effort.

With $566,499 in his campaign treasury at the start of 1991, Bevill did not have to worry about fund raising. Interest on his cash reserves accounted for 22 percent of his total receipts during the 1992 cycle.

To combat the Bevill juggernaut, Strickland made thirteen small radio buys and placed thirteen newspaper ads, for a total of $4,325 in media expenditures.

Campaign Expenditures	Bevill Amount Spent	Bevill % of Total	Strickland Amount Spent	Strickland % of Total
Overhead				
Office furniture/supplies	$ 10,169	1.98	$ 556	2.76
Rent/utilities	0		300	1.49
Salaries	0		25	.12
Taxes	14,528	2.82	0	
Bank/investment fees	0		0	
Lawyers/accountants	8,467	1.65	0	
Telephone	2,840	.55	2,239	11.13
Campaign automobile	0		0	
Computers/office equipment	902	.18	42	.21
Travel	67,965	13.21	1,685	8.38
Food/meetings	936	.18	0	
Subtotal	**105,807**	**20.57**	**4,847**	**24.09**
Fund Raising				
Events	19,328	3.76	50	.25
Direct mail	0		0	
Telemarketing	0		0	
Subtotal	**19,328**	**3.76**	**50**	**.25**
Polling	**32,500**	**6.32**	**0**	
Advertising				
Electronic media	206,129	40.07	2,789	13.86
Other media	2,186	.42	1,536	7.63
Subtotal	**208,315**	**40.50**	**4,325**	**21.50**
Other Campaign Activity				
Persuasion mail/brochures	1,447	.28	2,214	11.00
Actual campaigning	33,579	6.53	7,026	34.92
Staff/volunteers	0		0	
Subtotal	**35,026**	**6.81**	**9,239**	**45.92**
Constituent Gifts/ Entertainment	**18,404**	**3.58**	**0**	
Donations to				
Candidates from same state	1,000	.19	0	
Candidates from other states	3,800	.74	0	
Civic organizations	19,142	3.72	0	
Ideological groups	2,000	.39	60	.30
Political parties	32,555	6.33	105	.52
Subtotal	**58,497**	**11.37**	**165**	**.82**
Unitemized Expenses	**36,540**	**7.10**	**1,494**	**7.42**
Total Campaign Expenses	**$ 514,418**		**$ 20,119**	
PAC Contributions	$ 110,675		$ 2,500	
Individual Contributions	132,354		14,151	
Total Receipts*	318,198		20,114	

*Includes PAC and individual contributions as well as interest earned, party contributions, etc.

District 5 — ALABAMA

Rep. Robert E. "Bud" Cramer (D)

1992 Election Results
Robert E. "Bud" Cramer (D) — 160,060 (66%)
Terry Smith (R) — 77,951 (32%)

Although elected to his first term in 1990, Rep. Bud Cramer took no time getting used to running as an incumbent. Cramer spent $97,248 during 1991 to keep his permanent campaign primed, and he outspent his 1992 Republican challenger, Terry Smith, by a margin of nearly ten to one.

Cramer briefly closed his campaign office, but when it reopened in July 1991 his new landlord was the Cramer Corp., a company owned by his uncle. Travel was booked through Cramer Travel, his parent's travel agency. For his 1990 race, Cramer spent just $810 on his campaign car; once elected his campaign began paying $794 a month to lease a new 1991 Ford Explorer. The campaign mailed 2,500 holiday cards each December at a total cost of $3,223. He collected $6,619 in interest on the personal loans he had made to his 1990 campaign.

In 1990 Cramer raised a total of $573,685 from political action committees (PACs) and individual contributors in order to win the open seat vacated by former Democratic Rep. Ronnie G. Flippo. PACs accounted for $246,932, or 43 percent of that total. Without the need to raise extraordinary sums to finance his 1992 campaign, Cramer nevertheless collected $223,075 from PACS, or 57 percent of his total contributions.

Two of Cramer's Washington, D.C., PAC fundraisers were theater events: *Man of La Mancha* at the National Theater and the touring company production of *The Buddy Holly Musical* at the Kennedy Center. Press secretary Cindy Davis estimated that seventy-five people attended each of the post-performance receptions. "His consultants like to hold fundraisers that aren't just the standard reception-and-hors-d'oeuvres kind of events," Davis said.

Shortly before the November general election, Cramer made $500 donations to fellow Democratic incumbents Jim Bacchus (Fla.) and Les Aspin (Wis.). Democratic candidates Karen L. Thurman (Fla.), Carrie Meek (Fla.), George C. Wallace, Jr. (Ala.), Earl F. Hilliard (Ala.), and John Selph (Ohio) also received $500 donations. Incumbent George E. Brown, Jr. (Calif.), received $1,000.

Facing an opponent who could afford to spend only $2,050 on billboards and $1,276 on radio commercials, Cramer invested $63,620 in broadcast advertising and another $5,861 in newspaper and journal ads. Following a theme from his 1990 race, one of the three ads produced for him by the Campaign Group of Philadelphia, Pa., focused on Cramer's role in establishing the Child Advocacy Center, a shelter for abused children. Another ad highlighted his position on the Science, Space, and Technology Committee; his district is home to NASA's Huntsville Space Center.

Campaign Expenditures	Cramer Amount Spent	Cramer % of Total	Smith Amount Spent	Smith % of Total
Overhead				
Office furniture/supplies	$ 7,358	2.49	$ 1,670	5.59
Rent/utilities	7,899	2.67	625	2.09
Salaries	18,610	6.29	0	
Taxes	277	.09	0	
Bank/investment fees	6,803	2.30	349	1.17
Lawyers/accountants	126	.04	0	
Telephone	2,749	.93	1,470	4.92
Campaign automobile	20,878	7.06	0	
Computers/office equipment	4,677	1.58	120	.40
Travel	10,682	3.61	7,640	25.56
Food/meetings	1,149	.39	664	2.22
Subtotal	**81,209**	**27.45**	**12,537**	**41.95**
Fund Raising				
Events	90,617	30.63	706	2.36
Direct mail	0		0	
Telemarketing	0		0	
Subtotal	**90,617**	**30.63**	**706**	**2.36**
Polling	**4,700**	**1.59**	**0**	
Advertising				
Electronic media	63,620	21.50	1,276	4.27
Other media	5,861	1.98	2,050	6.86
Subtotal	**69,481**	**23.49**	**3,326**	**11.13**
Other Campaign Activity				
Persuasion mail/brochures	1,069	.36	2,477	8.29
Actual campaigning	27,149	9.18	6,532	21.85
Staff/volunteers	1,573	.53	0	
Subtotal	**29,792**	**10.07**	**9,010**	**30.14**
Constituent Gifts/Entertainment	**6,792**	**2.30**	**0**	
Donations to				
Candidates from same state	1,000	.34	150	.50
Candidates from other states	3,500	1.18	0	
Civic organizations	702	.24	0	
Ideological groups	1,420	.48	75	.25
Political parties	5,793	1.96	0	
Subtotal	**12,414**	**4.20**	**225**	**.75**
Unitemized Expenses	835	.28	4,086	13.67
Total Campaign Expenses	$ 295,839		$ 29,890	
PAC Contributions	$ 223,075		$ 1,523	
Individual Contributions	164,909		22,511	
Total Receipts*	400,693		28,545	

*Includes PAC and individual contributions as well as interest earned, party contributions, etc.

ALABAMA | District 6

Rep. Spencer Bachus (R)

1992 Election Results

Spencer Bachus (R)	146,599	(52%)
Ben Erdreich (D)	126,062	(45%)

Once Alabama's redistricting plan was approved, former state Republican party chairman Spencer Bachus knew Democratic Rep. Ben Erdreich was in trouble. Erdreich's old district had provided George Bush with 57 percent of the vote in 1988; the new District 6 had given Bush 77 percent in 1988.

During the primary, Bachus relied almost exclusively on Sterling Advertising & Public Relations of Birmingham. Sterling collected $49,280 for producing and placing Bachus's broadcast ads, $7,116 for purchasing billboard space, and $8,394 for coordinating direct-mail fund raising.

Bachus switched consultants for the primary runoff against former state Republican party executive director Marty Conhor, bringing in Bishop & Associates of Marietta, Ga., to handle his media. Bishop received $6,500 for ad production and $23,354 to place television commercials. The campaign spent $2,471 for radio and $2,964 for newspaper ads. Persuasion mail during the runoff cost $8,143. Bachus won the runoff with 59 percent of the vote.

Facing the better funded Erdreich, Bachus could not afford to waste any of his dwindling resources. "We've found that advertising in daily newspapers is virtually worthless today," noted media consultant Norm Bishop. "Radio can be almost as good as television, but it takes ten or twelve radio spots to get the same effectiveness as one TV spot, so we focused mostly on television."

Bachus's ads targeted the district's new Republican strongholds, attacking Erdreich for such things as his vote in support of a liberalized sex education bill for the District of Columbia. Another ad hit Erdreich for not supporting tougher penalties for Rep. Barney Frank (D-Mass.), who was reprimanded by the House for his relationship with a male prostitute. Yet another spot wondered why Erdreich's press secretary had been found rummaging through the dumpster behind Bachus's office.

Erdreich countered with his own $422,654 broadcast advertising campaign designed by Squier/Eskew/Knapp/Ochs Communications of Washington, D.C., and placed by its affiliate, The Communications Co. Among other things, Erdreich's ads charged Bachus with wanting to cut Social Security and Medicare.

Erdreich's six persuasion mailers, designed by Campaign Performance Group of San Francisco, Calif., largely echoed his broadcast ads. One charged Bachus with missing more than 3,000 votes during his tenure as an Alabama state legislator. Another attacked Bachus's role in the redistricting plan that "tore Tuscaloosa in two." Campaign Performance received $95,702.

	Bachus		Erdreich	
Campaign Expenditures	Amount Spent	% of Total	Amount Spent	% of Total
Overhead				
Office furniture/supplies	$ 10,102	2.06	$ 15,435	1.51
Rent/utilities	9,112	1.86	8,513	.83
Salaries	63,523	12.96	73,816	7.20
Taxes	23,444	4.78	6,471	.63
Bank/investment fees	116	.02	150	.01
Lawyers/accountants	225	.05	0	
Telephone	16,355	3.34	16,153	1.58
Campaign automobile	0		0	
Computers/office equipment	6,227	1.27	13,067	1.28
Travel	8,214	1.68	26,014	2.54
Food/meetings	43	.01	1,526	.15
Subtotal	**137,361**	**28.03**	**161,145**	**15.73**
Fund Raising				
Events	9,454	1.93	71,306	6.96
Direct mail	34,535	7.05	39,305	3.84
Telemarketing	6,750	1.38	0	
Subtotal	**50,740**	**10.35**	**110,611**	**10.79**
Polling	**12,381**	**2.53**	**76,380**	**7.45**
Advertising				
Electronic media	201,861	41.19	422,654	41.24
Other media	17,394	3.55	2,758	.27
Subtotal	**219,255**	**44.73**	**425,412**	**41.51**
Other Campaign Activity				
Persuasion mail/brochures	23,087	4.71	120,763	11.78
Actual campaigning	42,026	8.57	100,491	9.81
Staff/volunteers	94	.02	100	.01
Subtotal	**65,207**	**13.30**	**221,354**	**21.60**
Constituent Gifts/ Entertainment	**0**		**2,016**	**.20**
Donations to				
Candidates from same state	0		0	
Candidates from other states	1,000	.20	0	
Civic organizations	22	.00	4,207	.41
Ideological groups	0		3,273	.32
Political parties	0		10,180	.99
Subtotal	**1,022**	**.21**	**17,659**	**1.72**
Unitemized Expenses	**4,157**	**.85**	**10,171**	**.99**
Total Campaign Expenses	**$ 490,122**		**$ 1,024,748**	
PAC Contributions	**$ 150,307**		**$ 414,200**	
Individual Contributions	**329,694**		**227,959**	
Total Receipts*	**527,406**		**677,829**	

*Includes PAC and individual contributions as well as interest earned, party contributions, etc.

District 7 — ALABAMA

Rep. Earl F. Hilliard (D)

1992 Election Results

Earl F. Hilliard (D)	144,320	(70%)
Kervin Jones (R)	36,086	(17%)
James M. Lewis † (I)	12,461	(6%)

After winning the Democratic primary runoff by only 670 votes, state senator Earl F. Hilliard's November victory over Kervin Jones, a black Republican farmer, proved to be more a coronation than a contest. Prior to redistricting, 69 percent of District 7 residents were white; in the new District 7, 67 percent were black. Once Hilliard, a black Democrat, won the nomination, he coasted to victory, outspending Jones by nearly twenty to one.

To help him emerge from the six-person Democratic primary field, Hilliard secured the services of Direct Communications of Montgomery. "He didn't have much to spend on advertising," noted Direct Communications president Rick Heartsill. "It was a low-budget campaign." Low budget meant no television, so Heartsill developed a series of radio and newspaper ads that consumed $42,892 of Hilliard's budget during the primary and runoff campaigns.

The heart of Hilliard's primary and runoff campaigns was his grass-roots voter contact effort. For helping to distribute sample ballots, Hilliard paid $7,040 to the Jefferson County Democratic Conference, $6,000 to the Jefferson County Citizens Coalition, $4,000 to the Tuscaloosa County Democratic Committee, $4,000 to the Grace Temple Baptist Church, $3,040 to the Concerned Citizens of Bessemer political action committee (PAC), and a total of $9,460 to thirteen local Democratic party organizations. Hilliard's only other consultant, the Parker Group, collected $15,500 for running a phonebank.

For the general election campaign, Hilliard's advertising and get-out-the-vote expenditures were kept to a minimum. Between July and November Hilliard spent $12,426 on phonebanking and ballot distribution. Hilliard invested just $19,962 on his general election advertising, including $6,026 on newspaper ads and $13,936 on radio. Inexplicably, the Democratic Congressional Campaign Committee invested $37,599 in this lopsided race.

Bouyed by an influx of PAC checks following the runoff, Hilliard began putting more money into overhead. Before the runoff, Hilliard's brothers, Joel and Frederick, each received salary payments of $917; after the runoff they received checks for $3,500 and $3,450, respectively. Roderick Hilliard, another brother, was paid $1,515 after the runoff, but only $190 before. The campaign also paid $2,900 in travel expenses for his wife Mary to attend the Democratic National Convention. His son, Earl F. Hilliard, Jr., received salary payments totaling $2,000.

Hilliard donated $500 each to the Sixteenth Street Baptist Church and the Boy Scouts. Among his other donations was a $22 payment to a homeless woman for medicine and food.

Campaign Expenditures	Hilliard Amount Spent	Hilliard % of Total	Jones Amount Spent	Jones % of Total
Overhead				
Office furniture/supplies	$ 14,852	4.86	$ 627	4.08
Rent/utilities	16,098	5.27	0	
Salaries	42,956	14.06	1,056	6.87
Taxes	1,071	.35	0	
Bank/investment fees	0		107	.70
Lawyers/accountants	285	.09	332	2.16
Telephone	14,201	4.65	632	4.11
Campaign automobile	3,529	1.16	0	
Computers/office equipment	129	.04	719	4.69
Travel	20,608	6.75	4,171	27.16
Food/meetings	60	.02	99	.64
Subtotal	**113,789**	**37.26**	**7,742**	**50.42**
Fund Raising				
Events	15,177	4.97	0	
Direct mail	0		0	
Telemarketing	0		0	
Subtotal	**15,177**	**4.97**	**0**	
Polling	**0**		**0**	
Advertising				
Electronic media	44,352	14.53	2,522	16.42
Other media	18,503	6.06	1,811	11.79
Subtotal	**62,854**	**20.59**	**4,333**	**28.21**
Other Campaign Activity				
Persuasion mail/brochures	440	.14	1,480	9.64
Actual campaigning	107,836	35.32	1,751	11.41
Staff/volunteers	100	.03	0	
Subtotal	**108,376**	**35.49**	**3,232**	**21.04**
Constituent Gifts/ Entertainment	**0**		**0**	
Donations to				
Candidates from same state	0		0	
Candidates from other states	0		0	
Civic organizations	2,439	.80	0	
Ideological groups	185	.06	0	
Political parties	1,240	.41	0	
Subtotal	**3,864**	**1.27**	**0**	
Unitemized Expenses	**1,250**	**.41**	**50**	**.32**
Total Campaign Expenses	**$ 305,310**		**$ 15,356**	
PAC Contributions	$ 118,000		$ 0	
Individual Contributions	139,229		11,139	
Total Receipts*	362,942		13,281	

*Includes PAC and individual contributions as well as interest earned, party contributions, etc.

† No expenditures or receipts on file. Candidates raising or spending less than $5,000 are not required to file reports with the Federal Election Commission.

ALASKA — At Large

Rep. Don Young (R)

1992 Election Results

Don Young (R)	111,849	(47%)
John S. Devens (D)	102,378	(43%)

Following his narrow loss to Rep. Don Young in 1990, former Valdez mayor John S. Devens was anxious for a rematch. Unlike 1990, when Young outspent him by more than four to one, Devens approached 1992 with considerable financial resources and wide name recognition. Young had also presented Devens with an issue: fifty-seven overdrafts at the House bank.

Recognizing his vulnerability, Young invested $169,995 in his off-year campaign, including $78,912 for overhead, $52,256 for fund raising, and $14,187 for polls. In December 1991 the campaign also spent $13,591 on broadcast advertising. Press secretary Steven M. Hansen said these ads were meant to assure Alaskans that "things are getting better because there is peace around the world." Additional ads praising the Iditerod dogsled race were aired in February and March 1992.

Young wasted little time in going on the offensive, but his early attacks were aimed at the press, not at Devens. His attorney sent letters to reporters threatening libel suits against anyone who used the terms *bad check, bounced checks,* or *kited checks* when referring to Young's House bank overdrafts. Hansen said commercials aired prior to the September primary attacked the credibility of the press rather than his chief opponent, state senator Virginia Collins.

For the general election, one of Young's negative ads featured John Harris, the mayor of Valdez, reciting a list of "lavish expenses" supposedly incurred by Devens during his tenure as mayor of Valdez. Taxpayer-funded luxuries were contrasted with pictures of garbage-strewn streets as Harris described the "ridiculous job" Devens had done as mayor. However, as a local paper pointed out, one thing the ad did not say was that Young's supporters had littered the streets prior to shooting the street-scene footage.

Edmonds Powell Media of Washington, D.C., collected $302,832 from the campaign treasury, $39,801 from the National Republican Congressional Committee, and another $24,844 from the Republican National Committee to design and place Young's radio and television ads.

According to Hansen, Young's limited persuasion mail targeted military personnel, fishermen, blue collar workers, and rural constituents. The military mailer, which also included an absentee ballot, assailed Devens for seeking a 50 percent cut in the military budget.

Young also spent $34,296 on calendars for constituents and $5,500 for can openers, which were passed out at campaign events.

For his part, Devens noted that "the campaign became more sophisticated in 1992, and that took some of the fun out of it."

Campaign Expenditures	Young Amount Spent	Young % of Total	Devens Amount Spent	Devens % of Total
Overhead				
Office furniture/supplies	$ 11,596	1.29	$ 9,093	1.98
Rent/utilities	36,397	4.04	10,154	2.21
Salaries	87,811	9.74	58,690	12.76
Taxes	14,351	1.59	8,329	1.81
Bank/investment fees	173	.02	1,100	.24
Lawyers/accountants	26,941	2.99	2,559	.56
Telephone	14,311	1.59	9,512	2.07
Campaign automobile	3,506	.39	0	
Computers/office equipment	13,978	1.55	10,968	2.38
Travel	76,232	8.45	55,788	12.13
Food/meetings	2,992	.33	4,923	1.07
Subtotal	**288,288**	**31.97**	**171,115**	**37.20**
Fund Raising				
Events	98,104	10.88	37,125	8.07
Direct mail	26,657	2.96	13,994	3.04
Telemarketing	0		0	
Subtotal	**124,760**	**13.83**	**51,119**	**11.11**
Polling	**47,072**	**5.22**	**26,556**	**5.77**
Advertising				
Electronic media	329,059	36.49	125,546	27.29
Other media	9,366	1.04	11,831	2.57
Subtotal	**338,425**	**37.53**	**137,377**	**29.87**
Other Campaign Activity				
Persuasion mail/brochures	38,220	4.24	18,738	4.07
Actual campaigning	15,621	1.73	46,945	10.21
Staff/volunteers	30	.00	1,876	.41
Subtotal	**53,870**	**5.97**	**67,558**	**14.69**
Constituent Gifts/Entertainment	**34,296**	**3.80**	**0**	
Donations to				
Candidates from same state	0		0	
Candidates from other states	0		0	
Civic organizations	600	.07	1,252	.27
Ideological groups	0		25	.01
Political parties	3,000	.33	85	.02
Subtotal	**3,600**	**.40**	**1,362**	**.30**
Unitemized Expenses	**11,469**	**1.27**	**4,902**	**1.07**
Total Campaign Expenses	**$ 901,780**		**$ 459,988**	
PAC Contributions	$ 377,335		$ 98,851	
Individual Contributions	448,494		276,139	
Total Receipts*	867,848		468,027	

*Includes PAC and individual contributions as well as interest earned, party contributions, etc.

District 1 — ARIZONA

Rep. Sam Coppersmith (D)

1992 Election Results

Sam Coppersmith (D)	130,715	(51%)
John J. Rhodes (R)	113,613	(45%)

According to chief of staff Andrew S. Gordon, Sam Coppersmith's upset victory over Republican Rep. John J. Rhodes III could be chalked up to only one thing: "retail politics." In a district where the majority of voters are Republican, everything Democrat Coppersmith did was aimed at pressing the flesh.

Gordon said this philosophy extended to the campaign's Arizona fund-raising efforts, where Coppersmith preferred to ask for money "face to face." Tickets to these events generally ranged from $25 to $100. As a result, donations of less than $200 accounted for nearly one-third of the money Coppersmith raised from individual contributors.

However, small contributions from Arizonans alone would not have paid the bills. To help him tap into political action committee (PAC) money, Coppersmith paid Pederson & Thompson of Washington, D.C., $2,717 to arrange "general Washington fund-raisers." With their assistance, Coppersmith raised $66,183 from PACs, or 31 percent of his total contributions.

The Summit Group of Phoenix served as Coppersmith's general campaign consultant, collecting $44,240. President Mike Crusa said one of their first moves was to spend $19,411 to place 300 signs throughout the district. "It was a heck of a lot of signs, but a lot of people knew who Coppersmith was in a short time," noted Crusa. Crusa added that his company also handled collecting signatures on ballot petitions, phonebanking, and a get-out-the-vote mailing.

Emory, Young and Associates of Austin, Texas, was paid $21,250 for work on the campaign's persuasion mail. The campaign targeted pro-choice voters with one of its four mailings, paying $379 for a mailing list from Arizona Right to Choose.

Despite being outspent by nearly two to one, Coppersmith's outlays for broadcast advertising were just 21 percent less than Rhodes's. Progressive Communications of Tucson designed, produced, and placed Coppersmith's radio and television ads, including spots that sought to highlight his tenure as president of a local Planned Parenthood chapter.

While Coppersmith's personal campaigning may have made the difference, Rhodes entered the general campaign seriously wounded. He had cast votes in favor of both a congressional pay raise and income tax increases and had thirty-two overdrafts at the House bank totaling $60,000. Rhodes won the five-candidate Republican primary by only 1,500 votes.

Rhodes's media consultant, Winward Moody of Phoenix, developed three television and three radio spots for the general election. Campaign spokesman Gregg A. Houtz said the ads "tried to paint Coppersmith as a Ted Kennedy-type."

Campaign Expenditures	Coppersmith Amount Spent	Coppersmith % of Total	Rhodes Amount Spent	Rhodes % of Total
Overhead				
Office furniture/supplies	$ 4,116	1.64	$ 6,734	1.49
Rent/utilities	306	.12	9,022	1.99
Salaries	20,093	7.99	50,555	11.18
Taxes	7,539	3.00	15,337	3.39
Bank/investment fees	46	.02	8	.00
Lawyers/accountants	0		8,735	1.93
Telephone	839	.33	10,009	2.21
Campaign automobile	0		0	
Computers/office equipment	492	.20	6,693	1.48
Travel	851	.34	9,022	1.99
Food/meetings	117	.05	0	
Subtotal	**34,399**	**13.67**	**116,115**	**25.67**
Fund Raising				
Events	4,234	1.68	51,199	11.32
Direct mail	0		24,723	5.47
Telemarketing	0		0	
Subtotal	**4,234**	**1.68**	**75,922**	**16.78**
Polling	**22,359**	**8.89**	**2,483**	**.55**
Advertising				
Electronic media	109,313	43.44	137,581	30.41
Other media	574	.23	1,566	.35
Subtotal	**109,887**	**43.67**	**139,147**	**30.76**
Other Campaign Activity				
Persuasion mail/brochures	37,071	14.73	30,753	6.80
Actual campaigning	42,190	16.77	64,687	14.30
Staff/volunteers	835	.33	839	.19
Subtotal	**80,096**	**31.83**	**96,278**	**21.28**
Constituent Gifts/Entertainment	103	.04	4,906	1.08
Donations to				
Candidates from same state	0		500	.11
Candidates from other states	0		200	.04
Civic organizations	0		490	.11
Ideological groups	0		0	
Political parties	0		3,000	.66
Subtotal	**0**		**4,190**	**.93**
Unitemized Expenses	558	.22	13,315	2.94
Total Campaign Expenses	$ **251,635**		$ **452,355**	
PAC Contributions	$ **66,183**		$ **184,405**	
Individual Contributions	**142,693**		**265,061**	
Total Receipts*	**247,608**		**455,154**	

*Includes PAC and individual contributions as well as interest earned, party contributions, etc.

ARIZONA District 2

Rep. Ed Pastor (D)

1992 Election Results

Ed Pastor** (D)	90,693	(66%)
Don Shooter (R)	41,257	(30%)

In the September 1991 special election to fill the vacancy created by the retirement of Rep. Morris K. Udall, Maricopa County Supervisor Ed Pastor's greatest concern was voter turnout in the Hispanic community, which comprised 45 percent of the district's electorate. To help turn out the vote and ensure that he would become Arizona's first Hispanic representative, Pastor paid phonebankers Alexis Thompson & Associates of Phoenix and Roots Development of Tucson $37,190 and $12,540, respectively. Another $41,654 was invested in door-to-door canvassing; $12,164 was spent on food and drinks for volunteers. That was only the beginning of the special election spending.

First Tuesday of Malibu, Calif., collected $164,706 to produce and place Pastor's broadcast advertising, a sum that included a $10,000 victory bonus. The campaign also directly purchased $8,594 in TV air time and $2,274 in radio time. JRA Communications of Phoenix collected $116,154 for its work on Pastor's persuasion mail effort, including a $6,000 victory bonus.

Pastor maintained campaign offices in Phoenix, Tucson, and Yuma. Rent payments during this period totaled $10,062. Despite a largely volunteer staff, salary payments added $87,939 to Pastor's special election overhead. In all, Pastor spent more than $642,000 on the special election—nearly three-quarters of his spending for the two-year election cycle.

While the same level of intensity was not required in his 1992 race against farmer Don Shooter, the style of Pastor's campaign did not change. According to campaign manager Monica Lee, the campaign reviewed petition and precinct walking lists to better isolate areas where volunteers were needed. On election day the campaign employed poll watchers who contacted volunteers by two-way radio, informing them of precincts where turnout was light. The volunteers then fanned out with door hangers and campaign materials to encourage people to vote. Pastor also paid $13,797 to the Summit Group of Phoenix for phonebanking.

Lee said media production for the 1992 general election was a low-budget affair. Lee wrote most of the radio and television scripts herself; she used the Democratic party's Harriman Communications Center production facilities. The television ads aired mostly on cable stations aimed at reaching the district's Hispanic population.

To raise money, Lee said the campaign relied heavily on small events held in supporter's homes; 20 percent of Pastor's fund-raising event costs were paid directly by supporters. Lee added that the campaign also ran an in-house telephone fund-raising operation that she dubbed "dialing for dollars."

	Pastor		Shooter	
Campaign Expenditures	Amount Spent	% of Total	Amount Spent	% of Total
Overhead				
Office furniture/supplies	$ 24,309	2.74	$ 1,236	4.32
Rent/utilities	23,342	2.63	0	
Salaries	132,357	14.90	3,300	11.54
Taxes	6,334	.71	0	
Bank/investment fees	127	.01	90	.31
Lawyers/accountants	19,720	2.22	0	
Telephone	21,242	2.39	318	1.11
Campaign automobile	0		0	
Computers/office equipment	8,502	.96	0	
Travel	32,577	3.67	8,230	28.77
Food/meetings	1,866	.21	0	
Subtotal	**270,376**	**30.43**	**13,173**	**46.05**
Fund Raising				
Events	28,897	3.25	5,321	18.60
Direct mail	27,305	3.07	0	
Telemarketing	0		0	
Subtotal	**56,202**	**6.33**	**5,321**	**18.60**
Polling	**9,500**	**1.07**	**0**	
Advertising				
Electronic media	204,740	23.04	332	1.16
Other media	4,213	.47	290	1.01
Subtotal	**208,954**	**23.52**	**622**	**2.17**
Other Campaign Activity				
Persuasion mail/brochures	145,099	16.33	1,817	6.35
Actual campaigning	162,464	18.29	6,903	24.13
Staff/volunteers	25,245	2.84	50	.17
Subtotal	**332,808**	**37.46**	**8,770**	**30.66**
Constituent Gifts/ Entertainment	**3,692**	**.42**	**0**	
Donations to				
Candidates from same state	500	.06	0	
Candidates from other states	750	.08	0	
Civic organizations	1,327	.15	0	
Ideological groups	390	.04	0	
Political parties	2,115	.24	100	.35
Subtotal	**5,082**	**.57**	**100**	**.35**
Unitemized Expenses	**1,869**	**.21**	**620**	**2.17**
Total Campaign Expenses	**$ 888,483**		**$ 28,606**	
PAC Contributions	$ 350,310		$ 0	
Individual Contributions	508,749		29,846	
Total Receipts*	874,667		30,999	

*Includes PAC and individual contributions as well as interest earned, party contributions, etc.

**Totals include special election disbursements and receipts.

District 3 — ARIZONA

Rep. Bob Stump (R)

1992 Election Results

Bob Stump (R)	158,906	(62%)
Roger Hartstone (D)	88,830	(34%)

Rep. Bob Stump was not going to be surprised twice by businessman Roger Hartstone. Despite spending only $9,256 on his write-in campaign, Hartstone had captured 43 percent of the vote in his 1990 challenge to Stump and had never stopped running. For the 1992 campaign, Stump increased his overall spending by 37 percent, nearly doubled his advertising budget, and quadrupled his spending on brochures and persuasion mail over 1990 levels.

For the primary, which Stump won by a two-to-one margin, the campaign stuck exclusively with newspaper ads, which cost $4,871. In the general election, Stump spent $23,919 on newspaper and journal advertising. Radio spots cost $8,621. Including production costs, cable advertising totaled $10,027.

To encourage voter turnout, Stump invested $7,280 in the state party's phonebanking operation. Signs and posters cost another $2,006. The campaign spent $2,193 to buy fuzzy, green and white elephants that were used as promotional material. While the expenditures on signs and phonebanking were relatively low for an incumbent, Stump spent nothing on these items in 1990.

On the lighter side, Stump's expenditures for "constituent stroking" included $12,028 on Capitol calendars during the 1992 cycle, which was $6,091 more than the campaign spent on these gifts in 1989 and 1990. On the other hand, Stump's expenditure for year-end holiday cards dropped by $2,934 during the 1992 cycle to $4,903.

While he significantly increased spending on many aspects of the campaign, Stump's fund-raising expenditures for the 1992 cycle were 21 percent below the $46,934 he spent to raise money for his 1990 campaign.

As they had in 1990, political action committees (PACs) accounted for more than half of Stump's total receipts during the 1992 cycle. Administrative assistant Lisa A. Jackson said the campaign held two PAC events. Maxwell & Associates of Alexandria, Va., was paid $6,982 for coordinating the affairs.

Stump held only one major fund-raiser in Arizona during the 1992 cycle, a dinner at the Wigwam Resort that was timed to coincide with his sixty-fifth birthday. To celebrate the big day, as well as raise some money, the campaign spent $22,028.

Hartstone spent nearly $90,000 more on his 1992 challenge than he had in 1990 and did not do nearly as well. For one thing, Hartstone's additional effort was virtually offset by Stump's own $80,000 increase in expenditures. More importantly, Flagstaff, one of the state's more Democratic locales, was stripped from the district by the federal court, which redrew the boundaries for redistricting.

Campaign Expenditures	Stump Amount Spent	Stump % of Total	Hartstone Amount Spent	Hartstone % of Total
Overhead				
Office furniture/supplies	$ 6,032	1.99	$ 10,088	10.18
Rent/utilities	11,954	3.95	600	.61
Salaries	3,900	1.29	8,900	8.98
Taxes	0		0	
Bank/investment fees	0		42	.04
Lawyers/accountants	3,060	1.01	500	.50
Telephone	3,865	1.28	13,177	13.29
Campaign automobile	24,784	8.18	0	
Computers/office equipment	5,739	1.89	5,483	5.53
Travel	5,572	1.84	14,358	14.48
Food/meetings	1,302	.43	2,917	2.94
Subtotal	**66,208**	**21.86**	**56,065**	**56.55**
Fund Raising				
Events	37,039	12.23	3,562	3.59
Direct mail	0		0	
Telemarketing	0		0	
Subtotal	**37,039**	**12.23**	**3,562**	**3.59**
Polling	**4,700**	**1.55**	**0**	
Advertising				
Electronic media	18,887	6.24	11,718	11.82
Other media	28,790	9.51	3,232	3.26
Subtotal	**47,677**	**15.74**	**14,950**	**15.08**
Other Campaign Activity				
Persuasion mail/brochures	89,082	29.41	10,953	11.05
Actual campaigning	21,215	7.00	7,900	7.97
Staff/volunteers	341	.11	205	.21
Subtotal	**110,638**	**36.53**	**19,057**	**19.22**
Constituent Gifts/ Entertainment	**16,932**	**5.59**	**0**	
Donations to				
Candidates from same state	1,250	.41	0	
Candidates from other states	200	.07	0	
Civic organizations	200	.07	20	.02
Ideological groups	0		0	
Political parties	5,810	1.92	255	.26
Subtotal	**7,460**	**2.46**	**275**	**.28**
Unitemized Expenses	**12,210**	**4.03**	**5,229**	**5.27**
Total Campaign Expenses	**$ 302,863**		**$ 99,138**	
PAC Contributions	$ 136,092		$ 82,800	
Individual Contributions	79,162		17,410	
Total Receipts*	233,476		101,976	

*Includes PAC and individual contributions as well as interest earned, party contributions, etc.

ARIZONA — District 4

Rep. Jon Kyl (R)

1992 Election Results

Jon Kyl (R)	156,330	(59%)
Walter R. Mybeck † (D)	70,572	(27%)
Debbie Collings (I)	25,553	(10%)

In a district where registered Republicans comprised more than 50 percent of the electorate and registered Democrats accounted for only slightly more than 30 percent, Rep. John Kyl outspent his Democratic challenger, Walter R. Mybeck, by one hundred to one. Most of Kyl's efforts were directed at maintaining his permanent campaign organization, not at defeating the underfunded Mybeck.

In 1991 Kyl spent $104,785, including $60,219 on overhead, $29,321 on fund raising, and $3,989 on year-end holiday cards and constituent gifts. Over the two-year cycle, expenditures on these items accounted for 65 percent of Kyl's spending.

Kyl began 1991 with cash reserves of $335,703. By June 1992 his fund-raising drive had brought in another $532,264, and his cash balance stood at $620,270.

As in the 1990 cycle, Kyl maintained a "coffee cup club," which had annual dues of $19.91 and $19.92. Among his featured guests at the coffee meetings were Reps. Newt Gingrich (R-Ga.), Vin Weber (R-Minn.), and Dick Armey (R-Texas). The coffee cups given to each club member cost the campaign $4,987.

Big-ticket events featured White House Chief of Staff John Sununu and Secretary of Housing and Urban Development Jack Kemp. By far the most expensive of these was a reception held at the Registry Resort in Scottsdale in May 1992. Costs for the evening totaled $31,785, including $20,954 paid to the Registry, $3,500 for the band, and $535 for valet parking. The fact that individual contributors accounted for 70 percent of Kyl's receipts during this period is testimony to the success of these affairs.

While political action committees (PACs) were not the dominant focus of his fund raising, they were not ignored. Kyl held three Washington, D.C., events aimed at the PAC community during the first eighteen months of the campaign. With total expenses of $6,251 and receipts of $122,439, these fund-raisers were extremely cost effective.

Nelson/Ralston/Robb Communications of Phoenix served as Kyl's media adviser. With virtually no opposition, Kyl limited his media campaign to one television and two radio commercials. The TV spot credited the incumbent with forcing the House leadership to release of names of those who had overdrawn their accounts at the House bank. The ad also included a reference to his vote against the infamous 1990 budget compromise, which included several tax increases. Nelson/Ralston designed one brochure, which was mailed to households in the newly acquired portions of the district following redistricting. For its work Nelson/Ralston received $92,660.

Mybeck spent less than $5,000 and filed no reports with the Federal Election Commission.

Campaign Expenditures	Kyl Amount Spent	% of Total
Overhead		
Office furniture/supplies	$ 6,502	1.45
Rent/utilities	15,698	3.49
Salaries	55,874	12.43
Taxes	33,072	7.35
Bank/investment fees	138	.03
Lawyers/accountants	8,669	1.93
Telephone	7,296	1.62
Campaign automobile	0	
Computers/office equipment	4,700	1.05
Travel	29,883	6.65
Food/meetings	3,135	.70
Subtotal	164,967	36.69
Fund Raising		
Events	120,237	26.74
Direct mail	0	
Telemarketing	0	
Subtotal	120,237	26.74
Polling	25,100	5.58
Advertising		
Electronic media	73,921	16.44
Other media	1,612	.36
Subtotal	75,533	16.80
Other Campaign Activity		
Persuasion mail/brochures	23,356	5.19
Actual campaigning	17,265	3.84
Staff/volunteers	3,711	.83
Subtotal	44,332	9.86
Constituent Gifts/Entertainment	7,908	1.76
Donations to		
Candidates from same state	1,000	.22
Candidates from other states	0	
Civic organizations	0	
Ideological groups	0	
Political parties	1,538	.34
Subtotal	2,538	.56
Unitemized Expenses	9,053	2.01
Total Campaign Expenses	$ 449,668	
PAC Contributions	$ 163,168	
Individual Contributions	400,305	
Total Receipts*	616,410	

*Includes PAC and individual contributions as well as interest earned, party contributions, etc.

†No expenditures or receipts on file. Candidates raising or spending less than $5,000 are not required to file reports with the Federal Election Commission.

District 5 — ARIZONA

Rep. Jim Kolbe (R)

1992 Election Results

Jim Kolbe (R)	172,867	(67%)
Jim Toevs (D)	77,256	(30%)

Since narrowly winning his seat in 1984, Rep. Jim Kolbe had won reelection three times by margins of two to one, and 1992 proved to be no different. While George Bush saw his electoral totals drop in this district from 56 percent in 1988 to 37 percent in 1992, Kolbe garnered 67 percent of the vote against Democrat Jim Toevs.

However, Kolbe did not coast through the 1992 race. The $469,056 he spent in 1992 was $243,000 more than he had invested in his 1990 campaign. Compared with 1990, he spent $1,473 less on overhead but $95,395 more on brochures and persuasion mail. Having spent nothing on advertising in 1990, Kolbe invested $48,987 in the 1992 race on broadcast advertising and $3,015 on newspaper ads. Polling costs jumped from $4,995 in 1990 to $21,311 in 1992.

Much of this increased spending could be explained by the differences in his 1992 primary and general election challengers. "Jim had to redirect the campaign for each race," noted press secretary Robert Johnson. "In the primary, he was running against a right-wing family values candidate, and then in the general election he ran against Ted Kennedy's best friend on the left. Each time we had to rethink the whole campaign. Each time we had to get our message out."

To get that message out, Kolbe paid McNally, Temple & Associates of Sacramento, Calif., $71,656 to design and produce the campaign's persuasion mail. Hilton & Myers Advertising of Tucson received $48,601 for work on Kolbe's television and radio spots.

Kolbe increased his expenditures on fund raising by 42 percent over 1990 levels. Maxwell & Associates of Alexandria, Va., received $19,612 to arrange the campaign's Washington, D.C., events. Two sit-down dinners were held for members of the Kolbe Club, Kolbe's large-donor fund-raising organization. In addition to numerous receptions hosted by supporters, the campaign held two small-donor events: one in conjunction with a Pacific Coast League baseball game; another at Trail Dust Town, a western theme park. While the campaign mailed several fund-raising solicitations, Johnson said considerably more money was raised in response to their persuasion mail.

Overall, political action committees accounted for 36 percent of Kolbe's contributions and donations of $200 or more accounted for another 34 percent. Kolbe raised 29 percent of his donations from those who gave less than $200.

Among Toevs's biggest expenses was the $4,871 he spent for 500 copies of a ten-minute video, which he mailed to groups such as the Arizona Right to Choose Committee.

Campaign Expenditures	Kolbe Amount Spent	Kolbe % of Total	Toevs Amount Spent	Toevs % of Total
Overhead				
Office furniture/supplies	$ 13,675	2.92	$ 2,256	3.12
Rent/utilities	10,583	2.26	2,801	3.87
Salaries	46,869	9.99	3,873	5.35
Taxes	20,094	4.28	0	
Bank/investment fees	0		168	.23
Lawyers/accountants	2,940	.63	0	
Telephone	5,824	1.24	2,956	4.09
Campaign automobile	0		0	
Computers/office equipment	6,733	1.44	0	
Travel	9,045	1.93	5,682	7.86
Food/meetings	1,164	.25	106	.15
Subtotal	**116,928**	**24.93**	**17,842**	**24.67**
Fund Raising				
Events	51,343	10.95	2,385	3.30
Direct mail	26,348	5.62	0	
Telemarketing	10,157	2.17	0	
Subtotal	**87,848**	**18.73**	**2,385**	**3.30**
Polling	**21,311**	**4.54**	**8,500**	**11.75**
Advertising				
Electronic media	48,987	10.44	1,650	2.28
Other media	3,015	.64	5,698	7.88
Subtotal	**52,002**	**11.09**	**7,348**	**10.16**
Other Campaign Activity				
Persuasion mail/brochures	111,147	23.70	16,657	23.03
Actual campaigning	49,587	10.57	19,229	26.59
Staff/volunteers	1,232	.26	0	
Subtotal	**161,966**	**34.53**	**35,886**	**49.62**
Constituent Gifts/Entertainment	**5,853**	**1.25**	**0**	
Donations to				
Candidates from same state	1,000	.21	0	
Candidates from other states	250	.05	0	
Civic organizations	0		0	
Ideological groups	0		250	.35
Political parties	1,000	.21	117	.16
Subtotal	**2,250**	**.48**	**367**	**.51**
Unitemized Expenses	**20,897**	**4.46**	**0**	
Total Campaign Expenses	**$ 469,056**		**$ 72,328**	
PAC Contributions	$ 143,400		$ 26,000	
Individual Contributions	248,369		52,099	
Total Receipts*	409,883		104,313	

*Includes PAC and individual contributions as well as interest earned, party contributions, etc.

ARIZONA — District 6

Rep. Karan English (D)

1992 Election Results

Karan English (D)	124,251	(53%)
Doug Wead (R)	97,074	(41%)
Sarah Stannard † (I)	13,047	(6%)

State senator Karan English initially had difficulty raising money for her race against Republican Doug Wead, an Assemblies of God minister. So, in this "Year of the Woman," English turned to a host of women's organizations for help. "Women's groups were very helpful in the beginning," remarked staff fund-raiser Paul Kelly. "EMILY's List was responsible for jumpstarting the campaign when there was no interest in Karan or the race."

EMILY's List provided in-kind direct-mail fund-raising services totaling $9,246, and its president, Ellen Malcolm, was the featured guest at one of English's events. The Women's Campaign Fund donated $10,000. The National Women's Political Caucus contributed $6,500. The National Organization for Women gave $1,200, and the Hollywood Women's Political Committee added $1,000.

With EMILY's List taking care of the fund-raising mail, English's campaign concentrated on organizing countless in-home fund-raisers. "We didn't have a lot of money, so we really sought out people who supported Karan and asked them to have a fund-raiser in their home," said Kelly. These weekly events drew fifty to seventy-five people who paid $100 or less to attend.

Outspent on advertising by more than five to one, English had to rely heavily on persuasion mail to get her message out.

RO/LO Creative of Scottsdale developed a series of three mailings that targeted approximately 50,000 moderate Republicans, women, and registered Democrats. Striking an antiestablishment theme, the first mailer showed an overweight man sitting in a lawn chair, smoking a cigar. The tagline read: "Washington's been sitting down on the job again." The second mailing focused on Wead's close relationship with TV evangelists Jim and Tammy Faye Baker, while the third piece posed the question, "Who's better for Arizona?" Finally, a fourth piece summarizing the first three mailers was sent to 100,000 registered voters. For its work on these mailings, as well as for the production and placement of the campaign's radio ads, signs, and posters, RO/LO received $129,519.

In a move reminiscent of the Clinton-Gore bus tours, English toured the district twice—once in a rented recreational vehicle and a second time in "Ollie the Trolley." Noted Kelly, "If you pull a trolley into Apache, Arizona, you are going to have a ton of people come out, and the press will definitely be there, too."

Wead spent more than 45 percent of his funds on advertising, including $88,675 for copies of a seventeen-minute video mailed to potential supporters.

Campaign Expenditures	English Amount Spent	English % of Total	Wead Amount Spent	Wead % of Total
Overhead				
Office furniture/supplies	$ 15,714	3.56	$ 13,712	2.02
Rent/utilities	5,432	1.23	15,613	2.30
Salaries	79,534	18.00	34,353	5.06
Taxes	6,669	1.51	3,690	.54
Bank/investment fees	284	.06	0	
Lawyers/accountants	1,900	.43	0	
Telephone	19,587	4.43	9,198	1.36
Campaign automobile	0		0	
Computers/office equipment	5,880	1.33	8,493	1.25
Travel	13,045	2.95	21,642	3.19
Food/meetings	0		0	
Subtotal	**148,045**	**33.50**	**106,702**	**15.73**
Fund Raising				
Events	17,640	3.99	27,390	4.04
Direct mail	14,574	3.30	9,443	1.39
Telemarketing	0		0	
Subtotal	**32,214**	**7.29**	**36,833**	**5.43**
Polling	**28,131**	**6.37**	**0**	
Advertising				
Electronic media	56,624	12.81	215,986	31.83
Other media	3,320	.75	91,499	13.49
Subtotal	**59,943**	**13.57**	**307,485**	**45.32**
Other Campaign Activity				
Persuasion mail/brochures	91,946	20.81	106,956	15.76
Actual campaigning	81,298	18.40	101,837	15.01
Staff/volunteers	94	.02	962	.14
Subtotal	**173,338**	**39.23**	**209,756**	**30.91**
Constituent Gifts/ Entertainment	**0**		**0**	
Donations to				
Candidates from same state	0		0	
Candidates from other states	0		0	
Civic organizations	20	.00	10	.00
Ideological groups	0		0	
Political parties	0		0	
Subtotal	**20**	**.00**	**10**	**.00**
Unitemized Expenses	**202**	**.05**	**17,708**	**2.61**
Total Campaign Expenses	**$ 441,894**		**$ 678,495**	
PAC Contributions	**$ 135,087**		**$ 43,795**	
Individual Contributions	**221,882**		**499,069**	
Total Receipts*	**394,253**		**669,568**	

* Includes PAC and individual contributions as well as interest earned, party contributions, etc.

† No expenditures or receipts on file. Candidates raising or spending less than $5,000 are not required to file reports with the Federal Election Commission.

District 1 — ARKANSAS

Rep. Blanche Lambert (D)

1992 Election Results

Blanche Lambert (D)	149,558	(70%)
Terry Hayes (R)	64,618	(30%)

Blanche Lambert, a thirty-one-year-old former aide to Democratic Rep. Bill Alexander, saw both sides of the political money game during her 1992 campaign odyssey.

Lambert began her bid to unseat Alexander, who had served twenty-four years in the House, with virtually no money. However, she did have one very powerful campaign weapon: 487 overdrafts by Alexander at the House bank. In a year when "change" was the operative campaign buzzword and Washington insiders were running as "outsiders," Alexander's overdrafts were his undoing.

Lambert hired Strother-Duffy-Strother of Washington, D.C., to design her limited media campaign and provide general strategic advice, but she was able to pay them only $2,153 during the primary. To save money, the campaign opted not to do preprimary polls. In the three months prior to the primary, only $1,533 was spent on newspaper ads.

Ten days before the primary, Lambert unveiled a television commercial that focused on Alexander's initial denial that he had any overdrafts at the House bank. The spot opened with five seconds of footage showing Alexander's denial; his image was encased in a "Looney Tunes" cartoon box labeled "Bill Toons." Following the denial, a game show buzzer sounded, the Looney Tunes music started, and the words "Alexander had actually bounced 487 checks" appeared on the screen. At that point, the ad switched to a shot of Lambert, and the music shifted to Aaron Copeland's "Fanfare for the Common Man." The final twenty seconds was a positive pitch for her campaign.

Media Strategies of Falls Church, Va., collected $58,000 to buy preprimary air time, and the campaign directly purchased another $1,740. It clearly worked. Lambert carried twenty-three of the district's twenty-five counties and won 61 percent of the vote. Her primary victory cost $80,000. Immediately following the primary, Lambert spent $2,196 on "thank-you" newspaper ads.

With the nomination secured in an overwhelmingly Democratic district, Lambert quickly found herself in the role of the well-heeled incumbent. Over the last six months of 1992, contributions to Lambert totaled $310,404, including $159,950 from political action committees. On July 28, 1992 the Public Securities Association threw her an in-kind breakfast.

While Republican Terry Hayes had no money for advertising and spent $28,372 on his entire campaign, Lambert invested well over $100,000 in broadcast ads during the general election. Prior to the May primary, Lambert had conducted a districtwide, whistle-stop bus tour. In August she again toured the district, but this time she paid $410 for a chartered airplane to shuttle her between events.

	Lambert		Hayes	
Campaign Expenditures	Amount Spent	% of Total	Amount Spent	% of Total
Overhead				
Office furniture/supplies	$ 7,648	2.34	$ 1,413	4.98
Rent/utilities	3,494	1.07	748	2.64
Salaries	28,185	8.64	9,615	33.89
Taxes	0		0	
Bank/investment fees	72	.02	0	
Lawyers/accountants	0		0	
Telephone	19,649	6.02	2,297	8.09
Campaign automobile	0		0	
Computers/office equipment	1,917	.59	746	2.63
Travel	12,701	3.89	4,026	14.19
Food/meetings	0		0	
Subtotal	**73,666**	**22.57**	**18,844**	**66.42**
Fund Raising				
Events	6,698	2.05	267	.94
Direct mail	0		0	
Telemarketing	0		0	
Subtotal	**6,698**	**2.05**	**267**	**.94**
Polling	**12,319**	**3.78**	**0**	
Advertising				
Electronic media	190,627	58.42	0	
Other media	8,430	2.58	255	.90
Subtotal	**199,057**	**61.00**	**255**	**.90**
Other Campaign Activity				
Persuasion mail/brochures	445	.14	2,239	7.89
Actual campaigning	29,066	8.91	3,267	11.52
Staff/volunteers	220	.07	0	
Subtotal	**29,732**	**9.11**	**5,506**	**19.41**
Constituent Gifts/ Entertainment	**1,203**	**.37**	**0**	
Donations to				
Candidates from same state	0		0	
Candidates from other states	0		0	
Civic organizations	445	.14	0	
Ideological groups	0		0	
Political parties	1,000	.31	0	
Subtotal	**1,445**	**.44**	**0**	
Unitemized Expenses	2,196	.67	3,500	12.34
Total Campaign Expenses	$ 326,315		$ 28,372	
PAC Contributions	$ 176,400		$ 2,500	
Individual Contributions	247,049		27,635	
Total Receipts*	439,343		38,015	

*Includes PAC and individual contributions as well as interest earned, party contributions, etc.

ARKANSAS — District 2

Rep. Ray Thornton (D)

1992 Election Results

Ray Thornton (D)	154,946	(74%)
Dennis Scott (R)	53,978	(26%)

In the words of Lauren Gaddy, Rep. Ray Thornton's press secretary, the 1992 campaign was "not one of the most challenging races." Thornton faced no primary opposition and, as Gaddy diplomatically put it, "there was only a token opponent in the general."

In winning the 1990 race for what was then an open seat, Thornton had accumulated debts totaling $42,683. Yet, while congressional staff director Edward D. Fry II said donors in Arkansas were "pretty well worked over" by the presidential race, a Senate race, and contests for three open House seats, Thornton was able to easily retire his debts by the end of 1991.

According to Fry, Thornton held "two or three" fund-raisers each year in Washington, D.C. There were no set ticket prices; supporters were simply encouraged to contribute whatever they wanted. Political action committees accounted for $141,550, or 48 percent, of Thornton's contributions; $7,000 was raised from out-of-state donors who gave $200 or more.

While Fry said "the campaign was careful in its fund raising and didn't do a lot in the district," Thornton still managed to raise $132,975 from Arkansas residents who donated at least $200. An investment of $2,463 in direct-mail fund raising yielded $13,722 in contributions of less than $200, or 5 percent of Thornton's total donations.

Facing no significant opposition in Republican Dennis Scott, Thornton spent nothing on persuasion mail or brochures. The campaign invested just $4,861 in yard signs and posters. The $5,000 filing fee was one of the campaign's single biggest expenses. Newspaper ads cost the campaign only $1,126.

To remind voters that he was running and interested in their votes, Thornton ran three television ads. They focused on health care, his record in the House, and on jobs and economic development. Two radio ads encouraging people to vote were also run in the final days of the race.

Thornton paid $10,457 to Politics Inc. of Washington, D.C., and $5,071 to Like Dempictures & Post of Little Rock for creative and production work on the ad campaign. The Communications Group of Little Rock collected $45,253 to buy air time.

Immediately following the election, Thornton used campaign funds to pay for a retreat for some of his volunteers. According to Fry, between twenty-five and thirty volunteers were treated to dinner and an overnight stay at Gaston's, a fishing lodge. Fry dubbed the gesture a combination "thank you" and political strategy meeting where they discussed "the future of state and national politics."

	Thornton		Scott	
Campaign Expenditures	Amount Spent	% of Total	Amount Spent	% of Total
Overhead				
Office furniture/supplies	$ 7,629	4.68	$ 78	1.26
Rent/utilities	8,899	5.45	0	
Salaries	5,605	3.44	0	
Taxes	4,453	2.73	0	
Bank/investment fees	3,195	1.96	52	.84
Lawyers/accountants	1,050	.64	0	
Telephone	5,326	3.26	488	7.85
Campaign automobile	376	.23	0	
Computers/office equipment	9,235	5.66	0	
Travel	1,623	.99	827	13.31
Food/meetings	681	.42	0	
Subtotal	**48,073**	**29.47**	**1,446**	**23.27**
Fund Raising				
Events	18,999	11.64	120	1.93
Direct mail	2,463	1.51	0	
Telemarketing	0		0	
Subtotal	**21,462**	**13.15**	**120**	**1.93**
Polling	**0**		**0**	
Advertising				
Electronic media	65,839	40.35	0	
Other media	1,126	.69	205	3.30
Subtotal	**66,965**	**41.05**	**205**	**3.30**
Other Campaign Activity				
Persuasion mail/brochures	0		531	8.54
Actual campaigning	13,936	8.54	3,913	62.96
Staff/volunteers	2,161	1.32	0	
Subtotal	**16,096**	**9.87**	**4,444**	**71.50**
Constituent Gifts/Entertainment	2,340	1.43	0	
Donations to				
Candidates from same state	0		0	
Candidates from other states	0		0	
Civic organizations	0		0	
Ideological groups	140	.09	0	
Political parties	140	.09	0	
Subtotal	**280**	**.17**	**0**	
Unitemized Expenses	7,933	4.86	0	
Total Campaign Expenses	**$ 163,150**		**$ 6,215**	
PAC Contributions	$ 141,550		$ 500	
Individual Contributions	153,697		2,720	
Total Receipts*	303,430		5,724	

*Includes PAC and individual contributions as well as interest earned, party contributions, etc.

District 3 — ARKANSAS

Rep. Tim Hutchinson (R)

1992 Election Results

Tim Hutchinson (R)	125,295	(50%)
John VanWinkle (D)	117,775	(47%)

The contest between state representative Tim Hutchinson and attorney John VanWinkle for the open seat created by the retirement of Republican Rep. John Paul Hammerschmidt was waged largely on television. Virtually no money was spent on persuasion mail or grass-roots get-out-the-vote efforts. Both candidates held their fund-raising and overhead costs well below average. Every available dollar was funneled into broadcast advertising.

Hutchinson looked to Ron Fuller and Clint Albright, partners in Albright Ideas of Little Rock, for media consulting. Fuller also served as the campaign's general strategist.

Their first major decision was to forgo advertising on Little Rock stations, which fail to reach the district's northernmost counties. Instead, media buys were focused on Fayetteville, Fort Smith, and neighboring communities. This so-called Highway 71 Corridor—home to Wal-Mart and Tyson Foods—is by far the state's most Republican region. It was a strategy that "scared Tim a bit, but it was the way to go," noted Fuller. "The media won it."

To hold advertising costs down, the campaign used local broadcast production facilities. Albright Ideas created the newspaper ads, but had the campaign place them directly with local papers, which Albright described as "extraordinarily cheap." For its various services, Albright Ideas received $168,270.

Hutchinson's grass-roots efforts consisted largely of yard signs and posters that cost the campaign $10,531. The campaign also spent $1,239 on two bus tours of the district, which press secretary Samuel A. Sellars described as similar to the Clinton-Gore caravans, with rallies along the way. When Hammerschmidt decided to endorse Hutchinson, the campaign spent $495 to reprint the endorsement on postcards. Instead of spending money to mail them, Sellars said the postcards were passed on to local party officials for distribution.

Donna Hutchinson, former executive director of the state Republican party and Hutchinson's wife, was on the campaign payroll until August 1992 and was paid a total of $6,642. Sellars said that she left the payroll to "avoid any appearance of impropriety."

VanWinkle outspent Hutchinson by nearly $120,000, with roughly 60 percent of the difference used to buy additional advertising. McKinnon Media of Austin, Texas, received $57,114 for creating VanWinkle's ad campaign. Media Strategies and Research of Washington, D.C., collected $192,080 to place the broadcast ads.

VanWinkle's media campaign played to its geographic strength, which meant advertising more heavily on Little Rock and Springfield stations to reach Democratic strongholds.

Campaign Expenditures	Hutchinson Amount Spent	Hutchinson % of Total	VanWinkle Amount Spent	VanWinkle % of Total
Overhead				
Office furniture/supplies	$ 6,854	2.02	$ 4,909	1.07
Rent/utilities	5,164	1.52	5,954	1.30
Salaries	25,548	7.53	38,713	8.45
Taxes	5,062	1.49	2,446	.53
Bank/investment fees	0		0	
Lawyers/accountants	0		0	
Telephone	12,699	3.74	19,957	4.35
Campaign automobile	2,980	.88	0	
Computers/office equipment	0		1,292	.28
Travel	5,119	1.51	11,423	2.49
Food/meetings	0		35	.01
Subtotal	**63,426**	**18.68**	**84,729**	**18.49**
Fund Raising				
Events	11,304	3.33	4,207	.92
Direct mail	17,890	5.27	8,663	1.89
Telemarketing	0		0	
Subtotal	**29,194**	**8.60**	**12,869**	**2.81**
Polling	**9,700**	**2.86**	**27,100**	**5.91**
Advertising				
Electronic media	173,670	51.16	252,291	55.04
Other media	12,150	3.58	5,851	1.28
Subtotal	**185,820**	**54.74**	**258,142**	**56.32**
Other Campaign Activity				
Persuasion mail/brochures	9,879	2.91	3,201	.70
Actual campaigning	21,800	6.42	65,421	14.27
Staff/volunteers	0		0	
Subtotal	**31,680**	**9.33**	**68,622**	**14.97**
Constituent Gifts/ Entertainment	216	.06	0	
Donations to				
Candidates from same state	0		0	
Candidates from other states	0		0	
Civic organizations	0		0	
Ideological groups	0		0	
Political parties	0		480	.10
Subtotal	**0**		**480**	**.10**
Unitemized Expenses	19,436	5.73	6,415	1.40
Total Campaign Expenses	$ **339,472**		$ **458,358**	
PAC Contributions	$ 93,805		$ 160,362	
Individual Contributions	239,955		248,039	
Total Receipts*	344,017		495,863	

*Includes PAC and individual contributions as well as interest earned, party contributions, etc.

ARKANSAS — District 4

Rep. Jay Dickey (R)

1992 Election Results

Jay Dickey (R)	113,009	(52%)
W. J. "Bill" McCuen (D)	102,918	(48%)

As the owner of several small businesses, including two Taco Bell franchises, Jay Dickey knew a lot about marketing. He also knew he did not want his persuasion mail deposited in people's garbage along with their junk mail. To ensure his political "customers" actually read what he sent them, Dickey put a coupon for a free taco and large soft drink on the back of his campaign fliers. The campaign eventually paid Dickey's taco stands $2,500 to cover the cost of the promotion.

According to campaign office manager Glenda Peacock, the taco promotion was only one example of Dickey's "down-home" campaign style. There were weekly Sunday church appearances and a tour of the district in a rented recreational vehicle. And, like anyone who knows promotion, Dickey also knew the value of a strong television advertising campaign.

Dickey paid Sandler-Innocenzi of Washington, D.C., $124,226 to develop, produce, and place four television and five radio commercials. The commercials, which Peacock described as "comparison ads," focused on the differences between Dickey and his opponent, Arkansas Secretary of State W. J. "Bill" McCuen, on such issues as abortion rights and taxes. Another slammed McCuen for accepting a $324,000 no-bid contract on computers for his state office.

The Dickey campaign invested $20,089 in yard signs and posters, $16,530 on a phonebank, $5,398 on newspaper ads, $4,745 on T-shirts, $3,350 on billboards, and $2,818 on bumper stickers. The campaign's largest persuasion mailing went to registered voters in the district who belonged to the National Rifle Association (NRA) or had a hunting license. The mailing list of hunters cost $2,500.

McCuen secured the Democratic nomination by defeating Rep. Beryl Anthony, Jr., in a June 9 primary runoff. McCuen's media adviser, Jim Duffy of Washington, D.C.-based Strother-Duffy-Strother, described the campaign as a "media war" and added, "We begged, borrowed, and stole every available penny to buy television time."

For the primary and runoff, Duffy produced four television spots, including ads attacking Anthony's vote for a congressional pay raise and his 109 overdrafts at the House bank. Even those issues might not have derailed the seven-term incumbent had the NRA not spent $116,549 to blanket the district with radio and newspaper ads condemning Anthony for supporting the Brady Bill.

For the general election campaign, McCuen's ads focused on fines Dickey received for failing to pay the minimum wage to teenagers working at his two Taco Bell franchises. Strother-Duffy-Strother collected $220,051—68 percent of McCuen's entire expenditures—for designing and placing the ads.

Campaign Expenditures	Dickey Amount Spent	Dickey % of Total	McCuen Amount Spent	McCuen % of Total
Overhead				
Office furniture/supplies	$ 16,335	4.03	$ 3,917	1.22
Rent/utilities	3,171	.78	3,477	1.08
Salaries	32,358	7.99	4,535	1.41
Taxes	10,579	2.61	0	
Bank/investment fees	0		234	.07
Lawyers/accountants	5,590	1.38	0	
Telephone	9,372	2.31	6,843	2.12
Campaign automobile	0		0	
Computers/office equipment	503	.12	570	.18
Travel	9,137	2.26	9,266	2.88
Food/meetings	262	.06	172	.05
Subtotal	**87,309**	**21.55**	**29,014**	**9.01**
Fund Raising				
Events	4,284	1.06	3,267	1.01
Direct mail	21,881	5.40	0	
Telemarketing	0		0	
Subtotal	**26,165**	**6.46**	**3,267**	**1.01**
Polling	**12,250**	**3.02**	**0**	
Advertising				
Electronic media	140,773	34.75	245,695	76.28
Other media	8,748	2.16	6,812	2.12
Subtotal	**149,521**	**36.91**	**252,507**	**78.40**
Other Campaign Activity				
Persuasion mail/brochures	55,393	13.67	17,845	5.54
Actual campaigning	51,865	12.80	17,796	5.53
Staff/volunteers	258	.06	252	.08
Subtotal	**107,516**	**26.54**	**35,893**	**11.14**
Constituent Gifts/ Entertainment	**942**	**.23**	**55**	**.02**
Donations to				
Candidates from same state	0		75	.02
Candidates from other states	0		0	
Civic organizations	0		815	.25
Ideological groups	0		350	.11
Political parties	0		0	
Subtotal	**0**		**1,240**	**.39**
Unitemized Expenses	**21,439**	**5.29**	**100**	**.03**
Total Campaign Expenses	**$ 405,141**		**$ 322,076**	
PAC Contributions	$ 250		$ 184,150	
Individual Contributions	234,163		152,243	
Total Receipts*	412,465		373,085	

*Includes PAC and individual contributions as well as interest earned, party contributions, etc.

District 1 — CALIFORNIA

Rep. Dan Hamburg (D)

1992 Election Results

Dan Hamburg (D)	119,676	(48%)
Frank Riggs (R)	113,266	(45%)

Three weeks before the November general election, former Mendocino County Supervisor Dan Hamburg realized his campaign to unseat Rep. Frank Riggs was foundering and abruptly dropped his chief consultants, Directions by King & Associates and Hopcraft Communications, both of Sacramento. "We needed more punch," remarked campaign finance director Meg O'Donnell.

To provide that punch, Hamburg brought in the Campaign Group of Philadelphia to refocus his broadcast ads and the San Francisco-based Campaign Performance Group to concentrate on persuasion mail. Terris & Jaye of San Francisco worked with Campaign Performance on both the conceptualization and production of the mailing.

The Campaign Group produced two radio spots and one television spot, which ran only in the northern part of the district where, O'Donnell noted, "TV is accessible and inexpensive." All three ads focused on the economy. "With unemployment so high in this district, people didn't care about other issues," added O'Donnell. For its work the Campaign Group was paid $37,500.

Campaign Performance was given the task of communicating with voters in the southern part of the district, where broadcast advertising is more expensive. The company produced one mailer that asked, "What did they do with your money?" The answers included attacks on Riggs for accepting the congressional pay raise after railing against it in the 1990 campaign, for flying first class at taxpayer expense, and for availing himself of numerous congressional perks. Campaign Performance received $29,235 for its efforts. Terris & Jaye received $51,368.

The Democratic Congressional Campaign Committee (DCCC), which saw this race as imminently winnable, backed Hamburg's risky eleventh-hour move to reshuffle the campaign's braintrust. For the last three weeks, the DCCC dispatched a staffer to serve as Hamburg's new campaign manager.

Not all went smoothly in the transition. By the end of 1992, Hamburg had paid Directions $41,608; an additional bill for $8,321 was in dispute. While Hamburg had paid Hopcraft $96,971, he was disputing bills for an additional $38,883.

While musicians Bonnie Raitt and Holly Near held three benefit concerts to help fill Hamburg's coffers, the most novel fund-raising idea had to be Hamburg's invitation to "Sleep with the Candidate." For $150 each, ten couples stayed with Hamburg at a restored Victorian bed and breakfast inn.

Having won the 1990 race with only 43 percent of the vote, Riggs was in trouble from the outset. Nearly half his money was spent to raise money. He spent only 4 percent of his funds on advertising.

	Hamburg		Riggs	
Campaign Expenditures	Amount Spent	% of Total	Amount Spent	% of Total
Overhead				
Office furniture/supplies	$ 12,024	1.67	$ 12,101	1.81
Rent/utilities	9,419	1.31	5,522	.83
Salaries	31,670	4.40	9,370	1.40
Taxes	2,303	.32	405	.06
Bank/investment fees	1,254	.17	0	
Lawyers/accountants	42,805	5.94	58,118	8.69
Telephone	22,255	3.09	17,381	2.60
Campaign automobile	0		0	
Computers/office equipment	4,980	.69	3,491	.52
Travel	41,616	5.78	16,971	2.54
Food/meetings	427	.06	1,589	.24
Subtotal	**168,753**	**23.43**	**124,948**	**18.69**
Fund Raising				
Events	152,969	21.24	199,963	29.91
Direct mail	831	.12	124,023	18.55
Telemarketing	3,049	.42	0	
Subtotal	**156,848**	**21.78**	**323,986**	**48.47**
Polling	**13,338**	**1.85**	**13,000**	**1.94**
Advertising				
Electronic media	98,866	13.73	21,419	3.20
Other media	8,126	1.13	3,123	.47
Subtotal	**106,993**	**14.85**	**24,541**	**3.67**
Other Campaign Activity				
Persuasion mail/brochures	108,796	15.11	128,811	19.27
Actual campaigning	141,306	19.62	18,218	2.73
Staff/volunteers	97	.01	276	.04
Subtotal	**250,199**	**34.74**	**147,305**	**22.04**
Constituent Gifts/ Entertainment	**0**		**148**	**.02**
Donations to				
Candidates from same state	100	.01	0	
Candidates from other states	0		200	.03
Civic organizations	776	.11	47	.01
Ideological groups	0		0	
Political parties	5,750	.80	4,718	.71
Subtotal	**6,626**	**.92**	**4,965**	**.74**
Unitemized Expenses	**17,495**	**2.43**	**29,546**	**4.42**
Total Campaign Expenses	**$ 720,251**		**$ 668,438**	
PAC Contributions	**$ 185,507**		**$ 218,125**	
Individual Contributions	**405,421**		**479,838**	
Total Receipts*	**652,592**		**729,819**	

*Includes PAC and individual contributions as well as interest earned, party contributions, etc.

CALIFORNIA   District 2

Rep. Wally Herger (R)   *1992 Election Results*   Wally Herger (R)   167,247   (65%)
                                                                   Elliot Roy Freedman (D) 71,780   (28%)

Rep. Wally Herger spent $152,789 during 1991 to keep his permanent campaign running smoothly, including $68,975 on fund raising and $33,046 on overhead. Herger's off-year spending totaled roughly thirty times the amount Democrat Elliot Roy Freedman spent on his entire campaign.

"I wear all the hats," said campaign management consultant Brad Zerbe, and one of the hats he wore with distinction during the 1992 campaign was that of chief fund-raiser.

Slightly more than half of Herger's fund-raising expenses were invested in direct mail. During the off-year, Zerbe mailed four solicitations to the campaign's "house list" of past contributors. This list was tapped again in March, May, August, September, and October 1992. He also sent prospecting mailings that targeted agriculture and timber interests. Zerbe said another prospecting solicitation, mailed to Republicans in the newly acquired portions of the district following redistricting, broke even.

In March 1992 Zerbe organized a dinner at the Redding Convention Center. Zerbe said 560 people paid the modest $125 ticket price for the sit-down affair, and many paid an additional $250 to attend a predinner reception with Vice President Dan Quayle. The evening netted $121,000. While the campaign also occasionally sponsored smaller soirees, Zerbe said he was reluctant to make a habit of it because "it takes almost as much time to organize one of those things as a larger event."

Zerbe also orchestrated the campaign's four Washington, D.C., fund-raisers, which were held at the Capitol Hill Club. The $225,289 political action committees donated to Herger's campaign made Zerbe's East Coast trips well worth the effort.

In the primary, Herger ran television and radio commercials that sought to distance him from his Washington colleagues. The ads pointed out that he had no overdrafts at the House bank and that he had voted to close the bank, voted against the congressional pay raise, voted against tax increases, and voted for the amendment requiring a balanced federal budget. Ad production was done through the National Republican Congressional Committee. Huckaby Rodriguez of Sacramento received $20,000 to buy air time. Zerbe said he also blanketed the district with an "I'm not one of them" mailing that reached between 80,000 and 90,000 Republican households.

In the general election campaign, Wayne C. Johnson & Associates of Sacramento collected $47,260 to purchase air time for a series of commercials with the same anti-Washington theme. Against the underfunded Freedman, there was no need for any persuasion mail in the fall campaign.

For his efforts, Zerbe collected $93,939.

Campaign Expenditures	Herger Amount Spent	Herger % of Total	Freedman Amount Spent	Freedman % of Total
Overhead				
Office furniture/supplies	$ 13,560	2.55	$ 152	3.08
Rent/utilities	0		50	1.01
Salaries	3,445	.65	0	
Taxes	4,754	.90	0	
Bank/investment fees	415	.08	17	.34
Lawyers/accountants	24,648	4.64	0	
Telephone	8,529	1.61	424	8.57
Campaign automobile	0		0	
Computers/office equipment	4,124	.78	0	
Travel	13,927	2.62	605	12.22
Food/meetings	3,068	.58	0	
Subtotal	**76,470**	**14.40**	**1,248**	**25.22**
Fund Raising				
Events	94,857	17.86	80	1.62
Direct mail	95,035	17.89	0	
Telemarketing	0		0	
Subtotal	**189,892**	**35.75**	**80**	**1.62**
Polling	**27,540**	**5.19**	**0**	
Advertising				
Electronic media	82,277	15.49	30	.61
Other media	4,068	.77	874	17.66
Subtotal	**86,345**	**16.26**	**904**	**18.27**
Other Campaign Activity				
Persuasion mail/brochures	43,194	8.13	1,226	24.77
Actual campaigning	56,913	10.72	1,447	29.24
Staff/volunteers	0		0	
Subtotal	**100,107**	**18.85**	**2,673**	**54.01**
Constituent Gifts/ Entertainment	**2,562**	**.48**	**0**	
Donations to				
Candidates from same state	26,500	4.99	0	
Candidates from other states	6,200	1.17	0	
Civic organizations	1,875	.35	10	.20
Ideological groups	0		0	
Political parties	3,003	.57	34	.69
Subtotal	**37,578**	**7.08**	**44**	**.89**
Unitemized Expenses	**10,610**	**2.00**	**0**	
Total Campaign Expenses	**$ 531,104**		**$ 4,948**	
PAC Contributions	$ 225,289		$ 0	
Individual Contributions	389,183		5,785	
Total Receipts*	644,763		6,982	

*Includes PAC and individual contributions as well as interest earned, party contributions, etc.

District 3 — CALIFORNIA

Rep. Vic Fazio (D)

1992 Election Results

Vic Fazio (D)	122,149	(51%)
H. L. "Bill" Richardson (R)	96,092	(40%)
Ross Cain † (I)	20,444	(9%)

For the first time in fourteen years, Rep. Vic Fazio found himself facing a well-known, well-financed Republican challenger, former state senator H. L. "Bill" Richardson. However, million-dollar campaigns were nothing new to Fazio. In 1990 he had invested more than $1 million to defeat a little-known Republican challenger who spent $56,081. When it became clear that he was in for a fight, Fazio cranked his fund-raising machine up another notch.

While Fazio and Richardson succeeded in raising almost identical amounts from individual contributors, Fazio's role as chairman of the Democratic Congressional Campaign Committee and his seat on the Appropriations Committee provided him with virtually unlimited access to political action committee (PAC) money. Fazio's PAC donations accounted for 60 percent of his total contributions and 99 percent of his $1.1 million monetary advantage. In addition, the American Medical Association PAC spent $255,085 on an independent campaign in support of Fazio.

Contributions by union-affiliated PACs amounted to $230,376. Agriculture-related PACs anted up another $115,410. In all, twenty-eight PACs representing labor, agriculture, defense, health care, and financial interests gave Fazio the maximum legal contribution of $10,000.

Fazio invested much of his cash advantage in broadcast advertising. District director Richard Harris said the campaign aired eight television commercials, roughly divided into two phases. While early ads "focused on who Vic was," Harris said ads during the final three weeks of the campaign turned less positive, hitting Richardson for his "really right-wing" stand on abortion. Other ads attacked Richardson for accepting the perks associated with his tenure in the state senate while failing to show up for 90 percent of the votes.

There were also eight persuasion mailers, including three that juxtaposed Fazio's pro-choice stance on abortion with Richardson's proposal for a total ban, even in cases of rape. While all eight mailers referred to Richardson as "the face of extremism," the most inflammatory showed the laughing face of the challenger superimposed on a nuclear mushroom cloud. Beneath the image, the text of the mailer opened with: "Only H. L. Richardson wanted the unthinkable ... Full-scale nuclear war" in red, half-inch block type. It continued with remarks Richardson made after the Soviet Union shot down Korean Airlines flight 007.

Fazio paid Squier/Eskew/Knapp/Ochs Communications of Washington, D.C., $681,950 for strategic advice and for the design and placement of broadcast ads. Campaign Performance Group of San Francisco collected $275,801 for work on the persuasion mail.

Campaign Expenditures	Fazio Amount Spent	Fazio % of Total	Richardson Amount Spent	Richardson % of Total
Overhead				
Office furniture/supplies	$ 26,024	1.37	$ 14,219	1.63
Rent/utilities	13,764	.72	4,000	.46
Salaries	105,550	5.54	28,024	3.21
Taxes	60,406	3.17	7,176	.82
Bank/investment fees	525	.03	379	.04
Lawyers/accountants	37,563	1.97	14,152	1.62
Telephone	26,652	1.40	17,300	1.98
Campaign automobile	0		0	
Computers/office equipment	19,318	1.01	20,653	2.37
Travel	26,904	1.41	19,462	2.23
Food/meetings	8,833	.46	1,647	.19
Subtotal	325,540	17.08	127,012	14.57
Fund Raising				
Events	210,731	11.06	74,061	8.50
Direct mail	0		113,581	13.03
Telemarketing	0		5,395	.62
Subtotal	210,731	11.06	193,037	22.14
Polling	52,000	2.73	7,000	.80
Advertising				
Electronic media	672,444	35.28	192,822	22.12
Other media	5,377	.28	602	.07
Subtotal	677,822	35.57	193,423	22.19
Other Campaign Activity				
Persuasion mail/brochures	398,539	20.91	287,767	33.01
Actual campaigning	71,793	3.77	51,300	5.88
Staff/volunteers	1,122	.06	640	.07
Subtotal	471,454	24.74	339,707	38.97
Constituent Gifts/ Entertainment	15,717	.82	0	
Donations to				
Candidates from same state	6,750	.35	250	.03
Candidates from other states	7,000	.37	0	
Civic organizations	6,479	.34	0	
Ideological groups	8,450	.44	0	
Political parties	92,075	4.83	0	
Subtotal	120,754	6.34	250	.03
Unitemized Expenses	31,827	1.67	11,384	1.31
Total Campaign Expenses	$ 1,905,844		$ 871,813	
PAC Contributions	$ 1,148,438		$ 76,661	
Individual Contributions	777,118		728,478	
Total Receipts*	1,994,284		856,853	

*Includes PAC and individual contributions as well as interest earned, party contributions, etc.

† No expenditures or receipts on file. Candidates raising or spending less than $5,000 are not required to file reports with the Federal Election Commission.

CALIFORNIA — District 4

Rep. John T. Doolittle (R)

1992 Election Results

John T. Doolittle (R)	141,155	(50%)
Patricia Malberg (D)	129,489	(46%)

Rising costs forced Rep. John T. Doolittle to rethink his fund-raising strategy for his 1992 rematch with Patricia Malberg. Pointing to the fact that sit-down dinners were costing the campaign $30 per person, not including the invitations or the follow-up mail, congressional staff director David G. Lopez said the campaign formed the "Capitol Caucus," a fund-raising "club" aimed at well-heeled contributors.

In return for a $500 donation, Capitol Caucus members received invitations to selected events. For $1,000, contributors had an open invitation to all campaign social functions, which included a Christmas party, a "Dixieland Jazz Jubilee," a summertime barbecue, and a reception featuring Rep. Newt Gingrich (R-Ga.). In its inaugural year, Lopez said the Capitol Caucus raised roughly $50,000; in 1992 it raised nearly $110,000.

Lopez should know. Although he had no formal connection to the 1992 campaign, Lopez and his wife Cathy owned Event Planners of Roseville, Calif., a company Doolittle paid $48,774 for planning his fund-raisers. When queried about several campaign checks made out to him, Lopez chalked them up to his wife's fund-raising activities.

Doolittle spent 29 percent less on broadcast media in 1992 than he had in 1990. For one of his two television commercials, Doolittle paid $1,525 to acquire the "guts" of an ad produced for Rep. Rick Santorum (R-Pa.) by Brabender Cox of Pittsburgh. The ad, which focused on the House bank scandal, was retooled by Doolittle's media consultant, Wayne C. Johnson & Associates of Sacramento. A second Doolittle ad, aired for the ten days prior to the election, focused on his work in Congress. Doolittle also ran three radio spots, including two that attacked Malberg for failing to properly file her income taxes. In all, Doolittle spent $36,265 to air his radio commercials, $47,188 for air time on network affiliates, and another $4,548 for time on local cable outlets.

Persuasion mail cost Doolittle 18 percent more in 1992 than it had in 1990. Lopez said the campaign sent out six persuasion mailers, including one that focused on Doolittle's role as a member of the "Gang of Seven," a group of freshmen Republicans who demanded full disclosure of the House banking scandal and generally railed against House perks.

On the issue of perks, Doolittle was perhaps living in a glass house. In January 1991 Doolittle spent $9,206 from his campaign treasury to move his personal belongings from California to Washington.

When the votes were tallied, Malberg fell short by the same 4 percentage point margin in 1992 as she had in 1990, despite spending 71 percent more on her 1992 campaign.

Campaign Expenditures	Doolittle Amount Spent	Doolittle % of Total	Malberg Amount Spent	Malberg % of Total
Overhead				
Office furniture/supplies	$ 13,917	2.18	$ 4,814	1.28
Rent/utilities	2,296	.36	0	
Salaries	8,150	1.28	9,530	2.54
Taxes	0		0	
Bank/investment fees	0		0	
Lawyers/accountants	11,602	1.82	0	
Telephone	9,840	1.54	3,971	1.06
Campaign automobile	0		0	
Computers/office equipment	6,564	1.03	9,254	2.46
Travel	23,451	3.68	1,887	.50
Food/meetings	2,065	.32	0	
Subtotal	**77,885**	**12.21**	**29,456**	**7.84**
Fund Raising				
Events	72,775	11.41	5,513	1.47
Direct mail	49,379	7.74	42,494	11.30
Telemarketing	0		6,719	1.79
Subtotal	**122,154**	**19.15**	**54,726**	**14.56**
Polling	**20,212**	**3.17**	**17,228**	**4.58**
Advertising				
Electronic media	109,614	17.19	145,997	38.84
Other media	9,896	1.55	3,276	.87
Subtotal	**119,510**	**18.74**	**149,273**	**39.71**
Other Campaign Activity				
Persuasion mail/brochures	175,160	27.46	74,585	19.84
Actual campaigning	78,327	12.28	15,218	4.05
Staff/volunteers	47	.01	0	
Subtotal	**253,533**	**39.75**	**89,803**	**23.89**
Constituent Gifts/Entertainment	**728**	**.11**	**0**	
Donations to				
Candidates from same state	9,100	1.43	0	
Candidates from other states	1,400	.22	0	
Civic organizations	260	.04	0	
Ideological groups	80	.01	0	
Political parties	1,150	.18	0	
Subtotal	**11,990**	**1.88**	**0**	
Unitemized Expenses	**31,822**	**4.99**	**35,400**	**9.42**
Total Campaign Expenses	**$ 637,834**		**$ 375,887**	
PAC Contributions	$ 249,095		$ 121,357	
Individual Contributions	345,726		255,258	
Total Receipts*	610,104		385,906	

*Includes PAC and individual contributions as well as interest earned, party contributions, etc.

District 5 — CALIFORNIA

Rep. Robert T. Matsui (D)

1992 Election Results

Robert T. Matsui (D)	158,250	(69%)
Robert S. Dinsmore (R)	58,698	(25%)

Rep. Robert T. Matsui's campaign motto could have been, "If you have it, spend it."

Although occupied during the first six months of 1991 by an aborted bid for the Senate seat vacated by fellow Democrat Alan Cranston, Matsui still managed to invest $320,895 in maintaining his permanent House campaign during the off-year. Overhead in 1991 totaled $118,644; fund raising cost $37,612; donations to civic organizations, various ideological groups, other political candidates, and party organizations added $80,309. The $473,448 Matsui transferred from his House account to his Senate campaign in early 1991 is not included in the analysis of his reelection spending.

Against an opponent who ran no television, radio, or newspaper ads, Matsui spent $204,737 on advertising. Morris & Carrick of New York collected $197,000 for creating, producing, and placing the campaign's two 30-second television commercials and a 60-second radio spot.

While the ads focused on Matsui's efforts to foster better health care and create jobs, they did so in a way that underscored the fact that the incumbent was "just plain folks." The health care commercial showed Matsui touring a pediatric care unit and sitting with a group of senior citizens, singing "you are my sunshine, my only sunshine." To illustrate his commitment to job creation, his second ad showed him at a housing construction site, wearing a hard hat.

Clinton Reilly Campaigns of San Francisco, which also did work on Matsui's aborted Senate campaign, collected $40,591 for general campaign advice.

The $185,092 Matsui donated to other candidates and causes over the two-year cycle was eight times the amount Republican challenger Robert S. Dinsmore spent on his entire campaign. Matsui donated $66,688 to IMPAC 2000, the Democratic redistricting effort. Among his other donations to party organizations was a $10,000 gift to the Democratic Congressional Campaign Committee. Thirty-five House and Senate candidates received $1,000 contributions; Californians Jane Harman and Mark Takano received $3,000 and $2,000, respectively, for their unsuccessful House bids. Contributions to local candidates included $10,100 to Lloyd Connelly, a candidate for Superior Court judge, and $5,053 to Joe Serna, a candidate for mayor of Sacramento.

Matsui spent $16,469 on constituent gifts. "It was a wide variety, from pens and key chains to crystal bowls and clocks," noted Tomas Keaney, his administrative assistant. Keaney added that "books are the gift of choice," particularly books about former New York Yankee great, Mickey Mantle. Matsui also spent $3,042 on constituent meals, $1,898 on flowers, and $14,264 on year-end holiday cards.

Campaign Expenditures	Matsui Amount Spent	Matsui % of Total	Dinsmore Amount Spent	Dinsmore % of Total
Overhead				
Office furniture/supplies	$ 29,493	3.13	$ 840	3.62
Rent/utilities	6,996	.74	5,354	23.09
Salaries	84,080	8.91	0	
Taxes	25,371	2.69	0	
Bank/investment fees	3,105	.33	0	
Lawyers/accountants	35,168	3.73	0	
Telephone	10,579	1.12	259	1.12
Campaign automobile	15,091	1.60	0	
Computers/office equipment	8,298	.88	750	3.23
Travel	49,943	5.30	670	2.89
Food/meetings	16,519	1.75	0	
Subtotal	**284,643**	**30.18**	**7,873**	**33.95**
Fund Raising				
Events	79,024	8.38	1,968	8.49
Direct mail	7,716	.82	0	
Telemarketing	0		0	
Subtotal	**86,740**	**9.20**	**1,968**	**8.49**
Polling	**25,048**	**2.66**	**0**	
Advertising				
Electronic media	197,000	20.89	0	
Other media	7,737	.82	0	
Subtotal	**204,737**	**21.71**	**0**	
Other Campaign Activity				
Persuasion mail/brochures	4,565	.48	1,655	7.14
Actual campaigning	80,900	8.58	2,509	10.82
Staff/volunteers	86	.01	0	
Subtotal	**85,551**	**9.07**	**4,164**	**17.96**
Constituent Gifts/Entertainment	35,673	3.78	0	
Donations to				
Candidates from same state	39,403	4.18	0	
Candidates from other states	23,000	2.44	0	
Civic organizations	19,131	2.03	0	
Ideological groups	9,575	1.02	0	
Political parties	93,983	9.96	0	
Subtotal	**185,092**	**19.62**	**0**	
Unitemized Expenses	35,682	3.78	9,187	39.61
Total Campaign Expenses	**$ 943,167**		**$ 23,192**	
PAC Contributions	$ 365,100		$ 0	
Individual Contributions	170,210		18,754	
Total Receipts*	656,875		30,093	

*Includes PAC and individual contributions as well as interest earned, party contributions, etc.

CALIFORNIA — District 6

Rep. Lynn Woolsey (D)

1992 Election Results

Lynn Woolsey (D)	190,322	(65%)
Bill Filante (R)	98,171	(34%)

The race between Petaluma City Council member Lynn Woolsey and seven-term state representative Bill Filante looked as if it would develop into a barn-burner until Filante discovered he had a brain tumor. In late September Filante announced he would be unable to resume campaigning.

In the Democratic primary, Woolsey had emerged from a field of nine candidates that included Bennett Johnston, son of Louisiana Sen. J. Bennett Johnston. With considerable fund-raising assistance from his father, Johnston spent more than $600,000 on his failed bid. Woolsey spent less than $200,000 and prevailed with 26 percent of the vote.

Woolsey committed much of her primary budget to three persuasion mailers produced by Ambrosino & Muir of San Francisco. The first, mailed three weeks before the primary, linked Woolsey's candidacy to the treatment Anita Hill received during her testimony at the confirmation hearings for Supreme Court Justice Clarence Thomas. A second focused on education and her endorsement by both the National Education Association and the California Teachers Association. The third again played on Woolsey's gender and her status as a Washington outsider. Both the second and third mailings were sent during the final week of the primary campaign.

During the general election campaign, Ambrosino again produced three mailings for Woolsey. Instead of hitting the gender theme, which helped pull her through the primary, the mailings focused on the Democratic hot-buttons of health care and the economy. Woolsey also mailed absentee ballots in which she enclosed her general biographical piece. Ambrosino was paid a total of $94,227 for work in the primary and general election campaigns.

Trippi, McMahon & Squier of Alexandria, Va., developed two television commercials for the fall campaign. A biographical spot centered on Woolsey's background as a former "welfare mother" who could empathize with ordinary people. The second ad focused on jobs. For creating the ads and placing them on local cable outlets, Trippi collected $46,810.

As with many women candidates, Woolsey leaned heavily on other women to help her raise money. Gloria Steinem was the draw for an event that raised $20,000. EMILY's List provided her with $10,493 in direct-mail fund-raising assistance. The Women's Campaign Fund donated $8,500, the National Women's Political Caucus contributed $2,500, and the Women's Political Committee chipped in $2,000. The campaign formed a group called "Another Woman for Woolsey." Members could either make a single contribution or sign on for monthly payments. They also agreed to work as volunteers, host in-home fund-raisers, or recruit ten friends.

Campaign Expenditures	Woolsey Amount Spent	Woolsey % of Total	Filante Amount Spent	Filante % of Total
Overhead				
Office furniture/supplies	$ 10,454	1.68	$ 10,296	2.40
Rent/utilities	12,971	2.09	11,629	2.71
Salaries	108,984	17.52	122,312	28.55
Taxes	12,206	1.96	0	
Bank/investment fees	116	.02	0	
Lawyers/accountants	0		6,387	1.49
Telephone	11,140	1.79	17,091	3.99
Campaign automobile	0		0	
Computers/office equipment	4,506	.72	8,001	1.87
Travel	10,457	1.68	7,726	1.80
Food/meetings	0		0	
Subtotal	170,834	27.47	183,441	42.82
Fund Raising				
Events	28,108	4.52	94,128	21.97
Direct mail	43,695	7.03	53,233	12.43
Telemarketing	0		0	
Subtotal	71,803	11.55	147,361	34.40
Polling	38,554	6.20	6,286	1.47
Advertising				
Electronic media	47,161	7.58	0	
Other media	551	.09	0	
Subtotal	47,712	7.67	0	
Other Campaign Activity				
Persuasion mail/brochures	153,777	24.73	51,441	12.01
Actual campaigning	73,570	11.83	26,881	6.27
Staff/volunteers	0		0	
Subtotal	227,347	36.55	78,321	18.28
Constituent Gifts/ Entertainment	382	.06	0	
Donations to				
Candidates from same state	300	.05	0	
Candidates from other states	0		0	
Civic organizations	0		0	
Ideological groups	0		0	
Political parties	550	.09	0	
Subtotal	850	.14	0	
Unitemized Expenses	64,455	10.36	12,978	3.03
Total Campaign Expenses	$ 621,937		$ 428,387	
PAC Contributions	$ 186,853		$ 120,606	
Individual Contributions	313,587		308,337	
Total Receipts*	598,664		437,590	

*Includes PAC and individual contributions as well as interest earned, party contributions, etc.

District 7 — CALIFORNIA

Rep. George Miller (D)

1992 Election Results

George Miller (D)	153,320	(70%)
Dave Scholl (R)	54,822	(25%)

In his challenge to Rep. George Miller, Republican Dave Scholl spent 32 percent more than the incumbent's 1990 opponent. Unfortunately for Scholl, Miller increased his spending from 1990 to 1992 by 47 percent. Miller's off-year expenses alone were three times more than Scholl could muster for his entire campaign.

As a hedge against potential redistricting surprises, Miller raised $233,754 during the first six months of 1991, or 43 percent of his total receipts for the two-year election cycle. Despite the fact that he began the year with cash reserves of $438,229, Miller spent $80,798 during 1991 to raise additional funds.

Miller's 1991 fund-raising binge included an event at the Pleasant Hill Recreation Center in Pleasant Hill, Calif. The $26,575 tab included $15,238 for catering by Fantasy Foods. Miller's press secretary, Daniel Weiss, estimated that 700 people paid the $75 admission price to sample Italian, Mexican, and Oriental foods.

The campaign paid San Francisco-based fund-raisers Jerry Heather and Don Muir $5,000 each to stage a second 1991 event in the district; another $3,000 was spent on the food. Muir received $10,000 for arranging an event at the Beverly Hills Hilton; another $4,000 was paid directly to the hotel. Jim Wise Associates of Alexandria, Va., received $7,088 for arranging an event in Washington, D.C., to attract political action committee (PAC) donations; the Capitol Hill Club was paid $3,110 directly. Telemarketing added $10,785 to the cost of Miller's 1991 money chase.

In 1992 Miller held two district events, as well as receptions in Washington and Chicago. His fund-raising expenditures during 1992 totaled $64,661, including telemarketing costs of $6,054. Despite these efforts, Miller spent nearly $115,000 more than he raised.

Miller paid Ambrosino & Muir of San Francisco $84,750 for orchestrating the persuasion mail campaign. Paul Kinney Productions of Sacramento received $41,148 for creating, producing, and placing broadcast advertising. Solem/Loeb & Associates of San Francisco collected $54,401 for providing a variety of services, including $18,425 for polling.

Like many of his California colleagues, Miller was extremely generous with his campaign treasury. Among his donations to Democratic party organizations were a $10,000 gift to the Democratic Congressional Campaign Committee and a $22,688 contribution to IMPAC 2000, a PAC designed to assist Democrats in state reapportionment battles. His donations to charities and booster organizations included $330 to the East Bay Soccer League, $250 to the Contra Costa Child Care Council, and $200 to the Martinez Bocce Federation for Special Olympics.

	Miller		Scholl	
Campaign Expenditures	Amount Spent	% of Total	Amount Spent	% of Total
Overhead				
Office furniture/supplies	$ 6,493	.99	$ 968	1.59
Rent/utilities	0		400	.66
Salaries	57,385	8.73	2,931	4.82
Taxes	13,760	2.09	0	
Bank/investment fees	46	.01	0	
Lawyers/accountants	1,225	.19	0	
Telephone	219	.03	4,254	7.00
Campaign automobile	2,637	.40	0	
Computers/office equipment	2,513	.38	0	
Travel	23,119	3.52	225	.37
Food/meetings	7,787	1.18	0	
Subtotal	**115,184**	**17.53**	**8,778**	**14.45**
Fund Raising				
Events	128,620	19.57	1,447	2.38
Direct mail	0		0	
Telemarketing	16,838	2.56	0	
Subtotal	**145,458**	**22.13**	**1,447**	**2.38**
Polling	**18,425**	**2.80**	**0**	
Advertising				
Electronic media	41,148	6.26	0	
Other media	4,407	.67	0	
Subtotal	**45,555**	**6.93**	**0**	
Other Campaign Activity				
Persuasion mail/brochures	161,158	24.52	37,787	62.20
Actual campaigning	37,054	5.64	4,904	8.07
Staff/volunteers	2,945	.45	352	.58
Subtotal	**201,156**	**30.61**	**43,043**	**70.85**
Constituent Gifts/ Entertainment	**17,037**	**2.59**	**0**	
Donations to				
Candidates from same state	18,975	2.89	0	
Candidates from other states	12,600	1.92	0	
Civic organizations	20,752	3.16	0	
Ideological groups	11,613	1.77	0	
Political parties	45,289	6.89	0	
Subtotal	**109,229**	**16.62**	**0**	
Unitemized Expenses	**5,169**	**.79**	**7,480**	**12.31**
Total Campaign Expenses	**$ 657,215**		**$ 60,748**	
PAC Contributions	**$ 261,790**		**$ 3,500**	
Individual Contributions	**218,550**		**61,888**	
Total Receipts*	**542,532**		**66,731**	

*Includes PAC and individual contributions as well as interest earned, party contributions, etc.

CALIFORNIA — District 8

Rep. Nancy Pelosi (D)

1992 Election Results

Nancy Pelosi (D)	191,906	(83%)
Marc Wolin (R)	25,693	(11%)

Neither redistricting nor the supposed anti-incumbent mood of the electorate fazed Rep. Nancy Pelosi. The $442,243 she spent during the 1992 election cycle was just $8,765 more than she spent in 1990. In 1992 donations to charities, ideological groups, other candidates, and Democratic party organizations comprised 39 percent of Pelosi's expenditures; the comparable figure in 1990 was 44 percent. In both 1990 and 1992 she spent 9 percent of her money on overhead. Advertising accounted for 5 percent and 6 percent in 1992 and 1990, respectively. In virtually every aspect, her 1992 campaign was a carbon copy of her 1990 effort.

As in 1990, Pelosi's favorite political cause was IMPAC 2000, a political action committee formed to assist Democrats in state redistricting fights. During 1991 she donated $41,688 to IMPAC 2000.

Her generosity did not stop with IMPAC 2000. She contributed $10,000 to the Democratic Senatorial Campaign Committee, $7,000 to the Democratic Congressional Campaign Committee, $4,000 to California Lt. Gov. Leo McCarthy's unsuccessful primary Senate bid against Rep. Barbara Boxer, $3,100 to fellow California Democrat Dianne Feinstein's successful challenge to Sen. John Seymour, $2,000 each to Reps. Marty Russo (D-Ill.) and Anna G. Eshoo (D-Calif.), eight $1,000 contributions to various other candidates, and numerous smaller donations to candidates both in and out of California.

To benefit the Independent Federation of Chinese Students, Pelosi paid $800 for a painting by Li Ping, an organizer of the 1989 student demonstrations in Peking. She paid $2,000 for a dinner at the National Maritime Museum in San Francisco, $250 to attend a reception staged by EMILY's List, and $250 to attend the Anti-Defamation League's Award Dinner.

Only 22 percent of Pelosi's expenditures were devoted to contacting and persuading voters, and much of that served to help other Democrats as much as it helped her. She spent $6,800 for a series of slate mailers with local Democratic groups, the League of Conservation Voters, and Your Pro-Choice Voter Guide. According to Michael Yaki, her district director, the message in her one persuasion mailing was "pushing the Democratic agenda." She paid $11,411 to assist the state party's election day get-out-the-vote efforts.

On election night, Pelosi spent $399 of her campaign treasury to pay for lodging at the Arkansas Excelsior Hotel in Little Rock to celebrate the national ticket's triumph. Pelosi spent $9,470 from her 1992 campaign fund to attend various inaugural events, including $7,000 for tickets to the Inaugural Gala.

Marketing consultant Marc Wolin spent $83,550 less than Pelosi on direct appeals to voters and was never in the race.

	Pelosi		Wolin	
Campaign Expenditures	Amount Spent	% of Total	Amount Spent	% of Total
Overhead				
Office furniture/supplies	$ 6,459	1.46	$ 3,732	11.89
Rent/utilities	6,000	1.36	2,141	6.82
Salaries	2,000	.45	5,267	16.78
Taxes	0		0	
Bank/investment fees	0		0	
Lawyers/accountants	1,532	.35	0	
Telephone	2,833	.64	1,705	5.43
Campaign automobile	0		0	
Computers/office equipment	0		499	1.59
Travel	22,470	5.08	1,421	4.53
Food/meetings	149	.03	127	.40
Subtotal	**41,444**	**9.37**	**14,892**	**47.44**
Fund Raising				
Events	54,108	12.23	425	1.35
Direct mail	36,234	8.19	0	
Telemarketing	0		0	
Subtotal	**90,342**	**20.43**	**425**	**1.35**
Polling	**0**		**0**	
Advertising				
Electronic media	0		0	
Other media	21,094	4.77	5,434	17.31
Subtotal	**21,094**	**4.77**	**5,434**	**17.31**
Other Campaign Activity				
Persuasion mail/brochures	52,617	11.90	5,545	17.66
Actual campaigning	22,432	5.07	1,904	6.06
Staff/volunteers	291	.07	0	
Subtotal	**75,339**	**17.04**	**7,449**	**23.73**
Constituent Gifts/ Entertainment	**16,872**	**3.82**	**0**	
Donations to				
Candidates from same state	36,985	8.36	380	1.21
Candidates from other states	20,800	4.70	0	
Civic organizations	19,360	4.38	175	.56
Ideological groups	10,825	2.45	400	1.27
Political parties	85,338	19.30	59	.19
Subtotal	**173,308**	**39.19**	**1,014**	**3.23**
Unitemized Expenses	**23,842**	**5.39**	**2,179**	**6.94**
Total Campaign Expenses	**$ 442,243**		**$ 31,393**	
PAC Contributions	$ 204,689		$ 500	
Individual Contributions	193,533		19,997	
Total Receipts*	417,254		49,256	

*Includes PAC and individual contributions as well as interest earned, party contributions, etc.

District 9 — CALIFORNIA

Rep. Ronald V. Dellums (D)

1992 Election Results

Ronald V. Dellums (D)	164,265	(72%)
G. William Hunter (R)	53,707	(24%)
Dave Linn † (I)	10,472	(5%)

Rep. Ronald V. Dellums ran his 1992 campaign like most candidates: opening an office, sending out persuasion mail, and telephoning prospective voters to encourage turnout. Unlike most other candidates, Dellums did all this more for others than for himself.

According to Sandre Swanson, a congressional staff assistant, phonebanking is part of every Dellums campaign, even in years when he is not seriously challenged. Prior to every election, Dellums consults with an advisory committee that recommends which local candidates and ballot initiatives he should support. Once the decisions are made, teenagers hired by Dellums's campaign telephone district voters, urging them to vote and asking if they would like to hear the advisory committee's ballot recommendations. Dellums's 1992 phonebanking effort cost $43,508.

While Dellums does not bother with persuasion mail every election cycle, Swanson said he chose to do so in 1992 in order to support the Democratic presidential ticket and because "it was a historic opportunity to elect two women to the Senate."

Unlike 1990, Dellums opened a campaign office in 1992 and again the presidential and Senate races were prime motivating factors. Swanson added that since redistricting had altered the district somewhat, Dellums did not want his new constituents to think he was taking them for granted. Eight other candidates shared space in Dellums's headquarters, including both Dianne Feinstein and Barbara Boxer.

The Progressive Group of Northampton, Mass., provided telemarketing services and Mal Warwick & Associates of San Francisco handled direct-mail fund raising, as they had both done in 1990. Noting that responses to Dellums's nationwide direct-mail solicitations dropped as a result of increased fund-raising activity by other candidates, Swanson said local contributions carried the campaign in 1992.

The $66,186 Dellums donated from his campaign to other candidates, civic organizations, ideological groups, and Democratic party organization represented a 39 percent increase over 1990. IMPAC 2000, a political action committee devoted to assisting Democrats in state redistricting battles, received $41,688. He donated $5,000 to the Democratic Congressional Campaign Committee. He spent $1,650 on tickets to a Congressional Black Caucus event, $1,315 on tickets to the Black Filmmakers Hall of Fame, and $1,000 on tickets to a dinner sponsored by the Black Women Organized for Educational Development.

While Republican G. William Hunter spent roughly $70,000 more than Dellums's 1990 opponent, he received 15 percent less of the vote.

The fact that Dellums had 851 overdrafts at the House bank was never a factor in the race.

Campaign Expenditures	Dellums Amount Spent	Dellums % of Total	Hunter Amount Spent	Hunter % of Total
Overhead				
Office furniture/supplies	$ 17,090	2.16	$ 872	1.18
Rent/utilities	9,194	1.16	0	
Salaries	85,461	10.82	3,410	4.63
Taxes	3,120	.40	0	
Bank/investment fees	4,940	.63	0	
Lawyers/accountants	7,260	.92	0	
Telephone	9,952	1.26	769	1.04
Campaign automobile	0		0	
Computers/office equipment	6,901	.87	500	.68
Travel	58,416	7.40	513	.70
Food/meetings	5,357	.68	935	1.27
Subtotal	207,690	26.30	6,998	9.50
Fund Raising				
Events	53,061	6.72	5,293	7.19
Direct mail	242,564	30.71	0	
Telemarketing	30,024	3.80	0	
Subtotal	325,649	41.23	5,293	7.19
Polling	0		2,300	3.12
Advertising				
Electronic media	0		1,000	1.36
Other media	6,615	.84	2,084	2.83
Subtotal	6,615	.84	3,084	4.19
Other Campaign Activity				
Persuasion mail/brochures	29,500	3.73	41,690	56.60
Actual campaigning	55,078	6.97	3,805	5.17
Staff/volunteers	1,000	.13	0	
Subtotal	85,578	10.83	45,495	61.76
Constituent Gifts/ Entertainment	2,376	.30	0	
Donations to				
Candidates from same state	5,208	.66	0	
Candidates from other states	1,000	.13	0	
Civic organizations	3,649	.46	0	
Ideological groups	7,740	.98	0	
Political parties	48,589	6.15	0	
Subtotal	66,186	8.38	0	
Unitemized Expenses	95,740	12.12	10,489	14.24
Total Campaign Expenses	$ 789,834		$ 73,660	
PAC Contributions	$ 78,437		$ 2,200	
Individual Contributions	634,739		36,901	
Total Receipts*	854,478		76,530	

*Includes PAC and individual contributions as well as interest earned, party contributions, etc.

† No expenditures or receipts on file. Candidates raising or spending less than $5,000 are not required to file reports with the Federal Election Commission.

CALIFORNIA — District 10

Rep. Bill Baker (R)

1992 Election Results

Bill Baker (R) 145,702 (52%)
Wendell H. Williams (D) 134,635 (48%)

State representative Bill Baker's campaign was one of the few that conformed with conventional wisdom: he actually spent 70 percent of his funds on direct appeals to voters.

Baker funneled $337,435 of his spending through McNally, Temple & Associates of Sacramento. The company provided general strategic advice and designed, produced, and placed Baker's two radio commercials. However, 82 percent of the money McNally received was for work on the campaign's brochures and persuasion mail.

Rather than designing mailers that struck a single theme, much of Baker's literature took a shotgun approach. In one piece, McNally touched on Baker's pledges to fight for a constitutional amendment requiring a balanced federal budget, a presidential line-item veto to "cut wasteful pork barrel spending," and an immediate freeze on federal spending. The piece covered highlights of his career in the state legislature and underscored his authorship of a victims rights bill and his support for the death penalty and tougher mandatory sentencing for convicted criminals.

Another brochure touted Baker's votes against "every legislative pay raise in the state assembly," his record as a champion of "the angry taxpayer," his authorship of a bill to protect wetlands, and his displeasure with "the bounced checks, the staggering federal deficit, and the special privileges for members of Congress."

According to press secretary Alex Novak, the campaign also invested heavily in mail designed to encourage participation in the more than sixty coffees Baker attended throughout the district. Once the decision was made to hold one of these meet-and-greets, the campaign would saturate the surrounding precincts with persuasion mail and invitations. In some cases this would be followed up by a door-to-door literature drop. At the event itself, additional pamphlets were distributed but no donations were required.

While Baker spent only $2,712 on bumper stickers and buttons and $2,592 on posters and signs, he invested $12,780 to purchase refrigerator magnets and 4,000 retractable pens. The pens, which cost 80 cents apiece, were handed out to newly registered Republicans. The campaign also spent $2,232 on T-shirts.

Despite outspending Democrat Wendell H. Williams by nearly three to one, Baker was somewhat disheartened by the amount of money he raised, particularly during the primary. "He definitely thinks he should have raised more," noted Novak.

Williams, who had lost to Baker in two previous state legislature races, also spent more of his funds on persuasion mail than anything else, but he fell $332,383 short of Baker's mail effort and 11,000 votes short of victory.

Campaign Expenditures	Baker Amount Spent	Baker % of Total	Williams Amount Spent	Williams % of Total
Overhead				
Office furniture/supplies	$ 12,401	1.61	$ 20,500	7.89
Rent/utilities	16,590	2.16	3,960	1.52
Salaries	71,172	9.27	40,397	15.55
Taxes	30,008	3.91	5,902	2.27
Bank/investment fees	4	.00	243	.09
Lawyers/accountants	1,023	.13	0	
Telephone	16,704	2.17	4,483	1.73
Campaign automobile	0		0	
Computers/office equipment	8,006	1.04	4,158	1.60
Travel	256	.03	2,114	.81
Food/meetings	0		0	
Subtotal	156,164	20.33	81,759	31.47
Fund Raising				
Events	41,243	5.37	24,987	9.62
Direct mail	3,570	.46	4,729	1.82
Telemarketing	0		0	
Subtotal	44,813	5.83	29,717	11.44
Polling	20,600	2.68	2,500	.96
Advertising				
Electronic media	46,473	6.05	22,394	8.62
Other media	325	.04	2,593	1.00
Subtotal	46,798	6.09	24,987	9.62
Other Campaign Activity				
Persuasion mail/brochures	421,707	54.91	89,324	34.38
Actual campaigning	67,829	8.83	11,601	4.47
Staff/volunteers	518	.07	1,000	.38
Subtotal	490,054	63.80	101,925	39.23
Constituent Gifts/Entertainment	2,754	.36	0	
Donations to				
Candidates from same state	0		0	
Candidates from other states	1,000	.13	500	.19
Civic organizations	0		500	.19
Ideological groups	0		300	.12
Political parties	0		300	.12
Subtotal	1,000	.13	1,600	.62
Unitemized Expenses	5,883	.77	17,318	6.67
Total Campaign Expenses	$ 768,065		$ 259,805	
PAC Contributions	$ 178,550		$ 102,626	
Individual Contributions	453,249		93,146	
Total Receipts*	699,687		228,847	

*Includes PAC and individual contributions as well as interest earned, party contributions, etc.

District 11 — CALIFORNIA

Rep. Richard W. Pombo (R)

1992 Election Results

Richard W. Pombo (R)	94,453	(48%)
Patricia Garamendi (D)	90,539	(46%)
Christine Roberts † (I)	13,498	(7%)

Rancher and Tracy, Calif., City Council member Richard W. Pombo proved that victory does not always go to the candidate who spends the most. Businesswoman Patricia Garamendi, the wife of the state insurance commissioner, spent 48 percent more than her Republican opponent in a district where registered Democrats comprised 54 percent of the electorate, yet she came up 3,914 votes short. The important thing, as Pombo's press secretary Michael Hardiman put it, was to "raise enough to get your message across."

Hardiman might also have added that the pattern of spending was equally important. While Pombo invested just $71,318 in overhead, or 12 percent of his total outlays, Garamendi spent $202,370, or 23 percent of her treasury, on overhead. This $131,052 difference represented nearly half of Garamendi's monetary advantage. Garamendi managed to spend $18,038 more on broadcast advertising, but Pombo's strategy of rationing his early media buys meant that during the final few days of the campaign he was able to match Garamendi dollar for dollar.

Trippi, McMahon & Squier of Alexandria, Va., received $202,151 for designing and placing Garamendi's broadcast ads. One of the more effective television commercials opened with the word "extremist" written diagonally across the screen in large red letters and proceeded with attacks on Pombo's positions on gun control and abortion. Hardiman acknowledged that once Garamendi began airing the ad, Pombo's standing in the polls dropped.

Pombo struck back with ads designed and placed by Wayne C. Johnson & Associates of Sacramento. Over the last five days of the campaign, Pombo repeatedly aired one commercial that charged that 91 percent of Garamendi's money was raised outside the district. The ad went on to claim that Garamendi had moved three times in three years to run for political office.

Much of Pombo's early money was spent on persuasion mail, also designed and produced by Johnson. Striking the "family values" theme, one mailing criticized Time Warner for its release of "Cop Killer," a song by rapper Ice T. Other mailers centered on Pombo as a family man and a strong business leader.

When it came to persuasion mail, Garamendi outspent Pombo by $156,473. In addition to the standard biographical pieces, she mailed a "Women's Information Guide," which pitched her message and provided telephone numbers for a host of agencies and hotlines dealing with health care, violence against women, economic assistance, and education. A similar mailing targeting senior citizens carried the tagline: "A Belief in the Wisdom of Seniors."

Campaign Expenditures	Pombo Amount Spent	Pombo % of Total	Garamendi Amount Spent	Garamendi % of Total
Overhead				
Office furniture/supplies	$ 6,659	1.14	$ 11,350	1.32
Rent/utilities	4,086	.70	7,776	.90
Salaries	26,460	4.54	101,627	11.79
Taxes	0		20,847	2.42
Bank/investment fees	223	.04	0	
Lawyers/accountants	0		18,180	2.11
Telephone	8,924	1.53	16,624	1.93
Campaign automobile	0		0	
Computers/office equipment	5,972	1.02	14,437	1.67
Travel	17,937	3.08	11,195	1.30
Food/meetings	1,059	.18	334	.04
Subtotal	71,318	12.23	202,370	23.48
Fund Raising				
Events	72,913	12.50	58,776	6.82
Direct mail	65,828	11.29	21,663	2.51
Telemarketing	0		0	
Subtotal	138,741	23.79	80,439	9.33
Polling	28,936	4.96	22,950	2.66
Advertising				
Electronic media	184,113	31.57	202,151	23.45
Other media	437	.07	6,613	.77
Subtotal	184,550	31.64	208,764	24.22
Other Campaign Activity				
Persuasion mail/brochures	111,583	19.13	268,056	31.10
Actual campaigning	44,995	7.71	70,091	8.13
Staff/volunteers	72	.01	636	.07
Subtotal	156,651	26.86	338,783	39.30
Constituent Gifts/ Entertainment	0		0	
Donations to				
Candidates from same state	0		0	
Candidates from other states	0		0	
Civic organizations	220	.04	227	.03
Ideological groups	0		0	
Political parties	24	.00	0	
Subtotal	244	.04	227	.03
Unitemized Expenses	2,784	.48	8,444	.98
Total Campaign Expenses	$ 583,224		$ 861,977	
PAC Contributions	$ 152,486		$ 338,905	
Individual Contributions	360,709		483,051	
Total Receipts*	532,902		864,475	

*Includes PAC and individual contributions as well as interest earned, party contributions, etc.

† No expenditures or receipts on file. Candidates raising or spending less than $5,000 are not required to file reports with the Federal Election Commission.

CALIFORNIA — District 12

Rep. Tom Lantos (D)

1992 Election Results

Tom Lantos (D)	157,205	(69%)
Jim Tomlin (R)	53,278	(23%)

Rep. Tom Lantos ran the quintessential permanent campaign. Having received two-thirds or more of the vote in four successive contests and having been helped, if anything, by redistricting, Lantos nevertheless spent $600,660. His opponent, realtor Jim Tomlin, spent $5,555.

Very little of Lantos's investment was directed at his woefully underfunded challenger. Lantos spent $216,505 to keep his campaign machinery well oiled during 1991, including $73,025 on overhead and $112,934 on fund raising.

Throughout the two-year election cycle, direct-mail fund raising was by far the largest drain on Lantos's treasury, consuming 30 percent of his budget. Administrative assistant Robert R. King said at least six solicitations were mailed to a list of between 15,000 and 20,000 contributors who might be counted on to give $25 to $50. Intelligent Software Systems of San Carlos received $103,050 for maintaining the lists and coordinating the mailings.

While these mailings generated 51 percent of Lantos's total contributions, they were not cost effective. Lantos spent $179,238 on his direct-mail program and collected $228,451 in small donations. The net of $49,213 represented a return of $1.27 for every $1 invested.

A much better return was realized by the campaign's four Washington, D.C., events, which helped raise $112,850 from political action committees (PACs). For a total cost of $33,512, these PAC events returned $3.37 for each $1 invested. Robert H. Bassin Associates of Washington received $30,573 to cover their fees and various expenses.

Looking only at his campaign financial statements, it would be difficult to tell whether Lantos represented California or New Hampshire. While Lantos contributed a total of $16,296 to candidates and party organizations in California, he donated $33,500 to candidates and party organizations in New Hampshire. Lantos gave $12,500 to the New Hampshire Democratic party. He donated to three Democrats running for governor—$5,000 each to Ned Helms, Norman E. D'Amours, and the eventual nominee, Deborah Arnesen. He even contributed to both Democratic candidates for mayor of Nashua. Lantos's son-in-law, Rep. Dick Swett, represents the state's District 2, which includes Nashua.

As in 1990, Lantos's daughter, Katrina Lantos-Swett, served as his campaign treasurer. She was paid $22,600 during the 1992 cycle. Another $29,500 of Lantos's salary payments went to fifteen members of his congressional staff. These payments included $20,500 in bonuses, which ranged from $500 to $5,000. Nine of the staffers receiving bonuses had not been paid by the campaign previously.

Campaign Expenditures	Lantos Amount Spent	Lantos % of Total	Tomlin Amount Spent	Tomlin % of Total
Overhead				
Office furniture/supplies	$ 9,517	1.58	$ 245	4.42
Rent/utilities	3,600	.60	0	
Salaries	80,776	13.45	0	
Taxes	13,999	2.33	0	
Bank/investment fees	0		0	
Lawyers/accountants	39,898	6.64	0	
Telephone	1,140	.19	59	1.07
Campaign automobile	3,857	.64	0	
Computers/office equipment	0		0	
Travel	13,355	2.22	0	
Food/meetings	3,755	.63	39	.70
Subtotal	**169,897**	**28.28**	**344**	**6.19**
Fund Raising				
Events	66,722	11.11	245	4.41
Direct mail	179,238	29.84	0	
Telemarketing	0		0	
Subtotal	**245,960**	**40.95**	**245**	**4.41**
Polling	0		0	
Advertising				
Electronic media	291	.05	0	
Other media	10,409	1.73	381	6.85
Subtotal	**10,700**	**1.78**	**381**	**6.85**
Other Campaign Activity				
Persuasion mail/brochures	2,500	.42	446	8.04
Actual campaigning	59,513	9.91	462	8.32
Staff/volunteers	2,415	.40	0	
Subtotal	**64,428**	**10.73**	**908**	**16.35**
Constituent Gifts/Entertainment	15,838	2.64	0	
Donations to				
Candidates from same state	11,500	1.91	0	
Candidates from other states	33,000	5.49	0	
Civic organizations	6,270	1.04	0	
Ideological groups	736	.12	0	
Political parties	27,446	4.57	0	
Subtotal	**78,952**	**13.14**	**0**	
Unitemized Expenses	14,884	2.48	3,677	66.20
Total Campaign Expenses	**$ 600,660**		**$ 5,555**	
PAC Contributions	$ 112,850		$ 2,000	
Individual Contributions	334,531		815	
Total Receipts*	499,867		2,815	

*Includes PAC and individual contributions as well as interest earned, party contributions, etc.

District 13 — CALIFORNIA

Rep. Pete Stark (D)

1992 Election Results

Pete Stark (D)	123,795	(60%)
Verne Teyler (R)	64,953	(32%)
Roslyn A. Allen † (I)	16,768	(8%)

Having watched his percentage of the vote drop in 1990 below 60 percent for the first time in a decade, Rep. Pete Stark decided to get an early start on his 1992 campaign. Off-year spending totaled $181,280.

Despite ending the 1990 election cycle with cash reserves of $362,000, Stark spent $78,071 to raise $274,172 in 1991. Political action committees accounted for $160,190, or 58 percent of his total contributions. Individual contributors donating $200 or more provided another 30 percent. Stark spent little time or money pursuing small donations during the off-year, investing no money in direct mail and only $3,020 in telemarketing.

In March 1991 Stark retained persuasion mail consultant American Data Management, which began compiling mailing lists on areas acquired through redistricting. The campaign paid more than $6,000 to design and print a newsletter, which helped to push total off-year persuasion mail costs to $35,404.

Larry Tramutola of Oakland was paid $8,107 to organize a series of small, informal coffees designed to introduce the incumbent to his constituents. The campaign made payments totaling $5,405 to support the South Alameda County Voter Registration Project. In all, expenditures for such grass-roots organization amounted to $19,592 in 1991.

Representing a district where registered Democrats comprise 58 percent of the electorate and facing an underfunded Republican challenger, Stark continued to pour it on through election day. While foster-care home operator Verne Teyler managed to scrape together $43,439, Stark spent $406,523 in 1992 alone, nearly $200,000 of it during the final month of the campaign.

Stark paid $20,522 to Paul Kinney Productions of Sacramento for production and placement of two radio commercials. One ad extolled Stark's support for a national health care program; the other sought to portray Teyler as "a scary guy, a Pat Robertson clone," according to administrative assistant William K. Vaughan. Although reluctant to admit it, Vaughan said the negative ad "worked best."

In addition to one positive mailer focusing on health care, Vaughan said the campaign targeted senior citizens with a piece attacking Teyler for advocating the privatization of Medicare. Pro-choice voters and those identified as favoring gun control were also targeted with special mailings.

Stark was one of only five members of the California delegation who used campaign funds to lease or buy an automobile. Vaughan noted that two-thirds of the monthly lease on Stark's 1992 Cadillac Seville was paid by the campaign; the balance was paid directly by Stark.

Campaign Expenditures	Stark Amount Spent	Stark % of Total	Teyler Amount Spent	Teyler % of Total
Overhead				
Office furniture/supplies	$ 12,159	2.07	$ 1,351	3.11
Rent/utilities	0		0	
Salaries	940	.16	0	
Taxes	13,836	2.35	0	
Bank/investment fees	539	.09	46	.11
Lawyers/accountants	6,714	1.14	0	
Telephone	1,436	.24	883	2.03
Campaign automobile	16,737	2.85	0	
Computers/office equipment	13,209	2.25	1,844	4.24
Travel	6,681	1.14	1,421	3.27
Food/meetings	2,193	.37	0	
Subtotal	**74,445**	**12.66**	**5,545**	**12.76**
Fund Raising				
Events	144,952	24.66	2,431	5.60
Direct mail	0		0	
Telemarketing	43,858	7.46	0	
Subtotal	**188,810**	**32.12**	**2,431**	**5.60**
Polling	**10,308**	**1.75**	**0**	
Advertising				
Electronic media	20,522	3.49	14,220	32.74
Other media	5,573	.95	1,643	3.78
Subtotal	**26,095**	**4.44**	**15,863**	**36.52**
Other Campaign Activity				
Persuasion mail/brochures	180,135	30.65	6,053	13.93
Actual campaigning	59,047	10.05	11,571	26.64
Staff/volunteers	8,280	1.41	0	
Subtotal	**247,462**	**42.10**	**17,625**	**40.57**
Constituent Gifts/Entertainment	**3,913**	**.67**	**309**	**.71**
Donations to				
Candidates from same state	5,970	1.02	0	
Candidates from other states	3,000	.51	0	
Civic organizations	2,029	.35	0	
Ideological groups	2,769	.47	50	.12
Political parties	15,650	2.66	30	.07
Subtotal	**29,418**	**5.00**	**80**	**.18**
Unitemized Expenses	**7,353**	**1.25**	**1,586**	**3.65**
Total Campaign Expenses	**$ 587,803**		**$ 43,439**	
PAC Contributions	$ 349,444		$ 1,250	
Individual Contributions	178,756		28,483	
Total Receipts*	634,994		47,360	

*Includes PAC and individual contributions as well as interest earned, party contributions, etc.

† No expenditures or receipts on file. Candidates raising or spending less than $5,000 are not required to file reports with the Federal Election Commission.

CALIFORNIA — District 14

Rep. Anna G. Eshoo (D)

1992 Election Results

Anna G. Eshoo (D)	146,873	(57%)
Tom Huening (R)	101,202	(39%)

In the race to succeed retiring Rep. Tom Campbell, San Mateo County Supervisor Tom Huening got a running start. During 1991 Huening spent $93,384 to favorably position himself in the five-person Republican primary field, including $10,000 on polling, $14,324 on fund raising, and $44,420 on salaries, computer equipment, and other office overhead. He won 41 percent of the primary vote, spending $322,229 in the process.

Having expended $1.1 million on an unsuccessful race against Campbell in 1988, fellow San Mateo supervisor Anna G. Eshoo needed no such jump-start. She had both organizational strength and a demonstrated ability to raise huge sums of money. Once Eshoo joined the fray in early January 1992, she managed to raise and spend more than $300,000, outspending each of her seven Democratic primary opponents.

During the primary campaign, Eshoo spent $168,247 on brochures and persuasion mail. Ross Communications of Sacramento received $15,762 for designing the mail. Another $16,000 was spent on a slate mailer and voter guide. Campaign volunteers took care of the labor, so the remaining $136,485 was poured into printing, postage, and labels.

To help her secure the Democratic nomination, Eshoo also paid $10,416 to Sandi Polka of Sacramento for phonebanking. Her general campaign strategist, Staton & Hughes of San Francisco, collected $25,740 during the primary campaign. Seven campaign staffers were paid a total of $38,993.

The general election proved to be no contest in either a monetary or an electoral sense. Huening spent approximately $350,000 on the fall campaign; Eshoo spent more than $620,000.

Eshoo largely owed her spending advantage to the kindness of political action committees (PACs). During the primary campaign, PACs had accounted for 17 percent of her total contributions. Over the final six months of 1992, the comparable figure was 41 percent. Labor union PACs donated $125,550, or 42 percent of her total PAC contributions. Six PACs, including the Hollywood Women's Political Committee and the Women's Campaign Fund, gave Eshoo the maximum $10,000 contribution.

For the general election campaign, Eshoo spent $243,315 on persuasion mail. One of Eshoo's mailers was a sixty-page policy booklet that was sent to registered Democrats who had not voted in the primary. Other more traditional mailers dealt with gun control, her endorsement by the Sierra Club, and the voting records of the two candidates during their tenure as county supervisors. Ross Communications received $24,421 for work on the general election mailings.

	Eshoo		Huening	
Campaign Expenditures	Amount Spent	% of Total	Amount Spent	% of Total
Overhead				
Office furniture/supplies	$ 14,057	1.47	$ 14,282	2.12
Rent/utilities	23,083	2.41	24,209	3.59
Salaries	125,895	13.15	100,594	14.90
Taxes	53,926	5.63	41,088	6.09
Bank/investment fees	0		153	.02
Lawyers/accountants	19,264	2.01	8,300	1.23
Telephone	18,973	1.98	20,389	3.02
Campaign automobile	0		0	
Computers/office equipment	7,068	.74	10,597	1.57
Travel	11,092	1.16	7,239	1.07
Food/meetings	1,716	.18	476	.07
Subtotal	**275,073**	**28.74**	**227,327**	**33.68**
Fund Raising				
Events	37,782	3.95	28,305	4.19
Direct mail	31,348	3.28	14,609	2.16
Telemarketing	0		0	
Subtotal	**69,130**	**7.22**	**42,914**	**6.36**
Polling	**36,500**	**3.81**	**16,488**	**2.44**
Advertising				
Electronic media	49,815	5.20	62,863	9.31
Other media	165	.02	5,624	.83
Subtotal	**49,980**	**5.22**	**68,487**	**10.15**
Other Campaign Activity				
Persuasion mail/brochures	411,562	43.00	214,568	31.79
Actual campaigning	104,293	10.90	97,288	14.41
Staff/volunteers	0		220	.03
Subtotal	**515,855**	**53.90**	**312,076**	**46.23**
Constituent Gifts/ Entertainment	60	.01	0	
Donations to				
Candidates from same state	0		0	
Candidates from other states	0		0	
Civic organizations	615	.06	0	
Ideological groups	130	.01	0	
Political parties	5,250	.55	0	
Subtotal	**5,995**	**.63**	**0**	
Unitemized Expenses	4,510	.47	7,740	1.15
Total Campaign Expenses	$ 957,101		$ 675,031	
PAC Contributions	$ 296,322		$ 149,383	
Individual Contributions	610,938		457,744	
Total Receipts*	917,346		673,082	

*Includes PAC and individual contributions as well as interest earned, party contributions, etc.

District 15 — CALIFORNIA

Rep. Norman Y. Mineta (D)

1992 Election Results

Norman Y. Mineta (D)	168,617	(64%)
Robert Wick (R)	82,875	(31%)

Having run expensive, yet grass-roots oriented campaigns for years, Rep. Norman Y. Mineta wished he could personally talk with every new voter in his district. However, 40 percent of that electorate was new, and there was not enough time. The mail proved to be the next best option.

Campaign Performance Group of San Francisco designed an extensive persuasion mail effort. "Triumph of Spirit," which discussed his experiences in an internment camp for Japanese-Americans during World War II and the lessons it taught him, served to introduce Mineta to his new constituents. Later targeted mailings dealt with home ownership, education, health care, and his work as chairman of the Committee on Public Works and Transportation. One mailing was a nine-piece puzzle. Each piece had a Mineta accomplishment printed on one side and part of a picture on the other. When assembled, the nine pieces completed a picture that showed the smiling incumbent next to his promise to "keep making a difference for you in Congress." Campaign Performance received $171,325 for its efforts.

With his $1.1 million campaign treasury, Mineta did not need to limit himself to persuasion mail. Joe Slade White & Co. of New York received $69,127 for designing and producing two television spots on education and job creation. Shafto & Barton of Houston, Texas, collected $120,210 to place the commercials. Outlays for billboards and newspaper ads were $11,290 and $15,384, respectively.

Mineta spent 72 percent more in 1992 than he had in 1990, and that translated into significantly increased fund-raising activity. Hammelman Associates of Arlington, Va., which helped chase political action committee (PAC) donations, received $14,539 for coordinating two Washington, D.C., fund-raisers. Mineta paid the JDS Group of San Jose $19,105 for staging district events.

Overall, PACs accounted for 58 percent of his total contributions. Donations from PACs representing companies with interests in legislation before the Public Works and Transportation Committee totaled $170,984. Labor union PACs added $144,560.

Given the weak Republican opposition, not all of Mineta's spending was channeled directly into his re-election. He spent $15,783 on constiuent meals and $22,592 on year-end holiday cards. Constituent gifts, plaques, calendars, flowers, and other entertainment totaled $6,200. His $94,435 in donations included $10,500 to the Democratic Congressional Campaign Committee and $41,688 to IMPAC 2000, the PAC formed to assist Democrats in redistricting.

Republican Robert Wick refused to discuss his campaign unless he was given free advertising in the *Los Angeles Times*.

Campaign Expenditures	Mineta Amount Spent	Mineta % of Total	Wick Amount Spent	Wick % of Total
Overhead				
Office furniture/supplies	$ 14,025	1.27	$ 1,482	2.98
Rent/utilities	16,800	1.52	3,302	6.64
Salaries	98,380	8.92	2,000	4.02
Taxes	55,272	5.01	0	
Bank/investment fees	1,120	.10	108	.22
Lawyers/accountants	535	.05	10,000	20.09
Telephone	10,588	.96	2,866	5.76
Campaign automobile	0		0	
Computers/office equipment	9,473	.86	12,527	25.17
Travel	16,694	1.51	5,312	10.67
Food/meetings	4,341	.39	0	
Subtotal	**227,228**	**20.60**	**37,597**	**75.54**
Fund Raising				
Events	173,297	15.71	2,697	5.42
Direct mail	0		0	
Telemarketing	0		0	
Subtotal	**173,297**	**15.71**	**2,697**	**5.42**
Polling	**24,000**	**2.18**	**0**	
Advertising				
Electronic media	189,443	17.17	0	
Other media	33,308	3.02	0	
Subtotal	**222,751**	**20.19**	**0**	
Other Campaign Activity				
Persuasion mail/brochures	277,290	25.14	4,638	9.32
Actual campaigning	32,537	2.95	2,820	5.67
Staff/volunteers	4,670	.42	0	
Subtotal	**314,497**	**28.51**	**7,458**	**14.98**
Constituent Gifts/ Entertainment	**44,575**	**4.04**	**0**	
Donations to				
Candidates from same state	3,150	.29	0	
Candidates from other states	9,750	.88	0	
Civic organizations	15,011	1.36	0	
Ideological groups	2,693	.24	0	
Political parties	63,831	5.79	139	.28
Subtotal	**94,435**	**8.56**	**139**	**.28**
Unitemized Expenses	**2,264**	**.21**	**1,879**	**3.78**
Total Campaign Expenses	**$ 1,103,046**		**$ 49,770**	
PAC Contributions	$ 546,295		$ 3,260	
Individual Contributions	390,699		18,960	
Total Receipts*	967,049		62,391	

*Includes PAC and individual contributions as well as interest earned, party contributions, etc.

CALIFORNIA District 16

Rep. Don Edwards (D)

1992 Election Results

Don Edwards (D)	96,661	(62%)
Ted Bundesen † (R)	49,843	(32%)
Amani S. Kuumba † (I)	9,370	(6%)

In most respects, Rep. Don Edwards ran a fairly streamlined campaign in 1992. He paid no rent for the small office his campaign occupied in the Santa Clara Democratic Information Center. His monthly telephone bills averaged $52. There was no campaign car. Sarah Janigian, his campaign manager and only employee, also coordinated fund-raising events in the district. His total overhead amounted to less than $20,000.

Fund raising was also a largely bare-bones operation. Jim Wise Associates of Alexandria, Va., received $13,059 for coordinating the campaign's two Washington, D.C., events. The hors d'oeuvres and wine cost an additional $1,991 in 1991 and $2,093 in 1992. Political action committee donations amounted to $182,700, or 73 percent of his total receipts.

Advertising was virtually nonexistent. Edwards spent $1,340 on journal and program ads. For the Democratic primary, in which he faced electrical engineer Edward R. Dykes, Edwards paid $225 for an ad in the *San Jose Mercury News* and $500 for ads with La Ofreta Publishing, which puts out a local Spanish-language newspaper. General election advertising expenses consisted of a $203 ad in *Our Paper*, a small newspaper in San Jose, and $250 ads in both the *Mercury News* and the Spanish-language daily. Another $49 was spent on artwork. As usual, Edwards ran no television commercials; the cost of advertising in the San Francisco television market is prohibitive. In September he spent $13,299 on billboards that simply had his picture and the tagline: "Democrat Don Edwards. He Works for You."

There was a dearth of grass-roots campaigning, as well. To increase his name recognition in the newly acquired portions of the district following redistricting, Edwards spent $5,533 on yard signs. Only $2,404 was invested in get-out-the-vote efforts. Souvenir pens imprinted with "Don Edwards: 16th Congressional District" cost the campaign $444.

Edwards paid $4,581 to send year-end holiday cards to those his district coordinator jokingly referred to as "only his close, personal friends." Another $373 was spent on Capitol calendars. There were no expenditures for constituent meals or gifts.

In essence, persuasion mail was the campaign. High Tech Campaign Consultants of San Jose collected $100,392 for designing, printing, and mailing brochures, including $61,966 for preprimary work. To get the most bang for their modest buck, the mailings were tightly targeted to households in which all registered voters were Democrats who had voted in at least two of the previous three elections.

Edward's Republican challenger, aerospace analyst Ted Bundesen, spent less than $5,000 and filed no reports with the Federal Election Commission.

Campaign Expenditures	Edwards Amount Spent	% of Total
Overhead		
Office furniture/supplies	$ 3,262	1.13
Rent/utilities	0	
Salaries	7,925	2.75
Taxes	0	
Bank/investment fees	0	
Lawyers/accountants	2,670	.93
Telephone	1,255	.43
Campaign automobile	0	
Computers/office equipment	1,572	.54
Travel	2,339	.81
Food/meetings	904	.31
Subtotal	**19,927**	**6.91**
Fund Raising		
Events	53,481	18.54
Direct mail	0	
Telemarketing	0	
Subtotal	**53,481**	**18.54**
Polling	**0**	
Advertising		
Electronic media	0	
Other media	16,143	5.59
Subtotal	**16,143**	**5.59**
Other Campaign Activity		
Persuasion mail/brochures	107,186	37.15
Actual campaigning	12,466	4.32
Staff/volunteers	0	
Subtotal	**119,652**	**41.47**
Constituent Gifts/Entertainment	**4,954**	**1.72**
Donations to		
Candidates from same state	498	.17
Candidates from other states	0	
Civic organizations	8,751	3.03
Ideological groups	1,580	.55
Political parties	47,538	16.48
Subtotal	**58,367**	**20.23**
Unitemized Expenses	**16,003**	**5.55**
Total Campaign Expenses	**$ 288,527**	
PAC Contributions	$ 182,700	
Individual Contributions	61,631	
Total Receipts*	249,478	

*Includes PAC and individual contributions as well as interest earned, party contributions, etc.

† No expenditures or receipts on file. Candidates raising or spending less than $5,000 are not required to file reports with the Federal Election Commission.

District 17 — CALIFORNIA

Rep. Leon E. Panetta (D)

1992 Election Results

Leon E. Panetta (D)	151,565	(72%)
Bill McCampbell (R)	49,947	(24%)

Rep. Leon E. Panetta liked to show his appreciation with an annual Christmas card. The cards, which featured a photograph of Panetta and his wife Sylvia, are a collector's item in the district. According to Sylvia Panetta, a local butcher has a display in his shop with every card the incumbent has ever sent. During the 1992 election cycle, Christmas cards cost Panetta's campaign $12,387.

Panetta spent twice as much on his 1992 campaign as he had in 1990, despite facing little competition from attorney Bill McCampbell. Expenditures for advertising increased by more than $150,000. Persuasion mail cost Panetta $24,079 in 1992; in 1990 he spent nothing on such mail. Even his expenditures for constituent gifts and entertainment increased by more than $11,000 in the 1992 election cycle.

John Franzen was called upon once again to provide Panetta's media strategy, something Franzen said he had done for the past sixteen years. Franzen produced five television commercials, four of which began and ended with interviews of constituents discussing what Panetta had done for the district. One ad profiled Panetta's work to establish a bird sanctuary along a 250-mile stretch of California's coastline. Another focused on Panetta's plans to convert a local military base for civilian use. There was an ad focusing on health care and another on agriculture. The fifth commercial simply scrolled the names of Republicans in the district who were supporting Panetta.

Franzen also produced five radio spots, designed and placed virtually all the campaign's newspaper ads, and designed Panetta's one brochure. According to Franzen, the $259,948 paid to his Washington, D.C.-based firm included $165,000 for air time on local network affiliates and cable stations, $21,000 for radio placement, and $13,000 for newspaper ads. Production of the brochure cost $3,000, while broadcast ad production, travel expenses, and consulting fees accounted for the remaining $57,948.

The campaign directly placed $688 in newspaper ads and $300 in journal ads. Advertising production costs totaling $865 were also paid directly by the campaign.

In addition to his Christmas cards, other noncampaign related expenses included constituent meals totaling $4,005, $2,111 for constituent gifts, $6,089 for flowers sent to constituents, and $4,170 paid to the Hyatt Hotel in Washington, D.C., for lodging during the inaugural festivities. Panetta used campaign funds for a host of meals with his Washington staff, including a "staff Christmas dinner" for $991. The campaign paid for two meals totaling $101 at the King David Hotel in Jerusalem and for his $1,021 stay at the Maui Prince Hotel for "lodging and meals for conference with the Japanese Diet."

Campaign Expenditures	Panetta Amount Spent	Panetta % of Total	McCampbell Amount Spent	McCampbell % of Total
Overhead				
Office furniture/supplies	$ 5,110	.99	$ 1,750	2.61
Rent/utilities	0		900	1.35
Salaries	28,930	5.60	5,654	8.45
Taxes	34,620	6.70	0	
Bank/investment fees	115	.02	0	
Lawyers/accountants	583	.11	0	
Telephone	10,910	2.11	3,202	4.79
Campaign automobile	0		0	
Computers/office equipment	471	.09	0	
Travel	8,809	1.70	3,299	4.93
Food/meetings	2,183	.42	649	.97
Subtotal	**91,731**	**17.75**	**15,454**	**23.10**
Fund Raising				
Events	26,932	5.21	3,070	4.59
Direct mail	298	.06	0	
Telemarketing	0		2,100	3.14
Subtotal	**27,229**	**5.27**	**5,170**	**7.73**
Polling	0		0	
Advertising				
Electronic media	244,813	47.36	15,960	23.85
Other media	13,988	2.71	0	
Subtotal	**258,801**	**50.07**	**15,960**	**23.85**
Other Campaign Activity				
Persuasion mail/brochures	24,079	4.66	7,631	11.40
Actual campaigning	11,301	2.19	8,764	13.10
Staff/volunteers	10,469	2.03	0	
Subtotal	**45,849**	**8.87**	**16,395**	**24.50**
Constituent Gifts/Entertainment	30,390	5.88	0	
Donations to				
Candidates from same state	1,500	.29	0	
Candidates from other states	3,450	.67	0	
Civic organizations	2,678	.52	0	
Ideological groups	0		0	
Political parties	39,941	7.73	1,000	1.49
Subtotal	**47,569**	**9.20**	**1,000**	**1.49**
Unitemized Expenses	15,319	2.96	12,934	19.33
Total Campaign Expenses	$ 516,888		$ 66,912	
PAC Contributions	$ 239,250		$ 0	
Individual Contributions	150,874		52,698	
Total Receipts*	410,124		76,569	

*Includes PAC and individual contributions as well as interest earned, party contributions, etc.

CALIFORNIA — District 18

Rep. Gary A. Condit (D)

1992 Election Results

Gary A. Condit (D)	139,704	(85%)
Kim R. Almstrom † (I)	25,307	(15%)

With no opposition in the Democratic primary and no Republican opposition in the November general election, Rep. Gary A. Condit's election-year spending exceeded his off-year outlays by only $22,765. Less than $15,000 of Condit's $282,137 budget was invested in direct appeals to voters.

Condit did not open a campaign office in 1992. He sent out no persuasion mail, although the American Medical Association political action committee spent $2,500 for a slate mailer on his behalf. Campaign coordinator Donna Dami, the only full-time staffer, ran what little campaign there was out of a small office behind her home. Payments for electricity and water cost the campaign $400. The law firm that prepared Condit's campaign financial disclosure statements collected one of every seven dollars he spent.

Since he began the 1992 election cycle with debts totaling $45,326 from his 1989 special election and 1990 general election campaigns, fund raising was among Condit's principal concerns. He paid Jim Wise Associates of Alexandria, Va., $14,451 to coordinate events aimed at corralling political action committee donations. These efforts yielded $155,645, or 43 percent of Condit's total receipts.

Dami arranged a succession of receptions held at places like the Red Lion Hotel, the Elks Lodge, and the Merced Golf and Country Club. A picnic in Merced attracted more than 700 people who dined on hot dogs and hamburgers. With ticket prices to virtually all his district events ranging from $5 to $100, Condit managed to raise $116,265 in small donations.

Approximately 14 percent of Condit's expenses were related to his annual "Condit Country" fundraisers, which have been a part of Condit's campaign persona for more than fifteen years. Congressional chief of staff Mike Lynch estimated that in both 1991 and 1992 3,000 supporters paid $35 apiece to eat and enjoy the country western music provided by the band Drivin' Wheel. With staging costs of roughly $20,000, Lynch said each of these events netted between $60,000 and $70,000. "It's more of a local institution than a fund-raising event," demurred Lynch.

Continuing another fifteen-year tradition, Condit bought the prize-winning rabbits at the Stanislaus County Fair Junior Livestock Auction. The rabbits, which Condit returned to the children who raised them, cost $600 in 1991 and $990 in 1992.

For the 1991 Fourth of July parade circuit, Condit invested $3,685 in sun visors. In 1992 parade-goers received $612 worth of helium-filled balloons. Condit also purchased constituent gifts and plaques totaling $5,458. Flowers sent to express sympathy over the death of a constituent cost the campaign $6,534. "This is a very close-knit community," said Lynch.

	Condit	
Campaign Expenditures	Amount Spent	% of Total
Overhead		
Office furniture/supplies	$ 17,053	6.04
Rent/utilities	400	.14
Salaries	25,040	8.88
Taxes	0	
Bank/investment fees	63	.02
Lawyers/accountants	40,422	14.33
Telephone	3,974	1.41
Campaign automobile	0	
Computers/office equipment	6,212	2.20
Travel	9,938	3.52
Food/meetings	8,890	3.15
Subtotal	**111,993**	**39.69**
Fund Raising		
Events	102,875	36.46
Direct mail	0	
Telemarketing	0	
Subtotal	**102,875**	**36.46**
Polling	**0**	
Advertising		
Electronic media	0	
Other media	2,814	1.00
Subtotal	**2,814**	**1.00**
Other Campaign Activity		
Persuasion mail/brochures	2,500	.88
Actual campaigning	8,812	3.12
Staff/volunteers	0	
Subtotal	**11,312**	**4.00**
Constituent Gifts/Entertainment	**11,993**	**4.25**
Donations to		
Candidates from same state	4,500	1.59
Candidates from other states	0	
Civic organizations	2,224	.79
Ideological groups	0	
Political parties	12,850	4.55
Subtotal	**19,574**	**6.94**
Unitemized Expenses	**21,578**	**7.65**
Total Campaign Expenses	**$ 282,137**	
PAC Contributions	**$ 155,645**	
Individual Contributions	**192,603**	
Total Receipts*	**362,490**	

*Includes PAC and individual contributions as well as interest earned, party contributions, etc.

† No expenditures or receipts on file. Candidates raising or spending less than $5,000 are not required to file reports with the Federal Election Commission.

District 19 — CALIFORNIA

Rep. Richard H. Lehman (D)

1992 Election Results

Richard H. Lehman (D)	101,620	(47%)
Tal L. Cloud (R)	100,590	(46%)
Dorothy L. Wells † (I)	13,334	(6%)

The map Rep. Richard H. Lehman received under the redistricting plan mandated by the California Supreme Court was not a pleasant surprise. While Democrats comprised 58 percent of the registered voters in his old district, they made up only 48 percent of the electorate in his new one. Unopposed in 1990, Lehman had the fight of his political life in 1992 and prevailed by only 1,029 votes.

To introduce himself to the 50 percent of the electorate he gained through redistricting, Lehman hired Dalton Media Studios of Fresno to develop and place three television commercials and one radio ad for his primary campaign against laser salesman Curtis Youngs. Since the competition was weak, the ads stuck with positive themes. One showed ten-year-old footage of Lehman calling for an end to partisan politics. For this work, as well as the printing of primary brochures and signs, Dalton received $120,881.

In the general election against paper company executive Tal L. Cloud, Lehman added three new negative commercials to the mix. When Cloud hit the incumbent with a generic "tax-and-spend liberal" ad produced by the National Republican Congressional Committee, Lehman responded with an ad that depicted Cloud as a liar, turning into Pinocchio. Another ad showed Cloud's nose turning into a nuclear warhead. Dalton collected another $249,376 for work during the general election campaign.

While television advertising was extremely cost effective, Lehman also paid Campaign Performance Group of San Francisco $4,373 to provide a very limited persuasion mail component. Describing the experiment as "not extensive and not that well targeted," district representative David Brodie added that it amounted to a "real failed attempt."

To help him fund his campaign, Lehman leaned heavily on political action committees (PACs). Fraioli/Jost of Washington, D.C., arranged three PAC events at the National Democratic Club. With costs totaling $81,789, including $73,290 paid to Fraioli/Jost, the events proved highly successful.

PAC donations accounted for 65 percent of Lehman's contributions. Labor PACs provided the biggest boost, donating $159,250. Agriculture PACs added $52,970, but their clout had more far-reaching implications. When Vice President Dan Quayle attended an event to raise money for California Republicans, a number of powerful agriculture PACs attended only after it was agreed that none of the money raised at the event would go to Cloud.

With far fewer resources, Cloud ran a do-it-yourself campaign in the primary. Jim Orman Communications of Fresno collected $59,081 for coordinating media buys and general campaign strategy during the general election campaign.

	Lehman		Cloud	
Campaign Expenditures	Amount Spent	% of Total	Amount Spent	% of Total
Overhead				
Office furniture/supplies	$ 19,505	2.02	$ 1,752	1.14
Rent/utilities	7,320	.76	388	.25
Salaries	103,876	10.78	5,120	3.33
Taxes	14,439	1.50	0	
Bank/investment fees	0		0	
Lawyers/accountants	205	.02	0	
Telephone	24,540	2.55	1,503	.98
Campaign automobile	0		0	
Computers/office equipment	18,526	1.92	2,340	1.52
Travel	46,050	4.78	2,883	1.88
Food/meetings	5,555	.58	0	
Subtotal	240,016	24.91	13,987	9.10
Fund Raising				
Events	166,157	17.25	14,227	9.26
Direct mail	5,935	.62	0	
Telemarketing	0		0	
Subtotal	172,092	17.86	14,227	9.26
Polling	31,275	3.25	0	
Advertising				
Electronic media	355,535	36.90	49,127	31.98
Other media	1,054	.11	2,829	1.84
Subtotal	356,589	37.01	51,956	33.82
Other Campaign Activity				
Persuasion mail/brochures	57,471	5.97	12,159	7.91
Actual campaigning	28,527	2.95	52,867	34.41
Staff/volunteers	1,350	.14	0	
Subtotal	87,347	9.06	65,026	42.33
Constituent Gifts/ Entertainment	826	.09	0	
Donations to				
Candidates from same state	3,050	.32	0	
Candidates from other states	3,000	.31	0	
Civic organizations	2,861	.30	0	
Ideological groups	1,550	.16	0	
Political parties	39,550	4.11	0	
Subtotal	50,011	5.19	0	
Unitemized Expenses	25,232	2.62	8,438	5.49
Total Campaign Expenses	$ 963,388		$ 153,634	
PAC Contributions	$ 526,845		$ 32,975	
Individual Contributions	283,924		93,377	
Total Receipts*	826,532		157,053	

*Includes PAC and individual contributions as well as interest earned, party contributions, etc.

† No expenditures or receipts on file. Candidates raising or spending less than $5,000 are not required to file reports with the Federal Election Commission.

CALIFORNIA — District 20

Rep. Calvin Dooley (D)

1992 Election Results

Calvin Dooley (D)	72,679	(65%)
Ed Hunt (R)	39,388	(35%)

During his first term, Rep. Calvin Dooley quickly discovered that the power of incumbency could be carried all the way to the bank. While tickets to his 1991 Washington, D.C., fund-raisers cost political action committees (PACs) $350, by 1992 PACs were telling Dooley to raise his prices to $500. "PACs were telling us that they were willing to give us that much, so we said great," said chief of staff Lisa Quigley.

Dooley held three Washington PAC events during the two-year election cycle. In all, PACs donated $242,583, or 42 percent more than in his 1990 campaign. Since Dooley sat on the Agriculture Committee, Calcot Ltd., a cotton exporter in Bakersfield was also more than happy to sponsor an event. According to Quigley, 100 people paid $100 each to attend the affair, which cost Calcot $2,996.

In addition, Dooley held thirteen district fund-raisers. Among his largest was a 1991 dinner featuring House Speaker Thomas S. Foley (D-Wash). Guests paid $125 to attend the dinner and for $500 they could also buy their way into a private reception with the Speaker. Quigley said the event cleared $85,000. Donations of $200 or more amounted to $145,584, or 30 percent of Dooley's total contributions.

By far the largest share of Dooley's money was invested in a television advertising campaign designed and executed by Squier/Eskew/Knapp/Ochs Communications of Washington, D.C. One 60-second spot pointed out how "farmer Cal was getting things done for the farmers," as Quigley put it. Another showed Dooley working on his pickup truck, talking about how people had to "roll up their sleeves" to get the economy moving again. Squier/Eskew received $206,823 for creating and placing four commercials; a fifth commercial on health care never ran.

As a challenger in 1990, Dooley needed every penny he could lay his hands on to defeat then-Rep. Chip Pashayan. As a result, he donated just $646 to Democratic party organizations in 1990. However, once elected, Dooley found room in the next campaign budget for contributions totaling $38,188 to IMPAC 2000, the PAC established to help Democrats with redistricting.

He did not, however, fall into the habit of spending lavishly on travel and entertainment. The campaign was billed only $628 for expenses incurred at the Democratic National Convention. Holiday cards cost the campaign $1,347. Soft drinks were served at the party to celebrate his 1991 swearing-in; the party cost a grand total of $694. Campaign meals not associated with fund raising totaled $133.

Outspent on broadcast advertising by nearly twelve to one, District Attorney Ed Hunt failed to mount a serious challenge.

Campaign Expenditures	Dooley Amount Spent	Dooley % of Total	Hunt Amount Spent	Hunt % of Total
Overhead				
Office furniture/supplies	$ 5,802	1.14	$ 8,299	6.23
Rent/utilities	3,396	.67	4,397	3.30
Salaries	17,387	3.41	35,885	26.95
Taxes	9,621	1.89	0	
Bank/investment fees	128	.03	97	.07
Lawyers/accountants	16,256	3.19	0	
Telephone	7,225	1.42	5,869	4.41
Campaign automobile	0		0	
Computers/office equipment	6,302	1.24	891	.67
Travel	5,284	1.04	6,464	4.85
Food/meetings	133	.03	363	.27
Subtotal	71,533	14.02	62,265	46.76
Fund Raising				
Events	84,009	16.47	11,897	8.93
Direct mail	0		1,321	.99
Telemarketing	0		0	
Subtotal	84,009	16.47	13,218	9.93
Polling	29,500	5.78	0	
Advertising				
Electronic media	207,223	40.62	17,689	13.28
Other media	4,803	.94	1,218	.91
Subtotal	212,025	41.56	18,907	14.20
Other Campaign Activity				
Persuasion mail/brochures	29,458	5.77	13,863	10.41
Actual campaigning	26,379	5.17	23,621	17.74
Staff/volunteers	0		0	
Subtotal	55,837	10.94	37,484	28.15
Constituent Gifts/ Entertainment	2,713	.53	72	.05
Donations to				
Candidates from same state	2,250	.44	0	
Candidates from other states	0		0	
Civic organizations	1,880	.37	640	.48
Ideological groups	3,225	.63	0	
Political parties	38,688	7.58	24	.02
Subtotal	46,043	9.03	664	.50
Unitemized Expenses	8,508	1.67	550	.41
Total Campaign Expenses	$ 510,167		$ 133,160	
PAC Contributions	$ 242,583		$ 40,597	
Individual Contributions	241,239		133,563	
Total Receipts*	496,485		176,878	

*Includes PAC and individual contributions as well as interest earned, party contributions, etc.

District 21 — CALIFORNIA

Rep. Bill Thomas (R)

1992 Election Results

Bill Thomas (R)	127,758	(65%)
Deborah A. Vollmer (D)	68,058	(35%)

Prior to 1992, Rep. Bill Thomas had seen his winning percentage drop as low as 60 percent only once in six reelection bids. Yet, in a district carried comfortably by George Bush, Thomas spent $610,997 to defeat Democrat Deborah A. Vollmer, who managed to spend less than 4 percent of that total. "You never know what the results are going to be until election day," remarked Catherine M. Abernathy, Thomas's administrative assistant.

Thomas took no chances that his 119 overdrafts at the House bank would contribute to his political demise. His expenses for the 1992 election cycle were 23 percent higher than in 1990, and off-year expenses alone amounted to $168,769.

As was the case in 1990, Western Pacific Research of Bakersfield was responsible for every aspect of Thomas's campaign. The firm, owned by Abernathy and her husband Mark, provided day-to-day campaign management services and strategic advice; served as the campaign's sole fund-raising consultant; developed all of Thomas's advertising; conducted polls; provided posters, signs, and literature; handled the persuasion mail; coordinated volunteers; and organized phonebanks. Thomas paid Western Pacific $351,778.

In a year when many incumbents ran "outsider" campaigns, all four of Thomas's television commercials were testimonials to his work in Washington on behalf of constituents. A veteran talked about the incumbent's role in bringing a new veterans hospital to the district. A senior citizen spoke about Thomas's work on Medicare.

Prior to the primary, the ads aired on three Bakersfield stations and on one in Fresno. During the final week before the November general election, the ads were resurrected and shown four times each day on one station in Bakersfield. "A spot on the 'Cosby Show' costs $1,500 here when it would cost $25,000 in Los Angeles," noted Abernathy.

To further communicate its various messages, the campaign also spent $121,245 on brochures and persuasion mail, $23,700 on billboards, $8,856 on newspaper and journal ads, and another $14,930 to post signs in several thousand yards.

The campaign also invested more heavily in phonebanking than it had in past elections, a move Abernathy attributed to the deteriorating quality of available mailing lists and to escalating postage and printing costs. Instead of the blanket mailings they sent out in past campaigns, Western Pacific started with a phonebank to identify likely voters, who were then mailed brochures covering issues in which they had expressed an interest. The 1992 phonebank cost $67,327.

Campaign Expenditures	Thomas Amount Spent	Thomas % of Total	Vollmer Amount Spent	Vollmer % of Total
Overhead				
Office furniture/supplies	$ 8,882	1.44	$ 620	2.66
Rent/utilities	400	.07	0	
Salaries	2,253	.37	0	
Taxes	7,388	1.21	0	
Bank/investment fees	0		0	
Lawyers/accountants	1,250	.20	0	
Telephone	1,215	.20	0	
Campaign automobile	0		0	
Computers/office equipment	1,535	.25	445	1.91
Travel	19,843	3.25	0	
Food/meetings	442	.07	0	
Subtotal	43,148	7.06	1,064	4.57
Fund Raising				
Events	141,664	23.19	0	
Direct mail	0		0	
Telemarketing	0		0	
Subtotal	141,664	23.19	0	
Polling	11,100	1.82	0	
Advertising				
Electronic media	66,882	10.95	12,306	52.87
Other media	32,556	5.33	720	3.09
Subtotal	99,439	16.27	13,026	55.96
Other Campaign Activity				
Persuasion mail/brochures	121,245	19.84	2,538	10.90
Actual campaigning	169,632	27.76	1,845	7.92
Staff/volunteers	151	.02	0	
Subtotal	291,028	47.63	4,382	18.83
Constituent Gifts/Entertainment	235	.04	0	
Donations to				
Candidates from same state	3,000	.49	0	
Candidates from other states	4,000	.65	0	
Civic organizations	500	.08	0	
Ideological groups	0		0	
Political parties	1,500	.25	0	
Subtotal	9,000	1.47	0	
Unitemized Expenses	15,384	2.52	4,806	20.65
Total Campaign Expenses	$ 610,997		$ 23,279	
PAC Contributions	$ 277,436		$ 2,150	
Individual Contributions	252,161		11,185	
Total Receipts*	598,669		28,803	

*Includes PAC and individual contributions as well as interest earned, party contributions, etc.

CALIFORNIA — District 22

Rep. Michael Huffington (R)

1992 Election Results

Michael Huffington (R)	131,242	(53%)
Gloria Ochoa (D)	87,328	(35%)
Mindy Lorenz (I)	23,699	(10%)

Never having run for political office, Michael Huffington, a wealthy Santa Barbara Republican, embarked on a spending spree that was unparalleled in the history of House campaigns.

Huffington poured about $3.5 million into the Republican primary, virtually all of it his own money. The nonstop media blitz his money bought carried Huffington to a narrow upset victory over veteran Republican Rep. Robert J. Lagomarsino, who spent $747,536. In the fall campaign, Huffington again tapped his own checkbook, putting together a $1.9 million effort to dispatch Santa Barbara County Supervisor Gloria Ochoa.

When the last checks had been written, Huffington's was by far the most expensive House campaign in history. The previous record was the $2.6 million spent by then-Republican Rep. Jack Kemp. Huffington's expenditures exceeded the $4.1 million spent by the average incumbent senator in 1992 by a staggering $1.3 million.

Other than Huffington, the big winners in this cash bonanza were his media consultants. Ringe Media of Purcellville, Va., received $546,197 for creating the television commercials. Crest Films of New York was paid $280,501 for ad production. Specialized Media Services of Charlotte, N.C., collected $1,089,540 for buying air time; Target Enterprises of Hollywood received $151,648, also for buying time.

In a thirty-second spot, a family was shown sitting in a hospital room next to their dying relative as Huffington recounted the human cost of tobacco use. Arguing that the tobacco lobby has undo influence in Washington, Huffington called for a ban on tobacco advertisements and for a halt in price support payments. The spot ended with a close-up of the patient's face and the sound of a pumping respirator.

Huckaby Rodriguez of Sacramento served as his general campaign strategist, collecting $126,241. For spearheading the persuasion mail effort, McNally, Temple & Associates of Sacramento received $321,012. Huffington paid Mason Lundberg & Associates of Orange, Calif., $235,404 for phonebanking.

Even by Senate let alone House standards, the Huffington campaign spent a phenomenal amount on research. For conducting polls and providing research on a host of public policy issues, Hill Research Consultants of Woodlands, Texas, received $186,742. Benchmark Research Group of Sacramento collected $31,230 for conducting polls and voter research. Competitive Edge Research & Communication of San Diego was paid $10,196 for opposition research.

Outspent on advertising by twenty-three to one and on persuasion mail by twelve to one, Ochoa was simply overwhelmed.

Campaign Expenditures	Huffington Amount Spent	% of Total	Ochoa Amount Spent	% of Total
Overhead				
Office furniture/supplies	$ 103,378	1.90	$ 18,345	2.60
Rent/utilities	71,653	1.32	13,021	1.84
Salaries	424,215	7.81	69,372	9.82
Taxes	139,513	2.57	20,759	2.94
Bank/investment fees	160	.00	313	.04
Lawyers/accountants	94,480	1.74	58,480	8.28
Telephone	37,733	.69	27,945	3.96
Campaign automobile	0		5,834	.83
Computers/office equipment	48,985	.90	2,605	.37
Travel	48,322	.89	15,701	2.22
Food/meetings	14,539	.27	468	.07
Subtotal	**982,978**	**18.09**	**232,843**	**32.96**
Fund Raising				
Events	41,764	.77	27,551	3.90
Direct mail	0		54,511	7.72
Telemarketing	0		449	.06
Subtotal	**41,764**	**.77**	**82,510**	**11.68**
Polling	**160,039**	**2.94**	**47,000**	**6.65**
Advertising				
Electronic media	2,250,327	41.41	98,762	13.98
Other media	79,281	1.46	1,760	.25
Subtotal	**2,329,607**	**42.87**	**100,522**	**14.23**
Other Campaign Activity				
Persuasion mail/brochures	1,288,667	23.71	107,470	15.22
Actual campaigning	600,415	11.05	118,387	16.76
Staff/volunteers	1,140	.02	510	.07
Subtotal	**1,890,223**	**34.78**	**226,367**	**32.05**
Constituent Gifts/ Entertainment	0		300	.04
Donations to				
Candidates from same state	0		0	
Candidates from other states	0		0	
Civic organizations	5,735	.11	0	
Ideological groups	0		0	
Political parties	920	.02	2,500	.35
Subtotal	**6,655**	**.12**	**2,500**	**.35**
Unitemized Expenses	**23,302**	**.43**	**14,296**	**2.02**
Total Campaign Expenses	**$ 5,434,569**		**$ 706,338**	
PAC Contributions	$ 0		$ 152,663	
Individual Contributions	243,110		411,112	
Total Receipts*	5,443,247		657,375	

*Includes PAC and individual contributions as well as interest earned, party contributions, etc.

District 23 — CALIFORNIA

Rep. Elton Gallegly (R)

1992 Election Results

Elton Gallegly (R)   115,504   (54%)
Anita Perez Ferguson (D)   88,225   (41%)

Rep. Elton Gallegly had two significant problems that forced him to spend nearly twice as much on his 1992 campaign as he had in 1990. First, redistricting robbed him of almost three-quarters of his former constituency and handed him a new electorate in which registered Democrats slightly outnumbered Republicans. Perhaps more importantly, in a district where 30 percent of the population is Hispanic, Gallegly faced Democrat Anita Perez Ferguson, a Hispanic educational consultant who had taken 44 percent of the vote against Rep. Robert J. Lagomarsino in 1990.

Gallegly poured $309,745 into a persuasion mail campaign designed by Ben Key of James R. Foster & Associates in Carrollton, Texas. Key segmented the electorate into seven groups based on a combination of issue orientation and geography. Targeted groups included women, senior citizens, and likely voters. The message dealt with such issues as crime, education, and immigration. Foster & Associates collected $35,353 for Key's efforts.

According to Key, one of the campaign's most effective appeals was "the spouse letter." An initial letter touting Gallegly's accomplishments and signed by his wife Janet was mailed in early October, shortly before Ferguson hit the radio airwaves with her first attack ads. Once the negative charges hit, a second letter was mailed in which Janet Gallegly replead her husband's case. "They can say whatever they want about my husband, but I know him, and what they are saying is wrong." Key said he believed these letters worked because people felt they had "an emotional attachment" to Gallegly.

Gallegly also began airing his own radio ads in early October, charging that Ferguson had broken campaign contribution laws in her 1990 race against Lagomarsino and that she had the worst attendance on the Santa Barbara Planning Commission. "We can't afford your kind of carefree attitude in Congress," the commercial said. Radio buys totaled $24,150, of which $19,443 was spent in the fall campaign.

According to press secretary John Frith, the campaign produced two television commercials, including one focusing on Gallegly's endorsement by the sheriff of Ventura County. Air time on local cable outlets cost the campaign $35,888, more than twice the amount he spent on cable television in 1990. An additional $15,626 was spent to purchase time on an independent television station in Oxnard.

Ferguson opted to spend much more heavily on broadcast advertising than persuasion mail, paying the Campaign Group of Philadelphia, Pa., $127,694 for design and placement of the ads.

Campaign Expenditures	Gallegly Amount Spent	Gallegly % of Total	Ferguson Amount Spent	Ferguson % of Total
Overhead				
Office furniture/supplies	$ 22,497	2.64	$ 17,386	3.44
Rent/utilities	25,085	2.95	5,866	1.16
Salaries	91,286	10.72	72,214	14.28
Taxes	30,185	3.54	0	
Bank/investment fees	442	.05	759	.15
Lawyers/accountants	937	.11	4,203	.83
Telephone	15,892	1.87	24,788	4.90
Campaign automobile	0		0	
Computers/office equipment	43,424	5.10	5,720	1.13
Travel	18,657	2.19	9,048	1.79
Food/meetings	493	.06	352	.07
Subtotal	**248,898**	**29.22**	**140,337**	**27.75**
Fund Raising				
Events	87,495	10.27	24,269	4.80
Direct mail	30,554	3.59	43,383	8.58
Telemarketing	0		0	
Subtotal	**118,049**	**13.86**	**67,652**	**13.38**
Polling	**12,851**	**1.51**	**12,000**	**2.37**
Advertising				
Electronic media	76,674	9.00	132,226	26.14
Other media	12,939	1.52	0	
Subtotal	**89,613**	**10.52**	**132,226**	**26.14**
Other Campaign Activity				
Persuasion mail/brochures	309,745	36.37	125,550	24.82
Actual campaigning	48,955	5.75	27,645	5.47
Staff/volunteers	616	.07	329	.07
Subtotal	**359,315**	**42.19**	**153,524**	**30.35**
Constituent Gifts/ Entertainment	**889**	**.10**	**0**	
Donations to				
Candidates from same state	2,000	.23	0	
Candidates from other states	500	.06	0	
Civic organizations	890	.10	0	
Ideological groups	0		61	.01
Political parties	174	.02	0	
Subtotal	**3,564**	**.42**	**61**	**.01**
Unitemized Expenses	**18,523**	**2.17**	**0**	
Total Campaign Expenses	**$ 851,701**		**$ 505,799**	
PAC Contributions	**$ 195,705**		**$ 254,300**	
Individual Contributions	**421,257**		**254,227**	
Total Receipts*	**679,886**		**572,372**	

*Includes PAC and individual contributions as well as interest earned, party contributions, etc.

CALIFORNIA — District 24

Rep. Anthony C. Beilenson (D)

1992 Election Results

Anthony C. Beilenson (D)	141,742	(56%)
Tom McClintock (R)	99,835	(39%)
John Paul Lindblad † (I)	13,690	(5%)

Redistricting presented Rep. Anthony C. Beilenson with two unappealing and expensive alternatives—he could wage a race in his old west Hollywood district against fellow Democratic Rep. Henry A. Waxman or he could run in a newly created seat in a more Republican area. Beilenson chose what was undoubtedly the lesser of two evils and opted not to face Waxman.

Throughout the off-year and the first half of 1992 Beilenson continued to run his usual low-key campaign, spending a total of $141,558. His largest expense was a $35,000 gift to IMPAC 2000, the political action committee (PAC) established to assist Democrats with redistricting.

However, once the primary campaign was history, so was Beilenson's relaxed attitude. Over the next six months he invested $629,925 to defeat state representative Tom McClintock. Beilenson opened a $1,750-a-month campaign office and spent $2,500 on new computer software. By November, twenty-two people were drawing salary from the campaign, including campaign coordinator Matthew Petersen, who received a monthly salary of $3,000. During the final six months of 1992, Beilenson outspent McClintock by nearly $360,000.

Given the prohibitive cost of television and radio advertising in the Los Angeles market, Beilenson relied on a $368,049 persuasion mail campaign to communicate his message. One mailing touted the incumbent as "an independent leader for change." Another, the cover of which was emblazoned with "They Have Him in Their Pocket," pilloried McClintock for accepting $928,000 from PACs during his ten years in the state legislature and pointed to Beilenson's refusal to accept PAC money. The environmental vote was courted with two mailings—a positive piece crediting the incumbent with being the "Father of the Santa Monica Mountains" and a negative piece attacking McClintock for wanting to allow off-shore oil drilling. A fifth mailer cited "5 Reasons Why Republicans Are Supporting Congressman Beilenson." Yet another mailing juxtaposed Beilenson's pro-choice views with McClintock's anti-abortion stance. Below, Tobe & Associates of Bethesda, Md., received $59,884 for creating the mailings.

Unlike 1990, Beilenson ran ads on local cable television outlets. The ads, which cost $3,184 to produce and $5,995 to run, focused on Beilenson's pro-choice stance, his environmental record, and his refusal to accept PAC donations.

Beilenson spent $22,845 on potholders. He spent nothing on constituent entertainment and gifts.

The pattern of McClintock's campaign spending was virtually identical to Beilenson's, albeit on a considerably smaller scale.

	Beilenson		McClintock	
Campaign Expenditures	Amount Spent	% of Total	Amount Spent	% of Total
Overhead				
Office furniture/supplies	$ 25,908	3.36	$ 11,585	2.48
Rent/utilities	15,684	2.03	12,468	2.67
Salaries	58,836	7.63	52,423	11.22
Taxes	2,935	.38	21,367	4.57
Bank/investment fees	100	.01	0	
Lawyers/accountants	37,489	4.86	0	
Telephone	17,799	2.31	11,698	2.50
Campaign automobile	0		0	
Computers/office equipment	6,539	.85	29,374	6.29
Travel	8,628	1.12	796	.17
Food/meetings	7,877	1.02	0	
Subtotal	181,794	23.56	139,710	29.90
Fund Raising				
Events	96,642	12.53	7,180	1.54
Direct mail	12,225	1.58	30,319	6.49
Telemarketing	0		0	
Subtotal	108,867	14.11	37,498	8.03
Polling	0		4,896	1.05
Advertising				
Electronic media	9,178	1.19	16,046	3.43
Other media	1,456	.19	0	
Subtotal	10,634	1.38	16,046	3.43
Other Campaign Activity				
Persuasion mail/brochures	368,049	47.71	241,398	51.67
Actual campaigning	58,186	7.54	20,130	4.31
Staff/volunteers	0		0	
Subtotal	426,235	55.25	261,528	55.98
Constituent Gifts/Entertainment	0		0	
Donations to				
Candidates from same state	0		1,000	.21
Candidates from other states	0		0	
Civic organizations	370	.05	0	
Ideological groups	0		0	
Political parties	35,000	4.54	0	
Subtotal	35,370	4.58	1,000	.21
Unitemized Expenses	8,582	1.11	6,544	1.40
Total Campaign Expenses	$ 771,483		$ 467,223	
PAC Contributions	$ 0		$ 180,735	
Individual Contributions	682,406		222,809	
Total Receipts*	753,415		412,815	

* Includes PAC and individual contributions as well as interest earned, party contributions, etc.

† No expenditures or receipts on file. Candidates raising or spending less than $5,000 are not required to file reports with the Federal Election Commission.

District 25 — CALIFORNIA

Rep. Howard P. "Buck" McKeon (R)

1992 Election Results

Howard P. "Buck" McKeon (R)	113,611	(52%)
James H. "Gil" Gilmartin (D)	72,233	(33%)
Rick Pamplin † (I)	13,930	(6%)

Nearly 62,000 people voted in the Republican primary, and when all the ballots were tallied, businessman and former Santa Clarita mayor Howard P. "Buck" McKeon had defeated state representative Phillip D. Wyman by just 705 votes. In a district where 62 percent of the registered voters are Republican, that razor-thin margin hardly mattered; it was clear he was headed to Washington.

McKeon's primary victory cost roughly $358,000, 53 percent of which was invested in an extensive persuasion mail campaign created by Russo Marsh & Associates of Sacramento. In addition to twelve preprimary mailings, press secretary Armando Azarloza said McKeon and his staff handed out full-color brochures on walks that covered 80 percent of the precincts.

According to Azarloza, the campaign also ran two preprimary radio commercials. Targeting women, one ad criticized Wyman for not pushing domestic violence legislation. McKeon's other ad took a more positive approach, detailing his background and outlining his reasons for running. Production and placement of the ads totaled only $12,444.

Other preprimary costs included $13,700 for polls, $11,257 for opposition research, $7,234 for yard signs and posters, $5,195 for a slate mailer, and $489 for bumper stickers. By July 1 McKeon had accumulated campaign debts totaling more than $200,000.

To reduce those debts, McKeon retained Dan Morgan & Associates of Arlington, Va., to help him pursue political action committee (PAC) donations. Prior to the primary, McKeon collected only $15,750 from PACs. For increasing that total to $96,775, Morgan & Associates collected $4,077. The American Medical Association PAC also spent $2,500 to sponsor an event on McKeon's behalf.

McKeon held few postprimary events aimed at individual contributors. His largest event was a reception at the Sportsman Lodge in Studio City, which cost the campaign $10,114. Several supporters spent $1,932 to throw him another reception, but together these events yielded only $93,681.

The general election campaign was simply a scaled-back version of the primary. Russo Marsh collected $56,321 for developing four persuasion mailers, which targeted registered Republicans and independents. Another $12,500 was invested in mailing absentee ballots. Outlays for signs and posters amounted to $10,124. Opposition research cost the campaign $4,084. These general election expenses consumed all that McKeon raised following the primary, and he ended the cycle with debts of $201,102.

Democrat James H. "Gil" Gilmartin had no primary opposition, but in this safe Republican district his $68,322 treasury was still no match for McKeon's.

	McKeon		Gilmartin	
Campaign Expenditures	Amount Spent	% of Total	Amount Spent	% of Total
Overhead				
Office furniture/supplies	$ 23,417	4.44	$ 2,078	3.04
Rent/utilities	10,772	2.04	126	.18
Salaries	40,630	7.71	495	.72
Taxes	0		0	
Bank/investment fees	45	.01	3,969	5.81
Lawyers/accountants	23,123	4.39	0	
Telephone	11,115	2.11	153	.22
Campaign automobile	0		0	
Computers/office equipment	4,967	.94	0	
Travel	3,191	.61	3,825	5.60
Food/meetings	198	.04	0	
Subtotal	**117,458**	**22.28**	**10,646**	**15.58**
Fund Raising				
Events	39,565	7.50	3,177	4.65
Direct mail	0		0	
Telemarketing	0		0	
Subtotal	**39,565**	**7.50**	**3,177**	**4.65**
Polling	**23,692**	**4.49**	**0**	
Advertising				
Electronic media	12,444	2.36	17,336	25.37
Other media	1,844	.35	11,309	16.55
Subtotal	**14,288**	**2.71**	**28,645**	**41.93**
Other Campaign Activity				
Persuasion mail/brochures	279,997	53.11	14,844	21.73
Actual campaigning	47,714	9.05	9,046	13.24
Staff/volunteers	526	.10	250	.37
Subtotal	**328,238**	**62.26**	**24,140**	**35.33**
Constituent Gifts/ Entertainment	**0**		**0**	
Donations to				
Candidates from same state	0		0	
Candidates from other states	0		0	
Civic organizations	500	.09	0	
Ideological groups	0		50	.07
Political parties	200	.04	49	.07
Subtotal	**700**	**.13**	**99**	**.14**
Unitemized Expenses	3,305	.63	1,615	2.36
Total Campaign Expenses	$ 527,247		$ 68,322	
PAC Contributions	$ 96,775		$ 0	
Individual Contributions	230,497		62,403	
Total Receipts*	457,650		169,218	

*Includes PAC and individual contributions as well as interest earned, party contributions, etc.

† No expenditures or receipts on file. Candidates raising or spending less than $5,000 are not required to file reports with the Federal Election Commission.

CALIFORNIA — District 26

Rep. Howard L. Berman (D)

1992 Election Results

Howard L. Berman (D)	73,807	(61%)
Gary Forsch (R)	36,453	(30%)
Margery Hinds † (I)	7,180	(6%)

In one of the safest Democratic seats in the country, Rep. Howard L. Berman spent only 15 percent of his $720,810 campaign treasury on direct appeals to voters. While relatively small, this $108,649 investment in advertising, persuasion mail, and grass-roots campaigning looks gargantuan when compared with the $6,735 he spent for such campaign basics in 1990.

Principal among his 1992 expenditures for actual campaign activity was a $51,000 payment to B.A.D. Campaigns, a political consulting partnership that includes his brother and longtime adviser, Michael. "Really, for the first time since 1982, I ran a campaign," noted Berman. "I involved them very heavily in our plan—which district to run for, planning the campaign, writing the mail, and implementing the mail."

While Berman mounted a modest effort on his own behalf, most of his attention was focused on electing others. Sixty-one House and Senate candidates received donations ranging from $250 to $2,000. He donated $90,001 to the campaign of California state senator Herschel Rosenthal, who lost his June primary contest to state representative Tom Hayden. Other Californians benefiting from Berman's largess included state representatives Terry B. Friedman and Dave Elder, who received $25,000 and $22,000, respectively. State representative Teresa Hughes picked up $12,000 for her successful state senate bid.

To assist Democratic redistricting efforts, Berman donated $65,688 to IMPAC 2000. He gave $11,500 to the Democratic Congressional Campaign Committee and another $1,500 to the Democratic National Committee.

Not all of Berman's generosity was directed at candidates. He also paid the U.S. Capitol Historical Society $2,922 for Spanish translations of books about the Capitol that he distributed to Hispanic organizations and schools.

In the wake of the Los Angeles riots, the campaign paid for a banquet to honor Project Boyz—a Los Angeles street gang that had worked previously with the congressional office delivering gifts and food to the homeless and doing other community projects. During the riots, the gang members defended local merchants from looting. In recognition of their efforts, Berman's office threw a fancy banquet at a local restaurant, complete with $495 worth of flowers. "We made it a really fancy affair, so their girlfriends could get dressed up," said chief of staff Gene Smith.

Republican challenger Gary Forsch ran such a low-key campaign that he did not even have a listed campaign number. His son was getting obscene phone calls prior to his entering the race, Forsch said, so they did not want to publicize their phone number.

Campaign Expenditures	Berman Amount Spent	Berman % of Total	Forsch Amount Spent	Forsch % of Total
Overhead				
Office furniture/supplies	$ 3,428	.48	$ 1,255	1.57
Rent/utilities	0		0	
Salaries	3,513	.49	700	.88
Taxes	4,573	.63	0	
Bank/investment fees	0		61	.08
Lawyers/accountants	33,680	4.67	1,250	1.57
Telephone	737	.10	0	
Campaign automobile	0		0	
Computers/office equipment	541	.08	644	.81
Travel	46,872	6.50	328	.41
Food/meetings	6,495	.90	607	.76
Subtotal	**99,839**	**13.85**	**4,846**	**6.08**
Fund Raising				
Events	128,439	17.82	9,648	12.10
Direct mail	0		0	
Telemarketing	0		0	
Subtotal	**128,439**	**17.82**	**9,648**	**12.10**
Polling	**0**		**0**	
Advertising				
Electronic media	0		0	
Other media	3,031	.42	256	.32
Subtotal	**3,031**	**.42**	**256**	**.32**
Other Campaign Activity				
Persuasion mail/brochures	56,158	7.79	50,777	63.69
Actual campaigning	49,459	6.86	12,745	15.99
Staff/volunteers	0		0	
Subtotal	**105,618**	**14.65**	**63,522**	**79.67**
Constituent Gifts/ Entertainment	**12,610**	**1.75**	**0**	
Donations to				
Candidates from same state	185,001	25.67	0	
Candidates from other states	42,000	5.82	0	
Civic organizations	18,589	2.58	1,023	1.28
Ideological groups	19,150	2.66	103	.13
Political parties	88,688	12.30	24	.03
Subtotal	**353,428**	**49.03**	**1,150**	**1.44**
Unitemized Expenses	**17,846**	**2.48**	**309**	**.39**
Total Campaign Expenses	**$ 720,810**		**$ 79,731**	
PAC Contributions	$ 216,350		$ 2,525	
Individual Contributions	298,643		70,602	
Total Receipts*	548,212		76,578	

*Includes PAC and individual contributions as well as interest earned, party contributions, etc.

†No expenditures or receipts on file. Candidates raising or spending less than $5,000 are not required to file reports with the Federal Election Commission.

District 27 — CALIFORNIA

Rep. Carlos J. Moorhead (R)

1992 Election Results

Carlos J. Moorhead (R)	105,521	(50%)
Doug Kahn (D)	83,805	(39%)
Jesse A. Moorman (I)	11,003	(5%)

Redistricting turned Rep. Carlos J. Moorhead's comfortably safe Republican district into one in which a well-financed Democrat had a fighting chance. Fortunately for Moorhead, businessman Doug Kahn was only able to spend 18 percent as much as the ten-term incumbent.

Realizing that he faced the toughest electoral challenge since his initial House campaign in 1972, Moorhead spent 73 percent more in 1992 than he had in 1990. In January 1992 Moorhead retained the services of George Young & Associates of Marina Del Rey and over the next eleven months paid the firm $293,300 for providing general campaign strategy, polling, advertising production and placement, persuasion mail, posters, and yard signs.

Having served twenty years in the House, incumbency was not something Moorhead could easily run away from, so Young tried to turn it into an asset. The campaign's only television ad began with a recitation of the incumbent's accomplishments while in Congress and ended with Moorhead discussing his plans for the future. There were six mass mailings and a number of tightly targeted pieces, which Young said tended to be testimonials from district residents who recounted how Moorhead had helped solve their problems.

With a substantially altered constituency, research assumed a central role in the campaign. In 1990 Moorhead spent $9,700 on polling; in 1992 that figure jumped to $32,250. Payments to Young included $19,000 for focus groups and polls needed to shape the advertising and persuasion mail messages. Arnold Steinberg & Associates of Calabasas received $13,250 for conducting additional polls.

There was still room in Moorhead's budget to allow him to make more than $39,000 in donations. Fellow California Republican Reps. John T. Doolittle and Robert K. Dornan received $1,000 contributions, as did House candidates Ed Royce, H. L. "Bill" Richardson, Richard W. Pombo, Dick Rutan, and Joan Milke Flores.

Whenever a constituent was honored for public service, or just about anything else, the honoree received a small plaque paid for by the campaign. "There are hundreds of those things we try to cover," noted Moorhead. Plaques cost the campaign $1,956.

Moorhead spent $1,155 to buy congressional Christmas plates, which he gave to thirty-five of his volunteers. Congressional staffers received packages of pancake mix and syrup from L. L. Bean. "It was a little something different," Moorhead said of the gifts, which cost the campaign $532.

The campaign also paid for Moorhead's dues to the state bar of California, which were $498 in 1991 and $478 in 1992.

Campaign Expenditures	Moorhead Amount Spent	Moorhead % of Total	Kahn Amount Spent	Kahn % of Total
Overhead				
Office furniture/supplies	$ 5,876	.85	$ 1,692	1.35
Rent/utilities	5,000	.72	2,350	1.88
Salaries	23,712	3.43	12,415	9.93
Taxes	23,157	3.35	0	
Bank/investment fees	14	.00	0	
Lawyers/accountants	18,198	2.63	0	
Telephone	4,864	.70	3,553	2.84
Campaign automobile	0		0	
Computers/office equipment	1,544	.22	1,908	1.53
Travel	27,965	4.04	0	
Food/meetings	2,887	.42	0	
Subtotal	113,216	16.36	21,917	17.53
Fund Raising				
Events	78,765	11.38	2,500	2.00
Direct mail	32,773	4.74	5,799	4.64
Telemarketing	0		0	
Subtotal	111,537	16.12	8,299	6.64
Polling	32,250	4.66	11,887	9.51
Advertising				
Electronic media	90,333	13.05	12,311	9.84
Other media	37,311	5.39	65	.05
Subtotal	127,644	18.44	12,376	9.90
Other Campaign Activity				
Persuasion mail/brochures	148,623	21.48	53,407	42.71
Actual campaigning	87,169	12.60	15,381	12.30
Staff/volunteers	5,196	.75	0	
Subtotal	240,989	34.82	68,788	55.00
Constituent Gifts/Entertainment	10,458	1.51	0	
Donations to				
Candidates from same state	11,000	1.59	0	
Candidates from other states	500	.07	0	
Civic organizations	839	.12	0	
Ideological groups	100	.01	0	
Political parties	26,606	3.84	0	
Subtotal	39,045	5.64	0	
Unitemized Expenses	16,932	2.45	1,792	1.43
Total Campaign Expenses	$ 692,072		$ 125,060	
PAC Contributions	$ 260,025		$ 26,465	
Individual Contributions	94,316		56,821	
Total Receipts*	448,791		151,792	

*Includes PAC and individual contributions as well as interest earned, party contributions, etc.

CALIFORNIA — District 28

Rep. David Dreier (R)

1992 Election Results

David Dreier (R)	122,353	(58%)
Al Wachtel (D)	76,525	(37%)

Interest income on Rep. David Dreier's $2 million campaign cash reserves accounted for 38 percent of his total receipts during the 1992 election cycle. The $81,699 in taxes Dreier paid on that income was his largest expense. This was also more than three times the amount his Democratic opponent, professor Al Wachtel, spent on his entire campaign.

As in 1990, Dreier chose not to open a campaign office in 1992. He had no paid staff and no campaign car. Travel expenses totaled only $3,372. Less than $500 was spent on meals that were unrelated to fund raising. The campaign's new computer, laser printer, and software cost $5,522. "I think the days of spending a lot of money on overhead are gone," said chief of staff Brad Smith. While hardly an accurate generalization, it is clear that those days passed for Dreier some time ago.

With little competition, Dreier hired only two consultants. Robert Gouty Co., a general campaign consulting firm in Covina, received $6,000. Western Wats Center in Provo, Utah, was paid $5,200 for conducting one poll.

However, the lack of significant competition did not stop Dreier from raising money. While Smith was quick to point out that the incumbent held no Washington, D.C., events, the American Medical Association political action committee spent $2,500 to stage one on his behalf. The bulk of Dreier's money from individual contributors was raised through an annual breakfast at the Industry Hills Sheraton Resort in Industry, Calif. With annual attendance exceeding 400, costs of roughly $8 a piece, and ticket prices of $250, the events produced huge profits.

Dreier's cash reserves testify to the fact that he has routinely raised sums far exceeding his campaign needs. In each of the four elections prior to 1992, Dreier had spent an average of only 29 percent of the funds he collected. In 1992 that figure grew to 45 percent, partially on the strength of an increase in his donations to other candidates and party organizations.

Dreier gave away $73,250 during the 1992 election cycle, a 20 percent increase over 1990. He donated $30,000 to the National Republican Congressional Committee, $5,000 to Californians for Fair Reapportionment, $4,000 to a California assembly candidate, and $2,000 each to Senate candidate Paul Coverdell (Ga.) and Dick Rutan, a fellow House candidate from California. Another twenty-nine Republican House and Senate candidates across the country each received checks for $1,000. These donations exceeded Wachtel's total spending by a three-to-one margin.

Campaign Expenditures	Dreier Amount Spent	Dreier % of Total	Wachtel Amount Spent	Wachtel % of Total
Overhead				
Office furniture/supplies	$ 1,095	.38	$ 379	1.58
Rent/utilities	0		0	
Salaries	0		0	
Taxes	81,699	28.16	0	
Bank/investment fees	0		0	
Lawyers/accountants	12,190	4.20	0	
Telephone	756	.26	0	
Campaign automobile	0		0	
Computers/office equipment	5,843	2.01	0	
Travel	3,372	1.16	7,623	31.75
Food/meetings	462	.16	42	.17
Subtotal	105,416	36.33	8,044	33.50
Fund Raising				
Events	18,299	6.31	138	.57
Direct mail	0		0	
Telemarketing	0		0	
Subtotal	18,299	6.31	138	.57
Polling	5,200	1.79	0	
Advertising				
Electronic media	0		255	1.06
Other media	0		1,375	5.73
Subtotal	0		1,630	6.79
Other Campaign Activity				
Persuasion mail/brochures	59,006	20.34	7,415	30.88
Actual campaigning	16,688	5.75	2,042	8.51
Staff/volunteers	0		8	.03
Subtotal	75,694	26.09	9,465	39.42
Constituent Gifts/Entertainment	9,041	3.12	0	
Donations to				
Candidates from same state	27,250	9.39	0	
Candidates from other states	10,500	3.62	0	
Civic organizations	0		0	
Ideological groups	0		0	
Political parties	35,500	12.24	0	
Subtotal	73,250	25.25	0	
Unitemized Expenses	3,235	1.11	4,734	19.72
Total Campaign Expenses	$ 290,133		$ 24,012	
PAC Contributions	$ 131,350		$ 2,000	
Individual Contributions	260,755		20,500	
Total Receipts*	646,323		23,564	

*Includes PAC and individual contributions as well as interest earned, party contributions, etc.

District 29 — CALIFORNIA

Rep. Henry A. Waxman (D)

1992 Election Results

Henry A. Waxman (D)	160,312	(61%)
Mark A. Robbins (R)	67,141	(26%)
David Davis † (I)	15,445	(6%)

Rep. Henry A. Waxman proved to be something of a modern Robin Hood. He took from rich political action committees (PACs) and gave to poor candidates and party organizations.

As chairman of the subcommittee on Health and the Environment, Waxman was able to tap PACs representing health care interests for $177,800. In all, 203 PACs contributed a total of $402,915 to Waxman's coffers. This amounted to 64 percent of his donations. Small, individual donations accounted for only 6 percent of his total contributions.

With far more money than he needed, Waxman bestowed $67,688 on IMPAC 2000, the PAC established to assist Democrats in redistricting. He gave $55,000 to the Democratic Congressional Campaign Committee, $40,000 to the United Democratic Fund of Minnesota, $20,000 to the Democratic Senatorial Campaign Committee, and $5,000 to the California Democratic party.

Four days prior to his primary loss to California state representative Tom Hayden, state senator Herschel Rosenthal received a $50,000 check from Waxman's campaign. California state representative Terry B. Friedman received $10,000 for his race. Six House colleagues with whom he shared committee assignments each collected $2,000; another six received $1,000 donations.

Waxman's reasons for sharing his wealth with other candidates were simple. "First of all, they vote for or fight for the issues I care about," he noted. "Secondly, when you help somebody you develop a good working relationship with them."

Overhead for his permanent campaign totaled $112,008, or 16 percent of his spending. By far the largest portion of that overhead was the $47,294 he spent on travel. In March 1991 Waxman used $4,500 of his campaign funds to defray the costs of a trip he and his wife took to Jerusalem, including $753 for lodging at the King David Hotel and $3,699 for air fare. While there, Waxman attended a conference of Jewish parliamentarians from around the world. He also said he met with constituents and monitored the airlift of Ethiopian Jews, an issue of importance to his West Hollywood constituency.

What Waxman spent on his own campaign was largely invested in mail designed to introduce the eighteen-year incumbent to his new constituents. "One can't take these things for granted," Waxman said. "The old voters know me. The new ones need to get to know me."

Lawyer Mark A. Robbins, his Republican opponent, managed to spend roughly half as much as Waxman on direct appeals to voters, including nearly $43,000 on advertising. In this predominantly liberal Democratic district, it was largely a wasted effort.

	Waxman		Robbins	
Campaign Expenditures	Amount Spent	% of Total	Amount Spent	% of Total
Overhead				
Office furniture/supplies	$ 2,605	.36	$ 7,006	5.06
Rent/utilities	600	.08	1,036	.75
Salaries	10,150	1.41	27,207	19.67
Taxes	11,955	1.67	0	
Bank/investment fees	0		477	.34
Lawyers/accountants	34,051	4.74	0	
Telephone	2,793	.39	4,718	3.41
Campaign automobile	0		0	
Computers/office equipment	1,564	.22	1,846	1.33
Travel	47,294	6.59	2,566	1.86
Food/meetings	997	.14	878	.63
Subtotal	**112,008**	**15.61**	**45,734**	**33.06**
Fund Raising				
Events	90,343	12.59	2,521	1.82
Direct mail	0		6,629	4.79
Telemarketing	0		0	
Subtotal	**90,343**	**12.59**	**9,149**	**6.61**
Polling	**0**		**0**	
Advertising				
Electronic media	0		24,912	18.01
Other media	1,668	.23	17,934	12.96
Subtotal	**1,668**	**.23**	**42,845**	**30.97**
Other Campaign Activity				
Persuasion mail/brochures	154,722	21.56	18,506	13.38
Actual campaigning	7,945	1.11	19,124	13.83
Staff/volunteers	0		108	.08
Subtotal	**162,667**	**22.67**	**37,738**	**27.28**
Constituent Gifts/Entertainment	**3,301**	**.46**	**0**	
Donations to				
Candidates from same state	84,500	11.77	0	
Candidates from other states	39,000	5.43	0	
Civic organizations	1,150	.16	790	.57
Ideological groups	24,250	3.38	115	.08
Political parties	189,903	26.46	1,017	.74
Subtotal	**338,803**	**47.21**	**1,922**	**1.39**
Unitemized Expenses	**8,908**	**1.24**	**938**	**.68**
Total Campaign Expenses	**$ 717,698**		**$ 138,327**	
PAC Contributions	$ 402,915		$ 1,643	
Individual Contributions	227,228		122,803	
Total Receipts*	682,214		148,419	

*Includes PAC and individual contributions as well as interest earned, party contributions, etc.

† No expenditures or receipts on file. Candidates raising or spending less than $5,000 are not required to file reports with the Federal Election Commission.

CALIFORNIA — District 30

Rep. Xavier Becerra (D)

1992 Election Results

Xavier Becerra (D)	48,800	(58%)
Morry Waksberg (R)	20,034	(24%)
Blase Bonpane (I)	6,315	(8%)

After failing to convince long-time aide Henry Lozano to seek this seat, retiring Rep. Edward R. Roybal turned to thirty-four-year-old state representative Xavier Becerra, who had not yet finished his first term in the California assembly. With registered Democrats outnumbering Republicans by more than two to one, Becerra was quickly joined in the primary race by nine fellow Democrats, two of whom had powerful mentors of their own.

Backed by Los Angeles City Council member Richard Alatorre and state senator Art Torres, school board trustee Leticia Quezada spent $194,103 to garner 7,089 votes. Endorsed by state insurance commissioner John Garamendi, Los Angeles City Council member Michael Woo, and Los Angeles City Attorney James Hahn, lawyer Albert C. Lum spent $403,047, or nearly $79 for each of his 5,128 votes.

Added to the $282,137 Becerra invested to attract 10,417 votes and the $255,468 spent by educator Jeff J. Penichet to obtain 4,136 votes, the top four vote-getters spent a total of more than $1.1 million on an election in which fewer than 33,000 people voted.

Persuasion mail and brochures accounted for nearly half of Becerra's preprimary expenditures. According to administrative assistant Elsa Marquez, this preprimary effort consisted of between six and eight mass mailings to registered Democrats, as well as numerous smaller mailings targeted at groups such as senior citizens and members of environmental groups. Consultant Pat Bond of Pasadena received $17,500 for designing the various mailings and brochures.

In addition, Becerra paid Bond $22,500 for general consulting work. She, in turn, brought in consultant Martha Molina-Avila of Whittier, who received $4,250 for strategic advice. Consultant Janice Laruccia was paid $1,000 for precinct organization, absentee ballots, and other get-out-the-vote efforts. Precinct walk-lists cost $1,630. More than a dozen telephone lines were installed at Becerra's headquarters for an in-house phonebank, which ultimately cost the campaign $9,145 during the primary. Below, Tobe & Associates of Bethesda, Md., received $11,024 for work on a slate mailer.

Becerra's biggest preprimary fund-raiser was a tribute to Lozano, whose decision not to run had drawn Becerra into the race. Marquez said approximately 300 people attended the $100-a-plate dinner held at Stevens Steak House in Commerce, Calif.

The general election campaign against ophthalmologist Morry Waksberg was nothing more than a formality. Most of the $77,074 Becerra spent went to pay for overhead and fund raising. Fraioli/Jost of Washington, D.C., received $7,947 to help attract political action committee donations to help retire some of his $96,500 debt from the primary.

Campaign Expenditures	Becerra Amount Spent	Becerra % of Total	Waksberg Amount Spent	Waksberg % of Total
Overhead				
Office furniture/supplies	$ 12,654	3.52	$ 2,248	4.11
Rent/utilities	2,466	.69	0	
Salaries	71,476	19.90	11,888	21.70
Taxes	0		0	
Bank/investment fees	1,660	.46	209	.38
Lawyers/accountants	0		1,038	1.89
Telephone	3,601	1.00	489	.89
Campaign automobile	0		0	
Computers/office equipment	3,718	1.04	0	
Travel	0		7,625	13.92
Food/meetings	876	.24	553	1.01
Subtotal	**96,451**	**26.85**	**24,049**	**43.91**
Fund Raising				
Events	15,158	4.22	9,071	16.56
Direct mail	5,046	1.40	0	
Telemarketing	0		0	
Subtotal	**20,204**	**5.62**	**9,071**	**16.56**
Polling	**0**		**0**	
Advertising				
Electronic media	0		0	
Other media	0		3,906	7.13
Subtotal	**0**		**3,906**	**7.13**
Other Campaign Activity				
Persuasion mail/brochures	188,167	52.38	2,876	5.25
Actual campaigning	44,961	12.51	10,409	19.00
Staff/volunteers	539	.15	0	
Subtotal	**233,666**	**65.04**	**13,285**	**24.26**
Constituent Gifts/Entertainment	**260**	**.07**	**138**	**.25**
Donations to				
Candidates from same state	0		35	.06
Candidates from other states	0		0	
Civic organizations	0		746	1.36
Ideological groups	0		445	.81
Political parties	0		182	.33
Subtotal	**0**		**1,408**	**2.57**
Unitemized Expenses	**8,629**	**2.40**	**2,911**	**5.32**
Total Campaign Expenses	**$ 359,211**		**$ 54,769**	
PAC Contributions	$ 97,450		$ 2,150	
Individual Contributions	187,996		24,814	
Total Receipts*	387,385		58,197	

*Includes PAC and individual contributions as well as interest earned, party contributions, etc.

District 31 — CALIFORNIA

Rep. Matthew G. Martinez (D)

1992 Election Results

Matthew G. Martinez (D)	68,324	(63%)
Reuben D. Franco (R)	40,873	(37%)

In yet another of California's one-party districts in which registered Democrats outnumbered Republicans by nearly two to one, Rep. Matthew G. Martinez had nothing to fear from Republican challenger Reuben D. Franco, whom he had beaten by 21 percentage points in 1990. His only real concern was avoiding an upset by attorney Bonifacio Garcia in the Democratic primary.

Garcia mounted an aggressive campaign, attacking Martinez for missing nearly one of every five House votes during 1991 and for his nineteen overdrafts at the House bank. Garcia also accused Martinez of abusing his franking privilege by mailing letters to 95,000 district residents telling them how to register and urging them to vote. Garcia spent $125,425 on his campaign but managed to attract only 25 percent of the 35,250 primary votes cast.

Martinez countered by spending $88,517 during the first six months of 1992, running a primary campaign that largely tried to ignore Garcia. According to legislative director Maxine A. Grant, none of the four preprimary mailings mentioned Garcia. Instead, they touted Martinez's legislative achievements and recited endorsements from various groups, such as the Los Angeles County Federation of Labor and the California Teachers Association. In all, Martinez spent $59,168 on preprimary mailings, including $9,000 for his share of the costs of a slate mailer.

On April 6, 1992 Martinez opened his office for the primary campaign; on June 6 he closed it. An in-kind disbursement of $800 from one of his supporters covered the rent. There was no paid staff and no consultants were hired. Instead, he depended on a cadre of about forty supporters who manned the office, mostly on weekends and evenings. Grant said the campaign's phonebank consisted of ten people who worked out of their homes.

To express his thanks, Martinez spent $1,881 to feed his volunteers. Another $355 was spent on See's Candies, which he dispensed as Christmas presents in 1991. A 1992 Christmas party cost $238.

Five percent of Martinez's total spending was put into constituent stroking, including $3,136 in meals. Year-end holiday cards cost the campaign $4,416.

Martinez did not pay for a campaign car during the 1990 election cycle, but in July 1991 the campaign began making monthly car payments of $264 to the Congressional Federal Credit Union. In April 1992 the campaign stopped those payments and instead began leasing a Chevy Blazer from Executive Auto Leasing in Beltsville, Md. Monthly payments for the Blazer were $424. Repairs at Dave Pyles Lincoln Mercury in Annandale, Va., totaled $275.

In the end, Martinez extended his winning percentage over Franco to 26 points.

Campaign Expenditures	Martinez Amount Spent	Martinez % of Total	Franco Amount Spent	Franco % of Total
Overhead				
Office furniture/supplies	$ 2,756	1.83	$ 1,028	1.85
Rent/utilities	1,200	.80	4,000	7.19
Salaries	0		2,951	5.30
Taxes	0		0	
Bank/investment fees	0		168	.30
Lawyers/accountants	0		0	
Telephone	1,959	1.30	1,012	1.82
Campaign automobile	7,114	4.73	0	
Computers/office equipment	0		194	.35
Travel	1,784	1.19	2,000	3.59
Food/meetings	866	.58	0	
Subtotal	**15,678**	**10.42**	**11,352**	**20.39**
Fund Raising				
Events	7,353	4.89	361	.65
Direct mail	0		0	
Telemarketing	0		0	
Subtotal	**7,353**	**4.89**	**361**	**.65**
Polling	**0**		**0**	
Advertising				
Electronic media	0		10,563	18.97
Other media	725	.48	141	.25
Subtotal	**725**	**.48**	**10,703**	**19.23**
Other Campaign Activity				
Persuasion mail/brochures	79,349	52.74	10,167	18.26
Actual campaigning	5,177	3.44	7,220	12.97
Staff/volunteers	2,746	1.83	0	
Subtotal	**87,272**	**58.01**	**17,386**	**31.23**
Constituent Gifts/Entertainment	**7,888**	**5.24**	**0**	
Donations to				
Candidates from same state	3,000	1.99	0	
Candidates from other states	0		0	
Civic organizations	100	.07	150	.27
Ideological groups	50	.03	0	
Political parties	23,978	15.94	85	.15
Subtotal	**27,128**	**18.03**	**235**	**.42**
Unitemized Expenses	**4,400**	**2.92**	**15,631**	**28.08**
Total Campaign Expenses	**$ 150,444**		**$ 55,669**	
PAC Contributions	$ 77,450		$ 8,291	
Individual Contributions	41,564		25,345	
Total Receipts*	119,807		54,776	

*Includes PAC and individual contributions as well as interest earned, party contributions, etc.

CALIFORNIA — District 32

Rep. Julian C. Dixon (D)

1992 Election Results

Julian C. Dixon (D)	150,644	(87%)
Bob Weber † (I)	12,384	(7%)
William R. Williams † (I)	9,782	(6%)

Having won each of his seven previous House campaigns with at least 73 percent of the vote, Rep. Julian C. Dixon drew no Republican opposition. Like many safe incumbents, Dixon had absolutely no reason to mount an aggressive campaign effort in 1992. Unlike most safe incumbents, he actually chose not to do so.

He had no campaign office, no paid staff, no lawyers or accountants, and no campaign car. More than half his total travel costs were for expenses incurred during the Democratic National Convention in New York, including $3,853 at the Grand Hyatt Hotel and $700 for airline tickets.

Fund raising was also not a priority. The campaign staged only one event during the two-year cycle, a November 1991 dinner at the Bistro Restaurant in Beverly Hills. Expenses at the Bistro came to $7,899. Artwork and printing costs for the invitations totaled another $1,998. Music added $400. Dixon's only consultant for the campaign, fund-raiser Alescia Buford & Associates of Washington, D.C., received $2,984 for coordinating the affair. Dixon's only other fund-raising expense was the $3,800 he paid in April 1991 for pens, which he sent to contributors.

With these extremely modest efforts, Dixon succeeded in raising only $83,583 from political action committees (PACs) and individual contributors—$56,881 less than he spent on the race. PACs accounted for 66 percent of his total receipts. Individual donations of $200 or more amounted to $27,150, or 32 percent. Only 2 percent of his total contributions came from small donors.

Dixon's advertising had little to do with his own reelection. He purchased $455 in newspaper ads to commemorate Black History Month. Another $600 was spent on advertising to support the Ladera Little League in Culver City. He also paid $75 for a Los Angeles County Democratic party program ad.

With no campaign operation of his own, Dixon opted to pay $1,000 to LA Vote and $500 to the Unity Slate for slate mailers. The American Medical Association PAC also provided in-kind slate mailings valued at $2,500. This was his only voter contact mail.

More than anything else, Dixon simply gave his money away. IMPAC 2000, the PAC established to assist Democrats in redistricting, received $47,168. Dixon gave $10,000 to "No on 164," a committee set up to fight state term limits in California. Seven House and Senate candidates in California received contributions of $1,000, including Reps. Barbara Boxer and Mel Levine, who squared off in the Democratic primary for the seat of retiring Sen. Alan Cranston. Among the other beneficiaries were ten candidates for local and state offices in California and four members of the Congressional Black Caucus.

Campaign Expenditures	Dixon Amount Spent	% of Total
Overhead		
Office furniture/supplies	$ 3,797	2.70
Rent/utilities	0	
Salaries	0	
Taxes	0	
Bank/investment fees	0	
Lawyers/accountants	0	
Telephone	0	
Campaign automobile	0	
Computers/office equipment	745	.53
Travel	8,955	6.38
Food/meetings	6,937	4.94
Subtotal	**20,434**	**14.55**
Fund Raising		
Events	17,081	12.16
Direct mail	0	
Telemarketing	0	
Subtotal	**17,081**	**12.16**
Polling	**0**	
Advertising		
Electronic media	0	
Other media	1,130	.80
Subtotal	**1,130**	**.80**
Other Campaign Activity		
Persuasion mail/brochures	4,000	2.85
Actual campaigning	1,602	1.14
Staff/volunteers	1,677	1.19
Subtotal	**7,279**	**5.18**
Constituent Gifts/Entertainment	**1,487**	**1.06**
Donations to		
Candidates from same state	12,000	8.54
Candidates from other states	6,000	4.27
Civic organizations	5,270	3.75
Ideological groups	13,000	9.26
Political parties	49,167	35.00
Subtotal	**85,437**	**60.82**
Unitemized Expenses	**7,616**	**5.42**
Total Campaign Expenses	$ **140,464**	
PAC Contributions	$ **54,750**	
Individual Contributions	**28,833**	
Total Receipts*	**83,583**	

* Includes PAC and individual contributions as well as interest earned, party contributions, etc.

† No expenditures or receipts on file. Candidates raising or spending less than $5,000 are not required to file reports with the Federal Election Commission.

District 33 — CALIFORNIA

Rep. Lucille Roybal-Allard (D)

1992 Election Results

Lucille Roybal-Allard (D)	32,010	(63%)
Robert Guzman (R)	15,428	(30%)

From the moment she entered the race, state representative Lucille Roybal-Allard was considered a shoo-in. The state legislative district she had served since 1987 and the newly drawn congressional District 33 were largely the same. Her father, retiring Rep. Edward R. Roybal, had represented large portions of the district for thirty years. Nevertheless, Roybal-Allard took nothing for granted.

For the primary, Roybal-Allard sank $41,783 into voter contact mail, including $5,422 for her share of the costs of various slate mailers. Registered Democrats received a one-page letter detailing her reasons for running. A handwritten letter from her father was mailed to likely voters in 5,000 Hispanic households. Two brochures touched on the need for national health care, job programs, her record on environmental issues, and her belief in the need for tougher sentencing for convicted criminals. Postcards were mailed both to those who had been contacted through phonebanking and to people who were not at home when Royball-Allard or one of her volunteers came through on a precinct canvass.

In the general election, between 35,000 and 50,000 households received two mailings—one a recitation of endorsements by local officials, the other a description of her legislative achievements. Legislative director Maria Luisa Ochoa said that neither of these general election mailings was originally planned. However, rumors that anti-abortion groups were mounting an independent campaign in support of her Republican opponent, education consultant Robert Guzman, prompted Roybal-Allard to step up her efforts during the final two weeks of the campaign.

Consultant expenses were kept to a minimum. Pat Bond of Pasadena received $21,000 to provide general strategic advice. Pacific Communication Concepts of Commerce, Calif., was paid $7,522 for designing several glossy mailers.

Roybal-Allard gave away very little of her money. She donated $500 to Xavier Becerra, who ran successfully for another seat carved out of her father's old district, $250 to Rep. Vic Fazio (D-Calif.), and a total of $2,998 to three state assembly candidates. After the election, she contributed $2,000 to the Edward Roybal Foundation.

To fund her campaign, she relied heavily on political action committees (PACs), which accounted for 47 percent of her receipts. Union PACs contributed $30,500. PACs representing health care interests anted up $12,500. Various women's groups added $12,497, including $3,157 in fund-raising assistance from EMILY's List.

Rep. Bill Richardson, who served with the senior Roybal on the Select Aging Committee, spent $401 to sponsor a fund-raiser on her behalf.

Campaign Expenditures	Roybal-Allard Amount Spent	% of Total	Guzman Amount Spent	% of Total
Overhead				
Office furniture/supplies	$ 7,253	2.77	$ 8,902	5.30
Rent/utilities	6,981	2.66	9,826	5.85
Salaries	74,561	28.43	54,340	32.34
Taxes	0		0	
Bank/investment fees	0		0	
Lawyers/accountants	2,775	1.06	0	
Telephone	11,804	4.50	10,563	6.29
Campaign automobile	0		0	
Computers/office equipment	4,039	1.54	2,901	1.73
Travel	1,176	.45	1,413	.84
Food/meetings	0		171	.10
Subtotal	**108,588**	**41.41**	**88,117**	**52.44**
Fund Raising				
Events	8,819	3.36	1,643	.98
Direct mail	4,456	1.70	0	
Telemarketing	0		0	
Subtotal	**13,275**	**5.06**	**1,643**	**.98**
Polling	0		0	
Advertising				
Electronic media	0		375	.22
Other media	899	.34	1,000	.60
Subtotal	**899**	**.34**	**1,375**	**.82**
Other Campaign Activity				
Persuasion mail/brochures	84,605	32.26	30,054	17.89
Actual campaigning	37,523	14.31	43,543	25.92
Staff/volunteers	514	.20	883	.53
Subtotal	**122,642**	**46.77**	**74,480**	**44.33**
Constituent Gifts/ Entertainment	202	.08	0	
Donations to				
Candidates from same state	3,748	1.43	0	
Candidates from other states	0		0	
Civic organizations	2,100	.80	360	.21
Ideological groups	0		0	
Political parties	0		234	.14
Subtotal	**5,848**	**2.23**	**594**	**.35**
Unitemized Expenses	**10,779**	**4.11**	**1,810**	**1.08**
Total Campaign Expenses	**$ 262,233**		**$ 168,019**	
PAC Contributions	$ 133,587		$ 4,598	
Individual Contributions	141,580		12,082	
Total Receipts*	283,770		182,103	

*Includes PAC and individual contributions as well as interest earned, party contributions, etc.

CALIFORNIA — District 34

Rep. Esteban E. Torres (D)

1992 Election Results

Esteban E. Torres (D)	91,738	(61%)
J. "Jay" Hernandez (R)	50,907	(34%)
Carl M. Swinney † (I)	7,072	(5%)

Rep. Esteban E. Torres again chose to leave the management of his permanent campaign organization to his daughter, Carmen Garcia. Payments to Garcia, who also coordinated fund-raising events, crafted the persuasion mail, and wrote the campaign's direct-mail fund-raising solicitations, amounted to more than one-quarter of Torres's total expenditures for the two-year election cycle.

Prior to the June primary, the campaign spent $13,144 for printing, postage, and labels for two brochures. One was sent to 15,000 Democratic households drawn into the new District 34 under the court-imposed redistricting plan. The other was mailed to old constituents who remained in the redrawn district. Torres was unopposed in the primary.

Torres opened his general election campaign office in August and staffed it with one full-time employee. He spent $7,183 on signs and another $1,320 on a small, in-house phonebanking effort. Persuasion mail consumed by far the largest portion of his budget.

Garcia said the campaign mailed three brochures for the fall contest against businessman J. "Jay" Hernandez—one dealing with the need for congressional reform, another targeting senior citizens, and a third focusing on jobs and education. The campaign invested $80,143 to produce and mail these brochures to voters who the phonebank identified as having an interest in one or more of the subjects. The American Medical Association political action committee (PAC) ascribed $2,500 of its slate mailer costs to Torres's campaign.

Torres spent nothing on broadcast advertising and avoided the mainstream press for all his print advertising. Instead he spent $350 for a program ad with the Los Angeles County Federation of Labor and $800 for advertising in *Unidos: The Journal of Opportunity*. For a Mexican Independence Day parade, he bought a $750 ad with "Comite Mexicano Civico Patriotic." An ad in *La Opinion* cost $319.

Donations to other candidates and causes accounted for 9 percent of Torres's spending. To assist fellow Democrats in redistricting, he donated $13,000 to IMPAC 2000. He donated $5,000 each to the Democratic Congressional Campaign Committee, the California Democratic party, and Los Angeles County Supervisor Gloria Molina.

While he held no PAC events, Torres nevertheless collected one-third of his contributions from PACs. There were three fund-raisers aimed at individual contributors, including $15-a-plate barbecues held each summer. His only formal affair, held at the Industry Hills & Sheraton Resort in Industry, Calif., featured actress Rita Moreno. In addition to a $6,148 payment to the hotel, the campaign picked up her $140 limousine bill.

Campaign Expenditures	Torres Amount Spent	Torres % of Total	Hernandez Amount Spent	Hernandez % of Total
Overhead				
Office furniture/supplies	$ 3,770	1.47	$ 1,669	1.40
Rent/utilities	2,218	.86	1,800	1.51
Salaries	2,447	.95	25,854	21.67
Taxes	0		0	
Bank/investment fees	114	.04	0	
Lawyers/accountants	3,820	1.49	0	
Telephone	2,257	.88	3,059	2.56
Campaign automobile	0		0	
Computers/office equipment	3,443	1.34	1,254	1.05
Travel	13,742	5.36	450	.38
Food/meetings	1,634	.64	0	
Subtotal	**33,445**	**13.03**	**34,086**	**28.57**
Fund Raising				
Events	34,103	13.29	2,259	1.89
Direct mail	19,063	7.43	0	
Telemarketing	0		0	
Subtotal	**53,166**	**20.72**	**2,259**	**1.89**
Polling	0		6,250	5.24
Advertising				
Electronic media	0		2,008	1.68
Other media	3,294	1.28	2,493	2.09
Subtotal	**3,294**	**1.28**	**4,501**	**3.77**
Other Campaign Activity				
Persuasion mail/brochures	95,787	37.33	48,299	40.49
Actual campaigning	31,989	12.47	21,249	17.81
Staff/volunteers	745	.29	0	
Subtotal	**128,520**	**50.09**	**69,548**	**58.30**
Constituent Gifts/Entertainment	1,096	.43	0	
Donations to				
Candidates from same state	11,550	4.50	0	
Candidates from other states	1,500	.58	0	
Civic organizations	0		0	
Ideological groups	1,000	.39	0	
Political parties	23,024	8.97	0	
Subtotal	**37,074**	**14.45**	**0**	
Unitemized Expenses	0		2,644	2.22
Total Campaign Expenses	**$ 256,596**		**$ 119,289**	
PAC Contributions	$ 49,300		$ 1,750	
Individual Contributions	99,549		26,098	
Total Receipts*	**169,451**		**129,919**	

* *Includes PAC and individual contributions as well as interest earned, party contributions, etc.*

† *No expenditures or receipts on file. Candidates raising or spending less than $5,000 are not required to file reports with the Federal Election Commission.*

District 35 — CALIFORNIA

Rep. Maxine Waters (D)

1992 Election Results

Maxine Waters (D)	102,941	(83%)
Nate Truman (R)	17,417	(14%)

Rep. Maxine Waters coasted through the 1992 election, concerning herself more with helping to rebuild her district after the May 1992 Los Angeles riots than with campaigning. Waters had spent $637,064 in 1990 to steamroll a Republican opponent who spent less than $5,000. In her first re-election bid, she was able to accomplish similar results while spending only one-third as much.

While Waters ran a permanent campaign, it was extremely modest by congressional standards. During 1991 she closed her campaign office, which helped hold overhead costs to $31,819. Her total spending for the off-year was $81,729.

Off-year fund-raising expenditures totaled only $22,016, including $7,948 paid to the Beverly Hills Hotel in September 1991 for the campaign's lone fund-raising dinner. For organizing this soiree and several smaller cocktail parties, Waters paid Winner/Bragg of Los Angeles $10,208 in 1991.

In January 1991 Waters invited between 100 and 200 people to Washington to witness and celebrate her taking the oath of office. Guests paid their own transportation and lodging, and campaign funds paid for the party. A reception at the Washington Court Hotel cost her campaign $3,820; other miscellaneous expenses for the fete cost $550.

The campaign also paid expenses totaling $5,661 for the annual Congressional Black Caucus Weekend in September 1991. Bills at the Hyatt Regency and the Washington Hilton and Towers were $3,249 and $494, respectively. Limousine service added another $528; tickets to the evening gala cost $1,390.

In 1992 nearly two-thirds of the money Waters invested in persuasion mail was spent before the Democratic primary. She paid only one lump-sum payment of $2,826 for "office repairs and rent" in August. Winner/Bragg's fund-raising activity was limited to organizing several cocktail parties, for which the firm received $16,349.

Waters spent $623 from her campaign treasury on train tickets to ferry her and several staff members to and from the Democratic National Convention in New York. While there, the group spent $2,404 at the Intercontinental Hotel and $1,319 at the Grand Hyatt, all at campaign expense.

Several weeks before the November general election, Waters made contributions from her campaign funds to six fellow Democrats seeking House seats throughout California. During this eleventh-hour rush to donate, she also sent a check from her campaign account to California Senate candidate Barbara Boxer and to four House candidates from other states.

Television producer Nate Truman spent $6,919 on his campaign, none of which was itemized on his reports to the Federal Election Commission.

Campaign Expenditures	Waters Amount Spent	% of Total
Overhead		
Office furniture/supplies	$ 3,003	1.44
Rent/utilities	2,826	1.36
Salaries	0	
Taxes	946	.46
Bank/investment fees	582	.28
Lawyers/accountants	24,698	11.88
Telephone	676	.32
Campaign automobile	0	
Computers/office equipment	355	.17
Travel	23,120	11.12
Food/meetings	1,176	.57
Subtotal	57,381	27.59
Fund Raising		
Events	58,094	27.94
Direct mail	0	
Telemarketing	0	
Subtotal	58,094	27.94
Polling	0	
Advertising		
Electronic media	0	
Other media	600	.29
Subtotal	600	.29
Other Campaign Activity		
Persuasion mail/brochures	35,682	17.16
Actual campaigning	18,707	9.00
Staff/volunteers	0	
Subtotal	54,389	26.15
Constituent Gifts/Entertainment	5,949	2.86
Donations to		
Candidates from same state	7,074	3.40
Candidates from other states	4,299	2.07
Civic organizations	2,141	1.03
Ideological groups	5,090	2.45
Political parties	500	.24
Subtotal	19,104	9.19
Unitemized Expenses	12,439	5.98
Total Campaign Expenses	$ 207,957	
PAC Contributions	$ 91,890	
Individual Contributions	93,789	
Total Receipts*	191,510	

*Includes PAC and individual contributions as well as interest earned, party contributions, etc.

CALIFORNIA — District 36

Rep. Jane Harman (D)

1992 Election Results

Jane Harman (D)	125,751	(48%)
Joan Milke Flores (R)	109,684	(42%)
Richard H. Greene † (I)	13,297	(5%)

Lawyer and businesswoman Jane Harman declared her candidacy in October 1991, two months before the boundaries of her district were established. Over the next thirteen months Harman invested $823,000 of her own money to ensure primary and general election victories. Her win in the seven-candidate Democratic primary cost well over $500,000, including more than $200,000 of her own money.

Garin-Hart of Washington, D.C., was among the first to join Harman's braintrust, collecting $20,586 to conduct polls during the campaign's first month. Payments to Garin-Hart ultimately reached $76,445.

Harman had sufficient resources to do the unthinkable in a House campaign—run television ads in the pricey Los Angeles market. Doak, Shrum & Associates of Washington, D.C., was asked to develop two ads for the primary and, ultimately, another two for the general election campaign. Doak, Shrum's total billings for conceptualization, production, and placement of the ads were $429,190. The Media Co. of Washington received $201,808 for purchasing air time, mostly for the fall campaign.

In October 1992 Harman spent $600,000 of her own money to fund a television and persuasion-mail blitz. Her total spending over the final month of the campaign approached $1 million, well over twice the amount Los Angeles City Council member Joan Milke Flores was able to muster down the stretch.

Much of Harman's eleventh-hour spending was dedicated to attacking Flores. One mailer hit Flores for spending $50,000 of the city's money during her tenure on the city council to purchase three new cars for her use. She also criticized Flores for repeatedly supporting pay raises for council members: "Anytime Joan Milke Flores needs more money, she just votes herself a raise. Pretty neat, huh?"

Printing, postage, and labels for the October push totaled $286,121. Of the $30,297 Skelton Grover & Associates of Los Angeles collected for designing the mailers during the general election campaign, $18,297 was for work during this final onslaught.

Harman also invested $483,166 during the campaign's final weeks to produce and air two television commercials. In one, her pro-choice views on abortion were juxtaposed with Flores's statements that abortion should be banned except in cases of rape, incest, or when a woman's life is endangered by her pregnancy. The second ad mirrored her mailers on pay raise votes and perks.

Flores hit back with her own negative mailings, calling Harman a carpetbagger who collected most of her campaign funds on the East Coast and only moved into the district to run for office.

	Harman		Flores	
Campaign Expenditures	Amount Spent	% of Total	Amount Spent	% of Total
Overhead				
Office furniture/supplies	$ 28,848	1.72	$ 12,797	1.41
Rent/utilities	23,751	1.42	6,317	.70
Salaries	205,990	12.30	135,173	14.93
Taxes	32,970	1.97	0	
Bank/investment fees	446	.03	30	.00
Lawyers/accountants	20,747	1.24	1,995	.22
Telephone	24,274	1.45	17,633	1.95
Campaign automobile	0		0	
Computers/office equipment	9,046	.54	8,544	.94
Travel	15,091	.90	5,591	.62
Food/meetings	3,098	.18	798	.09
Subtotal	364,261	21.74	188,877	20.86
Fund Raising				
Events	31,689	1.89	99,388	10.98
Direct mail	32,467	1.94	4,281	.47
Telemarketing	5,675	.34	0	
Subtotal	69,831	4.17	103,668	11.45
Polling	76,445	4.56	47,650	5.26
Advertising				
Electronic media	630,998	37.67	0	
Other media	472	.03	6,646	.73
Subtotal	631,470	37.70	6,646	.73
Other Campaign Activity				
Persuasion mail/brochures	470,667	28.10	420,051	46.39
Actual campaigning	56,146	3.35	105,652	11.67
Staff/volunteers	721	.04	825	.09
Subtotal	527,535	31.49	526,527	58.15
Constituent Gifts/Entertainment	510	.03	0	
Donations to				
Candidates from same state	0		0	
Candidates from other states	0		0	
Civic organizations	25	.00	0	
Ideological groups	0		0	
Political parties	200	.01	0	
Subtotal	225	.01	0	
Unitemized Expenses	4,878	.29	32,087	3.54
Total Campaign Expenses	$ 1,675,155		$ 905,455	
PAC Contributions	$ 199,208		$ 267,429	
Individual Contributions	598,176		512,056	
Total Receipts*	1,628,376		812,022	

*Includes PAC and individual contributions as well as interest earned, party contributions, etc.

† No expenditures or receipts on file. Candidates raising or spending less than $5,000 are not required to file reports with the Federal Election Commission.

District 37 — CALIFORNIA

Rep. Walter R. Tucker III (D)

1992 Election Results

Walter R. Tucker III (D)   97,159   (86%)
B. Kwaku Duren (I)   16,178   (14%)

With Democrats comprising more than 75 percent of the district's registered voters, the election that mattered most was the five-candidate Democratic primary. In that contest, retiring Rep. Mervyn M. Dymally had thrown his support to his daughter Lynn, a Compton school board member. However, despite outspending her chief rival, Compton Mayor Walter R. Tucker III, by more than two to one, Dymally fell 1,103 votes short.

In an effort to reach younger, newly registered voters, Tucker wrote and produced his own campaign song with a decidedly upbeat tempo. "He's very artsy," said administrative assistant Marcus S. Mason.

While the song opened with a whimsical chorus of "Walter Tucker, Tucker for Congress, uh huh, uh huh," it carried a serious message. "It's time for us to rearrange our minds, it's time for us to create jobs where there was crime ... it's time for us to stop the killing." In addition to giving away cassette tapes of the tune, Tucker edited it into a sixty-second commercial that aired on two rhythm and blues radio stations.

For the older, more conservative crowd, Tucker developed what Mason described as "a more traditional commercial," which ran on CNN and Black Entertainment Television. The ad showed Tucker discussing various issues with constituents.

In all, Tucker spent about $123,000 on the primary, including $20,668 of his advertising budget. His preprimary expenditures for brochures and persuasion mail totaled roughly $30,000. Fund-raising costs through June 1992 totaled $24,274.

Tucker's largest preprimary fund-raiser was his own birthday party held at the Sheraton Long Beach Hotel. Tucker's wife Robin, a contemporary gospel singer, coordinated the affair, which was attended by Rep. Maxine Waters and singer Stephanie Mills. Mason said that while nearly 400 people paid between $40 and $250 to attend—depending upon their proximity to the honoree—high overhead cut into profits. Costs associated with the event totaled more than $10,000.

Tucker's general election campaign against Peace and Freedom party nominee B. Kwaku Duren resembled that of a safe incumbent. He held a $17,322 "Pirates of the Caribbean" fund-raiser at the Ritz Carlton Hotel. While he spent nearly $164,000, persuasion mail costs totaled only $22,852; total advertising amounted to $1,507. "Airfare for Congressional training" set the campaign back $4,601.

After the election, Tucker spent $1,576 of his campaign funds to help defray the costs of moving Mason and another staffer from California to Washington. Another $1,100 in campaign funds were spent to move Tucker's personal car to Washington.

Campaign Expenditures	Tucker Amount Spent	Tucker % of Total	Duren Amount Spent	Duren % of Total
Overhead				
Office furniture/supplies	$ 7,275	2.53	$ 0	
Rent/utilities	0		0	
Salaries	60,692	21.14	0	
Taxes	717	.25	0	
Bank/investment fees	21	.01[1]	0	
Lawyers/accountants	3,161	1.10	0	
Telephone	13,190	4.59	0	
Campaign automobile	0		0	
Computers/office equipment	354	.12	0	
Travel	11,156	3.89	0	
Food/meetings	32	.01	0	
Subtotal	**96,597**	**33.64**	**0**	
Fund Raising				
Events	64,088	22.32	0	
Direct mail	10,459	3.64	0	
Telemarketing	0		0	
Subtotal	**74,546**	**25.96**	**0**	
Polling	**0**		**0**	
Advertising				
Electronic media	4,127	1.44	2,225	59.96
Other media	18,048	6.29	100	2.70
Subtotal	**22,175**	**7.72**	**2,325**	**62.66**
Other Campaign Activity				
Persuasion mail/brochures	53,274	18.55	1,191	32.11
Actual campaigning	24,584	8.56	194	5.23
Staff/volunteers	3,653	1.27	0	
Subtotal	**81,511**	**28.39**	**1,386**	**37.34**
Constituent Gifts/Entertainment	1,731	.60	0	
Donations to				
Candidates from same state	229	.08	0	
Candidates from other states	0		0	
Civic organizations	5,962	2.08	0	
Ideological groups	1,445	.50	0	
Political parties	87	.03	0	
Subtotal	**7,723**	**2.69**	**0**	
Unitemized Expenses	**2,856**	**.99**	**0**	
Total Campaign Expenses	**$ 287,139**		**$ 3,711**	
PAC Contributions	$ 65,100		$ 0	
Individual Contributions	181,346		2,899	
Total Receipts*	283,230		4,129	

*Includes PAC and individual contributions as well as interest earned, party contributions, etc.

CALIFORNIA — District 38

Rep. Steve Horn (R)

1992 Election Results

Steve Horn (R)	92,038	(49%)
Evan Anderson Braude (D)	82,108	(43%)

California State University political science professor Steve Horn knew what was important. He did not open an office until October. His campaign staff consisted almost exclusively of volunteers. Day-to-day campaign management fell to his son, Steve Horn, Jr. Persuasion mail was designed by his wife, daughter, and son. Payments to consultants totaled only $46,426.

Instead, Horn spent a staggering 87 percent of his $458,310 campaign treasury on direct appeals to voters. This single-minded approach allowed Horn to upset state representative Dennis Brown by 105 votes in the Republican primary and defeat Long Beach City Council member Evan Anderson Braude in the fall campaign, despite the fact that registered Democrats outnumber Republicans in the district by about 30,000.

In the primary, Horn spent $43,636 to produce nearly 20,000 copies of an issue-oriented video, which the campaign mailed to registered Republicans in areas of the district where Horn appeared to be slightly behind or barely holding his own. This fifteen-minute video touched on seven topics, including crime, health care, abortion, foreign trade, and congressional reform.

Registered Republicans also received six major mailings prior to the June primary. Horn sent out 50,000 copies of a thirteen-page brochure, which included a three-page, postage-paid questionnaire soliciting opinions on various topics.

Another brochure outlined Horn's basic campaign themes and cited various endorsements. It opened into a poster that detailed his positions on seventeen issues. Large blank spaces were included for voters to tally their positions and those of the seven other Republicans. Over the blank spaces, in three-inch gray type, were the words, "You Be the Judge."

Horn's most creative preprimary mailer almost brought him a lawsuit. The brochure showed a beer can with the smiling, blond-haired, blue-eyed caricature of "Candidate Lite, King of Career Politicians." The can bore an unmistakable similarity to Budweiser's Bud Lite can. Unamused, Budweiser contacted Horn and insisted he cease using their image or face a copyright infringement suit.

Since Horn's campaign style worked in the primary, he simply repeated it in his race against Braude. Horn invested $55,984 to produce 49,000 copies of another video. There were numerous persuasion mailings but no broadcast ads. Instead, the campaign purchased the videotape of the debate between Horn and Braude and paid to rebroadcast it.

The $95,765 Braude spent on overhead more than consumed his modest monetary advantage.

Campaign Expenditures	Horn Amount Spent	Horn % of Total	Braude Amount Spent	Braude % of Total
Overhead				
Office furniture/supplies	$ 4,040	.88	$ 4,529	.88
Rent/utilities	200	.04	2,001	.39
Salaries	4,350	.95	58,647	11.40
Taxes	0		0	
Bank/investment fees	750	.16	6,173	1.20
Lawyers/accountants	0		12,578	2.44
Telephone	1,485	.32	7,420	1.44
Campaign automobile	0		1,914	.37
Computers/office equipment	0		724	.14
Travel	3,393	.74	1,615	.31
Food/meetings	0		165	.03
Subtotal	**14,218**	**3.10**	**95,765**	**18.61**
Fund Raising				
Events	10,363	2.26	19,857	3.86
Direct mail	17,271	3.77	0	
Telemarketing	0		11,502	2.24
Subtotal	**27,633**	**6.03**	**31,359**	**6.09**
Polling	**15,000**	**3.27**	**35,000**	**6.80**
Advertising				
Electronic media	350	.08	46,000	8.94
Other media	99,871	21.79	65	.01
Subtotal	**100,221**	**21.87**	**46,065**	**8.95**
Other Campaign Activity				
Persuasion mail/brochures	261,890	57.14	245,895	47.79
Actual campaigning	35,730	7.80	59,775	11.62
Staff/volunteers	0		433	.08
Subtotal	**297,621**	**64.94**	**306,104**	**59.49**
Constituent Gifts/ Entertainment	**0**		**0**	
Donations to				
Candidates from same state	0		0	
Candidates from other states	0		0	
Civic organizations	0		258	.05
Ideological groups	0		0	
Political parties	0		24	.00
Subtotal	**0**		**282**	**.05**
Unitemized Expenses	**3,618**	**.79**	**0**	
Total Campaign Expenses	**$ 458,310**		**$ 514,574**	
PAC Contributions	$ 3,000		$ 168,745	
Individual Contributions	361,847		129,324	
Total Receipts*	441,693		514,459	

*Includes PAC and individual contributions as well as interest earned, party contributions, etc.

District 39

CALIFORNIA

Rep. Ed Royce (R)

1992 Election Results

Ed Royce (R) 122,472 (57%)
Molly McClanahan (D) 81,728 (38%)

State senator Ed Royce got an eight-month head start on his Democratic challenger, Fullerton City Council member Molly McClanahan.

Royce announced his decision to run on August 11, 1991, and nine days later he made his first payment to fund-raising consultant Ann Hyde Co. of Glendale. During the final four months of 1991, Royce held three fund-raising events, including one that featured House Minority Whip Newt Gingrich (R-Ga.). The three receptions raised a total of $164,066 from individual contributors and political action committees (PACs), nearly twice as much as McClanahan would ultimately raise from these sources.

In September 1991 Royce opened a campaign office in Sacramento, paying monthly rent of $550. In January 1992 Royce brought in Huckaby, Rodriguez of Sacramento to provide day-to-day campaign management. Campaign Management Services of Washington, D.C., was hired in February to help increase PAC donations. In March he began paying monthly rent of $250 for an office in Fullerton. Throughout the spring, volunteers walked the district, passing out campaign literature and red, white, and blue cardboard fans with the words "I'm a Fan of State Senator Ed Royce" printed on them.

By the time McClanahan announced her candidacy on March 25, Royce had raised more than $180,000 and had cash reserves of more than $100,000. In this solidly Republican district, the race was over before it began.

According to Royce, most of his early efforts were designed more to discourage other Republicans from entering the race than to build a nest egg to combat his Democratic opponent. However, that did not mean he simply sat on his cash reserves.

During the final month of the general election campaign, Royce committed $310,207 to defeating McClanahan, including nearly $210,000 on his persuasion mail efforts. Cable television buys during this final push cost $10,757. Newspaper ads added $4,378. Mason, Lundberg & Associates of Orange, Calif., collected $9,397 for phonebanking.

By the end of the election cycle, Royce had paid Huckaby, Rodriguez a total of $56,611; Ann Hyde, $27,317; Campaign Management, $27,157; and pollster Arnold Steinberg & Associates of Calabasas, $15,500. The Padaro Group of Laguna Niguel also received $5,000 for organizing events.

This spending spree left his campaign with debts of $132,383, including $19,000 in loans he and other family members made to the campaign.

Unable to raise sufficient cash to make a real fight of it, McClanahan said her troubles were "nothing that a few hundred thousand dollars wouldn't solve."

Campaign Expenditures	Royce Amount Spent	Royce % of Total	McClanahan Amount Spent	McClanahan % of Total
Overhead				
Office furniture/supplies	$ 9,252	1.45	$ 2,822	3.13
Rent/utilities	10,623	1.66	3,000	3.33
Salaries	27,514	4.30	6,500	7.21
Taxes	1,101	.17	0	
Bank/investment fees	0		0	
Lawyers/accountants	0		0	
Telephone	6,310	.99	3,972	4.41
Campaign automobile	0		0	
Computers/office equipment	6,368	1.00	0	
Travel	6,699	1.05	127	.14
Food/meetings	0		0	
Subtotal	**67,868**	**10.61**	**16,421**	**18.22**
Fund Raising				
Events	107,215	16.76	0	
Direct mail	0		2,013	2.23
Telemarketing	0		0	
Subtotal	**107,215**	**16.76**	**2,013**	**2.23**
Polling	**15,500**	**2.42**	**0**	
Advertising				
Electronic media	11,571	1.81	0	
Other media	4,378	.68	6,829	7.58
Subtotal	**15,948**	**2.49**	**6,829**	**7.58**
Other Campaign Activity				
Persuasion mail/brochures	319,415	49.92	35,833	39.76
Actual campaigning	96,387	15.06	17,445	19.36
Staff/volunteers	0		0	
Subtotal	**415,802**	**64.99**	**53,279**	**59.12**
Constituent Gifts/ Entertainment	**0**		**0**	
Donations to				
Candidates from same state	2,950	.46	0	
Candidates from other states	0		0	
Civic organizations	0		0	
Ideological groups	0		0	
Political parties	0		0	
Subtotal	**2,950**	**.46**	**0**	
Unitemized Expenses	**14,549**	**2.27**	**11,573**	**12.84**
Total Campaign Expenses	**$ 639,833**		**$ 90,114**	
PAC Contributions	$ 200,562		$ 23,181	
Individual Contributions	262,215		61,750	
Total Receipts*	499,264		99,729	

*Includes PAC and individual contributions as well as interest earned, party contributions, etc.

CALIFORNIA — District 40

Rep. Jerry Lewis (R)

1992 Election Results

Jerry Lewis (R)	129,563	(63%)
Donald M. Rusk (D)	63,881	(31%)
Margie Akin † (I)	11,839	(6%)

After winning better than 60 percent of the vote in each of his previous seven House campaigns, Rep. Jerry Lewis was never overly concerned about the outcome of his 1992 contest with an underfunded Democratic opponent, Donald M. Rusk. What Lewis clearly was concerned about was maintaining his position as chairman of the House Republican Conference.

Lewis donated $110,864 to various Republican House and Senate candidates. He also spent $3,519 to attend campaign "schools" in Fair Oaks, Va., and Los Angeles, lending his expertise to Republican hopefuls from around the country. Unfortunately for Lewis, many of those he backed were not around to vote for him in December 1992 when he lost his leadership position to Rep. Dick Armey (Texas). He donated $40,500 to challengers and open seat candidates who lost their House bids and $5,000 to House incumbents who lost.

Lewis tapped his campaign treasury to pay for nearly $26,000 in meals that were unrelated to his fund-raising activities, many at posh restaurants on Capitol Hill. During the first six months of 1991, contributions to Lewis's campaign totaled only $4,810. During that same period, meals at the Monocle Restaurant amounted to $2,072, meals at La Brasserie came to $1,214, and a single dinner at Le Mistral cost the campaign $1,097. Bills at Gandels, a delicatessen near the Capitol, totaled $405. While he could not provide details on any specific meal, press secretary David M. LesStrang said they were for both business and constituent entertainment.

Lewis also invested considerable sums in constituent gifts. For example, in late 1991 he spent $2,525 on picture frames. He spent $5,442 in 1991 and $4,882 in 1992 to purchase and mail Christmas ornaments.

In July 1991 Lewis spent $9,150 of his campaign treasury on what LesStrang described as a "team building experience" for his congressional staff. Cabins for the three-night stay at Fort AP Hill, Va., cost $680; catering added $1,481. General campaign consultant Harlan-Evans of Stillwater, Minn., collected $6,989 for their participation.

Once the campaign got rolling, Lewis paid Piccirillo Productions of Stevenson Ranch, Calif., $29,445 for producing his television commercials. Quinn/Lamb Media of San Bernadino received $76,692 for purchasing both television and radio air time. Direct Communication of La Jolla was paid $23,725 for phonebanking. Charlton Research Co. of San Francisco received $20,500 for conducting the campaign's polls.

With no chance for an upset, Rusk raised only $2,201. Rusk supplied $18,300 of his own funds and received limited support from the Democratic party.

Campaign Expenditures	Lewis Amount Spent	Lewis % of Total	Rusk Amount Spent	Rusk % of Total
Overhead				
Office furniture/supplies	$ 11,237	2.06	$ 1,232	5.38
Rent/utilities	0		1,050	4.59
Salaries	7,125	1.30	1,128	4.93
Taxes	8,006	1.46	0	
Bank/investment fees	22	.00	0	
Lawyers/accountants	8,956	1.64	0	
Telephone	493	.09	1,272	5.56
Campaign automobile	0		0	
Computers/office equipment	0		2,569	11.22
Travel	27,248	4.99	0	
Food/meetings	25,840	4.73	0	
Subtotal	88,928	16.27	7,251	31.69
Fund Raising				
Events	66,752	12.21	0	
Direct mail	0		0	
Telemarketing	0		0	
Subtotal	66,752	12.21	0	
Polling	20,500	3.75	0	
Advertising				
Electronic media	106,707	19.52	2,889	12.62
Other media	954	.17	1,607	7.02
Subtotal	107,661	19.70	4,495	19.64
Other Campaign Activity				
Persuasion mail/brochures	61,539	11.26	2,571	11.23
Actual campaigning	38,719	7.08	6,041	26.40
Staff/volunteers	2,362	.43	0	
Subtotal	102,620	18.78	8,612	37.63
Constituent Gifts/Entertainment	14,844	2.72	0	
Donations to				
Candidates from same state	35,614	6.52	0	
Candidates from other states	81,250	14.87	0	
Civic organizations	1,700	.31	0	
Ideological groups	5,000	.91	0	
Political parties	5,000	.91	0	
Subtotal	128,564	23.52	0	
Unitemized Expenses	16,680	3.05	2,526	11.04
Total Campaign Expenses	$ 546,549		$ 22,884	
PAC Contributions	$ 358,045		$ 0	
Individual Contributions	88,599		2,201	
Total Receipts*	471,956		21,840	

*Includes PAC and individual contributions as well as interest earned, party contributions, etc.

† No expenditures or receipts on file. Candidates raising or spending less than $5,000 are not required to file reports with the Federal Election Commission.

District 41 — CALIFORNIA

Rep. Jay C. Kim (R)

1992 Election Results

Jay C. Kim (R)	101,753	(60%)
Bob Baker † (D)	58,777	(34%)
Mike Noonan † (I)	10,136	(6%)

Businessman Jay C. Kim, mayor of Diamond Bar, spent nearly half his $703,799 campaign treasury to defeat former state representative Charles W. Bader in the Republican primary, and that was apparently only the beginning.

In July 1993 the *Los Angeles Times* reported that records provided to the paper showed that Kim had violated federal law by using money from a company he owned, JayKim Engineers, to pay many of his 1992 campaign expenses. According to the *Times*, Kim used more than $400,000 of corporate money to pay for airline tickets, telephone service, free office space, staff salaries, and office supplies, among other items. Following these reports, both the Federal Bureau of Investigation and the Internal Revenue Service launched investigations. None of the corporate money in question is accounted for in this analysis.

Even without this additional cash flow, Kim outspent Bader by about $140,000. With that money, Kim was able to run four commercials on local cable television outlets, a luxury Bader could not afford. An ad decrying congressional inaction to improve business opportunities for women was run on the USA Network and the Lifetime channel. Two biographical spots and one attack ad aired on CNN and during NBA playoff games. Signature Entertainment of Rialto received $47,995 for designing and placing the ads on three cable systems.

For the primary, Kim also sank $185,946 into brochures and persuasion mail, including a $17,500 payment to Robert Gouty Co. of Covina for consultation and design fees. He paid Silver State Communication of Reno, Nev., $35,580 for phonebanking. He spent $10,254 on yard signs and posters, $4,997 on newspaper ads in the *Ontario Daily Bulietin,* $4,500 on bus ads, $4,189 on precinct walk-sheets, and $2,400 on a slate mailer. "We started with 3 percent name recognition in this district," explained campaign manager Sandra Garner.

While his Democratic opponent, intelligence analyst Bob Baker, spent less than $5,000, Kim continued to spend freely in the general election campaign. Robert Gouty received another $17,500 for putting together a $154,888 persuasion mail campaign. Kim spent another $14,376 on yard signs, $17,745 on an in-house phonebank, and $4,500 on bus signs. He ran numerous newspaper ads, paying $2,190 to the *Chinese Daily News,* $1,600 to the *Korean Central Daily,* $800 to *Korea Times,* $1,110 to the *Daily Bulletin,* and $700 to the *International Daily News.*

To sharpen his public speaking skills, Kim also used $3,350 of his campaign treasury for speech lessons.

Campaign Expenditures	Kim Amount Spent	% of Total
Overhead		
Office furniture/supplies	$ 18,723	2.66
Rent/utilities	0	
Salaries	82,012	11.65
Taxes	0	
Bank/investment fees	156	.02
Lawyers/accountants	4,395	.62
Telephone	8,239	1.17
Campaign automobile	0	
Computers/office equipment	604	.09
Travel	1,563	.22
Food/meetings	3,290	.47
Subtotal	**118,981**	**16.91**
Fund Raising		
Events	43,881	6.23
Direct mail	0	
Telemarketing	0	
Subtotal	**43,881**	**6.23**
Polling	**11,000**	**1.56**
Advertising		
Electronic media	49,709	7.06
Other media	23,122	3.29
Subtotal	**72,831**	**10.35**
Other Campaign Activity		
Persuasion mail/brochures	340,834	48.43
Actual campaigning	107,265	15.24
Staff/volunteers	143	.02
Subtotal	**448,243**	**63.69**
Constituent Gifts/Entertainment	**330**	**.05**
Donations to		
Candidates from same state	150	.02
Candidates from other states	0	
Civic organizations	1,180	.17
Ideological groups	0	
Political parties	514	.07
Subtotal	**1,844**	**.26**
Unitemized Expenses	**6,690**	**.95**
Total Campaign Expenses	$ **703,799**	
PAC Contributions	$ **91,900**	
Individual Contributions	**511,814**	
Total Receipts*	**791,483**	

*Includes PAC and individual contributions as well as interest earned, party contributions, etc.

† No expenditures or receipts on file. Candidates raising or spending less than $5,000 are not required to file reports with the Federal Election Commission.

CALIFORNIA District 42

Rep. George E. Brown, Jr. (D)

1992 Election Results

George E. Brown, Jr. (D)	79,780	(51%)
Dick Rutan (R)	69,251	(44%)
Fritz R. Ward † (I)	8,424	(5%)

One need look no further than Rep. George E. Brown, Jr.'s fund-raisers to see a link between his position as chairman of the Committee on Science, Space, and Technology and his ability to raise large sums of political action committee (PAC) money.

In early 1991 Brown held a $1,000-a-head event aimed at PACs representing aerospace companies, and in July Lockheed's PAC spent $763 to stage a small fund-raiser on his behalf. In May 1992 Brown drew close to one hundred contributors to a fund-raiser at Houston's Clear Lake Space Club. One month later he traveled to New York for a fund-raising breakfast thrown for him by the Loral Corporation. In all, PACs representing aerospace, science, and technology interests contributed $115,488 to Brown's reelection effort.

Brown had been held to 53 percent of the vote in 1990, and redistricting had given him a somewhat more Republican district. With twenty-six overdrafts at the House bank, Brown looked to be vulnerable in his race against Dick Rutan, a former air force pilot who in 1986 had flown around the world in a lightweight airplane of his own design on a single tank of fuel.

To combat this folk hero, Brown relied heavily on a persuasion mail campaign designed by Campaign Performance Group of San Francisco. "We didn't turn up much on Rutan from a negative research point of view," noted Campaign Performance president Richard M. Schlackman. "So we hit him with pieces focusing on choice and guns because he was a right-wing ideologue."

Brown's opposition research discovered that Rutan had arranged a $100,000 bank loan for a company he owned shortly after being named to the bank's board of directors. That discovery prompted a mailing that attempted to draw parallels between that loan and "the greedy and corrupt S&L gang in the 80s."

Austin-Sheinkopf of New York handled Brown's radio and cable television advertising. The highlight of the ad campaign was a radio commercial in which Jeana Yeager, Rutan's copilot on their around-the-world flight, endorsed Brown. "I flew around the world with Dick Rutan and he's not prepared to lead," Yeager began. Campaign manager Bobi Johnson said a similar television commercial never ran.

For their efforts, Campaign Performance and Austin-Sheinkopf received $224,376 and $92,147, respectively. Pollster Fairbank, Bregman & Maullin of San Francisco was paid $46,950. Brown paid four fund-raising consultants a total of $123,487.

To spread the word of his candidacy, Rutan sent out a nationwide mailing to 41,000 potential supporters in April 1992 asking them for money.

	Brown		Rutan	
Campaign Expenditures	Amount Spent	% of Total	Amount Spent	% of Total
Overhead				
Office furniture/supplies	$ 11,265	1.33	$ 7,401	1.62
Rent/utilities	10,680	1.26	6,000	1.31
Salaries	67,278	7.92	51,136	11.17
Taxes	13,339	1.57	2,049	.45
Bank/investment fees	369	.04	10	.00
Lawyers/accountants	4,798	.56	0	
Telephone	12,645	1.49	9,255	2.02
Campaign automobile	0		0	
Computers/office equipment	2,159	.25	5,869	1.28
Travel	8,559	1.01	5,155	1.13
Food/meetings	228	.03	0	
Subtotal	**131,321**	**15.45**	**86,874**	**18.98**
Fund Raising				
Events	109,083	12.84	55,744	12.18
Direct mail	61,710	7.26	29,301	6.40
Telemarketing	0		0	
Subtotal	**170,793**	**20.10**	**85,045**	**18.58**
Polling	**46,950**	**5.53**	**7,500**	**1.64**
Advertising				
Electronic media	96,132	11.31	29,568	6.46
Other media	8,269	.97	10,030	2.19
Subtotal	**104,401**	**12.29**	**39,598**	**8.65**
Other Campaign Activity				
Persuasion mail/brochures	283,992	33.42	155,872	34.06
Actual campaigning	20,529	2.42	74,084	16.19
Staff/volunteers	580	.07	0	
Subtotal	**305,101**	**35.90**	**229,956**	**50.25**
Constituent Gifts/Entertainment	**4,453**	**.52**	**39**	**.01**
Donations to				
Candidates from same state	7,284	.86	550	.12
Candidates from other states	0		0	
Civic organizations	1,663	.20	345	.08
Ideological groups	3,122	.37	99	.02
Political parties	28,443	3.35	127	.03
Subtotal	**40,511**	**4.77**	**1,121**	**.24**
Unitemized Expenses	**46,220**	**5.44**	**7,512**	**1.64**
Total Campaign Expenses	**$ 849,749**		**$ 457,645**	
PAC Contributions	$ 506,920		$ 69,065	
Individual Contributions	379,552		125,519	
Total Receipts*	908,348		468,862	

*Includes PAC and individual contributions as well as interest earned, party contributions, etc.

† No expenditures or receipts on file. Candidates raising or spending less than $5,000 are not required to file reports with the Federal Election Commission.

District 43 — CALIFORNIA

Rep. Ken Calvert (R)

1992 Election Results

Ken Calvert (R)   88,987   (47%)
Mark A. Takano (D)   88,468   (46%)

Real estate developer Ken Calvert spent nearly $507,000 on his campaign, but more than half that total was invested in the seven-candidate Republican primary. For the primary, Calvert spent more than $100,000 on persuasion mail alone and prevailed by less than 2,800 votes.

In the general election, perhaps Calvert's smartest investment was the $18,000 he spent to mail 40,000 absentee ballots. An apparent loser by 1,200 votes on election day, Calvert pulled out a 519-vote win over Mark A. Takano only after 17,000 absentee votes were counted.

Campaign strategist and media consultant Marty Wilson said Calvert embarked on this effort to find and turn out absentee voters simply "because we had the money to engage in voter contact activities six to eight weeks before the election." Wilson added that this group was targeted a second time, reminding them to return their marked ballots.

The campaign hired America Telemarketing of Concord just days before the election to undertake a last-minute phonebanking effort. "We panicked," said Wilson. "Takano got a lot of money toward the end, and we wanted to secure our base." America Telemarketing received $5,798 for their work.

Excluding fees paid to Wilson for designing the mailers and for the cost of the absentee ballots, Calvert spent about $77,000 on persuasion mail for the general election. Calvert invested nothing in television, but the campaign took advantage of extremely inexpensive radio air time to buy large blocks on both Colton and San Bernadino stations. On Sunday, Nov. 1—two days before the election—the campaign paid $7,669 for newspaper ads that listed endorsements Calvert had received from a host of local officials.

In both the primary and general election campaigns, Calvert's overhead expenses were largely driven by campaign salaries, which accounted for 19 percent of his total spending. Sue Miller, who subsequently became Calvert's district director, earned $40,000 for her work on the campaign. Linda Fisher, who moved into a staff assistant position on the district congressional staff, collected $18,300 from the campaign.

Following the election, Calvert used $2,514 of his treasury to help pay for moving his belongings to Washington.

Takano had a much easier path to the general election, spending only about $85,000 to secure the Democratic nomination. Initially given no chance in this solidly Republican district, Takano began by mailing thousands of copies of a twenty-four-page treatise outlining his ideas on reviving the economy. Hammering away at education and job creation, he almost pulled off the upset.

Campaign Expenditures	Calvert Amount Spent	Calvert % of Total	Takano Amount Spent	Takano % of Total
Overhead				
Office furniture/supplies	$ 8,664	1.71	$ 4,892	1.81
Rent/utilities	9,574	1.89	2,570	.95
Salaries	97,308	19.21	37,005	13.66
Taxes	0		0	
Bank/investment fees	0		438	.16
Lawyers/accountants	0		0	
Telephone	10,589	2.09	11,887	4.39
Campaign automobile	0		0	
Computers/office equipment	13,846	2.73	1,343	.50
Travel	5,160	1.02	3,456	1.28
Food/meetings	0		42	.02
Subtotal	**145,141**	**28.65**	**61,633**	**22.75**
Fund Raising				
Events	22,917	4.52	31,021	11.45
Direct mail	0		1,410	.52
Telemarketing	0		0	
Subtotal	**22,917**	**4.52**	**32,431**	**11.97**
Polling	**14,314**	**2.83**	**28,987**	**10.70**
Advertising				
Electronic media	21,316	4.21	11,907	4.39
Other media	7,948	1.57	1,190	.44
Subtotal	**29,264**	**5.78**	**13,097**	**4.83**
Other Campaign Activity				
Persuasion mail/brochures	200,312	39.54	117,021	43.19
Actual campaigning	83,604	16.50	14,793	5.46
Staff/volunteers	132	.03	91	.03
Subtotal	**284,048**	**56.07**	**131,905**	**48.68**
Constituent Gifts/ Entertainment	**511**	**.10**	**0**	
Donations to				
Candidates from same state	0		0	
Candidates from other states	0		0	
Civic organizations	0		40	.01
Ideological groups	0		100	.04
Political parties	0		50	.02
Subtotal	**0**		**190**	**.07**
Unitemized Expenses	**10,409**	**2.05**	**2,708**	**1.00**
Total Campaign Expenses	**$ 506,604**		**$ 270,951**	
PAC Contributions	**$ 138,485**		**$ 156,537**	
Individual Contributions	259,850		162,345	
Total Receipts*	423,001		344,361	

*Includes PAC and individual contributions as well as interest earned, party contributions, etc.

CALIFORNIA — District 44

Rep. Al McCandless (R)

1992 Election Results

Al McCandless (R)	110,333	(54%)
Georgia Smith (D)	81,693	(40%)
Phil Turner † (I)	11,515	(6%)

If Rep. Al McCandless learned anything from his close electoral shave in 1990, it was the value of a permanent campaign.

McCandless had won his 1984, 1986, and 1988 campaigns with 64 percent of the vote while spending an average of only $116,793. During those halcyon days, the off-year was just that—there was no campaign office, no staff, and no heavy fund-raising.

However, in 1990 actor Ralph Waite spent a total of $634,544 on his Democratic primary and general election campaigns and came within 5 percentage points of retiring McCandless. In the process, Waite may have changed the incumbent's campaign strategy forever. "At that point, he decided he would not be left holding the bag," said administrative assistant Signy Ellerton. "He decided to play the game."

To guard against a repeat of 1990, McCandless maintained an off-year campaign office for the first time in his congressional career. The $200-a-month space served as headquarters for his staff fund-raiser, James Moore. Expenditures for overhead and fund raising in 1991 amounted to $35,500 and $31,570, respectively. Although his total off-year campaign budget of $73,721 was modest when compared with most incumbents, it was remarkably high for McCandless.

While his district is littered with golf courses, McCandless had never held a golf event until March 1991. Food and green fees at the La Quinta Hotel Golf Club cost the campaign $999; prizes added $854. He spent $585 to purchase 207 porcelain coffee cups for two breakfast fund-raisers held in May 1991. Other off-year events included a summer picnic and an autumn reception at the Capitol Hill Club in Washington, D.C.

For the fourth straight campaign, McCandless increased his efforts to raise political action committee (PAC) money. PACs accounted for $44,478 of his receipts in 1982, $50,403 in 1984, $65,500 in 1986, $75,500 in 1988, $179,600 in his tough 1990 campaign, and $195,137 in 1992. The increase in 1992 was particularly significant since his total receipts were $233,477 less than in 1990. Dan Morgan & Associates of Arlington, Va., received $39,558 for coordinating PAC events, $25,264 of that total in 1991.

With an ample campaign treasury, McCandless paid Moore Information of Portland, Ore., a total of $18,500 to conduct one poll in late May 1992 and another in October. Russo, Marsh & Associates of Sacramento received $84,797 for coordinating the general election persuasion mail campaign.

Despite spending only $10,006 on her campaign, Democrat Georgia Smith received 40 percent of the vote.

Campaign Expenditures	McCandless Amount Spent	McCandless % of Total	Smith Amount Spent	Smith % of Total
Overhead				
Office furniture/supplies	$ 2,543	.98	$ 0	
Rent/utilities	2,164	.84	0	
Salaries	26,266	10.15	0	
Taxes	2,732	1.06	0	
Bank/investment fees	68	.03	0	
Lawyers/accountants	7,650	2.95	0	
Telephone	6,401	2.47	0	
Campaign automobile	0		0	
Computers/office equipment	3,693	1.43	0	
Travel	13,424	5.19	225	2.25
Food/meetings	0		0	
Subtotal	**64,941**	**25.08**	**225**	**2.25**
Fund Raising				
Events	65,890	25.45	0	
Direct mail	0		0	
Telemarketing	0		0	
Subtotal	**65,890**	**25.45**	**0**	
Polling	**18,500**	**7.15**	**0**	
Advertising				
Electronic media	0		348	3.48
Other media	1,436	.55	0	
Subtotal	**1,436**	**.55**	**348**	**3.48**
Other Campaign Activity				
Persuasion mail/brochures	88,890	34.34	4,017	40.15
Actual campaigning	5,639	2.18	3,696	36.94
Staff/volunteers	0		0	
Subtotal	**94,529**	**36.51**	**7,713**	**77.08**
Constituent Gifts/ Entertainment	**6,767**	**2.61**	**0**	
Donations to				
Candidates from same state	2,060	.80	0	
Candidates from other states	0		0	
Civic organizations	452	.17	0	
Ideological groups	0		0	
Political parties	1,524	.59	0	
Subtotal	**4,036**	**1.56**	**0**	
Unitemized Expenses	**2,785**	**1.08**	**1,720**	**17.19**
Total Campaign Expenses	**$ 258,884**		**$ 10,006**	
PAC Contributions	$ 195,137		$ 1,448	
Individual Contributions	120,634		2,552	
Total Receipts*	318,312		7,693	

*Includes PAC and individual contributions as well as interest earned, party contributions, etc.

† No expenditures or receipts on file. Candidates raising or spending less than $5,000 are not required to file reports with the Federal Election Commission.

District 45 — CALIFORNIA

Rep. Dana Rohrabacher (R)

1992 Election Results

Dana Rohrabacher (R)	123,731	(55%)
Patricia McCabe (D)	88,508	(39%)
Gary D. Copeland † (I)	14,777	(6%)

When California's redistricting plan was announced in December 1991, both Rep. Dana Rohrabacher and Rep. Robert K. Dornan coveted this highly Republican district, although neither actually lived within its boundaries. Rohrabacher won the ensuing argument, registered to vote in Orange County, and convinced Huntington Beach Mayor Jim Silva to stay on the sidelines. However, Rohrabacher was less persuasive with other Republicans and found himself in a difficult primary battle with Costa Mesa Council member Peter Buffa and Huntington Beach Council member Peter Green.

Buffa proved to be particularly pesky, running radio ads, investing heavily in persuasion mail, and littering the district with signs. One radio spot featured Michael Reagan, son of the former president, assailing Rohrabacher for his claim that he had been instrumental in helping to devise the policies that ended the Cold War. Buffa spent $155,374 on his campaign and received 28 percent of the primary votes.

Green spent only $34,196, but his attacks on Rohrabacher for having eight overdrafts at the House bank, for misusing congressional franking privileges, and for his "carpetbagger" move into the district dovetailed with Buffa's. This one-two punch succeeded in holding Rohrabacher to 48 percent of the vote.

Faced with what amounted to a $190,000 primary challenge from Buffa and Green, Rohrabacher spent $179,829 during the first six months of 1992. This spending flurry accounted for 58 percent of his overall spending for the election cycle and 75 percent of his spending during 1992.

For the primary, Rohrabacher spent $88,618 for a brochure with the words "Congressman Dana Rohrabacher: You Know Where He Stands" emblazoned across the cover. Inside, the incumbent's positions on various issues were detailed, including his desire to put more federal money into stopping the flood of illegal immigrants across the U.S.-Mexican border. As he put it in one of his speeches, "Pedro" should not expect to be able to cross the border to get a $50,000 heart-bypass operation for free. Mail consultant Below, Tobe & Associates of Bethesda, Md., collected more than $14,000 of its $19,130 total billings for work during the primary.

Prior to the primary, Rohrabacher also paid Arnold Steinberg & Associates of Calabasas $11,500 for conducting his lone survey. Rohrabacher's share of the cost for three slate mailers totaled $10,469.

In the fall campaign, accountant Patricia McCabe's $29,976 effort succeeded only to the degree that she held Rohrabacher to 55 percent of the vote, exactly the proportion of the district's voters who are registered Republicans.

Campaign Expenditures	Rohrabacher Amount Spent	Rohrabacher % of Total	McCabe Amount Spent	McCabe % of Total
Overhead				
Office furniture/supplies	$ 14,181	4.61	$ 1,185	3.95
Rent/utilities	7,300	2.37	400	1.33
Salaries	54,215	17.63	500	1.67
Taxes	410	.13	0	
Bank/investment fees	0		16	.05
Lawyers/accountants	0		0	
Telephone	4,068	1.32	404	1.35
Campaign automobile	0		0	
Computers/office equipment	11,691	3.80	0	
Travel	9,248	3.01	0	
Food/meetings	2,637	.86	9	.03
Subtotal	**103,750**	**33.74**	**2,514**	**8.39**
Fund Raising				
Events	44,428	14.45	700	2.34
Direct mail	0		0	
Telemarketing	0		449	1.50
Subtotal	**44,428**	**14.45**	**1,149**	**3.83**
Polling	**11,500**	**3.74**	**0**	
Advertising				
Electronic media	0		1,380	4.60
Other media	1,513	.49	150	.50
Subtotal	**1,513**	**.49**	**1,530**	**5.10**
Other Campaign Activity				
Persuasion mail/brochures	113,493	36.91	18,231	60.82
Actual campaigning	10,565	3.44	3,631	12.11
Staff/volunteers	0		111	.37
Subtotal	**124,058**	**40.35**	**21,973**	**73.30**
Constituent Gifts/Entertainment	**640**	**.21**	**0**	
Donations to				
Candidates from same state	10,850	3.53	0	
Candidates from other states	750	.24	0	
Civic organizations	0		225	.75
Ideological groups	795	.26	0	
Political parties	1,811	.59	99	.33
Subtotal	**14,206**	**4.62**	**324**	**1.08**
Unitemized Expenses	**7,371**	**2.40**	**2,485**	**8.29**
Total Campaign Expenses	**$ 307,466**		**$ 29,976**	
PAC Contributions	$ 108,926		$ 8,298	
Individual Contributions	199,367		19,089	
Total Receipts*	323,608		32,944	

*Includes PAC and individual contributions as well as interest earned, party contributions, etc.

† No expenditures or receipts on file. Candidates raising or spending less than $5,000 are not required to file reports with the Federal Election Commission.

CALIFORNIA
District 46

Rep. Robert K. Dornan (R)

1992 Election Results

Robert K. Dornan (R)	55,659	(50%)
Robert John Banuelos † (D)	45,435	(41%)
Richard G. Newhouse † (I)	9,712	(9%)

Targeted by the California Abortion Rights Action League (CARAL), Rep. Robert K. Dornan drew opposition in the Republican primary for the first time since 1984. He responded by calling supporters of his Republican opponent, retired judge Judith M. Ryan, "lesbian spear chuckers." He also responded by spending considerable sums on something other than his usual million-dollar direct-mail fund-raising effort.

Dornan never opened a campaign office during the 1990 cycle, but Ryan's $255,583 challenge and the $88,164 CARAL spent to defeat him forced Dornan to do so in 1992, if only for one month. He hired Campaign Telecommunications of New York and Mason Lundberg & Associates of Orange, Calif., for phonebanking and paid them $21,790 and $3,959, respectively.

Ryan's challenge prompted Dornan to spend $2,732 for an ad in the *Los Angeles Times;* in 1990 he spent nothing on advertising in either the primary or general election campaigns. During May and June 1992 Dornan put $172,626 into brochures and persuasion mail. He even invested $424 in T-shirts.

Immediately following his comfortable primary victory, Dornan reverted to his traditional Orange County campaign. With no threat of a Democratic upset by challenger Robert John Banuelos, he closed his campaign office and spent nothing more on newspaper or broadcast advertising, signs, posters, buttons, or bumper stickers. His persuasion mail for the general election cost $94,056.

As in 1990, the vast majority of Dornan's money was spent on direct-mail fund raising. During 1991 he spent a total of $403,929 on direct mail, or 87 percent of his total off-year expenditures. The $717,674 he spent on such fund raising in 1992 accounted for 66 percent of his election year outlays.

Each month the campaign mailed requests for money to a list of approximately 7,500 regular contributors. Four to six times each year the campaign also mailed "prospecting" letters in an effort to expand its regular donor base. Dornan paid Response Dynamics of Alexandria, Va., $967,650 for list rental, production, postage, and caging services. Robin Dornan Griffin, Dornan's daughter and chief creative consultant on the direct-mail program, said the average contribution was $11.50.

Griffin said she focused much of her attention on crafting the monthly mailings to the campaign's big-ticket donors, approximately 400 people who had donated a minimum of $500 to Dornan's past campaigns. Griffin also orchestrated the infrequent fund-raising events, including a reception at the Capitol Hill Club in Washington, D.C. For her efforts, Griffin received $55,353.

	Dornan	
Campaign Expenditures	Amount Spent	% of Total
Overhead		
Office furniture/supplies	$ 12,333	.79
Rent/utilities	450	.03
Salaries	285	.02
Taxes	0	
Bank/investment fees	0	
Lawyers/accountants	2,100	.14
Telephone	2,006	.13
Campaign automobile	0	
Computers/office equipment	1,209	.08
Travel	21,149	1.36
Food/meetings	389	.03
Subtotal	**39,920**	**2.57**
Fund Raising		
Events	28,834	1.86
Direct mail	1,121,604	72.26
Telemarketing	900	.06
Subtotal	**1,151,338**	**74.17**
Polling	**0**	
Advertising		
Electronic media	0	
Other media	2,732	.18
Subtotal	**2,732**	**.18**
Other Campaign Activity		
Persuasion mail/brochures	269,420	17.36
Actual campaigning	38,414	2.47
Staff/volunteers	0	
Subtotal	**307,834**	**19.83**
Constituent Gifts/Entertainment	**3,432**	**.22**
Donations to		
Candidates from same state	1,000	.06
Candidates from other states	0	
Civic organizations	0	
Ideological groups	0	
Political parties	0	
Subtotal	**1,000**	**.06**
Unitemized Expenses	**46,024**	**2.96**
Total Campaign Expenses	**$ 1,552,281**	
PAC Contributions	$ 75,978	
Individual Contributions	1,331,944	
Total Receipts*	1,443,564	

*Includes PAC and individual contributions as well as interest earned, party contributions, etc.

† No expenditures or receipts on file. Candidates raising or spending less than $5,000 are not required to file reports with the Federal Election Commission.

District 47 — CALIFORNIA

Rep. C. Christopher Cox (R)

1992 Election Results

C. Christopher Cox (R)	165,004	(65%)
John F. Anwiller † (D)	76,924	(30%)
Maxine B. Quirk † (I)	12,297	(5%)

Rep. C. Christopher Cox's flirtation with a possible 1994 Senate bid was clearly evident in his 1992 fund raising. Cox had ended the 1990 campaign with debts of $61,622 and cash reserves of only $5,113. By the end of 1992, he had managed to stash away 22 percent of the more than $500,000 he raised, leaving him with a cash-on-hand total of $118,668.

One of Cox's fund-raising events pulled together two people one would not normally expect to see in the same room. Reagan-Bush speech writer Peggy Noonan and liberal journalist P. J. O'Rourke were featured speakers at a dinner at the Anaheim Marriott Hotel in October 1991, which Cox spokesman Peter M. Slen said drew more than 500 people. "Both are friends of his," noted Slen. "He worked very hard to get them here." Payments to the Marriott totaled $21,362.

Actor Charlton Heston was the star of another major fund-raiser held in October 1992 at the Hyatt Hotel in Irvine. The event drew more than 1,000 supporters and cost the Cox campaign nearly $25,000, including $211 for a limousine to ferry Heston to and from the event.

The campaign held twenty smaller district fundraisers, many in supporters' homes. "It's a little more personal that way," said Slen. More personal did not necessarily translate into inexpensive, however. For one of these less formal gatherings, Cox paid $3,185 to fly in Dinesh D'Souza, author of the book *Illiberal Education*.

Pitted against Democrat John F. Anwiller, who spent less than $5,000, Cox had no reason to wage an extensive campaign. He spent less than 10 percent of his funds on direct appeals to voters. His only persuasion mail was a joint effort with state senator Marian Bergeson that focused on the issue of job creation. He spent just $16 on signs and $90 on research. Other than his modest mailing costs, his biggest expenses for actual campaigning were a $1,256 filing fee and a $2,000 payment to help defray the cost of a Republican party phonebank.

Overhead accounted for half of Cox's expenditures. Monthly rent on his permanent campaign headquarters in Newport Beach was $700. Salary payments to his lone staffer, campaign director Marcella McKenzie, amounted to $62,239. McKenzie also received $4,838 in commissions for her fund-raising work.

A graduate of Harvard Business School, Cox billed the campaign $60 for his dues to the "Harvard Business School of Orange County." He also was paid $8,826 in accrued interest on his 1989 loan to the campaign.

Campaign Expenditures	Cox Amount Spent	% of Total
Overhead		
Office furniture/supplies	$ 19,302	5.76
Rent/utilities	15,505	4.63
Salaries	68,747	20.51
Taxes	23,676	7.06
Bank/investment fees	9,284	2.77
Lawyers/accountants	2,350	.70
Telephone	9,555	2.85
Campaign automobile	0	
Computers/office equipment	11,823	3.53
Travel	5,028	1.50
Food/meetings	916	.27
Subtotal	**166,186**	**49.58**
Fund Raising		
Events	93,286	27.83
Direct mail	0	
Telemarketing	0	
Subtotal	**93,286**	**27.83**
Polling	**0**	
Advertising		
Electronic media	0	
Other media	0	
Subtotal	**0**	
Other Campaign Activity		
Persuasion mail/brochures	23,625	7.05
Actual campaigning	4,490	1.34
Staff/volunteers	3,657	1.09
Subtotal	**31,773**	**9.48**
Constituent Gifts/Entertainment	**7,755**	**2.31**
Donations to		
Candidates from same state	19,500	5.82
Candidates from other states	3,000	.89
Civic organizations	405	.12
Ideological groups	1,075	.32
Political parties	8,096	2.42
Subtotal	**32,076**	**9.57**
Unitemized Expenses	**4,132**	**1.23**
Total Campaign Expenses	**$ 335,208**	
PAC Contributions	**$ 155,500**	
Individual Contributions	**346,699**	
Total Receipts*	**515,754**	

*Includes PAC and individual contributions as well as interest earned, party contributions, etc.

† No expenditures or receipts on file. Candidates raising or spending less than $5,000 are not required to file reports with the Federal Election Commission.

CALIFORNIA — District 48

Rep. Ron Packard (R)

1992 Election Results

Ron Packard (R)	140,935	(61%)
Michael Farber (D)	67,415	(29%)
Donna White † (I)	13,396	(6%)

Redistricting provided Rep. Ron Packard with something he had not had since 1984—Republican primary opposition. Unlike 1990, Packard also had Democratic opposition in the general election and, as a result, his spending for the 1992 election cycle was more than double his expenditures in 1990.

Despite the fact that neither of his Republican primary opponents spent as much as $5,000, Packard invested $204,565 in his campaign during the first six months of 1992. This preprimary blitz accounted for 57 percent of his total spending for the two-year election cycle.

Packard briefly opened offices in San Clemente and Oceanside, paying $4,200 in rent. His one full-time primary campaign staffer earned $4,800. Pollster Moore Information of Portland, Ore., collected $14,648. Slate mailers cost the campaign $5,600. Another $3,500 was spent on a voter registration drive.

Most of Packard's preprimary spending was put into persuasion mail designed by Ellis-Hart Associates of Corona Del Mar. Among other things, the mailings touted Packard's opposition to off-shore oil drilling and his claim that he had never voted for a tax increase. According to consultant David Ellis, the mailings "were all positive and showed that he truly reflects his district, which is Republican, conservative, and middle-class." For their preprimary efforts, Ellis-Hart received $115,162.

In a district where registered Republicans outnumber Democrats by a margin of two to one, the general election campaign against Democrat Michael Farber, Peace and Freedom party nominee Donna White, and libertarian Ted Lowe was a relaxed affair. Packard did not need polls to tell him he would win. He did not need a campaign office from which to run. His staff costs totaled $240. Ellis-Hart was called upon to produce only a single tabloid mailer and collected just $29,927.

Seven percent of Packard's campaign spending took the form of donations to other candidates, causes, and political party organizations. He made $1,000 contributions to eleven California House candidates, including Reps. John T. Doolittle, Elton Gallegly, Frank Riggs, and Robert J. Lagomarsino. He also donated $2,000 and loaned another $4,300 of his campaign treasury to his son Scott, who successfully ran for a seat on the Vista, Calif., City Council.

To fund his campaign, Packard depended largely on political action committees (PACs). In all, 149 PACs donated a total of $191,832, accounting for 72 percent of Packard's total contributions.

Although Farber spent $64,646 on his campaign, $47,708 or nearly 74 percent of that total was invested in new computer equipment.

Campaign Expenditures	Packard Amount Spent	Packard % of Total	Farber Amount Spent	Farber % of Total
Overhead				
Office furniture/supplies	$ 8,018	2.22	$ 2,408	3.73
Rent/utilities	4,200	1.16	0	
Salaries	5,040	1.40	1,750	2.71
Taxes	5,500	1.52	0	
Bank/investment fees	0		89	.14
Lawyers/accountants	5,668	1.57	0	
Telephone	4,115	1.14	3,246	5.02
Campaign automobile	0		0	
Computers/office equipment	2,371	.66	47,708	73.80
Travel	14,488	4.02	954	1.47
Food/meetings	673	.19	615	.95
Subtotal	**50,072**	**13.88**	**56,769**	**87.82**
Fund Raising				
Events	59,734	16.56	20	.03
Direct mail	14,344	3.98	0	
Telemarketing	0		0	
Subtotal	**74,077**	**20.53**	**20**	**.03**
Polling	**14,648**	**4.06**	**0**	
Advertising				
Electronic media	0		850	1.31
Other media	652	.18	0	
Subtotal	**652**	**.18**	**850**	**1.31**
Other Campaign Activity				
Persuasion mail/brochures	176,634	48.95	750	1.16
Actual campaigning	9,916	2.75	4,850	7.50
Staff/volunteers	777	.22	7	.01
Subtotal	**187,327**	**51.92**	**5,607**	**8.67**
Constituent Gifts/Entertainment	**239**	**.07**	**0**	
Donations to				
Candidates from same state	20,000	5.54	0	
Candidates from other states	500	.14	0	
Civic organizations	3,000	.83	0	
Ideological groups	0		0	
Political parties	525	.15	350	.54
Subtotal	**24,025**	**6.66**	**350**	**.54**
Unitemized Expenses	**9,770**	**2.71**	**1,050**	**1.62**
Total Campaign Expenses	**$ 360,811**		**$ 64,646**	
PAC Contributions	$ 191,832		$ 500	
Individual Contributions	72,591		10,099	
Total Receipts*	292,021		66,495	

* *Includes PAC and individual contributions as well as interest earned, party contributions, etc.*

† *No expenditures or receipts on file. Candidates raising or spending less than $5,000 are not required to file reports with the Federal Election Commission.*

District 49 — CALIFORNIA

Rep. Lynn Schenk (D)

1992 Election Results

Lynn Schenk (D)	127,280	(51%)
Judy Jarvis (R)	106,170	(43%)

The contest between San Diego Port Commissioner Lynn Schenk and registered nurse Judy Jarvis was one of only five House races in which the Democratic and Republican nominees were both women. Unlike many races where the abortion issue distanced the opponents, both women took strong pro-choice stands. In the end, money may well have been the deciding factor.

Schenk had extensive experience in state Democratic politics and fund raising, and it showed. She covered the country, holding events in New York, Florida, Texas, and Washington, D.C. She traveled to Los Angeles in search of Hollywood's monetary blessing. EMILY's List provided $8,089 in fund-raising assistance. Political action committees donated more than $300,000 to her campaign, and individual contributions of $200 or more added $480,621.

With the fruit of these fund-raising labors, Schenk went shopping. She brought in the Campaign Group of Philadelphia, Pa., and paid them $470,292 to develop and place her broadcast advertising. She paid Roger Lee & Carol Beddo Associates of San Jose $80,699 for developing her preprimary persuasion mail effort. San Francisco-based Campaign Performance Group received $97,006 to develop the general election mailings.

Robbed of any advantage on the abortion issue, pollster Fairbank, Bregman & Maullin of San Francisco needed to find another effective wedge. After testing a number of themes, Schenk's advisers settled on taxes.

According to Richard M. Schlackman, president of Campaign Performance, the Schenk campaign began rolling out its negative mail three weeks prior to the election. The first piece attacked Jarvis's plan for a national sales tax and pointed out that her business, the California Nurses Bureau, had been suspended by the California Franchise Tax Board for failure to pay taxes and had been hit twice by federal tax liens. A second piece on the tax theme made these same points and sought to make certain that people did not mistakenly connect Jarvis with Howard Jarvis, a long-time antitax crusader in California. "We played the Republican's own tax game on her," noted Schlackman.

Chief of staff Laurie J. Black said the Campaign Group developed three television ads for the primary and another three for the general election campaign. Nearly $286,000 of the money paid to the Campaign Group was for work in the fall contest.

Outspent on advertising by roughly seven to one in the general election, Jarvis simply lacked the resources to pull out a win in this marginally Republican district.

Campaign Expenditures	Schenk Amount Spent	Schenk % of Total	Jarvis Amount Spent	Jarvis % of Total
Overhead				
Office furniture/supplies	$ 11,507	1.03	$ 7,195	1.91
Rent/utilities	13,320	1.19	6,342	1.68
Salaries	117,529	10.47	28,653	7.60
Taxes	9,911	.88	5,282	1.40
Bank/investment fees	98	.01	2,982	.79
Lawyers/accountants	9,023	.80	17,760	4.71
Telephone	15,738	1.40	9,132	2.42
Campaign automobile	0		0	
Computers/office equipment	13,554	1.21	10,982	2.91
Travel	11,765	1.05	4,833	1.28
Food/meetings	0		0	
Subtotal	**202,448**	**18.04**	**93,161**	**24.71**
Fund Raising				
Events	39,985	3.56	25,823	6.85
Direct mail	11,580	1.03	1,039	.28
Telemarketing	0		208	.06
Subtotal	**51,565**	**4.59**	**27,071**	**7.18**
Polling	**35,600**	**3.17**	**6,604**	**1.75**
Advertising				
Electronic media	470,292	41.90	40,973	10.87
Other media	3,382	.30	1,842	.49
Subtotal	**473,674**	**42.20**	**42,815**	**11.36**
Other Campaign Activity				
Persuasion mail/brochures	243,352	21.68	160,345	42.53
Actual campaigning	92,810	8.27	41,657	11.05
Staff/volunteers	2,054	.18	0	
Subtotal	**338,216**	**30.13**	**202,003**	**53.58**
Constituent Gifts/ Entertainment	227	.02	0	
Donations to				
Candidates from same state	250	.02	0	
Candidates from other states	0		0	
Civic organizations	1,000	.09	0	
Ideological groups	1,300	.12	0	
Political parties	7,550	.67	0	
Subtotal	**10,100**	**.90**	**0**	
Unitemized Expenses	10,674	.95	5,337	1.42
Total Campaign Expenses	$ 1,122,504		$ 376,990	
PAC Contributions	$ 300,129		$ 149,993	
Individual Contributions	653,104		87,799	
Total Receipts*	1,154,531		433,861	

*Includes PAC and individual contributions as well as interest earned, party contributions, etc.

CALIFORNIA — District 50

Rep. Bob Filner (D)

1992 Election Results

Bob Filner (D)	77,293	(57%)
Tony Valencia (R)	39,531	(29%)
Barbara Hutchinson (I)	15,489	(11%)

Once the District 50 boundaries were established, it seemed almost certain that the winner of the Democratic primary would move on to Washington. Former Rep. Jim Bates, who had lost his seat to Rep. Randy "Duke" Cunningham in 1990, was considered the front-runner, followed by state senator Wadie P. Deddeh. Early prognostications had city council member Bob Filner finishing third. So much for early prognostications.

Filner hired Roger Lee & Carol Beddo Associates of San Jose to provide general campaign strategy and to design the campaign's persuasion mail. Campaign Group of Philadelphia, Pa., designed, produced, and placed television commercials. Fairbank, Bregman & Maullin of San Francisco conducted polls, and Big Sky Consulting of Washington, D.C., provided opposition research. Telemark of Wilsonville, Ore., ran the campaign's phonebanks.

Three television ads were produced for Filner for the primary. Aired predominantly on local network affiliates over the final four weeks of the campaign, one ad focused on job creation and the economy while the other two attacked his opponents.

Bates was among the leaders in overdrafts at the House bank. When this was coupled with his 1989 rebuke by the House Ethics Committee on sexual harassment charges, his campaign sank. Filner said his preprimary attack ads centered on Deddeh, criticizing him for accepting more than $800,000 in special-interest campaign contributions during his previous seven years in the state senate, for being delinquent in paying property taxes owed by land-development companies in which he had an interest, and for accepting more than $50,000 in free trips and other gifts from lobbyists. The Campaign Group received $151,026 for their efforts in the primary.

Lee & Beddo produced five persuasion mail pieces for the primary, each of which was targeted to approximately 15,000 households. While it was clear that Bates's campaign was floundering, Filner's mail took the opportunity to remind voters of Bates's various scandals.

Filner received 26 percent of the votes in the six-candidate primary, defeating Deddeh by 1,086 votes.

In the general election, Tony Valencia offered little competition. However, afraid that in the "year of the woman" libertarian Barbara Hutchinson might run well enough to cause him problems, Filner devoted one of his two TV commercials to attacking what he described as her "strange" beliefs.

Filner ultimately funneled $546,316 of his spending through consultants, including payments of $313,104 to the Campaign Group; $150,165 to Lee & Beddo; $42,332 to Fairbank, Bregman; $32,229 to Telemark; and $6,736 to Big Sky Consulting.

	Filner		Valencia	
Campaign Expenditures	Amount Spent	% of Total	Amount Spent	% of Total
Overhead				
Office furniture/supplies	$ 12,984	1.54	$ 1,208	1.48
Rent/utilities	17,230	2.04	933	1.14
Salaries	124,414	14.71	2,000	2.45
Taxes	0		0	
Bank/investment fees	7,727	.91	0	
Lawyers/accountants	0		0	
Telephone	16,986	2.01	0	
Campaign automobile	0		0	
Computers/office equipment	9,060	1.07	0	
Travel	5,111	.60	5,844	7.17
Food/meetings	801	.09	250	.31
Subtotal	**194,313**	**22.97**	**10,236**	**12.55**
Fund Raising				
Events	7,706	.91	731	.90
Direct mail	8,582	1.01	0	
Telemarketing	0		0	
Subtotal	**16,288**	**1.93**	**731**	**.90**
Polling	**42,332**	**5.01**	**1,350**	**1.66**
Advertising				
Electronic media	313,434	37.06	2,023	2.48
Other media	6,542	.77	7,690	9.43
Subtotal	**319,976**	**37.83**	**9,713**	**11.91**
Other Campaign Activity				
Persuasion mail/brochures	178,773	21.14	0	
Actual campaigning	82,911	9.80	3,642	4.47
Staff/volunteers	0		0	
Subtotal	**261,684**	**30.94**	**3,642**	**4.47**
Constituent Gifts/ Entertainment	**1,596**	**.19**	**0**	
Donations to				
Candidates from same state	0		0	
Candidates from other states	0		0	
Civic organizations	0		32	.04
Ideological groups	300	.04	60	.07
Political parties	0		0	
Subtotal	**300**	**.04**	**92**	**.11**
Unitemized Expenses	**9,286**	**1.10**	**55,797**	**68.41**
Total Campaign Expenses	**$ 845,774**		**$ 81,561**	
PAC Contributions	$ 267,797		$ 0	
Individual Contributions	409,855		58,210	
Total Receipts*	856,869		63,504	

*Includes PAC and individual contributions as well as interest earned, party contributions, etc.

District 51 — CALIFORNIA

Rep. Randy "Duke" Cunningham (R)

1992 Election Results
Randy "Duke" Cunningham (R) 141,890 (56%)
Bea Herbert (D) 85,148 (34%)

Rep. Randy "Duke" Cunningham was only eleven months into his first term when California's redistricting plan was unveiled, presenting him with the unpleasant option of remaining in a district that had become more Democratic or running in a district where he would be forced to take on fellow Republican Rep. Bill Lowery. Despite the fact that Lowery had represented about 40 percent of the new District 51 while he had represented none of it, Cunningham decided fratricide provided his best chance for returning to Washington for a second term.

Having finished the 1990 election cycle with cash reserves of only $5,554, Cunningham spent $122,069 in 1991 to raise just $241,062, a return of slightly less than $2 for each dollar invested. At the time he chose to take on Lowery in what would clearly have been an expensive race, Cunningham had cash reserves of $76,000, so his first concern was money.

During the first three months of 1992, Cunningham raised $155,948, including $135,368 from individual contributors. A benefit concert by country-western star Johnny Cash drew 1,000 supporters who paid $25 each for an evening's entertainment. Former test pilot Chuck Yeager was the attraction at a $200-per-couple dinner attended by more than 400 couples.

Cunningham also moved quickly to assemble his team of campaign strategists. Pollster Arthur J. Finkelstein & Associates of New York was the first to join in January 1992. The campaign office in Glendale opened in February, and that same month Cunningham hired Russo, Marsh & Associates of Sacramento as his general strategist and media consultant. Payments to CMT Advertising of San Diego for radio buys began in March.

Russo, Marsh produced three 30-second television commercials, including a constituent testimonial and an endorsement by Yeager. Four of the five radio spots focused on Cunningham's positives; one hit Lowery for his vote in favor of the 1990 budget agreement, among other things.

For work in the primary, Russo, Marsh collected $47,963; Finkelstein, $29,850; CMT Advertising, $17,143; and Campaign Telecommunications of New York, $14,880 for phonebanking. However, all of this preparation proved unnecessary when on April 14, less than two months before the primary, Lowery announced his intention to retire and pulled out of the race.

In this overwhelmingly Republican district, Cunningham needed none of his high-priced consultants for his general election contest with accountant Bea Herbert. The underfunded Democrat never opened a campaign office and spent less than $3,000 on advertising.

Campaign Expenditures	Cunningham Amount Spent	Cunningham % of Total	Herbert Amount Spent	Herbert % of Total
Overhead				
Office furniture/supplies	$ 27,122	3.21	$ 2,560	10.98
Rent/utilities	12,253	1.45	0	
Salaries	19,929	2.36	895	3.84
Taxes	3,974	.47	0	
Bank/investment fees	589	.07	0	
Lawyers/accountants	2,684	.32	0	
Telephone	17,796	2.11	908	3.89
Campaign automobile	0		0	
Computers/office equipment	13,242	1.57	0	
Travel	25,013	2.96	1,254	5.38
Food/meetings	3,222	.38	0	
Subtotal	**125,824**	**14.91**	**5,617**	**24.09**
Fund Raising				
Events	161,944	19.19	667	2.86
Direct mail	273,308	32.39	0	
Telemarketing	0		0	
Subtotal	**435,252**	**51.57**	**667**	**2.86**
Polling	**29,850**	**3.54**	**0**	
Advertising				
Electronic media	93,992	11.14	2,600	11.15
Other media	12,145	1.44	314	1.35
Subtotal	**106,137**	**12.58**	**2,914**	**12.50**
Other Campaign Activity				
Persuasion mail/brochures	94,340	11.18	8,028	34.43
Actual campaigning	40,284	4.77	3,219	13.81
Staff/volunteers	0		444	1.90
Subtotal	**134,625**	**15.95**	**11,691**	**50.14**
Constituent Gifts/ Entertainment	**4,596**	**.54**	**0**	
Donations to				
Candidates from same state	1,000	.12	0	
Candidates from other states	0		0	
Civic organizations	2,255	.27	96	.41
Ideological groups	2,557	.30	0	
Political parties	578	.07	215	.92
Subtotal	**6,390**	**.76**	**311**	**1.33**
Unitemized Expenses	**1,248**	**.15**	**2,115**	**9.07**
Total Campaign Expenses	**$ 843,921**		**$ 23,315**	
PAC Contributions	$ 283,367		$ 949	
Individual Contributions	648,157		15,575	
Total Receipts*	967,013		23,315	

*Includes PAC and individual contributions as well as interest earned, party contributions, etc.

CALIFORNIA — District 52

Rep. Duncan Hunter (R)

1992 Election Results

Duncan Hunter (R)	112,995	(53%)
Janet M. Gastil (D)	88,076	(41%)

Rep. Duncan Hunter spent nearly half of his $558,577 campaign treasury on direct appeals to voters in 1992, a nearly 180-degree reversal of his 1990 campaign tactics, when he devoted most of his time and resources to electing fellow Republican Rep. Randy "Duke" Cunningham.

"Whenever money came in, we found a place to advertise," said campaign manager Valarie Snesko. Prior to the primary, Hunter spent $17,990 on broadcast advertising. Then, in the weeks leading up to the November general election against Janet M. Gastil, Hunter spent $51,763 to show a series of television commercials on local network affiliates, $46,154 to air the campaign's three radio spots, $4,250 for time on local cable television outlets, and $12,605 for newspaper ads. The campaign also spent $6,020 for copies of a campaign video, which were passed out by volunteers walking selected neighborhoods. Total advertising costs in 1990 were only $9,531.

According to Snesko, the theme running through all the ads was the same—jobs and, more particularly, that "buying American will keep jobs in America." One of the radio spots was a testimonial, with constituents reciting what Hunter had done to keep jobs in the district.

While it was not his principal means of communicating with voters, Hunter spent nearly twice as much in 1992 as he had in 1990 on brochures and persuasion mail.

Virtually none of this increased spending ended up in the pockets of consultants. Arthur J. Finkelstein & Associates of New York received $2,000 for general campaign advice. CMT Advertising of San Diego picked up $3,000 for advice on the media effort. His only fund-raising consultant, Dan Morgan & Associates of Arlington, Va., received $7,693. Campaign Telecommunications of New York received $20,000 for phonebanking. "He's never had lots of professional consultants," noted district chief of staff Wendell Cutting. "He doesn't believe in them."

Not all of Hunter's expenses were directly tied to wooing voters. He charged his $100 House Gym dues to the campaign in March 1991. He spent $8,238 of his campaign treasury on constituent meals and $5,791 on year-end holiday cards. Gifts for constituents totaled $4,855. Plaques and the framing of certificates to commemorate special events added another $1,158. Two Christmas parties cost the campaign $2,531. Hunter also spent $543 for tickets to Sea World, which were given to lucky constituents. Flowers for constituents cost $1,464.

Gastil ran her campaign out of her house until July 1992. This frugality allowed her to spend $79,250 on broadcast advertising, $6,936 on newspaper and journal ads, and $3,934 on billboards.

	Hunter		Gastil	
Campaign Expenditures	Amount Spent	% of Total	Amount Spent	% of Total
Overhead				
Office furniture/supplies	$ 26,774	4.79	$ 5,900	3.97
Rent/utilities	9,872	1.77	2,659	1.79
Salaries	66,271	11.86	5,475	3.68
Taxes	1,905	.34	627	.42
Bank/investment fees	94	.02	304	.20
Lawyers/accountants	2,500	.45	950	.64
Telephone	20,899	3.74	3,307	2.23
Campaign automobile	0		0	
Computers/office equipment	6,991	1.25	577	.39
Travel	31,590	5.66	1,483	1.00
Food/meetings	1,532	.27	9	.01
Subtotal	**168,429**	**30.15**	**21,291**	**14.33**
Fund Raising				
Events	79,637	14.26	725	.49
Direct mail	0		2,006	1.35
Telemarketing	0		0	
Subtotal	**79,637**	**14.26**	**2,731**	**1.84**
Polling	**0**		**2,500**	**1.68**
Advertising				
Electronic media	129,316	23.15	79,250	53.33
Other media	20,065	3.59	10,869	7.31
Subtotal	**149,382**	**26.74**	**90,119**	**60.64**
Other Campaign Activity				
Persuasion mail/brochures	37,681	6.75	14,890	10.02
Actual campaigning	67,233	12.04	14,898	10.02
Staff/volunteers	2,571	.46	347	.23
Subtotal	**107,485**	**19.24**	**30,135**	**20.28**
Constituent Gifts/Entertainment	**24,649**	**4.41**	**0**	
Donations to				
Candidates from same state	5,384	.96	0	
Candidates from other states	3,935	.70	0	
Civic organizations	5,300	.95	0	
Ideological groups	1,078	.19	0	
Political parties	385	.07	0	
Subtotal	**16,082**	**2.88**	**0**	
Unitemized Expenses	**12,912**	**2.31**	**1,838**	**1.24**
Total Campaign Expenses	**$ 558,577**		**$ 148,615**	
PAC Contributions	$ 201,107		$ 41,535	
Individual Contributions	248,593		78,451	
Total Receipts*	561,203		161,428	

*Includes PAC and individual contributions as well as interest earned, party contributions, etc.

District 1 — COLORADO

Rep. Patricia Schroeder (D)

1992 Election Results

Patricia Schroeder (D)   155,629   (69%)
Raymond Diaz Aragon † (R)   70,902   (31%)

Rep. Patricia Schroeder spent nearly $173,000 less in her 1992 campaign on direct-mail fund raising than she had in the 1990 election cycle. As a result, her overall spending dropped by nearly $120,000 despite the fact that she marginally increased her spending on overhead, persuasion mail, and donations to candidates and causes.

Redistricting added new suburban voters to Schroeder's constituency, a change that prompted her to alter her communication strategy. While she had relied almost exclusively on broadcast advertising in 1990, she abandoned it altogether in 1992. "We had to introduce Pat to a lot of new voters and that was done best through the newspaper and the mail," noted campaign accountant Max Snead.

Bachurski Associates of Washington, D.C., was paid $4,105 to develop a modest persuasion mail campaign. Snead said the campaign sent out three 40,000-piece mailings to increase Schroeder's visibility in the newly enlarged district, as well as one smaller mailing shortly before the general election.

Schroeder purchased newspaper ads throughout the election cycle, spending $3,593 in 1991 and another $16,645 in 1992. To target specific constituencies, Schroeder's campaign placed many of the ads in smaller publications such as the *Intermountain Jewish News, La Voz,* the *Colorado Labor Advocate,* and the *Urban Spectrum.*

Journal and program advertisements, which were as much contributions to causes as they were ads in support of her reelection, cost Schroeder's campaign $3,028. She purchased space from the Colorado AIDS Project, the Family Resource Guide, and the Denver Black Arts Festival, among others.

With Republican Raymond Diaz Aragon investing less than $5,000 in his perfunctory challenge, Schroeder chose to invest little in traditional grassroots campaigning. To get the general election campaign off the ground, she paid Snead $500 to rent space in his office during August and September. In October she invested $4,000 to rent a large office in Denver, which was closed immediately after the election. She spent $8,045 on signs, $4,006 on collateral material such as bumper stickers and buttons, and $3,003 on T-shirts. She gave $5,000 to the Denver Democratic party for sample ballots and spent $8,715 to have additional sample ballots printed.

Without the need to campaign intensely, there was plenty of room in the budget for other things. Schroeder donated $58,877 of her campaign funds to other candidates, causes, and party organizations, a 43 percent increase over 1990. Holiday cards cost the campaign $16,573. Tortilla Coast, a restaurant in Washington, D.C., was paid $277 for catering what Snead said was "just a party."

Campaign Expenditures	Schroeder Amount Spent	% of Total
Overhead		
Office furniture/supplies	$ 10,223	2.57
Rent/utilities	4,804	1.21
Salaries	35,869	9.01
Taxes	29,215	7.33
Bank/investment fees	368	.09
Lawyers/accountants	36,186	9.08
Telephone	3,150	.79
Campaign automobile	0	
Computers/office equipment	2,273	.57
Travel	19,151	4.81
Food/meetings	7,514	1.89
Subtotal	148,752	37.35
Fund Raising		
Events	53,098	13.33
Direct mail	23,749	5.96
Telemarketing	0	
Subtotal	76,847	19.29
Polling	0	
Advertising		
Electronic media	0	
Other media	24,746	6.21
Subtotal	24,746	6.21
Other Campaign Activity		
Persuasion mail/brochures	27,769	6.97
Actual campaigning	34,561	8.68
Staff/volunteers	0	
Subtotal	62,330	15.65
Constituent Gifts/Entertainment	16,895	4.24
Donations to		
Candidates from same state	5,500	1.38
Candidates from other states	26,478	6.65
Civic organizations	4,749	1.19
Ideological groups	2,115	.53
Political parties	20,035	5.03
Subtotal	58,877	14.78
Unitemized Expenses	9,864	2.48
Total Campaign Expenses	$ 398,310	
PAC Contributions	$ 134,147	
Individual Contributions	165,452	
Total Receipts*	361,845	

*Includes PAC and individual contributions as well as interest earned, party contributions, etc.

† No expenditures or receipts on file. Candidates raising or spending less than $5,000 are not required to file reports with the Federal Election Commission.

COLORADO   District 2

Rep. David E. Skaggs (D)

1992 Election Results

David E. Skaggs (D)	164,790	(61%)
Bryan Day (R)	88,470	(33%)
Vern Tharp † (I)	18,101	(7%)

In keeping with his 1990 pledge to hold down campaign spending, Rep. David E. Skaggs spent only $68,315 to run his permanent campaign in 1991. With additional expenditures of roughly $140,000 through the first seven months of 1992, Skaggs looked as though he might bring his spending for the entire cycle in well under $400,000.

However, that was before it was revealed that Skaggs had fifty-seven overdrafts at the House bank and before he found himself facing Republican Bryan Day, a southern Baptist minister with strong backing from the National Republican Congressional Committee (NRCC) and the evangelical Christian Coalition. Together, these two developments led Skaggs to spend more than $470,000 over the final months of the campaign. He committed approximately $350,000 to the effort in October alone.

As he had since his initial House race in 1986, Skaggs turned to John Franzen Multimedia of Washington, D.C., for his broadcast advertising. The centerpiece of the television campaign was a commercial dubbed "Where They Stand," which juxtaposed Skaggs's pro-choice stance on abortion with Day's antiabortion position. On tax policy, the ad also portrayed Day as a friend of the rich, with Skaggs cast in the role of champion of the middle class. "We made Day the issue in that campaign," noted Franzen.

A retooled ad dating back to 1988 touted the fact that Skaggs spends three days each week in the district while maintaining a 99 percent attendance record for House votes. As in past campaigns, Franzen also wanted to make use of the fact that Skaggs always donated his congressional pay raise to local charities, but his old ad simply would not work anymore.

"The old spot had a picture of him sitting at a desk writing a check and a voice-over talking about what he'd done for local charities with his pay raise," said Franzen. However, with Skaggs's overdrafts at the House bank, the campaign was reluctant to show any picture on television of Skaggs writing a check. Franzen reshot the commercial with a woman talking about how his pay-raise contributions had helped a community health clinic where she worked.

In all, Franzen developed four 30-second television commercials that aired with increasing regularity over the final three weeks of the campaign. Franzen also developed three 60-second radio spots, which aired a total of seventy-one times during the second week of October. Franzen billed the campaign $278,326, including nearly $217,000 for air time. Expenditures for the media campaign accounted for 41 percent of the incumbent's total spending.

In addition to the $113,732 spent by Day's campaign, the NRCC spent $52,601 on the race.

Campaign Expenditures	Skaggs Amount Spent	% of Total	Day Amount Spent	% of Total
Overhead				
Office furniture/supplies	$ 12,757	1.89	$ 4,938	4.34
Rent/utilities	9,395	1.39	2,081	1.83
Salaries	93,409	13.81	27,825	24.47
Taxes	33,950	5.02	490	.43
Bank/investment fees	894	.13	0	
Lawyers/accountants	15,192	2.25	0	
Telephone	15,010	2.22	4,545	4.00
Campaign automobile	0		0	
Computers/office equipment	9,574	1.42	3,036	2.67
Travel	22,151	3.27	1,535	1.35
Food/meetings	1,238	.18	0	
Subtotal	**213,572**	**31.57**	**44,449**	**39.08**
Fund Raising				
Events	50,188	7.42	4,191	3.68
Direct mail	30,686	4.54	0	
Telemarketing	0		0	
Subtotal	**80,873**	**11.95**	**4,191**	**3.68**
Polling	**23,268**	**3.44**	**1,970**	**1.73**
Advertising				
Electronic media	279,356	41.29	9,208	8.10
Other media	767	.11	24,257	21.33
Subtotal	**280,123**	**41.40**	**33,466**	**29.43**
Other Campaign Activity				
Persuasion mail/brochures	24,443	3.61	9,245	8.13
Actual campaigning	30,542	4.51	2,722	2.39
Staff/volunteers	1,785	.26	132	.12
Subtotal	**56,770**	**8.39**	**12,099**	**10.64**
Constituent Gifts/ Entertainment	**5,103**	**.75**	**0**	
Donations to				
Candidates from same state	0		0	
Candidates from other states	2,750	.41	0	
Civic organizations	176	.03	0	
Ideological groups	0		0	
Political parties	3,139	.46	300	.26
Subtotal	**6,066**	**.90**	**300**	**.26**
Unitemized Expenses	**10,789**	**1.59**	**17,257**	**15.17**
Total Campaign Expenses	**$ 676,563**		**$ 113,732**	
PAC Contributions	**$ 316,637**		**$ 2,225**	
Individual Contributions	**325,534**		**80,366**	
Total Receipts*	**659,719**		**93,846**	

*Includes PAC and individual contributions as well as interest earned, party contributions, etc.

†No expenditures or receipts on file. Candidates raising or spending less than $5,000 are not required to file reports with the Federal Election Commission.

District 3 — COLORADO

Rep. Scott McInnis (R)

1992 Election Results

Scott McInnis (R)	143,293	(55%)
Mike Callihan (D)	114,480	(44%)

State representative Scott McInnis spent $89,453 more than Lt. Gov. Mike Callihan, two-thirds of which was funneled into advertising and other forms of direct voter contact. This 26 percent overall spending differential might well have been enough to give McInnis the victory, but it does not begin to tell the story of this race.

The American Medical Association (AMA) spent $184,910 on his behalf, $102,800 of which was poured into an independent television advertising campaign designed by Sandler-Innocenzi of Washington, D.C. The AMA also paid John Maddox & Associates of Alexandria, Va., $43,690 for persuasion mail and $22,920 for phonebanking in support of McInnis. Public Opinion Strategies of Alexandria, Va., collected $15,500 from the AMA for polling.

The National Republican Congressional Committee invested $55,000 to support McInnis's advertising effort and another $2,500 to pay some of his polling expenses. The National Rifle Association and the National Federation of Independent Business also ran campaigns in support of McInnis totaling $12,393 and $899, respectively.

Callihan received $4,255 in independent help from the AFL-CIO and $10,522 in coordinated support from the Democratic Congressional Campaign Committee. What looks like a spending gap of less than $90,000 was actually a differential of $330,378.

McInnis pumped 36 percent of his campaign treasury into advertising, most of which was invested in three television and three radio commercials designed by Mike Murphy Media of Washington, D.C. Murphy received $132,657 for designing and placing the ads, $99,215 in October alone.

To spread his message, McInnis spent $13,574 for newspaper ads, $2,799 for car-toppers, and $2,380 for billboards. The campaign mailed four persuasion pieces—a general biographical piece, one focusing on McInnis's tenure in the state legislature, and mailings that touted his views on economic revival and water rights. Perhaps his most innovative approach was to put a "McInnis for Congress" message at the end of a telephone dial-in time-and-temperature report.

Overhead accounted for more than one-third of McInnis's expenses. In June 1992 he opened offices in Grand Junction and Pueblo, which cost the campaign a total of $850 each month. By election day eight people were on payroll. Campaign manager Nancy Hopper collected $18,800, including a $4,000 bonus. Stephannie Finley, now on McInnis's congressional staff, made $20,019, including her $4,000 bonus.

McInnis paid pollster Hill Research Consultants of Woodlands, Texas, $28,175. Patricia Price of Littleton received $22,850 for fund raising. Katy Atkinson collected $2,615 for providing strategic advice.

Campaign Expenditures	McInnis Amount Spent	McInnis % of Total	Callihan Amount Spent	Callihan % of Total
Overhead				
Office furniture/supplies	$ 13,704	3.16	$ 9,103	2.64
Rent/utilities	4,735	1.09	3,217	.93
Salaries	67,893	15.64	55,614	16.13
Taxes	18,968	4.37	19,333	5.61
Bank/investment fees	349	.08	345	.10
Lawyers/accountants	0		849	.25
Telephone	14,335	3.30	18,144	5.26
Campaign automobile	3,967	.91	0	
Computers/office equipment	2,648	.61	4,915	1.43
Travel	24,699	5.69	30,718	8.91
Food/meetings	811	.19	22	.01
Subtotal	**152,108**	**35.03**	**142,259**	**41.26**
Fund Raising				
Events	26,756	6.16	24,093	6.99
Direct mail	4,389	1.01	3,614	1.05
Telemarketing	0		0	
Subtotal	**31,145**	**7.17**	**27,707**	**8.04**
Polling	**28,175**	**6.49**	**15,852**	**4.60**
Advertising				
Electronic media	135,156	31.13	108,543	31.48
Other media	21,245	4.89	874	.25
Subtotal	**156,401**	**36.02**	**109,417**	**31.74**
Other Campaign Activity				
Persuasion mail/brochures	36,862	8.49	26,464	7.68
Actual campaigning	23,209	5.35	21,873	6.34
Staff/volunteers	2,495	.57	0	
Subtotal	**62,566**	**14.41**	**48,337**	**14.02**
Constituent Gifts/ Entertainment	**580**	**.13**	**31**	**.01**
Donations to				
Candidates from same state	750	.17	135	.04
Candidates from other states	0		0	
Civic organizations	78	.02	198	.06
Ideological groups	0		0	
Political parties	55	.01	77	.02
Subtotal	**883**	**.20**	**410**	**.12**
Unitemized Expenses	**2,346**	**.54**	**738**	**.21**
Total Campaign Expenses	**$ 434,203**		**$ 344,750**	
PAC Contributions	$ 144,614		$ 191,600	
Individual Contributions	270,305		99,234	
Total Receipts*	438,090		353,489	

*Includes PAC and individual contributions as well as interest earned, party contributions, etc.

COLORADO   District 4

Rep. Wayne Allard (R)   *1992 Election Results*   Wayne Allard (R)   139,884   (58%)
                                                              Tom Redder (D)   101,957   (42%)

Freshman Rep. Wayne Allard opted to run an extremely low-level permanent campaign in 1991. Monthly rent on his Ft. Collins campaign office was $275. The average monthly telephone bills totaled only $78, with charges for the campaign's cellular telephone accounting for roughly one-quarter of that amount. Allard's wife Judith served as one of the campaign's two part-time employees, drawing salary payments of $3,076. The second part-timer collected $3,125 for sporadic campaign work. Total off-year overhead expenses amounted to $15,415.

With cash reserves of only $3,428 at the start of 1991, Allard concentrated much of his off-year efforts on raising money. Here again, frugality was the watchword. Allard spent $2,559 to stage three events at the Capitol Hill Club, all without a fund-raising consultant. These events pushed his 1991 contributions from political action committees to $56,300, accounting for 60 percent of his off-year donations.

With no primary opposition, Allard continued to husband his resources in the first six months of 1992. Of the $55,513 he spent during this phase of the campaign, $13,318 was paid to Doug Benevento, legislative director on Allard's congressional staff. Benevento received a $6,000 lump-sum payment in January and in May began drawing a monthly campaign salary of $3,659.

However, once the general election contest against well-funded Democratic state representative Tom Redder began in earnest, Allard poured money into his campaign. Over the final six months of 1992, Allard spent $363,444, or 80 percent of his total outlays for the two-year election cycle. Allard spent $240,894 in October alone.

Nearly half of Allard's spending for the two-year cycle and 52 percent of his spending for 1992 was put into an advertising campaign developed by the Colorado Media Group of Englewood and Walt Klein & Associates of Winston-Salem, N.C. According to administrative assistant Roy Palmer, the campaign aired four television and six radio spots, including one ad juxtaposing Redder's legal background with Allard's experience as the owner of a small business. Colorado Media received $213,000 for creating and placing the ads. Walt Klein was paid $4,200 for his creative advice.

Redder countered with a $162,982 broadcast media campaign designed by Nordlinger Associates of Washington, D.C. As Nordlinger delicately phrased it, while all the ads promoted Redder's positives, "none were particularly positive on Allard." Nordlinger added that in a district where registered Republicans outnumber Democrats by roughly 22,000, Redder would have needed to spend three times as much as he did on media to pull out a victory.

Campaign Expenditures	Allard Amount Spent	Allard % of Total	Redder Amount Spent	Redder % of Total
Overhead				
Office furniture/supplies	$ 8,264	1.81	$ 10,591	2.77
Rent/utilities	7,195	1.58	1,850	.48
Salaries	30,802	6.76	62,607	16.39
Taxes	7,747	1.70	9,409	2.46
Bank/investment fees	1,299	.29	182	.05
Lawyers/accountants	1,168	.26	0	
Telephone	7,491	1.64	21,293	5.57
Campaign automobile	0		0	
Computers/office equipment	4,488	.98	1,671	.44
Travel	7,619	1.67	5,008	1.31
Food/meetings	1,062	.23	1,304	.34
Subtotal	**77,135**	**16.93**	**113,914**	**29.82**
Fund Raising				
Events	52,505	11.52	23,095	6.05
Direct mail	15,470	3.39	30,938	8.10
Telemarketing	0		0	
Subtotal	**67,975**	**14.92**	**54,033**	**14.15**
Polling	**14,725**	**3.23**	**8,796**	**2.30**
Advertising				
Electronic media	217,200	47.66	162,982	42.67
Other media	5,467	1.20	1,497	.39
Subtotal	**222,667**	**48.86**	**164,478**	**43.06**
Other Campaign Activity				
Persuasion mail/brochures	59,298	13.01	216	.06
Actual campaigning	7,036	1.54	33,593	8.79
Staff/volunteers	0		264	.07
Subtotal	**66,334**	**14.56**	**34,072**	**8.92**
Constituent Gifts/Entertainment	**96**	**.02**	**0**	
Donations to				
Candidates from same state	500	.11	450	.12
Candidates from other states	0		0	
Civic organizations	0		50	.01
Ideological groups	0		0	
Political parties	1,000	.22	25	.01
Subtotal	**1,500**	**.33**	**525**	**.14**
Unitemized Expenses	**5,272**	**1.16**	**6,162**	**1.61**
Total Campaign Expenses	**$ 455,705**		**$ 381,981**	
PAC Contributions	**$ 266,115**		**$ 163,449**	
Individual Contributions	**215,894**		**160,319**	
Total Receipts*	**565,311**		**384,648**	

*Includes PAC and individual contributions as well as interest earned, party contributions, etc.

District 5 — COLORADO

Rep. Joel Hefley (R)

1992 Election Results

Joel Hefley (R)	173,096	(71%)
Charles A. Oriez (D)	62,550	(26%)

Rep. Joel Hefley had nothing to worry about in 1992. His lowest winning percentage in three previous elections had been the 66 percent he received in 1990, and redistricting had done little to change the overwhelming Republican makeup of the district. As campaign manager John W. Jackson put it, with no opposition in the primary and no significant challenge in the general election, "It didn't make sense to run a full-blown campaign."

Hefley's only voter contact mail was a picture postcard of his family with Pike's Peak in the background. Jackson said the postcard format was chosen to minimize the chance that people would simply toss it into the garbage. The campaign also produced one brochure, which was distributed at campaign events and handed out to people who ventured by the campaign headquarters.

As insurance, the campaign developed two television and six radio commercials, which aired over the final week of the campaign. While most of these ads focused on the traditional incumbent theme of constituent service, one television spot designed to distinguish Hefley from the average politician was decidedly different. The ad opened with a man silhouetted against the dawn sky, playing a harmonica. As the sun rose, it became apparent the man was Hefley.

Overhead accounted for nearly half of Hefley's modest campaign spending. At a cost of only $29,350, his off-year effort was subsistence level. He had no office until June 1992, when he began renting space from the El Paso City Republicans. Although salary payments consumed 16 percent of his budget, they totaled only $26,178. Monthly payments on his Buick LeSabre cost the campaign $330 for the first fifteen months of the election cycle; in April 1992 he began leasing a new car for $390 per month.

With the help of Tucker & Associates of Washington, D.C., which received $8,241 for its efforts, Hefley raised 78 percent of his total contributions from political action committees. Little effort was expended to collect money from district residents, who added $24,996 to Hefley's coffers.

According to Jackson, there were no district events in 1991 and perhaps as many as ten in 1992. Tickets to these small, in-home events tended to cost about $20. Individual contributions of less than $200 amounted to $13,996.

Democratic challenger Charles A. Oriez had little fund-raising success, assembling a campaign treasury of less than $15,000. He received $31,132 in assistance from the Democratic Congressional Campaign Committee for broadcast advertising and $8,352 from the Democratic National Committee for polling, but this influx of money had little impact.

	Hefley		Oriez	
Campaign Expenditures	Amount Spent	% of Total	Amount Spent	% of Total
Overhead				
Office furniture/supplies	$ 8,931	5.52	$ 1,497	10.24
Rent/utilities	1,200	.74	225	1.54
Salaries	26,178	16.19	1,350	9.24
Taxes	3,910	2.42	0	
Bank/investment fees	114	.07	0	
Lawyers/accountants	5,174	3.20	0	
Telephone	4,352	2.69	3,010	20.59
Campaign automobile	12,779	7.90	0	
Computers/office equipment	2,479	1.53	0	
Travel	7,287	4.51	738	5.05
Food/meetings	1,248	.77	0	
Subtotal	73,652	45.54	6,819	46.66
Fund Raising				
Events	19,450	12.03	725	4.96
Direct mail	5,903	3.65	0	
Telemarketing	0		0	
Subtotal	25,353	15.68	725	4.96
Polling	0		0	
Advertising				
Electronic media	18,196	11.25	2,450	16.76
Other media	1,026	.63	1,043	7.14
Subtotal	19,221	11.89	3,493	23.90
Other Campaign Activity				
Persuasion mail/brochures	24,697	15.27	1,181	8.08
Actual campaigning	9,759	6.03	1,373	9.39
Staff/volunteers	751	.46	62	.42
Subtotal	35,206	21.77	2,616	17.90
Constituent Gifts/ Entertainment	3,498	2.16	0	
Donations to				
Candidates from same state	2,000	1.24	0	
Candidates from other states	0		0	
Civic organizations	163	.10	10	.07
Ideological groups	0		0	
Political parties	1,396	.86	17	.12
Subtotal	3,559	2.20	27	.18
Unitemized Expenses	1,233	.76	936	6.40
Total Campaign Expenses	$ 161,723		$ 14,615	
PAC Contributions	$ 99,515		$ 2,310	
Individual Contributions	27,196		10,832	
Total Receipts*	137,757		14,817	

*Includes PAC and individual contributions as well as interest earned, party contributions, etc.

COLORADO   District 6

Rep. Dan Schaefer (R)   *1992 Election Results*   Dan Schaefer (R)   142,021   (61%)
                                                                Tom Kolbe (D)   91,073   (39%)

Rep. Dan Schaefer spent less than 10 percent of his $351,901 campaign treasury on advertising and persuasion mail. Combined expenditures for these direct appeals to voters amounted to less than Schaefer's payments to his accountant. Payments to lease and maintain his campaign car exceeded his advertising expenditures by $844, and the $13,431 spent on advertising was just $281 more than he invested in computers and other office equipment. In short, his 1992 effort was nearly a carbon copy of his 1990 campaign.

To keep his campaign running smoothly in the off-year, Schaefer spent $110,146, including $37,045 on fund raising. Despite having no office or telephone expenses and spending only $1,782 on travel, overhead totaled $43,893 during 1991.

The $11,121 the campaign spent on newspaper ads was not concentrated around the general election. The campaign spent $3,763 for ads during 1991, slightly more than the $3,690 it invested in ads during October and November 1992.

Schaefer held three fund-raisers in Washington, D.C., including a St. Patrick's Day party and a "Rocky Mountain Roundup" in 1992. Dan Morgan & Associates of Arlington, Va., received $53,750 to stage these highly successful events, which helped push political action committee contributions to $269,984—80 percent of his total contributions.

Sports played a big role in Schaefer's district fund-raising activities. Joining the frenzy over Denver's new major league baseball franchise, Schaefer invested $2,493 of his 1992 campaign treasury to buy season tickets to see the Colorado Rockies. The tickets were passed out to contributors. Each year the campaign also held an event at a minor league baseball game. The $400 in tickets for the event were donated by one of his supporters. Additional expenses for food at the games cost the campaign $329 in 1991 and $587 in 1992. Frank Layden, owner of the National Basketball Association's Utah Jazz, was the featured speaker at a June 1992 event.

Other district fund-raising efforts cost as much as they raised. An annual party was held to coincide with Schaefer's birthday. With a ticket price of $5, the monetary goal was simply to break even. Schaefer also staged five breakfasts for his "coffee club." For $19.91 in 1991 and $19.92 in 1992, members received a commemorative coffee mug and a chance to meet with Schaefer. Attendees paid for their own breakfast, but artwork, shipping, and the mugs themselves cost the campaign $1,809. Room rentals and miscellaneous facility costs added $3,229. Together, Schaefer's ten district events raised only $61,810.

Democrat Tom Kolbe spent only $9,691 on his campaign, 43 percent of which was unitemized.

	Schaefer		Kolbe	
Campaign Expenditures	Amount Spent	% of Total	Amount Spent	% of Total
Overhead				
Office furniture/supplies	$ 7,714	2.19	$ 5	.05
Rent/utilities	11,853	3.37	1,000	10.32
Salaries	22,808	6.48	0	
Taxes	9,707	2.76	0	
Bank/investment fees	615	.17	0	
Lawyers/accountants	39,577	11.25	0	
Telephone	3,621	1.03	103	1.06
Campaign automobile	14,275	4.06	0	
Computers/office equipment	13,150	3.74	0	
Travel	8,364	2.38	0	
Food/meetings	2,404	.68	0	
Subtotal	**134,088**	**38.10**	**1,108**	**11.43**
Fund Raising				
Events	89,789	25.52	422	4.36
Direct mail	0		0	
Telemarketing	0		0	
Subtotal	**89,789**	**25.52**	**422**	**4.36**
Polling	**12,000**	**3.41**	**0**	
Advertising				
Electronic media	0		400	4.13
Other media	13,431	3.82	0	
Subtotal	**13,431**	**3.82**	**400**	**4.13**
Other Campaign Activity				
Persuasion mail/brochures	21,071	5.99	2,739	28.26
Actual campaigning	23,862	6.78	876	9.04
Staff/volunteers	2,373	.67	0	
Subtotal	**47,307**	**13.44**	**3,614**	**37.30**
Constituent Gifts/ Entertainment	**7,310**	**2.08**	**0**	
Donations to				
Candidates from same state	12,937	3.68	0	
Candidates from other states	4,500	1.28	0	
Civic organizations	5,797	1.65	0	
Ideological groups	0		0	
Political parties	11,100	3.15	0	
Subtotal	**34,334**	**9.76**	**0**	
Unitemized Expenses	**13,642**	**3.88**	**4,146**	**42.79**
Total Campaign Expenses	**$ 351,901**		**$ 9,691**	
PAC Contributions	**$ 269,984**		**$ 500**	
Individual Contributions	**69,060**		**6,864**	
Total Receipts*	**357,020**		**10,316**	

*Includes PAC and individual contributions as well as interest earned, party contributions, etc.

District 1 — CONNECTICUT

Rep. Barbara B. Kennelly (D)

1992 Election Results

Barbara B. Kennelly (D)   164,735   (67%)
Philip L. Steele (R)   75,113   (31%)

Despite the fact that local radio celebrity Philip L. Steele spent only $360 more on his entire campaign than Rep. Barbara B. Kennelly paid for basic telephone service, Kennelly apparently viewed him as a viable challenger.

Instead of running the campaign out of her home and garage as she had in past elections, Kennelly opened a formal campaign headquarters in August 1992. Campaign manager David Kozak said that with seven full-time staffers and a large number of volunteers, the campaign had outgrown the house. With monthly rent of only $200, the space was a bargain. She then spent $3,264 on new computer equipment, $3,000 on a fax machine, and $2,775 for a copier.

Kennelly paid the Campaign Group of Philadelphia, Pa., $225,000 to develop and place six television commercials and one radio spot. Kozak said the television ads all focused on economic issues, such as job creation, tax relief, health care, and welfare reform. While production began in July, the entire media buy was focused between Oct. 1 and Nov. 3, when it was clear that Steele would not be a threat.

Following a custom from past elections, Kennelly also spent $29,152 to put "Kennelly for Congress" signs on one hundred buses. Newspaper ads for the fall campaign, including one that listed the names of prominent women supporting Kennelly, cost $8,420.

Campaign Performance Group of San Francisco, Calif., received $29,341 for production and mailing costs associated with the campaign's lone brochure. On the cover, the phrase "I'll always remember..." was superimposed on a picture of Kennelly sitting in a congressional hearing. Inside, pictures of Kennelly talking with veterans, visiting a retirement home, meeting with Russian President Boris Yeltsin, and attending her children's double wedding were arranged beneath the phrase "...this is my home." In addition to the payment to Campaign Performance, Kennelly spent another $12,309 on postage to mail the feel-good brochure one week before the election.

Not all of Kennelly's expenses were directed toward defeating the woefully underfunded Steele. She spent $5,000 of her campaign treasury to settle expenses incurred during the four-day Democratic National Convention—$2,535 at the Helmsley Hotel and another $2,465 at the New York Hilton. Constituent flowers for funerals, weddings, and simple thank-yous cost the campaign $4,063. Donations to other candidates, party organizations, and causes totaled nearly five times the amount Steele spent on his entire campaign. In 1991 she paid $1,300 for tickets to the Connecticut inaugural ball and $1,500 for tickets to the mayoral inauguration in Hartford, Conn.

Campaign Expenditures	Kennelly Amount Spent	Kennelly % of Total	Steele Amount Spent	Steele % of Total
Overhead				
Office furniture/supplies	$ 9,022	1.58	$ 1,284	18.21
Rent/utilities	1,200	.21	0	
Salaries	29,902	5.22	200	2.84
Taxes	17,831	3.11	0	
Bank/investment fees	176	.03	0	
Lawyers/accountants	0		0	
Telephone	6,693	1.17	0	
Campaign automobile	0		0	
Computers/office equipment	10,473	1.83	0	
Travel	23,524	4.11	1,222	17.32
Food/meetings	15,189	2.65	0	
Subtotal	**114,009**	**19.91**	**2,706**	**38.37**
Fund Raising				
Events	36,340	6.35	220	3.12
Direct mail	3,432	.60	0	
Telemarketing	0		0	
Subtotal	**39,772**	**6.95**	**220**	**3.12**
Polling	**23,431**	**4.09**	**0**	
Advertising				
Electronic media	226,886	39.62	85	1.21
Other media	45,615	7.97	1,146	16.25
Subtotal	**272,500**	**47.59**	**1,231**	**17.46**
Other Campaign Activity				
Persuasion mail/brochures	43,970	7.68	1,696	24.04
Actual campaigning	37,892	6.62	1,200	17.01
Staff/volunteers	272	.05	0	
Subtotal	**82,135**	**14.34**	**2,896**	**41.06**
Constituent Gifts/Entertainment	**5,920**	**1.03**	**0**	
Donations to				
Candidates from same state	1,685	.29	0	
Candidates from other states	7,500	1.31	0	
Civic organizations	2,306	.40	0	
Ideological groups	890	.16	0	
Political parties	22,452	3.92	0	
Subtotal	**34,833**	**6.08**	**0**	
Unitemized Expenses	**0**		**0**	
Total Campaign Expenses	**$ 572,602**		**$ 7,053**	
PAC Contributions	**$ 336,281**		**$ 0**	
Individual Contributions	**161,472**		**4,267**	
Total Receipts*	**523,025**		**5,927**	

*Includes PAC and individual contributions as well as interest earned, party contributions, etc.

CONNECTICUT — District 2

Rep. Sam Gejdenson (D)

1992 Election Results

Sam Gejdenson (D)	123,291 (51%)
Edward W. Munster (R)	119,416 (49%)

As chairman of the House Administration Committee task force on congressional campaign finance reform, Rep. Sam Gejdenson has been the Democratic point-man on legislation that would establish a $600,000 voluntary spending limit in House campaigns. Had he adhered to that limit in 1992, Gejdenson would in all likelihood no longer be a member of Congress.

With off-year spending of $117,701, Gejdenson seemed headed toward a repeat of 1990, when he spent $486,246 to secure his sixth term. He raised only $89,362 during 1991 and at year's end had cash reserves of just $5,826. "We didn't want anyone to twist our actions around on us, so we didn't do any organized fund raising until after the veto," explained administrative assistant Bob Baskin.

While that was something of an overstatement, Gejdenson clearly held back prior to President Bush's June 1992 veto of the campaign finance bill. During the first six months of 1992 he raised $179,137 and in the process built his cash-on-hand total to $99,453.

However, after the veto, Gejdenson began raising money with a vengeance, collecting $519,518 during the next five months. "We sold T-shirts and had small-donor events, pancake breakfasts, picnics, and rallies," noted Baskin. "I really couldn't say how many events we had. We had a lot of small receptions and two or three big events—just a lot."

Gejdenson invested $392,253 in a broadcast media campaign designed by Galanty & Co. of Santa Monica, Calif., that included both radio and television commercials suggesting that his opponent, state senator Edward W. Munster, had not paid his property taxes. Galanty collected $52,445 for design and production of the ads. Media Placement of San Rafael, Calif., was paid $338,656 for placing the spots.

To ensure that he was literally a household name, Gejdenson mailed out more than 85,000 potholders. Gejdenson spent $40,728 for the potholders, which were stamped both with his name and the union label.

Munster had few resources but made the most of what he had. "We had 600 volunteers who made phone calls, passed out literature, and did everything we couldn't afford to do," recalled Munster. At $3 apiece, Munster bought thousands of time-slots on CNN and ESPN attacking Gejdenson for his fifty-one overdrafts at the House bank and his vote for the congressional pay raise. "If you don't request a specific time-slot and just saturate the channel, you are virtually guaranteed some prime-time spots," Munster explained. "We bought a lot of cheap time and sure enough the strategy worked."

Gejdenson defeated Munster by less than 4,000 votes and his victory percentage dropped from 20 to 2 percentage points.

Campaign Expenditures	Gejdenson Amount Spent	Gejdenson % of Total	Munster Amount Spent	Munster % of Total
Overhead				
Office furniture/supplies	$ 17,303	1.93	$ 6,450	4.52
Rent/utilities	17,421	1.94	1,700	1.19
Salaries	60,053	6.68	19,341	13.55
Taxes	24,983	2.78	0	
Bank/investment fees	2,539	.28	446	.31
Lawyers/accountants	0		0	
Telephone	9,832	1.09	8,104	5.68
Campaign automobile	15,324	1.71	0	
Computers/office equipment	73,759	8.21	6,155	4.31
Travel	29,223	3.25	546	.38
Food/meetings	12,919	1.44	514	.36
Subtotal	**263,355**	**29.31**	**43,256**	**30.31**
Fund Raising				
Events	31,812	3.54	1,079	.76
Direct mail	34,017	3.79	5,840	4.09
Telemarketing	0		0	
Subtotal	**65,829**	**7.33**	**6,919**	**4.85**
Polling	**5,400**	**.60**	**980**	**.69**
Advertising				
Electronic media	392,253	43.65	36,423	25.52
Other media	2,137	.24	17,423	12.21
Subtotal	**394,391**	**43.89**	**53,846**	**37.73**
Other Campaign Activity				
Persuasion mail/brochures	53,984	6.01	25,410	17.80
Actual campaigning	98,476	10.96	8,887	6.23
Staff/volunteers	1,010	.11	215	.15
Subtotal	**153,470**	**17.08**	**34,512**	**24.18**
Constituent Gifts/ Entertainment	**14,254**	**1.59**	**93**	**.06**
Donations to				
Candidates from same state	0		0	
Candidates from other states	0		0	
Civic organizations	700	.08	70	.05
Ideological groups	63	.01	0	
Political parties	100	.01	241	.17
Subtotal	**863**	**.10**	**311**	**.22**
Unitemized Expenses	**1,000**	**.11**	**2,802**	**1.96**
Total Campaign Expenses	**$ 898,562**		**$ 142,719**	
PAC Contributions	$ 336,601		$ 13,891	
Individual Contributions	471,673		82,318	
Total Receipts*	1,024,091		140,416	

*Includes PAC and individual contributions as well as interest earned, party contributions, etc.

District 3 — CONNECTICUT

Rep. Rosa DeLauro (D)

1992 Election Results

Rosa DeLauro (D)	162,568	(66%)
Tom Scott (R)	84,952	(34%)

With 1990 campaign debts of $100,000, first-term Rep. Rosa DeLauro's first order of business was fund raising, and she found numerous political action committees (PACs) willing to help her out. During the first six months of 1991, DeLauro raised $116,762, 74 percent of which was donated by PACs. Principal among her early benefactors was KIDSPAC, which donated $10,000. The American Federation of Teachers, the Machinists Non-Partisan Political League, and the United Auto Workers all gave at least $5,000 in early money. By July 1, 1991 DeLauro's debt load had been reduced to $10,000.

DeLauro could have paid that debt off entirely had she not spent $10,237 to celebrate her inauguration. To ferry supporters in for the big day, she spent $2,950 from the campaign treasury to charter a bus. A party at America, a restaurant near the Capitol, cost the campaign $5,734. A second reception at the Hyatt Hotel cost another $1,553.

The 1992 campaign was a reprise of 1990 in virtually every respect. Former state senator Tom Scott was again the Republican nominee. Outspent by more than three to one in 1990, Scott was monetarily buried by four to one in 1992.

As in 1990, DeLauro's broadcast advertising was handled by Greer, Margolis, Mitchell & Associates of Washington, D.C. The $394,496 Greer, Margolis received for developing and placing the commercials was $24,026 more than they received in 1990.

Campaign Performance Group of San Francisco, Calif., once again handled DeLauro's persuasion mail effort. One piece juxtaposed her pro-choice position on abortion with Scott's antiabortion stance; another was a straightforward attack on Scott's abortion views that did not bother to mention DeLauro's name. "For Them" and "Every Day Counts" were mailers touting her efforts on behalf of middle-class families, including votes for the Highway Transportation Bill, for an extension of unemployment benefits, and against a five-cent increase in the gasoline tax. DeLauro paid Campaign Performance $84,360.

DeLauro spent $112,000 less on overhead in 1992 than she had in 1990, largely by keeping her staff to a minimum throughout the first eighteen months of the cycle and by waiting until October to open her campaign headquarters. By October she had fourteen paid staffers.

Scott's first bid for this seat was considerably stronger than his second. While his fund-raising events featured such Republican luminaries as Housing and Urban Development Secretary Jack Kemp, Rep. Newt Gingrich (Ga.), Rep. Robert K. Dornan (Calif.), and columnist William F. Buckley, Jr., Scott raised $81,931 less in 1992 than he had in 1990.

	DeLauro		Scott	
Campaign Expenditures	Amount Spent	% of Total	Amount Spent	% of Total
Overhead				
Office furniture/supplies	$ 22,666	2.30	$ 11,214	4.64
Rent/utilities	5,499	.56	7,300	3.02
Salaries	109,210	11.07	60,079	24.87
Taxes	33,051	3.35	15,843	6.56
Bank/investment fees	371	.04	526	.22
Lawyers/accountants	11,666	1.18	0	
Telephone	23,882	2.42	16,844	6.97
Campaign automobile	0		0	
Computers/office equipment	11,253	1.14	5,977	2.47
Travel	9,010	.91	7,314	3.03
Food/meetings	0		1,286	.53
Subtotal	**226,609**	**22.97**	**126,383**	**52.31**
Fund Raising				
Events	99,264	10.06	6,120	2.53
Direct mail	49,085	4.98	20,842	8.63
Telemarketing	0		0	
Subtotal	**148,350**	**15.04**	**26,962**	**11.16**
Polling	**34,395**	**3.49**	**0**	
Advertising				
Electronic media	395,542	40.10	48,137	19.92
Other media	6,299	.64	8,000	3.31
Subtotal	**401,841**	**40.74**	**56,137**	**23.24**
Other Campaign Activity				
Persuasion mail/brochures	97,360	9.87	5,578	2.31
Actual campaigning	35,024	3.55	24,412	10.10
Staff/volunteers	2,768	.28	1,073	.44
Subtotal	**135,152**	**13.70**	**31,063**	**12.86**
Constituent Gifts/ Entertainment	**11,425**	**1.16**	**43**	**.02**
Donations to				
Candidates from same state	0		40	.02
Candidates from other states	938	.10	0	
Civic organizations	900	.09	336	.14
Ideological groups	0		24	.01
Political parties	2,045	.21	296	.12
Subtotal	**3,883**	**.39**	**696**	**.29**
Unitemized Expenses	**24,710**	**2.51**	**310**	**.13**
Total Campaign Expenses	**$ 986,363**		**$ 241,595**	
PAC Contributions	**$ 494,781**		**$ 48,088**	
Individual Contributions	**514,400**		**144,741**	
Total Receipts*	**1,026,034**		**207,430**	

*Includes PAC and individual contributions as well as interest earned, party contributions, etc.

CONNECTICUT   District 4

Rep. Christopher Shays (R)

1992 Election Results

Christopher Shays (R)	147,816 (67%)
Dave Schropfer (D)	58,666 (27%)
Al Smith (I)	11,679 (5%)

Having won his two reelection contests by margins of approximately three to one in a district unaffected by reapportionment, Rep. Christopher Shays had nothing to worry about in 1992. As a result, only about one-third of his campaign spending was invested in direct appeals to voters.

While the other five members of the Connecticut House delegation spent an average of $266,601 on broadcast advertising, Shays spent nothing. "I know what it takes to win the district, and [television] isn't necessary," argued Shays. "If I get my job done, re-electing me should be a pretty easy thing to accept."

Shays spent little on other forms of advertising. Billboards cost $17,821 and bus signs added $3,556. He also spent $505 to place program and journal ads with the Mid-Fairfield Substance Abuse Committee, the Mount Aery Baptist Church, the Republican State Central Committee, and the Connecticut Abortion Rights Action League, among others. One week before the November general election, Shays invested 96 percent of the $1,164 he spent on newspaper advertising to purchase ad space from the *Connecticut Jewish Ledger,* the *Fairfield Press,* Hometown Publications, and the *New Canaan Advertiser.*

The campaign produced one persuasion mailer, which was sent out two weeks before the election. Wayman Productions of Westport received $16,377 for producing the piece. Mailing labels cost $4,004, and the campaign paid $45,300 to the Connecticut Republican party to mail the brochure.

At the grass-roots level, Shays toured the district in a rented recreational vehicle (RV), holding rallies at train stations and shopping centers. Frequently accompanied by his family, Shays said their days began at 4:45 a.m. and ended after 8:00 p.m. "It was an intense period," noted Shays. "But my daughter didn't want it to end. She cried when the campaign was over." Shays's whistle-stop tour cost $7,598, including $3,836 for the RV and $236 for "presents for Mr. & Mrs. Moon for providing free accommodations for RV driver." He spent $8,729 on an in-house phonebank and $5,006 on yard signs and posters.

While his investments in direct voter-contact were relatively small, Shays's spending on overhead was anything but restrained. Total overhead amounted to $218,052, or 57 percent of his total outlays. Thirty-nine cents of every dollar was spent on salaries and payroll taxes. Richard Slawsky, district director on Shays's congressional staff, received $13,961 for his campaign work. Three other congressional staff members joined the reelection effort in October, collecting a total of $7,473 for their efforts.

Challenger Dave Schropfer spent 46 percent of his treasury on direct appeals to voters.

Campaign Expenditures	Shays Amount Spent	Shays % of Total	Schropfer Amount Spent	Schropfer % of Total
Overhead				
Office furniture/supplies	$ 14,807	3.90	$ 604	2.08
Rent/utilities	22,953	6.04	600	2.07
Salaries	111,796	29.42	0	
Taxes	36,707	9.66	0	
Bank/investment fees	293	.08	0	
Lawyers/accountants	0		0	
Telephone	16,835	4.43	1,227	4.24
Campaign automobile	0		0	
Computers/office equipment	5,977	1.57	0	
Travel	8,111	2.13	345	1.19
Food/meetings	572	.15	0	
Subtotal	218,052	57.38	2,776	9.58
Fund Raising				
Events	9,774	2.57	569	1.96
Direct mail	18,960	4.99	0	
Telemarketing	0		0	
Subtotal	28,734	7.56	569	1.96
Polling	0		9,500	32.79
Advertising				
Electronic media	0		2,906	10.03
Other media	23,046	6.06	0	
Subtotal	23,046	6.06	2,906	10.03
Other Campaign Activity				
Persuasion mail/brochures	71,365	18.78	4,661	16.09
Actual campaigning	30,879	8.13	5,635	19.45
Staff/volunteers	1,884	.50	0	
Subtotal	104,129	27.40	10,296	35.54
Constituent Gifts/ Entertainment	2,625	.69	0	
Donations to				
Candidates from same state	124	.03	0	
Candidates from other states	0		0	
Civic organizations	20	.01	0	
Ideological groups	0		0	
Political parties	1,140	.30	0	
Subtotal	1,284	.34	0	
Unitemized Expenses	2,152	.57	2,927	10.10
Total Campaign Expenses	$ 380,021		$ 28,974	
PAC Contributions	$ 56,800		$ 0	
Individual Contributions	328,174		14,770	
Total Receipts*	402,100		29,443	

*Includes PAC and individual contributions as well as interest earned, party contributions, etc.

District 5 — CONNECTICUT

Rep. Gary A. Franks (R)

1992 Election Results

Gary A. Franks (R)	104,891	(44%)
James J. Lawlor (D)	74,791	(31%)
Lynn H. Taborsak (I)	54,022	(23%)

After a shaky first term in which he was plagued by high staff turnover, sued by a savings and loan for defaulting on loans totaling $471,000, and sued by his 1990 campaign manager for back wages, it looked like Rep. Gary A. Franks would need both help and luck to retain his position as the only black Republican House member. He got plenty of both.

On the fund-raising side of the campaign equation, Franks twice called upon Vice President Dan Quayle to speak at large-donor events in Connecticut. Former secretary of state Henry Kissinger was also featured twice. Yet another big-ticket event featured Texas Sen. Phil Gramm. In all, these Republican heavyweights helped Franks raise $217,222 from individuals who gave at least $200.

Franks received $293,259, 47 percent of his total contributions, from political action committees (PACs). As a member of the Armed Services Committee, Franks received $62,050 from PACs representing defense interests.

Dan Morgan & Associates of Arlington, Va., received $3,751 for coordinating PAC events. Odell, Roper & Associates of Golden, Colo., was paid $17,891 for direct-mail fund raising. However, Franks's most active fund-raising consultant was his wife Donna, who was paid $23,890.

While Franks spent a total of $589,991, $134,616 of that total was spent during 1991 and another $146,500 was invested prior to the September 1992 Connecticut primary. That left about $309,000 for the final push. Franks sank most of this money into a broadcast media campaign designed and placed by the Stuart Stevens Group of New York. According to Rus Schirefer of Stuart Stevens, the media effort consisted of three television commercials and five radio spots. The centerpiece of the campaign was an ad in which Franks argued that he was unlike other politicians—"I was elected to get things done." Stuart Stevens billed the campaign $221,789.

These ads were not the only pro-Franks messages circulating through the district. While Franks spent just $19,655 on brochures and voter contact mail, the American Medical Association Political Action Committee undertook its own $81,256 campaign on Franks's behalf, spending $10,500 on polls by American Viewpoint of Alexandria, Va., $39,009 to air radio spots, and $31,747 on mailings. The National Association of Realtors and the National Rifle Association spent $14,916 and $3,209, respectively, in support of Franks.

Franks's biggest assist may have come from state representative Lynn H. Taborsak, who ran as an independent after losing an expensive Democratic primary battle with probate judge James J. Lawlor.

	Franks		Lawlor	
Campaign Expenditures	Amount Spent	% of Total	Amount Spent	% of Total
Overhead				
Office furniture/supplies	$ 8,736	1.48	$ 6,144	1.63
Rent/utilities	9,115	1.55	7,850	2.09
Salaries	35,438	6.01	16,136	4.29
Taxes	8,345	1.41	1,374	.37
Bank/investment fees	85	.01	82	.02
Lawyers/accountants	1,968	.33	4,199	1.12
Telephone	15,334	2.60	16,936	4.50
Campaign automobile	0		5,072	1.35
Computers/office equipment	19,833	3.36	10,825	2.88
Travel	19,670	3.33	3,486	.93
Food/meetings	644	.11	1,583	.42
Subtotal	**119,170**	**20.20**	**73,686**	**19.59**
Fund Raising				
Events	122,014	20.68	25,235	6.71
Direct mail	22,433	3.80	9,243	2.46
Telemarketing	0		0	
Subtotal	**144,447**	**24.48**	**34,478**	**9.17**
Polling	14,500	2.46	24,500	6.51
Advertising				
Electronic media	245,756	41.65	113,510	30.18
Other media	3,050	.52	4,492	1.19
Subtotal	**248,806**	**42.17**	**118,002**	**31.38**
Other Campaign Activity				
Persuasion mail/brochures	19,655	3.33	72,268	19.22
Actual campaigning	27,707	4.70	35,123	9.34
Staff/volunteers	2,510	.43	243	.06
Subtotal	**49,872**	**8.45**	**107,634**	**28.62**
Constituent Gifts/Entertainment	2,500	.42	0	
Donations to				
Candidates from same state	250	.04	0	
Candidates from other states	250	.04	0	
Civic organizations	2,347	.40	540	.14
Ideological groups	325	.06	0	
Political parties	800	.14	300	.08
Subtotal	**3,972**	**.67**	**840**	**.22**
Unitemized Expenses	**6,723**	**1.14**	**16,923**	**4.50**
Total Campaign Expenses	**$ 589,991**		**$ 376,062**	
PAC Contributions	$ 293,259		$ 61,200	
Individual Contributions	295,331		252,521	
Total Receipts*	644,632		352,779	

*Includes PAC and individual contributions as well as interest earned, party contributions, etc.

CONNECTICUT

District 6

Rep. Nancy L. Johnson (R)

1992 Election Results

Nancy L. Johnson (R)	166,967	(70%)
Eugene F. Slason (D)	60,373	(25%)

With little serious opposition, Rep. Nancy L. Johnson decided to forgo the three television commercials her campaigns generally run. Instead, the campaign spent $28,514 to produce and copy a 45-minute video that was sent to every library and civic organization in the district. Congressional district director and campaign manager Cheryl Lounsbury said that 165 tapes were ultimately distributed.

Johnson spent $72,569 on three 60-second radio spots. Newspaper ads cost the campaign $19,204 and billboard ads cost $11,828. Makiaris Media Services of Bloomfield received $97,612 for producing and placing the radio spots, as well as placing most of the newspaper and billboard advertising.

To keep her name prominent in voters' minds, Johnson mailed a brochure to every household in the district. Yard signs and posters cost the campaign $10,891. The campaign also spent $10,436 to buy "chip clips," plastic clips used to keep bags of potato chips and other snacks closed. According to Lounsbury, the clips imprinted with Johnson's name were passed out at local fairs, parades, and campaign events and were "the hottest thing in town."

Johnson's senior campaign staff included three members of her congressional staff. Lounsbury received $38,517 for her work as campaign manager. Donna Mullen, a part-time congressional staffer, was paid $34,317 by the campaign. Congressional staff assistant Marianne Calen collected $13,717 from the campaign, and other congressional staffers were paid a total of $2,778. Altogether, congressional staff members received $89,329 of the $99,041 Johnson paid out in campaign salaries.

Donations to other candidates, political party organizations, and causes cost Johnson's campaign $28,737, a 48 percent increase over 1990. She gave $5,000 to the Republican Leaders Fund, a political action committee (PAC) established by Rep. Robert H. Michel (R-Ill.). She donated $5,000 to the National Republican Congressional Committee's "generic media account." Sixteen Republican candidates received contributions of $1,000.

Johnson held no fund-raising events in Connecticut during 1991. The Washington, D.C., PAC community accounted for 83 percent of the $119,727 she raised during the off-year. Lounsbury said the campaign's only in-state receipts for the year were in response to several direct-mail solicitations.

With the help of Dan Morgan & Associates of Arlington, Va., which received $9,078, Johnson was able to raise $339,312 from PACs over the two-year election cycle, which amounted to 58 percent of her total contributions. In-state donors contributing $200 or more accounted for another 14 percent.

Campaign Expenditures	Johnson Amount Spent	Johnson % of Total	Slason Amount Spent	Slason % of Total
Overhead				
Office furniture/supplies	$ 7,690	1.36	$ 1,385	5.88
Rent/utilities	3,461	.61	0	
Salaries	99,041	17.48	1,770	7.51
Taxes	51,572	9.10	0	
Bank/investment fees	0		15	.06
Lawyers/accountants	1,225	.22	0	
Telephone	11,466	2.02	1,882	7.98
Campaign automobile	0		0	
Computers/office equipment	14,998	2.65	28	.12
Travel	10,283	1.81	179	.76
Food/meetings	8,834	1.56	37	.16
Subtotal	**208,571**	**36.80**	**5,296**	**22.47**
Fund Raising				
Events	47,851	8.44	292	1.24
Direct mail	15,451	2.73	0	
Telemarketing	0		0	
Subtotal	**63,302**	**11.17**	**292**	**1.24**
Polling	**40,842**	**7.21**	**0**	
Advertising				
Electronic media	72,569	12.81	9,493	40.27
Other media	61,666	10.88	2,068	8.77
Subtotal	**134,235**	**23.69**	**11,561**	**49.04**
Other Campaign Activity				
Persuasion mail/brochures	52,964	9.35	3,099	13.15
Actual campaigning	35,015	6.18	2,498	10.60
Staff/volunteers	335	.06	0	
Subtotal	**88,314**	**15.58**	**5,597**	**23.74**
Constituent Gifts/ Entertainment	**1,608**	**.28**	**30**	**.13**
Donations to				
Candidates from same state	4,000	.71	0	
Candidates from other states	13,457	2.37	0	
Civic organizations	0		0	
Ideological groups	6,000	1.06	0	
Political parties	5,280	.93	117	.50
Subtotal	**28,737**	**5.07**	**117**	**.50**
Unitemized Expenses	**1,100**	**.19**	**680**	**2.89**
Total Campaign Expenses	**$ 566,709**		**$ 23,574**	
PAC Contributions	$ 339,312		$ 6,000	
Individual Contributions	242,737		8,942	
Total Receipts*	596,412		39,706	

*Includes PAC and individual contributions as well as interest earned, party contributions, etc.

At Large — DELAWARE

Rep. Michael N. Castle (R)

1992 Election Results

Michael N. Castle (R)	153,037	(55%)
S. B. Woo (D)	117,426	(43%)

It was a case of political musical chairs. In one of the more unusual political scenarios of 1992, Democratic Rep. Thomas R. Carper gave up his House seat to make a successful bid for governor. Republican Gov. Michael N. Castle, who could not run for a third term, announced he would seek Carper's House seat. His opponent, Democrat S. B. Woo, was Castle's former lieutenant governor.

Both Castle and Woo depended heavily on out-of-state money to fund their campaigns. Castle collected $206,868 from political action committees, or 30 percent of his total contributions. He held fund-raisers in New York and nearby Philadelphia that helped push his large donations from nonconstituents to $128,750. As he had in previous campaigns, Woo tapped into Chinese-American communities throughout the country, holding events in San Francisco; Philadelphia; Houston; New York; Bellevue, Wash.; and Columbus, Ohio. He also paid $2,100 to air cable television ads in California that were aimed at raising money from Chinese-Americans. Woo received 995 contributions of $200 or more, and only 60 of those were made by residents of Delaware.

While Woo outspent Castle by $213,423, most of that spending advantage was put into overhead, fund raising, and polling. When it came to advertising, persuasion mail, and other direct voter contacts, Castle was only outspent by $50,393.

Castle invested $280,705 of his campaign treasury to get through the four-candidate Republican primary. He paid $78,270 to media adviser Smith & Harroff of Alexandria, Va., for developing and placing his preprimary broadcast ads. Another $20,053 was spent on brochures and persuasion mail. Payco American Corp. of Brookfield, Wis., received $14,078 for phonebanking. He spent $10,985 on yard signs and posters, $2,819 on tabloid-style newspaper inserts, $612 on newspaper ads, $3,245 on sun visors and bumper stickers, and $2,256 on T-shirts.

Castle focused nearly 60 percent of his spending into the final three months of the election cycle. Payments to Smith & Harroff totaled $254,183 during this final drive. Outlays for persuasion mail and brochures amounted to $40,850. Newspaper inserts cost $17,602 and newspaper ads totaled $15,718.

Woo countered with expenditures of $500,436 over the final three months, which amounted to 55 percent of his total spending for the election cycle. Broadcast advertising accounted for 61 percent of this final splurge, or $304,271. During this period, media adviser Trippi, McMahon & Squier of Alexandria, Va., received $237,387 of the $382,867 it collected for developing and placing Woo's broadcast ads.

	Castle		Woo	
Campaign Expenditures	Amount Spent	% of Total	Amount Spent	% of Total
Overhead				
Office furniture/supplies	$ 15,162	2.20	$ 8,075	.89
Rent/utilities	6,513	.94	10,416	1.15
Salaries	45,800	6.63	85,061	9.41
Taxes	19,476	2.82	28,047	3.10
Bank/investment fees	18	.00	216	.02
Lawyers/accountants	1,749	.25	0	
Telephone	6,278	.91	18,766	2.08
Campaign automobile	2,234	.32	0	
Computers/office equipment	11,985	1.74	16,101	1.78
Travel	7,225	1.05	26,237	2.90
Food/meetings	3,833	.55	3,454	.38
Subtotal	**120,273**	**17.41**	**196,374**	**21.72**
Fund Raising				
Events	64,069	9.28	75,612	8.36
Direct mail	9,980	1.44	27,594	3.05
Telemarketing	0		0	
Subtotal	**74,048**	**10.72**	**103,206**	**11.41**
Polling	**19,050**	**2.76**	**52,794**	**5.84**
Advertising				
Electronic media	335,324	48.55	432,714	47.86
Other media	37,037	5.36	26,491	2.93
Subtotal	**372,361**	**53.91**	**459,205**	**50.79**
Other Campaign Activity				
Persuasion mail/brochures	60,903	8.82	25,088	2.77
Actual campaigning	40,775	5.90	40,405	4.47
Staff/volunteers	375	.05	108	.01
Subtotal	**102,052**	**14.77**	**65,601**	**7.26**
Constituent Gifts/ Entertainment	295	.04	0	
Donations to				
Candidates from same state	0		645	.07
Candidates from other states	0		0	
Civic organizations	2,125	.31	2,630	.29
Ideological groups	145	.02	0	
Political parties	270	.04	764	.08
Subtotal	**2,540**	**.37**	**4,039**	**.45**
Unitemized Expenses	125	.02	22,950	2.54
Total Campaign Expenses	$ 690,745		$ 904,168	
PAC Contributions	$ 206,868		$ 37,600	
Individual Contributions	472,769		750,322	
Total Receipts*	708,671		1,018,360	

*Includes PAC and individual contributions as well as interest earned, party contributions, etc.

FLORIDA — District 1

Rep. Earl Hutto (D)

1992 Election Results

Earl Hutto (D)	118,753	(52%)
Terry Ketchel (R)	100,136	(44%)

In 1990 attorney Terry Ketchel marginally outspent Rep. Earl Hutto and in the process captured 48 percent of the vote in a losing effort. Redistricting then robbed Hutto of his Panama City political base, and when Ketchel announced he would challenge Hutto a second time, the seven-term incumbent appeared vulnerable.

However, by providing evidence of Hutto's potential weakness in 1990, Ketchel succeeded in drawing state representative Tom Banjanin into the Republican primary. While Ketchel emerged with 54 percent of the votes, the difficult primary cost him roughly $93,000, or 61 percent of his total spending.

Hutto was also much better prepared for the challenge than he had been in 1990. Overall, his spending increased from $158,277 in 1990 to $308,424 in 1992, a 95 percent rise. Hutto increased his advertising budget by 30 percent over 1990 levels, and outlays for brochures and persuasion mail jumped by 369 percent. He more than doubled his expenditures for both overhead and fund raising.

As a former sportscaster and advertising agency executive, Hutto had no need for media consultants. He wrote and produced all his ads.

Representing a district that is heavily dependent on military spending, Hutto said many of his ads focused on his senior position on the Armed Services Committee and on the attendant economic advantages that flow from that leadership position. When Ketchel attacked him for voting too frequently with liberal members of the Armed Services Committee, such as Rep. Patricia Schroeder (D-Colo.), Hutto rolled out an ad that used the *Congressional Record* to show that on the particular vote Ketchel had cited, Hutto had opposed Schroeder.

Hutto also developed spots heralding his record of constituent service on such issues as Social Security and veterans benefits. Broadcast advertising production cost Hutto $9,947. The remaining 85 percent of his broadcast budget was invested in air time—$40,632 on network television affiliates, $6,053 on cable television, and $9,744 on radio. An investment of $9,705 in newspaper ads rounded out the general election advertising budget.

To reach constituents added by redistricting, Hutto also spent $59,869 on persuasion mail. Another $7,956 was spent to print brochures that were dispensed at campaign events and handed out to people who stopped by campaign headquarters.

Hutto hired only one consultant, pollster Frederick/Schneiders of Washington, D.C. "It saves money, and with the small amount I raise, I try to guard my funds," noted Hutto in explaining the paucity of outside advisers.

Campaign Expenditures	Hutto Amount Spent	Hutto % of Total	Ketchel Amount Spent	Ketchel % of Total
Overhead				
Office furniture/supplies	$ 10,613	3.44	$ 5,635	3.70
Rent/utilities	2,716	.88	4,895	3.21
Salaries	19,045	6.18	22,786	14.96
Taxes	2,339	.76	5,720	3.75
Bank/investment fees	206	.07	5,469	3.59
Lawyers/accountants	0		0	
Telephone	1,670	.54	10,207	6.70
Campaign automobile	0		0	
Computers/office equipment	11,159	3.62	1,760	1.16
Travel	15,804	5.12	7,375	4.84
Food/meetings	1,149	.37	117	.08
Subtotal	**64,701**	**20.98**	**63,964**	**41.98**
Fund Raising				
Events	23,320	7.56	10,822	7.10
Direct mail	0		1,909	1.25
Telemarketing	0		0	
Subtotal	**23,320**	**7.56**	**12,730**	**8.36**
Polling	**12,000**	**3.89**	**2,489**	**1.63**
Advertising				
Electronic media	66,376	21.52	7,685	5.04
Other media	10,428	3.38	809	.53
Subtotal	**76,804**	**24.90**	**8,495**	**5.58**
Other Campaign Activity				
Persuasion mail/brochures	67,825	21.99	27,028	17.74
Actual campaigning	21,189	6.87	25,667	16.85
Staff/volunteers	1,495	.48	0	
Subtotal	**90,509**	**29.35**	**52,695**	**34.59**
Constituent Gifts/Entertainment	**9,289**	**3.01**	**0**	
Donations to				
Candidates from same state	0		0	
Candidates from other states	100	.03	0	
Civic organizations	4,377	1.42	20	.01
Ideological groups	376	.12	0	
Political parties	8,206	2.66	0	
Subtotal	**13,059**	**4.23**	**20**	**.01**
Unitemized Expenses	**18,741**	**6.08**	**11,965**	**7.85**
Total Campaign Expenses	**$ 308,424**		**$ 152,357**	
PAC Contributions	**$ 144,704**		**$ 27,786**	
Individual Contributions	**126,033**		**124,932**	
Total Receipts*	**298,700**		**164,581**	

*Includes PAC and individual contributions as well as interest earned, party contributions, etc.

District 2 — FLORIDA

Rep. Pete Peterson (D)

1992 Election Results

Pete Peterson (D)	167,151	(73%)
Ray Wagner (R)	60,378	(27%)

Following his 1990 victory over Republican incumbent Bill Grant, who outspent him by nearly $500,000, Rep. Pete Peterson was undoubtedly relieved by the lack of strong opposition in 1992. "This was a standard, size 42, off-the-rack campaign," remarked administrative assistant Suzanne Farmer.

Peterson began the 1992 election cycle with debts of $62,141 and cash reserves of only $324, so fund raising was high on the list of priorities for his otherwise nonexistent permanent campaign. During 1991, Peterson spent only $23,813, and $11,828 of that total was invested in fund raising. Over the first six months of 1992, total campaign outlays were $78,809, of which $51,058 was devoted to raising money. Springer Associates of Falls Church, Va., received $44,362 during this eighteen-month period for helping to raise $170,850 from political action committees. By the end of June 1992 Peterson had whittled his debts down to $22,505 and increased his cash reserves to $97,156.

Over the final six months of 1992, Peterson invested $209,434 to defeat farmer Buster Smith in the September Democratic primary and contractor Ray Wagner in the November general election. While actual campaigning replaced fund raising as the primary focus of Peterson's efforts, he still spent $44,741 during this period to raise money. Springer received $34,893 of the total fund-raising outlays.

In the primary, Smith spent $116,463 in his failed bid. Peterson countered with his own $111,612 effort, including $50,348 for two television commercials described by Farmer as "Pete in Washington profiles." Peterson also spent $4,026 to place ads in twenty-six newspapers and $1,734 for phonebanking run by the Florida Lawyers Action Group. Peterson prevailed easily with 69 percent of the vote.

Given that Wagner could muster only $22,640 for the race, the fall campaign was even easier for Peterson. He spent $34,117 to air the same ads he had used in the primary as well as a third spot urging people to vote. Advertisements placed in twenty-two newspapers cost Peterson $3,519, including design costs of $500. Beasley Associates of Tallahassee collected $3,500 for designing one brochure and for running a small phonebank. The Florida Lawyers Action Group was also paid $988 for phonebanking.

For creating the television spots, which never bothered to mention either of Peterson's opponents, Andrews Plus of Tallahassee collected $21,473. Simons Media Techniques of Tallahassee billed the campaign $60,348 to cover the cost of air time and their fees for placing the ads.

Campaign Expenditures	Peterson Amount Spent	Peterson % of Total	Wagner Amount Spent	Wagner % of Total
Overhead				
Office furniture/supplies	$ 5,296	1.70	$ 0	
Rent/utilities	1,238	.40	1,507	6.66
Salaries	15,377	4.93	4,700	20.76
Taxes	5,009	1.61	0	
Bank/investment fees	316	.10	0	
Lawyers/accountants	7,786	2.50	0	
Telephone	5,151	1.65	0	
Campaign automobile	0		0	
Computers/office equipment	11,760	3.77	0	
Travel	5,612	1.80	0	
Food/meetings	178	.06	0	
Subtotal	**57,721**	**18.50**	**6,207**	**27.42**
Fund Raising				
Events	104,227	33.40	0	
Direct mail	3,400	1.09	0	
Telemarketing	0		0	
Subtotal	**107,627**	**34.49**	**0**	
Polling	**3,610**	**1.16**	**0**	
Advertising				
Electronic media	84,465	27.07	0	
Other media	10,568	3.39	0	
Subtotal	**95,033**	**30.45**	**0**	
Other Campaign Activity				
Persuasion mail/brochures	7,476	2.40	3,400	15.02
Actual campaigning	34,006	10.90	10,187	44.99
Staff/volunteers	0		0	
Subtotal	**41,482**	**13.29**	**13,586**	**60.01**
Constituent Gifts/ Entertainment	**3,475**	**1.11**	**0**	
Donations to				
Candidates from same state	0		0	
Candidates from other states	0		0	
Civic organizations	153	.05	0	
Ideological groups	0		0	
Political parties	1,150	.37	0	
Subtotal	**1,303**	**.42**	**0**	
Unitemized Expenses	**1,806**	**.58**	**2,847**	**12.57**
Total Campaign Expenses	**$ 312,056**		**$ 22,640**	
PAC Contributions	**$ 282,350**		**$ 0**	
Individual Contributions	**112,007**		**6,550**	
Total Receipts*	**400,867**		**23,425**	

*Includes PAC and individual contributions as well as interest earned, party contributions, etc.

FLORIDA — District 3

Rep. Corrine Brown (D)

1992 Election Results

Corrine Brown (D)	91,877	(59%)
Don Weidner (R)	63,070	(41%)

Snaking through fourteen counties, District 3 is a horseshoe-shaped monument to the art of racial gerrymandering. Registered Democrats make up 78 percent of the district's electorate; 58 percent of its registered voters are black. Once state representative Corrine Brown captured the Democratic nomination, Florida was assured of having at least one black in its congressional delegation for the first time in more than one hundred years.

Brown's spending was well below the average invested by open seat candidates, in part because she did not enter the race until July 1992. By October 1 she had spent $153,211 to wage her primary and run-off campaigns, $37,404 more than she would commit to defeating Republican Don Weidner, general counsel for the Florida Physicians Association.

Brown invested 35 percent of her campaign treasury in advertising, primarily in three radio and three television commercials designed by Austin-Sheinkopf of New York. The most effective of Brown's television spots focused on a job-training program that Brown had helped to implement during her tenure in the state legislature. Presenting a series of photos of Brown at work in the community, the ad ended with the tagline: "Corrine Fights, Corrine Works, Corrine Delivers, Corrine Makes It Happen."

"Corrine was out in Gainesville knocking on doors, and as she walked away from one house, a child started saying Corrine this and Corrine that and then said 'Corrine delivers,'" recalled Austin-Sheinkopf's David Hellar. "And his mother said to him, 'and that's why we're voting for her.' At that point, Corrine came back and told us to up the TV budget."

Another ad, dubbed "Respect," highlighted Brown's commitment to public works projects in the district. "Ships" focused on trade as the means to increasing employment. Three radio spots were used to reach the district's rural population with messages similar to the television commercials. For producing and placing the spots, Austin-Sheinkopf received $81,862—$48,218 through the primary, $10,287 for the run-off, and $23,357 for the general election campaign.

To ensure a high turnout among the district's black voters, Brown spent $20,808 on various get-out-the-vote efforts. "You're talking about a woman who was outspent almost two to one by her white Republican opponent on the air," noted Hellar. "This was a campaign won primarily in the field."

Apparently, Weidner agreed. "We didn't have a lot of money, and we weren't running enough points to have the impact we needed," Weidner said of his television campaign. "Looking back, I would have cut it and invested the money in mail."

Campaign Expenditures	Brown Amount Spent	Brown % of Total	Weidner Amount Spent	Weidner % of Total
Overhead				
Office furniture/supplies	$ 4,755	1.77	$ 2,792	1.00
Rent/utilities	2,000	.74	3,814	1.36
Salaries	17,235	6.41	10,562	3.78
Taxes	0		2,968	1.06
Bank/investment fees	0		378	.14
Lawyers/accountants	0		0	
Telephone	4,038	1.50	3,942	1.41
Campaign automobile	0		0	
Computers/office equipment	0		4,249	1.52
Travel	11,914	4.43	16,074	5.75
Food/meetings	0		441	.16
Subtotal	39,941	14.85	45,219	16.17
Fund Raising				
Events	9,302	3.46	150	.05
Direct mail	1,419	.53	7,607	2.72
Telemarketing	0		0	
Subtotal	10,722	3.99	7,757	2.77
Polling	8,500	3.16	11,250	4.02
Advertising				
Electronic media	84,454	31.39	103,514	37.02
Other media	10,427	3.88	210	.08
Subtotal	94,881	35.27	103,724	37.09
Other Campaign Activity				
Persuasion mail/brochures	63,458	23.59	68,922	24.65
Actual campaigning	41,925	15.58	32,346	11.57
Staff/volunteers	0		0	
Subtotal	105,383	39.17	101,268	36.22
Constituent Gifts/Entertainment	275	.10	0	
Donations to				
Candidates from same state	0		0	
Candidates from other states	0		0	
Civic organizations	738	.27	30	.01
Ideological groups	250	.09	0	
Political parties	0		393	.14
Subtotal	988	.37	423	.15
Unitemized Expenses	8,329	3.10	9,987	3.57
Total Campaign Expenses	$ 269,018		$ 279,627	
PAC Contributions	$ 147,363		$ 24,500	
Individual Contributions	123,121		208,538	
Total Receipts*	289,260		258,431	

*Includes PAC and individual contributions as well as interest earned, party contributions, etc.

District 4 — FLORIDA

Rep. Tillie Fowler (R)

1992 Election Results

Tillie Fowler (R)	135,772	(57%)
Mattox Hair (D)	103,484	(43%)

When Rep. Charles E. Bennett abruptly reversed his decision to seek a twenty-third term, Republican Tillie Fowler, a Jacksonville City Council member, was already running hard. Fowler, who announced her own candidacy just one week before Bennett's surprise withdrawal, had been working for months to assemble a high-profile finance committee. By the time former Democratic state legislator and judge Mattox Hair got into the race, Fowler had already lined up the support of twenty-two people who had helped Hair raise money for his 1984 state senate race. With eighty people committed to raising between $5,000 and $10,000 each, Fowler knew money would not be her problem.

Fowler spent only $31,670 to raise $524,951, and $18,360 of her fund-raising outlays were accounted for by in-kind events thrown by members of her finance committee. Her only direct-mail fund-raising expense was also an in-kind donation. What little Fowler spent from her treasury was for invitations to these in-kind affairs. "The committee raised every dime," noted administrative assistant David Gilliland.

Freed from the burden of raising money, Fowler was able to concentrate 74 percent of her resources on advertising, persuasion mail, and other direct appeals to voters. Overhead consumed only 12 percent of her budget during the six-month campaign.

Fowler paid the William Cook Agency of Jacksonville $30,710 to develop six television commercials and a similar number of radio spots. Production costs totaled $37,282. The campaign placed the ads directly, investing $119,138 to buy time on local network affiliates, $11,280 for time on local cable systems, and another $28,577 to air its radio spots.

Bennett's retirement robbed Fowler of the chance to run an "outsider" campaign against an individual incumbent, so instead she ran an outsider campaign against the entire Congress. One of her television commercials simply scrolled across the screen the names of all congressional staffers with annual salaries of $100,000 or more. She also scored with attacks on Hair for having supported the state's service tax, which was passed and then almost immediately repealed in response to the public's angry outcry.

Tolbert Inc. of Jacksonville collected $12,567 for designing Fowler's persuasion mailers. Gilliland said the largest piece—both in size and audience—was a tabloid-style newspaper that carried an endorsement from Senate Minority Leader Bob Dole (R-Kan.).

Even without his twenty-two former supporters, Hair was financially competitive. Strother-Duffy-Strother of Washington, D.C., collected $52,183 for designing and producing five radio and five television commercials. Media Targeting of Orlando was paid $3,625 for advice on ad placement.

Campaign Expenditures	Fowler Amount Spent	Fowler % of Total	Hair Amount Spent	Hair % of Total
Overhead				
Office furniture/supplies	$ 9,719	1.86	$ 7,447	1.77
Rent/utilities	9,396	1.80	8,629	2.05
Salaries	28,428	5.44	36,162	8.59
Taxes	0		0	
Bank/investment fees	475	.09	499	.12
Lawyers/accountants	0		240	.06
Telephone	9,171	1.76	9,769	2.32
Campaign automobile	0		0	
Computers/office equipment	2,314	.44	2,175	.52
Travel	2,260	.43	1,194	.28
Food/meetings	160	.03	0	
Subtotal	**61,923**	**11.85**	**66,114**	**15.70**
Fund Raising				
Events	30,696	5.88	42,295	10.04
Direct mail	975	.19	12,930	3.07
Telemarketing	0		0	
Subtotal	**31,670**	**6.06**	**55,226**	**13.11**
Polling	**36,762**	**7.04**	**18,600**	**4.42**
Advertising				
Electronic media	226,986	43.45	167,293	39.73
Other media	22,414	4.29	8,000	1.90
Subtotal	**249,401**	**47.74**	**175,294**	**41.63**
Other Campaign Activity				
Persuasion mail/brochures	69,452	13.30	68,073	16.17
Actual campaigning	68,616	13.14	35,641	8.46
Staff/volunteers	410	.08	0	
Subtotal	**138,479**	**26.51**	**103,714**	**24.63**
Constituent Gifts/Entertainment	**0**		**0**	
Donations to				
Candidates from same state	0		0	
Candidates from other states	0		0	
Civic organizations	85	.02	229	.05
Ideological groups	0		0	
Political parties	0		0	
Subtotal	**85**	**.02**	**229**	**.05**
Unitemized Expenses	**4,043**	**.77**	**1,922**	**.46**
Total Campaign Expenses	**$ 522,363**		**$ 421,098**	
PAC Contributions	$ 115,350		$ 144,050	
Individual Contributions	386,382		279,019	
Total Receipts*	524,951		428,706	

*Includes PAC and individual contributions as well as interest earned, party contributions, etc.

FLORIDA — District 5

Rep. Karen L. Thurman (D)

1992 Election Results

Karen L. Thurman (D)	129,678	(49%)
Tom Hogan (R)	114,331	(43%)
Cindy Munkittrick † (I)	19,459	(7%)

State senator Karen L. Thurman had the good fortune to chair the Florida Senate Subcommittee on Congressional Reapportionment, so it came as no surprise that the boundaries of the new District 5 overlapped much of her state senate district. Her November victory over Republican attorney Tom Hogan also seemed preordained, since she had beaten him in the 1990 state senate race. Nevertheless, the race turned out to be anything but easy.

To get her message out, Thurman spent 31 percent of her treasury to produce and air four television commercials and six radio spots hitting such basic Democratic themes as education, the environment, and health care. One ad focused heavily on her opposition to the North American Free Trade Agreement; another answered charges that her campaign signs were made in Brazil, suggesting that she did not adequately support American businesses after all.

Joseph L. Lander of Cross City received $10,605 for creating most of the ads; Bob White Productions of Gainesville collected $80,479 for ad production and placement. New York-based Austin-Sheinkopf was paid $23,869 for producing and placing one television and one radio spot.

Rather than bring in a persuasion mail consultant, the campaign mailed out a steady stream of postcards and letters outlining Thurman's positions and answering charges made by both her primary opponents and by Hogan. Printing bills totaled $48,147; postage, $16,343; mailing lists, $3,350.

To fund her campaign, Thurman depended heavily on political action committees (PACs), including strong support from various women's organizations. EMILY's List provided her with $7,495 of in-kind fund-raising assistance. The National Organization for Women contributed $5,083, including $1,485 of in-kind printing and staff support services shortly before the November general election. Women's Campaign Fund gave $5,000.

Labor PACs weighed in with $50,000. Proving the cliché that politics creates strange bedfellows, the National Education Association provided her with $10,000 while the National Rifle Association kicked in $9,900. In all, Thurman collected 59 percent of her money from PACs. For coordinating her PAC fund-raising events, Robert H. Bassin Associates of Washington, D.C., received $15,430.

While Thurman spent much of her time campaigning against Congress and politics-as-usual, her reliance on PAC money provided Hogan with an issue. One of the television spots produced by Mike Bernos Media of Ocala juxtaposed Thurman's plentiful PAC donations with his own rejection of PAC money. Bernos collected $27,520 for creating the ads and planning the placement strategy.

Campaign Expenditures	Thurman Amount Spent	Thurman % of Total	Hogan Amount Spent	Hogan % of Total
Overhead				
Office furniture/supplies	$ 5,057	1.36	$ 1,983	1.37
Rent/utilities	4,102	1.11	1,947	1.34
Salaries	46,435	12.52	0	
Taxes	3,593	.97	0	
Bank/investment fees	311	.08	18	.01
Lawyers/accountants	0		0	
Telephone	15,477	4.17	4,254	2.94
Campaign automobile	2,807	.76	0	
Computers/office equipment	3,946	1.06	0	
Travel	7,529	2.03	0	
Food/meetings	278	.07	50	.03
Subtotal	**89,535**	**24.15**	**8,253**	**5.70**
Fund Raising				
Events	23,981	6.47	3,401	2.35
Direct mail	7,132	1.92	0	
Telemarketing	0		0	
Subtotal	**31,113**	**8.39**	**3,401**	**2.35**
Polling	**11,000**	**2.97**	**0**	
Advertising				
Electronic media	114,953	31.00	48,440	33.45
Other media	3,293	.89	2,633	1.82
Subtotal	**118,246**	**31.89**	**51,072**	**35.27**
Other Campaign Activity				
Persuasion mail/brochures	67,839	18.30	56,802	39.23
Actual campaigning	27,906	7.53	20,755	14.33
Staff/volunteers	500	.13	0	
Subtotal	**96,245**	**25.96**	**77,557**	**53.56**
Constituent Gifts/ Entertainment	**517**	**.14**	**0**	
Donations to				
Candidates from same state	0		0	
Candidates from other states	0		0	
Civic organizations	0		39	.03
Ideological groups	0		0	
Political parties	0		0	
Subtotal	**0**		**39**	**.03**
Unitemized Expenses	**24,148**	**6.51**	**4,489**	**3.10**
Total Campaign Expenses	**$ 370,805**		**$ 144,810**	
PAC Contributions	**$ 206,401**		**$ 0**	
Individual Contributions	**123,801**		**19,067**	
Total Receipts*	**360,160**		**145,470**	

*Includes PAC and individual contributions as well as interest earned, party contributions, etc.

† No expenditures or receipts on file. Candidates raising or spending less than $5,000 are not required to file reports with the Federal Election Commission.

District 6 — FLORIDA

Rep. Cliff Stearns (R)

1992 Election Results

Cliff Stearns (R)	144,120	(65%)
Phil Denton (D)	76,396	(35%)

In his second reelection campaign, Rep. Cliff Stearns faced Democrat Phil Denton, a diaper service operator who spent only $2,335 on his token challenge. Denton devoted just $617 to advertising, including $517 on radio ads that proclaimed: "I'm Phil Denton, the diaper man. People tell me I'm prepared for Congress because I've been up to my elbows in it."

Yet despite such weak competition, Stearns still spent $270,944, including $60,933 to maintain his permanent campaign operation in 1991. Approximately three-quarters of this off-year investment was put into overhead and fund raising.

Reflecting the lack of opposition, Stearns spent $54,660 less on advertising than he had in 1990, a decrease of 60 percent. Ad production was handled in-house with an assist from the National Republican Congressional Committee. Production costs totaled only $1,223. During the first week of October, the campaign spent $8,115 to air its first radio spots, and over the final month of the campaign invested another $15,659 in radio ads. Cable television buys added $7,440.

However, this reduction in advertising was more than offset by increases in persuasion mail. Having spent nothing on voter contact mail in 1990, Stearns shifted gears in 1992, investing $78,661 to mail three such pieces. The largest of the mailings was a tabloid-style piece sent to registered voters throughout the district. One campaign staffer described it as having pictures of Stearns "in the office doing stuff." Direct Mail Systems of St. Petersburg and Campaign Mail & Data of Falls Church, Va., received $47,314 and $7,910, respectively, for orchestrating the persuasion mail effort. For its creative input, Karl Rove & Co. of Austin, Texas, received $4,852.

This shift in communication strategy resulted in a net increase of $24,001 in spending on direct appeals to voters. In contrast, Denton spent only $1,271 on advertising and persuasion mail—$8,274 less than Stearn's 1990 opponent had spent.

Stearns dramatically cut back on his fund-raising effort in 1992, spending $92,467 less than he had in 1990. By far the largest reduction was in direct-mail expenses, which dropped from $87,411 to $21,180, a 76 percent reduction. Stearns paid Direct Mail Systems $13,631 for producing three prospecting letters. As a result of this reduced activity, Stearns's contributions of less than $200 totaled only $67,410 in 1992, down from $104,773 in 1990.

To keep his finger on the public's pulse, Stearns paid pollster Tarrance & Associates of Alexandria, Va., $3,100. The American Medical Association's political action committee provided him with an in-kind poll valued at $4,700.

	Stearns		Denton	
Campaign Expenditures	Amount Spent	% of Total	Amount Spent	% of Total
Overhead				
Office furniture/supplies	$ 11,118	4.10	$ 44	1.89
Rent/utilities	5,520	2.04	0	
Salaries	10,573	3.90	0	
Taxes	4,608	1.70	0	
Bank/investment fees	87	.03	10	.43
Lawyers/accountants	6,058	2.24	0	
Telephone	5,453	2.01	455	19.49
Campaign automobile	0		0	
Computers/office equipment	5,701	2.10	0	
Travel	8,960	3.31	555	23.77
Food/meetings	86	.03	0	
Subtotal	**58,165**	**21.47**	**1,064**	**45.58**
Fund Raising				
Events	43,395	16.02	0	
Direct mail	21,180	7.82	0	
Telemarketing	0		0	
Subtotal	**64,575**	**23.83**	**0**	
Polling	**7,800**	**2.88**	**0**	
Advertising				
Electronic media	32,437	11.97	517	22.13
Other media	3,602	1.33	100	4.28
Subtotal	**36,039**	**13.30**	**617**	**26.42**
Other Campaign Activity				
Persuasion mail/brochures	78,661	29.03	654	28.00
Actual campaigning	22,242	8.21	0	
Staff/volunteers	14	.01	0	
Subtotal	**100,917**	**37.25**	**654**	**28.00**
Constituent Gifts/ Entertainment	**3,117**	**1.15**	**0**	
Donations to				
Candidates from same state	0		0	
Candidates from other states	0		0	
Civic organizations	0		0	
Ideological groups	0		0	
Political parties	50	.02	0	
Subtotal	**50**	**.02**	**0**	
Unitemized Expenses	**280**	**.10**	**0**	
Total Campaign Expenses	**$ 270,944**		**$ 2,335**	
PAC Contributions	$ 171,239		$ 0	
Individual Contributions	158,205		1,860	
Total Receipts*	374,016		1,860	

*Includes PAC and individual contributions as well as interest earned, party contributions, etc.

FLORIDA — District 7

Rep. John L. Mica (R)

1992 Election Results

John L. Mica (R)	125,790	(56%)
Dan Webster (D)	96,926	(44%)

Republican businessman John L. Mica came late to this race, declaring his candidacy at the end of May 1992. However, a $100,000 personal loan to his campaign got him rolling, and within two weeks he had tapped his various business and political connections for another $100,000.

Mica was no stranger to politics, having served four years in the Florida legislature. He had also worked as chief of staff for former U.S. senator Paula Hawkins (R-Fla.) and as a lobbyist. For Mica, the 1992 campaign was "the culmination of years of campaigning and learning from my mistakes."

Before turning his attention to Democrat Dan Webster, Mica first had to dispose of state representative Dick Graham and Vaughn S. Forrest, chief of staff for Rep. Bill McCollum (R-Fla.), in the Republican primary. Mica handily won the primary, but it cost more than $194,000, including $45,500 for television commercials and $17,284 for radio ads.

Media consultant Sandler-Innocenzi of Washington, D.C., was brought in to develop the television advertising. Two commercials were developed for the primary; three were produced for the general election. Mica said the ads focused primarily on jobs and health care with several "comparison ads" among the mix. Unlike many who took great pains to distance themselves from Washington, Mica said he accentuated his Washington connections and experience. For producing and placing the five ads, Sandler-Innocenzi received $123,830.

Mica also spent heavily on radio advertising developed by Todd Persons Communications of Orlando. Mica had three spots developed for the primary and two produced for the general election. Mica noted that one of the more controversial primary spots, which attacked Graham's support for early-release programs for prisoners, was reminiscent of the infamous 1988 Willie Horton ad in the Bush/Dukakis presidential campaign. Persons collected $46,390 for producing and placing the five spots.

Production of Mica's voter contact mail was handled by Direct Mail Systems of St. Petersburg. According to Mica, they also handled about 60 percent of the creative work. Richard Morris of West Redding, Conn., who also served as the campaign's pollster and general consultant, was responsible for the balance of the design and copywriting. Direct Mail received $73,405 for its efforts; Morris collected $10,000 for his various consulting roles.

One lesson Mica said he learned from previous unsuccessful campaigns for state and federal offices was the value of phonebanking. Cherry Communications of Gainesville was paid $12,958 for making more than 25,000 telephone calls. Another $18,963 was spent on an in-house phonebank.

	Mica		Webster	
Campaign Expenditures	Amount Spent	% of Total	Amount Spent	% of Total
Overhead				
Office furniture/supplies	$ 23,017	5.13	$ 13,185	3.88
Rent/utilities	2,379	.53	11,028	3.24
Salaries	19,614	4.37	31,198	9.17
Taxes	0		10,063	2.96
Bank/investment fees	4,305	.96	489	.14
Lawyers/accountants	0		0	
Telephone	6,263	1.39	21,115	6.21
Campaign automobile	0		6,351	1.87
Computers/office equipment	0		11,441	3.36
Travel	0		4,694	1.38
Food/meetings	0		266	.08
Subtotal	55,579	12.38	109,832	32.30
Fund Raising				
Events	25,393	5.65	42,203	12.41
Direct mail	17,371	3.87	7,169	2.11
Telemarketing	0		0	
Subtotal	42,765	9.52	49,372	14.52
Polling	3,333	.74	7,500	2.21
Advertising				
Electronic media	171,939	38.28	80,192	23.58
Other media	15,306	3.41	2,260	.66
Subtotal	187,245	41.69	82,452	24.25
Other Campaign Activity				
Persuasion mail/brochures	76,738	17.09	58,605	17.23
Actual campaigning	58,644	13.06	18,719	5.50
Staff/volunteers	0		521	.15
Subtotal	135,382	30.14	77,845	22.89
Constituent Gifts/ Entertainment	0		171	.05
Donations to				
Candidates from same state	0		0	
Candidates from other states	0		0	
Civic organizations	0		330	.10
Ideological groups	0		0	
Political parties	0		210	.06
Subtotal	0		540	.16
Unitemized Expenses	24,801	5.52	12,354	3.63
Total Campaign Expenses	$ 449,104		$ 340,065	
PAC Contributions	$ 145,700		$ 133,595	
Individual Contributions	154,256		131,605	
Total Receipts*	465,407		310,201	

*Includes PAC and individual contributions as well as interest earned, party contributions, etc.

District 8 — FLORIDA

Rep. Bill McCollum (R)

1992 Election Results

Bill McCollum (R)	141,925	(69%)
Chuck Kovaleski (D)	65,132	(31%)

Redistricting left seven-term Republican Rep. Bill McCollum with only half of his former constituents, but the new voters were no less Republican than the old. Having won reelection with 60 percent of the vote in 1990, McCollum garnered 69 percent in 1992—21 percentage points ahead of the Republican presidential ticket.

Despite the eventual lopsided result, Democrat Chuck Kovaleski presented a credible challenge. While refusing to accept political action committee donations and imposing a $1,000 ceiling on his individual contributions, Kovaleski still managed to mount a $153,524 campaign. In contrast, McCollum's 1990 challenger had managed to spend just $18,662 on a token effort.

To meet the challenge, McCollum spent $246,838 on radio and television advertising designed by Chesapeake Media of Cordova, Md. Of that total, slightly more than $170,000 was spent on airing the commercials. Production of the ads cost $39,029 and consultant fees totaled $37,451, of which $22,476 went to Chesapeake Media. The balance of the consultant fee was paid to Donald J. Morrissey of Severna Park, Md., who placed some of the spots. McCollum's broadcast advertising expenses were $130,149 higher in 1992 than in 1990.

McCollum also increased his spending on voter contact mail from $40,191 in 1990 to $63,184 in 1992, a 57 percent rise. His two mailings—one before the primary and another before the general election—were sent to all registered Republicans. The general election mailing also targeted Democrats in new areas of the district.

In-house phonebanks cost the campaign $17,141. During the final weeks of the campaign, fifteen telephone lines were in operation from 9:00 a.m. to 9:00 p.m. While volunteers pulled some of the telephone duty, the campaign also hired temporary employees to make certain the phones were never idle.

Staff salaries took a hefty 15 percent of McCollum's campaign budget, largely because he paid two congressional staffers a total of $56,815. As he had in 1990, chief of staff Vaughn S. Forrest drew large, lump-sum payments from the campaign for "consulting" in addition to his congressional salary. Between April 16, 1991 and June 1, 1992, Forrest received four campaign checks totaling $38,190.

Forrest's last check from the McCollum campaign came just three months before Forrest waged his own unsuccessful House race against John L. Mica in Florida's District 7 Republican primary. It also came just before his request that he be allowed to remain on the congressional payroll while campaigning for the District 7 seat. "I am not a millionaire. Millionaires quit to run," Forrest told a local newspaper.

Campaign Expenditures	McCollum Amount Spent	McCollum % of Total	Kovaleski Amount Spent	Kovaleski % of Total
Overhead				
Office furniture/supplies	$ 11,540	1.72	$ 3,129	2.04
Rent/utilities	22,691	3.38	4,566	2.97
Salaries	103,397	15.38	56,271	36.65
Taxes	24,958	3.71	17,821	11.61
Bank/investment fees	9,248	1.38	95	.06
Lawyers/accountants	3,479	.52	0	
Telephone	5,402	.80	7,698	5.01
Campaign automobile	0		0	
Computers/office equipment	6,874	1.02	2,773	1.81
Travel	11,290	1.68	2,562	1.67
Food/meetings	3,390	.50	679	.44
Subtotal	**202,270**	**30.09**	**95,594**	**62.27**
Fund Raising				
Events	69,381	10.32	3,916	2.55
Direct mail	3,687	.55	7,555	4.92
Telemarketing	0		0	
Subtotal	**73,068**	**10.87**	**11,471**	**7.47**
Polling	**25,058**	**3.73**	**11,050**	**7.20**
Advertising				
Electronic media	246,838	36.71	17,945	11.69
Other media	2,038	.30	0	
Subtotal	**248,876**	**37.02**	**17,945**	**11.69**
Other Campaign Activity				
Persuasion mail/brochures	63,184	9.40	3,503	2.28
Actual campaigning	35,759	5.32	12,987	8.46
Staff/volunteers	931	.14	0	
Subtotal	**99,874**	**14.86**	**16,490**	**10.74**
Constituent Gifts/ Entertainment	**6,562**	**.98**	**0**	
Donations to				
Candidates from same state	2,650	.39	0	
Candidates from other states	2,000	.30	0	
Civic organizations	370	.06	590	.38
Ideological groups	0		60	.04
Political parties	3,723	.55	24	.02
Subtotal	**8,743**	**1.30**	**674**	**.44**
Unitemized Expenses	**7,869**	**1.17**	**300**	**.20**
Total Campaign Expenses	**$ 672,319**		**$ 153,524**	
PAC Contributions	$ 301,830		$ 0	
Individual Contributions	296,141		132,661	
Total Receipts*	642,785		174,941	

*Includes PAC and individual contributions as well as interest earned, party contributions, etc.

FLORIDA — District 9

Rep. Michael Bilirakis (R)

1992 Election Results

Michael Bilirakis (R)	157,822	(59%)
Cheryl Davis Knapp (D)	110,023	(41%)

Democrat Cheryl Davis Knapp spent $180,791 more in 1992 than she had in 1990 to challenge Rep. Michael Bilirakis. Her increased spending yielded 1 percent *less* of the votes.

Forced to spend $816,699 to defeat Knapp the first time, Bilirakis entered the 1992 election cycle with cash reserves of only $2,617. With Knapp poised for a better funded reprise, the incumbent's first order of business was fund raising.

According to campaign manager Robert Meyers, Bilirakis held twenty fund-raising events, including one celebrating his Greek heritage and another featuring Minority Whip Newt Gingrich (R-Ga.). However, most of the fund-raisers were small affairs, sponsored by Bilirakis's supporters. "No major celebrities or party people were involved," said Meyers. "No Hollywood stars. Just small events with a dozen people on up."

To supplement his events, Bilirakis paid Tucker & Associates of Washington, D.C., $4,680 to coordinate direct-mail solicitations. While he declined to give an exact number, Meyers said the campaign sent out fund-raising letters "whenever the campaign needed money."

By mid-August 1992 Bilirakis had raised 60 percent of the $779,124 he would ultimately collect and had spent just 30 percent of the $774,096 he would spend to defeat Knapp. At that point he had cash reserves of $133,740 compared with Knapp's $8,645.

From the middle of August until November, Bilirakis poured his money into television, voter contact mail, and a phonebanking operation. He also increased his campaign staff from three to ten.

National Media of Alexandria, Va., received $213,244 for developing and placing four television commercials: two comparative ads and two biographical spots. Radio air time was purchased directly by the campaign. The $237,684 Bilirakis spent on broadcast ads represented a 40 percent increase over his 1990 spending for such advertising.

Direct Mail Systems of St. Petersburg collected $114,519 for handling Bilirakis's persuasion mail. Meyers said the incumbent sent out six or seven mailings, all heavily targeted toward voters who were fifty-five years old or older.

To ensure that his voters made their way to the polls on election day, Bilirakis invested $29,106 in his phonebank. National Call Center of Clearwater and Campaign Telecommunications of New York received $16,106 and $13,000, respectively.

Bilirakis still found time to wine-and-dine his constituents. He invested $7,519 in his annual picnics to thank supporters and spent $14,362 on constituent meals, entertainment, and gifts. Year-end holiday cards mailed to his supporters added another $7,242.

	Bilirakis		Knapp	
Campaign Expenditures	Amount Spent	% of Total	Amount Spent	% of Total
Overhead				
Office furniture/supplies	$ 14,758	1.91	$ 8,744	3.28
Rent/utilities	13,518	1.75	2,365	.89
Salaries	77,218	9.98	8,216	3.08
Taxes	8,492	1.10	0	
Bank/investment fees	330	.04	15	.01
Lawyers/accountants	14,785	1.91	0	
Telephone	8,323	1.08	6,825	2.56
Campaign automobile	0		0	
Computers/office equipment	5,074	.66	3,937	1.48
Travel	30,555	3.95	28,447	10.67
Food/meetings	1,501	.19	0	
Subtotal	**174,554**	**22.55**	**58,549**	**21.96**
Fund Raising				
Events	31,507	4.07	23,466	8.80
Direct mail	52,381	6.77	9,869	3.70
Telemarketing	0		0	
Subtotal	**83,888**	**10.84**	**33,336**	**12.50**
Polling	**21,350**	**2.76**	**14,482**	**5.43**
Advertising				
Electronic media	237,684	30.70	118,009	44.27
Other media	5,958	.77	6,654	2.50
Subtotal	**243,642**	**31.47**	**124,663**	**46.76**
Other Campaign Activity				
Persuasion mail/brochures	130,436	16.85	16,490	6.19
Actual campaigning	73,930	9.55	14,901	5.59
Staff/volunteers	5,615	.73	256	.10
Subtotal	**209,980**	**27.13**	**31,647**	**11.87**
Constituent Gifts/Entertainment	**29,123**	**3.76**	**0**	
Donations to				
Candidates from same state	0		50	.02
Candidates from other states	0		0	
Civic organizations	6,244	.81	1,295	.49
Ideological groups	264	.03	1,194	.45
Political parties	4,209	.54	1,157	.43
Subtotal	**10,717**	**1.38**	**3,696**	**1.39**
Unitemized Expenses	**841**	**.11**	**212**	**.08**
Total Campaign Expenses	**$ 774,096**		**$ 266,586**	
PAC Contributions	$ 313,210		$ 115,659	
Individual Contributions	450,143		84,067	
Total Receipts*	779,124		271,378	

*Includes PAC and individual contributions as well as interest earned, party contributions, etc.

District 10 — FLORIDA

Rep. C. W. Bill Young (R)

1992 Election Results

C. W. Bill Young (R)	149,347	(57%)
Karen Moffitt (D)	114,637	(43%)

This was the most expensive campaign ever waged by Rep. C. W. Bill Young. It cost more than twice as much as his 1990 race, when he ran unopposed and spent very little on direct appeals to voters. In fact, the $458,366 Young invested in his 1992 effort was just $984 less than he spent on his three previous reelection bids combined.

Not coincidentally, Young's comfortable 14-point margin of victory over Democrat Karen Moffitt was also his narrowest ever. First elected in 1970, Young had never received less than 65 percent of the vote and had run unopposed four times.

Advertising and persuasion mail accounted for all of Young's increased spending and then some. While his overall spending rose by $264,323 from 1990 to 1992, his spending on voter contact mail and advertising rose by $307,397. Pressed for the first time, Young actually reduced his spending on overhead by $34,474, essentially the amount the campaign paid in 1990 to purchase, license, and insure his baby-blue Lincoln Town Car. Young also reduced his fund-raising costs from $21,215 in 1990 to an astonishingly low $15,806 in 1992, choosing to fund much of his campaign with money left over from previous elections.

Young's increased spending did not benefit any consultants. According to his administrative assistant, Douglas M. Gregory, Young believes that "after being in politics for thirty-two years, if he doesn't know what his constituents want, then how will some consultant know?" In that spirit, Young personally wrote all his voter contact mail, television and radio commercials, and newspaper ad copy. The campaign bought the air time and placed the newspaper ads directly, leaving only the production to be done by others.

Unlike many incumbents who tried to minimize their Washington-insider status, Gregory said the focus of Young's advertising was his ability to "get the job done." Young spent $72,252 to air his television ads and $12,126 on radio. Another $22,803 was spent to place ads in publications such as the *Gulfport Gabber,* the *Weekly Challenger,* the *Jewish Press,* and the *Senior Voice.*

Gregory noted that in District 10, like most congressional districts, the most effective way to communicate Young's "simple message" was through the mail. Printing and postage for a continuous barrage of persuasion mail cost the campaign $191,620.

Moffitt, an associate professor at the University of South Florida, matched Young nearly dollar for dollar on broadcast advertising expeditures. She paid Squier/Eskew/Knapp/Ochs Communications of Washington, D.C., $95,679 for producing and placing her ads. However, Moffitt was outspent by more than nine to one on persuasion mail.

Campaign Expenditures	Young Amount Spent	Young % of Total	Moffitt Amount Spent	Moffitt % of Total
Overhead				
Office furniture/supplies	$ 3,727	.81	$ 2,422	1.09
Rent/utilities	900	.20	1,169	.53
Salaries	0		20,714	9.32
Taxes	8,719	1.90	0	
Bank/investment fees	105	.02	261	.12
Lawyers/accountants	20,662	4.51	0	
Telephone	8,503	1.86	799	.36
Campaign automobile	3,572	.78	0	
Computers/office equipment	280	.06	2,170	.98
Travel	22,247	4.85	3,427	1.54
Food/meetings	727	.16	0	
Subtotal	**69,441**	**15.15**	**30,962**	**13.93**
Fund Raising				
Events	12,990	2.83	25,691	11.55
Direct mail	2,816	.61	3,939	1.77
Telemarketing	0		0	
Subtotal	**15,806**	**3.45**	**29,630**	**13.33**
Polling	**0**		**15,615**	**7.02**
Advertising				
Electronic media	104,769	22.86	96,679	43.48
Other media	24,603	5.37	1,498	.67
Subtotal	**129,373**	**28.22**	**98,177**	**44.16**
Other Campaign Activity				
Persuasion mail/brochures	191,620	41.80	21,153	9.51
Actual campaigning	12,519	2.73	24,429	10.99
Staff/volunteers	2,471	.54	180	.08
Subtotal	**206,609**	**45.08**	**45,762**	**20.58**
Constituent Gifts/ Entertainment	**21,571**	**4.71**	**0**	
Donations to				
Candidates from same state	0		0	
Candidates from other states	0		125	.06
Civic organizations	2,922	.64	0	
Ideological groups	850	.19	0	
Political parties	2,980	.65	0	
Subtotal	**6,752**	**1.47**	**125**	**.06**
Unitemized Expenses	**8,813**	**1.92**	**2,071**	**.93**
Total Campaign Expenses	**$ 458,366**		**$ 222,342**	
PAC Contributions	**$ 165,250**		**$ 102,711**	
Individual Contributions	63,449		71,630	
Total Receipts*	274,122		202,132	

*Includes PAC and individual contributions as well as interest earned, party contributions, etc.

FLORIDA — District 11

Rep. Sam M. Gibbons (D)

1992 Election Results

Sam M. Gibbons (D)	100,962	(53%)
Mark Sharpe (R)	77,625	(41%)
Joe De Minico † (I)	12,729	(7%)

Rep. Sam M. Gibbons spent $419,603 on overhead, 44 percent of his total campaign outlays. Gibbons's overhead alone was more than eight times the amount Republican challenger Mark Sharpe invested in his entire campaign.

Driving those phenomenal overhead expenditures were campaign salary and benefits payments totaling $189,218. To run his campaign, Gibbons hired Reggie Garcia, the husband of his public affairs assistant, Lisa M. Garcia. Over the two-year election cycle, Garcia received salary payments totaling $116,258. He also received $848 to pay for health insurance, $425 to cover the cost of his life insurance, and $1,500 for child care. The campaign also picked up the tab for Garcia's automobile insurance. Lisa Garcia received $5,864 for her general election campaign efforts.

As in past campaigns, Gibbons maintained two permanent campaign offices. A fund-raising office in Washington, D.C., cost the campaign $65,772 to maintain, including $26,545 for rent and $27,848 to cover the part-time salary of Patricia Stringer, who was also a part-time employee in Gibbons's congressional office. A new laser printer cost $2,704, telephone bills amounted to $2,243, utilities added $2,282, rent on the office copier totaled $1,544, and insurance premiums amounted to $1,034. Rounding out the expenses for the Washington office were payments for moving the office in 1992, office security, pest control, some electrical work, office supplies, and cleaning services. In contrast, rent on Gibbons's Florida office totaled just $5,304 for the two-year cycle.

Lease payments and registration fees on the campaign car came to $15,175. Gibbons's wife was reimbursed $12,290 for her travel. Gibbons paid his son's law firm a total of $12,478 for secretarial support and various office expenses. MCA Accounting Service of Tampa collected $15,823 and Primary Systems of Falls Church, Va., received $10,000 for providing computer-support services.

With the ability to tap political action committees for $427,161 and cash reserves at the beginning of 1991 totaling $278,961, Gibbons had enough left over to wage an expensive voter contact effort. Trippi, McMahon & Squier of Alexandria, Va., collected $215,867 for developing and placing Gibbons's broadcast ads. Another $7,820 was invested in newspaper ads. The November Group of Washington, D.C., received $33,038 for developing brochures and coordinating the persuasion mail effort.

With little money to fend off the Gibbons juggernaut, Sharpe said he walked various parts of the district every day from January through September 1992. He also wrote what little advertising he could afford to put on the air.

Campaign Expenditures	Gibbons Amount Spent	Gibbons % of Total	Sharpe Amount Spent	Sharpe % of Total
Overhead				
Office furniture/supplies	$ 10,231	1.07	$ 2,624	5.29
Rent/utilities	34,439	3.59	3,834	7.72
Salaries	189,218	19.72	1,450	2.92
Taxes	84,350	8.79	0	
Bank/investment fees	0		13	.03
Lawyers/accountants	15,823	1.65	0	
Telephone	13,795	1.44	2,519	5.07
Campaign automobile	15,175	1.58	0	
Computers/office equipment	27,265	2.84	550	1.11
Travel	27,215	2.84	194	.39
Food/meetings	2,094	.22	269	.54
Subtotal	**419,603**	**43.73**	**11,453**	**23.07**
Fund Raising				
Events	62,374	6.50	1,209	2.43
Direct mail	6,508	.68	5,015	10.10
Telemarketing	0		0	
Subtotal	**68,883**	**7.18**	**6,224**	**12.54**
Polling	**40,020**	**4.17**	**0**	
Advertising				
Electronic media	224,867	23.43	10,528	21.21
Other media	8,345	.87	125	.25
Subtotal	**233,211**	**24.30**	**10,653**	**21.46**
Other Campaign Activity				
Persuasion mail/brochures	125,019	13.03	11,451	23.07
Actual campaigning	29,014	3.02	9,152	18.43
Staff/volunteers	1,694	.18	221	.44
Subtotal	**155,727**	**16.23**	**20,824**	**41.94**
Constituent Gifts/Entertainment	**2,317**	**.24**	**0**	
Donations to				
Candidates from same state	2,140	.22	0	
Candidates from other states	1,750	.18	0	
Civic organizations	8,240	.86	39	.08
Ideological groups	1,455	.15	0	
Political parties	12,700	1.32	0	
Subtotal	**26,285**	**2.74**	**39**	**.08**
Unitemized Expenses	**13,535**	**1.41**	**454**	**.91**
Total Campaign Expenses	**$ 959,581**		**$ 49,646**	
PAC Contributions	$ 427,161		$ 750	
Individual Contributions	249,465		43,589	
Total Receipts*	722,678		51,952	

*Includes PAC and individual contributions as well as interest earned, party contributions, etc.

† No expenditures or receipts on file. Candidates raising or spending less than $5,000 are not required to file reports with the Federal Election Commission.

District 12 — FLORIDA

Rep. Charles T. Canady (R)

1992 Election Results

Charles T. Canady (R)	100,468	(52%)
Tom Mims (D)	92,333	(48%)

Financial records filed by the campaigns of Democrat Tom Mims and Republican Charles T. Canady showed Mims outspending Canady by more than two to one. Unfortunately for Mims, these numbers badly distort the dynamics of the race.

While he won the Democratic primary with 68 percent of the vote, the effort cost Mims $155,262, leaving him $175,344 with which to tackle Canady. The Democratic Congressional Campaign Committee's (DCCC) coordinated campaign added $24,418 to his effort. Unopposed in the Republican primary, Canady was able to concentrate his entire $155,671 budget on the fall campaign, and the National Republican Congressional Committee (NRCC) provided another $54,418. In their head-to-head general election battle, Canady outspent Mimms by $10,327.

Without a strong media market, both candidates relied heavily on persuasion mail to spread their messages. To develop his mail, Mims turned to Ambrosino & Muir of San Francisco, Calif. Of the $99,230 Ambrosino & Muir received, $41,800 was for work during the fall campaign. Other postage and printing associated with Mims's general election voter contact mail totaled $26,790.

In contrast, Canady created his mailings in-house, funneling nothing through consultants. Virtually all of the NRCC's coordinated effort was put into persuasion mail and, as a result, Canady managed to outspend Mims on persuasion mail over the final weeks of the campaign.

Canady made his first payment to National Media of Alexandria, Va., on October 1 and over the final weeks of the campaign attacked Mims for being both pro-tax and antibusiness. In one ad, Mims was shown getting all F's on a mock report card. Perhaps not surprisingly, postelection comments by Mims and various Democratic officials credited Canady's negative campaign with turning the tide.

Using virtually all the money provided by the DCCC's coordinated campaign effort, Mims countered with a $82,254 broadcast advertising campaign. He paid Joe Slade White & Co. of New York $3,038 for creative efforts. Production costs were picked up by the DCCC and totaled $4,316. Shafto & Barton of Houston, Texas, received $54,900 from Mims and another $20,000 from the DCCC to place the spots.

Mims also invested considerably more than Canady in measuring public sentiment. Mims relied on two pollsters. Kitchens, Powell & Kitchens of Orlando collected $8,500. Cooper & Secrest Associates of Alexandria, Va., received $3,202. The American Medical Association PAC donated a poll to Mims valued at $4,700. Canady's only polling expense was a $1,959 in-kind survey provided by the NRCC.

	Canady		Mims	
Campaign Expenditures	Amount Spent	% of Total	Amount Spent	% of Total
Overhead				
Office furniture/supplies	$ 4,544	2.92	$ 4,349	1.32
Rent/utilities	4,348	2.79	4,393	1.33
Salaries	10,355	6.65	12,011	3.63
Taxes	0		0	
Bank/investment fees	0		436	.13
Lawyers/accountants	0		0	
Telephone	4,608	2.96	5,478	1.66
Campaign automobile	0		0	
Computers/office equipment	655	.42	2,971	.90
Travel	2,937	1.89	3,554	1.07
Food/meetings	250	.16	0	
Subtotal	**27,697**	**17.79**	**33,191**	**10.04**
Fund Raising				
Events	7,326	4.71	23,695	7.17
Direct mail	0		3,806	1.15
Telemarketing	0		0	
Subtotal	**7,326**	**4.71**	**27,501**	**8.32**
Polling	**1,959**	**1.26**	**16,402**	**4.96**
Advertising				
Electronic media	56,370	36.21	57,938	17.52
Other media	0		200	.06
Subtotal	**56,370**	**36.21**	**58,137**	**17.59**
Other Campaign Activity				
Persuasion mail/brochures	39,217	25.19	165,735	50.13
Actual campaigning	9,540	6.13	14,521	4.39
Staff/volunteers	0		0	
Subtotal	**48,757**	**31.32**	**180,255**	**54.52**
Constituent Gifts/ Entertainment	**0**		**0**	
Donations to				
Candidates from same state	0		0	
Candidates from other states	0		0	
Civic organizations	0		0	
Ideological groups	0		0	
Political parties	0		0	
Subtotal	**0**		**0**	
Unitemized Expenses	**13,563**	**8.71**	**15,120**	**4.57**
Total Campaign Expenses	**$ 155,671**		**$ 330,606**	
PAC Contributions	**$ 53,311**		**$ 96,195**	
Individual Contributions	**94,757**		**93,155**	
Total Receipts*	**158,777**		**351,200**	

*Includes PAC and individual contributions as well as interest earned, party contributions, etc.

FLORIDA — District 13

Rep. Dan Miller (R)

1992 Election Results

Dan Miller (R)	158,836	(58%)
Rand Snell (D)	115,741	(42%)

The five-candidate Republican primary and the subsequent primary runoff between businessmen Dan Miller and Brad Baker were the only contests of consequence in this heavily Republican district. Of the $459,682 Miller spent to win this seat, $314,673 was spent to defeat his fellow Republicans. Baker pumped $438,577 into his losing effort.

More than half the money Miller invested to secure the Republican nomination was spent on persuasion mail and broadcast advertising. Direct Mail Systems of St. Petersburg collected $66,457 for developing six mailings. National Media of Alexandria, Va., received $56,935 for designing and placing preprimary radio and television commercials; the firm was paid an additional $28,475 during the abbreviated runoff campaign.

Miller paid American Viewpoint of Alexandria, Va., $16,000 for conducting polls before the primary and runoff. Payco American Corp. of Brookfield, Wis., collected $14,500 for phonebanking. Payments for yard signs and posters totaled $6,805. Bumper stickers cost $2,080. T-shirts and sun visors added $1,375 and $492, respectively.

With Republicans outnumbering Democrats by approximately 69,000, Miller ran a dramatically scaled-down campaign against Rand Snell, a former aide to Gov. Lawton Chiles. Miller paid National Media $22,335; Direct Mail Systems, $42,880; Payco, $6,336; and American Viewpoint, $5,000. He invested only $1,581 in signs and $1,130 in lapel pins.

Following Miller's April 1992 entry into the race, chief of staff Katherine Calhoun Wood said the campaign held at least two small, formal fund-raising receptions each month. Wood noted that ticket prices ranged between $50 and $250, since Miller preferred to personally ask for his larger donations. Sandi Lake Productions of Sarasota received $1,573 for helping to arrange several district events.

Miller paid Nancy Bocskor of Arlington, Va., $2,154 for helping him raise money from political action committees (PACs). Direct Mail Systems received $27,447 for its work on three mail solicitations. Wood said the small mailings targeted groups such as the alumni of Miller's alma mater.

Ultimately, Miller raised $156,931 from individual contributors who gave at least $200. Small donations amounted to $100,216. PACs contributed only $70,400. Miller also tapped his own bank account for loans totaling $122,500.

Snell sank 52 percent of his funds into advertising, narrowly outspending Miller on broadcast commercials and significantly outspending him on newspaper ads. Media Strategies & Research of Washington, D.C., collected $35,000 for buying time and another $10,000 for polling.

	Miller		Snell	
Campaign Expenditures	Amount Spent	% of Total	Amount Spent	% of Total
Overhead				
Office furniture/supplies	$ 7,990	1.74	$ 7,061	2.37
Rent/utilities	6,330	1.38	3,407	1.14
Salaries	31,623	6.88	12,575	4.22
Taxes	4,963	1.08	4,992	1.67
Bank/investment fees	534	.12	138	.05
Lawyers/accountants	760	.17	0	
Telephone	6,358	1.38	5,278	1.77
Campaign automobile	0		0	
Computers/office equipment	740	.16	4,457	1.49
Travel	2,271	.49	6,202	2.08
Food/meetings	59	.01	207	.07
Subtotal	**61,627**	**13.41**	**44,317**	**14.86**
Fund Raising				
Events	19,356	4.21	35,697	11.97
Direct mail	30,355	6.60	3,065	1.03
Telemarketing	0		0	
Subtotal	**49,710**	**10.81**	**38,762**	**12.99**
Polling	**21,000**	**4.57**	**10,000**	**3.35**
Advertising				
Electronic media	117,006	25.45	124,004	41.57
Other media	2,930	.64	30,555	10.24
Subtotal	**119,936**	**26.09**	**154,559**	**51.81**
Other Campaign Activity				
Persuasion mail/brochures	127,250	27.68	17,238	5.78
Actual campaigning	76,127	16.56	28,156	9.44
Staff/volunteers	127	.03	0	
Subtotal	**203,504**	**44.27**	**45,394**	**15.22**
Constituent Gifts/ Entertainment	**0**		**0**	
Donations to				
Candidates from same state	0		0	
Candidates from other states	0		0	
Civic organizations	225	.05	86	.03
Ideological groups	0		0	
Political parties	126	.03	0	
Subtotal	**351**	**.08**	**86**	**.03**
Unitemized Expenses	**3,554**	**.77**	**5,195**	**1.74**
Total Campaign Expenses	**$ 459,682**		**$ 298,314**	
PAC Contributions	**$ 70,400**		**$ 38,300**	
Individual Contributions	257,147		109,851	
Total Receipts*	453,193		298,372	

*Includes PAC and individual contributions as well as interest earned, party contributions, etc.

District 14 — FLORIDA

Rep. Porter J. Goss (R)

1992 Election Results

Porter J. Goss (R)	220,324	(82%)
James H. King (I)	48,156	(18%)

Rep. Porter J. Goss does not suffer competition gladly. In his initial House campaign in 1988, Goss invested $836,224—four times more than his Democratic opponent—and won with 71 percent of the vote. Unopposed in 1990, Goss still spent $170,854 on his campaign. When faced with a 1992 challenger who spent only $16,885, Goss nevertheless increased his own outlays to $407,490.

While most incumbents invested the bulk of their off-year spending in overhead and fund raising, 43 percent of Goss's 1991 spending was put into voter contact mail. According to chief of staff Sheryl V. Wooley, the October mailer "touched base" with 170,000 people who had voted in the 1988 Republican primary. James R. Foster & Associates of Carrollton, Texas, collected $56,679 for designing and mailing the piece. Goss had no primary opponent.

For the general election campaign against James H. King, an independent candidate, Goss paid Mike Murphy Media of Washington, D.C., $76,782 to produce and place three television commercials. Despite the fact that Goss was seeking his third House term, Wooley said the central theme of all the ads was change. As Wooley put it, "We wanted to show he was not the usual incumbent."

To keep constituents and supporters informed of Goss's activities in Washington, the campaign periodically mailed newsletters written by Goss's wife. Closer to the election, the campaign sent out 15,000 absentee ballots and mailed brochures to the relatively small number of new voters acquired through redistricting.

Goss invested $8,582 in yard signs, and on election night volunteers criss-crossed the district pasting "thank-you" stickers on all the signs. The campaign paid $297 to print the stickers and $23 to mail them to people who lived in outlying areas.

Not all of Goss's expenditures were tied to his 1992 reelection effort. Because he continued to receive contributions after the 1990 election, Wooley said Goss decided to stage a series of "thank-you" parties for contributors in mid-1991. These parties cost the campaign a total of $6,277, including $3,488 for food, $760 for music, and $1,179 for invitations and postage.

Goss enlisted college students from across the district, spent $1,414 of his campaign money to outfit them in white shorts and a Porter Goss T-shirt, and put them to work on a variety of community service projects. In addition to using campaign funds to absorb the miscellaneous expenses associated with these projects, Goss spent $3,600 of his campaign treasury to reward the college students for their good deeds.

	Goss		King	
Campaign Expenditures	Amount Spent	% of Total	Amount Spent	% of Total
Overhead				
Office furniture/supplies	$ 5,646	1.39	$ 1,135	6.72
Rent/utilities	4,133	1.01	0	
Salaries	69,758	17.12	0	
Taxes	21,782	5.35	0	
Bank/investment fees	40	.01	294	1.74
Lawyers/accountants	3,479	.85	0	
Telephone	6,582	1.62	0	
Campaign automobile	0		0	
Computers/office equipment	18,782	4.61	0	
Travel	3,961	.97	6,455	38.23
Food/meetings	552	.14	93	.55
Subtotal	**134,716**	**33.06**	**7,977**	**47.24**
Fund Raising				
Events	10,170	2.50	932	5.52
Direct mail	11,603	2.85	0	
Telemarketing	0		0	
Subtotal	**21,773**	**5.34**	**932**	**5.52**
Polling	**24,210**	**5.94**	**0**	
Advertising				
Electronic media	76,782	18.84	0	
Other media	0		0	
Subtotal	**76,782**	**18.84**	**0**	
Other Campaign Activity				
Persuasion mail/brochures	91,824	22.53	5,151	30.50
Actual campaigning	36,877	9.05	2,587	15.32
Staff/volunteers	438	.11	0	
Subtotal	**129,139**	**31.69**	**7,738**	**45.83**
Constituent Gifts/ Entertainment	**14,198**	**3.48**	**0**	
Donations to				
Candidates from same state	0		0	
Candidates from other states	0		0	
Civic organizations	333	.08	178	1.06
Ideological groups	0		50	.30
Political parties	6,065	1.49	10	.06
Subtotal	**6,398**	**1.57**	**238**	**1.41**
Unitemized Expenses	**273**	**.07**	**0**	
Total Campaign Expenses	**$ 407,490**		**$ 16,885**	
PAC Contributions	**$ 41,900**		**$ 0**	
Individual Contributions	**371,912**		**7,171**	
Total Receipts*	**419,508**		**17,382**	

*Includes PAC and individual contributions as well as interest earned, party contributions, etc.

FLORIDA   District 15

Rep. Jim Bacchus (D)

1992 Election Results

Jim Bacchus (D)	132,385	(51%)
Bill Tolley (R)	128,830	(49%)

Freshman Democratic Rep. Jim Bacchus ran 20 percentage points ahead of his party's presidential ticket, and in this heavily Republican district it was just barely enough. "Our biggest challenge was trying to get people to realize it was okay to vote for a Democrat," said Linda O. Hennessee, his congressional chief of staff. "It was an enormous task."

Bacchus's first task was to refill his campaign treasury, which contained only $2,112 at the beginning of 1991. Over the next eighteen months Bacchus spent $66,880 to raise $408,515. By June 30, 1992 he had reimbursed himself for a $30,000 loan he made to the 1990 campaign and had managed to build cash reserves of $292,243.

In the September 1 primary Bacchus faced Larry Bessinger, who he largely ignored. "We had a primary opponent, a right to life candidate, but we made the decision not to engage," remarked Hennessee. "Instead, we made the decision to spend our money in the general election." And spend it they did. Over the next two months, Bacchus committed $520,348 to his second bout with Republican Bill Tolley.

Bacchus sank $373,059 into a broadcast media campaign designed by Strother-Duffy-Strother of Washington, D.C. Because radio time is very inexpensive in this district, Hennessee said two radio spots aired almost continuously throughout the final weeks of the campaign. Five television commercials were aired that focused on issues including education and Bacchus's efforts on behalf of veterans. Another ad focused on his "Citizen Saturdays," events where Bacchus led volunteers in some community-betterment project such as painting a local drug treatment center.

For designing and producing the ads, Strother received $35,782. Media Strategies & Research of Washington, D.C., billed the campaign $318,567 to cover the cost of air time and their fees for placing the ads. "They are the best buyers in America," said Hennessee. "What most people don't seem to realize is that placement is the key to effective advertising."

Another $111,198 was spent on brochures and persuasion mail. Campaign Performance Group of San Francisco, Calif., received $92,825 for producing and sending six persuasion mailers, which included brochures focusing on the economy and on Bacchus's pro-choice stance on abortion.

Tolley's 1992 campaign cost $150,904 less than his 1990 effort. He spent $74,468 less on overhead and nearly $13,000 less on fund raising. Most importantly, his advertising budget was sliced by $31,098, a 32 percent reduction that might have made the difference in a race decided by only 3,555 votes.

	Bacchus		Tolley	
Campaign Expenditures	Amount Spent	% of Total	Amount Spent	% of Total
Overhead				
Office furniture/supplies	$ 7,577	.97	$ 3,170	1.47
Rent/utilities	1,144	.15	1,989	.92
Salaries	45,964	5.86	6,700	3.10
Taxes	18,542	2.36	0	
Bank/investment fees	21	.00	178	.08
Lawyers/accountants	0		0	
Telephone	13,542	1.73	1,763	.82
Campaign automobile	0		0	
Computers/office equipment	1,405	.18	1,027	.48
Travel	23,925	3.05	54	.03
Food/meetings	633	.08	233	.11
Subtotal	**112,754**	**14.38**	**15,114**	**7.00**
Fund Raising				
Events	99,236	12.65	11,534	5.34
Direct mail	0		1,125	.52
Telemarketing	0		0	
Subtotal	**99,236**	**12.65**	**12,659**	**5.86**
Polling	**29,750**	**3.79**	**5,000**	**2.32**
Advertising				
Electronic media	373,059	47.57	64,395	29.83
Other media	2,540	.32	3,073	1.42
Subtotal	**375,599**	**47.89**	**67,468**	**31.25**
Other Campaign Activity				
Persuasion mail/brochures	111,198	14.18	75,507	34.98
Actual campaigning	43,297	5.52	33,307	15.43
Staff/volunteers	247	.03	144	.07
Subtotal	**154,743**	**19.73**	**108,958**	**50.47**
Constituent Gifts/ Entertainment	**745**	**.10**	**0**	
Donations to				
Candidates from same state	575	.07	0	
Candidates from other states	3,000	.38	0	
Civic organizations	514	.07	54	.03
Ideological groups	100	.01	80	.04
Political parties	1,375	.18	200	.09
Subtotal	**5,564**	**.71**	**334**	**.15**
Unitemized Expenses	**5,910**	**.75**	**6,352**	**2.94**
Total Campaign Expenses	**$ 784,301**		**$ 215,886**	
PAC Contributions	**$ 460,597**		**$ 54,615**	
Individual Contributions	**354,523**		**105,362**	
Total Receipts*	**841,298**		**216,346**	

*Includes PAC and individual contributions as well as interest earned, party contributions, etc.

District 16 — FLORIDA

Rep. Tom Lewis (R)

1992 Election Results

Tom Lewis (R)	157,253	(61%)
John P. Comerford (D)	101,217	(39%)

Republican Rep. Tom Lewis had something in 1992 he had not had since his initial House campaign in 1982—Democratic opposition. With the exception of the 1990 campaign, Lewis had not even drawn Republican primary opposition in his four previous reelection bids. His was undoubtedly the safest seat in the House.

However, while he attracted both primary and general election opponents in 1992, Lewis spent 10 percent *less* in 1992 than he had in 1990. An increase of $30,606 in his advertising budget was more than offset by a $39,605 decrease in spending for persuasion mail and a $24,387 drop in overhead expenses.

Before he could worry about potential opponents, Lewis first had to make sure he had a district in which to run. He paid $3,479 to the law firm of Ervin, Varn, Jacobs & Odom, $3,000 to Southern Campaign Resources, and $2,324 to Susan Powers, all of Tallahassee, Fla., for help with the redistricting fight. "It was pretty hot and heavy," said press secretary Karen Hogan. "At one point they eliminated the district. Then they didn't even finish the process until June. It just didn't make for much fun."

Once the district lines were set, Lewis faced both his primary challenger and Hurricane Andrew, and the latter was clearly more trouble than the former. The campaign ran two preprimary radio spots that highlighted Lewis's role in defeating legislation that would have eliminated the air force's Hurricane Hunter program and stressed how much worse the situation might have been had Andrew not been tracked as extensively as it was. Lewis spent $6,912 to air the commercials and another $3,523 on companion newspaper ads.

For the general election contest with investment manager John P. Comerford, Lewis ran the same two radio spots and for the final three days of the campaign added a similar television commercial to the mix. Lewis spent another $6,256 for radio time prior to the general election. Time on network affiliates for his three-day television push cost $15,359. Cable television time added $846. "The hurricane was a big deal in the district and it was important to show Tom's role in protecting Florida," understated Hogan.

Hogan said the campaign mailed at least ten persuasion pieces prior to both the primary and general elections. The bulk of these mailings were tightly targeted, each reaching between 100 and 1,000 households. Cherry Communications of Gainesville received $17,540 for designing the mailings and another $3,105 for phonebanking.

American Viewpoint of Alexandria, Va., conducted the campaign's polls.

Comerford spent only $32,974 on direct appeals to voters.

Campaign Expenditures	Lewis Amount Spent	Lewis % of Total	Comerford Amount Spent	Comerford % of Total
Overhead				
Office furniture/supplies	$ 16,634	4.60	$ 2,899	2.79
Rent/utilities	9,876	2.73	4,657	4.48
Salaries	35,628	9.86	24,791	23.82
Taxes	18,394	5.09	1,071	1.03
Bank/investment fees	137	.04	113	.11
Lawyers/accountants	3,479	.96	0	
Telephone	15,684	4.34	5,410	5.20
Campaign automobile	0		0	
Computers/office equipment	8,510	2.35	1,829	1.76
Travel	12,863	3.56	5,212	5.01
Food/meetings	4,074	1.13	670	.64
Subtotal	**125,279**	**34.66**	**46,653**	**44.83**
Fund Raising				
Events	24,276	6.72	17,574	16.89
Direct mail	7,636	2.11	1,110	1.07
Telemarketing	0		0	
Subtotal	**31,911**	**8.83**	**18,684**	**17.96**
Polling	**19,200**	**5.31**	**5,500**	**5.29**
Advertising				
Electronic media	32,199	8.91	10,218	9.82
Other media	9,983	2.76	2,457	2.36
Subtotal	**42,182**	**11.67**	**12,675**	**12.18**
Other Campaign Activity				
Persuasion mail/brochures	86,930	24.05	4,643	4.46
Actual campaigning	29,661	8.20	15,656	15.05
Staff/volunteers	2,632	.73	0	
Subtotal	**119,223**	**32.98**	**20,299**	**19.51**
Constituent Gifts/Entertainment	**4,291**	**1.19**	**0**	
Donations to				
Candidates from same state	0		0	
Candidates from other states	0		0	
Civic organizations	2,800	.77	110	.11
Ideological groups	0		0	
Political parties	1,849	.51	0	
Subtotal	**4,649**	**1.29**	**110**	**.11**
Unitemized Expenses	**14,764**	**4.08**	**138**	**.13**
Total Campaign Expenses	**$ 361,499**		**$ 104,058**	
PAC Contributions	$ 129,015		$ 40,200	
Individual Contributions	146,609		26,686	
Total Receipts*	296,405		99,097	

*Includes PAC and individual contributions as well as interest earned, party contributions, etc.

FLORIDA — District 17

Rep. Carrie Meek (D)

1992 Election Results Carrie Meek (D) 102,732 (100%)

State senator Carrie Meek invested more than $430,000 to defeat two Democratic primary opponents whose combined spending totaled less than $30,000 and who together received only 17 percent of the vote. No Republican candidate bothered to contest this majority-black seat and a write-in candidate garnered only a few votes.

In an inner-city district that press secretary Jeff Mell described as "difficult to organize," Meek's campaign was vintage grass-roots politics. She spent more than $48,000 to pay workers for distributing campaign literature door-to-door. "Our volunteer base was huge, but we didn't want to depend on them," noted Mell. "We wanted to hire people to pay for their accountability."

Cox & Associates of Coral Gables received $4,690 for running the campaign's phonebank, which delivered a prerecorded telephone message from Meek. A second phonebank with live operators cost $6,400. Meek invested $11,601 in posters and signs and another $2,422 was spent on campaign buttons.

Mell estimated that by the end of the primary campaign every Democrat in the district had received at least three pieces of campaign mail; some voters received as many as five mailings. There was a letter of introduction from the candidate and position papers highlighting her pro-choice stance on abortion and her support for legislation to control the sale of guns. The campaign also mailed postcard endorsements from retiring Reps. Dante B. Fascell and William Lehman, whose old districts overlapped portions of the newly drawn District 17. Phil-Jac Productions of Miami received $27,647 for creating the various persuasion mailers.

Phil-Jac also collected $7,707 for producing six radio commercials for the primary, four of which focused on various relief efforts in the wake of Hurricane Andrew. Newspaper ads for the primary cost $17,131.

Her wide lead in the polls coupled with the high cost of advertising in the Miami market made it easy for Meek to forgo television. However, Mell said time on local cable access channels was so inexpensive that the campaign could not resist running an ad consisting of still photos of Meek and a voice-over touting her record. Mell also said that Phil-Jac urged them not to waste the $375 it cost to air the ad.

In the wake of Hurricane Andrew, Meek spent $5,220 to rent soundtrucks that drove through the most devastated areas of the district announcing that the primary had been postponed and giving people instructions on where to vote. These expenses have been included as "other advertising."

Ron Lester & Associates of Washington, D.C., collected $17,852 for conducting the campaign's polls.

Campaign Expenditures	Meek Amount Spent	% of Total
Overhead		
Office furniture/supplies	$ 18,183	3.96
Rent/utilities	7,011	1.53
Salaries	77,036	16.78
Taxes	0	
Bank/investment fees	164	.04
Lawyers/accountants	0	
Telephone	10,319	2.25
Campaign automobile	0	
Computers/office equipment	2,711	.59
Travel	9,638	2.10
Food/meetings	25	.01
Subtotal	**125,087**	**27.25**
Fund Raising		
Events	39,717	8.65
Direct mail	4,315	.94
Telemarketing	0	
Subtotal	**44,032**	**9.59**
Polling	**17,852**	**3.89**
Advertising		
Electronic media	30,183	6.58
Other media	23,037	5.02
Subtotal	**53,220**	**11.60**
Other Campaign Activity		
Persuasion mail/brochures	113,458	24.72
Actual campaigning	102,213	22.27
Staff/volunteers	533	.12
Subtotal	**216,204**	**47.11**
Constituent Gifts/Entertainment	**48**	**.01**
Donations to		
Candidates from same state	500	.11
Candidates from other states	0	
Civic organizations	613	.13
Ideological groups	630	.14
Political parties	0	
Subtotal	**1,743**	**.38**
Unitemized Expenses	**781**	**.17**
Total Campaign Expenses	**$ 458,967**	
PAC Contributions	$ 158,615	
Individual Contributions	414,452	
Total Receipts*	574,719	

*Includes PAC and individual contributions as well as interest earned, party contributions, etc.

District 18 — FLORIDA

Rep. Ileana Ros-Lehtinen (R)

1992 Election Results

Ileana Ros-Lehtinen (R)	104,715	(67%)
Magda Montiel Davis (D)	52,095	(33%)

Rep. Ileana Ros-Lehtinen began the 1992 election cycle with cash reserves of only $14,387. Over the next eighteen months, she invested $163,954 in a nonstop search for cash and raised $485,618. By the end of June 1992 her campaign treasury contained $296,772.

Ros-Lehtinen's financial reports indicated that she held at least fifteen events in Florida during her fundraising blitz. Senate Minority Leader Bob Dole (R-Kan.), House Minority Whip Newt Gingrich (R-Ga.), Secretary of Housing and Urban Development Jack Kemp, and Secretary of Health and Human Services Louis W. Sullivan were among her featured guests. In July 1991 Ros-Lehtinen paid White House chef Henry Haller $2,175 for his assistance.

Fund-raising costs accounted for 79 percent of Ros-Lehtinen's spending during the first eighteen months of the election cycle. Hebrock & Associates of Tallahassee received $63,755 for organizing the 1991 events. The campaign paid Dan Morgan & Associates of Arlington, Va., $3,066 for event consultation during the first six months of 1992, 46 percent of their 1992 total.

Unopposed in the Republican primary, Ros-Lehtinen focused all her attention on attorney Magda Montiel Davis, her general election opponent. During the final month of the campaign, the incumbent committed $376,905 to her reelection effort, or 56 percent of her outlays for the entire two-year cycle.

J.G.R. & Associates of Miami received $211,469 for producing and placing English and Spanish-language versions of one television commercial and a companion radio spot. Ros-Lehtinen spent $11,016 to place ads on bus-stop benches. Advertisements in newspapers such as *La Prensa, Prensa Libre,* and the *Miami Herald* added $5,864 to her advertising bill.

Ros-Lehtinen paid Cherry Communications of Gainesville $30,941 for phonebanking, and another $10,490 was invested in an in-house phonebank. Brochures and persuasion mail cost her $107,454. By the time Ros-Lehtinen was finished with her direct appeals for votes, her campaign bank account had been drained of all but $7,076.

Since Davis spent virtually nothing to raise money, Ros-Lehtinen's spending advantage was not nearly as potent as the bottom-line difference suggests. Davis spent just $33,996 less than Ros-Lehtinen on broadcast advertising. Strother-Duffy-Strother of Washington, D.C., received $12,109 from Davis for designing two English and two Spanish television spots. Hamilton & Staff of Washington, D.C., billed the campaign $159,000 to cover the cost of air time and their fee for placing the ads. One 60-second radio spot aired on Spanish-language stations called Ros-Lehtinen "the leading clown in the Capitol Hill circus."

Campaign Expenditures	Ros-Lehtinen Amount Spent	Ros-Lehtinen % of Total	Davis Amount Spent	Davis % of Total
Overhead				
Office furniture/supplies	$ 13,505	2.02	$ 3,552	1.06
Rent/utilities	6,171	.92	3,300	.98
Salaries	14,798	2.22	23,898	7.12
Taxes	3,668	.55	0	
Bank/investment fees	300	.05	315	.09
Lawyers/accountants	9,725	1.46	6,903	2.06
Telephone	3,394	.51	2,827	.84
Campaign automobile	0		0	
Computers/office equipment	13,958	2.09	1,689	.50
Travel	7,735	1.16	9,087	2.71
Food/meetings	0		18	.01
Subtotal	**73,253**	**10.98**	**51,588**	**15.38**
Fund Raising				
Events	183,122	27.44	9,367	2.79
Direct mail	0		2,834	.84
Telemarketing	0		0	
Subtotal	**183,122**	**27.44**	**12,201**	**3.64**
Polling	**0**		**14,062**	**4.19**
Advertising				
Electronic media	213,700	32.02	179,704	53.58
Other media	17,030	2.55	7,425	2.21
Subtotal	**230,730**	**34.57**	**187,129**	**55.79**
Other Campaign Activity				
Persuasion mail/brochures	107,454	16.10	38,800	11.57
Actual campaigning	63,479	9.51	30,375	9.06
Staff/volunteers	1,223	.18	232	.07
Subtotal	**172,155**	**25.80**	**69,407**	**20.69**
Constituent Gifts/ Entertainment	**0**		**0**	
Donations to				
Candidates from same state	0		60	.02
Candidates from other states	0		0	
Civic organizations	750	.11	100	.03
Ideological groups	0		15	.00
Political parties	1,050	.16	0	
Subtotal	**1,800**	**.27**	**175**	**.05**
Unitemized Expenses	**6,316**	**.95**	**848**	**.25**
Total Campaign Expenses	**$ 667,376**		**$ 335,410**	
PAC Contributions	**$ 149,344**		**$ 38,150**	
Individual Contributions	**487,927**		**163,667**	
Total Receipts*	**662,069**		**338,147**	

*Includes PAC and individual contributions as well as interest earned, party contributions, etc.

FLORIDA District 19

Rep. Harry A. Johnston (D)

1992 Election Results

Harry A. Johnston (D)	177,411	(63%)
Larry Metz (R)	103,848	(37%)

Facing limited opposition, Rep. Harry A. Johnston spent only 57 percent as much in 1992 as he had in 1990. He had no campaign office and no paid staff. Travel costs amounted to only $3,393. However, that did not mean he reduced his fund-raising effort to a similar degree—he raised 1.5 times as much as he spent.

As in 1990, Kimberly A. Scott of Washington, D.C., arranged fund-raising events targeted at political action committees (PACs). With PAC donations totaling $180,300 and accounting for 54 percent of Johnston's contributions, the $27,860 Scott received was money well spent.

According to Suzanne M. Stoll, Johnston's congressional chief of staff, in-state fund raising was held to a minimum. Supporters spent a total of $3,176 to host a series of small in-kind receptions. A barbecue and several direct-mail solicitations rounded out the in-state activity, which yielded $31,796 in small contributions and $113,346 in contributions of $200 or more. The Kara Group of Jupiter, Fla., received $24,247 for coordinating local events in 1992.

Johnston had little need to campaign actively. His Republican opponent, attorney Larry Metz, spent just $54,074 and more than one-third of that was invested in overhead. Metz spent nothing on broadcast advertising. Instead, the campaign printed up a tabloid they called *New Congress*. Metz said they created two different issues of the tabloid and printed a total of 300,000 copies, 250,000 of which were distributed as newspaper inserts. The remainder were mailed or handed out at campaign events.

As inoculation against a potential upset, Johnston spent $13,482 to run newspaper ads and invested another $11,111 in yard signs and posters. He also redid the voice-over on one of his 1990 television commercials and picked up a second generic ad from the Democratic Congressional Campaign Committee's archives. The campaign also produced two radio spots that were simply the voice-overs from the two television commercials. Broadcast production costs at the Harriman Communications Center in Washington, D.C., totaled $998. Cable television air time over the final week of the campaign cost $8,245; another $5,237 was spent to air the radio spots. "We were trying to be very economical," noted Stoll.

Johnston's largest expense for the cycle was for the production and mailing of 125,000 tabloid-style brochures. Artwork on the mailer cost $4,063; $16,447 was spent on printing; postage added $15,000; mailing lists cost another $2,382.

To keep tabs on public opinion, Johnston paid pollster Kitchens, Powell & Kitchens of Orlando $22,100.

	Johnston		Metz	
Campaign Expenditures	Amount Spent	% of Total	Amount Spent	% of Total
Overhead				
Office furniture/supplies	$ 3,487	1.50	$ 682	1.26
Rent/utilities	0		2,125	3.93
Salaries	0		8,849	16.37
Taxes	1,605	.69	1,845	3.41
Bank/investment fees	46	.02	66	.12
Lawyers/accountants	175	.08	0	
Telephone	0		2,590	4.79
Campaign automobile	0		0	
Computers/office equipment	70	.03	766	1.42
Travel	3,393	1.45	2,125	3.93
Food/meetings	138	.06	0	
Subtotal	**8,913**	**3.82**	**19,048**	**35.23**
Fund Raising				
Events	74,177	31.81	2,013	3.72
Direct mail	4,588	1.97	3,025	5.59
Telemarketing	0		0	
Subtotal	**78,765**	**33.77**	**5,038**	**9.32**
Polling	**22,100**	**9.48**	**0**	
Advertising				
Electronic media	14,680	6.29	0	
Other media	14,156	6.07	11,910	22.03
Subtotal	**28,836**	**12.36**	**11,910**	**22.03**
Other Campaign Activity				
Persuasion mail/brochures	37,892	16.25	4,880	9.02
Actual campaigning	33,031	14.16	7,358	13.61
Staff/volunteers	0		0	
Subtotal	**70,923**	**30.41**	**12,238**	**22.63**
Constituent Gifts/ Entertainment	**2,150**	**.92**	**0**	
Donations to				
Candidates from same state	0		0	
Candidates from other states	0		0	
Civic organizations	1,472	.63	0	
Ideological groups	0		0	
Political parties	12,278	5.26	0	
Subtotal	**13,750**	**5.90**	**0**	
Unitemized Expenses	**7,782**	**3.34**	**5,840**	**10.80**
Total Campaign Expenses	**$ 233,219**		**$ 54,074**	
PAC Contributions	$ 180,300		$ 0	
Individual Contributions	153,642		25,936	
Total Receipts*	348,039		62,630	

*Includes PAC and individual contributions as well as interest earned, party contributions, etc.

District 20 — FLORIDA

Rep. Peter Deutsch (D)

1992 Election Results

Peter Deutsch (D)	130,946	(55%)
Beverly Kennedy (R)	91,573	(39%)
James M. Blackburn † (I)	15,340	(6%)

State representative Peter Deutsch entered the race on May 12, 1992, and over the next four months spent $540,943 to win a bitter Democratic primary battle with Broward County Commissioner Nicki Grossman. His ability to tap his own bank account for $358,241 allowed Deutsch to outspend Grossman by nearly $233,000.

Grossman's first mass mailing in mid-August set the tone for the final weeks of the campaign. Mailed to 55,000 households, the brochure criticized Deutsch's attendance record in the state legislature and attacked his views on abortion and gun control. It was a fight she did not have the money to finish.

Over the next three weeks, Deutsch hit her with an avalanche of negative mail and broadcast advertising. Bates & Associates of Washington, D.C., collected $118,476 for producing preprimary mailings. Preprimary payments to Nordlinger Associates of Washington for production and placement of radio and television commercials totaled $160,588.

To paint her as a junket-mad politician who had allowed garbage fees at county incinerators to skyrocket, one brochure showed a lobster-and-champagne dinner on the front and sea gulls gliding over piles of garbage on the back. The mailer mentioned Deutsch only once and Grossman fifteen times, once turning the S's in her name into dollar signs. A companion television commercial featured a woman complaining about Grossman's trips, her job at the Gulfstream, Fla., racetrack, and the incinerators. The ad ended with the woman saying, "Vote for Nicki Grossman? Not on your life."

Deutsch invested $12,948 to sponsor rallies, free picnics, and other events during the late summer. He spent $15,294 on yard signs and $1,136 on buttons. Frederick/Schneiders of Washington, D.C., received $12,499 for preprimary polling. In all, Deutsch spent $18.81 for each of his 28,753 primary votes.

Following the primary, Deutsch paid Washington-based Kimberly A. Scott $8,724 to help him raise money from political action committees (PACs). While he had attracted only $19,750 in PAC donations prior to his primary victory, Deutsch received $142,849 from PACs once he won the nomination.

Aided by this influx of PAC money, Deutsch was able to focus $270,331 on the general election campaign against Beverly Kennedy. He paid Nordlinger another $112,583, which accounted for 42 percent of his total outlays during the fall campaign. Frederick/Schneiders collected $28,000 for general election polling. Bates & Associates received $1,750.

Kennedy's longshot campaign unraveled in October. Norman Gross, president of Spencer Research Associates, bailed out as campaign strategist in a dispute over money he said his company was owed.

Campaign Expenditures	Deutsch Amount Spent	Deutsch % of Total	Kennedy Amount Spent	Kennedy % of Total
Overhead				
Office furniture/supplies	$ 15,246	1.88	$ 1,700	1.72
Rent/utilities	5,005	.62	2,815	2.85
Salaries	32,192	3.97	5,200	5.27
Taxes	5,158	.64	0	
Bank/investment fees	479	.06	0	
Lawyers/accountants	300	.04	0	
Telephone	13,299	1.64	1,466	1.48
Campaign automobile	0		0	
Computers/office equipment	9,530	1.17	0	
Travel	17,048	2.10	200	.20
Food/meetings	3,923	.48	0	
Subtotal	**102,180**	**12.60**	**11,381**	**11.52**
Fund Raising				
Events	21,258	2.62	1,000	1.01
Direct mail	4,206	.52	1,472	1.49
Telemarketing	0		0	
Subtotal	**25,464**	**3.14**	**2,472**	**2.50**
Polling	**40,499**	**4.99**	**0**	
Advertising				
Electronic media	279,801	34.49	18,268	18.50
Other media	6,730	.83	2,120	2.15
Subtotal	**286,532**	**35.32**	**20,388**	**20.65**
Other Campaign Activity				
Persuasion mail/brochures	279,427	34.44	10,476	10.61
Actual campaigning	66,495	8.20	31,393	31.79
Staff/volunteers	2,203	.27	0	
Subtotal	**348,125**	**42.91**	**41,869**	**42.40**
Constituent Gifts/Entertainment	107	.01	0	
Donations to				
Candidates from same state	0		0	
Candidates from other states	0		0	
Civic organizations	290	.04	0	
Ideological groups	915	.11	0	
Political parties	500	.06	0	
Subtotal	**1,705**	**.21**	**0**	
Unitemized Expenses	6,662	.82	22,644	22.93
Total Campaign Expenses	$ 811,274		$ 98,753	
PAC Contributions	$ 162,599		$ 10,350	
Individual Contributions	323,771		60,051	
Total Receipts*	856,210		90,009	

*Includes PAC and individual contributions as well as interest earned, party contributions, etc.

† No expenditures or receipts on file. Candidates raising or spending less than $5,000 are not required to file reports with the Federal Election Commission.

FLORIDA   District 21

Rep. Lincoln Diaz-Balart (R)   *1992 Election Results*   Lincoln Diaz-Balart** (R)

The winner of the September Republican primary between state senators Lincoln Diaz-Balart and Javier D. Souto was assured of becoming the second Hispanic member of the House from Dade County. No Democrat bothered to run in this overwhelmingly Republican district.

Diaz-Balart announced his candidacy on April 2, 1992, and over the next several months paid Hebrock & Associates of Tallahassee $6,640 for what district director Ana M. Carbonell described as "setting the base for the campaign and helping to set up our finance committee." By the end of June Diaz-Balart had raised $141,542 and had cash reserves of $106,951, indicating that Hebrock did their job well.

Souto got a much later start, entering the race in early June. While he was able to transfer $21,192 from his state senate campaign funds into his House campaign treasury, he ended June with cash reserves of less than $23,000 and never caught up. His total expenditures amounted to $97,143.

Both candidates were fervently anti-Castro, supported federal budget cuts, and opposed both new taxes and the North American Free Trade Agreement. The difference came down in large part to the fact that only one could afford to get his message out.

With his insurmountable cash advantage, Diaz-Balart invested $111,381 in advertising, most of which aired on Spanish-language stations. The campaign directly placed $40,065 in radio ads, including $22,971 with Radio Mambi. Television commercials placed by the campaign amounted to $12,364, including $8,330 with the local Univision station and $3,824 with the local Telemundo affiliate. The Robert Goodman Agency of Baltimore, Md., received $41,237 for producing the ads and purchasing additional air time. In all, Carbonell said the campaign aired fifteen radio spots and five television commercials. Diaz-Balart also invested $8,603 in newspaper ads and $2,547 in billboards.

When Souto aired a radio spot suggesting that Diaz-Balart favored allowing minors to work in bars because he had voted for legislation allowing Disney World to serve liquor at several of its restaurants, Diaz-Balart was able to answer with two commercials. According to Carbonell, one ad accused Souto of lying and closed with Diaz-Balart inviting people to call the state's Department of Business Regulation to discover for themselves what the law allowed. The second ad used a mock discussion between a mother and daughter to make the same points.

Three persuasion mailings cost the Diaz-Balart campaign $58,441. Carbonell said a twelve-page tabloid mailed following Hurricane Andrew targeted older voters because "after the hurricane, only the staunch voted."

Campaign Expenditures	Diaz-Balart Amount Spent	% of Total
Overhead		
Office furniture/supplies	$ 6,069	2.15
Rent/utilities	754	.27
Salaries	13,805	4.88
Taxes	0	
Bank/investment fees	1,465	.52
Lawyers/accountants	0	
Telephone	4,762	1.68
Campaign automobile	0	
Computers/office equipment	1,104	.39
Travel	11,828	4.18
Food/meetings	0	
Subtotal	39,786	14.07
Fund Raising		
Events	19,894	7.04
Direct mail	0	
Telemarketing	0	
Subtotal	19,894	7.04
Polling	0	
Advertising		
Electronic media	99,386	35.16
Other media	11,995	4.24
Subtotal	111,381	39.40
Other Campaign Activity		
Persuasion mail/brochures	58,441	20.67
Actual campaigning	45,188	15.99
Staff/volunteers	4,393	1.55
Subtotal	108,022	38.21
Constituent Gifts/Entertainment	104	.04
Donations to		
Candidates from same state	1,500	.53
Candidates from other states	500	.18
Civic organizations	475	.17
Ideological groups	100	.04
Political parties	186	.07
Subtotal	2,761	.98
Unitemized Expenses	736	.26
Total Campaign Expenses	$ 282,683	
PAC Contributions	$ 83,800	
Individual Contributions	190,478	
Total Receipts*	279,773	

*Includes PAC and individual contributions as well as interest earned, party contributions, etc.

**In Florida votes are not tallied for unopposed candidates.

District 22 — FLORIDA

Rep. E. Clay Shaw, Jr. (R)

1992 Election Results

E. Clay Shaw, Jr. (R)	128,376	(52%)
Gwen Margolis (D)	91,605	(37%)
Richard "Even" Stephens † (I)	15,467	(6%)

To defeat state senate president Gwen Margolis, Rep. E. Clay Shaw, Jr., spent nearly four times the $294,985 average cost of his previous six campaigns. His $1.1 million campaign was ten times the amount he invested in 1990, when he had no major party opposition.

Shaw invested 48 percent of his campaign treasury in hard-hitting broadcast advertising designed by National Media of Alexandria, Va. One television commercial attacked Margolis for poor management of the state senate and for ignoring Florida's problems while jockeying for national office. Another spot ended with the picture of a cash register and the tagline: "We can't afford Gwen Margolis." National Media received $543,424 for producing and placing five television and three radio spots.

Direct Mail Systems of St. Petersburg handled Shaw's voter contact mail. Press secretary Amy Stromberg described three of the seven persuasion mailers as negative pieces, attacking Margolis for flying first class at taxpayer expense and for her pro-choice stance on abortion. Another mailing depicted Margolis as the quintessential tax-and-spend liberal.

In a more positive vein, the campaign mailed copies of a handwritten letter by Shaw's wife that included a picture of the family as well as a brochure outlining Shaw's opposition to the Brady Bill and his support for a line-item veto. A third positive piece highlighting Shaw's "Watchdog of the Treasury Award" targeted senior citizens. Direct Mail received $157,508 for its work on the persuasion mail.

Shaw invested $25,952 in yard signs and posters, $4,546 in taxi-top signs, $3,185 in bumper stickers, $905 in T-shirts, and $397 in campaign buttons.

To pay for it all, Stromberg said the campaign held "cocktail parties, coffees and lunches—sometimes as many as three a week." His most lucrative district events were a series of $250-a-person receptions held in supporter's homes, which pushed his in-state large-donor contribution total to $292,980.

A Ways and Means Committee member, Shaw collected 49 percent of his contributions from political action committees (PACs). In April 1991 thirteen groups representing the insurance industry banded together to host an in-kind fund-raiser. Five other PACs hosted separate in-kind events. Maxwell & Associates of Alexandria, Va., and Dan Morgan & Associates of Arlington, Va., received $4,470 and $9,091, respectively, for coordinating still more PAC events.

The National Association of Realtors waged a $125,208 independent campaign in support of Shaw, which included a $97,508 payment to Public Opinion Strategies of Alexandria, Va., for persuasion mail.

Margolis spent $932,420 and held Shaw to 52 percent—his lowest winning percentage ever.

Campaign Expenditures	Shaw Amount Spent	Shaw % of Total	Margolis Amount Spent	Margolis % of Total
Overhead				
Office furniture/supplies	$ 15,056	1.32	$ 15,313	1.64
Rent/utilities	9,774	.86	4,180	.45
Salaries	64,868	5.71	48,068	5.16
Taxes	10,066	.89	0	
Bank/investment fees	79	.01	12	.00
Lawyers/accountants	15,233	1.34	0	
Telephone	17,846	1.57	6,036	.65
Campaign automobile	0		0	
Computers/office equipment	12,131	1.07	2,080	.22
Travel	23,940	2.11	11,631	1.25
Food/meetings	1,707	.15	952	.10
Subtotal	**170,698**	**15.02**	**88,272**	**9.47**
Fund Raising				
Events	62,041	5.46	67,742	7.27
Direct mail	20,581	1.81	10,940	1.17
Telemarketing	0		0	
Subtotal	**82,622**	**7.27**	**78,682**	**8.44**
Polling	**40,200**	**3.54**	**17,100**	**1.83**
Advertising				
Electronic media	544,178	47.89	483,254	51.83
Other media	6,185	.54	28,724	3.08
Subtotal	**550,363**	**48.43**	**511,978**	**54.91**
Other Campaign Activity				
Persuasion mail/brochures	170,770	15.03	123,625	13.26
Actual campaigning	94,773	8.33	96,698	10.37
Staff/volunteers	0		627	.07
Subtotal	**265,543**	**23.36**	**220,951**	**23.70**
Constituent Gifts/ Entertainment	**9,802**	**.86**	**776**	**.08**
Donations to				
Candidates from same state	0		0	
Candidates from other states	1,000	.09	0	
Civic organizations	1,702	.15	1,004	.11
Ideological groups	0		520	.06
Political parties	1,000	.09	896	.10
Subtotal	**3,702**	**.33**	**2,420**	**.26**
Unitemized Expenses	**13,489**	**1.19**	**12,240**	**1.31**
Total Campaign Expenses	**$ 1,136,419**		**$ 932,420**	
PAC Contributions	$ 441,663		$ 250,242	
Individual Contributions	452,278		465,948	
Total Receipts*	948,514		939,410	

*Includes PAC and individual contributions as well as interest earned, party contributions, etc.

† No expenditures or receipts on file. Candidates raising or spending less than $5,000 are not required to file reports with the Federal Election Commission.

FLORIDA — District 23

Rep. Alcee L. Hastings (D)

1992 Election Results

Alcee L. Hastings (D)	84,232	(59%)
Ed Fielding (R)	44,800	(31%)
Al Woods † (I)	14,873	(10%)

One might think that impeachment by the House of Representatives, conviction by the Senate on bribery charges, and removal from the federal bench would not be good resume-builders for someone seeking a House seat. According to campaign manager Art W. Kennedy, that scenario probably *helped* Alcee Hastings. "People were either for him of against him," Kennedy said. "It wasn't a matter of getting support. It was about getting people to vote."

Outspent by a margin of five to one by state representative Lois Frankel in the Democratic primary and primary runoff, Hastings prevailed by pouring money and energy into his grass-roots get-out-the-vote efforts. "We had him out there on floats, bandstands, everywhere in the district," noted Kennedy. "Walking and radio were the keys."

To ensure a big turnout, Hastings paid Strata-Tech of Lantana, Fla., $26,425 to coordinate the campaign's in-house phonebank. Other miscellaneous phonebanking charges added $13,283. Campaign staffers also visited dozens of churches and local civic groups, handing out telephone lists to people who made calls from their homes.

Hastings hired more than twenty people to put up signs, pass out campaign literature, canvass neighborhoods, and ferry people to and from the polls for both the primary and general elections. Many of these workers were local college students like Sophia Sappleton, who now works on Hastings's congressional staff. Organizations such as the Urban League and the NAACP also assisted Hastings in turning out the vote. In all, payments to these individuals and organizations totaled $37,640.

Kennedy said the campaign advertised only during the final four days of each campaign—primary, runoff, and general. Beginning on the Saturday preceding the election, the campaign aired spots on rhythm and blues stations. On Sunday they would buy time during gospel broadcasts. On Monday and Tuesday the best option was drive-time talk shows.

Kennedy said Hastings's first ad in the primary responded to a statement by Frankel, who is white, that blacks do not vote. The ad, written by Hastings, called on voters to prove her wrong. Later ads featured ministers, politicians, friends, and other community leaders asking people to vote, along with a Hastings campaign number they could call for a ride to the polls. Kennedy said the campaign did not need to do additional advertising because of Hastings's high name recognition and the free publicity he had received.

In the overwhelmingly Democratic district, Republican Ed Fielding spent less than $16,000 on his token campaign.

Campaign Expenditures	Hastings Amount Spent	Hastings % of Total	Fielding Amount Spent	Fielding % of Total
Overhead				
Office furniture/supplies	$ 6,176	2.61	$ 0	
Rent/utilities	5,578	2.36	0	
Salaries	26,655	11.27	0	
Taxes	0		0	
Bank/investment fees	0		0	
Lawyers/accountants	0		0	
Telephone	5,061	2.14	0	
Campaign automobile	0		0	
Computers/office equipment	3,450	1.46	0	
Travel	3,419	1.45	0	
Food/meetings	0		0	
Subtotal	**50,338**	**21.29**	**0**	
Fund Raising				
Events	19,229	8.13	0	
Direct mail	0		0	
Telemarketing	0		0	
Subtotal	**19,229**	**8.13**	**0**	
Polling	**0**		**0**	
Advertising				
Electronic media	19,292	8.16	0	
Other media	4,871	2.06	629	4.03
Subtotal	**24,163**	**10.22**	**629**	**4.03**
Other Campaign Activity				
Persuasion mail/brochures	18,073	7.64	12,621	80.77
Actual campaigning	111,762	47.27	1,047	6.70
Staff/volunteers	788	.33	0	
Subtotal	**130,623**	**55.24**	**13,668**	**87.47**
Constituent Gifts/ Entertainment	**500**	**.21**	**0**	
Donations to				
Candidates from same state	0		0	
Candidates from other states	0		0	
Civic organizations	1,000	.42	0	
Ideological groups	685	.29	0	
Political parties	35	.01	0	
Subtotal	**1,720**	**.73**	**0**	
Unitemized Expenses	**9,873**	**4.18**	**1,329**	**8.51**
Total Campaign Expenses	**$ 236,446**		**$ 15,626**	
PAC Contributions	$ 98,200		$ 2,250	
Individual Contributions	273,706		10,090	
Total Receipts*	417,158		15,626	

*Includes PAC and individual contributions as well as interest earned, party contributions, etc.

† No expenditures or receipts on file. Candidates raising or spending less than $5,000 are not required to file reports with the Federal Election Commission.

District 1   GEORGIA

Rep. Jack Kingston (R)

1992 Election Results

Jack Kingston (R)	103,932	(58%)
Barbara Christmas (D)	75,808	(42%)

Less than a week before the election, most observers saw the contest between two-term state senator Jack Kingston and elementary school principal Barbara Christmas as a tossup. Instead, with the help of a negative advertising campaign that turned Christmas's own campaign slogan against her, Kingston emerged with a resounding 16-point victory.

Christmas built her entire campaign around the fact that she was a political outsider. To blunt that message, Kingston aired commercials that hit her as too inexperienced for the job. Another Kingston ad took Christmas's campaign slogan, "Christmas in November," and used it to attack her as an old-style, tax-and-spend liberal. "Can we afford Christmas in November?" the commercial asked.

In all, Kingston sank 63 percent of his resources into advertising. The Farwell Group of New Orleans, La., received $54,232 for developing the broadcast ads. Monroe Marketing of Savannah collected $189,861 from Kingston's campaign treasury and another $25,000 from the National Republican Congressional Committee to cover the cost of air time and placement fees. "We ran television ads in the Jacksonville market, and those stations are mega-bucks," noted company president Rick Monroe. Monroe was also paid $28,414 for placing newspaper ads.

When Christmas received contributions totaling $6,250 from the National Organization for Women (NOW), Kingston jumped on those donations as proof that Christmas had a liberal, feminist agenda that was outside the conservative, mainstream views of her would-be constituents. A Kingston flier noted that NOW supported gay and lesbian rights.

Printing, postage, and distribution costs for Kingston's various campaign fliers and mailers totaled $23,151, including $197 to purchase mailing labels from the American Family Association. The campaign invested $750 in a mailing to members of Citizens for Safe Government and another $450 to purchase mailing lists of farmers from the Georgia Department of Agriculture. Voter Outreach received $8,000 for placing fliers on parked cars during the final days of the campaign.

Kingston raised 68 percent of his money in Georgia, relying mostly on fish fries and barbecues in the district. While there was never a required price of admission, many of his contributors came with sizable checks in hand. In-state donations of $200 or more accounted for 45 percent of his total receipts.

Christmas's own media budget fell more than $100,000 short of Kingston's, but in an attempt to save the seat the Democratic Congressional Campaign Committee pumped in an additional $40,925, much of it to cover the cost of producing her commercials.

Campaign Expenditures	Kingston Amount Spent	Kingston % of Total	Christmas Amount Spent	Christmas % of Total
Overhead				
Office furniture/supplies	$ 4,907	1.13	$ 4,968	1.54
Rent/utilities	6,357	1.46	5,327	1.65
Salaries	16,015	3.68	24,004	7.42
Taxes	6,153	1.41	7,551	2.33
Bank/investment fees	239	.05	144	.04
Lawyers/accountants	0		0	
Telephone	8,773	2.01	7,527	2.33
Campaign automobile	0		0	
Computers/office equipment	2,550	.59	2,675	.83
Travel	10,747	2.47	4,618	1.43
Food/meetings	981	.23	0	
Subtotal	**56,722**	**13.02**	**56,815**	**17.56**
Fund Raising				
Events	22,993	5.28	9,501	2.94
Direct mail	0		0	
Telemarketing	0		0	
Subtotal	**22,993**	**5.28**	**9,501**	**2.94**
Polling	**11,200**	**2.57**	**9,125**	**2.82**
Advertising				
Electronic media	244,537	56.12	148,387	45.86
Other media	29,385	6.74	15,628	4.83
Subtotal	**273,922**	**62.87**	**164,014**	**50.68**
Other Campaign Activity				
Persuasion mail/brochures	23,151	5.31	14,520	4.49
Actual campaigning	43,739	10.04	52,487	16.22
Staff/volunteers	0		0	
Subtotal	**66,890**	**15.35**	**67,006**	**20.71**
Constituent Gifts/Entertainment	850	.20	0	
Donations to				
Candidates from same state	0		0	
Candidates from other states	0		0	
Civic organizations	0		132	.04
Ideological groups	0		0	
Political parties	0		400	.12
Subtotal	**0**		**532**	**.16**
Unitemized Expenses	**3,147**	**.72**	**16,606**	**5.13**
Total Campaign Expenses	**$ 435,723**		**$ 323,600**	
PAC Contributions	$ 113,985		$ 106,050	
Individual Contributions	303,940		200,803	
Total Receipts*	439,846		332,113	

*Includes PAC and individual contributions as well as interest earned, party contributions, etc.

GEORGIA   District 2

Rep. Sanford D. Bishop, Jr. (D)

1992 Election Results

Sanford D. Bishop, Jr. (D) 95,789 (64%)
Jim Dudley (R) 54,593 (36%)

Six-term incumbent Rep. Charles Hatcher had two strikes against him. He had 819 overdrafts at the House bank, making him the sixth worst offender. Pushed by the Justice Department to take more aggressive steps to comply with the Voting Rights Act, the state legislature had transformed Hatcher's district from one in which 62 percent of the residents were white into one in which 52 percent were black.

Spurred into action by these developments, state senator Sanford D. Bishop, Jr., opted to enter what turned out to be a six-candidate Democratic primary. After holding Hatcher to 40 percent in the primary, Bishop prevailed in a runoff, capturing 53 percent of the vote.

Of the $377,525 Bishop spent on his campaign, $164,803 was invested to defeat Hatcher. His media adviser, Austin-Sheinkopf of New York, collected 61 percent of Bishop's outlays during the primary and runoff campaigns, or $100,329. Bishop also spent $3,174 to air additional radio spots, $2,197 on newspaper ads, $5,600 on yard signs and posters, $4,667 on brochures, $3,591 on bumper stickers, $1,300 on various get-out-the-vote efforts, and $872 on T-shirts.

Bishop said the most effective television commercial produced by Austin-Sheinkopf was one in which a "grandmotherly looking" woman spoke directly into the camera. "You know, I always thought I was a pretty good judge of character," the woman began. "Charles Hatcher, I forgive you for writing 819 bad checks. I forgive you for voting yourself a pay raise. I forgive you for taking trips to posh resorts. Yes, I'll forgive you, but I'm not going to vote for you," she concluded.

While the outcome of the general election contest with Republican Jim Dudley was never in doubt in this heavily Democratic district, Bishop took nothing for granted. He paid Austin-Sheinkopf $107,570 to design and place additional radio and television commercials. Newspaper ads cost $3,272, and the campaign directly bought radio air time totaling $980.

Bishop was not shy about asking for strategic advice. He paid Beth Shapiro & Associates of Atlanta $1,000 for advice on women's issues. "In the 'Year of the Woman,' I wanted to make sure I had all my bases covered," Bishop said. Peggy Neilson & Associates of Albany, Ga., collected $5,000. Tommy Coleman, former executive director of the Georgia Democratic party, received $5,554 for his input. Christopher Jeffries, a professor at Columbus College in Columbus, Ga., was paid $3,750 to prepare the campaign's policy papers on education and economic development.

Campaign Expenditures	Bishop Amount Spent	Bishop % of Total	Dudley Amount Spent	Dudley % of Total
Overhead				
Office furniture/supplies	$ 7,296	1.93	$ 2,874	1.60
Rent/utilities	8,056	2.13	6,609	3.69
Salaries	13,904	3.68	10,969	6.12
Taxes	0		0	
Bank/investment fees	1,022	.27	1,694	.95
Lawyers/accountants	0		0	
Telephone	9,211	2.44	5,926	3.31
Campaign automobile	7,179	1.90	0	
Computers/office equipment	2,924	.77	4,686	2.61
Travel	1,653	.44	1,615	.90
Food/meetings	280	.07	0	
Subtotal	51,526	13.65	34,374	19.18
Fund Raising				
Events	12,240	3.24	824	.46
Direct mail	0		3,440	1.92
Telemarketing	0		0	
Subtotal	12,240	3.24	4,264	2.38
Polling	13,400	3.55	0	
Advertising				
Electronic media	218,674	57.92	107,572	60.01
Other media	6,094	1.61	2,446	1.36
Subtotal	224,768	59.54	110,019	61.38
Other Campaign Activity				
Persuasion mail/brochures	28,611	7.58	9,262	5.17
Actual campaigning	42,300	11.20	14,483	8.08
Staff/volunteers	998	.26	0	
Subtotal	71,909	19.05	23,745	13.25
Constituent Gifts/ Entertainment	2,581	.68	0	
Donations to				
Candidates from same state	0		0	
Candidates from other states	0		0	
Civic organizations	100	.03	0	
Ideological groups	1,000	.26	0	
Political parties	0		0	
Subtotal	1,100	.29	0	
Unitemized Expenses	0		6,847	3.82
Total Campaign Expenses	$ 377,525		$ 179,249	
PAC Contributions	$ 142,100		$ 20,100	
Individual Contributions	161,062		111,911	
Total Receipts*	353,162		223,736	

*Includes PAC and individual contributions as well as interest earned, party contributions, etc.

District 3 — GEORGIA

Rep. Mac Collins (R)

1992 Election Results

Mac Collins (R)	114,107	(55%)
Richard Ray (D)	94,271	(45%)

Redistricting was not kind to Rep. Richard Ray. Not only did it rob him of about two-thirds of his political base, but the redrawn district included the home of fellow Democrat David Worley, who had lost a 1990 House race to Minority Whip Newt Gingrich by just 974 votes. Sensing that Ray was vulnerable, Worley entered the fray.

The primary proved brutal. Worley's advertising, designed and placed by Squier/Eskew/Knapp/Ochs Communications of Washington, D.C., and his mail, orchestrated by the Campaign Performance Group of San Francisco, Calif., blasted Ray's record as Georgia's leading congressional "junketeer," his vote for a congressional pay raise, and for lying in his campaign ads.

Ray responded with a $149,642 advertising campaign created by Fenn & King Communications of Washington, D.C, which attacked Worley as a career candidate who still had not paid off the debts from his last campaign. A similar $216,439 persuasion mail effort was designed by Fenn & King and executed by Blaemire Communications of Reston, Va. Ray avoided a runoff against Worley by capturing 51 percent of the vote in the four-candidate race.

In the fall campaign, Republican state senator Mac Collins picked up where Worley had left off. He attacked Ray for his votes in favor of the congressional pay raise and the 1990 budget compromise, which included tax increases. He hit repeatedly with a commercial reviving a 1980s allegation that Ray had accepted an illegal contribution from the Unisys Corp., a charge Ray heatedly denied. Collins even attacked Ray for having accumulated $1.5 million in pension benefits during his tenure in Washington. In all, Collins invested $69,108 in advertising aimed at Ray, $67,000 of which went to Mentzer Media Services of Baltimore, Md. The National Republican Congressional Committee paid Mentzer another $45,273 to augment Collins's advertising budget.

Over the final month of the campaign, Collins spent $137,535. In addition to his outlays for television and radio advertising, he invested $7,284 in voter contact mail and brochures, $3,448 in newspaper advertising, and $4,125 in signs and posters. He also spent $2,520 to purchase 2,000 full-sized brooms—a symbol of sweeping Washington clean—each one affixed with a "Mac Collins for Congress" sticker.

Ray answered by investing $298,429 during October in a last-ditch effort to save his seat. More than three-quarters of that investment, or $229,344, was paid to Fenn & King for advertising. Using a negative newspaper editorial as fodder, one television ad attacked Collins's supposedly suspect business dealings and asked, "This man wants us to send him to Congress?" In the end, it was not enough.

	Collins		Ray	
Campaign Expenditures	Amount Spent	% of Total	Amount Spent	% of Total
Overhead				
Office furniture/supplies	$ 3,261	1.35	$ 17,518	1.85
Rent/utilities	7,150	2.97	13,904	1.47
Salaries	25,225	10.47	67,116	7.10
Taxes	0		3,995	.42
Bank/investment fees	110	.05	9,551	1.01
Lawyers/accountants	0		0	
Telephone	5,678	2.36	12,177	1.29
Campaign automobile	0		23,091	2.44
Computers/office equipment	4,225	1.75	18,599	1.97
Travel	5,760	2.39	18,867	2.00
Food/meetings	41	.02	2,665	.28
Subtotal	**51,450**	**21.37**	**187,482**	**19.83**
Fund Raising				
Events	21,231	8.82	56,698	6.00
Direct mail	0		0	
Telemarketing	0		0	
Subtotal	**21,231**	**8.82**	**56,698**	**6.00**
Polling	**0**		**40,000**	**4.23**
Advertising				
Electronic media	73,581	30.56	379,016	40.09
Other media	4,595	1.91	2,314	.24
Subtotal	**78,177**	**32.46**	**381,330**	**40.34**
Other Campaign Activity				
Persuasion mail/brochures	33,123	13.75	241,169	25.51
Actual campaigning	55,061	22.86	26,432	2.80
Staff/volunteers	0		299	.03
Subtotal	**88,185**	**36.62**	**267,900**	**28.34**
Constituent Gifts/ Entertainment	934	.39	9,449	1.00
Donations to				
Candidates from same state	0		12	
Candidates from other states	0		0	
Civic organizations	630	.26	1,376	.15
Ideological groups	30	.01	758	.08
Political parties	0		300	.03
Subtotal	**660**	**.27**	**2,446**	**.26**
Unitemized Expenses	177	.07	0	
Total Campaign Expenses	**$ 240,813**		**$ 945,304**	
PAC Contributions	$ 50,272		$ 353,971	
Individual Contributions	133,509		281,028	
Total Receipts*	255,683		1,036,440	

*Includes PAC and individual contributions as well as interest earned, party contributions, etc.

GEORGIA — District 4

Rep. John Linder (R)

1992 Election Results

John Linder (R)	126,495	(51%)
Cathey Steinberg (D)	123,819	(49%)

For businessman and former state representative John Linder, the second time was the charm. After spending more than $650,000 in a narrow loss to Rep. Ben Jones in 1990, Linder was prepared to take a second shot at the incumbent in 1992 until redistricting moved Jones's home into District 10. Linder's 1992 victory ultimately cost $164,606 less than his 1990 loss.

Before moving on to the general election campaign against state senator Cathey Steinberg, Linder first had to dispatch five other Republican hopefuls, a process that cost $207,612. Over the course of the primary and succeeding runoff campaigns, Linder spent $69,410 on radio and television commercials, $60,100 on persuasion mail, $10,068 on phonebanking, $7,000 on billboards, $4,336 on yard signs, and $1,058 on newspaper ads.

Steinberg had an easier time in the Democratic primary, spending slightly less than $170,000 to defeat District Attorney Bob Wilson. Through the July 21 primary, Steinberg spent $59,693 on persuasion mail and only $21,291 to develop and air her radio commercials. Steinberg ultimately spent $148,601 more than Linder in their head-to-head competition, and her ability to save resources in the primary enabled her to outspend him on broadcast advertising by $107,356.

Fortunately for Linder, the redistricting that moved Jones to District 10 also moved a good number of Democrats with him. Despite a huge drop in the district's support for the Republican presidential ticket, Linder managed to overcome Steinberg's sizable monetary advantage.

Throughout the fall, Linder and Steinberg traded negative charges. She called him an extremist and "Pat Robertson with a southern drawl" for his views on abortion. When he discovered that she had taken money from EMILY's List, a political action committee that raises money for women candidates, he ran ads labeling her a liberal extremist. He also slammed her for voting in favor of a pay raise for Georgia legislators.

To foster his "outsider" image, a television commercial dubbed "The Piggy Bank" was rolled out. The ad showed Linder helping a group of children pick up the pieces of a broken piggy bank that they had dropped. Noting that the federal government had "broken the bank," the voice-over reminded voters that Linder would "help pick up the pieces."

For designing Linder's advertising campaign, Beacher & Co. of Alpharetta received $8,516. Western International Media Corp. of Los Angeles, Calif., collected $45,000 for buying air time in the primary. Air time for both the runoff and fall campaigns was purchased directly by the campaign.

	Linder		Steinberg	
Campaign Expenditures	Amount Spent	% of Total	Amount Spent	% of Total
Overhead				
Office furniture/supplies	$ 6,056	1.24	$ 10,505	1.75
Rent/utilities	4,050	.83	4,800	.80
Salaries	77,974	15.96	94,900	15.83
Taxes	0		0	
Bank/investment fees	0		354	.06
Lawyers/accountants	0		0	
Telephone	3,073	.63	7,603	1.27
Campaign automobile	0		0	
Computers/office equipment	5,626	1.15	9,104	1.52
Travel	4,100	.84	8,726	1.46
Food/meetings	0		339	.06
Subtotal	**100,879**	**20.65**	**136,331**	**22.74**
Fund Raising				
Events	9,572	1.96	6,089	1.02
Direct mail	0		21,869	3.65
Telemarketing	0		0	
Subtotal	**9,572**	**1.96**	**27,958**	**4.66**
Polling	**8,200**	**1.68**	**29,387**	**4.90**
Advertising				
Electronic media	190,009	38.89	249,246	41.57
Other media	11,479	2.35	2,649	.44
Subtotal	**201,488**	**41.24**	**251,895**	**42.02**
Other Campaign Activity				
Persuasion mail/brochures	121,020	24.77	86,419	14.41
Actual campaigning	41,898	8.58	59,231	9.88
Staff/volunteers	0		634	.11
Subtotal	**162,918**	**33.35**	**146,284**	**24.40**
Constituent Gifts/ Entertainment	0		0	
Donations to				
Candidates from same state	0		0	
Candidates from other states	0		0	
Civic organizations	1,000	.20	0	
Ideological groups	0		0	
Political parties	1,000	.20	0	
Subtotal	**2,000**	**.41**	**0**	
Unitemized Expenses	3,493	.72	7,670	1.28
Total Campaign Expenses	$ 488,551		$ 599,526	
PAC Contributions	$ 187,978		$ 151,832	
Individual Contributions	279,162		462,702	
Total Receipts*	543,357		621,771	

*Includes PAC and individual contributions as well as interest earned, party contributions, etc.

District 5 — GEORGIA

Rep. John Lewis (D)

1992 Election Results

John Lewis (D)	147,445	(72%)
Paul R. Stabler (R)	56,960	(28%)

With 125 overdrafts at the House bank, Rep. John Lewis knew he had better not take either his primary or general election opponent for granted. As in each of his previous House campaigns, Lewis emerged with more than 70 percent of the vote, but not before spending nearly $39,000 more than he had on his two previous contests combined.

Lewis did not run a permanent campaign. He waited until June 1992 to open his headquarters and hire campaign manager Melvin Collins. Befitting the overwhelming Democratic nature of the district, Collins was retained only until the middle of September, when it was clear Lewis had nothing to fear from real estate investor Paul R. Stabler. Collins collected $10,914 in salary for his three-month effort.

For the July 21 primary against state representative "Able" Mable Thomas, Lewis paid Harnell-Cohen Associates of Atlanta $17,700 for placement of his radio commercials. Strother-Duffy-Strother of Washington, D.C., received $1,729 for producing the spots. Lewis also invested $3,225 in newspaper advertising—$1,410 with the *Atlanta Journal and Constitution,* $1,313 with the *Atlanta Daily World,* and $502 with the *Atlanta Tribune.* Poll watchers cost the campaign $4,000.

In the general election, Lewis paid Harnell-Cohen another $21,653 for radio buys. Advertisements in the *Atlanta Bulletin* and the *Northside Neighbor* cost $403 and $752, respectively.

Throughout the late summer and fall, Lewis peppered the district with campaign literature. The $50,583 he spent on brochures and mailings was nearly six times the amount he invested in such items during the 1990 campaign. Posters and signs cost the campaign $3,847.

However, not all of Lewis's spending was directly related to his campaign. His travel costs included $3,040 in expenses related to Congressional Black Caucus (CBC) meetings, including $1,076 for a CBC retreat for spouses at the Contemporary Resort Hotel in Orlando, Fla. The campaign picked up Lewis's $7,554 tab for food and lodging at the New York Hilton during the Democratic National Convention. The campaign also reimbursed his wife Lillian, staff assistant James Waller, and press secretary Ronald Roach for convention expenses totaling $1,580, $700, and $335, respectively.

Lewis donated $1,475 to 100 Black Men of America, paid $350 for a table at a "Salute to Fathers" staged by the Concerned Black Clergy, and spent $250 for ten tickets to an awards ceremony for the Georgia Coalition of Black Women. Among his other donations were gifts to the Democratic Congressional Campaign Committee totaling $6,000.

Campaign Expenditures	Lewis Amount Spent	Lewis % of Total	Stabler Amount Spent	Stabler % of Total
Overhead				
Office furniture/supplies	$ 8,934	3.59	$ 2,376	3.75
Rent/utilities	5,024	2.02	2,040	3.22
Salaries	24,766	9.96	15,468	24.41
Taxes	0		0	
Bank/investment fees	0		283	.45
Lawyers/accountants	250	.10	0	
Telephone	8,100	3.26	361	.57
Campaign automobile	5,147	2.07	0	
Computers/office equipment	1,089	.44	95	.15
Travel	16,255	6.54	45	.07
Food/meetings	75	.03	1,369	2.16
Subtotal	**69,641**	**28.02**	**22,037**	**34.78**
Fund Raising				
Events	26,624	10.71	3,478	5.49
Direct mail	0		2,178	3.44
Telemarketing	0		0	
Subtotal	**26,624**	**10.71**	**5,656**	**8.93**
Polling	**0**		**0**	
Advertising				
Electronic media	41,273	16.61	3,981	6.28
Other media	9,300	3.74	1,773	2.80
Subtotal	**50,573**	**20.35**	**5,754**	**9.08**
Other Campaign Activity				
Persuasion mail/brochures	50,583	20.35	21,791	34.39
Actual campaigning	16,644	6.70	7,458	11.77
Staff/volunteers	489	.20	15	.02
Subtotal	**67,716**	**27.25**	**29,265**	**46.19**
Constituent Gifts/ Entertainment	3,739	1.50	0	
Donations to				
Candidates from same state	3,845	1.55	238	.38
Candidates from other states	4,200	1.69	0	
Civic organizations	5,248	2.11	235	.37
Ideological groups	6,375	2.57	25	.04
Political parties	6,930	2.79	50	.08
Subtotal	**26,598**	**10.70**	**548**	**.86**
Unitemized Expenses	**3,645**	**1.47**	**101**	**.16**
Total Campaign Expenses	**$ 248,535**		**$ 63,361**	
PAC Contributions	$ 225,195		$ 8,000	
Individual Contributions	73,392		43,051	
Total Receipts*	300,865		58,966	

*Includes PAC and individual contributions as well as interest earned, party contributions, etc.

GEORGIA District 6

Rep. Newt Gingrich (R)

1992 Election Results

Newt Gingrich (R)	158,761	(58%)
Tony Center (D)	116,196	(42%)

Having survived reelection in 1990 by only 974 votes, Rep. Newt Gingrich expected—and got—a strong challenge in 1992.

The Democratic-controlled Georgia legislature proved to be one of his chief opponents. "The redistricting committee was instructed to break up the Sixth District and design the rest of the state after that," argued Barry Hutchinson, Gingrich's campaign director.

The new district was uncharted territory for Gingrich, and his decision to run there set up an acrimonious primary with Herman Clark, who had resigned his seat in the state legislature to run. Clark spent more than $188,000, much of it on negative advertising. He also benefited from independent campaigns waged against Gingrich by the Democratic Congressional Campaign Committee (DCCC) and Ralph Nader's Public Citizen, a watchdog group.

Clark's companion sixty-second television and radio spots, sung to the tune of "Old MacDonald Had a Farm," blasted Gingrich for his twenty-two overdrafts at the House bank and for accepting the congressional pay raise. Public Citizen spent more than $59,000 to defeat Gingrich in the primary, most of which was put into television commercials labeling Gingrich a hypocrite for criticizing Congress for its excesses while taking all the perks. The DCCC aired radio spots on his overdrafts.

Between January 1, 1992 and the July 21 primary, Gingrich spent nearly $665,000 of his campaign treasury. His primary expenses included payments of $23,930 to The Farwell Group of New Orleans, La., for designing his advertising and $135,973 to SFM Media for placing most of the spots. The campaign directly bought $21,318 of air time. Campaign Telecommunications of New York and Cherry Communications of Gainesville, Fla., collected $45,096 and $6,160, respectively, for phonebanking. Persuasion mail added another $68,569.

After defeating Clark by only 980 votes in this heavily Republican district, Gingrich was expected to coast to victory over attorney Tony Center in November. Instead, the two redefined negative campaigning.

Center spent $122,341 on broadcast advertising, which included attacks on Gingrich for delivering divorce papers to his wife the day after a cancer operation. Public Citizen weighed in with another $23,302 independent campaign.

Gingrich struck back with a $256,022 broadcast advertising campaign that included charges that Center had tried to strip child support payments from a client in order to cover his fees. The Farwell Group and SFM Media received $38,648 and $150,000, respectively, for their work in the general election campaign.

Campaign Expenditures	Gingrich Amount Spent	Gingrich % of Total	Center Amount Spent	Center % of Total
Overhead				
Office furniture/supplies	$ 18,206	.98	$ 3,231	.91
Rent/utilities	37,834	2.03	5,699	1.60
Salaries	229,477	12.31	28,673	8.06
Taxes	47,981	2.57	7,822	2.20
Bank/investment fees	2,246	.12	55	.02
Lawyers/accountants	6,638	.36	0	
Telephone	45,653	2.45	8,968	2.52
Campaign automobile	1,216	.07	0	
Computers/office equipment	54,767	2.94	4,390	1.23
Travel	66,547	3.57	4,880	1.37
Food/meetings	3,075	.16	39	.01
Subtotal	**513,640**	**27.56**	**63,756**	**17.91**
Fund Raising				
Events	156,902	8.42	10,129	2.85
Direct mail	160,507	8.61	1,342	.38
Telemarketing	0		0	
Subtotal	**317,409**	**17.03**	**11,472**	**3.22**
Polling	**84,338**	**4.53**	**9,550**	**2.68**
Advertising				
Electronic media	440,321	23.62	122,341	34.37
Other media	6,619	.36	1,646	.46
Subtotal	**446,940**	**23.98**	**123,987**	**34.83**
Other Campaign Activity				
Persuasion mail/brochures	145,364	7.80	121,758	34.21
Actual campaigning	279,274	14.98	16,387	4.60
Staff/volunteers	1,099	.06	178	.05
Subtotal	**425,736**	**22.84**	**138,323**	**38.86**
Constituent Gifts/ Entertainment	10,489	.56	0	
Donations to				
Candidates from same state	0		0	
Candidates from other states	3,000	.16	0	
Civic organizations	1,559	.08	0	
Ideological groups	150	.01	0	
Political parties	1,875	.10	0	
Subtotal	**6,584**	**.35**	**0**	
Unitemized Expenses	58,682	3.15	8,840	2.48
Total Campaign Expenses	**$ 1,863,818**		**$ 355,927**	
PAC Contributions	$ 653,712		$ 129,650	
Individual Contributions	1,314,363		164,329	
Total Receipts*	1,962,935		410,786	

*Includes PAC and individual contributions as well as interest earned, party contributions, etc.

District 7 — GEORGIA

Rep. George "Buddy" Darden (D)

1992 Election Results

George "Buddy" Darden (D) 111,374 (57%)
Al Beverly (R) 82,915 (43%)

The rematch between Rep. George "Buddy" Darden and Republican Al Beverly was waged in a significantly redrawn district. Gone from District 7 was most of heavily Republican Cobb County, which would have strengthened Darden's position had the lost territory been replaced by Democratic strongholds. Instead, the lost Republicans were largely replaced by Republicans formerly represented by Minority Whip Newt Gingrich.

As a result, Darden dramatically increased his communication budget for the 1992 race. Expenditures for advertising and persuasion mail increased by 42 percent, from $187,523 in 1990 to $266,325 in 1992. Outlays for broadcast advertising more than doubled, from $71,467 in 1990 to $155,435 in 1992.

Darden relied more heavily on big-name consultants for his 1992 effort. In August 1992 Darden hired McKinnon Media of Austin, Texas, to handle broadcast media. Produced in-house during the 1990 campaign, persuasion mail was handled in 1992 by Austin-based Gold Communications Co. Kitchens, Powell & Kitchens of Orlando, Fla., conducted the campaign's polls; no polls were done in 1990.

The majority of the broadcast media budget was put into three 30-second television spots, including a basic biographical piece, an ad focusing on Darden's efforts to bring jobs to the district, and one touting the incumbent's commitment to agriculture and the family farm. For producing and placing these spots, McKinnon Media collected $143,850. The campaign spent $11,385 to purchase radio air time to better reach selected rural areas of the district.

Gold Communications received $29,250 for designing two persuasion mailers that dovetailed with Darden's television ads. Both mailers combined the requisite biographical material with his messages on jobs and agriculture.

With monthly rent of only $160, Darden could easily afford to maintain a small office in Marietta throughout the cycle. He opened a large campaign headquarters in July 1992 but, with monthly rent of $1,250, he chose to close it immediately after the election. His off-year staff of one grew to nine by election day.

In all, Darden spent $381,038 over the final six months of the two-year election cycle. More than $239,000 of this was spent during October. In addition to the bulk of his broadcast advertising and mail expenses, Darden's October push included $7,420 for ads in such newspapers as the *Rome News-Tribune,* the *Douglas County Sentinel,* and the *Chattooga Press.*

Beverly spent more than twice what he had invested in the 1990 campaign, and he drew 3 percent more of the vote.

Campaign Expenditures	Darden Amount Spent	Darden % of Total	Beverly Amount Spent	Beverly % of Total
Overhead				
Office furniture/supplies	$ 6,359	1.25	$ 2,057	5.04
Rent/utilities	9,515	1.87	0	
Salaries	33,382	6.56	5,955	14.60
Taxes	9,995	1.97	0	
Bank/investment fees	185	.04	71	.17
Lawyers/accountants	810	.16	250	.61
Telephone	8,086	1.59	1,413	3.47
Campaign automobile	17,823	3.50	0	
Computers/office equipment	5,897	1.16	34	.08
Travel	5,831	1.15	483	1.18
Food/meetings	1,185	.23	0	
Subtotal	**99,068**	**19.48**	**10,263**	**25.17**
Fund Raising				
Events	36,262	7.13	1,941	4.76
Direct mail	0		0	
Telemarketing	0		0	
Subtotal	**36,262**	**7.13**	**1,941**	**4.76**
Polling	**18,100**	**3.56**	**0**	
Advertising				
Electronic media	155,435	30.56	9,974	24.46
Other media	17,283	3.40	2,036	4.99
Subtotal	**172,718**	**33.96**	**12,009**	**29.45**
Other Campaign Activity				
Persuasion mail/brochures	93,607	18.41	5,815	14.26
Actual campaigning	60,269	11.85	10,404	25.51
Staff/volunteers	1,458	.29	0	
Subtotal	**155,334**	**30.54**	**16,218**	**39.77**
Constituent Gifts/ Entertainment	**10,360**	**2.04**	**0**	
Donations to				
Candidates from same state	0		0	
Candidates from other states	2,250	.44	0	
Civic organizations	6,551	1.29	0	
Ideological groups	500	.10	0	
Political parties	7,406	1.46	350	.86
Subtotal	**16,707**	**3.29**	**350**	**.86**
Unitemized Expenses	**0**		**0**	
Total Campaign Expenses	**$ 508,550**		**$ 40,781**	
PAC Contributions	**$ 226,940**		**$ 4,200**	
Individual Contributions	**161,540**		**16,034**	
Total Receipts*	**410,958**		**40,956**	

*Includes PAC and individual contributions as well as interest earned, party contributions, etc.

GEORGIA District 8

Rep. J. Roy Rowland (D)

1992 Election Results

J. Roy Rowland (D)	108,472	(56%)
Bob Cunningham (R)	86,220	(44%)

Elected without Republican opposition in three of his five previous House campaigns, Rep. J. Roy Rowland was clearly unaccustomed to electoral competition. However, when redistricting placed 40 percent of his black constituents in other districts and added new territory, Rowland drew both primary and general election opposition.

To meet the challenges, Rowland increased spending on virtually every aspect of his campaign. Overhead went from $98,628 in the 1990 election cycle to $153,347 in 1992. Fund-raising expenses increased to $41,573 from $29,701. He spent $24,090 on polls in 1992 compared with $17,755 in 1990. Advertising increased from $189,682 to $260,666. Expenditures for persuasion mail and brochures totaled $21,854 in 1992; in 1990 he spent nothing on such material. In all, Rowland's 1992 spending was 48 percent higher in 1992 than in 1990.

In the primary against teacher Bill Lightle, Rowland could afford to take the high road. Lightle brought only $14,030 to the fight and had no money to advertise, so Rowland's ads centered on his effectiveness in Congress, his conservatism, and his work on health care issues.

In the general election campaign things turned more negative. Republican challenger Bob Cunningham was no match for Rowland financially, but 63 percent of what he had was invested in advertising that painted the conservative Rowland as too liberal for the district. Cunningham's ads also charged that Rowland had made little attempt to save a local military base from the base closure committee's ax.

According to administrative assistant Selby L. McCash, Rowland responded with ads calling Cunningham "a liar who was uninformed and spreading misinformation." On a positive front, McCash said the campaign also ran ads focusing on Rowland's "fiscal responsibility."

Rowland spent more than $9,000 on newspaper ads in both the primary and general election campaigns. McCash said the campaign advertised in every newspaper in the district both because it was a way of "maintaining good relationships" with the papers and because it was "still the best way to reach the movers and shakers in the district."

For designing and placing Rowland's advertising, Shorr Associates of Philadelphia, Pa., received $217,843. Complete Pictures of Philadelphia collected $35,638 for producing the broadcast spots.

Anticipating that he might undertake a heavy persuasion mail effort, Rowland paid Campaign Performance Group of San Francisco, Calif., $3,750 for advice. Instead, the campaign sent one 65,000-piece mailer to those areas of the district not covered by television.

	Rowland		Cunningham	
Campaign Expenditures	Amount Spent	% of Total	Amount Spent	% of Total
Overhead				
Office furniture/supplies	$ 19,294	3.57	$ 2,005	1.08
Rent/utilities	18,883	3.50	3,500	1.88
Salaries	45,944	8.51	19,965	10.74
Taxes	11,218	2.08	0	
Bank/investment fees	140	.03	586	.32
Lawyers/accountants	0		0	
Telephone	6,218	1.15	2,095	1.13
Campaign automobile	0		0	
Computers/office equipment	8,170	1.51	2,172	1.17
Travel	41,879	7.75	3,062	1.65
Food/meetings	1,602	.30	904	.49
Subtotal	**153,347**	**28.40**	**34,290**	**18.45**
Fund Raising				
Events	38,986	7.22	264	.14
Direct mail	2,586	.48	4,789	2.58
Telemarketing	0		0	
Subtotal	**41,573**	**7.70**	**5,053**	**2.72**
Polling	**24,090**	**4.46**	**8,700**	**4.68**
Advertising				
Electronic media	237,849	44.04	105,568	56.79
Other media	22,817	4.23	11,008	5.92
Subtotal	**260,666**	**48.27**	**116,576**	**62.71**
Other Campaign Activity				
Persuasion mail/brochures	21,854	4.05	4,172	2.24
Actual campaigning	19,285	3.57	15,608	8.40
Staff/volunteers	464	.09	13	.01
Subtotal	**41,602**	**7.70**	**19,793**	**10.65**
Constituent Gifts/ Entertainment	**4,333**	**.80**	**0**	
Donations to				
Candidates from same state	1,000	.19	0	
Candidates from other states	250	.05	0	
Civic organizations	3,055	.57	0	
Ideological groups	455	.08	0	
Political parties	9,502	1.76	0	
Subtotal	**14,262**	**2.64**	**0**	
Unitemized Expenses	150	.03	1,474	.79
Total Campaign Expenses	$ **540,023**		$ **185,885**	
PAC Contributions	$ 286,099		$ 5,000	
Individual Contributions	113,764		126,525	
Total Receipts*	454,319		215,170	

*Includes PAC and individual contributions as well as interest earned, party contributions, etc.

District 9 — GEORGIA

Rep. Nathan Deal (D)

1992 Election Results

Nathan Deal (D)	113,024	(59%)
Daniel Becker (R)	77,919	(41%)

On the eve of the primary runoff between state senators Nathan Deal and Thomas P. Ramsey III, Deal pulled off an innovative advertising coup.

Ramsey had purchased a thirty-minute block of television time to conduct a call-in show, so Deal bought the two minutes immediately preceding Ramsey's time-slot. With his first minute, Deal aired a standard commercial; with the second minute, he ran a color test pattern, hoping people would change channels before Ramsey's show began. In case that failed, Deal also bought the first minute after Ramsey's show ended and, as campaign manager Andrew W. Maddox remembered it, announced, "What you have just watched was a fake TV call-in show which was the act of a desperate politician."

For the primary and runoff campaigns, Deal spent $106,219 on television and radio advertising, much of it on stations in Chattanooga, Tenn., which reached the northernmost parts of the district. Due to the high cost, almost no time was purchased in the Atlanta market to reach voters in the southern parts of the district. For creating the ads and buying most of the air time, Shorr Associates of Philadelphia, Pa., received $99,143.

The principal communication tool to reach potential primary and runoff voters, particularly in the district's southern counties, was persuasion mail created by the Campaign Performance Group of San Francisco, Calif. "No one in the district knew any of the candidates, and you had to define yourself before you were defined by someone else," Maddox noted. "With $100,000 you can send out four pieces of mail, but $100,000 would hardly be a blip on TV." Campaign Performance received $94,740 for designing and mailing four brochures. Direct payments for printing campaign literature and postage amounted to $42,956. Maddox said that no persuasion mail was done during the fall campaign.

To secure the nomination, Deal also invested $6,334 in billboards scattered throughout the northwest portion of the district where no mail was sent. Signs cost the campaign $8,784. Newspaper ads cost $8,284, and an in-house phonebank added $3,868. In all, Deal spent about $347,000 to defeat Ramsey.

In the general election, Deal faced Daniel Becker, who ran thirty-minute antiabortion infomercials. After internal polls showed that the abortion ads were having little impact, the decision was made not to answer them. Deal spent $45,065 with Shorr in the general election and directly placed $270 in radio ads and $653 in cable television ads. The campaign also spent $6,848 on newspaper ads.

Campaign Expenditures	Deal Amount Spent	Deal % of Total	Becker Amount Spent	Becker % of Total
Overhead				
Office furniture/supplies	$ 2,866	.56	$ 6,032	3.94
Rent/utilities	11,152	2.18	1,700	1.11
Salaries	46,749	9.16	19,498	12.74
Taxes	18,431	3.61	2,385	1.56
Bank/investment fees	2,374	.47	439	.29
Lawyers/accountants	0		0	
Telephone	8,819	1.73	5,029	3.28
Campaign automobile	0		0	
Computers/office equipment	4,433	.87	452	.30
Travel	8,071	1.58	3,126	2.04
Food/meetings	405	.08	479	.31
Subtotal	**103,300**	**20.24**	**39,140**	**25.57**
Fund Raising				
Events	15,559	3.05	0	
Direct mail	0		118	.08
Telemarketing	0		0	
Subtotal	**15,559**	**3.05**	**118**	**.08**
Polling	**35,350**	**6.93**	**0**	
Advertising				
Electronic media	148,482	29.09	51,750	33.80
Other media	24,275	4.76	14,383	9.39
Subtotal	**172,757**	**33.85**	**66,133**	**43.20**
Other Campaign Activity				
Persuasion mail/brochures	137,696	26.98	13,340	8.71
Actual campaigning	36,652	7.18	29,052	18.98
Staff/volunteers	100	.02	113	.07
Subtotal	**174,448**	**34.18**	**42,504**	**27.76**
Constituent Gifts/ Entertainment	161	.03	0	
Donations to				
Candidates from same state	0		0	
Candidates from other states	0		0	
Civic organizations	268	.05	0	
Ideological groups	0		0	
Political parties	0		0	
Subtotal	**268**	**.05**	**0**	
Unitemized Expenses	8,591	1.68	5,203	3.40
Total Campaign Expenses	$ 510,434		$ 153,098	
PAC Contributions	$ 136,250		$ 3,174	
Individual Contributions	228,817		110,443	
Total Receipts*	543,942		161,110	

*Includes PAC and individual contributions as well as interest earned, party contributions, etc.

GEORGIA — District 10

Rep. Don Johnson (D)

1992 Election Results

Don Johnson (D)	108,426	(54%)
Ralph Hudgens (R)	93,059	(46%)

When Democratic Rep. Doug Barnard, Jr., decided to retire after sixteen years in the House, state senator Don Johnson made sure that the redrawn District 10 would include his own political base in Banks, Franklin, Hart, and Jackson counties. That accomplished, he easily won a bitter Democratic nomination fight with Rep. Ben Jones, whose home had been moved into the redrawn district.

Johnson ran a heavily negative, "outsider" campaign against Jones. Nearly $68,000 was put into ads attacking Jones for his votes in favor of a congressional pay raise and other perks. While Jones had only seven overdrafts at the House bank, he was vulnerable to attacks on the issue because of his vote against releasing bank documents to a special prosecutor.

One radio spot made not-so-subtle references to Jones's former acting career (he once had a role in the television series "Dukes of Hazzard") and marital problems. The ad began with a glib introduction: "Don Johnson, is that Don Johnson of 'Miami Vice'?" "No," came the reply. "Not the actor, Don Johnson the state senator running for Congress." The ad then talked about Johnson as the family man, a move district director Jane Kidd described as "a subtle jab" at Jones, who by then was married to his fifth wife.

Johnson spent another $65,577 on preprimary persuasion mail designed by Bates & Associates of Washington, D.C., including one that employed the ever-popular broom as a symbol of sweeping clean the Washington mess. Other mailers hit Jones for his check overdrafts and attacked him for his opposition to organized prayer in the public schools.

After dispatching Jones by nearly two to one in the five-candidate primary, Johnson focused on Republican Ralph Hudgens, former head of Georgia's Agricultural Stabilization and Conservation Service.

Hudgens received considerable help from the Christian Coalition, which placed comparative newspaper ads and passed out fliers showing "for" and "against" columns on issues such as abortion and gun control. "We felt there was little we could do without coming across as defensive," Kidd lamented.

Kidd added that while the campaign hesitated, it did not completely demure from painting Hudgens as "scary and dangerous." Their ads attacked Hudgens for wanting to do away with the Department of Education and rebutted Hudgens's charges that Johnson favored third trimester abortions.

For designing Johnson's advertising campaigns and for placing many of the spots, Shorr Associates of Philadelphia, Pa., collected $82,854. Bates & Associates received $108,895 for persuasion mail. Parrish-Smith Associates of Atlanta was paid $36,121 for fund raising.

Campaign Expenditures	Johnson Amount Spent	Johnson % of Total	Hudgens Amount Spent	Hudgens % of Total
Overhead				
Office furniture/supplies	$ 6,192	1.04	$ 3,779	2.13
Rent/utilities	6,307	1.06	4,000	2.25
Salaries	50,825	8.55	17,198	9.68
Taxes	14,810	2.49	5,404	3.04
Bank/investment fees	2,552	.43	242	.14
Lawyers/accountants	0		0	
Telephone	18,598	3.13	7,306	4.11
Campaign automobile	5,271	.89	0	
Computers/office equipment	7,718	1.30	2,650	1.49
Travel	11,870	2.00	8,954	5.04
Food/meetings	914	.15	198	.11
Subtotal	**125,056**	**21.04**	**49,731**	**28.00**
Fund Raising				
Events	74,713	12.57	10,224	5.76
Direct mail	2,534	.43	615	.35
Telemarketing	0		0	
Subtotal	**77,247**	**13.00**	**10,839**	**6.10**
Polling	**40,824**	**6.87**	**0**	
Advertising				
Electronic media	106,660	17.95	14,085	7.93
Other media	14,600	2.46	36,378	20.48
Subtotal	**121,261**	**20.40**	**50,463**	**28.41**
Other Campaign Activity				
Persuasion mail/brochures	191,280	32.18	47,664	26.83
Actual campaigning	22,713	3.82	17,464	9.83
Staff/volunteers	0		147	.08
Subtotal	**213,994**	**36.00**	**65,275**	**36.75**
Constituent Gifts/ Entertainment	**1,010**	**.17**	**31**	**.02**
Donations to				
Candidates from same state	0		0	
Candidates from other states	0		0	
Civic organizations	0		0	
Ideological groups	0		175	.10
Political parties	0		760	.43
Subtotal	**0**		**935**	**.53**
Unitemized Expenses	**14,980**	**2.52**	**367**	**.21**
Total Campaign Expenses	**$ 594,372**		**$ 177,641**	
PAC Contributions	$ 161,235		$ 24,318	
Individual Contributions	349,284		97,176	
Total Receipts*	629,607		189,780	

*Includes PAC and individual contributions as well as interest earned, party contributions, etc.

GEORGIA — District 11

Rep. Cynthia A. McKinney (D)

1992 Election Results

Cynthia A. McKinney (D) 120,168 (73%)
Woodrow Lovett (R) 44,221 (27%)

In this new majority-black district, the five-way Democratic primary was the only election of significance. In that contest, state representative Cynthia A. McKinney received a plurality of 31 percent, setting up a runoff with former Waynesboro mayor George L. DeLoach, the only white candidate in the field. McKinney easily won the runoff before trouncing underfunded Republican farmer Woodrow Lovett in the general election.

To get to the runoff, McKinney had to dispatch state senator Eugene P. Walker and state representative Michael Thurmond, a feat she accomplished at least in part by playing racial politics. Her sixty-second radio spots accused Walker and Thurmond of selling out black voters by not fighting for a third majority-black district—a district that the Justice Department ultimately forced the state legislature to create. Morgan/Fletcher & Co. received nearly $59,000 during the primary and runoff campaigns for producing and placing her radio spots.

To ensure that black voters did not take the runoff with DeLoach for granted, McKinney's supporters saturated selected precincts with campaign literature. "We put more people on the streets than anyone else in Georgia," boasted her father and general campaign strategist, Billy McKinney.

McKinney spent more than $173,000, or 49 percent of her budget, to win the nomination. In addition to her media campaign, McKinney's larger expenses included $17,082 for payroll, $12,679 for rent and utilities, $9,673 for travel, $9,500 for a poll conducted by Ron Lester & Associates of Washington, D.C., $9,371 for yard signs and posters, $8,165 for T-shirts, and $4,426 for printing tabloid-style handouts.

McKinney's general election campaign mirrored her primary effort in both scope and style. Morgan/Fletcher received another $36,500 and the campaign directly purchased $673 of radio time. McKinney paid $2,899 to advertise in twenty-five local newspapers, spent $2,518 to print the campaign's tabloid handouts, and invested $6,537 in T-shirts.

While political action committees (PACs) supplied 54 percent of McKinney's total contributions, she became increasingly dependent upon them as the campaign wore on. During the primary, PACs gave only 11 percent of her contributions. However, for the runoff, when her election was all but assured, PACs accounted for 61 percent of her donations. That figure grew to 65 percent in the fall campaign.

On November 25 McKinney paid out bonuses to fifty staff members and volunteers. The bonuses, which ranged from $100 to $5,000, totaled $38,750, or 11 percent of her total outlays. For serving as the campaign's scheduler, McKinney's mother collected a $2,500 bonus.

Campaign Expenditures	McKinney Amount Spent	McKinney % of Total	Lovett Amount Spent	Lovett % of Total
Overhead				
Office furniture/supplies	$ 7,418	2.10	$ 55	.20
Rent/utilities	17,221	4.88	0	
Salaries	66,982	18.97	0	
Taxes	0		0	
Bank/investment fees	128	.04	12	.05
Lawyers/accountants	5,000	1.42	0	
Telephone	8,789	2.49	518	1.94
Campaign automobile	0		0	
Computers/office equipment	3,032	.86	0	
Travel	42,259	11.97	2,940	11.00
Food/meetings	624	.18	0	
Subtotal	**151,453**	**42.90**	**3,525**	**13.19**
Fund Raising				
Events	21,455	6.08	0	
Direct mail	1,237	.35	0	
Telemarketing	0		0	
Subtotal	**22,692**	**6.43**	**0**	
Polling	**9,500**	**2.69**	**0**	
Advertising				
Electronic media	101,533	28.76	8,406	31.46
Other media	4,949	1.40	2,387	8.93
Subtotal	**106,482**	**30.16**	**10,793**	**40.39**
Other Campaign Activity				
Persuasion mail/brochures	17,944	5.08	3,208	12.01
Actual campaigning	42,431	12.02	7,227	27.05
Staff/volunteers	472	.13	0	
Subtotal	**60,847**	**17.23**	**10,435**	**39.05**
Constituent Gifts/Entertainment	247	.07	0	
Donations to				
Candidates from same state	0		0	
Candidates from other states	0		0	
Civic organizations	0		0	
Ideological groups	750	.21	0	
Political parties	0		0	
Subtotal	**750**	**.21**	**0**	
Unitemized Expenses	1,094	.31	1,968	7.37
Total Campaign Expenses	$ 353,065		$ 26,721	
PAC Contributions	$ 166,642		$ 2,250	
Individual Contributions	138,014		11,238	
Total Receipts*	311,365		27,801	

*Includes PAC and individual contributions as well as interest earned, party contributions, etc.

District 1 — HAWAII

Rep. Neil Abercrombie (D)

1992 Election Results

Neil Abercrombie (D) 129,332 (73%)
Warner C. Kimo Sutton (R) 41,575 (23%)

It did not take freshman Rep. Neil Abercrombie long to learn the game. In winning his 1990 open seat contest against well-funded Republican Mike Liu, Abercrombie had spent $357,271, sinking 74 percent of that total into advertising and persuasion mail. His 1990 overhead had amounted to only $19,315, or 5 percent of his total outlays. However, once elected Abercrombie immediately settled into the permanent campaign mode.

Despite the fact that he closed his campaign headquarters during the off-year, Abercrombie's permanent campaign cost him $107,835 in 1991. While he spent just $41,731 to raise $455,954 in 1990, Abercrombie invested $49,800 to raise $127,153 in 1991. During the off-year he spent $6,767 on a new computer and software. Constituent meals, gifts, and year-end holiday cards cost $7,830. He donated $12,594 to other politicians, Democratic party organizations, and causes, including $5,000 to the Democratic Congressional Campaign Committee (DCCC).

Unopposed in the Democratic primary, Abercrombie faced Warner C. Kimo Sutton in the general election. Although Sutton spent only $16,105 and posed no threat, Abercrombie poured $215,266 into his campaign during 1992. However, unlike the 1990 campaign, only 41 percent of his election-year spending was put into advertising and voter contact mail.

Fund-raising expenses during 1992 totaled $50,395, only $4,249 less than Abercrombie spent on broadcast advertising. He spent $4,895 on year-end holiday cards—$1,531 more than he spent on newspaper advertising. Constituent meals and gifts added another $2,221 to his 1992 totals—$618 more than his combined office rent and telephone bills for the year. The $12,998 he gave away included another $5,000 gift to the DCCC.

When all the bills were totaled, Abercrombie's combined spending over the two-year election cycle for polling, advertising, persuasion mail, and other campaign activities amounted to $121,985, or $18,748 less than his combined outlays for fund raising, constituent gifts and entertainment, and donations.

To fund his campaign, Abercrombie relied much more heavily on political action committees (PACs) than he had in 1990. He held three PAC events in Washington, D.C., during the two-year cycle, which helped push PAC donations to $192,019, or 62 percent of his total contributions. Donations from PACs represented only 31 percent of his 1990 contributions.

Susan Hunter of Falls Church, Va., received $42,267 for spearheading his fund-raising efforts. Loomis & Pollock of Honolulu collected $87,424 for handling his advertising, persuasion mail, and some local fund raising.

Campaign Expenditures	Abercrombie Amount Spent	Abercrombie % of Total	Sutton Amount Spent	Sutton % of Total
Overhead				
Office furniture/supplies	$ 5,890	1.82	$ 916	5.69
Rent/utilities	1,000	.31	1,933	12.00
Salaries	8,270	2.56	450	2.79
Taxes	2,589	.80	0	
Bank/investment fees	1,041	.32	0	
Lawyers/accountants	959	.30	0	
Telephone	1,727	.53	913	5.67
Campaign automobile	0		0	
Computers/office equipment	7,573	2.34	396	2.46
Travel	8,901	2.75	529	3.28
Food/meetings	1,086	.34	37	.23
Subtotal	**39,036**	**12.08**	**5,174**	**32.13**
Fund Raising				
Events	100,196	31.01	670	4.16
Direct mail	0		0	
Telemarketing	0		0	
Subtotal	**100,196**	**31.01**	**670**	**4.16**
Polling	**11,258**	**3.48**	**0**	
Advertising				
Electronic media	54,644	16.91	2,530	15.71
Other media	5,106	1.58	3,390	21.05
Subtotal	**59,749**	**18.49**	**5,920**	**36.76**
Other Campaign Activity				
Persuasion mail/brochures	29,390	9.10	1,867	11.60
Actual campaigning	20,358	6.30	850	5.28
Staff/volunteers	1,230	.38	358	2.23
Subtotal	**50,978**	**15.78**	**3,076**	**19.10**
Constituent Gifts/Entertainment	**14,946**	**4.63**	**412**	**2.56**
Donations to				
Candidates from same state	3,140	.97	273	1.70
Candidates from other states	3,800	1.18	0	
Civic organizations	4,636	1.43	580	3.60
Ideological groups	1,740	.54	0	
Political parties	12,275	3.80	0	
Subtotal	**25,591**	**7.92**	**854**	**5.30**
Unitemized Expenses	**21,346**	**6.61**	**0**	
Total Campaign Expenses	**$ 323,101**		**$ 16,105**	
PAC Contributions	$ 192,019		$ 0	
Individual Contributions	119,194		3,510	
Total Receipts*	359,336		16,103	

*Includes PAC and individual contributions as well as interest earned, party contributions, etc.

District 2 — HAWAII

Rep. Patsy T. Mink (D)

1992 Election Results

Patsy T. Mink (D)	131,454	(73%)
Kamuela Price (R)	40,070	(22%)
Lloyd "Jeff" Mallan † (I)	9,431	(5%)

When asked to compare her 1992 and 1990 campaign efforts, Rep. Patsy T. Mink barely paused. "The two elections were like night and day," she said. "I spent three times as much money last time as I did this time."

Forced to win three elections—a special election to fill a vacancy, then the primary and general—in three months against well-funded opponents, Mink spent nearly $659,000 on her 1990 campaigns, including $521,221 on advertising. However, faced with only a weak challenge in the 1992 Democratic primary and a Republican opponent who had less than $800 to spend, Mink could afford to coast.

Mink ended the 1990 campaign with cash reserves of only $288 and debts totaling $188,256. Since $170,000 of the debts were loans she had made to the campaign, Mink had strong reason to devote considerable time and resources to raising money.

She held at least one large event on each of Hawaii's four main islands—Oahu, Maui, Hawaii, and Kauai. However, with ticket prices ranging from $10 on Kauai to $50 in Honolulu, she was unable to reduce the campaign's debts substantially. At the end of 1992, the campaign still owed her $136,590.

To help her wage her modest primary and general election campaigns, Mink turned to Chun & Yonamine, the same Honolulu-based ad agency she used in 1990. The firm developed and placed her broadcast advertising, designed her brochures, handled persuasion mail, placed some of her newspaper ads, and furnished fund-raising invitations.

Without major opposition, Mink stuck with campaign themes that stressed the positives of incumbency. Her brochures all bore the message: "A record of achievement, a legacy of service." One television spot detailed her work on the Higher Education Bill.

For the primary contest with attorney David L. Bourgoin, Mink spent $34,375 with Chun & Yonamine, most of which was put into broadcast advertising. The campaign also invested $6,823 in newspaper ads. Following her overwhelming victory, Mink spent $2,439 to place "thank you" ads.

In the fall campaign against Republican Kamuela Price, Mink paid Chun & Yonamine $21,041 for persuasion mail, $20,156 for creating and placing broadcast ads, and $7,334 for placing newspaper ads. Mink also paid $4,600 to the Hawaii County Democratic party for their coordinated get-out-the-vote efforts. Following the election, she paid Chun & Yonamine another $4,108 for placing more "thank you" newspaper ads.

In September 1991 the campaign paid a $3,800 fine levied by the Federal Election Commission for failure to promptly report last-minute contributions to her 1990 effort.

Campaign Expenditures	Mink Amount Spent	Mink % of Total	Price Amount Spent	Price % of Total
Overhead				
Office furniture/supplies	$ 4,288	1.86	$ 13	1.65
Rent/utilities	7,715	3.35	0	
Salaries	3,000	1.30	0	
Taxes	308	.13	0	
Bank/investment fees	65	.03	0	
Lawyers/accountants	3,800	1.65	0	
Telephone	2,724	1.18	0	
Campaign automobile	0		0	
Computers/office equipment	1,497	.65	0	
Travel	4,578	1.99	10	1.29
Food/meetings	389	.17	0	
Subtotal	**28,362**	**12.33**	**23**	**2.95**
Fund Raising				
Events	45,347	19.71	0	
Direct mail	0		0	
Telemarketing	0		0	
Subtotal	**45,347**	**19.71**	**0**	
Polling	0		0	
Advertising				
Electronic media	61,822	26.87	0	
Other media	30,185	13.12	0	
Subtotal	**92,007**	**39.98**	**0**	
Other Campaign Activity				
Persuasion mail/brochures	29,003	12.60	300	38.81
Actual campaigning	26,189	11.38	400	51.75
Staff/volunteers	0		0	
Subtotal	**55,192**	**23.99**	**700**	**90.56**
Constituent Gifts/Entertainment	2,943	1.28	0	
Donations to				
Candidates from same state	0		0	
Candidates from other states	0		0	
Civic organizations	370	.16	0	
Ideological groups	0		0	
Political parties	5,000	2.17	50	6.47
Subtotal	**5,370**	**2.33**	**50**	**6.47**
Unitemized Expenses	886	.39	0	
Total Campaign Expenses	$ 230,107		$ 773	
PAC Contributions	$ 113,425		$ 0	
Individual Contributions	205,887		195	
Total Receipts*	336,089		745	

*Includes PAC and individual contributions as well as interest earned, party contributions, etc.

† No expenditures or receipts on file. Candidates raising or spending less than $5,000 are not required to file reports with the Federal Election Commission.

IDAHO — District 1

Rep. Larry LaRocco (D)

1992 Election Results

Larry LaRocco (D)	140,985	(58%)
Rachel S. Gilbert (R)	90,983	(38%)

In the wake of his 1990 victory over C. A. "Skip" Smyser, freshman Rep. Larry LaRocco began 1991 with cash reserves of only $1,523 and debts of $71,316. By the end of 1991, he had raised $236,358, repaid all his debts, and had more than $100,000 in the bank. The $623,847 he collected over the two-year election cycle was $174,428 more than he raised in 1990.

He accomplished this feat largely with the help of political action committees (PACs) and out-of-state donors. A debt retirement fund-raiser was held at the Ridpath Hotel in Spokane, Wash. An employee of the Walt Disney Co. in Burbank, Calif., sponsored another reception. The Oppenheimer Co. sponsored yet another fund-raiser in New York.

As a member of the Water, Power and Offshore Energy Subcommittee, LaRocco found the Water Power Federal Political Action Committee eager to serve as co-host of a fund-raising breakfast in Spokane. Having landed a seat on the Banking, Finance and Urban Affairs Committee, he benefited from events sponsored by Bankers Trust Co. in New York and the Oregon Bankers PAC. LaRocco held more than a half dozen receptions in Washington, D.C., aimed at still more PAC contributions. In all, nearly two-thirds of the money he raised was donated by PACs and out-of-state contributors.

Approximately half of LaRocco's spending was devoted to direct appeals to voters. As in 1990, Fenn & King Communications of Washington, D.C., handled the broadcast media. "Taking care of Idaho was still our message," explained Peter Fenn. "But to combat the anti-incumbency problem, we also needed to show he was part of the solution, not part of the problem."

To do that one commercial highlighted LaRocco's citation by the National Taxpayers Union as one of the more frugal members of Congress. Another focused on the fact that he had not used $60,000 of his congressional franking privileges and that he had no overdrafts at the House bank. When his Republican opponent, former state senator Rachel S. Gilbert, attacked him for being a tax-and-spend liberal, LaRocco fired back with an ad citing all her previous votes in favor of increasing state taxes. In all, Fenn produced at least eight television commercials and several companion radio spots. All but $26,928 of the media budget was committed to the fall campaign.

LaRocco also spent $29,102 on brochures and limited persuasion mailings. He invested $13,090 in yard signs, $10,000 in the state Democratic party's phonebanking effort, and $6,545 in campaign buttons and bumper stickers.

Outspent by nearly three to one, Gilbert spent more on her staff salaries than on advertising.

Campaign Expenditures	LaRocco Amount Spent	LaRocco % of Total	Gilbert Amount Spent	Gilbert % of Total
Overhead				
Office furniture/supplies	$ 9,357	1.59	$ 7,235	3.47
Rent/utilities	6,911	1.17	87	.04
Salaries	87,352	14.83	46,378	22.25
Taxes	3,803	.65	1,691	.81
Bank/investment fees	1,326	.23	47	.02
Lawyers/accountants	2,150	.36	210	.10
Telephone	14,435	2.45	10,777	5.17
Campaign automobile	4,300	.73	1,671	.80
Computers/office equipment	10,541	1.79	6,031	2.89
Travel	49,209	8.35	5,995	2.88
Food/meetings	3,899	.66	0	
Subtotal	193,283	32.81	80,123	38.44
Fund Raising				
Events	52,346	8.89	12,972	6.22
Direct mail	0		32,692	15.68
Telemarketing	0		0	
Subtotal	52,346	8.89	45,664	21.91
Polling	25,325	4.30	0	
Advertising				
Electronic media	230,572	39.14	44,350	21.27
Other media	527	.09	410	.20
Subtotal	231,099	39.23	44,759	21.47
Other Campaign Activity				
Persuasion mail/brochures	29,102	4.94	17,040	8.17
Actual campaigning	43,479	7.38	17,802	8.54
Staff/volunteers	298	.05	0	
Subtotal	72,879	12.37	34,843	16.71
Constituent Gifts/ Entertainment	458	.08	0	
Donations to				
Candidates from same state	1,000	.17	0	
Candidates from other states	1,000	.17	0	
Civic organizations	1,134	.19	18	.01
Ideological groups	0		0	
Political parties	3,650	.62	40	.02
Subtotal	6,784	1.15	58	.03
Unitemized Expenses	6,882	1.17	3,015	1.45
Total Campaign Expenses	$ 589,056		$ 208,461	
PAC Contributions	$ 408,955		$ 47,110	
Individual Contributions	176,495		142,698	
Total Receipts*	623,847		222,858	

*Includes PAC and individual contributions as well as interest earned, party contributions, etc.

District 2 — IDAHO

Rep. Michael D. Crapo (R)

1992 Election Results

Michael D. Crapo (R)	139,783	(61%)
J. D. Williams (D)	81,450	(35%)

Republican state senator Michael D. Crapo knew he would need help to win the seat vacated by Democratic Rep. Richard Stallings, who resigned to wage an unsuccessful Senate campaign. "Mike was a first-time candidate, and most of the people around him hadn't been involved in a congressional campaign before," explained chief of staff John Hoehne. "We made sure we had the help we needed when we needed it."

To help him overcome the problem of raising money in Idaho, Crapo hired three fund-raising consultants. Rich, Smith & Rich of Boise received $43,287 for arranging in-state events and for work on direct-mail fund-raising solicitations. Direct Mail Systems of St. Petersburg, Fla., was paid $24,364 for assisting Rich with production of the direct mail. Ziebart Associates of Washington, D.C., received $26,181 for coordinating Washington events that targeted political action committee money.

To frame his message, Crapo hired media consultants Sandler-Innocenzi of Washington, D.C., and Elgin, Syferd, Drake of Boise. Sandler-Innocenzi collected $61,194 from Crapo for work on the campaign's broadcast advertising. Elgin, Syferd, Drake received $59,139 for work on the radio and television spots, as well as the design of Crapo's newspaper ads.

Payco American Corp. of Brookfield, Wis., and Telemark of Wilsonville, Ore., were paid $17,835 and $9,715, respectively, for phonebanking. For providing general strategic advice, John Maddox & Associates of Alexandria, Va., received $16,173 and Ruder-Finn of New York collected $17,539. The Farwell Group of New Orleans, La., was paid $6,500 for brochure design. Public Opinion Strategies of Alexandria, Va., conducted polls for $12,997.

In all, eleven consultants billed the campaign $294,924. Sandler-Innocenzi also picked up $27,620 from the National Republican Congressional Committee. "We left no stone unturned," noted Hoehne.

Crapo's message in both the primary and general election campaigns was one of reform. Given his position as president pro tem of the state senate, he did not need to run commercials introducing himself to voters. Instead, his radio and television spots touted his support for a constitutional amendment to require a balanced federal budget, his opposition to further increases in the national debt limit, and his support for a presidential line-item veto and twelve-year congressional term limits.

Democrat J. D. Williams's campaign stalled badly when it was revealed he had made improper campaign-related telephone calls from his state auditor's office. By the second week of October, Williams lacked the funds to advertise, leaving Crapo to run virtually unanswered advertising for two weeks.

Campaign Expenditures	Crapo Amount Spent	Crapo % of Total	Williams Amount Spent	Williams % of Total
Overhead				
Office furniture/supplies	$ 12,452	2.20	$ 2,992	1.13
Rent/utilities	6,411	1.13	2,691	1.02
Salaries	74,303	13.11	72,617	27.45
Taxes	37,889	6.69	0	
Bank/investment fees	1,083	.19	0	
Lawyers/accountants	500	.09	0	
Telephone	18,568	3.28	9,307	3.52
Campaign automobile	7,743	1.37	0	
Computers/office equipment	6,332	1.12	3,143	1.19
Travel	22,773	4.02	20,270	7.66
Food/meetings	1,651	.29	0	
Subtotal	**189,706**	**33.48**	**111,020**	**41.96**
Fund Raising				
Events	60,981	10.76	19,989	7.56
Direct mail	48,544	8.57	11,337	4.29
Telemarketing	0		0	
Subtotal	**109,525**	**19.33**	**31,326**	**11.84**
Polling	**22,397**	**3.95**	**24,085**	**9.10**
Advertising				
Electronic media	123,705	21.83	60,912	23.02
Other media	24,057	4.25	1,286	.49
Subtotal	**147,762**	**26.08**	**62,198**	**23.51**
Other Campaign Activity				
Persuasion mail/brochures	20,314	3.59	4,536	1.71
Actual campaigning	73,404	12.96	22,415	8.47
Staff/volunteers	589	.10	25	.01
Subtotal	**94,308**	**16.65**	**26,977**	**10.20**
Constituent Gifts/Entertainment	34	.01	0	
Donations to				
Candidates from same state	0		0	
Candidates from other states	0		0	
Civic organizations	170	.03	250	.09
Ideological groups	0		0	
Political parties	900	.16	0	
Subtotal	**1,070**	**.19**	**250**	**.09**
Unitemized Expenses	**1,751**	**.31**	**8,714**	**3.29**
Total Campaign Expenses	**$ 566,553**		**$ 264,570**	
PAC Contributions	$ 234,599		$ 126,075	
Individual Contributions	270,948		112,056	
Total Receipts*	554,691		253,051	

*Includes PAC and individual contributions as well as interest earned, party contributions, etc.

ILLINOIS — District 1

Rep. Bobby L. Rush (D)

1992 Election Results
Bobby L. Rush (D)   209,258   (83%)
Jay Walker (R)   43,453   (17%)

For nearly three months prior to the March 17 Democratic primary, Chicago alderman and former Black Panther Bobby L. Rush hammered away at Rep. Charles A. Hayes for his inability to deliver for the district during his eight years in Congress.

The cover of one of Rush's persuasion mailers showed Hayes's face in the center of a mock $100 bill. Emblazoned across one corner of the bill was a block of type that read, "Since 1986, Congressman Charlie Hayes Has Pocketed $55,980." Inside, the mailing slammed Hayes for accepting $55,980 in honoraria, for spending $35,000 on congressional fact-finding junkets, for accepting $7,100 in contributions from a Chicago company that received millions of dollars in federal contracts, and for voting for the congressional pay raise. "Enough is enough," the mailer concluded.

However, Rush did not seem to be making much progress with his anti-incumbent drumbeat until it was revealed that Hayes had 716 overdrafts at the House bank. Rush jumped on the checks as proof that Hayes was part of an institution that needed changing. Enough of the voters agreed, as they handed him a narrow victory in the seven-candidate primary.

Rush spent only $104,815 to retire Hayes, including the $18,550 he paid his persuasion mail consultants, Ambrosino & Muir of San Francisco, Calif. Additional postage and printing charges totaled $13,584. He spent $5,000 on billboards, $2,451 on signs and posters, and $1,100 on campaign buttons. For their primary day efforts, seven people collected checks totaling $2,000. Advertising in the *Southwest Messenger,* the *Chicago Defender,* and the *Independent Bulletin* added $1,822.

Much of the money to fund the primary campaign was raised at a single event held at the Chicago Historical Society in February. Expenses for the affair totaled $16,951, including $8,115 for catering, $1,500 to rent the museum for the evening, and $5,021 to cover expenses incurred by Planning Experts of Chicago.

Through the primary, political action committee (PAC) contributions to Rush's campaign amounted to only $21,350, or 19 percent of his total donations. After his primary victory, PACs contributed $110,950 to his coffers, or 76 percent of the money he raised during the last nine months of 1992. Lori Ann Bass of Chicago received $16,214 for coordinating Rush's postprimary fund raising.

In this overwhelmingly Democratic district, Rush spent $178,604 to dispatch administrative law judge Jay Walker, including another $10,000 to Ambrosino & Muir. He also spent $950 on a "ministers breakfast" and $450 to help defray funeral costs for a staff member's son.

Campaign Expenditures	Rush Amount Spent	Rush % of Total	Walker Amount Spent	Walker % of Total
Overhead				
Office furniture/supplies	$ 8,551	3.02	$ 13	.07
Rent/utilities	12,001	4.23	0	
Salaries	62,466	22.04	8,145	41.58
Taxes	0		0	
Bank/investment fees	960	.34	0	
Lawyers/accountants	2,000	.71	0	
Telephone	7,788	2.75	0	
Campaign automobile	0		0	
Computers/office equipment	1,105	.39	0	
Travel	16,025	5.65	415	2.12
Food/meetings	1,050	.37	21	.11
Subtotal	**111,946**	**39.50**	**8,595**	**43.87**
Fund Raising				
Events	34,771	12.27	736	3.76
Direct mail	0		0	
Telemarketing	0		0	
Subtotal	**34,771**	**12.27**	**736**	**3.76**
Polling	**9,300**	**3.28**	**0**	
Advertising				
Electronic media	0		85	.43
Other media	7,331	2.59	3,430	17.51
Subtotal	**7,331**	**2.59**	**3,515**	**17.94**
Other Campaign Activity				
Persuasion mail/brochures	89,202	31.47	3,452	17.62
Actual campaigning	22,867	8.07	3,157	16.12
Staff/volunteers	541	.19	0	
Subtotal	**112,611**	**39.73**	**6,609**	**33.74**
Constituent Gifts/ Entertainment	**0**		**0**	
Donations to				
Candidates from same state	0		0	
Candidates from other states	0		0	
Civic organizations	1,431	.50	0	
Ideological groups	270	.10	0	
Political parties	1,590	.56	0	
Subtotal	**3,291**	**1.16**	**0**	
Unitemized Expenses	**4,169**	**1.47**	**135**	**.69**
Total Campaign Expenses	**$ 283,419**		**$ 19,590**	
PAC Contributions	$ 132,300		$ 6,250	
Individual Contributions	125,155		3,400	
Total Receipts*	257,455		14,050	

*Includes PAC and individual contributions as well as interest earned, party contributions, etc.

District 2 — ILLINOIS

Rep. Mel Reynolds (D)

1992 Election Results

Mel Reynolds (D)	182,614	(78%)
Ron Blackstone (R)	31,957	(14%)
Louanner Peters † (I)	19,293	(8%)

After two failed attempts to unseat Rep. Gus Savage, Roosevelt University professor Mel Reynolds received a crucial assist from three federal judges called upon to redraw the Illinois political map. The new map removed voters from Savage's South Side Chicago base and replaced them with suburban voters less open to Savage's message.

Reynolds never closed his 1990 campaign office. Once the district's boundaries were set, he immediately opened a suburban headquarters. His off-year spending totaled $88,548.

During the first three months of 1992, Reynolds committed $389,997 to defeating Savage. Even though Reynolds is a Baptist, Savage saw his spending as evidence of a Jewish conspiracy against blacks. At a candidates' forum one week before the March 17 primary, Savage warned of a "danger of genocide" against blacks, adding that "the Jewish population is contributing to this pending disaster." Savage went on to say of Reynolds, "He'll spend five times the money I can raise, most of it coming from Jews."

Reynolds paid Fenn & King Communications of Washington, D.C., $107,623 for developing and placing two preprimary radio commercials. Noting that in 1990 Savage had portrayed him as "a traitor to the black cause," Reynolds said one ad recounted his birth in Mississippi, his childhood poverty, and its impact on his political views. The second ad attacked Savage's job performance, juxtaposing the $400,000 in federal contracts Savage had helped bring to the district with the millions of dollars received by other districts represented by Chicago's black House members. "In this campaign we vowed not to go after Gus on any personal matters—just on his responsiveness to the district," Reynolds said.

Reynolds sank $95,288 into preprimary persuasion mail, including a $2,500 consulting fee paid to the Campaign Performance Group of San Francisco, Calif. After that initial consultation, Reynolds said he decided to handle the mail in-house.

Few of Savage's House colleagues were sorry to see him go. Shortly after his upset primary victory, Reynolds flew to Washington, D.C. where Rep. Dan Rostenkowski (D-Ill.), House Speaker Thomas S. Foley (D-Wash.), Majority Leader Richard A. Gephardt (D-Mo.), Majority Whip David E. Bonior (D-Mich.), Democratic Congressional Campaign Committee Chairman Vic Fazio (D-Calif.), and a host of other Democratic leaders attended a fundraiser to help retire Reynold's campaign debt.

The general election campaign was anticlimatic. Reynolds spent just $62,791 to defeat Republican businessman Ron Blackstone and Savage's administrative assistant, Louanner Peters, who ran as an independent. Fenn & King collected $22,500 of that total.

Campaign Expenditures	Reynolds Amount Spent	Reynolds % of Total	Blackstone Amount Spent	Blackstone % of Total
Overhead				
Office furniture/supplies	$ 10,843	2.00	$ 306	.85
Rent/utilities	50,376	9.31	550	1.53
Salaries	66,866	12.35	8,097	22.59
Taxes	0		0	
Bank/investment fees	0		0	
Lawyers/accountants	6,250	1.15	1,650	4.60
Telephone	9,343	1.73	742	2.07
Campaign automobile	12,326	2.28	0	
Computers/office equipment	6,832	1.26	0	
Travel	8,730	1.61	824	2.30
Food/meetings	0		0	
Subtotal	171,566	31.69	12,169	33.94
Fund Raising				
Events	27,360	5.05	2,590	7.23
Direct mail	0		0	
Telemarketing	0		0	
Subtotal	27,360	5.05	2,590	7.23
Polling	20,000	3.69	0	
Advertising				
Electronic media	130,123	24.04	2,910	8.12
Other media	5,488	1.01	3,179	8.87
Subtotal	135,611	25.05	6,089	16.99
Other Campaign Activity				
Persuasion mail/brochures	140,324	25.92	6,872	19.17
Actual campaigning	37,215	6.87	4,935	13.77
Staff/volunteers	3,100	.57	0	
Subtotal	180,639	33.37	11,807	32.94
Constituent Gifts/ Entertainment	0		0	
Donations to				
Candidates from same state	0		50	.14
Candidates from other states	0		0	
Civic organizations	540	.10	280	.78
Ideological groups	254	.05	60	.17
Political parties	0		320	.89
Subtotal	794	.15	710	1.98
Unitemized Expenses	5,366	.99	2,484	6.93
Total Campaign Expenses	$ 541,336		$ 35,849	
PAC Contributions	$ 195,772		$ 1,000	
Individual Contributions	323,158		25,070	
Total Receipts*	532,031		36,075	

* *Includes PAC and individual contributions as well as interest earned, party contributions, etc.*

† *No expenditures or receipts on file. Candidates raising or spending less than $5,000 are not required to file reports with the Federal Election Commission.*

ILLINOIS District 3

Rep. William O. Lipinski (D)

1992 Election Results

William O. Lipinski (D)   162,165   (64%)
Harry C. Lepinske (R)   93,128   (36%)

Forced into a primary confrontation by a federal court's imposition of a Republican-dominated redistricting plan, Democratic Reps. William O. Lipinski and Marty Russo waged one of the more acrimonious campaigns of 1992.

Considering the stakes, the campaign began on a relatively cordial, positive note. Using taxpayer dollars, not money from their campaign treasuries, both candidates peppered their new constituents with franked mail. An eight-term veteran, Russo touted his health cares initiatives and his support for a middle-class tax cut. A five-term incumbent, Lipinski touted his opposition to new civil rights legislation and his record of constituent service. However, things went down hill quickly.

With far less money to spend, Lipinski relied heavily on persuasion mail. His first effort slammed Russo as a wealthy carpetbagger, juxtaposing his own modest home in the district with Russo's large home outside the district. Other mailings painted Russo as a junketeering tool of special interests and charged that he "voted funding for art considered obscene."

One particularly harsh attack accused Russo of engineering tax breaks for insurance companies as part of the 1986 Tax Reform Act. The cover of the mailing depicted Russo as the man in the moon, looking down at the Capitol dome. "At 4:00 o'clock in the morning on September 25, 1986, Marty Russo used his influence as a Congressman to help some lobbyists," the text began.

Lipinski sank $157,367 into his preprimary persuasion mail. James Strong & Associates of Chicago collected $3,750 for producing radio spots and $51,022 was spent to air them over the final three weeks of the primary campaign. Shirley Reid of Washington, D.C., received $7,363 for providing the opposition research on Russo, and McKeon & Associates were paid $7,000 for polling. Yard signs and posters cost $7,875 and payments to election day workers added $6,200. Lipinski's total expenses for the primary exceeded $275,000.

With the backing of fellow Illinois Rep. Dan Rostenkowski and most of the House Democratic leadership, Russo did not go quietly. Russo spent nearly $700,000 during the three-month primary campaign, including more than $361,000 on persuasion mail and nearly $200,000 on broadcast advertising. Among other things, Russo charged Lipinski with exacting illegal campaign contributions from his congressional staff and using campaign funds to enrich himself by renting campaign office space in a building he owned.

After his 21-point primary win, Lipinski breezed through the general election against international trade consultant and Lyons Township supervisor Harry C. Lepinske.

Campaign Expenditures	Lipinski Amount Spent	Lipinski % of Total	Lepinske Amount Spent	Lepinske % of Total
Overhead				
Office furniture/supplies	$ 11,557	2.18	$ 1,328	1.80
Rent/utilities	9,904	1.86	1,275	1.73
Salaries	13,914	2.62	5,839	7.90
Taxes	0		0	
Bank/investment fees	72	.01	232	.31
Lawyers/accountants	4,350	.82	1,233	1.67
Telephone	11,302	2.13	1,423	1.93
Campaign automobile	3,357	.63	0	
Computers/office equipment	567	.11	647	.88
Travel	3,898	.73	1,645	2.23
Food/meetings	3,128	.59	90	.12
Subtotal	**62,050**	**11.68**	**13,712**	**18.55**
Fund Raising				
Events	40,966	7.71	7,481	10.12
Direct mail	9,500	1.79	4,953	6.70
Telemarketing	0		0	
Subtotal	**50,466**	**9.50**	**12,434**	**16.83**
Polling	**12,000**	**2.26**	**1,996**	**2.70**
Advertising				
Electronic media	58,871	11.08	0	
Other media	6,436	1.21	1,029	1.39
Subtotal	**65,307**	**12.30**	**1,029**	**1.39**
Other Campaign Activity				
Persuasion mail/brochures	224,271	42.22	30,765	41.63
Actual campaigning	37,326	7.03	13,870	18.77
Staff/volunteers	3,142	.59	0	
Subtotal	**264,739**	**49.84**	**44,635**	**60.40**
Constituent Gifts/ Entertainment	**16,340**	**3.08**	**0**	
Donations to				
Candidates from same state	6,525	1.23	75	.10
Candidates from other states	0		0	
Civic organizations	8,696	1.64	19	.03
Ideological groups	1,580	.30	0	
Political parties	11,550	2.17	0	
Subtotal	**28,351**	**5.34**	**94**	**.13**
Unitemized Expenses	**31,897**	**6.01**	**0**	
Total Campaign Expenses	**$ 531,150**		**$ 73,900**	
PAC Contributions	**$ 316,350**		**$ 9,999**	
Individual Contributions	**231,746**		**33,356**	
Total Receipts*	**561,335**		**67,070**	

*Includes PAC and individual contributions as well as interest earned, party contributions, etc.

District 4 — ILLINOIS

Rep. Luis V. Gutierrez (D)

1992 Election Results

Luis V. Gutierrez (D)	90,452	(78%)
Hildegarde Rodriguez-Schieman (R)	26,154	(22%)

Chicago Alderman Luis V. Gutierrez became the first Hispanic elected to the House from Illinois without much of a fight. The day after he announced his candidacy, he was endorsed by Mayor Richard M. Daley. After his two most serious challengers dropped out of the Democratic primary, Gutierrez captured 60 percent of the primary vote before pummeling Hildegarde Rodriguez-Schieman, who spent $3,575.

While he was considered the overwhelming favorite from the outset, Gutierrez left nothing to chance. He began in September 1991 and over the next six months spent $292,961 to secure the nomination.

His first step was to hire the Strategy Group, a Chicago-based campaign management consulting firm. During the six months before the primary, the Strategy Group collected $32,759 for providing office space, staff, and day-to-day campaign strategy.

To increase his name identification, Gutierrez spent $120,796 on brochures and persuasion mail, including $30,174 for postage and $8,263 for mailing lists and labels. Ambrosino & Muir of San Francisco, Calif., received $82,359 for designing and producing the mailers. "We did a lot of mail focusing on crime and economic development," remarked chief of staff Doug Scofield.

Urban Strategy of Orland Park collected $4,000 for creating the campaign's radio and television commercials. Scofield said the ads ran primarily on Spanish-language stations and hit the same themes covered in the mail. The campaign spent $18,925 to air its television ads and $11,480 on radio.

Frederick/Schneiders of Washington, D.C., received $12,549 for conducting a survey used to refine the campaign's message. Big Sky Consulting of Washington, D.C., was paid $16,500 for providing opposition research.

The general election campaign was a formality. Over the last nine months of 1992, Gutierrez spent $125,299, with only $2,225 going to advertising. By far his biggest expense was the $31,766 he invested in brochures and persuasion mail, including payments to Ambrosino & Muir totaling $19,250. With less need for a campaign organization, Gutierrez paid the Strategy Group only $23,548.

After the election, Gutierrez spent $990 of his campaign funds to purchase sixty copies of the book *Adventures in Pork Land*, which he gave to other Democratic freshmen.

Gutierrez employed three fund-raising consultants. Erickson & Co. of Washington, D.C., was paid $15,868 for their assistance in raising $187,945 from political action committees. Chicago-area events were coordinated by local fund-raisers Q&A Partners and Lori Ann Bass for $5,582 and $26,199, respectively.

Campaign Expenditures	Gutierrez Amount Spent	Gutierrez % of Total	Rodriguez-Schieman Amount Spent	Rodriguez-Schieman % of Total
Overhead				
Office furniture/supplies	$ 2,016	.48	$ 291	8.13
Rent/utilities	1,966	.47	230	6.43
Salaries	5,375	1.29	0	
Taxes	0		0	
Bank/investment fees	0		0	
Lawyers/accountants	486	.12	0	
Telephone	777	.19	0	
Campaign automobile	0		0	
Computers/office equipment	0		638	17.85
Travel	18,275	4.37	0	
Food/meetings	213	.05	0	
Subtotal	**29,108**	**6.96**	**1,159**	**32.41**
Fund Raising				
Events	63,711	15.23	50	1.40
Direct mail	0		0	
Telemarketing	0		0	
Subtotal	**63,711**	**15.23**	**50**	**1.40**
Polling	**12,549**	**3.00**	**0**	
Advertising				
Electronic media	43,743	10.46	0	
Other media	2,265	.54	0	
Subtotal	**46,007**	**11.00**	**0**	
Other Campaign Activity				
Persuasion mail/brochures	152,562	36.48	1,121	31.36
Actual campaigning	91,367	21.84	428	11.98
Staff/volunteers	0		0	
Subtotal	**243,929**	**58.32**	**1,549**	**43.34**
Constituent Gifts/Entertainment	**10,579**	**2.53**	**0**	
Donations to				
Candidates from same state	250	.06	0	
Candidates from other states	3,250	.78	0	
Civic organizations	0		265	7.41
Ideological groups	0		50	1.40
Political parties	0		25	.70
Subtotal	**3,500**	**.84**	**340**	**9.51**
Unitemized Expenses	**8,878**	**2.12**	**477**	**13.34**
Total Campaign Expenses	**$ 418,260**		**$ 3,575**	
PAC Contributions	**$ 187,945**		**$ 741**	
Individual Contributions	**242,881**		**1,198**	
Total Receipts*	**438,253**		**3,857**	

*Includes PAC and individual contributions as well as interest earned, party contributions, etc.

ILLINOIS District 5

Rep. Dan Rostenkowski (D)

1992 Election Results

Dan Rostenkowski (D)   132,889   (57%)
Elias R. Zenkich (R)   90,738   (39%)

Rep. Dan Rostenkowski had more than his share of troubles. Seventy percent of the voters in his redrawn district were new to him, and after seventeen terms in the House, he was the embodiment of the Washington establishment. Concerned that he might become a casualty of an anti-incumbent backlash, Rostenkowski poured $1,454,462 into his campaign—nearly five times the amount he spent on his 1990 reelection campaign.

During the first three months of 1992, Rostenkowski spent $764,940 to beat back a serious primary challenge mounted by former Chicago alderman Dick Simpson, who committed $236,579 to the race. Rostenkowski's media adviser for the primary campaign, Axelrod & Associates of Chicago, collected $235,716. His Chicago-based persuasion mail consultant, Kevin B. Tynan & Associates, received $133,320 for designing eleven persuasion mailers. Postage charges amounted to $75,000.

Rather than running from incumbency, Rostenkowski embraced it. "I went to Congress with one thing in mind—to fight for Chicago and for ways to ease the burden on working families and retirees," he proclaimed in one radio commercial. "Now I'm in a position to lead that fight." David Axelrod produced eight radio spots that focused largely on the incumbent's ability to deliver federal dollars to Chicago. "We used the spots to educate people about who Rostenkowski is and the influence he brings to Chicago from his position in Washington," Axelrod explained.

For the primary, Rostenkowski paid Sarafin & Associates of Chicago $20,131 for handling press relations and designing newspaper advertising. He spent $15,745 to place the newspaper ads, $28,232 on an in-house phonebank, $10,021 on signs and posters, and $47,308 on polls conducted by Target Research Associates of Chicago and KRC Research of New York.

The general election against Republican Elias R. Zenkich, who legally changed his name to include "Non-Incumbent," proved much more placid. Rostenkowski paid Sarafin & Associates another $85,874, including $54,000 for placing radio ads. Printing and postage for one persuasion mailer sent to every registered voter in the district totaled $89,924. Billboard ads cost $32,710.

Not all of Rostenkowski's campaign spending was crucial to his reelection. His campaign paid $30,000 to rent an office in a building he and his sister owned. Five golf pros listed as "consultants" collected a total of $1,600 from the campaign. He spent $28,734 for meals at expensive Washington, D.C., and Chicago-area restaurants. Legal fees associated with a federal investigation into his possible misuse of campaign funds totaled $156,953; they consumed 11 percent of his total campaign spending.

Campaign Expenditures	Rostenkowski Amount Spent	Rostenkowski % of Total	Zenkich Amount Spent	Zenkich % of Total
Overhead				
Office furniture/supplies	$ 15,294	1.05	$ 4,178	2.72
Rent/utilities	34,283	2.36	3,897	2.54
Salaries	43,052	2.96	4,547	2.96
Taxes	26,877	1.85	0	
Bank/investment fees	79,256	5.45	352	.23
Lawyers/accountants	156,953	10.79	0	
Telephone	5,582	.38	2,545	1.66
Campaign automobile	8,446	.58	0	
Computers/office equipment	14,250	.98	5,237	3.41
Travel	11,131	.77	3,249	2.12
Food/meetings	28,734	1.98	0	
Subtotal	**423,858**	**29.14**	**24,005**	**15.65**
Fund Raising				
Events	85,623	5.89	10,004	6.52
Direct mail	0		0	
Telemarketing	0		0	
Subtotal	**85,623**	**5.89**	**10,004**	**6.52**
Polling	**59,517**	**4.09**	**2,046**	**1.33**
Advertising				
Electronic media	289,716	19.92	7,660	4.99
Other media	102,130	7.02	20,086	13.09
Subtotal	**391,847**	**26.94**	**27,746**	**18.09**
Other Campaign Activity				
Persuasion mail/brochures	347,164	23.87	38,148	24.87
Actual campaigning	94,566	6.50	45,655	29.76
Staff/volunteers	1,486	.10	0	
Subtotal	**443,216**	**30.47**	**83,803**	**54.63**
Constituent Gifts/Entertainment	**4,364**	**.30**	**0**	
Donations to				
Candidates from same state	3,750	.26	1,300	.85
Candidates from other states	0		0	
Civic organizations	5,705	.39	0	
Ideological groups	0		0	
Political parties	11,000	.76	0	
Subtotal	**20,455**	**1.41**	**1,300**	**.85**
Unitemized Expenses	**25,583**	**1.76**	**4,498**	**2.93**
Total Campaign Expenses	**$ 1,454,462**		**$ 153,401**	
PAC Contributions	$ 962,937		$ 0	
Individual Contributions	371,634		31,790	
Total Receipts*	1,587,108		95,447	

*Includes PAC and individual contributions as well as interest earned, party contributions, etc.

District 6 — ILLINOIS

Rep. Henry J. Hyde (R)

1992 Election Results

Henry J. Hyde (R)	165,009	(66%)
Barry W. Watkins (D)	86,891	(34%)

Businessman Barry W. Watkins spent $62,426 on his 1992 challenge to Rep. Henry J. Hyde, or $61,370 more than Democrat Robert J. Cassidy had spent on his 1990 bid. With this additional spending, Watkins succeeded in reducing Hyde's winning percentage in this overwhelmingly Republican district from 67 to 66 percent.

To meet the challenge, Hyde increased his spending from $267,951 in 1990 to $408,991 in 1992, a 53 percent rise. He increased his outlays for advertising from $20,668 to $35,140. Spending on voter contact mail grew from $46,108 to $121,354.

Unable to afford network rates in the pricey Chicago media market, Hyde spent $7,605 to air two spots on local cable television systems, something he avoided completely in 1990. Newspaper advertising cost the campaign $21,044. With little competition, his message was positive. Ads trumpeted the fact that he had been named a "Taxpayer Hero" by Citizens Against Government Waste and had received the "Bulldog Award" from Voters to Cut Government Spending. "We didn't have any reason to be negative," remarked press secretary Sam Stratman.

The campaign's principal persuasion mailer was an eight-page, tabloid-style piece that contained reprints of several speeches, as well as issue papers prepared for him by his two speech writers. Hyde paid the speech writers a total of $16,500 during the two-year election cycle.

Hyde invested $3,278 in plastic bags imprinted with his campaign logo, which he filled with campaign literature and hung on the door of virtually every home in the district. He paid the Republican Organization of Cook County $6,620 for sample ballots. Another $5,000 was invested in DuPage Republican Central Committee Candidate Guides.

As in past campaigns, Hyde purchased a variety of promotional items. Coffee mugs cost the campaign $3,569. The campaign invested $6,611 in paper fans that were given away at county fairs. "Everyone walks around cooling off to Henry Hyde," noted Stratman. "It's a hell of a name recognition tool, not that we needed it."

Hyde spent $12,386 on calendars from the U.S. Capitol Historical Society and on the postage needed to mail them to supporters. Expenditures for other constituent gifts and flowers amounted to $2,407.

Hyde kept his overhead low by not opening a campaign office until August 1992. Of the $31,563 he paid in salaries, $28,611 went to four members of his congressional staff.

Watkins had little luck raising money and ultimately contributed $57,200 of his own money to the futile cause.

Campaign Expenditures	Hyde Amount Spent	Hyde % of Total	Watkins Amount Spent	Watkins % of Total
Overhead				
Office furniture/supplies	$ 4,926	1.20	$ 2,374	3.80
Rent/utilities	1,861	.46	1,700	2.72
Salaries	31,563	7.72	24,688	39.55
Taxes	4,682	1.14	0	
Bank/investment fees	0		145	.23
Lawyers/accountants	10,877	2.66	0	
Telephone	2,535	.62	2,085	3.34
Campaign automobile	591	.14	0	
Computers/office equipment	1,592	.39	608	.97
Travel	6,922	1.69	0	
Food/meetings	6,284	1.54	0	
Subtotal	**71,833**	**17.56**	**31,600**	**50.62**
Fund Raising				
Events	51,260	12.53	361	.58
Direct mail	0		0	
Telemarketing	0		0	
Subtotal	**51,260**	**12.53**	**361**	**.58**
Polling	0		0	
Advertising				
Electronic media	10,345	2.53	3,695	5.92
Other media	24,794	6.06	2,321	3.72
Subtotal	**35,140**	**8.59**	**6,016**	**9.64**
Other Campaign Activity				
Persuasion mail/brochures	121,354	29.67	12,872	20.62
Actual campaigning	51,821	12.67	7,812	12.51
Staff/volunteers	1,169	.29	0	
Subtotal	**174,344**	**42.63**	**20,684**	**33.13**
Constituent Gifts/ Entertainment	14,793	3.62	0	
Donations to				
Candidates from same state	7,430	1.82	0	
Candidates from other states	5,750	1.41	0	
Civic organizations	2,200	.54	0	
Ideological groups	400	.10	0	
Political parties	17,036	4.17	0	
Subtotal	**32,816**	**8.02**	**0**	
Unitemized Expenses	28,806	7.04	3,765	6.03
Total Campaign Expenses	$ 408,991		$ 62,426	
PAC Contributions	$ 170,882		$ 0	
Individual Contributions	163,424		4,811	
Total Receipts*	355,851		62,534	

*Includes PAC and individual contributions as well as interest earned, party contributions, etc.

ILLINOIS — District 7

Rep. Cardiss Collins (D)

1992 Election Results

Cardiss Collins (D)	182,811	(81%)
Norman G. Boccio (R)	35,346	(16%)

Worried that the creation of a new Hispanic district would split her district in two, Rep. Cardiss Collins paid Chicago attorney James D. Montgomery $12,480 for advice. However, in the end, the federal court ultimately responsible for setting the boundaries left her old district largely intact.

As she had in past election cycles, Collins ran a year-round campaign operation that cost $107,336 during 1991. Overhead expenses amounted to $50,250 in 1991, including $15,685 for rent on her Chicago headquarters, $5,100 for payroll, and $3,487 for a new computer. In January 1991 Collins paid $4,181 to the Four Seasons in Washington, D.C., for a reception to honor three incoming House members: Barbara Rose Collins (D-Mich.), Maxine Waters (D-Calif.), and Eleanor Holmes Norton (D-D.C). Overhead again dominated Collins's spending in 1992, accounting for 28 percent of her total outlays.

Collins's eighteen overdrafts at the House bank caused her no problems in either the primary or general election campaigns. She spent nothing on television advertising and only $12,022 to run radio commercials in the primary. For the general contest with Republican Norman G. Boccio, Collins increased her radio buys marginally to $18,629. Limited persuasion mail cost her campaign $3,196 for the primary and $26,545 for the fall campaign. Newspaper advertising added $5,122 to the cost of her primary efforts and $1,382 to her general election expenses.

Whichever medium Collins chose, the message delivered was basically the same. "We told of her fight against the Bush administration and his budget cuts to people-programs," said administrative assistant Bud Myers. Her mail also highlighted the positive ratings given her by the League of Women Voters and the AFL-CIO.

Constituent entertainment and gifts cost the Collins's campaign $50,201 during the 1992 election cycle, a 68 percent increase over 1990. Her annual senior citizens picnic cost $3,750 in 1991 and $11,336 in 1992, with half the difference in cost accounted for by the $3,870 in aprons she passed out in 1992. She spent a total of $25,634 on the four bingo events she staged during the two-year cycle. A brunch for local ministers cost the campaign $3,869. She spent $1,810 on Easter cards and $2,554 on year-end holiday cards.

Collins relied almost exclusively on political action committee donations to fund her campaign. Interest earned on her cash reserves amounted to $26,142, far outdistancing the $17,436 she raised from individual contributors in Illinois. Collins raised only $1,336 from small donors who gave less than $200.

Boccio spent only $6,979 on his token challenge.

Campaign Expenditures	Collins Amount Spent	Collins % of Total	Boccio Amount Spent	Boccio % of Total
Overhead				
Office furniture/supplies	$ 8,763	2.64	$ 0	
Rent/utilities	23,937	7.22	0	
Salaries	12,600	3.80	0	
Taxes	1,179	.36	0	
Bank/investment fees	115	.03	0	
Lawyers/accountants	37,435	11.29	0	
Telephone	4,046	1.22	0	
Campaign automobile	0		0	
Computers/office equipment	7,851	2.37	0	
Travel	9,803	2.96	0	
Food/meetings	6,492	1.96	0	
Subtotal	**112,221**	**33.83**	**0**	
Fund Raising				
Events	33,875	10.21	1,530	21.92
Direct mail	0		0	
Telemarketing	0		0	
Subtotal	**33,875**	**10.21**	**1,530**	**21.92**
Polling	**0**		**0**	
Advertising				
Electronic media	32,708	9.86	0	
Other media	7,784	2.35	1,942	27.83
Subtotal	**40,492**	**12.21**	**1,942**	**27.83**
Other Campaign Activity				
Persuasion mail/brochures	29,740	8.97	2,200	31.52
Actual campaigning	19,343	5.83	480	6.88
Staff/volunteers	466	.14	0	
Subtotal	**49,550**	**14.94**	**2,680**	**38.40**
Constituent Gifts/Entertainment	50,201	15.13	0	
Donations to				
Candidates from same state	11,623	3.50	0	
Candidates from other states	3,000	.90	0	
Civic organizations	5,490	1.66	0	
Ideological groups	7,389	2.23	0	
Political parties	16,950	5.11	0	
Subtotal	**44,452**	**13.40**	**0**	
Unitemized Expenses	910	.27	827	11.85
Total Campaign Expenses	$ 331,701		$ 6,979	
PAC Contributions	$ 235,518		$ 0	
Individual Contributions	26,462		7,695	
Total Receipts*	289,196		7,695	

*Includes PAC and individual contributions as well as interest earned, party contributions, etc.

District 8 — ILLINOIS

Rep. Philip M. Crane (R)

1992 Election Results

Philip M. Crane (R)	132,887	(56%)
Sheila A. Smith (D)	96,419	(40%)

Rep. Philip M. Crane had failed to capture at least 70 percent of the vote only twice in his previous ten reelection contests. In 1990 Crane attracted no primary opposition and faced only an independent challenger in the fall. As a result, he spent nothing on broadcast advertising or persuasion mail.

That changed in 1992, when Crane faced serious challenges in both the primary and general election campaigns. He was forced to spend $168,200 during the first three months of 1992 just to garner 55 percent of the vote against developer Gary Skoien, who invested $189,911 in their primary battle. Over the final nine months of the 1992 election cycle, Crane spent another $269,935 to defeat businesswoman Sheila A. Smith, who held the veteran incumbent to 56 percent. In all, Crane spent more than three times as much during the 1992 election cycle as he had in the 1990 cycle.

Crane built his 1992 campaign around the slogan "the taxpayer's best friend" and delivered that message primarily through the mail. Crane's preprimary mailers touted the high ratings his voting record had received from the National Taxpayers Union. They also highlighted his record as a social conservative, including his stances against abortion and gun control. According to legislative assistant Kirt G. Johnson, the campaign sent mailings to members of the National Rifle Association, local chapters of the National Taxpayers Union, and "to as many churches and Christian organizations as we could." Preprimary persuasion mail costs amounted to $56,965.

Other primary election expenses included $6,465 for radio ads, which Johnson said aired on Christian radio broadcasts; $22,966 for a phonebank run by Campaign Tele-Resources of Omaha, Neb.; $15,674 for newspaper ads; and $8,080 for sample ballots.

The fall campaign was essentially a carbon copy of the primary effort. Persuasion mail expenses totaled $56,860. Radio spots and newspaper ads cost $9,723 and $12,169, respectively. Costs associated with an in-house phonebank amounted to $8,525.

As in past campaigns, mail was also Crane's principal fund-raising mechanism. Johnson said about one dozen solicitations were put together by several Raleigh firms associated with Sen. Jesse Helms's consulting empire. Sixty-eight percent of his total contributions came from individual donors who gave less than $200. Crane did not accept political action committee donations.

Strapped for cash during the campaign, Smith still spent $2,140 at Neiman Marcus after the election to purchase glass paperweights in the shape of Illinois, which she had imprinted with her campaign logo and presented to her staff.

	Crane		Smith	
Campaign Expenditures	Amount Spent	% of Total	Amount Spent	% of Total
Overhead				
Office furniture/supplies	$ 2,934	.56	$ 4,611	3.33
Rent/utilities	11,779	2.23	5,544	4.01
Salaries	53,699	10.18	22,299	16.12
Taxes	18,812	3.57	0	
Bank/investment fees	302	.06	54	.04
Lawyers/accountants	15,130	2.87	0	
Telephone	7,218	1.37	5,583	4.04
Campaign automobile	0		0	
Computers/office equipment	4,964	.94	909	.66
Travel	32,036	6.07	3,363	2.43
Food/meetings	9,025	1.71	179	.13
Subtotal	**155,898**	**29.54**	**42,543**	**30.76**
Fund Raising				
Events	35,061	6.64	10,163	7.35
Direct mail	56,899	10.78	0	
Telemarketing	0		0	
Subtotal	**91,960**	**17.43**	**10,163**	**7.35**
Polling	**0**		**6,000**	**4.34**
Advertising				
Electronic media	16,188	3.07	30,120	21.78
Other media	36,905	6.99	8,107	5.86
Subtotal	**53,093**	**10.06**	**38,227**	**27.64**
Other Campaign Activity				
Persuasion mail/brochures	113,825	21.57	31,278	22.62
Actual campaigning	58,803	11.14	6,764	4.89
Staff/volunteers	0		3,114	2.25
Subtotal	**172,628**	**32.72**	**41,157**	**29.76**
Constituent Gifts/ Entertainment	**4,393**	**.83**	**0**	
Donations to				
Candidates from same state	1,570	.30	0	
Candidates from other states	0		0	
Civic organizations	900	.17	53	.04
Ideological groups	1,150	.22	0	
Political parties	24,010	4.55	110	.08
Subtotal	**27,630**	**5.24**	**163**	**.12**
Unitemized Expenses	**22,068**	**4.18**	**42**	**.03**
Total Campaign Expenses	**$ 527,670**		**$ 138,295**	
PAC Contributions	$ 0		$ 71,557	
Individual Contributions	450,188		51,863	
Total Receipts*	477,110		140,239	

*Includes PAC and individual contributions as well as interest earned, party contributions, etc.

ILLINOIS District 9

Rep. Sidney R. Yates (D)

1992 Election Results

Sidney R. Yates (D)	162,942	(68%)
Herb Sohn (R)	64,760	(27%)
Sheila A. Jones † (I)	12,001	(5%)

In the 1990 election cycle Rep. Sidney R. Yates spent $839,100, largely to counter a $641,971 primary challenge from Chicago Alderman Edwin W. Eisendrath. In 1992 no well-funded challenger emerged, so Yates cut his spending by $610,584.

Yates accomplished this dramatic reduction largely by slicing his advertising budget by 90 percent. While he paid Squier/Eskew Communications $305,946 to create and place his radio and television commercials in 1990, Yates ran no television ads in 1992. His 1992 radio spots were produced in-house, and the campaign spent just $35,253 to air them. Newspaper and other advertising costs fell from $113,127 in 1990 to $4,374 in 1992.

Yates spent only $14,187 during the off-year, $11,150 of which was simply given away. Tickets to Democratic Congressional Campaign Committee fund-raisers cost $4,500. Tickets to events staged by the Democratic party of Illinois totaled $1,100. He donated $100 to the National Organization for Women and $400 to Voters for Choice.

In January 1992 Yates began making monthly payments to the state Democratic party to cover the cost of office space, staff, and other overhead expenses. Over the next twelve months the party collected $15,000 for these services, including $7,500 to cover office rent.

Bates & Associates of Washington, D.C., collected $18,105 for designing and sending one preprimary persuasion mailer. According to administrative assistant Mary Anderson Bain, the mailing covered Yates's legislative resume and his efforts on behalf of Chicago, targeting new voters with the message that Yates was "an old friend of the family."

John and Engel of Chicago received $17,785 for placing radio spots during the final two weeks of the primary campaign. The ads consisted of endorsements from local officials and ended with Yates's comment, "I'm proud of the people who have endorsed me, and I hope you will, too."

Yates's spending over the first three months of 1992 totaled $92,201, which was about $49,000 less than his Democratic primary opponent, restaurateur Glenn T. Sugiyama, invested in the race. Proving that more money does not always translate into more votes, Yates received 65 percent of the 97,990 primary votes.

In the general election, Yates defeated urologist Herb Sohn for the third time by running a campaign that was virtually a carbon copy of his primary campaign effort. Killian & Co. Advertising of Chicago received $17,468 for placing radio spots recycled from the primary. Persuasion mail cost Yates $57,997, including payments to Bates & Associates totaling $30,826.

Campaign Expenditures	Yates Amount Spent	Yates % of Total	Sohn Amount Spent	Sohn % of Total
Overhead				
Office furniture/supplies	$ 2,233	.98	$ 0	
Rent/utilities	8,725	3.82	0	
Salaries	18,634	8.15	0	
Taxes	0		0	
Bank/investment fees	0		243	1.93
Lawyers/accountants	1,081	.47	0	
Telephone	1,298	.57	0	
Campaign automobile	0		0	
Computers/office equipment	0		0	
Travel	751	.33	0	
Food/meetings	0		0	
Subtotal	**32,722**	**14.32**	**243**	**1.93**
Fund Raising				
Events	7,518	3.29	0	
Direct mail	0		0	
Telemarketing	0		0	
Subtotal	**7,518**	**3.29**	**0**	
Polling	**18,000**	**7.88**	**0**	
Advertising				
Electronic media	35,745	15.64	3,565	28.29
Other media	4,374	1.91	3,449	27.37
Subtotal	**40,119**	**17.56**	**7,014**	**55.66**
Other Campaign Activity				
Persuasion mail/brochures	97,840	42.82	4,580	36.34
Actual campaigning	5,776	2.53	0	
Staff/volunteers	0		0	
Subtotal	**103,616**	**45.34**	**4,580**	**36.34**
Constituent Gifts/ Entertainment	**0**		**0**	
Donations to				
Candidates from same state	2,096	.92	0	
Candidates from other states	1,000	.44	0	
Civic organizations	9,269	4.06	0	
Ideological groups	500	.22	0	
Political parties	10,642	4.66	765	6.07
Subtotal	**23,507**	**10.29**	**765**	**6.07**
Unitemized Expenses	**3,034**	**1.33**	**0**	
Total Campaign Expenses	**$ 228,516**		**$ 12,603**	
PAC Contributions	$ 34,350		$ 1,000	
Individual Contributions	190,298		9,640	
Total Receipts*	227,671		12,140	

*Includes PAC and individual contributions as well as interest earned, party contributions, etc.

† No expenditures or receipts on file. Candidates raising or spending less than $5,000 are not required to file reports with the Federal Election Commission.

District 10 — ILLINOIS

Rep. John Edward Porter (R)

1992 Election Results

John Edward Porter (R)	155,230	(65%)
Michael J. Kennedy (D)	85,400	(35%)

Rep. John Edward Porter's toughest battle was the Republican primary, which pit the pro-choice Porter against Kathleen M. Sullivan, an abortion foe and founder of Project Respect, an organization dedicated to the promotion of sexual abstinence among teenagers.

During the first three months of 1992, Porter spent $170,285 to dispatch Sullivan. Brochure printing and postage amounted to $57,701. Porter's only consultant, Unistat of Willowbrook, Ill., collected $42,228 for phonebanking. He invested $4,244 in newspaper advertising, $2,247 in radio spots, and $1,349 in posters. He paid the Suburban Republican Organization of Cook County $5,840 for its coordinated campaign efforts and spent $750 on sample ballots.

Porter worked suburban train stations, passing out his campaign literature to Chicago-bound commuters. Mailings invited constituents to "issue conferences," where they could meet with Porter. The phonebank generated lists for other mailings that touted the incumbent's record as a fiscal conservative and his pro-choice stance. A separate mailing targeted senior citizens. Porter's efforts yielded him 60 percent of the primary votes.

While Democrat Michael J. Kennedy posed less of a threat, Porter took nothing for granted. He invested another $57,250 in brochures and persuasion mail. Newspaper advertising and radio spots cost $4,330 and $3,300, respectively. He spent $4,650 on sample ballots, $2,500 on a voter guide, and $1,170 on local party coordinated campaign efforts.

Overhead consumed 38 percent of Porter's budget over the two-year cycle, even though he did not open a campaign office until March 1992. Porter's staff consisted of three part-time employees during the off-year and as many as five part-timers during 1992. Campaign manager Bill Cadigan received salary payments totaling $17,733. Erbe Inc., an accounting firm in Skokie collected $39,990. Travel expenses totaled $31,794. The campaign's fax machine, new computer, software, and supplies added $10,224.

Porter raised 60 percent of his funds from Illinois residents. For a $100 donation, supporters could join his congressional club, which entitled them to attend three or four events each year. In addition, Cadigan said the campaign held six or seven receptions over the two-year cycle, one of which featured former Surgeon General C. Everett Koop.

The campaign staged one Washington, D.C., event each year targeting political action committees (PACs). Attendees received a Chicago Bulls mug and food supplied by Well Dunn Catering in return for their donations. With costs totaling just $6,175, the two events proved well worth the investment, helping to raise $160,649 from PACs.

Campaign Expenditures	Porter Amount Spent	Porter % of Total	Kennedy Amount Spent	Kennedy % of Total
Overhead				
Office furniture/supplies	$ 4,788	.99	$ 1,369	3.93
Rent/utilities	6,290	1.30	2,282	6.55
Salaries	63,576	13.10	0	
Taxes	22,907	4.72	0	
Bank/investment fees	268	.06	0	
Lawyers/accountants	39,990	8.24	0	
Telephone	5,008	1.03	2,141	6.15
Campaign automobile	0		0	
Computers/office equipment	10,224	2.11	0	
Travel	31,794	6.55	0	
Food/meetings	1,919	.40	315	.90
Subtotal	**186,763**	**38.49**	**6,108**	**17.53**
Fund Raising				
Events	42,074	8.67	0	
Direct mail	4,595	.95	0	
Telemarketing	0		0	
Subtotal	**46,669**	**9.62**	**0**	
Polling	**4,700**	**.97**	**0**	
Advertising				
Electronic media	5,947	1.23	2,669	7.66
Other media	10,397	2.14	14,349	41.18
Subtotal	**16,344**	**3.37**	**17,018**	**48.84**
Other Campaign Activity				
Persuasion mail/brochures	117,160	24.15	8,455	24.26
Actual campaigning	64,888	13.37	2,967	8.52
Staff/volunteers	785	.16	0	
Subtotal	**182,833**	**37.68**	**11,422**	**32.78**
Constituent Gifts/ Entertainment	287	.06	0	
Donations to				
Candidates from same state	2,010	.41	0	
Candidates from other states	0		0	
Civic organizations	400	.08	0	
Ideological groups	0		0	
Political parties	17,085	3.52	0	
Subtotal	**19,495**	**4.02**	**0**	
Unitemized Expenses	**28,142**	**5.80**	**298**	**.86**
Total Campaign Expenses	**$ 485,233**		**$ 34,846**	
PAC Contributions	$ 160,649		$ 0	
Individual Contributions	285,258		28,945	
Total Receipts*	453,794		37,334	

*Includes PAC and individual contributions as well as interest earned, party contributions, etc.

ILLINOIS — District 11

Rep. George E. Sangmeister (D)

1992 Election Results
George E. Sangmeister (D)   135,387   (56%)
Robert T. Herbolsheimer (R)   107,860   (44%)

Outspent in 1990 by nearly $194,000 and facing a redistricting battle that would ultimately replace most of his suburban Cook County district with rural territory, Rep. George E. Sangmeister nevertheless chose not to spend 1991 in a frenzied chase for money. Instead, he closed his office, got rid of his campaign staff, and largely bided his time. Of the $28,407 his campaign spent during the off-year, only $6,656 was invested in fund raising. He raised just $42,500.

Without an opponent in the March 17 Democratic primary, Sangmeister continued his frugal ways. Between January 1 and March 31, he spent $24,457, including $8,195 on billboard advertising, $1,309 on posters, and $1,548 to purchase ads in twenty local newspapers. During the second quarter of 1992, his spending amounted to $33,321, including payments totaling $4,831 to Washington, D.C., fund-raising consultant Fraioli/Jost. Another $2,036 was spent at the National Democratic Club for his April political action committee fund-raiser.

Sangmeister cranked up his campaign in May, opening an office in Joliet. He hired three people to staff the office, including campaign manager Matt Ryan, who earned a monthly salary of $3,800. In June he spent $1,281 on furniture and office equipment. He leased a computer for $849 each month. Computer software cost another $6,000.

Due to the new rural character of the district, the general election contest with attorney Robert T. Herbolsheimer was waged primarily through the mail. Hoping for an anti-incumbent backlash, Herbolsheimer's persuasion mail and radio advertising portrayed Sangmeister as a career politician and a tax-and-spend liberal. Sangmeister returned fire with mail and advertising that accused Herbolsheimer of being a carpetbagger for having moved into the district only one month before the filing deadline. Not surprisingly, Sangmeister's press secretary, Christopher A. Ganschow, said his mail portrayed the incumbent as "a long-time member of the community and a public servant."

While Sangmeister spent $17,419 to produce and air his radio commercials during the final three weeks of the campaign, that was only 21 percent of the amount he invested in such ads during the 1990 campaign. Sangmeister invested an additional $6,483 in billboard advertising for the fall campaign. In October he spent $8,808 on newspaper ads. Door-hangers cost the campaign $2,053. Expenditures for promotional material included $665 for "campaign rain bonnets," $612 for campaign buttons, $362 for lapel stickers, and $300 for fortune cookies that included the message "Sangmeister for Congress."

Campaign Expenditures	Sangmeister Amount Spent	Sangmeister % of Total	Herbolsheimer Amount Spent	Herbolsheimer % of Total
Overhead				
Office furniture/supplies	$ 6,139	1.81	$ 4,106	1.43
Rent/utilities	6,148	1.81	6,055	2.11
Salaries	34,054	10.05	56,194	19.62
Taxes	0		0	
Bank/investment fees	82	.02	0	
Lawyers/accountants	0		952	.33
Telephone	3,703	1.09	9,971	3.48
Campaign automobile	0		0	
Computers/office equipment	9,287	2.74	14,653	5.12
Travel	7,510	2.22	7,381	2.58
Food/meetings	914	.27	1,032	.36
Subtotal	**67,836**	**20.02**	**100,343**	**35.03**
Fund Raising				
Events	49,220	14.53	22,540	7.87
Direct mail	0		0	
Telemarketing	0		0	
Subtotal	**49,220**	**14.53**	**22,540**	**7.87**
Polling	**12,000**	**3.54**	**0**	
Advertising				
Electronic media	17,419	5.14	21,453	7.49
Other media	28,480	8.41	5,111	1.78
Subtotal	**45,900**	**13.55**	**26,565**	**9.27**
Other Campaign Activity				
Persuasion mail/brochures	108,568	32.05	84,466	29.49
Actual campaigning	17,641	5.21	37,143	12.97
Staff/volunteers	1,498	.44	102	.04
Subtotal	**127,706**	**37.69**	**121,711**	**42.49**
Constituent Gifts/ Entertainment	**5,466**	**1.61**	**0**	
Donations to				
Candidates from same state	4,561	1.35	1,485	.52
Candidates from other states	0		0	
Civic organizations	12,782	3.77	642	.22
Ideological groups	5,128	1.51	0	
Political parties	7,591	2.24	220	.08
Subtotal	**30,063**	**8.87**	**2,347**	**.82**
Unitemized Expenses	**600**	**.18**	**12,946**	**4.52**
Total Campaign Expenses	**$ 338,790**		**$ 286,451**	
PAC Contributions	$ 252,210		$ 97,272	
Individual Contributions	66,306		146,103	
Total Receipts*	339,478		283,199	

*Includes PAC and individual contributions as well as interest earned, party contributions, etc.

District 12 — ILLINOIS

Rep. Jerry F. Costello (D)

1992 Election Results

Jerry F. Costello (D)	168,762	(71%)
Mike Starr (R)	68,115	(29%)

With Illinois losing two congressional districts, Rep. Jerry F. Costello made sure his interests in the redistricting process were well taken care of. He paid his attorney, Grey Chatham of Belleville $84,000 in 1991 for legal assistance on the redistricting fight. Campaigns, Research & Demographics of St. Louis, Mo., received $44,600 in 1991 for redistricting work, which included identifying new voters and preparing new mailing lists.

This was only the beginning of Costello's off-year spending. In January he paid Executive Services of Collinsville, Ill., $30,100 for providing office facilities, staff, and bookkeeping services until the campaign moved to a larger office. In December the campaign paid $12,000 to a local law firm to cover rent and utilities on yet another space, which was needed to tide the campaign over until it could move to its larger headquarters.

To introduce himself to a host of new constituents acquired through redistricting, Costello spent $6,471 on newspaper advertising and another $1,765 on program ads in 1991. He also invested $18,116 of his treasury to mail newsletters and postcards asking constituents about their views. He spent $1,784 on St. Louis Cardinal baseball tickets, which were passed out to volunteers. Another $1,261 was spent on tickets to St. Louis Blues hockey games, also for volunteers. In all, Costello invested $307,505 in his off-year permanent campaign, or 51 percent of his total outlays for the two-year cycle.

The new headquarters was finally opened in August 1992. Costello's press secretary, Brian Lott, took a leave of absence from the congressional staff and collected $7,500 for managing the campaign. Costello paid Richard Day Research of Chicago $12,204 for conducting a benchmark survey of the district. The Democratic National Committee paid Greenberg-Lake of Washington, D.C., $11,736 for additional polling.

Costello spent $45,837 to produce and air five television and five radio commercials, $33,701 more than he had invested in such advertising during the 1990 campaign. In-house production, coupled with $4,235 in production help from the Democratic Congressional Campaign Committee, allowed Costello to sink most of his media budget into air time. He spent $30,831 for time on television network affiliates, $2,510 for time on local cable systems, and $2,732 on radio. Lott said that 75 percent of the television buys were put into airing a "real soft" sixty-second biographical ad.

Republican Mike Starr spent 40 percent of his limited budget on overhead, leaving him with only $16,310 to spend on direct voter contact.

	Costello		Starr	
Campaign Expenditures	Amount Spent	% of Total	Amount Spent	% of Total
Overhead				
Office furniture/supplies	$ 7,957	1.32	$ 624	1.90
Rent/utilities	18,650	3.09	2,250	6.87
Salaries	27,049	4.48	500	1.53
Taxes	18,414	3.05	0	
Bank/investment fees	0		108	.33
Lawyers/accountants	85,683	14.19	0	
Telephone	18,332	3.04	2,497	7.62
Campaign automobile	0		0	
Computers/office equipment	2,167	.36	0	
Travel	25,893	4.29	6,746	20.59
Food/meetings	9,563	1.58	252	.77
Subtotal	**213,707**	**35.39**	**12,977**	**39.60**
Fund Raising				
Events	64,357	10.66	433	1.32
Direct mail	0		0	
Telemarketing	0		0	
Subtotal	**64,357**	**10.66**	**433**	**1.32**
Polling	**12,204**	**2.02**	**1,000**	**3.05**
Advertising				
Electronic media	45,837	7.59	1,554	4.74
Other media	25,086	4.15	963	2.94
Subtotal	**70,923**	**11.74**	**2,516**	**7.68**
Other Campaign Activity				
Persuasion mail/brochures	58,953	9.76	7,476	22.82
Actual campaigning	115,664	19.15	6,277	19.16
Staff/volunteers	3,045	.50	42	.13
Subtotal	**177,662**	**29.42**	**13,794**	**42.10**
Constituent Gifts/ Entertainment	1,584	.26	0	
Donations to				
Candidates from same state	10,700	1.77	635	1.94
Candidates from other states	2,000	.33	0	
Civic organizations	9,961	1.65	0	
Ideological groups	300	.05	60	.18
Political parties	20,000	3.31	0	
Subtotal	**42,961**	**7.11**	**695**	**2.12**
Unitemized Expenses	**20,487**	**3.39**	**1,351**	**4.12**
Total Campaign Expenses	**$ 603,886**		**$ 32,766**	
PAC Contributions	$ 145,175		$ 0	
Individual Contributions	327,223		10,250	
Total Receipts*	503,778		21,177	

*Includes PAC and individual contributions as well as interest earned, party contributions, etc.

ILLINOIS — District 13

Rep. Harris W. Fawell (R)

1992 Election Results

Harris W. Fawell (R)	179,257	(68%)
Dennis Michael Temple (D)	82,985	(32%)

Rep. Harris W. Fawell loves his nickname, "The Porkbuster." He used the phrase in one of his billboard ads. Small plastic pigs eating dollar bills were used as centerpieces on all the tables at a barbecue fund-raiser. He spent $4,873 of his campaign treasury to purchase copies of the book *Adventures in Porkland,* which he gave to contributors.

While he took pride in his image of rooting out waste in the federal budget, Fawell was not above lavish spending when it came to his campaign. Having won his four previous general election campaigns by margins of two to one or better in this safe Republican district, Fawell nevertheless spent $176,564 to maintain his campaign operation during 1991.

Over the course of the two-year election cycle, Fawell spent $8,079 on constituent stroking, including $4,338 for tickets to Chicago White Sox games. Year-end holiday cards cost $2,810; flowers, $462; and gifts, $262. Expenses associated with the congressional art contest amounted to $207.

Fawell also spent $10,692 to provide his constituents with mementos of the campaign. He paid $5,348 for 20,000 customized parade fans, $1,818 for headbands, and $1,564 for engraved pencils.

Health care association executive Stewart A. Wesbury's $314,642 Republican primary challenge provided Fawell with his only electoral test. He responded by spending $206,975 during the first three months of 1992, including $38,958 for printing, labeling, and sending a glossy brochure and a tabloid-style mailer. He invested $14,458 in newspaper ads, $9,764 in billboards, $6,103 in cable television ads, and $1,436 in radio spots. Broadcast production charges amounted to $3,196. Yard signs cost the campaign $8,389; door-hangers, $7,941; and buttons, $487. Fawell received 73 percent of the primary votes.

Fawell faced off against woefully underfunded Democrat Dennis Michael Temple in the general election. Although Fawell spent about $41,000 on persuasion mail, he ran no broadcast ads and spent $2,042 on newspaper ads. Yard signs for the fall campaign cost $3,900.

Attention! of Naperville collected $188,200 for providing complete campaign management services throughout the election cycle. The firm created and placed all Fawell's advertising, provided office space and staff, and handled all the campaign's printing, including 200,000 brochures and 170,000 tabloid-style persuasion mailers.

Marketing Strategies of Naperville received $60,510 for coordinating Fawell's twelve fund-raisers, including an annual baseball event. Tickets for the 100 donors who attended the 1991 event at Cominski Park cost $927. In 1992 Fawell received an in-kind donation of $2,500 to cover the cost of a sky box.

Campaign Expenditures	Fawell Amount Spent	Fawell % of Total	Temple Amount Spent	Temple % of Total
Overhead				
Office furniture/supplies	$ 6,629	1.23	$ 290	6.69
Rent/utilities	3,000	.56	0	
Salaries	25,976	4.83	0	
Taxes	2,103	.39	0	
Bank/investment fees	477	.09	0	
Lawyers/accountants	4,185	.78	0	
Telephone	6,019	1.12	134	3.09
Campaign automobile	755	.14	0	
Computers/office equipment	6,502	1.21	0	
Travel	8,227	1.53	305	7.05
Food/meetings	4,479	.83	0	
Subtotal	68,352	12.70	728	16.82
Fund Raising				
Events	162,690	30.23	173	4.00
Direct mail	16,746	3.11	0	
Telemarketing	0		0	
Subtotal	179,436	33.34	173	4.00
Polling	1,325	.25	0	
Advertising				
Electronic media	10,735	1.99	0	
Other media	27,667	5.14	1,399	32.31
Subtotal	38,402	7.14	1,399	32.31
Other Campaign Activity				
Persuasion mail/brochures	80,322	14.93	1,227	28.35
Actual campaigning	139,060	25.84	43	.99
Staff/volunteers	2,188	.41	0	
Subtotal	221,570	41.17	1,270	29.34
Constituent Gifts/Entertainment	8,078	1.50	0	
Donations to				
Candidates from same state	1,980	.37	0	
Candidates from other states	1,400	.26	0	
Civic organizations	1,421	.26	0	
Ideological groups	87	.02	0	
Political parties	15,668	2.91	0	
Subtotal	20,556	3.82	0	
Unitemized Expenses	444	.08	759	17.53
Total Campaign Expenses	$ 538,163		$ 4,328	
PAC Contributions	$ 216,917		$ 0	
Individual Contributions	331,096		3,339	
Total Receipts*	563,194		4,327	

*Includes PAC and individual contributions as well as interest earned, party contributions, etc.

District 14 ILLINOIS

Rep. Dennis Hastert (R)

1992 Election Results

Dennis Hastert (R) 155,271 (67%)
Jonathan Abram Reich † (D) 75,294 (33%)

In 1990 Rep. Dennis Hastert won reelection with 67 percent of the vote, spending $312,568 against a challenger who spent less than $5,000. In 1992 Hastert once again garnered 67 percent of the vote against Democrat Jonathan Abram Reich, who also spent less than $5,000, but Hastert's spending nearly doubled to $613,623.

Hastert relied on political action committees (PACs) to supply his additional campaign funds. While contributions from individuals dropped from $258,477 in 1990 to $251,828 in 1992, PAC donations jumped from $181,074 to $317,656.

The PAC money was particularly attractive given the small investment required to raise it. Over the course of the 1992 election cycle, Hastert held four Washington, D.C., PAC events, which cost a total of only $11,898. Bills for three events held at the Powers Court restaurant on Capitol Hill amounted to $4,066. The Capitol Hill Club was paid $1,332 to cover the cost of food and beverages for the fourth affair. J.A.G. Associates of Washington, D.C., collected $6,500 for coordinating the four events.

Hastert held two major events in Illinois each year. One, a summer picnic, was aimed at his rural supporters and in 1991 featured Agriculture Secretary Edward Madigan. The second was a far more upscale affair held at the Pheasant Run Resort in Chicago. Charges at the Pheasant Run came to $16,279 in 1991 and $25,028 in 1992.

Hastert's congressional club members were treated to three or four local events each year, as well as a trip to the nation's capital. In 1991 the campaign spent $3,908 on the Washington excursion, including $817 for lodging at the J.W. Marriott, $827 for dinner at Gadsby's Tavern in Alexandria, Va., and another $641 for food at the House restaurant. In 1992 expenses for the Washington briefing totaled $3,852, including $1,630 for lodging at the Mt. Vernon Inn and $625 at the House restaurant. Congressional club members also received gifts worth $2,887.

Because of redistricting, Hastert spent more heavily on actual campaign activity than he had in 1990. During the off-year, he paid $37,500 each to Information Research Associates of Sycamore and McKeon & Associates of Joliet for polls of his new constituents. McKeon & Associates picked up another $28,000 in 1992. In September 1992 the campaign brought on Kathy Mankivsky of Weaton who collected $48,554 for phonebanking. Lists for the phonebank cost another $10,461. Hastert's advertising budget increased from $2,535 in 1990 to a still modest $35,646 in 1992. He invested $13,323 in signs and $9,784 on fans that were handed out at parades.

Campaign Expenditures	Hastert Amount Spent	% of Total
Overhead		
Office furniture/supplies	$ 9,381	1.53
Rent/utilities	13,245	2.16
Salaries	74,035	12.07
Taxes	539	.09
Bank/investment fees	619	.10
Lawyers/accountants	0	
Telephone	7,547	1.23
Campaign automobile	13,581	2.21
Computers/office equipment	7,036	1.15
Travel	26,793	4.37
Food/meetings	5,992	.98
Subtotal	**158,768**	**25.87**
Fund Raising		
Events	122,662	19.99
Direct mail	15,382	2.51
Telemarketing	0	
Subtotal	**138,045**	**22.50**
Polling	**103,000**	**16.79**
Advertising		
Electronic media	13,302	2.17
Other media	22,344	3.64
Subtotal	**35,646**	**5.81**
Other Campaign Activity		
Persuasion mail/brochures	27,212	4.43
Actual campaigning	94,914	15.47
Staff/volunteers	3,273	.53
Subtotal	**125,399**	**20.44**
Constituent Gifts/Entertainment	**6,448**	**1.05**
Donations to		
Candidates from same state	8,464	1.38
Candidates from other states	3,250	.53
Civic organizations	822	.13
Ideological groups	0	
Political parties	13,996	2.28
Subtotal	**26,531**	**4.32**
Unitemized Expenses	**19,786**	**3.22**
Total Campaign Expenses	$ **613,623**	
PAC Contributions	$ **317,656**	
Individual Contributions	**251,828**	
Total Receipts*	**601,812**	

*Includes PAC and individual contributions as well as interest earned, party contributions, etc.

† No expenditures or receipts on file. Candidates raising or spending less than $5,000 are not required to file reports with the Federal Election Commission.

ILLINOIS — District 15

Rep. Thomas W. Ewing (R)

1992 Election Results

Thomas W. Ewing** (R)   142,167   (59%)
Charles D. Mattis (D)   97,190   (41%)

When the 1991 special election to replace Rep. Edward Madigan was scheduled for July 2, Republican state representative Thomas W. Ewing realized his greatest problem would be turnout, not Democrat Gerald Bradley. Knowing that many voters would get an early start on their Fourth of July travel, the campaign looked for ways to grab the attention of those who remained in the district.

Rather than mail standard brochures, Russo Marsh & Associates of Sacramento, Calif., opted to send slick, colored postcards that did not need to be opened to deliver their highly tailored messages. Residents of Kankakee, where unemployment was high, received a postcard stressing job creation. Voters in the eastern half of the district received a postcard focusing on anticrime legislation. A basic biographical mailer was sent to those who had never been represented by Ewing in the state legislature.

Ewing's total outlays for the special election amounted to $299,550. Russo Marsh collected $29,282 of the $117,686 Ewing spent on campaign literature and persuasion mail. While he ran no television commercials, Ewing spent $19,322 on radio advertising described by chief of staff Mike Stokke as "folksy" requests for support. McKeon & Associates of Joliet received $17,000 for polling. An in-house phonebank cost $16,130, yard signs added $4,455, and newspaper ads cost $1,277. With fewer than 39,000 people bothering to vote, Ewing won the special election by a two-to-one margin.

For the 1992 campaign against Charles D. Mattis, Russo Marsh was busy working for Texas billionaire Ross Perot, so Ewing hired the Penta Corporation of Champaign to coordinate persuasion mail and advertising. According to Stokke, Ewing originally planned a major advertising effort but changed his mind. "Bush was doing terribly in our district, and we thought a lower profile would be better," explained Stokke. "We wanted to be as independent from Bush as possible."

As a result, Ewing spent $16,869 on radio spots and $60,247 on brochures and voter contact mail. The Penta Corporation received $46,233 of that total. Despite the fact that Mattis mounted virtually no campaign, Ewing was sufficiently concerned about negative coattails from the Bush reelection effort that he paid McKeon & Associates another $32,500 for polling. For their efforts, son Sam and daughter Jane Ewing received $5,000 and $3,000, respectively.

Fund raising was a constant concern throughout both campaigns. Most of Ewing's district events were low-dollar, in-home affairs with ticket prices of $100 or less. The campaign's largest event was a $5-a-head bean dinner attended by 1,000 supporters.

Campaign Expenditures	Ewing Amount Spent	Ewing % of Total	Mattis Amount Spent	Mattis % of Total
Overhead				
Office furniture/supplies	$ 8,062	1.40	$ 39	.65
Rent/utilities	4,311	.75	0	
Salaries	58,448	10.14	0	
Taxes	237	.04	0	
Bank/investment fees	32	.01	0	
Lawyers/accountants	26,066	4.52	0	
Telephone	17,113	2.97	0	
Campaign automobile	0		0	
Computers/office equipment	5,167	.90	0	
Travel	35,468	6.15	0	
Food/meetings	2,362	.41	0	
Subtotal	**157,265**	**27.27**	**39**	**.65**
Fund Raising				
Events	92,650	16.07	0	
Direct mail	2,375	.41	0	
Telemarketing	0		0	
Subtotal	**95,025**	**16.48**	**0**	
Polling	**50,750**	**8.80**	**0**	
Advertising				
Electronic media	36,191	6.28	1,451	24.47
Other media	1,597	.28	0	
Subtotal	**37,789**	**6.55**	**1,451**	**24.47**
Other Campaign Activity				
Persuasion mail/brochures	177,933	30.86	201	3.39
Actual campaigning	26,537	4.60	3,166	53.43
Staff/volunteers	343	.06	0	
Subtotal	**204,813**	**35.52**	**3,367**	**56.82**
Constituent Gifts/ Entertainment	**13,678**	**2.37**	**0**	
Donations to				
Candidates from same state	3,620	.63	0	
Candidates from other states	0		0	
Civic organizations	167	.03	0	
Ideological groups	110	.02	0	
Political parties	86	.01	0	
Subtotal	**3,983**	**.69**	**0**	
Unitemized Expenses	**13,362**	**2.32**	**1,070**	**18.05**
Total Campaign Expenses	**$ 576,666**		**$ 5,927**	
PAC Contributions	$ 323,776		$ 2,600	
Individual Contributions	325,865		3,288	
Total Receipts*	700,868		6,338	

*Includes PAC and individual contributions as well as interest earned, party contributions, etc.

**Totals include special election disbursements and receipts.

District 16 — ILLINOIS

Rep. Donald Manzullo (R)

1992 Election Results

Donald Manzullo (R) 142,388 (56%)
John W. Cox, Jr. (D) 113,555 (44%)

As the only Democrat ever to represent this district, freshman Rep. John W. Cox, Jr., was a very vulnerable incumbent from the day he won the 1990 election. When redistricting made his territory even more Republican, Cox's fate was all but sealed.

On the Republican side, conservative Donald Manzullo was not supposed to make it past his primary date with state senator Jack Schaffer, who had the backing of former Rep. Lynn Martin and Illinois Gov. Jim Edgar. However, with a treasury of slightly more than $79,000 and a substantial assist from an army of evangelical volunteers, Manzullo won by a comfortable 12-point margin, despite being outspent by more than two to one.

Manzullo invested two-thirds of his meager primary budget on direct appeals to voters. He spent $10,836 to buy time on television network affiliates, $1,668 on cable television buys, and $6,540 on radio. Billboard and newspaper advertising amounted to $4,910 and $3,978, respectively. Persuasion mail and campaign literature cost $19,391, and $4,427 was spent on signs.

In a preview of his general election campaign, Manzullo's advertising and mail attacked Schaffer for supporting a pay raise for state legislators; for supporting increases in gasoline, cigarette, and business taxes; and for being too liberal for the district.

Over the final nine months of 1992, Manzullo spent more than $377,000 to defeat Cox. In June he hired Associated Public Affairs Professionals of Fairfax, Va., and paid them $22,461 for providing strategic advice. Marketing Research Institute of Jackson, Miss., received $6,700 for polling. Nolte Communications of Rockford was paid $20,941 for placing radio commercials, and the campaign directly purchased additional air time, spending $23,537 on radio, $9,983 on network TV, and $7,639 on cable television. The campaign spent $7,336 on newspaper advertising, $23,751 on yard signs, $2,717 on T-shirts, $1,522 on buttons, and $1,447 on bumper stickers.

Cox played to Manzullo's strength by proposing increases in the federal gasoline tax. To the sound of quarters falling on a table, one of Manzullo's radio spots labeled him a tax-and-spend liberal. Produced in-house, Manzullo's mail targeted abortion opponents and gun owners. The Right to Work Political Action Committee also spent $1,361 on a mailer to its members on Manzullo's behalf.

Cox responded with a $126,816 advertising campaign and a $69,705 persuasion mail effort designed to woo moderate Republicans and independents. "We naively thought we had the Democrats with us, so we tried to reach the undecided voters," lamented Cox's press secretary, Mary Ann Presman.

Campaign Expenditures	Manzullo Amount Spent	Manzullo % of Total	Cox Amount Spent	Cox % of Total
Overhead				
Office furniture/supplies	$ 21,016	4.60	$ 13,170	2.76
Rent/utilities	8,629	1.89	8,725	1.83
Salaries	48,800	10.68	58,969	12.37
Taxes	11,524	2.52	23,146	4.86
Bank/investment fees	440	.10	954	.20
Lawyers/accountants	0		0	
Telephone	16,663	3.65	15,009	3.15
Campaign automobile	0		9,303	1.95
Computers/office equipment	25,271	5.53	15,419	3.23
Travel	15,533	3.40	25,534	5.36
Food/meetings	600	.13	2,734	.57
Subtotal	**148,476**	**32.49**	**172,962**	**36.29**
Fund Raising				
Events	33,314	7.29	39,863	8.36
Direct mail	13,520	2.96	832	.17
Telemarketing	0		0	
Subtotal	**46,834**	**10.25**	**40,695**	**8.54**
Polling	**6,700**	**1.47**	**17,844**	**3.74**
Advertising				
Electronic media	86,788	18.99	122,323	25.66
Other media	18,887	4.13	4,493	.94
Subtotal	**105,675**	**23.12**	**126,816**	**26.61**
Other Campaign Activity				
Persuasion mail/brochures	74,064	16.21	69,705	14.62
Actual campaigning	71,527	15.65	33,777	7.09
Staff/volunteers	371	.08	2,036	.43
Subtotal	**145,962**	**31.94**	**105,518**	**22.14**
Constituent Gifts/Entertainment	**146**	**.03**	**3,569**	**.75**
Donations to				
Candidates from same state	170	.04	1,878	.39
Candidates from other states	0		0	
Civic organizations	1,210	.26	553	.12
Ideological groups	413	.09	590	.12
Political parties	679	.15	1,919	.40
Subtotal	**2,472**	**.54**	**4,940**	**1.04**
Unitemized Expenses	**728**	**.16**	**4,315**	**.91**
Total Campaign Expenses	**$ 456,994**		**$ 476,660**	
PAC Contributions	$ 123,598		$ 338,389	
Individual Contributions	259,431		149,084	
Total Receipts*	440,379		506,523	

*Includes PAC and individual contributions as well as interest earned, party contributions, etc.

ILLINOIS District 17

Rep. Lane Evans (D)

1992 Election Results

Lane Evans (D)	156,233	(60%)
Ken Schloemer (R)	103,719	(40%)

Rep. Lane Evans ran largely the same campaign in 1992 as he had in 1990. "We base our campaigns on how strongly we are contested," noted Dennis J. King, Evans's administrative assistant. "We didn't take any chances, and we were prepared to expand our campaign if someone strongly contested for the seat, but in this race we didn't even have to do any polling."

Overhead and fund raising consumed 72 percent of Evans's budget. Monthly rent on his year-round campaign office was $376 in 1991 and $401 in 1992, and even during the off-year it was staffed by two people. He spent $6,861 on new computer equipment and $6,815 on software and other computer supplies.

While Evans raised 52 percent of his contributions from political action committees, he held only one event in Washington, D.C., which cost $444. In contrast, King said the campaign held "a ton" of small-donor district events, none of which raised more than $25,000. "We do them to keep people involved," he added. Lori Ann Bass of Chicago received $10,656 for coordinating the in-state events. Meyer Associates of St. Cloud, Minn., was paid $24,504 for telemarketing.

In the Democratic primary, Evans faced a token challenge by Richard E. Maynard, who spent only $546 on the effort. During the first three months of 1992, Evans countered with expenditures of approximately $52,000. He paid his media consultant, Zimmerman & Markman of Santa Monica, Calif., $9,520 for creating, producing, and buying television time for ads aimed more at introducing Evans to his new constituents than at combating Maynard. The campaign handled radio ad production in-house and directly purchased $984 of radio time.

Evans's only persuasion mailers of 1992 were sent out prior to the primary and targeted households in the territory acquired through redistricting. Johnson & Associates of Tolland, Conn., received $7,598 for creating three slightly tailored versions of an introductory piece, and Advertising Consultants of DePue collected $4,776 for mailing them. "We had produced our mail in-house in past elections, but we wanted to see what an outside firm could do for us," King said.

For the fall campaign against restauranteur Ken Schloemer, Evans paid Zimmerman $33,387 for creating two television spots. According to King, these "soft, positive messages" focused on Evans's constituent service, both at home and in Washington. In addition, the campaign produced six radio spots, all testimonials from local public officials. A total of $1,158 was spent to air them.

Despite redistricting that made the district more Republican and Schloemer's $116,514 investment in the challenge, he failed to cut into Evans's support.

Campaign Expenditures	Evans Amount Spent	Evans % of Total	Schloemer Amount Spent	Schloemer % of Total
Overhead				
Office furniture/supplies	$ 6,607	1.77	$ 3,204	2.75
Rent/utilities	10,660	2.85	469	.40
Salaries	60,154	16.10	24,544	21.07
Taxes	23,395	6.26	0	
Bank/investment fees	109	.03	4	
Lawyers/accountants	0		5,033	4.32
Telephone	13,655	3.66	2,886	2.48
Campaign automobile	0		0	
Computers/office equipment	20,763	5.56	2,646	2.27
Travel	31,709	8.49	7,722	6.63
Food/meetings	200	.05	946	.81
Subtotal	**167,253**	**44.78**	**47,454**	**40.73**
Fund Raising				
Events	38,460	10.30	3,450	2.96
Direct mail	30,581	8.19	9,586	8.23
Telemarketing	31,094	8.32	0	
Subtotal	**100,135**	**26.81**	**13,036**	**11.19**
Polling	**0**		**0**	
Advertising				
Electronic media	46,872	12.55	17,264	14.82
Other media	688	.18	13,365	11.47
Subtotal	**47,560**	**12.73**	**30,628**	**26.29**
Other Campaign Activity				
Persuasion mail/brochures	12,374	3.31	10,762	9.24
Actual campaigning	9,271	2.48	4,958	4.26
Staff/volunteers	1,134	.30	108	.09
Subtotal	**22,778**	**6.10**	**15,827**	**13.58**
Constituent Gifts/ Entertainment	**2,785**	**.75**	**0**	
Donations to				
Candidates from same state	2,173	.58	0	
Candidates from other states	3,500	.94	0	
Civic organizations	584	.16	49	.04
Ideological groups	85	.02	295	.25
Political parties	170	.05	0	
Subtotal	**6,511**	**1.74**	**344**	**.29**
Unitemized Expenses	**26,496**	**7.09**	**9,224**	**7.92**
Total Campaign Expenses	**$ 373,519**		**$ 116,514**	
PAC Contributions	**$ 188,260**		**$ 34,994**	
Individual Contributions	**171,401**		**73,641**	
Total Receipts*	**370,096**		**117,626**	

*Includes PAC and individual contributions as well as interest earned, party contributions, etc.

District 18 — ILLINOIS

Rep. Robert H. Michel (R)

1992 Election Results

Robert H. Michel (R)	156,533	(58%)
Ronald C. Hawkins † (D)	114,413	(42%)

After more than thirty-five years in the House, Minority Leader Robert H. Michel had long since passed the point where he personally worried about his reelection campaigns. Campaign manager MaryAlice Erickson and her associates at Campaigns & Elections of Peoria were left to run things for him. However, the work was not without its rewards. Over the course of the 1992 election cycle, Campaigns & Elections collected $188,433.

Other than his payments to Campaigns & Elections, the biggest drain on Michel's budget was his fund-raising operation, which incorporated his passion for golf. Michel paid $69,082 for costs relating to his five golf events, including green fees, prizes, and catering expenses. He held only one Washington, D.C., fund-raiser, a reception at the Capitol Hill Club that cost $22,527, including $8,674 paid to Jerry Rapp & Associates of Washington for organizing the affair. Erickson produced one direct-mail solicitation, which cost the campaign $8,241.

To stroke his volunteers and long-time political allies, Michel spent $12,868 on meals and receptions, including Christmas parties that cost a total of $4,615. Gifts for volunteers, including cans of caramel corn, cost $5,283. He spent $1,031 for flowers. Sodas and bottled water added $1,567 to the tab.

Michel spent $17,799 of his campaign treasury to mail 20,000 year-end holiday cards over the two-year cycle. He also spent $8,606 to purchase and mail calendars from the Capitol Historical Society.

Approximately one of every nine dollars Michel spent was simply given away to other candidates, Republican party organizations, and causes. He made $1,000 contributions to thirty-seven House candidates, including Minority Whip Newt Gingrich (Ga.). He also gave $5,000 to the National Republican Congressional Committee.

For the actual campaign, such as it was, Michel spent $7,235 on billboard ads and $4,953 on ads in newspapers such as the *Limestone Independent News, Lincoln Courier,* and *Peoria Heights Herald.* He ran no radio commercials and aired only one television spot, which ran the day before the election and urged people to vote. For placing the ads, which highlighted Michel's ability to deliver federal dollars to the district, Ross Inc. of Peoria collected $3,916.

Michel also paid WEEK TV in Peoria $3,570 to run an ad he recorded in support of Bradley University, his alma mater. The ad showed Michel, a member of Bradley's Board of Trustees, strolling across campus, extolling the virtues of the university and its basketball team.

Ronald C. Hawkins, the Democratic nominee, spent less than $5,000 and filed no reports with the Federal Election Commission.

Campaign Expenditures	Michel Amount Spent	% of Total
Overhead		
Office furniture/supplies	$ 16,209	2.56
Rent/utilities	12,544	1.98
Salaries	0	
Taxes	4,671	.74
Bank/investment fees	140	.02
Lawyers/accountants	20,770	3.27
Telephone	6,960	1.10
Campaign automobile	0	
Computers/office equipment	9,999	1.58
Travel	20,274	3.20
Food/meetings	3,593	.57
Subtotal	**95,160**	**15.00**
Fund Raising		
Events	100,443	15.83
Direct mail	8,241	1.30
Telemarketing	0	
Subtotal	**108,683**	**17.13**
Polling	**15,000**	**2.36**
Advertising		
Electronic media	7,418	1.17
Other media	30,336	4.78
Subtotal	**37,754**	**5.95**
Other Campaign Activity		
Persuasion mail/brochures	46,475	7.33
Actual campaigning	204,989	32.31
Staff/volunteers	21,594	3.40
Subtotal	**273,057**	**43.04**
Constituent Gifts/Entertainment	**26,643**	**4.20**
Donations to		
Candidates from same state	6,502	1.02
Candidates from other states	31,000	4.89
Civic organizations	8,529	1.34
Ideological groups	0	
Political parties	22,663	3.57
Subtotal	**68,693**	**10.83**
Unitemized Expenses	**9,389**	**1.48**
Total Campaign Expenses	**$ 634,380**	
PAC Contributions	**$ 404,027**	
Individual Contributions	**215,412**	
Total Receipts*	**646,637**	

*Includes PAC and individual contributions as well as interest earned, party contributions, etc.

† No expenditures or receipts on file. Candidates raising or spending less than $5,000 are not required to file reports with the Federal Election Commission.

ILLINOIS District 19

Rep. Glenn Poshard (D)

1992 Election Results

Glenn Poshard (D)	187,156	(69%)
Douglas E. Lee (R)	83,526	(31%)

Rep. Terry L. Bruce seemed to hold most of the cards in his primary battle with Rep. Glenn Poshard. Their redrawn district contained more of Bruce's old constituents. In January 1992 Bruce had cash reserves of $699,486, and over the next three months he spent more than $740,000. Poshard began 1992 with just $17,272 in the bank and was able to spend only about $150,000 in the primary. However, Poshard emerged with 62 percent of the vote.

Poshard accomplished this nearly impossible feat by turning his financial weakness into an asset. "We were the underdog, fighting the good fight," explained press secretary David D. Stricklin. "We were able to set up the contrast between our opponent's reliance on PAC contributions and our refusal to accept them."

In addition to tying Bruce to special interest money, Poshard's ads highlighted his ideas about deficit reduction and pay-as-you-go government, themes that played well to the 1992 electorate. In an area where coal mining is a major industry, Poshard's commercials juxtaposed his vote against the Clean Air Act with Bruce's vote for it. Biographical ads introduced him to voters in the fourteen counties he had never represented.

Poshard held down his advertising costs by creating his own commercials, with some advice from close friends. "He's his own campaign manager, strategist, and creative designer," said Stricklin. He ran television ads only for the final three days of the campaign, and much of the time he bought was in preemptable time-slots around local newscasts. Through this careful budgeting, Poshard spent only $38,056 to air commercials on network television affiliates. He also spent $34,272 on newspaper ads, $14,778 on radio spots, and $2,185 on cable television.

In contrast, Bruce poured $340,241 into a media campaign designed and executed by Fenn & King Communications of Washington, D.C. Bay Communications of Edgewater, Md., collected $108,892 of the $179,322 he spent on persuasion mail. Bruce repeatedly hammered Poshard for his vote in favor of the 1990 budget compromise, which included increased gasoline taxes and Medicare cuts.

"Terry made that vote the overriding issue in the campaign," explained Poshard. "They mailed thousands of slick brochures tying me to President Bush, and I spent all my time explaining my position on deficit reduction and entitlements. In the end, people showed they were more scared of the debt."

In the general election Poshard took on Douglas E. Lee, who had only $25,000 to spend. Poshard cut back for this race, spending $22,146 on television ads, $6,932 on radio spots, and $12,510 on newspaper ads.

	Poshard		Lee	
Campaign Expenditures	Amount Spent	% of Total	Amount Spent	% of Total
Overhead				
Office furniture/supplies	$ 1,917	.64	$ 59	.23
Rent/utilities	4,820	1.61	171	.68
Salaries	17,625	5.87	931	3.68
Taxes	0		0	
Bank/investment fees	518	.17	0	
Lawyers/accountants	4,430	1.48	0	
Telephone	9,399	3.13	499	1.97
Campaign automobile	0		0	
Computers/office equipment	1,599	.53	912	3.60
Travel	20,955	6.98	2,510	9.92
Food/meetings	656	.22	250	.99
Subtotal	**61,919**	**20.64**	**5,331**	**21.07**
Fund Raising				
Events	30,631	10.21	1,958	7.74
Direct mail	0		0	
Telemarketing	0		0	
Subtotal	**30,631**	**10.21**	**1,958**	**7.74**
Polling	**0**		**0**	
Advertising				
Electronic media	84,097	28.03	6,252	24.71
Other media	48,841	16.28	0	
Subtotal	**132,938**	**44.31**	**6,252**	**24.71**
Other Campaign Activity				
Persuasion mail/brochures	26,128	8.71	2,742	10.84
Actual campaigning	24,395	8.13	2,848	11.25
Staff/volunteers	0		0	
Subtotal	**50,523**	**16.84**	**5,590**	**22.09**
Constituent Gifts/ Entertainment	**6,336**	**2.11**	**0**	
Donations to				
Candidates from same state	0		0	
Candidates from other states	0		0	
Civic organizations	250	.08	0	
Ideological groups	1,000	.33	0	
Political parties	1,171	.39	0	
Subtotal	**2,421**	**.81**	**0**	
Unitemized Expenses	**15,267**	**5.09**	**6,173**	**24.39**
Total Campaign Expenses	**$ 300,034**		**$ 25,304**	
PAC Contributions	**$ 0**		**$ 0**	
Individual Contributions	**290,666**		**19,484**	
Total Receipts*	**317,043**		**27,203**	

Includes PAC and individual contributions as well as interest earned, party contributions, etc.

ILLINOIS District 20

Rep. Richard J. Durbin (D)

1992 Election Results

Richard J. Durbin (D)   154,869   (57%)
John M. Shimkus (R)   119,219   (43%)

Redistricting did more than give Rep. Richard J. Durbin a host of new constituents. It also added a new media market. "Seventy percent of our district is now in the St. Louis market, and that means it's four times as expensive to advertise as before," lamented district staff director Michael E. Daly. As a result of this unfortunate development and the fact that Durbin attracted a reasonably well-funded Republican challenger, his expenditures for broadcast advertising rose from $10,690 in 1990 to $378,052 in 1992.

Approximately half of Durbin's constituents were new to him, so he also increased his voter contact efforts. Durbin spent nothing on persuasion mail in 1990, but in 1992 he invested $150,907 in brochures and voter contact mail. Travel costs rose from $29,476 to $51,656 and his payroll increased from $7,021 to $46,364. With only token opposition in 1990, Durban spent nothing on polls, but to help formulate his message and strategy in 1992 he invested $43,500 in surveys conducted by Garin-Hart of Washington, D.C. In all, he spent $713,829 more in 1992 than in 1990.

In April 1992 Durbin hired Shorr Associates of Philadelphia, Pa., and over the next eight months paid them $340,265 for designing and placing ten television and radio commercials. One negative spot hit Republican county treasurer John M. Shimkus for wasting taxpayer money by purchasing new furniture for his office.

Durbin paid Campaign Performance Group of San Francisco, Calif., $83,509 for four persuasion mailers. One attacked Shimkus for advocating cuts in Social Security benefits; another labeled him as "big oil's candidate in this race." Additional brochure and voter contact mail charges included $48,080 for postage, $15,723 for printing, and $3,595 for mailing lists.

To pay for his spending spree, Durbin held twenty-three fund-raisers and mailed ten direct-mail solicitations. Fraioli/Jost of Washington, D.C., received $29,521 for coordinating four Washington events that helped push his political action committee contributions to $420,402, or 67 percent of his total donations.

For most of the two-year election cycle, Durbin ran his permanent campaign out of the Sangamon County Democratic Central Committee office. For the final month of the campaign he opened a large headquarters, which by election day was staffed by six employees.

Shimkus put 72 percent of his limited funds into direct appeals to voters. The Illinois Republican State Central Committee spent $55,000 to augment his television and radio buys, but that still left him more than $270,000 short of Durbin's broadcast budget.

Campaign Expenditures	Durbin Amount Spent	Durbin % of Total	Shimkus Amount Spent	Shimkus % of Total
Overhead				
Office furniture/supplies	$ 13,731	1.49	$ 4,195	2.39
Rent/utilities	6,547	.71	3,453	1.97
Salaries	46,364	5.04	17,543	10.00
Taxes	6,845	.74	7,265	4.14
Bank/investment fees	343	.04	235	.13
Lawyers/accountants	10,082	1.10	0	
Telephone	21,570	2.34	5,880	3.35
Campaign automobile	0		0	
Computers/office equipment	15,373	1.67	358	.20
Travel	51,656	5.62	1,591	.91
Food/meetings	2,417	.26	0	
Subtotal	174,927	19.02	40,518	23.11
Fund Raising				
Events	68,691	7.47	8,068	4.60
Direct mail	20,405	2.22	0	
Telemarketing	0		0	
Subtotal	89,095	9.69	8,068	4.60
Polling	43,500	4.73	1,000	.57
Advertising				
Electronic media	378,052	41.10	49,586	28.28
Other media	20,711	2.25	8,193	4.67
Subtotal	398,763	43.35	57,779	32.95
Other Campaign Activity				
Persuasion mail/brochures	150,907	16.40	49,199	28.06
Actual campaigning	23,994	2.61	18,700	10.66
Staff/volunteers	2,860	.31	0	
Subtotal	177,761	19.32	67,899	38.72
Constituent Gifts/ Entertainment	4,423	.48	0	
Donations to				
Candidates from same state	4,605	.50	0	
Candidates from other states	3,500	.38	0	
Civic organizations	1,996	.22	95	.05
Ideological groups	945	.10	0	
Political parties	20,410	2.22	0	
Subtotal	31,456	3.42	95	.05
Unitemized Expenses	0		0	
Total Campaign Expenses	$ 919,925		$ 175,359	
PAC Contributions	$ 420,402		$ 44,271	
Individual Contributions	202,415		120,413	
Total Receipts*	666,110		281,184	

*Includes PAC and individual contributions as well as interest earned, party contributions, etc.

INDIANA — District 1

Rep. Peter J. Visclosky (D)

1992 Election Results

Peter J. Visclosky (D)   147,054   (69%)
David J. Vucich † (R)   64,770   (31%)

While redistricting added Republican voters from suburban Lake and Porter counties to District 1, their presence did little to change the overwhelmingly Democratic nature of the district. Elected by two-to-one margins or better in each of his four House races, Rep. Peter J. Visclosky had few worries.

Visclosky ran no radio or television commercials in Chicago's pricey media market. As in 1990, he depended almost exclusively on persuasion mail designed by Campaign Performance Group of San Francisco, Calif., to get his message out.

"The anti-incumbent mood caused us to change our thinking on biographical mailers," said Campaign Performance president Richard M. Schlackman. "A bio piece institutionalizes the candidate, and the goal in 1992 was to make incumbents seem different."

To accomplish this feat, Schlackman designed a mailer that pictured five headless men in suits and ties. Schlackman replaced the heads with mock newspaper stories headlined "Politician's vacations that you paid for," "They gave themselves a raise," "Bounced check scandal widens," "No plans for ailing economy," and "Politicians more out of touch than ever." Beneath this was the phrase "You want something different from government." Inside was a picture of Visclosky striding purposefully forward, shirt-sleeves rolled up, beneath the phrase "Pete Visclosky is something different." "No bounced checks," "No Junkets, " "Voted against giving himself a pay raise" the mailer trumpeted in red lettering.

A fluttering American flag and the phrase "What America buys ..." adorned the cover of a second mailer. Inside, the phrase concluded "... should have an American face on it." The mailer encouraged people to "Buy American" and vote for Visclosky.

Campaign Performance collected $33,728 for preprimary work and $25,569 for its general election efforts. The campaign spent another $14,680 on postage and $2,075 to print campaign fliers.

To make sure his constituents were surrounded by reminders of his campaign, Visclosky spent $7,829 on promotional material, including $1,837 on signature glasses. Yard signs and posters cost the campaign $9,615. He paid the Gary Democratic Precinct Organization $7,240 for coordinated campaign efforts prior to the May 5 primary.

Each year, Visclosky invited some constituents to join him for a Christmas dinner. These small gatherings and occasional meals with constituents cost the campaign a total of $4,987. Year-end holiday cards cost $2,100.

Accountant David J. Vucich spent less than $5,000 on his token challenge and never filed financial reports with the Federal Election Commission.

Campaign Expenditures	Visclosky Amount Spent	% of Total
Overhead		
Office furniture/supplies	$ 4,148	1.54
Rent/utilities	4,498	1.67
Salaries	8,307	3.09
Taxes	2,316	.86
Bank/investment fees	172	.06
Lawyers/accountants	500	.19
Telephone	3,437	1.28
Campaign automobile	0	
Computers/office equipment	20,724	7.71
Travel	16,866	6.27
Food/meetings	3,120	1.16
Subtotal	**64,088**	**23.84**
Fund Raising		
Events	27,157	10.10
Direct mail	0	
Telemarketing	0	
Subtotal	**27,157**	**10.10**
Polling	**15,400**	**5.73**
Advertising		
Electronic media	0	
Other media	1,033	.38
Subtotal	**1,033**	**.38**
Other Campaign Activity		
Persuasion mail/brochures	76,052	28.29
Actual campaigning	28,353	10.55
Staff/volunteers	0	
Subtotal	**104,405**	**38.84**
Constituent Gifts/Entertainment	**7,087**	**2.64**
Donations to		
Candidates from same state	3,400	1.26
Candidates from other states	1,500	.56
Civic organizations	350	.13
Ideological groups	290	.11
Political parties	27,045	10.06
Subtotal	**32,585**	**12.12**
Unitemized Expenses	**17,034**	**6.34**
Total Campaign Expenses	**$ 268,789**	
PAC Contributions	**$ 175,715**	
Individual Contributions	**82,420**	
Total Receipts*	**275,278**	

*Includes PAC and individual contributions as well as interest earned, party contributions, etc.

† No expenditures or receipts on file. Candidates raising or spending less than $5,000 are not required to file reports with the Federal Election Commission.

District 2 — INDIANA

Rep. Philip R. Sharp (D)

1992 Election Results

Philip R. Sharp (D)	130,881	(57%)
William G. Frazier (R)	90,593	(40%)

Having defeated him in 1976, 1978, and 1980, Rep. Philip R. Sharp was all too familiar with former Republican state senator William G. Frazier. However, with 120 overdrafts at the House bank, Sharp could not afford to take Frazier's fourth challenge lightly.

Over the final six months of the two-year election cycle Sharp spent $483,079—$290,500 of which was paid to the Campaign Group of Philadelphia, Pa., for creating, producing, and placing his broadcast advertising. The campaign spent another $5,058 to directly place radio commercials.

According to campaign manager Joe Fuld, the advertising effort began on a positive note, focusing on job creation, economic growth, and Sharp's efforts to secure federal money for the district. One of these early commercials stressed that Sharp would support the North American Free Trade Agreement only if he could be convinced that it would not cost American's their jobs.

Fuld was quick to add that a strictly positive campaign was impossible. Noting that Frazier had sought several state offices in addition to his three House bids, one of Sharp's negative spots branded Frazier a "perennial candidate" who missed numerous votes while a member of the state senate. When Frazier began running commercials attacking Sharp for his overdrafts, Sharp was quick to respond with an ad focusing on his letter of exoneration from special counsel Malcolm Wilkey.

Since 95 percent of the district could be reached through a limited number of television stations, Sharp opted not to do much persuasion mail. Blaemire Communications of Reston, Va., received $6,637 for designing the campaign's brochures.

To keep tabs on the mood of the electorate and provide input to the advertising campaign, Sharp hired pollster Cooper & Secrest Associates of Alexandria, Va. The firm conducted a benchmark survey of the redrawn district in January 1992, a midcourse poll in June, and two additional surveys during the fall campaign. Cooper & Secrest collected $48,716 for their efforts.

Sharp received $449,549 from political action committees (PACs), which accounted for 74 percent of his total contributions. Christine Koerner Associates of Alexandria, Va., was paid $30,437 for arranging PAC events.

Frazier was able to invest $112,102—nearly two-thirds of his entire budget—in broadcast advertising, much of it placed on local cable television systems. "We bought for as little as $1 or $2 a spot, but when something is cheap, there's usually a reason," he noted. "It just didn't reach the right people."

Campaign Expenditures	Sharp Amount Spent	Sharp % of Total	Frazier Amount Spent	Frazier % of Total
Overhead				
Office furniture/supplies	$ 5,849	.94	$ 832	.48
Rent/utilities	10,346	1.66	248	.14
Salaries	62,677	10.06	12,951	7.51
Taxes	31,314	5.02	1,869	1.08
Bank/investment fees	120	.02	17	.01
Lawyers/accountants	2,859	.46	0	
Telephone	8,902	1.43	3,503	2.03
Campaign automobile	0		0	
Computers/office equipment	9,287	1.49	728	.42
Travel	19,495	3.13	6,158	3.57
Food/meetings	1,075	.17	0	
Subtotal	**151,925**	**24.38**	**26,306**	**15.26**
Fund Raising				
Events	58,191	9.34	1,250	.73
Direct mail	12,041	1.93	2,721	1.58
Telemarketing	0		0	
Subtotal	**70,232**	**11.27**	**3,971**	**2.30**
Polling	**48,716**	**7.82**	**0**	
Advertising				
Electronic media	295,558	47.43	112,102	65.05
Other media	1,116	.18	10,250	5.95
Subtotal	**296,674**	**47.60**	**122,352**	**71.00**
Other Campaign Activity				
Persuasion mail/brochures	25,466	4.09	6,993	4.06
Actual campaigning	21,890	3.51	6,086	3.53
Staff/volunteers	22		0	
Subtotal	**47,378**	**7.60**	**13,079**	**7.59**
Constituent Gifts/ Entertainment	52	.01	0	
Donations to				
Candidates from same state	350	.06	0	
Candidates from other states	0		0	
Civic organizations	0		0	
Ideological groups	0		0	
Political parties	5,775	.93	480	.28
Subtotal	**6,125**	**.98**	**480**	**.28**
Unitemized Expenses	**2,100**	**.34**	**6,149**	**3.57**
Total Campaign Expenses	**$ 623,204**		**$ 172,338**	
PAC Contributions	$ 449,549		$ 6,515	
Individual Contributions	153,785		22,492	
Total Receipts*	624,265		176,488	

*Includes PAC and individual contributions as well as interest earned, party contributions, etc.

INDIANA   District 3

Rep. Tim Roemer (D)

1992 Election Results　　Tim Roemer (D)　　121,269　(57%)
　　　　　　　　　　　　　　Carl H. Baxmeyer (R)　89,834　(43%)

Philosophically, freshman Rep. Tim Roemer's 1992 campaign mirrored his 1990 effort, when he defeated five-term Republican Rep. John Hiler. "We were still running as the challenger and an agent of change," remarked John Franzen, Roemer's Washington, D.C.-based media consultant.

That outsider message was delivered almost exclusively through broadcast advertising, which accounted for 47 percent of his spending. His five television commercials included one calling for a new Marshall Plan to rebuild America. A spot focusing on Roemer's efforts to improve day care and public schools declared that "children don't hire lobbyists." Other ads trumpeted Roemer's constituent outreach program, including his mobile office, the eighty town meetings he held during his first term, and his successful fight to save a firm that employed 400 district residents. Companion radio spots ran for the final seven weeks of the campaign, and none of the ads mentioned his opponent, Republican city planner Carl H. Baxmeyer.

At the grass-roots level, Roemer spent $5,639 on signs and posters, $3,910 on campaign literature, $1,763 on newspaper and program ads, $1,114 for T-shirts, $1,109 on lapel stickers, and $877 for bumper stickers. His principal campaign handouts were 20,000 "Seeds of Change" packets, which contained seeds of flowers indigenous to the state and cost the campaign $2,295. On the back of each packet was a synopsis of Roemer's platform.

Roemer paid for delivering his outsider message with a thoroughly insider fund-raising operation. Political action committees accounted for 70 percent of the $457,596 he raised. He collected $105,027 from individual contributors who gave $200 or more, and $41,050 of that total was donated by out-of-state residents. Those giving less than $200 accounted for only $24,710 of the money he raised.

Fraioli/Jost of Washington, D.C., received $15,825 for organizing two fund-raising events at the National Democratic Club. Payments to the club for food and beverages added $4,048. The Independent Insurance Agents Political Action Committee also sponsored an in-kind event, which it valued at $798.

Although Roemer held at least ten fund-raisers in the district during the two-year election cycle, these receptions were not geared toward making money. According to administrative assistant Bernard R. Toon, the most successful of these events was a $20-a-plate dinner attended by 500 supporters. However, with catering costs alone of $3,500, the campaign realized a very small profit.

Baxmeyer plowed 40 percent of the $228,950 he spent into overhead. His payroll was nearly $9,000 higher than Roemer's.

Campaign Expenditures	Roemer Amount Spent	% of Total	Baxmeyer Amount Spent	% of Total
Overhead				
Office furniture/supplies	$ 9,750	2.35	$ 2,475	1.08
Rent/utilities	12,381	2.98	3,665	1.60
Salaries	35,481	8.55	44,094	19.26
Taxes	24,448	5.89	23,438	10.24
Bank/investment fees	65	.02	37	.02
Lawyers/accountants	0		6,396	2.79
Telephone	6,134	1.48	8,117	3.55
Campaign automobile	3,576	.86	0	
Computers/office equipment	4,778	1.15	3,024	1.32
Travel	21,265	5.12	1,086	.47
Food/meetings	1,942	.47	74	.03
Subtotal	**119,821**	**28.86**	**92,407**	**40.36**
Fund Raising				
Events	41,315	9.95	7,531	3.29
Direct mail	0		11,922	5.21
Telemarketing	0		0	
Subtotal	**41,315**	**9.95**	**19,453**	**8.50**
Polling	**14,500**	**3.49**	**14,200**	**6.20**
Advertising				
Electronic media	193,313	46.56	74,633	32.60
Other media	1,763	.42	8,007	3.50
Subtotal	**195,075**	**46.98**	**82,640**	**36.10**
Other Campaign Activity				
Persuasion mail/brochures	3,910	.94	9,067	3.96
Actual campaigning	27,041	6.51	10,338	4.52
Staff/volunteers	2,132	.51	26	.01
Subtotal	**33,083**	**7.97**	**19,431**	**8.49**
Constituent Gifts/ Entertainment	7,273	1.75	99	.04
Donations to				
Candidates from same state	280	.07	0	
Candidates from other states	1,000	.24	0	
Civic organizations	576	.14	0	
Ideological groups	18		0	
Political parties	1,738	.42	0	
Subtotal	**3,612**	**.87**	**0**	
Unitemized Expenses	520	.13	721	.31
Total Campaign Expenses	**$ 415,200**		**$ 228,950**	
PAC Contributions	$ 320,249		$ 16,706	
Individual Contributions	129,737		195,883	
Total Receipts*	467,094		245,862	

*Includes PAC and individual contributions as well as interest earned, party contributions, etc.

District 4 — INDIANA

Rep. Jill L. Long (D)

1992 Election Results

Jill L. Long (D)   134,907   (62%)
Charles W. Pierson (R)   82,468   (38%)

After spending a total of $1.2 million to win a 1989 special election and her initial reelection bid in 1990, Rep. Jill L. Long largely coasted through the 1992 campaign. While she had twenty-one overdrafts at the House bank, neither her Democratic primary opponent, bookkeeper J. Carolyn Williams, nor her Republican challenger, marketing executive Charles W. Pierson, had sufficient resources to exploit the issue.

During 1991 Long spent $51,546 to maintain her permanent campaign operation, including $20,576 on overhead and $16,661 on fund raising. Considering that she ended the 1990 campaign with debts of $57,049 and that Vice President Dan Quayle and Republican Sen. Daniel R. Coats had held the District 4 seat for a dozen years prior to her 1989 victory, Long's 1991 outlays were remarkably low.

Long spent nearly $66,000 to secure the Democratic nomination. Her expenses for the primary campaign included $17,821 to Campaign Performance Group of San Francisco, Calif., for consultation, production, and mailing costs associated with the campaign's lone persuasion mailing. Greenberg-Lake of Washington, D.C., collected $22,554 for consulting and preprimary polls. They received another $6,198 for work on the general election.

According to Brad Senden, Long's chief campaign strategist, the campaign's early emphasis on polling was driven by anxiety over the electorate's anti-incumbent mood. "We were really concerned about the dynamic of anti-incumbency, but our polling showed us we had no real problem."

As in 1990, Long found herself running against a conservative ideologue in the fall campaign. "We weren't really running against a candidate," remarked Senden. "We were running against some of the insane statements he occasionally made."

One of Pierson's television spots showed him standing with an assault-style weapon. Proclaiming himself a friend of the National Rifle Association, Pierson used the weapon to riddle a picture of Long. "We should have run that spot ourselves," noted Senden.

Long paid Sautter Communications of Washington, D.C., $20,496 for developing four television commercials that Senden said focused on Long's work on the Agriculture Committee and foreign trade. None of the spots mentioned Pierson. Axelrod & Associates of Chicago, Ill., received $25,949 to cover production costs and ad placement. The Media Group of Columbus, Ohio, was also paid $6,780 for ad production.

To repay her 1990 debts and fund her 1992 campaign, Long turned to political action committees, which accounted for 72 percent of her receipts. She paid Christine Koerner Associates of Alexandria, Va., $46,639 for organizing Washington, D.C., events.

Campaign Expenditures	Long Amount Spent	Long % of Total	Pierson Amount Spent	Pierson % of Total
Overhead				
Office furniture/supplies	$ 3,798	1.32	$ 975	6.69
Rent/utilities	5,851	2.03	0	
Salaries	20,914	7.25	0	
Taxes	18,078	6.27	0	
Bank/investment fees	440	.15	0	
Lawyers/accountants	1,009	.35	0	
Telephone	8,325	2.89	2,533	17.39
Campaign automobile	0		0	
Computers/office equipment	17,469	6.06	0	
Travel	10,220	3.55	938	6.44
Food/meetings	115	.04	52	.35
Subtotal	**86,220**	**29.91**	**4,497**	**30.87**
Fund Raising				
Events	62,858	21.81	154	1.06
Direct mail	0		0	
Telemarketing	0		0	
Subtotal	**62,858**	**21.81**	**154**	**1.06**
Polling	**28,752**	**9.97**	**0**	
Advertising				
Electronic media	54,022	18.74	1,992	13.68
Other media	0		231	1.58
Subtotal	**54,022**	**18.74**	**2,223**	**15.26**
Other Campaign Activity				
Persuasion mail/brochures	23,338	8.10	2,198	15.09
Actual campaigning	24,522	8.51	5,312	36.47
Staff/volunteers	471	.16	154	1.05
Subtotal	**48,331**	**16.77**	**7,664**	**52.61**
Constituent Gifts/ Entertainment	**3,157**	**1.10**	**0**	
Donations to				
Candidates from same state	0		0	
Candidates from other states	0		0	
Civic organizations	0		0	
Ideological groups	0		0	
Political parties	1,350	.47	30	.21
Subtotal	**1,350**	**.47**	**30**	**.21**
Unitemized Expenses	**3,575**	**1.24**	**0**	
Total Campaign Expenses	**$ 288,266**		**$ 14,568**	
PAC Contributions	$ 263,182		$ 500	
Individual Contributions	93,100		676	
Total Receipts*	366,814		6,094	

*Includes PAC and individual contributions as well as interest earned, party contributions, etc.

INDIANA District 5

Rep. Steve Buyer (R)

1992 Election Results

Steve Buyer (R)	112,492	(51%)
Jim Jontz (D)	107,973	(49%)

Attorney Steve Buyer had sufficient resources to compete with Rep. Jim Jontz, but he had little room for budgetary mistakes. While Jontz could afford to spend $140,288 on his advertising campaign and $200,092 on brochures and persuasion mail, Buyer had to limit himself to one method of delivering his message. He decided to go with broadcast advertising.

Outspent by $204,359, Buyer funneled 40 percent of his resources into radio and television commercials created by Mike Murphy Media of Washington, D.C. As a result, Buyer actually spent $15,546 more than Jontz on such ads. "We had to say no to other things that came up during the campaign in order to save our money for TV at the end," noted administrative assistant Kelly Craven.

Murphy created two television and two radio commercials for Buyer, all of which hit on the anti-incumbent, outsider theme. "Steve had never run for office before while Jim Jontz had been in public office for eighteen years," Craven explained.

Rather than spreading his advertising budget over the entire fall campaign, Buyer decided to hold his fire until the final three weeks, when he unveiled his radio spots. His television buys were limited to the campaign's final ten days. "We saw other candidates on the air earlier and wondered if we should be on," recalled Craven. "But we held off until the end."

Throughout September and October Buyer and his staff walked the district, handing out campaign literature. Buyer spent $37,236 to print and mail campaign newsletters. The National Republican Congressional Committee spent $24,925 to send additional persuasion mail. Yard signs cost $9,795. Buyer paid $1,161 for T-shirts, $771 for bumper stickers, and $336 for lapel pins.

To save money, Buyer ran the campaign out of his home, donating office space he valued at $1,875. Other than Murphy, his only consultant was Public Opinion Strategies of Alexandria, Va., which received $10,038 for conducting polls. However, with twenty counties in the district, he could not afford to be too frugal with his paid staff, which by election day had grown to six.

Looking back on his failed reelection bid, Jontz said he "should have gone with a more negative message and started earlier." Instead, he chose to focus one of his two television commercials on a scholarship fund he started with part of his congressional pay raise. His lone attack ad, a spot criticizing Buyer for waffling on the North American Free Trade Agreement, was not enough to carry him in a district he had won with 56 percent of the vote or less in three previous campaigns.

Campaign Expenditures	Buyer Amount Spent	Buyer % of Total	Jontz Amount Spent	Jontz % of Total
Overhead				
Office furniture/supplies	$ 6,475	1.66	$ 8,558	1.44
Rent/utilities	1,875	.48	7,315	1.23
Salaries	48,485	12.43	56,524	9.51
Taxes	17,560	4.50	18,676	3.14
Bank/investment fees	70	.02	622	.10
Lawyers/accountants	2,500	.64	1,300	.22
Telephone	18,816	4.83	26,252	4.42
Campaign automobile	0		0	
Computers/office equipment	8,406	2.16	6,353	1.07
Travel	13,195	3.38	17,641	2.97
Food/meetings	0		1,492	.25
Subtotal	117,382	30.10	144,732	24.35
Fund Raising				
Events	14,847	3.81	17,614	2.96
Direct mail	10,629	2.73	25,234	4.25
Telemarketing	0		0	
Subtotal	25,476	6.53	42,847	7.21
Polling	10,038	2.57	41,429	6.97
Advertising				
Electronic media	155,834	39.97	140,288	23.61
Other media	2,761	.71	0	
Subtotal	158,595	40.67	140,288	23.61
Other Campaign Activity				
Persuasion mail/brochures	53,518	13.73	200,092	33.67
Actual campaigning	14,121	3.62	10,408	1.75
Staff/volunteers	2,383	.61	13	
Subtotal	70,022	17.96	210,513	35.42
Constituent Gifts/ Entertainment	422	.11	0	
Donations to				
Candidates from same state	500	.13	0	
Candidates from other states	0		0	
Civic organizations	0		0	
Ideological groups	0		35	.01
Political parties	0		0	
Subtotal	500	.13	35	.01
Unitemized Expenses	7,477	1.92	14,428	2.43
Total Campaign Expenses	$ 389,913		$ 594,272	
PAC Contributions	$ 135,834		$ 352,065	
Individual Contributions	201,400		221,790	
Total Receipts*	395,825		598,531	

*Includes PAC and individual contributions as well as interest earned, party contributions, etc.

District 6 — INDIANA

Rep. Dan Burton (R)

1992 Election Results

Dan Burton (R)	186,499	(72%)
Natalie M. Bruner (D)	71,952	(28%)

Rep. Dan Burton received 63 percent of the vote or better in each of his five previous House races, and redistricting made his solidly Republican district even more Republican. Nevertheless, Burton spent $399,952 on his 1992 campaign, nearly fifteen times as much as Democrat Natalie M. Bruner was able to spend on her challenge.

Burton spent $123,484 to keep his permanent campaign going during 1991, including $73,298 on overhead and $24,809 on fund raising. He spent $11,743 in 1991 on meals apparently unrelated to his fund-raising efforts.

Over the two-year election cycle, Burton invested $11,238 in constituent stroking. The campaign invested $2,403 in constituent gifts, $3,768 in holiday greeting cards, $1,782 in flowers, $3,031 in meals and other constituent entertainment, and $254 in the congressional art contest.

Burton's campaign spent $5,094 to insure and repair his 1948 antique fire truck, which was emblazoned with his name and used in local parades. Fire hats, which were distributed to children along the parade route whenever Burton made an appearance with his fire truck, cost $6,078. Clowns for various campaign events, including parades, set the campaign back another $2,229 and the mini-car they rode in cost $628.

Burton spent nothing on persuasion mail and only 20 percent of his spending was devoted to advertising. As in 1990, Burton wrote his lone television commercial and several radio spots, most of which were produced at the National Republican Congressional Committee's broadcast studio. Kevin Binger, Burton's press secretary, described the television commercial as "a simple shoulder and head shot," which featured Burton talking about the need to hold the line on taxes and spending.

While the campaign spent $4,098 to air radio commercials and $4,925 to run the television spot before the primary, the bulk of Burton's limited media budget was devoted to the fall campaign. The Perkins Group of Indianapolis received $54,544 for placing the television ad. The campaign spent an additional $5,257 to place the television spot on a local cable system and $6,255 for radio advertising. Newspaper ads cost $2,583.

Burton's campaign treasury never dropped below $400,000, and over the two-year cycle that hefty balance earned $49,099 in interest. Sheehan Associates of Washington, D.C., received $6,000 for organizing Burton's Washington fund-raisers, which helped him raise $213,385 from political action committees. Out-of-state donors who contributed at least $200 pumped another $135,252 into his coffers.

	Burton		Bruner	
Campaign Expenditures	Amount Spent	% of Total	Amount Spent	% of Total
Overhead				
Office furniture/supplies	$ 6,486	1.62	$ 225	.84
Rent/utilities	4,400	1.10	0	
Salaries	70,335	17.59	0	
Taxes	50,147	12.54	0	
Bank/investment fees	175	.04	55	.21
Lawyers/accountants	2,816	.70	0	
Telephone	3,154	.79	58	.22
Campaign automobile	0		0	
Computers/office equipment	6,160	1.54	2,221	8.32
Travel	10,161	2.54	4,555	17.06
Food/meetings	24,154	6.04	0	
Subtotal	**177,989**	**44.50**	**7,113**	**26.65**
Fund Raising				
Events	47,754	11.94	2,834	10.61
Direct mail	19,390	4.85	6,926	25.94
Telemarketing	0		0	
Subtotal	**67,145**	**16.79**	**9,759**	**36.56**
Polling	**417**	**.10**	**0**	
Advertising				
Electronic media	78,420	19.61	2,375	8.90
Other media	3,083	.77	642	2.41
Subtotal	**81,503**	**20.38**	**3,017**	**11.30**
Other Campaign Activity				
Persuasion mail/brochures	0		500	1.87
Actual campaigning	20,561	5.14	2,569	9.62
Staff/volunteers	250	.06	0	
Subtotal	**20,811**	**5.20**	**3,069**	**11.50**
Constituent Gifts/ Entertainment	**11,238**	**2.81**	**0**	
Donations to				
Candidates from same state	11,100	2.78	0	
Candidates from other states	4,250	1.06	0	
Civic organizations	1,000	.25	0	
Ideological groups	0		0	
Political parties	10,850	2.71	140	.52
Subtotal	**27,200**	**6.80**	**140**	**.52**
Unitemized Expenses	**13,650**	**3.41**	**3,597**	**13.47**
Total Campaign Expenses	**$ 399,952**		**$ 26,696**	
PAC Contributions	$ 213,385		$ 0	
Individual Contributions	350,404		22,950	
Total Receipts*	629,390		32,156	

*Includes PAC and individual contributions as well as interest earned, party contributions, etc.

INDIANA District 7

Rep. John T. Myers (R)

1992 Election Results

John T. Myers (R)	129,189	(59%)
Ellen E. Wedum (D)	88,005	(41%)

Held to 58 percent of the vote in 1990 by a Democratic challenger who spent only $282 and saddled with the burden of sixty-one overdrafts at the House bank, Rep. John T. Myers chose not to take anything for granted in 1992. While chemist Ellen E. Wedum was able to spend only $48,129 on her campaign, Myers's effort totaled $356,840—$150,119 more than he had spent in 1990.

Myers put most of that increased spending into direct appeals for votes. He increased his broadcast advertising budget from $18,876 in 1990 to $110,343 in 1992. Outlays for newspaper and program ads increased from $1,259 to $7,312. Although his expenditures for brochures and persuasion mail amounted to a modest $35,494 in 1992, he spent nothing on such mailings in 1990.

According to administrative assistant Ronald L. Hardman, Brockmeyer/Allen & Associates of Baltimore, Md., developed ten broadcast ads for Myers. Most of the campaign's early ads sought to paint Wedum as a tax-and-spend liberal. Pointing to her support for federally funded universal health care, one ad noted that Wedum had not offered a plan to pay for it. During the three weeks before the election, Hardman said the campaign switched to ads touting Myers's ability to deliver federal projects to the district. Brockmeyer/Allen received $12,828 for developing the commercials; Mentzer Media Service of Baltimore collected $96,515 to place them.

At the grass-roots level, Myers spent $3,870 for yard signs and posters, $1,243 for balloons and helium, $1,226 for bumper stickers, and $484 for lapel labels. He spent $2,679 on visor caps; $1,348 on refrigerator magnets; $1,074 on sewing kits; $1,070 on potholders; $1,042 on red, white, and blue match books; and $963 on orange antenna balls, all of which were handed out at parades and other events.

Not all of Myers's spending was devoted directly to his reelection effort. In both 1991 and 1992 the campaign paid for sixteen season tickets to Indianapolis Colts football games and four season tickets to Purdue University football games, which Myers and his wife used to entertain constituents, campaign volunteers, and county Republican officials. Total cost to the campaign: $10,153. The campaign also spent $10,695 on holiday greeting cards.

Myers invested $19,635 of his treasury in a new Chrysler LeBaron convertible. In addition to the registration and license fees for the new car, the campaign also picked up the tab for insurance premiums and upkeep on three others—a 1970 Impala convertible, a 1989 Plymouth Sundance, and a 1984 Chrysler.

	Myers		Wedum	
Campaign Expenditures	Amount Spent	% of Total	Amount Spent	% of Total
Overhead				
Office furniture/supplies	$ 3,505	.98	$ 395	.82
Rent/utilities	3,400	.95	0	
Salaries	4,800	1.35	7,093	14.74
Taxes	2,803	.79	0	
Bank/investment fees	93	.03	0	
Lawyers/accountants	3,445	.97	0	
Telephone	2,833	.79	1,119	2.32
Campaign automobile	28,250	7.92	0	
Computers/office equipment	4,861	1.36	0	
Travel	28,961	8.12	226	.47
Food/meetings	5,221	1.46	0	
Subtotal	**88,174**	**24.71**	**8,832**	**18.35**
Fund Raising				
Events	40,989	11.49	0	
Direct mail	12,049	3.38	0	
Telemarketing	0		0	
Subtotal	**53,038**	**14.86**	**0**	
Polling	**11,640**	**3.26**	**0**	
Advertising				
Electronic media	110,343	30.92	25,168	52.29
Other media	7,312	2.05	0	
Subtotal	**117,656**	**32.97**	**25,168**	**52.29**
Other Campaign Activity				
Persuasion mail/brochures	35,494	9.95	1,837	3.82
Actual campaigning	16,969	4.76	6,222	12.93
Staff/volunteers	949	.27	0	
Subtotal	**53,412**	**14.97**	**8,059**	**16.75**
Constituent Gifts/ Entertainment	**21,602**	**6.05**	**0**	
Donations to				
Candidates from same state	0		0	
Candidates from other states	0		0	
Civic organizations	4,872	1.37	0	
Ideological groups	283	.08	0	
Political parties	4,184	1.17	0	
Subtotal	**9,339**	**2.62**	**0**	
Unitemized Expenses	**1,979**	**.55**	**6,070**	**12.61**
Total Campaign Expenses	**$ 356,840**		**$ 48,129**	
PAC Contributions	$ 199,784		$ 7,550	
Individual Contributions	88,657		8,378	
Total Receipts*	329,387		51,495	

*Includes PAC and individual contributions as well as interest earned, party contributions, etc.

District 8 — INDIANA

Rep. Frank McCloskey (D)

1992 Election Results

Frank McCloskey (D)	125,244	(53%)
Richard E. Mourdock (R)	108,054	(45%)

Coal mining executive Richard E. Mourdock held Rep. Frank McCloskey to 55 percent of the vote in 1990, and McCloskey's sixty-five overdrafts at the House bank appeared to strengthen the challenger's hand as he prepared for their 1992 rematch. Yet, despite raising 69 percent more and spending 63 percent more on the rematch, Mourdock collected an identical 45 percent of the vote.

Mourdock's increased campaign activity certainly grabbed McCloskey's attention. The incumbent increased his spending from $439,910 in 1990 to $512,414 in 1992, and his advertising budget jumped from $151,793 to $200,306.

For designing his five television and two radio commercials, McCloskey paid Sautter Communications of Washington, D.C., $26,830. The Media Group of Columbus, Ohio, collected $11,693 for ad production, and Axelrod & Associates of Chicago, Ill., received $159,450 for placing the spots.

According to Chris Sautter, most of the ads centered on the theme "working hard for working families," detailing McCloskey's efforts to secure federal highway construction dollars and new federal contracts for military bases in the district. One ad simply scrolled across the screen a list of the jobs these projects had generated.

However, not all McCloskey's ads focused on the spoils of incumbency. Hammered by Mourdock for his overdrafts, McCloskey responded with a radio commercial that began, "After running for Congress twice, you'd think Richard Mourdock would have something positive to say about himself." The ad went on to remind voters that one of Mourdock's coal mines had been slapped with health and safety code violations and concluded, "No wonder he doesn't have anything positive to say."

One of McCloskey's negative television spots attacked Mourdock for supporting a capital gains tax cut for the rich while failing to come up with a plan to create more jobs. As Mourdock's picture slowly turned into a picture of George Bush, the announcer asked, "Sound familiar?"

McCloskey sent out only one, narrowly targeted persuasion mailer. With a number of competitive races in the state, Sautter said fund raising became difficult and plans for a more aggressive mail effort were scrapped.

An in-house phonebank cost McCloskey $5,381 and 10,000 yard signs added $2,810. He spent $3,984 on small American flags, which he passed out at the three Fourth of July parades he attended annually.

McCloskey paid pollster Cooper & Secrest Associates of Alexandria, Va., $42,149. For helping him raise $329,569 from political action committees, Diane Gould of Washington, D.C., received $10,045.

Campaign Expenditures	McCloskey Amount Spent	McCloskey % of Total	Mourdock Amount Spent	Mourdock % of Total
Overhead				
Office furniture/supplies	$ 3,674	.72	$ 3,955	1.62
Rent/utilities	5,242	1.02	3,437	1.41
Salaries	51,832	10.12	45,694	18.69
Taxes	20,754	4.05	3,756	1.54
Bank/investment fees	62	.01	0	
Lawyers/accountants	0		0	
Telephone	11,018	2.15	10,230	4.18
Campaign automobile	7,852	1.53	5,436	2.22
Computers/office equipment	4,913	.96	3,664	1.50
Travel	19,352	3.78	3,128	1.28
Food/meetings	5,609	1.09	331	.14
Subtotal	**130,308**	**25.43**	**79,632**	**32.57**
Fund Raising				
Events	33,018	6.44	7,675	3.14
Direct mail	11,406	2.23	7,670	3.14
Telemarketing	0		0	
Subtotal	**44,424**	**8.67**	**15,344**	**6.28**
Polling	**42,149**	**8.23**	**2,700**	**1.10**
Advertising				
Electronic media	198,530	38.74	119,350	48.82
Other media	1,776	.35	240	.10
Subtotal	**200,306**	**39.09**	**119,590**	**48.92**
Other Campaign Activity				
Persuasion mail/brochures	23,422	4.57	9,369	3.83
Actual campaigning	18,487	3.61	4,657	1.90
Staff/volunteers	0		0	
Subtotal	**41,909**	**8.18**	**14,025**	**5.74**
Constituent Gifts/ Entertainment	**10,939**	**2.13**	**0**	
Donations to				
Candidates from same state	5,200	1.01	200	.08
Candidates from other states	4,000	.78	0	
Civic organizations	250	.05	0	
Ideological groups	0		0	
Political parties	7,210	1.41	1,850	.76
Subtotal	**16,660**	**3.25**	**2,050**	**.84**
Unitemized Expenses	**25,720**	**5.02**	**11,139**	**4.56**
Total Campaign Expenses	**$ 512,414**		**$ 244,481**	
PAC Contributions	$ 329,569		$ 0	
Individual Contributions	144,626		232,650	
Total Receipts*	498,192		248,777	

*Includes PAC and individual contributions as well as interest earned, party contributions, etc.

INDIANA   District 9

Rep. Lee H. Hamilton (D)

1992 Election Results

Lee H. Hamilton (D)	160,980	(70%)
Michael E. Bailey (R)	70,057	(30%)

In 1990 Rep. Lee H. Hamilton's Republican challenger spent less than $5,000 and received 31 percent of the vote. In 1992 Republican Michael E. Bailey, a vocal opponent of abortion and the founder of Christian Media Ministries, spent $175,489 on his longshot bid and received 30 percent of the vote.

Bailey invested more than $54,000 of his campaign treasury to secure the Republican nomination, including $34,554 to produce and air several controversial television commercials that purported to show pictures of second and third trimester aborted fetuses. On the strength of his evangelical support, Bailey captured 60 percent of the 29,920 primary votes cast.

In the general election contest against Hamilton, Bailey poured $69,635 into broadcast advertising. His six television spots for the fall campaign included two that focused on abortion. These two ads proved so inflammatory that conservative Republican Pat Buchanan canceled plans to attend a Bailey fund-raiser in September. Since Hamilton personally opposes abortion, favors some state-mandated restrictions, and had voted to bar federal funds for abortions except in cases where the woman's life was endangered, Bailey's message ultimately had little more than shock value. However, other Republican candidates paid Bailey $50 to acquire the controversial footage for inclusion in their own ads.

Unopposed in the primary, Hamilton countered Bailey's ads with a $73,106 broadcast advertising effort of his own. Robert Winningham of New Albany collected $18,891 for designing the ads, and production costs totaled another $14,394. The campaign spent $21,672 to air the television commercials, all of which ran on Louisville, Kentucky, stations that reach the southernmost portions of the district. Radio buys cost the campaign another $18,149, more than half of which went to Louisville stations.

Hamilton invested $9,112 on billboard advertising and $3,199 on newspaper ads. Postage and printing charges associated with campaign literature and persuasion mail amounted to $86,987.

In 1991 Hamilton paid Sheehy, Knopf & Shaver of Louisville $16,832 for promotional shopping bags. In May 1992 he spent another $22,588 to purchase 125,000 additional shopping bags from Heldman Packaging in Fairfield, Ohio. He also invested $2,418 in T-shirts.

Hamilton paid DeSisti & Associates of Washington, D.C., $41,888 for helping to fill his campaign coffers. In addition to his Washington events, Hamilton's search for funds took him to New York, Chicago, San Francisco, Los Angeles, San Diego, New Orleans, and Baton Rouge. Political action committees and out-of-state contributors who donated at least $200 accounted for 63 percent of his contributions.

	Hamilton		Bailey	
Campaign Expenditures	Amount Spent	% of Total	Amount Spent	% of Total
Overhead				
Office furniture/supplies	$ 8,648	1.81	$ 2,850	1.62
Rent/utilities	13,465	2.82	0	
Salaries	42,680	8.94	0	
Taxes	19,956	4.18	0	
Bank/investment fees	0		0	
Lawyers/accountants	13,775	2.88	4,967	2.83
Telephone	10,328	2.16	8,926	5.09
Campaign automobile	0		0	
Computers/office equipment	26,488	5.55	1,974	1.12
Travel	25,147	5.27	3,045	1.74
Food/meetings	953	.20	0	
Subtotal	**161,440**	**33.80**	**21,762**	**12.40**
Fund Raising				
Events	65,430	13.70	10,479	5.97
Direct mail	0		2,602	1.48
Telemarketing	0		0	
Subtotal	**65,430**	**13.70**	**13,081**	**7.45**
Polling	**6,000**	**1.26**	**0**	
Advertising				
Electronic media	73,106	15.31	104,189	59.37
Other media	12,881	2.70	4,602	2.62
Subtotal	**85,987**	**18.00**	**108,792**	**61.99**
Other Campaign Activity				
Persuasion mail/brochures	86,987	18.21	10,637	6.06
Actual campaigning	53,388	11.18	12,718	7.25
Staff/volunteers	0		0	
Subtotal	**140,375**	**29.39**	**23,355**	**13.31**
Constituent Gifts/ Entertainment	**5,806**	**1.22**	**0**	
Donations to				
Candidates from same state	0		0	
Candidates from other states	0		0	
Civic organizations	0		0	
Ideological groups	0		0	
Political parties	500	.10	0	
Subtotal	**500**	**.10**	**0**	
Unitemized Expenses	**12,058**	**2.52**	**8,498**	**4.84**
Total Campaign Expenses	**$ 477,596**		**$ 175,489**	
PAC Contributions	$ 199,150		$ 6,400	
Individual Contributions	271,644		115,222	
Total Receipts*	484,849		175,189	

*Includes PAC and individual contributions as well as interest earned, party contributions, etc.

District 10 — INDIANA

Rep. Andrew Jacobs, Jr. (D)

1992 Election Results

Andrew Jacobs, Jr. (D)	117,604	(64%)
Janos Horvath (R)	64,378	(35%)

Rep. Andrew Jacobs, Jr., has a decidedly different approach to campaigning. "I am willing to lose before I take PAC contributions," Jacobs remarked. "It's obscene that lobbyists are able to make campaign contributions."

With that philosophy, Jacobs rarely raises or spends much on his campaigns, and his 1992 rematch with economics professor Janos Horvath was no exception. Jacobs spent just $14,376 to dispatch Horvath, which was $294 less than Jacobs invested to beat him the first time. Among incumbents, only William H. Natcher (D-Ky.) spent less than Jacobs on his 1992 reelection campaign.

Jacobs raised his small treasury primarily from a list of 700 "friends" who had responded to past direct-mail solicitations. However, even there, Jacobs drew the line. When, in September 1992, he realized that his campaign bank account had risen to more than $39,000, the nine-term incumbent mailed out a letter asking his supporters not to send more money. "It's fall and time for a solicitation, but this time we don't need any money, so thank you," Jacobs remembered writing.

Jacobs ran the same radio spots in 1992 that he has been running for the past several elections. "Gregory Peck recorded several ads a few years ago that were suitably self-indulgent and said nothing negative about me," Jacobs remarked. He added that his ads said nothing negative about Horvath because "I don't do that, and we can't afford it anyway."

His grass-roots campaign effort consisted of a $992 expenditure for signs and a $4,000 payment to the Marion County Democratic Committee for his share of the cost of a slate mailer. While Jacobs said he no longer depends on their endorsement, he continues to pay to be included on the slate mailer "out of gratitude." He paid the county party committee $200 for his share of the cost for multicandidate brochures the party distributed. His share of the cost of a pre-election party for precinct workers was also $200.

Jacobs paid $100 to attend the NAACP's Freedom Fund Dinner and $150 to attend the Indianapolis Chamber of Commerce Black Expo Luncheon. He spent $100 for tickets to an Urban league dinner and $24 to attend the Equality Recognition breakfast.

Horvath spent nearly $19,000 more in 1992 than he had in 1990 and increased his share of the vote by an insignificant 1 percentage point. He spent $3,641 to air his four television commercials and $2,242 to air his three radio spots. Billboard advertising cost him $7,672.

Undaunted by his poor showings, Horvath has begun planning for his third challenge to Jacobs in 1994.

	Jacobs		Horvath	
Campaign Expenditures	Amount Spent	% of Total	Amount Spent	% of Total
Overhead				
Office furniture/supplies	$ 856	5.95	$ 1,649	3.21
Rent/utilities	0		6,621	12.89
Salaries	1,332	9.27	0	
Taxes	918	6.39	0	
Bank/investment fees	0		0	
Lawyers/accountants	0		0	
Telephone	0		2,447	4.76
Campaign automobile	0		0	
Computers/office equipment	0		2,914	5.67
Travel	0		0	
Food/meetings	0		220	.43
Subtotal	**3,106**	**21.61**	**13,850**	**26.97**
Fund Raising				
Events	0		4,672	9.10
Direct mail	485	3.37	3,089	6.01
Telemarketing	0		0	
Subtotal	**485**	**3.37**	**7,761**	**15.11**
Polling	**0**		**0**	
Advertising				
Electronic media	2,207	15.35	6,539	12.73
Other media	2,554	17.77	9,817	19.12
Subtotal	**4,761**	**33.12**	**16,356**	**31.85**
Other Campaign Activity				
Persuasion mail/brochures	0		6,419	12.50
Actual campaigning	5,392	37.51	4,306	8.39
Staff/volunteers	0		0	
Subtotal	**5,392**	**37.51**	**10,725**	**20.89**
Constituent Gifts/Entertainment	67	.46	0	
Donations to				
Candidates from same state	0		0	
Candidates from other states	0		0	
Civic organizations	150	1.04	0	
Ideological groups	224	1.56	0	
Political parties	165	1.15	0	
Subtotal	**539**	**3.75**	**0**	
Unitemized Expenses	**25**	**.17**	**2,659**	**5.18**
Total Campaign Expenses	**$ 14,376**		**$ 51,351**	
PAC Contributions	$ 0		$ 0	
Individual Contributions	12,776		20,234	
Total Receipts*	15,690		67,192	

Includes PAC and individual contributions as well as interest earned, party contributions, etc.

IOWA District 1

Rep. Jim Leach (R)

1992 Election Results

Jim Leach (R)	178,042	(68%)
Jan J. Zonneveld † (D)	81,600	(31%)

Redistricting brought Republican Rep. Jim Leach a slightly more Democratic constituency. This, in turn, brought him something he had not had in 1990—a Democratic opponent. While retired actuary Jan J. Zonneveld had less than $5,000 for the challenge, his candidacy prompted Leach to spend $171,453 more in 1992 than in 1990.

Much of that increase was devoted to overhead. Unlike 1990, Leach opened a campaign office. In August 1991 he hired a part-time campaign manager, Tom Cope, who received $20,119 over the remainder of the election cycle. While hardly exorbitant, Cope's salary helped push Leach's payroll from $4,989 in the 1990 election cycle to $40,662 in 1992. A new computer and printer cost $4,770. His most unusual overhead expense was the $90 he paid for a subscription to *Current Comedy*.

Schreurs & Associates of Waterloo collected $32,214 for producing and placing two television and three radio commercials. Another three radio spots were produced and placed by the campaign. According to Cope, the television spots featured constituent testimonials, while the radio ads dealt with such issues as deficit reduction and his strong support for campaign finance reform. Leach invested $21,778 in billboard advertising. He spent $6,798 on dozens of ads in newspapers such as the *Cedar Rapids Gazette,* the *Clinton Herald,* the *Daily Iowan,* the *Monticello Express,* and the *West Branch Times.* Yard signs cost the campaign $7,131.

Leach hired several high school students to assemble "Jim Leach" headbands, which he passed out at parades and various political events. The total cost for the headbands was $3,651. He spent $2,100 on commemorative notepads, $1,738 on T-shirts, $1,232 on bumper stickers, and $340 on lapel stickers.

As in past campaigns, Leach took no political action committee money. He raised only $58,583 from contributors who gave $200 or more, and 94 percent of that total was raised in Iowa. Donations of less than $200 accounted for 70 percent of Leach's total contributions.

While Leach's campaign held a number of small, moderately priced in-home events, his largest fundraisers were his annual garden parties, which attracted more than 500 people in both 1991 and 1992. However, with combined costs of more than $30,000 and a $40 price of admission, these backyard picnics produced more fun than money.

Leach also invested $20,484 in direct-mail fund raising, something he had not done in 1990. Campaign Services of Canton, Ohio, received $3,276 for producing most of the letters.

Campaign Expenditures	Leach Amount Spent	% of Total
Overhead		
Office furniture/supplies	$ 6,764	2.62
Rent/utilities	1,750	.68
Salaries	40,662	15.74
Taxes	16,651	6.44
Bank/investment fees	1,173	.45
Lawyers/accountants	0	
Telephone	5,973	2.31
Campaign automobile	0	
Computers/office equipment	9,097	3.52
Travel	20,792	8.05
Food/meetings	353	.14
Subtotal	**103,215**	**39.94**
Fund Raising		
Events	42,249	16.35
Direct mail	20,484	7.93
Telemarketing	0	
Subtotal	**62,732**	**24.28**
Polling	**2,100**	**.81**
Advertising		
Electronic media	37,930	14.68
Other media	29,344	11.36
Subtotal	**67,274**	**26.03**
Other Campaign Activity		
Persuasion mail/brochures	923	.36
Actual campaigning	16,923	6.55
Staff/volunteers	0	
Subtotal	**17,846**	**6.91**
Constituent Gifts/Entertainment	**4,828**	**1.87**
Donations to		
Candidates from same state	0	
Candidates from other states	0	
Civic organizations	20	.01
Ideological groups	0	
Political parties	324	.13
Subtotal	**344**	**.13**
Unitemized Expenses	**72**	**.03**
Total Campaign Expenses	**$ 258,411**	
PAC Contributions	**$ 0**	
Individual Contributions	**195,092**	
Total Receipts*	**213,649**	

*Includes PAC and individual contributions as well as interest earned, party contributions, etc.

† No expenditures or receipts on file. Candidates raising or spending less than $5,000 are not required to file reports with the Federal Election Commission.

District 2 — IOWA

Rep. Jim Nussle (R)

1992 Election Results

Jim Nussle (R)	134,536	(50%)
Dave Nagle (D)	131,570	(49%)

Freshman Rep. Jim Nussle's victory over three-term Rep. Dave Nagle in a race set up by the state's loss of on House seat provided ample testimony to the power of negative campaigning and outsider politics. While Nagle campaigned on his ability to deliver federal highway and dam construction projects to the district, Nussle positioned himself as a congressional reformer and attacked Nagle as the consummate insider.

To orchestrate his outsider campaign, Nussle assembled a team of ten consultants, including American Viewpoint of Alexandria, Va., which collected $49,700 for polling. James R. Foster & Associates of Carrollton, Texas, received $41,023 for direct-mail fund raising and $84,308 for handling persuasion mail. Gannon, McCarthy, Mason of Washington, D.C., collected $47,850 for developing Nussle's broadcast advertising. Schreurs & Associates of Waterloo received $190,566 from the campaign, $40,477 from the National Republican Congressional Committee, and $6,248 from the Republican National Committee for placing the ads.

In mid-September Nussle began airing television commercials slamming Nagle for his four overdrafts at the House bank and for his initial denial of having any overdrafts. One particularly damaging ad featured Nagle saying "public opinion be damned" on the House floor, a statement he made in arguing that release of House banking records would violate members' constitutional rights. The projects Nagle pointed to as proof that he was delivering jobs for the district Nussle attacked as wasteful, pork-barrel spending.

While he paid Fenn & King Communications of Washington, D.C.,$288,072 for developing and placing his broadcast ads, for much of the campaign Nagle ignored their advice to attack Nussle. With polls by the *Des Moines Register* showing him leading by 14 percentage points in mid-September, Nagle was content to stick with his pro-incumbency pitch.

One ad showed Nagle standing near the Mississippi River talking about the need to maintain the locks and dams. "There are some who say this is pork-barrel spending," Nagle said. Kneeling next to an oinking pig he concluded, "This is a river. This is pork. If you're going to represent Iowa in Congress, you'd better know the difference." While cute, the ad was no match for Nussle's negative bombardment.

By mid-October polls showed that Nagle had lost his lead and actually trailed Nussle by 6 percentage points, a 20-point swing in just one month. Nagle went on the offensive with ads attacking Nussle for failing to fulfill his promise to give back his congressional pay raise and for giving huge raises to members of his congressional staff. While the attacks helped close the gap, it was too little, too late.

Campaign Expenditures	Nussle Amount Spent	Nussle % of Total	Nagle Amount Spent	Nagle % of Total
Overhead				
Office furniture/supplies	$ 17,676	2.07	$ 14,318	1.70
Rent/utilities	14,462	1.69	8,700	1.03
Salaries	88,631	10.37	162,436	19.31
Taxes	35,447	4.15	0	
Bank/investment fees	1,329	.16	439	.05
Lawyers/accountants	0		0	
Telephone	17,616	2.06	17,267	2.05
Campaign automobile	0		5,721	.68
Computers/office equipment	13,880	1.62	7,715	.92
Travel	56,499	6.61	51,563	6.13
Food/meetings	4,110	.48	480	.06
Subtotal	**249,650**	**29.21**	**268,639**	**31.94**
Fund Raising				
Events	52,705	6.17	97,800	11.63
Direct mail	57,330	6.71	19,233	2.29
Telemarketing	0		0	
Subtotal	**110,035**	**12.87**	**117,032**	**13.92**
Polling	**52,096**	**6.09**	**42,850**	**5.10**
Advertising				
Electronic media	245,783	28.76	304,846	36.25
Other media	7,035	.82	14,237	1.69
Subtotal	**252,818**	**29.58**	**319,083**	**37.94**
Other Campaign Activity				
Persuasion mail/brochures	128,063	14.98	38,075	4.53
Actual campaigning	58,707	6.87	38,770	4.61
Staff/volunteers	32		861	.10
Subtotal	**186,801**	**21.85**	**77,706**	**9.24**
Constituent Gifts/ Entertainment	**1,450**	**.17**	**5,629**	**.67**
Donations to				
Candidates from same state	0		725	.09
Candidates from other states	1,100	.13	1,000	.12
Civic organizations	0		275	.03
Ideological groups	0		0	
Political parties	560	.07	5,852	.70
Subtotal	**1,660**	**.19**	**7,852**	**.93**
Unitemized Expenses	**232**	**.03**	**2,200**	**.26**
Total Campaign Expenses	**$ 854,742**		**$ 840,991**	
PAC Contributions	$ 350,565		$ 486,347	
Individual Contributions	471,532		221,950	
Total Receipts*	867,359		835,449	

*Includes PAC and individual contributions as well as interest earned, party contributions, etc.

IOWA District 3

Rep. Jim Ross Lightfoot (R)

1992 Election Results

Jim Ross Lightfoot (R)	125,931	(49%)
Elaine Baxter (D)	121,063	(47%)

On paper, it did not look good for Republican Rep. Jim Ross Lightfoot. He had represented only ten of the twenty-eight counties drawn into his new district, and registered Democrats outnumbered Republicans by 25,000. He had 105 overdrafts at the House bank. Businessman and political neophyte Ronald J. Long had held him to 58 percent in the Republican primary, and his Democratic challenger was two-term Iowa Secretary of State Elaine Baxter, who was unopposed in the Democratic primary.

During the first eighteen months of the election cycle, Lightfoot spent nearly $260,000, most of it on overhead and fund raising. His expenditures for preprimary broadcast advertising totaled just $20,200, including a $6,000 payment to Smith & Harroff of Alexandria, Va., for creating his radio spots. After his wakeup call in the primary, Lightfoot began pouring money into direct voter contact. He hired Brockmeyer/Allen & Associates of Baltimore, Md., and over the next five months paid them $52,534 for developing four television commercials and several radio spots. Schreurs & Associates of Waterloo billed the campaign $141,618 to cover the cost of air time and their fees for placing the ads. The Republican National Committee paid Schreurs $15,000 for additional media buys.

While Lightfoot ran one biographical television spot, introducing his adoptive parents and outlining his military service, most of his television advertising was highly negative. He attacked Baxter for voting in favor of tax increases while a member of the Iowa legislature, for taking taxpayer-funded junkets around the country to further her political career, and for wasting taxpayer money on redecorating her state office. His radio ads featured fellow Iowa Republicans, Sen. Charles E. Grassley and Rep. Jim Leach, endorsing their "colleague and friend."

Lightfoot also received considerable help from the Christian Coalition, which peppered the district with fliers echoing charges made by Lightfoot that Baxter favored abortions for purposes of sex selection. Phyllis Schlafly, Pat Buchanan, and Ralph Reed, head of the Christian Coalition, all stumped the district on Lightfoot's behalf.

Baxter returned fire with her own highly negative advertising campaign, designed by Joe Slade White & Co. of New York. The firm collected $67,917 for producing eight television and five radio commercials, including spots that attacked Lightfoot for his 105 overdrafts and his antiabortion stance. Shafto & Barton of Houston, Texas, received $177,366 from Baxter, $11,500 from the Iowa Democratic party, and another $5,000 from the Democratic Congressional Campaign Committee for placing the ads.

	Lightfoot		Baxter	
Campaign Expenditures	Amount Spent	% of Total	Amount Spent	% of Total
Overhead				
Office furniture/supplies	$ 13,956	1.85	$ 7,977	1.23
Rent/utilities	14,665	1.94	5,000	.77
Salaries	106,014	14.04	99,341	15.32
Taxes	41,275	5.47	38,076	5.87
Bank/investment fees	193	.03	0	
Lawyers/accountants	0		0	
Telephone	29,671	3.93	10,289	1.59
Campaign automobile	0		1,500	.23
Computers/office equipment	9,410	1.25	16,318	2.52
Travel	91,407	12.10	21,279	3.28
Food/meetings	392	.05	0	
Subtotal	**306,984**	**40.65**	**199,780**	**30.80**
Fund Raising				
Events	41,743	5.53	35,582	5.49
Direct mail	25,554	3.38	34,749	5.36
Telemarketing	36,046	4.77	0	
Subtotal	**103,343**	**13.68**	**70,331**	**10.84**
Polling	**24,998**	**3.31**	**43,540**	**6.71**
Advertising				
Electronic media	217,909	28.86	248,977	38.39
Other media	2,511	.33	365	.06
Subtotal	**220,420**	**29.19**	**249,342**	**38.45**
Other Campaign Activity				
Persuasion mail/brochures	33,771	4.47	11,925	1.84
Actual campaigning	49,557	6.56	56,023	8.64
Staff/volunteers	0		0	
Subtotal	**83,329**	**11.03**	**67,948**	**10.48**
Constituent Gifts/ Entertainment	**615**	**.08**	**0**	
Donations to				
Candidates from same state	0		0	
Candidates from other states	0		0	
Civic organizations	0		0	
Ideological groups	0		0	
Political parties	250	.03	0	
Subtotal	**250**	**.03**	**0**	
Unitemized Expenses	**15,243**	**2.02**	**17,596**	**2.71**
Total Campaign Expenses	**$ 755,181**		**$ 648,537**	
PAC Contributions	**$ 260,302**		**$ 287,902**	
Individual Contributions	**316,535**		**351,045**	
Total Receipts*	**623,098**		**657,055**	

*Includes PAC and individual contributions as well as interest earned, party contributions, etc.

District 4 — IOWA

Rep. Neal Smith (D)

1992 Election Results

Neal Smith (D)	158,610	(62%)
Paul Lunde (R)	94,045	(37%)

Running in a district that was 50 percent new to him, Rep. Neal Smith ran a decidedly different campaign in 1992 than he had in 1990. However, by congressional standards his effort was still extremely low key.

As the third-ranking Democrat on the Appropriations Committee, Smith found it easy to get political action committees (PACs) to fill his campaign coffers. He spent $5,814 at the National Democratic Club to hold his PAC events and paid the Democratic House and Senate Council $4,375 for planning and promoting the affairs. These modest efforts helped yield $210,300 in PAC donations, or 65 percent of his total receipts.

As in 1990, Smith spent little time or resources on in-state fund raising. Nearly half of his large, individual donations, which totaled $24,950, were raised outside of Iowa. He held a few small, in-home events in the district, as well as a reception at the Cub Club in Des Moines, but his total in-state receipts amounted to only $34,830. Interest earned on his substantial cash reserves was $49,834.

Smith invested more than three times as much in his 1992 campaign as he had in 1990, but the impetus clearly was redistricting, not his primary challengers or his general election opponent, Republican Paul Lunde, who spent $11,180 on his entire campaign. Instead of relying on the Iowa Democratic party for polling, as he had in 1990, Smith paid Cooper & Secrest Associates of Washington, D.C., $14,650 to bring him up to speed on what his new constituents were thinking. The Democratic National Committee also paid Lauer, Lalley & Associates of Washington, D.C., $8,935 to provide Smith with polling data.

J. D. Evans & Associates of Des Moines collected $39,453 for producing and placing several positive television commercials aimed primarily at introducing Smith to newly acquired voters. He also spent $20,303 on billboards.

Virtually unchallenged in the primary—he received 99 percent of the vote—Smith nevertheless spent $22,469 to print and mail brochures to his new constituents. In the fall campaign, he paid the Iowa Democratic party $17,060 for printing and mailing campaign literature. He also spent $1,996 to print additional brochures that were handed out. He paid the Polk County Democratic party $2,500 for phonebanking.

Unlike 1990, Smith opted to open a campaign headquarters and hire one part-time employee. The doors opened in August and closed immediately after the election. By far his largest overhead expense was the $22,041 he paid to travel to and from the district. He also paid $6,692 in taxes on the campaign's interest income.

Campaign Expenditures	Smith Amount Spent	Smith % of Total	Lunde Amount Spent	Lunde % of Total
Overhead				
Office furniture/supplies	$ 1,814	.93	$ 1,380	12.35
Rent/utilities	600	.31	0	
Salaries	4,432	2.28	0	
Taxes	6,692	3.44	0	
Bank/investment fees	0		135	1.21
Lawyers/accountants	0		0	
Telephone	800	.41	683	6.11
Campaign automobile	0		0	
Computers/office equipment	698	.36	1,200	10.73
Travel	22,041	11.32	5,755	51.48
Food/meetings	0		0	
Subtotal	**37,077**	**19.05**	**9,153**	**81.87**
Fund Raising				
Events	16,744	8.60	0	
Direct mail	0		0	
Telemarketing	0		0	
Subtotal	**16,744**	**8.60**	**0**	
Polling	**14,650**	**7.53**	**0**	
Advertising				
Electronic media	39,453	20.27	170	1.52
Other media	20,303	10.43	1,100	9.84
Subtotal	**59,756**	**30.70**	**1,270**	**11.36**
Other Campaign Activity				
Persuasion mail/brochures	41,525	21.33	0	
Actual campaigning	8,020	4.12	757	6.77
Staff/volunteers	0		0	
Subtotal	**49,545**	**25.45**	**757**	**6.77**
Constituent Gifts/ Entertainment	**216**	**.11**	**0**	
Donations to				
Candidates from same state	0		0	
Candidates from other states	2,000	1.03	0	
Civic organizations	0		0	
Ideological groups	0		0	
Political parties	10,000	5.14	0	
Subtotal	**12,000**	**6.16**	**0**	
Unitemized Expenses	**4,675**	**2.40**	**0**	
Total Campaign Expenses	**$ 194,662**		**$ 11,180**	
PAC Contributions	**$ 210,300**		**$ 0**	
Individual Contributions	**59,780**		**1,286**	
Total Receipts*	**324,231**		**11,178**	

*Includes PAC and individual contributions as well as interest earned, party contributions, etc.

IOWA — District 5

Rep. Fred Grandy (R)

1992 Election Results   Fred Grandy (R)   196,942   (99%)

Without a challenger in either the primary or general election, Rep. Fred Grandy spent the 1992 election cycle preparing for a gubernatorial bid in 1994. "It's clear the real change in this country is happening at the state level," he told the *Des Moines Register* editorial board.

"We weren't real aggressive in the fund-raising arena," argued his administrative assistant, Craig W. Tufte. Even so, Grandy succeeded in raising nearly $383,000 over the two-year election cycle. In so doing, he reduced his previous campaign debts from $101,069 to $43,772 and increased his cash reserves from $84,849 to $174,722.

Unlike 1990, when he raised roughly one-third of his money in Iowa, Grandy made almost no effort in 1992 to tap the wallets of his home-state constituents. Instead, he collected $296,149 from political action committees (PACs) and another $17,450 from out-of-state donors who gave at least $200. At most, Iowans contributed $56,006 to his coffers—$38,510 in large contributions and $17,496 in amounts under $200.

In May 1991 "Hogs on the Hill" catered his largest PAC event of the election cycle, which Tufte said drew at least 200 people. In October Grandy's campaign staged another fund-raiser at the Capitol Hill Club. In December the Mutual of Omaha PAC sponsored an event on his behalf. Two additional PAC fund-raisers were staged in 1992, including one sponsored jointly by the Iowa Medical Association PAC and the American Medical Association PAC. For helping to coordinate the bulk of Grandy's PAC events, Elizabeth Montgomery & Associates of Alexandria, Va., received $35,304. Tracy Warren & Associates of Washington, D.C., received $1,583 in 1991.

Grandy spent about half as much on direct-mail fund raising as he did in 1990. The Lukens Co. of Arlington, Va., received $5,186 for soliciting the campaign's list of 4,000 past donors and for preparing limited prospecting mailings.

Monthly rent on the campaign's permanent headquarters was only $100, but his one full-time campaign staffer received salary payments totaling $50,809. Part-time staffers who maintained the campaign's mailing lists added $6,018 to the payroll.

Grandy also used $1,809 of his campaign treasury to pay for part of the production costs of a satellite "community conference" on health care. Rep. Bill Gradison (R-Ohio) also picked up part of the expense.

His contributions of other candidates, causes, and Republican party organizations more than doubled from $14,181 in 1990 to $32,097 in 1992. The Republican party of Iowa received $10,000, and nineteen fellow Republican House candidates collected donations of at least $1,000.

Campaign Expenditures	Grandy Amount Spent	% of Total
Overhead		
Office furniture/supplies	$ 5,654	2.40
Rent/utilities	3,000	1.28
Salaries	56,827	24.16
Taxes	10,233	4.35
Bank/investment fees	0	
Lawyers/accountants	1,221	.52
Telephone	15,399	6.55
Campaign automobile	0	
Computers/office equipment	2,071	.88
Travel	19,952	8.48
Food/meetings	421	.18
Subtotal	**114,778**	**48.79**
Fund Raising		
Events	44,402	18.88
Direct mail	13,504	5.74
Telemarketing	0	
Subtotal	**57,906**	**24.62**
Polling	**0**	
Advertising		
Electronic media	0	
Other media	771	.33
Subtotal	**771**	**.33**
Other Campaign Activity		
Persuasion mail/brochures	0	
Actual campaigning	22,036	9.37
Staff/volunteers	0	
Subtotal	**22,036**	**9.37**
Constituent Gifts/Entertainment	**7,619**	**3.24**
Donations to		
Candidates from same state	1,954	.83
Candidates from other states	20,000	8.50
Civic organizations	143	.06
Ideological groups	0	
Political parties	10,000	4.25
Subtotal	**32,097**	**13.64**
Unitemized Expenses	**30**	**.01**
Total Campaign Expenses	**$ 235,237**	
PAC Contributions	**$ 296,149**	
Individual Contributions	**73,456**	
Total Receipts*	**382,626**	

*Includes PAC and individual contributions as well as interest earned, party contributions, etc.

District 1 — KANSAS

Rep. Pat Roberts (R)

1992 Election Results

Pat Roberts (R)	194,912	(68%)
Duane West (D)	83,620	(29%)

In 1990 administrative assistant Leroy D. Towns was able to boast that Rep. Pat Roberts had not run a television commercial since 1982. However, spurred by what Towns described as "the perilous times for incumbents and redistricting," Roberts spent nearly $200,000 to buy television air time in 1992.

New York-based media consultants Dresner, Sykes, Jordan & Townsend created four television and five radio commercials that focused on health care, campaign finance reform, Roberts's opposition to tax increases for the middle class, and agriculture policy. Democrat Duane West, who was making his second bid to unseat Roberts, was never mentioned.

Dresner, Sykes received $63,742 for creating the spots and for conducting the polls needed to sharpen the campaign's message. Creative Media Planning of New York billed the campaign $196,844 to cover the cost of airing the television ads and the firm's placement fees. High Plains Advertising Agency of Dodge City, Kan., collected $48,853 for placing the radio spots.

With a district that was roughly 40 percent new to him, Roberts vastly increased his spending in other areas, as well. While he spent nothing on persuasion mail in 1990, he paid High Plains Advertising $52,936 for coordinating a $155,646 voter contact mail effort in 1992. The firm also collected $31,770 for placing most of the campaign's newspaper ads.

Roberts kept his overhead to a minimum, waiting until August 1992 to open a campaign office. Even then, he shared space with two Republican county organizations. His part-time staff of two cost him only $3,036.

In all, Roberts spent nearly four times as much in 1992 as he had in the previous campaign. The $493,131 he spent on direct appeals to voters was $396,672 more than he spent on such activities in 1990.

To pay for his advertising and persuasion mail, Roberts raised $185,085 from political action committees, or 59 percent of his total receipts. Five percent of his money was raised from out-of-state donors who contributed at least $200. No more than $67,718 was raised from individual contributors in Kansas.

Roberts began the election cycle with $399,529 in his campaign bank account, and this cushion proved invaluable. His fund-raising efforts yielded $267,140, and interest on his cash reserves amounted to $43,450. He also drew $288,638 from his cash-on-hand to fund his increased voter contact.

West began the campaign hoping to raise $120,000 but raised only 30 percent of that goal. To get his message out, he was forced to put $27,500 of his own money into the campaign.

Campaign Expenditures	Roberts Amount Spent	Roberts % of Total	West Amount Spent	West % of Total
Overhead				
Office furniture/supplies	$ 3,544	.59	$ 682	1.05
Rent/utilities	498	.08	84	.13
Salaries	3,036	.50	0	
Taxes	11,573	1.92	0	
Bank/investment fees	0		74	.11
Lawyers/accountants	500	.08	0	
Telephone	919	.15	2,886	4.45
Campaign automobile	0		0	
Computers/office equipment	24		0	
Travel	41,146	6.84	7,671	11.82
Food/meetings	4,314	.72	145	.22
Subtotal	**65,554**	**10.90**	**11,542**	**17.78**
Fund Raising				
Events	17,464	2.90	0	
Direct mail	6,313	1.05	1,471	2.27
Telemarketing	0		0	
Subtotal	**23,777**	**3.95**	**1,471**	**2.27**
Polling	**12,500**	**2.08**	**0**	
Advertising				
Electronic media	298,897	49.68	27,597	42.52
Other media	33,114	5.50	15,105	23.27
Subtotal	**332,011**	**55.18**	**42,702**	**65.80**
Other Campaign Activity				
Persuasion mail/brochures	155,646	25.87	3,456	5.33
Actual campaigning	5,473	.91	5,611	8.65
Staff/volunteers	0		0	
Subtotal	**161,120**	**26.78**	**9,067**	**13.97**
Constituent Gifts/ Entertainment	3,576	.59	0	
Donations to				
Candidates from same state	0		0	
Candidates from other states	108	.02	0	
Civic organizations	1,946	.32	30	.05
Ideological groups	0		0	
Political parties	1,070	.18	0	
Subtotal	**3,123**	**.52**	**30**	**.05**
Unitemized Expenses	**0**		**87**	**.13**
Total Campaign Expenses	**$ 601,661**		**$ 64,899**	
PAC Contributions	$ 185,085		$ 0	
Individual Contributions	82,055		34,741	
Total Receipts*	313,020		64,899	

*Includes PAC and individual contributions as well as interest earned, party contributions, etc.

KANSAS   District 2

Rep. Jim Slattery (D)   *1992 Election Results*   Jim Slattery (D)   151,019   (56%)
                                                     Jim Van Slyke (R) 109,801   (41%)

	Slattery		Slyke	
Campaign Expenditures	Amount Spent	% of Total	Amount Spent	% of Total
Overhead				
Office furniture/supplies	$ 18,204	2.46	$ 459	1.25
Rent/utilities	7,060	.95	0	
Salaries	113,163	15.29	0	
Taxes	19,138	2.59	0	
Bank/investment fees	40	.01	0	
Lawyers/accountants	6,926	.94	0	
Telephone	13,574	1.83	672	1.83
Campaign automobile	6,310	.85	4,182	11.40
Computers/office equipment	11,634	1.57	314	.86
Travel	55,297	7.47	67	.18
Food/meetings	9,674	1.31	0	
Subtotal	**261,019**	**35.28**	**5,695**	**15.52**
Fund Raising				
Events	58,056	7.85	978	2.66
Direct mail	0		1,329	3.62
Telemarketing	0		0	
Subtotal	**58,056**	**7.85**	**2,307**	**6.29**
Polling	**47,928**	**6.48**	**0**	
Advertising				
Electronic media	211,390	28.57	17,091	46.58
Other media	24,415	3.30	1,765	4.81
Subtotal	**235,805**	**31.87**	**18,856**	**51.40**
Other Campaign Activity				
Persuasion mail/brochures	34,248	4.63	3,650	9.95
Actual campaigning	62,048	8.39	2,778	7.57
Staff/volunteers	1,742	.24	0	
Subtotal	**98,038**	**13.25**	**6,428**	**17.52**
Constituent Gifts/Entertainment	**14,915**	**2.02**	**0**	
Donations to				
Candidates from same state	1,275	.17	0	
Candidates from other states	500	.07	0	
Civic organizations	753	.10	0	
Ideological groups	20		0	
Political parties	17,725	2.40	0	
Subtotal	**20,273**	**2.74**	**0**	
Unitemized Expenses	3,885	.52	3,402	9.27
Total Campaign Expenses	$ 739,918		$ 36,687	
PAC Contributions	$ 439,021		$ 4,870	
Individual Contributions	251,963		26,989	
Total Receipts*	701,965		36,704	

Rep. Jim Slattery had no reason to fear Republican challenger Jim Van Slyke and chose not to mention him in his $235,805 advertising campaign. However, Slattery was very concerned with both his fifty overdrafts at the House bank and redistricting, which added most of the old District 5 to his territory. As a result, Slattery spent $235,172 more in 1992 than he had in 1990.

In January 1992 Slattery retained Shorr Associates of Philadelphia, Pa., and over the next eleven months Shorr received $138,648 for creating and placing ten television and five radio commercials. Complete Pictures of Philadelphia collected $62,826 for producing the spots. Hinkle & Scannel Advertising of Topeka was paid $5,894, primarily for supplying film footage of Slattery's speeches for use in the ad campaign. Other miscellaneous production costs and direct ad placements amounted to $4,022.

Since Van Slyke had little money for advertising and Slattery's polls showed that the challenger was not a threat, Shorr developed ads that completely ignored his fifty overdrafts. Instead, administrative assistant Howard P. Bauleke said the ads focused on Democratic themes such as the economy and on Slattery's efforts in Congress on behalf of the district.

Other major consultants to Slattery's campaign included Campaign Performance Group of San Francisco, Calif., which collected $19,436 for producing one persuasion mailer. Pollster Cooper & Secrest Associates of Alexandria, Va., received $47,928, and JASA Associates of Topeka was paid $31,889 for providing strategic advice because they were familiar with the new portions of the district.

Full page ads in most of the district's newspapers and one-quarter page layouts in the others cost the campaign $22,093. The campaign spent $12,566 on various get-out-the-vote efforts.

Not all of Slattery's expenses were directly related to his reelection effort. As in past election cycles, he staged Irish coffee receptions at Washington Day, an annual gathering of Kansas Democrats. Costs for these receptions amounted to $7,028, including $1,618 for the Irish coffee, $1,973 for room rentals, $750 to the New Caledonian Bagpipers, and $271 for whipped cream. The campaign paid $537 for Slattery's tuxedo rentals.

With the exception of the $11,711 he spent on year-end holiday cards, Slattery spent little on constituent stroking. Constituent meals cost only $649, while gifts and flowers amounted to $2,439. His investment in the congressional art contest totaled $116.

Although Van Slyke was able to muster only about $37,000 for his ill-fated challenge, he found room in his budget to make five $647 payments on his 1991 Chevrolet Corsica.

*Includes PAC and individual contributions as well as interest earned, party contributions, etc.

District 3 — KANSAS

Rep. Jan Meyers (R)

1992 Election Results

Jan Meyers (R)	169,929	(58%)
Tom Love † (D)	110,071	(38%)

Republican Rep. Jan Meyers had to overcome several obstacles to win her fifth term. Her votes in favor of the 1986 tax reform bill and the 1990 budget compromise, which included tax increases, left her open to a challenge from her party's right wing. That challenge came in the form of Republican state representative Kerry Patrick, a conservative who sought to brand Meyers as too willing to compromise with tax-happy liberal Democrats.

Then, in July 1992, a House task force reported that between 1986 and 1988 House Post Office employees had delivered responses to Meyers's fund-raising solicitations, in violation of both federal law and House rules. Patrick jumped on that revelation, painting her as a typical, scandal-ridden incumbent.

Meyers could not afford to take Patrick's $164,176 challenge lightly. She spent more than $167,000 of her campaign treasury between July 1 and the August 4 primary, including $60,125 paid to Ruth Burke & Associates of Kansas City, Mo., for placing television and radio commercials.

To combat Patrick's attacks on her House Post Office problems, Meyers ran radio ads that focused on her integrity and her clean record at the House bank. Another radio ad rebutted Patrick's claims that Meyers had voted against the balanced budget amendment, while a third trumpeted awards she had received from Citizens Against Government Waste and the National Taxpayers Union. Meyers's lone television commercial touted her ability to deliver federal dollars to the district.

Meyers also invested $56,248 in preprimary persuasion mail. In addition to several more general pieces echoing her broadcast ads, Meyers targeted pro-choice groups and heath care professionals. Each mailer had a response card people could return if they wanted to post a campaign sign in their yard or add their name to one of the campaign's local-endorsement newspaper ads. Signs and newspaper ads for the primary cost $10,703 and $6,550, respectively.

A fifteen-line phonebank was in operation for the last thirty days before the primary, at a cost of $10,360. Public Opinion Strategies of Alexandria, Va., was paid $23,400 for preprimary polling, and Jayhawk Consulting of Overland Park collected $2,300 for a tracking poll.

Following her 23-point victory over Patrick, the general election campaign against state representative Tom Love proved easier. Ruth Burke received only $10,720 for placing radio commercials, and newspapers ads cost $11,621. A limited persuasion mail effort cost $16,089. Seeing no danger in Love's challenge, the campaign opted not to do any polling.

Love spent less than $5,000 and filed no financial documents with the Federal Election Commission.

Campaign Expenditures	Meyers Amount Spent	% of Total
Overhead		
Office furniture/supplies	$ 9,836	2.13
Rent/utilities	17,155	3.71
Salaries	77,346	16.72
Taxes	28,667	6.20
Bank/investment fees	248	.05
Lawyers/accountants	2,746	.59
Telephone	6,279	1.36
Campaign automobile	0	
Computers/office equipment	19,586	4.23
Travel	5,960	1.29
Food/meetings	3,508	.76
Subtotal	171,332	37.04
Fund Raising		
Events	17,245	3.73
Direct mail	26,191	5.66
Telemarketing	0	
Subtotal	43,436	9.39
Polling	25,700	5.56
Advertising		
Electronic media	75,060	16.23
Other media	20,315	4.39
Subtotal	95,376	20.62
Other Campaign Activity		
Persuasion mail/brochures	72,337	15.64
Actual campaigning	33,698	7.28
Staff/volunteers	104	.02
Subtotal	106,139	22.94
Constituent Gifts/Entertainment	6,138	1.33
Donations to		
Candidates from same state	250	.05
Candidates from other states	100	.02
Civic organizations	1,244	.27
Ideological groups	200	.04
Political parties	250	.05
Subtotal	2,044	.44
Unitemized Expenses	12,447	2.69
Total Campaign Expenses	$ 462,610	
PAC Contributions	$ 209,895	
Individual Contributions	200,612	
Total Receipts*	431,501	

*Includes PAC and individual contributions as well as interest earned, party contributions, etc.

† No expenditures or receipts on file. Candidates raising or spending less than $5,000 are not required to file reports with the Federal Election Commission.

KANSAS District 4

Rep. Dan Glickman (D)

1992 Election Results

Dan Glickman (D)	143,671	(52%)
Eric R. Yost (R)	117,070	(42%)
Seth L. Warren † (I)	17,275	(6%)

Anticipating a hard-fought general election contest, Democratic Rep. Dan Glickman and freshman Republican Rep. Dick Nichols began firing salvos at each other well before the August primary. Nichols spent $45,000 to air three television commercials that labeled Glickman a tax-and-spend liberal and slammed him for his 105 overdrafts at the House bank. Glickman returned fire with a $15,000 television buy labeling Nichols a carpetbagger for moving into the district in order to avoid a primary contest with fellow Republican Pat Roberts.

Unfortunately for Nichols, he should have spent his money attacking his Republican primary opponent, state senator Eric R. Yost. Using the same carpetbagger ploy, Yost spent $182,228 and emerged with a comfortable 12-point primary victory.

Unopposed in the Democratic primary, Glickman had all he could handle in the fall campaign. Not only did he have to face the well-funded Yost, but he also had to fend off four independent campaigns that targeted him for defeat.

Following Glickman's vote in favor of imposing federal regulations on the cable television industry, Multimedia Cablevision of Wichita began airing editorials denouncing the incumbent and urging viewers to vote for Yost. The editorials aired at least one hundred times a day on as many as ten cable stations, including CNN. Because Multimedia Cablevision called the spots "editorials," they did not have to report the cost to the Federal Election Commission.

After Glickman voted in favor of the Brady Bill, the National Rifle Association spent $68,983 to attack him, most of which was spent on radio commercials and newspaper ads. Also targeting Glickman were the National Right to Life Political Action Committee and the Eagle Forum Political Action Committee, which spent $7,889 and $5,390, respectively.

Glickman responded by running a $1,046,776 campaign, which was three times as much as he spent in 1990. Nearly $670,000 of his spending was focused into the final six months of the two-year election cycle, giving him a cash advantage of more than a three to one in his head-to-head competition with Yost.

For developing the preprimary commercial and three additional television spots for the fall campaign, Doak, Shrum & Associates of Washington, D.C., received $117,556. The Media Co. of Washington, D.C., collected $304,747 to cover the cost of air time and placement fees.

Glickman paid $10,790 in legal fees to Perkins Coie for their work in reaching an agreement with Multimedia Cablevision, which allowed him to run 600 free spots over the campaign's final week as retribution for the previous "editorial" attacks.

	Glickman		Yost	
Campaign Expenditures	Amount Spent	% of Total	Amount Spent	% of Total
Overhead				
Office furniture/supplies	$ 12,345	1.18	$ 8,401	2.15
Rent/utilities	11,829	1.13	9,318	2.38
Salaries	84,707	8.09	45,778	11.71
Taxes	36,072	3.45	10,206	2.61
Bank/investment fees	116	.01	154	.04
Lawyers/accountants	13,100	1.25	0	
Telephone	7,680	.73	11,356	2.91
Campaign automobile	0		0	
Computers/office equipment	14,203	1.36	4,788	1.23
Travel	25,798	2.46	5,560	1.42
Food/meetings	7,486	.72	1,034	.26
Subtotal	**213,335**	**20.38**	**96,595**	**24.72**
Fund Raising				
Events	162,133	15.49	11,626	2.97
Direct mail	10,414	.99	26,698	6.83
Telemarketing	0		3,625	.93
Subtotal	**172,547**	**16.48**	**41,949**	**10.73**
Polling	**94,000**	**8.98**	**1,500**	**.38**
Advertising				
Electronic media	427,627	40.85	123,599	31.63
Other media	5,610	.54	730	.19
Subtotal	**433,237**	**41.39**	**124,329**	**31.81**
Other Campaign Activity				
Persuasion mail/brochures	28,239	2.70	63,597	16.27
Actual campaigning	58,598	5.60	56,385	14.43
Staff/volunteers	290	.03	237	.06
Subtotal	**87,126**	**8.32**	**120,219**	**30.76**
Constituent Gifts/ Entertainment	**11,804**	**1.13**	**56**	**.01**
Donations to				
Candidates from same state	120	.01	0	
Candidates from other states	1,750	.17	0	
Civic organizations	626	.06	0	
Ideological groups	500	.05	0	
Political parties	19,464	1.86	350	.09
Subtotal	**22,460**	**2.15**	**350**	**.09**
Unitemized Expenses	**12,267**	**1.17**	**5,795**	**1.48**
Total Campaign Expenses	**$ 1,046,776**		**$ 390,792**	
PAC Contributions	$ 421,726		$ 76,011	
Individual Contributions	406,856		284,658	
Total Receipts*	873,194		397,565	

*Includes PAC and individual contributions as well as interest earned, party contributions, etc.

†No expenditures or receipts on file. Candidates raising or spending less than $5,000 are not required to file reports with the Federal Election Commission.

District 1 — KENTUCKY

Rep. Tom Barlow (D)

1992 Election Results

Tom Barlow (D)	128,524	(61%)
Steve Hamrick (R)	83,088	(39%)

Few pundits initially gave Tom Barlow much chance of winning the Democratic primary against nine-term incumbent Rep. Carroll Hubbard, Jr. After all, Barlow had challenged Hubbard in 1986 and received only 19 percent of the vote.

However, that was before the revelation that Hubbard had 152 overdrafts at the House bank. The overdrafts took on added significance in Hubbard's case because he had publicly denied having any. For forty days, Barlow pounded away at the issue.

Barlow invested $31,748, or roughly 60 percent of his $55,000 primary campaign budget, in newspaper ads. Because of its relatively high cost, Barlow shied away from the *Louisville Courier Journal* and instead hit small daily and weekly newspapers such as the *Todd County Standard*, the *Lake News*, the *Sebree Banner*, the *Murray Ledger & Times*, and the *Franklin Favorite*. As campaign spokesman Bobby Miller put it, "We advertised everywhere."

Besides his check problems, Hubbard was chairman of the House Banking Subcommittee on General Oversight, which put him squarely in the middle of the savings and loan debacle. Barlow's newspaper ads also charged Hubbard with failing to foresee the disaster that was costing taxpayers billions.

Barlow invested $6,908 in radio spots, most of which aired during the final week of the primary campaign. Over the final ten days, he sank $6,305 into television commercials. While touching on Hubbard's weaknesses, Miller said the broadcast ads focused more on defining Barlow.

For his part, Hubbard apparently failed to recognize the extent of his vulnerability. While he spent $161,907 through the first six months of 1992, or about three times what Barlow invested, Hubbard still had cash reserves of $244,957 after his loss. He spent $39,629 on television commercials, $21,878 on radio spots, $22,020 on newspaper ads, and $20,744 on persuasion mail.

Barlow funded his primary campaign effort on his own, loaning the campaign $53,000. After Barlow dethroned Hubbard with a 3-point primary win, Miller said the campaign "tapped into traditional Democratic givers, particularly PACs." That effort was spearheaded by Fraioli/Jost of Washington, D.C., which collected $9,312 for its fund-raising efforts. Political action committees ultimately accounted for 48 percent of Barlow's receipts.

Even though no Republican had been elected to represent the district since 1863, Barlow continued to advertise during the fall campaign against Steve Hamrick. "Our message in the general was to pull the Democratic lever," noted Miller. "The Clinton campaign was making a big push at that time and we wanted to tap into that."

Campaign Expenditures	Barlow Amount Spent	Barlow % of Total	Hamrick Amount Spent	Hamrick % of Total
Overhead				
Office furniture/supplies	$ 6,887	3.70	$ 1,212	1.75
Rent/utilities	5,818	3.12	1,679	2.42
Salaries	14,969	8.04	13,730	19.78
Taxes	0		0	
Bank/investment fees	0		134	.19
Lawyers/accountants	375	.20	1,000	1.44
Telephone	6,025	3.23	8,990	12.95
Campaign automobile	912	.49	0	
Computers/office equipment	1,681	.90	2,021	2.91
Travel	553	.30	7,611	10.97
Food/meetings	689	.37	128	.18
Subtotal	**37,909**	**20.35**	**36,505**	**52.60**
Fund Raising				
Events	17,832	9.57	1,578	2.27
Direct mail	2,718	1.46	0	
Telemarketing	0		0	
Subtotal	**20,550**	**11.03**	**1,578**	**2.27**
Polling	**7,000**	**3.76**	**0**	
Advertising				
Electronic media	42,615	22.87	20,233	29.15
Other media	50,024	26.85	505	.73
Subtotal	**92,639**	**49.73**	**20,737**	**29.88**
Other Campaign Activity				
Persuasion mail/brochures	7,841	4.21	4,117	5.93
Actual campaigning	14,445	7.75	5,771	8.32
Staff/volunteers	22	.01	0	
Subtotal	**22,309**	**11.97**	**9,888**	**14.25**
Constituent Gifts/ Entertainment	**300**	**.16**	**0**	
Donations to				
Candidates from same state	0		0	
Candidates from other states	0		0	
Civic organizations	266	.14	155	.22
Ideological groups	0		0	
Political parties	0		235	.34
Subtotal	**266**	**.14**	**390**	**.56**
Unitemized Expenses	**5,328**	**2.86**	**300**	**.43**
Total Campaign Expenses	**$ 186,301**		**$ 69,399**	
PAC Contributions	$ 104,825		$ 13,500	
Individual Contributions	43,478		44,277	
Total Receipts*	218,358		67,051	

*Includes PAC and individual contributions as well as interest earned, party contributions, etc.

KENTUCKY   District 2

Rep. William H. Natcher (D)   *1992 Election Results*   William H. Natcher (D)   126,894   (61%)
                                                                Bruce R. Bartley (R)   79,684   (39%)

As he had since his initial House race in 1953, Rep. William H. Natcher paid for his entire campaign—all $6,625 of it—from his own pocket. After thirty-nine years of refusing to take political contributions of any kind, Natcher had no reason to change.

As in the past, he ran no television commercials. He had no campaign office and no paid or unpaid campaign staff. As the second-ranking Democrat and acting chair of the Appropriations Committee, he had no reason to curry favor with fellow House members by contributing to their campaigns.

Instead, Natcher's campaign was a throwback to the 1950s. His office was his Chevrolet Citation, which he drove through all twenty counties in the district. Campaign stops consisted of conversations in coffee shops and drug stores. Since he never reported what he spent on the coffee he drank or the gasoline he put in his car, the true cost of his campaign was undoubtedly somewhat higher than listed here.

Natcher's spending was almost entirely devoted to dispatching his two Democratic primary opponents. Between April 20 and the May 26 primary, Natcher spent $6,580 to run fifty small ads in twenty-seven newspapers. Each ad simply advised readers that he was the incumbent and was seeking reelection. Items listed on his campaign financial statements as "miscellaneous and postage" amounted to $19.47. He received 71 percent of the 49,851 primary votes.

In twenty previous House campaigns, Natcher had run without opposition seven times and had received less than 60 percent of the general election vote only three times. Republican Martin A. Tori spent a combined total of more than $228,000 on his unsuccessful campaigns in 1988 and 1990. Yet, while he outspent Natcher by seventeen to one, Tori could not hold the incumbent under 60 percent.

With that electoral history, it was not surprising that the only Republican to step forward in 1992 was Bruce R. Bartley, a twenty-five-year-old college student. Bartley spent $133 to print some campaign stationery and $979 on bumper stickers and buttons.

Natcher completely ignored Bartley's candidacy. After May 27, Natcher reported expenses to the Federal Election Commission totaling just $25.20.

However, while Natcher was thoroughly disinterested in Republican activity in his district, national Democratic party organizations were intensely concerned. The Democratic National Committee paid Lauer, Lalley & Associates of Washington, D.C., $17,633 for polling in the district, ostensibly on behalf of Natcher. Garin-Hart of Washington, D.C., collected $137 from the Democratic Congressional Campaign Committee for looking at some polling data.

Campaign Expenditures	Natcher Amount Spent	Natcher % of Total	Bartley Amount Spent	Bartley % of Total
Overhead				
Office furniture/supplies	$ 45	.67	$ 133	11.81
Rent/utilities	0		0	
Salaries	0		0	
Taxes	0		0	
Bank/investment fees	0		0	
Lawyers/accountants	0		0	
Telephone	0		0	
Campaign automobile	0		0	
Computers/office equipment	0		0	
Travel	0		0	
Food/meetings	0		0	
Subtotal	**45**	**.67**	**133**	**11.81**
Fund Raising				
Events	0		0	
Direct mail	0		0	
Telemarketing	0		0	
Subtotal	**0**		**0**	
Polling	**0**		**0**	
Advertising				
Electronic media	0		0	
Other media	6,580	99.32	0	
Subtotal	**6,580**	**99.32**	**0**	
Other Campaign Activity				
Persuasion mail/brochures	0		0	
Actual campaigning	0		979	87.06
Staff/volunteers	0		0	
Subtotal	**0**		**979**	**87.06**
Constituent Gifts/ Entertainment	**0**		**0**	
Donations to				
Candidates from same state	0		0	
Candidates from other states	0		0	
Civic organizations	0		0	
Ideological groups	0		0	
Political parties	0		0	
Subtotal	**0**		**0**	
Unitemized Expenses	**0**		**13**	**1.16**
Total Campaign Expenses	**$ 6,625**		**$ 1,125**	
PAC Contributions	$ 0		$ 0	
Individual Contributions	0		0	
Total Receipts*	**6,624**		**1,125**	

*Includes PAC and individual contributions as well as interest earned, party contributions, etc.

KENTUCKY

District 3

Rep. Romano L. Mazzoli (D)

1992 Election Results

Romano L. Mazzoli (D)   148,066   (53%)
Susan B. Stokes (R)   132,689   (47%)

Rep. Romano L. Mazzoli was one of only ten victorious House incumbents who were outspent by their challengers, but his financial difficulties were entirely of his own making. In December 1989 Mazzoli announced he would no longer accept donations from political action committees. Then, in February 1992, he announced he would only accept individual contributions of $100 or less. As a result, small contributions comprised 93 percent of his donations, or $202,157.

Mazzoli said he imposed these rigid limits because of his strong belief in campaign finance reform. It certainly was not because he was swimming in money and could easily afford to take the moral stand. He began the election cycle with only $291 in his campaign account and his cash reserves never topped the $33,579 he had at the beginning of September 1992.

With her large monetary advantage, Republican Susan B. Stokes hired the Farwell Group of New Orleans, La., and over the final two months of the campaign paid them $194,134 for creating and placing four television and two radio commercials. Stokes directly purchased $3,145 in TV air time and spent $2,614 on additional advertising production. The National Republican Congressional Committee augmented her advertising budget with a $45,000 payment to the Farwell Group.

Stokes's television commercials attacked Mazzoli as an extremist because he opposes abortion even in cases of incest and rape. Other ads attacked Mazzoli for his vote in favor of a congressional pay raise and touted Stokes's outsider status. She also ran ads attacking the incumbent for voting in favor of a campaign finance reform bill that included partial public financing of congressional campaigns, a point that played directly into Mazzoli's strength.

With little money, Mazzoli let Stokes's charges go largely unanswered for weeks, and when he finally went on the air it was with a $20,000 radio campaign designed and placed by Sheehy, Knopf & Shaver of Louisville. His ads focused on his support for campaign finance reform and juxtaposed his lack of money to wage an expensive media campaign with Stokes's negative media bombardment. Sheehy, Knopf also collected $11,000 for placing newspaper ads that struck the same themes.

Mazzoli received no coordinated advertising help from the Democratic Congressional Campaign Committee. When the Kentucky Right to Life Association began airing radio and television ads in support of Mazzoli, he asked them to stop. A total of $5,973 was spent by Kentucky and national right-to-life groups.

After his hard fought victory, Mazzoli announced he would not seek reelection in 1994.

Campaign Expenditures	Mazzoli Amount Spent	Mazzoli % of Total	Stokes Amount Spent	Stokes % of Total
Overhead				
Office furniture/supplies	$ 6,154	3.44	$ 3,978	1.09
Rent/utilities	1,282	.72	1,938	.53
Salaries	8,239	4.61	20,560	5.66
Taxes	2,022	1.13	8,109	2.23
Bank/investment fees	2,864	1.60	185	.05
Lawyers/accountants	0		0	
Telephone	5,777	3.23	5,197	1.43
Campaign automobile	0		0	
Computers/office equipment	8,980	5.03	6,890	1.90
Travel	11,940	6.68	5,405	1.49
Food/meetings	470	.26	337	.09
Subtotal	**47,727**	**26.71**	**52,599**	**14.47**
Fund Raising				
Events	16,118	9.02	11,126	3.06
Direct mail	18,018	10.08	34,572	9.51
Telemarketing	0		0	
Subtotal	**34,136**	**19.10**	**45,698**	**12.57**
Polling	0		23,800	6.55
Advertising				
Electronic media	20,000	11.19	199,893	55.00
Other media	14,674	8.21	639	.18
Subtotal	**34,674**	**19.40**	**200,532**	**55.17**
Other Campaign Activity				
Persuasion mail/brochures	49,827	27.88	23,733	6.53
Actual campaigning	9,187	5.14	14,426	3.97
Staff/volunteers	750	.42	0	
Subtotal	**59,764**	**33.45**	**38,160**	**10.50**
Constituent Gifts/ Entertainment	56	.03	0	
Donations to				
Candidates from same state	0		0	
Candidates from other states	0		0	
Civic organizations	140	.08	0	
Ideological groups	50	.03	0	
Political parties	2,087	1.17	0	
Subtotal	**2,277**	**1.27**	**0**	
Unitemized Expenses	57	.03	2,661	.73
Total Campaign Expenses	$ 178,692		$ 363,448	
PAC Contributions	$ 0		$ 170,123	
Individual Contributions	217,057		260,633	
Total Receipts*	223,091		446,807	

*Includes PAC and individual contributions as well as interest earned, party contributions, etc.

KENTUCKY   District 4

Rep. Jim Bunning (R)   *1992 Election Results*   Jim Bunning (R)   139,634   (62%)
                                                                  Floyd G. Poore (D) 86,890   (38%)

Faced with a Democratic challenger who had more than three times the resources of his 1990 opponent and fighting the effects of redistricting, which added large numbers of Democrats to his constituency, Rep. Jim Bunning spent nearly $1 million on his third reelection campaign.

Bunning, a former major league pitcher, started advertising early, investing more than $100,000 in broadcast ads by the end of September 1992. Chief of staff Dave York said the ad campaign began positively, focusing on Bunning's background. But things quickly turned nasty. A spoof of the Grey Poupon mustard commercials showed someone resembling Floyd G. Poore, his Democratic opponent, sitting in the back of a Rolls Royce, which York said was meant to "show that this was a rich guy who used to collect Rolls Royces but was trying to pass himself off as a man of the people." Another ad charged that Poore was a hypocrite for discussing children's issues because he had missed child support payments in the early 1970s. A third spot attacked him for taking five-month vacations. The Media Team of Alexandria, Va., received $84,302 for creating six television and six radio commercials. National Media, also of Alexandria, received $438,137 for placing the ads.

Bunning invested $35,375 in newspaper advertising, hitting every weekly paper in the district, as well as several community magazines. He also spent $8,430 to place ads with organizations such as Right to Life of Louisville, the Campbell County Farm Bureau, the Kidney Foundation, the North Kentucky Chamber of Commerce, the Kenton County Republican party, and the District 4 Republican party.

Bunning spent $100,952 on an in-house persuasion mail effort. Yard signs cost the campaign $17,428. Faeth & Faeth of Covington was paid $10,022 to make certain his supporters turned out to vote.

Bunning ran a sizable permanent campaign. Monthly rent on his campaign office rose from $695 to $719 during the election cycle, and a second office opened in July 1992. In July 1991 Debbie McKinney, district administrator on Bunning's congressional staff, began receiving a monthly campaign salary of slightly more than $1,000. According to York, McKinney split her time between her government and campaign duties, a task made easier by the fact that the campaign rents its office down the hall from Bunning's congressional office. By election day, his campaign staff had grown to five, including two other congressional staffers.

Poore, an unsuccessful candidate for governor in 1991, put $107,177 into advertising but failed to make any headway despite the fact that registered Democrats outnumbered Republicans in the district by more than two to one.

Campaign Expenditures	Bunning Amount Spent	Bunning % of Total	Poore Amount Spent	Poore % of Total
Overhead				
Office furniture/supplies	$ 10,224	1.05	$ 6,197	2.00
Rent/utilities	19,817	2.03	5,642	1.82
Salaries	34,340	3.52	16,264	5.26
Taxes	18,892	1.94	6,262	2.02
Bank/investment fees	1,578	.16	214	.07
Lawyers/accountants	0		2,418	.78
Telephone	15,008	1.54	5,182	1.67
Campaign automobile	20,395	2.09	0	
Computers/office equipment	15,801	1.62	159	.05
Travel	28,143	2.88	16,293	5.27
Food/meetings	1,092	.11	723	.23
Subtotal	**165,289**	**16.94**	**59,353**	**19.18**
Fund Raising				
Events	52,986	5.43	28,499	9.21
Direct mail	25,901	2.65	0	
Telemarketing	3,171	.32	0	
Subtotal	**82,059**	**8.40**	**28,499**	**9.21**
Polling	**0**		**18,278**	**5.91**
Advertising				
Electronic media	522,451	53.53	81,839	26.45
Other media	43,805	4.49	25,338	8.19
Subtotal	**566,256**	**58.02**	**107,177**	**34.64**
Other Campaign Activity				
Persuasion mail/brochures	100,952	10.34	49,225	15.91
Actual campaigning	37,520	3.84	46,318	14.97
Staff/volunteers	1,191	.12	13	
Subtotal	**139,663**	**14.31**	**95,556**	**30.88**
Constituent Gifts/Entertainment	9,327	.96	0	
Donations to				
Candidates from same state	6,678	.68	0	
Candidates from other states	0		0	
Civic organizations	390	.04	540	.17
Ideological groups	0		0	
Political parties	3,225	.33	0	
Subtotal	**10,293**	**1.05**	**540**	**.17**
Unitemized Expenses	3,037	.31	0	
Total Campaign Expenses	$ **975,925**		$ **309,403**	
PAC Contributions	$ 439,491		$ 106,573	
Individual Contributions	454,791		186,455	
Total Receipts*	946,781		311,111	

*Includes PAC and individual contributions as well as interest earned, party contributions, etc.

District 5 — KENTUCKY

Rep. Harold Rogers (R)

1992 Election Results

Harold Rogers (R)	115,255	(55%)
John Doug Hays (D)	95,760	(45%)

Running unopposed in 1986, 1988, and 1990, Rep. Harold Rogers spent a combined total of $484,046. In 1991 his low-key permanent campaign cost only $49,075. However, when redistricting transformed his safe Republican district into one in which 55 percent of the registered voters were Democrats, Roger's days of relaxed campaigning quickly drew to a close.

During the first six months of 1992, Rogers spent nearly $209,000, despite being unopposed in the May primary. He paid One Acorn Management of Somerset $25,000 to provide strategic advice. Sandler-Innocenzi of Washington, D.C., collected $92,537 for preprimary radio and television commercials, including $50,000 to cover the cost of air time.

Rogers then invested $627,624 over the final six months of the election cycle to defeat former state senator John Doug Hays, more than half of which was spent in October. Sandler-Innocenzi and One Acorn Management collected $267,943 and $25,000, respectively, for their work in the general election campaign.

The six television commercials Sandler-Innocenzi developed took the high road, focusing on Rogers's ability to deliver federal dollars to the district for flood control, highway tunnel construction, and the Big South Fork National River and Recreation area. "In the year of the anti-incumbent, we ran against the grain," explained district administrator and campaign manager Robert L. Mitchell. "Rogers likes to work on projects, and he gets things done for the district, so we ran on that. Some people call it pork barrel, but we don't."

Rogers used radio spots to deliver his attacks. Based on polls that showed the district to be strongly antiabortion, he aired radio ads criticizing Hays for his pro-choice stance. Another radio commercial pointed to the numerous votes Hays had missed during his tenure in the state senate.

Telemark America of London, Ky., collected $63,333 from Rogers's campaign and $34,077 from the National Republican Congressional Committee for its massive phonebanking effort. Rather than targeting Republican households, the phonebank was directed predominantly at Democratic households in order to find people Mitchell described as "philosophically in tune" with Rogers. Once identified, these voters received follow-up persuasion mailers.

The phonebank was so effective that even Hays was impressed. "They went on night after night," Hays lamented. "People got several calls, and they were calling me a baby killer. That issue probably hurt me more than anything else. I wish I'd had the money to do phonebanks, but I didn't and couldn't respond."

Campaign Expenditures	Rogers Amount Spent	Rogers % of Total	Hays Amount Spent	Hays % of Total
Overhead				
Office furniture/supplies	$ 14,071	1.59	$ 3,931	1.42
Rent/utilities	4,633	.52	3,988	1.44
Salaries	36,206	4.09	21,794	7.87
Taxes	21,376	2.41	7,819	2.82
Bank/investment fees	433	.05	73	.03
Lawyers/accountants	0		0	
Telephone	12,163	1.37	6,580	2.38
Campaign automobile	0		0	
Computers/office equipment	10,311	1.16	2,080	.75
Travel	19,790	2.24	9,729	3.51
Food/meetings	3,441	.39	0	
Subtotal	**122,425**	**13.83**	**55,993**	**20.22**
Fund Raising				
Events	33,411	3.77	5,125	1.85
Direct mail	55,368	6.25	4,354	1.57
Telemarketing	0		0	
Subtotal	**88,778**	**10.03**	**9,479**	**3.42**
Polling	**23,015**	**2.60**	**5,000**	**1.81**
Advertising				
Electronic media	360,502	40.72	96,711	34.93
Other media	22,651	2.56	44,635	16.12
Subtotal	**383,153**	**43.28**	**141,346**	**51.05**
Other Campaign Activity				
Persuasion mail/brochures	27,038	3.05	8,237	2.98
Actual campaigning	145,513	16.44	56,690	20.48
Staff/volunteers	4,265	.48	27	.01
Subtotal	**176,816**	**19.97**	**64,953**	**23.46**
Constituent Gifts/ Entertainment	**20,360**	**2.30**	**0**	
Donations to				
Candidates from same state	0		0	
Candidates from other states	0		0	
Civic organizations	1,305	.15	0	
Ideological groups	0		0	
Political parties	1,050	.12	0	
Subtotal	**2,355**	**.27**	**0**	
Unitemized Expenses	**68,397**	**7.73**	**89**	**.03**
Total Campaign Expenses	**$ 885,300**		**$ 276,861**	
PAC Contributions	$ 233,890		$ 58,150	
Individual Contributions	371,001		187,218	
Total Receipts*	651,821		280,313	

*Includes PAC and individual contributions as well as interest earned, party contributions, etc.

KENTUCKY   District 6

Rep. Scotty Baesler (D)

1992 Election Results

Scotty Baesler (D)	135,613	(61%)
Charles W. Ellinger (R)	87,816	(39%)

Three-term Lexington Mayor Scotty Baesler was prepared for a tough, expensive campaign against Republican Rep. Larry J. Hopkins. While Hopkins had been soundly thrashed in his 1991 gubernatorial bid, collecting only 38 percent of the vote in his own congressional district, the district remained marginally Republican and the seven-term incumbent retained a $665,000 campaign treasury.

However, the big race never materialized. Wounded by accusations that he had misrepresented his military record and with eighty-three overdrafts at the House bank, Hopkins opted to retire rather than face voters again. That decision was made much easier by the fact that Hopkins was able to pocket his entire campaign treasury as his own personal retirement account.

Baesler began preparing in January 1992 for the May primary battle by hiring media consultant Fenn & King Communications of Washington, D.C., but with Hopkins out of the way, Baesler coasted to victory. He won 82 percent of the vote in the five-candidate Democratic primary before pasting county council member Charles W. Ellinger in November.

With little meaningful opposition, more than half of Baesler's campaign spending was funneled into overhead. Salary payments to his four campaign staffers accounted for one-quarter of his spending. In addition to the $31,420 he paid campaign manager Chuck Atkins, Baesler paid his daughter $7,195.

For designing a preprimary get-out-the-vote postcard and general consultation, Fenn & King collected $6,167. One month before the primary, the firm was also reimbursed $4,283 for the purchase of sunflower seeds, which Baesler handed out on his tours of the district. During the fall campaign, the company billed Baesler $32,652 for placing one television spot and $8,090 to cover its retainer and miscellaneous expenses.

Baesler spent $1,592 before the primary to advertise in every weekly newspaper in the district. Blaemire Communications of Reston, Va., received $7,000 for producing the reminder postcard designed by Fenn & King.

For the contest with Ellinger, Baesler spent $11,088 on radio spots and $2,963 on newspaper ads. The campaign also produced another reminder postcard for $2,695.

Harrison & Goldberg of Cambridge, Mass., received $8,000 for conducting a poll shortly before the general election. Atkins said that despite winning the race handily, "You don't take anything for granted when you get that close." Apparently, the Democratic National Committee had the same philosophy because they paid Lauer, Lalley & Associates of Washington, D.C., $17,633 for polling on Baesler's behalf.

	Baesler		Ellinger	
Campaign Expenditures	Amount Spent	% of Total	Amount Spent	% of Total
Overhead				
Office furniture/supplies	$ 6,018	2.21	$ 1,825	2.78
Rent/utilities	5,106	1.88	4,445	6.77
Salaries	67,661	24.87	5,336	8.13
Taxes	34,295	12.61	0	
Bank/investment fees	729	.27	114	.17
Lawyers/accountants	0		0	
Telephone	8,636	3.17	4,059	6.18
Campaign automobile	0		0	
Computers/office equipment	3,422	1.26	1,241	1.89
Travel	13,134	4.83	1,590	2.42
Food/meetings	545	.20	20	.03
Subtotal	**139,545**	**51.30**	**18,631**	**28.38**
Fund Raising				
Events	7,632	2.81	1,123	1.71
Direct mail	15,377	5.56	2,616	3.99
Telemarketing	0		0	
Subtotal	**23,009**	**8.46**	**3,739**	**5.70**
Polling	**8,000**	**2.94**	**0**	
Advertising				
Electronic media	55,519	20.41	11,367	17.32
Other media	4,765	1.75	3,708	5.65
Subtotal	**60,284**	**22.16**	**15,075**	**22.96**
Other Campaign Activity				
Persuasion mail/brochures	12,965	4.77	16,100	24.53
Actual campaigning	25,680	9.44	11,132	16.96
Staff/volunteers	264	.10	215	.33
Subtotal	**38,909**	**14.30**	**27,447**	**41.81**
Constituent Gifts/ Entertainment	**2,018**	**.74**	**0**	
Donations to				
Candidates from same state	0		0	
Candidates from other states	0		0	
Civic organizations	101	.04	50	.08
Ideological groups	0		0	
Political parties	160	.06	0	
Subtotal	**261**	**.10**	**50**	**.08**
Unitemized Expenses	**0**		**702**	**1.07**
Total Campaign Expenses	**$ 272,027**		**$ 65,644**	
PAC Contributions	**$ 0**		**$ 9,291**	
Individual Contributions	**295,963**		**44,422**	
Total Receipts*	**301,557**		**70,095**	

*Includes PAC and individual contributions as well as interest earned, party contributions, etc.

District 1 — LOUISIANA

Rep. Robert L. Livingston (R)

1992 Election Results

Robert L. Livingston (R)	83,685	(73%)
Anne Thompson † (R)	11,620	(10%)
Vincent J. Bruno † (R)	7,847	(7%)

Since his special election victory in 1977, Rep. Robert L. Livingston had seen his winning percentage drop below 80 percent only once, and while redistricting added new territory and about 100,000 new voters, it left the political tenor of District 1 largely unchanged. With no overdrafts at the House bank, he also had little need to worry about an anti-incumbent backlash. Nevertheless, when five challengers entered the open primary, Livingston decided to take no chances and invested three times as much in his 1992 campaign as he had in 1990.

Although Beuerman Consultants of New Orleans was hired in July 1992 to assemble the necessary campaign infrastructure, the bulk of Livingston's direct appeals to voters was restricted to the final six weeks of the primary campaign.

Early polls showed Livingston drawing 75 percent of the vote in suburban New Orleans, so Greg Beuerman focused the campaign's initial radio buys on the outlying parishes where a sixty-second spot can be bought for as little as $5. With comparable radio spots in New Orleans costing up to $155, Beurman opted to avoid that market until the final week of the campaign.

Beuerman also designed a twelve-page tabloid-style persuasion piece that was both mailed and used as a newspaper insert, primarily in newly acquired areas of the district. Among other things, the mailer covered Livingston's sponsorship of a bill that would "lock the door and throw away the key" on those convicted three times of a violent crime and highlighted his high ratings from the American Conservative Union, the National Tax Limitation Committee, and the National Federation of Independent Businesses. In all, Beuerman collected $37,325.

Issues Management Group of New Orleans received $56,011 for designing and placing the campaign's three television commercials, including a spot covering his anticrime bill. Rather than running from incumbency, his other ads embraced its power, in one case relating how Livingston had intervened to convince the Internal Revenue Service to reverse a decision that had cost a constituent $40,000.

In August 1991 Livingston threw a party for volunteers and past contributors that cost the campaign $7,541, including $5,000 for catering and $2,000 for music. Livingston paid $2,796 for "Mardis Gras in Washington" expenses over the two years. Doubloons, which he threw out during Mardis Gras parades, cost $1,307.

Livingston's five challengers spent a combined total of $23,965. Anne Thompson and Vincent J. Bruno, who finished second and third, respectively, in the open primary, never filed financial reports with the Federal Election Commission.

Campaign Expenditures	Livingston Amount Spent	% of Total
Overhead		
Office furniture/supplies	$ 1,922	.60
Rent/utilities	7,099	2.21
Salaries	0	
Taxes	6,574	2.05
Bank/investment fees	0	
Lawyers/accountants	0	
Telephone	1,645	.51
Campaign automobile	0	
Computers/office equipment	5,433	1.69
Travel	7,174	2.24
Food/meetings	0	
Subtotal	**29,848**	**9.30**
Fund Raising		
Events	39,819	12.41
Direct mail	14,855	4.63
Telemarketing	0	
Subtotal	**54,675**	**17.03**
Polling	**19,700**	**6.14**
Advertising		
Electronic media	69,188	21.55
Other media	12,870	4.01
Subtotal	**82,059**	**25.56**
Other Campaign Activity		
Persuasion mail/brochures	9,378	2.92
Actual campaigning	26,658	8.31
Staff/volunteers	0	
Subtotal	**36,037**	**11.23**
Constituent Gifts/Entertainment	**10,817**	**3.37**
Donations to		
Candidates from same state	8,700	2.71
Candidates from other states	22,000	6.85
Civic organizations	2,309	.72
Ideological groups	1,300	.40
Political parties	26,000	8.10
Subtotal	**60,309**	**18.79**
Unitemized Expenses	**27,546**	**8.58**
Total Campaign Expenses	**$ 320,991**	
PAC Contributions	$ 133,247	
Individual Contributions	170,424	
Total Receipts*	337,316	

*Includes PAC and individual contributions as well as interest earned, party contributions, etc.

† No expenditures or receipts on file. Candidates raising or spending less than $5,000 are not required to file reports with the Federal Election Commission.

LOUISIANA — District 2

Rep. William J. Jefferson (D)

1992 Election Results

William J. Jefferson (D)	67,030	(73%)
Wilma Knox Irvin (D)	14,121	(15%)
Roger C. Johnson † (I)	10,090	(11%)

Rep. William J. Jefferson's 1992 reelection campaign was considerably easier than his initial race in 1990, when he spent more than $500,000 to defeat eleven other candidates seeking to succeed retiring Rep. Lindy Boggs. Challenged only by fellow Democrat Wilma Knox Irvin and independent Roger C. Johnson, who together spent less than $28,000, Jefferson garnered 73 percent of the vote in the open primary and avoided having to run in the November general election.

To help retire his 1990 campaign debts of more than $150,000, Jefferson immediately turned to the Washington, D.C., political action committee (PAC) community. A Washington reception in April 1991 helped generate $64,200 in PAC contributions, which accounted for 75 percent of his donations for the first six months of 1991. Over the two-year election cycle, PACs accounted for 61 percent of Jefferson's funds.

Jefferson kept his overhead down by housing his campaign at the headquarters of Progressive Democrats, a local political organization that he founded. While he spent $24,960 on travel, $5,895 of that total was incurred during his stay in New York for the Democratic National Convention, including $2,610 for a party at the New York Hilton.

Donations to other candidates, Democratic party organizations, and various causes amounted to twice what Jefferson invested in advertising. The chief beneficiary was the NACCP, which received four contributions totaling $1,250. The Alumni Association at Southern University, Jefferson's alma mater, received $500, as did the Rev. James Landrum. Young Democrats of America received two checks totaling $650. Jefferson gave $250 to the Close-Up Foundation, $340 to the Veterans of Foreign Wars, $400 to the Greater St. Matthew Chapel Baptist Church, $202 to the Louisiana Association of the Deaf, and $300 to the Anti-Defamation League of B'nai Brith. He also bought a $218 videocassette recorder for the Flint-Goodrich Hospital in New Orleans.

The campaign itself was largely a grass-roots operation. With the help of volunteers, Jefferson distributed $28,160 worth of campaign literature. Persuasion mail added $16,136. Jefferson spent $14,125 on yard signs, $9,767 on his in-house phonebank, and $2,522 on buttons and other campaign paraphernalia.

Payments to consultants were relatively low. Enterprise Consultants of New Orleans collected $27,100 for general campaign advice and coordination. Col-Sol of New Orleans received $5,450 for creating and placing radio commercials, and Silas Lee & Associates of New Orleans was paid $9,800 for polling.

	Jefferson		Irvin	
Campaign Expenditures	Amount Spent	% of Total	Amount Spent	% of Total
Overhead				
Office furniture/supplies	$ 5,370	1.83	$ 0	
Rent/utilities	0		200	.87
Salaries	20,287	6.91	548	2.38
Taxes	0		0	
Bank/investment fees	2,306	.79	0	
Lawyers/accountants	22,300	7.60	0	
Telephone	0		1,270	5.51
Campaign automobile	0		0	
Computers/office equipment	0		0	
Travel	24,960	8.51	0	
Food/meetings	922	.31	0	
Subtotal	**76,146**	**25.95**	**2,018**	**8.76**
Fund Raising				
Events	37,235	12.69	0	
Direct mail	0		0	
Telemarketing	0		0	
Subtotal	**37,235**	**12.69**	**0**	
Polling	**9,800**	**3.34**	**0**	
Advertising				
Electronic media	6,050	2.06	5,000	21.70
Other media	3,858	1.31	868	3.77
Subtotal	**9,908**	**3.38**	**5,868**	**25.47**
Other Campaign Activity				
Persuasion mail/brochures	44,296	15.10	8,996	39.04
Actual campaigning	60,027	20.46	6,159	26.73
Staff/volunteers	0		0	
Subtotal	**104,323**	**35.56**	**15,154**	**65.77**
Constituent Gifts/Entertainment	**4,116**	**1.40**	**0**	
Donations to				
Candidates from same state	2,650	.90	0	
Candidates from other states	3,300	1.12	0	
Civic organizations	5,531	1.89	0	
Ideological groups	3,490	1.19	0	
Political parties	4,887	1.67	0	
Subtotal	**19,858**	**6.77**	**0**	
Unitemized Expenses	**32,027**	**10.92**	**0**	
Total Campaign Expenses	**$ 293,412**		**$ 23,041**	
PAC Contributions	**$ 223,735**		**$ 0**	
Individual Contributions	**139,981**		**10,290**	
Total Receipts*	**376,227**		**44,246**	

*Includes PAC and individual contributions as well as interest earned, party contributions, etc.

† No expenditures or receipts on file. Candidates raising or spending less than $5,000 are not required to file reports with the Federal Election Commission.

LOUISIANA

District 3

Rep. W. J. "Billy" Tauzin (D)

1992 Election Results

W. J. "Billy" Tauzin (D)	82,047	(82%)
Paul I. Boynton † (R)	18,402	(18%)

In six previous reelection bids, Rep. W. J. "Billy" Tauzin had never received less than 85 percent of the vote and had run unopposed three times. Unaffected by redistricting, Tauzin nevertheless felt it necessary to spend $294,430 to defeat Republican Paul I. Boynton, who spent less than $5,000 and garnered only 18 percent of the vote.

Having used nearly $276,000 of his 1990 House campaign funds to pay off old debts associated with his failed 1987 gubernatorial bid, Tauzin began 1991 with campaign cash reserves of only $48,412. With the uncertainties of redistricting looming, he spent $34,968 during 1991 in search of funds to replenish his bank account.

The principal targets of Tauzin's off-year fundraising efforts were political action committees (PACs). He spent $23,760 on a Washington, D.C., event that helped push his PAC contributions for the year to $157,050. The remainder of his off-year fundraising outlays were put into his annual riverboat party for members of his congressional club, known as the "Billy Club Society." Individual contributions during 1991 amounted to only $44,700.

Tauzin's fund raising picked up in 1992 where it left off in 1991. He spent a total of $61,239 to raise $285,509 from PACs and $85,105 from individual contributors. By the close of the two-year cycle, Tauzin had increased his cash reserves to $327,478.

Only 19 percent of Tauzin's expenditures for the cycle went into direct appeals for votes. He invested $6,909 to air commercials on local cable television systems and another $7,061 to run his radio spots. Numerous ads in small papers such as the *Assumption Pioneer*, the *Morgan City Daily Review*, the *Cajun Gazette*, and the *Donaldsonville Chief* cost the campaign $21,367. Printing charges for his campaign literature and postage for limited persuasion mailings totaled only $17,461. The campaign spent just $898 on yard signs and posters.

Tauzin invested $23,051, or 8 percent of his campaign outlays, in constituent stroking. Each year he tapped his campaign treasury to pay for a "Washington, D.C., Mardi Gras," a party primarily for Louisianans living in Washington who were unable to attend the real thing. The 1991 and 1992 events cost the campaign $6,455 and $6,558, respectively. Other constituent social events cost the campaign $3,415. The campaign spent $4,322 on holiday cards, $1,770 on inaugural tickets, $476 on flowers for constituents, and $55 for the congressional art contest.

Transfers of funds from Tauzin's House campaign to cover remaining debts from his 1987 gubernatorial bid totaled $15,922 and were not included in this analysis.

Campaign Expenditures	Tauzin Amount Spent	% of Total
Overhead		
Office furniture/supplies	$ 6,989	2.37
Rent/utilities	10,696	3.63
Salaries	33,499	11.38
Taxes	2,324	.79
Bank/investment fees	66	.02
Lawyers/accountants	0	
Telephone	4,513	1.53
Campaign automobile	0	
Computers/office equipment	16,739	5.69
Travel	17,633	5.99
Food/meetings	2,328	.79
Subtotal	**94,788**	**32.19**
Fund Raising		
Events	96,207	32.68
Direct mail	0	
Telemarketing	0	
Subtotal	**96,207**	**32.68**
Polling	**0**	
Advertising		
Electronic media	13,970	4.74
Other media	22,258	7.56
Subtotal	**36,228**	**12.30**
Other Campaign Activity		
Persuasion mail/brochures	17,461	5.93
Actual campaigning	3,421	1.16
Staff/volunteers	124	.04
Subtotal	**21,005**	**7.13**
Constituent Gifts/Entertainment	**23,051**	**7.83**
Donations to		
Candidates from same state	1,100	.37
Candidates from other states	2,850	.97
Civic organizations	2,520	.86
Ideological groups	100	.03
Political parties	16,500	5.60
Subtotal	**23,070**	**7.84**
Unitemized Expenses	**81**	**.03**
Total Campaign Expenses	**$ 294,430**	
PAC Contributions	**$ 442,559**	
Individual Contributions	**129,805**	
Total Receipts*	**590,179**	

*Includes PAC and individual contributions as well as interest earned, party contributions, etc.

† No expenditures or receipts on file. Candidates raising or spending less than $5,000 are not required to file reports with the Federal Election Commission.

LOUISIANA — District 4

Rep. Cleo Fields (D)

1992 Election Results

Cleo Fields (D)	143,980	(74%)
Charles Jones (D)	50,851	(26%)

Meandering through twenty-eight parishes and five of the state's largest cities, the Z-shaped District 4 was specifically drawn to elect one of two Democratic black state senators, thirteen-year incumbent Charles Jones or Cleo Fields, who chaired the state senate's reapportionment committee. Fields outspent Jones by more than two to one and coasted to easy wins in the open primary and subsequent election day runoff.

Field's financial advantage enabled him to put more money into his advertising than Jones spent on his entire campaign. Fields paid Roy Fletcher of Baton Rouge $96,791 for producing and placing a series of positive television commercials, which district director Johnny G. Anderson said focused on job creation, education, improving access to and reducing the cost of health care, and the need to slice foreign aid to pay for domestic spending. National Management Consultants of Baton Rouge received $10,914 for placing companion radio spots, and the campaign directly purchased $15,014 of radio time.

Billboards reading "Leadership You Can Trust" and "For Our Children and Our Jobs. Cleo Fields for Congress" cost the campaign $17,050. The campaign spent $6,475 to have sky writers spell out "Vote Cleo" or pull banners reading "Cleo Fields for Congress" over Saturday afternoon football crowds. Only $605 was invested in newspaper and journal advertising.

Instead of sending out persuasion mail, "We wore out our shoes," Anderson said. Fields and hundreds of student volunteers walked door to door, handing out the campaign's brochure. Other volunteers put up yard signs, which cost the campaign $13,041.

To ensure that his efforts did not go to waste, Fields invested heavily in his get-out-the-vote effort. For the October 3 primary, he paid 380 individuals a total of $20,995 to walk door to door, reminding people to vote. A scaled-down effort on November 3 employed 174 people and cost $13,120. To make certain that the canvassers would be heard, the campaign spent $152 on bullhorns.

Fields's modest overhead expenses would have been considerably lower had he not spent $7,884 on chartered flights to ferry him around a district that takes four hours to traverse by automobile.

Kimberly A. Scott of Washington, D.C., received $2,330 for helping to raise money from political action committees, which accounted for only 19 percent of Fields's total contributions. Fields raised 76 percent of his money from individual contributors who gave at least $200, and most of that was raised by various fund-raising committees such as "Women for Fields." Small contributions, most of which were collected by volunteers during their precinct canvassing, totaled $13,973, or 5 percent of his receipts.

Campaign Expenditures	Fields Amount Spent	Fields % of Total	Jones Amount Spent	Jones % of Total
Overhead				
Office furniture/supplies	$ 1,707	.59	$ 150	.12
Rent/utilities	1,000	.34	7,968	6.18
Salaries	14,127	4.85	3,440	2.67
Taxes	0		0	
Bank/investment fees	229	.08	0	
Lawyers/accountants	669	.23	1,500	1.16
Telephone	2,305	.79	3,088	2.39
Campaign automobile	0		0	
Computers/office equipment	265	.09	0	
Travel	20,849	7.16	10,721	8.31
Food/meetings	1,503	.52	0	
Subtotal	**42,653**	**14.66**	**26,867**	**20.83**
Fund Raising				
Events	12,135	4.17	9,731	7.54
Direct mail	0		0	
Telemarketing	0		0	
Subtotal	**12,135**	**4.17**	**9,731**	**7.54**
Polling	**0**		**0**	
Advertising				
Electronic media	123,051	42.28	50,879	39.44
Other media	24,130	8.29	4,350	3.37
Subtotal	**147,181**	**50.57**	**55,229**	**42.81**
Other Campaign Activity				
Persuasion mail/brochures	9,314	3.20	8,809	6.83
Actual campaigning	70,333	24.17	8,768	6.80
Staff/volunteers	312	.11	0	
Subtotal	**79,959**	**27.47**	**17,577**	**13.62**
Constituent Gifts/Entertainment	4,587	1.58	0	
Donations to				
Candidates from same state	130	.04	0	
Candidates from other states	0		0	
Civic organizations	1,382	.47	0	
Ideological groups	0		0	
Political parties	0		0	
Subtotal	**1,512**	**.52**	**0**	
Unitemized Expenses	**3,014**	**1.04**	**19,602**	**15.19**
Total Campaign Expenses	**$ 291,042**		**$ 129,005**	
PAC Contributions	$ 49,020		$ 4,400	
Individual Contributions	208,523		43,464	
Total Receipts*	304,719		85,552	

*Includes PAC and individual contributions as well as interest earned, party contributions, etc.

District 5 — LOUISIANA

Rep. Jim McCrery (R)

1992 Election Results

Jim McCrery (R)	153,501	(63%)
Jerry Huckaby (D)	90,079	(37%)

Redistricting and the electorate's anger over congressional perks were simply too much for Democratic Rep. Jerry Huckaby to overcome in his incumbent-versus-incumbent battle with Republican Rep. Jim McCrery. Having survived for sixteen years in a district where 31 percent of the population was black, Huckaby found himself running in a new district in which blacks made up only 22 percent of the population. With eighty-eight overdrafts at the House bank, Huckaby could not afford the loss of this key Democratic constituency.

With no overdrafts at the House bank, McCrery had a clear tactical advantage. His problem was financial. McCrery's campaign bank account contained $151,252 on June 30, 1992; Huckaby had cash reserves of $343,579.

Huckaby went for an early knockout, investing $403,808 in his campaign between July 1 and September 13. During this period, Politics Inc. of Washington, D.C., received 70 percent of the $99,291 it earned for designing and producing ads that attacked McCrery for his votes in favor of a congressional pay raise and against higher unemployment benefits. Another ad slammed McCrery for voting to cut Medicare benefits, which was something of a stretch since the vote had actually been to cut Medicare reimbursements to hospitals and doctors. Huckaby also paid Media Strategies & Research of Washington, D.C., 74 percent of the $269,140 it ultimately billed his campaign for placing the ads.

With far less to spend, McCrery was forced to hold off on his ad campaign, letting Huckaby's charges go unanswered for more than a month. When he finally hit back, McCrery's ads attacked Huckaby for his eighty-eight overdrafts, pointing out that Huckaby had initially admitted to having only three. Other ads pointed out that Huckaby lived in McLean, Va., and no longer had a home in the district. McCrery's positive spots touted his votes as "principle, not politics." From July 1 to September 13, McCrery was able to put only $128,890 into his advertising effort. To save money, the campaign placed most of the ads directly rather than using its media consultants, Roy Fletcher of Baton Rouge and Evets Management Services of Shreveport.

The October 3 open primary failed to produce a winner, but McCrery's 44 percent showing started money flowing his direction for the general election. Over the final month of the campaign, McCrery poured more than $280,000 into his reelection effort. Having garnered only 29 percent of the primary vote, Huckaby was able to counter with expenditures of about $187,000.

Campaign Expenditures	McCrery Amount Spent	McCrery % of Total	Huckaby Amount Spent	Huckaby % of Total
Overhead				
Office furniture/supplies	$ 6,685	.90	$ 1,330	.17
Rent/utilities	7,438	1.00	2,635	.33
Salaries	98,227	13.22	22,781	2.88
Taxes	0		6,263	.79
Bank/investment fees	0		55	.01
Lawyers/accountants	2,000	.27	0	
Telephone	7,200	.97	4,244	.54
Campaign automobile	0		4,992	.63
Computers/office equipment	8,271	1.11	1,117	.14
Travel	6,027	.81	28,165	3.55
Food/meetings	142	.02	1,675	.21
Subtotal	**135,990**	**18.30**	**73,257**	**9.25**
Fund Raising				
Events	65,533	8.82	45,749	5.77
Direct mail	45,119	6.07	0	
Telemarketing	0		0	
Subtotal	**110,653**	**14.89**	**45,749**	**5.77**
Polling	0		41,648	5.26
Advertising				
Electronic media	341,606	45.96	395,528	49.92
Other media	8,395	1.13	58,572	7.39
Subtotal	**350,000**	**47.09**	**454,099**	**57.31**
Other Campaign Activity				
Persuasion mail/brochures	0		12,965	1.64
Actual campaigning	78,433	10.55	48,398	6.11
Staff/volunteers	0		0	
Subtotal	**78,433**	**10.55**	**61,363**	**7.74**
Constituent Gifts/Entertainment	**6,399**	**.86**	**34,382**	**4.34**
Donations to				
Candidates from same state	1,250	.17	250	.03
Candidates from other states	0		0	
Civic organizations	3,667	.49	13,404	1.69
Ideological groups	789	.11	0	
Political parties	0		5,000	.63
Subtotal	**5,706**	**.77**	**18,654**	**2.35**
Unitemized Expenses	**56,075**	**7.54**	**63,170**	**7.97**
Total Campaign Expenses	**$ 743,255**		**$ 792,322**	
PAC Contributions	$ 225,593		$ 232,241	
Individual Contributions	505,786		212,660	
Total Receipts*	768,933		519,141	

*Includes PAC and individual contributions as well as interest earned, party contributions, etc.

LOUISIANA — District 6

Rep. Richard H. Baker (R)

1992 Election Results

Richard H. Baker (R)	123,953	(51%)
Clyde C. Holloway (R)	121,225	(49%)

Rep. Richard H. Baker knew changes had to be made for the one-month general election campaign against fellow Republican Rep. Clyde C. Holloway. Through the October 3 open primary, Baker had outspent Holloway by nearly $300,000 and had come up 5,022 votes short in the three-way race, although his tally was enough to force a November runoff. The confrontation had been set up by Louisiana's loss of one House seat and redistricting that created a second black-majority district.

Baker's solution was to fire his media consultant for the primary, Gus Weil & Associates of Baton Rouge, and bring in Baton Rouge-based Weiner & Weiner. "We didn't feel Weil's ads were hard-hitting enough," noted administrative assistant Christina Kyle Casteel.

That clearly was not a problem with Weiner & Weiner. The firm created one spot that accused Holloway of having used improper influence to obtain a farm loan. Another charged that he had failed to pay payroll taxes at one of his businesses. Yet another said "Clyde lied" but never actually told what he had lied about. Over the final four weeks of the campaign, Baker paid Weiner & Weiner $133,618.

Despite collecting $167,265 from Baker, Weil apparently did not take his firing well. Almost immediately, he joined the Holloway campaign and produced its only negative ad, which detailed how Baker's real estate development company had filed for bankruptcy protection when a land deal turned sour. Weil received $2,000 for producing the spot, which Holloway never ran. "I guess now I probably should have run it," Holloway lamented. "I certainly don't have any love for him after the campaign he ran."

Among the ads Holloway did run was a thirty-minute commercial highlighting his conservative approach on issues such as crime and welfare reform. In a more conventional thirty-second spot, Holloway's wife described him as "the ultimate public servant."

To make certain that his supporters turned out for the primary and general election, Baker spent $48,735 on phonebanking, including $34,533 with Campaign Telecommunications of New York. He invested $10,795 in yard signs and posters. Election day poll watchers cost the campaign $3,300.

Those were expenditures Holloway could not match. He spent $10,275 on yard signs, but could funnel only $5,679 into his get-out-the-vote efforts.

Baker spent significantly more than Holloway on persuasion mail and campaign handouts. Karl Rove & Company of Austin, Texas, received $43,063 for coordinating Baker's mail efforts; Holloway handled his limited mail campaign in-house.

During the campaign's final month, Baker outspent Holloway by 132,987.

Campaign Expenditures	Baker Amount Spent	Baker % of Total	Holloway Amount Spent	Holloway % of Total
Overhead				
Office furniture/supplies	$ 29,114	3.58	$ 4,164	1.08
Rent/utilities	27,384	3.36	13,148	3.42
Salaries	37,412	4.59	34,607	9.01
Taxes	9,794	1.20	7,692	2.00
Bank/investment fees	1,325	.16	501	.13
Lawyers/accountants	4,754	.58	3,866	1.01
Telephone	15,142	1.86	11,532	3.00
Campaign automobile	15,543	1.91	8,654	2.25
Computers/office equipment	25,328	3.11	2,281	.59
Travel	24,918	3.06	1,797	.47
Food/meetings	6,377	.78	1,119	.29
Subtotal	197,091	24.20	89,360	23.27
Fund Raising				
Events	49,407	6.07	30,981	8.07
Direct mail	23,636	2.90	6,776	1.76
Telemarketing	17,274	2.12	0	
Subtotal	90,316	11.09	37,757	9.83
Polling	31,842	3.91	47,196	12.29
Advertising				
Electronic media	312,783	38.41	140,984	36.71
Other media	4,591	.56	17,638	4.59
Subtotal	317,374	38.97	158,622	41.30
Other Campaign Activity				
Persuasion mail/brochures	58,846	7.23	13,528	3.52
Actual campaigning	94,104	11.56	31,947	8.32
Staff/volunteers	98	.01	2,689	.70
Subtotal	153,048	18.79	48,164	12.54
Constituent Gifts/Entertainment	3,827	.47	368	.10
Donations to				
Candidates from same state	700	.09	1,000	.26
Candidates from other states	500	.06	0	
Civic organizations	90	.01	848	.22
Ideological groups	100	.01	116	.03
Political parties	400	.05	50	.01
Subtotal	1,790	.22	2,014	.52
Unitemized Expenses	19,077	2.34	557	.15
Total Campaign Expenses	$ 814,366		$ 384,039	
PAC Contributions	$ 268,350		$ 193,475	
Individual Contributions	428,540		160,692	
Total Receipts*	711,147		374,471	

*Includes PAC and individual contributions as well as interest earned, party contributions, etc.

District 7 — LOUISIANA

Rep. Jimmy Hayes (D)

1992 Election Results

Jimmy Hayes (D)	84,149	(73%)
Fredric Hayes (R)	23,870	(21%)
Robert J. Nain † (R)	7,184	(6%)

Hollywood could not have scripted a more entertaining scenario. Three-term Democratic Rep. Jimmy Hayes's 1992 Republican opponent was his older brother, Fredric. Fredric Hayes said he decided to run because he was disappointed that his brother had "become part of the tax-and-spend Democratic elite which has bankrupted the nation." Upon learning of her eldest son's intentions, Jewell Hayes issued a statement calling on him to reconsider. In part, her statement said that Fredric Hayes had "been experiencing a personally difficult period in his life, during which he has developed problems with the family."

While Fredric Hayes did not reconsider, neither did he mount a serious challenge. He spent $8,398 on newspaper ads and $1,310 to air radio commercials. Other than that, his largest single expense was a $900 filing fee.

Jimmy Hayes was another story entirely. Having spent a very modest $53,444 to keep his permanent campaign running during the off-year, Hayes invested $261,092 during 1992. Between July 1 and September 30 he put $143,000 into routing his older brother in the October 3 open primary.

Virtually all of the $83,609 the incumbent spent on television, radio, and newspaper ads was committed to the final two weeks of the primary campaign. He ran ads promising to refuse future congressional pay raises, fight for a balanced budget, and help preserve Louisiana's wetlands. He promised not to participate in the congressional retirement system. Roy Fletcher of Baton Rouge collected $61,235 for creating the spots and handling most of the ad placement. The campaign directly purchased $7,260 of air time.

Jimmy Hayes's campaign spent $6,674 on yard signs and posters; Fredric Hayes spent $300 on signs. The incumbent spent $2,965 on T-shirts and $2,147 on buttons, bumper stickers, and other campaign paraphernalia. Without any real opposition, Jimmy Hayes spent $24,500 on polls conducted by Garin-Hart of Washington, D.C. Jimmy Clark & Associates of Lafayette provided its polling expertise for $4,050. The purchase and installation of a new computer system cost the incumbent $13,638, or $2,300 more than Fredric Hayes spent on his entire campaign.

To fund his spending spree, which amounted to nearly twice what he invested in his 1990 campaign, Jimmy Hayes turned to political action committees (PACs). Over the two-year election cycle, PACs accounted for 64 percent of his total contributions. Out-of-state donors accounted for $28,550 of the $81,450 he raised from individuals who gave at least $200. Contributions of less than $200 amounted to only $41,040.

	J. Hayes		F. Hayes	
Campaign Expenditures	Amount Spent	% of Total	Amount Spent	% of Total
Overhead				
Office furniture/supplies	$ 12,577	4.00	$ 162	1.43
Rent/utilities	33,203	10.56	0	
Salaries	505	.16	0	
Taxes	0		0	
Bank/investment fees	25,040	7.96	0	
Lawyers/accountants	0		0	
Telephone	3,828	1.22	0	
Campaign automobile	0		0	
Computers/office equipment	13,698	4.35	0	
Travel	21,748	6.91	184	1.62
Food/meetings	8,064	2.56	6	.05
Subtotal	118,663	37.73	353	3.11
Fund Raising				
Events	27,417	8.72	0	
Direct mail	0		0	
Telemarketing	0		0	
Subtotal	27,417	8.72	0	
Polling	28,550	9.08	0	
Advertising				
Electronic media	68,495	21.78	1,310	11.56
Other media	15,113	4.80	8,398	74.07
Subtotal	83,609	26.58	9,708	85.62
Other Campaign Activity				
Persuasion mail/brochures	0		71	.63
Actual campaigning	32,686	10.39	1,207	10.64
Staff/volunteers	696	.22	0	
Subtotal	33,382	10.61	1,277	11.27
Constituent Gifts/ Entertainment	1,476	.47	0	
Donations to				
Candidates from same state	0		0	
Candidates from other states	100	.03	0	
Civic organizations	3,169	1.01	0	
Ideological groups	160	.05	0	
Political parties	1,000	.32	0	
Subtotal	4,429	1.41	0	
Unitemized Expenses	17,010	5.41	0	
Total Campaign Expenses	$ 314,536		$ 11,338	
PAC Contributions	$ 240,552		$ 0	
Individual Contributions	122,500		5,858	
Total Receipts*	429,546		18,675	

*Includes PAC and individual contributions as well as interest earned, party contributions, etc.

† No expenditures or receipts on file. Candidates raising or spending less than $5,000 are not required to file reports with the Federal Election Commission.

MAINE   District 1

Rep. Thomas H. Andrews (D)

1992 Election Results

Thomas H. Andrews (D) 232,696 (65%)
Linda Bean (R) 125,236 (35%)

Rep. Thomas H. Andrews had good reason to worry about Republican challenger Linda Bean. In October 1991 Bean hired pollster Fabrizio, McLaughlin & Associates of Alexandria, Va., best known for helping to develop such negative television commercials as the infamous Willie Horton spot from the Bush/Dukakis presidential campaign and an ad attacking Senate opponents of Supreme Court Justice Clarence Thomas, which aired during his confirmation hearings. As the granddaughter of the late retailer L. L. Bean, she also had the resources to follow their advice.

By the end of the campaign, Bean had invested more than $1.2 million of her own money, much of it in a withering barrage of distorted advertising designed by Fabrizio, McLaughlin and the Robert Goodman Agency of Baltimore, Md. One ad presented David Pelletier, a disabled veteran who attacked Andrews for refusing to help him find a job. Andrews was able to produce a file showing dozens of verbal and written exchanges with Pelletier, including a thirty-minute meeting they had in December 1991.

Another of Bean's television spots featured a woman who had lost her job at Bath Iron Works and implied her unemployment was the result of Andrews's failure to fight harder to secure contracts for the company. In fact, the woman had lost her job as part of a planned downsizing announced before Andrews was elected.

Realizing that her negative ads were ineffective, Bean shifted gears in October. She hired VP Film & Tape of South Portland to develop several positive spots, including an endorsement from Housing and Urban Development Secretary Jack Kemp. While softer, the ads apparently worked no better.

Fortunately for Andrews, he did not have to spend any of his own advertising budget to denounce the inaccuracies in Bean's commercials. The local news media did that for free.

Instead, Andrews paid Joe Slade White & Co. of New York $335,986 for developing and placing a series of soft, positive commercials, including one that touted Andrews's work on the Small Business Economic Opportunity Enhancement Act of 1991. While the ads began airing occasionally as early as June, roughly half of the advertising budget was spent during the final month of the campaign.

Andrews held fund-raisers in Riverside, Calif.; New York; and Boston. His financing plan called for one hundred in-state, in-home events. It was hoped that each event would draw fifty people willing to pay $50. According to chief of staff Craig S. Brown, the campaign almost met those goals. Noris Weiss received $46,844 for coordinating political action committee fund-raisers, which helped yield $392,357.

Campaign Expenditures	Andrews Amount Spent	% of Total	Bean Amount Spent	% of Total
Overhead				
Office furniture/supplies	$ 12,939	1.65	$ 10,358	.72
Rent/utilities	12,808	1.64	12,635	.88
Salaries	127,941	16.36	124,886	8.66
Taxes	285	.04	31,240	2.17
Bank/investment fees	4,378	.56	71	
Lawyers/accountants	0		3,398	.24
Telephone	9,668	1.24	12,735	.88
Campaign automobile	0		0	
Computers/office equipment	8,911	1.14	21,605	1.50
Travel	26,730	3.42	11,651	.81
Food/meetings	337	.04	100	.01
Subtotal	203,998	26.09	228,680	15.86
Fund Raising				
Events	81,670	10.44	81,175	5.63
Direct mail	56,733	7.25	0	
Telemarketing	0		0	
Subtotal	138,403	17.70	81,175	5.63
Polling	39,774	5.09	69,740	4.84
Advertising				
Electronic media	336,088	42.98	572,833	39.73
Other media	867	.11	46,593	3.23
Subtotal	336,954	43.09	619,426	42.97
Other Campaign Activity				
Persuasion mail/brochures	13,086	1.67	348,362	24.16
Actual campaigning	44,864	5.74	80,844	5.61
Staff/volunteers	2,780	.36	695	.05
Subtotal	60,730	7.77	429,901	29.82
Constituent Gifts/ Entertainment	300	.04	0	
Donations to				
Candidates from same state	0		0	
Candidates from other states	0		0	
Civic organizations	0		20	
Ideological groups	1,600	.20	0	
Political parties	75	.01	35	
Subtotal	1,675	.21	55	
Unitemized Expenses	200	.03	12,716	.88
Total Campaign Expenses	$ 782,034		$ 1,441,694	
PAC Contributions	$ 392,357		$ 57,176	
Individual Contributions	455,995		183,370	
Total Receipts*	861,564		1,469,959	

*Includes PAC and individual contributions as well as interest earned, party contributions, etc.

District 2 — MAINE

Rep. Olympia J. Snowe (R)

1992 Election Results

Olympia J. Snowe (R)	153,022	(49%)
Patrick K. McGowan (D)	130,824	(42%)
Jonathan K. Carter (I)	27,526	(9%)

Former Democratic state representative Patrick K. McGowan came within 4,906 of defeating Rep. Olympia J. Snowe in 1990, but she was not about to be surprised a second time. While McGowan increased his spending by $153,780 for their 1992 rematch, Snowe upped her spending by $428,819.

Snowe's overhead costs increased from $87,413 in the 1990 election cycle to $219,847 in 1992. She opted to maintain a campaign office throughout the 1992 cycle, a move that increased her rent payments more than four-fold. In February 1991 she hired campaign manager James Tobin and over the next twenty-three months paid him $37,773. By election day her campaign staff had grown to thirteen, producing a payroll that was $76,013 higher than in 1990.

For the rematch, McGowan increased his advertising budget by $77,595. Designed and placed by MacWilliams/Cosgrove of Somerville, Mass., his six television commercials included a biographical sketch and an attack on Snowe and her husband, Maine Gov. John R. McKernan, Jr., for their ties to President George Bush and for allowing the state's economy to flounder on their watch.

Snowe increased her advertising expenditures by $171,692, flooding the district's three major media markets with radio and television commercials that sought to tar McGowan with the brush of incumbency. "We weren't going to let McGowan get away with running as a fresh new face, as he had in 1990," remarked Edward Blakely, vice president of Smith & Harroff of Alexandria, Va.

According to Blakely, Smith & Harroff produced at least eight radio and television spots, including one that attacked McGowan for supporting increases in state taxes while a member of the state legislature. Another ad pointed to McGowan's apparent flip-flops on issues ranging from military base closings to a balanced budget amendment in an attempt to show that he would say anything to get elected.

On the positive side, one commercial featured endorsements from actress Kirstie Alley, a Democrat, and her Republican husband, actor Parker Stevens. "We needed to hammer home that she was not a partisan representative, but was willing to go against the president and do what's right for Maine," Blakely explained. Snowe paid Smith & Harroff $292,982 for its work.

As in 1990, Snowe invested nothing in persuasion mail. She left that expense to the National Republican Congressional Committee, which spent $44,360 to send mail on her behalf.

Cherry Communications of Gainesville, Fla., received $16,750 for coordinating Snowe's $32,396 phonebanking effort. Public Opinion Strategies of Alexandria, Va., collected $43,981 for polling.

Campaign Expenditures	Snowe Amount Spent	Snowe % of Total	McGowan Amount Spent	McGowan % of Total
Overhead				
Office furniture/supplies	$ 9,630	1.30	$ 6,322	1.64
Rent/utilities	10,917	1.47	6,682	1.74
Salaries	104,069	14.05	46,555	12.10
Taxes	32,429	4.38	14,087	3.66
Bank/investment fees	1,566	.21	27	.01
Lawyers/accountants	0		0	
Telephone	14,440	1.95	26,771	6.96
Campaign automobile	0		9,614	2.50
Computers/office equipment	8,960	1.21	5,505	1.43
Travel	34,813	4.70	15,466	4.02
Food/meetings	3,021	.41	0	
Subtotal	**219,847**	**29.68**	**131,028**	**34.07**
Fund Raising				
Events	27,799	3.75	20,397	5.30
Direct mail	53,572	7.23	3,774	.98
Telemarketing	0		0	
Subtotal	**81,371**	**10.99**	**24,171**	**6.28**
Polling	**45,481**	**6.14**	**13,700**	**3.56**
Advertising				
Electronic media	301,107	40.66	169,798	44.15
Other media	9,836	1.33	3,083	.80
Subtotal	**310,944**	**41.98**	**172,881**	**44.95**
Other Campaign Activity				
Persuasion mail/brochures	0		7,427	1.93
Actual campaigning	67,212	9.08	24,830	6.46
Staff/volunteers	694	.09	0	
Subtotal	**67,906**	**9.17**	**32,257**	**8.39**
Constituent Gifts/Entertainment	858	.12	0	
Donations to				
Candidates from same state	0		0	
Candidates from other states	250	.03	0	
Civic organizations	0		0	
Ideological groups	0		0	
Political parties	255	.03	0	
Subtotal	**505**	**.07**	**0**	
Unitemized Expenses	13,702	1.85	10,598	2.76
Total Campaign Expenses	**$ 740,614**		**$ 384,635**	
PAC Contributions	$ 246,095		$ 134,462	
Individual Contributions	465,681		208,280	
Total Receipts*	746,628		382,445	

*Includes PAC and individual contributions as well as interest earned, party contributions, etc.

MARYLAND   District 1

Rep. Wayne T. Gilchrest (R)   *1992 Election Results*   Wayne T. Gilchrest (R)   120,084   (52%)
                                                                          Tom McMillen (D)   112,771   (48%)

In a battle created by redistricting, freshman Rep. Wayne T. Gilchrest knew he would be vastly outspent by Democratic Rep. Tom McMillen. However, having bested incumbent Rep. Roy Dyson in 1990 despite being outspent by $418,691, Gilchrest knew he could turn McMillen's $1,128,349 spending advantage into a liability. "We couldn't match his ability to raise money all over the country, so we turned that fact into a campaign issue," remarked administrative assistant Anthony P. Caligiuri.

Gilchrest first had to get past four Republican primary challengers, including businesswoman Lisa G. Renshaw. Renshaw scored with charges that Gilchrest was a closet liberal, citing his votes against easing restrictions on wetlands development and in favor of overturning a Bush administration policy against allowing personnel at federally funded clinics to discuss abortion with patients. Between January 1, 1992 and the March 3 primary Gilchrest was forced to spend $51,876, including $29,915 of his media budget, to secure a 47 percent plurality.

For the fall campaign, Gilchrest aired six radio and two television commercials, several of which questioned McMillen's dependence on special interest money. When McMillen was cited as one of the top one hundred representatives who accepted free travel, Gilchrest attacked with a radio spot depicting McMillen being pampered by a flight attendant: "Fluff your pillow, Mr. McMillen? More champagne, Mr. McMillen? More sushi, Mr. McMillen?" Companion newspaper ads cost $6,004.

Gilchrest's persuasion mail was limited to a single piece targeted at households in the newly acquired portion of the district. "Radio is the only efficient way to communicate in this district," explained Caligiuri.

For creating and placing the broadcast advertising, Sandler-Innocenzi of Washington, D.C., collected $173,332 from Gilchrest and $8,972 from the Republican National Committee. Welch Communications of Arlington, Va., received $4,000 from Gilchrest and $9,337 from the National Republican Congressional Committee for coordinating the persuasion mail effort. A poll conducted by Public Opinion Strategies of Alexandria, Va., cost Gilchrest $5,500.

Running in a district that was more new to him than it was to Gilchrest, McMillen invested $98,101 in polls conducted by Cooper & Secrest Associates of Alexandria, Va. Shorr Associates of Philadelphia, Pa., collected $409,015 for creating and placing his broadcast ads, including one that depicted a thumb-sucking child with the words, "Who would lie to this child?" The ad proceeded to charge Gilchrest with doing just that. Campaign Performance Group of San Francisco, Calif., received $101,621 for a highly negative persuasion mail campaign.

Campaign Expenditures	Gilchrest Amount Spent	Gilchrest % of Total	McMillen Amount Spent	McMillen % of Total
Overhead				
Office furniture/supplies	$ 1,457	.36	$ 14,403	.94
Rent/utilities	6,850	1.71	44,483	2.91
Salaries	28,263	7.07	119,391	7.81
Taxes	10,907	2.73	36,258	2.37
Bank/investment fees	0		5	
Lawyers/accountants	5,105	1.28	10,135	.66
Telephone	10,040	2.51	34,856	2.28
Campaign automobile	0		0	
Computers/office equipment	1,847	.46	36,140	2.37
Travel	1,842	.46	58,558	3.83
Food/meetings	0		2,762	.18
Subtotal	**66,311**	**16.60**	**356,991**	**23.36**
Fund Raising				
Events	40,162	10.05	210,787	13.80
Direct mail	26,328	6.59	20,970	1.37
Telemarketing	0		0	
Subtotal	**66,490**	**16.64**	**231,757**	**15.17**
Polling	**5,500**	**1.38**	**102,801**	**6.73**
Advertising				
Electronic media	174,317	43.63	451,494	29.55
Other media	8,826	2.21	33,634	2.20
Subtotal	**183,143**	**45.84**	**485,128**	**31.75**
Other Campaign Activity				
Persuasion mail/brochures	25,793	6.46	166,825	10.92
Actual campaigning	12,543	3.14	111,616	7.31
Staff/volunteers	1,700	.43	3,815	.25
Subtotal	**40,037**	**10.02**	**282,257**	**18.47**
Constituent Gifts/ Entertainment	**577**	**.14**	**9,346**	**.61**
Donations to				
Candidates from same state	0		2,615	.17
Candidates from other states	0		0	
Civic organizations	0		7,381	.48
Ideological groups	0		3,049	.20
Political parties	300	.08	7,079	.46
Subtotal	**300**	**.08**	**20,123**	**1.32**
Unitemized Expenses	**37,195**	**9.31**	**39,501**	**2.59**
Total Campaign Expenses	**$ 399,554**		**$ 1,527,903**	
PAC Contributions	**$ 94,529**		**$ 699,296**	
Individual Contributions	250,073		498,961	
Total Receipts*	394,794		1,256,666	

*Includes PAC and individual contributions as well as interest earned, party contributions, etc.

District 2 — MARYLAND

Rep. Helen Delich Bentley (R)

1992 Election Results

Helen Delich Bentley (R)	165,443	(65%)
Michael C. Hickey, Jr. (D)	88,658	(35%)

In her final race before retiring to run for governor, four-term Rep. Helen Delich Bentley spent $956,201 to defeat primary challenger Robert T. Petr, who received 13 percent of the vote, and Democratic challenger Michael C. Hickey, Jr., who spent only $45,715. As campaign manager Thomas K. O'Neil put it, Bentley "never takes anything for granted."

Bentley's permanent campaign was enormous, costing $308,352 during 1991 alone. Overhead in the off-year amounted to $212,610, including monthly payments for rent and utilities that averaged $2,103. Her permanent staff of eight collected salaries totaling $91,269. Payroll and income taxes amounted to $47,815. New office equipment and computer software for the off-year effort added $13,538.

During the first three months of 1992, Bentley put $151,547 into her campaign, but only $1,504 of that was spent on advertising for the March 3 primary. M.E.M. & Associates of Austin, Texas, received $11,636 for coordinating her $13,636 preprimary phonebanking effort. Bentley's office payroll for the first three months of 1992 was $30,725.

Over the final nine months of the election cycle, Bentley's campaign spent $496,302, with a significant share directed at appealing to voters. Hottman Edwards Advertising received $54,513 for creating and placing radio commercials that touted her record of constituent and community service. O'Neil said the spots largely targeted new voters acquired through redistricting, a group he said comprised between 20 and 25 percent of her constituency. The campaign invested $4,661 to advertise in small, community newspapers. M.E.M. collected $62,675 for phonebanking. Printing and postage charges for campaign literature totaled $39,297. Yard signs and posters cost $11,409. Still, her largest single expense was the $96,196 she paid out in salaries.

Like virtually all incumbents, Bentley set aside some of her treasury for constituent stroking. Over the two-year cycle, Bentley spent $13,890 to purchase calendars and mail them to supporters. The campaign shelled out $2,371 to pay for assorted gifts. Meals, commemorative plaques, and flowers added $449.

Having argued that Serbs in the former Yugoslavia have received unfair treatment in the American press, Bentley was not hesitant to turn to the Serbian-American community for money. She held fundraisers at the Serbian Orthodox Church in New York, the Serbian Social Center in Lansing, Ill., and the American Serbian Memorial Hall in Detroit.

Hickey's central focus was an unsuccessful attempt to exploit Bentley's Serbian ties, running ads critical of her pro-Serbian stand on five cable television systems.

	Bentley		Hickey	
Campaign Expenditures	Amount Spent	% of Total	Amount Spent	% of Total
Overhead				
Office furniture/supplies	$ 15,456	1.62	$ 614	1.34
Rent/utilities	53,978	5.65	0	
Salaries	218,190	22.82	3,450	7.55
Taxes	110,150	11.52	0	
Bank/investment fees	207	.02	175	.38
Lawyers/accountants	3,997	.42	0	
Telephone	16,222	1.70	1,685	3.69
Campaign automobile	12,748	1.33	0	
Computers/office equipment	24,247	2.54	129	.28
Travel	29,783	3.11	0	
Food/meetings	6,186	.65	25	.05
Subtotal	491,163	51.37	6,078	13.30
Fund Raising				
Events	144,386	15.10	1,470	3.21
Direct mail	16,483	1.72	0	
Telemarketing	0		0	
Subtotal	160,869	16.82	1,470	3.21
Polling	500	.05	0	
Advertising				
Electronic media	55,538	5.81	17,585	38.47
Other media	12,168	1.27	2,355	5.15
Subtotal	67,705	7.08	19,940	43.62
Other Campaign Activity				
Persuasion mail/brochures	59,778	6.25	8,081	17.68
Actual campaigning	150,340	15.72	5,828	12.75
Staff/volunteers	1,000	.10	0	
Subtotal	211,118	22.08	13,909	30.42
Constituent Gifts/ Entertainment	16,710	1.75	0	
Donations to				
Candidates from same state	135	.01	25	.05
Candidates from other states	1,500	.16	0	
Civic organizations	588	.06	304	.67
Ideological groups	0		147	.32
Political parties	644	.07	375	.82
Subtotal	2,867	.30	852	1.86
Unitemized Expenses	5,268	.55	3,467	7.58
Total Campaign Expenses	$ 956,201		$ 45,715	
PAC Contributions	$ 240,620		$ 4,000	
Individual Contributions	700,987		36,630	
Total Receipts*	959,100		49,031	

*Includes PAC and individual contributions as well as interest earned, party contributions, etc.

MARYLAND — District 3

Rep. Benjamin L. Cardin (D)

1992 Election Results

Benjamin L. Cardin (D) 163,354 (74%)
William T. S. Bricker (R) 58,869 (26%)

Rep. Benjamin L. Cardin spent $284,329 more on his 1992 campaign than he had in 1990 and in the process outspent attorney William T. S. Bricker by nearly sixty to one. Cardin's $149,768 off-year investment was nearly fourteen times as much as Bricker's total outlays.

Monthly rent on Cardin's permanent campaign office was $525. Salary payments and payroll taxes for three permanent, part-time employees amounted to $44,758. Taxes on the campaign's interest income came to $5,023. He paid $11,935 for computer equipment and software, which helped to push his total off-year overhead costs to $74,687.

Fund raising during 1991 consisted of two large-donor events staged by the campaign and an in-kind luncheon sponsored by the National Good Government Fund in Houston, Texas. With an investment of $36,905, the campaign raised $255,127.

During 1991 Cardin spent $2,400 on program ads from groups such as the Save-a-Heart Foundation, the Talmudical Academy of Baltimore, and the Polish-American Citizens Committee. He also spent $498 for an ad in the *Baltimore Jewish Times*. Media consultant Struble-Totten Communications of Washington, D.C, collected $7,052 for work done in 1990 but not billed until 1991.

Broadcast advertising accounted for half of Cardin's election-year outlays. Since the entire district could be reached with Baltimore television and one-third of the district was new to him, Cardin spent more than twice as much on broadcast advertising as he had in 1990. "Television was the most influential method of getting our message out," explained campaign director Debbie Weiss.

Struble-Totten was paid $18,500 for producing three television commercials—one highlighting Cardin's work on health care, another on congressional reform, and a third on reordering federal budget priorities to allow for investment in other areas, such as education. Media Strategies & Research of Washington, D.C., collected $230,000 for placing the spots. The firm also received $10,000 from the campaign and $4,700 from the American Medical Association Political Action Committee for polling.

For the primary, Cardin spent $3,250 to place ads in eleven publications, including the *Baltimore Chronicle*, the *Community Times*, and the *East Baltimore Guide*. Another $3,798 was spent on newspaper ads prior to the general election.

Since his first election in 1986, Cardin has held a swearing-in celebration for volunteers and contributors after each victory. The 1991 edition cost $2,901. According to Weiss, the proximity of the district to Washington makes it easy for Cardin to maintain this tradition. Holiday cards cost the campaign $2,338.

Campaign Expenditures	Cardin Amount Spent	Cardin % of Total	Bricker Amount Spent	Bricker % of Total
Overhead				
Office furniture/supplies	$ 5,661	.88	$ 19	.17
Rent/utilities	16,184	2.50	0	
Salaries	78,234	12.10	0	
Taxes	45,148	6.98	0	
Bank/investment fees	141	.02	56	.51
Lawyers/accountants	610	.09	0	
Telephone	4,445	.69	174	1.60
Campaign automobile	0		0	
Computers/office equipment	13,855	2.14	150	1.38
Travel	2,120	.33	0	
Food/meetings	674	.10	0	
Subtotal	**167,072**	**25.84**	**398**	**3.67**
Fund Raising				
Events	99,656	15.41	3,566	32.85
Direct mail	15,775	2.44	0	
Telemarketing	0		0	
Subtotal	**115,431**	**17.85**	**3,566**	**32.85**
Polling	**14,700**	**2.27**	**0**	
Advertising				
Electronic media	255,644	39.53	0	
Other media	12,511	1.93	2,311	21.29
Subtotal	**268,155**	**41.47**	**2,311**	**21.29**
Other Campaign Activity				
Persuasion mail/brochures	25,802	3.99	739	6.81
Actual campaigning	19,432	3.00	2,864	26.38
Staff/volunteers	1,693	.26	12	.11
Subtotal	**46,928**	**7.26**	**3,615**	**33.30**
Constituent Gifts/ Entertainment	**6,566**	**1.02**	**0**	
Donations to				
Candidates from same state	3,070	.47	0	
Candidates from other states	6,000	.93	0	
Civic organizations	1,161	.18	0	
Ideological groups	370	.06	0	
Political parties	15,327	2.37	790	7.28
Subtotal	**25,928**	**4.01**	**790**	**7.28**
Unitemized Expenses	**1,900**	**.29**	**176**	**1.62**
Total Campaign Expenses	**$ 646,679**		**$ 10,857**	
PAC Contributions	$ 292,553		$ 0	
Individual Contributions	220,741		1,236	
Total Receipts*	591,234		6,635	

*Includes PAC and individual contributions as well as interest earned, party contributions, etc.

District 4 — MARYLAND

Rep. Albert R. Wynn (D)

1992 Election Results

Albert R. Wynn (D)	136,902	(75%)
Michele Dyson (R)	45,166	(25%)

In this majority black, overwhelmingly Democratic district, the only contest of significance was the thirteen-candidate Democratic primary. While State's Attorney Alexander Williams, Jr., was pronounced the early front runner, state senator Albert R. Wynn waged an aggressive, well-funded campaign and emerged with a 1,286-vote victory.

Wynn launched his campaign in August 1991 and over the next six months spent nearly $206,000 to secure the Democratic nomination. For the March primary he invested $60,716 in persuasion mail, $4,996 in other campaign literature, $20,000 in broadcast media, $15,774 in polls, $5,930 in bus signs, and a total of $1,742 in yard signs, bumper stickers, nail files, combs, and hats.

With his considerable campaign treasury, Wynn put together what administrative assistant Luis A. Navarro described as a "fully integrated, professional campaign" orchestrated by leading Democratic consultants. Campaign Performance Group of San Francisco, Calif., collected $41,509 for producing two persuasion mailers and coordinating the mail effort. "George Bush doesn't want to hear your problems, but there is a leader who cares," began an eight-page brochure that focused on education, crime, and health care. The second brochure focused entirely on education, attacking the Bush administration for having "abandoned our youth."

Austin-Sheinkopf received $20,000 for producing three radio spots and a companion television commercial that ran on local cable outlets prior to the primary. The ads touted Wynn's authorship of legislation to ban the sale of assault weapons in Maryland and denounced Bush administration policies.

Wynn did not rely soley on consultants. During the five months leading up to the primary he spent every weekend knocking on doors. He greeted voters in shopping malls and at bus stops throughout the district.

Given the high stakes, Wynn paid the Feldman Group of Washington, D.C., to conduct preprimary polls, something he did not do for the November general election.

Although he spent more than $170,000, Wynn's campaign against Republican businesswoman Michele Dyson proved far easier. He handled the extremely limited mailing effort in-house. He held his media buys until the final two weeks, paying Austin-Sheinkopf $2,500 for consulting, $28,348 for placing radio commercials, and $59,894 for TV buys, including a pro-choice spot that Navarro said was targeted primarily at white, female voters. He invested $7,685 in bus signs and $4,183 to air his ads prior to movies shown at National Cinema theaters.

	Wynn		Dyson	
Campaign Expenditures	Amount Spent	% of Total	Amount Spent	% of Total
Overhead				
Office furniture/supplies	$ 4,910	1.30	$ 1,634	1.19
Rent/utilities	5,919	1.57	1,800	1.31
Salaries	33,027	8.77	38,765	28.25
Taxes	8		7,116	5.19
Bank/investment fees	97	.03	287	.21
Lawyers/accountants	500	.13	0	
Telephone	5,643	1.50	1,065	.78
Campaign automobile	0		0	
Computers/office equipment	1,075	.29	0	
Travel	726	.19	0	
Food/meetings	320	.08	0	
Subtotal	**52,226**	**13.86**	**50,666**	**36.92**
Fund Raising				
Events	51,942	13.79	9,907	7.22
Direct mail	0		4,712	3.43
Telemarketing	0		0	
Subtotal	**51,942**	**13.79**	**14,619**	**10.65**
Polling	**15,774**	**4.19**	**1,200**	**.87**
Advertising				
Electronic media	114,658	30.44	27,881	20.32
Other media	19,732	5.24	16,583	12.09
Subtotal	**134,390**	**35.67**	**44,464**	**32.40**
Other Campaign Activity				
Persuasion mail/brochures	95,887	25.45	18,451	13.45
Actual campaigning	20,869	5.54	7,680	5.60
Staff/volunteers	2,504	.66	11	.01
Subtotal	**119,260**	**31.66**	**26,142**	**19.05**
Constituent Gifts/ Entertainment	**364**	**.10**	**0**	
Donations to				
Candidates from same state	0		0	
Candidates from other states	0		0	
Civic organizations	1,982	.53	0	
Ideological groups	260	.07	0	
Political parties	150	.04	125	.09
Subtotal	**2,392**	**.63**	**125**	**.09**
Unitemized Expenses	**375**	**.10**	**0**	
Total Campaign Expenses	**$ 376,722**		**$ 137,216**	
PAC Contributions	**$ 238,477**		**$ 18,192**	
Individual Contributions	**181,581**		**54,238**	
Total Receipts*	**571,408**		**137,717**	

*Includes PAC and individual contributions as well as interest earned, party contributions, etc.

MARYLAND District 5

Rep. Steny H. Hoyer (D)

1992 Election Results
Steny H. Hoyer (D)   118,312   (53%)
Lawrence J. Hogan, Jr. (R)   97,982   (44%)

Rep. Steny H. Hoyer, chairman of the Democratic Caucus, faced several significant hurdles in his attempt to win a seventh term. In order to carve out a new majority-black district, Maryland legislators had significantly altered the boundaries of District 5, and the new territory Hoyer was given in southern Maryland was decidedly more conservative. His Republican opponent, Lawrence J. Hogan, Jr., was the son of a former House member and Prince George's County executive. As a result, Hoyer spent $1,577,485 during the 1992 election cycle, more than twice what he spent on his 1990 campaign.

Recognizing that the 1992 effort would not mirror his five previous reelection campaigns, which he won with 72 percent of the vote or more, Hoyer wasted no time in laying the foundation of his voter persuasion efforts. In August 1991 he hired media consultant Brown Inc. of Santa Fe, N.M., and over the next seven months paid the firm $99,841 for the design and initial execution of persuasion mail, broadcast advertising, and limited newspaper advertising campaigns that introduced him to his new constituents. By January 1992 Mellman & Lazarus had collected $16,400 for conducting the campaign's benchmark poll.

For the fall campaign, Brown Inc. received $482,410 for creating and placing three television commercials and one radio spot, producing three districtwide persuasion mailings, placing newspaper ads, and preparing lists for the campaign's phonebank operation. Fenn & King Communications of Washington, D.C., collected $39,289 for producing and placing one radio commercial.

Hoyer had little reason to air negative spots since Hogan's relatively meager resources prevented him from airing television commercials entirely and severely limited his radio buys. Instead, Hoyer's ads delivered the message that his incumbency was an asset. A television spot asked voters to imagine what life would be like without the wildlife preserve he had fought to bring to the district or without the thousands of jobs created by the federal projects he secured for the district. Two weeks before the November 3 election, Hoyer rolled out his only negative radio ad, which accused Hogan of distorting the facts and of being willing to say anything to get elected.

Given Hoyer's leadership position, it would have been surprising if Hogan had run anything but an outsider campaign. Hogan aired three radio commercials produced by the Robert Goodman Agency of Baltimore that attacked Hoyer for his $28,000 in overdrafts at the House bank and for being named by Ralph Nader as the biggest congressional junketeer.

Campaign Expenditures	Hoyer Amount Spent	Hoyer % of Total	Hogan Amount Spent	Hogan % of Total
Overhead				
Office furniture/supplies	$ 25,533	1.62	$ 4,567	1.93
Rent/utilities	25,013	1.59	4,750	2.00
Salaries	118,660	7.52	49,040	20.69
Taxes	46,913	2.97	0	
Bank/investment fees	2,201	.14	141	.06
Lawyers/accountants	11,826	.75	1,200	.51
Telephone	30,123	1.91	9,055	3.82
Campaign automobile	10,511	.67	0	
Computers/office equipment	7,855	.50	8,702	3.67
Travel	28,224	1.79	4,533	1.91
Food/meetings	9,382	.59	1,099	.46
Subtotal	**316,241**	**20.05**	**83,089**	**35.06**
Fund Raising				
Events	275,483	17.46	15,644	6.60
Direct mail	0		16,602	7.01
Telemarketing	0		0	
Subtotal	**275,483**	**17.46**	**32,246**	**13.61**
Polling	**52,114**	**3.30**	**4,355**	**1.84**
Advertising				
Electronic media	530,084	33.60	44,211	18.66
Other media	18,629	1.18	1,300	.55
Subtotal	**548,713**	**34.78**	**45,511**	**19.20**
Other Campaign Activity				
Persuasion mail/brochures	182,548	11.57	36,315	15.32
Actual campaigning	94,811	6.01	25,424	10.73
Staff/volunteers	4,008	.25	594	.25
Subtotal	**281,367**	**17.84**	**62,334**	**26.30**
Constituent Gifts/ Entertainment	**21,471**	**1.36**	**0**	
Donations to				
Candidates from same state	1,370	.09	0	
Candidates from other states	18,000	1.14	0	
Civic organizations	21,869	1.39	0	
Ideological groups	14,535	.92	60	.03
Political parties	22,622	1.43	1,820	.77
Subtotal	**78,395**	**4.97**	**1,880**	**.79**
Unitemized Expenses	**3,699**	**.23**	**7,564**	**3.19**
Total Campaign Expenses	**$ 1,577,485**		**$ 236,980**	
PAC Contributions	**$ 711,367**		**$ 51,409**	
Individual Contributions	**535,995**		**138,701**	
Total Receipts*	**1,304,867**		**267,271**	

*Includes PAC and individual contributions as well as interest earned, party contributions, etc.

District 6 — MARYLAND

Rep. Roscoe G. Bartlett (R)

1992 Election Results

Roscoe G. Bartlett (R) 125,564 (54%)
Thomas H. Hattery (D) 106,224 (46%)

Retired teacher Roscoe G. Bartlett beat Democratic state representative Thomas H. Hattery at his own game. Hattery had upset seven-term Rep. Beverly B. Byron in the Democratic primary by spending nearly $230,000 on a highly negative campaign that emphasized the anti-incumbent theme. In the general election contest, Bartlett returned the favor and tarred Hattery with the negatives of incumbency.

Given little chance of defeating Byron, Hattery spent $74,265 on persuasion mail and broadcast advertising during the final two weeks of the primary campaign. Campaign Performance Group of San Francisco, Calif., received $45,504 for three persuasion mailers, including a general anti-incumbency piece that opened with a picture of the Capitol and the words, "No room for families here." The other two mailers attacked Byron for voting against increasing the minimum wage while voting for the congressional pay raise, for taking congressional junkets to Barbados and twelve other foreign destinations, and for joining the rest of Congress "in letting the S&L profiteers run wild." Austin-Sheinkopf of Washington, D.C., collected $27,376 for designing and placing companion radio and cable television spots. The campaign bought another $3,885 of air time on its own. Hattery carried all six counties in the district and won with 56 percent of the vote.

Bartlett spent nearly $124,000 to secure the Republican nomination, surviving the primary by only 646 votes. Having dispatched fellow Republicans Michael Downey and Frank K. Nethken, Bartlett immediately went on the offensive, holding a press conference to accuse Hattery of falsifying meal, hotel, and other travel expenses on his legislative expense account as part of an "embezzlement scheme." While Hattery vehemently denied the charges, they clearly hurt his chances. "It was enough to make people mad," lamented Hattery.

With less than $150,000 in his coffers for the general election, Bartlett spent considerable time touring the district in a mobile home to get his message out. He paid $34,066 to air radio spots attacking Hattery for supporting tax increases in the Maryland legislature and for failing to buy workers' compensation insurance for the employees of his family-owned printing business. Air time for his companion television spots cost $12,250, including $7,317 for time on local cable outlets.

Hattery had considerably more resources and struck back with a sharply negative campaign of his own designed by Campaign Performance and Austin-Sheinkopf. "I was told by my consultants that the only way to beat Bartlett was to totally trash him," Hattery said.

Campaign Expenditures	Bartlett Amount Spent	Bartlett % of Total	Hattery Amount Spent	Hattery % of Total
Overhead				
Office furniture/supplies	$ 8,758	3.28	$ 9,736	1.78
Rent/utilities	4,171	1.56	9,521	1.74
Salaries	72,772	27.22	21,638	3.95
Taxes	0		461	.08
Bank/investment fees	133	.05	137	.02
Lawyers/accountants	0		0	
Telephone	5,774	2.16	9,111	1.66
Campaign automobile	0		0	
Computers/office equipment	9,627	3.60	6,963	1.27
Travel	585	.22	1,142	.21
Food/meetings	997	.37	0	
Subtotal	**102,815**	**38.45**	**58,709**	**10.71**
Fund Raising				
Events	42,713	15.98	55,713	10.16
Direct mail	0		15,212	2.77
Telemarketing	0		0	
Subtotal	**42,713**	**15.98**	**70,925**	**12.94**
Polling	**2,119**	**.79**	**30,423**	**5.55**
Advertising				
Electronic media	55,946	20.92	179,414	32.73
Other media	7,565	2.83	4,015	.73
Subtotal	**63,511**	**23.75**	**183,429**	**33.46**
Other Campaign Activity				
Persuasion mail/brochures	15,049	5.63	182,635	33.31
Actual campaigning	38,963	14.57	16,886	3.08
Staff/volunteers	150	.06	244	.04
Subtotal	**54,162**	**20.26**	**199,765**	**36.44**
Constituent Gifts/ Entertainment	37	.01	0	
Donations to				
Candidates from same state	0		0	
Candidates from other states	0		0	
Civic organizations	102	.04	113	.02
Ideological groups	0		122	.02
Political parties	873	.33	1,442	.26
Subtotal	**975**	**.36**	**1,677**	**.31**
Unitemized Expenses	**1,035**	**.39**	**3,283**	**.60**
Total Campaign Expenses	**$ 267,366**		**$ 548,210**	
PAC Contributions	**$ 90,500**		**$ 279,492**	
Individual Contributions	**100,741**		**193,603**	
Total Receipts*	**311,819**		**598,213**	

*Includes PAC and individual contributions as well as interest earned, party contributions, etc.

MARYLAND   District 7

Rep. Kweisi Mfume (D)

1992 Election Results

Kweisi Mfume (D)	152,689	(85%)
Kenneth Kondner † (R)	26,304	(15%)

Facing a weak primary opponent and then the same underfunded Republican challenger he walloped in 1990, Rep. Kweisi Mfume spent only 36 percent of his $214,937 campaign treasury on direct appeals for votes. The $32,845 he spent on broadcast advertising was $1,386 less than he invested in constituent entertainment and gifts.

In the spring of 1991 and 1992 the campaign rented tents, tables, and chairs; set them up in a parking lot near the main congressional office in Baltimore; and invited district residents to a free open house. The campaign hired magicians and supplied face painting and balloons for the children. Parents received a picture of Mfume. Attendees were fed by local caterers and entertained by musicians from Morgan State University. The two events cost the campaign a total of $10,798.

The campaign hosted an annual year-end holiday reception at the Walters Art Gallery in Baltimore, where local elected officials and other invited guests celebrated the season. No one paid to attend the affairs, which together cost $7,566.

Mfume spent $6,286 of his treasury on holiday cards. Plaques given in recognition of various constituent achievements cost $1,155. Lunches with visiting constituents, primarily at the House restaurant, cost $1,364. Assorted gifts added $4,883.

As in past years, Mfume used campaign funds to frame the winning entry in the district's congressional art contest. In 1991 the campaign also passed out cash awards of $500 to the winner, $200 to the runner-up, and $100 to the third-place entrant. A catered party to celebrate the winners cost $200. In 1992 Mfume increased the prizes for finishing second and third to $300 and $200, respectively.

Constituents were not the only ones who partied at campaign expense. Mfume treated his congressional staff to an annual Christmas party at Stouffer's Harbour Place Hotel in Baltimore, which cost the campaign $1,000 in 1991 and $955 in 1992. Mfume spent $7,350 of his campaign treasury to attend the annual Congressional Black Caucus weekend retreat in 1991 and $5,950 to attend a similar event in 1992.

Actual campaign expenses were extremely modest. Outlays for the primary included $13,797 for production and placement of radio spots, $2,637 for newspaper ads, $5,079 for sample ballots, and $3,289 for yard signs. For the fall campaign against dental technician Kenneth Kondner, Mfume spent $17,231 on broadcast ads, $11,988 on billboards, $2,715 on yard signs, $2,383 on sample ballots, and $1,546 on newspaper ads.

Kondner spent less than $5,000 on his campaign and filed no financial statements with the Federal Election Commission.

Campaign Expenditures	Mfume Amount Spent	% of Total
Overhead		
Office furniture/supplies	$ 2,777	1.29
Rent/utilities	1,200	.56
Salaries	3,645	1.70
Taxes	0	
Bank/investment fees	1,201	.56
Lawyers/accountants	0	
Telephone	7,647	3.56
Campaign automobile	0	
Computers/office equipment	2,799	1.30
Travel	3,571	1.66
Food/meetings	22,181	10.32
Subtotal	**45,022**	**20.95**
Fund Raising		
Events	49,548	23.05
Direct mail	0	
Telemarketing	0	
Subtotal	**49,548**	**23.05**
Polling	**0**	
Advertising		
Electronic media	32,845	15.28
Other media	23,050	10.72
Subtotal	**55,895**	**26.01**
Other Campaign Activity		
Persuasion mail/brochures	0	
Actual campaigning	20,770	9.66
Staff/volunteers	0	
Subtotal	**20,770**	**9.66**
Constituent Gifts/Entertainment	**34,231**	**15.93**
Donations to		
Candidates from same state	2,100	.98
Candidates from other states	1,750	.81
Civic organizations	2,172	1.01
Ideological groups	3,450	1.61
Political parties	0	
Subtotal	**9,472**	**4.41**
Unitemized Expenses	**0**	
Total Campaign Expenses	**$ 214,937**	
PAC Contributions	**$ 131,687**	
Individual Contributions	**113,669**	
Total Receipts*	**255,269**	

*Includes PAC and individual contributions as well as interest earned, party contributions, etc.

†No expenditures or receipts on file. Candidates raising or spending less than $5,000 are not required to file reports with the Federal Election Commission.

District 8 — MARYLAND

Rep. Constance A. Morella (R)

1992 Election Results

Constance A. Morella (R) 203,377 (73%)
Edward J. Heffernan (D) 77,042 (27%)

While Rep. Constance A. Morella spent roughly the same amount on her 1992 campaign as she had in 1990, redistricting caused her to spend a bit more of her 1992 budget on direct appeals to voters. Advertising and persuasion mail costs during the 1992 campaign amounted to $68,092, accounting for 21 percent of her total outlays. By comparison, Morella spent just $30,676 on such items in 1990.

As in 1990, Smith & Harroff of Alexandria, Va., handled her limited broadcast advertising campaign, collecting $16,730 for creating and placing two new radio spots. Noting that they had run against "a very inexperienced challenger," campaign manager William C. Miller said Morella's ads stressed her "longtime roots in the district" and the fact that she was "an independent voice in Montgomery county." Miller added that Morella closed each of the thirty-second spots by stating that she "enjoyed representing the county and hoped to be reelected."

To reach her new constituents, Morella sent out a persuasion mailer prior to the general election, something she had not done in 1990. According to Miller, Republican and independent voters in the district received an introductory piece on the three-term incumbent that included her legislative accomplishments, endorsements by various local officials, and a personal appeal by Morella for their votes.

Morella spent $5,058 to run a series of ads in newspapers such as the *Washington Jewish Week*, the *Montgomery County Sentinel*, the *Montgomery County Express*, and the *Frederick News Post*. She also placed one ad in the *Washington Post*.

A much less expensive form of advertising was the $420 she invested in cardboard fans, which were passed out a fairs and parades. One version had Morella's picture with the phrase "I'm a Connie Morella fan." Another asked people to "Join the Connie Morella fan club" and listed the campaign headquarters phone number.

As in 1990, Morella's biggest expense was her campaign overhead, which consumed 50 percent of her 1992 budget. She had four part-time employees throughout the two-year election cycle. Rent on her permanent campaign office amounted to $26,433 and parking fees added $6,330.

To fund her permanent campaign, Morella held a dozen fund-raisers, including a $75-a-head dinner that raised additional money by auctioning off donated items, such as a day on a boat, a balloon ride, and a golf outing.

Edward J. Heffernan, a former aide to Rep. Richard J. Durbin (D-Ill.), largely waged a door-to-door campaign, distributing 25,000 brochures during the primary and general election campaigns.

Campaign Expenditures	Morella Amount Spent	Morella % of Total	Heffernan Amount Spent	Heffernan % of Total
Overhead				
Office furniture/supplies	$ 6,230	1.90	$ 2,798	3.37
Rent/utilities	32,763	9.98	6,073	7.32
Salaries	85,143	25.94	11,172	13.46
Taxes	21,535	6.56	0	
Bank/investment fees	65	.02	0	
Lawyers/accountants	0		0	
Telephone	7,270	2.21	2,108	2.54
Campaign automobile	0		0	
Computers/office equipment	9,285	2.83	0	
Travel	510	.16	340	.41
Food/meetings	968	.29	0	
Subtotal	**163,769**	**49.89**	**22,491**	**27.11**
Fund Raising				
Events	28,073	8.55	7,588	9.14
Direct mail	30,590	9.32	0	
Telemarketing	0		0	
Subtotal	**58,663**	**17.87**	**7,588**	**9.14**
Polling	**10,695**	**3.26**	**0**	
Advertising				
Electronic media	16,730	5.10	6,544	7.89
Other media	6,616	2.02	6,148	7.41
Subtotal	**23,346**	**7.11**	**12,692**	**15.30**
Other Campaign Activity				
Persuasion mail/brochures	44,746	13.63	21,312	25.69
Actual campaigning	5,680	1.73	11,231	13.54
Staff/volunteers	446	.14	0	
Subtotal	**50,872**	**15.50**	**32,543**	**39.22**
Constituent Gifts/Entertainment	**5,941**	**1.81**	**0**	
Donations to				
Candidates from same state	0		0	
Candidates from other states	0		0	
Civic organizations	0		0	
Ideological groups	0		0	
Political parties	80	.02	150	.18
Subtotal	**80**	**.02**	**150**	**.18**
Unitemized Expenses	**14,900**	**4.54**	**7,508**	**9.05**
Total Campaign Expenses	**$ 328,266**		**$ 82,972**	
PAC Contributions	**$ 184,373**		**$ 10,606**	
Individual Contributions	**227,352**		**57,626**	
Total Receipts*	**430,301**		**75,483**	

*Includes PAC and individual contributions as well as interest earned, party contributions, etc.

MASSACHUSETTS District 1

Rep. John W. Olver (D)

1992 Election Results

John W. Olver** (D)	135,049	(52%)
Patrick Larkin (R)	113,828	(43%)

After thirty-two years in the House, Rep. Silvio O. Conte died in February 1991, setting up a free-for-all to fill the seat no Democrat had held during the twentieth century.

Ten candidates entered the Democratic melee, including state senator John W. Olver. Olver pumped nearly $240,000 into his two-month primary effort, bringing in Squier/Eskew/Knapp/Ochs Communications of Washington, D.C., to handle broadcast media; Johnson and Associates of Tolland, Conn., for persuasion mail; and Boston-based pollsters Harrison & Goldberg. Olver received 31 percent of the vote and emerged with a 12-point win.

Olver's opponent in the June 4 special election was former state representative Steven D. Pierce, who put more than $575,000 into their head-to-head battle. Throughout their five-week duel Pierce slammed Olver as a tax-and-spend liberal who had helped former Democratic governor Michael Dukakis ruin the state's economy. Senate Minority Leader Bob Dole (R-Kan.) echoed that theme, calling Olver "a taller Mike Dukakis."

Pierce also benefited from independent campaigns waged against Olver by the Massachusetts Citizens for Life and the National Right to Life Political Action Committee, which together reported spending $19,708. One brochure charged that Olver favored legislation allowing "tax-funded abortion on demand even up until the moment of birth."

Olver responded by spending nearly $497,000, much of it on advertising that attacked Pierce as a right-wing ideologue. His ads included a spot slamming Pierce for his opposition to abortion and his support of a constitutional amendment that would allow public money to go to parochial schools. Olver benefited greatly from a $144,091 independent campaign waged against Pierce by the National Abortion Rights Action League. Olver prevailed by fewer than 2,000 votes out of the nearly 140,000 votes cast.

Olver's 1991 victories cost $736,723, or 54 percent of his spending for the entire 1992 election cycle. Squier/Eskew received $314,589 for designing and placing broadcast ads during the 1991 campaigns.

In 1992 Olver faced Patrick Larkin, Conte's former administrative assistant. Television advertising dominated Olver's spending, with Squier/Eskew collecting $235,967. Olver's worst investment was the $13,633 he paid NK Associates for opposition research. Based on their work Olver charged Larkin with holding a no-show job with former New Jersey Rep. Jim Courter at the same time he was collecting a government salary from Conte. Courter immediately produced documents showing his payments had been made to different Patrick J. Larkin, prompting an embarrassed Olver to apologize.

	Olver		Larkin	
Campaign Expenditures	Amount Spent	% of Total	Amount Spent	% of Total
Overhead				
Office furniture/supplies	$ 20,022	1.42	$ 7,828	2.03
Rent/utilities	18,723	1.33	8,738	2.26
Salaries	167,419	11.88	27,755	7.18
Taxes	46,516	3.30	0	
Bank/investment fees	476	.03	355	.09
Lawyers/accountants	1,236	.09	0	
Telephone	16,478	1.17	7,530	1.95
Campaign automobile	3,550	.25	0	
Computers/office equipment	26,486	1.88	8,541	2.21
Travel	13,800	.98	2,755	.71
Food/meetings	820	.06	106	.03
Subtotal	315,525	22.39	63,607	16.46
Fund Raising				
Events	123,081	8.73	12,973	3.36
Direct mail	2,440	.17	1,728	.45
Telemarketing	9,986	.71	0	
Subtotal	135,508	9.62	14,701	3.80
Polling	84,532	6.00	35,615	9.22
Advertising				
Electronic media	574,120	40.74	165,748	42.90
Other media	5,994	.43	19,332	5.00
Subtotal	580,114	41.17	185,080	47.90
Other Campaign Activity				
Persuasion mail/brochures	149,616	10.62	25,288	6.55
Actual campaigning	133,467	9.47	51,570	13.35
Staff/volunteers	1,861	.13	187	.05
Subtotal	284,945	20.22	77,044	19.94
Constituent Gifts/ Entertainment	2,480	.18	0	
Donations to				
Candidates from same state	620	.04	0	
Candidates from other states	0		0	
Civic organizations	25		1,321	.34
Ideological groups	135	.01	0	
Political parties	275	.02	130	.03
Subtotal	1,055	.07	1,451	.38
Unitemized Expenses	4,927	.35	8,866	2.29
Total Campaign Expenses	$ 1,409,086		$ 386,365	
PAC Contributions	$ 296,780		$ 96,685	
Individual Contributions	286,294		248,242	
Total Receipts*	705,906		398,618	

*Includes PAC and individual contributions as well as interest earned, party contributions, etc.

**Totals include special election disbursements and receipts.

District 2 — MASSACHUSETTS

Rep. Richard E. Neal (D)

1992 Election Results

Richard E. Neal (D)	131,215	(53%)
Anthony W. Ravosa, Jr. (R)	76,795	(31%)
Thomas R. Sheehan † (I)	38,963	(16%)

Rep. Richard E. Neal had every reason to increase his spending in 1992. One-third of the constituents in his redrawn district were new to him. He had eighty-seven overdrafts at the House bank. He attracted two Democratic primary opponents who spent a total of $104,092 and together captured 52 percent of the votes. His Republican challenger, Anthony W. Ravosa, Jr., spent $131,542 on the campaign and captured 31 percent of the general election votes. For the People party nominee Thomas R. Sheehan mounted a strong third-party challenge and received 16 percent. Nevertheless, Neal spent $225,930 less on his 1992 reelection effort than he had in 1990.

Neal reduced his spending on overhead from $133,825 in the 1990 election cycle to $59,911 in 1992, a drop of 55 percent. Outlays for salaries and taxes dropped by $57,020, primarily because congressional staff assistants who had drawn salaries from the campaign in 1990 opted to volunteer their time in 1992. "The campaign was not nearly as intense as in 1990," explained Kevin Kennedy, one such staff assistant.

With less need to raise money, fund-raising expenses declined from $90,632 to $58,973, a drop of 35 percent. Neal paid Robert H. Bassin Associates of Washington, D.C., $4,597 for coordinating the campaign's two political action committee (PAC) receptions. PAC contributions accounted for 54 percent of Neal's receipts. Numerous receptions in his district raised $162,651, including $108,182 from individuals who gave less than $200.

Neal spent $70,596 of his campaign budget during 1991, and more than $180,000 of the remaining $233,993 he spent was invested in winning the September 15 primary. The campaign's lone persuasion mailing was sent out before the primary. Four of the campaign's five television commercials and all eight of its radio spots were aired before the primary. The ads focused on Neal's ability to deliver federal projects to the district and never mentioned his opponents or his House bank overdrafts.

For providing general strategic advice, Joseph Napolitan Associates received $62,509, which accounted for most of the expenses listed under "actual campaigning." Campaign Performance Group of San Francisco, Calif., collected $19,630 for its work on the low-key persuasion mail effort, and the Rendon Co. of Boston received $12,806 for designing his advertising.

One area in which Neal increased his spending over 1990 was constituent entertainment and gifts, which increased from an almost nonexistent $662 in 1990 to a still modest $4,882 in 1992. His largest constituent expense was a free family picnic in 1991 that cost $1,568.

	Neal		Ravosa	
Campaign Expenditures	Amount Spent	% of Total	Amount Spent	% of Total
Overhead				
Office furniture/supplies	$ 2,818	.93	$ 2,273	1.73
Rent/utilities	6,000	1.97	1,877	1.43
Salaries	0		12,570	9.56
Taxes	11,045	3.63	0	
Bank/investment fees	2,710	.89	361	.27
Lawyers/accountants	2,512	.82	0	
Telephone	6,704	2.20	2,234	1.70
Campaign automobile	18,828	6.18	0	
Computers/office equipment	4,670	1.53	36	.03
Travel	2,604	.85	7,830	5.95
Food/meetings	2,020	.66	0	
Subtotal	59,911	19.67	27,180	20.66
Fund Raising				
Events	58,973	19.36	5,949	4.52
Direct mail	0		2,189	1.66
Telemarketing	0		0	
Subtotal	58,973	19.36	8,138	6.19
Polling	3,000	.98	0	
Advertising				
Electronic media	31,209	10.25	18,701	14.22
Other media	3,576	1.17	10,776	8.19
Subtotal	34,785	11.42	29,477	22.41
Other Campaign Activity				
Persuasion mail/brochures	33,721	11.07	28,946	22.00
Actual campaigning	69,636	22.86	37,198	28.28
Staff/volunteers	2,792	.92	189	.14
Subtotal	106,148	34.85	66,332	50.43
Constituent Gifts/ Entertainment	4,882	1.60	0	
Donations to				
Candidates from same state	0		0	
Candidates from other states	0		0	
Civic organizations	0		50	.04
Ideological groups	0		0	
Political parties	0		0	
Subtotal	0		50	.04
Unitemized Expenses	36,891	12.11	365	.28
Total Campaign Expenses	$ 304,590		$ 131,542	
PAC Contributions	$ 208,395		$ 7,550	
Individual Contributions	170,901		66,214	
Total Receipts*	384,741		108,758	

*Includes PAC and individual contributions as well as interest earned, party contributions, etc.

† No expenditures or receipts on file. Candidates raising or spending less than $5,000 are not required to file reports with the Federal Election Commission.

MASSACHUSETTS   District 3

Rep. Peter I. Blute (R)

1992 Election Results
Peter I. Blute (R)   131,473   (50%)
Joseph D. Early (D)   115,587   (44%)

Unopposed in both 1988 and 1990, nine-term Rep. Joseph D. Early presented an inviting target in 1992. He had 140 overdrafts at the House bank and had voted for both the congressional pay raise and the 1990 budget agreement, which included several tax hikes. When redistricting presented him with 270,000 new voters who knew little about him other than the fact that he had "bounced" numerous checks, four Democrats and three Republicans, including state representative Peter I. Blute, jumped into the fray.

The primary campaign was particularly draining on Early, who spent more than $337,000 between January 1 and September 15, 1992 to secure the Democratic nomination. Having also spent $182,128 during the off-year to keep his permanent campaign humming, Early was able to commit only $397,881 of his $917,389 campaign treasury to the general election contest with Blute.

Blute, on the other hand, spent only about $150,000 to win the Republican nomination. A coordinated expenditure of $53,229 by the National Republican Congressional Committee helped pay for four persuasion mailers, so Blute was able to focus $389,836 on the fall campaign.

During the final weeks of the campaign, Blute put $107,829 into radio and television commercials, many of them negative. He aired spots that slammed Early for his overdrafts and his vote for the congressional pay raise. One ad charged that Early had "a terrible addiction: perkomania," while another labeled him "Tahiti Joe" for taking taxpayer-funded junkets to Tahiti and other exotic locales. In one radio spot, Early was portrayed as a Bart Simpson-like character who shunned responsibility for his mistakes.

Early returned fire with a $142,000 ad campaign that attacked Blute for running a negative campaign. Early's ads also skewered Blute for standing "with his conservative right-wing cronies who spend their time trying to define a family rather than help one." He accused Blute of favoring "trickle-down economics," and, in an effort to tie himself to Bill Clinton's coattails, convinced his chief Democratic primary rival to cut an ad stating that a vote for Blute would be "a vote for George Bush." Another spot accused Blute of voting in the state legislature to cut off unemployment benefits, reduce job training funds, and slash college scholarships.

While Early put $24,380 into yard signs and posters and another $17,732 into buttons and bumper stickers, Blute spent just $3,157 on such items. Instead, Blute put $29,000 into a phonebank operation run by Groundswell Direct of Worcester. Early spent $9,144 on his get-out-the-vote efforts.

Campaign Expenditures	Blute Amount Spent	Blute % of Total	Early Amount Spent	Early % of Total
Overhead				
Office furniture/supplies	$ 8,347	1.71	$ 15,459	1.69
Rent/utilities	4,652	.95	5,914	.64
Salaries	28,426	5.83	102,598	11.18
Taxes	0		39,630	4.32
Bank/investment fees	225	.05	261	.03
Lawyers/accountants	0		5,307	.58
Telephone	15,552	3.19	5,913	.64
Campaign automobile	0		24,214	2.64
Computers/office equipment	12,418	2.55	4,944	.54
Travel	1,618	.33	10,306	1.12
Food/meetings	209	.04	13,133	1.43
Subtotal	**71,446**	**14.66**	**227,681**	**24.82**
Fund Raising				
Events	58,767	12.06	221,066	24.10
Direct mail	67,514	13.85	0	
Telemarketing	0		0	
Subtotal	**126,280**	**25.91**	**221,066**	**24.10**
Polling	**3,500**	**.72**	**32,500**	**3.54**
Advertising				
Electronic media	145,867	29.93	173,891	18.95
Other media	17,657	3.62	23,912	2.61
Subtotal	**163,524**	**33.56**	**197,803**	**21.56**
Other Campaign Activity				
Persuasion mail/brochures	77,630	15.93	117,852	12.85
Actual campaigning	38,628	7.93	66,397	7.24
Staff/volunteers	0		1,621	.18
Subtotal	**116,258**	**23.86**	**185,870**	**20.26**
Constituent Gifts/ Entertainment	0		31,963	3.48
Donations to				
Candidates from same state	0		350	.04
Candidates from other states	0		0	
Civic organizations	285	.06	6,863	.75
Ideological groups	0		125	.01
Political parties	0		0	
Subtotal	**285**	**.06**	**7,338**	**.80**
Unitemized Expenses	**6,035**	**1.24**	**13,169**	**1.44**
Total Campaign Expenses	**$ 487,328**		**$ 917,389**	
PAC Contributions	$ 43,900		$ 220,725	
Individual Contributions	388,439		606,118	
Total Receipts*	438,994		829,258	

*Includes PAC and individual contributions as well as interest earned, party contributions, etc.

District 4 — MASSACHUSETTS

Rep. Barney Frank (D)

1992 Election Results

Barney Frank (D)	182,633	(68%)
Edward J. McCormick III (R)	70,665	(26%)
Luke Lumina † (I)	13,670	(5%)

Neither redistricting nor the electorate's anti-incumbent mood had any effect on Rep. Barney Frank's 1992 campaign. Frank spent $341,275 less in 1992 than he had in 1990.

Frank's 1990 spending had been driven largely by the fallout from the investigation and subsequent reprimand by the House ethics committee for his relationship with male prostitute Stephen Gobie. He had tapped his campaign treasury for $118,151 to cover legal expenses. To monitor public reaction to the storm of negative publicity, Frank had invested $35,200 in polls. Nearly $148,000 was put into advertising to thwart Republican John R. Soto, who continuously denounced Frank for his relationship with Gobie, railed against gay rights laws, and called upon Frank to be tested for AIDS and reveal the results.

The 1992 campaign offered Frank welcome relief. Attorney Edward J. McCormick III chose to fight Frank on issues of public policy, calling efforts to raise the issue of sexual misconduct "character assassination." When a heckler began hurling charges of sexual misconduct at Frank during one of their debates, McCormick took the microphone and told the heckler to stop.

McCormick's problem was that he had no money to get his message out. With only $51,624 to spend, he could not afford television advertising. He could afford to place only one round of newspaper ads. He had no money to print or mail glossy brochures, so he printed palm cards, which campaign volunteers handed out.

Without the need to defend himself against caustic, personal attacks or to counter his opponent's positive message, Frank could afford to take it easy. He spent nothing on polls. Daniel B. Payne & Co. of Boston received $27,533 for creating and producing broadcast and newspaper ads; Boston-based Yellin Media Services collected $44,545 for placing the ads. Frank chose not to hire a persuasion mail consultant, opting instead to handle the $69,048 effort in-house. He spent only $2,343 on buttons and bumper stickers. Signs and posters cost $2,268. He also gave $2,000 to the state Democratic party's coordinated get-out-the-vote drive.

As in previous campaigns, Frank wrote his own fund-raising solicitations, several of which were mailed to a list of more than 16,000 frequent contributors. Over the two-year election cycle, these appeals helped raise $184,093 from donors who gave less than $200.

Frank's $21,539 travel budget included $728 for airfare to attend a conference sponsored by the International Gay and Lesbian Human Rights Caucus.

Campaign Expenditures	Frank Amount Spent	Frank % of Total	McCormick Amount Spent	McCormick % of Total
Overhead				
Office furniture/supplies	$ 3,565	.95	$ 225	.44
Rent/utilities	6,442	1.71	800	1.55
Salaries	48,966	13.02	14,750	28.57
Taxes	3,913	1.04	0	
Bank/investment fees	113	.03	227	.44
Lawyers/accountants	3,450	.92	0	
Telephone	4,887	1.30	368	.71
Campaign automobile	0		0	
Computers/office equipment	21,332	5.67	0	
Travel	21,539	5.73	2,632	5.10
Food/meetings	1,620	.43	0	
Subtotal	**115,827**	**30.79**	**19,002**	**36.81**
Fund Raising				
Events	36,849	9.80	2,394	4.64
Direct mail	40,848	10.86	0	
Telemarketing	0		0	
Subtotal	**77,698**	**20.65**	**2,394**	**4.64**
Polling	**0**		**0**	
Advertising				
Electronic media	45,267	12.03	0	
Other media	29,853	7.94	17,363	33.63
Subtotal	**75,120**	**19.97**	**17,363**	**33.63**
Other Campaign Activity				
Persuasion mail/brochures	69,048	18.36	2,618	5.07
Actual campaigning	8,421	2.24	10,248	19.85
Staff/volunteers	50	.01	0	
Subtotal	**77,519**	**20.61**	**12,866**	**24.92**
Constituent Gifts/ Entertainment	525	.14	0	
Donations to				
Candidates from same state	1,000	.27	0	
Candidates from other states	13,473	3.58	0	
Civic organizations	1,360	.36	0	
Ideological groups	250	.07	0	
Political parties	13,365	3.55	0	
Subtotal	**29,448**	**7.83**	**0**	
Unitemized Expenses	42	.01	0	
Total Campaign Expenses	**$ 376,179**		**$ 51,624**	
PAC Contributions	$ 185,360		$ 0	
Individual Contributions	300,761		27,301	
Total Receipts*	498,997		51,540	

*Includes PAC and individual contributions as well as interest earned, party contributions, etc.

† No expenditures or receipts on file. Candidates raising or spending less than $5,000 are not required to file reports with the Federal Election Commission.

MASSACHUSETTS — District 5

Rep. Martin T. Meehan (D)

1992 Election Results

Martin T. Meehan (D)	133,844	(52%)
Paul W. Cronin (R)	96,206	(38%)
Mary J. Farmelli † (I)	19,077	(7%)

Attorney Martin T. Meehan waited until three months before the September 15 primary to officially launch his campaign against Rep. Chester G. Atkins. It was August before Meehan pulled together his team of consultants. Yet despite his late start, Meehan cruised to a two-to-one victory.

Meehan's 30-point primary victory cost more than $400,000, 87 percent of which was spent on the design and delivery of his direct appeals to voters. The Campaign Group of Philadelphia, Pa., received $280,000 for creating and placing radio and television commercials. Campaign Performance Group of San Francisco, Calif., collected $36,612 for creating two brochures. Barry Kaplovitz Associates of Boston was paid $17,420 for conducting preprimary polls and the Sinsheimer Group of Durham, N.C., received $5,552 for conducting opposition research that fueled the advertising and persuasion mail.

Both Meehan's broadcast ads and brochures pounded home the anti-incumbent theme, pointing to Meehan's local roots and his tenure as a county prosecuting attorney while portraying Atkins as an unethical Washington insider who had lost touch with his district. Atkins had opened himself up to the latter charge by working unsuccessfully to convince state legislators to remove the towns of Lawrence and Lowell from the district's boundaries. Atkins was further wounded by his support for a congressional pay raise and his 127 overdrafts at the House bank, facts that quickly made their way into Meehan's advertising and mail. The brochures also charged that Atkins had "put a political operative on his taxpayer-financed congressional payroll at a salary of $90,000 to help with his reelection campaign."

The general election contest with Paul W. Cronin, who had served one term in the House before losing his seat to Democrat Paul S. Tsongas in 1974, was equally bitter. Meehan's advertising and mail pointed out that in 1980 the Internal Revenue Service had placed a tax lien against his property for failing to pay his federal taxes, that his company had polluted two Superfund sites, and that Cronin had paid a $50,000 criminal fine because the company had mishandled hazardous waste. Referring to Cronin as representing "25 years of politics as usual," Meehan's one persuasion mailer also labeled Cronin "ineffective," "deceptive," and "hypocritical." The Campaign Group collected $360,000 for creating and placing general election broadcast ads. Campaign Performance Group received $1,886 from Meehan, $17,186 from the state Democratic party, and $5,000 from the Democratic Congressional Campaign Committee.

Cronin ran ads questioning the legality of the home loan Meehan used to help finance his campaign and attacking Meehan for negative campaigning.

	Meehan		Cronin	
Campaign Expenditures	Amount Spent	% of Total	Amount Spent	% of Total
Overhead				
Office furniture/supplies	$ 5,313	.64	$ 3,768	.65
Rent/utilities	2,801	.33	2,400	.41
Salaries	4,600	.55	39,704	6.85
Taxes	0		15,341	2.65
Bank/investment fees	4,820	.58	98	.02
Lawyers/accountants	0		0	
Telephone	6,164	.74	5,090	.88
Campaign automobile	0		3,042	.52
Computers/office equipment	2,901	.35	24,528	4.23
Travel	2,339	.28	5,770	1.00
Food/meetings	0		0	
Subtotal	28,937	3.46	99,742	17.20
Fund Raising				
Events	37,993	4.54	17,314	2.99
Direct mail	0		26,594	4.59
Telemarketing	5,839	.70	0	
Subtotal	43,832	5.24	43,908	7.57
Polling	33,618	4.02	15,138	2.61
Advertising				
Electronic media	640,000	76.51	297,671	51.34
Other media	8,623	1.03	11,636	2.01
Subtotal	648,623	77.54	309,307	53.34
Other Campaign Activity				
Persuasion mail/brochures	51,225	6.12	79,839	13.77
Actual campaigning	29,933	3.58	21,770	3.75
Staff/volunteers	200	.02	413	.07
Subtotal	81,357	9.73	102,022	17.59
Constituent Gifts/ Entertainment	71	.01	0	
Donations to				
Candidates from same state	0		0	
Candidates from other states	0		0	
Civic organizations	50	.01	0	
Ideological groups	0		0	
Political parties	0		0	
Subtotal	50	.01	0	
Unitemized Expenses	0		9,728	1.68
Total Campaign Expenses	$ 836,487		$ 579,845	
PAC Contributions	$ 0		$ 0	
Individual Contributions	628,704		414,464	
Total Receipts*	832,266		565,565	

*Includes PAC and individual contributions as well as interest earned, party contributions, etc.

† No expenditures or receipts on file. Candidates raising or spending less than $5,000 are not required to file reports with the Federal Election Commission.

District 6 — MASSACHUSETTS

Rep. Peter Torkildsen (R)

1992 Election Results

Peter Torkildsen (R)   159,165   (55%)
Nicholas Mavroules (D)   130,248   (45%)

Former state representative and state commissioner of labor and industries Peter G. Torkildsen ran few negative ads in his battle with seven-term Democratic Rep. Nicholas Mavroules. Daily media coverage of a federal grand jury investigation of Mavroules and his indictment in August 1992 on seventeen counts of racketeering, bribery, and tax evasion provided all the negatives any challenger could hope for.

However, before he could afford to worry about Mavroules, Torkildsen first had to get past former state party executive director Alexander T. Tennant in the Republican primary. Tennant spent more than $468,000 on the contest, outspending Torkildsen by nearly three to one.

Among the most hard-hitting of Tennant's ads was one that claimed Torkildsen had switched from an anti-abortion position to a pro-choice stance in April 1992 only after reviewing polls showing that such a switch would improve his electoral chances. Tennant pulled the commercial after Torkildsen's pollster, Williams & Associates of Salem provided evidence that the poll in question had been conducted after Torkildsen announced his change of heart. Torkildsen ran no television ads and spent just $16,590 on radio spots for the primary but emerged with 56 percent of the votes.

Mavroules invested $140,377 in his permanent campaign in 1991. During the first nine months of 1992, his legal problems consumed $78,148 of his campaign treasury. He was forced to devote $222,502 to his September primary contest with state representative Barbara Hildt, which he won by fewer than 700 votes. Only $277,231 of Mavroules's total outlays were directly focused on Torkildsen, or about $58,000 less than Torkildsen put into his final push.

According to campaign manager Eugene Hartigan, Torkildsen's polls showed that their biggest challenge was "to make Peter more 'congressional,' to take him from a state representative to a congressional candidate in people's minds." Torkildsen paid Severin/Aviles Associates of New York $114,718 over the final month of the campaign to place a television commercial featuring close-up shots of the candidate telling viewers that he wanted to change and clean up government. Adnet Associates of Framingham received $19,663 for buying time to air two radio commercials.

Mavroules countered with a $127,000 broadcast advertising campaign consisting of one television and five radio commercials created by McDougall Associates of Peabody. The television spot was a personal plea to voters to keep an open mind concerning his innocence. After the election, he was convicted and sent to prison.

Campaign Expenditures	Torkildsen Amount Spent	Torkildsen % of Total	Mavroules Amount Spent	Mavroules % of Total
Overhead				
Office furniture/supplies	$ 3,661	.74	$ 4,488	.62
Rent/utilities	14,855	3.00	8,392	1.17
Salaries	98,912	20.00	70,465	9.81
Taxes	0		1,071	.15
Bank/investment fees	974	.20	75	.01
Lawyers/accountants	0		101,148	14.08
Telephone	7,590	1.53	23,127	3.22
Campaign automobile	3,501	.71	14,408	2.01
Computers/office equipment	6,988	1.41	2,214	.31
Travel	1,342	.27	2,260	.31
Food/meetings	92	.02	2,966	.41
Subtotal	**137,915**	**27.89**	**230,613**	**32.11**
Fund Raising				
Events	37,143	7.51	140,035	19.50
Direct mail	20,050	4.05	0	
Telemarketing	0		0	
Subtotal	**57,192**	**11.56**	**140,035**	**19.50**
Polling	**24,670**	**4.99**	**15,568**	**2.17**
Advertising				
Electronic media	157,117	31.77	149,613	20.83
Other media	2,326	.47	15,305	2.13
Subtotal	**159,443**	**32.24**	**164,918**	**22.96**
Other Campaign Activity				
Persuasion mail/brochures	61,878	12.51	57,224	7.97
Actual campaigning	33,368	6.75	54,574	7.60
Staff/volunteers	261	.05	5,527	.77
Subtotal	**95,507**	**19.31**	**117,325**	**16.33**
Constituent Gifts/Entertainment	**389**	**.08**	**4,115**	**.57**
Donations to				
Candidates from same state	0		0	
Candidates from other states	0		1,000	.14
Civic organizations	300	.06	2,125	.30
Ideological groups	0		0	
Political parties	0		1,800	.25
Subtotal	**300**	**.06**	**4,925**	**.69**
Unitemized Expenses	**19,160**	**3.87**	**40,758**	**5.67**
Total Campaign Expenses	**$ 494,576**		**$ 718,258**	
PAC Contributions	$ 0		$ 249,125	
Individual Contributions	421,779		353,599	
Total Receipts*	463,007		612,064	

Includes PAC and individual contributions as well as interest earned, party contributions, etc.

MASSACHUSETTS District 7

Rep. Edward J. Markey (D)

1992 Election Results

Edward J. Markey (D)	174,837	(62%)
Stephen A. Sohn (R)	78,262	(28%)
Robert B. Antonelli † (I)	28,421	(10%)

Democratic Rep. Edward J. Markey had not faced a primary or general election opponent since 1984 and had emerged virtually unscathed from the redistricting process. He did, however, have ninety-two overdrafts at the House bank, and that prompted plastic surgeon Stephen A. Sohn to take up the challenge.

Initially, Sohn fought an uphill battle to get press coverage of his long-shot campaign. According to campaign manager Dennis O'Connor, Jr., that problem was solved by what he termed "the pig ad." The television commercial opened with pigs eating at a trough. Charging that Markey had "voted time and again to raise his pay and your taxes," the ad concluded by slamming Markey for his overdrafts.

Sohn expanded on the theme by renting a pig costume, dressing campaign workers as "Les Pork," and sending them into the streets with a sign that called for "less pork in congress" and Markey's defeat. The campaign also rented a chicken costume, which Sohn dubbed "The Markey Chicken." Campaign workers wore the outfit on walks through the district to dramatize Markey's refusal to debate. "We were sending out serious press releases on the issues for weeks, but got not one iota of coverage," recalled O'Connor. "But as soon as the pig ad ran and the chicken showed up, we were in the paper every day."

Markey countered with a $891,977 campaign. Marttila & Kiley of Boston received $398,178 for creating and placing broadcast ads, conducting polls, and providing general strategic advice. Among Markey's ads was a television commercial touting his work on legislation to reregulate the cable television industry. A radio spot slammed Sohn for the pig spot: "Had enough mud? Say 'no' to Stephen Sohn's negative campaign."

While the Markey campaign had no office until July 1992, it did have a campaign manager throughout the election cycle. Maura Donlan, his former legislative assistant, assumed the post in January 1991 and collected $34,057 over the next two years. The campaign had offices in Chelsea, Framingham, and Waltham. By election day, the campaign staff had grown considerably, with a dozen people assigned to organize what Dan Rabinovitz, Markey's administrative assistant, described as "field community outreach."

There was also room in the budget for items not directly tied to Markey's reelection efforts. The campaign spent $10,362 on holiday cards, $1,047 on constituent flowers, $3,881 on a Christmas party for volunteers and supporters, $6,370 on tickets to presidential inaugural events, and $3,745 at the Democratic National Convention.

Campaign Expenditures	Markey Amount Spent	Markey % of Total	Sohn Amount Spent	Sohn % of Total
Overhead				
Office furniture/supplies	$ 15,686	1.76	$ 8,605	3.33
Rent/utilities	9,450	1.06	10,730	4.16
Salaries	75,777	8.50	26,605	10.31
Taxes	16,175	1.81	10,921	4.23
Bank/investment fees	0		11	
Lawyers/accountants	21,364	2.40	0	
Telephone	4,471	.50	3,089	1.20
Campaign automobile	0		0	
Computers/office equipment	5,723	.64	3,574	1.38
Travel	20,668	2.32	130	.05
Food/meetings	1,645	.18	20	.01
Subtotal	**170,959**	**19.17**	**63,684**	**24.67**
Fund Raising				
Events	128,951	14.46	6,033	2.34
Direct mail	0		6,880	2.67
Telemarketing	0		6,563	2.54
Subtotal	**128,951**	**14.46**	**19,476**	**7.55**
Polling	**9,178**	**1.03**	**8,000**	**3.10**
Advertising				
Electronic media	359,000	40.25	89,493	34.67
Other media	18,900	2.12	1,747	.68
Subtotal	**377,900**	**42.37**	**91,240**	**35.35**
Other Campaign Activity				
Persuasion mail/brochures	60,685	6.80	28,337	10.98
Actual campaigning	60,290	6.76	44,628	17.29
Staff/volunteers	1,147	.13	111	.04
Subtotal	**122,121**	**13.69**	**73,076**	**28.31**
Constituent Gifts/ Entertainment	22,319	2.50	0	
Donations to				
Candidates from same state	1,250	.14	0	
Candidates from other states	6,750	.76	0	
Civic organizations	3,400	.38	0	
Ideological groups	0		0	
Political parties	6,800	.76	50	.02
Subtotal	**18,200**	**2.04**	**50**	**.02**
Unitemized Expenses	42,349	4.75	2,587	1.00
Total Campaign Expenses	$ 891,977		$ 258,113	
PAC Contributions	$ 0		$ 0	
Individual Contributions	394,179		170,646	
Total Receipts*	450,926		289,756	

*Includes PAC and individual contributions as well as interest earned, party contributions, etc.

† No expenditures or receipts on file. Candidates raising or spending less than $5,000 are not required to file reports with the Federal Election Commission.

District 8 — MASSACHUSETTS

Rep. Joseph P. Kennedy II (D)

1992 Election Results

Joseph P. Kennedy II (D)	149,903	(83%)
Alice Harriett Nakash † (I)	30,402	(17%)

Rep. Joseph P. Kennedy II spent $766,014 on his 1992 reelection effort, but only 15 percent of that total was invested in direct appeals to voters. No Republican bothered to contest the seat, and neither his Democratic primary challenger nor his general election opponent, independent Alice Harriett Nakash, spent more than $5,000 on the race.

Kennedy spent a staggering $355,317 in 1991 to keep his permanent campaign operation running smoothly, including $183,510 on overhead and $134,834 on fund raising.

Over the two-year election cycle, the $353,745 Kennedy invested in overhead exceeded the total campaign outlays of 452 candidates, including 90 incumbents, 80 open-seat candidates, and 282 challengers. Kennedy's spending on staff salaries and benefits alone exceeded the total outlays of 201 challengers.

Chief of staff Michael Powell said the campaign held more than fifty fund-raising events. In all, the campaign invested $239,646 in its fund-raisers, staging dozens of events in the Boston area, at least a half dozen receptions in and around Washington, D.C., and multiple events in California, New York, Illinois, and Ohio. While Kennedy succeeded in raising $171,820 from out-of-state contributors who gave at least $200, that total was $116,074 less than he collected from such donors in the 1990 election cycle.

Despite all this fund-raising activity, Kennedy spent virtually nothing on fund-raising consultants. Fraioli/Jost of Washington, D.C., and T-Catalyst of Charlestown, Mass., received $1,191 and $3,000, respectively.

With no real opposition, Kennedy gave away more of his campaign funds than he invested in advertising. The campaign even spent more on constituent stroking than on broadcast advertising. Holiday greeting cards and meals for constituents cost $11,168 and $1,807, respectively. Expenditures on flowers for constituents and supporters totaled $4,012.

Redistricting handed Kennedy a constituency that was nearly 40 percent minority, which prompted Charles Calvin Yancy, a black Boston City Council member, to challenge Kennedy in the primary. Kennedy responded with four radio spots, including one touting his work to combat redlining by banks and insurance companies. Two persuasion mailers focused on Kennedy's legislative efforts to promote affordable housing and health care. Marttila & Kiley of Boston received $7,500 for designing the preprimary broadcast ads and persuasion mail and another $22,500 for general consulting. Austin-Sheinkopf of New York collected $7,600 for ad production. No such efforts were undertaken for the fall campaign.

Campaign Expenditures	Kennedy Amount Spent	% of Total
Overhead		
Office furniture/supplies	$ 16,610	2.17
Rent/utilities	22,806	2.98
Salaries	126,771	16.55
Taxes	29,174	3.81
Bank/investment fees	123	.02
Lawyers/accountants	6,000	.78
Telephone	46,070	6.01
Campaign automobile	17,749	2.32
Computers/office equipment	20,122	2.63
Travel	60,402	7.89
Food/meetings	7,918	1.03
Subtotal	**353,745**	**46.18**
Fund Raising		
Events	239,646	31.28
Direct mail	0	
Telemarketing	0	
Subtotal	**239,646**	**31.28**
Polling	**0**	
Advertising		
Electronic media	14,324	1.87
Other media	13,482	1.76
Subtotal	**27,806**	**3.63**
Other Campaign Activity		
Persuasion mail/brochures	55,311	7.22
Actual campaigning	29,776	3.89
Staff/volunteers	413	.05
Subtotal	**85,500**	**11.16**
Constituent Gifts/Entertainment	**17,044**	**2.22**
Donations to		
Candidates from same state	1,400	.18
Candidates from other states	6,900	.90
Civic organizations	5,845	.76
Ideological groups	3,220	.42
Political parties	18,510	2.42
Subtotal	**35,875**	**4.68**
Unitemized Expenses	**6,399**	**.84**
Total Campaign Expenses	**$ 766,014**	
PAC Contributions	**$ 146,030**	
Individual Contributions	**588,799**	
Total Receipts*	**769,635**	

*Includes PAC and individual contributions as well as interest earned, party contributions, etc.

† No expenditures or receipts on file. Candidates raising or spending less than $5,000 are not required to file reports with the Federal Election Commission.

MASSACHUSETTS — District 9

Rep. Joe Moakley (D)

1992 Election Results

Joe Moakley (D)	175,550	(69%)
Martin D. Conboy (R)	54,291	(21%)
Lawrence C. Mackin † (I)	15,637	(6%)

Rep. Joe Moakley had run unopposed in three of his nine previous reelection bids and had not faced a Republican challenger since 1982. His 1992 Republican opponent, insurance agent Martin D. Conboy, was able to spend just $12,619 on his long-shot challenge. Nevertheless, Moakley poured $1,070,769 into the contest, more than three times what he spent in 1990. "Our race was not 100 percent focused on the challenger," noted Frederick W. Clark, Washington liaison in Moakley's district office.

Overhead expenses accounted for 55 percent of Moakley's total outlays. In addition to office space he periodically rented in Boston's World Trade Center, Moakley opened campaign offices in Brockton and West Roxbury.

To keep the campaign engine humming during the off-year, Moakley paid eight part-time employees a total of $35,491. By election day the paid staff had grown to nineteen, pushing payroll costs for the two years to $247,780. A field staff coordinated the activities of 3,000 volunteers, while a separate fund-raising staff worked to fill the campaign's coffers. Six congressional staffers provided the leadership and drew campaign salaries totaling $57,986.

In the wake of reapportionment, which cost Massachusetts one of its eleven House seats, Moakley was concerned that redistricting might present him with a choice between a race in largely unknown territory and a contest with fellow Democratic Rep. Joseph P. Kennedy II. To ensure that his interests would be well represented, Moakley retained the Chicago law firm of Jenner & Block in October 1991. Over the next eleven months, the firm's advice cost the campaign $38,418. While redistricting provided Moakley with a constituency that was 45 percent new to him, the district's overwhelmingly Democratic character was maintained.

Moakley's advertising campaign consisted of three radio commercials and three companion newspaper ads that touted his success at delivering federal projects to the district, his efforts to end human rights abuses in El Salvador, and the need for comprehensive health care reform. The campaign developed two tabloid handouts and mailed a letter of introduction to new constituents.

Three Weymouth firms handled the bulk of his ad campaign. Michael P. Shea collected $15,000 for creating the radio spots and helping to design the tabloids and persuasion mail. Creative Concepts received $23,000 for its work on the tabloids and mailing. Yellin Media Services collected $30,937 for placing the radio spots and $57,533 for designing and placing the newspaper ads. The campaign also directly placed $6,826 of newspaper advertising.

	Moakley		Conboy	
Campaign Expenditures	Amount Spent	% of Total	Amount Spent	% of Total
Overhead				
Office furniture/supplies	$ 31,088	2.90	$ 712	5.64
Rent/utilities	19,364	1.81	125	.99
Salaries	247,780	23.14	0	
Taxes	100,702	9.40	0	
Bank/investment fees	1,532	.14	64	.51
Lawyers/accountants	76,016	7.10	0	
Telephone	8,603	.80	534	4.23
Campaign automobile	7,102	.66	0	
Computers/office equipment	51,118	4.77	0	
Travel	34,079	3.18	18	.14
Food/meetings	8,703	.81	0	
Subtotal	**586,088**	**54.74**	**1,452**	**11.51**
Fund Raising				
Events	62,086	5.80	0	
Direct mail	2,850	.27	0	
Telemarketing	12,644	1.18	0	
Subtotal	**77,581**	**7.25**	**0**	
Polling	**6,800**	**.64**	**0**	
Advertising				
Electronic media	41,641	3.89	1,459	11.56
Other media	66,449	6.21	507	4.02
Subtotal	**108,089**	**10.09**	**1,965**	**15.58**
Other Campaign Activity				
Persuasion mail/brochures	95,363	8.91	5,501	43.60
Actual campaigning	58,146	5.43	3,531	27.98
Staff/volunteers	14,259	1.33	0	
Subtotal	**167,769**	**15.67**	**9,032**	**71.58**
Constituent Gifts/ Entertainment	**22,515**	**2.10**	**0**	
Donations to				
Candidates from same state	9,870	.92	0	
Candidates from other states	3,500	.33	0	
Civic organizations	27,487	2.57	0	
Ideological groups	3,200	.30	0	
Political parties	16,700	1.56	69	.54
Subtotal	**60,757**	**5.67**	**69**	**.54**
Unitemized Expenses	**41,170**	**3.84**	**100**	**.79**
Total Campaign Expenses	**$ 1,070,769**		**$ 12,619**	
PAC Contributions	**$ 430,075**		**$ 2,159**	
Individual Contributions	378,357		12,445	
Total Receipts*	855,533		15,105	

*Includes PAC and individual contributions as well as interest earned, party contributions, etc.

† No expenditures or receipts on file. Candidates raising or spending less than $5,000 are not required to file reports with the Federal Election Commission.

District 10 — MASSACHUSETTS

Rep. Gerry E. Studds (D)

1992 Election Results

Gerry E. Studds (D)	189,342	(61%)
Daniel W. Daly (R)	75,887	(24%)
Jon L. Bryan (I)	39,265	(13%)

Rep. Gerry E. Studds, a ten-term incumbent, appeared vulnerable at the outset of the 1992 campaign. Republican Jon L. Bryan, a pilot for U.S. Air, had captured 47 percent of the vote in 1990. Redistricting had robbed Studds of his base of support in New Bedford and replaced it with more conservative, blue-collar communities such as Quincy. However, Studds's problems quickly faded amid the flurry of a $1,503,088 campaign.

Studds began the election cycle with cash reserves of only $21,912, so fund raising was a constant concern. He raised $666,026 from individual contributors who gave less than $200 and $413,068 from political action committees (PACs). Individual donations of $200 or more amounted to $342,845, 55 percent of which came from out-of-state contributors.

In 1991 Goldman Associates of Boston and Sean Strub of New York coordinated a relatively modest $67,697 direct-mail fund-raising effort, targeted primarily at supporters within District 10. In 1992 that low-key approach gave way to a $173,042 direct-mail program spearheaded by Malchow & Co. of Washington, D.C. For their work, Malchow, Goldman, and Strub received $156,939, $6,399, and $5,606, respectively. Goldman received an additional $8,000 for coordinating numerous small-donor events.

Studds paid Kurz & Volk of Washington, D.C., $24,119 for handling his 1991 PAC receptions, but in 1992 those duties were passed on to Susan Hunter of Falls Church, Va., who received $23,668. Labor Union PACs contributed $174,430 to Studds's coffers, and health care-related PACs added $60,550.

Challenged in the primary by state senator Paul Harold and in the general election by Republican Daniel W. Daly and Bryan, who ran as an independent rather than pass up a third consecutive shot at the seat, Studds paid MacWilliams/Cosgrove of Somerville $418,042 to create and place two television and three radio commercials. It was the first time in eleven House campaigns that Studds had felt the need to air television spots.

In part, Studds felt the need because Bryan invested more than $170,000 in a highly negative campaign. Recalling Studds's 1983 censure for having sex with a seventeen-year-old male page, Bryan repeatedly referred to the incumbent as a "rapist" and a "child molester." "It was a very nasty, sustained attack," noted administrative assistant Steven C. Schwadrown.

While Daly had the backing of Republican Gov. William F. Weld and the resources to run three radio and three television ads, his campaign never took off. "I think that even if we had doubled the amount spent on television, it wouldn't have made any difference," Daly lamented.

Campaign Expenditures	Studds Amount Spent	Studds % of Total	Daly Amount Spent	Daly % of Total
Overhead				
Office furniture/supplies	$ 11,303	.75	$ 2,286	.85
Rent/utilities	13,944	.93	10,000	3.73
Salaries	162,371	10.80	48,821	18.19
Taxes	22,743	1.51	12,370	4.61
Bank/investment fees	408	.03	265	.10
Lawyers/accountants	9,658	.64	0	
Telephone	7,899	.53	8,745	3.26
Campaign automobile	0		0	
Computers/office equipment	31,426	2.09	4,318	1.61
Travel	50,064	3.33	333	.12
Food/meetings	976	.06	94	.03
Subtotal	**310,792**	**20.68**	**87,232**	**32.51**
Fund Raising				
Events	97,969	6.52	21,779	8.12
Direct mail	240,739	16.02	7,242	2.70
Telemarketing	0		1,170	.44
Subtotal	**338,709**	**22.53**	**30,191**	**11.25**
Polling	**64,234**	**4.27**	**4,470**	**1.67**
Advertising				
Electronic media	429,161	28.55	91,556	34.12
Other media	3,894	.26	11,170	4.16
Subtotal	**433,056**	**28.81**	**102,726**	**38.28**
Other Campaign Activity				
Persuasion mail/brochures	233,951	15.56	12,586	4.69
Actual campaigning	86,158	5.73	28,239	10.52
Staff/volunteers	202	.01	0	
Subtotal	**320,312**	**21.31**	**40,825**	**15.21**
Constituent Gifts/Entertainment	**0**		**0**	
Donations to				
Candidates from same state	500	.03	0	
Candidates from other states	0		0	
Civic organizations	1,578	.10	0	
Ideological groups	0		0	
Political parties	1,500	.10	90	.03
Subtotal	**3,577**	**.24**	**90**	**.03**
Unitemized Expenses	**32,409**	**2.16**	**2,818**	**1.05**
Total Campaign Expenses	**$ 1,503,088**		**$ 268,351**	
PAC Contributions	$ 413,068		$ 8,160	
Individual Contributions	1,008,871		164,099	
Total Receipts*	1,438,264		241,250	

*Includes PAC and individual contributions as well as interest earned, party contributions, etc.

MICHIGAN District 1

Rep. Bart Stupak (D)

1992 Election Results

Bart Stupak (D)	144,857	(54%)
Philip E. Ruppe (R)	117,056	(44%)

Republican Rep. Robert W. Davis seemed perfectly safe at the outset of the 1992 election cycle. In six previous reelection campaigns, his vote tallies had fallen below 60 percent only once, and redistricting did little to alter the political landscape. However, following the revelation that he had 878 overdrafts at the House bank, Davis discovered how quickly high poll ratings can dissipate. He opted to retire rather than face an angry electorate.

Three Democrats immediately jumped into the race, including former state representative Bart Stupak and restaurateur Mike McElroy. While McElroy was able to put $176,572 into the race, Stupak struggled to come up with $42,627.

Stupak's low-budget campaign allowed him to invest only $12,366 in the production and placement of preprimary broadcast advertising, including $8,148 for air time on three television stations and $1,454 for spots on four radio stations. Nevertheless, Stupak emerged with the 2,730-vote victory.

On the Republican side, state and national party officials agreed that the two declared candidates, former county commissioner Bill Kurtz and state representative Stephen P. Dresch, could not win. Former six-term Rep. Philip E. Ruppe was coaxed into seeking the seat he had relinquished in 1978. After spending about $133,000, Ruppe won the primary with 47 percent of the vote.

Stupak began to reap the rewards of his hard-fought primary victory almost immediately. Having raised virtually nothing from political action committees (PACs) over the first three months of his candidacy, he collected nearly $50,000 from PACs during the ten weeks following the primary. By the end of the election cycle, PACs had donated more than $100,000, nearly half of what Stupak spent on his head-to-head confrontation with Ruppe. Pederson & Thompson of Washington, D.C., received $3,000 for coordinating the PAC fund raising.

With his new fund-raising ability, Stupak could afford to hire Trippi, McMahon & Squier of Alexandria, Va., to develop and place his general election advertising. Stupak's ads juxtaposed his support for a national health insurance system with Ruppe's opposition to such a system, one of the few issues on which there was strong disagreement. Stupak also labeled Ruppe a carpetbagger who had moved back to the district from Washington in order to run. Trippi received $84,468 from Stupak's campaign and $15,000 from the Democratic Congressional Campaign Committee.

The ads were clearly effective. While late summer polls showed him trailing Ruppe, Stupak opened up a 10-point margin by election day.

Campaign Expenditures	Stupak Amount Spent	Stupak % of Total	Ruppe Amount Spent	Ruppe % of Total
Overhead				
Office furniture/supplies	$ 741	.28	$ 3,468	.81
Rent/utilities	2,800	1.07	11,877	2.77
Salaries	63,237	24.19	33,636	7.83
Taxes	5,069	1.94	16,211	3.77
Bank/investment fees	0		70	.02
Lawyers/accountants	1,000	.38	7,712	1.80
Telephone	11,899	4.55	5,962	1.39
Campaign automobile	0		2,462	.57
Computers/office equipment	2,068	.79	6,803	1.58
Travel	18,274	6.99	5,277	1.23
Food/meetings	213	.08	101	.02
Subtotal	**105,301**	**40.29**	**93,580**	**21.79**
Fund Raising				
Events	5,125	1.96	10,757	2.50
Direct mail	0		12,668	2.95
Telemarketing	0		0	
Subtotal	**5,125**	**1.96**	**23,425**	**5.45**
Polling	**5,000**	**1.91**	**22,838**	**5.32**
Advertising				
Electronic media	97,118	37.16	200,478	46.68
Other media	486	.19	5,277	1.23
Subtotal	**97,604**	**37.34**	**205,756**	**47.91**
Other Campaign Activity				
Persuasion mail/brochures	16,332	6.25	36,054	8.39
Actual campaigning	18,794	7.19	23,563	5.49
Staff/volunteers	0		36	.01
Subtotal	**35,126**	**13.44**	**59,653**	**13.89**
Constituent Gifts/ Entertainment	**0**		**0**	
Donations to				
Candidates from same state	0		225	.05
Candidates from other states	0		0	
Civic organizations	0		45	.01
Ideological groups	0		140	.03
Political parties	0		405	.09
Subtotal	**0**		**815**	**.19**
Unitemized Expenses	**13,221**	**5.06**	**23,403**	**5.45**
Total Campaign Expenses	**$ 261,377**		**$ 429,469**	
PAC Contributions	**$ 104,950**		**$ 131,250**	
Individual Contributions	**89,302**		**151,496**	
Total Receipts*	**225,699**		**458,270**	

*Includes PAC and individual contributions as well as interest earned, party contributions, etc.

District 2 | MICHIGAN

Rep. Peter Hoekstra (R)

1992 Election Results

Peter Hoekstra (R)	155,577	(63%)
John H. Miltner (D)	86,265	(35%)

As head of the National Republican Congressional Committee, Rep. Guy Vander Jagt toured the country throughout the first seven months of 1992 arguing that voters were fed up with Washington and about to retire dozens of House members involuntarily. When Peter Hoekstra, a businessman with no prior political experience, knocked him out in the August 4 primary, Vander Jagt discovered just how right he had been.

Like most challengers, Hoekstra had difficulty raising money. He borrowed $24,300 from a local bank. Forty supporters agreed to send personal letters to one hundred acquaintances asking for donations, a process that yielded between $10,000 and $15,000.

Unable to afford television advertising, Hoekstra invested $7,471 to print his campaign literature and $3,057 in signs and posters. Postage for several small mailings and a 15,000-piece mailing to past Republican primary voters totaled $4,371. Arguing that Vander Jagt had lost touch with his constituents, Hoekstra bicycled thirty miles through the heart of the district to underscore his own commitment to talk personally with voters. For parade appearances, Hoekstra rode in a 1966 Nash Rambler, made the year Vander Jagt first went to Washington. The sign on the car read, "Isn't it time for a change?"

Hoekstra spent $7,539 during the final week of the primary campaign to air three radio spots, including one that highlighted the incumbent's reliance on contributions from political action committees (PACs) and out-of-state donors. Another ad focused on Vander Jagt's junket to Barbados, which was entirely paid for by lobbyists and unflatteringly profiled on television. "Who does Guy Vander Jagt represent?" the ads asked. The third ad featured an endorsement from Hoekstra's mother. "I think my son would make a good congressman," she intone in her thick Dutch brogue. All three ads included references to his fifteen years of business experience.

Realizing he was in trouble, Vander Jagt spent $60,130 on an eleventh-hour broadcast media blitz. Ironically, having railed against tax-and-spend Democrats for months, Vander Jagt's ad campaign focused on his ability to deliver pork-barrel projects for the district. It was a hard sell, and he fell 4,369 votes short in the primary. "There is a ferocious tide against incumbents running across the country, and I could not swim strongly enough to offset it," he told reporters the next day.

The general election campaign against John H. Miltner was low key. Hoekstra invested another $5,265 in signs, $2,116 in radio advertising, and $1,498 on campaign hats. Eschewing PAC contributions, he raised money through personal letters and an auction of items donated by supporters.

Campaign Expenditures	Hoekstra Amount Spent	Hoekstra % of Total	Miltner Amount Spent	Miltner % of Total
Overhead				
Office furniture/supplies	$ 903	.93	$ 561	1.98
Rent/utilities	0		300	1.06
Salaries	30,850	31.88	4,000	14.11
Taxes	0		0	
Bank/investment fees	53	.05	0	
Lawyers/accountants	0		0	
Telephone	1,864	1.93	1,524	5.37
Campaign automobile	0		0	
Computers/office equipment	542	.56	549	1.94
Travel	776	.80	2,357	8.31
Food/meetings	0		0	
Subtotal	**34,988**	**36.15**	**9,291**	**32.77**
Fund Raising				
Events	5,389	5.57	0	
Direct mail	2,520	2.60	0	
Telemarketing	0		0	
Subtotal	**7,909**	**8.17**	**0**	
Polling	**0**		**0**	
Advertising				
Electronic media	9,655	9.98	5,570	19.65
Other media	2,556	2.64	3,537	12.48
Subtotal	**12,212**	**12.62**	**9,107**	**32.12**
Other Campaign Activity				
Persuasion mail/brochures	15,716	16.24	5,285	18.64
Actual campaigning	12,868	13.30	4,667	16.46
Staff/volunteers	0		0	
Subtotal	**28,584**	**29.54**	**9,953**	**35.11**
Constituent Gifts/Entertainment	**0**		**0**	
Donations to				
Candidates from same state	0		0	
Candidates from other states	0		0	
Civic organizations	0		0	
Ideological groups	0		0	
Political parties	0		0	
Subtotal	**0**		**0**	
Unitemized Expenses	**13,088**	**13.52**	**0**	
Total Campaign Expenses	**$ 96,781**		**$ 28,350**	
PAC Contributions	$ 0		$ 6,000	
Individual Contributions	64,086		1,031	
Total Receipts*	104,861		21,447	

*Includes PAC and individual contributions as well as interest earned, party contributions, etc.

MICHIGAN — District 3

Rep. Paul B. Henry (R)

1992 Election Results

Paul B. Henry (R)	162,451	(61%)
Carol S. Kooistra (D)	95,927	(36%)

The late Rep. Paul B. Henry and his Democratic challenger, former Republican Carol S. Kooistra, had been friends for more than twenty years, and that friendship reverberated throughout the campaign. In one of their debates, Henry went so far as to whisper congratulations to Kooistra on the strength of her opening statement. When Henry was hospitalized with a brain tumor in October, Kooistra refused to make his health an issue and offered to withdraw from the race. Henry's campaign staff convinced Kooistra to continue, but she canceled the print order on a persuasion mailer that attacked Henry's voting record, saying that such attacks would be unfair since he could not respond.

Despite the fact that Kooistra had all but given up her challenge, Henry invested $23,901 in advertising to let his constituents know that he was still running and interested in their votes. During the final two weeks of the campaign, he spent $9,199 to produce and air radio commercials. Three ads in the *Grand Rapids Press* cost $8,880, and single ads in the *Grand Rapids Times*, the *Hastings Banner*, the *Ionia Sentinel-Standard*, the *Lowell Ledger*, and several weekly newspapers added $2,706. He also invested $27,224 in campaign literature, $5,112 in yard signs and posters, $2,088 in bumper stickers and signs, and $1,663 in Oh Henry candy bars, which were given out at parades and fund-raisers.

Although Henry did not open his campaign office until April 1992, overhead accounted for 39 percent of his spending for the two-year election cycle. Henry looked to Beth Bandstra, a special assistant in his Grand Rapids congressional office, to run his reelection effort. Over the last eight months of the campaign, Bandstra collected payroll checks totaling $21,378. By election day, the campaign's part-time staff had grown to five. Salaries and payroll taxes accounted for approximately 30 percent of Henry's election-year spending.

As in past campaigns, Henry raised most of his money from his constituents. Uncomfortable with the traditional Washington, D.C., cocktail receptions, Henry raised only $72,650 from political action committees. Only $500 of his treasury came from out-of-state contributors who gave at least $200. In contrast, in-state donations of $200 or more amounted to $112,375 and small donations totaled $137,509.

By far his biggest events were his annual "Henry's Hurrah" picnics, which each attracted well over 1,200 supporters. Together the two picnics cost the campaign $32,977, or 12 percent of his total spending.

Henry died in July 1993.

Campaign Expenditures	Henry Amount Spent	Henry % of Total	Kooistra Amount Spent	Kooistra % of Total
Overhead				
Office furniture/supplies	$ 8,518	3.02	$ 721	1.52
Rent/utilities	7,600	2.69	2,250	4.75
Salaries	40,493	14.34	7,515	15.85
Taxes	24,902	8.82	0	
Bank/investment fees	110	.04	0	
Lawyers/accountants	5,950	2.11	0	
Telephone	5,769	2.04	484	1.02
Campaign automobile	6,073	2.15	0	
Computers/office equipment	7,853	2.78	427	.90
Travel	1,338	.47	0	
Food/meetings	2,613	.92	0	
Subtotal	**111,218**	**39.37**	**11,397**	**24.04**
Fund Raising				
Events	82,174	29.09	1,281	2.70
Direct mail	0		0	
Telemarketing	0		0	
Subtotal	**82,174**	**29.09**	**1,281**	**2.70**
Polling	**14,770**	**5.23**	**0**	
Advertising				
Electronic media	9,199	3.26	0	
Other media	14,702	5.20	19,612	41.36
Subtotal	**23,901**	**8.46**	**19,612**	**41.36**
Other Campaign Activity				
Persuasion mail/brochures	27,224	9.64	2,998	6.32
Actual campaigning	12,078	4.28	8,734	18.42
Staff/volunteers	114	.04	0	
Subtotal	**39,416**	**13.95**	**11,732**	**24.75**
Constituent Gifts/ Entertainment	**3,161**	**1.12**	**0**	
Donations to				
Candidates from same state	0		0	
Candidates from other states	0		0	
Civic organizations	544	.19	0	
Ideological groups	0		0	
Political parties	1,615	.57	0	
Subtotal	**2,159**	**.76**	**0**	
Unitemized Expenses	**5,677**	**2.01**	**3,390**	**7.15**
Total Campaign Expenses	**$ 282,476**		**$ 47,412**	
PAC Contributions	$ 72,650		$ 20,600	
Individual Contributions	250,384		21,288	
Total Receipts*	349,444		43,258	

*Includes PAC and individual contributions as well as interest earned, party contributions, etc.

District 4 — MICHIGAN

Rep. Dave Camp (R)

1992 Election Results

Dave Camp (R)	157,337	(63%)
Lisa A. Donaldson (D)	87,573	(35%)

With 1990 campaign debts totaling more than $100,000, cash reserves of only $10,484, and facing uncertain electoral prospects following Michigan's loss of two House seats in reapportionment, freshman Rep. Dave Camp put a lot of effort into raising money. During the 1992 election cycle, he invested $44,404 in fund-raising events and $22,567 in direct-mail solicitations that together brought in $487,952. By the end of 1992, Camp had spent $401,290 on his campaign while reducing his debt to less than $4,000.

Many of Camp's events were traditional cocktail receptions. Events at the Capitol Hill Club and a reception hosted by the American Medical Association Political Action Committee helped pull in $204,537 from PACs and $15,850 from out-of-state donors who gave at least $200. In-state receptions at locales such as the Germania Town & Country Club and the Holiday Inn in Mount Pleasant raised nearly $148,226.

Camp held his share of less formal events, as well. An annual picnic in Midland featured hot dogs from Pizza Sams and frozen yogurt. Together with numerous in-home, in-kind receptions and his direct-mail effort, Camp's small-donor program raised $119,339.

When Michigan's new political map was unveiled, Camp learned that his old District 10 had become the new District 4, with only minor boundary changes. With no Republican primary opposition, a weak Democratic opponent, and a district almost identical to the one that had given him 65 percent of the vote in 1990, Camp was virtually assured of reelection.

Nevertheless, Camp took nothing for granted. He paid Research/Strategy/Management of Washington, D.C., $178,590 for providing general strategic advice, supplying campaign buttons and bumper stickers, and creating and placing broadcast advertising. The campaign aired radio and television versions of a biographical sketch, as well as companion radio and television commercials touting Camp's low congressional office expenses and his commitment to reducing the federal budget deficit.

Brochures and limited persuasion mailings cost the campaign $14,011. Camp spent $5,847 to place ads in dozens of daily and weekly newspapers, including the *Cadillac Evening News,* the *Clare County Review,* the *Midland Daily News,* the *Ogemaw County Herald,* and the *Shiawassee County Independent.* Yard signs added $5,505. In all, Camp devoted $208,867 to direct voter appeals.

Democratic nominee Lisa A. Donaldson lacked the resources to wage an effective campaign. Her outlays for advertising, campaign literature, and other forms of voter contact amounted to only $7,548. The Democratic Congressional Campaign Committee opted not to financially support her campaign.

	Camp		Donaldson	
Campaign Expenditures	Amount Spent	% of Total	Amount Spent	% of Total
Overhead				
Office furniture/supplies	$ 4,736	1.18	$ 663	4.38
Rent/utilities	1,890	.47	0	
Salaries	14,225	3.54	0	
Taxes	8,261	2.06	0	
Bank/investment fees	10,739	2.68	6	.04
Lawyers/accountants	22,594	5.63	0	
Telephone	8,603	2.14	868	5.73
Campaign automobile	0		0	
Computers/office equipment	202	.05	0	
Travel	18,526	4.62	4,875	32.17
Food/meetings	250	.06	0	
Subtotal	**90,028**	**22.43**	**6,413**	**42.32**
Fund Raising				
Events	44,404	11.07	163	1.08
Direct mail	22,567	5.62	0	
Telemarketing	0		0	
Subtotal	**66,971**	**16.69**	**163**	**1.08**
Polling	**17,000**	**4.24**	**0**	
Advertising				
Electronic media	123,341	30.74	1,269	8.37
Other media	6,075	1.51	1,372	9.05
Subtotal	**129,417**	**32.25**	**2,640**	**17.43**
Other Campaign Activity				
Persuasion mail/brochures	14,011	3.49	3,342	22.05
Actual campaigning	65,440	16.31	1,537	10.14
Staff/volunteers	0		30	.20
Subtotal	**79,450**	**19.80**	**4,908**	**32.39**
Constituent Gifts/ Entertainment	**818**	**.20**	**0**	
Donations to				
Candidates from same state	0		0	
Candidates from other states	1,000	.25	0	
Civic organizations	1,737	.43	0	
Ideological groups	0		0	
Political parties	228	.06	0	
Subtotal	**2,965**	**.74**	**0**	
Unitemized Expenses	**14,642**	**3.65**	**1,027**	**6.78**
Total Campaign Expenses	**$ 401,290**		**$ 15,152**	
PAC Contributions	**$ 204,537**		**$ 2,500**	
Individual Contributions	**283,415**		**5,301**	
Total Receipts*	**507,855**		**15,650**	

*Includes PAC and individual contributions as well as interest earned, party contributions, etc.

MICHIGAN District 5

Rep. James A. Barcia (D)

1992 Election Results

James A. Barcia (D)	147,618	(60%)
Keith Muxlow (R)	93,098	(38%)

Democratic state senator James A. Barcia had several advantages over Republican state representative Keith Muxlow. The redrawn District 5 consisted largely of territory inherited from retiring Democratic Rep. Bob Traxler, and registered Democrats comprised about 54 percent of the district's electorate. As a member of the state senate, Barcia already represented about half of the district's 580,000 residents; Muxlow's state house district included only about 88,000 District 5 residents. Barcia not only had a head start on positive name recognition, but also three times as much money to spend.

However, before he could turn his attention to Muxlow, Barcia first had to win the August 4 Democratic primary against state senator John D. Cherry, Jr., and Don Hare, Traxler's former congressional chief of staff. Together, Cherry and Hare put more than $161,000 into the race, and much of their energy was devoted to attacking Barcia. Hare ran radio and newspaper ads labeling Barcia's legislative voting record as more Republican than Democratic. Seeking to capitalize on the anti-incumbent mood, both Hare and Cherry painted Barcia as a career politician.

Barcia spent nearly $84,000 to secure the nomination, including $42,166 on campaign literature and persuasion mail, $18,423 on broadcast advertising, $9,392 on an absentee ballot mailing, and $8,389 on yard signs and posters. He invested $7,891 for ads in seven daily and weekly newspapers, including the *Thumb Area Senior News,* the *Saginaw Banner,* the *Flint Journal,* and the *Catholic Weekly.*

With the nomination in hand, Barcia had better luck raising money for the general election campaign. In October he opened a fund-raising office in Washington, D.C., and over the final three months of the campaign raised $104,250 from political action committees (PACs). During this period, he raised $74,853 more from PACs than from individual contributors.

This influx of cash allowed Barcia to radically alter his communication strategy. For the general election campaign, Barcia spent $53,219 on radio and television commercials, $24,719 on persuasion mail, $4,430 on yard signs, and $3,743 on newspaper ads.

Over the eight-month campaign, Winning Strategies of Flushing, Mich., collected $69,905 for producing Barcia's campaign literature, creating his broadcast ads, and buying most of the air time. During the general election campaign, Barcia paid Professional Management of Laytonsville, Md., $10,741 for providing day-to-day campaign management services. Susie Bruster of McLean, Va., received $5,885 for coordinating the PAC fund-raising effort.

Muxlow's limited budget allowed him to spend only $14,615 on airing his radio commercials, $10,501 on billboard ads, and $9,268 on yard signs.

	Barcia		Muxlow	
Campaign Expenditures	Amount Spent	% of Total	Amount Spent	% of Total
Overhead				
Office furniture/supplies	$ 1,882	.69	$ 2,057	2.28
Rent/utilities	4,399	1.61	1,482	1.64
Salaries	16,643	6.10	6,366	7.06
Taxes	1,957	.72	0	
Bank/investment fees	41	.02	0	
Lawyers/accountants	0		0	
Telephone	5,151	1.89	1,112	1.23
Campaign automobile	0		2,942	3.26
Computers/office equipment	218	.08	0	
Travel	7,501	2.75	0	
Food/meetings	155	.06	0	
Subtotal	**37,947**	**13.91**	**13,960**	**15.48**
Fund Raising				
Events	28,176	10.33	9,663	10.72
Direct mail	0		4,973	5.52
Telemarketing	0		0	
Subtotal	**28,176**	**10.33**	**14,636**	**16.23**
Polling	**2,000**	**.73**	**0**	
Advertising				
Electronic media	71,642	26.25	15,337	17.01
Other media	13,504	4.95	12,033	13.35
Subtotal	**85,146**	**31.20**	**27,370**	**30.36**
Other Campaign Activity				
Persuasion mail/brochures	66,886	24.51	10,448	11.59
Actual campaigning	40,325	14.78	11,761	13.04
Staff/volunteers	0		0	
Subtotal	**107,211**	**39.29**	**22,209**	**24.63**
Constituent Gifts/ Entertainment	**0**		**0**	
Donations to				
Candidates from same state	0		0	
Candidates from other states	0		0	
Civic organizations	0		0	
Ideological groups	0		0	
Political parties	0		0	
Subtotal	**0**		**0**	
Unitemized Expenses	**12,393**	**4.54**	**11,983**	**13.29**
Total Campaign Expenses	**$ 272,872**		**$ 90,158**	
PAC Contributions	**$ 138,251**		**$ 14,906**	
Individual Contributions	110,026		49,448	
Total Receipts*	289,443		93,876	

*Includes PAC and individual contributions as well as interest earned, party contributions, etc.

District 6 — MICHIGAN

Rep. Fred Upton (R)

1992 Election Results

Fred Upton (R)	144,083	(62%)
Andy Davis (D)	89,020	(38%)

Unopposed in the Republican primary and challenged by underfunded geologist Andy Davis in the general election, Rep. Fred Upton spent $134,594 less on his 1992 campaign than he had in 1990. However, while he reduced his advertising outlays by $114,782, his overhead expenses rose by $14,415. Over the two-year election cycle, overhead accounted for 47 percent of Upton's spending.

An advocate of campaign finance reform, Upton spent $97,614 to maintain his permanent campaign during 1991, including $57,068 on overhead. He paid monthly rent of $250 for office space in a community center run by the St. Joseph public school system. Throughout the off-year Upton's office was staffed by three part-time employees, who collected salaries totaling $28,207.

Fund-raising activities continued unabated throughout the cycle, although the rate of return was somewhat smaller than in 1990. Upton spent $42,571 on fund-raising receptions, an increase of 40 percent over 1990. Individual contributions of $200 or more rose by 18 percent, while political action committee donations fell by 2 percent.

Although Upton's campaign sent small, targeted mailings to business leaders, senior citizens, and constituents acquired through redistricting, every piece had a dual purpose. "We did no pure voter contact mail in 1992," noted finance director Liz Garey. "It always contained a fund-raising pitch." In spite of this increased effort, Upton raised $26,718 less in small contributions in 1992 than he had in 1990.

Upton invested only 19 percent of his treasury in direct appeals for votes. His broadcast advertising effort was limited to three upbeat radio commercials that included a call for an end to partisan politics, a constituent testimonial, and a spot focusing on his work in Washington to secure federal dollars and jobs for the district.

The campaign paid $12,429 to place ads in several dozen daily and weekly newspapers, including the *Dowagiac Daily News*, the *Herald Palladium*, the *Kalamazoo Gazette*, and the *Three Rivers Community News*. He spent $5,143 for billboard ads in the new portions of the district, $4,648 on yard signs and posters, and $2,046 on campaign buttons and bumper stickers.

Perry Ballard Advertising of St. Joseph received $22,340 for creating two of the radio spots, designing the newspaper ads, handling much of the placement, and consulting on the direct-mail effort. Brockmeyer/Allen & Associates of Baltimore, Md., collected $1,111 for creating one radio ad. Public Opinion Strategies of Alexandria, Va., received $9,000 for polling. Marmen Computing of Menominee was paid $18,270 for work on the fund-raising mail.

	Upton		Davis	
Campaign Expenditures	Amount Spent	% of Total	Amount Spent	% of Total
Overhead				
Office furniture/supplies	$ 7,390	2.01	$ 530	1.30
Rent/utilities	6,052	1.65	1,867	4.59
Salaries	90,094	24.51	8,635	21.24
Taxes	39,712	10.80	3,344	8.22
Bank/investment fees	181	.05	4	.01
Lawyers/accountants	610	.17	200	.49
Telephone	9,685	2.63	2,633	6.48
Campaign automobile	0		0	
Computers/office equipment	5,526	1.50	0	
Travel	14,089	3.83	12	.03
Food/meetings	646	.18	13	.03
Subtotal	**173,985**	**47.33**	**17,238**	**42.39**
Fund Raising				
Events	42,571	11.58	409	1.00
Direct mail	52,966	14.41	0	
Telemarketing	0		0	
Subtotal	**95,537**	**25.99**	**409**	**1.00**
Polling	**9,000**	**2.45**	**0**	
Advertising				
Electronic media	40,371	10.98	7,614	18.73
Other media	18,734	5.10	1,552	3.82
Subtotal	**59,105**	**16.08**	**9,166**	**22.54**
Other Campaign Activity				
Persuasion mail/brochures	0		4,356	10.71
Actual campaigning	9,550	2.60	8,027	19.74
Staff/volunteers	0		392	.96
Subtotal	**9,550**	**2.60**	**12,775**	**31.42**
Constituent Gifts/Entertainment	**6,727**	**1.83**	**75**	**.18**
Donations to				
Candidates from same state	0		0	
Candidates from other states	0		0	
Civic organizations	0		0	
Ideological groups	0		25	.06
Political parties	345	.09	0	
Subtotal	**345**	**.09**	**25**	**.06**
Unitemized Expenses	**13,352**	**3.63**	**975**	**2.40**
Total Campaign Expenses	**$ 367,601**		**$ 40,663**	
PAC Contributions	**$ 149,585**		**$ 19,600**	
Individual Contributions	**275,665**		**14,935**	
Total Receipts*	**432,851**		**42,048**	

*Includes PAC and individual contributions as well as interest earned, party contributions, etc.

MICHIGAN — District 7

Rep. Nick Smith (R)

1992 Election Results

Nick Smith (R)	133,972 (88%)
Kenneth L. Proctor † (I)	18,751 (12%)

Since no Democrat even bothered to vie for the seat in this heavily Republican district, the race was essentially decided by the four-candidate Republican primary on August 4. Benefiting from a bitter fight between state senator John Schwarz and 1990 congressional candidate Brad Haskins, state senator Nick Smith emerged victorious with 43 percent of the vote.

Schwarz was the prohibitive early favorite. He had the backing of the party regulars, was running in a district primarily composed of territory he already represented in the state senate, and had a proven ability to raise large sums of money. Ultimately, Schwarz spent nearly $335,000 on the primary and outspent Smith by a nearly two-to-one margin. Haskins had little money to put into the race, but most of what he had was invested in airing a single radio spot that resurrected a two-year charge that Schwarz had assaulted a security guard.

Smith entrusted $105,982 of his $180,000 primary campaign budget to Mike Murphy Media of Washington, D.C., which created the campaign's one television commercial and one of its two radio spots. Taking a gamble, the firm decided to completely abandon the Grand Rapids media market and scale back its buys in Lansing. Instead, they bought heavily on stations in Toledo, Ohio, which reached areas of the district that the campaign's polls showed were winnable.

At the core of Smith's ad campaign was his refusal to accept political action committee (PAC) contributions, which Schwarz aggressively sought. An antitax theme was added to the mix to help round out Smith's Republican credentials, and the whole package was wrapped into a commercial filmed with Smith's tractor as the backdrop to underscore his agricultural roots. As Smith put it, the message they delivered was that "I was an independent who did not take any PAC funds and was responsible to the people."

Rather than sending armies of volunteers door-to-door, Smith said his canvassing effort was predominantly a family affair. His four children, two grandchildren, twenty-one first cousins, and all of their children fanned out across targeted areas with stacks of brochures.

Smith said contributions to his campaign "came in very slowly." He largely avoided traditional fund-raising receptions, preferring instead to attend in-home events where he could make a more personal appeal. While he was able to raise $100,000, he had to loan the campaign another $100,000 to make ends meet.

Facing only Libertarian Kenneth L. Proctor in the general election, Smith spent just $10,303 on his advertising campaign.

Campaign Expenditures	Smith Amount Spent	% of Total
Overhead		
Office furniture/supplies	$ 5,243	2.42
Rent/utilities	3,762	1.74
Salaries	23,578	10.89
Taxes	1,247	.58
Bank/investment fees	95	.04
Lawyers/accountants	0	
Telephone	4,170	1.93
Campaign automobile	0	
Computers/office equipment	1,789	.83
Travel	5,427	2.51
Food/meetings	44	.02
Subtotal	**45,356**	**20.95**
Fund Raising		
Events	3,555	1.64
Direct mail	8,559	3.95
Telemarketing	0	
Subtotal	**12,114**	**5.59**
Polling	**6,057**	**2.80**
Advertising		
Electronic media	116,490	53.79
Other media	4,462	2.06
Subtotal	**120,952**	**55.86**
Other Campaign Activity		
Persuasion mail/brochures	24,313	11.23
Actual campaigning	7,431	3.43
Staff/volunteers	138	.06
Subtotal	**31,883**	**14.72**
Constituent Gifts/Entertainment	**40**	**.02**
Donations to		
Candidates from same state	0	
Candidates from other states	0	
Civic organizations	10	
Ideological groups	0	
Political parties	135	.06
Subtotal	**145**	**.07**
Unitemized Expenses	**0**	
Total Campaign Expenses	**$ 216,547**	
PAC Contributions	**$ 0**	
Individual Contributions	**127,826**	
Total Receipts*	**242,908**	

*Includes PAC and individual contributions as well as interest earned, party contributions, etc.

†No expenditures or receipts on file. Candidates raising or spending less than $5,000 are not required to file reports with the Federal Election Commission.

District 8 — MICHIGAN

Rep. Bob Carr (D)

1992 Election Results

Bob Carr (D)	135,517	(48%)
Dick Chrysler (R)	131,906	(46%)

Unopposed in 1990, Rep. Bob Carr still managed to spend $222,601 on his permanent campaign, only 13 percent of which was put into direct appeals for votes. He spent $98,108 on overhead, $17,000 on polling, $14,489 on fund raising, and donated $38,698 to other candidates, organizations, and causes. As it turned out, Carr could have made better use of that money in 1992.

Running in a drastically redrawn, significantly more Republican district, Carr would have been forced to spend more than he had in 1990 under almost any circumstances. However, when businessman Dick Chrysler entered the race for the Republican nomination, it was clear that Carr would need to spend considerably more.

Already well known as a result of his unsuccessful 1986 gubernatorial bid, Chrysler invested nearly $1.8 million of his own money in the campaign. Chrysler poured $849,340 into his broadcast ads, one of which slammed Carr for his dependence on political action committee (PAC) contributions and depicted the eight-term incumbent as the familiar yellow "Pac-Man" character, busily devouring dollar bills. Chrysler also invested $384,838 in brochures and persuasion mail, $67,000 in phonebanking, $65,000 in polls, $40,976 in newspaper ads, $37,304 in yard signs, $7,973 in buttons and bumper stickers, and $3,394 in billboard advertising. Marketing Resource Group of Lansing received $1,294,249 for supplying Chrysler with the bulk of these materials and services.

Chrysler was only one of Carr's problems. In the Republican primary, John Mangopoulos spent as much time and money attacking Carr as he spent campaigning against Chrysler. Mangopoulos's ads attacked Carr's pro-choice abortion stance, using pictures of aborted fetuses to make his point. Ads showing two men kissing and pictures of naked boys were used to attack Carr for supporting government funding for the arts. In the general election campaign, Ralph Nader's Public Citizen Fund for a Clean Congress spent more than $40,000 on commercials attacking Carr for accepting huge amounts of PAC contributions.

Carr returned fire with a $1,353,305 campaign, and unlike 1990 he invested 62 percent of his campaign treasury in voter contact. He paid the Campaign Group of Philadelphia, Pa., $637,000 for creating and placing broadcast ads. He spent $97,292 on campaign literature and persuasion mail, $45,989 on various get-out-the-vote efforts, $13,053 on yard signs and posters, and $6,473 on T-shirts.

To keep tabs on the electorate, Carr paid pollster Greenberg-Lake of Washington, D.C., $104,907. Big Sky Consulting, also of Washington, collected $22,470 for providing opposition research.

	Carr		Chrysler	
Campaign Expenditures	Amount Spent	% of Total	Amount Spent	% of Total
Overhead				
Office furniture/supplies	$ 14,054	1.04	$ 7,332	.42
Rent/utilities	25,880	1.91	29,042	1.65
Salaries	128,968	9.53	135,889	7.71
Taxes	27,034	2.00	57,276	3.25
Bank/investment fees	307	.02	485	.03
Lawyers/accountants	1,815	.13	0	
Telephone	11,060	.82	13,897	.79
Campaign automobile	2,449	.18	0	
Computers/office equipment	35,015	2.59	8,494	.48
Travel	28,019	2.07	12,588	.71
Food/meetings	4,631	.34	304	.02
Subtotal	**279,232**	**20.63**	**265,306**	**15.06**
Fund Raising				
Events	58,155	4.30	16,295	.92
Direct mail	0		0	
Telemarketing	0		0	
Subtotal	**58,155**	**4.30**	**16,295**	**.92**
Polling	**104,907**	**7.75**	**65,000**	**3.69**
Advertising				
Electronic media	637,000	47.07	849,340	48.20
Other media	8,088	.60	47,975	2.72
Subtotal	**645,088**	**47.67**	**897,315**	**50.92**
Other Campaign Activity				
Persuasion mail/brochures	97,292	7.19	384,838	21.84
Actual campaigning	100,002	7.39	129,643	7.36
Staff/volunteers	2,372	.18	129	.01
Subtotal	**199,666**	**14.75**	**514,611**	**29.20**
Constituent Gifts/ Entertainment	10,316	.76	0	
Donations to				
Candidates from same state	450	.03	25	
Candidates from other states	1,000	.07	0	
Civic organizations	2,530	.19	102	.01
Ideological groups	250	.02	0	
Political parties	7,630	.56	210	.01
Subtotal	**11,860**	**.88**	**337**	**.02**
Unitemized Expenses	**44,082**	**3.26**	**3,265**	**.19**
Total Campaign Expenses	**$ 1,353,305**		**$ 1,762,128**	
PAC Contributions	$ 568,003		$ 0	
Individual Contributions	479,127		163,612	
Total Receipts*	1,107,973		1,763,305	

*Includes PAC and individual contributions as well as interest earned, party contributions, etc.

MICHIGAN — District 9

Rep. Dale E. Kildee (D)

1992 Election Results

Dale E. Kildee (D)	133,956	(54%)
Megan O'Neill (R)	111,798	(45%)

Democratic Rep. Dale E. Kildee had three strikes against his 1992 reelection prospects. He had 100 overdrafts at the House bank. His redrawn district was 49 percent new to him. In the political "Year of the Woman," his Republican opponent was Megan O'Neill, a former member of the advance team for President George Bush and Vice President Dan Quayle.

Kildee responded to the challenge by spending $867,703, nearly seven times the amount spent by O'Neill. Kildee's prodigious effort cost nearly four times as much as his 1990 campaign and $144,290 more than he had invested in his previous eight campaigns combined.

Kildee ran his usual low-key campaign throughout 1991. He had no office or paid staff. Most of his fundraising efforts targeted political action committees (PACs), which accounted for $125,530 of the $164,472 he raised. Springer Associates of Falls Church, Va., received $23,071 for coordinating PAC events.

However, once the state's redistricting plan was announced in April 1992, Kildee immediately opened two campaign offices. By June he had opened two others. By the end of 1992, his payroll had ballooned to $92,263. Over the final nine months of 1992, Kildee committed $748,248 to his reelection effort.

Prior to 1992, Kildee had found it unnecessary to invest in television advertising. In 1992 he put his entire $219,905 broadcast budget into three television commercials designed by Nordlinger Associates of Washington, D.C. Using the tagline: "Washington may not be working, but Congressman Kildee is," one spot highlighted the fact that he had taken no taxpayer-funded foreign junkets, had never voted for a congressional pay raise, and had rarely missed a vote. A second positive spot focused on children's issues, while the lone attack ad accused O'Neill of flip-flopping on the North American Free Trade Agreement, which Kildee strongly opposed.

Kildee's massive campaign treasury allowed him to buy time in both the Flint and Detroit media markets. While buys in Detroit cost about four times as much as comparable time in Flint, the Detroit market was crucial to reaching voters in the redrawn district's newly acquired suburban areas. With only $26,900 to spend on broadcast ads, O'Neill was forced to limit her buys to stations in the more Democratic Flint market, foregoing the opportunity to reach the voters most likely to support her candidacy.

Campaign literature and targeted persuasion mailers on trade issues, the environment, and health care cost Kildee $127,776. He spent $27,660 on 8,000 yard signs and 300 4' × 8' signs.

Campaign Expenditures	Kildee Amount Spent	Kildee % of Total	O'Neill Amount Spent	O'Neill % of Total
Overhead				
Office furniture/supplies	$ 7,187	.83	$ 485	.39
Rent/utilities	24,934	2.87	1,250	1.00
Salaries	92,263	10.63	12,300	9.86
Taxes	203	.02	0	
Bank/investment fees	172	.02	0	
Lawyers/accountants	2,035	.23	1,102	.88
Telephone	10,502	1.21	1,222	.98
Campaign automobile	0		0	
Computers/office equipment	10,617	1.22	569	.46
Travel	19,686	2.27	227	.18
Food/meetings	13,208	1.52	67	.05
Subtotal	**180,807**	**20.84**	**17,223**	**13.80**
Fund Raising				
Events	97,050	11.18	13,063	10.47
Direct mail	28,453	3.28	0	
Telemarketing	0		0	
Subtotal	**125,503**	**14.46**	**13,063**	**10.47**
Polling	**40,333**	**4.65**	**0**	
Advertising				
Electronic media	219,905	25.34	26,900	21.56
Other media	22,048	2.54	12,412	9.95
Subtotal	**241,952**	**27.88**	**39,312**	**31.50**
Other Campaign Activity				
Persuasion mail/brochures	127,776	14.73	30,516	24.45
Actual campaigning	102,482	11.81	16,549	13.26
Staff/volunteers	1,252	.14	200	.16
Subtotal	**231,510**	**26.68**	**47,265**	**37.88**
Constituent Gifts/ Entertainment	**3,152**	**.36**	**0**	
Donations to				
Candidates from same state	1,630	.19	0	
Candidates from other states	250	.03	0	
Civic organizations	3,774	.43	0	
Ideological groups	1,625	.19	0	
Political parties	4,070	.47	0	
Subtotal	**11,349**	**1.31**	**0**	
Unitemized Expenses	33,097	3.81	7,927	6.35
Total Campaign Expenses	$ 867,703		$ 124,790	
PAC Contributions	$ 464,970		$ 13,751	
Individual Contributions	238,611		98,204	
Total Receipts*	762,758		135,192	

*Includes PAC and individual contributions as well as interest earned, party contributions, etc.

District 10 — MICHIGAN

Rep. David E. Bonior (D)

1992 Election Results

David E. Bonior (D)	138,193	(53%)
Douglas Carl (R)	114,918	(44%)

Rep. David E. Bonior had failed to get as much as 60 percent of the vote in four of his seven previous reelection bids, including a 1988 contest with conservative state senator Douglas Carl. As Majority Whip, he was potentially vulnerable to a strong "outsider" campaign, a problem made all the more acute by his seventy-six overdrafts at the House bank. When redistricting added 90,000 new constituents to Bonior's turf, Carl decided to try his luck again.

Bonior's only comfortable wins had come in 1982, 1986, and 1990, when there was no Republican presidential candidate at the top of the ballot to provide coattails. With George Bush riding high in the polls throughout much of 1991, Bonior never stopped running.

Bonior's campaign spent $339,097 during 1991, including $82,139 on overhead and $52,856 on fund raising. He used $94,319 of his campaign treasury to pay for television advertising in support of a proposed ballot initiative that would have mandated a $500 property tax cut for middle-income homeowners. The initiative was sponsored by the Michigan Homeowners Tax Break Committee, which Bonior co-chaired, and his spending on its behalf has been included here as a contribution to an ideological organization.

To meet the challenge posed by Carl, who lacked money to advertise but had the strong backing of religious fundamentalists and antiabortion activists, Bonior invested another $1,005,894 in his reelection effort during 1992. Fifty-five percent of Bonior's election year splurge was put into broadcast advertising.

Reflecting the fact that the district is economically dependent on the auto industry and that political action committees representing unions gave Bonior's campaign $274,748, two of his four television commercials focused on trade. Referring to the North American Free Trade Agreement as "the Mexican Free Trade Agreement," Bonior attacked it as "a terrible agreement for workers." Another spot argued that "on trade, you've got to get tough, because when you get tough, you get results."

The campaign shifted its focus in the final weeks to health care. A positive spot dubbed "Kitchen" featured Bonior, seated at a kitchen table, discussing the importance of affordable health care. The campaign's only negative spot slammed Carl for opposing universal health care while his service in the state legislature entitled him to free health insurance for life. Fenn & King Communications of Washington, D.C., received $523,463 for creating and placing the ads.

Bonior paid Greenberg-Lake of Washington, D.C., $135,691 for polling. The Research Group of Chicago, Ill., supplied opposition research for $14,242.

	Bonior		Carl	
Campaign Expenditures	Amount Spent	% of Total	Amount Spent	% of Total
Overhead				
Office furniture/supplies	$ 13,771	1.02	$ 6,614	4.35
Rent/utilities	18,570	1.38	3,201	2.11
Salaries	108,528	8.07	19,670	12.93
Taxes	62,282	4.63	0	
Bank/investment fees	0		821	.54
Lawyers/accountants	9,174	.68	1,867	1.23
Telephone	13,212	.98	4,900	3.22
Campaign automobile	0		0	
Computers/office equipment	1,411	.10	2,724	1.79
Travel	36,134	2.69	1,830	1.20
Food/meetings	2,850	.21	402	.26
Subtotal	**265,932**	**19.77**	**42,029**	**27.64**
Fund Raising				
Events	111,003	8.25	25,726	16.92
Direct mail	10,597	.79	12,117	7.97
Telemarketing	0		0	
Subtotal	**121,599**	**9.04**	**37,843**	**24.88**
Polling	135,691	10.09	0	
Advertising				
Electronic media	557,521	41.45	1,141	.75
Other media	882	.07	800	.53
Subtotal	**558,403**	**41.52**	**1,941**	**1.28**
Other Campaign Activity				
Persuasion mail/brochures	17,726	1.32	36,119	23.75
Actual campaigning	39,912	2.97	32,801	21.57
Staff/volunteers	9,797	.73	643	.42
Subtotal	**67,436**	**5.01**	**69,563**	**45.74**
Constituent Gifts/Entertainment	2,324	.17	74	.05
Donations to				
Candidates from same state	4,200	.31	100	.07
Candidates from other states	36,350	2.70	0	
Civic organizations	1,675	.12	145	.10
Ideological groups	98,014	7.29	0	
Political parties	10,740	.80	0	
Subtotal	**150,979**	**11.23**	**245**	**.16**
Unitemized Expenses	42,628	3.17	381	.25
Total Campaign Expenses	$ 1,344,991		$ 152,077	
PAC Contributions	$ 934,613		$ 19,562	
Individual Contributions	281,909		199,092	
Total Receipts*	1,295,553		253,607	

*Includes PAC and individual contributions as well as interest earned, party contributions, etc.

MICHIGAN   District 11

Rep. Joe Knollenberg (R)

1992 Election Results

Joe Knollenberg (R)	168,940	(58%)
Walter Briggs (D)	117,725	(40%)

When Republican Rep. William S. Broomfield announced he would not seek a nineteenth term, it was a foregone conclusion that his successor would emerge from the Republican primary. With registered Republicans comprising about 58 percent of the electorate, Oakland County circuit judge Alice L. Gilbert, state senator Dave Honigman, and insurance agent Joe Knollenberg waged an expensive, bitter fight for the nomination.

Although Knollenberg had served as both chairman of the local Republican party and as Broomfield's campaign chairman, he ran as an outsider, challenging Gilbert and Honigman to join him in a pledge to spend no more than $250,000. While the challenge was couched in terms of campaign finance reform, Knollenberg had little choice. Honigman and Gilbert were both millionaires; Knollenberg was not. Honigman ultimately put $1,142,282 of his own money into his $1,332,422 campaign. Gilbert self-financed $214,930 of her $436,371 effort. Knollenberg invested less than $2,000 of his own money and spent about $180,000 on the primary.

Gilbert's television and radio ads attacked Honigman as an overly ambitious, untrustworthy career politician who was attempting to buy his way into Congress. Honigman struck back with an ad calling Gilbert lazy, pointing out that she had recessed a high profile murder trial in order to attend the 1991 opening day game at Tigers Stadium. While Gilbert attacked Knollenberg for his belief that abortion should only be allowed to save the life of the mother, Knollenberg largely escaped the personal attacks.

For running Knollenberg's limited primary campaign effort, Creative Media of East Lansing received $118,204. Lacking money for television advertising, the campaign put about $46,000 into radio ads, which included an endorsement by Broomfield and attacks on his opponents for trying to buy the election. The firm pumped out three targeted mailings that cost nearly $18,000 apiece and put more than $13,000 into signs, billboards, buttons, and bumper stickers.

Spurred by the active support of the antiabortion movement and a voter backlash that forced Honigman to take out a newspaper ad apologizing for his negative campaign, Knollenberg won with 43 percent of the vote, surprising some of his own advisers. "We didn't have enough money for polling at the end," noted Creative Media account manager Gary Naeyaert. "We had no idea how we were doing."

In the general election campaign, accountant Walter Briggs spent nearly $213,000 on persuasion mail and advertising, but could not crack the Republican lock on the district.

	Knollenberg		Briggs	
Campaign Expenditures	Amount Spent	% of Total	Amount Spent	% of Total
Overhead				
Office furniture/supplies	$ 3,712	.79	$ 1,077	.38
Rent/utilities	3,719	.79	4,800	1.68
Salaries	32,039	6.83	31,894	11.15
Taxes	0		0	
Bank/investment fees	491	.10	1,551	.54
Lawyers/accountants	0		0	
Telephone	4,590	.98	5,457	1.91
Campaign automobile	0		0	
Computers/office equipment	3,009	.64	2,129	.74
Travel	5,601	1.19	1,387	.48
Food/meetings	642	.14	0	
Subtotal	**53,804**	**11.48**	**48,295**	**16.88**
Fund Raising				
Events	35,266	7.52	3,854	1.35
Direct mail	2,862	.61	0	
Telemarketing	0		0	
Subtotal	**38,129**	**8.13**	**3,854**	**1.35**
Polling	**15,000**	**3.20**	**12,800**	**4.47**
Advertising				
Electronic media	129,923	27.71	37,500	13.11
Other media	8,386	1.79	588	.21
Subtotal	**138,309**	**29.50**	**38,088**	**13.31**
Other Campaign Activity				
Persuasion mail/brochures	167,333	35.69	174,729	61.07
Actual campaigning	49,402	10.54	4,312	1.51
Staff/volunteers	2,155	.46	0	
Subtotal	**218,890**	**46.69**	**179,041**	**62.57**
Constituent Gifts/ Entertainment	**0**		**0**	
Donations to				
Candidates from same state	30	.01	0	
Candidates from other states	0		0	
Civic organizations	526	.11	0	
Ideological groups	105	.02	0	
Political parties	0		1,150	.40
Subtotal	**662**	**.14**	**1,150**	**.40**
Unitemized Expenses	**4,024**	**.86**	**2,895**	**1.01**
Total Campaign Expenses	**$ 468,817**		**$ 286,122**	
PAC Contributions	$ 116,436		$ 78,350	
Individual Contributions	324,841		124,345	
Total Receipts*	496,036		272,984	

*Includes PAC and individual contributions as well as interest earned, party contributions, etc.

District 12 — MICHIGAN

Rep. Sander M. Levin (D)

1992 Election Results

Sander M. Levin (D)	137,514	(53%)
John Pappageorge (R)	119,357	(46%)

Rep. Sander M. Levin expected to be hit hard by redistricting, so he spent 1991 preparing for the worst. During the off-year Levin spent $241,851 to maintain his permanent campaign, including $85,953 on overhead. For the first seven months of 1991 Levin paid rent of $125 to the Oakland County Democratic party. In May he began paying $410 for a larger space in Southfield. Three people received salary payments totaling $47,091, including Levin's son Matthew, who collected $13,426.

Levin spent $103,051 on an off-year fund-raising frenzy that raised $550,556. Springer Associates of Falls Church, Va., received $49,757 for coordinating events that helped raise $319,932 from political action committees. His fund-raising itinerary took him beyond his district boundaries, helping him bring in $157,648 from individual donors who gave at least $200. A. B. Data of Milwaukee received $12,771 for a direct-mail effort that helped collect $72,977 in small contributions. Coupled with the $31,847 in interest earned on his cash reserves, Levin's campaign treasury swelled from $255,205 to $601,236.

Throughout the first four months of 1992, Levin invested heavily to ensure that his interests in the redistricting process would be well served. He turned to Sonosky, Chamber, Sachs & Endreson of Washington, D.C., and George Brookover of East Lansing for legal advice, paying them $15,692 and $17,029, respectively. Data Base Graphics of East Lansing received $4,909 for providing mapping services. Legal fees at the federal district court in Detroit amounted to $3,224.

The map that emerged from the redistricting process set the stage for a primary confrontation between Levin and fellow Democratic Rep. Dennis M. Hertel. However, Hertel had 547 overdrafts at the House bank; Levin had none. Levin had $717,804 in his campaign account on March 31; Hertel had $346,117. Four days after the redistricting plan was unveiled, Hertel announced his retirement.

Levin had avoided a costly primary battle, but he could not afford to let down his guard against Oakland County commissioner John Pappageorge. To communicate with the thousands of new constituents added to his radically redrawn district, Levin paid Struble-Totten Communications of Washington, D.C., $412,620 for creating and placing broadcast ads. Additional production costs amounted to $5,056. Levin also spent $82,695 on brochures and persuasion mail and $12,355 on an in-house phonebanking operation. Mellman & Lazarus of Washington, D.C, collected $49,028 for polling.

For their fund-raising efforts in 1992, Springer Associates and A. B. Data received $50,932 and $8,341, respectively.

Campaign Expenditures	Levin Amount Spent	Levin % of Total	Pappageorge Amount Spent	Pappageorge % of Total
Overhead				
Office furniture/supplies	$ 21,551	1.82	$ 5,834	3.27
Rent/utilities	18,222	1.54	4,068	2.28
Salaries	132,854	11.21	36,359	20.38
Taxes	20,210	1.71	4,406	2.47
Bank/investment fees	70	.01	0	
Lawyers/accountants	35,945	3.03	0	
Telephone	19,011	1.60	5,729	3.21
Campaign automobile	5,302	.45	0	
Computers/office equipment	16,756	1.41	4,497	2.52
Travel	28,999	2.45	658	.37
Food/meetings	2,142	.18	2	
Subtotal	**301,062**	**25.41**	**61,553**	**34.50**
Fund Raising				
Events	152,630	12.88	8,117	4.55
Direct mail	56,362	4.76	1,978	1.11
Telemarketing	0		0	
Subtotal	**208,992**	**17.64**	**10,095**	**5.66**
Polling	**49,028**	**4.14**	**0**	
Advertising				
Electronic media	417,676	35.26	0	
Other media	6,474	.55	4,176	2.34
Subtotal	**424,150**	**35.80**	**4,176**	**2.34**
Other Campaign Activity				
Persuasion mail/brochures	82,695	6.98	60,539	33.93
Actual campaigning	55,306	4.67	35,579	19.94
Staff/volunteers	149	.01	125	.07
Subtotal	**138,151**	**11.66**	**96,243**	**53.95**
Constituent Gifts/ Entertainment	**16,510**	**1.39**	**0**	
Donations to				
Candidates from same state	8,567	.72	0	
Candidates from other states	8,437	.71	0	
Civic organizations	4,717	.40	0	
Ideological groups	3,413	.29	0	
Political parties	17,007	1.44	0	
Subtotal	**42,141**	**3.56**	**0**	
Unitemized Expenses	**4,621**	**.39**	**6,338**	**3.55**
Total Campaign Expenses	**$ 1,184,654**		**$ 178,405**	
PAC Contributions	$ 504,521		$ 16,800	
Individual Contributions	454,110		97,642	
Total Receipts*	1,028,481		192,095	

*Includes PAC and individual contributions as well as interest earned, party contributions, etc.

MICHIGAN — District 13

Rep. William D. Ford (D)

1992 Election Results

William D. Ford (D)	127,642	(52%)
R. Robert Geake (R)	105,169	(43%)

Democratic Rep. William D. Ford's winning percentage had dropped as low as 60 percent only once in fourteen previous House races, including his initial campaign in 1964. He had garnered at least 70 percent of the vote eight times. However, redistricting and negative publicity over his love of first-class air travel and fine dining at taxpayer expense nearly cost him his seat in 1992.

Faced with his first serious challenge in more than a decade, Ford spent $572,012 more on his 1992 campaign than he had in 1990. Ford's overhead expenses nearly tripled, rising from $77,317 in the 1990 election cycle to $216,283 in 1992. Outlays for broadcast advertising increased from $48,592 to $164,369. Persuasion mail costs jumped from $73,808 to $264,962, and expenditures on such items as phonebanking, yard signs, buttons, and bumper stickers increased from $21,891 to $56,611.

Ford's increased spending did not prove to be a bonanza for consultants. While he paid Politics Inc. of Washington, D.C., $21,043 for designing his campaign literature, all the printing was done by local print shops. An army of volunteers saw to it that the mail was addressed, stamped, and sent on its way. Television and radio commercials were produced at the Democratic party's Harriman Communication Center and placed directly by the campaign. Pollster Garin-Hart of Washington, D.C., collected $5,000 from Ford's treasury and another $5,137 from the Democratic Congressional Campaign Committee. Fraioli/Jost, also of Washington, received $12,489 for coordinating political action committee fund-raising efforts.

Expenditures for constituent stroking rose from $5,771 during the 1990 election cycle to $13,461 in 1992. He spent $1,364 on trees that he donated to local schools on Arbor Day. He spent $2,562 on poinsettias, which he sent to volunteers and local elected officials each Christmas. Annual Christmas parties catered by the Culinary Arts Department at the William D. Ford Vocational Tech Center cost a total of $3,192, and year-end holiday cards cost the campaign $4,388.

In February 1991 the campaign made its last $411 payment on a car used by Ford in Washington, D.C. That same month, the campaign made a $2,603 down payment on a new car from Dave Pyle's Lincoln Mercury in Annandale, Va., and began making monthly loan payments of $732. The campaign also spent $16,416 on a new car in Michigan.

State senator R. Robert Geake put 62 percent of his much smaller budget into direct appeals for votes. He held Ford to 52 percent—a 9-point drop from 1990.

	Ford		Geake	
Campaign Expenditures	Amount Spent	% of Total	Amount Spent	% of Total
Overhead				
Office furniture/supplies	$ 3,706	.40	$ 1,238	.56
Rent/utilities	12,331	1.33	6,022	2.73
Salaries	72,741	7.85	34,306	15.54
Taxes	31,343	3.38	0	
Bank/investment fees	0		92	.04
Lawyers/accountants	0		0	
Telephone	2,556	.28	2,586	1.17
Campaign automobile	40,778	4.40	0	
Computers/office equipment	20,647	2.23	3,692	1.67
Travel	26,927	2.91	844	.38
Food/meetings	5,255	.57	0	
Subtotal	**216,283**	**23.34**	**48,781**	**22.09**
Fund Raising				
Events	79,096	8.53	23,341	10.57
Direct mail	0		3,788	1.72
Telemarketing	0		0	
Subtotal	**79,096**	**8.53**	**27,129**	**12.29**
Polling	**5,000**	**.54**	**2,000**	**.91**
Advertising				
Electronic media	164,369	17.74	65,857	29.83
Other media	13,943	1.50	7,592	3.44
Subtotal	**178,312**	**19.24**	**73,449**	**33.27**
Other Campaign Activity				
Persuasion mail/brochures	264,962	28.59	47,283	21.42
Actual campaigning	56,611	6.11	16,950	7.68
Staff/volunteers	0		27	.01
Subtotal	**321,574**	**34.70**	**64,260**	**29.11**
Constituent Gifts/ Entertainment	**13,461**	**1.45**	**0**	
Donations to				
Candidates from same state	2,700	.29	0	
Candidates from other states	2,000	.22	0	
Civic organizations	6,790	.73	55	.02
Ideological groups	1,750	.19	0	
Political parties	7,900	.85	0	
Subtotal	**21,140**	**2.28**	**55**	**.02**
Unitemized Expenses	**91,875**	**9.91**	**5,100**	**2.31**
Total Campaign Expenses	**$ 926,741**		**$ 220,773**	
PAC Contributions	$ 520,850		$ 35,031	
Individual Contributions	124,204		104,692	
Total Receipts*	681,981		188,860	

*Includes PAC and individual contributions as well as interest earned, party contributions, etc.

District 14   MICHIGAN

Rep. John Conyers, Jr. (D)

1992 Election Results

John Conyers, Jr. (D)	165,496	(82%)
John W. Gordon † (R)	32,036	(16%)

In fourteen previous House campaigns, Rep. John Conyers, Jr., had faced few primary opponents and never received less than 84 percent of the general election vote. In 1990 he had spent only $155,975, and just $16,425 of that total had been invested in direct appeals to voters.

However, with 273 overdrafts totaling $108,000 at the House bank, Conyers was one of twenty-two House members who were found by the Committee on Standards of Official Conduct to have abused banking privileges. He also had redistricting to worry about. While 18 percent of his old constituency was white, redistricting had increased that figure to 29 percent. As a result, Conyers, who is black, upped his spending to $246,774 during the 1992 election cycle, putting $85,927 into direct voter contact.

Conyers drew three challengers in the Democratic primary, including state senator John Kelly. With less than $52,000 to spend, Kelly reached out to fellow whites in Grosse Point Woods with a letter that asked, "Did you know that unless you vote on August 4, you will be represented by John Conyers in Congress as part of the new 14th District?" Kelly captured 26 percent of the vote, a figure that closely mirrored the percentage of whites in the district.

Conyers did not take the challenge by Kelly lightly. Between May 1 and August 4 Conyers pumped $120,925 into his campaign, which was only $35,050 less than he spent on his entire 1990 bid. As Conyers told the local press, "I'm not taking anything for granted. It's the full-court press."

He opened two campaign offices and staffed them with ten part-time employees. The staffers helped Conyers send out $36,951 in voter persuasion mail, something he did not do in 1990. Conyers also paid $250 to put his name on the "Eastside Slate" mailer.

Two weeks before the primary, Conyers paid $5,000 to Coley and Associates of Detroit for placing radio commercials, which were produced for $600 in Washington, D.C., at the Democrat's Harriman Communications Center. He spent $6,948 on newspaper ads and $5,281 on signs.

To ensure that his supporters turned out for the primary, Conyers spent $14,995 on an in-house phonebank. Vans to ferry voters to the polls cost $1,950, and gasoline to fuel them added $547.

Conyers took the general election campaign against computer operator John W. Gordon much more lightly. He spent nothing on broadcast advertising, $2,561 on newspaper ads, and $2,767 on persuasion mail. Only $1,659 was put into the in-house phonebank.

Conyers awarded his volunteers and supporters by throwing a $5,398 party at the end of 1992.

	Conyers	
Campaign Expenditures	Amount Spent	% of Total
Overhead		
Office furniture/supplies	$ 1,721	.70
Rent/utilities	9,916	4.02
Salaries	14,175	5.74
Taxes	0	
Bank/investment fees	0	
Lawyers/accountants	5,846	2.37
Telephone	995	.40
Campaign automobile	0	
Computers/office equipment	0	
Travel	14,251	5.77
Food/meetings	574	.23
Subtotal	**47,478**	**19.24**
Fund Raising		
Events	58,378	23.66
Direct mail	0	
Telemarketing	0	
Subtotal	**58,378**	**23.66**
Polling	**0**	
Advertising		
Electronic media	5,600	2.27
Other media	10,679	4.33
Subtotal	**16,279**	**6.60**
Other Campaign Activity		
Persuasion mail/brochures	39,968	16.20
Actual campaigning	29,680	12.03
Staff/volunteers	0	
Subtotal	**69,648**	**28.22**
Constituent Gifts/Entertainment	**6,563**	**2.66**
Donations to		
Candidates from same state	0	
Candidates from other states	0	
Civic organizations	3,050	1.24
Ideological groups	500	.20
Political parties	3,050	1.24
Subtotal	**6,600**	**2.67**
Unitemized Expenses	**41,828**	**16.95**
Total Campaign Expenses	$ **246,774**	
PAC Contributions	$ **215,008**	
Individual Contributions	**125,508**	
Total Receipts*	**309,396**	

*Includes PAC and individual contributions as well as interest earned, party contributions, etc.

† No expenditures or receipts on file. Candidates raising or spending less than $5,000 are not required to file reports with the Federal Election Commission.

MICHIGAN — District 15

Rep. Barbara-Rose Collins (D)

1992 Election Results

Barbara-Rose Collins (D) 148,908 (81%)
Charles C. Vincent (R) 31,849 (17%)

Rep. Barbara-Rose Collins spent $226,735 on her initial reelection campaign, but eighteen cents of every dollar were put into constituent entertainment and gifts. She invested $25,064 of her campaign funds to celebrate her January 1991 inauguration, including $13,364 for a pre-inaugural prayer breakfast, $3,561 to transport supporters to Washington, and $7,603 for food and room rental at the Hyatt Regency Hotel in Washington. At the end of the election cycle, the campaign spent $4,500 for tickets to the presidential inaugural ball. Flowers and telegrams to express sympathy over a constituent's death or to celebrate a new constituent's birth cost the campaign $1,222. The campaign spent $5,463 on constituent meals, $2,875 on receptions for senior citizens and other groups, $1,433 on "oval pen stands" and other gifts, and $215 on commemorative plaques.

These were not Collins's only outlays that had little or nothing to do with her reelection effort. One-third of her $15,790 travel budget was spent in New York during the four-day Democratic National Convention. After investing more than $7,000 of her 1990 campaign funds in clothes and image consulting, Collins spent more than $1,800 to finish off her wardrobe in early 1991.

In the Democratic primary, accountant Tom Barrow tried in vain to capitalize on Collins's less than spectacular first term. Collins had admitted accepting illegal campaign contributions, pleading ignorance of federal campaign finance law. She was named by the National Taxpayers Union as one of the biggest users of franked mail in the House. She had high staff turnover and few legislative accomplishments. However, with less than $5,000 to spend on the race, Barrow lacked the funds to get his anti-incumbent message out.

Collins had no such problems. She spent about $100,000 during the two months prior to the August 4 primary. She invested $41,054 on campaign literature and persuasion mail, $15,653 on billboard advertising, $8,242 on signs and posters, and $7,513 to air radio commercials touting her work to secure federal mass transit funds for Detroit.

In this heavily democratic district, Collins had little to fear in the general election from Republican nominee Charles C. Vincent, a physician who had finished third behind Collins and Barrow in the 1990 Democratic primary before switching his party allegiance. Although Vincent spent at least $84,000 more than Collins's 1990 Republican challenger, he received an identical 17 percent of the vote.

Collins countered Vincent's weak challenge by spending only $5,781 on campaign pamphlets, $3,000 to air her radio spots, and $602 on additional signs.

Campaign Expenditures	Collins Amount Spent	Collins % of Total	Vincent Amount Spent	Vincent % of Total
Overhead				
Office furniture/supplies	$ 6,346	2.80	$ 1,742	1.95
Rent/utilities	2,897	1.28	3,884	4.35
Salaries	12,333	5.44	25,705	28.80
Taxes	0		0	
Bank/investment fees	767	.34	3	
Lawyers/accountants	860	.38	4,071	4.56
Telephone	3,454	1.52	1,824	2.04
Campaign automobile	0		0	
Computers/office equipment	2,601	1.15	0	
Travel	15,790	6.96	1,088	1.22
Food/meetings	3,177	1.40	0	
Subtotal	**48,225**	**21.27**	**38,317**	**42.93**
Fund Raising				
Events	19,106	8.43	6,557	7.35
Direct mail	0		1,338	1.50
Telemarketing	0		0	
Subtotal	**19,106**	**8.43**	**7,895**	**8.85**
Polling	**0**		**0**	
Advertising				
Electronic media	10,513	4.64	10,305	11.54
Other media	20,797	9.17	1,147	1.28
Subtotal	**31,310**	**13.81**	**11,452**	**12.83**
Other Campaign Activity				
Persuasion mail/brochures	46,835	20.66	19,870	22.26
Actual campaigning	22,112	9.75	10,017	11.22
Staff/volunteers	1,800	.79	620	.69
Subtotal	**70,747**	**31.20**	**30,507**	**34.18**
Constituent Gifts/ Entertainment	**40,772**	**17.98**	**0**	
Donations to				
Candidates from same state	820	.36	0	
Candidates from other states	1,450	.64	0	
Civic organizations	2,589	1.14	50	.06
Ideological groups	1,475	.65	0	
Political parties	2,230	.98	0	
Subtotal	**8,564**	**3.78**	**50**	**.06**
Unitemized Expenses	**8,012**	**3.53**	**1,041**	**1.17**
Total Campaign Expenses	**$ 226,735**		**$ 89,262**	
PAC Contributions	**$ 121,721**		**$ 10,020**	
Individual Contributions	**109,769**		**67,029**	
Total Receipts*	**278,723**		**98,434**	

*Includes PAC and individual contributions as well as interest earned, party contributions, etc.

District 16 — MICHIGAN

Rep. John D. Dingell (D)

1992 Election Results

John D. Dingell (D)	156,964	(65%)
Frank Beaumont (R)	75,694	(31%)

Rep. John D. Dingell's 1992 campaign was a study in excess. First elected in 1955, Dingell had never received less than 63 percent of the vote and he had not been hurt by the latest round of redistricting. The 1992 election was a rematch with Republican Frank Beaumont, who had spent only $3,775 on his 1990 campaign. Nevertheless, Dingell spent $1,085,395—$488,804 more than the $596,591 he spent in 1990.

This massive increase was reflected in virtually every aspect of Dingell's effort. Overhead rose from $124,441 in 1990 to $244,744 in 1992, an increase of 97 percent. His 1992 fund-raising costs increased 73 percent to $161,127 from $92,890. Broadcast advertising more than doubled from $100,981 to $211,779. In fact, the only exception to the trend was Dingell's outlays for constituent entertainment and gifts, which declined from $57,921 to $54,707.

In 1991 alone Dingell spent $364,960—nearly sixty-eight times what Beaumont would spend on his entire campaign. Overhead amounted to $106,480, including $32,368 to the Washington, D.C., law firm of Perkins Coie. Reflecting his heavy reliance on political action committee (PAC) contributions, Dingell invested $96,797 in his off-year fund-raising activities, including a $14,250 event at the Washington Court Hotel and a $13,641 soiree at the Sheraton Carlton Hotel in Washington.

Over the cycle, one-quarter of Dingell's spending was funneled through consultants. Morris & Carrick of New York received $211,000 for producing and placing broadcast advertising. Never seriously challenged, Dingell still paid Garin-Hart of Washington, D.C., $45,000 for conducting polls. Fraioli/Jost of Washington, D.C., received $16,761 for helping him raise $767,931 from PACs.

Dingell contributed to dozens of state and local politicians, including candidates for mayor, county sheriff, county clerk, and probate judge. Twenty-nine congressional candidates each received $1,000.

About 10 percent of Dingell's spending was either unitemized or so vaguely described that it was impossible to tell how the money was spent. In accordance with federal regulations, Dingell chose not to itemize $67,801 in expenditures of less than $200. Reimbursements to individuals for "campaign expenses" amounted to $27,991, including $17,593 paid to Dingell. Payments for "petty cash" totaled $12,000.

While Dingell clearly did not need their assistance, the Democratic National Committee (DNC) spent $16,039 on his behalf for additional polls. As was the case with other safe incumbents who received this help, the DNC's payments went to Greenberg-Lake of Washington, D.C., a key member of presidential candidate Bill Clinton's braintrust.

	Dingell		Beaumont	
Campaign Expenditures	Amount Spent	% of Total	Amount Spent	% of Total
Overhead				
Office furniture/supplies	$ 10,088	.93	$ 283	5.24
Rent/utilities	13,940	1.28	350	6.48
Salaries	64,004	5.90	0	
Taxes	31,742	2.92	0	
Bank/investment fees	2,036	.19	53	.98
Lawyers/accountants	34,500	3.18	0	
Telephone	5,658	.52	389	7.21
Campaign automobile	0		0	
Computers/office equipment	10,194	.94	25	.46
Travel	48,917	4.51	444	8.22
Food/meetings	23,666	2.18	0	
Subtotal	**244,744**	**22.55**	**1,544**	**28.58**
Fund Raising				
Events	161,127	14.85	0	
Direct mail	0		0	
Telemarketing	0		0	
Subtotal	**161,127**	**14.85**	**0**	
Polling	**45,000**	**4.15**	**0**	
Advertising				
Electronic media	211,779	19.51	0	
Other media	15,682	1.44	304	5.64
Subtotal	**227,461**	**20.96**	**304**	**5.64**
Other Campaign Activity				
Persuasion mail/brochures	100,645	9.27	1,797	33.27
Actual campaigning	44,433	4.09	893	16.53
Staff/volunteers	5,387	.50	0	
Subtotal	**150,465**	**13.86**	**2,690**	**49.80**
Constituent Gifts/ Entertainment	**54,707**	**5.04**	**0**	
Donations to				
Candidates from same state	22,569	2.08	64	1.18
Candidates from other states	24,000	2.21	0	
Civic organizations	8,829	.81	53	.98
Ideological groups	1,800	.17	102	1.88
Political parties	36,901	3.40	44	.81
Subtotal	**94,099**	**8.67**	**263**	**4.86**
Unitemized Expenses	**107,792**	**9.93**	**600**	**11.11**
Total Campaign Expenses	**$ 1,085,395**		**$ 5,402**	
PAC Contributions	$ 767,931		$ 0	
Individual Contributions	281,312		570	
Total Receipts*	1,112,141		5,402	

*Includes PAC and individual contributions as well as interest earned, party contributions, etc.

MINNESOTA   District 1

Rep. Timothy J. Penny (D)

1992 Election Results Timothy J. Penny (D) 206,369 (74%)
                        Timothy R. Droogsma (R) 72,367 (26%)

After collecting more than 70 percent of the votes in three consecutive campaigns, Rep. Timothy J. Penny spent the first sixteen months of the 1992 election cycle exploring a possible confrontation with Sen. Dave Durenberger in 1996. "It was no secret we were looking at a potential statewide race," noted administrative assistant Steven T. Bosacker.

Penny closed his campaign office following the 1990 election and did not reopen it until April 1992. However, during that period Penny paid Bosacker—who at the time had temporarily left the congressional staff—a campaign salary of $49,364 plus expenses. This salary was $7,649 more than Penny spent on payroll during the entire 1990 election cycle.

In March 1992 Penny hired telemarketing fundraiser Meyer Associates of St. Cloud to help expand his political base. "We needed new blood," explained Bosacker.

In April Penny refocused his attention on the 1992 reelection campaign, which he thought might be tougher than he had become accustomed to. He was pitted against Timothy R. Droogsma, who had promised to make Penny's vote against the Gulf War a campaign issue. Droogsma's credentials as a former press secretary to both Gov. Arne Carlson and former Sen. Rudy Boschwitz suggested he might be able to assemble a substantial campaign treasury.

However, Droogsma never succeeded in turning his political connections into contributions, and the Gulf War vote failed to excite much anger in a campaign dominated by economic issues.

While Penny spent 67 percent more on advertising than he had in 1990, his $26,933 advertising budget represented only about 9 percent of his total spending. Penny did not feel the need to send out persuasion mail and invested just $6,460 in fliers that were primarily distributed during district walking tours.

As he had in the past, Penny campaigned on the importance of deficit reduction. One of his two radio spots, recycled from 1990, criticized pork-barrel politics and featured the sound of pigs oinking in the background. Several rounds of ads in seventy-six weekly newspapers and eight dailies consisted of pictures of his family, references to his fourth-generation roots in the district, and recitations of the high ratings accorded his voting record by a number of taxpayer watchdog organizations. Coleman & Christison of St. Paul received $26,369 for creating and placing the various radio and newspaper ads.

Penny's only other major voter contact expenses were the $39,500 he paid to the Minnesota Democratic-Farm-Labor party for its coordinated voter identification effort and the $6,106 he invested in yard signs.

Campaign Expenditures	Penny Amount Spent	% of Total	Droogsma Amount Spent	% of Total
Overhead				
Office furniture/supplies	$ 3,767	1.29	$ 2,114	2.06
Rent/utilities	2,209	.75	2,950	2.87
Salaries	74,523	25.44	10,937	10.64
Taxes	22,868	7.81	1,181	1.15
Bank/investment fees	196	.07	0	
Lawyers/accountants	0		0	
Telephone	5,517	1.88	4,662	4.53
Campaign automobile	0		0	
Computers/office equipment	1,594	.54	5,667	5.51
Travel	15,718	5.37	11,330	11.02
Food/meetings	1,926	.66	215	.21
Subtotal	**128,319**	**43.81**	**39,056**	**37.98**
Fund Raising				
Events	29,298	10.00	3,037	2.95
Direct mail	16,623	5.68	3,483	3.39
Telemarketing	9,113	3.11	0	
Subtotal	**55,035**	**18.79**	**6,520**	**6.34**
Polling	**0**		**0**	
Advertising				
Electronic media	12,421	4.24	0	
Other media	14,512	4.95	15,820	15.38
Subtotal	**26,933**	**9.20**	**15,820**	**15.38**
Other Campaign Activity				
Persuasion mail/brochures	6,460	2.21	19,502	18.96
Actual campaigning	47,435	16.20	13,440	13.07
Staff/volunteers	0		25	.02
Subtotal	**53,895**	**18.40**	**32,967**	**32.06**
Constituent Gifts/ Entertainment	**4,969**	**1.70**	**0**	
Donations to				
Candidates from same state	2,200	.75	0	
Candidates from other states	3,226	1.10	0	
Civic organizations	1,000	.34	0	
Ideological groups	75	.03	0	
Political parties	13,156	4.49	0	
Subtotal	**19,657**	**6.71**	**0**	
Unitemized Expenses	**4,092**	**1.40**	**8,472**	**8.24**
Total Campaign Expenses	**$ 292,900**		**$ 102,835**	
PAC Contributions	$ 92,743		$ 10,981	
Individual Contributions	117,646		74,897	
Total Receipts*	244,518		96,568	

*Includes PAC and individual contributions as well as interest earned, party contributions, etc.

District 2 — MINNESOTA

Rep. David Minge (D)

1992 Election Results

David Minge (D)	132,156 (48%)
Cal R. Ludeman (R)	131,587 (48%)

When Republican Rep. Vin Weber decided to retire rather than face voters with his 125 House bank overdrafts, prognosticators anointed Cal R. Ludeman, a former state legislator and the 1986 Republican gubernatorial nominee, as Weber's likely successor.

According to the pundits, attorney David Minge's pro-choice stance on abortion, his lack of political experience, and his lackluster 53 percent victory in the Democratic primary spelled disaster in the conservative district held for twelve years by Weber. Less than one week before the November general election, one such newspaper pundit noted that Ludeman was "set to win this seat." However, when the 275,889 votes were counted, Minge eked out a 569-vote victory.

According to Minge's son Olaf, who worked on the campaign for nine months without pay, the turning point was Minge's nine-day, 478-mile September bicycle ride through the district's twenty-seven counties. "Before that, we had no exposure, but local papers took pictures and wrote about the ride, which helped attract an infusion of campaign workers in the last month," explained the younger Minge.

To ensure that his volunteers had a place to work, Minge opened five satellite offices in addition to his main office in Montevideo. Twelve phonebanking operations, most with no more than four telephone lines, were set up by volunteers in businesses throughout the district. Telephone bills for these phonebanks amounted to $23,330. Since name recognition was a problem, $12,738 was invested in signs.

Overall, Minge was outspent by $75,167, but he invested more than twice as much as Ludeman in broadcast advertising. Initially, Minge put his money into radio commercials, airing a biographical spot, an ad targeting farmers that ran on the Farm News Network, and spots that featured letters he had received from children. The latter ads served as a means to segue into discussions of his ideas on job creation and health care reform. Having set the stage with positive spots, Minge unleashed a round of negative ads that attacked Ludeman's state legislative voting record, including one that pointed to his vote against funding a program to help find missing children.

For the final three days of the campaign, Minge aired his lone television commercial, which showed him walking through a small, rural town discussing how he would help save it if sent to Washington. Austin-Sheinkopf of New York received $102,018 for creating and placing the broadcast ads.

Ludeman opted not to use television, a decision he later described as his "biggest tactical mistake."

	Minge		Ludeman	
Campaign Expenditures	Amount Spent	% of Total	Amount Spent	% of Total
Overhead				
Office furniture/supplies	$ 1,393	.39	$ 9,609	2.24
Rent/utilities	3,984	1.13	5,242	1.22
Salaries	42,985	12.15	58,464	13.63
Taxes	14,792	4.18	22,161	5.17
Bank/investment fees	33	.01	62	.01
Lawyers/accountants	1,900	.54	1,830	.43
Telephone	7,542	2.13	3,578	.83
Campaign automobile	0		1,340	.31
Computers/office equipment	3,548	1.00	8,292	1.93
Travel	37,458	10.59	21,981	5.12
Food/meetings	37	.01	1,162	.27
Subtotal	**113,671**	**32.13**	**133,720**	**31.18**
Fund Raising				
Events	27,604	7.80	39,191	9.14
Direct mail	17,297	4.89	17,310	4.04
Telemarketing	1,455	.41	22,076	5.15
Subtotal	**46,356**	**13.10**	**78,578**	**18.32**
Polling	**14,886**	**4.21**	**4,250**	**.99**
Advertising				
Electronic media	104,672	29.59	46,000	10.72
Other media	5,277	1.49	32,844	7.66
Subtotal	**109,950**	**31.08**	**78,844**	**18.38**
Other Campaign Activity				
Persuasion mail/brochures	12,592	3.56	104,152	24.28
Actual campaigning	43,157	12.20	13,910	3.24
Staff/volunteers	0		0	
Subtotal	**55,749**	**15.76**	**118,062**	**27.53**
Constituent Gifts/ Entertainment	**0**		**0**	
Donations to				
Candidates from same state	0		750	.17
Candidates from other states	0		0	
Civic organizations	0		0	
Ideological groups	0		1,000	.23
Political parties	1,000	.28	750	.17
Subtotal	**1,000**	**.28**	**2,500**	**.58**
Unitemized Expenses	**12,138**	**3.43**	**12,964**	**3.02**
Total Campaign Expenses	**$ 353,750**		**$ 428,917**	
PAC Contributions	**$ 159,958**		**$ 14,415**	
Individual Contributions	**148,491**		**382,156**	
Total Receipts*	**365,394**		**432,038**	

*Includes PAC and individual contributions as well as interest earned, party contributions, etc.

MINNESOTA — District 3

Rep. Jim Ramstad (R)

1992 Election Results

Jim Ramstad (R)	200,240	(64%)
Paul Mandell (D)	104,606	(33%)

After garnering 67 percent of the vote to win an open seat in 1990, freshman Rep. Jim Ramstad immediately settled into the permanent campaign mode. Off-year expenses totaled $151,776, including $600 a month rent on his campaign office. Campaign manager Tim Berkness was hired in May 1991 and by the end of the cycle had collected salary payments totaling $43,926, including a $1,307 bonus. Two part-time staffers were hired in September 1991 and three others were added before the election.

Ramstad began 1991 with debts of $122,580 and cash reserves of only $2,448. Twenty-four months later he had whittled his debts to $21,793 and increased his cash on hand to $317,719. He raised $486,967 from individual contributors who gave at least $200, $270,772 from donors who gave less than $200, and $260,016 from political action committees (PACs). He accomplished this by sinking 41 percent of his $599,672 campaign outlays into fund raising.

Kay Weinstock-Rose of Golden Valley received $45,709 for coordinating Ramstad's thirty-six district fund-raising events. Six receptions held at the Capitol Hill Club cost a total of $5,082. For mailing fund-raising solicitations, Campaign Services Group of Austin, Texas, and Campaign Support Services of Minneapolis received $32,517 and $15,000, respectively. Strategic Telecommunications of St. Paul was paid $46,282 for telemarketing.

Although nearly 50 percent of the district was new to him, Ramstad invested only 22 percent of his campaign expenditures in direct appeals to voters. Unopposed in the primary and faced with a $18,166 challenge by Democrat Paul Mandell, Ramstad had no reason to worry.

National Media of Alexandria, Va., collected $74,788 for creating, producing, and placing one television commercial and a companion radio spot. According to press secretary Dean P. Peterson, the ads sought to remind voters that they had "sent Jim Ramstad to Washington to shake things up." The ads listed endorsements from such groups as the Sierra Club, Citizens Against Government Waste, and the Crime Victims Group.

Ramstad spent $27,540 on billboards with the slogan, "an energetic new voice for Minnesota." Newspaper ads cost $5,222; T-shirts, $2,043; and promotional sunglasses, $950. Cherry Communications of Gainesville, Fla., collected $4,139 for what Peterson described as a voter identification program undertaken with other local candidates.

A poll of district residents by Tarrance & Associates of Alexandria, Va., cost Ramstad $8,000. The American Medical Association Political Action Committee picked up $4,700 of his polling costs.

	Ramstad		Mandell	
Campaign Expenditures	Amount Spent	% of Total	Amount Spent	% of Total
Overhead				
Office furniture/supplies	$ 8,948	1.49	$ 680	3.74
Rent/utilities	14,400	2.40	0	
Salaries	73,815	12.31	0	
Taxes	35,921	5.99	0	
Bank/investment fees	75	.01	16	.09
Lawyers/accountants	21,484	3.58	0	
Telephone	15,283	2.55	0	
Campaign automobile	0		0	
Computers/office equipment	11,334	1.89	0	
Travel	10,943	1.82	242	1.33
Food/meetings	1,895	.32	30	.16
Subtotal	**194,099**	**32.37**	**968**	**5.33**
Fund Raising				
Events	87,525	14.60	0	
Direct mail	111,776	18.64	0	
Telemarketing	46,282	7.72	0	
Subtotal	**245,583**	**40.95**	**0**	
Polling	**12,700**	**2.12**	**0**	
Advertising				
Electronic media	74,984	12.50	3,223	17.74
Other media	33,447	5.58	5,921	32.60
Subtotal	**108,432**	**18.08**	**9,144**	**50.34**
Other Campaign Activity				
Persuasion mail/brochures	0		3,893	21.43
Actual campaigning	22,153	3.69	4,064	22.37
Staff/volunteers	1,411	.24	97	.53
Subtotal	**23,564**	**3.93**	**8,054**	**44.33**
Constituent Gifts/ Entertainment	**9,096**	**1.52**	**0**	
Donations to				
Candidates from same state	2,500	.42	0	
Candidates from other states	0		0	
Civic organizations	1,000	.17	0	
Ideological groups	0		0	
Political parties	108	.02	0	
Subtotal	**3,608**	**.60**	**0**	
Unitemized Expenses	**2,591**	**.43**	**0**	
Total Campaign Expenses	**$ 599,672**		**$ 18,166**	
PAC Contributions	$ 260,016		$ 8,670	
Individual Contributions	739,739		7,083	
Total Receipts*	1,010,791		18,609	

*Includes PAC and individual contributions as well as interest earned, party contributions, etc.

District 4 — MINNESOTA

Rep. Bruce F. Vento (D)

1992 Election Results

Bruce F. Vento (D)	159,796	(58%)
Ian Maitland (R)	101,744	(37%)

Republican Ian Maitland, a professor at the University of Minnesota, does not give up easily. For the third consecutive time, Maitland challenged Democratic Rep. Bruce F. Vento, who had received less than 60 percent of the vote only twice in eight previous House campaigns. While the results were only marginally different, Maitland was moving in the right direction. Having received 27 percent of the vote in 1988 and 35 percent in 1990, Maitland grabbed 37 percent in 1992.

Vento presented a mixed target for Maitland's anti-incumbent campaign theme. While Vento had only three overdrafts at the House bank and had voted against the 1990 budget summit plan for spending and taxing, he had voted for the congressional pay raise in 1989 and routinely collected more than 70 percent of his campaign funds from political action committees.

Perhaps Vento's biggest problem was the less than spectacular showing by the Clinton/Gore team at the top of the ticket. Although the district had been held by the Democratic-Farm-Labor party (DFL) since 1948 and their strength had been only mildly diluted by redistricting, the 1992 Democratic presidential ticket carried a smaller percentage of the vote than the Dukakis/Bentsen ticket in 1988, the Mondale/Ferraro ticket in 1984, or the Carter/Mondale tickets in 1980 and 1976.

Vento responded by radically altering his approach to voter communication. In 1990 he spent $51,849 to produce and air four radio commercials and $39,485 on newspaper, bus, and program ads. In 1992 he put $110,764 into television commercials, ran no radio spots, and reduced his investment in newspaper ads, bus signs, and program ads to $11,710. Chief of staff Lawrence J. Romans said the television campaign focused primarily on Vento's environmental record and never mentioned Maitland. Coleman & Christison of St. Paul received $120,706 for creating and placing the various ads.

Vento also more than doubled his investment in persuasion mail and campaign literature, from $8,924 in 1990 to $21,375 in 1992. In addition to sharing the cost of several mailings by the local DFL party organization, the Vento campaign sent mailings to more targeted audiences, including members of the Sierra Club.

Maitland's scant budget forced him to generate free media. For one stunt he spent $3,500 to rent a billboard that carried the message: "Change has a name—Maitland." He then set up a tent, a chair, and a coffee table on the billboard's twenty-five foot high platform and camped out for several days so that drivers on Interstate 94 could see him sitting in suit and tie next to his message.

	Vento		Maitland	
Campaign Expenditures	Amount Spent	% of Total	Amount Spent	% of Total
Overhead				
Office furniture/supplies	$ 1,763	.51	$ 779	.95
Rent/utilities	1,910	.55	526	.64
Salaries	17,346	4.99	11,240	13.71
Taxes	10,667	3.07	2,686	3.28
Bank/investment fees	20	.01	0	
Lawyers/accountants	2,874	.83	0	
Telephone	2,390	.69	1,192	1.45
Campaign automobile	0		0	
Computers/office equipment	64	.02	3,000	3.66
Travel	2,949	.85	0	
Food/meetings	2,398	.69	0	
Subtotal	**42,381**	**12.19**	**19,423**	**23.69**
Fund Raising				
Events	48,951	14.08	1,221	1.49
Direct mail	0		16,777	20.46
Telemarketing	0		0	
Subtotal	**48,951**	**14.08**	**17,998**	**21.95**
Polling	**11,000**	**3.16**	**0**	
Advertising				
Electronic media	110,764	31.86	12,610	15.38
Other media	11,710	3.37	6,757	8.24
Subtotal	**122,474**	**35.23**	**19,366**	**23.62**
Other Campaign Activity				
Persuasion mail/brochures	21,375	6.15	15,900	19.40
Actual campaigning	15,317	4.41	5,739	7.00
Staff/volunteers	294	.08	0	
Subtotal	**36,986**	**10.64**	**21,639**	**26.40**
Constituent Gifts/ Entertainment	**3,142**	**.90**	**0**	
Donations to				
Candidates from same state	2,200	.63	0	
Candidates from other states	1,000	.29	0	
Civic organizations	590	.17	0	
Ideological groups	0		0	
Political parties	73,400	21.11	0	
Subtotal	**77,190**	**22.20**	**0**	
Unitemized Expenses	**5,509**	**1.58**	**3,553**	**4.33**
Total Campaign Expenses	**$ 347,633**		**$ 81,981**	
PAC Contributions	$ 207,495		$ 0	
Individual Contributions	52,373		81,674	
Total Receipts*	280,123		83,114	

*Includes PAC and individual contributions as well as interest earned, party contributions, etc.

MINNESOTA — District 5

Rep. Martin Olav Sabo (D)

1992 Election Results

Martin Olav Sabo (D)	174,139	(63%)
Stephen A. Moriarty (R)	77,093	(28%)

Representing the state's most Democratic constituency, Rep. Martin Olav Sabo's only significant hurdle of the 1992 campaign was winning the Democratic-Farm-Labor party's nomination. Despite having won consistently high ratings from liberal organizations such as the Americans for Democratic Action, the seven-term incumbent found himself challenged from the left by Lisa Niebauer-Stall, co-founder of the Minnesota Women's Political Alliance. Niebauer-Stall's coalition of feminists, those eager to see deeper defense cuts than supported by Sabo, and backers of Democratic Sen. Paul Wellstone succeeded in keeping Sabo from obtaining the endorsement of those attending the district party convention until the eighth ballot.

Employing the slogan "A Woman for a Change," Niebauer-Stall carried the fight on to the three-candidate Democratic primary, where she lacked the resources to communicate her anti-incumbent message. Sabo easily prevailed with 67 percent of the vote.

Although voters had paid little attention to Niebauer-Stall's message that Democrats did not want "fourteen more years of do-nothing, tread-softly, make-no-waves, career politicians," Sabo had heard her loud and clear. Between July 1 and the September 15 primary, he spent $342,936 on securing the Democratic nomination, or 59 percent of his spending for the entire two-year election cycle.

After sticking exclusively with radio for seven House campaigns, Sabo asked his media adviser, John Franzen Multimedia of Washington, D.C., to create a television commercial. "Incumbency was a dirty word in 1992, and TV seemed the best medium to get our message out," explained administrative assistant Michael S. Erlandson.

The ad sought to blunt Niebauer-Stall's message and convince voters that there was no reason to change simply for the sake of change. Since Sabo's record reflected his constituent's thinking, they ought to send him back to Washington. Of the $112,857 Franzen received for creating and placing the ad, all but about $3,500 was for preprimary work.

Sabo paid Coleman & Christison of St. Paul $32,031 to create and place the bulk of his radio commercials and to design several small ads that ran in community newspapers throughout the district. Of that total, $29,164 was spent before the primary.

Sabo paid Bates & Associates of Washington, D.C., $47,000 for producing persuasion mailers detailing his pro-choice stance on abortion and his leadership on defense issues. Lauer, Lalley & Associates of Washington, D.C., received $15,000 for polling.

In the general election contest against Republican challenger Stephen A. Moriarty, Sabo took things much easier, spending less than $70,000.

Campaign Expenditures	Sabo Amount Spent	Sabo % of Total	Moriarty Amount Spent	Moriarty % of Total
Overhead				
Office furniture/supplies	$ 4,492	.77	$ 225	1.34
Rent/utilities	3,267	.56	0	
Salaries	24,145	4.14	0	
Taxes	13,195	2.26	0	
Bank/investment fees	918	.16	0	
Lawyers/accountants	7,553	1.30	0	
Telephone	3,940	.68	70	.41
Campaign automobile	0		0	
Computers/office equipment	7,939	1.36	0	
Travel	12,045	2.07	0	
Food/meetings	5,062	.87	158	.94
Subtotal	**82,557**	**14.16**	**452**	**2.69**
Fund Raising				
Events	32,387	5.56	577	3.44
Direct mail	0		0	
Telemarketing	7,525	1.29	0	
Subtotal	**39,912**	**6.85**	**577**	**3.44**
Polling	**15,000**	**2.57**	**0**	
Advertising				
Electronic media	146,230	25.09	11,200	66.74
Other media	26,957	4.63	0	
Subtotal	**173,187**	**29.71**	**11,200**	**66.74**
Other Campaign Activity				
Persuasion mail/brochures	145,591	24.98	4,164	24.82
Actual campaigning	76,525	13.13	367	2.19
Staff/volunteers	1,289	.22	0	
Subtotal	**223,405**	**38.33**	**4,532**	**27.00**
Constituent Gifts/ Entertainment	**6,604**	**1.13**	**0**	
Donations to				
Candidates from same state	2,249	.39	0	
Candidates from other states	6,500	1.12	0	
Civic organizations	1,230	.21	0	
Ideological groups	500	.09	0	
Political parties	19,155	3.29	20	.12
Subtotal	**29,634**	**5.08**	**20**	**.12**
Unitemized Expenses	**12,537**	**2.15**	**0**	
Total Campaign Expenses	**$ 582,835**		**$ 16,781**	
PAC Contributions	**$ 247,703**		**$ 1,742**	
Individual Contributions	**112,262**		**15,002**	
Total Receipts*	**408,981**		**16,870**	

*Includes PAC and individual contributions as well as interest earned, party contributions, etc.

District 6 — MINNESOTA

Rep. Rod Grams (R)

1992 Election Results

Rod Grams (R)	133,564	(44%)
Gerry Sikorski (D)	100,016	(33%)
Dean Barkley (I)	48,329	(16%)

In 1990 Rep. Gerry Sikorski had spent $90,385 to produce and air a television commercial designed specifically to answer criticism over his vote in favor of the budget summit plan for spending and taxing. That controversy paled in comparison with the publicity generated by the revelation in 1992 of his 697 overdrafts at the House bank. When coupled with his 1989 vote in favor of a congressional pay raise and his switch from a strong anti-abortion stance to a pro-choice position, Sikorski's problems had become too much to overcome.

In the primary, Hennepin County Commissioner Tad Jude softened up the five-term incumbent with a $182,123 effort, attacking Sikorski for his overdrafts and his change of heart on abortion. Jude also benefited from a $53,295 independent campaign waged by Minnesota Citizens Concerned for Life. The centerpiece of the group's effort was a 200,000-piece mailing that hammered Sikorski for his overdrafts, not for his abortion stance.

With the revelation of his overdrafts, Sikorski began pouring money into his reelection effort. Between April 1 and the September 15 primary, Sikorski spent $596,793, including more than $200,000 on an advertising blitz created and placed by Fenn & King Communications of Washington, D.C. Among other things, his ads accused Jude of favoring jail terms for women who had abortions, a charge Jude heatedly denied. Sikorski emerged with 49 percent of the vote, a mere 3-point primary victory.

In the general election campaign, real estate developer and former television news anchor Rod Grams opted not to attack Sikorski for his overdrafts, leaving that job to the local media. The Grams campaign paid Brockmeyer/Allen & Associates of Baltimore, Md., $11,447 for designing and placing three television and two radio commercials. In addition to a basic biographical piece, the television spots focused on Grams's proposals for deficit reduction and congressional reform. Cottington & Marti of Edina, Minn., collected $114,531 from Grams and $41,327 from the National Republican Congressional Committee for placing the ads.

Having invested nearly $170,000 in the primary, Grams did not send out any persuasion mail prior to the general election. Instead, volunteers canvassed the district and distributed brochures.

As in the primary, Minnesota Citizens Concerned for Life weighed in with its own $45,157 campaign to defeat Sikorski, much of it spent on mailings.

Sikorski countered with another $321,814 media push, but to no avail. Independent candidates were an additional force in the race, accruing more than 22 percent of the votes.

Campaign Expenditures	Grams Amount Spent	Grams % of Total	Sikorski Amount Spent	Sikorski % of Total
Overhead				
Office furniture/supplies	$ 5,978	1.23	$ 6,363	.52
Rent/utilities	8,037	1.65	6,750	.54
Salaries	68,631	14.10	104,167	8.36
Taxes	16,187	3.33	37,205	2.98
Bank/investment fees	1,111	.23	0	
Lawyers/accountants	150	.03	52,858	4.34
Telephone	4,490	.92	3,003	.24
Campaign automobile	0		0	
Computers/office equipment	6,501	1.34	27,402	2.20
Travel	13,768	2.83	22,238	1.78
Food/meetings	1,253	.26	1,113	.09
Subtotal	126,107	25.91	261,099	20.94
Fund Raising				
Events	47,467	9.75	50,925	4.08
Direct mail	26,981	5.54	0	
Telemarketing	29,866	6.14	0	
Subtotal	104,314	21.43	50,925	4.08
Polling	20,817	4.28	73,802	5.92
Advertising				
Electronic media	127,258	26.14	554,401	44.47
Other media	1,188	.24	10,041	.81
Subtotal	128,447	26.39	564,442	45.27
Other Campaign Activity				
Persuasion mail/brochures	38,372	7.88	130,211	10.44
Actual campaigning	60,053	12.34	80,672	6.47
Staff/volunteers	2,085	.43	0	
Subtotal	100,511	20.65	210,883	16.91
Constituent Gifts/ Entertainment	4,364	.90	7,791	.62
Donations to				
Candidates from same state	133	.03	250	.02
Candidates from other states	0		5,000	.40
Civic organizations	0		0	
Ideological groups	0		500	.04
Political parties	0		5,000	.40
Subtotal	133	.03	10,750	.86
Unitemized Expenses	2,080	.43	37,044	2.97
Total Campaign Expenses	$ 486,771		$ 1,216,736	
PAC Contributions	$ 138,784		$ 607,683	
Individual Contributions	299,044		226,241	
Total Receipts*	464,693		905,875	

*Includes PAC and individual contributions as well as interest earned, party contributions, etc.

MINNESOTA — District 7

Rep. Collin C. Peterson (D)

1992 Election Results

Collin C. Peterson (D)	133,886	(50%)
Bernie Omann (R)	130,396	(49%)

Rep. Collin C. Peterson had waged four unsuccessful campaigns for the District 7 seat before finally defeating a scandal-tainted Rep. Arlan Stangeland in 1990. In 1992, despite being outspent by a margin of nearly two to one, Republican state representative Bernie Omann came within 3,490 votes of retiring Peterson after one term.

With 1990 campaign debts of $79,406 and cash reserves of only $9,233, Peterson made fund raising a top priority. During 1991, 55 percent of the $53,942 spent to maintain his permanent campaign was invested in raising money. Those efforts yielded contributions totaling $199,677, including political action committee donations of $154,985. By January 1992 Peterson had eliminated his debts and increased his cash-on-hand to $100,431.

Peterson's first electoral hurdle was the Minnesota Democratic-Farm-Labor (DFL) party's district nominating convention, where he faced a challenge from businesswoman Lorelei Kraft. As an abortion rights supporter and a state board member of Planned Parenthood, Kraft took umbrage at Peterson's vote to sustain President Bush's veto of legislation that would have lifted the ban on abortion counseling at federally funded health clinics. Only after three ballots and a vague statement promising that he had gotten "the message" did Peterson emerge with the endorsement of party regulars. Within two months, he again voted against lifting the counseling ban.

Kraft carried her challenge through to the September 15 Democratic primary. While she collected only 29 percent of the primary votes, Kraft forced Peterson to spend $165,229 during the three-month campaign, including $25,417 to air television commercials, $13,686 to air radio spots, $18,513 for a phonebank operation run by Meyer Associates of St. Cloud, $9,418 for an in-house phonebank, $16,266 for campaign literature and persuasion mail, $7,919 for newspaper ads, $3,308 for billboards, and $2,163 for yard signs.

Peterson was left with slightly more than $140,000 for the general election contest with Omann, who spent $132,257 to secure the Republican nomination.

Peterson opted to focus his limited budget on broadcast media, investing $45,943 and $25,829 to air his television and radio ads, respectively. Outlays for campaign literature were sliced to $4,188. He paid $8,850 to the DFL for coordinated get-out-the-vote efforts and spent $9,171 on phonebanking.

Omann spent his entire $34,919 broadcast advertising budget in the general election. He was able to match Peterson's broadcast budget down the stretch thanks to a $26,995 assist from the National Republican Congressional Committee and a $15,000 television buy by the state Republican party.

Campaign Expenditures	Peterson Amount Spent	Peterson % of Total	Omann Amount Spent	Omann % of Total
Overhead				
Office furniture/supplies	$ 5,406	1.26	$ 5,819	2.51
Rent/utilities	1,561	.36	4,355	1.88
Salaries	37,133	8.62	24,842	10.70
Taxes	8,704	2.02	6,227	2.68
Bank/investment fees	581	.13	539	.23
Lawyers/accountants	0		247	.11
Telephone	3,699	.86	2,851	1.23
Campaign automobile	0		0	
Computers/office equipment	19,034	4.42	1,840	.79
Travel	11,328	2.63	10,462	4.50
Food/meetings	524	.12	110	.05
Subtotal	**87,972**	**20.42**	**57,291**	**24.67**
Fund Raising				
Events	61,721	14.33	11,016	4.74
Direct mail	0		14,494	6.24
Telemarketing	119	.03	21,360	9.20
Subtotal	**61,840**	**14.36**	**46,870**	**20.18**
Polling	**0**		**11,056**	**4.76**
Advertising				
Electronic media	121,421	28.19	34,919	15.03
Other media	25,995	6.04	6,350	2.73
Subtotal	**147,415**	**34.22**	**41,269**	**17.77**
Other Campaign Activity				
Persuasion mail/brochures	20,454	4.75	28,387	12.22
Actual campaigning	66,290	15.39	43,945	18.92
Staff/volunteers	0		98	.04
Subtotal	**86,745**	**20.14**	**72,430**	**31.19**
Constituent Gifts/ Entertainment	**4,094**	**.95**	**38**	**.02**
Donations to				
Candidates from same state	1,070	.25	0	
Candidates from other states	0		0	
Civic organizations	237	.06	0	
Ideological groups	55	.01	0	
Political parties	21,184	4.92	0	
Subtotal	**22,547**	**5.23**	**0**	
Unitemized Expenses	**20,115**	**4.67**	**3,303**	**1.42**
Total Campaign Expenses	**$ 430,729**		**$ 232,257**	
PAC Contributions	$ 321,507		$ 35,300	
Individual Contributions	121,113		150,245	
Total Receipts*	488,844		218,216	

*Includes PAC and individual contributions as well as interest earned, party contributions, etc.

District 8 — MINNESOTA

Rep. James L. Oberstar (D)

1992 Election Results

James L. Oberstar (D)	167,104	(59%)
Phil Herwig (R)	83,823	(30%)
Harry Robb Welty † (I)	22,619	(8%)

Reflecting the general concern over anti-incumbent sentiment and redistricting, which gave him about 55,000 new constituents, Rep. James L. Oberstar spent $155,978 more on his 1992 campaign than he had in 1990, an increase of 68 percent. While he spent marginally more on overhead, polling, and grass-roots campaigning, about half of the increased spending was pumped into advertising.

Little advertising was needed in the Democratic primary, where Oberstar faced convicted murderer Leonard J. Richards, who was in prison for killing his attorney. However, in the general election against Republican Phil Herwig, Ross Perot supporter Harry Robb Welty, and term-limits advocate Floyd A. Henspeter, Oberstar decided not to take any chances.

Unlike 1990, when he used retooled television commercials from the archives of the Democratic Congressional Campaign Committee's Harriman Communications Center, Oberstar invested $25,990 to produce new spots. "We needed to intensify our message," explained communications director James A. Berard, who also served as the campaign's media consultant. "In a presidential election year, we did not want our ads to get lost."

Over the final month of the campaign, Oberstar invested $77,058 in broadcast ads and $11,030 in newspaper ads. To be most cost effective, the campaign limited its advertising on network television to those stations whose audience was entirely within district boundaries. Radio, cable television, and newspaper ads were concentrated in the newly acquired portions of the district between St. Cloud and Minneapolis/St. Paul.

In a highly unusual arrangement for a government employee, the campaign funneled its media buys through Berard's company, Jim Berard Media Services of Washington, D.C. His company also received $2,664 for coordinating press access to Oberstar during the Democratic National Convention.

As in 1990, Oberstar's day-to-day campaign operations were intertwined with those of the Minnesota Democratic-Farm-Labor (DFL) party. Oberstar did not maintain a campaign office during the first eighteen months of the election cycle, but he paid $14,800 to rent office space from the DFL between June 1992 and election day. He paid the DFL's United Democratic Fund (UDF) $16,000 to cover his share of coordinated mailings and phonebanking. Between December 1991 and November 1992, Oberstar paid the UDF $51,250 to help cover its general operating costs. Together, these payments accounted for 21 percent of Oberstar's total expenditures.

With $121,068 less to spend on advertising in a strongly Democratic district, Herwig managed to attract just 30 percent of the vote.

Campaign Expenditures	Oberstar Amount Spent	Oberstar % of Total	Herwig Amount Spent	Herwig % of Total
Overhead				
Office furniture/supplies	$ 4,551	1.18	$ 700	1.36
Rent/utilities	14,800	3.84	315	.61
Salaries	0		646	1.25
Taxes	8,588	2.23	0	
Bank/investment fees	24	.01	0	
Lawyers/accountants	8,995	2.33	0	
Telephone	694	.18	1,512	2.93
Campaign automobile	0		0	
Computers/office equipment	1,389	.36	530	1.03
Travel	24,842	6.45	7,806	15.10
Food/meetings	2,991	.78	131	.25
Subtotal	**66,873**	**17.36**	**11,640**	**22.52**
Fund Raising				
Events	18,466	4.79	776	1.50
Direct mail	0		3,795	7.34
Telemarketing	0		0	
Subtotal	**18,466**	**4.79**	**4,570**	**8.84**
Polling	**13,350**	**3.47**	**0**	
Advertising				
Electronic media	103,108	26.76	14,306	27.68
Other media	34,398	8.93	2,132	4.12
Subtotal	**137,506**	**35.69**	**16,438**	**31.80**
Other Campaign Activity				
Persuasion mail/brochures	19,342	5.02	7,750	14.99
Actual campaigning	40,385	10.48	7,044	13.63
Staff/volunteers	391	.10	0	
Subtotal	**60,118**	**15.60**	**14,794**	**28.62**
Constituent Gifts/ Entertainment	**1,567**	**.41**	**0**	
Donations to				
Candidates from same state	3,000	.78	0	
Candidates from other states	14,500	3.76	0	
Civic organizations	719	.19	0	
Ideological groups	0		0	
Political parties	68,322	17.73	0	
Subtotal	**86,541**	**22.46**	**0**	
Unitemized Expenses	**829**	**.22**	**4,248**	**8.22**
Total Campaign Expenses	**$ 385,250**		**$ 51,690**	
PAC Contributions	$ 202,005		$ 500	
Individual Contributions	72,787		33,095	
Total Receipts*	340,642		41,039	

*Includes PAC and individual contributions as well as interest earned, party contributions, etc.

†No expenditures or receipts on file. Candidates raising or spending less than $5,000 are not required to file reports with the Federal Election Commission.

MISSISSIPPI District 1

Rep. Jamie L. Whitten (D)

1992 Election Results

Jamie L. Whitten (D)   121,664   (59%)
Clyde E. Whitaker (R)   82,952   (41%)

For fifty years Rep. Jamie L. Whitten's biennial reelection had been the closest thing imaginable to a sure thing in politics. First elected in 1941, Whitten faced Republican opposition only three times between 1942 and 1976. Only one of the seven Republicans that Whitten faced between 1978 and 1990 spent as much as $100,000; two spent less than $5,000. The 1992 campaign was another story.

Sensing that Whitten's advanced age and failing health made him vulnerable, former Tupelo mayor Clyde E. Whitaker spent $229,285 on his challenge. The National Republican Congressional Committee apparently agreed with Whitaker's assessment and devoted $48,503 to the race, $45,000 of which went to the Swinehart Political Agency in Atlanta, Ga., for media buys. With this cash transfusion, Whitaker was able to spend more than twice as much as Whitten on broadcast advertising.

Threatened but not bowed, Whitten steadfastly refused Whitaker's challenges to debate, just as he had refused each of his previous opponents. He made few public appearances. Nevertheless, the 1992 reelection effort was Whitten's most aggressive campaign ever. While extremely modest by modern standards, the $267,227 he spent was nearly $100,000 more than he had invested in any previous campaign. "We felt the need to do more to show he was healthy and fit for office," explained press secretary Steven C. Burtt.

To counter Whitaker's efforts, Whitten leaned almost exclusively on his media adviser, Bill Miles Associates of Tupelo. In addition to creating and placing the campaign's radio and television commercials, the firm was responsible for developing and placing ads in virtually every newspaper in the district, creating tabloid-style newspaper inserts, placing billboard advertising, supplying yard signs and posters, and handling Whitten's persuasion mail effort. For all this, Miles received $184,674, or 69 percent of Whitten's total outlays.

Given Whitten's seniority in the House, his proven track record for delivering federal public works projects to the state and district, and the fact that he had no overdrafts at the House bank or any other major flaws associated with incumbency to defend, his advertising strategy was simple. As Miles put, the campaign's only message was "Stand up for Jamie Whitten. He stands up for Mississippi."

Whitten paid for the campaign without holding a single fund-raiser. His historically easy path to reelection had allowed him to gradually build cash reserves of $435,724, which supplied $184,554 of the capital he needed for the 1992 campaign. Interest earned on his cash reserves amounted to $37,037.

Campaign Expenditures	Whitten Amount Spent	% of Total	Whitaker Amount Spent	% of Total
Overhead				
Office furniture/supplies	$ 1,428	.53	$ 1,589	.69
Rent/utilities	1,000	.37	0	
Salaries	19,923	7.46	12,703	5.54
Taxes	21,354	7.99	0	
Bank/investment fees	0		0	
Lawyers/accountants	3,000	1.12	650	.28
Telephone	958	.36	3,544	1.55
Campaign automobile	0		0	
Computers/office equipment	1,044	.39	0	
Travel	1,848	.69	777	.34
Food/meetings	628	.24	0	
Subtotal	**51,183**	**19.15**	**19,263**	**8.40**
Fund Raising				
Events	0		5,574	2.43
Direct mail	0		2,285	1.00
Telemarketing	0		0	
Subtotal	**0**		**7,859**	**3.43**
Polling	**0**		**3,800**	**1.66**
Advertising				
Electronic media	67,014	25.08	108,266	47.22
Other media	58,736	21.98	32,176	14.03
Subtotal	**125,750**	**47.06**	**140,442**	**61.25**
Other Campaign Activity				
Persuasion mail/brochures	56,906	21.29	4,593	2.00
Actual campaigning	16,768	6.27	39,005	17.01
Staff/volunteers	0		0	
Subtotal	**73,674**	**27.57**	**43,598**	**19.01**
Constituent Gifts/ Entertainment	**0**		**0**	
Donations to				
Candidates from same state	0		0	
Candidates from other states	0		0	
Civic organizations	1,320	.49	0	
Ideological groups	0		0	
Political parties	15,300	5.73	0	
Subtotal	**16,620**	**6.22**	**0**	
Unitemized Expenses	**0**		**14,324**	**6.25**
Total Campaign Expenses	**$ 267,227**		**$ 229,285**	
PAC Contributions	**$ 30,700**		**$ 6,400**	
Individual Contributions	**5,937**		**137,122**	
Total Receipts*	**82,667**		**229,172**	

*Includes PAC and individual contributions as well as interest earned, party contributions, etc.

District 2 — MISSISSIPPI

Rep. Mike Espy (D)

1992 Election Results

Mike Espy (D)	133,361	(76%)
Dorothy Benford † (R)	41,248	(24%)

In December 1992, one month before resigning to become secretary of agriculture in the Clinton administration, Rep. Mike Espy spent $16,325 of his campaign treasury to help celebrate the inauguration of his future boss. A $15,000 check was written to the Presidential Inaugural Committee to cover the deposit on a table at the inaugural dinner. To make certain that he looked sharp for the evening, Espy spent $1,325 of his campaign funds to buy a new tuxedo.

Espy's Republican opponent in 1992 was Dorothy Benford, a teacher making her second consecutive bid to unseat the popular three-term incumbent. As in 1990, Benford spent less than $5,000 on her token challenge and was never a factor in the race. Unconcerned about his 191 overdrafts at the House bank, Espy spent $59,280 less during the 1992 election cycle than he had in 1990.

Perhaps the best measure of Espy's lack of concern over the outcome of the race was the fact that he spent just $9,787 more in 1992 than he invested in his permanent campaign during 1991. His off-year overhead expenses of $49,656 actually exceeded his election year outlays for overhead by $28,319. The $18,728 he spent on fund raising in 1992 was $16,813 less than he spent to raise money during the off-year. Only $13,280 of the $32,487 he invested in "actual campaigning" was spent in 1992, and that included the cost of his tuxedo.

Payments to his brother Tom and to Reliance Consultants, a Jackson-based firm run by Tom Espy, amounted to $66,369, or 26 percent of Espy's total spending. Neither of the Espy brothers returned calls to clarify precisely what services Tom Espy performed for the campaign. In an attempt to give them the maximum benefit of the doubt, a lump-sum $43,459 payment made to Reliance on Oct. 22, 1992 has been coded as a media buy, since there were documented payments for media production made to other companies and no other indications of media placement.

As in past campaigns, Espy collected most of his money from political action committees (PACs). As a member of the Agriculture Committee, Espy was able to tap PACs representing agriculture interests for $55,975. Labor PACs kicked in $87,150. The $235,960 Espy pulled in from PACs accounted for 79 percent of his total receipts. Espy received ninety-two contributions totaling $42,383 from individuals who gave at least $200, but only thirty-three of those contributions, amounting to $15,883, came from Mississippi residents.

Campaign Expenditures	Amount Spent	% of Total
Overhead		
Office furniture/supplies	$ 4,898	1.91
Rent/utilities	1,936	.76
Salaries	4,786	1.87
Taxes	0	
Bank/investment fees	2,263	.88
Lawyers/accountants	7,729	3.02
Telephone	6,206	2.42
Campaign automobile	0	
Computers/office equipment	3,289	1.28
Travel	37,310	14.56
Food/meetings	2,575	1.00
Subtotal	**70,993**	**27.70**
Fund Raising		
Events	54,269	21.17
Direct mail	0	
Telemarketing	0	
Subtotal	**54,269**	**21.17**
Polling	**0**	
Advertising		
Electronic media	45,933	17.92
Other media	2,818	1.10
Subtotal	**48,751**	**19.02**
Other Campaign Activity		
Persuasion mail/brochures	0	
Actual campaigning	32,487	12.67
Staff/volunteers	0	
Subtotal	**32,487**	**12.67**
Constituent Gifts/Entertainment	**19,981**	**7.80**
Donations to		
Candidates from same state	100	.04
Candidates from other states	8,250	3.22
Civic organizations	1,700	.66
Ideological groups	1,600	.62
Political parties	12,650	4.94
Subtotal	**24,300**	**9.48**
Unitemized Expenses	**5,528**	**2.16**
Total Campaign Expenses	$ **256,309**	
PAC Contributions	$ **235,960**	
Individual Contributions	**63,550**	
Total Receipts*	**299,560**	

*Includes PAC and individual contributions as well as interest earned, party contributions, etc.

† No expenditures or receipts on file. Candidates raising or spending less than $5,000 are not required to file reports with the Federal Election Commission.

MISSISSIPPI District 3

Rep. G. V. "Sonny" Montgomery (D)

1992 Election Results
G. V. "Sonny" Montgomery (D)   162,864   (81%)
Michael E. Williams † (R)   37,710   (19%)

Rep. G. V. "Sonny" Montgomery had no need for a high-powered, permanent campaign organization. Republicans had failed to mount a challenge in six of his previous twelve reelection bids. He had received less than 90 percent of the vote only three times in his twenty-six-year House career.

As a result, Montgomery spent only $38,584 on his off-year campaign activities. Excluding the $2,200 he paid his accountant and the $1,368 in taxes he paid on the interest income generated by his campaign cash reserves, Montgomery's 1991 overhead amounted to just $1,307—$588 for supplies, $548 for travel, and $171 for meals unrelated to fund raising or constituent entertainment. He spent nothing on fund raising.

During 1991 Montgomery invested $9,007 in constituent gifts and entertainment, including $1,575 to print and distribute *The Sonny Montgomery Cookbook* and $1,804 for cheese that he gave as Christmas gifts. In September he paid $958 to sponsor a tennis tournament, including $525 for commemorative T-shirts and $300 for food from Chick-Fil-A. Year-end holiday cards cost $2,538.

Montgomery donated $16,950 to Democratic party organizations, other candidates, and charities in 1991. He gave $6,500 to the Democratic Congressional Campaign Committee (DCCC), $4,900 to the Mississippi Democratic party, and $500 to the Young Democrats of Mississippi. Tickets to a DCCC fund-raising dinner cost the campaign $1,500. Democratic Reps. Dick Swett (N.H.), William Lehman (Fla.), and Bill Alexander (Ark.) received contributions of $250, $200, and $100, respectively. Montgomery gave $450 to the Boy Scouts Choctaw Council, $100 to the War Memorial Fund in Yazoo City, and $100 to the Close-Up Foundation, among others.

In most respects, Montgomery's election-year spending mirrored his 1991 spending. He never opened an office or hired any employees and he spent virtually nothing on fund raising. He again sponsored the tennis tournament, purchased cheese for Christmas gifts, and mailed year-end holiday cards, investing $7,009 in constituent gifts and entertainment. He gave away $19,930, including $5,000 to the DCCC.

Montgomery also put $78,864 into advertising, excluding program ads. He committed $14,521 of that to his primary contest with farmer Henry P. Clayton. Advertising outlays for the general election campaign against paralegal Michael E. Williams totaled $64,343. With the exception of $11,443 designated as radio ads, none of the $76,581 paid to his media consultant, the Gianakos & Chalk Agency of Meridian, was itemized. When both Montgomery and the ad agency refused to cooperate in this study, the unitemized portion was assigned to "other media."

Campaign Expenditures	Montgomery Amount Spent	% of Total
Overhead		
Office furniture/supplies	$ 929	.53
Rent/utilities	0	
Salaries	0	
Taxes	2,481	1.42
Bank/investment fees	0	
Lawyers/accountants	3,400	1.95
Telephone	0	
Campaign automobile	0	
Computers/office equipment	0	
Travel	2,965	1.70
Food/meetings	171	.10
Subtotal	9,947	5.71
Fund Raising		
Events	2,008	1.15
Direct mail	5,487	3.15
Telemarketing	0	
Subtotal	7,495	4.30
Polling	4,700	2.70
Advertising		
Electronic media	11,443	6.57
Other media	70,452	40.45
Subtotal	81,894	47.02
Other Campaign Activity		
Persuasion mail/brochures	3,365	1.93
Actual campaigning	9,386	5.39
Staff/volunteers	0	
Subtotal	12,752	7.32
Constituent Gifts/Entertainment	16,016	9.20
Donations to		
Candidates from same state	1,050	.60
Candidates from other states	5,700	3.27
Civic organizations	5,080	2.92
Ideological groups	0	
Political parties	25,050	14.38
Subtotal	36,880	21.17
Unitemized Expenses	4,485	2.57
Total Campaign Expenses	$ 174,168	
PAC Contributions	$ 97,600	
Individual Contributions	60,763	
Total Receipts*	172,603	

*Includes PAC and individual contributions as well as interest earned, party contributions, etc.

† No expenditures or receipts on file. Candidates raising or spending less than $5,000 are not required to file reports with the Federal Election Commission.

District 4 — MISSISSIPPI

Rep. Mike Parker (D)

1992 Election Results

Mike Parker (D)	130,927	(67%)
Jack L. McMillan † (R)	43,705	(23%)
Liz Gilchrist † (I)	10,523	(5%)

Faced with only a token challenge from Republican Jack L. McMillan, Rep. Mike Parker was able to bank more than 60 percent of the money he raised. While he began the election cycle with only $48,162 in his campaign treasury, his cash reserves had risen to $307,873 by the end of 1992.

Like many politicians, Parker depended on his professional contacts to help fund his campaign. His most lucrative event was a gathering of 300 fellow funeral home directors, held in conjunction with their 1992 convention in Houston, Texas. The event was largely responsible for his $50,750 in out-of-state contributions and cost the campaign $12,696, including $5,750 for food and beverages, $2,844 for gifts given to volunteers who worked on the reception, $1,822 for air fare for Parker and his wife, and $850 for the band.

While Parker raised a substantial proportion of his funds through direct-mail solicitations, the target audience was not exclusively small donors. Twice each year, the campaign mailed solicitations to approximately 3,000 political action committees (PACs). These efforts helped push Parker's PAC contributions to $240,200 despite the fact that he hosted just one Washington, D.C., PAC reception.

Parker held only three receptions in his district, including a $25-a-head event featuring Rep. Ben Jones (D-Ga.). Two in-home, in-kind receptions rounded out his Mississippi fund-raisers. Twice each year, fund-raising letters were mailed to between 4,000 and 5,000 individual donors who had contributed to Parker's past campaigns. At most, $79,772 was raised in Mississippi.

Parker's actual reelection effort did not begin until October. He ran the campaign out of his funeral home. A part-time funeral home employee did double duty as his only paid campaign staffer. His grass-roots campaign activity consisted of a $2,835 payment for bumper stickers, $2,500 for the state party's coordinated get-out-the-vote effort, and a $1,000 in-house effort to increase turnout.

Over the final four weeks of the campaign, Parker paid Maggie Clark Media Services of Jackson $31,341 to place three radio commercials and companion newspaper ads. Administrative assistant Arthur D. Rhodes said the message was, "Mike Parker was born and raised here, he has served two terms in Congress, and he wants to go back."

Parker sent year-end greetings in the form of a one-page letter rather than the traditional card. He also spent $1,132 for thirty-five crystal candy jars engraved with the Capitol seal, which he gave to volunteers.

Campaign Expenditures	Parker Amount Spent	% of Total
Overhead		
Office furniture/supplies	$ 1,844	1.48
Rent/utilities	0	
Salaries	15,850	12.68
Taxes	1,436	1.15
Bank/investment fees	243	.19
Lawyers/accountants	0	
Telephone	306	.25
Campaign automobile	0	
Computers/office equipment	3,932	3.15
Travel	3,726	2.98
Food/meetings	970	.78
Subtotal	28,308	22.65
Fund Raising		
Events	25,668	20.54
Direct mail	4,365	3.49
Telemarketing	0	
Subtotal	30,033	24.03
Polling	0	
Advertising		
Electronic media	19,922	15.94
Other media	17,730	14.19
Subtotal	37,652	30.13
Other Campaign Activity		
Persuasion mail/brochures	0	
Actual campaigning	6,900	5.52
Staff/volunteers	2,072	1.66
Subtotal	8,972	7.18
Constituent Gifts/Entertainment	3,383	2.71
Donations to		
Candidates from same state	250	.20
Candidates from other states	9,250	7.40
Civic organizations	425	.34
Ideological groups	0	
Political parties	6,700	5.36
Subtotal	16,625	13.30
Unitemized Expenses	0	
Total Campaign Expenses	$ 124,973	
PAC Contributions	$ 240,200	
Individual Contributions	130,522	
Total Receipts*	416,677	

* Includes PAC and individual contributions as well as interest earned, party contributions, etc.

† No expenditures or receipts on file. Candidates raising or spending less than $5,000 are not required to file reports with the Federal Election Commission.

MISSISSIPPI — District 5

Rep. Gene Taylor (D)

1992 Election Results

Gene Taylor (D)	120,766	(63%)
Paul Harvey (R)	67,619	(35%)

When Rep. Gene Taylor voted against the 1991 measure authorizing the use of force against Iraq, District 5 Republicans thought they had found their campaign issue for 1992. In a district dominated by the defense industry, retired air force general Paul Harvey, retired naval officer Will Bramlett, Gulf War veteran Chris Roosa, and real estate broker Billy Hewes lined up for the chance to use Taylor's vote against him.

The four-candidate Republican primary field virtually guaranteed a runoff, since state election law requires nominees to win a majority of their party's votes. By the time Harvey had dispatched Hewes in the March 31 runoff, he had spent $86,475, including $20,960 of his modest advertising budget.

By November, the public cared more about economics than the Gulf War, and with less than $30,000 to spend on advertising, Harvey's general election campaign never took off. Taylor's conservative voting record gave Harvey little else to criticize.

Over the two-year election cycle, Taylor invested nearly half his campaign treasury in overhead. He maintained a permanent campaign headquarters in Bay St. Louis and opened offices in Gulfport and Pascgoula for the final three months of the campaign. During the off-year, he had one part-time employee, but by election day his paid staff had grown to six.

Taylor's television and radio advertising virtually ignored Harvey, focusing instead on the need for deficit reduction and the fact that Taylor donated his pay raise to a scholarship fund at a local community college. As a hedge against negative reaction to his Gulf War vote, several of the ads stressed his efforts to maintain a strong national defense. "We did get Gene on TV looking at a ship saying, 'I did that,'" noted his campaign manager and father-in-law, Carroll Gordon.

Fosterfilm Inc. of Gulfport received $24,074 for creating the spots. The campaign spent $30,607 to air the ads on television network affiliates and $2,091 for air time on local cable systems. Radio air time cost $2,843.

Although Taylor relied primarily on broadcast advertising to deliver his message, he spent $2,796 on billboards and $3,598 for ads in newspapers such as the *Biloxi Sun Herald,* the *Sea Coast Echo,* and the *Hattiesburg Advertiser News.* He invested $7,009 in yard signs and $4,497 in buttons and bumper stickers.

Initially concerned that the race might be closer, Taylor hired pollster Hickman-Brown Research of Washington, D.C., and paid $2,000 for advice. The race was ultimately so lopsided that no polls were needed.

	Taylor		Harvey	
Campaign Expenditures	Amount Spent	% of Total	Amount Spent	% of Total
Overhead				
Office furniture/supplies	$ 5,298	1.84	$ 4,095	1.83
Rent/utilities	8,092	2.81	6,409	2.87
Salaries	38,300	13.31	48,072	21.50
Taxes	20,263	7.04	10,156	4.54
Bank/investment fees	1,855	.64	1,740	.78
Lawyers/accountants	10,426	3.62	0	
Telephone	3,044	1.06	14,163	6.33
Campaign automobile	0		0	
Computers/office equipment	41,462	14.41	5,579	2.50
Travel	6,311	2.19	7,709	3.45
Food/meetings	657	.23	512	.23
Subtotal	**135,708**	**47.17**	**98,434**	**44.02**
Fund Raising				
Events	39,385	13.69	13,515	6.04
Direct mail	0		19,107	8.55
Telemarketing	0		0	
Subtotal	**39,385**	**13.69**	**32,621**	**14.59**
Polling	**2,000**	**.70**	**8,000**	**3.58**
Advertising				
Electronic media	59,615	20.72	38,727	17.32
Other media	6,895	2.40	11,611	5.19
Subtotal	**66,510**	**23.12**	**50,338**	**22.51**
Other Campaign Activity				
Persuasion mail/brochures	271	.09	6,440	2.88
Actual campaigning	23,623	8.21	12,033	5.38
Staff/volunteers	84	.03	0	
Subtotal	**23,978**	**8.33**	**18,473**	**8.26**
Constituent Gifts/ Entertainment	**5,708**	**1.98**	**0**	
Donations to				
Candidates from same state	0		0	
Candidates from other states	0		0	
Civic organizations	200	.07	0	
Ideological groups	0		0	
Political parties	0		0	
Subtotal	**200**	**.07**	**0**	
Unitemized Expenses	**14,378**	**5.00**	**15,722**	**7.03**
Total Campaign Expenses	**$ 287,867**		**$ 223,588**	
PAC Contributions	$ 158,535		$ 20,310	
Individual Contributions	166,041		148,686	
Total Receipts*	340,357		237,123	

*Includes PAC and individual contributions as well as interest earned, party contributions, etc.

District 1 — MISSOURI

Rep. William L. Clay (D)

1992 Election Results

William L. Clay (D)	158,693 (68%)
Arthur S. Montgomery (R)	74,482 (32%)

Rep. William L. Clay maintains two campaign committees—one that is used for actual campaigning and one that is used to pay for things that have little or nothing to do with seeking the office he holds. The latter committee is named the "D.C. Friends of Bill Clay."

Funds from the second committee were used to pay the $799 monthly lease and repair bills on a car he drove in Washington, D.C. That committee picked up the tab for season tickets to Washington Redskins games in 1991. When he traveled to New Jersey for meetings with the board of Benedict College and with the United Negro College Fund, the hotel bills were paid by the D.C. Friends of Bill Clay. The committee paid for Clay's $310 dues at the Robin Hood Swim Club in Silver Spring, Md. It paid for virtually all his constituent gifts and entertainment, including a $425 meal at the Lobster House Restaurant in Fayetteville, N.C.; his expenses at the annual Congressional Black Caucus weekend retreats; expenses incurred on trips to Jamaica, N.Y., for meetings of the Clay Scholarship Board; and a reception for former Rep. William H. Gray III. About the only campaign-related expenses contained in the financial reports filed by this committee were related to the political action committee fund-raisers he held in Washington. In all, the D.C. Friends of Bill Clay committee reported spending $113,151 over the two-year election cycle.

Clay's investment in direct appeals for votes was $48,119 higher in 1992 than in the 1990 campaign. Courtesy of an agreement worked out prior to the 1990 election with Reps. Richard A. Gephardt and Jack Buechner, Clay knew who his new constituents would be even before redistricting had begun. Despite the fact that Buechner, a Republican, lost his 1990 race by 54 votes to Democrat Joan Kelly Horn, Clay and Gephardt refused to cede back to Horn any of the Democratic voters Buechner had agreed to give away. By January 1991, Clay was busy courting his soon-to-be constituents.

During the first week of January, canvassers began criss-crossing the district's new neighborhoods, telling voters that they would be represented by Clay. In February Clay aired his only radio commercial of the election cycle. "We do the same thing for each election after redistricting," noted district assistant Pearlie I. Evans. "You'll see the same thing in our reports in 2001."

With only $19,859 to spend, Republican Arthur S. Montgomery was unable to mount an advertising campaign to make an issue of Clay's 328 House bank overdrafts.

	Clay		Montgomery	
Campaign Expenditures	Amount Spent	% of Total	Amount Spent	% of Total
Overhead				
Office furniture/supplies	$ 5,265	1.76	$ 0	
Rent/utilities	1,747	.58	0	
Salaries	4,750	1.59	2,325	11.71
Taxes	3,485	1.16	0	
Bank/investment fees	902	.30	0	
Lawyers/accountants	1,750	.58	0	
Telephone	837	.28	235	1.18
Campaign automobile	19,176	6.41	0	
Computers/office equipment	172	.06	0	
Travel	31,014	10.36	0	
Food/meetings	12,012	4.01	0	
Subtotal	**81,110**	**27.09**	**2,560**	**12.89**
Fund Raising				
Events	29,594	9.89	0	
Direct mail	0		0	
Telemarketing	0		0	
Subtotal	**29,594**	**9.89**	**0**	
Polling	0		0	
Advertising				
Electronic media	242	.08	0	
Other media	6,254	2.09	0	
Subtotal	**6,496**	**2.17**	**0**	
Other Campaign Activity				
Persuasion mail/brochures	24,018	8.02	8,809	44.36
Actual campaigning	46,386	15.50	3,729	18.78
Staff/volunteers	0		0	
Subtotal	**70,404**	**23.52**	**12,538**	**63.14**
Constituent Gifts/Entertainment	14,100	4.71	0	
Donations to				
Candidates from same state	25,885	8.65	0	
Candidates from other states	7,800	2.61	0	
Civic organizations	7,605	2.54	0	
Ideological groups	4,405	1.47	0	
Political parties	26,070	8.71	0	
Subtotal	**71,765**	**23.97**	**0**	
Unitemized Expenses	**25,888**	**8.65**	**4,761**	**23.97**
Total Campaign Expenses	**$ 299,357**		**$ 19,859**	
PAC Contributions	$ 251,680		$ 550	
Individual Contributions	40,681		15,900	
Total Receipts*	300,187		20,587	

*Includes PAC and individual contributions as well as interest earned, party contributions, etc.

MISSOURI — District 2

Rep. James M. Talent (R)

1992 Election Results

James M. Talent (R)	157,594	(50%)
Joan Kelly Horn (D)	148,729	(48%)

Eight weeks before the November 3 general election, state representative James M. Talent's own polls showed him trailing freshman Rep. Joan Kelly Horn by more than 20 percentage points. However, Horn's razor-thin, fifty-four-vote victory over Rep. Jack Buechner in 1990, coupled with the fact that redistricting had made the district somewhat more Republican, gave Talent hope.

Talent had beaten long odds in the primary, pulling down 58 percent of the vote in a four-candidate field that included George Herbert Walker III, a cousin of President George Bush. Although Walker outspent Talent by more than $220,000, Walker's $550,000 campaign brought him only 32 percent of the vote. Talent's strong grass-roots organization pulled him through.

Over the final three weeks of the primary campaign, Talent's door-to-door canvassers blanketed the district. Potential supporters received follow-up mailings cranked out by volunteers. The campaign put nearly $15,000 into buttons, bumper stickers, and yard signs. "There were so many signs it really helped us win," argued media adviser and persuasion mail consultant Steven K. Boriss of St. Louis. Only 25 percent of the campaign's $455,285 broadcast advertising budget was invested in the primary.

To close the early 20-point gap with Horn in the fall campaign, Talent put $342,382 into broadcast advertising. One commercial pointed out that Horn had signed on as a cosponsor to the balanced budget amendment only to vote against it. Another ad highlighted Horn's opposition to the Gulf War and congressional term limits.

Horn had proven in 1990 that she was quite willing to run a negative campaign. Her toughest ad had opened with a shot of Buechner saying that congressional service amounted to "a public trust, not a public trough." It then recounted the personal benefits Buchner had enjoyed during his congressional tenure, as a picture of hogs wallowing in the mud played in the background.

When one of Horn's 1992 spots attacked Talent's legislative attendance record, Talent responded with an ad attacking Horn for her negative campaign style. Borrowing footage from Horn's 1990 "hog" spot, Talent reminded viewers of Horn's past tactics and promised to "focus on the real issues and fight for the middle class."

With only marginal Democratic primary opposition, Horn was able to focus most of her resources on Talent. In addition to taking swipes at Talent for his missed votes, she ran ads juxtaposing her pro-choice views with Talent's opposition to abortion except in cases of rape, incest, or when the mother's life was endangered.

	Talent		Horn	
Campaign Expenditures	Amount Spent	% of Total	Amount Spent	% of Total
Overhead				
Office furniture/supplies	$ 9,439	1.04	$ 7,241	.89
Rent/utilities	9,307	1.03	16,390	2.01
Salaries	57,643	6.36	56,882	6.98
Taxes	19,492	2.15	7,036	.86
Bank/investment fees	208	.02	0	
Lawyers/accountants	0		700	.09
Telephone	7,061	.78	9,496	1.16
Campaign automobile	0		0	
Computers/office equipment	8,607	.95	9,833	1.21
Travel	3,269	.36	4,846	.59
Food/meetings	817	.09	501	.06
Subtotal	**115,842**	**12.79**	**112,924**	**13.85**
Fund Raising				
Events	45,460	5.02	68,104	8.35
Direct mail	39,443	4.35	22,651	2.78
Telemarketing	0		0	
Subtotal	**84,904**	**9.37**	**90,755**	**11.13**
Polling	**35,227**	**3.89**	**20,817**	**2.55**
Advertising				
Electronic media	455,285	50.25	371,898	45.62
Other media	6,922	.76	7,523	.92
Subtotal	**462,208**	**51.02**	**379,421**	**46.55**
Other Campaign Activity				
Persuasion mail/brochures	134,975	14.90	176,405	21.64
Actual campaigning	49,628	5.48	28,130	3.45
Staff/volunteers	0		84	.01
Subtotal	**184,603**	**20.38**	**204,619**	**25.10**
Constituent Gifts/ Entertainment	**0**		**898**	**.11**
Donations to				
Candidates from same state	0		0	
Candidates from other states	0		0	
Civic organizations	0		0	
Ideological groups	0		2,200	.27
Political parties	0		450	.06
Subtotal	**0**		**2,650**	**.33**
Unitemized Expenses	**23,237**	**2.56**	**3,063**	**.38**
Total Campaign Expenses	**$ 906,021**		**$ 815,147**	
PAC Contributions	$ 213,472		$ 372,427	
Individual Contributions	639,058		420,818	
Total Receipts*	920,895		827,576	

*Includes PAC and individual contributions as well as interest earned, party contributions, etc.

District 3 — MISSOURI

Rep. Richard A. Gephardt (D)

1992 Election Results

Richard A. Gephardt (D)   174,000   (64%)
Malcolm L. Holekamp (R)   90,006   (33%)

Riding a wave of anti-incumbent sentiment, Republican Malcolm L. Holekamp received 43 percent of the vote against Majority Leader Richard A. Gephardt in 1990, despite the fact that Gephardt spent $522,735 more than Holekamp on direct appeals for votes. However, redistricting had strengthened Gephardt's position, and when Holekamp made a second, significantly better funded try in 1992, Gephardt buried him under a $1,283,711 avalanche of advertising and persuasion mail.

Gephardt paid Doak, Shrum & Associates of Washington, D.C., $97,632 for creating six television commercials and two radio spots that pointed to various federal projects he had brought the district and his leadership on health care reform. As campaign manager Joyce Aboussie put it, the ad campaign sought to show that "while he's a national figure and majority leader, he's also a local congressman." The Media Company of Washington, D.C., was paid $703,217 for air time and placement fees.

Gold Communications Co. of Austin, Texas, received $140,099 for designing and coordinating Gephardt's persuasion mail campaign, which was tightly targeted by geography and age. Gold got the job after Gephardt dropped the November Group, which collected $16,946 for its early efforts.

While Gephardt's ads and brochures underscored his role as the district's representative, his fund-raising operation belied that image. Throughout the election cycle he maintained a Washington, D.C., fund-raising office with a staff of eight, including Richard Sullivan, a fund-raiser for the Democratic Senatorial Campaign Committee (DSCC) and Donald J. Foley, political director at the DSCC. Among the stops on his fund-raising itinerary were Minneapolis, New York, Atlanta, Los Angeles, Chicago, San Francisco, Las Vegas, New Orleans, and Houston. On his travels, Gephardt collected $1,240,597 from political action committees (PACs). Philip Morris, Southern California Edison, the American Trucking Political Action Committee, the American Council of Life Insurance, and Circus Circus Enterprises were among the organizations that hosted events. He took in $1,237,598 from out-of-state donors who gave at least $200. Even assuming that all the receipts from his national direct-mail efforts came from Missouri residents, at most he raised $624,766 in-state.

Gephardt's travel bills included $38,877 in reimbursements to corporations for the use of private jets. Archer, Daniels, Midland of Decatur, Ill.; Benjamin Franklin Properties of North Miami Beach, Fla.; Healthsouth Corporation of Birmingham, Ala.; Perot Company of Dallas, Texas; and Katz Investments of Houston, Texas, were among the firms that put their jets at Gephardt's disposal.

Campaign Expenditures	Gephardt Amount Spent	Gephardt % of Total	Holekamp Amount Spent	Holekamp % of Total
Overhead				
Office furniture/supplies	$ 60,482	1.97	$ 9,691	2.72
Rent/utilities	79,677	2.60	17,982	5.05
Salaries	413,335	13.48	49,049	13.79
Taxes	133,482	4.35	10,543	2.96
Bank/investment fees	1,670	.05	1,078	.30
Lawyers/accountants	98,335	3.21	0	
Telephone	61,460	2.00	7,236	2.03
Campaign automobile	0		0	
Computers/office equipment	48,212	1.57	6,474	1.82
Travel	191,711	6.25	4,327	1.22
Food/meetings	7,539	.25	1,789	.50
Subtotal	1,095,904	35.75	108,170	30.40
Fund Raising				
Events	380,933	12.43	3,418	.96
Direct mail	52,567	1.71	22,209	6.24
Telemarketing	0		0	
Subtotal	433,500	14.14	25,627	7.20
Polling	207,745	6.78	0	
Advertising				
Electronic media	818,691	26.71	163,093	45.84
Other media	7,848	.26	5,915	1.66
Subtotal	826,539	26.96	169,008	47.50
Other Campaign Activity				
Persuasion mail/brochures	323,479	10.55	27,333	7.68
Actual campaigning	131,136	4.28	15,021	4.22
Staff/volunteers	2,558	.08	630	.18
Subtotal	457,172	14.91	42,985	12.08
Constituent Gifts/Entertainment	1,845	.06	0	
Donations to				
Candidates from same state	2,731	.09	0	
Candidates from other states	0		0	
Civic organizations	100		0	
Ideological groups	200	.01	0	
Political parties	9,445	.31	302	.09
Subtotal	12,476	.41	302	.09
Unitemized Expenses	30,258	.99	9,695	2.73
Total Campaign Expenses	$ 3,065,439		$ 355,787	
PAC Contributions	$ 1,240,597		$ 18,529	
Individual Contributions	1,862,364		246,105	
Total Receipts*	3,237,531		426,168	

*Includes PAC and individual contributions as well as interest earned, party contributions, etc.

MISSOURI — District 4

Rep. Ike Skelton (D)

1992 Election Results

Ike Skelton (D)	176,977	(70%)
John Carley (R)	74,475	(30%)

Rep. Ike Skelton had no need to alter his campaign style in 1992. In the wake of four successive lopsided victories, Skelton drew only scant opposition from Republican John Carley, a semiretired handyman who had never run for public office.

Faced with this token challenge, Skelton invested only about one-third of his $426,872 budget in direct appeals for votes. His off-year permanent campaign cost $106,519, including $23,882 for overhead and $28,091 for fund raising.

As he had in 1990, Skelton spent much of the 1992 election cycle stroking his constituents. Skelton tapped his campaign treasury for $24,600 to pay for constituent meals, including $3,683 for meals at the House dining room and $2,228 for seven dinners at Maison Blanche near the White House. He spent at least $5,371 on dinners with constituents at restaurants near his home in McLean, Va., including a $1,414 Turkish feast at the Kazan Restaurant.

The campaign paid $11,939 for various constituent gifts, including $1,272 for congressional club cookbooks, $350 for Christmas ornaments from the White House Historical Society, and $327 for edibles from Burger's Smokehouse in California, Mo. He spent $4,221 on holiday greeting cards and $6,229 on various parties.

To communicate his accomplishments to new constituents, Skelton spent $41,120 more on advertising in 1992 than he had in 1990, an increase of 60 percent. Still, his $109,975 advertising budget represented just 26 percent of his total expenditures.

Skelton invested more than two-thirds of his advertising budget and virtually all of his grass-roots campaign budget in the Democratic primary, where he was challenged by Ron Beller, a former local police chief, and Lewis E. Seay, a retired army officer. Skelton spent $48,592 to air commercials on thirty-one radio stations throughout the district. New Sounds Inc. of New York collected $15,243 for creating the spots. Preprimary newspaper ads cost $10,603. He spent $4,339 on yard signs and $2,342 on campaign tote bags. Neither Beller nor Seay spent as much as $5,000 on their campaigns, and Skelton easily prevailed with 79 percent of the vote.

Skelton took things much easier against Carley, who reported spending $4,629 but did not itemize his expenditures. The Skelton campaign spent $20,981 to air his radio spots and paid New Sounds another $5,644. Newspaper ads for the general election cost $8,612, but there were no additional expenditures for signs or campaign paraphernalia.

Rowan & Michaels of New York was paid $31,100 for polls and $21,846 for general strategic advice, despite the lack of competition.

Campaign Expenditures	Skelton Amount Spent	% of Total
Overhead		
Office furniture/supplies	$ 2,857	.67
Rent/utilities	5,722	1.34
Salaries	44,624	10.45
Taxes	14,677	3.44
Bank/investment fees	0	
Lawyers/accountants	0	
Telephone	2,977	.70
Campaign automobile	0	
Computers/office equipment	3,420	.80
Travel	22,550	5.28
Food/meetings	963	.23
Subtotal	97,790	22.91
Fund Raising		
Events	62,684	14.68
Direct mail	0	
Telemarketing	0	
Subtotal	62,684	14.68
Polling	31,100	7.29
Advertising		
Electronic media	90,461	21.19
Other media	19,515	4.57
Subtotal	109,975	25.76
Other Campaign Activity		
Persuasion mail/brochures	0	
Actual campaigning	32,913	7.71
Staff/volunteers	0	
Subtotal	32,913	7.71
Constituent Gifts/Entertainment	46,989	11.01
Donations to		
Candidates from same state	1,900	.45
Candidates from other states	1,000	.23
Civic organizations	80	.02
Ideological groups	1,000	.23
Political parties	14,525	3.40
Subtotal	18,505	4.34
Unitemized Expenses	26,916	6.31
Total Campaign Expenses	$ 426,872	
PAC Contributions	$ 211,391	
Individual Contributions	96,929	
Total Receipts*	310,017	

*Includes PAC and individual contributions as well as interest earned, party contributions, etc.

District 5 — MISSOURI

Rep. Alan Wheat (D)

1992 Election Results

Alan Wheat (D)	151,014 (59%)
Edward "Gomer" Moody (R)	93,562 (37%)

Democratic Rep. Alan Wheat had not faced a serious challenge since his initial victory in 1982. However, when it was revealed that he had eighty-six overdrafts at the House bank, four members of his own party jumped into the race.

Concerned primarily over the candidacy of Fred Arbanas, who had played in two Super Bowls with the Kansas City Chiefs before beginning a twenty-year career in Kansas City politics, Wheat spent nearly $218,000 in the four months preceding the August 4 primary. That investment was just $20,000 less than Wheat's entire spending for the 1990 election cycle.

During the preprimary push, Wheat paid Trippi, McMahon & Squier of Alexandria, Va., $45,751 for creating and placing broadcast ads. Hunt Communications of Philadelphia, Pa., received $10,327 for ad placement. Simmons & Co. of Kansas City collected $25,315 for coordinating a preprimary phonebanking effort and sending out follow-up mailings to likely supporters. Cooper & Secrest Associates of Alexandria, Va., received $19,400 for polling.

In additional to salary payments to his staff of eight, Wheat spent $4,375 on per diem wages for dozens of field workers, who combed the district looking for primary supporters and distributing $7,924 worth of campaign literature. Wheat invested $11,349 in yard signs and $5,427 in buttons and bumper stickers. T-shirts given to campaign volunteers, field workers, and office staff cost $3,571. Wheat grabbed 58 percent of the primary vote. Arbanas spent $77,277 and finished second with 38 percent.

Wheat continued his free spending in the general election campaign against businessman Edward "Gomer" Moody. While Moody put just $56,053 into his challenge, Wheat countered with a $319,291 effort.

Trippi, McMahon & Squier received $132,397 for their work down the stretch. Hunt picked up $3,577 for additional ad placement and pollsters Cooper & Secrest received $16,147. Wheat paid Ambrosino & Muir of San Francisco, Calif., $27,240 for persuasion mail. In a solidly Democratic district, Wheat spent only $7,334 on his general election get-out-the-vote efforts.

To help pay for his campaign, which cost nearly three times as much as his 1990 effort and $185,463 more than he raised during the 1992 cycle, Wheat relied heavily on political action committees (PACs). Over the two-year cycle, PACs accounted for 75 percent of Wheat's total contributions. He raised only $71,818 from individual donors who gave at least $200, and $31,720 of that total came from out-of-state contributors. Donations of less that $200 amounted to just $44,546. For coordinating the PAC events, Pederson & Thompson of Washington, D.C., received $44,315.

Campaign Expenditures	Wheat Amount Spent	Wheat % of Total	Moody Amount Spent	Moody % of Total
Overhead				
Office furniture/supplies	$ 12,162	1.80	$ 169	.30
Rent/utilities	17,298	2.57	1,000	1.78
Salaries	86,670	12.86	0	
Taxes	20,674	3.07	0	
Bank/investment fees	20		0	
Lawyers/accountants	4,990	.74	0	
Telephone	10,430	1.55	440	.78
Campaign automobile	11,571	1.72	0	
Computers/office equipment	9,279	1.38	0	
Travel	24,110	3.58	726	1.30
Food/meetings	2,040	.30	273	.49
Subtotal	**199,243**	**29.57**	**2,608**	**4.65**
Fund Raising				
Events	75,301	11.17	650	1.16
Direct mail	0		1,617	2.88
Telemarketing	0		0	
Subtotal	**75,301**	**11.17**	**2,267**	**4.04**
Polling	**35,547**	**5.27**	**0**	
Advertising				
Electronic media	192,540	28.57	21,889	39.05
Other media	6,871	1.02	16,890	30.13
Subtotal	**199,411**	**29.59**	**38,779**	**69.18**
Other Campaign Activity				
Persuasion mail/brochures	67,401	10.00	0	
Actual campaigning	58,336	8.66	12,177	21.72
Staff/volunteers	6,472	.96	0	
Subtotal	**132,209**	**19.62**	**12,177**	**21.72**
Constituent Gifts/Entertainment	3,771	.56	0	
Donations to				
Candidates from same state	5,394	.80	0	
Candidates from other states	3,500	.52	0	
Civic organizations	2,215	.33	0	
Ideological groups	3,660	.54	0	
Political parties	13,550	2.01	0	
Subtotal	**28,319**	**4.20**	**0**	
Unitemized Expenses	**101**	**.01**	**223**	**.40**
Total Campaign Expenses	**$ 673,902**		**$ 56,053**	
PAC Contributions	$ 344,588		$ 2,000	
Individual Contributions	116,364		51,339	
Total Receipts*	488,439		55,395	

*Includes PAC and individual contributions as well as interest earned, party contributions, etc.

MISSOURI — District 6

Rep. Pat Danner (D)

1992 Election Results

Pat Danner (D)	148,887	(55%)
Tom Coleman (R)	119,637	(45%)

Throughout the three-month general election campaign, state senator Pat Danner and Republican Rep. Tom Coleman traded broadcast advertising salvos, slamming each other for taking advantage of the spoils of incumbency. Each had plenty of outside help.

Held to 52 percent of the vote in 1990 by a little-known farmer and truck driver who spent just $22,429, Coleman came out swinging with a television commercial that accused Danner of spending $11,000 of taxpayer money to redecorate her senate office and of supporting pay raises that benefited both she and her son Steve, who was also a state senator. The ad went on to charge that Danner had been forced to return illegal campaign money she took from her son, who was also her chief fund-raiser.

Another ad accused Danner of supporting the construction of a hazardous waste site in the district. A third commercial slammed her for voting "time and again against requiring the Missouri state government to buy American." National Media of Alexandria, Va., collected $249,639 for creating and placing five television commercials and a similar number of radio spots for Coleman.

Danner did not sit quietly on the sidelines. She paid Politics Inc. of Washington, D.C., $34,996 for creating five television commercials and four radio ads, including one that criticized Coleman for his 1989 vote in favor of the congressional pay raise, his frequent taxpayer-funded junkets, and his extensive use of the franking privilege.

In fact, Coleman did not need to spend much of his campaign treasury on persuasion mail. Unopposed in the primary, he had flooded the district with franked mailings worth $109,379. The National Republican Congressional Committee also paid Jantsch Communications of Kansas City, Mo., $28,450 for persuasion mailings on Coleman's behalf and picked up $15,760 of the postage charges.

Over the last ten days of the campaign, Danner benefited greatly from a $94,502 independent campaign waged against Coleman by the National Rifle Association (NRA). Angered by Coleman's vote in favor of the Brady Bill, the NRA paid Edmonds Powell Media of Washington, D.C., $30,110 for producing and placing radio spots that attacked Coleman for his congressional junkets and his vote on the pay raise. Ackerman, Hood & McQueen of Oklahoma City collected $31,101 for placing full-page newspaper ads hitting the same themes. These ads and companion persuasion mailers listed the National Victory Committee as the organization responsible for paying for the campaign, never informing the viewer or recipient that the organization was an arm of the NRA.

Campaign Expenditures	Danner Amount Spent	Danner % of Total	Coleman Amount Spent	Coleman % of Total
Overhead				
Office furniture/supplies	$ 2,219	.54	$ 5,908	1.08
Rent/utilities	2,826	.68	3,488	.64
Salaries	18,500	4.48	31,456	5.73
Taxes	0		5,916	1.08
Bank/investment fees	30	.01	81	.01
Lawyers/accountants	0		0	
Telephone	4,024	.97	3,141	.57
Campaign automobile	0		3,862	.70
Computers/office equipment	0		897	.16
Travel	7,592	1.84	9,001	1.64
Food/meetings	0		1,031	.19
Subtotal	**35,191**	**8.52**	**64,781**	**11.80**
Fund Raising				
Events	10,089	2.44	59,300	10.80
Direct mail	2,020	.49	5,670	1.03
Telemarketing	0		8,178	1.49
Subtotal	**12,108**	**2.93**	**73,149**	**13.33**
Polling	**33,089**	**8.01**	**36,600**	**6.67**
Advertising				
Electronic media	252,423	61.08	276,105	50.30
Other media	4,685	1.13	10,290	1.87
Subtotal	**257,108**	**62.22**	**286,395**	**52.18**
Other Campaign Activity				
Persuasion mail/brochures	57,219	13.85	39,095	7.12
Actual campaigning	13,774	3.33	21,997	4.01
Staff/volunteers	0		89	.02
Subtotal	**70,993**	**17.18**	**61,181**	**11.15**
Constituent Gifts/ Entertainment	**0**		**5,404**	**.98**
Donations to				
Candidates from same state	0		0	
Candidates from other states	0		0	
Civic organizations	0		0	
Ideological groups	0		0	
Political parties	0		0	
Subtotal	**0**		**0**	
Unitemized Expenses	**4,757**	**1.15**	**21,393**	**3.90**
Total Campaign Expenses	**$ 413,246**		**$ 548,902**	
PAC Contributions	$ 183,992		$ 343,299	
Individual Contributions	149,538		133,328	
Total Receipts*	486,277		501,200	

*Includes PAC and individual contributions as well as interest earned, party contributions, etc.

District 7 — MISSOURI

Rep. Mel Hancock (R)

1992 Election Results

Mel Hancock (R)	160,303	(62%)
Thomas Patrick Deaton (D)	99,762	(38%)

Held to 52 percent by Democrat Thomas Patrick Deaton in 1990, two-term Republican Rep. Mel Hancock was more than prepared for their 1992 rematch. While Deaton, a Springfield attorney, spent $217,675 more in 1992 than he had in 1990, Hancock increased his spending by $242,503.

In 1990 Deaton's lone strategist, Cathryne Simmons of Kansas City, Mo., had joined the campaign just forty-six days before the November general election. With little time and very little money, Simmons had opted to produce and place the campaign's ads herself.

The 1992 campaign was a different story entirely, with Deaton funneling $226,149 through his team of professional consultants. Simmons joined the campaign in January 1992, and over the next eleven months earned $35,909 for providing general strategic advice. Media Strategies of Falls Church, Va., came on board in April, earning $32,304 for polling. Trippi, McMahon & Squier of Alexandria, Va., joined the effort in June and over the next six months collected $155,936 for creating and placing one television commercial and a companion radio spot.

In an area hard-hit by unemployment, Deaton's ads focused on the economy. His television spot ripped Hancock for voting against the family leave bill and in support of "fast-track" negotiations with Mexico on what would become the North American Free Trade Agreement. The ad implied that Hancock's vote had contributed to a decision by Zenith Electronics Corp. to close a local plant and shift 1,500 manufacturing jobs to Mexico. "Gracias, Señor Hancock," intoned an actor in the ad.

Hancock quickly pointed out that the Zenith decision had predated the trade agreement and struck back with an ad depicting Deaton as soft on crime. The ad pointed out that Deaton had served as the defense attorney for a man convicted of killing a state highway patrolman, convincing the jury to sentence him to life in prison without parole rather than hand down the death penalty. Hancock paid Brockmeyer/Allen & Associates of Baltimore, Md., $43,017 for creating his ads and spent $155,606 to place them. Additional production costs totaled $4,987.

To spread his message, Hancock spent $14,100 on billboards and $18,162 on newspaper ads. He invested $11,969 in signs that touted him as the "taxpayer's choice" and placed them along roadways throughout the district.

In a reversal of the usual trend, Hancock collected less from political action committees (PACs) than his challenger. In addition to the $164,430 Hancock picked up from PACs, he collected $120,804 from individuals who gave at least $200. Smaller donations amounted to $78,681.

Campaign Expenditures	Hancock Amount Spent	Hancock % of Total	Deaton Amount Spent	Deaton % of Total
Overhead				
Office furniture/supplies	$ 3,282	.77	$ 1,934	.60
Rent/utilities	7,550	1.77	7,015	2.19
Salaries	14,714	3.45	5,830	1.82
Taxes	8,676	2.04	2,066	.64
Bank/investment fees	388	.09	0	
Lawyers/accountants	0		0	
Telephone	6,336	1.49	2,635	.82
Campaign automobile	0		0	
Computers/office equipment	2,241	.53	4,288	1.34
Travel	9,260	2.17	9,747	3.04
Food/meetings	870	.20	0	
Subtotal	**53,316**	**12.51**	**33,516**	**10.44**
Fund Raising				
Events	22,383	5.25	4,286	1.34
Direct mail	10,007	2.35	8,608	2.68
Telemarketing	0		6,901	2.15
Subtotal	**32,389**	**7.60**	**19,795**	**6.17**
Polling	**28,018**	**6.58**	**32,304**	**10.07**
Advertising				
Electronic media	203,611	47.78	157,936	49.21
Other media	32,262	7.57	14,527	4.53
Subtotal	**235,872**	**55.35**	**172,463**	**53.74**
Other Campaign Activity				
Persuasion mail/brochures	19,335	4.54	994	.31
Actual campaigning	20,683	4.85	42,662	13.29
Staff/volunteers	0		1,348	.42
Subtotal	**40,018**	**9.39**	**45,003**	**14.02**
Constituent Gifts/ Entertainment	**906**	**.21**	**0**	
Donations to				
Candidates from same state	1,500	.35	100	.03
Candidates from other states	5,000	1.17	0	
Civic organizations	365	.09	0	
Ideological groups	250	.06	0	
Political parties	0		0	
Subtotal	**7,115**	**1.67**	**100**	**.03**
Unitemized Expenses	**28,495**	**6.69**	**17,759**	**5.53**
Total Campaign Expenses	**$ 426,130**		**$ 320,941**	
PAC Contributions	**$ 164,430**		**$ 183,268**	
Individual Contributions	**199,485**		**117,013**	
Total Receipts*	**393,638**		**309,432**	

*Includes PAC and individual contributions as well as interest earned, party contributions, etc.

MISSOURI   District 8

Rep. Bill Emerson (R)   *1992 Election Results*   Bill Emerson (R)   147,398   (63%)
                                                                    Thad Bullock (D)   86,730   (37%)

Thad Bullock's challenge to Republican Rep. Bill Emerson was, if nothing else, a testimonial to perseverance. After six unsuccessful attempts, the seventy-five-year-old Bullock finally grabbed the Democratic nomination. However, with only $6,062 to spend, Bullock played the role of sacrificial lamb.

Reflecting his easy path to a seventh term, Emerson spent $209,990 less on his 1992 reelection effort than he had in 1990, a decrease of 30 percent. He sliced his broadcast advertising budget by $123,471 and his overhead by $76,081. In 1990 he invested $51,727 in brochures and targeted persuasion mailings; in 1992 he spent nothing on such items.

However, as chief of staff Lloyd F. Smith put it, "Things were going wrong at the top of the ticket in Missouri, and we didn't want to take anything for granted." In that spirit, Emerson paid Smith & Harroff of Alexandria, Va., $28,916 for creating radio and television spots that highlighted his constituent service and work on the Agriculture and the Public Works & Transportation committees. For placing the spots, Smith & Harroff and Harry Lightfoot Advertising of Cape Girardeau collected $54,744 and $59,442, respectively.

In 1990 Emerson had used persuasion mail to reach areas of the district not covered by one of four broadcast media markets. To reach those areas in 1992, Emerson significantly increased his newspaper advertising budget. He spent $18,272 on newspaper ads and $37,597 on tabloid-style newspaper inserts, which were customized for different areas of the district.

To help spread his name, Emerson spent $18,928 to purchase more than 5,000 signs. Bumper stickers, lapel stickers, and other campaign paraphernalia cost $4,005.

With little opposition in either the primary or general elections, Emerson had plenty of room in the budget for constituent stroking. He spent $6,414 on holiday cards and $1,970 on calendars from the U.S. Capitol Historical Society. Constituent meals, flowers, and gifts added $1,783.

As in 1990, political action committees (PACs) accounted for more than half of Emerson's total receipts. He paid Sheehan Associates of Washington, D.C., $7,520 to coordinate PAC fund-raisers in 1991 that helped raise $99,817, but in 1992 he handed the PAC fund-raising responsibilities over to HTH & Associates of Alexandria, Va. "HTH offered us a package better tailored to what we thought we were facing in 1992," noted Smith. "We didn't want a Cadillac when a Caprice Chevrolet would do."

Campaign Expenditures	Emerson Amount Spent	Emerson % of Total	Bullock Amount Spent	Bullock % of Total
Overhead				
Office furniture/supplies	$ 9,718	1.99	$ 0	
Rent/utilities	4,400	.90	0	
Salaries	38,383	7.86	0	
Taxes	14,171	2.90	0	
Bank/investment fees	81	.02	0	
Lawyers/accountants	0		0	
Telephone	7,286	1.49	0	
Campaign automobile	0		0	
Computers/office equipment	808	.17	0	
Travel	40,215	8.23	1,136	18.74
Food/meetings	10,295	2.11	0	
Subtotal	**125,357**	**25.66**	**1,136**	**18.74**
Fund Raising				
Events	74,251	15.20	0	
Direct mail	17,567	3.60	0	
Telemarketing	0		0	
Subtotal	**91,818**	**18.80**	**0**	
Polling	**17,500**	**3.58**	**0**	
Advertising				
Electronic media	144,568	29.60	2,983	49.22
Other media	58,074	11.89	1,552	25.61
Subtotal	**202,642**	**41.49**	**4,536**	**74.83**
Other Campaign Activity				
Persuasion mail/brochures	0		90	1.49
Actual campaigning	28,072	5.75	150	2.47
Staff/volunteers	0		0	
Subtotal	**28,072**	**5.75**	**240**	**3.96**
Constituent Gifts/ Entertainment	**10,167**	**2.08**	**0**	
Donations to				
Candidates from same state	0		0	
Candidates from other states	1,550	.32	0	
Civic organizations	1,435	.29	0	
Ideological groups	200	.04	0	
Political parties	456	.09	0	
Subtotal	**3,641**	**.75**	**0**	
Unitemized Expenses	**9,261**	**1.90**	**150**	**2.47**
Total Campaign Expenses	**$ 488,457**		**$ 6,062**	
PAC Contributions	$ 299,188		$ 6,000	
Individual Contributions	213,453		400	
Total Receipts*	518,998		12,650	

*Includes PAC and individual contributions as well as interest earned, party contributions, etc.

District 9 — MISSOURI

Rep. Harold L. Volkmer (D)

1992 Election Results

Harold L. Volkmer (D)	124,694	(48%)
Rick Hardy (R)	118,811	(45%)

On paper, redistricting appeared to have made Democratic Rep. Harold L. Volkmer's political life easier by removing solidly Republican Osage County from District 9. In addition, Volker did not appear particularly vulnerable to an anti-incumbent campaign. While he had voted in favor of the congressional pay raise, he had only one overdraft at the House bank, had voted against the 1990 budget compromise that included several tax increases, and had voted for a constitutional amendment requiring a balanced federal budget. However, things did not work out quite as smoothly as Volkmer might have hoped.

In the Democratic primary, a real estate broker, a tax adjuster, a salesman, a construction worker, and a music company owner combined to take 43 percent of the vote from Volkmer. Their showing forced Volkmer to spend $52,962 of his advertising budget to secure the nomination. The FMR Group of Washington, D.C., received $12,158 for creating radio commercials, which Volkmer then spent $11,528 to air. Preprimary newspaper ads cost $29,276. Volkmer also invested $13,908 in targeted persuasion mailings.

Despite Volkmer's lackluster showing in the primary, few observers initially took Republican challenger Rick Hardy seriously. "I had hired a twenty-two-year-old former student as my campaign manager," recalled Hardy, a political science professor at the University of Missouri. "It was a suicide mission."

With the help of nearly 500 former students who volunteered to knock on doors, Hardy waged an aggressive anti-incumbent campaign. He called for term limits, using lines such as, "I believe Congress and diapers should be changed regularly." Lacking the money to advertise heavily, he began holding press conferences to blast Volkmer for accepting political action committee contributions, counting on the free media to spread his message. Over the final two weeks of the campaign, when it became clear that the race had tightened, Hardy's $31,206 advertising budget was augmented by a $40,000 infusion from the National Republican Congressional Committee.

Volkmer countered by putting $133,993 into his broadcast media. FMR collected $30,418 for producing both television and radio commercials. Television and radio air time cost $86,658 and $16,640, respectively. Ads in newspapers such as the *Hannibal Courier Post,* the *Moberly Monitor Index,* the *Palmyra Spectator,* and the *Mark Twain Regional News* cost $37,903. Volkmer spent $36,222 on persuasion mail, $12,259 on yard signs, and $2,581 on buttons and bumper stickers.

With two independent candidates siphoning off nearly 7 percent of the anti-incumbent vote, Volkmer pulled out a 5,883-vote victory.

	Volkmer		Hardy	
Campaign Expenditures	Amount Spent	% of Total	Amount Spent	% of Total
Overhead				
Office furniture/supplies	$ 3,419	.67	$ 6,087	4.14
Rent/utilities	7,296	1.43	4,830	3.28
Salaries	41,473	8.11	28,036	19.05
Taxes	14,316	2.80	9,357	6.36
Bank/investment fees	146	.03	90	.06
Lawyers/accountants	0		0	
Telephone	9,338	1.83	7,554	5.13
Campaign automobile	0		0	
Computers/office equipment	4,696	.92	4,227	2.87
Travel	19,529	3.82	7,233	4.92
Food/meetings	5,854	1.14	200	.14
Subtotal	**106,066**	**20.73**	**67,613**	**45.95**
Fund Raising				
Events	43,285	8.46	1,794	1.22
Direct mail	0		17,657	12.00
Telemarketing	0		0	
Subtotal	**43,285**	**8.46**	**19,451**	**13.22**
Polling	**33,677**	**6.58**	**0**	
Advertising				
Electronic media	157,679	30.82	31,206	21.21
Other media	68,739	13.44	779	.53
Subtotal	**226,418**	**44.26**	**31,984**	**21.74**
Other Campaign Activity				
Persuasion mail/brochures	50,130	9.80	2,034	1.38
Actual campaigning	19,001	3.71	15,793	10.73
Staff/volunteers	231	.05	144	.10
Subtotal	**69,363**	**13.56**	**17,972**	**12.21**
Constituent Gifts/ Entertainment	**723**	**.14**	**0**	
Donations to				
Candidates from same state	695	.14	0	
Candidates from other states	0		0	
Civic organizations	428	.08	30	.02
Ideological groups	0		0	
Political parties	13,383	2.62	0	
Subtotal	**14,506**	**2.84**	**30**	**.02**
Unitemized Expenses	**17,516**	**3.42**	**10,089**	**6.86**
Total Campaign Expenses	**$ 511,554**		**$ 147,139**	
PAC Contributions	$ 247,010		$ 0	
Individual Contributions	81,974		130,697	
Total Receipts*	354,612		144,157	

*Includes PAC and individual contributions as well as interest earned, party contributions, etc.

MONTANA   At Large

Rep. Pat Williams (D)

1992 Election Results

Pat Williams (D)	203,711	(50%)
Ron Marlenee (R)	189,570	(47%)

Montana's population grew by only 12,375 between 1980 and 1990, resulting in the loss of one of its two House seats. Together, Democratic Rep. Pat Williams and Republican Rep. Ron Marlenee spent nearly $2.7 million to woo 403,735 voters in one of the most hotly contested incumbent battles of 1992.

To reach voters spread across 147,046 square miles, both candidates depended largely on broadcast advertising. Williams paid New York-based Joe Slade White & Co. $114,244 for developing twelve television commercials and more than two dozen radio spots. For placing the ads, Williams paid Shafto and Barton of Houston, Texas, and Sage Advertising of Billings $318,359 and $28,436, respectively.

Marlenee countered with a $498,301 broadcast campaign of his own, $473,465 of which went to Edmonds Powell Media of Washington, D.C. Campaign manager Will Brooke said they aired between fifteen and twenty radio commercials and five television spots, including ads attacking Williams for his reliance on political action committee (PAC) donations and his heavy investment in television commercials.

Campaign Performance Group of San Francisco, Calif., collected $34,850 from Williams and $48,584 from the Montana Democratic Central Committee for producing and mailing three persuasion mailers. One attacked Marlenee for supporting tax breaks for corporations and the wealthy, for voting against a middle-class tax cut, and for voting to cut funding for college scholarships and loans. Another slammed Marlenee as "bankrolled by big oil" and "the polluters' pal." The third focused on Williams's support for health care reform, protection of Social Security cost-of-living adjustments, and strong veterans benefits. In all, Campaign Performance mailed about 200,000 brochures. Williams spent $43,491 to mail thousands of additional pieces of campaign literature.

Marlenee spent slightly more than Williams on broadcast advertising but roughly $26,000 less on persuasion mail. The National Republican Congressional Committee spent $32,503 to augment Marlenee's mail effort, which largely offset the help Williams received from the state Democratic party.

Williams invested substantially more than Marlenee in traditional grass-roots campaigning. Williams spent $40,300 on various get-out-the-vote efforts, $9,734 on 35,000 yard signs, and $6,068 on bumper stickers and promotional materials. Marlenee spent just $4,123 on such grass-roots campaigning.

Both candidates depended heavily on PACs for contributions. Williams paid Fraioli/Jost of Washington, D.C., $36,282 to set up his PAC fund-raisers. Ziebart Associates of Washington, D.C., received $52,536 for coordinating Marlenee's PAC soirees.

	Williams		Marlenee	
Campaign Expenditures	Amount Spent	% of Total	Amount Spent	% of Total
Overhead				
Office furniture/supplies	$ 24,799	1.83	$ 25,765	1.98
Rent/utilities	14,560	1.07	22,348	1.72
Salaries	154,365	11.39	148,620	11.42
Taxes	67,163	4.95	46,386	3.56
Bank/investment fees	780	.06	372	.03
Lawyers/accountants	3,644	.27	551	.04
Telephone	11,387	.84	41,368	3.18
Campaign automobile	0		28,507	2.19
Computers/office equipment	21,231	1.57	9,394	.72
Travel	74,306	5.48	119,392	9.17
Food/meetings	5,513	.41	3,301	.25
Subtotal	**377,748**	**27.87**	**446,006**	**34.26**
Fund Raising				
Events	111,307	8.21	109,386	8.40
Direct mail	57,341	4.23	136,632	10.49
Telemarketing	25,959	1.91	0	
Subtotal	**194,607**	**14.36**	**246,018**	**18.90**
Polling	**75,389**	**5.56**	**11,563**	**.89**
Advertising				
Electronic media	482,474	35.59	498,301	38.27
Other media	22,634	1.67	12,469	.96
Subtotal	**505,108**	**37.26**	**510,770**	**39.23**
Other Campaign Activity				
Persuasion mail/brochures	78,341	5.78	52,185	4.01
Actual campaigning	71,655	5.29	22,093	1.70
Staff/volunteers	0		917	.07
Subtotal	**149,996**	**11.06**	**75,195**	**5.78**
Constituent Gifts/ Entertainment	**7,997**	**.59**	**4,064**	**.31**
Donations to				
Candidates from same state	0		0	
Candidates from other states	0		0	
Civic organizations	673	.05	2,855	.22
Ideological groups	45		595	.05
Political parties	15,100	1.11	1,261	.10
Subtotal	**15,818**	**1.17**	**4,711**	**.36**
Unitemized Expenses	**28,947**	**2.14**	**3,605**	**.28**
Total Campaign Expenses	**$ 1,355,610**		**$ 1,301,930**	
PAC Contributions	$ 501,505		$ 384,885	
Individual Contributions	632,329		782,471	
Total Receipts*	1,190,716		1,220,494	

*Includes PAC and individual contributions as well as interest earned, party contributions, etc.

District 1 — NEBRASKA

Rep. Doug Bereuter (R)

1992 Election Results

Doug Bereuter (R)	142,713	(60%)
Gerry Finnegan (D)	96,309	(40%)

With thirty-nine overdrafts at the House bank and a struggling Republican president at the top of the ballot, Rep. Doug Bereuter opted to invest in television advertising for the first time since his initial House campaign in 1978. As a result, he spent about $140,000 more on his 1992 reelection effort than he had in 1990.

Bereuter's off-year campaign was virtually nonexistent. He had no campaign office. Travel and meals unrelated to fund raising amounted to only $783 and $354, respectively. Computer equipment and software cost $6,454. Salaries for part-time staffers amounted to $9,044, which was nearly half of the $19,272 he spent on overhead.

Off-year fund raising cost Bereuter $11,802 and yielded just $52,206. After paying for various campaign expenditures, this low-key fund-raising effort produced a $21,512 increase in his modest cash reserves, from $54,731 to $76,243.

Bereuter wasted little of his resources on the May 12 Republican primary, which he won with 99 percent of the vote. His only office space during the primary campaign was provided in-kind by the state Republican party. David Shively, district assistant in Bereuter's Lincoln congressional office, coordinated day-to-day campaign activities for $2,450. By far his largest preprimary expense was the $20,867 he spent on campaign literature and one large persuasion mailing sent to past Republican primary voters.

The campaign began in earnest in June, when Bereuter hired Bailey-Lauerman & Associates of Lincoln to design and place the bulk of his newspaper ads and consult on persuasion mail. Over the next five months, the firm was paid $33,365. In July Bereuter hired Smith & Harroff of Alexandria, Va., and over the final four months of the campaign paid them $144,774 for creating and placing four television and two radio commercials.

According to administrative assistant Susan L. Olson, Bereuter's broadcast advertising emphasized his efforts to foster agricultural exports and his work to secure federal community development projects for the district. None of the ads mentioned Democrat Gerry Finnegan, who unsuccessfully sought to tar Bereuter with the negatives of incumbency. "Finnegan's media buy was too small to have an impact, so we never had to respond to it," explained Olson.

Bereuter devoted 11 percent of his campaign budget to newspaper advertising, but that expenditure apparently had little to do with the effectiveness of such ads. "Doug feels very strongly about newspaper advertising because smaller community papers depend on advertising to survive," noted Olson. She added that the campaign placed ads in every daily newspaper and most weeklies in the district.

Campaign Expenditures	Bereuter Amount Spent	Bereuter % of Total	Finnegan Amount Spent	Finnegan % of Total
Overhead				
Office furniture/supplies	$ 3,907	1.07	$ 1,742	1.90
Rent/utilities	2,180	.60	2,883	3.15
Salaries	31,356	8.58	20,150	22.00
Taxes	11,157	3.05	0	
Bank/investment fees	12		0	
Lawyers/accountants	0		0	
Telephone	4,453	1.22	3,987	4.35
Campaign automobile	2,162	.59	0	
Computers/office equipment	7,675	2.10	2,258	2.46
Travel	6,844	1.87	3,945	4.31
Food/meetings	699	.19	0	
Subtotal	**70,445**	**19.28**	**34,964**	**38.17**
Fund Raising				
Events	34,702	9.50	6,367	6.95
Direct mail	7,735	2.12	1,976	2.16
Telemarketing	0		10,922	11.92
Subtotal	**42,437**	**11.61**	**19,266**	**21.03**
Polling	**13,000**	**3.56**	**0**	
Advertising				
Electronic media	144,849	39.64	14,092	15.38
Other media	41,304	11.30	506	.55
Subtotal	**186,154**	**50.95**	**14,599**	**15.94**
Other Campaign Activity				
Persuasion mail/brochures	28,850	7.90	8,163	8.91
Actual campaigning	9,892	2.71	9,010	9.84
Staff/volunteers	0		0	
Subtotal	**38,742**	**10.60**	**17,173**	**18.75**
Constituent Gifts/ Entertainment	**4,301**	**1.18**	**0**	
Donations to				
Candidates from same state	0		0	
Candidates from other states	0		0	
Civic organizations	0		0	
Ideological groups	0		0	
Political parties	0		0	
Subtotal	**0**		**0**	
Unitemized Expenses	**10,314**	**2.82**	**5,606**	**6.12**
Total Campaign Expenses	**$ 365,391**		**$ 91,608**	
PAC Contributions	$ 194,482		$ 27,521	
Individual Contributions	112,443		47,985	
Total Receipts*	315,824		86,028	

*Includes PAC and individual contributions as well as interest earned, party contributions, etc.

NEBRASKA District 2

Rep. Peter Hoagland (D)

1992 Election Results

Peter Hoagland (D) 119,512 (51%)
Ronald L. Staskiewicz (R) 113,828 (49%)

Having captured this seat in a marginally Republican district by fewer than 3,000 votes in 1988 and having been held to 58 percent of the vote in 1990, Democratic Rep. Peter Hoagland knew he would face a stiff challenge in 1992. He was not disappointed. Restauranteur Ronald L. Staskiewicz waged an aggressive anti-incumbent campaign and came within 5,684 votes of denying Hoagland a third term.

Despite his tenuous hold on the seat, Hoagland invested only $60,504 in his off-year permanent campaign, including $17,304 in overhead and $21,291 in fund raising. However, Hoagland's campaign quickly picked up steam in 1992. Between January 1 and the May 12 primary, Hoagland spent $164,959 to dispatch fellow Democrat Jess M. Pritchett. He paid media consultant Joe Slade White & Co. of New York $23,433 for creating broadcast ads and spent $18,206 to place them. Hoagland emerged with 85 percent of the primary votes.

For the general election campaign, Hoagland paid White $51,044 for creating additional commercials, including one that charged Staskiewicz with refusing to pay debts owed to former employees and creditors of a bar he owned in Vermillion, S.D. Hoagland spent $132,833 to air his ads on local network affiliates and $3,480 for air time on cable television systems. Radio spots cost the campaign $28,437.

Hoagland paid Campaign Performance Group of San Francisco, Calif., $58,682 for producing and printing three persuasion mailings. One highly negative piece opened with a picture of a laughing Staskiewicz next to the phrase, "I want to outlaw abortion—even for victims of rape and incest." The piece concluded by labeling Staskiewicz as "the face of extremism." A second mailing accused Staskiewicz of scheming "to become rich by funneling campaign donations into his own bank accounts," citing as examples campaign payments to him for the lease of his own car and the lease of office space in a building he owned. A positive mailer touted the fact that Hoagland had no bounced checks and had voted against the congressional pay raise.

Hoagland also invested $10,056 in opposition research conducted by the Research Group of Chicago, Ill., $8,872 in signs and posters, and $6,911 in various get-out-the-vote efforts.

Unopposed in the Republican primary, Staskiewicz was able to focus his entire media budget on Hoagland. With a $44,999 assist from the National Republican Congressional Committee, he was able to put $163,271 into producing and airing four television commercials and four radio spots, half of which were negative.

Campaign Expenditures	Hoagland Amount Spent	Hoagland % of Total	Staskiewicz Amount Spent	Staskiewicz % of Total
Overhead				
Office furniture/supplies	$ 8,493	1.23	$ 8,357	2.25
Rent/utilities	11,567	1.67	27,949	7.52
Salaries	47,660	6.90	58,194	15.65
Taxes	19,564	2.83	18,173	4.89
Bank/investment fees	1,973	.29	2,482	.67
Lawyers/accountants	31,340	4.53	0	
Telephone	10,982	1.59	8,187	2.20
Campaign automobile	0		0	
Computers/office equipment	5,595	.81	2,052	.55
Travel	19,559	2.83	15,565	4.19
Food/meetings	1,885	.27	648	.17
Subtotal	**158,619**	**22.95**	**141,607**	**38.09**
Fund Raising				
Events	26,967	3.90	7,699	2.07
Direct mail	11,557	1.67	6,913	1.86
Telemarketing	21,768	3.15	0	
Subtotal	**60,291**	**8.72**	**14,612**	**3.93**
Polling	**49,750**	**7.20**	**13,150**	**3.54**
Advertising				
Electronic media	257,483	37.25	118,272	31.81
Other media	1,748	.25	2,111	.57
Subtotal	**259,231**	**37.51**	**120,382**	**32.38**
Other Campaign Activity				
Persuasion mail/brochures	82,402	11.92	49,320	13.27
Actual campaigning	41,143	5.95	18,603	5.00
Staff/volunteers	490	.07	208	.06
Subtotal	**124,035**	**17.95**	**68,131**	**18.33**
Constituent Gifts/ Entertainment	**5,832**	**.84**	**0**	
Donations to				
Candidates from same state	1,050	.15	0	
Candidates from other states	1,750	.25	0	
Civic organizations	851	.12	1,940	.52
Ideological groups	423	.06	0	
Political parties	17,145	2.48	80	.02
Subtotal	**21,219**	**3.07**	**2,020**	**.54**
Unitemized Expenses	**12,193**	**1.76**	**11,857**	**3.19**
Total Campaign Expenses	**$ 691,171**		**$ 371,759**	
PAC Contributions	$ 457,190		$ 83,110	
Individual Contributions	225,283		261,858	
Total Receipts*	701,282		379,153	

*Includes PAC and individual contributions as well as interest earned, party contributions, etc.

District 3 — NEBRASKA

Rep. Bill Barrett (R)

1992 Election Results

Bill Barrett (R)	170,857	(72%)
Lowell Fisher (D)	67,457	(28%)

Despite winning a 1990 open seat contest by only 4,373 votes, Republican Rep. Bill Barrett had few worries in his first reelection campaign. Barrett's predecessor, Republican Virginia Smith, had held the seat from 1974 until her retirement in 1990. President George Bush had carried the district by a two-to-one margin in 1988. Perhaps more impressively, Bush carried District 3 by 23 points in 1992, with independent presidential candidate Ross Perot finishing second. Barrett's 1992 Democratic challenger, farmer Lowell Fisher, had no prior political experience and little money.

Facing an easy path to reelection, Barrett spent $242,768 less on his 1992 campaign than he had in 1990, a decrease of 39 percent. He spent $85,276 less on advertising and $82,064 less on other direct appeals for votes. With the outcome of the 1990 race in doubt, Barrett had invested $34,041 in polls; with the 1992 race never in doubt, he spent just $9,700 on polls. Overhead expenses dropped from $165,640 in 1990 to $81,919 in 1992.

Barrett ended the 1990 election cycle with debts of $70,000 and a campaign bank balance of only $19,982, so raising money was a top priority. During 1991, fund-raising expenses accounted for 57 percent of the $67,768 he spent to keep his permanent campaign running smoothly. These efforts reaped individual contributions totaling $81,598 and political action committee (PAC) donations of $74,775. He began 1992 with no debts and cash reserves of $27,847.

While PACs accounted for 41 percent of Barrett's total receipts for the two-year election cycle, he also placed heavy emphasis on his small-donor program. To get more people involved with the campaign, a half dozen barbecues were held for those who could not afford a $200 donation. Campaign Tele-Resources of Omaha was paid $6,000 for its telemarketing services. As a result, donations of less than $200 amounted to $137,042, or 28 percent of Barrett's receipts.

For the campaign itself, Barrett paid Brockmeyer/Allan & Associates of Baltimore, Md., $16,890 for developing four television and six radio commercials. Fearing an anti-incumbent backlash, the ads avoided any mention of federal projects Barrett had sought for the district. Instead, they focused on such things as the numerous town meetings he had held, the fact that he spent nearly every weekend in the district, and the citations his voting record had received from various taxpayer watchdog groups. Cottington & Marti of Edina, Minn., collected $123,252 for placing the broadcast ads and $13,661 for placing companion newspaper ads.

Campaign Expenditures	Barrett Amount Spent	Barrett % of Total	Fisher Amount Spent	Fisher % of Total
Overhead				
Office furniture/supplies	$ 5,167	1.39	$ 2,442	2.56
Rent/utilities	4,206	1.13	839	.88
Salaries	40,855	10.99	21,046	22.08
Taxes	1,825	.49	3,586	3.76
Bank/investment fees	4,007	1.08	24	.03
Lawyers/accountants	0		0	
Telephone	8,548	2.30	8,800	9.23
Campaign automobile	0		0	
Computers/office equipment	9,547	2.57	1,710	1.79
Travel	7,214	1.94	12,519	13.13
Food/meetings	550	.15	0	
Subtotal	**81,919**	**22.03**	**50,967**	**53.46**
Fund Raising				
Events	71,642	19.27	13,115	13.76
Direct mail	20,179	5.43	16,967	17.80
Telemarketing	6,000	1.61	0	
Subtotal	**97,821**	**26.31**	**30,082**	**31.56**
Polling	**9,700**	**2.61**	**0**	
Advertising				
Electronic media	143,930	38.71	2,881	3.02
Other media	14,517	3.90	917	.96
Subtotal	**158,446**	**42.61**	**3,798**	**3.98**
Other Campaign Activity				
Persuasion mail/brochures	6,266	1.69	3,149	3.30
Actual campaigning	13,346	3.59	6,911	7.25
Staff/volunteers	393	.11	0	
Subtotal	**20,005**	**5.38**	**10,061**	**10.55**
Constituent Gifts/ Entertainment	**41**	**.01**	**0**	
Donations to				
Candidates from same state	0		0	
Candidates from other states	0		0	
Civic organizations	20	.01	0	
Ideological groups	0		0	
Political parties	425	.11	150	.16
Subtotal	**445**	**.12**	**150**	**.16**
Unitemized Expenses	**3,482**	**.94**	**270**	**.28**
Total Campaign Expenses	**$ 371,860**		**$ 95,328**	
PAC Contributions	$ 197,875		$ 19,400	
Individual Contributions	242,372		64,281	
Total Receipts*	485,326		92,706	

*Includes PAC and individual contributions as well as interest earned, party contributions, etc.

NEVADA District 1

Rep. James Bilbray (D)

1992 Election Results

James Bilbray (D) 128,278 (58%)
Jimmy Coy Pettyjohn (R) 84,217 (38%)

Following a mutually beneficial redistricting deal between Democratic Rep. James Bilbray and Republican Rep. Barbara F. Vucanovich, Bilbray found himself running in a district with a Democratic registration edge of more than 50,000. However, when state representative and former air force officer Jimmy Coy Pettyjohn entered the race, Bilbray decided that 1992 was not the year to significantly reduce his campaign spending. While Pettyjohn spent $43,986 less than Bilbray's 1990 challenger, Bilbray reduced his spending by just $8,995.

According to Dan Geary, Bilbray's executive assistant, the campaign aired five television commercials and three companion radio ads that touted his fight against a proposed nuclear waste dump, his efforts to keep mining companies out of the Red Rock Conservation Area, and his work to secure a new veterans hospital for the district. In response to Pettyjohn's attempts to tie Bilbray to the House banking scandal, Bilbray aired spots pointing out that he had no overdrafts at the bank, had voted to close it, and had voted to reduce the House operating budget. Former press secretary Mark Fierro, who left Bilbray's congressional staff in April 1992, collected $14,000 for his creative input to the ad campaign. Altimira Communications of Las Vegas received $78,853 for producing and placing the ads.

Bilbray spent $6,047 to advertise in newspapers and magazines such as the *Las Vegas Sentinel-Voice, Jewish Reporter, Senior Times, Las Vegas Woman,* and *Nevada Today.* Program ads purchased from organizations such as the Nevada Youth Assistance Foundation, the Las Vegas Jaycees, and the Nevada Conference of Police and Sheriffs added $3,335.

Kent Industries of Las Vegas received $45,400 for coordinating day-to-day campaign operations, which accounted for 62 percent of the $72,817 Bilbray invested in grass-roots campaigning. He spent $9,211 on yard signs and posters, $2,715 on research, and $2,501 on T-shirts. Grass Roots Association of Las Vegas collected $3,283 for organizing precinct walks to distribute $9,865 worth of campaign literature. Phonebanking cost $3,222.

As in 1990, Bilbray maintained a line of bank credit, which he regularly tapped to even out his cash flow. Over the two-year election cycle, he borrowed and repaid more than $200,000. To avoid double-counting his expenditures, these loan repayments have been excluded from our analysis.

Pettyjohn had difficulty raising money for his long-shot campaign and spent only $15,821 to produce and air two television commercials. "He did a great deal of campaigning on street corners," noted campaign manager Julia Willis.

Campaign Expenditures	Bilbray Amount Spent	Bilbray % of Total	Pettyjohn Amount Spent	Pettyjohn % of Total
Overhead				
Office furniture/supplies	$ 9,943	2.44	$ 3,099	2.83
Rent/utilities	7,534	1.85	3,128	2.85
Salaries	29,488	7.23	24,119	22.01
Taxes	6,659	1.63	6,862	6.26
Bank/investment fees	4,496	1.10	136	.12
Lawyers/accountants	18,725	4.59	0	
Telephone	4,166	1.02	2,064	1.88
Campaign automobile	9,652	2.37	0	
Computers/office equipment	671	.16	1,242	1.13
Travel	21,209	5.20	264	.24
Food/meetings	3,529	.86	45	.04
Subtotal	**116,072**	**28.45**	**40,959**	**37.37**
Fund Raising				
Events	47,960	11.75	7,515	6.86
Direct mail	0		16,457	15.02
Telemarketing	0		948	.86
Subtotal	**47,960**	**11.75**	**24,919**	**22.74**
Polling	**0**		**2,000**	**1.82**
Advertising				
Electronic media	99,836	24.47	15,821	14.44
Other media	9,382	2.30	4,645	4.24
Subtotal	**109,218**	**26.77**	**20,465**	**18.67**
Other Campaign Activity				
Persuasion mail/brochures	11,142	2.73	2,599	2.37
Actual campaigning	72,817	17.85	15,621	14.25
Staff/volunteers	327	.08	294	.27
Subtotal	**84,287**	**20.66**	**18,514**	**16.89**
Constituent Gifts/Entertainment	**1,394**	**.34**	**144**	**.13**
Donations to				
Candidates from same state	0		0	
Candidates from other states	1,700	.42	0	
Civic organizations	7,199	1.76	909	.83
Ideological groups	1,547	.38	300	.27
Political parties	10,500	2.57	50	.05
Subtotal	**20,946**	**5.13**	**1,259**	**1.15**
Unitemized Expenses	**28,141**	**6.90**	**1,331**	**1.21**
Total Campaign Expenses	**$ 408,019**		**$ 109,592**	
PAC Contributions	$ 228,534		$ 9,613	
Individual Contributions	196,666		91,234	
Total Receipts*	698,431		114,361	

*Includes PAC and individual contributions as well as interest earned, party contributions, etc.

District 2 — NEVADA

Rep. Barbara F. Vucanovich (R)

1992 Election Results

Barbara F. Vucanovich (R)	129,575	(48%)
Pete Sferrazza (D)	117,199	(43%)
Daniel M. Hansen (I)	13,285	(5%)

Despite a redistricting deal that added Republican voters to her already Republican-leaning constituency, Rep. Barbara F. Vucanovich captured only 48 percent of the vote in 1992. In a five-candidate field, that proved to be enough.

Reno Mayor Pete Sferrazza poured 92 percent of his $198,391 treasury into advertising and persuasion mail. Although he had served as mayor for nearly a decade, Sferrazza ran an outsider campaign, slamming Vucanovich for her 1989 vote in favor of the congressional pay raise and for her acceptance of political action committee donations. In an attempt to pull votes from moderate Republican women, Sferrazza criticized Vucanovich for her antiabortion stance and cited an article in *McCall* magazine that named Vucanovich as one of the top ten congressional enemies of women's issues.

Vucanovich countered by spending $315,455 more on her 1992 campaign than she had in 1990, a 76 percent increase. She more than quadrupled her investment in broadcast advertising from $48,052 to $216,415. Her spending on brochures and persuasion mail went from $4,389 to $38,368.

To counter Sferrazza's outsider message, Vucanovich developed ads that pointed to his long service in government and attacked him for supporting a pay increase for Reno government employees during his tenure as mayor. The ads accused Sferrazza of violating election laws, of being an "absentee mayor" who missed numerous mayoral commission meetings, and of allowing spending by the Reno city government to increase by nearly 60 percent during his tenure. Given that "change" was the catch-phrase of 1992, Vucanovich's ads let voters know she supported congressional reform. Jay Bryant Communications of Upper Marlboro, Md., received $43,575 for creating the television and radio spots.

According to Bill Martin, president of Bill Martin Public Relations in Reno, most of Vucanovich's persuasion mail targeted Republicans "to make sure our base was solid." Independents and some Democrats in suburban Las Vegas received mailers that Martin described as "anti-Pete more than anything." In addition to handling the persuasion mail, Martin produced and placed the campaign's broadcast ads, placed newspaper and billboard ads, wrote and produced fund-raising solicitations, printed fund-raising invitations, and supplied most of the campaign's signs. Martin collected $272,706 from Vucanovich, $30,000 from the National Republican Congressional Committee, and $25,000 from the Republican National Committee for his efforts.

Vucanovich paid Tony Payton & Associates of Arlington, Va., $35,665 for providing general strategic advice.

	Vucanovich		Sferrazza	
Campaign Expenditures	Amount Spent	% of Total	Amount Spent	% of Total
Overhead				
Office furniture/supplies	$ 13,845	1.90	$ 0	
Rent/utilities	4,754	.65	200	.10
Salaries	71,691	9.83	0	
Taxes	23,229	3.18	0	
Bank/investment fees	345	.05	0	
Lawyers/accountants	0		0	
Telephone	9,560	1.31	339	.17
Campaign automobile	2,097	.29	0	
Computers/office equipment	6,600	.90	0	
Travel	58,981	8.08	1,419	.72
Food/meetings	6,020	.83	250	.13
Subtotal	**197,122**	**27.02**	**2,207**	**1.12**
Fund Raising				
Events	84,164	11.54	681	.34
Direct mail	54,786	7.51	0	
Telemarketing	0		0	
Subtotal	**138,950**	**19.04**	**681**	**.34**
Polling	**35,767**	**4.90**	**0**	
Advertising				
Electronic media	216,415	29.66	145,988	73.59
Other media	33,998	4.66	11,039	5.56
Subtotal	**250,413**	**34.32**	**157,027**	**79.15**
Other Campaign Activity				
Persuasion mail/brochures	38,368	5.26	24,929	12.57
Actual campaigning	54,964	7.53	5,645	2.85
Staff/volunteers	1,471	.20	0	
Subtotal	**94,802**	**12.99**	**30,574**	**15.42**
Constituent Gifts/ Entertainment	**2,869**	**.39**	**0**	
Donations to				
Candidates from same state	10		0	
Candidates from other states	1,850	.25	0	
Civic organizations	5,496	.75	0	
Ideological groups	1,363	.19	0	
Political parties	690	.09	0	
Subtotal	**9,409**	**1.29**	**0**	
Unitemized Expenses	**300**	**.04**	**7,903**	**3.98**
Total Campaign Expenses	**$ 729,633**		**$ 198,391**	
PAC Contributions	$ 256,119		$ 19,100	
Individual Contributions	357,191		43,618	
Total Receipts*	686,022		207,252	

*Includes PAC and individual contributions as well as interest earned, party contributions, etc.

NEW HAMPSHIRE District 1

Rep. Bill Zeliff (R)

1992 Election Results   Bill Zeliff (R)   135,936   (53%)
                          Bob Preston (D)   108,578   (42%)

After spending $820,965 on his 1990 campaign, freshman Republican Rep. Bill Zeliff had hoped to dramatically reduce his spending in 1992. Virtually unknown at the outset of his 1990 bid, Zeliff had invested heavily in television advertising to increase his name recognition, something he thought would be unnecessary in 1992. "Frankly, I think that I will have to spend no more than half as much as I did in 1990," he predicted. As it turned out, Zeliff's prediction was about $280,000 too low.

To get through the five-candidate Republican primary in 1990, Zeliff had waged a heavily negative campaign, at one point referring to one of his fellow Republicans as "a foreign agent." That caustic style had left its mark, and Zeliff again faced strong primary opposition in 1992. Manchester lawyer Ovide Lamontagne invested $131,812, attacking Zeliff for accepting money from political action committees, for spending more of his taxpayer-funded office account than necessary, and for his pro-choice stance on abortion.

Having spent $141,200 through the first fifteen months of the election cycle, Zeliff was forced to spend another $239,464 between April 1 and the September 8 primary. O'Neil, Griffin & Associates of Manchester collected $85,146 for creating and placing two television and two radio commercials. These spots focused on his fiscal conservatism and constituent service; they never mentioned Lamontagne. Each ad closed with the tagline: "No one works harder, no one cares more."

To combat the endorsement of Lamontagne by the *Manchester Union*, Zeliff spent $10,158 on persuasion mailers targeted at those areas where the *Union's* circulation was the highest. Zeliff garnered 50 percent of the vote, Lamontagne picked up 35 percent, and a third candidate received 15 percent.

O'Neil, Griffin received $168,783 for creating and placing five television and four radio ads for Zeliff's general election contest with former state senate minority leader Bob Preston. The firm also collected $13,802 for designing and placing newspaper ads.

Not all of Zeliff's spending was directly tied to his reelection. Following the 1990 campaign, Democrat Joseph F. Keefe filed a nuisance complaint with the Federal Election Commission, charging that a $150,000 loan Zeliff had made to his campaign was improper. Since the loan was made using proceeds from the sale of property Zeliff and his wife jointly owned, Keefe argued that half the loan was really an illegal campaign contribution made by Zeliff's wife. The Washington, D.C., law firm Wiley, Rein & Fielding collected $40,250 from Zeliff's 1992 campaign treasury for its work on the complaint.

Campaign Expenditures	Zeliff Amount Spent	Zeliff % of Total	Preston Amount Spent	Preston % of Total
Overhead				
Office furniture/supplies	$ 4,407	.64	$ 2,188	1.36
Rent/utilities	4,620	.67	3,810	2.36
Salaries	45,945	6.63	16,396	10.17
Taxes	16,332	2.36	0	
Bank/investment fees	561	.08	202	.13
Lawyers/accountants	72,441	10.46	0	
Telephone	7,686	1.11	4,379	2.72
Campaign automobile	0		0	
Computers/office equipment	3,340	.48	900	.56
Travel	1,675	.24	5,099	3.16
Food/meetings	132	.02	496	.31
Subtotal	**157,139**	**22.69**	**33,470**	**20.75**
Fund Raising				
Events	121,457	17.54	6,659	4.13
Direct mail	10,844	1.57	4,896	3.04
Telemarketing	0		0	
Subtotal	**132,301**	**19.10**	**11,555**	**7.16**
Polling	**21,450**	**3.10**	**0**	
Advertising				
Electronic media	254,892	36.80	72,384	44.88
Other media	18,067	2.61	4,364	2.71
Subtotal	**272,959**	**39.41**	**76,748**	**47.58**
Other Campaign Activity				
Persuasion mail/brochures	30,699	4.43	19,199	11.90
Actual campaigning	64,046	9.25	16,934	10.50
Staff/volunteers	0		300	.19
Subtotal	**94,745**	**13.68**	**36,433**	**22.59**
Constituent Gifts/ Entertainment	**1,068**	**.15**	**105**	**.06**
Donations to				
Candidates from same state	0		0	
Candidates from other states	0		0	
Civic organizations	0		50	.03
Ideological groups	0		40	.02
Political parties	0		110	.07
Subtotal	**0**		**200**	**.12**
Unitemized Expenses	**12,983**	**1.87**	**2,779**	**1.72**
Total Campaign Expenses	**$ 692,646**		**$ 161,290**	
PAC Contributions	**$ 325,915**		**$ 62,287**	
Individual Contributions	**412,832**		**81,508**	
Total Receipts*	**776,283**		**174,566**	

*Includes PAC and individual contributions as well as interest earned, party contributions, etc.

District 2 — NEW HAMPSHIRE

Rep. Dick Swett (D)

1992 Election Results

Dick Swett (D)	157,328	(62%)
Bill Hatch (R)	91,126	(36%)

As the first Democrat elected to represent District 2 since 1912, Rep. Dick Swett was thought to be a marked man from the moment he upset Republican Rep. Chuck Douglas in 1990. Determined not to be a one-term aberration, Swett spent $319,578 more to defend his seat than he spent to win it—a 69 percent increase. Much of that increase was the result of a dramatic shift in his approach to raising money.

In 1990 Swett had invested less than 1 percent of his $465,540 treasury in fund raising, a remarkable feat made possible by his wife's political connections. Katrina Lantos-Swett, the daughter of Rep. Tom Lantos (D-Calif.), had long served as a fund-raiser for her father. To fill her husband's treasury, Lantos-Swett simply picked up the telephone and tapped into a network of donors across the country. The campaign augmented her efforts by holding in-home receptions that cost a total of only $3,463.

For the 1992 campaign, Swett followed his father-in-law's example and turned to Robert H. Bassin Associates of Washington, D.C., for help with political action committee (PAC) fund raising. Over the two-year election cycle, Swett paid Bassin $53,884 for coordinating PAC receptions that helped raise $403,900—a significant increase over the $186,000 he raised from PACs in 1990.

Trips to New York, Atlanta, and Hillsborough, Calif., helped raise $317,968 from individual out-of-state donors who gave at least $200, which accounted for 85 percent of his large donations. To tap small donors, Swett initially turned to Intelligent Software Systems of San Carlos, Calif., a direct-mail consultant used by his father-in-law. As the need for money intensified, Swett also brought in A.B. Data of Milwaukee, Wis. Together, these firms helped push Swett's small contributions to $71,360. Intelligent Software and A.B. Data received $11,571 and $11,629, respectively.

The overlap between the Swett and Lantos campaigns was made virtually complete when Swett retained Rowan & Michaels of New York to provide general strategic advice and polling. For its efforts, the firm collected $42,538.

Swett increased his outlays for broadcast advertising by only 11 percent, from $192,398 to $214,481. He began airing recycled ads from 1990 on local cable systems during the 1992 Republican National Convention. Merv Weston Marketing of Manchester collected $197,740 for creating and placing Swett's commercials.

Former state representative Bill Hatch struggled to win the bitter Republican primary and lacked the resources to compete with Swett. "After the primary, we knew it was futile," Hatch lamented.

	Swett		Hatch	
Campaign Expenditures	Amount Spent	% of Total	Amount Spent	% of Total
Overhead				
Office furniture/supplies	$ 5,703	.73	$ 8,969	3.39
Rent/utilities	3,475	.44	4,050	1.53
Salaries	77,006	9.81	66,135	25.02
Taxes	343	.04	14,151	5.35
Bank/investment fees	12		0	
Lawyers/accountants	35,914	4.57	0	
Telephone	10,757	1.37	3,903	1.48
Campaign automobile	0		0	
Computers/office equipment	12,766	1.63	7,156	2.71
Travel	35,216	4.49	10,832	4.10
Food/meetings	3,060	.39	864	.33
Subtotal	184,252	23.47	116,060	43.91
Fund Raising				
Events	124,640	15.88	12,742	4.82
Direct mail	30,685	3.91	38,172	14.44
Telemarketing	0		3,236	1.22
Subtotal	155,326	19.78	54,150	20.49
Polling	15,426	1.96	30,291	11.46
Advertising				
Electronic media	214,481	27.32	42,123	15.94
Other media	8,175	1.04	300	.11
Subtotal	222,657	28.36	42,423	16.05
Other Campaign Activity				
Persuasion mail/brochures	69,593	8.86	0	
Actual campaigning	77,676	9.89	9,775	3.70
Staff/volunteers	391	.05	0	
Subtotal	147,659	18.81	9,775	3.70
Constituent Gifts/ Entertainment	6,072	.77	0	
Donations to				
Candidates from same state	1,300	.17	0	
Candidates from other states	250	.03	0	
Civic organizations	7,429	.95	150	.06
Ideological groups	0		0	
Political parties	18,600	2.37	150	.06
Subtotal	27,580	3.51	300	.11
Unitemized Expenses	26,146	3.33	11,327	4.29
Total Campaign Expenses	$ 785,118		$ 264,326	
PAC Contributions	$ 403,900		$ 35,118	
Individual Contributions	444,502		125,740	
Total Receipts*	872,187		231,226	

*Includes PAC and individual contributions as well as interest earned, party contributions, etc.

NEW JERSEY   District 1

Rep. Robert E. Andrews (D)

1992 Election Results

Robert E. Andrews (D)	153,525 (67%)
Lee A. Solomon (R)	65,123 (29%)

Rep. Robert E. Andrews had good reason to take the 1992 campaign seriously. Despite outspending his 1990 Republican opponent by nearly $500,000, Andrews had captured just 54 percent of the vote in the open seat battle set off by Democrat James J. Florio's 1989 move to the governor's mansion. Throughout 1990, Andrews had struggled to overcome anger over tax increases engineered by Florio, and the anger had not subsided by 1992.

The competition also promised to be considerably more intense. Andrews's 1990 opponent had spent only $74,790, switched his position on abortion, and claimed to have attended a college he never attended. Andrews's 1992 challenger, Republican state assemblyman Lee A. Solomon, was a veteran campaigner, and Andrews knew Solomon would have considerable resources. In response to this threat, Andrews spent $720,209—$685,745 of this during 1992.

Andrews paid the Campaign Group of Philadelphia, Pa., $300,000 to create and place three television commercials. Campaign Performance Group of San Francisco, Calif., received $175,974 for persuasion mail, and Greenberg-Lake of Washington, D.C., collected $48,486 for polling. The Research Group of Chicago, Ill., was paid $10,000 for opposition research. Robert H. Bassin Associates and Fraioli/Jost, both of Washington, D.C., received $37,839 and $6,978, respectively, for coordinating political action committee fund-raisers.

The ads and persuasion mail both sought to balance the benefits of incumbency with an outsider theme. Emblematic of that effort was the television spot dubbed "Workers." "Finally, someone in public office who keeps his word," the ad began. "Andrews promised not to raise taxes. He voted against every tax increase. Andrews promised not to take the congressional pay raise. He gave the raise to scholarships. And Andrews promised to fight for hard-working, middle-class families. He led the fight to keep the navy yard open and opposed the trade agreement with Mexico because it hurts American workers and jobs. Democrat Rob Andrews, a fighter for change. Committed to South Jersey."

Two comparison spots repeated these points and slammed Solomon for waffling on whether he would accept the congressional pay raise, for accepting contributions from the National Rifle Association, and for being a "career politician" who had voted for tax increases, increases in prescription drug copayments by senior citizens, and against an increase in the state's minimum wage. "With that record, let's make this Lee Solomon's last campaign," one spot stated.

Outspent by more than three to one, Solomon's campaign received virtually no financial support from the National Republican Congressional Committee.

	Andrews		Solomon	
Campaign Expenditures	Amount Spent	% of Total	Amount Spent	% of Total
Overhead				
Office furniture/supplies	$ 2,715	.38	$ 647	.30
Rent/utilities	4,000	.56	3,241	1.53
Salaries	8,459	1.17	21,100	9.95
Taxes	3,426	.48	0	
Bank/investment fees	5,212	.72	330	.16
Lawyers/accountants	0		0	
Telephone	730	.10	0	
Campaign automobile	0		0	
Computers/office equipment	0		3,100	1.46
Travel	1,266	.18	1,750	.82
Food/meetings	128	.02	0	
Subtotal	25,936	3.60	30,169	14.22
Fund Raising				
Events	116,715	16.21	16,153	7.61
Direct mail	0		1,404	.66
Telemarketing	0		0	
Subtotal	116,715	16.21	17,557	8.28
Polling	48,486	6.73	15,100	7.12
Advertising				
Electronic media	301,600	41.88	112,365	52.97
Other media	0		7,024	3.31
Subtotal	301,600	41.88	119,388	56.28
Other Campaign Activity				
Persuasion mail/brochures	203,456	28.25	13,444	6.34
Actual campaigning	18,848	2.62	4,922	2.32
Staff/volunteers	0		0	
Subtotal	222,304	30.87	18,366	8.66
Constituent Gifts/ Entertainment	1,000	.14	0	
Donations to				
Candidates from same state	1,000	.14	0	
Candidates from other states	0		0	
Civic organizations	600	.08	0	
Ideological groups	0		0	
Political parties	0		0	
Subtotal	1,600	.22	0	
Unitemized Expenses	2,568	.36	11,544	5.44
Total Campaign Expenses	$ 720,209		$ 212,123	
PAC Contributions	$ 345,800		$ 22,631	
Individual Contributions	323,832		147,047	
Total Receipts*	758,301		176,601	

*Includes PAC and individual contributions as well as interest earned, party contributions, etc.

District 2 — NEW JERSEY

Rep. William J. Hughes (D)

1992 Election Results

William J. Hughes (D)	132,465	(56%)
Frank A. LoBiondo (R)	98,315	(42%)

In nine previous House campaigns, Rep. William J. Hughes had never found it necessary to hire a media consultant, preferring instead to develop his ads in-house. To hold down costs in 1990, Hughes had simply recycled spots from his 1988 campaign. "For eighteen years he ran a mom-and-pop operation," noted administrative assistant Mark H. Brown.

That low-key campaign style changed dramatically in 1992. Concerned over the rising tide of anti-incumbent sentiment in New Jersey and faced with a well-funded challenge from Republican state representative Frank A. LoBiondo, Hughes paid the Campaign Group of Philadelphia, Pa., $210,030 for creating and placing four television commercials.

A spot dubbed "Ocean" pointed to Hughes's efforts to stop 300 companies and 100 municipalities from dumping sewage sludge into the Atlantic Ocean. To tap voter fears on crime, another spot focused on Hughes's work on forty anticrime laws, including legislation that allowed federal agents to seize property of suspected drug dealers. A third spot focused on his efforts to secure federal dollars for the district, reminding voters that "next year, Bill Hughes will become New Jersey's senior member of Congress, opening up even more opportunities." All three spots ended with the tagline: "Standing up for South Jersey." Hughes's final ad featured an endorsement by Jim and Sarah Brady, who cautioned voters that LoBiondo and the National Rifle Association were working jointly to defeat the nine-term incumbent.

That ad was but one salvo in the campaign's bitter flurry of charges and countercharges. Midway through the fall campaign, Hughes filed a formal complaint with the Federal Election Commission, charging that LoBiondo and his supporters had distributed a campaign poster comparing Hughes to Adolph Hitler without properly disclosing who had paid for the poster. The poster showed a picture of Hitler with the words: "Everyone in favor of gun control raise your right hand." While he had blasted Hughes for his stance on gun control, LoBiondo denied responsibility for the poster and accused Hughes's campaign of distributing it to drum up sympathy.

In addition to his television ads, Hughes spent $53,192 to directly place radio commercials, $8,373 on newspaper ads, $1,609 on billboards, and $3,303 on yard signs. To make certain that his supporters turned out, he invested $16,559 in his in-house phonebank and $9,097 in the state party's get-out-the-vote effort.

To celebrate his hard-fought victory and that of the Clinton/Gore presidential ticket, Hughes spent $8,462 of his campaign treasury on inaugural festivities.

Campaign Expenditures	Hughes Amount Spent	Hughes % of Total	LoBiondo Amount Spent	LoBiondo % of Total
Overhead				
Office furniture/supplies	$ 6,350	1.06	$ 4,107	1.38
Rent/utilities	7,087	1.18	1,515	.51
Salaries	16,050	2.67	74,306	25.01
Taxes	4,642	.77	0	
Bank/investment fees	995	.17	281	.09
Lawyers/accountants	10,073	1.67	0	
Telephone	4,591	.76	8,561	2.88
Campaign automobile	0		882	.30
Computers/office equipment	6,653	1.11	5,918	1.99
Travel	9,172	1.52	9,309	3.13
Food/meetings	3,882	.65	113	.04
Subtotal	**69,495**	**11.55**	**104,992**	**35.34**
Fund Raising				
Events	50,130	8.33	6,467	2.18
Direct mail	9,242	1.54	8,530	2.87
Telemarketing	0		0	
Subtotal	**59,372**	**9.87**	**14,997**	**5.05**
Polling	**19,500**	**3.24**	**16,200**	**5.45**
Advertising				
Electronic media	263,904	43.85	15,275	5.14
Other media	14,783	2.46	2,381	.80
Subtotal	**278,687**	**46.31**	**17,656**	**5.94**
Other Campaign Activity				
Persuasion mail/brochures	77,810	12.93	126,023	42.42
Actual campaigning	48,831	8.11	9,933	3.34
Staff/volunteers	5,673	.94	0	
Subtotal	**132,314**	**21.99**	**135,956**	**45.77**
Constituent Gifts/ Entertainment	**17,965**	**2.99**	**0**	
Donations to				
Candidates from same state	6,284	1.04	0	
Candidates from other states	0		1,000	.34
Civic organizations	8,754	1.45	0	
Ideological groups	360	.06	0	
Political parties	8,138	1.35	0	
Subtotal	**23,536**	**3.91**	**1,000**	**.34**
Unitemized Expenses	**936**	**.16**	**6,271**	**2.11**
Total Campaign Expenses	**$ 601,805**		**$ 297,072**	
PAC Contributions	$ 223,125		$ 39,862	
Individual Contributions	256,047		255,200	
Total Receipts*	513,720		324,027	

*Includes PAC and individual contributions as well as interest earned, party contributions, etc.

NEW JERSEY — District 3

H. James Saxton (R)

1992 Election Results

H. James Saxton (R)	151,368	(59%)
Timothy E. Ryan (D)	94,012	(37%)

Rep. H. James Saxton spent $315,900 less on his 1992 campaign than his 1990 effort and received 1 percent more of the vote. In 1990 Saxton spent $730,406 to beat back a $210,360 challenge by John H. Adler, a former member of the Cherry Hill City Council. Against 1992 challenger Timothy E. Ryan, a funeral home director who was neither well funded nor well known, Saxton sliced his spending by 43 percent to $414,506.

In 1990 Saxton spent 60 percent of his sizable campaign treasury on direct appeals for votes, investing $342,457 in television and radio advertising, $46,118 in brochures and persuasion mail, and $46,713 in other grass-roots campaigning. That changed radically in 1992, with only 42 percent of Saxton's much reduced budget going to direct voter appeals.

When his polls indicated that Ryan would pose little problem, Saxton opted to forgo television advertising entirely and limit his radio buys to Ryan's home turf in Ocean County. The Media Team of Alexandria, Va., charged Saxton $23,735 for consulting and design work. National Media, also of Arlington, collected $5,057 for buying air time. Additional production costs were provided in-kind by the National Republican Congressional Committee.

Persuasion mail was virtually the only aspect of voter outreach Saxton increased in 1992. Two mass mailings focused on the economy and his constituent service activities. Targeted mailings dealt with health care reform, social security, and other issues of concern to senior citizens. Volunteers walked door-to-door distributing $22,830 worth of literature. In all, Saxton put $136,462 into handouts, brochures, and mailings, an increase of nearly 200 percent over 1990.

Saxton's 1990 campaign cost $102,264 more than he raised, forcing him to tap his cash reserves. Not knowing when he might need the additional funds again, Saxton took advantage of his relatively easy contest in 1992 to fatten his campaign treasury. During the off-year he invested $63,120 to raise $275,745, building his cash reserves from $48,862 to $224,795. In 1992 he spent $58,257 to raise $349,747, leaving him with $279,382 at the close of the election cycle.

Saxton put considerable resources into attracting small contributions. He spent $72,988 on direct-mail solicitations. He held annual all-you-can-eat lobster feeds that attracted about 250 people each year. The lobsters were donated by local fisherman, so he could afford to put a $75 ticket price on the events. Donations of less than $200 amounted to $185,295.

With only $30,018 to spend, Ryan had no hope of being competitive.

Campaign Expenditures	Saxton Amount Spent	Saxton % of Total	Ryan Amount Spent	Ryan % of Total
Overhead				
Office furniture/supplies	$ 6,058	1.46	$ 603	2.01
Rent/utilities	9,550	2.30	0	
Salaries	36,124	8.70	5,300	17.66
Taxes	11,893	2.86	0	
Bank/investment fees	311	.07	138	.46
Lawyers/accountants	450	.11	1,500	5.00
Telephone	5,480	1.32	2,187	7.29
Campaign automobile	0		0	
Computers/office equipment	4,265	1.03	0	
Travel	3,139	.76	1,073	3.58
Food/meetings	2,796	.67	0	
Subtotal	**80,067**	**19.27**	**10,802**	**35.98**
Fund Raising				
Events	49,289	11.87	2,805	9.34
Direct mail	72,988	17.57	0	
Telemarketing	0		0	
Subtotal	**122,277**	**29.44**	**2,805**	**9.34**
Polling	**14,450**	**3.48**	**2,000**	**6.66**
Advertising				
Electronic media	28,951	6.97	3,315	11.04
Other media	1,497	.36	287	.96
Subtotal	**30,448**	**7.33**	**3,602**	**12.00**
Other Campaign Activity				
Persuasion mail/brochures	136,462	32.85	6,610	22.02
Actual campaigning	7,712	1.86	3,249	10.82
Staff/volunteers	573	.14	0	
Subtotal	**144,747**	**34.84**	**9,859**	**32.84**
Constituent Gifts/Entertainment	**6,556**	**1.58**	**0**	
Donations to				
Candidates from same state	2,000	.48	0	
Candidates from other states	1,000	.24	0	
Civic organizations	0		0	
Ideological groups	30	.01	0	
Political parties	250	.06	0	
Subtotal	**3,280**	**.79**	**0**	
Unitemized Expenses	**13,581**	**3.27**	**950**	**3.16**
Total Campaign Expenses	**$ 415,406**		**$ 30,018**	
PAC Contributions	**$ 278,875**		**$ 6,950**	
Individual Contributions	**343,978**		**23,011**	
Total Receipts*	**647,329**		**30,561**	

*Includes PAC and individual contributions as well as interest earned, party contributions, etc.

District 4 — NEW JERSEY

Rep. Christopher H. Smith (R)

1992 Election Results

Christopher H. Smith (R) 149,095 (62%)
Brian M. Hughes (D) 84,514 (35%)

Although Republican Rep. Christopher H. Smith had captured more than 60 percent of the vote in his previous four campaigns, Democrats had reason to be hopeful in 1992. As a result of redistricting, one-third of Smith's constituents were new to him. Even though the new map brought additional Republicans into District 4, the Democratic challenger, Brian M. Hughes, was the son of popular former governor Richard J. Hughes. The Hughes legacy seemed likely to produce a substantial campaign treasury.

Hughes came out swinging. He charged that Smith wanted to "spend public money on private schools," attacked him for refusing to take a strong position on health care reform, and tried to tie Smith to the Bush administration's economic policies. As each of Smith's past Democratic challengers had done, Hughes also attacked Smith for his belief that abortion should be allowed only to save the life of the mother. Referring to Smith as a "zealot" and a "fanatic," Hughes charged that the incumbent had used his congressional office account to finance antiabortion activities. Unfortunately for Hughes, the abortion issue proved to be of no greater concern to Smith's new constituents than it had been to his old.

Having spent just $34,559 to keep his campaign running during the off-year, Smith responded to Hughes's challenge with a $379,833 burst during 1992. The $414,392 Smith spent during the two-year cycle was $76,148 more than he had invested in any of his previous House campaigns.

Most of Smith's increased spending was put into persuasion mail. In 1990 Smith invested $66,132, 23 percent of his total spending, in printing and sending his campaign literature. In 1992 his $164,407 in-house persuasion mail effort represented 40 percent of his reelection expenses. The mailings touted his constituent service, his sponsorship of legislation to benefit veterans, his efforts to prevent polluters from suing municipalities to help defray their cleanup costs, and his position on the Foreign Affairs Committee. The mailings also included accusations that Hughes padded his resume by falsely claiming to have testified before a congressional committee.

Smith also reduced his outlays for broadcast advertising, from $42,326 in 1990 to $39,962 in 1992. As in 1990, both the radio and cable television commercials were produced and placed without the aid of a media consultant.

Smith's only consultant, pollster Tarrance & Associates of Alexandria, Va., collected $11,738 from Smith and $3,750 from the National Republican Congressional Committee.

Campaign Expenditures	Smith Amount Spent	Smith % of Total	Hughes Amount Spent	Hughes % of Total
Overhead				
Office furniture/supplies	$ 10,008	2.42	$ 2,831	1.58
Rent/utilities	5,682	1.37	5,852	3.27
Salaries	41,071	9.91	23,772	13.30
Taxes	21,650	5.22	0	
Bank/investment fees	0		170	.10
Lawyers/accountants	5,423	1.31	0	
Telephone	2,363	.57	3,065	1.71
Campaign automobile	0		0	
Computers/office equipment	5,895	1.42	4,034	2.26
Travel	9,115	2.20	4,114	2.30
Food/meetings	229	.06	0	
Subtotal	101,436	24.48	43,839	24.52
Fund Raising				
Events	12,138	2.93	18,284	10.23
Direct mail	18,552	4.48	2,290	1.28
Telemarketing	0		9,266	5.18
Subtotal	30,690	7.41	29,841	16.69
Polling	15,487	3.74	23,489	13.14
Advertising				
Electronic media	39,962	9.64	17,038	9.53
Other media	10,272	2.48	12	.01
Subtotal	50,234	12.12	17,049	9.54
Other Campaign Activity				
Persuasion mail/brochures	164,407	39.67	18,864	10.55
Actual campaigning	21,333	5.15	33,152	18.54
Staff/volunteers	138	.03	56	.03
Subtotal	185,879	44.86	52,072	29.13
Constituent Gifts/ Entertainment	7,808	1.88	0	
Donations to				
Candidates from same state	4,375	1.06	0	
Candidates from other states	5,000	1.21	25	.01
Civic organizations	500	.12	65	.04
Ideological groups	0		400	.22
Political parties	6,194	1.49	1,076	.60
Subtotal	16,069	3.88	1,566	.88
Unitemized Expenses	6,788	1.64	10,475	5.86
Total Campaign Expenses	$ 414,392		$ 178,773	
PAC Contributions	$ 110,958		$ 23,761	
Individual Contributions	225,611		144,657	
Total Receipts*	369,949		176,898	

*Includes PAC and individual contributions as well as interest earned, party contributions, etc.

NEW JERSEY — District 5

Rep. Marge Roukema (R)

1992 Election Results

Marge Roukema (R)	196,198	(72%)
Frank R. Lucas (D)	67,579	(25%)

Campaign Expenditures	Roukema Amount Spent	Roukema % of Total	Lucas Amount Spent	Lucas % of Total
Overhead				
Office furniture/supplies	$ 5,666	1.03	$ 90	7.39
Rent/utilities	18,310	3.32	0	
Salaries	76,983	13.95	0	
Taxes	31,766	5.76	0	
Bank/investment fees	72	.01	0	
Lawyers/accountants	5,315	.96	0	
Telephone	5,594	1.01	0	
Campaign automobile	0		0	
Computers/office equipment	10,267	1.86	0	
Travel	7,537	1.37	0	
Food/meetings	64	.01	0	
Subtotal	161,574	29.28	90	7.39
Fund Raising				
Events	54,716	9.92	0	
Direct mail	17,991	3.26	0	
Telemarketing	0		0	
Subtotal	72,707	13.18	0	
Polling	0		0	
Advertising				
Electronic media	6,863	1.24	0	
Other media	16,223	2.94	0	
Subtotal	23,086	4.18	0	
Other Campaign Activity				
Persuasion mail/brochures	238,645	43.25	220	18.06
Actual campaigning	17,261	3.13	630	51.72
Staff/volunteers	81	.01	0	
Subtotal	255,987	46.39	850	69.79
Constituent Gifts/ Entertainment	0		0	
Donations to				
Candidates from same state	630	.11	0	
Candidates from other states	0		0	
Civic organizations	26,468	4.80	0	
Ideological groups	1,110	.20	0	
Political parties	5,765	1.04	0	
Subtotal	33,973	6.16	0	
Unitemized Expenses	4,435	.80	278	22.81
Total Campaign Expenses	$ 551,762		$ 1,218	
PAC Contributions	$ 224,598		$ 0	
Individual Contributions	199,599		1,000	
Total Receipts*	439,150		2,080	

*Includes PAC and individual contributions as well as interest earned, party contributions, etc.

Landslide victories had become the norm for Rep. Marge Roukema. First elected in 1980, Roukema had collected at least 65 percent of the vote in each of her five reelection bids. In 1986, 1988, and 1990 she had garnered 75 percent or better. The 1992 campaign was simply more of the same.

Roukema spent $106,361 to keep her campaign running during the off-year, including $57,917 on overhead. Rent on her permanent campaign headquarters amounted to $9,660. Salaries for her three part-time employees totaled $26,989. Taxes added $12,284. Helbring, Lindman, Goldstein & Seigal of Newark collected $5,000 for representing Roukema's interests in the redistricting process.

Redistricting added Warren County to her domain, but this did little to change the district's solidly Republican character. Roukema's bout with anti-incumbency was limited to the Republican primary, where she faced opposition for the first time since 1986. Attorney Lou Sette spent $63,565 on his challenge, attacking Roukema for favoring abortion rights and voting in favor of excessive government spending.

To counter Sette's attacks, as well as an independent campaign launched by religious fundamentalists, Roukema spent $99,516 on preprimary persuasion mail, including $34,736 to David J. Murray & Associates of Princeton for producing the mailers. One piece defending her stance on abortion was targeted to women. To reach voters in the least densely populated areas, the campaign spent $6,863 to place ads on five radio stations during the final days of the campaign. An in-house phonebank added $3,837.

While the general election campaign against Frank R. Lucas proved uneventful, Roukema took nothing for granted. She invested $139,129 in persuasion mail that touted her record as a fiscal conservative and pointed to her leadership on the Family and Medical Leave Act. Murray collected $43,136 for producing the brochures. Phonebanking over the final month of the fall campaign cost $4,026.

Roukema spent virtually nothing on newspaper advertising. Her expenses for "other media" consisted almost entirely of program ads purchased from organizations such as the Girl Scout Council of Bergen County, the Women's Rights Information Center, the Anti-Defamation League, Hackensack Medical Center, and the William Paterson College Foundation.

While she spent none of her campaign funds on constituent entertainment and gifts, Roukema donated $26,468 to charities and civic organizations, including the American Red Cross, the Eastern Christian Children's Retreat, the National Organization of Italian Women, and the Family Counseling Service. She also gave $6,265 to various state and local Republican party organizations.

District 6 — NEW JERSEY

Rep. Frank Pallone, Jr.

1992 Election Results

Frank Pallone, Jr. (D)	118,266	(52%)
Joseph M. Kyrillos (R)	100,949	(45%)

Before the state's redistricting plan was announced in March 1992, Rep. Frank Pallone, Jr., knew he would face an uphill reelection battle. Having won his District 3 seat in 1988 with 52 percent of the vote, Pallone had prevailed by only 4,258 votes in 1990. Despite outspending his 1990 Republican challenger by more than five to one, Pallone had captured just 49 percent of the vote in a five-candidate field. Redistricting appeared to seal Pallone's fate when mapmakers dismembered his old district and set up a Democratic primary confrontation with Rep. Bernard J. Dwyer in District 6.

However, Dwyer retired, and instead of facing a six-term incumbent on his home turf, Pallone found himself facing state representative Bob Smith, homemaker Barbara Jensen, and systems analyst Jeffrey R. Gorman in the June primary. During the two-month campaign, Pallone spent more than $390,000, including $102,215 on broadcast advertising created and placed by Message & Media of New Brunswick. He spent $92,237 on campaign literature and persuasion mail. Expenditures for various get-out-the-vote efforts amounted to $53,006, including per diem payments of $23,000 to election day workers. Yard signs and posters added $22,638.

With the campaign slogan "Our best hope—their worst nightmare," Pallone presented himself as an outsider. He toured the district in a 1974 Ford Maverick to symbolize that he had frequently taken positions in opposition to the House Democratic leadership, pointing to his 1989 vote against the congressional pay raise as one example. Although Smith was able to match Pallone's spending and had Dwyer's endorsement, Pallone received 55 percent of the vote.

Pallone's off-year spending and preprimary splurge left him with about $400,000 for the fall campaign against Republican state senator Joseph M. Kyrillos. As he had in the primary, Pallone ran as an outsider, drawing up a "Declaration of Independence" that cited examples of his breaking ranks with the House Democratic leadership. He sank $166,346 into brochures and persuasion mail, including $71,776 paid to the Campaign Design Group of Washington, D.C. He paid Message & Media another $80,567 for broadcast advertising.

Kyrillos spent about $145,000 on the Republican primary, which allowed him to devote more than $275,000 to the head-to-head contest with Pallone. With infusions of $22,920 from the Republican National Committee, $14,492 from the National Republican Congressional Committee, and $17,000 from the New Jersey Republican State Committee, Kyrillos was financially competitive, but his campaign suffered considerably from President George Bush's 39 percent showing in the district.

Campaign Expenditures	Pallone Amount Spent	Pallone % of Total	Kyrillos Amount Spent	Kyrillos % of Total
Overhead				
Office furniture/supplies	$ 13,510	1.51	$ 971	.23
Rent/utilities	14,360	1.61	5,228	1.24
Salaries	146,855	16.42	47,178	11.21
Taxes	17,414	1.95	14,552	3.46
Bank/investment fees	312	.03	0	
Lawyers/accountants	1,000	.11	0	
Telephone	3,307	.37	9,184	2.18
Campaign automobile	0		0	
Computers/office equipment	6,565	.73	8,142	1.93
Travel	7,596	.85	719	.17
Food/meetings	241	.03	0	
Subtotal	**211,159**	**23.61**	**85,974**	**20.43**
Fund Raising				
Events	75,089	8.40	32,235	7.66
Direct mail	0		0	
Telemarketing	0		9,672	2.30
Subtotal	**75,089**	**8.40**	**41,907**	**9.96**
Polling	**24,653**	**2.76**	**16,956**	**4.03**
Advertising				
Electronic media	182,782	20.44	105,424	25.05
Other media	3,746	.42	12,341	2.93
Subtotal	**186,528**	**20.86**	**117,765**	**27.98**
Other Campaign Activity				
Persuasion mail/brochures	258,583	28.91	115,726	27.50
Actual campaigning	104,863	11.73	26,402	6.27
Staff/volunteers	6,307	.71	157	.04
Subtotal	**369,753**	**41.34**	**142,285**	**33.81**
Constituent Gifts/Entertainment	**3,724**	**.42**	**0**	
Donations to				
Candidates from same state	2,135	.24	500	.12
Candidates from other states	0		0	
Civic organizations	3,149	.35	0	
Ideological groups	5,501	.62	0	
Political parties	4,907	.55	800	.19
Subtotal	**15,692**	**1.75**	**1,300**	**.31**
Unitemized Expenses	**7,753**	**.87**	**14,657**	**3.48**
Total Campaign Expenses	**$ 894,352**		**$ 420,844**	
PAC Contributions	**$ 531,079**		**$ 97,881**	
Individual Contributions	**375,665**		**297,304**	
Total Receipts*	**932,079**		**408,460**	

*Includes PAC and individual contributions as well as interest earned, party contributions, etc.

NEW JERSEY District 7

Rep. Bob Franks (R)

1992 Election Results

Bob Franks (R) 132,174 (53%)
Leonard R. Sendelsky (D) 105,761 (43%)

Ten-term Republican Rep. Matthew J. Rinaldo appeared headed toward an easy victory when he announced his retirement less than two months before the November 3 election. Rinaldo's eleventh-hour replacement on the ballot was state representative Bob Franks, who grabbed the nomination at a special convention of party leaders held September 15. "The short campaign was actually a benefit," noted Greg M. Edwards, Franks's congressional chief of staff. "There was a real sense of urgency."

Given the prohibitive cost of television advertising in New Jersey, Franks invested 26 percent of his treasury in brochures and persuasion mailers. Registered Republicans and unaffiliated voters received a general biographical piece touting Franks's leadership role in the unsuccessful fight to block Democratic Gov. James J. Florio's unpopular plan to raise taxes. Women and registered Democrats received a mailer pointing out that Franks's Democratic opponent, real estate developer Leonard R. Sendelsky, had been endorsed by the National Rifle Association. Anticipating that Sendelsky would attack him for his attendance record in the state assembly, Franks struck first with a mailer that slammed Sendelsky's attendance record during his tenure on the state Building Authority. Welch Communications of Arlington, Va., collected $87,013 from Franks, $20,700 from the New Jersey State Republican party, and $11,200 from the National Republican Congressional Committee for producing six mailers and a brochure that was distributed by door-to-door canvassers. The state party also augmented Franks's budget for the mailings with stamp purchases totaling $4,286.

Franks paid Mike Murphy Media of Washington, D.C., $99,186 for two radio commercials, one of which focused on his antitax stance. To increase his name recognition in portions of the district he had not represented in the state legislature, Franks invested $13,997 in billboard ads, $3,711 in signs, and $3,009 in buttons and bumper stickers. To publicize his campaign rallies, Franks spent $4,217 on newspaper ads.

Considerable resources were devoted to identifying Franks's supporters and making certain they turned out on election day. Franks spent $4,347 for computer tapes containing the names and telephone numbers of district residents and paid Payco American Corp. of Brookfield, Wis., $22,000 for phone-banking. He spent $6,780 on an election day mailing to Republicans and unaffiliated voters in precincts where Republican turnout had been high in past elections, reminding them to vote. Another $5,000 was spent on miscellaneous election day expenses.

Despite his reputation as one of the state's top Democratic fund-raisers, Sandelsky was unable to match Franks's six-week spending blitz.

Campaign Expenditures	Franks Amount Spent	Franks % of Total	Sendelsky Amount Spent	Sendelsky % of Total
Overhead				
Office furniture/supplies	$ 1,773	.37	$ 6,115	2.64
Rent/utilities	5,671	1.20	4,722	2.04
Salaries	49,376	10.43	15,691	6.78
Taxes	29,028	6.13	0	
Bank/investment fees	0		102	.04
Lawyers/accountants	0		0	
Telephone	11,717	2.48	5,533	2.39
Campaign automobile	2,038	.43	0	
Computers/office equipment	2,960	.63	945	.41
Travel	7,323	1.55	3,788	1.64
Food/meetings	1,042	.22	26	.01
Subtotal	**110,929**	**23.44**	**36,921**	**15.96**
Fund Raising				
Events	19,404	4.10	29,085	12.57
Direct mail	4,271	.90	2,286	.99
Telemarketing	0		0	
Subtotal	**23,675**	**5.00**	**31,371**	**13.56**
Polling	**21,444**	**4.53**	**20,300**	**8.78**
Advertising				
Electronic media	100,475	21.23	40,199	17.38
Other media	18,434	3.90	9,100	3.93
Subtotal	**118,909**	**25.13**	**49,298**	**21.31**
Other Campaign Activity				
Persuasion mail/brochures	123,867	26.17	57,888	25.03
Actual campaigning	59,384	12.55	28,136	12.16
Staff/volunteers	2,230	.47	536	.23
Subtotal	**185,480**	**39.19**	**86,561**	**37.42**
Constituent Gifts/Entertainment	**3,736**	**.79**	**0**	
Donations to				
Candidates from same state	4,100	.87	0	
Candidates from other states	0		0	
Civic organizations	100	.02	274	.12
Ideological groups	1,525	.32	0	
Political parties	3,150	.67	1,170	.51
Subtotal	**8,875**	**1.88**	**1,444**	**.62**
Unitemized Expenses	**204**	**.04**	**5,403**	**2.34**
Total Campaign Expenses	**$ 473,253**		**$ 231,298**	
PAC Contributions	**$ 131,032**		**$ 36,965**	
Individual Contributions	304,576		152,289	
Total Receipts*	460,998		224,844	

*Includes PAC and individual contributions as well as interest earned, party contributions, etc.

District 8 — NEW JERSEY

Rep. Herbert C. Klein (D)

1992 Election Results

Herbert C. Klein (D)	96,742	(47%)
Joseph L. Bubba (R)	84,674	(41%)
Gloria J. Kolodziej (I)	16,170	(8%)

When Democratic Rep. Robert A. Roe decided not to seek a thirteenth term, attorney and former state representative Herbert C. Klein decided to turn his talents as a prodigious Democratic fund-raiser to his own advantage. Despite entering the race just six months before the November 3 election, Klein was the only New Jersey candidate to spend more than $1 million.

Klein spent less than $75,000 through the June 2 Democratic primary. He paid Bay Communications of Edgewater, Md., $26,925 to produce one persuasion mailer and spent $10,625 on postage. Pollster Penn & Schoen Associates of New York collected a $1,363 consulting fee and $6,500 for preprimary phonebanking to identify and turn out Klein's supporters. Fenn & King Communications of Washington, D.C., received $3,750 for initial consultations on Klein's general election advertising campaign. Klein paid Jackie Yustein of Glen Ridge $6,125 for coordinating in-state fund-raisers. Klein won the five-candidate primary with 39 percent of the vote.

Over the next six months, Fenn & King billed Klein's campaign $356,867 for creating and placing four radio commercials and a single television ad, which ran exclusively on local cable systems. Bay Communications collected $186,628 for persuasion mail. Penn & Schoen received $32,000 for polling and $16,831 for phonebanking. Klein spent $13,937 for opposition research provided by the Research Group of Chicago, Ill. He paid Yustein another $20,318 for staging in-state fund-raisers. Assets Consulting Services received $11,659 for coordinating political action committee receptions in Washington, D.C.

Over the final month of the general election campaign, Klein and his opponent, state senator Joseph L. Bubba, traded punches over ethics. Unfortunately for Bubba, Klein had nearly three times the money to invest in advertising and persuasion mail.

Bubba hit first with a radio ad and mailer charging that Klein had used political connections to win changes in state regulations governing wetlands that benefited a real estate developer his law firm represented. "No wonder he's a millionaire," the ad noted.

Klein returned fire, attacking Bubba for accepting $46,000 in campaign contributions "from a known felon convicted of bribery." While the dollar amount was correct, the ad failed to note that Bubba had received the contributions over several years before the bribery charges were filed. In other ads and mailers Klein attacked Bubba for failing to pay property taxes on an addition to his house, for voting in favor of legislation in which he had a financial stake, and for taking money from the National Rifle Association.

Independent Gloria Kolodziej spent $3,850 and siphoned off 8 percent of the vote.

Campaign Expenditures	Klein Amount Spent	Klein % of Total	Bubba Amount Spent	Bubba % of Total
Overhead				
Office furniture/supplies	$ 6,582	.66	$ 2,018	.49
Rent/utilities	7,816	.78	6,500	1.59
Salaries	42,844	4.28	30,721	7.53
Taxes	11,364	1.14	14,093	3.45
Bank/investment fees	0		35	.01
Lawyers/accountants	0		0	
Telephone	9,157	.92	3,259	.80
Campaign automobile	0		0	
Computers/office equipment	10,571	1.06	5,903	1.45
Travel	1,914	.19	4,553	1.12
Food/meetings	33		2,542	.62
Subtotal	**90,281**	**9.02**	**69,625**	**17.06**
Fund Raising				
Events	68,021	6.80	29,956	7.34
Direct mail	0		1,523	.37
Telemarketing	0		0	
Subtotal	**68,021**	**6.80**	**31,479**	**7.72**
Polling	**33,363**	**3.33**	**20,200**	**4.95**
Advertising				
Electronic media	361,043	36.08	82,000	20.10
Other media	3,609	.36	1,144	.28
Subtotal	**364,653**	**36.44**	**83,144**	**20.38**
Other Campaign Activity				
Persuasion mail/brochures	365,700	36.54	177,715	43.56
Actual campaigning	65,075	6.50	21,559	5.28
Staff/volunteers	2,413	.24	1,008	.25
Subtotal	**433,188**	**43.29**	**200,282**	**49.09**
Constituent Gifts/Entertainment	0		0	
Donations to				
Candidates from same state	0		0	
Candidates from other states	0		0	
Civic organizations	0		377	.09
Ideological groups	0		440	.11
Political parties	3,500	.35	322	.08
Subtotal	**3,500**	**.35**	**1,140**	**.28**
Unitemized Expenses	**7,695**	**.77**	**2,150**	**.53**
Total Campaign Expenses	**$ 1,000,701**		**$ 408,021**	
PAC Contributions	$ 173,920		$ 115,849	
Individual Contributions	423,134		236,014	
Total Receipts*	1,291,518		435,590	

*Includes PAC and individual contributions as well as interest earned, party contributions, etc.

NEW JERSEY   District 9

Rep. Robert G. Torricelli (D)

1992 Election Results   Robert G. Torricelli (D)   139,188   (58%)
                           Patrick J. Roma (R)   88,179   (37%)

Like all Democrats in New Jersey, Rep. Robert G. Torricelli had to be concerned with lingering voter anger over the $2.8 billion tax increase engineered in 1990 by Democratic Gov. James J. Florio. Twenty-seven overdrafts at the House bank—the most by any member of the New Jersey delegation—gave Torricelli additional food for thought. His insurance policy was a $996,795 campaign, which was $145,131 more than he had invested in his previous two campaigns, combined.

In 1990 Torricelli had spent just $36,534 on broadcast advertising, but fears of an anti-incumbent backlash prompted him to spend $313,760 on such ads in 1992. In addition to radio commercials, which are the advertising staple of New Jersey politics, Torricelli opted to air television spots on local cable outlets. Joe Slade White & Co. of New York collected $62,314 for creating the ads. Shafto & Barton of Houston, Texas, billed the campaign $250,824 to cover the cost of air time and the firm's placement fees.

Torricelli more than doubled his spending on campaign literature and persuasion mail, from $100,798 in 1990 to $233,064 in 1992. To personalize and soften his image, Torricelli's biographical piece featured a boyhood picture of the five-term incumbent with his mother. To distance himself from the Washington establishment, his mailers stressed his commitment to work for "change," his integrity, and his willingness to buck conventional wisdom. While they sought to avoid a "pork barrel" image, the mailers portrayed Torricelli as a House member who worked hard for the district. One piece criticized Republican state representative Patrick J. Roma for his stance on gun control and pointed to Roma's endorsement by the National Rifle Association. Torricelli paid Media Plus of Washington, D.C., $135,197 for designing and producing most of the mailers. The November Group, also of Washington, collected $10,690 for creating several targeted mailings.

Outspent by nearly six to one, Roma nevertheless waged an aggressive anti-incumbent campaign. He passed out thousands of rubber checks that read "Bouncy Savings & Loan; Bounce Torricelli—Elect Roma." The cover of one Roma mailer showed a picture of a sleeping baby with the words, "Bob Torricelli could have helped crack babies survive. But he helped himself instead." Inside, the mailer attacked Torricelli for voting against an appropriations bill that would have transferred $45 million of the budget for franked mail to a fund established to care for babies born with an addiction to crack cocaine. Roma's $79,721 persuasion mail budget received a $24,328 boost from the National Republican Congressional Committee.

Campaign Expenditures	Torricelli Amount Spent	Torricelli % of Total	Roma Amount Spent	Roma % of Total
Overhead				
Office furniture/supplies	$ 7,669	.77	$ 1,605	.93
Rent/utilities	22,901	2.30	1,800	1.05
Salaries	62,817	6.30	17,631	10.24
Taxes	18,316	1.84	13,755	7.99
Bank/investment fees	178	.02	105	.06
Lawyers/accountants	8,171	.82	0	
Telephone	11,611	1.16	1,620	.94
Campaign automobile	11,482	1.15	0	
Computers/office equipment	4,325	.43	3,362	1.95
Travel	9,761	.98	1,342	.78
Food/meetings	2,287	.23	56	.03
Subtotal	**159,517**	**16.00**	**41,275**	**23.98**
Fund Raising				
Events	174,697	17.53	7,261	4.22
Direct mail	0		18,621	10.82
Telemarketing	0		430	.25
Subtotal	**174,697**	**17.53**	**26,311**	**15.28**
Polling	**26,275**	**2.64**	**2,500**	**1.45**
Advertising				
Electronic media	313,760	31.48	0	
Other media	27,882	2.80	3,666	2.13
Subtotal	**341,643**	**34.27**	**3,666**	**2.13**
Other Campaign Activity				
Persuasion mail/brochures	233,064	23.38	79,721	46.31
Actual campaigning	32,052	3.22	15,658	9.10
Staff/volunteers	4,240	.43	0	
Subtotal	**269,355**	**27.02**	**95,379**	**55.41**
Constituent Gifts/ Entertainment	7,286	.73	0	
Donations to				
Candidates from same state	0		0	
Candidates from other states	4,250	.43	0	
Civic organizations	2,200	.22	2,540	1.48
Ideological groups	0		25	.01
Political parties	700	.07	0	
Subtotal	**7,150**	**.72**	**2,565**	**1.49**
Unitemized Expenses	**10,871**	**1.09**	**446**	**.26**
Total Campaign Expenses	**$ 996,795**		**$ 172,142**	
PAC Contributions	**$ 350,495**		**$ 29,550**	
Individual Contributions	**698,325**		**128,385**	
Total Receipts*	**1,190,045**		**176,768**	

*Includes PAC and individual contributions as well as interest earned, party contributions, etc.

District 10 — NEW JERSEY

Rep. Donald M. Payne (D)

1992 Election Results

Donald M. Payne (D)   117,287   (78%)
Alfred D. Palermo (R)   30,160   (20%)

Rep. Donald M. Payne had little reason to wage an aggressive campaign in 1992. After winning the seat with 77 percent of the general election vote in 1988, Payne had no opposition in the 1990 Democratic primary and grabbed 81 percent of the general election vote. Redistricting had marginally increased the black population in his already majority-black district from 58 percent to 60 percent. While he attracted three primary opponents in 1992, none spent as much as $5,000.

In this perfectly safe political environment, Payne devoted only 16 percent of his $285,219 budget to direct appeals for votes. He spent nothing on radio or television advertising and only $185 on newspaper ads. The remainder of his $5,343 advertising budget was spent on program ads that were as much contributions to charitable and ideological organizations as they were advertisements. Among the dozens of program ads he purchased in 1991 was a $100 ad with Essex County College, a $75 ad with the National Organization of Black Law Enforcement Executives, a $162 ad with the Newark chapter of the NAACP, and a $150 ad with the Industrial Union Council of Crawford, N.J. The pattern was repeated and escalated in 1992.

Virtually all of the $24,062 Payne invested to print and mail campaign literature was spent before the Democratic primary. Payne spent only $2,839 on signs and $1,353 on buttons and other campaign handouts. Per diem payments to election day workers added $4,800.

Payne's biggest expense by far was the $147,862 he invested in raising money, which accounted for 52 percent of his total expenditures. These costs were driven largely by the $68,024 Payne paid his brother William for serving as the campaign's fund-raising consultant.

To attract political action committee (PAC) contributions, Payne held at least five fund-raisers in Washington, D.C., including an annual event at the National Democratic Club, a reception at the United Brotherhood of Carpenter's Hall, and an evening at Ford's Theater. PAC donations amounted to $183,606, or 51 percent of his total receipts.

To celebrate his reelection in 1990, Payne spent $4,166 on an inaugural party in January 1991. Various awards and plaques given to constituents cost $1,550. He spent $1,343 on flowers for constituents and $856 to entertain them. He gave away a total of $45,240—$525 more than he invested in appeals for votes.

Insurance agent Alfred D. Palermo had no opposition in the Republican primary and spent only $24,678 on his long-shot campaign.

Campaign Expenditures	Payne Amount Spent	Payne % of Total	Palermo Amount Spent	Palermo % of Total
Overhead				
Office furniture/supplies	$ 3,790	1.33	$ 19	.08
Rent/utilities	8,400	2.95	400	1.62
Salaries	0		0	
Taxes	2,173	.76	0	
Bank/investment fees	34	.01	0	
Lawyers/accountants	0		0	
Telephone	1,752	.61	0	
Campaign automobile	0		0	
Computers/office equipment	3,500	1.23	0	
Travel	10,077	3.53	0	
Food/meetings	9,761	3.42	0	
Subtotal	39,486	13.84	419	1.70
Fund Raising				
Events	147,862	51.84	0	
Direct mail	0		0	
Telemarketing	0		0	
Subtotal	147,862	51.84	0	
Polling	0		0	
Advertising				
Electronic media	0		2,681	10.86
Other media	5,343	1.87	3,286	13.31
Subtotal	5,343	1.87	5,966	24.18
Other Campaign Activity				
Persuasion mail/brochures	24,062	8.44	17,456	70.73
Actual campaigning	15,259	5.35	674	2.73
Staff/volunteers	51	.02	163	.66
Subtotal	39,372	13.80	18,293	74.13
Constituent Gifts/ Entertainment	7,915	2.78	0	
Donations to				
Candidates from same state	4,240	1.49	0	
Candidates from other states	19,500	6.84	0	
Civic organizations	11,790	4.13	0	
Ideological groups	1,610	.56	0	
Political parties	8,100	2.84	0	
Subtotal	45,240	15.86	0	
Unitemized Expenses	0		0	
Total Campaign Expenses	$ 285,219		$ 24,678	
PAC Contributions	$ 183,606		$ 1,305	
Individual Contributions	142,750		15,110	
Total Receipts*	358,688		26,277	

*Includes PAC and individual contributions as well as interest earned, party contributions, etc.

NEW JERSEY — District 11

Rep. Dean A. Gallo (R)

1992 Election Results

Dean A. Gallo (R)	188,165	(70%)
Ona Spiridellis (D)	68,871	(26%)

In three previous reelection campaigns, Rep. Dean A. Gallo had not received less than 65 percent of the vote. Gallo's combined spending in those three races was $1,839,499; his three opponents had spent a combined total of $272,807. Neither redistricting nor anti-incumbent sentiment gave him any reason to alter his nonstop, free-spending campaign style in 1992.

Gallo spent $176,943 to maintain his permanent campaign operation during 1991—$62,222 more than Democrat Ona Spiridellis was able to muster for her entire campaign. Gallo's 1991 overhead expenses totaled $52,428, or only about $14,000 less than Spiridellis put into direct appeals for votes. His off-year fund-raising outlays of $105,462 amounted to $39,100 more than Spiridellis spent on direct voter appeals.

As in past campaigns, Gallo's fund-raising efforts were inefficient by design. While he held an annual high-yield reception for political action committees (PACs) in Washington, D.C., and staged both periodic dinners and an annual Christmas party for his $1,000 donors, many of Gallo's events were designed primarily to get more people involved in the campaign and to maintain contact with loyal supporters.

His low-dollar events included an annual golf outing, which cost $11,863 in 1991 and $11,552 in 1992. To make sure that lucky participants did not carry off what little profits the golf outings generated, Gallo spent a total of $1,331 on hole-in-one insurance for the two events. Once each year Gallo rented a luxury box at the Meadowlands Racetrack and invited supporters to join him for an evening of horse racing. The two catered events cost the campaign $18,261 and raised little more than they cost. An afternoon of professional football at Giants Stadium cost $1,802 in 1991 and $2,501 in 1992. Souvenir shirts and mugs given away at the golf tournament and other events added $3,651.

For organizing these events, as well as several small receptions, Gallo paid Lynn Shapiro of Red Bank $82,649. Odell, Roper & Associates of Golden, Colo., received $33,951 for direct-mail fund raising. Over the two-year election cycle, Gallo's fund-raising expenses amounted to $247,603, or 40 percent of his total spending. He raised $243,730 from individuals who gave $200 or more, $187,284 from PACs, and $130,385 from individuals who gave less than $200.

Only 32 percent of Gallo's spending was committed to direct appeals for votes. Welch Communications of Arlington, Va., collected $116,996 for creating and placing Gallo's one radio commercial, producing his persuasion mailers, and supplying yard signs, bumper stickers, and other campaign paraphernalia.

Campaign Expenditures	Gallo Amount Spent	Gallo % of Total	Spiridellis Amount Spent	Spiridellis % of Total
Overhead				
Office furniture/supplies	$ 8,559	1.39	$ 1,892	1.65
Rent/utilities	18,100	2.93	327	.28
Salaries	33,820	5.48	13,497	11.77
Taxes	13,822	2.24	0	
Bank/investment fees	75	.01	0	
Lawyers/accountants	24,283	3.93	200	.17
Telephone	10,174	1.65	2,786	2.43
Campaign automobile	0		0	
Computers/office equipment	8,879	1.44	678	.59
Travel	1,500	.24	1,755	1.53
Food/meetings	4,911	.80	0	
Subtotal	**124,123**	**20.09**	**21,137**	**18.42**
Fund Raising				
Events	210,227	34.03	6,757	5.89
Direct mail	37,376	6.05	7,933	6.92
Telemarketing	0		3,694	3.22
Subtotal	**247,603**	**40.08**	**18,384**	**16.02**
Polling	**12,255**	**1.98**	**7,500**	**6.54**
Advertising				
Electronic media	20,990	3.40	57,465	50.09
Other media	13,386	2.17	430	.37
Subtotal	**34,375**	**5.57**	**57,895**	**50.47**
Other Campaign Activity				
Persuasion mail/brochures	146,855	23.77	5,542	4.83
Actual campaigning	14,575	2.36	2,925	2.55
Staff/volunteers	1,990	.32	0	
Subtotal	**163,420**	**26.46**	**8,467**	**7.38**
Constituent Gifts/ Entertainment	**3,462**	**.56**	**0**	
Donations to				
Candidates from same state	5,800	.94	0	
Candidates from other states	0		0	
Civic organizations	5,881	.95	0	
Ideological groups	500	.08	0	
Political parties	9,849	1.59	0	
Subtotal	**22,030**	**3.57**	**0**	
Unitemized Expenses	**10,433**	**1.69**	**1,338**	**1.17**
Total Campaign Expenses	**$ 617,701**		**$ 114,721**	
PAC Contributions	$ 187,284		$ 21,150	
Individual Contributions	374,115		97,487	
Total Receipts*	567,280		123,342	

*Includes PAC and individual contributions as well as interest earned, party contributions, etc.

District 12 — NEW JERSEY

Rep. Dick Zimmer (R)

1992 Election Results

Dick Zimmer (R)	174,216	(64%)
Frank G. Abate (D)	83,035	(30%)

Freshman Republican Rep. Dick Zimmer had few electoral concerns in 1992. Although more than half his constituency was new to him following redistricting, the district remained solidly Republican. His Democratic challenger, former Marlboro City Council member Frank G. Abate, had only $59,439 to spend—$1,225,696 less than Zimmer's 1990 opponent. Nevertheless, Zimmer took no chances. While he spent $563,084 less than he had in 1990, Zimmer still outspent Abate by $704,276.

Zimmer invested 53 percent of his treasury in direct appeals for votes, including $159,444 on broadcast advertising and $204,831 on brochures and persuasion mail. Citing the high ratings accorded his voting record by both Citizens Against Government Waste and the National Taxpayer's Union, Zimmer's two radio and two cable television commercials reminded voters that he had remained true to his 1990 campaign pledge to vote against taxes and additional deficit spending. Three districtwide mailings and several tightly targeted pieces presented variations on the fiscal conservatism theme. A fourth mass mailing slammed Abate for having voted to increase city council members' salaries at a time when local taxes were rising. Jamestown Associates of South Orange collected $266,705 for creating and placing the broadcast ads, producing the persuasion mail, and providing general strategic advice.

Saddled with 1990 campaign debts totaling $208,000 and determined to wage an aggressive campaign in 1992, Zimmer pumped $246,516 into fund raising. This investment represented a $94,566 increase over what he spent to raise $1,106,088 in 1990. Alan Zakin Associates of Basking Ridge and Mark Husik & Associates of Trenton received $74,861 and $36,531, respectively, for helping to raise $532,792 from individual contributors who donated $200 or more. Zimmer paid Dan Morgan & Associates of Arlington, Va., $31,600 for orchestrating political action committee events that raised $214,214. Odell, Roper & Associates of Golden, Colo., received $15,168 for its work on direct-mail solicitations that helped raise $91,605 from individuals who gave less than $200.

As the only House member from New Jersey to vote against the Brady Bill, Zimmer received fundraising assistance from the National Rifle Association, which issued a mailer urging its members to make contributions directly to Zimmer so the "liberal media" would not be able to tarnish him with the pro-gun label. Democratic attempts to turn the letter into a campaign issue failed to sway many voters.

During his first two years in office, Zimmer spent $13,952 on constituent entertainment and gifts, including $10,793 on year-end holiday cards, $764 on flowers, and $340 on meals.

Campaign Expenditures	Zimmer Amount Spent	Zimmer % of Total	Abate Amount Spent	Abate % of Total
Overhead				
Office furniture/supplies	$ 9,678	1.27	$ 1,278	2.15
Rent/utilities	14,145	1.85	925	1.56
Salaries	19,823	2.60	6,640	11.17
Taxes	413	.05	0	
Bank/investment fees	363	.05	42	.07
Lawyers/accountants	9,041	1.18	0	
Telephone	16,577	2.17	3,407	5.73
Campaign automobile	0		0	
Computers/office equipment	6,153	.81	764	1.28
Travel	6,254	.82	780	1.31
Food/meetings	645	.08	518	.87
Subtotal	**83,091**	**10.88**	**14,356**	**24.15**
Fund Raising				
Events	204,926	26.83	7,874	13.25
Direct mail	41,590	5.45	2,300	3.87
Telemarketing	0		0	
Subtotal	**246,516**	**32.28**	**10,173**	**17.12**
Polling	**7,723**	**1.01**	**11,035**	**18.57**
Advertising				
Electronic media	159,444	20.88	5,946	10.00
Other media	4,793	.63	140	.24
Subtotal	**164,238**	**21.51**	**6,086**	**10.24**
Other Campaign Activity				
Persuasion mail/brochures	204,831	26.82	6,635	11.16
Actual campaigning	32,180	4.21	9,867	16.60
Staff/volunteers	0		0	
Subtotal	**237,011**	**31.03**	**16,502**	**27.76**
Constituent Gifts/ Entertainment	**13,952**	**1.83**	**0**	
Donations to				
Candidates from same state	1,633	.21	30	.05
Candidates from other states	0		0	
Civic organizations	778	.10	352	.59
Ideological groups	100	.01	605	1.02
Political parties	3,660	.48	300	.50
Subtotal	**6,171**	**.81**	**1,287**	**2.17**
Unitemized Expenses	**5,014**	**.66**	**0**	
Total Campaign Expenses	**$ 763,715**		**$ 59,439**	
PAC Contributions	$ 214,214		$ 19,970	
Individual Contributions	624,397		34,014	
Total Receipts*	943,548		63,184	

*Includes PAC and individual contributions as well as interest earned, party contributions, etc.

NEW JERSEY — District 13

Rep. Robert Menendez (D)

1992 Election Results

Robert Menendez (D)   93,670   (64%)
Fred J. Theemling, Jr. (R)   44,529   (31%)

When Democratic Rep. Frank J. Guarini decided to step aside after fourteen years in the House, it was assumed that his successor would emerge from the Democratic primary between state senator Robert Menendez and attorney Robert P. Haney, Jr. Given that redistricting had nearly doubled the Hispanic population of District 13 to 41 percent, Menendez was the clear favorite.

In the two months leading up to the June 2 primary, Menendez spent more than $400,000, including $126,619 on television and radio commercials. Preprimary outlays for campaign literature and persuasion mailings totaled $115,802. Ads in newspapers such as the *Italian Tribune News, El Diario, La Voz,* and the *Bayonne Community News* cost $25,322.

Menendez aired three radio ads that focused on crime and jobs. Because he was not well known outside his Hudson County base, the campaign ran one television spot covering the same themes, primarily to show voters what Menendez looked like.

Haney spent nearly $200,000 on his unsuccessful bid, attacking Menendez as a "machine politician" and "former protege of political power-broker and convicted felon William Musto." Musto, who served as Union City's mayor for thirty-five years, was convicted on federal racketeering charges in 1983.

Not to be outdone, Menendez accused Haney of having "made a pact with the devil," for accepting the support of former Jersey City mayor Gerald McCann, who had been forced to resign following his conviction on fraud and tax evasion charges. Having outspent Haney by about two to one, Menendez emerged with a two-to-one primary victory.

For the general election contest with Republican Fred J. Theemling, Jr., and three independent candidates, Menendez could afford to take things considerably easier. He spent $82,415 on broadcast media, $82,620 on brochures and persuasion mail, and $30,187 on newspaper advertising. Theemling spent only $7,815 on his campaign, none of which was itemized on the Federal Election Commission reports.

Menendez funneled $267,028 through consultants. Message & Media of New Brunswick collected $174,659 for producing his broadcast ads, buying most of the air time, and creating persuasion mail. C&C Advertising of North Bergen received $24,626 for placing ads on Spanish-language radio stations. Kimberly A. Scott of Washington, D.C., was paid $29,144 for coordinating his political action committee fund-raisers. His pollster, Bill Johnson Survey Research of Mt. Vernon, N.Y., collected $23,100.

To celebrate his victory, Menendez spent $8,300 on a luncheon at the J. W. Marriott in Washington, D.C., where 1,000 supporters watched on big-screen televisions as he took the oath of office.

Campaign Expenditures	Menendez Amount Spent	% of Total
Overhead		
Office furniture/supplies	$ 2,485	.39
Rent/utilities	9,195	1.44
Salaries	23,589	3.69
Taxes	0	
Bank/investment fees	400	.06
Lawyers/accountants	8,750	1.37
Telephone	2,797	.44
Campaign automobile	0	
Computers/office equipment	3,165	.50
Travel	8,368	1.31
Food/meetings	124	.02
Subtotal	58,873	9.21
Fund Raising		
Events	68,416	10.71
Direct mail	0	
Telemarketing	0	
Subtotal	68,416	10.71
Polling	23,100	3.62
Advertising		
Electronic media	209,034	32.72
Other media	56,259	8.81
Subtotal	265,293	41.52
Other Campaign Activity		
Persuasion mail/brochures	198,422	31.05
Actual campaigning	13,901	2.18
Staff/volunteers	250	.04
Subtotal	212,573	33.27
Constituent Gifts/Entertainment	8,445	1.32
Donations to		
Candidates from same state	1,000	.16
Candidates from other states	0	
Civic organizations	400	.06
Ideological groups	100	.02
Political parties	400	.06
Subtotal	1,900	.30
Unitemized Expenses	342	.05
Total Campaign Expenses	$ 638,942	
PAC Contributions	$ 226,497	
Individual Contributions	433,908	
Total Receipts*	668,659	

*Includes PAC and individual contributions as well as interest earned, party contributions, etc.

District 1 — NEW MEXICO

Rep. Steven H. Schiff (R)

1992 Election Results

Steven H. Schiff (R)	128,426	(63%)
Robert J. Aragon (D)	76,600	(37%)

In a district where Democrats comprise 55 percent of the electorate and registered Republicans account for only 38 percent, two-term Republican Rep. Steven H. Schiff chose not to take his reelection for granted. Unopposed in the Republican primary and faced with an $81,295 challenge from Democrat Robert J. Aragon, Schiff pumped $596,838 into his campaign.

Having spent $493,624 in 1990, Schiff began 1991 with cash reserves of only $20,541, so fund raising was a top priority. During the off-year, Schiff devoted 53 percent of the $90,518 he spent on his permanent campaign to raising money. Spurred by a $30,024 investment in direct-mail solicitations, his contributions of $200 or less totaled $85,922. Donations from political action committees and individuals who gave at least $200 amounted to $51,800 and $37,575, respectively. Schiff had built his campaign treasury to $104,419 by January 1, 1992.

Schiff had only one overdraft at the House bank and had voted against the 1989 congressional pay raise. His vote in favor of the 1990 budget summit plan for spending and taxing had not hurt him in 1990 and showed no signs of causing him problems in 1992. He did not have to wage a primary battle and seemed to be virtually immune to the kind of anti-incumbent campaign that would require early media buys. Nevertheless, he paid Sandler-Innocenzi of Washington, D.C., $16,316 to create preprimary television commercials and another $30,286 to place them. "I don't know why we did that, but we won't do it again," remarked campaign manager Jim Altwies.

For the general election campaign against Aragon, Schiff paid Sandler-Innocenzi $34,183 in creative and production fees and $87,167 for placing both television and radio commercials. Altwies said the television spots centered on Schiff's concerns over the ballooning national debt, his tenure as a former district attorney, and his work on federal anti-crime bills. To guard against any anti-incumbent backlash, his ads also sought to underscore his image as a family man, pointed out that he was a longtime resident of Albuquerque, and noted that he was a member of the national guard. To show he was different than many of his colleagues, one spot noted that he had not taken honoraria. Companion radio spots aired primarily during morning and evening drive-times.

Schiff also spent $23,293 on persuasion mail, $8,014 on signs, and $5,039 to advertise in weekly newspapers. He paid Telemark of Wilsonville, Ore., $13,705 for phonebanking. Diana Daggett of Albuquerque collected $35,213 for general consulting and fund-raising services.

Campaign Expenditures	Schiff Amount Spent	Schiff % of Total	Aragon Amount Spent	Aragon % of Total
Overhead				
Office furniture/supplies	$ 5,026	.84	$ 274	.34
Rent/utilities	6,710	1.12	2,550	3.14
Salaries	99,032	16.59	10,270	12.63
Taxes	43,072	7.22	0	
Bank/investment fees	16		35	.04
Lawyers/accountants	0		0	
Telephone	5,381	.90	1,036	1.27
Campaign automobile	0		0	
Computers/office equipment	4,451	.75	257	.32
Travel	10,621	1.78	480	.59
Food/meetings	3,917	.66	80	.10
Subtotal	178,226	29.86	14,983	18.43
Fund Raising				
Events	37,835	6.34	3,382	4.16
Direct mail	91,961	15.41	0	
Telemarketing	0		0	
Subtotal	129,797	21.75	3,382	4.16
Polling	19,443	3.26	0	
Advertising				
Electronic media	170,376	28.55	14,574	17.93
Other media	6,549	1.10	4,237	5.21
Subtotal	176,926	29.64	18,811	23.14
Other Campaign Activity				
Persuasion mail/brochures	23,293	3.90	18,793	23.12
Actual campaigning	45,086	7.55	25,317	31.14
Staff/volunteers	0		0	
Subtotal	68,379	11.46	44,110	54.26
Constituent Gifts/ Entertainment	1,549	.26	0	
Donations to				
Candidates from same state	250	.04	0	
Candidates from other states	1,500	.25	0	
Civic organizations	1,284	.22	0	
Ideological groups	113	.02	0	
Political parties	4,985	.84	0	
Subtotal	8,132	1.36	0	
Unitemized Expenses	14,387	2.41	10	.01
Total Campaign Expenses	$ 596,838		$ 81,295	
PAC Contributions	$ 186,910		$ 0	
Individual Contributions	380,696		31,790	
Total Receipts*	573,884		81,585	

*Includes PAC and individual contributions as well as interest earned, party contributions, etc.

NEW MEXICO   District 2

Rep. Joe Skeen (R)

1992 Election Results

Joe Skeen (R)	94,838	(56%)
Dan Sosa, Jr. (D)	73,157	(44%)

Rep. Joe Skeen had not faced either primary or general election opposition since 1986. His 1988 and 1990 campaigns had cost $67,727 and $81,070, respectively. However, when redistricting added more than 65,000 Hispanic constituents to his district, Skeen was forced to run hard. Although Skeen outspent him by nearly seven to one, former state supreme court chief justice Dan Sosa, Jr., who is Hispanic, grabbed 44 percent of the vote.

Unopposed in the June 2 primary, Skeen began preparing for the general election campaign early. In March he brought in Smith & Harroff of Alexandria, Va., to produce two biographical television commercials that began airing shortly after the primary. Two other television spots focused on his ability to deliver federal dollars for projects that aided the district's tourism industry, including one to restore historic forts.

To combat any anti-incumbenct undercurrents, Smith & Harroff produced a commercial consisting of constituent endorsements, including one from a woman who said, "A politician votes for the next election. A statesman votes for the next generation. Joe Skeen is a statesman and that's why I'm voting for him." When Sosa's hometown newspaper endorsed Skeen, a sixth commercial touting that fact was rushed on the air. Smith & Harroff collected $204,787 for creating and placing the commercials.

Skeen invested $9,885 in newspaper ads, including $6,779 paid to Smith & Harroff. He spent $30,981 on brochures and voter contact mailings, including postcards reminding people to vote. Telemark of Wilsonville, Ore., collected $14,755 for phone-banking. Skeen also spent $9,258 on signs, $7,128 on buttons and bumper stickers, and $1,193 on engraved gifts for his most active volunteers.

Skeen's fund raising was handled entirely in-house. Two events in Washington, D.C., helped raise $160,125, or 41 percent of his total receipts, from political action committees. He spent $4,455 on commemorative plaques, which were given to members of his congressional club who donated $1,000. Contributions of $200 or more amounted to $84,663.

Special emphasis was put into attracting smaller donations. Skeen invested $30,072 in direct-mail solicitations, including $8,100 for White House Historical Society Christmas ornaments that were used as inducements to increase the returns. Supporters could join his congressional club for as little as $25, and while that small donation did not entitle them to an engraved plaque, it did earn them a campaign key chain. Those who gave $50 received a special license plate cover. These efforts enabled Skeen to raise $109,788 from donors who gave less than $200.

	Skeen		Sosa	
Campaign Expenditures	Amount Spent	% of Total	Amount Spent	% of Total
Overhead				
Office furniture/supplies	$ 7,165	1.46	$ 520	.71
Rent/utilities	2,501	.51	168	.23
Salaries	35,331	7.18	2,000	2.72
Taxes	21,937	4.46	0	
Bank/investment fees	0		0	
Lawyers/accountants	10,875	2.21	0	
Telephone	6,105	1.24	3,306	4.49
Campaign automobile	0		0	
Computers/office equipment	15,839	3.22	693	.94
Travel	28,159	5.72	3,904	5.30
Food/meetings	2,343	.48	122	.17
Subtotal	**130,255**	**26.45**	**10,714**	**14.55**
Fund Raising				
Events	16,354	3.32	1,529	2.08
Direct mail	30,072	6.11	7,284	9.89
Telemarketing	0		0	
Subtotal	**46,426**	**9.43**	**8,813**	**11.97**
Polling	**24,700**	**5.02**	**2,665**	**3.62**
Advertising				
Electronic media	205,519	41.74	38,694	52.55
Other media	10,160	2.06	7,265	9.87
Subtotal	**215,679**	**43.80**	**45,959**	**62.41**
Other Campaign Activity				
Persuasion mail/brochures	30,981	6.29	0	
Actual campaigning	32,292	6.56	4,984	6.77
Staff/volunteers	2,386	.48	0	
Subtotal	**65,659**	**13.33**	**4,984**	**6.77**
Constituent Gifts/ Entertainment	**0**		**0**	
Donations to				
Candidates from same state	0		0	
Candidates from other states	0		0	
Civic organizations	0		0	
Ideological groups	0		0	
Political parties	2,525	.51	500	.68
Subtotal	**2,525**	**.51**	**500**	**.68**
Unitemized Expenses	**7,168**	**1.46**	**0**	
Total Campaign Expenses	**$ 492,412**		**$ 73,635**	
PAC Contributions	$ 160,125		$ 1,750	
Individual Contributions	194,451		35,437	
Total Receipts*	387,893		39,561	

*Includes PAC and individual contributions as well as interest earned, party contributions, etc.

District 3 — NEW MEXICO

Rep. Bill Richardson (D)

1992 Election Results

Bill Richardson (D)	122,850	(67%)
F. Greg Bemis, Jr. (R)	54,569	(30%)

From the outset, Rep. Bill Richardson knew his contest with Republican F. Greg Bemis, Jr., would not prove difficult. In May 1992 Richardson told a newspaper reporter that he did not plan to begin campaigning before September and that he hoped to spend no more than half his campaign treasury, which at that time contained about $450,000.

On one level, Richardson's spending prediction was accurate. Between July 1 and the November 3 election, Richardson committed $184,970 to broadcast advertising. He invested $3,344 in signs, $3,105 in parade materials, and $2,500 for the state party's coordinated get-out-the-vote effort. However, while he spent only $211,840 on direct appeals for votes, his campaign treasury was tapped for $598,334 over the two-year election cycle.

At the time Richardson made his spending prediction, he had already spent approximately $200,000. Maintenance of his off-year campaign had cost $166,678, including $41,645 for overhead, $68,404 for fund raising, and $23,850 for contributions to other candidates, Democratic party organizations, charities, and causes.

Richardson invested $146,088 in overhead over the two-year cycle. His travel costs of $96,788 included $4,676 spent in conjunction with the Democratic National Convention in August 1992. His meal charges of $11,200 included a $399 farewell dinner at The Palm in Washington, D.C., for a departing member of his congressional staff; a $704 meal at LaFonda, another Washington, D.C., restaurant, to entertain guests attending a conference of Hispanic elected officials; and a $1,107 repast at Doe's Eat Place in Little Rock, Ark., which Richardson said was a dinner with North American tribal chiefs who had met with presidential candidate Bill Clinton.

As one of four Democratic deputy whips, Richardson spread his campaign largess to other candidates and party organizations. The Democratic Congressional Campaign Committee and the Democratic Leadership Council received $10,000 and $1,000, respectively. He made contributions totaling $35,312 to dozens of House and Senate candidates. He donated $13,850 to local Democratic party organizations throughout the district, $7,500 to state and local candidates, $3,900 to the state Democratic party, $5,976 to various charitable organizations, and $5,984 to organizations such as the Speaker's House Leadership Fund, a political action committee established by House Speaker Thomas S. Foley (D-Wash.).

For the campaign, Richardson turned to Brown, Inc., of Santa Fe, which collected $177,925 for designing broadcast ads and buying most of the time.

Outspent by more than twelve to one, Bemis's campaign never got off the ground.

Campaign Expenditures	Richardson Amount Spent	Richardson % of Total	Bemis Amount Spent	Bemis % of Total
Overhead				
Office furniture/supplies	$ 9,009	1.51	$ 542	1.13
Rent/utilities	235	.04	3,325	6.92
Salaries	5,324	.89	1,184	2.46
Taxes	10,330	1.73	0	
Bank/investment fees	56	.01	52	.11
Lawyers/accountants	9,446	1.58	0	
Telephone	1,200	.20	3,067	6.38
Campaign automobile	0		0	
Computers/office equipment	2,500	.42	1,165	2.42
Travel	96,788	16.18	1,833	3.81
Food/meetings	11,200	1.87	64	.13
Subtotal	**146,088**	**24.42**	**11,234**	**23.37**
Fund Raising				
Events	64,898	10.85	1,067	2.22
Direct mail	33,255	5.56	962	2.00
Telemarketing	34,713	5.80	0	
Subtotal	**132,867**	**22.21**	**2,028**	**4.22**
Polling	**0**		**0**	
Advertising				
Electronic media	184,970	30.91	24,247	50.44
Other media	1,747	.29	691	1.44
Subtotal	**186,717**	**31.21**	**24,938**	**51.88**
Other Campaign Activity				
Persuasion mail/brochures	0		4,625	9.62
Actual campaigning	24,085	4.03	3,493	7.27
Staff/volunteers	1,038	.17	0	
Subtotal	**25,123**	**4.20**	**8,118**	**16.89**
Constituent Gifts/ Entertainment	**3,020**	**.50**	**37**	**.08**
Donations to				
Candidates from same state	9,600	1.60	0	
Candidates from other states	33,212	5.55	0	
Civic organizations	5,976	1.00	0	
Ideological groups	5,984	1.00	0	
Political parties	29,750	4.97	0	
Subtotal	**84,523**	**14.13**	**0**	
Unitemized Expenses	**19,996**	**3.34**	**1,713**	**3.56**
Total Campaign Expenses	**$ 598,334**		**$ 48,068**	
PAC Contributions	$ 387,551		$ 1,000	
Individual Contributions	235,455		20,590	
Total Receipts*	680,154		49,879	

*Includes PAC and individual contributions as well as interest earned, party contributions, etc.

NEW YORK — District 1

Rep. George J. Hochbrueckner (D)

1992 Election Results

George J. Hochbrueckner (D)	117,940	(52%)
Edward P. Romaine (R)	110,043	(48%)

In a district where registered Republicans outnumber Democrats by two to one, Democratic Rep. George J. Hochbrueckner had survived three hard-fought campaigns. Elected in both 1986 and 1988 with 51 percent of the vote, Hochbrueckner had outspent his 1990 challenger by $572,501 and still garnered only 56 percent of the vote. When Suffolk County Clerk Edward P. Romaine, Hochbrueckner's 1988 opponent, decided to try again, it was clear Hochbrueckner would face another difficult test.

Although he had spent nearly $1.8 million over the three previous campaigns, Hochbrueckner approached the 1992 election cycle in a surprisingly low-key manner. During 1991, he invested just $69,123 to maintain his campaign operation, including $39,152 on overhead. While he began the cycle with cash reserves of only $15,836, Hochbrueckner devoted just $9,371 to off-year fund raising. With political action committees (PACs) accounting for two-thirds of the $102,929 he raised, Hochbrueckner increased his cash-on-hand to $50,700 by year's end.

Hochbrueckner invested 26 percent of his budget in brochures and persuasion mailers designed by Campaign Performance Group of San Francisco, Calif. The cover of one mailer pictured a stack of books, including *The Robber Barons, Honest Graft*, and *Scandal*. Next to these books stood a fictitious book entitled *True Stories from Brookhaven*. Inside, the mailer labeled Romaine "a product of the corrupt Brookhaven Town Republican organization," slamming him for, among other things, taking "over a thousand dollars and a free car as a campaign contribution" from a man who had admitted bribing local politicians. Other mailers touted Hochbrueckner's health care reform proposals and juxtaposed his pro-choice stance on abortion with Romaine's "extremist" antiabortion position. Campaign Performance collected $96,940 for producing the mailers.

Fenn & King Communications of Washington, D.C., received $105,630 for creating and placing three television commercials and companion radio spots. Rather than avoiding the issue of incumbency, Hochbrueckner's first commercial embraced it, focusing on his efforts to save the F14 jet fighter program, create high-tech jobs, stop offshore dumping, and clean up Peconic Bay. Two commercials delivered attacks identical to those in the mailers.

Romaine countered by stressing change. "We had radio and TV ads that called for an end to the Five P's—perks, PACs, paralysis, privilege, and patronage," recalled Fred Towle, Romaine's press secretary. Romaine received a $50,259 infusion from the National Republican Congressional Committee, which was invested in broadcast advertising, newspaper ads, and persuasion mail.

Campaign Expenditures	Hochbrueckner Amount Spent	% of Total	Romaine Amount Spent	% of Total
Overhead				
Office furniture/supplies	$ 5,929	1.06	$ 3,921	1.74
Rent/utilities	8,181	1.46	4,061	1.80
Salaries	76,084	13.57	32,852	14.60
Taxes	996	.18	0	
Bank/investment fees	0		33	.01
Lawyers/accountants	0		0	
Telephone	26,709	4.76	5,851	2.60
Campaign automobile	19,431	3.47	2,164	.96
Computers/office equipment	14,447	2.58	2,455	1.09
Travel	17,568	3.13	3,863	1.72
Food/meetings	3,286	.59	74	.03
Subtotal	**172,629**	**30.79**	**55,274**	**24.56**
Fund Raising				
Events	55,901	9.97	28,588	12.70
Direct mail	2,397	.43	38,741	17.22
Telemarketing	0		0	
Subtotal	**58,298**	**10.40**	**67,329**	**29.92**
Polling	**38,150**	**6.81**	**5,580**	**2.48**
Advertising				
Electronic media	106,400	18.98	23,085	10.26
Other media	750	.13	13,758	6.11
Subtotal	**107,150**	**19.11**	**36,843**	**16.37**
Other Campaign Activity				
Persuasion mail/brochures	147,347	26.28	7,153	3.18
Actual campaigning	1,502	.27	51,137	22.72
Staff/volunteers	210	.04	1,050	.47
Subtotal	**149,059**	**26.59**	**59,340**	**26.37**
Constituent Gifts/Entertainment	**3,222**	**.57**	**40**	**.02**
Donations to				
Candidates from same state	6,050	1.08	0	
Candidates from other states	3,000	.54	0	
Civic organizations	980	.17	425	.19
Ideological groups	252	.05	125	.06
Political parties	1,700	.30	40	.02
Subtotal	**11,982**	**2.14**	**590**	**.26**
Unitemized Expenses	**20,124**	**3.59**	**41**	**.02**
Total Campaign Expenses	**$ 560,615**		**$ 225,037**	
PAC Contributions	**$ 296,600**		**$ 26,761**	
Individual Contributions	**248,585**		**171,228**	
Total Receipts*	**628,248**		**235,259**	

*Includes PAC and individual contributions as well as interest earned, party contributions, etc.

District 2 — NEW YORK

Rep. Rick A. Lazio (R)

1992 Election Results

Rick A. Lazio (R)	109,386	(53%)
Thomas J. Downey (D)	96,328	(47%)

A member of the Watergate class of 1974, Democratic Rep. Thomas J. Downey had managed to win eight reelection bids comfortably in a district that had voted Republican in each of the previous four presidential campaigns. In 1992 Downey fell victim to the collective weight of his own insider baggage, which included 151 overdrafts at the House bank, his wife's job as "House bank auditor," and a 1990 junket to Barbados that was paid for by lobbyists and detailed on television on *PrimeTime Live*, complete with pictures of Downey on a jet-ski.

Outspent by more than five to one, Suffolk County legislator Rick A. Lazio worked with the National Republican Congressional Committee (NRCC) to develop three television commercials—one that featured Lazio discussing his goals and two that hammered Downey for the Barbados excursion and his overdrafts. Lazio hired no consultants, allowing him to funnel $51,152 of his limited broadcast advertising budget into air time. Rainbow Advertising of Independence, Ohio, and National Media of Alexandria, Va., received $33,178 and $2,027, respectively, for placing cable television spots over the final eight weeks of the campaign. Ray Adell Media Enterprises of Greenlawn collected $15,947 for buying radio air time. Miscellaneous production charges amounted to $2,793.

Sensing an upset in the making, the NRCC and the Republican National Committee together spent $54,130 to augment Lazio's $60,952 investment in campaign leaflets and persuasion mail. Lazio flooded the district with eight mailers during the final two weeks. A wrap-up piece modeled after *Time* magazine's "Man of the Year" issue dubbed Downey "Greed Man of the Decade." Other attack pieces slammed Downey over the Barbados trip, his overdrafts, and his wife's purported role as House bank auditor. "We also printed a huge number of handouts, which we passed out at supermarkets and door-to-door," recalled Philip Boyle, Lazio's administrative assistant. "We hit Downey with our mail pieces and kept the handouts positive, pro-Rick Lazio."

Although Downey spent $282,725 during the off-year to keep his permanent campaign running smoothly—more than Lazio spent on his entire campaign—he had more than enough left over to get his message out in 1992. He paid Joe Slade White & Co. of New York $80,929 for creating broadcast ads; Shafto & Barton of Dallas, Texas, $325,203 for placing the commercials; and the November Group of Washington, D.C., $181,570 for producing persuasion mailers. Fully realizing the depth of his problems, Downey paid Greenberg-Lake, also of Washington, $109,873 to keep tabs on the electorate's mood.

Campaign Expenditures	Lazio Amount Spent	Lazio % of Total	Downey Amount Spent	Downey % of Total
Overhead				
Office furniture/supplies	$ 2,702	.99	$ 16,812	1.18
Rent/utilities	4,939	1.82	53,914	3.79
Salaries	26,123	9.60	188,203	13.22
Taxes	0		10,919	.77
Bank/investment fees	0		0	
Lawyers/accountants	0		16,955	1.19
Telephone	9,260	3.40	23,461	1.65
Campaign automobile	0		23,698	1.66
Computers/office equipment	2,193	.81	37,179	2.61
Travel	3,753	1.38	39,767	2.79
Food/meetings	0		2,412	.17
Subtotal	**48,970**	**18.00**	**413,321**	**29.03**
Fund Raising				
Events	41,920	15.41	101,115	7.10
Direct mail	1,039	.38	22,094	1.55
Telemarketing	0		0	
Subtotal	**42,959**	**15.79**	**123,209**	**8.65**
Polling	**5,000**	**1.84**	**109,873**	**7.72**
Advertising				
Electronic media	53,945	19.83	407,010	28.59
Other media	14,279	5.25	6,339	.45
Subtotal	**68,224**	**25.07**	**413,350**	**29.03**
Other Campaign Activity				
Persuasion mail/brochures	60,952	22.40	276,291	19.41
Actual campaigning	35,032	12.87	24,066	1.69
Staff/volunteers	31	.01	661	.05
Subtotal	**96,015**	**35.29**	**301,018**	**21.14**
Constituent Gifts/ Entertainment	**1,673**	**.61**	**10,746**	**.75**
Donations to				
Candidates from same state	0		1,500	.11
Candidates from other states	0		6,000	.42
Civic organizations	0		6,125	.43
Ideological groups	0		550	.04
Political parties	0		5,200	.37
Subtotal	**0**		**19,375**	**1.36**
Unitemized Expenses	9,256	3.40	32,851	2.31
Total Campaign Expenses	$ 272,097		$ 1,423,743	
PAC Contributions	$ 43,663		$ 457,222	
Individual Contributions	197,873		564,219	
Total Receipts*	276,487		1,085,414	

*Includes PAC and individual contributions as well as interest earned, party contributions, etc.

NEW YORK — District 3

Rep. Peter T. King (R)

1992 Election Results

Peter T. King (R)	124,727	(50%)
Steve A. Orlins (D)	116,915	(46%)

Democrat Steve A. Orlins spent $775,000 of his own money in his unsuccessful bid to succeed retiring Republican Rep. Norman F. Lent. In the process, Orlins outspent his Republican opponent, Nassau County comptroller Peter T. King, by more than four to one in this open seat contest. In a year supposedly marked by antagonism toward career politicians, King ran as a political insider whose experience would allow him to get things done, while Orlins portrayed himself as an agent of change. Outspent by $643,132 on direct voter appeals, King won by 7,812 votes.

With his massive cash advantage, Orlins paid Shorr Associates of Philadelphia, Pa., $327,281 for creating and placing his broadcast ads. Given the expense of television advertising in the New York City market, Orlins invested heavily in airing six radio commercials, two of which focused on his pro-choice stance on abortion.

Orlins paid Campaign Performance Group of San Francisco, Calif., $257,284 for blanketing the district with eight persuasion mailers, four of which attacked King for his strong opposition to abortion. Two mailers focused on "change," the mantra of 1992. Rounding out the mail was a biographical piece introducing Orlins to district residents and a mailer blaming King for a 41 percent increase in county taxes.

Three other consultants brought Orlins's total investment in professional advice and services to $724,570. Lunde & Burger of Alexandria, Va., collected $67,970 for providing general strategic advice; Garin-Hart of Washington, D.C., received $52,035 for polling; and Penn & Schoen of New York collected $20,000 for phonebanking.

Although he lacked Orlins's resources, King did not sit quietly on the sidelines. He slammed Orlins as "a carpetbagging millionaire" who had moved to the district from New York City "to buy the election." To counter attacks that he was responsible for the sorry state of the local economy, King touted his belief in tax cuts and supply-side economics. King paid Fabrizio, McLaughlin & Associates of Alexandria, Va., $14,000 for creating his radio commercials and $9,700 for conducting polls that fed those ads. The firm collected another $15,000 from the Republican National Committee. Multi Media Services Corp., also of Alexandria, received $74,500 from King and $38,981 from the National Republican Congressional Committee for placing the spots.

While Orlins sank $27,003 in rent and utilities and $107,166 in staff salaries, King invested only $600 in rent, $254 in utilities, and $5,000 in payroll. As a result, overhead consumed just 4 percent of King's budget. King's persuasion mail was created in-house to hold down costs.

	King		Orlins	
Campaign Expenditures	Amount Spent	% of Total	Amount Spent	% of Total
Overhead				
Office furniture/supplies	$ 140	.05	$ 2,839	.25
Rent/utilities	854	.33	27,003	2.40
Salaries	5,000	1.91	107,166	9.51
Taxes	0		20,097	1.78
Bank/investment fees	0		0	
Lawyers/accountants	1,818	.69	3,500	.31
Telephone	1,267	.48	11,023	.98
Campaign automobile	0		0	
Computers/office equipment	472	.18	12,014	1.07
Travel	1,324	.50	2,082	.18
Food/meetings	250	.10	0	
Subtotal	**11,126**	**4.24**	**185,723**	**16.48**
Fund Raising				
Events	5,713	2.18	8,643	.77
Direct mail	15,720	5.99	11,446	1.02
Telemarketing	0		0	
Subtotal	**21,432**	**8.17**	**20,089**	**1.78**
Polling	**14,157**	**5.40**	**52,035**	**4.62**
Advertising				
Electronic media	110,570	42.15	327,281	29.05
Other media	1,071	.41	32,896	2.92
Subtotal	**111,641**	**42.55**	**360,177**	**31.97**
Other Campaign Activity				
Persuasion mail/brochures	96,247	36.69	394,099	34.98
Actual campaigning	6,579	2.51	103,323	9.17
Staff/volunteers	0		0	
Subtotal	**102,826**	**39.19**	**497,422**	**44.15**
Constituent Gifts/ Entertainment	**0**		**0**	
Donations to				
Candidates from same state	0		0	
Candidates from other states	0		0	
Civic organizations	0		0	
Ideological groups	0		0	
Political parties	0		0	
Subtotal	**0**		**0**	
Unitemized Expenses	**1,164**	**.44**	**11,305**	**1.00**
Total Campaign Expenses	**$ 262,347**		**$ 1,126,751**	
PAC Contributions	**$ 117,550**		**$ 0**	
Individual Contributions	**121,302**		**328,543**	
Total Receipts*	**244,526**		**1,142,476**	

*Includes PAC and individual contributions as well as interest earned, party contributions, etc.

District 4 — NEW YORK

Rep. David A. Levy (R)

1992 Election Results

David A. Levy (R)	110,710	(50%)
Philip M. Schiliro (D)	100,386	(45%)

The road to the general election was bumpy for both Republican David A. Levy, a member of the Hempstead Town Council, and Democrat Philip M. Schiliro, a top aide to Rep. Henry A. Waxman (D-Calif.). Levy and Schiliro spent about $85,000 and $179,000, respectively, to secure their party's nominations to vie for the vacancy created by the retirement of Republican Rep. Raymond J. McGrath.

The Republican primary pitted Levy, a political protege of Nassau County Republican party chairman Joseph Mondello, against state representative Daniel Frisa, who had the backing of Joseph N. Margiatta, a former Nassau County Republican party chairman who had been convicted of extortion and sent to prison.

Levy invested $56,872 of his preprimary spending in handouts and at least six advocacy mailings that focused on taxes, economic development, and government waste. He accused Frisa of missing more than 1,000 votes in the state assembly between 1989 and 1992 and of being Margiatta's puppet. Levy spent $4,208 on signs, many of which featured a picture of Levy standing with McGrath on the Capitol steps.

Frisa countered with an $87,588 campaign, virtually all of which was invested in persuasion mailings to the district's 148,000 registered Republicans. The mailings touted his staunch opposition to increases in both the county sales tax and property taxes. Not to be outdone in the name-calling game, he accused Levy of being Mondello's puppet. With only 23,946 Republicans voting, Levy prevailed with 53 percent.

In the Democratic primary, Schiliro faced attorney and business consultant Joan F. Axinn, who spent $479,296 attacking Shiliro as a carpetbagging Washington insider. Schiliro invested $98,626 of his budget in advocacy mailings, including one that proclaimed, "In the Year of the Woman, the best candidate for the job is a man." The mailer went on to list his pro-choice stance and positions on a variety of other issues, including increased funding for breast cancer research. He spent $16,436 on phonebanking to turn out the vote and emerged with a 426-vote victory.

With registered Republicans outnumbering Democrats by nearly 70,000, Levy entered the general election campaign with a clear advantage. To make sure it held up, he invested $52,743 in persuasion mail and paid Ryan & Ryan Public Relations of Farmingdale $67,849 to create and place television ads. The Republican National Committee paid Ryan & Ryan $12,000 for additional air time. He attacked Schiliro for sharing Waxman's "ultraliberal philosophy," among other things.

Schiliro countered with a $298,256 campaign and nearly overcame the party registration gap.

	Levy		Schiliro	
Campaign Expenditures	Amount Spent	% of Total	Amount Spent	% of Total
Overhead				
Office furniture/supplies	$ 1,348	.60	$ 5,405	1.13
Rent/utilities	3,835	1.70	11,781	2.47
Salaries	0		58,414	12.24
Taxes	0		0	
Bank/investment fees	340	.15	318	.07
Lawyers/accountants	0		0	
Telephone	1,517	.67	7,903	1.66
Campaign automobile	0		0	
Computers/office equipment	1,189	.53	4,043	.85
Travel	675	.30	4,274	.90
Food/meetings	0		0	
Subtotal	8,905	3.94	92,139	19.30
Fund Raising				
Events	13,446	5.95	16,425	3.44
Direct mail	3,178	1.41	0	
Telemarketing	0		0	
Subtotal	16,624	7.36	16,425	3.44
Polling	0		0	
Advertising				
Electronic media	67,849	30.02	5,011	1.05
Other media	5,407	2.39	944	.20
Subtotal	73,256	32.41	5,955	1.25
Other Campaign Activity				
Persuasion mail/brochures	109,615	48.50	311,696	65.30
Actual campaigning	11,275	4.99	46,685	9.78
Staff/volunteers	3,453	1.53	1,082	.23
Subtotal	124,343	55.02	359,464	75.30
Constituent Gifts/ Entertainment	0		0	
Donations to				
Candidates from same state	0		0	
Candidates from other states	0		0	
Civic organizations	0		0	
Ideological groups	0		40	.01
Political parties	0		500	.10
Subtotal	0		540	.11
Unitemized Expenses	2,867	1.27	2,841	.60
Total Campaign Expenses	$ 225,995		$ 477,364	
PAC Contributions	$ 60,880		$ 258,530	
Individual Contributions	138,636		205,380	
Total Receipts*	217,319		506,217	

*Includes PAC and individual contributions as well as interest earned, party contributions, etc.

NEW YORK   District 5

Rep. Gary L. Ackerman (D)   *1992 Election Results*   Gary L. Ackerman (D)   110,476   (52%)
                                                                          Allan E. Binder (R)   94,907   (45%)

One week before the November 3 general election, Democratic Rep. Gary L. Ackerman's campaign began running radio commercials touting his endorsement by the *New York Times*. Unfortunately for Ackerman, several days after his ads hit the airwaves, the *Times* officially endorsed his opponent, Republican Allan E. Binder. Noting that his staff had queried the paper before airing the spots and had been led to believe that he would receive its endorsement, an embarrassed Ackerman immediately pulled the ads. He also canceled a mailing that trumpeted the phantom endorsement, wasting $15,000 of his resources. It was a rough end to a rough campaign.

The state's loss of three House seats through reapportionment coupled with the need to create a new Hispanic-majority seat in New York City had produced a new political map that obliterated Ackerman's old district. His new constituency, which was about 90 percent new to him, was considerably more suburban and Republican.

In the Democratic primary, Ackerman faced Rita-Louise A. Morris, a college librarian who had never run for office but who had a son in the political consulting business. Morris spent $200,000 of her own money, running commercials criticizing Ackerman for his 111 overdrafts at the House bank and for spending too much of the taxpayers' money.

In addition to spending $137,739 during the off-year, Ackerman invested nearly $540,000 to secure the Democratic nomination. He spent $430,000 between July 1 and the September 15 primary, alone. During this push, Ackerman sank $206,003 into brochures and mailings that touted his record for constituent service and cited endorsements he had received. "We didn't state 'you should reelect the incumbent,' but we stressed things he had done for the district," recalled Jedd I. Moskowitz, Ackerman's administrative assistant. Ackerman spent $16,332 on newspaper ads and $13,698 on phonebanking. He collected 62 percent of the primary votes.

In the general election, Binder spent $19,000 on radio commercials and $41,455 on campaign literature that attacked Ackerman as a check-bouncing career politician who had consistently voted for racial quotas and to use taxpayer money to fund obscene art. The National Republican Congressional Committee and the Republican National Committee spent $31,108 to augment Binder's mail effort.

Ackerman pulled out the victory by spending $70,587 on additional mailers, $49,869 on broadcast advertising, and $15,304 on newspaper ads.

Over the two-year cycle, Ackerman spent $31,131 of his campaign funds to lease and maintain a Lincoln Towncar.

	Ackerman		Binder	
Campaign Expenditures	Amount Spent	% of Total	Amount Spent	% of Total
Overhead				
Office furniture/supplies	$ 8,781	.96	$ 2,419	1.65
Rent/utilities	16,934	1.85	2,836	1.93
Salaries	71,219	7.76	13,379	9.12
Taxes	13,236	1.44	7,082	4.83
Bank/investment fees	115	.01	0	
Lawyers/accountants	9,888	1.08	0	
Telephone	12,764	1.39	7,037	4.80
Campaign automobile	31,131	3.39	0	
Computers/office equipment	9,782	1.07	3,819	2.60
Travel	24,276	2.65	376	.26
Food/meetings	5,694	.62	0	
Subtotal	**203,821**	**22.22**	**36,949**	**25.18**
Fund Raising				
Events	131,293	14.31	6,588	4.49
Direct mail	0		0	
Telemarketing	0		0	
Subtotal	**131,293**	**14.31**	**6,588**	**4.49**
Polling	**75,000**	**8.18**	**0**	
Advertising				
Electronic media	49,869	5.44	19,000	12.95
Other media	50,359	5.49	4,305	2.93
Subtotal	**100,228**	**10.93**	**23,305**	**15.88**
Other Campaign Activity				
Persuasion mail/brochures	276,590	30.15	41,455	28.25
Actual campaigning	59,613	6.50	31,554	21.51
Staff/volunteers	3,896	.42	0	
Subtotal	**340,099**	**37.08**	**73,009**	**49.76**
Constituent Gifts/ Entertainment	**12,849**	**1.40**	**0**	
Donations to				
Candidates from same state	7,750	.84	0	
Candidates from other states	1,250	.14	0	
Civic organizations	8,780	.96	725	.49
Ideological groups	1,411	.15	0	
Political parties	25,707	2.80	0	
Subtotal	**44,898**	**4.89**	**725**	**.49**
Unitemized Expenses	**9,129**	**1.00**	**6,147**	**4.19**
Total Campaign Expenses	**$ 917,318**		**$ 146,723**	
PAC Contributions	$ 342,775		$ 9,250	
Individual Contributions	259,241		80,245	
Total Receipts*	674,901		125,965	

*Includes PAC and individual contributions as well as interest earned, party contributions, etc.

District 6 — NEW YORK

Rep. Floyd H. Flake (D)

1992 Election Results

Floyd H. Flake (D)	96,972	(81%)
Dianand D. Bhagwandin (R)	22,687	(19%)

After four unsuccessful bids for the Republican nomination, Dianand D. Bhagwandin had no illusions of an upset victory over Rep. Floyd H. Flake. Sexual harassment charges leveled against Flake in 1988 had done nothing to shake voter confidence in him. Flake had coasted through the 1990 campaign with virtually no opposition, despite his indictment on federal charges of income tax evasion and embezzling $141,000 from the church where he had served as pastor for fifteen years. "This was a no-win situation," recalled Bhagwandin. "But this is a district with a high population of minority residents that do not get involved. I keep running to get out the message that they have to become U.S. citizens and vote."

Bhagwandin spent $3,864 to advertise on a local public access cable television channel aimed at the district's Indian community. He placed ads in *India Today* and the *India News*. Lacking the money to mail brochures, he printed approximately 300,000 leaflets, which canvassers distributed door-to-door.

Flake invested 38 percent of his $263,256 budget in overhead. He paid $13,500 in rent to the Allen African Methodist Episcopal Church—the church he had served as pastor. Flake depended heavily on two congressional staffers to keep the campaign running smoothly, although he did not pay them a salary. Willie Armstrong, a community aide in his Queens congressional office, received expense reimbursements totaling $5,971 for food, gasoline, tolls, and parking. Edwin C. Reed, executive staff director in Flake's Washington, D.C., office, collected expenses totaling $3,304. Flake also racked up $11,902 in legal bills.

At war with the Queens Democratic party, Flake initially sought to run his own slate of candidates for various elective and local party offices in the primary. In turn, party leaders tried to block Flake's access to the ballot by filing a challenge to his petitions. Both sides backed down, but not before the local party had formally endorsed Flake's Democratic primary opponent, Simeon Golar. In the end, Golar's $21,809 challenge proved ineffective and Flake emerged with 75 percent of the vote.

Flake could hardly afford to completely ignore the challenge posed by his own party leaders. In October 1991 Flake hired Bill Johnson Survey Research of Mt. Vernon, N.Y., and over the next year paid the firm $36,750 to keep tabs on the mood of the electorate. This expenditure was $29,250 more than he spent on polls in 1990, and all but $2,500 of these polling costs were incurred before the primary. All his persuasion mail was sent prior to the primary, as well.

	Flake		Bhagwandin	
Campaign Expenditures	Amount Spent	% of Total	Amount Spent	% of Total
Overhead				
Office furniture/supplies	$ 4,990	1.90	$ 1,396	2.47
Rent/utilities	17,421	6.62	9,179	16.20
Salaries	6,225	2.36	0	
Taxes	430	.16	0	
Bank/investment fees	2,017	.77	603	1.06
Lawyers/accountants	11,902	4.52	0	
Telephone	4,513	1.71	3,468	6.12
Campaign automobile	21,899	8.32	0	
Computers/office equipment	510	.19	1,470	2.60
Travel	19,690	7.48	8,365	14.77
Food/meetings	3,785	1.44	0	
Subtotal	**93,381**	**35.47**	**24,481**	**43.22**
Fund Raising				
Events	51,084	19.40	6,324	11.16
Direct mail	0		0	
Telemarketing	4,250	1.61	0	
Subtotal	**55,334**	**21.02**	**6,324**	**11.16**
Polling	**36,750**	**13.96**	**0**	
Advertising				
Electronic media	1,615	.61	3,864	6.82
Other media	8,428	3.20	2,851	5.03
Subtotal	**10,043**	**3.82**	**6,715**	**11.86**
Other Campaign Activity				
Persuasion mail/brochures	52,704	20.02	9,216	16.27
Actual campaigning	2,887	1.10	9,288	16.40
Staff/volunteers	305	.12	95	.17
Subtotal	**55,896**	**21.23**	**18,599**	**32.83**
Constituent Gifts/ Entertainment	**444**	**.17**	**0**	
Donations to				
Candidates from same state	3,000	1.14	25	.04
Candidates from other states	1,500	.57	0	
Civic organizations	5,165	1.96	130	.23
Ideological groups	235	.09	25	.04
Political parties	1,395	.53	345	.61
Subtotal	**11,295**	**4.29**	**525**	**.93**
Unitemized Expenses	**112**	**.04**	**0**	
Total Campaign Expenses	**$ 263,256**		**$ 56,645**	
PAC Contributions	$ 142,490		$ 1,379	
Individual Contributions	75,482		37,670	
Total Receipts*	272,263		50,090	

*Includes PAC and individual contributions as well as interest earned, party contributions, etc.

NEW YORK — District 7

Rep. Thomas J. Manton (D)

1992 Election Results

Thomas J. Manton (D)	72,280	(57%)
Dennis C. Shea (R)	54,639	(43%)

Attorney Dennis C. Shea got off to a quick start in his bid to unseat Rep. Thomas J. Manton. Seven months before the November general election, Shea paid Multi Media Services Corp. of Alexandria, Va., $17,950 to place radio commercials attacking Manton for his seventeen overdrafts at the House bank. Shea also paid New York-based media consultant Severin/Aviles Associates $3,000 for consultations in July, but he did not have the resources to implement that campaign advice.

Manton had no such monetary problems, although he chose not to spend any of his $1,013,639 treasury on broadcast ads in the pricey New York market. Instead, he pumped $413,954 into brochures, leaflets, and persuasion mailers that touted his constituent service and ability to deliver federal projects to the district. When it became apparent that Shea's anti-incumbent message was having an impact, several Manton mailers slammed Shea as a carpetbagger who had moved to the district in order to run. Clinton Reilly Campaigns of San Francisco, Calif., collected $241,524 for its work on the advocacy mail. Postage for the mailers amounted to $126,252, including a $50,000 payment on October 7.

To keep his name constantly before the public, Manton ran ads throughout the two-year cycle in community newspapers such as the *Tablet,* the *Times Newsweekly,* the *Irish Echo,* the *Irish Voice,* the *Queens Tribune,* and the *Bronx Times Reporter.* "This area is festooned with small, local papers," noted campaign spokesman Martin J. McLaughlin. In all, these ads cost $25,397. McLaughlin received $27,500 for handling the campaign's public relations chores.

Every weekend between July 20 and November 3, Manton climbed aboard a trolley car rented from Manhattan Neighborhood Trolley and toured the district, holding what McLaughlin referred to as "mini rallies." Payments for the trolley, which has been a campaign tradition since Manton's first successful House campaign in 1984, totaled $11,620. Other rally and campaign event expenses added $27,070. Manton spent $10,127 on yard signs and posters. Pins, buttons, balloons, refrigerator magnets, and other campaign paraphernalia cost $15,967.

Manton's ample treasury allowed him to invest $42,911 in constituent stroking. His annual Christmas parties cost a total of $15,146. He spent $9,846 on year-end holiday cards; $4,693 on floral arrangements for constituents; $2,918 on gifts; $1,158 on constituent meals and other entertainment, including an $802 meal at Le Triomphe in Long Island City; $1,053 on plaques and awards; and $246 on the congressional art contest. In January 1991 Manton spent $7,851 of his campaign treasury to celebrate his swearing in.

Campaign Expenditures	Manton Amount Spent	Manton % of Total	Shea Amount Spent	Shea % of Total
Overhead				
Office furniture/supplies	$ 18,227	1.80	$ 6,062	2.73
Rent/utilities	11,424	1.13	4,850	2.19
Salaries	45,862	4.52	26,851	12.11
Taxes	13,939	1.38	0	
Bank/investment fees	0		19	.01
Lawyers/accountants	8,245	.81	1,500	.68
Telephone	10,135	1.00	8,182	3.69
Campaign automobile	6,069	.60	0	
Computers/office equipment	24,024	2.37	5,878	2.65
Travel	8,100	.80	1,943	.88
Food/meetings	6,512	.64	370	.17
Subtotal	**152,537**	**15.05**	**55,655**	**25.10**
Fund Raising				
Events	85,553	8.44	14,493	6.54
Direct mail	0		12,322	5.56
Telemarketing	0		0	
Subtotal	**85,553**	**8.44**	**26,815**	**12.09**
Polling	**50,500**	**4.98**	**8,700**	**3.92**
Advertising				
Electronic media	0		22,822	10.29
Other media	61,652	6.08	1,065	.48
Subtotal	**61,652**	**6.08**	**23,887**	**10.77**
Other Campaign Activity				
Persuasion mail/brochures	413,954	40.84	73,038	32.94
Actual campaigning	87,285	8.61	30,933	13.95
Staff/volunteers	2,358	.23	1,360	.61
Subtotal	**503,598**	**49.68**	**105,332**	**47.51**
Constituent Gifts/ Entertainment	**42,911**	**4.23**	**565**	**.25**
Donations to				
Candidates from same state	21,200	2.09	0	
Candidates from other states	7,250	.72	0	
Civic organizations	16,449	1.62	85	.04
Ideological groups	1,100	.11	0	
Political parties	36,861	3.64	22	.01
Subtotal	**82,860**	**8.17**	**108**	**.05**
Unitemized Expenses	**34,027**	**3.36**	**659**	**.30**
Total Campaign Expenses	**$ 1,013,639**		**$ 221,721**	
PAC Contributions	$ 427,492		$ 25,832	
Individual Contributions	144,908		168,644	
Total Receipts*	643,780		216,128	

*Includes PAC and individual contributions as well as interest earned, party contributions, etc.

District 8

NEW YORK

Rep. Jerrold Nadler (D)

1992 Election Results

Jerrold Nadler (D)	138,296	(81%)
David L. Askren (R)	25,548	(15%)

One day before the September 15 primary, Democratic Rep. Ted Weiss died of heart failure. Weiss had been considered a lock for reelection after eight consecutive victories in which he had received 80 percent of the vote or more. Weiss's only primary opponent was attorney Arthur Block, a member of the New Alliance party who local Democratic party leaders found unacceptable. At the urging of party officials, 88 percent of the primary voters opted to renominate Weiss.

In this overwhelmingly Democratic district, that move paved the way for party leaders to designate not only Weiss's replacement on the general election ballot but also his replacement in Congress. The beneficiary of this arrangement was state representative Jerrold Nadler, whose insider credentials allowed him to maneuver through a field of rivals that included former Rep. Bella Abzug, New York City Council member Ronnie Eldridge, and Weiss's widow.

Nadler immediately began working the telephones, talking personally with nearly all the 1,000 Democratic committee members. "He did a lot of one-on-one talking with people," recalled Amy E. Green, Nadler's administrative assistant. He also fed the delegates well, investing $3,591 of his campaign funds in a dinner at the Tribeca Grill several days prior to the convention. Sandwiches and beverages supplied to delegates the night of the convention cost his campaign $4,278. In all, he spent $7,943, or 15 percent of his total outlays, courting the delegates.

For the general election, Nadler spent only $225 on advertising—a single ad placed in a small weekly newspaper. He spent $16,498 on campaign literature and advocacy mailings, $541 for buttons, and $3,898 on his election night victory party.

Overhead accounted for the remainder of Nadler's outlays. Office rent for the six-week campaign came to $1,500. On December 31 Nadler paid $500 to the Community Free Democrats to cover the initial rent and security deposit for a small office that would become the base of operations for his permanent campaign. Telephone service for the office cost $1,459 and cellular phone bills added $866. He invested $3,689 in computer hardware, $1,431 in software, and $701 on other office equipment. His campaign staff of three collected salaries totaling $3,875.

Nadler had no time to arrange elaborate fund-raising events and raised what little money he needed through his personal contacts. "He just got on the phone and called people he knew," Green noted. "He had a solid, progressive record in Albany and knew a lot of people in the community."

Republican David L. Askren reported spending $2,150, but he did not itemize the expenditures.

	Nadler	
Campaign Expenditures	Amount Spent	% of Total
Overhead		
Office furniture/supplies	$ 1,781	3.27
Rent/utilities	2,315	4.26
Salaries	3,875	7.12
Taxes	0	
Bank/investment fees	207	.38
Lawyers/accountants	0	
Telephone	2,325	4.27
Campaign automobile	0	
Computers/office equipment	5,821	10.70
Travel	6,540	12.02
Food/meetings	0	
Subtotal	22,864	42.02
Fund Raising		
Events	0	
Direct mail	0	
Telemarketing	0	
Subtotal	0	
Polling	0	
Advertising		
Electronic media	0	
Other media	225	.41
Subtotal	225	.41
Other Campaign Activity		
Persuasion mail/brochures	16,498	30.32
Actual campaigning	13,588	24.98
Staff/volunteers	0	
Subtotal	30,087	55.30
Constituent Gifts/Entertainment	0	
Donations to		
Candidates from same state	0	
Candidates from other states	0	
Civic organizations	0	
Ideological groups	0	
Political parties	0	
Subtotal	0	
Unitemized Expenses	1,230	2.26
Total Campaign Expenses	$ 54,406	
PAC Contributions	$ 37,750	
Individual Contributions	8,035	
Total Receipts*	49,685	

*Includes PAC and individual contributions as well as interest earned, party contributions, etc.

NEW YORK — District 9

Rep. Charles E. Schumer (D)

1992 Election Results

Charles E. Schumer (D)   116,545   (89%)
Alice E. Gaffney † (I)   14,985   (11%)

Rep. Charles E. Schumer had spent a decade preparing for the 1992 Democratic primary. Fearing that redistricting following the 1990 census would force him into a battle with Rep. Stephen J. Solarz, Schumer had spent less than $100,000 on each of the last four campaigns but routinely raised huge sums. By January 1992, Schumer had $1.8 million in his campaign treasury.

Schumer began laying the groundwork for the campaign in late 1991, spending $19,000 for a benchmark poll conducted by Marttila & Kiley of Boston, Mass. In May 1992 Schumer opened a campaign office in Brooklyn. His part-time staff of six included three people responsible for field organization. That same month Schumer paid the first half of a $20,000 retainer to media consultants Morris & Carrick of New York and paid Bell Strategic Research of Washington, D.C., $1,500 for opposition research.

In June Schumer sent out a direct-mail fund-raising solicitation put together by Baraff/Lawrence of Yorktown. According to Larry Schwartz, Schumer's campaign management consultant, virtually everyone in the district received the plea for funds. Schwartz added that had Solarz opted to take on Schumer, the campaign would have broadened its search for donors in order to raise another $500,000. The campaign spent $6,000 on opposition research conducted by Shirley Reid of Washington, D.C. KRC Research of New York was paid $16,000 for conducting focus groups, and Morris & Carrick received the balance of its retainer.

The campaign paid $957 for district phone lists and conducted an in-house phonebank. Once the district's boundaries were set, the campaign called Schumer's new Democratic constituents to let them know Schumer was their new representative and to identify potential Schumer supporters. Once identified, these voters received a follow-up mailing.

When Solarz decided to seek the newly created Hispanic-majority District 12 seat, Schumer quickly abandoned all his plans. He was unopposed in the primary and faced only a Conservative party challenger in the general election.

Schumer spent much of October giving his money away. On October 16 alone, he donated a total of $10,500 to thirteen different federal candidates, including $1,000 each to Democratic Reps. Ronald D. Coleman (Texas), George E. Sangmeister (Ill.), John W. Cox, Jr. (Ill.), Stephen L. Neal (N.C.), Sam Gejdenson (Conn.), and Peter H. Kostmayer (Pa.). Thirty candidates running in state assembly and senate races each received $250 on October 22.

He gave $10,500 to the Democratic Congressional Campaign Committee and $5,000 to the New York State Democratic Senate Campaign Committee.

Campaign Expenditures	Schumer Amount Spent	% of Total
Overhead		
Office furniture/supplies	$ 1,027	.27
Rent/utilities	5,250	1.37
Salaries	41,285	10.76
Taxes	43,240	11.27
Bank/investment fees	0	
Lawyers/accountants	14,222	3.71
Telephone	5,312	1.38
Campaign automobile	0	
Computers/office equipment	9,815	2.56
Travel	240	.06
Food/meetings	0	
Subtotal	120,391	31.38
Fund Raising		
Events	2,419	.63
Direct mail	39,168	10.21
Telemarketing	0	
Subtotal	41,586	10.84
Polling	35,512	9.25
Advertising		
Electronic media	20,000	5.21
Other media	791	.21
Subtotal	20,791	5.42
Other Campaign Activity		
Persuasion mail/brochures	13,015	3.39
Actual campaigning	57,483	14.98
Staff/volunteers	0	
Subtotal	70,498	18.37
Constituent Gifts/Entertainment	379	.10
Donations to		
Candidates from same state	26,943	7.02
Candidates from other states	14,500	3.78
Civic organizations	6,426	1.67
Ideological groups	1,750	.46
Political parties	32,685	8.52
Subtotal	82,304	21.45
Unitemized Expenses	12,252	3.19
Total Campaign Expenses	$ 383,714	
PAC Contributions	$ 187,114	
Individual Contributions	537,346	
Total Receipts*	923,272	

* Includes PAC and individual contributions as well as interest earned, party contributions, etc.

† No expenditures or receipts on file. Candidates raising or spending less than $5,000 are not required to file reports with the Federal Election Commission.

District 10 — NEW YORK

Rep. Edolphus Towns (D)

1992 Election Results

Edolphus Towns (D)	97,509	(96%)
Owen Augustin † (I)	4,315	(4%)

Democratic Rep. Edolphus Towns had coasted though the 1990 campaign, investing only 7 percent of his $280,840 budget on direct appeals for votes. He had spent nothing on either broadcast advertising or persuasion mail. In 1992 Towns spent $713,723, including $106,430 for campaign literature and advocacy mailings and $5,290 to produce and air radio commercials. In all, direct appeals for votes accounted for 36 percent of his 1992 outlays.

With expenditures of less than $5,000, Conservative party nominee Owen Augustin clearly had nothing to do with Town's increased spending. In an overwhelmingly Democratic district where 61 percent of the residents are black, Towns's chief protagonist was Democratic city council member Susan D. Alter, who is white. Alter pumped $257,500 of her own money into her long-shot primary challenge, swelling her campaign treasury to $409,260.

Alter invested heavily in radio commercials and persuasion mail, accusing Towns of ignoring his constituents to defend the interests of tobacco, cable television, and pharmaceutical companies that supported his campaign through political action committee donations. On at least one mailing, Alter did not bother to let recipients know that Alter's campaign had paid the bills. When she was asked by local reporters to explain her clear violation of federal election law, she made an almost incredible statement: "The idea was to catch the voters' attention and not be dismissed because it was someone's campaign piece."

Towns countered with his own barrage of advocacy mailings and a $5,015 radio buy. Prior to the September 15 primary, he paid W. F. Doring & Co. of Jersey City, N.J., $14,132 for phonebanking and spent $33,720 on an in-house phonebank and other get-out-the-vote efforts. On election day, he dispensed $24,769 to fund an army of workers who served as poll watchers and canvassers, much of it dispensed through party precinct captains. He spent $5,952 on signs and $6,289 on buttons and other promotional materials. Although Towns appeared concerned over the large number of voters identified by polls as undecided just one week before the primary, he grabbed 62 percent of the 53,775 primary votes cast. The fact that he donated $44,750 to district Democratic party organizations in the two months leading up to the primary could not have hurt his cause.

Over the two-year cycle, Towns spent $30,738 on constituent stroking, including $7,151 on constituent events, such as Christmas parties for senior citizens, $6,979 on awards and plaques, $5,120 on year-end holiday cards, and $3,088 on meals with constituents.

Towns felt no need to actively campaign against the underfunded Augustin.

Campaign Expenditures	Amount Spent (Towns)	% of Total
Overhead		
Office furniture/supplies	$ 21,935	3.07
Rent/utilities	5,700	.80
Salaries	64,049	8.97
Taxes	3,773	.53
Bank/investment fees	0	
Lawyers/accountants	6,400	.90
Telephone	5,982	.84
Campaign automobile	0	
Computers/office equipment	19,195	2.69
Travel	31,779	4.45
Food/meetings	15,336	2.15
Subtotal	**174,150**	**24.40**
Fund Raising		
Events	113,315	15.88
Direct mail	0	
Telemarketing	0	
Subtotal	**113,315**	**15.88**
Polling	**15,000**	**2.10**
Advertising		
Electronic media	5,290	.74
Other media	35,711	5.00
Subtotal	**41,001**	**5.74**
Other Campaign Activity		
Persuasion mail/brochures	106,430	14.91
Actual campaigning	106,503	14.92
Staff/volunteers	1,057	.15
Subtotal	**213,990**	**29.98**
Constituent Gifts/Entertainment	**30,738**	**4.31**
Donations to		
Candidates from same state	18,700	2.62
Candidates from other states	5,000	.70
Civic organizations	25,034	3.51
Ideological groups	9,034	1.27
Political parties	59,390	8.32
Subtotal	**117,158**	**16.42**
Unitemized Expenses	**8,370**	**1.17**
Total Campaign Expenses	**$ 713,723**	
PAC Contributions	$ 241,165	
Individual Contributions	260,061	
Total Receipts*	560,977	

*Includes PAC and individual contributions as well as interest earned, party contributions, etc.

† No expenditures or receipts on file. Candidates raising or spending less than $5,000 are not required to file reports with the Federal Election Commission.

NEW YORK   District 11

Rep. Major R. Owens (D)   *1992 Election Results*   Major R. Owens (D)   80,028   (94%)
                                                          Michael Gaffney † (I)   4,287   (5%)

In five previous House campaigns, Rep. Major R. Owens had never received less than 91 percent of the general election vote. He had not faced Democratic primary opposition since 1986, when he prevailed with 78 percent of the vote over Roy Innis, chairman of the Congress of Racial Equality. Despite his forty-eight overdrafts at the House bank, Owens had no reason to worry about anti-incumbent sentiment. While he spent $173,374 on his 1992 campaign, only $13,501 was invested in communicating with voters.

Owens spent $98,803 to maintain his campaign during 1991—$24,232 more than he spent during the election year itself. He invested 53 percent of his off-year spending in raising money. Owen's campaign spent $32,898 on an dinner at the Sheraton Center in New York, including $22,000 paid to the hotel for the food and beverages. Dorothy Jackson of Samdor Enterprises in Washington, D.C., received $7,993 for organizing the soiree. A political action committee (PAC) reception in Washington, D.C., cost $8,411, half of which went to Morgans Seafood. Owens's return on these investments was relatively low—$46,664 from individual contributors and $59,108 from PACs.

Challenged only by Conservative party candidate Michael Gaffney and New Alliance nominee Ernest N. Foster, neither of whom spent as much as $5,000, Owens took a very low-key approach to fund raising during 1992. Total fund-raising costs for the year were $13,674; total contributions from PACs and individuals were $55,710.

Owens donated $35,947 of his campaign treasury to other candidates, Democratic party organizations, and various causes. He gave a total of $11,120 to numerous candidates for state and local offices. He gave only $1,500 to House and Senate candidates from other states—$1,000 to Rep. Charles A. Hayes (Ill.), who lost a bitter primary contest with Bobby L. Rush, and $500 to Sanford D. Bishop, Jr. (Ga.), who defeated Rep. Charles Hatcher in the primary. Owens dispensed $10,717 to charitable and booster organizations, including $120 to Parents of Crown Heights Youth in July 1991 and $190 to the Grace Baptist Church in October 1992. In May 1992 he gave Save Our Children $1,100 to rent a bus to ferry people to a demonstration in Washington, D.C.

Constituent stroking consumed $9,729 of Owens's budget, $8,113 of which was spent on constituent meals. He spent $528 on plaques and awards and $497 on floral arrangements.

For the campaign itself, Owens spent only $2,440 to print and send campaign literature. The $860 he spent on advertising was for program ads. His petition drive cost $1,616.

Campaign Expenditures	Owens Amount Spent	% of Total
Overhead		
Office furniture/supplies	$ 5,100	2.94
Rent/utilities	1,115	.64
Salaries	3,125	1.80
Taxes	0	
Bank/investment fees	862	.50
Lawyers/accountants	10,040	5.79
Telephone	0	
Campaign automobile	0	
Computers/office equipment	1,585	.91
Travel	19,026	10.97
Food/meetings	3,098	1.79
Subtotal	**43,952**	**25.35**
Fund Raising		
Events	66,274	38.23
Direct mail	0	
Telemarketing	0	
Subtotal	**66,274**	**38.23**
Polling	**0**	
Advertising		
Electronic media	0	
Other media	860	.50
Subtotal	**860**	**.50**
Other Campaign Activity		
Persuasion mail/brochures	2,440	1.41
Actual campaigning	6,405	3.69
Staff/volunteers	3,796	2.19
Subtotal	**12,641**	**7.29**
Constituent Gifts/Entertainment	**9,729**	**5.61**
Donations to		
Candidates from same state	11,120	6.41
Candidates from other states	1,500	.87
Civic organizations	10,717	6.18
Ideological groups	9,000	5.19
Political parties	3,610	2.08
Subtotal	**35,947**	**20.73**
Unitemized Expenses	**3,972**	**2.29**
Total Campaign Expenses	**$ 173,374**	
PAC Contributions	**$ 89,972**	
Individual Contributions	**71,510**	
Total Receipts*	**173,365**	

* Includes PAC and individual contributions as well as interest earned, party contributions, etc.

† No expenditures or receipts on file. Candidates raising or spending less than $5,000 are not required to file reports with the Federal Election Commission.

District 12 — NEW YORK

Rep. Nydia M. Velazquez (D)

1992 Election Results

Nydia M. Velazquez (D)   55,926   (77%)
Angel Diaz (R)   14,976   (20%)

When political mapmakers snaked the boundaries of District 11 through parts of Manhattan, Brooklyn, and Queens in order to create a Hispanic-majority district, it was assumed that a Hispanic would be elected to represent it. It clearly was not assumed that Rep. Stephen J. Solarz, a nine-term incumbent whose largely Jewish district was obliterated by redistricting, would spend his $3,158,822 treasury in pursuit of the seat.

Yet, with only 33,230 people bothering to vote in the six-candidate Democratic primary, Solarz's vast resources brought him within 1,869 votes of victory. In the process, he spent an average of $346 for each of the 9,138 votes he received. Nydia M. Velazquez, who bested Solarz and four Hispanic contenders, spent nearly $425,000 on the primary, or approximately $39 for each of the 11,007 votes she garnered.

Solarz poured $1,166,813 into broadcast advertising created and placed by Fenn & King Communications of Washington, D.C. In a district where 49 percent of the registered Democrats were Hispanic, he targeted Spanish television and radio stations with ads touting his ability to deliver for his constituents. "Congressman Solarz has a record of taking on the tough problems of our neighborhoods," began one Spanish-language spot. "Hundreds of millions of dollars for new housing. Hospitals. And new jobs.... Congressman Solarz: a fighter who gets results."

Velazquez could not afford television advertising and spent only $21,400 to air radio spots that were produced in-house. She invested $210,799 in brochures, leaflets, and advocacy mailings. Bates & Associates of Washington, D.C., received $44,379 for creating the mailers.

Velazquez benefited greatly from a massive grassroots campaign orchestrated largely by Local 1199 of the Hospital and Health Care Workers union. The union undertook a phonebank effort, canvassed targeted precincts, and paid an army of election day workers to pass out campaign literature near polling locations. "I don't remember how many people there were, but it was a lot," explained Karen Ackerman, Velazquez's campaign manager and current chief of staff. "I believe that made it possible for her to win."

The outcome of the general election was a foregone conclusion in this overwhelmingly Democratic district. Velazquez spent nothing more on persuasion mail or broadcast advertising. With additional canvassing help from her union supporters, she grabbed 77 percent of the vote. On election day, her campaign wrote a $106,082 check to the Hospital and Health Care Workers Local to cover the cost of its efforts on her behalf.

Angel Diaz did not itemize any of the $4,059 he reported spending on his longshot campaign.

Campaign Expenditures	Velazquez Amount Spent	% of Total
Overhead		
Office furniture/supplies	$ 734	.13
Rent/utilities	6,535	1.18
Salaries	66,516	12.01
Taxes	0	
Bank/investment fees	1,175	.21
Lawyers/accountants	13,000	2.35
Telephone	6,623	1.20
Campaign automobile	0	
Computers/office equipment	2,963	.54
Travel	6,394	1.15
Food/meetings	0	
Subtotal	103,940	18.77
Fund Raising		
Events	43,978	7.94
Direct mail	0	
Telemarketing	0	
Subtotal	43,978	7.94
Polling	**15,500**	**2.80**
Advertising		
Electronic media	21,400	3.86
Other media	3,174	.57
Subtotal	24,574	4.44
Other Campaign Activity		
Persuasion mail/brochures	210,799	38.07
Actual campaigning	150,143	27.12
Staff/volunteers	0	
Subtotal	360,942	65.19
Constituent Gifts/Entertainment	2,024	.37
Donations to		
Candidates from same state	100	.02
Candidates from other states	0	
Civic organizations	135	.02
Ideological groups	0	
Political parties	0	
Subtotal	235	.04
Unitemized Expenses	2,500	.45
Total Campaign Expenses	$ 553,694	
PAC Contributions	$ 155,000	
Individual Contributions	205,154	
Total Receipts*	480,174	

*Includes PAC and individual contributions as well as interest earned, party contributions, etc.

NEW YORK District 13

Rep. Susan Molinari (R)

1992 Election Results

Susan Molinari (R)	107,903	(56%)
Sal F. Albanese (D)	73,520	(38%)
Kathleen M. Murphy (I)	10,825	(6%)

During the first eighteen months of her first full term, Republican Rep. Susan Molinari devoted considerable resources to raising money. Between January 1, 1991 and June 30, 1992, Molinari spent $126,602 to maintain her campaign organization, $36,494 of which was invested in fund-raising events. This effort allowed her to wipe out $12,124 in debts from the 1990 campaign and increase her cash reserves from $16,013 to $175,040.

Molinari had opted not to maintain a permanent campaign office, but when her pro-choice stance on abortion attracted a primary challenge from fellow attorney Kathleen M. Murphy, Molinari quickly shifted her approach. In July 1992 she opened her $1,000-a-month campaign office. While Murphy could afford to put only about $30,000 into the race, Molinari pumped $63,967 into campaign literature and three advocacy mailings, alone. She paid Cherry Communications of Gainesville, Fla., $13,101 for phonebanking, spent another $7,316 on an in-house phonebank, and invested $1,235 in voter lists for her canvassing efforts. She spent $6,493 on yard signs and $3,339 on newspaper ads. Between July 1 and September 30, Molinari invested $171,791 in her re-election effort. She garnered 71 percent of the primary votes.

Not all her early efforts were directed at the underfunded Murphy. A letter, written on her behalf by former district attorney Rudolph Giuliani and mailed in August to voters in heavily Italian neighborhoods where New York City Mayor David Dinkins was highly unpopular, noted that Democratic nominee Sal F. Albanese "was and still is a major supporter of David Dinkins" and had even headed an organization called Italian-Americans for Dinkins.

For the general election, Molinari used the National Republican Congressional Committee's facilities to produce two television commercials touting her accomplishments during her first term. Air time on local cable systems cost the campaign $8,093. Campaign literature and two persuasion mailings cost $108,016. "We did a ton of lit drops," recalled Paul Lobo, Molinari's legislative assistant. "With a district this size, you can walk a lot of it." Molinari spent $3,928 on an in-house phonebank.

Albanese invested 41 percent of his budget in leaflets, brochures, and advocacy mailings. He spent $5,775 on newspaper ads, $3,872 on signs, and $3,320 on his phonebank. He paid Austin-Sheinkopf of New York $1,000 for initial discussions on developing an advertising campaign, but he ultimately lacked the resources to carry out their advice. "We had planned both radio and billboard ads, but we never raised the money," Albanese lamented.

Campaign Expenditures	Molinari Amount Spent	Molinari % of Total	Albanese Amount Spent	Albanese % of Total
Overhead				
Office furniture/supplies	$ 7,901	1.60	$ 2,129	.75
Rent/utilities	11,676	2.36	11,923	4.21
Salaries	14,364	2.90	49,583	17.49
Taxes	0		0	
Bank/investment fees	157	.03	161	.06
Lawyers/accountants	120	.02	0	
Telephone	4,610	.93	5,582	1.97
Campaign automobile	0		0	
Computers/office equipment	5,664	1.15	8,476	2.99
Travel	5,724	1.16	1,868	.66
Food/meetings	2,242	.45	0	
Subtotal	**52,459**	**10.61**	**79,721**	**28.12**
Fund Raising				
Events	132,183	26.73	43,389	15.30
Direct mail	0		11,784	4.16
Telemarketing	0		3,709	1.31
Subtotal	**132,183**	**26.73**	**58,882**	**20.77**
Polling	**10,550**	**2.13**	**0**	
Advertising				
Electronic media	11,344	2.29	0	
Other media	41,597	8.41	5,775	2.04
Subtotal	**52,941**	**10.71**	**5,775**	**2.04**
Other Campaign Activity				
Persuasion mail/brochures	171,983	34.78	118,128	41.66
Actual campaigning	44,666	9.03	11,065	3.90
Staff/volunteers	677	.14	0	
Subtotal	**217,327**	**43.95**	**129,192**	**45.56**
Constituent Gifts/ Entertainment	**8,865**	**1.79**	**0**	
Donations to				
Candidates from same state	1,005	.20	0	
Candidates from other states	0		0	
Civic organizations	5,449	1.10	0	
Ideological groups	255	.05	0	
Political parties	11,185	2.26	0	
Subtotal	**17,894**	**3.62**	**0**	
Unitemized Expenses	**2,298**	**.46**	**9,964**	**3.51**
Total Campaign Expenses	**$ 494,518**		**$ 283,534**	
PAC Contributions	$ 195,775		$ 94,500	
Individual Contributions	279,884		135,690	
Total Receipts*	523,755		251,248	

*Includes PAC and individual contributions as well as interest earned, party contributions, etc.

District 14 — NEW YORK

Rep. Carolyn B. Maloney (D)

1992 Election Results

Carolyn B. Maloney (D)	101,652	(50%)
Bill Green (R)	97,215	(48%)

Rep. Bill Green spent $1,140,564 during the 1992 election cycle—more than twice what he had invested in his 1990 reelection effort and nearly three times as much as his 1992 Democratic challenger, New York City Council member Carolyn B. Maloney, spent on her campaign. It was not enough to overcome the effects of redistricting and the 70 percent landslide scored in the district by Democratic presidential nominee Bill Clinton. While Green bested Maloney in the affluent Manhattan precincts he had served for fourteen years, she prevailed by an almost two-to-one margin among voters in the newly added neighborhoods in Brooklyn and Queens, which made up about one-fifth of the redrawn district.

With his substantial financial edge, Green poured $562,423 into persuasion mailers and leaflets that touted his pro-choice stance on abortion, his support for gun control, and his strong record on environmental issues—positions that helped him outpoll President George Bush by twenty-five points in the district. He paid Sann Communications of New York $125,124 for producing the mailers and for placing cable television commercials that aired during the campaign's final week.

Green invested $50,487 in bus and subway signs and paid National Telecommunications Services of Washington, D.C., $25,342 for phonebanking. He paid pollsters Raritan Associates of Highland Park, N.J., Public Opinion Strategies of Alexandria, Va., and American Viewpoint, also of Alexandria, $28,782, $5,915, and $3,000, respectively.

Maloney countered with a $32,000 broadcast advertising campaign created and placed by John Houston Communications of Washington, D.C. According to John Wade, Maloney's chief of staff, one of the three television spots was an animated takeoff on the "Where's Waldo" children's books. The ad depicted in cartoon form events where Green should have been present to represent the district's interests but failed to show up. "Where's Bill Green," the commercial repeatedly asked, showing that he was nowhere to be found. Newspaper ads cost the campaign $10,526.

While Green buried the district in mail, Maloney could afford to spend only $98,481 on her brochures, leaflets, and mail. As a result, she spent much of her time standing on street corners and canvassing the newly acquired, less affluent portions of the district. "We knew we couldn't compete with Green's mail, so we went to the streets and outworked him," Wade said. Maloney could not afford to contract out her phonebanking effort and depended on volunteers to make the calls. She spent only $4,475 on signs. Election day poll watchers cost the campaign $17,184.

	Maloney		Green	
Campaign Expenditures	Amount Spent	% of Total	Amount Spent	% of Total
Overhead				
Office furniture/supplies	$ 2,104	.64	$ 15,495	1.36
Rent/utilities	2,713	.82	14,405	1.26
Salaries	41,193	12.45	152,322	13.35
Taxes	0		55,847	4.90
Bank/investment fees	454	.14	0	
Lawyers/accountants	25,422	7.69	44,069	3.86
Telephone	6,370	1.93	3,786	.33
Campaign automobile	0		0	
Computers/office equipment	1,698	.51	5,963	.52
Travel	7,642	2.31	7,119	.62
Food/meetings	715	.22	831	.07
Subtotal	**88,310**	**26.70**	**299,837**	**26.29**
Fund Raising				
Events	39,509	11.94	58,294	5.11
Direct mail	0		26,502	2.32
Telemarketing	1,716	.52	0	
Subtotal	**41,225**	**12.46**	**84,796**	**7.43**
Polling	**5,635**	**1.70**	**37,697**	**3.31**
Advertising				
Electronic media	32,000	9.67	17,969	1.58
Other media	10,526	3.18	60,143	5.27
Subtotal	**42,526**	**12.86**	**78,112**	**6.85**
Other Campaign Activity				
Persuasion mail/brochures	98,481	29.77	562,423	49.31
Actual campaigning	47,404	14.33	61,595	5.40
Staff/volunteers	2,876	.87	0	
Subtotal	**148,761**	**44.97**	**624,017**	**54.71**
Constituent Gifts/Entertainment	**0**		**0**	
Donations to				
Candidates from same state	2,000	.60	0	
Candidates from other states	0		0	
Civic organizations	0		0	
Ideological groups	0		0	
Political parties	275	.08	0	
Subtotal	**2,275**	**.69**	**0**	
Unitemized Expenses	2,039	.62	16,105	1.41
Total Campaign Expenses	$ 330,771		$ 1,140,564	
PAC Contributions	$ 73,935		$ 211,300	
Individual Contributions	184,224		570,973	
Total Receipts*	283,909		850,661	

*Includes PAC and individual contributions as well as interest earned, party contributions, etc.

NEW YORK
District 15

Rep. Charles B. Rangel (D)

1992 Election Results

Charles B. Rangel (D)   105,011   (95%)
Jose A. Suero † (I)   4,345   (4%)

While eleven-term Rep. Charles B. Rangel faced two primary opponents and was challenged in the general election by Jose A. Suero, who had both the Conservative and Independent Fusion party nominations, none of Rangel's three opponents spent as much as $5,000. As Rangel's treasurer, Richard A. Brown, put it, "It was not a serious race." Nevertheless, Rangel spent $669,096 during the 1992 election cycle, an increase of $71,716 over 1990. Only 14 percent of his 1992 outlays were directed at anything remotely connected with direct appeals for votes.

Rangel simply gave away $197,018 to other candidates, Democratic party organizations, and various causes, which represented 29 percent of his total outlays. He gave $72,950 to candidates for various state and local offices, including $6,500 to New York City Mayor David Dinkins. He donated a total of $13,600 to fellow New Yorkers seeking House and Senate seats, including $5,000 to Rep. Edolphus Towns and $1,000 to Rev. Al Sharpton, who waged an unsuccessful bid for the Democratic nomination for the Senate. Candidates across the country collected checks from Rangel's campaign totaling $20,250, including a $500 donation to Angela Stokes, the daughter of Rep. Louis Stokes, who ran for judge in Ohio. The $16,285 he gave to national Democratic party committees included a $10,000 check to the Democratic Congressional Campaign Committee. He gave $10,725 to state party committees and $6,245 to local party organizations. The $49,013 he gave to charitable and booster organizations included a $500 donation to the Addicts Rehabilitation Center in March 1991 and a $3,133 contribution to Harlem Hospital in November 1991. Among the ideological groups cashing in on Rangel's generosity were the American Civil Liberties Union and the Americans for Democratic Action.

Fund-raising expenses accounted for 24 percent of Rangel's total outlays. The campaign's largest fundraiser in 1991 was held at Tavern on the Green in Central Park. Staged to coincide with Rangel's birthday, the event cost $31,006. In 1992 Rangel traveled to Puerto Rico for a reception sponsored by "Amigos de Charlie." Including the $1,022 Rangel spent on lodging for himself and his executive assistant at the Condado Beach Hotel in San Juan, the $5,862 he spent at the same hotel for the reception, and the $8,223 he paid Premier, Maldonado & Associates of Hato Rey for arranging the affair, Rangel's campaign spent $15,107 on the event. These and other events enabled Rangel to raise $325,850 from political action committees and $151,364 from individuals who gave at least $200.

Campaign Expenditures	Rangel Amount Spent	% of Total
Overhead		
Office furniture/supplies	$ 11,069	1.66
Rent/utilities	0	
Salaries	29,709	4.45
Taxes	0	
Bank/investment fees	110	.02
Lawyers/accountants	7,923	1.19
Telephone	4,436	.66
Campaign automobile	11,951	1.79
Computers/office equipment	1,622	.24
Travel	56,233	8.42
Food/meetings	10,082	1.51
Subtotal	**133,134**	**19.93**
Fund Raising		
Events	157,830	23.62
Direct mail	0	
Telemarketing	0	
Subtotal	**157,830**	**23.62**
Polling	**0**	
Advertising		
Electronic media	0	
Other media	10,524	1.58
Subtotal	**10,524**	**1.58**
Other Campaign Activity		
Persuasion mail/brochures	14,198	2.13
Actual campaigning	64,252	9.62
Staff/volunteers	2,810	.42
Subtotal	**81,260**	**12.16**
Constituent Gifts/Entertainment	**18,644**	**2.79**
Donations to		
Candidates from same state	86,550	12.96
Candidates from other states	20,250	3.03
Civic organizations	49,013	7.34
Ideological groups	7,950	1.19
Political parties	33,255	4.98
Subtotal	**197,018**	**29.50**
Unitemized Expenses	**70,686**	**10.58**
Total Campaign Expenses	**$ 669,096**	
PAC Contributions	**$ 325,850**	
Individual Contributions	**203,043**	
Total Receipts*	**539,183**	

*Includes PAC and individual contributions as well as interest earned, party contributions, etc.

† No expenditures or receipts on file. Candidates raising or spending less than $5,000 are not required to file reports with the Federal Election Commission.

District 16 — NEW YORK

Rep. Jose E. Serrano (D)

1992 Election Results

Jose E. Serrano (D)	85,222	(91%)
Michael Walters † (R)	7,975	(9%)

Elected in a March 1990 special election and re-elected to a full term just nine months later, Rep. Jose E. Serrano was already solidly entrenched by 1992. Redistricting had strengthened his position by making this overwhelmingly Democratic district more Hispanic. For the third consecutive campaign, Serrano coasted to victory with more than 90 percent of the general election vote.

While Serrano spent $47,266 during the off-year, $12,197 of that was for printing charges incurred during the 1990 campaign but not billed until 1991. In April 1991 he closed his campaign office and did not reopen it until August 1992. Immediately following the election, he closed it again. His only salary payments for the cycle were two checks totaling $525 to Lisa Principato of Staten Island for data entry.

Representing the South Bronx, with its median per capita income of $7,102 and household income of $15,060, Serrano's fund-raising efforts were aimed almost exclusively at political action committees (PACs) in Washington, D.C. He raised $93,350 from PACs, which accounted for 83 percent of his total receipts. He raised only $16,050 from individual donors who gave $200 or more, and $5,550 of that came from out-of-state donors. Contributions of $200 or less amounted to just $3,140. Fraioli/Jost of Washington, D.C., Serrano's only consultant, received $10,145 for coordinating PAC receptions.

Given the expense of New York media and the almost total lack of competition presented by Republican Michael Walters, Serrano's advertising consisted largely of program ads purchased from organizations such as the East Bronx NAACP, Family Support Services Inc., the DeCatur Democratic Club, and the James Monroe Senior Center. In all, such ads cost Serrano $1,705, accounting for 53 percent of his advertising outlays. Newspaper ads in various neighborhood weeklies cost $1,170. His only broadcast expense was a $370 payment to the Democratic Congressional Campaign Committee's Harriman Communications Center for production of a public service announcement.

Although the numbers show that Serrano spent $20,371 on persuasion mail and other grass-roots activity, the tardy bill from 1990 represents the entire entry for persuasion mail. For the 1992 campaign, Serrano's grass-roots campaign activity included a $2,360 petition drive to get his name on the ballot; $3,138 in parade expenses, including a $750 bus rental for the Puerto Rican Day parade; and $300 for election day poll watchers.

Serrano gave away far more than he spent on direct appeals for votes. He donated $6,635 to various local Democratic organizations and purchased $820 worth of tickets to their events.

Campaign Expenditures	Amount Spent (Serrano)	% of Total
Overhead		
Office furniture/supplies	$ 3,186	3.40
Rent/utilities	7,223	7.71
Salaries	525	.56
Taxes	0	
Bank/investment fees	29	.03
Lawyers/accountants	4,972	5.31
Telephone	1,436	1.53
Campaign automobile	0	
Computers/office equipment	1,700	1.81
Travel	3,319	3.54
Food/meetings	793	.85
Subtotal	**23,183**	**24.74**
Fund Raising		
Events	25,149	26.84
Direct mail	0	
Telemarketing	0	
Subtotal	**25,149**	**26.84**
Polling	**0**	
Advertising		
Electronic media	370	.39
Other media	2,875	3.07
Subtotal	**3,245**	**3.46**
Other Campaign Activity		
Persuasion mail/brochures	12,197	13.01
Actual campaigning	7,569	8.08
Staff/volunteers	605	.65
Subtotal	**20,371**	**21.74**
Constituent Gifts/Entertainment	**4,874**	**5.20**
Donations to		
Candidates from same state	3,325	3.55
Candidates from other states	500	.53
Civic organizations	917	.98
Ideological groups	1,950	2.08
Political parties	10,005	10.68
Subtotal	**16,697**	**17.82**
Unitemized Expenses	199	.21
Total Campaign Expenses	$ 93,718	
PAC Contributions	$ 93,350	
Individual Contributions	19,190	
Total Receipts*	112,982	

*Includes PAC and individual contributions as well as interest earned, party contributions, etc.

† No expenditures or receipts on file. Candidates raising or spending less than $5,000 are not required to file reports with the Federal Election Commission.

NEW YORK — District 17

Rep. Eliot L. Engel (D)

1992 Election Results

Eliot L. Engel (D)	98,068	(80%)
Martin Richman † (R)	16,511	(13%)

In 1990 Rep. Eliot L. Engel had spent $318,645 to dispatch two general election challengers who spent less than $5,000 apiece. In 1992 Engel drew a primary challenge from a convicted felon. None of his four general election opponents spent as much as $5,000. In response, Engel spent $459,685—a 44 percent increase over 1990.

Engel's only real concern was the Democratic primary against former Rep. Mario Biaggi. Biaggi had been convicted in 1987 of illegally accepting a Florida vacation from a local Democratic party official and had lost his seat to Engel in 1988. In 1989 Biaggi had been convicted of taking $1.8 million in bribes and sentenced to eight years in prison. Released from prison early because of concerns over his health, Biaggi had decided he was feeling sufficiently well to make a run at winning back his old seat.

Apprehensive over both Biaggi's lingering popularity and his $100,034 campaign budget, Engel invested more than $230,000 in the primary. He paid Austin-Sheinkopf of New York $20,000 for creating and placing radio spots that focused on the federal dollars he had brought back to the district and his constituent outreach efforts. "Biaggi tried to portray himself as better at providing constituent service—things like arranging the installation of traffic lights—so we made our advertising case-work oriented," recalled Frank M. Pizzurro, Engel's press secretary.

Engel pumped $142,393 into preprimary persuasion mailers, including the $90,207 Branford Communications of New York billed the campaign for brochure production. General pieces echoing the radio spots featured the pictures and stories of six people whose problems Engel had helped solve. Among the negative pieces was one that focused on the two candidates' "records." "Biaggi had gotten out of prison just for this race, so we compared their records—his prison record with Eliot's constituent work," Pizzurro noted. Additional positive pieces targeted senior citizens, Irish-Americans, and blacks.

Engel's lone survey of voters, conducted by Penn & Schoen Associates of New York, was done before the primary. As Engel told local reporters, "He comes with a lot of baggage, but I don't take him lightly." Engel collected 74 percent of the primary votes.

The general election campaign was anticlimactic. Engel spent nothing on broadcast advertising and only $22,159 on campaign literature and mailings, including $14,739 paid to Branford for brochures.

Over the two-year cycle, Engel invested $11,219 in constituent stroking, including $4,211 on holiday parties and $4,089 on holiday cards. He spent $1,055 on awards and plaques and $1,040 on constituent meals.

Campaign Expenditures	Engel Amount Spent	% of Total
Overhead		
Office furniture/supplies	$ 6,217	1.35
Rent/utilities	2,130	.46
Salaries	9,316	2.03
Taxes	0	
Bank/investment fees	708	.15
Lawyers/accountants	36,832	8.01
Telephone	4,755	1.03
Campaign automobile	0	
Computers/office equipment	2,089	.45
Travel	13,266	2.89
Food/meetings	2,646	.58
Subtotal	**77,959**	**16.96**
Fund Raising		
Events	48,897	10.64
Direct mail	2,520	.55
Telemarketing	0	
Subtotal	**51,417**	**11.19**
Polling	**15,000**	**3.26**
Advertising		
Electronic media	20,000	4.35
Other media	25,843	5.62
Subtotal	**45,843**	**9.97**
Other Campaign Activity		
Persuasion mail/brochures	164,552	35.80
Actual campaigning	28,010	6.09
Staff/volunteers	1,927	.42
Subtotal	**194,489**	**42.31**
Constituent Gifts/Entertainment	**11,219**	**2.44**
Donations to		
Candidates from same state	10,875	2.37
Candidates from other states	1,500	.33
Civic organizations	13,547	2.95
Ideological groups	3,250	.71
Political parties	34,335	7.47
Subtotal	**63,507**	**13.82**
Unitemized Expenses	**250**	**.05**
Total Campaign Expenses	**$ 459,685**	
PAC Contributions	**$ 285,450**	
Individual Contributions	**146,347**	
Total Receipts*	**465,735**	

*Includes PAC and individual contributions as well as interest earned, party contributions, etc.

† No expenditures or receipts on file. Candidates raising or spending less than $5,000 are not required to file reports with the Federal Election Commission.

District 18 — NEW YORK

Rep. Nita M. Lowey (D)

1992 Election Results

Nita M. Lowey (D)	115,841	(56%)
Joseph J. DioGuardi (R)	92,687	(44%)

Two-term Democratic Rep. Nita M. Lowey and Republican Joseph J. DioGuardi were not the best of friends. Lowey had won the seat from DioGuardi in 1988, employing an eleventh-hour negative media blitz that questioned DioGuardi's ethics. Following revelations that a member of DioGuardi's 1988 finance committee had illegally funneled $57,000 in corporate contributions to the campaign through his employees, Lowey had pumped $250,000 of her own money into television and radio ads slamming DioGuardi over the controversy. Four years later, DioGuardi's bitter memory of that loss had not mellowed.

DioGuardi immediately went on the offensive, vowing not to wait for Lowey to cast the first stone. He attacked her as a tax-and-spend liberal who had voted against the Persian Gulf War but for federal funding of obscene art. He accused her of being soft on crime and of pressuring New York lawyers into giving her campaign $100,000. On the positive side, he touted his own background as an accountant who could help reduce the federal budget deficit. DioGuardi invested only one-third of his $571,947 budget in advertising and persuasion mail to communicate those messages.

Lowey's budget was roughly twice as large as DioGuardi's, and she spent 62 percent of it on direct appeals for votes. She paid Fenn & King Communications of Washington, D.C., $286,561 for creating radio commercials and providing general strategic advice. Bates & Associates, also of Washington, collected $153,288 for producing persuasion mailers targeting women, senior citizens, Jewish constituents, and new voters acquired through redistricting.

Lowey spent only $12,225 on newspaper ads, $3,580 on program and journal ads, $2,570 on signs, and $2,158 on buttons, bumper stickers, and other campaign paraphernalia. An in-house phonebank cost $11,005.

To pay for her voter communication, Lowey invested $147,244 of her resources in fund raising. In addition, three of her staff devoted their time to organizing numerous events and writing direct-mail solicitations. Share Systems of Cambridge, Mass., collected $2,577 for telemarketing.

For legal advice on redistricting, Lowey paid Stanley Schlein of New York and Paul, Weiss, Rifkind, Warton, and Garrison of Washington, D.C., $21,000 and $5,000, respectively. The Washington law firm of Perkins Coie received $21,347 to assist Lowey in negotiating with the Federal Election Commission over violations of election law, including her failure to promptly report money she had put into her final 1988 advertising blitz. She then tapped the campaign for $8,000 to cover the negotiated fines.

	Lowey		DioGuardi	
Campaign Expenditures	Amount Spent	% of Total	Amount Spent	% of Total
Overhead				
Office furniture/supplies	$ 6,909	.67	$ 22,594	3.95
Rent/utilities	6,045	.58	16,393	2.87
Salaries	66,258	6.41	64,390	11.26
Taxes	16,530	1.60	4,919	.86
Bank/investment fees	65	.01	1,222	.21
Lawyers/accountants	55,347	5.35	34,517	6.03
Telephone	7,719	.75	31,667	5.54
Campaign automobile	0		5,038	.88
Computers/office equipment	7,821	.76	8,894	1.55
Travel	2,149	.21	11,216	1.96
Food/meetings	292	.03	5,500	.96
Subtotal	**169,134**	**16.35**	**206,349**	**36.08**
Fund Raising				
Events	37,734	3.65	52,060	9.10
Direct mail	106,933	10.34	14,522	2.54
Telemarketing	2,577	.25	0	
Subtotal	**147,244**	**14.24**	**66,582**	**11.64**
Polling	**31,350**	**3.03**	**95,729**	**16.74**
Advertising				
Electronic media	284,636	27.52	148,537	25.97
Other media	15,805	1.53	2,042	.36
Subtotal	**300,441**	**29.05**	**150,579**	**26.33**
Other Campaign Activity				
Persuasion mail/brochures	312,032	30.17	33,828	5.91
Actual campaigning	26,320	2.54	9,571	1.67
Staff/volunteers	147	.01	499	.09
Subtotal	**338,499**	**32.73**	**43,898**	**7.68**
Constituent Gifts/ Entertainment	**14,145**	**1.37**	**0**	
Donations to				
Candidates from same state	5,340	.52	1,345	.24
Candidates from other states	0		60	.01
Civic organizations	975	.09	2,318	.41
Ideological groups	0		155	.03
Political parties	24,370	2.36	4,732	.83
Subtotal	**30,685**	**2.97**	**8,609**	**1.51**
Unitemized Expenses	**2,684**	**.26**	**200**	**.03**
Total Campaign Expenses	**$ 1,034,182**		**$ 571,947**	
PAC Contributions	$ 307,977		$ 79,357	
Individual Contributions	766,922		402,593	
Total Receipts*	1,153,696		583,458	

*Includes PAC and individual contributions as well as interest earned, party contributions, etc.

NEW YORK
District 19

Rep. Hamilton Fish, Jr. (R)

1992 Election Results

Hamilton Fish, Jr. (R)	139,610	(60%)
Neil McCarthy (D)	92,854	(40%)

Rep. Hamilton Fish, Jr., does not believe in taking chances. Democrat Richard Barbuto had spent less than $1,000 on his 1990 campaign; Fish had invested $411,677. In 1992 redistricting had made his constituency significantly less Republican, and his Democratic challenger, attorney Neil McCarthy, had $139,800 to spend. Fish increased his spending to $614,787.

As in past election cycles, Fish never stopped running after his 1990 victory. He spent $118,212 to maintain his campaign during 1991, including $74,061 on overhead. Off-year payroll amounted to $37,599, including $16,600 paid to John Barry, Fish's campaign manager since his election in 1968. Pilgrim Business Management of Poughkeepsie, his accountant since 1968, collected $24,086. "It was the same old campaign," noted Nicholas Hayes, Fish's administrative assistant. "We did nothing new."

While that was largely true with respect to overhead, it was something of an understatement in other respects. In 1990 Fish had not felt the need to survey a constituency that had provided him with 70 percent of the vote or better in nine of his ten reelection bids. For the 1992 campaign, he paid $10,000 each to pollsters Arthur J. Finkelstein & Associates of New York and Strategic Planning Services of Clifton Park. The American Medical Association Political Action Committee supplemented his polling budget with an in-kind donation of $3,750.

In 1990 Fish had spent $74,847 on direct appeals for votes. In 1992 he poured $245,557 into such activities. He spent $55,162 to produce and air three television and four radio commercials. According to Hayes, the spots touted Fish's "experience in government and constituent service." Multi Media Services Corp. of Alexandria, Va., collected $38,515 for placing the television spots. In 1990 Fish had invested only $19,918 on campaign literature and advocacy mailings. To introduce himself to his new constituents, Fish spent $161,873 to print and mail literature in 1992. Fish invested $2,355 in yard signs and $4,597 in buttons, bumper stickers, and other promotional items. He spent 41 percent of his budget over the final month of the campaign.

Over the two-year cycle, Fish spent $15,815 on constituent stroking. He held an annual Christmas party at West Point that cost $3,466 in 1991 and $5,771 in 1992. He spent $2,836 on year-end holiday cards, $1,655 on constituent meals, $1,177 on flowers, and $910 on gifts, including $755 on tie tacks.

With a $15,000 infusion from the Democratic Congressional Campaign Committee, McCarthy ran ads urging voters to retire the "Bush-Fish" team. While unsuccessful, he held Fish to his lowest winning percentage since 1968.

	Fish		McCarthy	
Campaign Expenditures	Amount Spent	% of Total	Amount Spent	% of Total
Overhead				
Office furniture/supplies	$ 5,560	.90	$ 4,721	3.38
Rent/utilities	6,592	1.07	3,269	2.34
Salaries	118,433	19.26	24,839	17.77
Taxes	0		0	
Bank/investment fees	49	.01	256	.18
Lawyers/accountants	64,289	10.46	0	
Telephone	8,433	1.37	4,524	3.24
Campaign automobile	3,111	.51	0	
Computers/office equipment	5,694	.93	2,688	1.92
Travel	23,483	3.82	1,337	.96
Food/meetings	1,841	.30	83	.06
Subtotal	**237,485**	**38.63**	**41,717**	**29.84**
Fund Raising				
Events	46,531	7.57	200	.14
Direct mail	2,240	.36	2,452	1.75
Telemarketing	0		0	
Subtotal	**48,771**	**7.93**	**2,652**	**1.90**
Polling	**23,750**	**3.86**	**19,726**	**14.11**
Advertising				
Electronic media	55,162	8.97	3,050	2.18
Other media	9,548	1.55	645	.46
Subtotal	**64,711**	**10.53**	**3,695**	**2.64**
Other Campaign Activity				
Persuasion mail/brochures	161,873	26.33	64,626	46.23
Actual campaigning	18,973	3.09	6,950	4.97
Staff/volunteers	0		0	
Subtotal	**180,846**	**29.42**	**71,576**	**51.20**
Constituent Gifts/ Entertainment	**15,815**	**2.57**	**0**	
Donations to				
Candidates from same state	7,181	1.17	0	
Candidates from other states	3,450	.56	0	
Civic organizations	4,317	.70	100	.07
Ideological groups	350	.06	0	
Political parties	23,936	3.89	35	.03
Subtotal	**39,233**	**6.38**	**135**	**.10**
Unitemized Expenses	**4,177**	**.68**	**300**	**.21**
Total Campaign Expenses	**$ 614,787**		**$ 139,800**	
PAC Contributions	**$ 229,000**		**$ 14,100**	
Individual Contributions	187,810		113,068	
Total Receipts*	489,831		131,097	

*Includes PAC and individual contributions as well as interest earned, party contributions, etc.

District 20 — NEW YORK

Rep. Benjamin A. Gilman (D)

1992 Election Results

Benjamin A. Gilman (R) 150,301 (66%)
Jonathan L. Levine (D) 66,826 (29%)

An advocate of spending limits, Rep. Benjamin A. Gilman spent $482,690 in 1990 and captured 69 percent of the vote; his Democratic challenger spent $4,058. When his 1992 Democratic challenger, attorney Jonathan L. Levine, spent $18,709, Gilman pumped $573,886 into the race and took 66 percent of the votes in a district largely untouched by redistricting. It marked the fifth consecutive contest in which Gilman had received 66 percent or more of the vote.

Well known to his constituents and running with virtually no opposition, Gilman sliced his expenditures for broadcast advertising from $48,811 in 1990 to $37,998 in 1992, a 22 percent drop. In a year when anti-incumbent sentiment was supposedly running rampant, Gilman's press secretary, Andrew J. Zarutskie, explained that the decision was made to reduce the radio buys because "we didn't have the budget for it." The limited ads the campaign ran focused on Gilman's experience and his ability to use that experience for the benefit of the district.

Gilman also trimmed his outlays for print and billboard advertising from $67,404 in 1990 to $58,095 in 1992. Several rounds of ads in virtually every daily and weekly newspaper in the district cost $51,405. Billboards reminding voters that "his experience works for all of us" cost $3,971. Potholders with the same message added $3,574.

With little need to actively campaign, Gilman spent just 17 percent of his budget on consultants. Ingrid Large/Studio Advertising of Florida, N.Y., billed the campaign $48,000 to cover creative and placement fees for the broadcast and newspaper ads. Bryant Seaman Voter Communications of Briarcliff, N.J., collected $33,262 for phonebanking that targeted Republican and independent voters. Fabrizio, McLaughlin & Associates of Alexandria, Va., received $10,000 for offering strategic advice. Pollster Arthur J. Finkelstein & Associates of New York collected $6,500.

Over the two-year election cycle, Gilman spent $13,609 on cards to commemorate both the Jewish New Year and Christmas. He also invested $5,789 of his treasury in gifts. "Every Christmas he goes from one end of the district to the other, visiting everyone who contributed, volunteered, or helped in any way and gives them a gift," Zarutskie explained.

Gilman filled his campaign coffers by hosting a variety of events. He held a fashion show with table favors provided by designer Oleg Cassini. He rented buses for an $80-a-head trip to a Catskill mountains resort for a day of tennis and golf, followed by a floor show. He raised $192,281 from individual contributors who gave at least $200 and $146,836 from small donors.

Campaign Expenditures	Gilman Amount Spent	Gilman % of Total	Levine Amount Spent	Levine % of Total
Overhead				
Office furniture/supplies	$ 9,746	1.70	$ 642	3.43
Rent/utilities	12,468	2.17	150	.80
Salaries	85,812	14.95	6,020	32.18
Taxes	35,242	6.14	0	
Bank/investment fees	312	.05	176	.94
Lawyers/accountants	0		0	
Telephone	17,696	3.08	2,088	11.16
Campaign automobile	6,557	1.14	0	
Computers/office equipment	15,209	2.65	700	3.74
Travel	3,014	.53	1,400	7.48
Food/meetings	7,828	1.36	61	.32
Subtotal	**193,882**	**33.78**	**11,237**	**60.06**
Fund Raising				
Events	110,332	19.23	0	
Direct mail	9,598	1.67	0	
Telemarketing	0		0	
Subtotal	**119,929**	**20.90**	**0**	
Polling	**6,500**	**1.13**	**0**	
Advertising				
Electronic media	37,998	6.62	0	
Other media	58,095	10.12	2,910	15.55
Subtotal	**96,093**	**16.74**	**2,910**	**15.55**
Other Campaign Activity				
Persuasion mail/brochures	35,726	6.23	165	.88
Actual campaigning	50,485	8.80	875	4.68
Staff/volunteers	275	.05	0	
Subtotal	**86,486**	**15.07**	**1,040**	**5.56**
Constituent Gifts/ Entertainment	**19,709**	**3.43**	**0**	
Donations to				
Candidates from same state	580	.10	0	
Candidates from other states	250	.04	0	
Civic organizations	1,814	.32	0	
Ideological groups	0		0	
Political parties	2,339	.41	0	
Subtotal	**4,983**	**.87**	**0**	
Unitemized Expenses	**46,303**	**8.07**	**3,523**	**18.83**
Total Campaign Expenses	**$ 573,886**		**$ 18,709**	
PAC Contributions	$ 212,397		$ 0	
Individual Contributions	339,117		20,935	
Total Receipts*	566,773		30,135	

*Includes PAC and individual contributions as well as interest earned, party contributions, etc.

NEW YORK — District 21

Rep. Michael R. McNulty (D)

1992 Election Results

Michael R. McNulty (D) 166,371 (63%)
Nancy Norman (R) 91,184 (34%)

In his third consecutive lopsided win, Rep. Michael R. McNulty spent less on advertising than he gave away to other candidates, Democratic party organizations, and charitable causes. Over the two-year election cycle, McNulty's campaign wrote 630 checks—329 of which were donations.

McNulty contributed $14,500 to the Democratic Congressional Campaign Committee (DCCC). Donations and tickets to state party fund-raisers amounted to $7,700. Local party organizations, including the Green Island Democratic Organization, the Duanesburg Democrats, the Niskayuna Democratic Committee, and the Albany County Democratic Committee, received checks totaling $11,502. McNulty's contributions to party organizations rose from $18,189 in 1990 to $34,202 in 1992—an 88 percent increase.

Responding to an almost endless stream of requests, McNulty's contributions to charitable and booster organizations increased from $11,234 in 1990 to $14,011 in 1992. He gave $50 to the Latham Fire Department, $100 to the Hope House Foundation, $25 to Literacy Volunteers of America, and $25 to the Albany Teen Pageants, among many others.

Assured of reelection, McNulty donated $30,788 to other candidates. In October 1992 he gave $1,000 to fellow Democratic Reps. Les Aspin (Wis.), Vic Fazio (Calif.), David E. Bonior (Mich.), and New Yorkers George J. Hochbrueckner and Gary L. Ackerman. In all, McNulty doubled his contributions from $40,033 in 1990 to $80,291 in 1992. Donations accounted for 32 percent of his campaign outlays.

McNulty sank $8,510, or 11 percent of his advertising budget, into ads that were essentially contributions. He placed dozens of program ads with political party organizations, including a $2,000 ad with the Conservative party of New York. Two ads with the Cohoes Catholic Athletic Fund cost $85 and an ad in the Islander '92 Yearbook cost $80.

Unaffected by redistricting and facing Nancy Norman, a Republican challenger who had only $15,463 to spend, McNulty tripled his investment in broadcast advertising from $19,672 in 1990 to $61,997 in 1992. McNulty opted not to hire a media consultant. He spent $1,653 to produce his own commercials touting his experience and constituent service. The campaign spent $48,822 for air time on local television network affiliates and cable systems. Radio air time cost $11,522.

While McNulty was liberally spending his treasury on a variety of things that had virtually nothing to do with the campaign, the DCCC wasted $18,052 of its resources to pick up production costs accumulated by McNulty at the Harriman Communications Center in Washington, D.C.

Campaign Expenditures	McNulty Amount Spent	McNulty % of Total	Norman Amount Spent	Norman % of Total
Overhead				
Office furniture/supplies	$ 3,161	1.25	$ 505	3.27
Rent/utilities	0		0	
Salaries	0		3,895	25.19
Taxes	369	.15	0	
Bank/investment fees	0		149	.96
Lawyers/accountants	5,000	1.98	0	
Telephone	2,310	.91	558	3.61
Campaign automobile	0		0	
Computers/office equipment	3,842	1.52	878	5.68
Travel	3,530	1.40	252	1.63
Food/meetings	4,050	1.60	0	
Subtotal	**22,262**	**8.81**	**6,238**	**40.34**
Fund Raising				
Events	39,282	15.54	2,233	14.44
Direct mail	0		0	
Telemarketing	0		0	
Subtotal	**39,282**	**15.54**	**2,233**	**14.44**
Polling	**0**		**0**	
Advertising				
Electronic media	61,997	24.53	6,748	43.64
Other media	15,923	6.30	0	
Subtotal	**77,920**	**30.83**	**6,748**	**43.64**
Other Campaign Activity				
Persuasion mail/brochures	12,868	5.09	0	
Actual campaigning	7,692	3.04	244	1.57
Staff/volunteers	0		0	
Subtotal	**20,560**	**8.14**	**244**	**1.57**
Constituent Gifts/ Entertainment	**1,627**	**.64**	**0**	
Donations to				
Candidates from same state	25,988	10.28	0	
Candidates from other states	4,800	1.90	0	
Civic organizations	14,011	5.54	0	
Ideological groups	1,290	.51	0	
Political parties	34,202	13.53	0	
Subtotal	**80,291**	**31.77**	**0**	
Unitemized Expenses	**10,784**	**4.27**	**0**	
Total Campaign Expenses	**$ 252,726**		**$ 15,463**	
PAC Contributions	**$ 126,386**		**$ 0**	
Individual Contributions	**79,396**		**15,463**	
Total Receipts*	**220,997**		**15,463**	

*Includes PAC and individual contributions as well as interest earned, party contributions, etc.

District 22 — NEW YORK

Rep. Gerald B. H. Solomon (R)

1992 Election Results

Gerald B. H. Solomon (R)	164,436	(65%)
David Roberts (D)	86,896	(35%)

Elected in 1978, Rep. Gerald B. H. Solomon had never received less than 67 percent of the vote in six previous reelection bids, and redistricting had done nothing to change the district's basic political character. His Democratic opponent, businessman David Roberts, had made seven previous bids for local elective office, losing four times. Roberts had $61,138 less to spend than Solomon's 1990 opponent, who had received 32 percent of the vote. Nevertheless, Solomon opted to spend $284,585 on his campaign, a 20 percent increase over 1990.

Solomon paid Cookfair Associates of Buffalo $85,627 for creating and placing broadcast advertising, including one television commercial touting Solomon as supportive of environmental causes. While he had voted for the 1989 Clean Air Act, Solomon was not considered by many to be a strong advocate for the environment. Solomon refused to pull the spot, saying he would instead return to the Sierra Club a medal the group had given him to commemorate his vote in favor of the Clean Air Act. Solomon's 1992 investment in broadcast ads was $10,980 less than in 1990, an 11 percent drop.

He more than made up for the decline in broadcast advertising expenditures by dramatically increasing his outlays for other forms of advertising. Ads in newspapers such as the *Saratogian,* the *Poughkeepsie Journal,* the *Adirondack Daily Enterprise,* and the *Moreau Sun* cost Solomon's campaign $5,828; Solomon spent less than $2,000 on such ads in 1990. He spent $13,687 on billboards in 1992, something he had eschewed altogether in 1990.

As he had in 1990, Solomon spent virtually nothing on campaign literature, but he put $7,252 into signs and posters. Again, that was an expense he had not incurred in 1990. Solomon decided to pay Public Opinion Strategies of Alexandria, Va., $15,050 to poll his constituents, who would ultimately be just one of nine of New York's thirty-one congressional districts that went for President George Bush in 1992.

Solomon's congressional office refused to explain some of the less obvious expenses, but his records indicate that over the two-year election cycle he spent $12,262 on constituent stroking, including $7,729 to print and mail year-end holiday cards. Outlays for gifts and entertainment accounted for the remaining $4,533.

Roberts operated his campaign out of his barn and toured the district in an old pickup truck. He paid Schnurr & Jackson of Troy $15,578 to produce and place broadcast ads. He spent $2,733 on newspaper ads, $3,719 on yard signs and posters, $2,537 on bumper stickers and other campaign paraphernalia, and $1,604 on his get-out-the-vote efforts.

Campaign Expenditures	Solomon Amount Spent	Solomon % of Total	Roberts Amount Spent	Roberts % of Total
Overhead				
Office furniture/supplies	$ 4,188	1.47	$ 190	.57
Rent/utilities	2,000	.70	0	
Salaries	13,006	4.57	0	
Taxes	0		0	
Bank/investment fees	150	.05	11	.03
Lawyers/accountants	0		0	
Telephone	3,439	1.21	300	.89
Campaign automobile	14,811	5.20	0	
Computers/office equipment	2,245	.79	0	
Travel	12,119	4.26	0	
Food/meetings	4,068	1.43	0	
Subtotal	**56,026**	**19.69**	**502**	**1.49**
Fund Raising				
Events	39,363	13.83	431	1.28
Direct mail	5,874	2.06	0	
Telemarketing	0		0	
Subtotal	**45,237**	**15.90**	**431**	**1.28**
Polling	**15,050**	**5.29**	**0**	
Advertising				
Electronic media	85,627	30.09	15,678	46.63
Other media	20,448	7.19	2,733	8.13
Subtotal	**106,075**	**37.27**	**18,411**	**54.75**
Other Campaign Activity				
Persuasion mail/brochures	1,265	.44	5,692	16.93
Actual campaigning	11,635	4.09	8,350	24.83
Staff/volunteers	426	.15	140	.42
Subtotal	**13,326**	**4.68**	**14,182**	**42.18**
Constituent Gifts/Entertainment	**12,262**	**4.31**	**0**	
Donations to				
Candidates from same state	7,000	2.46	0	
Candidates from other states	4,000	1.41	0	
Civic organizations	573	.20	0	
Ideological groups	0		0	
Political parties	7,711	2.71	0	
Subtotal	**19,284**	**6.78**	**0**	
Unitemized Expenses	**17,325**	**6.09**	**100**	**.30**
Total Campaign Expenses	**$ 284,585**		**$ 33,625**	
PAC Contributions	**$ 283,180**		**$ 0**	
Individual Contributions	**88,601**		**23,025**	
Total Receipts*	**382,251**		**33,625**	

*Includes PAC and individual contributions as well as interest earned, party contributions, etc.

NEW YORK   District 23

Rep. Sherwood Boehlert (R)

1992 Election Results
Sherwood Boehlert (R)   139,774   (64%)
Paula DiPerna (D)   61,835   (28%)

Running in a district that was roughly 25 percent new to him following redistricting and initially concerned over the candidacy of anti-abortion zealot Randall A. Terry, five-term Republican Rep. Sherwood Boehlert spent $99,321 more than he had during the 1990 election cycle. However, only 32 percent of Boehlert's spending was channeled into direct appeals for votes.

Terry, the Right to Life party candidate, never actively campaigned. He invested his energy in organizing protests at the Democratic and Republican national conventions and garnered just 4 percent of the vote. Writer Paula DiPerna, the Democratic standard-bearer, had no political experience and few resources. She attracted 28 percent of the votes. Boehlert coasted to his fifth consecutive landslide victory.

Boehlert spent $89,987 during the off-year to maintain his permanent campaign, 46 percent of which was invested in overhead. He paid the Eisenhower Club in Utica $2,400 for "administrative rent." Periodic payments to several part-time employees, including district director Randall L. Wilcox, amounted to $15,118. He paid the Washington law firm of Brand & Lowell $6,220 and spent $6,989 on computer hardware and software.

Boehlert invested $30,146 in constituent stroking over the two-year cycle. He spent $8,362 on meals with constituents, including an annual dinner for cadets at Griffiss Air Force Base that cost $761 in 1991 and $1,067 in 1992. Year-end holiday cards cost $6,273. He spent $5,883 on gifts and awards, including Congressional Medal of Merit awards given annually to a deserving graduating senior at each of the district's high schools. Expenses for the annual congressional art contest amounted to $1,094. He spent $5,745 on tickets to various sporting events, including the annual National Baseball Hall of Fame game in Cooperstown. Each year he invited local military personnel to take in a Utica Blue Sox baseball game, a courtesy that cost his campaign $4,080 during the 1992 cycle. A Christmas party at the Fort Schuyler Club in 1992 cost the campaign $1,926. Flowers added $863.

For the campaign itself, Boehlert paid Cookfair Associates of Buffalo $68,555 for creating and placing his broadcast advertising, placing one round of ads in most of the district's daily and weekly newspapers, and providing general strategic advice. None of his three television and two radio spots mentioned his opponents. They focused instead on his promise to fight against new taxes and for deficit reduction.

DiPerna invested 81 percent of her budget in direct appeals for votes, but that amounted to only $9,139 more than Boehlert spent on constituent entertainment.

Campaign Expenditures	Boehlert Amount Spent	% of Total	DiPerna Amount Spent	% of Total
Overhead				
Office furniture/supplies	$ 7,742	2.08	$ 1,056	2.19
Rent/utilities	5,400	1.45	0	
Salaries	50,430	13.57	596	1.24
Taxes	3,924	1.06	0	
Bank/investment fees	466	.13	43	.09
Lawyers/accountants	6,220	1.67	0	
Telephone	7,672	2.06	678	1.41
Campaign automobile	0		0	
Computers/office equipment	14,465	3.89	0	
Travel	5,613	1.51	2,366	4.91
Food/meetings	3,402	.92	77	.16
Subtotal	105,334	28.35	4,816	9.99
Fund Raising				
Events	47,427	12.76	2,652	5.50
Direct mail	4,231	1.14	785	1.63
Telemarketing	0		0	
Subtotal	51,658	13.90	3,436	7.13
Polling	19,528	5.26	0	
Advertising				
Electronic media	53,456	14.39	20,536	42.59
Other media	12,297	3.31	1,880	3.90
Subtotal	65,753	17.70	22,416	46.49
Other Campaign Activity				
Persuasion mail/brochures	35,622	9.59	770	1.60
Actual campaigning	15,556	4.19	16,099	33.39
Staff/volunteers	206	.06	0	
Subtotal	51,384	13.83	16,869	34.98
Constituent Gifts/ Entertainment	30,146	8.11	0	
Donations to				
Candidates from same state	3,732	1.00	0	
Candidates from other states	1,400	.38	0	
Civic organizations	3,870	1.04	0	
Ideological groups	0		0	
Political parties	19,216	5.17	0	
Subtotal	28,218	7.59	0	
Unitemized Expenses	19,537	5.26	685	1.42
Total Campaign Expenses	$ 371,558		$ 48,222	
PAC Contributions	$ 197,496		$ 5,500	
Individual Contributions	142,560		34,652	
Total Receipts*	368,179		64,018	

*Includes PAC and individual contributions as well as interest earned, party contributions, etc.

District 24 — NEW YORK

Rep. John M. McHugh (R)

1992 Elections Results

John M. McHugh (R)	122,257	(61%)
Margaret M. Ravenscroft (D)	47,675	(24%)
Morrison J. Hosley, Jr. (I)	26,763	(13%)

The open seat race to fill the vacancy created by the retirement of Republican Rep. David O'B. Martin proved to be no contest at all. In the Republican primary, state senator John M. McHugh coasted to a forty-point victory over businessman Morrison J. Hosley, Jr. In the general election, McHugh grabbed 61 percent of vote against Democrat Margaret M. Ravenscroft, a retired teacher; Hosley, who ran on the Conservative and Right to Life slates; and Stephen Burke, the Liberal party nominee.

McHugh's $170,749 budget was less than half the amount spent by the typical open seat candidate. Since the state senate district he had represented since 1985 included most of the redrawn District 24, McHugh did not need to spend money introducing himself to voters.

As a result, McHugh invested less than $49,000 in the September 15 primary. He waited until August to open his campaign headquarters. Prior to the primary, he spent $13,669 on persuasion mailings, $6,788 to produce and place radio commercials, $1,672 on palm cards, $1,408 on posters, $1,017 on bumper stickers, and $444 on an ad in the *Watertown Times*. Balloons, pencils, and emery boards emblazoned with McHugh's name cost $3,652.

For the general election contest, McHugh spent $43,773 to produce and place television and radio spots. He invested $24,797 in advocacy mailings, $3,129 in palm cards and bumper stickers, and $388 in pencils. A second newspaper ad cost $444. Together with his primary expenses, McHugh spent only $115,574 on direct appeals for votes.

Without much competition, McHugh depended less than many other open seat candidates on consultants. His limited fund-raising efforts were handled in-house, as was his persuasion mail. McHugh wrote his own commercials and paid Multi Media Services Corp. of Alexandria, Va., $43,916 for producing and placing the spots. Strategic Planning Service of Clifton Park collected $10,000 for providing general strategic advice.

A career politician considered a certain winner, McHugh had no difficulty tapping political action committees (PACs) to fund his campaign. The National Association of Realtors PAC donated $10,000 and the National Rifle Association (NRA) Political Victory Fund gave him $9,900. With debate on health care reform looming on the horizon, PACs representing health care interests donated $16,145. The American Medical Association's PAC gave $4,700 before the election and spent $195 to host a breakfast fund-raiser for McHugh after the election. The NRA and the National Association of Realtors also waged independent advertising campaigns on his behalf valued at $10,780 and $6,645, respectively.

Campaign Expenditures	McHugh Amount Spent	McHugh % of Total	Ravenscroft Amount Spent	Ravenscroft % of Total
Overhead				
Office furniture/supplies	$ 1,925	1.13	$ 0	
Rent/utilities	1,500	.88	0	
Salaries	0		0	
Taxes	0		0	
Bank/investment fees	0		0	
Lawyers/accountants	4,953	2.90	0	
Telephone	5,581	3.27	0	
Campaign automobile	0		0	
Computers/office equipment	0		0	
Travel	15,582	9.13	0	
Food/meetings	73	.04	0	
Subtotal	**29,613**	**17.34**	**0**	
Fund Raising				
Events	5,594	3.28	0	
Direct mail	6,731	3.94	0	
Telemarketing	0		0	
Subtotal	**12,326**	**7.22**	**0**	
Polling	**5,000**	**2.93**	**0**	
Advertising				
Electronic media	50,561	29.61	1,778	22.44
Other media	1,038	.61	0	
Subtotal	**51,599**	**30.22**	**1,778**	**22.44**
Other Campaign Activity				
Persuasion mail/brochures	42,177	24.70	2,038	25.71
Actual campaigning	21,798	12.77	0	
Staff/volunteers	0		0	
Subtotal	**63,975**	**37.47**	**2,038**	**25.71**
Constituent Gifts/Entertainment	**0**		**0**	
Donations to				
Candidates from same state	0		0	
Candidates from other states	0		0	
Civic organizations	0		0	
Ideological groups	0		0	
Political parties	0		0	
Subtotal	**0**		**0**	
Unitemized Expenses	8,237	4.82	4,109	51.85
Total Campaign Expenses	$ **170,749**		$ **7,925**	
PAC Contributions	$ 96,351		$ 0	
Individual Contributions	50,210		7,925	
Total Receipts*	177,033		7,925	

*Includes PAC and individual contributions as well as interest earned, party contributions, etc.

NEW YORK

District 25

Rep. James T. Walsh (R)

1992 Election Results

James T. Walsh (R)	135,076	(56%)
Rhea Jezer (D)	107,310	(44%)

Rep. James T. Walsh spent $49,799 less than he had in 1990, despite the fact that teacher Rhea Jezer spent $64,145 more than his 1990 Democrat challenger. While Walsh outspent Jezer by $215,837, he committed only 20 percent of his budget to direct appeals for votes; as a result, he invested just $13,969 more than Jezer in such appeals.

Walsh spent $89,630 during 1991, including $54,490 on overhead. Monthly rent on his year-round campaign office was $223. The office was staffed by one full-time employee who collected $26,303 in after-tax salary for her efforts. Off-year fund-raising expenses amounted to $20,758, including a golf tournament at the Bellevue Country Club that cost $11,373.

Overhead and fund raising continued to dominate Walsh's spending throughout most of 1992. Rent jumped to $558 a month and salaries climbed slightly to $28,601, as additional part-time employees were added during the fall campaign. Fund-raising costs more than doubled to $52,617—driven in large part by the $14,091 he spent on the 1992 golf tournament. Over the two-year cycle, overhead and fund raising accounted for 67 percent of Walsh's spending.

For the campaign itself, Walsh paid Cookfair Associates of Buffalo $29,771 for creating and placing three positive television commercials and companion radio spots. "We tried to convey the message that James was the same guy they sent to Washington in 1988, a moderate who doesn't always vote the party line," recalled James H. O'Connor, Walsh's executive assistant. Among other things, the ads touted Walsh's record of voting against tax increases. The Republican National Committee paid Cookfair $25,000 for additional air time.

When Jezer attacked him for his thirty overdrafts at the House bank, the decision was made to rely on free media to deliver the response. A similar decision was made when Jezer attacked him for supporting "fast track" negotiations on the North American Free Trade Agreement (NAFTA) at a time when jobs were being moved from the district to Mexico. "We used free media to explain that voting for the fast track did not equate with supporting NAFTA. James ended up voting against it," noted O'Connor.

Walsh invested $16,198 in campaign literature and advocacy mailings that targeted Republicans who had voted in the three previous elections, urging them to get out and support the party's ticket. He paid Public Opinion Strategies of Alexandria, Va., $8,540 for a benchmark survey of the district. Walsh paid Syracuse University professor Jeff Stonecash $1,256 to supply a tracking poll conducted by his students.

	Walsh		Jezer	
Campaign Expenditures	Amount Spent	% of Total	Amount Spent	% of Total
Overhead				
Office furniture/supplies	$ 6,255	2.14	$ 977	1.28
Rent/utilities	9,368	3.21	0	
Salaries	54,904	18.81	13,360	17.56
Taxes	26,773	9.17	0	
Bank/investment fees	726	.25	0	
Lawyers/accountants	1,500	.51	0	
Telephone	7,825	2.68	1,234	1.62
Campaign automobile	0		0	
Computers/office equipment	4,867	1.67	201	.26
Travel	8,189	2.81	0	
Food/meetings	2,316	.79	0	
Subtotal	122,723	42.04	15,773	20.73
Fund Raising				
Events	64,606	22.13	4,029	5.30
Direct mail	8,769	3.00	0	
Telemarketing	0		0	
Subtotal	73,375	25.14	4,029	5.30
Polling	9,796	3.36	9,500	12.49
Advertising				
Electronic media	29,800	10.21	29,000	38.12
Other media	658	.23	0	
Subtotal	30,457	10.43	29,000	38.12
Other Campaign Activity				
Persuasion mail/brochures	16,198	5.55	10,248	13.47
Actual campaigning	5,066	1.74	5,089	6.69
Staff/volunteers	6,585	2.26	0	
Subtotal	27,849	9.54	15,337	20.16
Constituent Gifts/ Entertainment	4,497	1.54	0	
Donations to				
Candidates from same state	500	.17	0	
Candidates from other states	0		0	
Civic organizations	2,675	.92	0	
Ideological groups	0		0	
Political parties	3,325	1.14	0	
Subtotal	6,500	2.23	0	
Unitemized Expenses	16,724	5.73	2,447	3.22
Total Campaign Expenses	$ 291,922		$ 76,085	
PAC Contributions	$ 82,495		$ 22,345	
Individual Contributions	190,736		30,510	
Total Receipts*	284,162		99,340	

*Includes PAC and individual contributions as well as interest earned, party contributions, etc.

District 26 — NEW YORK

Rep. Maurice D. Hinchey (D)

1992 Election Results

Maurice D. Hinchey (D) 119,557 (50%)
Bob Moppert (R) 110,738 (47%)

The battle to fill the vacancy created by the retirement of Democratic Rep. Matthew F. McHugh proved to be a local version of the presidential campaign. While Democratic state representative Maurice D. Hinchey argued that government should play an active role in revitalizing the economy, Republican Broome County legislator Bob Moppert portrayed government regulation as the root of the district's economic woes. Democratic presidential nominee Bill Clinton pulled in 45 percent of the district's vote in his three-way race; Hinchey garnered 50 percent in his three-way contest.

However, before he could get to the general election, Hinchey first had to dispatch Binghamton Mayor Juanita M. Crabb. It was a race that few prognosticators believed he could win. Hinchey pulled off the mild upset by spending approximately $170,000, including $62,745 on television and radio ads that focused on his record, particularly in the area of environmental protection. His forty-line phonebank operation attempted to contact every registered Democrat in the district.

When Crabb went on the offensive, accusing Hinchey of not pressing for stronger laws on toxic waste disposal because he was considering a career move into that business, Hinchey shot back with an ad that touted his work on solid and toxic waste disposal and noted that his integrity had never been questioned during an eighteen-year career in the New York Assembly. When Crabb suggested that she was the true agent of change in the "Year of the Woman," Hinchey responded with a television ad listing endorsements from female legislators and a radio spot featuring actress Mary Tyler Moore.

Baraff/Lawrence of Yorktown collected $15,016 for creating his preprimary ads. Peggy Stein Media of Binghamton received $45,431 for placing the spots and $9,440 for placing billboard ads. Hinchey garnered 54 percent of the primary vote.

For the general election, MacWilliams/Cosgrove of Takoma Park, Md., collected $81,072 from Hinchey and $5,000 from the Democratic Congressional Campaign Committee for producing and placing ads that focused on national health care reform, economic development, education, and the environment. His persuasion pieces included a twenty-nine-page proposal for "demilitarizing" the economy.

Moppert had built his campaign strategy on the assumption that he would face Crabb, so he quickly had to regroup. Having exhausted his opposition research budget on Crabb's background, that proved exceedingly difficult. "We took the position that he was a tax-and-spend Democrat, but we were never able to get specific because we didn't know him very well," Moppert lamented.

Campaign Expenditures	Hinchey Amount Spent	Hinchey % of Total	Moppert Amount Spent	Moppert % of Total
Overhead				
Office furniture/supplies	$ 10,169	2.70	$ 2,088	1.05
Rent/utilities	4,968	1.32	3,510	1.76
Salaries	25,162	6.67	9,443	4.73
Taxes	0		0	
Bank/investment fees	696	.18	0	
Lawyers/accountants	0		0	
Telephone	4,605	1.22	1,969	.99
Campaign automobile	0		0	
Computers/office equipment	2,022	.54	4,006	2.01
Travel	17,620	4.67	2,811	1.41
Food/meetings	969	.26	0	
Subtotal	**66,212**	**17.56**	**23,827**	**11.94**
Fund Raising				
Events	23,118	6.13	13,767	6.90
Direct mail	5,355	1.42	44,167	22.14
Telemarketing	0		0	
Subtotal	**28,473**	**7.55**	**57,934**	**29.04**
Polling	**24,600**	**6.52**	**0**	
Advertising				
Electronic media	156,445	41.49	71,890	36.04
Other media	23,924	6.34	10,151	5.09
Subtotal	**180,369**	**47.83**	**82,041**	**41.13**
Other Campaign Activity				
Persuasion mail/brochures	40,637	10.78	0	
Actual campaigning	22,228	5.90	10,037	5.03
Staff/volunteers	1,000	.27	0	
Subtotal	**63,865**	**16.94**	**10,037**	**5.03**
Constituent Gifts/Entertainment	1,903	.50	0	
Donations to				
Candidates from same state	0		0	
Candidates from other states	0		0	
Civic organizations	0		0	
Ideological groups	0		0	
Political parties	0		115	.06
Subtotal	**0**		**115**	**.06**
Unitemized Expenses	11,645	3.09	25,536	12.80
Total Campaign Expenses	$ 377,067		$ 199,490	
PAC Contributions	$ 145,258		$ 32,750	
Individual Contributions	202,043		94,901	
Total Receipts*	374,264		209,386	

*Includes PAC and individual contributions as well as interest earned, party contributions, etc.

NEW YORK

District 27

Rep. Bill Paxon (R)

1992 Election Results

Bill Paxon (R)	156,596	(64%)
W. Douglas Call (D)	89,906	(36%)

After his initial election in 1988, Rep. Bill Paxon had immediately begun to worry about the upcoming redistricting battle. The state's loss of three House seats following reapportionment in 1990, coupled with Paxon's brief House tenure, made his district a likely candidate for extinction. Rather than sit on the sidelines and quietly await his fate, Paxon stepped forward with a pledge of $10,000 each year for ten years to the New York State Senate Republican Committee, if he kept his seat.

Paxon made good on his pledge in both the 1990 and 1992 election cycles, dipping into his campaign treasury for a total of $40,000. He met personally with the thirty-five Republican state senators who controlled his fate, proposed his own redistricting plan, and worked to raise money above and beyond his pledge. When the final map was approved in 1992, senate Republicans had seen to it that Paxon would not face another incumbent in either the primary or general election. Instead, they drew the district boundaries in such a way that fifteen-term Republican Rep. Frank Horton, the dean of New York's delegation, would face Democratic Rep. Louise M. Slaughter in November. Horton chose to retire rather than fight, while Paxon skated through with a two-to-one victory.

Concerned with his ninety-six overdrafts at the House bank and his status as the twelfth biggest user of the franking privilege in the House, Paxon poured $1,015,082 into his second reelection campaign. He was unopposed in the primary and in the general election faced former county sheriff W. Douglas Call, who managed to scrape together $68,062 for the race.

Paxon paid Smith & Harroff of Alexandria, Va., $356,051 for creating and placing television and radio commercials touting his staunch opposition to tax increases. Miscellaneous production costs added $666. He spent $101,280 on brochures, leaflets, and advocacy mailings that included accusations that Call supported a 50 percent payroll tax increase and a 20 percent increase in federal income taxes. He paid Cherry Communications of Gainesville, Fla., $30,000 for phonebanking. Pollster Tarrance & Associates of Alexandria, Va., received $31,000. Paxon's general strategic adviser, Harry Spector Associates of Buffalo, collected $32,015.

During the off-year, Paxon invested $67,560 in overhead and $68,246 in fund raising. Over the two-year cycle, such expenses accounted for 37 percent of his spending. The $372,926 he sank into overhead and fund raising was more than five times as much as Call spent on his entire campaign and eighteen times as much as Call invested in broadcast advertising, campaign literature, and persuasion mail.

	Paxon		Call	
Campaign Expenditures	Amount Spent	% of Total	Amount Spent	% of Total
Overhead				
Office furniture/supplies	$ 11,173	1.10	$ 4,321	6.35
Rent/utilities	15,438	1.52	1,710	2.51
Salaries	59,962	5.91	8,907	13.09
Taxes	36,615	3.61	2,606	3.83
Bank/investment fees	110	.01	61	.09
Lawyers/accountants	0		0	
Telephone	23,805	2.35	2,300	3.38
Campaign automobile	8,924	.88	0	
Computers/office equipment	8,223	.81	0	
Travel	23,109	2.28	1,804	2.65
Food/meetings	6,737	.66	0	
Subtotal	**194,096**	**19.12**	**21,710**	**31.90**
Fund Raising				
Events	123,746	12.19	4,713	6.92
Direct mail	55,084	5.43	1,776	2.61
Telemarketing	0		0	
Subtotal	**178,830**	**17.62**	**6,489**	**9.53**
Polling	**31,000**	**3.05**	**0**	
Advertising				
Electronic media	356,717	35.14	14,479	21.27
Other media	150	.01	5,899	8.67
Subtotal	**356,867**	**35.16**	**20,378**	**29.94**
Other Campaign Activity				
Persuasion mail/brochures	101,280	9.98	5,781	8.49
Actual campaigning	68,889	6.79	13,365	19.64
Staff/volunteers	1,165	.11	0	
Subtotal	**171,335**	**16.88**	**19,146**	**28.13**
Constituent Gifts/ Entertainment	**586**	**.06**	**0**	
Donations to				
Candidates from same state	8,980	.88	0	
Candidates from other states	4,750	.47	0	
Civic organizations	1,765	.17	0	
Ideological groups	5,000	.49	0	
Political parties	31,884	3.14	339	.50
Subtotal	**52,379**	**5.16**	**339**	**.50**
Unitemized Expenses	**29,989**	**2.95**	**0**	
Total Campaign Expenses	**$ 1,015,082**		**$ 68,062**	
PAC Contributions	$ 329,412		$ 11,900	
Individual Contributions	472,835		45,539	
Total Receipts*	845,163		72,481	

*Includes PAC and individual contributions as well as interest earned, party contributions, etc.

District 28 — NEW YORK

Rep. Louise M. Slaughter (D)

1992 Election Results

Louise M. Slaughter (D) 140,908 (55%)
William P. Polito (R) 112,273 (44%)

Redistricting had added more Democrats to Rep. Louise M. Slaughter's constituency, yet her winning percentage slid from 59 percent in 1990 to 55 percent in 1992. Although she had no overdrafts at the House bank, Slaughter struggled to overcome the hard-hitting, outsider campaign waged by Monroe County legislator William P. Polito.

Polito spent $111,356 to produce and air four radio and five television commercials, each of which consisted of three attacks on Slaughter's record. By segmenting the commercials into thirds, Polito was able to re-edit the spots, mixing and matching the segments to create new commercials.

One spot opened with a shot of Polito dropping off a balcony a thirty-foot piece of paper that purported to list all of Slaughter's political action committee (PAC) contributions. As it unfurled, Polito noted that Slaughter had accepted $1.5 million from special interests during her six years in Congress. When it hit the ground, the voice-over exclaimed, "Geez, Louise," then Polito noted that he took no PAC money. The second segment showed a toy train, with a voice-over stating that Slaughter had voted to build a twenty-mile experimental railroad from Rochester to Manchester that would have cost $22 million per mile. Again, the voice-over exclaimed, "Geez, Louise." The third segment noted that the railroad industry was Slaughter's second largest source of campaign contributions, slammed her for the experimental railroad, and once again concluded with "Geez, Louise."

Polito went on to enshrine his catchy tagline in a country-western-style campaign song. "Geez, Louise, you've brought us to our knees, spending money any way you please," the song lamented.

Slaughter countered these attacks with a $305,376 broadcast advertising campaign, most of which was invested in television ads. She chose not to spend her advertising dollars on direct responses to Polito's attacks, relying on the local media to critique their accuracy. Instead, a testimonial told how she had helped a woman with breast cancer cut through bureaucratic red tape to secure medical benefits. Another testimonial described her intervention to help restore electricity to a constituent's home following an ice storm. Other spots touted her work on a childhood immunization bill and her endorsement by the president of the local Chamber of Commerce. Struble-Totten Communications of Washington, D.C., collected $65,204 for creating the spots. Pro Media of Needham, Mass., received $240,032 to cover the cost of air time and placement fees. The Democratic Congressional Campaign Committee picked up $26,882 of the production costs.

Campaign Expenditures	Slaughter Amount Spent	Slaughter % of Total	Polito Amount Spent	Polito % of Total
Overhead				
Office furniture/supplies	$ 4,605	.89	$ 2,989	1.13
Rent/utilities	3,600	.70	4,791	1.80
Salaries	34,558	6.68	10,682	4.02
Taxes	18,935	3.66	1,731	.65
Bank/investment fees	658	.13	37	.01
Lawyers/accountants	0		358	.13
Telephone	4,640	.90	6,109	2.30
Campaign automobile	0		0	
Computers/office equipment	1,524	.29	310	.12
Travel	7,903	1.53	0	
Food/meetings	1,003	.19	76	.03
Subtotal	77,426	14.96	27,082	10.20
Fund Raising				
Events	17,656	3.41	9,138	3.44
Direct mail	15,835	3.06	6,668	2.51
Telemarketing	0		0	
Subtotal	33,491	6.47	15,807	5.95
Polling	27,047	5.23	16,520	6.22
Advertising				
Electronic media	305,376	59.00	111,356	41.94
Other media	1,467	.28	6,880	2.59
Subtotal	306,843	59.29	118,235	44.53
Other Campaign Activity				
Persuasion mail/brochures	37,580	7.26	72,625	27.35
Actual campaigning	16,853	3.26	15,195	5.72
Staff/volunteers	0		0	
Subtotal	54,432	10.52	87,819	33.08
Constituent Gifts/Entertainment	2,732	.53	0	
Donations to				
Candidates from same state	500	.10	0	
Candidates from other states	0		0	
Civic organizations	0		15	.01
Ideological groups	300	.06	0	
Political parties	5,142	.99	30	.01
Subtotal	5,942	1.15	45	.02
Unitemized Expenses	9,643	1.86	0	
Total Campaign Expenses	$ 517,557		$ 265,508	
PAC Contributions	$ 297,050		$ 0	
Individual Contributions	156,740		132,113	
Total Receipts*	473,871		245,768	

*Includes PAC and individual contributions as well as interest earned, party contributions, etc.

NEW YORK   District 29

Rep. John J. LaFalce (D)   *1992 Election Results*   John J. LaFalce (D)   128,230   (54%)
William E. Miller, Jr. (R)   98,031   (42%)

On January 1, 1991 Rep. John J. LaFalce had campaign cash reserves of $645,139, significantly more than any member of the New York delegation except fellow Democrats Stephen J. Solarz and Charles E. Schumer, who were worried about facing each other in a redistricting-induced intraparty slugfest. With New York's loss of three House seats, LaFalce had his own redistricting fears—a general election showdown with Republican Rep. Bill Paxon. Preparing for the worst, LaFalce pumped $101,211 into his campaign operation during 1991 and raised his cash-on-hand to $842,672.

Paxon was equally concerned about an incumbent versus incumbent match-up and, courtesy of his pledge to reward the New York State Senate Republican Committee with $100,000 over ten years if he kept his seat, Paxon had succeeded in shifting the lines to his liking. In so doing, Paxon saved both himself and LaFalce from an extremely costly campaign.

Relieved of that concern, LaFalce still had problems. After garnering 60 percent of the general election vote in his initial House campaign and 67 percent of the vote or better in seven consecutive reelection bids, LaFalce had seen his winning percentage drop to 55 percent in 1990. That encouraged Republican William E. Miller, Jr., the son of the party's 1964 vice presidential nominee, to challenge LaFalce in 1992. With the presumed strong backing of the national Republican party, Miller seemed likely to wage a well-funded campaign.

However, "presumed" turned out to be the operative word. Miller spent $92,866 on his own behalf, but the National Republican Congressional Committee spent only $2,988 to augment his polling budget.

Miller sank 37 percent of his $92,866 budget into broadcast advertising that portrayed him as an agent of change, while painting LaFalce as a career politician who had voted for the congressional pay raise, for the 1990 budget compromise that included several tax increases, and against a proposed constitutional amendment requiring a balanced federal budget. However, without any financial boost from the party, Miller was outspent by four to one on broadcast advertising.

LaFalce paid Shorr Associates of Philadelphia, Pa., $114,190 for creating and placing his broadcast advertising campaign, which stressed the importance of having a senior member in Congress to represent the district's interests. Pollster Cooper & Secrest Associates of Alexandria, Va., collected $33,993.

While LaFalce was struggling to get his winning percentage back up toward 60 percent, he opted to invest $20,297 in constituent stroking, including more than $12,000 for his biennial free picnic held during the off-year.

Campaign Expenditures	LaFalce Amount Spent	LaFalce % of Total	Miller Amount Spent	Miller % of Total
Overhead				
Office furniture/supplies	$ 10,881	2.33	$ 1,587	1.71
Rent/utilities	2,984	.64	3,112	3.35
Salaries	16,490	3.53	10,400	11.20
Taxes	23,106	4.95	0	
Bank/investment fees	1,406	.30	62	.07
Lawyers/accountants	0		237	.26
Telephone	7,620	1.63	6,206	6.68
Campaign automobile	0		0	
Computers/office equipment	24,236	5.19	2,300	2.48
Travel	17,146	3.67	0	
Food/meetings	5,425	1.16	0	
Subtotal	**109,296**	**23.41**	**23,904**	**25.74**
Fund Raising				
Events	48,968	10.49	3,587	3.86
Direct mail	0		0	
Telemarketing	0		0	
Subtotal	**48,968**	**10.49**	**3,587**	**3.86**
Polling	**33,993**	**7.28**	**0**	
Advertising				
Electronic media	135,036	28.92	34,327	36.96
Other media	10,311	2.21	695	.75
Subtotal	**145,346**	**31.13**	**35,022**	**37.71**
Other Campaign Activity				
Persuasion mail/brochures	36,522	7.82	7,493	8.07
Actual campaigning	17,554	3.76	7,953	8.56
Staff/volunteers	1,542	.33	0	
Subtotal	**55,618**	**11.91**	**15,445**	**16.63**
Constituent Gifts/Entertainment	**20,297**	**4.35**	**0**	
Donations to				
Candidates from same state	11,775	2.52	0	
Candidates from other states	0		0	
Civic organizations	3,310	.71	400	.43
Ideological groups	175	.04	0	
Political parties	25,955	5.56	0	
Subtotal	**41,215**	**8.83**	**400**	**.43**
Unitemized Expenses	**12,211**	**2.62**	**14,507**	**15.62**
Total Campaign Expenses	**$ 466,946**		**$ 92,866**	
PAC Contributions	$ 312,570		$ 1,000	
Individual Contributions	197,300		55,999	
Total Receipts*	588,616		83,924	

*Includes PAC and individual contributions as well as interest earned, party contributions, etc.

District 30 — NEW YORK

Rep. Jack Quinn (R)

1992 Election Results

Jack Quinn (R)	125,734	(52%)
Dennis T. Gorski (D)	111,445	(46%)

Considering the fact that Democrat Bill Clinton ran 20 points ahead of President George Bush in the presidential balloting in District 30, Republican Jack Quinn's victory was stunning. Given that Erie County executive Dennis Gorski outspent him by more than two to one, Quinn's victory was miraculous.

Quinn's upset was the result of an aggressive outsider campaign. While he ran on the Republican ticket, he also secured a place on the ballot under the banner of a party he founded—the Change Congress party. He sank 70 percent of his budget into four television commercials and companion radio spots that featured calls for congressional reforms, including reduced spending on franked mail and taxpayer-funded junkets. Administrative assistant Mary Lou Palmer said the ads also pointed to Quinn's support of term limits and stricter limits on political action committee (PAC) contributions. Quinn hammered Gorski as another career politician who would give voters "more of the same." Harry Spector Associates of Buffalo collected $136,846 from Quinn's coffers, $34,999 from the National Republican Congressional Committee, and $16,700 from the Republican National Committee for creating and placing the ads. Miscellaneous production charges added $3,500.

Having invested so heavily in television advertising, there was little room in Quinn's budget for other types of voter communication. He spent nothing on newspaper ads or billboards. Outlays for yard signs, buttons, and bumper stickers amounted to $3,198. He could not afford to operate an in-house phonebank. Quinn spent $9,214 on campaign literature, $5,608 of which went to Spector for design and production, but the campaign opted not to invest money in postage to send it out. Instead, Quinn and his volunteers knocked on thousands of doors. "It was that grassroots effort that won it for us," Palmer noted.

With little money to spare, Quinn chose not to invest in fund-raising direct mail. The bulk of his contributions were raised through three large events—a reception at the Brierwood Country Club in Hamburg, a dinner at Connor's Restaurant in West Seneca, and a reception at the Radisson Hotel in Buffalo. These events and several smaller affairs helped Quinn raise $123,950 from individual contributors who gave at least $200 and $58,276 from donors who gave less than $200. Given his desire to restrict their participation, Quinn raised only $10,665 from PACs.

With his significantly larger budget, Gorski paid $198,798 to Trippi, McMahon & Squier of Alexandria, Va., for creating and placing the broadcast ads. Cooper & Secrest Associates provided polls for $17,390. His $100,283 persuasion mail operation was handled entirely in-house.

Campaign Expenditures	Quinn Amount Spent	Quinn % of Total	Gorski Amount Spent	Gorski % of Total
Overhead				
Office furniture/supplies	$ 658	.33	$ 7,236	1.56
Rent/utilities	5,131	2.55	9,999	2.15
Salaries	0		19,400	4.18
Taxes	0		0	
Bank/investment fees	280	.14	783	.17
Lawyers/accountants	0		0	
Telephone	1,760	.88	2,493	.54
Campaign automobile	0		0	
Computers/office equipment	733	.36	11,678	2.52
Travel	966	.48	3,724	.80
Food/meetings	0		622	.13
Subtotal	9,528	4.74	55,935	12.05
Fund Raising				
Events	29,988	14.92	24,975	5.38
Direct mail	0		0	
Telemarketing	0		0	
Subtotal	29,988	14.92	24,975	5.38
Polling	2,500	1.24	17,390	3.75
Advertising				
Electronic media	140,346	69.82	207,647	44.72
Other media	253	.13	2,524	.54
Subtotal	140,598	69.95	210,171	45.26
Other Campaign Activity				
Persuasion mail/brochures	9,214	4.58	100,283	21.60
Actual campaigning	6,693	3.33	35,227	7.59
Staff/volunteers	0		1,122	.24
Subtotal	15,908	7.91	136,632	29.42
Constituent Gifts/Entertainment	0		105	.02
Donations to				
Candidates from same state	0		1,445	.31
Candidates from other states	0		0	
Civic organizations	0		2,500	.54
Ideological groups	0		0	
Political parties	0		100	.02
Subtotal	0		4,045	.87
Unitemized Expenses	2,487	1.24	15,088	3.25
Total Campaign Expenses	$ 201,010		$ 464,341	
PAC Contributions	$ 10,665		$ 119,525	
Individual Contributions	182,226		254,920	
Total Receipts*	205,843		456,099	

*Includes PAC and individual contributions as well as interest earned, party contributions, etc.

NEW YORK — District 31

Rep. Amo Houghton (R)

1992 Election Results

Amo Houghton (R)	150,696	(71%)
Joseph P. Leahey (D)	52,010	(24%)
Gretchen S. McManus † (I)	10,846	(5%)

Rep. Amo Houghton had spent $172,442 on his 1990 campaign, dedicating $37,414 to direct appeals for votes. His Democratic challenger, retired federal employee Joseph P. Leahey, had spent $6,592. Two years later, Houghton found himself in a rematch with Leahey, who had even less to spend. Nevertheless, Houghton pumped $452,834 into his campaign. "1992 was very different from 1990," recalled Brian A. Fitzpatrick, Houghton's staff director. "The Bush campaign was falling like a rock, and we were worried about reverse coattails."

Those concerns prompted Houghton to spend $46,862 on positive radio commercials that touted his accomplishments in Washington and his efforts to bring jobs to the district. Houghton spent $13,616 to place ads in every daily and weekly newspaper in the district, including $4,320 for "thank-you ads" following his landslide victory. Billboard ads cost $5,555. Determined to spend money on air time if necessary, the campaign produced several companion television spots. The spots were shelved when it became clear that Houghton was going to coast to another big win.

Houghton's main form of communication with voters, particularly those acquired through redistricting, was persuasion mail. The targeted mailings, which cost $96,073, focused on federal highway projects Houghton had delivered and economic development. The cost of printing palm cards and other campaign leaflets added $8,800. "We had annexed two counties and several townships through redistricting, and people had to get to know who we were," Fitzpatrick noted. Stuart Stevens of New York collected $44,399 for creating and placing the broadcast advertising and designing the advocacy mailers.

To provide constant reminders that he was seeking reelection, Houghton invested $3,564 in key chains produced by Level Enterprises in Los Angeles, Calif. As the name of the firm implies, the key rings were attached to a miniature carpenters level, imprinted with Houghton's name. "The built-in message was 'we're on the level,'" Fitzpatrick explained. Houghton spent $2,654 on yard signs, $2,038 on buttons and bumper stickers, and $1,278 on hats.

Houghton maintained a three-tiered congressional fund-raising club. Donors received a memento to commemorate thir membership, ranging from a piece of jewelry to an etched drinking glass. Houghton raised $180,298 from individual donors who gave $200 or more and $37,468 from smaller donors. While paying for the campaign was important, fund-raising events served other purposes, as well. "Sens. Dole and D'Amato came in for events that were designed as party-builders. All the local party chairs were there, as well, and we probably broke even," said Fitzpatrick.

Campaign Expenditures	Houghton Amount Spent	Houghton % of Total	Leahey Amount Spent	Leahey % of Total
Overhead				
Office furniture/supplies	$ 6,215	1.37	$ 644	11.05
Rent/utilities	2,489	.55	0	
Salaries	95,811	21.16	0	
Taxes	3,573	.79	0	
Bank/investment fees	972	.21	46	.78
Lawyers/accountants	0		0	
Telephone	8,105	1.79	443	7.60
Campaign automobile	0		0	
Computers/office equipment	13,616	3.01	0	
Travel	34,990	7.73	1,378	23.63
Food/meetings	1,542	.34	273	4.68
Subtotal	**167,314**	**36.95**	**2,784**	**47.73**
Fund Raising				
Events	51,988	11.48	0	
Direct mail	2,284	.50	0	
Telemarketing	0		0	
Subtotal	**54,272**	**11.98**	**0**	
Polling	**20,866**	**4.61**	**0**	
Advertising				
Electronic media	46,862	10.35	648	11.11
Other media	20,565	4.54	668	11.46
Subtotal	**67,428**	**14.89**	**1,316**	**22.57**
Other Campaign Activity				
Persuasion mail/brochures	104,873	23.16	295	5.07
Actual campaigning	21,291	4.70	68	1.17
Staff/volunteers	1,078	.24	100	1.71
Subtotal	**127,242**	**28.10**	**463**	**7.95**
Constituent Gifts/ Entertainment	**665**	**.15**	**0**	
Donations to				
Candidates from same state	6,875	1.52	0	
Candidates from other states	5,350	1.18	0	
Civic organizations	0		0	
Ideological groups	0		0	
Political parties	1,906	.42	222	3.81
Subtotal	**14,131**	**3.12**	**222**	**3.81**
Unitemized Expenses	**916**	**.20**	**1,046**	**17.94**
Total Campaign Expenses	**$ 452,834**		**$ 5,831**	
PAC Contributions	**$ 117,060**		**$ 500**	
Individual Contributions	**217,766**		**1,463**	
Total Receipts*	**359,995**		**5,849**	

*Includes PAC and individual contributions as well as interest earned, party contributions, etc.

† No expenditures or receipts on file. Candidates raising or spending less than $5,000 are not required to file reports with the Federal Election Commission.

NORTH CAROLINA   District 1

Rep. Eva Clayton (D)

1992 Election Results

Eva Clayton (D)	116,078	(67%)
Ted Tyler (R)	54,457	(31%)

The only contest that mattered in District 1 was the battle for the Democratic nomination. Snaking through parts of twenty-eight counties, the district was specifically drawn to elect a new black representative. However, when five black candidates and two whites entered the Democratic fray, it was unclear whether the mapmaker's intent would be realized.

The race quickly became a contest between former Warren County commissioner Eva Clayton and Walter B. Jones, Jr., the son of Democratic Rep. Walter B. Jones, who represented much of District 1 until his death in September 1992. Jones benefited from a reservoir of good will built by his father, the strong support of white voters, and an ability to raise $122,895 for the May 5 primary and $131,440 for the June 2 runoff. Clayton had a strong grass-roots organization and the backing of labor and women's groups, which anted up most of the $56,126 she raised from political action committees (PACs) prior to the primary. EMILY's List, a PAC created to help women candidates raise money, weighed in with early direct-mail fund-raising support.

Clayton spent $126,269 on the primary, including $36,650 on radio and television commercials, $15,505 on targeted persuasion mailings, $2,135 on newspaper ads, and $1,676 on signs. To make certain that black voters turned out, Clayton invested $8,991 in phonebanking and door-to-door canvassing. Although Jones won the primary with 38 percent of the vote, that was 2 percentage points short of what he needed to avoid a runoff. Clayton's grass-roots efforts pulled her into second place with 31 percent.

Once it was certain that Clayton would be in the runoff, PACs delivered an additional $106,000, or 76 percent of the $140,130 she spent in the runoff. She pumped $45,400 into her broadcast ads, $32,510 into persuasion mail, $24,494 into her get-out-the-vote efforts, and $3,069 into newspaper ads. Endorsed by three of the four black candidates she had bested in the primary, Clayton emerged with 55 percent of the runoff votes.

Assured of victory, Clayton did not let up for the fall campaign. While Republican Ted Tyler spent just $6,132 on the race, Clayton poured an additional $282,671 into the contest, including $33,608 on broadcast ads and $33,828 on persuasion mail.

For creating her ads and buying most of the air time during the campaign's three phases, Shorr Associates of Philadelphia, Pa., collected $106,008. Roger Lee & Carol Beddo Associates of San Jose, Calif., received $40,525 for producing the persuasion mailers.

	Clayton		Tyler	
Campaign Expenditures	Amount Spent	% of Total	Amount Spent	% of Total
Overhead				
Office furniture/supplies	$ 14,893	2.71	$ 0	
Rent/utilities	6,839	1.25	0	
Salaries	58,091	10.58	0	
Taxes	4,368	.80	0	
Bank/investment fees	796	.14	23	.37
Lawyers/accountants	220	.04	0	
Telephone	13,869	2.53	92	1.50
Campaign automobile	5,562	1.01	0	
Computers/office equipment	13,271	2.42	0	
Travel	29,451	5.36	264	4.31
Food/meetings	4,012	.73	0	
Subtotal	**151,372**	**27.57**	**379**	**6.18**
Fund Raising				
Events	62,968	11.47	0	
Direct mail	12,860	2.34	0	
Telemarketing	0		0	
Subtotal	**75,828**	**13.81**	**0**	
Polling	**0**		**0**	
Advertising				
Electronic media	115,658	21.06	0	
Other media	20,061	3.65	1,178	19.21
Subtotal	**135,719**	**24.72**	**1,178**	**19.21**
Other Campaign Activity				
Persuasion mail/brochures	81,843	14.91	952	15.52
Actual campaigning	78,948	14.38	3,496	57.01
Staff/volunteers	1,549	.28	34	.55
Subtotal	**162,340**	**29.57**	**4,481**	**73.08**
Constituent Gifts/ Entertainment	341	.06	0	
Donations to				
Candidates from same state	6,545	1.19	0	
Candidates from other states	400	.07	0	
Civic organizations	1,179	.21	0	
Ideological groups	690	.13	0	
Political parties	1,167	.21	60	.98
Subtotal	**9,982**	**1.82**	**60**	**.98**
Unitemized Expenses	**13,488**	**2.46**	**34**	**.55**
Total Campaign Expenses	**$ 549,070**		**$ 6,132**	
PAC Contributions	$ 281,665		$ 0	
Individual Contributions	201,333		7,055	
Total Receipts*	**551,491**		**7,055**	

*Includes PAC and individual contributions as well as interest earned, party contributions, etc.

NORTH CAROLINA — District 2

Rep. Tim Valentine (D)

1992 Election Results

Tim Valentine (D)	113,693	(54%)
Don Davis (R)	93,893	(44%)

Elected in 1982 with 54 percent of the vote, Rep. Tim Valentine had parlayed his moderate-to-conservative voting record and constituent service into a safe seat. In four reelection campaigns, Valentine had never received less than 68 percent of the vote. However, when redistricting moved large numbers of his black constituents into District 1 and replaced them with conservative white Democrats, Valentine was back to square one. Among his new constituents was retired army officer Don Davis, who had captured 41 percent of the vote against Democratic Rep. H. Martin Lancaster in 1990.

Davis received fund-raising help from televangelist Pat Robertson and conservative commentator Patrick Buchanan and was able to invest $176,991 in his challenge to Valentine, or about twice what he spent to combat Lancaster. Davis put $52,040 into producing and airing one television and three radio commercials that criticized Valentine for his 1989 vote in favor of a congressional pay raise and attempted to paint him as a tax-and-spend liberal. The National Republican Congressional Committee spent $19,850 to purchase additional television air time.

Valentine responded with a $164,170 broadcast advertising campaign. According to administrative assistant A. B. Swindell, the four television and two radio spots focused on Valentine's ability to deliver federal projects to the district. "We played up the importance of incumbency, even though it was supposedly an anti-incumbent year," noted Swindell. GVA Productions of Charlotte collected $161,854 for creating the spots and buying most of the air time.

During the final week of the campaign, Valentine also spent $5,645 to buy a round of ads in newspapers throughout the district. "You do it because it's expected, not because you get more bang for the buck," Swindell explained.

To keep tabs on the mood of the electorate, Valentine paid Mellman & Lazarus of Washington, D.C., $16,127. For providing general campaign advice and helping Valentine prepare for interviews, Robert S. Havely of Raleigh, Pope McCorkle III of Durham, and David Smith of Durham collected $3,750, $1,857, and $500, respectively. Valentine paid Creative Campaign Consultant of Washington, D.C., $36,809 for coordinating political action committee fund raising. DWD Software Development Corp. received $14,146 for producing the campaign's lone direct-mail solicitation.

Valentine spent 5 percent of his funds on various gifts and constituent entertainment, including $11,727 on meals, $5,541 on year-end holiday cards, and $1,606 on flowers. Valentine's Day cookies passed out to other House members cost $711 in 1991 and $810 in 1992.

	Valentine		Davis	
Campaign Expenditures	Amount Spent	% of Total	Amount Spent	% of Total
Overhead				
Office furniture/supplies	$ 5,762	1.26	$ 4,387	2.48
Rent/utilities	1,379	.30	4,434	2.51
Salaries	39,728	8.68	13,686	7.73
Taxes	2,122	.46	0	
Bank/investment fees	155	.03	5,339	3.02
Lawyers/accountants	6,027	1.32	600	.34
Telephone	4,930	1.08	2,987	1.69
Campaign automobile	0		0	
Computers/office equipment	7,684	1.68	8,313	4.70
Travel	20,882	4.56	2,502	1.41
Food/meetings	2,674	.58	87	.05
Subtotal	**91,343**	**19.95**	**42,336**	**23.92**
Fund Raising				
Events	96,126	20.99	6,871	3.88
Direct mail	21,264	4.64	8,756	4.95
Telemarketing	0		1,909	1.08
Subtotal	**117,390**	**25.64**	**17,536**	**9.91**
Polling	**16,127**	**3.52**	**10,875**	**6.14**
Advertising				
Electronic media	164,170	35.86	52,040	29.40
Other media	6,085	1.33	2,369	1.34
Subtotal	**170,255**	**37.18**	**54,409**	**30.74**
Other Campaign Activity				
Persuasion mail/brochures	0		33,415	18.88
Actual campaigning	21,775	4.76	17,076	9.65
Staff/volunteers	795	.17	0	
Subtotal	**22,570**	**4.93**	**50,491**	**28.53**
Constituent Gifts/Entertainment	**23,424**	**5.12**	**0**	
Donations to				
Candidates from same state	250	.05	0	
Candidates from other states	500	.11	0	
Civic organizations	2,497	.55	30	.02
Ideological groups	275	.06	95	.05
Political parties	7,701	1.68	305	.17
Subtotal	**11,223**	**2.45**	**430**	**.24**
Unitemized Expenses	**5,532**	**1.21**	**913**	**.52**
Total Campaign Expenses	**$ 457,863**		**$ 176,991**	
PAC Contributions	**$ 237,040**		**$ 19,110**	
Individual Contributions	**171,597**		**138,942**	
Total Receipts*	**443,499**		**180,889**	

*Includes PAC and individual contributions as well as interest earned, party contributions, etc.

District 3 — NORTH CAROLINA

Rep. H. Martin Lancaster (D)

1992 Election Results

H. Martin Lancaster (D)	101,739	(54%)
Tommy Pollard (R)	80,759	(43%)

Rep. H. Martin Lancaster had little trouble winning his first three House campaigns, a fact that was clearly reflected in his campaign style. Against a 1990 opponent who spent just $11,024 on broadcast advertising, Lancaster had aired seven television commercials that focused on constituent service, his work on the Armed Services Committee, and his town meetings. Positive ads touted his efforts to foster better rural health care and to bring disaster relief to draught-plagued farmers. However, the 1992 campaign was a different story entirely.

Redistricting radically altered the boundaries of District 3 and attracted a well-funded challenge by Republican state senator Tommy Pollard. To meet that challenge, Lancaster began airing his television commercials in late August.

Initially, Lancaster's ads struck the same positive themes he had articulated in 1990. His first spot, "Town Meetings," noted that he had held more than 100 such events during his six years in office and stressed that he had listened to the concerns about rural health care expressed in those forums. A second commercial, dubbed "Values," focused on his work to secure increased funding for rural hospitals, disaster relief for farmers, and increased veterans benefits. A third spot hit these same themes and pointed out that Lancaster had grown up on a tobacco farm, was a family man, and served in the naval reserve.

In late September, Pollard began airing spots that attacked Lancaster for his five overdrafts at the House bank and his use of franked mail. One spot depicted a fat, cigar-smoking representative enjoying the beach while on a taxpayer-funded junket. Another accused Lancaster of lying about his overdrafts because he initially claimed not to have any.

Pollard's attacks prompted Lancaster to leave the high road. Lancaster first counterattacked with a commercial dubbed "Kids," which noted that Pollard had refused to pay child support after his divorce until ordered to do so by the courts. The ad gave viewers an address where they could write for a copy of the court order. Another ad slammed Pollard for failing to pay his property taxes on four occasions, touched on Pollard's child-support problems, pointed out that a company Pollard owned had violated wastewater treatment standards, and dredged up the fact that Pollard had been convicted of assault for shooting his former wife's new husband at a truck stop in 1975.

The Campaign Group of Philadelphia, Pa., collected $175,000 for creating and placing Lancaster's commercials. The Sinsheimer Group of Durham received $11,083 for providing the opposition research that fed the advertising.

Campaign Expenditures	Lancaster Amount Spent	Lancaster % of Total	Pollard Amount Spent	Pollard % of Total
Overhead				
Office furniture/supplies	$ 7,577	1.39	$ 3,622	1.68
Rent/utilities	4,100	.75	3,217	1.50
Salaries	36,755	6.73	14,826	6.89
Taxes	16,980	3.11	1,795	.83
Bank/investment fees	146	.03	223	.10
Lawyers/accountants	400	.07	0	
Telephone	7,651	1.40	5,184	2.41
Campaign automobile	0		0	
Computers/office equipment	7,757	1.42	3,556	1.65
Travel	27,549	5.04	7,334	3.41
Food/meetings	4,557	.83	245	.11
Subtotal	113,473	20.77	40,001	18.60
Fund Raising				
Events	71,795	13.14	4,713	2.19
Direct mail	16,025	2.93	0	
Telemarketing	0		0	
Subtotal	87,820	16.07	4,713	2.19
Polling	24,101	4.41	0	
Advertising				
Electronic media	178,468	32.66	104,421	48.54
Other media	30,784	5.63	8,545	3.97
Subtotal	209,252	38.29	112,966	52.52
Other Campaign Activity				
Persuasion mail/brochures	38,456	7.04	41,157	19.13
Actual campaigning	37,463	6.86	14,675	6.82
Staff/volunteers	153	.03	19	.01
Subtotal	76,072	13.92	55,850	25.96
Constituent Gifts/ Entertainment	8,006	1.47	22	.01
Donations to				
Candidates from same state	0		300	.14
Candidates from other states	200	.04	0	
Civic organizations	1,129	.21	236	.11
Ideological groups	200	.04	70	.03
Political parties	12,950	2.37	0	
Subtotal	14,479	2.65	606	.28
Unitemized Expenses	13,259	2.43	952	.44
Total Campaign Expenses	$ 546,463		$ 215,110	
PAC Contributions	$ 300,165		$ 0	
Individual Contributions	271,582		184,480	
Total Receipts*	588,664		238,256	

*Includes PAC and individual contributions as well as interest earned, party contributions, etc.

NORTH CAROLINA — District 4

Rep. David Price (D)

1992 Election Results

David Price (D)	171,299	(65%)
LaVinia "Vicky" Goudie (R)	89,345	(34%)

First elected in 1986, Rep. David Price had been forced to spend a total of more than $1.8 million to hold on to the seat, winning 58 percent of the vote against well-funded Republican challengers in each of his first two reelection bids. Redistricting paved the way to a much more comfortable victory in 1992 by moving heavily Republican Randolph County into District 6.

In 1990 Raleigh businessman John Carrington had personally funded most of his $831,228 challenge, forcing Price to invest 62 percent of his $820,821 treasury in direct appeals for votes. With the new political map in 1992, the only Republican challenger to step forward was LaVinia "Vicky" Goudie, a state employee who spent only $13,188 on her campaign.

As a result, Price slashed his spending for the 1992 election cycle to $373,629 and put only 36 percent of that into direct voter contact. As administrative assistant Paul H. Feldman succinctly put it, "When you're not having $800,000 spent against you, you change the way you spend your money."

Without the pressure of a hotly contested race, Price's fund-raising efforts proved considerably less efficient than his efforts during the 1990 campaign. In 1989 and 1990 Price had invested a total of $103,762 to raise $729,196 from political action committees (PACs) and individual contributors, a return of $7.03 for each dollar invested. In 1991 and 1992 the campaign spent $109,157 to raise $459,524 from nonparty sources, a return of only $4.21 for each dollar invested.

Over the two-year cycle, PAC donations to Price's campaign totaled $275,211, or 60 percent of his total contributions. Creative Campaign Consultant of Washington, D.C., received $46,803 for coordinating the PAC events. With the help of a $40,162 direct-mail effort, Price raised $138,928 from donors who gave less than $200. DWD Software Development Corp. of Raleigh received $13,115 for designing the direct-mail solicitations. Donations from individuals who gave $200 or more amounted to only $45,385.

Despite Goudie's anemic challenge, Price was sufficiently concerned about an anti-incumbent backlash to put $114,612 into television advertising. One spot focused on Price's sponsorship of legislation aimed at improving job training programs offered by community colleges. While Goudie's gender never became an issue in the race, Price was careful to run ads touting his pro-choice stance on abortion to guard against any drop in his support among women. Shorr Associates of Philadelphia, Pa., received $91,316 for designing and placing the ads. Production costs amounted to $23,296.

	Price		Goudie	
Campaign Expenditures	Amount Spent	% of Total	Amount Spent	% of Total
Overhead				
Office furniture/supplies	$ 3,197	.86	$ 1,163	8.82
Rent/utilities	8,375	2.24	0	
Salaries	18,331	4.91	2,675	20.28
Taxes	14,416	3.86	0	
Bank/investment fees	1,394	.37	268	2.03
Lawyers/accountants	43,445	11.63	0	
Telephone	1,771	.47	213	1.62
Campaign automobile	0		0	
Computers/office equipment	4,774	1.28	331	2.51
Travel	7,503	2.01	355	2.69
Food/meetings	1,563	.42	283	2.15
Subtotal	**104,769**	**28.04**	**5,288**	**40.10**
Fund Raising				
Events	68,995	18.47	1,858	14.09
Direct mail	40,162	10.75	0	
Telemarketing	0		0	
Subtotal	**109,157**	**29.22**	**1,858**	**14.09**
Polling	**14,981**	**4.01**	**0**	
Advertising				
Electronic media	114,612	30.68	350	2.66
Other media	5,340	1.43	425	3.23
Subtotal	**119,952**	**32.10**	**776**	**5.89**
Other Campaign Activity				
Persuasion mail/brochures	1,349	.36	2,367	17.95
Actual campaigning	13,355	3.57	2,899	21.99
Staff/volunteers	105	.03	0	
Subtotal	**14,809**	**3.96**	**5,266**	**39.94**
Constituent Gifts/ Entertainment	463	.12	0	
Donations to				
Candidates from same state	75	.02	0	
Candidates from other states	0		0	
Civic organizations	425	.11	0	
Ideological groups	55	.01	0	
Political parties	8,930	2.39	0	
Subtotal	**9,485**	**2.54**	**0**	
Unitemized Expenses	13		0	
Total Campaign Expenses	$ 373,629		$ 13,188	
PAC Contributions	$ 275,211		$ 1,486	
Individual Contributions	184,313		5,485	
Total Receipts*	480,758		12,330	

*Includes PAC and individual contributions as well as interest earned, party contributions, etc.

District 5 — NORTH CAROLINA

Rep. Stephen L. Neal (D)

1992 Election Results

Stephen L. Neal (D)	117,835	(53%)
Richard M. Burr (R)	102,086	(46%)

Rep. Stephen L. Neal's hold on District 5 had been tenuous, to say the least. Neal had received 54 percent of the vote or less in seven of his nine previous campaigns, so a permanent campaign was a necessity.

In the 1990 election cycle Neal's campaign had paid $40,568 to lease and maintain a building Neal himself owned. After paying himself $2,167 for rent in January 1991, Neal evidently decided the rental income he was receiving was not worth the negative publicity the arrangement had generated, and he discontinued the rent payments. His official campaign headquarters reopened in August 1992 in a building he did not own. Excluding utilities, the new space cost his campaign just $1,950 for the entire three months he leased it, or only $547 more than Neal had charged his campaign for each of the twenty-four months of the 1990 election cycle.

Locked in a difficult battle with Republican businessman Richard M. Burr, Neal invested 65 percent of his $519,521 treasury in direct appeals to voters. The Campaign Group of Philadelphia, Pa., received $249,500 for creating and placing television commercials. Terris & Jaye of San Francisco, Calif., collected $14,912 for producing persuasion mailers that targeted voters in areas of the district not easily reached by the television ads. Billboards conveying the simple message "Steve Neal for Congress" cost $8,569. Neal spent $24,734 to place ads in several daily papers and full-page ads in virtually every weekly newspaper in the district.

A television spot dubbed "Environment" touted the high ratings he had received from the Sierra Club and other environmental groups. Stating that Neal had "stood alone against the big oil and chemical companies to force them to come clean and disclose whether they were discharging dangerous chemicals," the ad proclaimed that he had "fought the toughest special interests and beat them."

When Burr aired an ad charging that Neal had been "caught in the check bouncing scandal," Neal's media team responded with an ad that began with video of Burr's ad framed with the words, "Richard Burr's Deceptive Negative TV Ad." Interrupting the video, an announcer demanded, "Hold it a second, Mr. Burr. That's just not true and you know it." The ad then pointed out that Neal had been cleared of any wrongdoing by special investigator Malcolm Wilkey.

Burr invested 55 percent of his $188,132 budget in television advertising. Rotterman & Associates of Raleigh received $17,490 for creating the ads. Strapped for cash, the campaign placed the ads directly.

	Neal		Burr	
Campaign Expenditures	Amount Spent	% of Total	Amount Spent	% of Total
Overhead				
Office furniture/supplies	$ 7,083	1.36	$ 1,068	.57
Rent/utilities	5,043	.97	0	
Salaries	28,543	5.49	14,473	7.69
Taxes	11,709	2.25	3,021	1.61
Bank/investment fees	479	.09	231	.12
Lawyers/accountants	1,615	.31	0	
Telephone	4,018	.77	5,950	3.16
Campaign automobile	0		0	
Computers/office equipment	1,354	.26	6,199	3.29
Travel	18,651	3.59	325	.17
Food/meetings	1,300	.25	161	.09
Subtotal	79,796	15.36	31,428	16.71
Fund Raising				
Events	38,710	7.45	10,556	5.61
Direct mail	25,087	4.83	9,904	5.26
Telemarketing	0		0	
Subtotal	63,797	12.28	20,460	10.88
Polling	15,050	2.90	2,368	1.26
Advertising				
Electronic media	252,552	48.61	104,145	55.36
Other media	41,356	7.96	1,701	.90
Subtotal	293,908	56.57	105,846	56.26
Other Campaign Activity				
Persuasion mail/brochures	25,179	4.85	6,969	3.70
Actual campaigning	21,118	4.06	11,461	6.09
Staff/volunteers	48	.01	0	
Subtotal	46,346	8.92	18,430	9.80
Constituent Gifts/ Entertainment	1,715	.33	0	
Donations to				
Candidates from same state	100	.02	0	
Candidates from other states	0		0	
Civic organizations	2,113	.41	900	.48
Ideological groups	2,263	.44	0	
Political parties	8,955	1.72	0	
Subtotal	13,431	2.59	900	.48
Unitemized Expenses	5,478	1.05	8,701	4.62
Total Campaign Expenses	$ 519,521		$ 188,132	
PAC Contributions	$ 339,570		$ 18,134	
Individual Contributions	139,814		158,010	
Total Receipts*	493,627		188,189	

*Includes PAC and individual contributions as well as interest earned, party contributions, etc.

NORTH CAROLINA — District 6

Rep. Howard Coble (R)

1992 Election Results

Howard Coble (R)	162,822	(71%)
Robin Hood (D)	67,200	(29%)

Redistricting cemented Republican Rep. Howard Coble's hold on District 6 by adding heavily Republican Randolph County and moving black neighborhoods in Greensboro into the newly created majority-minority District 12. As a result, Coble was able to spend $86,544 less than he had in 1990 and he captured 4 percent more of the vote.

Following the 1990 election, Coble had indicated a desire to reduce his campaign spending. He began by closing his campaign office for the first six months of the 1992 election cycle. That move saved $6,396 in rent and utilities. He sliced his campaign payroll from $108,863 in 1990 to $86,249 in 1992. In all, Coble spent $35,181 less on overhead than he had in 1990.

Coble's 1992 fund-raising costs were $52,183 lower than in 1990, a 35 percent drop. These savings were realized almost entirely as a result of a $50,466 decrease in spending on direct mail. Fund-raising events were virtually identical to those held during the 1990 election cycle and cost $1,716 less. An annual event was held to coincide with Coble's birthday and the campaign also sponsored an annual golf outing. "It gets a little boring, but the tried-and-true seems to work," explained administrative assistant Edward F. McDonald.

Operating from a strengthened base, Coble paid Tarrance & Associates of Alexandria, Va., $9,086 for polling. Coble's polling budget was $17,950 in 1990.

Having reduced these operating costs by $96,228, Coble plowed some of the savings into radio and television commercials. The $76,694 he spent on such ads represented a 52 percent increase over 1990.

To keep costs down, Coble recycled television ads from 1990, including one spot that showed pigs wallowing in the mud while a narrator noted that Coble had refused to participate in the congressional pension plan. McDonald said four radio spots focused on "what a great guy he is and what he's done for the district."

Coble also paid $1,871 to the Greensboro Professional Baseball Club to rent advertising space on their outfield wall. Newspaper and program ads cost $2,168. Signs added $1,336.

In his first campaign in 1984 Coble had promised to "take a sharp pencil to Congress" and work to reduce the budget deficit. In 1992 he invested $611 to buy 5,000 souvenir pencils to underscore that pledge.

In another act of symbolism, Coble's challenger, Roberta Ann Hood, campaigned under the nickname of "Robin" Hood in the hope that voters would rally behind the play on words. They did not.

Campaign Expenditures	Coble Amount Spent	Coble % of Total	Hood Amount Spent	Hood % of Total
Overhead				
Office furniture/supplies	$ 6,147	1.42	$ 1,125	4.26
Rent/utilities	16,772	3.87	2,461	9.32
Salaries	86,249	19.90	1,300	4.92
Taxes	42,480	9.81	0	
Bank/investment fees	293	.07	0	
Lawyers/accountants	2,200	.51	0	
Telephone	11,967	2.76	1,037	3.93
Campaign automobile	0		0	
Computers/office equipment	16,920	3.91	1,824	6.91
Travel	5,069	1.17	937	3.55
Food/meetings	0		0	
Subtotal	**188,098**	**43.42**	**8,684**	**32.88**
Fund Raising				
Events	87,012	20.09	1,237	4.68
Direct mail	11,143	2.57	0	
Telemarketing	0		0	
Subtotal	**98,155**	**22.66**	**1,237**	**4.68**
Polling	**9,086**	**2.10**	**0**	
Advertising				
Electronic media	76,694	17.71	2,689	10.18
Other media	4,039	.93	555	2.10
Subtotal	**80,733**	**18.64**	**3,245**	**12.28**
Other Campaign Activity				
Persuasion mail/brochures	25,973	6.00	353	1.34
Actual campaigning	19,179	4.43	7,162	27.12
Staff/volunteers	72	.02	0	
Subtotal	**45,224**	**10.44**	**7,515**	**28.46**
Constituent Gifts/Entertainment	**8,178**	**1.89**	**0**	
Donations to				
Candidates from same state	0		0	
Candidates from other states	0		0	
Civic organizations	892	.21	0	
Ideological groups	425	.10	0	
Political parties	20		128	.48
Subtotal	**1,337**	**.31**	**128**	**.48**
Unitemized Expenses	**2,366**	**.55**	**5,605**	**21.22**
Total Campaign Expenses	**$ 433,177**		**$ 26,413**	
PAC Contributions	$ 207,135		$ 8,300	
Individual Contributions	278,236		14,060	
Total Receipts*	504,213		28,046	

*Includes PAC and individual contributions as well as interest earned, party contributions, etc.

District 7 — NORTH CAROLINA

Rep. Charlie Rose (D)

1992 Election Results

Charlie Rose (D)	92,414	(57%)
Robert C. Anderson (R)	66,536	(41%)

Having raised only $21,459 for his 1990 challenge to Rep. Charlie Rose, retired army officer Robert C. Anderson tried again in 1992. This time Anderson could muster only $12,537. Nevertheless, Rose felt it necessary to increase his spending for the rematch by $103,515.

Rose ploughed $106,173 into overhead, an increase of $45,252 over his 1990 outlays. As it had in 1990, overhead consumed more than 40 percent of his total budget, primarily due to costs associated with the purchase and maintenance of various vehicles.

In June 1991 the campaign paid $38,661 to Allsport RV Center in Fayetteville for "mobile campaign office, gas, propane, title and license." Repair costs for the recreational vehicle, which served as Rose's only campaign office, added another $195, and a mobile radio cost $282.

Rose had spent $8,288 of his 1990 campaign treasury to purchase a campaign car. In June 1992 the campaign bought a $13,821 car from Fair Bluff Motors in Fair Bluff. Six months later, the campaign shelled out $10,594 to Valley Motors in Fayetteville for another car. The $6,786 he spent to insure, maintain, and fuel his various automobiles included a $272 bill at Precision Tune in Alexandria, Va.

For the rematch with Anderson, Rose also increased his grass-roots campaign expenses by $40,146. Umbrellas stamped with the campaign's logo cost $11,615. He invested $14,462 in potholders; $13,175 in rose-colored hats stitched with "Charlie Rose"; $3,692 in campaign magnets; $2,956 in an assortment of buttons, stickers, and badges; and $1,929 in T-shirts. Rose also spent $2,925 on new campaign portraits, which had not been updated since the 1970s.

Rose's advertising budget increased by only $2,150. He spent $7,650 to air his ads on local network affiliates and another $2,108 on cable spots. Campaign spokesman Bill Oldaker said the ads were created by Rose and his wife. Advertising production costs of $13,522 were paid by the Democratic Congressional Campaign Committee.

Constituent stroking expenses amounted to $6,998. Rose spent $3,700 on assorted gifts, $319 on flowers, and only $289 on meals. Year-end holiday cards cost $2,690.

Rose relied primarily on political action committees (PACs) and out-of-state contributors to fund his campaign. PACs accounted for $251,535 of his total receipts. Contributions of at least $200 amounted to $61,650, and $47,650 of that amount came from outside of North Carolina. At most, Rose raised $33,783 from in-state donors.

Anderson put only $1,620 into advertising, but he held Rose to a career low winning percentage.

	Rose		Anderson	
Campaign Expenditures	Amount Spent	% of Total	Amount Spent	% of Total
Overhead				
Office furniture/supplies	$ 2,290	.90	$ 316	2.52
Rent/utilities	39,138	15.43	0	
Salaries	0		0	
Taxes	10,488	4.14	0	
Bank/investment fees	18	.01	66	.52
Lawyers/accountants	10,067	3.97	400	3.19
Telephone	1,644	.65	317	2.53
Campaign automobile	31,201	12.30	0	
Computers/office equipment	1,745	.69	0	
Travel	6,392	2.52	1,573	12.55
Food/meetings	3,190	1.26	0	
Subtotal	**106,173**	**41.87**	**2,671**	**21.31**
Fund Raising				
Events	33,080	13.04	2,459	19.61
Direct mail	0		0	
Telemarketing	0		0	
Subtotal	**33,080**	**13.04**	**2,459**	**19.61**
Polling	**0**		**0**	
Advertising				
Electronic media	9,758	3.85	626	4.99
Other media	3,401	1.34	994	7.93
Subtotal	**13,159**	**5.19**	**1,620**	**12.92**
Other Campaign Activity				
Persuasion mail/brochures	0		3,899	31.10
Actual campaigning	61,564	24.28	1,864	14.87
Staff/volunteers	0		25	.20
Subtotal	**61,564**	**24.28**	**5,788**	**46.17**
Constituent Gifts/ Entertainment	**6,998**	**2.76**	**0**	
Donations to				
Candidates from same state	0		0	
Candidates from other states	3,000	1.18	0	
Civic organizations	3,165	1.25	0	
Ideological groups	1,260	.50	0	
Political parties	9,275	3.66	0	
Subtotal	**16,700**	**6.59**	**0**	
Unitemized Expenses	**15,910**	**6.27**	**0**	
Total Campaign Expenses	**$ 253,584**		**$ 12,537**	
PAC Contributions	$ 251,535		$ 0	
Individual Contributions	81,433		7,703	
Total Receipts*	395,280		14,280	

*Includes PAC and individual contributions as well as interest earned, party contributions, etc.

NORTH CAROLINA — District 8

Rep. W. G. "Bill" Hefner (D)

1992 Election Results

W. G. "Bill" Hefner (D)	113,162	(58%)
Coy C. Privette (R)	71,842	(37%)
J. Wendell Drye † (I)	10,447	(5%)

Having received as much as 60 percent of the vote only once in eight previous reelection campaigns, Rep. W. G. "Bill" Hefner took no chances with his 1992 Republican challenger, state representative Coy C. Privette. While Privette put only $4,510 of his $109,593 treasury into broadcast advertising, Hefner poured $272,000 into television and radio commercials created and placed by the Campaign Group of Philadelphia, Pa.

Although Hefner ran five television commercials, most of the budget for air time was put into three spots—one on jobs, one on the environment, and one on drugs. All three ads began with an attack on Privette and ended by touting Hefner's achievements. Each ad also delivered the secondary messages that Privette was a politician and an extremist. "We found our opponent's weaknesses and exploited them," noted Hefner's campaign manager Billy Paul.

For instance, the ad on jobs began by attacking Privette for blocking a Pace Warehouse store from moving into his hometown because "they sold something he didn't like." While the ad never said what that "something" was, attentive voters knew that the veiled reference was to alcoholic beverages. The ad continued with a charge that Privette's actions had resulted in "225 jobs lost. Over $2 million in annual taxes down the drain. For politician Coy Privette, the economy takes a back seat to his own narrow personal agenda." The spot concluded with the positive message that Hefner had written "the buy-American amendment that saves jobs in the textile industry and protects American jobs from unfair competition."

Similarly, the environmental spot began not with a statement about the environment, but with the declaration that "Coy Privette is a politician and paid lobbyist." It went on to slam him for voting in the state legislature "against legislation to hold hazardous waste transporters liable for damages." Before getting to Hefner's positives, the ad charged that "Privette spent his time trying to legislate morality" and that he would "try to get the federal government to regulate your daily personal life." The ad concluded by stating that Hefner had fought against the construction of a hazardous waste incinerator and had "consistently worked to protect the environment."

Hefner paid pollsters Penn & Schoen of New York and Greenberg-Lake of Washington, D.C., $9,000 and $6,787, respectively, for keeping tabs on the electorate. The Sinsheimer Group of Durham received $11,104 for conducting opposition research.

Privette put 37 percent of his limited budget into persuasion mail designed by Blackwelder Communications of Greensboro, N.C.

	Hefner		Privette	
Campaign Expenditures	Amount Spent	% of Total	Amount Spent	% of Total
Overhead				
Office furniture/supplies	$ 4,458	.75	$ 2,154	1.97
Rent/utilities	5,968	1.00	0	
Salaries	68,943	11.61	10,208	9.31
Taxes	30,848	5.20	5,910	5.39
Bank/investment fees	0		56	.05
Lawyers/accountants	1,906	.32	0	
Telephone	3,299	.56	3,556	3.24
Campaign automobile	30,373	5.12	0	
Computers/office equipment	3,164	.53	1,497	1.37
Travel	10,555	1.78	1,441	1.32
Food/meetings	0		351	.32
Subtotal	**159,514**	**26.87**	**25,174**	**22.97**
Fund Raising				
Events	51,848	8.73	1,516	1.38
Direct mail	8,680	1.46	9,125	8.33
Telemarketing	8,354	1.41	0	
Subtotal	**68,882**	**11.60**	**10,640**	**9.71**
Polling	**20,727**	**3.49**	**0**	
Advertising				
Electronic media	272,000	45.81	4,510	4.12
Other media	9,255	1.56	13,075	11.93
Subtotal	**281,255**	**47.37**	**17,585**	**16.05**
Other Campaign Activity				
Persuasion mail/brochures	4,277	.72	40,581	37.03
Actual campaigning	26,847	4.52	13,102	11.96
Staff/volunteers	551	.09	0	
Subtotal	**31,676**	**5.33**	**53,683**	**48.98**
Constituent Gifts/ Entertainment	**1,526**	**.26**	**0**	
Donations to				
Candidates from same state	0		82	.07
Candidates from other states	1,500	.25	0	
Civic organizations	1,850	.31	35	.03
Ideological groups	1,550	.26	12	.01
Political parties	5,000	.84	0	
Subtotal	**9,900**	**1.67**	**129**	**.12**
Unitemized Expenses	**20,338**	**3.42**	**2,382**	**2.17**
Total Campaign Expenses	**$ 593,817**		**$ 109,593**	
PAC Contributions	$ 356,179		$ 8,505	
Individual Contributions	172,268		75,621	
Total Receipts*	566,530		108,333	

*Includes PAC and individual contributions as well as interest earned, party contributions, etc.

† No expenditures or receipts on file. Candidates raising or spending less than $5,000 are not required to file reports with the Federal Election Commission.

District 9 — NORTH CAROLINA

Rep. Alex McMillan (R)

1992 Election Results

Alex McMillan (R)	153,650	(67%)
Rory Blake (D)	74,583	(33%)

After razor-thin victories in 1984 and 1986, Rep. Alex McMillan's campaigns had grown progressively easier. In keeping with his fiscal conservatism, McMillan had spent progressively less. The 1990 campaign cost $57,553 less than his 1988 effort; in 1992 the costs were reduced another $146,212.

Fearing that the negative campaign tactics of Sen. Jesse Helms would create a general anti-Republican backlash in 1990, McMillan had paid Severin/Aviles Associates of New York $201,685 for television commercials showcasing McMillan's work ethic. A secondary reason for the advertising push was redistricting. "We wanted to make a big push in 1990 to drive up the margin of victory," noted chief of staff Frank H. Hill. "We didn't want to give Democrats in the state legislature a reason to split up the district." The strategy apparently worked, since redistricting gave McMillan a more Republican constituency.

With no such worries in 1992, McMillan opted to spend nothing on either television or radio commercials. That decision was influenced by the campaign's assessment of the voter's anti-incumbent mood. "We decided that the more you plaster your face all over the TV, the more people will equate you with incumbency," noted Hill.

Instead, McMillan paid Severin/Aviles $49,124 for a persuasion mailer sent to about 50,000 households. The mailer focused on his views concerning health care reform, the budget deficit, and ways to stimulate economic growth. It targeted voters in two counties acquired through redistricting and those areas of the district where McMillan was thought to be weakest. Data processing charges for producing the targeted mailing lists and miscellaneous printing charges amounted to $7,004. The $56,128 McMillan invested in this effort was $39,386 more than he had spent on persuasion mail in 1990.

McMillan leaned heavily on political action committees (PACs) to finance his campaign. Dan Morgan & Associates of Arlington, Va., received $6,503 for coordinating PAC events that helped raise $268,000, or 82 percent of his total contributions. Hill said the campaign held no major events in the district because McMillan "didn't want to bug people for money." McMillan raised only $55,694 from North Carolina residents.

Although the Democratic Congressional Campaign Committee spent $7,585 to help pharmacist Rory Blake produce one television and one radio commercial, his limited budget prevented him from airing them enough to have any impact.

In November 1993, citing frustration with "the suppression of creative ideas and gridlock," McMillan announced he would not seek reelection in 1994.

	McMillan		Blake	
Campaign Expenditures	Amount Spent	% of Total	Amount Spent	% of Total
Overhead				
Office furniture/supplies	$ 8,766	3.71	$ 317	.96
Rent/utilities	19,008	8.04	0	.00
Salaries	20,868	8.83	500	1.51
Taxes	11,712	4.96	0	.00
Bank/investment fees	570	.24	35	.11
Lawyers/accountants	7,075	2.99	0	.00
Telephone	4,341	1.84	0	.00
Campaign automobile	0	.00	0	.00
Computers/office equipment	5,129	2.17	1,266	3.83
Travel	11,583	4.90	900	2.72
Food/meetings	99	.04	0	.00
Subtotal	**89,152**	**37.73**	**3,018**	**9.12**
Fund Raising				
Events	13,759	5.82	0	.00
Direct mail	6,857	2.90	0	.00
Telemarketing	0	.00	0	.00
Subtotal	**20,616**	**8.72**	**0**	**.00**
Polling	0	.00	0	.00
Advertising				
Electronic media	0	.00	14,550	43.98
Other media	4,441	1.88	807	2.44
Subtotal	**4,441**	**1.88**	**15,357**	**46.42**
Other Campaign Activity				
Persuasion mail/brochures	56,128	23.75	1,021	3.09
Actual campaigning	45,576	19.29	3,253	9.83
Staff/volunteers	0	.00	67	.20
Subtotal	**101,705**	**43.04**	**4,341**	**13.12**
Constituent Gifts/ Entertainment	8,569	3.63	0	.00
Donations to				
Candidates from same state	1,200	.51	0	.00
Candidates from other states	7,500	3.17	0	.00
Civic organizations	250	.11	0	.00
Ideological groups	1,000	.42	0	.00
Political parties	1,230	.52	0	.00
Subtotal	**11,180**	**4.73**	**0**	**.00**
Unitemized Expenses	655	.28	10,364	31.33
Total Campaign Expenses	$ 236,317		$ 33,080	
PAC Contributions	$ 268,000		$ 2,350	
Contributions	59,444		2,475	
Total Receipts*	345,961		31,720	

*Includes PAC and individual contributions as well as interest earned, party contributions, etc.

NORTH CAROLINA — District 10

Rep. Cass Ballenger (R)

1992 Election Results

Cass Ballenger (R)	148,033 (63%)
Ben Neill (D)	79,206 (34%)

Representing the most Republican district in North Carolina, Rep. Cass Ballenger had little to worry about in 1992. Comfortable with his reelection prospects, Ballenger spent only about half as much as the typical incumbent.

During 1991, Ballenger spent $51,209 to maintain his campaign operation. He had no office and his payroll totaled $3,927. He made no donations to other candidates, party organizations, or causes. He spent $1,727 on year-end holiday cards and $53 on flowers for a constituent's funeral. Fund-raising costs amounted to $35,292, or 69 percent of his off-year spending.

Unopposed in the Republican primary, Ballenger spent just $26,019 through the first six months of 1992, including his $1,250 filing fee and a $2,500 payment to Citizens for Voting Rights to help defray legal expenses incurred in conjunction with an unsuccessful lawsuit the group filed over the state's redistricting plan. Ballenger did not open his campaign headquarters until June 26.

However, once the campaign began, Ballenger quickly shifted gears. Over the final six months of the election cycle, Ballenger invested $201,739 to defeat his underfunded Democratic challenger, retired teacher Ben Neill. Nearly $125,000 of Ballenger's budget was spent during October.

Although Neill spent about $17,000 less than Ballenger's 1990 challenger, redistricting prompted Ballenger to increase his spending on advertising by nearly $20,000. He spent $30,468 to air two commercials on local cable television systems and $10,360 to run companion radio spots. Production costs and creative fees added $12,066. According to Patrick M. Murphy, Ballenger's administrative assistant, the commercials sought to communicate one simple message: that the three-term incumbent was the best candidate to solve the nation's problems. "They were based on [President] Reagan's 'Morning in America' ad," explained Murphy. "There were no specifics, just general statements."

Ballenger invested $5,971 in billboards, $2,300 in newspaper ads, $3,231 in signs, $2,660 in bumper stickers and other campaign paraphernalia, and $6,871 in get-out-the-vote efforts. Two weeks before the election, he spent $26,463 to send a combination fund-raising solicitation and persuasion mailer to 75,800 constituents.

One-third of Ballenger's spending was funneled through Bradford Communications of Hickory, N.C., which collected $91,262 for creating and placing the broadcast ads, placing the billboard and newspaper ads, and designing and producing campaign literature, signs, and fund-raising solicitations.

Campaign Expenditures	Ballenger Amount Spent	Ballenger % of Total	Neill Amount Spent	Neill % of Total
Overhead				
Office furniture/supplies	$ 4,247	1.52	$ 40	.19
Rent/utilities	1,517	.54	0	
Salaries	21,563	7.73	0	
Taxes	6,922	2.48	0	
Bank/investment fees	0		4	.02
Lawyers/accountants	0		0	
Telephone	2,320	.83	304	1.48
Campaign automobile	0		0	
Computers/office equipment	4,971	1.78	393	1.91
Travel	6,430	2.30	0	
Food/meetings	239	.09	0	
Subtotal	**48,208**	**17.28**	**741**	**3.60**
Fund Raising				
Events	52,097	18.67	559	2.71
Direct mail	48,156	17.26	0	
Telemarketing	0		0	
Subtotal	**100,253**	**35.94**	**559**	**2.71**
Polling	**9,750**	**3.50**	**0**	
Advertising				
Electronic media	52,894	18.96	5,446	26.43
Other media	10,744	3.85	7,592	36.85
Subtotal	**63,637**	**22.81**	**13,038**	**63.28**
Other Campaign Activity				
Persuasion mail/brochures	10,360	3.71	636	3.09
Actual campaigning	19,698	7.06	1,952	9.48
Staff/volunteers	0		0	
Subtotal	**30,057**	**10.77**	**2,588**	**12.56**
Constituent Gifts/ Entertainment	**3,474**	**1.25**	**0**	
Donations to				
Candidates from same state	750	.27	300	1.46
Candidates from other states	0		0	
Civic organizations	575	.21	0	
Ideological groups	0		200	.97
Political parties	21,419	7.68	678	3.29
Subtotal	**22,744**	**8.15**	**1,178**	**5.72**
Unitemized Expenses	**845**	**.30**	**2,500**	**12.14**
Total Campaign Expenses	**$ 278,967**		**$ 20,604**	
PAC Contributions	$ 167,925		$ 6,500	
Individual Contributions	99,087		10,781	
Total Receipts*	277,122		25,660	

*Includes PAC and individual contributions as well as interest earned, party contributions, etc.

District 11 — NORTH CAROLINA

Rep. Charles H. Taylor (R)

1992 Election Results

Charles H. Taylor (R)	130,158	(55%)
John S. Stevens (D)	108,003	(45%)

Freshman Republican Rep. Charles H. Taylor looked extremely vulnerable in early 1992. In 1988 Taylor had lost to Rep. James McClure Clarke by 1,529 of the 215,343 votes cast. In 1990 Taylor returned the favor, defeating Clarke by 2,673 votes, marking the fifth time in six elections that voters in District 11 had cast aside the incumbent. Following redistricting, Democrats comprised more than 60 percent of the registered voters in the district.

Taylor began 1991 with campaign debts totaling $434,467, including $323,157 he had loaned his campaigns. When his advisers told him it would look bad if he paid himself interest on the loans, Taylor took out bank loans totaling $350,000. He paid himself back and began making interest payments to the bank. Since this money had already been spent in previous campaigns, these loan repayments have not been included in this analysis.

Virtually all of Taylor's $87,902 spending advantage over former Democratic state representative John S. Stevens was the result of off-year spending. Taylor spent $96,674 on his permanent campaign during 1991; Stevens spent $17,020. In their head-to-head contest, Taylor's monetary advantage was an insignificant $8,248.

Realizing the race would be close, both parties weighed in with sizable coordinated campaign efforts. The National Republican Congressional Committee spent $48,575 on Taylor's behalf, including $44,831 on persuasion mail. The Democratic Congressional Campaign Committee (DCCC) provided Stevens with a $42,575 infusion, $37,769 of which was spent on broadcast advertising.

With the DCCC's help, Stevens spent $100,661 more than Taylor on television and radio advertising. Stevens waited until September to begin airing his three television and six radio spots, something he came to regret. "The polls showed Taylor wasn't liked, but I wasn't well known," lamented Stevens. "I should have spent the money I had and borrowed more in order to go on television in June to up my name recognition."

One thing Taylor clearly had going for him was his status as one of the "Gang of Seven," Republican freshmen who had fought to force the House leadership to reveal the names of members who had overdrafts at the House bank. According to administrative assistant Roger France, all seven of Taylor's television commercials and their companion radio spots were created in-house and struck the theme of congressional reform. Each closed with the tagline: "He's fighting our fight." The campaign bought air time directly to eliminate ad placement fees.

Taylor spent $9,790 on phonebanking, trying to contact every Republican household in the district.

Campaign Expenditures	Taylor Amount Spent	Taylor % of Total	Stevens Amount Spent	Stevens % of Total
Overhead				
Office furniture/supplies	$ 3,086	.60	$ 6,981	1.62
Rent/utilities	28,422	5.48	4,942	1.15
Salaries	29,879	5.76	27,659	6.42
Taxes	728	.14	10,133	2.35
Bank/investment fees	68,256	13.17	129	.03
Lawyers/accountants	1,200	.23	0	
Telephone	10,541	2.03	5,410	1.26
Campaign automobile	0		0	
Computers/office equipment	2,266	.44	8,477	1.97
Travel	3,619	.70	2,484	.58
Food/meetings	84	.02	104	.02
Subtotal	**148,081**	**28.56**	**66,320**	**15.40**
Fund Raising				
Events	62,859	12.12	16,994	3.95
Direct mail	32,766	6.32	16,885	3.92
Telemarketing	0		0	
Subtotal	**95,625**	**18.44**	**33,879**	**7.87**
Polling	**15,200**	**2.93**	**16,400**	**3.81**
Advertising				
Electronic media	210,845	40.67	274,237	63.70
Other media	6,925	1.34	11,462	2.66
Subtotal	**217,770**	**42.00**	**285,699**	**66.36**
Other Campaign Activity				
Persuasion mail/brochures	15,127	2.92	9,527	2.21
Actual campaigning	14,794	2.85	16,489	3.83
Staff/volunteers	0		0	
Subtotal	**29,921**	**5.77**	**26,016**	**6.04**
Constituent Gifts/ Entertainment	1,625	.31	279	.06
Donations to				
Candidates from same state	0		473	.11
Candidates from other states	0		0	
Civic organizations	0		70	.02
Ideological groups	0		17	
Political parties	0		50	.01
Subtotal	**0**		**610**	**.14**
Unitemized Expenses	**10,227**	**1.97**	**1,342**	**.31**
Total Campaign Expenses	**$ 518,448**		**$ 430,546**	
PAC Contributions	$ 298,425		$ 113,595	
Individual Contributions	397,516		271,247	
Total Receipts*	1,216,256		431,367	

*Includes PAC and individual contributions as well as interest earned, party contributions, etc.

NORTH CAROLINA   District 12

Rep. Melvin Watt (D)

1992 Election Results
Melvin Watt (D)   127,262   (70%)
Barbara Gore Washington (R)   49,402   (27%)

Spurred by the Justice Department to create two black-majority districts and loathe to wound any white Democratic incumbents, the Democratic-controlled state legislature created District 12. Stretching 134 miles along Interstate 85, the district is no wider than the highway in some places. With a 57 percent black majority and a four-to-one Democratic edge in registration, the Democratic primary winner was assured of victory in November.

Having run Harvey Gantt's $7.8 million challenge to Sen. Jesse Helms in 1990, attorney and former state senator Melvin Watt knew how to raise money. While state representative Mickey Michaux, former Winston-Salem alderman Larry D. Little, and Greensboro City Council member Earl Jones spent a combined $51,472 on their campaigns, Watt spent $291,028 to secure the nomination.

Unlike his opponents, Watt could afford to run television and radio advertising. Doak, Shrum & Associates of Washington, D.C., worked with Watt to create the spots and collected $10,000 for its efforts. "Mel did most of it himself," noted district director Don Baker. Castleberry & Co. of Charlotte received $99,736 for producing and placing the spots, which referred to Watt as "everybody's choice" and ended with the catch-phrase: "Give 'em Mel." Designed principally to increase Watt's name recognition, the ads never mentioned his opponents.

Watt sank $51,903 into preprimary persuasion mailings, including $8,662 to Castleberry to cover design and production costs. Baker said the campaign targeted three mailings at black constituents and two mailings at white constituents. Watt spent $5,342 on newspaper ads, $2,312 on yard signs and posters, $1,218 on bumper stickers, and $870 on T-shirts for his volunteers. Door-to-door canvassing expenses amounted to $5,597, including $870 in $30 per diem payments to twenty-nine election day workers, $375 for pagers, and $494 for a van to shuttle voters to and from the polls. Watt grabbed 47 percent of the primary vote; Michaux finished second with 29 percent.

The general election campaign against Greensboro attorney Barbara Gore Washington was a scaled-back version of the primary. Given the virtual certainty of his victory, Watt opted not to retain Doak, Shrum. Castleberry received $42,525 for placing radio and television ads. Watt invested $13,014 in campaign literature and persuasion mail, $3,939 in newspaper ads, and $3,698 in signs and bumper stickers. In an effort to turn out votes for the Clinton/Gore presidential ticket, Watt spent $6,442 on canvassing.

Campaign overhead to support Watt's grass-roots efforts in the primary and general election campaigns amounted to $209,911. For serving as campaign manager, Watt's son Brian collected $15,398.

Campaign Expenditures	Watt Amount Spent	Watt % of Total	Washington Amount Spent	Washington % of Total
Overhead				
Office furniture/supplies	$ 8,962	1.74	$ 1,218	4.37
Rent/utilities	16,600	3.23	0	
Salaries	94,780	18.41	0	
Taxes	21,139	4.11	0	
Bank/investment fees	218	.04	16	.06
Lawyers/accountants	12,000	2.33	0	
Telephone	17,048	3.31	1,883	6.75
Campaign automobile	0		0	
Computers/office equipment	7,035	1.37	624	2.24
Travel	31,302	6.08	5,513	19.77
Food/meetings	826	.16	221	.79
Subtotal	**209,911**	**40.78**	**9,476**	**33.98**
Fund Raising				
Events	28,468	5.53	4,845	17.37
Direct mail	14,716	2.86	0	
Telemarketing	0		0	
Subtotal	**43,184**	**8.39**	**4,845**	**17.37**
Polling	**0**		**0**	
Advertising				
Electronic media	153,084	29.74	0	
Other media	13,233	2.57	3,009	10.79
Subtotal	**166,317**	**32.31**	**3,009**	**10.79**
Other Campaign Activity				
Persuasion mail/brochures	64,917	12.61	4,167	14.94
Actual campaigning	23,841	4.63	6,244	22.39
Staff/volunteers	1,568	.30	0	
Subtotal	**90,327**	**17.55**	**10,412**	**37.33**
Constituent Gifts/ Entertainment	**900**	**.17**	**0**	
Donations to				
Candidates from same state	70	.01	40	.14
Candidates from other states	0		0	
Civic organizations	490	.10	6	.02
Ideological groups	1,290	.25	0	
Political parties	1,110	.22	100	.36
Subtotal	**2,960**	**.58**	**146**	**.52**
Unitemized Expenses	**1,118**	**.22**	**0**	
Total Campaign Expenses	**$ 514,717**		**$ 27,888**	
PAC Contributions	$ 208,732		$ 506	
Individual Contributions	226,789		17,341	
Total Receipts*	483,601		25,388	

*Includes PAC and individual contributions as well as interest earned, party contributions, etc.

At Large — NORTH DAKOTA

Rep. Earl Pomeroy (D)

1992 Election Results

Earl Pomeroy (D)	169,273	(57%)
John T. Korsmo (R)	117,442	(39%)

When Democratic Rep. Byron L. Dorgan decided to seek the open Senate seat created by the temporary retirement of Democratic Sen. Kent Conrad, state insurance commissioner Earl Pomeroy shelved plans to join the Peace Corps and announced he would seek Dorgan's House seat. Having served as president of the National Association of Insurance Commissioners, Pomeroy knew where to go for money.

Within three weeks of opening his campaign headquarters, Pomeroy traveled to Washington, D.C., where the political action committee (PAC) of the Independent Insurance Agents of America, INSUR PAC, spent $1,238 to sponsor a fund-raiser on his behalf. During the six-month campaign, PACs representing MetLife, Continental Insurance, the Principal Group, the American International Group, and the Alliance of American Insurers also sponsored in-kind fund-raising events for Pomeroy. Together these six insurance PACs picked up $9,112 of Pomeroy's event costs, or 35 percent of his total event expenses.

To make certain that a steady stream of PAC dollars continued to flow, Pomeroy opened a Washington, D.C., fund-raising office in June, less than one month after opening his Bismarck headquarters. Over the next six months, rent on the Washington office amounted to $3,200—$1,200 more than he paid to rent his in-state office. Salaries and bonuses for his Washington staff of two amounted to $25,871, or 46 percent of his total staff salaries. Telephone bills and a fax machine for the Washington office added $2,966 and $472, respectively. With PAC contributions accounting for 69 percent of his total receipts, the office proved well worth the expense.

Pomeroy raised $61,904 from individuals who gave at least $200, but only $7,077 was collected from North Dakota residents. Donors from twenty-three states anted up $54,827, with at least $15,900 coming from insurance company executives. Even assuming that all of the $57,967 he raised from small donors came from North Dakotans, Pomeroy raised just 15 percent of his money in-state.

Pomeroy hired two Washington, D.C.-based consultants to orchestrate his victory. Squier/Eskew/Knapp/Ochs Communications received $230,947 for creating and placing one television and two radio commercials that hit all the big themes of 1992: congressional reform, health care reform, and jobs. Garin-Hart of Washington, D.C., collected $18,000 for polling.

Although his $71,388 advertising budget got a $10,000 infusion from the National Republican Congressional Committee, Fargo businessman John T. Korsmo's campaign was overwhelmed by Pomeroy's three-to-one cash advantage.

Campaign Expenditures	Pomeroy Amount Spent	Pomeroy % of Total	Korsmo Amount Spent	Korsmo % of Total
Overhead				
Office furniture/supplies	$ 1,622	.35	$ 1,373	.95
Rent/utilities	5,200	1.14	450	.31
Salaries	55,969	12.24	9,319	6.47
Taxes	24,533	5.37	3,654	2.54
Bank/investment fees	23	.01	10	.01
Lawyers/accountants	0		40	.03
Telephone	10,395	2.27	1,010	.70
Campaign automobile	0		0	
Computers/office equipment	7,113	1.56	0	
Travel	9,684	2.12	1,804	1.25
Food/meetings	132	.03	0	
Subtotal	**114,670**	**25.08**	**17,661**	**12.26**
Fund Raising				
Events	26,315	5.76	11,967	8.30
Direct mail	7,450	1.63	13,515	9.38
Telemarketing	0		0	
Subtotal	**33,765**	**7.39**	**25,482**	**17.68**
Polling	**18,000**	**3.94**	**0**	
Advertising				
Electronic media	230,947	50.52	55,328	38.40
Other media	4,225	.92	16,060	11.15
Subtotal	**235,172**	**51.45**	**71,388**	**49.54**
Other Campaign Activity				
Persuasion mail/brochures	20,265	4.43	17,078	11.85
Actual campaigning	22,764	4.98	10,731	7.45
Staff/volunteers	0		0	
Subtotal	**43,029**	**9.41**	**27,809**	**19.30**
Constituent Gifts/Entertainment	**1,118**	**.24**	**0**	
Donations to				
Candidates from same state	0		0	
Candidates from other states	0		0	
Civic organizations	0		0	
Ideological groups	0		0	
Political parties	0		0	
Subtotal	**0**		**0**	
Unitemized Expenses	**11,378**	**2.49**	**1,757**	**1.22**
Total Campaign Expenses	**$ 457,132**		**$ 144,096**	
PAC Contributions	$ 296,260		$ 58,532	
Individual Contributions	119,871		80,677	
Total Receipts*	431,979		143,817	

*Includes PAC and individual contributions as well as interest earned, party contributions, etc.

OHIO District 1

Rep. David Mann (D)

1992 Election Results
David Mann (D)   120,190   (51%)
Steve Grote (I)   101,498   (43%)

After spending $649,546 to win the seat in 1990, freshman Democratic Rep. Charles Luken won renomination without opposition on June 2, 1992. Twenty-seven days later he abruptly changed course, announcing he was disenchanted with Congress and would rather spend more time with his family than seek a second term. Assuming Luken would be easily reelected, no Republican candidate had entered the race.

With Luken's withdrawal, Democrats immediately scheduled a special election to replace him on the November ballot. The party also launched efforts to stop Republicans from holding their own special election, on the grounds that they had passed up the opportunity to field a candidate in the primary. Republican Secretary of State Bob Taft and the state's Supreme Court sided with the Democrats.

Seven Democrats jumped at the opportunity to replace Luken: Cincinnati City Council member David Mann, state senator William F. Bowen, Cincinnati School Board member Virginia Rhodes, and four political novices. In the abbreviated campaign leading up the August 4 special primary, only Mann and Bowen had the resources to compete.

Mann invested approximately $106,000 in the special primary. He paid Galvin, Siegel, Kemper Advertising of Cincinnati $66,205 for creating and placing television commercials. Preprimary persuasion mail cost $16,639. Fliers and lapel stickers added $13,187. Mann outspent Bowen by roughly $20,000 and emerged with a 418-vote victory.

Bakery executive Steve Grote had originally sought to run as a Republican but had been ruled off the June 2 primary ballot for filing invalid nominating petitions. He successfully filed as an independent candidate and inherited Republican support when the party was not allowed to stage its own special primary election. Without the distraction of a primary campaign, Grote was able to devote virtually all his relatively limited resources to the head-to-head contest with Mann. He spent $13,600 to air his one television ad and two radio spots during the campaign's final two weeks.

Mann countered by spending more than $180,000. He paid Galvin, Siegel another $94,393, virtually all of which was put into the design and placement of television spots. Penn & Schoen Associates of New York collected $23,000 for polling. He spent $10,521 on yard signs, $8,590 on leaflets and advocacy mailers, $1,600 on radio commercials, and $1,702 on newspaper ads.

While he could not afford to give away much of his money, Mann realized the value of a well-placed contribution. One such donation was a $100 gift to the Black Family Reunion Fund for "cake ingredients."

Campaign Expenditures	Mann Amount Spent	Mann % of Total	Grote Amount Spent	Grote % of Total
Overhead				
Office furniture/supplies	$ 1,804	.63	$ 737	.90
Rent/utilities	1,275	.44	2,709	3.32
Salaries	23,115	8.03	4,000	4.91
Taxes	0		0	
Bank/investment fees	115	.04	188	.23
Lawyers/accountants	4,379	1.52	0	
Telephone	1,237	.43	434	.53
Campaign automobile	0		0	
Computers/office equipment	0		2,665	3.27
Travel	4,420	1.54	918	1.13
Food/meetings	503	.17	0	
Subtotal	**36,849**	**12.80**	**11,652**	**14.29**
Fund Raising				
Events	6,399	2.22	8,461	10.38
Direct mail	3,526	1.22	2,898	3.55
Telemarketing	0		0	
Subtotal	**9,925**	**3.45**	**11,359**	**13.93**
Polling	**23,000**	**7.99**	**450**	**.55**
Advertising				
Electronic media	160,267	55.68	17,144	21.03
Other media	1,772	.62	6,890	8.45
Subtotal	**162,039**	**56.29**	**24,034**	**29.48**
Other Campaign Activity				
Persuasion mail/brochures	35,640	12.38	12,800	15.70
Actual campaigning	17,793	6.18	19,687	24.15
Staff/volunteers	1,803	.63	677	.83
Subtotal	**55,236**	**19.19**	**33,164**	**40.68**
Constituent Gifts/ Entertainment	**47**	**.02**	**0**	
Donations to				
Candidates from same state	325	.11	0	
Candidates from other states	0		0	
Civic organizations	210	.07	500	.61
Ideological groups	215	.07	0	
Political parties	0		360	.44
Subtotal	**750**	**.26**	**860**	**1.05**
Unitemized Expenses	**0**		**0**	
Total Campaign Expenses	**$ 287,846**		**$ 81,519**	
PAC Contributions	**$ 107,550**		**$ 8,752**	
Individual Contributions	**165,048**		**58,537**	
Total Receipts*	**281,158**		**83,526**	

*Includes PAC and individual contributions as well as interest earned, party contributions, etc.

District 2 — OHIO

Rep. Bill Gradison (R)

1992 Election Results

Bill Gradison (R)	177,720	(70%)
Thomas R. Chandler (D)	75,924	(30%)

Just two months after easily winning his tenth term, Rep. Bill Gradison resigned in January 1993 to become head of the Health Insurance Association of America.

Donations to Republican party organizations, other candidates, and various causes accounted for 39 percent of Gradison's modest spending in what turned out to be his final House campaign. Much of that money was invested in Ohio, including donations of $10,000 to the Republican Senate Campaign Committee in Columbus and $4,000 to the Republican Finance Committee of Hamilton County. He made contributions to seventeen candidates for state senate, city council, county commissioner, county prosecutor, and the local judiciary. On the national level, Gradison donated $1,000 to the Bush/Quayle campaign. Eight House and Senate candidates received contributions of $1,000 or less.

Gradison's various direct appeals for votes cost him $24,651. At the grass-roots level, he spent a total of $209 to rent a community center and a theater for town meetings in the newly acquired portions of his district. Amity Unlimited of Cincinnati was paid $7,376 for sending out the meeting announcements and collected another $11,424 for mailing a questionnaire to new constituents.

Gradison paid Hogan, Nolan & Stites of Cincinnati $8,465 for a variety of campaign-related services, including $3,093 to cover the printing of brochures and $2,578 for billboard ads. As they had since 1974, the billboards simply said, "Gradison for Congress" in red, white, and blue lettering. Included in Hogan, Nolan & Stite's fees was the cost of district maps and photographs of Gradison, which were hung in Republican booths at county fairs. The firm also collected $1,376 for television advertising production associated with the 1990 campaign but not billed until 1991.

Gradison spent $1,571 for the design and placement of his newspaper advertising. He spent nothing on yard signs or posters, only $482 on items such as buttons and bumper stickers, and $832 on fans. He paid $1,000 to the state party for its coordinated get-out-the-vote effort and celebrated his victory with a small party that cost $901.

While he traditionally held one large fund-raising event in the district each year, Gradison opted not to do so in 1991. His sole campaign income for that year was the $29,022 in interest he collected on his cash reserves. The 1992 event was shelved by the need to campaign for the presidential ticket.

Democrat Thomas R. Chandler reported spending only $105 on the race, none of which was itemized.

Campaign Expenditures	Gradison Amount Spent	% of Total
Overhead		
Office furniture/supplies	$ 1,820	1.91
Rent/utilities	0	
Salaries	0	
Taxes	5,261	5.53
Bank/investment fees	0	
Lawyers/accountants	2,000	2.10
Telephone	0	
Campaign automobile	0	
Computers/office equipment	2,656	2.79
Travel	7,804	8.21
Food/meetings	909	.96
Subtotal	**20,450**	**21.51**
Fund Raising		
Events	1,036	1.09
Direct mail	10,617	11.17
Telemarketing	0	
Subtotal	**11,653**	**12.26**
Polling	0	
Advertising		
Electronic media	0	
Other media	4,599	4.84
Subtotal	**4,599**	**4.84**
Other Campaign Activity		
Persuasion mail/brochures	13,163	13.85
Actual campaigning	6,473	6.81
Staff/volunteers	416	.44
Subtotal	**20,052**	**21.09**
Constituent Gifts/Entertainment	**611**	**.64**
Donations to		
Candidates from same state	9,045	9.52
Candidates from other states	5,764	6.06
Civic organizations	325	.34
Ideological groups	1,500	1.58
Political parties	20,153	21.20
Subtotal	**36,787**	**38.70**
Unitemized Expenses	**905**	**.95**
Total Campaign Expenses	$ **95,056**	
PAC Contributions	$ 0	
Individual Contributions	68,939	
Total Receipts*	111,258	

*Includes PAC and individual contributions as well as interest earned, party contributions, etc.

OHIO　　District 3

Rep. Tony P. Hall (D)

1992 Election Results

Tony P. Hall (D)	146,072	(60%)
Peter W. Davis (R)	98,733	(40%)

In five consecutive campaigns, Rep. Tony P. Hall had received 74 percent of the vote or more, running unopposed in both 1984 and 1990. Redistricting had done nothing to change the solidly Democratic character of his constituency. Nevertheless, after voting against authorizing the use of force against Iraq, Hall found himself on the list of incumbents targeted by the National Republican Congressional Committee.

Peter W. Davis, a corporate attorney and Gulf War veteran, found the Gulf War issue of little concern to voters by November 1992, but he found many voters open to an anti-incumbent message. His television ads slammed Hall for having a home in suburban Washington, D.C., but no home in the district. He attacked Hall for his 1989 vote in favor of the congressional pay raise and for his acceptance of political action committee donations.

Realizing he would have his toughest race in twelve years, Hall hired Washington heavyweights Fenn & King Communications in June 1991 to be his media consultant. With his sizable cash advantage, Hall launched his ad campaign seven weeks before the general election, and in just the first three weeks invested more than $75,000 in air time. His initial television spots touted his efforts to launch a program to provide meals to senior citizens and to prevent the closing of a local plant that employed 2,000 of his constituents. Hall's only negative spot criticized Davis for having failed to vote in eight previous elections.

To counter Davis's criticism that he had not done enough to close the House bank when he first went to Washington, Hall rolled out an ad dubbed "Haircut."

"When I first went to Congress, they said, 'You should bank at the House bank. It's a great deal. There's no penalty for bounced checks.' It didn't sound right to me," the spot began. After noting that he had never had an account at the bank and had therefore never bounced any checks, the ad continued on a more humorous vein. "They also told me about this great haircut I could get in the House barbershop. They said, 'Try it, it's a great deal,' and I went there, and they put a hole here in the back of my hair. I went home, and my wife saw it. She said, 'Don't go there any more.'" As Hall finished speaking, the words "No Bounced Checks. One Bad Haircut," flashed on the screen. Fenn & King collected $244,989 for creating and placing the commercials. Production costs added $26,696.

Hall blanketed 382 of the roughly 600 precincts in the district with brochures that his canvassers handed out door-to-door. "I don't think I would do the brochures again—they were large, four-color, too expensive," noted Rick Carney, Hall's chief of staff and campaign manager.

Campaign Expenditures	Hall Amount Spent	Hall % of Total	Davis Amount Spent	Davis % of Total
Overhead				
Office furniture/supplies	$ 13,568	2.28	$ 2,192	1.25
Rent/utilities	12,632	2.12	6,344	3.63
Salaries	48,775	8.18	14,150	8.10
Taxes	24,306	4.08	0	
Bank/investment fees	0		0	
Lawyers/accountants	32,852	5.51	0	
Telephone	8,351	1.40	5,188	2.97
Campaign automobile	0		0	
Computers/office equipment	11,392	1.91	89	.05
Travel	17,109	2.87	909	.52
Food/meetings	2,032	.34	54	.03
Subtotal	**171,017**	**28.68**	**28,927**	**16.55**
Fund Raising				
Events	34,146	5.73	12,898	7.38
Direct mail	0		3,876	2.22
Telemarketing	0		0	
Subtotal	**34,146**	**5.73**	**16,774**	**9.60**
Polling	**17,828**	**2.99**	**3,057**	**1.75**
Advertising				
Electronic media	271,685	45.56	61,989	35.46
Other media	700	.12	0	
Subtotal	**272,385**	**45.68**	**61,989**	**35.46**
Other Campaign Activity				
Persuasion mail/brochures	33,447	5.61	38,253	21.88
Actual campaigning	27,654	4.64	14,266	8.16
Staff/volunteers	406	.07	0	
Subtotal	**61,507**	**10.32**	**52,519**	**30.05**
Constituent Gifts/ Entertainment	**0**		**0**	
Donations to				
Candidates from same state	5,800	.97	0	
Candidates from other states	500	.08	0	
Civic organizations	4,175	.70	0	
Ideological groups	2,900	.49	0	
Political parties	9,350	1.57	500	.29
Subtotal	**22,725**	**3.81**	**500**	**.29**
Unitemized Expenses	**16,668**	**2.80**	**11,027**	**6.31**
Total Campaign Expenses	**$ 596,276**		**$ 174,793**	
PAC Contributions	**$ 235,200**		**$ 0**	
Individual Contributions	**69,937**		**149,318**	
Total Receipts*	**342,116**		**174,717**	

*Includes PAC and individual contributions as well as interest earned, party contributions, etc.

District 4 — OHIO

Rep. Michael G. Oxley (R)

1992 Election Results

Michael G. Oxley (R)	147,346	(61%)
Raymond M. Ball (D)	92,608	(39%)

Faced with a 1990 Democratic challenger who spent $19,104, Rep. Michael G. Oxley had pumped $330,530 into his campaign. In 1992 Democrat Raymond M. Ball managed to assemble $65,827 for his challenge, so Oxley upped his spending to $645,629.

After narrowly winning a 1981 special election to fill the vacancy created by the death of Republican Rep. Tennyson Guyer, Oxley had been reelected with 65 percent of the vote or more in each of his next four campaigns. In 1988 district Democrats had not bothered to mount a challenge. However, Oxley had been held to 62 percent in 1990 by Thomas E. Burkhart, a bus factory worker. Oxley was not about to take chances in 1992.

Oxley spent $119,338 to maintain his campaign during 1991, despite the fact that he opted not to keep a campaign office open. Part-time payroll amounted to $13,195 and travel, largely to and from the district, added $14,739. He sank $21,601 into his fund-raising events, which added only $38,159 to his cash reserves. However, with $222,716 in the bank on January 1, 1992, Oxley could have outspent Ball by more than three to one in 1992 without raising another dime.

Instead, Oxley accelerated his fund-raising efforts in 1992, bringing in $323,371 in nonparty contributions. Oxley refused to take more than $1,000 from any political action committee (PAC) and further limited contributions from PACs "with no presence in the state of Ohio" to $500. Those seemingly strict limitations still allowed him to raise $281,775 from PACs over the two-year cycle, which accounted for 60 percent of his nonparty contributions.

Oxley paid Chris Mottola of Philadelphia, Pa., $133,200 for creating, producing, and placing broadcast advertising. Miscellaneous production costs added $524. Oxley spent $26,761 to advertise in such newspapers as the *Lima News,* the *Wapakoneta Daily News,* the *Bucyrus Telegraph Forum,* the *Bellefontaine Examiner,* and the *Marion Star.* Billboard ads cost $17,179.

Campaign Technology Corp., a company formerly located in Alexandria, Va., billed Oxley's campaign $98,186 for a variety of services. Although the company's telephone number is no longer in service and Oxley's congressional and campaign offices refused to cooperate in this project, his campaign financial statements indicate that the company supplied computer hardware, computer consulting services, and provided mailing lists and brochures. American Viewpoint, also of Alexandria, collected $22,400 for polling.

Oxley spent $19,746 on constituent stroking, including $11,255 on gifts, including baubles from B&C Jewelers in Alexandria, Va. Year-end holiday cards added $7,531.

Campaign Expenditures	Oxley Amount Spent	Oxley % of Total	Ball Amount Spent	Ball % of Total
Overhead				
Office furniture/supplies	$ 8,234	1.28	$ 870	1.32
Rent/utilities	2,230	.35	2,800	4.25
Salaries	44,059	6.82	6,071	9.22
Taxes	4,319	.67	1,142	1.73
Bank/investment fees	90	.01	25	.04
Lawyers/accountants	0		250	.38
Telephone	4,171	.65	2,214	3.36
Campaign automobile	7,397	1.15	0	
Computers/office equipment	25,050	3.88	818	1.24
Travel	46,989	7.28	6,089	9.25
Food/meetings	7,501	1.16	0	
Subtotal	**150,040**	**23.24**	**20,281**	**30.81**
Fund Raising				
Events	45,803	7.09	2,950	4.48
Direct mail	10,771	1.67	0	
Telemarketing	0		0	
Subtotal	**56,574**	**8.76**	**2,950**	**4.48**
Polling	**22,400**	**3.47**	**7,100**	**10.79**
Advertising				
Electronic media	133,724	20.71	15,140	23.00
Other media	43,990	6.81	2,102	3.19
Subtotal	**177,714**	**27.53**	**17,242**	**26.19**
Other Campaign Activity				
Persuasion mail/brochures	132,512	20.52	4,354	6.61
Actual campaigning	29,992	4.65	9,562	14.53
Staff/volunteers	190	.03	789	1.20
Subtotal	**162,695**	**25.20**	**14,705**	**22.34**
Constituent Gifts/ Entertainment	**19,746**	**3.06**	**0**	
Donations to				
Candidates from same state	1,800	.28	391	.59
Candidates from other states	3,250	.50	0	
Civic organizations	775	.12	0	
Ideological groups	325	.05	0	
Political parties	39,404	6.10	250	.38
Subtotal	**45,554**	**7.06**	**641**	**.97**
Unitemized Expenses	**10,906**	**1.69**	**2,908**	**4.42**
Total Campaign Expenses	**$ 645,629**		**$ 65,827**	
PAC Contributions	$ 281,775		$ 46,125	
Individual Contributions	187,544		10,929	
Total Receipts*	491,631		68,810	

*Includes PAC and individual contributions as well as interest earned, party contributions, etc.

OHIO District 5

Rep. Paul E. Gillmor (R) *1992 Election Results* Paul E. Gillmor (R) 187,860 (100%)

Rep. Paul E. Gillmor spent $179,777 in 1990; neither Democrat P. Scott Mange nor independent John E. Jackson spent as much as $5,000 against him. In 1992 Gillmor ran unopposed in both the Republican primary and the November general election but still managed to spend $251,741. Only 6 percent of his 1992 outlays were devoted in any way to appealing to his constituents for votes.

Gillmor used his campaign as an auxiliary fund for his wife Karen, who waged a successful campaign of her own for the Ohio state senate. Gillmor donated $72,000 of his treasury to his wife's campaign, including a $22,000 loan he later forgave. He spent $13,198 of his campaign funds on postage, which he then gave to his wife's campaign as an in-kind contribution. In all, Gillmor tapped his campaign for 55 percent of the $155,282 Karen Gillmor reported spending on her campaign.

While Gillmor dispensed money to candidates other than his wife, he was far less generous. He donated $1,000 each to fellow Ohio Reps. Ralph Regula and Paul Coverdell, who defeated Georgia Sen. Wyche Fowler, Jr. Republican Reps. Mickey Edwards (Okla.), Newt Gingrich (Ga.), Jim McCrery (La.), Don Young (Alaska), C. W. Bill Young (Fla.), Ronald K. Machtley (R.I.), and John J. Rhodes III (Ariz.) each received $500, as did Margaret R. Mueller and Deborah Pryce, who contested open seats in Ohio. Excluding contributions to his wife, Gillmor gave only $8,600 to fellow Republicans seeking local, state, and federal offices.

Overhead accounted for 28 percent of Gillmor's spending. Rent on his permanent campaign headquarters amounted to $17,790 and utilities added $2,443. He spent $20,774 on travel, including $3,981 for charter flights and $1,348 for expenses incurred during the 1992 Republican National Convention in Houston, Texas. Meals and meetings unconnected to fund raising amounted to $4,336, including a $1,222 meal at the House restaurant described in his campaign financial reports as "Capitol luncheon."

Gillmor's investment in constituent stroking totaled $20,118—$4,779 more than he spent on direct appeals for votes. He gave away $5,585 in "favors" distributed at annual Lincoln Day events. Various constituent events cost $4,774, including a $2,068 "district constituent lunch" held in May 1992 at the Seaport Inn in Alexandria, Va. While Gillmor's office failed to return three telephone calls to discuss their spending, it appeared that he spent $9,545 to print and mail year-end holiday cards.

Political action committee contributions accounted for 68 percent of the money Gillmor raised to pay for this spending spree.

Campaign Expenditures	Gillmor Amount Spent	% of Total
Overhead		
Office furniture/supplies	$ 2,482	.99
Rent/utilities	20,233	8.04
Salaries	9,384	3.73
Taxes	1,028	.41
Bank/investment fees	66	.03
Lawyers/accountants	0	.00
Telephone	2,908	1.15
Campaign automobile	0	.00
Computers/office equipment	9,345	3.71
Travel	20,774	8.25
Food/meetings	4,336	1.72
Subtotal	70,555	28.03
Fund Raising		
Events	34,500	13.70
Direct mail	13,024	5.17
Telemarketing	0	.00
Subtotal	47,525	18.88
Polling	0	.00
Advertising		
Electronic media	0	.00
Other media	65	.03
Subtotal	65	.03
Other Campaign Activity		
Persuasion mail/brochures	9,903	3.93
Actual campaigning	5,371	2.13
Staff/volunteers	0	.00
Subtotal	15,274	6.07
Constituent Gifts/Entertainment	20,118	7.99
Donations to		
Candidates from same state	88,548	35.17
Candidates from other states	5,250	2.09
Civic organizations	0	.00
Ideological groups	0	.00
Political parties	1,487	.59
Subtotal	95,285	37.85
Unitemized Expenses	2,919	1.16
Total Campaign Expenses	$ 251,741	
PAC Contributions	$ 160,137	
Individual Contributions	72,904	
Total Receipts*	244,817	

*Includes PAC and individual contributions as well as interest earned, party contributions, etc.

District 6 — OHIO

Rep. Ted Strickland (D)

1992 Election Results
Ted Strickland (D) 122,720 (51%)
Bob McEwen (R) 119,252 (49%)

Defeated in three previous House campaigns, including a 1980 loss to Rep. Bob McEwen, Shawnee State University professor Ted Strickland had plenty of campaign experience and enough money to be competitive. Nevertheless, in more placid times, Strickland might well have been swamped by McEwen's sizable cash advantage.

However, the times were anything but placid. As a result of redistricting, McEwen and fellow Republican Rep. Clarence E. Miller found themselves locked in a bitter primary battle. Comparing McEwen to Pinocchio, Miller continuously blasted his colleague for having 166 overdrafts at the House bank and for initially denying that he had any. After preliminary vote tallies showed him losing by 297 votes and a recount closed the gap to 286 votes, Miller filed a lawsuit claiming that ballots had been mishandled and asking the courts to declare him the winner.

The real winner was Strickland. "We ran the whole time holding our breath that Miller wasn't going to come out with a big endorsement of McEwen at the end," recalled Frances Strickland, who served as her husband's campaign manager. "If Miller had spoken up for him, things could have gone the other way."

Strickland sunk 62 percent of his money in broadcast advertising and persuasion mail, a decision that was not always popular with his supporters. "It made the troops nervous," noted Frances Strickland. "They wanted a lot of signs, but signs don't win campaigns. I fought down suggestions that we spend money on billboards and just kept telling people we had to save our money for television in the last few weeks."

With a limited budget, Strickland could afford only one low-tech television commercial, which featured still photos and hammered McEwen for his checks, for taking congressional junkets, and for voting himself a pay raise. The ad then touted Strickland's support of health care reform, his commitment to education, and, as his wife put it, "Ted's lifetime of helping people." When McEwen began airing ads accusing him of flip-flopping on abortion and gun control, Strickland answered with radio spots featuring actors discounting the accuracy of McEwen's charges. Austin-Sheinkopf of New York collected $82,409 from Strickland and $29,000 from the Democratic Congressional Campaign Committee for creating and placing the various spots.

Realizing that McEwen was in trouble, the National Republican Congressional Committee and the Republican National Committee pumped $53,188 into the campaign, most of which was invested in persuasion mail. It was not enough to overcome the impact of McEwen's overdrafts and intraparty feuding, as Strickland eked out a 3,468-vote victory.

Campaign Expenditures	Strickland Amount Spent	% of Total	McEwen Amount Spent	% of Total
Overhead				
Office furniture/supplies	$ 2,450	.96	$ 5,139	.65
Rent/utilities	3,527	1.37	3,150	.40
Salaries	15,799	6.16	45,738	5.83
Taxes	0		3,153	.40
Bank/investment fees	59	.02	524	.07
Lawyers/accountants	0		11,888	1.52
Telephone	8,272	3.22	3,965	.51
Campaign automobile	0		10,509	1.34
Computers/office equipment	655	.26	7,034	.90
Travel	3,640	1.42	68,268	8.70
Food/meetings	1,001	.39	1,349	.17
Subtotal	**35,403**	**13.80**	**160,717**	**20.48**
Fund Raising				
Events	31,864	12.42	36,667	4.67
Direct mail	9,413	3.67	13,532	1.72
Telemarketing	0		0	
Subtotal	**41,277**	**16.09**	**50,199**	**6.40**
Polling	**14,690**	**5.73**	**15,300**	**1.95**
Advertising				
Electronic media	91,330	35.60	319,983	40.78
Other media	656	.26	20,880	2.66
Subtotal	**91,986**	**35.86**	**340,863**	**43.44**
Other Campaign Activity				
Persuasion mail/brochures	67,039	26.13	77,218	9.84
Actual campaigning	5,128	2.00	69,815	8.90
Staff/volunteers	508	.20	0	
Subtotal	**72,675**	**28.33**	**147,032**	**18.74**
Constituent Gifts/Entertainment	**69**	**.03**	**19,363**	**2.47**
Donations to				
Candidates from same state	0		900	.11
Candidates from other states	0		5,500	.70
Civic organizations	15	.01	2,550	.32
Ideological groups	40	.02	0	
Political parties	40	.02	14,241	1.81
Subtotal	**95**	**.04**	**23,191**	**2.96**
Unitemized Expenses	**326**	**.13**	**28,012**	**3.57**
Total Campaign Expenses	**$ 256,521**		**$ 784,676**	
PAC Contributions	$ 112,457		$ 273,355	
Individual Contributions	93,064		303,246	
Total Receipts*	240,391		598,006	

*Includes PAC and individual contributions as well as interest earned, party contributions, etc.

OHIO — District 7

Rep. David L. Hobson (R)

1992 Election Results

David L. Hobson (R)	164,195	(71%)
Clifford S. Heskett † (D)	66,237	(29%)

Rep. David L. Hobson had spent nearly $164,000 less than the average open seat candidate in 1990, en route to winning his first term with 62 percent of the vote. In the first defense of his seat, Hobson grabbed 71 percent of the vote, while spending nearly $240,000 less than the typical freshman.

Unopposed in the primary and challenged in the general election by Democrat Clifford S. Heskett, a retired teacher who spent less than $5,000, Hobson invested just 34 percent of his $266,760 budget in direct appeals for votes. While he paid Wilson Communications of Washington, D.C., $17,756 for creating and placing radio commercials, $4,191 of that was for work done in 1990 but not billed until 1991. Miscellaneous production costs for the 1992 spots amounted to only $116. To raise the level of his name identification, primarily among constituents he acquired through redistricting, Hobson spent $1,544 on billboards, $14,466 on yard signs, and $4,209 on T-shirts, sun visors, and caps emblazoned with his name. He invested $4,208 in newspaper ads, most of which were placed through the Ohio Newspaper Association.

Overhead consumed 29 percent of Hobson's budget. His $300-a-month campaign office remained open throughout the two-year cycle, with monthly utilities averaging $140. His payroll totaled $34,858, but while he listed the payments as "salary," he paid no payroll taxes.

Hobson began 1991 with cash reserves of only $603 and 1990 debts of $14,008. By the end of 1992, his relaxed campaign had allowed him to build a cushion of $81,974. Political action committees (PACs) had accounted for 52 percent of the money Hobson raised for his initial campaign, and he picked up in the 1992 cycle right where he had left off. Without a fund-raising consultant, he raised $78,050 from PACs during the first fifteen months of the 1992 cycle. With assistance from Nancy Bocskor of Arlington, Va., who received $5,476 for her efforts, Hobson raised another $118,925 from PACs over the final eight months of the campaign.

Hobson's cash reserves would have been considerably higher had he not given $30,368 of his treasury to other candidates, Republican party organizations, and various causes. He donated $2,000 to Minority Whip Newt Gingrich (Ga.), who was locked in a bitter battle to retain his seat. When Hobson's predecessor in District 7, Lt. Gov. Mike DeWine, decided to challenge Sen. John Glenn, Hobson gave his campaign $1,100. He spent $4,110 on livestock purchased at fairs and 4-H Club events. "Coming from a rural district, that's what you do," noted Joyce McGarry, Hobson's press secretary.

Campaign Expenditures	Hobson Amount Spent	% of Total
Overhead		
Office furniture/supplies	$ 9,582	3.59
Rent/utilities	10,552	3.96
Salaries	34,858	13.07
Taxes	511	.19
Bank/investment fees	1,030	.39
Lawyers/accountants	5,364	2.01
Telephone	6,760	2.53
Campaign automobile	1,810	.68
Computers/office equipment	5,061	1.90
Travel	1,459	.55
Food/meetings	131	.05
Subtotal	77,119	28.91
Fund Raising		
Events	48,419	18.15
Direct mail	0	
Telemarketing	0	
Subtotal	48,419	18.15
Polling	6,000	2.25
Advertising		
Electronic media	17,872	6.70
Other media	6,607	2.48
Subtotal	24,479	9.18
Other Campaign Activity		
Persuasion mail/brochures	38,825	14.55
Actual campaigning	26,040	9.76
Staff/volunteers	845	.32
Subtotal	65,710	24.63
Constituent Gifts/Entertainment	10,484	3.93
Donations to		
Candidates from same state	7,263	2.72
Candidates from other states	6,135	2.30
Civic organizations	5,765	2.16
Ideological groups	1,200	.45
Political parties	10,005	3.75
Subtotal	30,368	11.38
Unitemized Expenses	4,180	1.57
Total Campaign Expenses	$ 266,760	
PAC Contributions	$ 196,975	
Individual Contributions	151,627	
Total Receipts*	380,267	

*Includes PAC and individual contributions as well as interest earned, party contributions, etc.

† No expenditures or receipts on file. Candidates raising or spending less than $5,000 are not required to file reports with the Federal Election Commission.

District 8 — OHIO

Rep. John A. Boehner (R)

1992 Election Results

John A. Boehner (R)	176,362	(74%)
Fred Sennet (D)	62,033	(26%)

Freshman Rep. John A. Boehner spent 1991 hoping for the best and preparing for the worst. "We didn't think reelection would be that tough because this has generally been a conservative-leaning district where as long as you keep yourself honest and clean you won't get into trouble," noted Barry Jackson, Boehner's chief of staff. "However, one of the early [redistricting] maps took away all of the district but John's home town, so we had to gear up like it was our first race."

With 1990 campaign debts of $191,055, including personal loans of $140,000, Boehner placed considerable emphasis on fund raising, which accounted for 40 percent of his spending over the two-year election cycle. He spent $44,987 on direct-mail solicitations. He held several dozen events in the district, including annual golf outings that cost the campaign $14,535 in 1991 and $13,953 in 1992, a birthday reception, a series of $25-a-head "pork buster" events, and numerous in-home cocktail parties. Five events were held in Washington, D.C., and its suburbs to attract political action committee (PAC) contributions, including one sponsored by the National Association of Home Builders. In all, Boehner raised $238,854 from PACs, $107,699 from contributors who gave $200 or more, and $200,786 in smaller donations.

Redistricting proved uneventful, and Boehner cruised to victory in what remained a solidly Republican district. Unopposed in the primary and facing underfunded Democrat Fred Sennet in the general election, Boehner spent just 20 percent of his $405,908 budget on direct appeals for votes. He paid Smith & Harroff of Alexandria, Va., $1,832 for creating radio spots that were aimed at raising his name recognition in two counties acquired through redistricting. Air time and miscellaneous production costs amounted to $3,756 and $107, respectively.

Boehner invested $13,253 in billboard ads and $9,941 in yard signs. The signs not only served to remind constituents that he was running but also provided a phonetic spelling of his name so that they might learn the correct pronunciation (BAY ner). He invested $1,256 in T-shirts and $2,783 in buttons and bumper stickers.

Two persuasion mailers—one to introduce Boehner to his new constituents and one designed to boost Republican turnout—cost the campaign a total of $28,290. He paid the Miami County Republican Men's Club $2,208 for his share of a slate mailer. A tabloid-style walk-piece distributed door-to-door cost the campaign $1,200.

Boehner gave away nearly three times as much as he spent on advertising. He donated $53,309 of his treasury to other candidates, political party organizations, and various causes.

Campaign Expenditures	Boehner Amount Spent	Boehner % of Total	Sennet Amount Spent	Sennet % of Total
Overhead				
Office furniture/supplies	$ 2,909	.72	$ 379	5.63
Rent/utilities	2,400	.59	600	8.91
Salaries	33,490	8.25	0	
Taxes	8,270	2.04	0	
Bank/investment fees	69	.02	10	.15
Lawyers/accountants	1,655	.41	0	
Telephone	6,267	1.54	278	4.13
Campaign automobile	0		0	
Computers/office equipment	9,226	2.27	0	
Travel	24,593	6.06	0	
Food/meetings	609	.15	113	1.68
Subtotal	**89,488**	**22.05**	**1,380**	**20.50**
Fund Raising				
Events	116,536	28.71	927	13.77
Direct mail	44,987	11.08	0	
Telemarketing	0		0	
Subtotal	**161,522**	**39.79**	**927**	**13.77**
Polling	**4,700**	**1.16**	**0**	
Advertising				
Electronic media	5,695	1.40	0	
Other media	13,963	3.44	50	.74
Subtotal	**19,658**	**4.84**	**50**	**.74**
Other Campaign Activity				
Persuasion mail/brochures	31,698	7.81	294	4.36
Actual campaigning	29,678	7.31	314	4.66
Staff/volunteers	1,599	.39	0	
Subtotal	**62,976**	**15.51**	**607**	**9.02**
Constituent Gifts/ Entertainment	**1,004**	**.25**	**0**	
Donations to				
Candidates from same state	9,411	2.32	0	
Candidates from other states	25,162	6.20	0	
Civic organizations	4,491	1.11	30	.45
Ideological groups	640	.16	0	
Political parties	13,606	3.35	0	
Subtotal	**53,309**	**13.13**	**30**	**.45**
Unitemized Expenses	**13,252**	**3.26**	**3,737**	**55.52**
Total Campaign Expenses	**$ 405,908**		**$ 6,731**	
PAC Contributions	$ 238,854		$ 4,500	
Individual Contributions	308,485		2,230	
Total Receipts*	557,539		6,730	

*Includes PAC and individual contributions as well as interest earned, party contributions, etc.

OHIO — District 9

Rep. Marcy Kaptur (D)

1992 Election Results

Marcy Kaptur (D)	178,879	(74%)
Ken D. Brown (R)	53,011	(22%)

First elected in 1982 with 58 percent of the vote, Rep. Marcy Kaptur entered the 1992 election cycle with a string of three consecutive wins in which she had garnered 78 percent of the general election vote or more. She had no overdrafts at the House bank, was unopposed in the Democratic primary, and faced a Republican challenger, Ken D. Brown, who spent only $43,933. Even so, Kaptur spent $335,097—a 63 percent increase over her 1990 expenditures.

While Brown invested $600 on broadcast advertising production and $3,209 on air time, Kaptur paid her media adviser, William Morgan & Co. of Baton Rouge, La., $109,834 for creating and placing her broadcast ads. Miscellaneous production costs and air time purchased directly by the campaign added $425 and $292, respectively. Kaptur's budget also allowed room for billboard ads costing $12,144 and newspaper ads costing $3,723. Brown found room in his budget for $1,969 worth of newspaper ads.

Kaptur spent little on campaign literature or advocacy mailings. She invested $6,482 in campaign photographs, which was nearly six times as much as Brown could afford to spend on yard signs. In fact, the $1,218 Kaptur spent on T-shirts for her volunteers was $88 more than Brown's investment in signs. Kaptur spent $6,954 on balloons, buttons, bumper stickers, and other campaign paraphernalia.

Kaptur gave away $23,166 of her treasury to other candidates, Democratic party organizations, and various causes. Fellow Ohio Democrats received a total of $8,871, all but $200 of which went to candidates for state and local offices, not House and Senate candidates. The chief beneficiary of this largess was state representative Vernal G. Riffe, Jr., whose position as majority leader had made him an important ally in a redistricting process that had to reduce the number of congressional districts by two.

Constituent stroking consumed $6,392 of Kaptur's budget. She spent $2,928 on year-end holiday cards, $1,432 on calendars and other constituent gifts, $1,329 on flowers, and $703 on entertainment.

With a seat on the Appropriations Committee, Kaptur knew where to turn for the money she needed to fund her campaign. In 1991 Kaptur spent just $17,144 to raise $97,855, a return of $5.71 for each dollar invested. Political action committees (PACs) accounted for $83,050 of her off-year receipts. Her 1992 fund-raising efforts proved even more cost effective, with a return of $8.55 for each of the $21,673 she spent. PAC donations during 1992 amounted to $125,255. Over the two-year cycle, PACs accounted for 74 percent of her nonparty contributions.

	Kaptur		Brown	
Campaign Expenditures	Amount Spent	% of Total	Amount Spent	% of Total
Overhead				
Office furniture/supplies	$ 4,839	1.44	$ 3,117	7.09
Rent/utilities	2,845	.85	0	
Salaries	23,906	7.13	4,800	10.93
Taxes	674	.20	0	
Bank/investment fees	0		0	
Lawyers/accountants	0		0	
Telephone	5,815	1.74	241	.55
Campaign automobile	0		0	
Computers/office equipment	638	.19	0	
Travel	12,825	3.83	10,522	23.95
Food/meetings	2,139	.64	0	
Subtotal	**53,680**	**16.02**	**18,680**	**42.52**
Fund Raising				
Events	35,408	10.57	5,626	12.81
Direct mail	3,409	1.02	0	
Telemarketing	0		0	
Subtotal	**38,817**	**11.58**	**5,626**	**12.81**
Polling	**43,756**	**13.06**	**0**	
Advertising				
Electronic media	110,551	32.99	3,809	8.67
Other media	20,430	6.10	1,969	4.48
Subtotal	**130,981**	**39.09**	**5,778**	**13.15**
Other Campaign Activity				
Persuasion mail/brochures	9,354	2.79	4,727	10.76
Actual campaigning	21,275	6.35	5,735	13.05
Staff/volunteers	0		0	
Subtotal	**30,629**	**9.14**	**10,462**	**23.81**
Constituent Gifts/ Entertainment	**6,392**	**1.91**	**0**	
Donations to				
Candidates from same state	8,871	2.65	0	
Candidates from other states	1,550	.46	0	
Civic organizations	2,181	.65	0	
Ideological groups	1,125	.34	0	
Political parties	9,439	2.82	0	
Subtotal	**23,166**	**6.91**	**0**	
Unitemized Expenses	**7,676**	**2.29**	**3,387**	**7.71**
Total Campaign Expenses	**$ 335,097**		**$ 43,933**	
PAC Contributions	$ 208,305		$ 8,650	
Individual Contributions	74,750		20,606	
Total Receipts*	290,940		44,782	

*Includes PAC and individual contributions as well as interest earned, party contributions, etc.

District 10 — OHIO

Rep. Martin R. Hoke (R)

1992 Election Results

Martin R. Hoke (R)	136,433	(57%)
Mary Rose Oakar (D)	103,788	(43%)

Rep. Mary Rose Oakar had significant problems heading into the 1992 campaign. She had 213 overdrafts at the House bank and had been named one of the bank's twenty-two worst abusers. The *Cleveland Plain Dealer* reported allegations that she had placed phantom employees on the House Post Office staff at the time she chaired the subcommittee charged with overseeing its operations. While the reported allegations proved baseless, she was undoubtedly damaged by them. To top it all off, redistricting had provided her with a constituency that was 50 percent new to her.

Encouraged by Oakar's difficulties, six Democrats challenged her in the primary. Despite investing more than $700,000, Oakar prevailed with just 39 percent of the vote. Having spent more than $114,000 during 1991, Oakar's preprimary splurge left her with less than $500,000 to funnel into her head-to-head battle with Republican Martin R. Hoke.

Hoke's Republican primary victory had cost about $150,000. The Oppidan Group of Cleveland received $132,169 for creating and placing broadcast advertising that touted his business experience and called for change. This easier path to the general election left Hoke with enough resources to slightly outspend Oakar over the final six months of the campaign.

Hoke came out swinging, hammering Oakar as "the most persuasive argument for term limitation." When Oakar ran commercials admitting that she had done things "I'm not proud of," Hoke countered with a radio spot featuring a female announcer who noted, "Saying I'm sorry is nothing new for Oakar." The spot concluded, "I'm sorry, but it's time for a change." While Oakar ran commercials depicting Hoke and his ideas as being from "outer space," he slammed her for her overdrafts and various ethical difficulties. The Henry Woodward Co. of Cleveland received $268,680 for creating and placing the majority of Hoke's general election broadcast ads. Rainbow Advertising of Independence, Ohio, collected $4,433 for placing some cable television spots.

Hoke spent $13,640 on billboard ads, one of which proclaimed, "You can make a difference. Martin Hoke." The campaign spent $5,105 for 5,000 yard signs. He invested $3,883 in various promotional materials, including packets of aspirin that advised voters to "take two of these" and vote for Hoke if Congress gave them a headache. Buttons and bumper stickers cost $3,022. An in-house phonebank added $8,069. In all, 67 percent of Hoke's outlays were pumped into direct appeals for votes.

Hoke's election night victory party cost $3,236. The musical selection for the event was "Ding, dong, the witch is dead" from the *Wizard of Oz*.

Campaign Expenditures	Hoke Amount Spent	Hoke % of Total	Oakar Amount Spent	Oakar % of Total
Overhead				
Office furniture/supplies	$ 12,129	1.74	$ 16,699	1.31
Rent/utilities	11,787	1.69	14,366	1.13
Salaries	67,973	9.73	71,259	5.58
Taxes	36,954	5.29	25,156	1.97
Bank/investment fees	0		4,034	.32
Lawyers/accountants	750	.11	28,960	2.27
Telephone	6,358	.91	9,237	.72
Campaign automobile	0		0	
Computers/office equipment	9,786	1.40	28,652	2.24
Travel	2,301	.33	20,400	1.60
Food/meetings	20		3,037	.24
Subtotal	**148,057**	**21.20**	**221,800**	**17.38**
Fund Raising				
Events	12,169	1.74	77,264	6.05
Direct mail	38,712	5.54	518	.04
Telemarketing	0		0	
Subtotal	**50,881**	**7.28**	**77,782**	**6.09**
Polling	17,500	2.51	41,001	3.21
Advertising				
Electronic media	412,937	59.12	454,218	35.58
Other media	15,565	2.23	31,350	2.46
Subtotal	**428,502**	**61.35**	**485,568**	**38.04**
Other Campaign Activity				
Persuasion mail/brochures	13,098	1.88	175,075	13.72
Actual campaigning	28,923	4.14	112,903	8.85
Staff/volunteers	0		3,923	.31
Subtotal	**42,021**	**6.02**	**291,901**	**22.87**
Constituent Gifts/Entertainment	0		23,493	1.84
Donations to				
Candidates from same state	0		2,250	.18
Candidates from other states	0		2,000	.16
Civic organizations	20		3,616	.28
Ideological groups	0		0	
Political parties	950	.14	5,400	.42
Subtotal	**970**	**.14**	**13,266**	**1.04**
Unitemized Expenses	10,530	1.51	121,630	9.53
Total Campaign Expenses	**$ 698,460**		**$ 1,276,442**	
PAC Contributions	$ 0		$ 529,853	
Individual Contributions	405,258		434,439	
Total Receipts*	684,560		1,237,668	

*Includes PAC and individual contributions as well as interest earned, party contributions, etc.

OHIO — District 11

Rep. Louis Stokes (D)

1992 Election Results

Louis Stokes (D)	154,718	(69%)
Beryl E. Rothschild (R)	43,866	(20%)
Edmund Gudenas † (I)	19,773	(9%)

Rep. Louis Stokes outspent Republican challenger Beryl E. Rothschild by a total of $254,238. When it came to direct appeals for votes, Stokes outspent Rothschild by just $15,673, as Rothschild sunk 61 percent of his funds in advertising and other campaign activities while Stokes allocated just 19 percent to these expenditures.

Stokes invested $21,594 in constituent stroking, which was only $4,221 less than Rothschild spent on advertising. Annual Labor Day picnics cost the campaign a total of $10,153. He spent $3,861 on floral arrangements for constituents, $2,134 on constituent receptions and meals, $2,085 on holiday cards, $1,856 on gifts, and $1,505 on various awards and plaques.

Stokes entertained more than just constituents at campaign expense. In September 1991 he spent $4,111 on a reception at the House restaurant for attendees of the National Baptist Convention. The campaign also paid for lunches with other members of the Ohio delegation, interns, and House pages.

Much of Stokes's travel had nothing to do with campaigning. In January 1991 he tapped his campaign treasury for $1,841 to pay the bill at the Washington Hilton and Towers for "candidate and family hotel accommodations." Two months later Stokes spent $1,285 of his campaign funds to pay for him and his family to participate in "the New York Congressional Tour." In September 1991 the campaign picked up another $1,861 tab at the Washington Hilton and Towers for "candidate and family hotel accommodations." In April 1992 the campaign paid $351 for his family's hotel accommodations at Walt Disney World Resorts in Orlando, Fla., and $2,385 for "candidate's family air fare." He spent $2,343 of his treasury to take his family to New York for the Democratic National Convention in July 1992. In October there was another $555 expense for his family's air fare and a $3,199 hotel bill at the Washington Hilton and Towers, where he and his family stayed during the Congressional Black Caucus's (CBC) annual weekend bash. Stokes closed out the election cycle with December payments of $682 and $4,270 to cover "candidate and family hotel accommodations" at the Marriott Hotel in Cleveland and "candidate's family air fare," respectively.

Stokes gave away $57,467, including $9,775 for tickets to a dinner and fashion show sponsored by the CBC Foundation and staged during the CBC's 1991 celebration. He gave $10,000 to the Democratic Congressional Campaign Committee and $2,500 to his daughter's campaign for a judgeship in Cleveland. Stokes dipped into his cash reserves to make a $50,000 loan to the Angela R. Stokes for Judge Committee. Since it was a loan, this $50,000 outlay has not been included as part of Stokes's spending.

Campaign Expenditures	Stokes Amount Spent	Stokes % of Total	Rothschild Amount Spent	Rothschild % of Total
Overhead				
Office furniture/supplies	$ 9,298	2.74	$ 2,314	2.72
Rent/utilities	6,655	1.96	1,703	2.00
Salaries	31,226	9.21	11,261	13.26
Taxes	13,103	3.86	3,733	4.39
Bank/investment fees	0		239	.28
Lawyers/accountants	11,467	3.38	750	.88
Telephone	2,588	.76	1,939	2.28
Campaign automobile	0		0	
Computers/office equipment	3,517	1.04	833	.98
Travel	26,681	7.87	922	1.09
Food/meetings	11,212	3.31	55	.06
Subtotal	**115,747**	**34.12**	**23,748**	**27.96**
Fund Raising				
Events	31,474	9.28	6,684	7.87
Direct mail	0		1,802	2.12
Telemarketing	0		0	
Subtotal	**31,474**	**9.28**	**8,486**	**9.99**
Polling	**0**		**0**	
Advertising				
Electronic media	39,762	11.72	24,990	29.42
Other media	5,736	1.69	825	.97
Subtotal	**45,498**	**13.41**	**25,815**	**30.39**
Other Campaign Activity				
Persuasion mail/brochures	9,421	2.78	17,818	20.97
Actual campaigning	12,203	3.60	7,916	9.32
Staff/volunteers	100	.03	0	
Subtotal	**21,724**	**6.40**	**25,734**	**30.29**
Constituent Gifts/Entertainment	**21,594**	**6.37**	**0**	
Donations to				
Candidates from same state	8,850	2.61	25	.03
Candidates from other states	5,600	1.65	0	
Civic organizations	2,605	.77	680	.80
Ideological groups	26,162	7.71	0	
Political parties	14,250	4.20	0	
Subtotal	**57,467**	**16.94**	**705**	**.83**
Unitemized Expenses	**45,685**	**13.47**	**462**	**.54**
Total Campaign Expenses	**$ 339,188**		**$ 84,950**	
PAC Contributions	$ 149,293		$ 2,260	
Individual Contributions	141,445		50,912	
Total Receipts*	391,172		79,879	

*Includes PAC and individual contributions as well as interest earned, party contributions, etc.

† No expenditures or receipts on file. Candidates raising or spending less than $5,000 are not required to file reports with the Federal Election Commission.

District 12 — OHIO

Rep. John R. Kasich (R)

1992 Election Results

John R. Kasich (R)	170,297	(71%)
Bob Fitrakis (D)	68,761	(29%)

Rep. John R. Kasich was one of those rare incumbents who committed more than half his spending to the final month of the campaign.

He spent $41,658 for air time on local network affiliates, $3,468 for time on cable television systems, and $4,811 for radio ads. According to press secretary Bruce Cuthbertson, the ads delivered the message that Kasich "was a guy who fought against special interests," citing his efforts to kill the B-2 Bomber as an example. To ensure that he got the maximum mileage out of his limited advertising budget, Kasich created the ads in-house and directly placed them.

During the final push, $19,382 was spent to print brochures, which Kasich and numerous volunteers handed out while canvassing door-to-door. When a door was not answered, the material was left in one of the plastic door-hangers, which cost $1,157. To reach rural voters, Kasich paid $2,985 to have his campaign material included in a packet of local ads.

Another $12,286 was spent on yard signs. Cuthbertson said the campaign has always been "big on yard signs" and keeps a catalog of people who have expressed interest in placing a yard sign on their lawn.

The campaign spent $3,304 on full-page ads in community newspapers such as the *Licking Courtian*, the *Rocky Fork Enterprise*, the *Pataskala Standard*, and the *Granville Booster*.

As in past campaigns, Kasich held an election eve torchlight parade through his hometown. He paid a total of $1,850 to three high school bands, the Republican Glee Club, and two bagpipers for marching in the parade.

Kasich waited until August 1992 to open his office and hire his two campaign staffers. While he spent $48,642 during 1991, 46 percent of that total was invested in raising money.

Fund-raiser Carla Saunders of Washington, D.C., was Kasich's only consultant and received $5,435 for organizing events to attract donations from political action committees (PACs). Her efforts helped the five-term incumbent raise $116,470 from PACs, or 42 percent of his total contributions.

Not all of the campaign expenses were related to his reelection effort. Season tickets and parking privileges for Ohio State University football games cost the campaign $1,160 over the two years. Cuthbertson said Kasich used these tickets himself.

Democrat Bob Fitrakis said he intentionally sought to make his limited advertising campaign controversial in the hopes of generating free media. In one ad, which aired on MTV, a simulated music video was interrupted by a group of armed men who Fistrakis said where making "an all-out assault on the Reagan-Bush-Kasich years." However, by early October Fitrakis knew it was a lost cause.

Campaign Expenditures	Kasich Amount Spent	Kasich % of Total	Fitrakis Amount Spent	Fitrakis % of Total
Overhead				
Office furniture/supplies	$ 2,427	1.01	$ 276	.66
Rent/utilities	2,400	1.00	1,925	4.59
Salaries	9,278	3.87	587	1.40
Taxes	3,193	1.33	0	
Bank/investment fees	0		31	.07
Lawyers/accountants	0		0	
Telephone	6,656	2.78	993	2.37
Campaign automobile	3,132	1.31	0	
Computers/office equipment	4,415	1.84	85	.20
Travel	1,727	.72	0	
Food/meetings	651	.27	0	
Subtotal	33,878	14.14	3,896	9.28
Fund Raising				
Events	49,489	20.65	4,995	11.90
Direct mail	0		4,440	10.58
Telemarketing	0		0	
Subtotal	49,489	20.65	9,435	22.48
Polling	0		10,000	23.83
Advertising				
Electronic media	59,419	24.80	6,819	16.25
Other media	13,335	5.57	2,383	5.68
Subtotal	72,755	30.37	9,201	21.93
Other Campaign Activity				
Persuasion mail/brochures	23,660	9.87	3,946	9.40
Actual campaigning	24,079	10.05	4,353	10.37
Staff/volunteers	2,720	1.14	0	
Subtotal	50,459	21.06	8,298	19.77
Constituent Gifts/ Entertainment	6,839	2.85	0	
Donations to				
Candidates from same state	6,640	2.77	0	
Candidates from other states	4,500	1.88	0	
Civic organizations	9,039	3.77	0	
Ideological groups	410	.17	0	
Political parties	5,591	2.33	0	
Subtotal	26,180	10.93	0	
Unitemized Expenses	0		1,135	2.70
Total Campaign Expenses	$ 239,600		$ 41,966	
PAC Contributions	$ 116,470		$ 17,200	
Individual Contributions	161,196		7,570	
Total Receipts*	279,301		44,702	

*Includes PAC and individual contributions as well as interest earned, party contributions, etc.

OHIO — District 13

Rep. Sherrod Brown (D)

1992 Election Results

Sherrod Brown (D)	134,486	(53%)
Margaret R. Mueller (R)	88,889	(35%)
Mark Miller † (I)	20,320	(8%)

The fourth time was not the charm for Margaret R. Mueller, a millionaire who had lost three previous bids to oust Rep. Dennis E. Eckart in District 11. Despite spending $141,148 more than former state representative and Ohio secretary of state Sherrod Brown, Mueller suffered her fourth lopsided loss in this open seat contest to succeed retiring Rep. Don J. Pease.

To win the right to meet Mueller, Brown first had to dispatch seven fellow Democrats in the June 2 primary, a process that cost him slightly more than $100,000. He paid Burges & Burges of Cleveland $57,381, virtually all of which was invested in creating and placing one television and two radio commercials. Miscellaneous production costs added $3,794. The clear favorite from the outset, Brown grabbed 45 percent of the primary votes and scored a 23-point victory.

Mueller had a much more difficult time shedding five fellow Republicans. Former state representative Jeffrey P. Jacobs, whose family owns the Cleveland Indians baseball team, pumped $389,875 into the race and came within 5,000 votes of denying Mueller the nomination. His candidacy forced Mueller to invest more than $260,000 in the primary, wiping out her cash advantage over Brown.

Both candidates began the general election campaign on a positive note and, according to Jeff Rusnak, a vice president at Burges & Burges, that was creating problems for Brown. "Our polling showed she had cut our lead way down with positive ads, pulling within the margin of error," Rusnak recalled. "She may not have realized it because she then went negative about two and a half weeks out, and dropped badly."

Brown paid Burges & Burges another $232,311 for creating and placing five television and four radio commercials, developing persuasion mailers, and providing strategic advice for the general election campaign. Austin-Sheinkopf of New York received $16,131 for consulting on the spots, which touted Brown's opposition to the free-trade agreement, his support for a five-day waiting period for handgun purchases, his pro-choice stance on abortion, and his support for increased taxes on the wealthy. When Mueller began airing television and radio commercials attacking Brown over his handling of his divorce, Brown answered through the free media and rolled out a radio spot featuring a woman announcer. "She only knows how to run one kind of race," Brown's radio spot charged. "If there were awards for the dirtiest campaign in Ohio, Margaret Mueller would win first, second, and third place all by herself."

Campaign Expenditures	Brown Amount Spent	Brown % of Total	Mueller Amount Spent	Mueller % of Total
Overhead				
Office furniture/supplies	$ 3,783	.69	$ 1,727	.25
Rent/utilities	4,775	.88	0	
Salaries	59,403	10.89	40,213	5.86
Taxes	0		1,320	.19
Bank/investment fees	0		2,801	.41
Lawyers/accountants	14,159	2.60	19,151	2.79
Telephone	13,003	2.38	9,284	1.35
Campaign automobile	2,492	.46	0	
Computers/office equipment	3,531	.65	6,167	.90
Travel	8,635	1.58	3,554	.52
Food/meetings	628	.12	370	.05
Subtotal	**110,408**	**20.25**	**84,586**	**12.32**
Fund Raising				
Events	20,766	3.81	9,392	1.37
Direct mail	9,476	1.74	0	
Telemarketing	0		0	
Subtotal	**30,242**	**5.55**	**9,392**	**1.37**
Polling	**34,000**	**6.24**	**7,000**	**1.02**
Advertising				
Electronic media	272,125	49.91	397,140	57.86
Other media	5,125	.94	265	.04
Subtotal	**277,250**	**50.84**	**397,405**	**57.89**
Other Campaign Activity				
Persuasion mail/brochures	60,995	11.19	125,419	18.27
Actual campaigning	21,112	3.87	61,487	8.96
Staff/volunteers	238	.04	0	
Subtotal	**82,344**	**15.10**	**186,906**	**27.23**
Constituent Gifts/ Entertainment	**1,423**	**.26**	**0**	
Donations to				
Candidates from same state	1,000	.18	0	
Candidates from other states	0		0	
Civic organizations	179	.03	55	.01
Ideological groups	150	.03	32	
Political parties	25		0	
Subtotal	**1,354**	**.25**	**87**	**.01**
Unitemized Expenses	**8,264**	**1.52**	**1,056**	**.15**
Total Campaign Expenses	**$ 545,284**		**$ 686,432**	
PAC Contributions	**$ 263,816**		**$ 43,721**	
Individual Contributions	**224,646**		**121,173**	
Total Receipts*	**495,275**		**866,740**	

*Includes PAC and individual contributions as well as interest earned, party contributions, etc.

† No expenditures or receipts on file. Candidates raising or spending less than $5,000 are not required to file reports with the Federal Election Commission.

District 14 — OHIO

Rep. Tom Sawyer (D)

1992 Election Results

Tom Sawyer (D)	165,335	(68%)
Robert Morgan (R)	78,659	(32%)

Spurred into action by concerns over his 1989 vote in favor of a congressional pay raise, Rep. Tom Sawyer had spent $267,137 on his 1990 campaign, despite the fact that neither his primary opponent nor his challenger in the general election had spent as much as $5,000. Having dispelled that issue and faced with equally underfunded challengers in 1992, Sawyer scaled back his spending to $209,238, a drop of 22 percent. In a year when anti-incumbent sentiment was supposedly running rampant throughout the country, Sawyer spent considerably less than he had in any of his three previous House campaigns.

Sawyer significantly sliced his spending on overhead, fund raising, and advertising. He cut his spending on overhead by $8,376, a 14 percent decline. His fund-raising costs plummeted by $22,745, a 38 percent drop. Against a 1990 opponent who spent just $2,604 on her campaign, Sawyer had invested $71,098 in advertising to inoculate himself against any anti-incumbent backlash, including $52,219 in television and radio commercials. Against Republican Robert Morgan, who spent $2,260, Sawyer apparently felt no need to maintain that sort of presence in 1992. He spent nothing on broadcast advertising and only $4,379 on program and newspaper ads.

A 40 percent increase in spending on persuasion mail partially offset Sawyer's dramatic reductions in other parts of the budget. Burges & Burges of Cleveland, which had provided both strategic advice and media services to Sawyer in 1990, found themselves displaced by New York-based media consultant Austin-Sheinkopf in 1992. However, Sawyer came to Burges & Burges in 1992 for mailing lists that cost $4,334. Sawyer paid $39,037 to print and mail his campaign literature.

Beginning in March 1992, Sawyer paid Austin-Sheinkopf a $2,250-a-month retainer that rose to $2,500 in August. A campaign spokesman said the $26,250 Austin-Sheinkopf received was for general consulting, not for planning a media campaign that was never launched. These payments have been coded as "actual campaigning." To make certain that his popularity had not slipped, Sawyer paid Decision Research Corp. of Cleveland $10,000 for polling.

Assured that there was little chance of a constituent revolt, Sawyer invested virtually nothing in grassroots campaigning. He spent $7,258 on signs, buttons, bumper stickers, and other campaign paraphernalia. He paid $1,500 for his share of the cost of the Summit County Democratic party's coordinated get-out-the-vote effort. Candy and other parade expenses came to $1,011. On election night, the campaign spent $301 to cover its share of a victory party staged by the local Democratic party.

	Sawyer		Morgan	
Campaign Expenditures	Amount Spent	% of Total	Amount Spent	% of Total
Overhead				
Office furniture/supplies	$ 3,893	1.86	$ 0	
Rent/utilities	5,620	2.69	0	
Salaries	26,212	12.53	0	
Taxes	5,695	2.72	0	
Bank/investment fees	47	.02	36	1.61
Lawyers/accountants	0		0	
Telephone	4,011	1.92	0	
Campaign automobile	0		0	
Computers/office equipment	2,575	1.23	0	
Travel	3,993	1.91	0	
Food/meetings	1,454	.69	0	
Subtotal	53,499	25.57	36	1.61
Fund Raising				
Events	36,661	17.52	172	7.61
Direct mail	0		0	
Telemarketing	0		0	
Subtotal	36,661	17.52	172	7.61
Polling	**10,000**	**4.78**	**0**	
Advertising				
Electronic media	0		0	
Other media	4,379	2.09	0	
Subtotal	4,379	2.09	0	
Other Campaign Activity				
Persuasion mail/brochures	43,371	20.73	1,163	51.46
Actual campaigning	38,761	18.52	0	
Staff/volunteers	0		0	
Subtotal	82,133	39.25	1,163	51.46
Constituent Gifts/ Entertainment	**3,902**	**1.86**	**0**	
Donations to				
Candidates from same state	1,000	.48	0	
Candidates from other states	0		0	
Civic organizations	1,370	.65	0	
Ideological groups	465	.22	0	
Political parties	12,845	6.14	0	
Subtotal	15,680	7.49	0	
Unitemized Expenses	**2,985**	**1.43**	**889**	**39.31**
Total Campaign Expenses	**$ 209,238**		**$ 2,260**	
PAC Contributions	$ 148,625		$ 0	
Individual Contributions	39,863		2,260	
Total Receipts*	195,200		2,260	

*Includes PAC and individual contributions as well as interest earned, party contributions, etc.

OHIO   District 15

Rep. Deborah Pryce (R)

1992 Election Results

Deborah Pryce (R)	110,390	(44%)
Richard Cordray (D)	94,907	(38%)
Linda S. Reidelbach (I)	44,906	(18%)

After twenty-six years in the House, Republican Rep. Chalmers P. Wylie decided he had had enough. While he denied that his 515 overdrafts at the House bank were a factor, his decision came soon after his check problems were revealed. Redistricting had left Wylie's constituency largely intact and apparently had no impact on his decision to retire.

Franklin County Municipal Court judge Deborah Pryce secured the Republican nomination without a primary fight by convincing antiabortion activists at the district nominating convention that she was on their side. Her nomination was not assured until the sixth ballot. With the nomination in hand, Pryce decided to clarify her views for the rest of the electorate, revealing that she would "never back off my belief that every woman in America must have the right to choose." She explained that convention delegates must have misunderstood her comments.

That apparent change of heart brought Linda S. Reidelbach, a strong opponent of abortion, into the race as an independent. It also gave Democratic nominee Richard Cordray a glimmer of hope in this solidly Republican district.

Although she had no opposition in the primary, Pryce launched her advertising campaign with a $29,067 television buy in May that focused on her career as a judge and introduced her to district voters. Other positive spots focused on job creation and the need to reduce the federal budget deficit. "We wanted to run on our message and never planned to mention our opponents," noted Tom Wolfe, Pryce's chief of staff. That proved impossible when both Cordray and Reidelbach began hammering her over the apparent abortion flip-flop. Pryce quickly commissioned a sixty-second commercial on the issue.

Pryce invested $31,832 in campaign literature and persuasion mailers that included pieces outlining her positions on abortion, child care, and family leave. She spent $25,297 on newspaper ads, $9,246 on yard signs, and $3,932 on T-shirts. All of Pryce's campaign literature, newspaper ads, signs, and T-shirts carried the same message: "The Change We Need." To identify her supporters and encourage them to vote, Pryce paid Payco American Corp. of Brookfield, Wis., $7,918 for phonebanking.

Smith & Harroff of Alexandria, Va., collected $229,210 for creating and placing Pryce's television and radio commercials for the general election and for designing persuasion mailers. Pollsters Tarrance & Associates, also of Alexandria, and Spencer Market Research of Columbus received $21,477 and $3,930, respectively. Fund-raisers Shelby/Blaskeg of Washington, D.C., and Flourney & Associates of Hilliard received $23,032 and $15,300, respectively.

	Pryce		Cordray	
Campaign Expenditures	Amount Spent	% of Total	Amount Spent	% of Total
Overhead				
Office furniture/supplies	$ 8,534	1.47	$ 4,722	1.52
Rent/utilities	4,900	.84	900	.29
Salaries	65,206	11.22	36,533	11.77
Taxes	7,373	1.27	0	
Bank/investment fees	439	.08	132	.04
Lawyers/accountants	0		0	
Telephone	12,313	2.12	1,856	.60
Campaign automobile	0		0	
Computers/office equipment	8,292	1.43	2,357	.76
Travel	3,664	.63	0	
Food/meetings	735	.13	289	.09
Subtotal	111,455	19.18	46,789	15.08
Fund Raising				
Events	66,078	11.37	9,583	3.09
Direct mail	13,460	2.32	1,573	.51
Telemarketing	0		806	.26
Subtotal	79,537	13.69	11,962	3.85
Polling	25,407	4.37	10,500	3.38
Advertising				
Electronic media	265,775	45.73	134,479	43.33
Other media	25,945	4.46	30,989	9.98
Subtotal	291,720	50.20	165,468	53.31
Other Campaign Activity				
Persuasion mail/brochures	31,832	5.48	52,461	16.90
Actual campaigning	37,375	6.43	12,744	4.11
Staff/volunteers	1,044	.18	0	
Subtotal	70,250	12.09	65,205	21.01
Constituent Gifts/ Entertainment	2,245	.39	0	
Donations to				
Candidates from same state	0		0	
Candidates from other states	0		0	
Civic organizations	480	.08	935	.30
Ideological groups	0		0	
Political parties	65	.01	32	.01
Subtotal	545	.09	967	.31
Unitemized Expenses	0		9,481	3.05
Total Campaign Expenses	$ 581,160		$ 310,373	
PAC Contributions	$ 211,227		$ 129,810	
Individual Contributions	317,217		172,543	
Total Receipts*	558,617		312,488	

*Includes PAC and individual contributions as well as interest earned, party contributions, etc.

District 16 — OHIO

Rep. Ralph Regula (R)

1992 Election Results
Ralph Regula (R)   158,489   (64%)
Warner D. Mendenhall (D)   90,224   (36%)

For the first time in his twenty-year congressional career, Rep. Ralph Regula ran a television commercial in 1992. Helped by rising anti-incumbent sentiment, underfunded college professor Warner D. Mendenhall had held Regula to 59 percent of the vote in 1990—a drop of 20 points from the 1988 results. The incumbent worked hard to make certain that their 1992 rematch would not be as close.

To reach voters in two counties that had been added by redistricting, Regula invested about $25,000 to air his thirty-second spot on Cleveland television stations. The ad, which dealt with his views on foreign trade and job creation, showed him on his farm, at a local steel mill, and at a trade school he helped establish. "It was an experiment," noted Regula in explaining his more aggressive campaign style. "This was the most expensive campaign I've ever been involved in."

Wern, Rausch, Locke Advertising of North Canton designed, produced, and placed the television spot and handled Regula's radio and newspaper advertising. The firm designed what Regula described as a "get to know Ralph Regula" mailer, which was sent to 60,000 constituents in the newly added portion of the district. Wern, Rausch printed shopping bags and a cookbook put together by Regula's wife that contained recipes from other politicians' wives. For its efforts, the company collected a total of $95,550.

While Regula continued to refuse political action committee donations, the need for greater financial resources occasioned his first-ever Washington, D.C., fund-raiser. The in-kind event helped Regula raise $10,400 from out-of-state contributors, up from $3,000 in 1990.

Regula raised most of his money from his eleventh biennial fund-raiser and rally, held in September 1992. Although ticket prices held steady at $50-a-plate, Regula said attendance rose from about 500 in 1990 to 1,600 in 1992. "We give a great meal," Regula boasted.

The balance of Regula's in-state fund-raisers were donated in-kind. An Akron couple spent $1,855 to host a dinner, a luncheon cost another supporter $206, and an ice cream social cost a third supporter $504. Regula raised $58,713 from Ohio residents who gave $200 or more and a total of $82,477 in donations of less than $200.

Mendenhall spent more money in the rematch and received a smaller percentage of the vote. "In 1990, we took him by surprise," explained media consultant Nick Finn of Cleveland-based Burges & Burges. "By 1992, he had a chance to see how the race would play out, time to insulate himself from us, and he ran a more effective campaign."

Campaign Expenditures	Regula Amount Spent	Regula % of Total	Mendenhall Amount Spent	Mendenhall % of Total
Overhead				
Office furniture/supplies	$ 1,028	.50	$ 2,795	2.65
Rent/utilities	1,944	.95	942	.89
Salaries	0		27,173	25.78
Taxes	1,074	.52	51	.05
Bank/investment fees	0		270	.26
Lawyers/accountants	0		0	
Telephone	643	.31	3,047	2.89
Campaign automobile	2,877	1.40	0	
Computers/office equipment	3,523	1.72	1,968	1.87
Travel	488	.24	1,679	1.59
Food/meetings	3,135	1.53	0	
Subtotal	**14,710**	**7.17**	**37,925**	**35.98**
Fund Raising				
Events	19,373	9.44	2,099	1.99
Direct mail	0		586	.56
Telemarketing	0		0	
Subtotal	**19,373**	**9.44**	**2,685**	**2.55**
Polling	**0**		**4,000**	**3.80**
Advertising				
Electronic media	96,273	46.91	17,689	16.78
Other media	15,235	7.42	848	.80
Subtotal	**111,508**	**54.34**	**18,537**	**17.59**
Other Campaign Activity				
Persuasion mail/brochures	18,698	9.11	8,261	7.84
Actual campaigning	21,795	10.62	31,487	29.87
Staff/volunteers	0		170	.16
Subtotal	**40,493**	**19.73**	**39,918**	**37.87**
Constituent Gifts/Entertainment	**2,430**	**1.18**	**0**	
Donations to				
Candidates from same state	0		5	
Candidates from other states	0		0	
Civic organizations	90	.04	0	
Ideological groups	0		0	
Political parties	0		30	.03
Subtotal	**90**	**.04**	**35**	**.03**
Unitemized Expenses	**16,605**	**8.09**	**2,299**	**2.18**
Total Campaign Expenses	**$ 205,210**		**$ 105,399**	
PAC Contributions	$ 0		$ 50,975	
Individual Contributions	151,590		52,364	
Total Receipts*	168,665		109,794	

*Includes PAC and individual contributions as well as interest earned, party contributions, etc.

OHIO — District 17

Rep. James A. Traficant (D)

1992 Election Results

James A. Traficant, Jr. (D)	216,503	(84%)
Salvatore Pansino (R)	40,743	(16%)

Rep. James A. Traficant, Jr., did not need to spend much on broadcast advertising. He received what amounted to thirty minutes of free advertising every week.

Each week of the two-year election cycle, as he had for the previous six years, Traficant hosted a popular Sunday morning show that aired on WYTV, an ABC affiliate in Youngstown. According to press secretary H. West Richards, who wrote and produced the broadcasts as part of his congressional duties, Traficant occasionally had guests but more often spent his half hour discussing the previous week's congressional actions. Since the show aired as a public service, Traficant paid nothing for the time. Over the two-year election cycle, the campaign did pay $4,211 to cover the recording charges at the studio.

Facing only token opposition from Republican Salvatore Pansino and relieved of the need to advertise extensively, Traficant spent only $3,590 to air radio spots on a weekly polka program. Newspaper ads cost the campaign $2,618 and program ads totaled $230.

One of every nine dollars Traficant spent was devoted to constituent stroking. Various gifts cost the campaign $9,811. He gave away coffee mugs and paper weights. He spent $185 to purchase videotapes of the White House tour, which were given to people who had failed to get tour tickets. "He likes trinkets," Richards explained.

Traficant made numerous small donations, most of which went to local candidates and Democratic party organizations. He gave $500 to Rep. John P. Murtha (D-Pa.) and $200 to Rep. Barbara Boxer (D-Calif.) for her successful Senate bid. Reps. Les AuCoin (D-Ore.) and Jim Moody (D-Wis.) received $400 and $150, respectively, for their unsuccessful Senate campaigns. A former high school and college football star, Traficant gave $350 to the Young Disciples Football Organization for their league uniforms. He also donated $250 to the Poland Community Baseball League to help pay for lights.

Unconcerned by Pansino's challenge, Traficant reported spending nothing for the first fourteen days of October. He invested only $6,338 in his campaign from October 15 through November 23, including $1,380 for print advertising.

To pay for his low-key campaign, Traficant held three fund-raisers during the 1992 election cycle—two golf outings and a Washington, D.C., reception for political action committees (PACs). While Richards indicated that Traficant preferred events like the golf outings because "it's money he's raising from constituents," the incumbent raised 55 percent of his funds from PACs. Contributions of less than $200 totaled $38,382, or 25 percent of his total receipts.

	Traficant		Pansino	
Campaign Expenditures	Amount Spent	% of Total	Amount Spent	% of Total
Overhead				
Office furniture/supplies	$ 145	.15	$ 134	7.40
Rent/utilities	0		0	
Salaries	0		0	
Taxes	0		0	
Bank/investment fees	0		3	.17
Lawyers/accountants	0		0	
Telephone	1,310	1.34	55	3.02
Campaign automobile	0		0	
Computers/office equipment	499	.51	75	4.12
Travel	11,980	12.22	119	6.56
Food/meetings	2,637	2.69	29	1.60
Subtotal	**16,570**	**16.91**	**414**	**22.86**
Fund Raising				
Events	33,078	33.75	0	
Direct mail	0		0	
Telemarketing	0		0	
Subtotal	**33,078**	**33.75**	**0**	
Polling	**0**		**0**	
Advertising				
Electronic media	7,801	7.96	316	17.44
Other media	2,848	2.91	40	2.21
Subtotal	**10,649**	**10.87**	**356**	**19.65**
Other Campaign Activity				
Persuasion mail/brochures	0		380	20.98
Actual campaigning	1,779	1.82	468	25.82
Staff/volunteers	0		117	6.48
Subtotal	**1,779**	**1.82**	**966**	**53.29**
Constituent Gifts/Entertainment	**10,993**	**11.22**	**0**	
Donations to				
Candidates from same state	1,670	1.70	0	
Candidates from other states	1,450	1.48	0	
Civic organizations	1,300	1.33	76	4.22
Ideological groups	500	.51	0	
Political parties	3,579	3.65	0	
Subtotal	**8,499**	**8.67**	**76**	**4.22**
Unitemized Expenses	**16,426**	**16.76**	**0**	
Total Campaign Expenses	$ **97,996**		$ **1,812**	
PAC Contributions	$ 85,120		$ 0	
Individual Contributions	66,782		135	
Total Receipts*	155,474		3,488	

*Includes PAC and individual contributions as well as interest earned, party contributions, etc.

District 18 — OHIO

Rep. Douglas Applegate (D)

1992 Election Results

Douglas Applegate (D)	166,189	(68%)
Bill Ress (R)	77,229	(32%)

Rep. Douglas Applegate spent only $8,364 on advertising and campaign literature, but that was $6,316 more than he had invested in such direct voter contact in 1990.

To reach the four new counties added to his territory by redistricting, Applegate spent $2,275 to air radio spots that focused on his constituent service, veterans issues, and economic development. Applegate had not purchased a billboard ad since 1980, but in 1992 he spent $5,457 on such ads to inform his new constituents that they were now part of District 18 and that he was their representative. According to administrative assistant James R. Hart, none of the incumbent's previous constituents were targeted by advertising.

Facing only limited opposition from the Republican candidate, former state senator Bill Ress, Applegate restricted his grass-roots campaigning to $4,554 in yard signs and posters and a $632 expenditure for business-size cards with the incumbent's picture on one side and his congressional office telephone numbers on the other. Campaign photos added $748.

Applegate's budget had plenty of room for expenses that had little or nothing to do with his reelection. The campaign spent $13,845 to purchase and maintain a new Chevrolet—$180 more than was invested in all of Applegate's direct appeals to voters. Applegate consumed 171 meals at campaign expense, or an average of one meal every four days for the entire two-year cycle. He spent $2,094 on 83 meals in Ohio, including a $135 dinner at the Stone Crab Inn in St. Clairsville. Forty-five meals in Washington, D.C., and its suburbs cost the campaign $1,785, including a $114 dinner at the Chart House in Alexandria, Va. He spent $466 at restaurants in Pennsylvania, including a $6.98 meal at a Red Lobster in Pittsburgh. Meals in West Virginia cost the campaign $617. Hart said most of these meals were in connection with various speaking engagements when Applegate "can't use his official House account."

Applegate simply gave away 28 percent of his money, primarily to various charitable and booster organizations. He also gave $2,500 to the Democratic party of Ohio and $500 to Rep. Harley O. Staggers, Jr. (W.Va.).

Although he spent less than $26,000, Ress hired Republican heavyweight Arthur J. Finkelstein & Associates of New York to provide polling and strategic advice. "Arthur said, 'Bill, you can't win,' and it took the wind out of my sails," recalled Ress. As a result of that conversation, Ress opted not to hold any fundraisers. "I just couldn't get excited about the race, and then I just went through the motions of running for office," Ress added.

	Applegate		Ress	
Campaign Expenditures	Amount Spent	% of Total	Amount Spent	% of Total
Overhead				
Office furniture/supplies	$ 784	.77	$ 465	1.79
Rent/utilities	0		0	
Salaries	0		1,095	4.21
Taxes	2,869	2.80	0	
Bank/investment fees	40	.04	86	.33
Lawyers/accountants	4,500	4.40	0	
Telephone	0		851	3.28
Campaign automobile	13,845	13.53	0	
Computers/office equipment	241	.24	250	.96
Travel	1,651	1.61	0	
Food/meetings	4,962	4.85	0	
Subtotal	**28,891**	**28.23**	**2,747**	**10.57**
Fund Raising				
Events	13,022	12.72	0	
Direct mail	0		12,709	48.90
Telemarketing	0		0	
Subtotal	**13,022**	**12.72**	**12,709**	**48.90**
Polling	**0**		**7,900**	**30.40**
Advertising				
Electronic media	2,275	2.22	942	3.62
Other media	5,457	5.33	997	3.83
Subtotal	**7,732**	**7.56**	**1,939**	**7.46**
Other Campaign Activity				
Persuasion mail/brochures	632	.62	0	
Actual campaigning	5,301	5.18	595	2.29
Staff/volunteers	0		0	
Subtotal	**5,933**	**5.80**	**595**	**2.29**
Constituent Gifts/ Entertainment	**1,210**	**1.18**	**0**	
Donations to				
Candidates from same state	500	.49	0	
Candidates from other states	1,750	1.71	0	
Civic organizations	23,609	23.07	0	
Ideological groups	0		0	
Political parties	3,050	2.98	100	.38
Subtotal	**28,909**	**28.25**	**100**	**.38**
Unitemized Expenses	**16,642**	**16.26**	**0**	
Total Campaign Expenses	**$ 102,339**		**$ 25,989**	
PAC Contributions	$ 88,170		$ 250	
Individual Contributions	7,525		21,038	
Total Receipts*	117,262		27,288	

*Includes PAC and individual contributions as well as interest earned, party contributions, etc.

OHIO
District 19

Rep. Eric D. Fingerhut (D)

1992 Election Results

Eric D. Fingerhut (D)	138,465	(53%)
Robert A. Gardner (R)	124,606	(47%)

Named one of the House bank's twenty-two worst abusers, Democratic Rep. Edward F. Feighan opted to retire rather than seek a sixth term. Nine Democrats, including state senator Eric D. Fingerhut, Cuyahoga County auditor Tim McCormack, and former Cleveland mayor Dennis Kucinich, lined up to take Feighan's place.

Fingerhut called for change and congressional reform, including campaign finance reform. Ironically, he delivered his message of reform by spending more than $200,000 in just two months. Television and radio advertising created by Axelrod & Associates of Chicago, Ill., largely produced by The Media Group of Columbus and placed by Burges & Burges of Cleveland, accounted for more than $120,000 of his preprimary investment. Fingerhut defeated McCormack by 4,876 votes.

Lake County commissioner Robert A. Gardner spent only about $36,000 to defeat four primary opponents and secure the Republican nomination. While the Democratic Congressional Campaign Committee spent $11,648 on the race, the National Republican Congressional Committee pumped in $55,149, allowing Gardner to close his spending gap with Fingerhut to about $47,000 in their head-to-head contest.

The battle was waged primarily on television. It began on a civil note. Gardner claimed responsibility for the creation of more than 3,000 jobs. Fingerhut countered with a spot focusing on a ten-point program he dubbed "New Deal for the 19th," which focused on trade, economic reform, jobs, and health care reform. One of Fingerhut's radio commercials featured women who credited him with creating job programs that had helped them move off welfare. "The issues changed from the primary to the general election," recalled David Fleshler, Fingerhut's chief of staff. "Where the primary was about change, the general election was about, as James Carville put it, 'the economy, stupid.'"

As election day drew closer, both candidates took off the gloves and talked of things other than the economy. A Fingerhut commercial accused Gardner of flip-flopping on abortion and gun control. Gardner recalled that one of his commercials urged voters not to elect Fingerhut because he was an attorney—"something Congress has too many of." Each accused the other of negative campaigning.

Fingerhut paid Axelrod $58,510 for its work. Burges & Burges received $313,685 for placing the spots and for providing limited production services, general strategic advice, designing two persuasion mailers, placing a single billboard ad, and providing precinct walk-lists. The Media Group collected $12,121 for ad production. Decision Research Corp. of Cleveland provided polls for $38,000.

	Fingerhut		Gardner	
Campaign Expenditures	Amount Spent	% of Total	Amount Spent	% of Total
Overhead				
Office furniture/supplies	$ 7,556	1.07	$ 3,660	.84
Rent/utilities	12,245	1.73	4,346	1.00
Salaries	87,908	12.40	22,468	5.17
Taxes	21,727	3.06	8,893	2.05
Bank/investment fees	65	.01	135	.03
Lawyers/accountants	0		4,464	1.03
Telephone	9,428	1.33	2,227	.51
Campaign automobile	0		0	
Computers/office equipment	2,497	.35	6,645	1.53
Travel	2,999	.42	5,722	1.32
Food/meetings	435	.06	1,705	.39
Subtotal	**144,861**	**20.43**	**60,264**	**13.87**
Fund Raising				
Events	15,232	2.15	17,231	3.96
Direct mail	11,681	1.65	0	
Telemarketing	0		5,601	1.29
Subtotal	**26,912**	**3.80**	**22,833**	**5.25**
Polling	**38,000**	**5.36**	**15,872**	**3.65**
Advertising				
Electronic media	379,362	53.51	220,310	50.69
Other media	6,253	.88	22,810	5.25
Subtotal	**385,615**	**54.39**	**243,120**	**55.94**
Other Campaign Activity				
Persuasion mail/brochures	58,642	8.27	55,997	12.88
Actual campaigning	47,871	6.75	34,200	7.87
Staff/volunteers	167	.02	0	
Subtotal	**106,680**	**15.05**	**90,196**	**20.75**
Constituent Gifts/ Entertainment	**1,200**	**.17**	**0**	
Donations to				
Candidates from same state	0		0	
Candidates from other states	0		0	
Civic organizations	90	.01	235	.05
Ideological groups	185	.03	0	
Political parties	250	.04	95	.02
Subtotal	**525**	**.07**	**329**	**.08**
Unitemized Expenses	**5,174**	**.73**	**2,020**	**.46**
Total Campaign Expenses	**$ 708,967**		**$ 434,634**	
PAC Contributions	$ 210,017		$ 63,815	
Individual Contributions	395,521		366,438	
Total Receipts*	617,946		460,938	

*Includes PAC and individual contributions as well as interest earned, party contributions, etc.

District 1 — OKLAHOMA

Rep. James M. Inhofe (R)

1992 Election Results

James M. Inhofe (R)	119,211	(53%)
John Selph (D)	106,619	(47%)

In three previous campaigns Rep. James M. Inhofe had never topped 56 percent in the general election, and while redistricting had seemingly strengthened his position by adding Republicans to his constituency, he entered the 1992 campaign on the defensive. "We had some fairly high negatives," admitted Bruce V. Thompson, Inhofe's administrative assistant. "Had we not had the new district, we might have lost."

Tulsa County Commissioner John Selph invested $223,954 in broadcast advertising, $63,730 of which was put into preprimary ads created and placed by Don Hoover & Associates of Oklahoma City. For the fall campaign, Selph aired six television spots, most of which centered on his record in local government. He did not shy away from negative advertising, however.

In early 1992 Inhofe had lost a lawsuit filed by the Federal Deposit Insurance Corporation (FDIC), which sought to recover $588,238 in proceeds from a loan default occasioned by the bankruptcy of an insurance company Inhofe owned. Selph jumped on Inhofe's legal problems with an ad charging that the incumbent was refusing to repay the taxpayers despite the fact that he had previously won a $3 million lawsuit against his brother and clearly had the money. The ad did not mention that Inhofe had not repaid the FDIC because he was still appealing the decision. The Watershed Group of Tulsa collected $160,224 from Selph and $25,000 from the Democratic Congressional Campaign Committee for creating and placing the general election spots.

Inhofe responded in kind. "I'd guess about 85 percent of our advertising budget was spent on negative ads," Thompson recalled. "Selph's attacks were affecting our numbers, and we needed to get back at him. We painted him as a tax-and-spend liberal."

Inhofe did not respond directly to Selph's negative spot. "It was too much of a mess," explained Thompson. "Every time we tried to respond, it didn't work." Instead, Inhofe convinced former president Ronald Reagan to record a radio commercial on his behalf. "That played real well in Tulsa," Thompson added. Wiseman Public Relations of Tulsa received $42,739 from Inhofe and $5,316 from the Republican National Committee (RNC) for creating the spots and buying radio air time. J. L. Media, also of Tulsa, collected $141,923 from Inhofe for placing most of the ads.

National Republican party organizations heavily augmented Inhofe's $24,776 investment in brochures and persuasion mail. Wiseman collected $16,352 from the RNC and $21,697 from the National Republican Congressional Committee for production and postage charges associated with Inhofe's tightly targeted attack pieces.

	Inhofe		Selph	
Campaign Expenditures	Amount Spent	% of Total	Amount Spent	% of Total
Overhead				
Office furniture/supplies	$ 7,123	1.74	$ 3,126	.92
Rent/utilities	14,138	3.46	5,000	1.47
Salaries	35,155	8.60	19,285	5.66
Taxes	12,748	3.12	7,800	2.29
Bank/investment fees	185	.05	207	.06
Lawyers/accountants	9,961	2.44	0	
Telephone	7,863	1.92	2,721	.80
Campaign automobile	0		0	
Computers/office equipment	5,172	1.27	1,638	.48
Travel	10,328	2.53	697	.20
Food/meetings	849	.21	0	
Subtotal	**103,521**	**25.33**	**40,473**	**11.88**
Fund Raising				
Events	46,342	11.34	8,847	2.60
Direct mail	510	.12	0	
Telemarketing	0		0	
Subtotal	**46,851**	**11.46**	**8,847**	**2.60**
Polling	**3,563**	**.87**	**20,097**	**5.90**
Advertising				
Electronic media	184,972	45.26	223,954	65.75
Other media	8,132	1.99	4,505	1.32
Subtotal	**193,104**	**47.25**	**228,459**	**67.07**
Other Campaign Activity				
Persuasion mail/brochures	24,776	6.06	9,610	2.82
Actual campaigning	24,659	6.03	27,003	7.93
Staff/volunteers	3,707	.91	264	.08
Subtotal	**53,141**	**13.00**	**36,877**	**10.83**
Constituent Gifts/ Entertainment	**178**	**.04**	**0**	
Donations to				
Candidates from same state	0		0	
Candidates from other states	0		0	
Civic organizations	655	.16	0	
Ideological groups	495	.12	0	
Political parties	3,055	.75	80	.02
Subtotal	**4,205**	**1.03**	**80**	**.02**
Unitemized Expenses	**4,091**	**1.00**	**5,783**	**1.70**
Total Campaign Expenses	**$ 408,654**		**$ 340,615**	
PAC Contributions	$ 227,931		$ 56,775	
Individual Contributions	176,273		259,526	
Total Receipts*	425,361		331,132	

*Includes PAC and individual contributions as well as interest earned, party contributions, etc.

OKLAHOMA   District 2

Rep. Mike Synar (D)

1992 Election Results

Mike Synar (D)	118,542	(56%)
Jerry Hill (R)	87,657	(41%)

As always, the only real battle for Rep. Mike Synar was the Democratic primary. In his unsuccessful bid to unseat the seven-term incumbent, former Muskogee district attorney Drew Edmondson spent $836,742. This splurge helped carry Edmondson to a second-place finish in the four-candidate primary and to within 5 percentage points of unseating Synar in the subsequent runoff.

Edmondson received more than $150,000 in contributions from political action committees representing tobacco, health insurance, petroleum, and ranching interests—groups Synar had angered during his tenure in the House. The son of the late Rep. Ed Edmondson and the nephew of a former governor and senator, Edmondson collected as much as $100,000 from individual ranchers irritated by Synar's votes to raise the fees they paid to graze their cattle on federal lands. This proved to be just the beginning of the anti-Synar money flowing into District 2.

Enraged by Synar's vote in favor of the Brady Bill, the National Rifle Association (NRA) poured $226,088 into an independent campaign to oust Synar. The NRA spent $127,561 on broadcast advertising, took out full-page newspaper ads costing $43,479, opened an office in the district, and spent $14,007 on travel. A series of letters attacking Synar and endorsing Edmondson cost $13,887.

Synar countered by spending $823,675 during the first nine months of 1992. Fenn & King Communications of Washington, D.C., collected $346,809 for developing and placing television commercials for the primary and runoff and for consulting on the persuasion mail effort. Clary & Associates of Tulsa received $36,873 for producing and placing radio spots and $14,075 for placing most of the preprimary and runoff newspaper ads. The Tyson Organization of Fort Worth, Texas, received $81,340 for phonebanking. Blaemire Communications of Reston, Va., collected $27,583 for coordinating the persuasion mail effort and $3,877 for providing phonebanking lists.

Synar turned the special-interest onslaught into a campaign issue. Both his ads and mail noted the influx of cash from the insurance, oil, and health care lobbyists. "I'd rather lose this election by doing what's right than win by turning my back on Oklahoma," Synar offered in one spot. Other ads slammed Edmondson for having let "ninety sex offenders go without a day in jail" during his tenure as district attorney. He did not have to take on either the NRA or the ranchers directly because the free media did it for him.

Having survived the runoff, Synar easily defeated Republican Jerry Hill. Fenn & King collected $33,493 and Clary received $10,603 for their efforts in the general election.

	Synar		Hill	
Campaign Expenditures	Amount Spent	% of Total	Amount Spent	% of Total
Overhead				
Office furniture/supplies	$ 8,929	.75	$ 299	1.23
Rent/utilities	11,234	.95	0	
Salaries	52,865	4.46	0	
Taxes	22,619	1.91	0	
Bank/investment fees	52		22	.09
Lawyers/accountants	1,200	.10	0	
Telephone	13,515	1.14	1,700	6.99
Campaign automobile	0		0	
Computers/office equipment	10,827	.91	25	.10
Travel	33,058	2.79	0	
Food/meetings	4,889	.41	0	
Subtotal	**159,190**	**13.43**	**2,045**	**8.40**
Fund Raising				
Events	174,880	14.75	0	
Direct mail	3,717	.31	0	
Telemarketing	0		0	
Subtotal	**178,597**	**15.06**	**0**	
Polling	**80,500**	**6.79**	**0**	
Advertising				
Electronic media	479,033	40.40	3,175	13.05
Other media	28,973	2.44	1,596	6.56
Subtotal	**508,006**	**42.85**	**4,772**	**19.61**
Other Campaign Activity				
Persuasion mail/brochures	69,502	5.86	6,540	26.88
Actual campaigning	122,701	10.35	8,732	35.88
Staff/volunteers	237	.02	0	
Subtotal	**192,440**	**16.23**	**15,272**	**62.76**
Constituent Gifts/ Entertainment	**4,289**	**.36**	**0**	
Donations to				
Candidates from same state	0		0	
Candidates from other states	0		75	.31
Civic organizations	500	.04	0	
Ideological groups	0		0	
Political parties	897	.08	0	
Subtotal	**1,397**	**.12**	**75**	**.31**
Unitemized Expenses	**61,256**	**5.17**	**2,169**	**8.91**
Total Campaign Expenses	**$ 1,185,676**		**$ 24,333**	
PAC Contributions	$ 0		$ 0	
Individual Contributions	1,170,261		21,978	
Total Receipts*	1,191,392		32,044	

*Includes PAC and individual contributions as well as interest earned, party contributions, etc.

District 3 — OKLAHOMA

Rep. Bill Brewster (D)

1992 Election Results

Bill Brewster (D)	155,934	(75%)
Robert W. Stokes (R)	51,725	(25%)

Having served eight years in the Oklahoma legislature before coming to Washington in 1990, freshman Rep. Bill Brewster had no trouble adjusting to his incumbent status. In his 1990 open seat contest, Brewster had invested 73 percent of his $445,020 budget in direct appeals for votes. Unopposed in the 1992 Democratic primary and challenged in November by a Republican opponent who spent just $5,723, Brewster spent 49 percent of his $351,147 treasury on voter contact.

In 1990 Brewster donated just $890 to charities and Democratic party organizations. Two years later he gave away $22,465. Fellow House Democrats Beryl Anthony, Jr. (Ark.), Thomas J. Downey (N.Y.), James A. Barcia (Mich.), Andy Fox (Va.), Laurie Williams (Okla.), and Sam Gejdenson (Conn.) each received checks for $1,000. Eight others received checks for $500.

Constituent stroking, which cost Brewster just $89 in 1990, cost his 1992 campaign $8,368. He spent $1,810 on year-end holiday cards, $1,293 on meals at the House restaurant, $880 on commemorative certificates, $700 on various Christmas gifts, $409 on U.S. flags, $360 on congressional cookbooks, and $202 on calendars purchased from the Oklahoma Democratic party. Tickets to the presidential inaugural festivities cost the campaign $2,370.

During the 1990 campaign, Brewster invested $7,054 in short-term auto leases. Less than six months after taking office, he began making $391 monthly lease payments to Ford Credit. Over the course of the election cycle, those payments totaled $10,436. The campaign spent $1,375 on automobile repairs, $1,107 to insure and register the car, and $2,654 on gasoline.

Brewster had been forced to take out a $35,000 loan and donate another $45,995 of his own money to cover the cost of his 1990 effort. In 1992 he paid off his loan, invested none of his own money, and still had $39,867 left at the end of the election cycle. Political action committees accounted for 40 percent of his total contributions in 1990; the comparable figure in 1992 was 64 percent. In September 1991 the American Pharmaceutical Association sponsored a fundraiser for Brewster, the only pharmacist in Congress.

In all, Brewster spent more than sixty-one times as much as Republican Robert W. Stokes. While Stokes put $1,186 into advertising, Brewster spent $86,236 on broadcast advertising, $44,517 on newspaper ads, $7,000 on billboards, and $6,371 on newspaper inserts, including $1,000 paid to the Southeastern Oklahoma State University baseball team for inserting them into the newspapers. Brewster spent $17,597 to blanket the district with yard signs. T-shirts, caps, and bandanas for volunteers cost $3,234.

	Brewster		Stokes	
Campaign Expenditures	Amount Spent	% of Total	Amount Spent	% of Total
Overhead				
Office furniture/supplies	$ 3,681	1.05	$ 53	.93
Rent/utilities	2,178	.62	0	
Salaries	34,929	9.95	0	
Taxes	4,810	1.37	0	
Bank/investment fees	6,422	1.83	0	
Lawyers/accountants	400	.11	0	
Telephone	5,633	1.60	0	
Campaign automobile	15,572	4.43	0	
Computers/office equipment	9,192	2.62	0	
Travel	13,047	3.72	0	
Food/meetings	2,943	.84	0	
Subtotal	**98,806**	**28.14**	**53**	**.93**
Fund Raising				
Events	32,038	9.12	0	
Direct mail	0		0	
Telemarketing	0		0	
Subtotal	**32,038**	**9.12**	**0**	
Polling	**0**		**0**	
Advertising				
Electronic media	86,236	24.56	0	
Other media	58,055	16.53	1,186	20.73
Subtotal	**144,292**	**41.09**	**1,186**	**20.73**
Other Campaign Activity				
Persuasion mail/brochures	2,057	.59	1,376	24.04
Actual campaigning	26,666	7.59	763	13.33
Staff/volunteers	280	.08	0	
Subtotal	**29,003**	**8.26**	**2,139**	**37.37**
Constituent Gifts/ Entertainment	**8,368**	**2.38**	**0**	
Donations to				
Candidates from same state	1,400	.40	0	
Candidates from other states	9,600	2.73	0	
Civic organizations	425	.12	0	
Ideological groups	0		0	
Political parties	11,040	3.14	0	
Subtotal	**22,465**	**6.40**	**0**	
Unitemized Expenses	**16,173**	**4.61**	**2,345**	**40.98**
Total Campaign Expenses	**$ 351,147**		**$ 5,723**	
PAC Contributions	$ 266,973		$ 0	
Individual Contributions	148,177		3,592	
Total Receipts*	423,953		6,338	

*Includes PAC and individual contributions as well as interest earned, party contributions, etc.

OKLAHOMA District 4

Rep. Dave McCurdy (D)

1992 Election Results

Dave McCurdy (D)	140,841	(71%)
Howard Bell † (R)	58,235	(29%)

Rep. Dave McCurdy spent $226,689 more on his 1992 campaign than he had in 1990. However, he reduced his investment in direct voter appeals by $62,802. During the 1992 election cycle, McCurdy put 72 percent of his $584,211 budget into overhead and fund raising. Only 15 percent of his budget was devoted to direct appeals for votes.

McCurdy spent considerable time and money exploring a possible presidential bid, at one point devoting a month to visiting swing districts around the country. Although he opted not to enter the race, McCurdy continued to travel extensively for Democratic presidential nominee Bill Clinton, accumulating travel expenses of $61,390 in the process. With presidential aspirations of his own, McCurdy was not about to let all that travel go to waste.

McCurdy hired Tim Phillips of Washington, D.C., to serve as a one-man advance team. Phillips planned the travel, set up meetings with supporters, and introduced McCurdy to people that chief of staff Stephen K. Patterson described as "potential contributors and people who could help us down the road." Added Patterson, "Dave felt he should be taking advantage of his travel to help himself as well as Clinton." Phillips collected $48,053 for his efforts, which have been included in McCurdy's fund-raising costs.

In addition to Phillips, McCurdy hired three professional fund-raisers to help fill his coffers. He paid Mary Pat Bonner of Springfield, Va., $80,394. Barbara Silby & Associates of Potomac, Md., and SWT Associates of Bethesda, Md., received $26,158 and $9,300, respectively. Together, Phillips and these three firms helped raise $270,250 from political action committees and $115,950 from out-of-state donors who gave at least $200. Large donations from in-state residents amounted to $93,700. Assuming that all his $59,650 in smaller contributions came from Oklahoma residents, McCurdy raised no more than 28 percent of his contributions from individual donors in Oklahoma.

McCurdy had little need to spend much on actual campaigning in this rematch with Democrat Howard Bell, who had been walloped by a margin of three to one in 1990 and had less than $5,000 to spend on this campaign. McCurdy paid Strother-Duffy-Strother of Washington, D.C., $13,507 to create two television commercials and one radio spot touting his constituent service and his ability to deliver federal economic development projects to the district. Media Strategies & Research, also of Washington, collected $50,891 for producing and placing the spots.

Constituent stroking cost McCurdy $17,547, including $9,246 for various inaugural parties and $6,389 for holiday cards.

Campaign Expenditures	McCurdy Amount Spent	% of Total
Overhead		
Office furniture/supplies	$ 9,200	1.57
Rent/utilities	5,770	.99
Salaries	51,514	8.82
Taxes	24,085	4.12
Bank/investment fees	148	.03
Lawyers/accountants	2,693	.46
Telephone	11,688	2.00
Campaign automobile	3,329	.57
Computers/office equipment	16,128	2.76
Travel	61,390	10.51
Food/meetings	4,493	.77
Subtotal	**190,437**	**32.60**
Fund Raising		
Events	229,060	39.21
Direct mail	2,553	.44
Telemarketing	0	
Subtotal	**231,613**	**39.65**
Polling	**18,000**	**3.08**
Advertising		
Electronic media	64,758	11.08
Other media	0	
Subtotal	**64,758**	**11.08**
Other Campaign Activity		
Persuasion mail/brochures	6,609	1.13
Actual campaigning	15,133	2.59
Staff/volunteers	459	.08
Subtotal	**22,200**	**3.80**
Constituent Gifts/Entertainment	**17,547**	**3.00**
Donations to		
Candidates from same state	2,800	.48
Candidates from other states	5,500	.94
Civic organizations	174	.03
Ideological groups	1,500	.26
Political parties	21,050	3.60
Subtotal	**31,024**	**5.31**
Unitemized Expenses	**8,632**	**1.48**
Total Campaign Expenses	**$ 584,211**	
PAC Contributions	$ 270,250	
Individual Contributions	269,300	
Total Receipts*	556,174	

*Includes PAC and individual contributions as well as interest earned, party contributions, etc.

† No expenditures or receipts on file. Candidates raising or spending less than $5,000 are not required to file reports with the Federal Election Commission.

District 5 — OKLAHOMA

Rep. Ernest Jim Istook, Jr. (R)

1992 Election Results

Ernest Jim Istook, Jr. (R)	123,237	(53%)
Laurie Williams (D)	107,579	(47%)

When the House bank scandal broke, eight-term Republican Rep. Mickey Edwards joined the chorus demanding full disclosure of those who had abused their accounts. Ironically, when the ethics committee released its list of the bank's twenty-two worst abusers, Edwards's name was on it with 386 checks totaling $54,000. Almost immediately four Republicans announced they would challenge Edwards in the primary, including 1990 gubernatorial nominee Bill Price and state representative Ernest Jim Istook, Jr. Few observers thought Edwards could avoid a primary runoff, and most viewed Price as his likely opponent.

Edwards entered the primary campaign with cash reserves of just $2,052, having spent approximately $219,000 during the first fifteen months of the election cycle. However, he quickly refilled his coffers and poured about $323,000 into the August 25 primary. He ran radio and television spots admitting that he had erred, but asked voters to return him to Washington to continue the fight "against liberal big spenders."

Price spent more than $260,000 on the primary, hammering Edwards for his overdrafts and for flooding the district with more than 500,000 pieces of franked mail in 1991, an amount exceeded by only twenty-four House members. Price's barrage of radio and television commercials carried him into the runoff and knocked Edwards into third place and out of the race.

With less than $110,000 to spend, Istook waged a much quieter primary campaign. He spent $39,564 on targeted persuasion mailings, $13,104 to produce and air one television commercial, $7,507 on radio ads, and $6,474 on yard signs. His advertising focused primarily on his votes in the state legislature against taxes and for tougher anticrime laws. "Based on Price's past campaigns, we knew he would attack Edwards," recalled district director Dwight A. Dissler. "Since polls showed Mickey just wasn't going to make it, we wanted to run a positive campaign."

That strategy paid off in the September 15 runoff. Although Price had won the primary with 37 percent of the vote, his attacks had alienated many of Edwards's supporters. Ishtook collected most of those Edwards votes and won the runoff with 56 percent. That victory cost Istook another $70,000, including $30,067 for persuasion mail, $23,804 to air two television ads, and $5,297 for radio air time.

Attorney Laurie Williams spent $110,372 to win the Democratic primary, giving her a cash advantage of more than two to one in her matchup with Istook. Labeling Istook an "extremist," she promised "change"—a message that won her a larger share of the vote than any Democrat had received since 1976.

Campaign Expenditures	Istook Amount Spent	Istook % of Total	Williams Amount Spent	Williams % of Total
Overhead				
Office furniture/supplies	$ 8,554	2.99	$ 1,960	.58
Rent/utilities	5,850	2.04	2,708	.80
Salaries	38,417	13.42	36,313	10.74
Taxes	0		1,385	.41
Bank/investment fees	1,604	.56	0	
Lawyers/accountants	0		7,760	2.30
Telephone	2,327	.81	4,286	1.27
Campaign automobile	2,109	.74	0	
Computers/office equipment	3,551	1.24	1,667	.49
Travel	4,193	1.46	4,046	1.20
Food/meetings	163	.06	0	
Subtotal	66,767	23.32	60,124	17.78
Fund Raising				
Events	2,310	.81	8,910	2.64
Direct mail	10,341	3.61	0	
Telemarketing	2,630	.92	0	
Subtotal	15,280	5.34	8,910	2.64
Polling	0		8,000	2.37
Advertising				
Electronic media	109,811	38.35	227,202	67.19
Other media	4,348	1.52	9,161	2.71
Subtotal	114,159	39.86	236,363	69.90
Other Campaign Activity				
Persuasion mail/brochures	71,006	24.80	949	.28
Actual campaigning	14,808	5.17	19,094	5.65
Staff/volunteers	195	.07	314	.09
Subtotal	86,009	30.03	20,357	6.02
Constituent Gifts/Entertainment	0		0	
Donations to				
Candidates from same state	0		0	
Candidates from other states	0		0	
Civic organizations	0		0	
Ideological groups	0		0	
Political parties	0		0	
Subtotal	0		0	
Unitemized Expenses	4,150	1.45	4,372	1.29
Total Campaign Expenses	$ 286,365		$ 338,125	
PAC Contributions	$ 72,277		$ 19,060	
Individual Contributions	162,428		191,791	
Total Receipts*	365,630		349,220	

*Includes PAC and individual contributions as well as interest earned, party contributions, etc.

OKLAHOMA — District 6

Rep. Glenn English (D)

1992 Election Results

Glenn English (D)	134,734	(68%)
Bob Anthony (R)	64,068	(32%)

Blessed with a succession of easy reelection campaigns, Rep. Glenn English had accumulated a $324,042 campaign nest egg by the end of 1990. When state corporation commissioner Bob Anthony mounted a $375,785 anti-incumbent campaign against him in 1992, English tapped those cash reserves for $173,240 of the money he needed to counterattack.

Anthony invested $293,131 in broadcast ads that focused on his support of a free trade agreement with Mexico, touted his business experience and fiscal conservatism, pointed to his support for term limits, and blasted English for his dependence on political action committee donations. The Farwell Group of New Orleans, La., collected $55,315 for creating Anthony's television commercials and buying some air time. Campaign Compendium of Oklahoma City was paid $44,681 for creating radio ads. J. L. Media of Tulsa received $189,003 for placing both the television and radio spots.

English struck back with a $299,184 broadcast advertising campaign that began on a positive note but quickly turned negative. A television spot dubbed "Independence" featured English decrying the level of partisan politics in Washington and ended with the tagline: "Glenn English, independent leadership for our Oklahoma." Negative ads pounded Anthony for driving his family's business into bankruptcy through the use of junk-bond financing, thus driving "hundreds of loyal employees out of work." One response ad accused Anthony of distorting English's record and pointed out that English had "voted against every pay raise," "voted against $600 billion in tax increases," and "returned half a million dollars in office funds to the U.S. Treasury." The ad returned to the bankruptcy issue before ending with "Bob Anthony, running for Congress while he runs from his record."

When a local television station graded Anthony's attack ads a "D for distorted," English's advisers rolled out a spot with the tagline: "That 'D' is for more than distortion. That's a 'D' for disgrace." For creating and placing the television commercials and three companion radio ads, Fenn & King Communications of Washington, D.C., received $290,691. Miscellaneous production expenses totaled $8,493.

Newspaper and billboard ads cost English $14,664 and $8,190, respectively. He invested $11,785 in yard signs and posters. Pollster Kitchens, Powell & Kitchens of Orlando, Fla., collected $41,300.

Not all of English's expenses were connected to his appeals for votes. In October 1991 he spent $26,140 of his campaign treasury to purchase a new Buick. The campaign paid $2,111 for expenses during the 1992 Democratic National Convention in New York. Year-end holiday cards cost $2,970.

Campaign Expenditures	English Amount Spent	English % of Total	Anthony Amount Spent	Anthony % of Total
Overhead				
Office furniture/supplies	$ 2,378	.43	$ 2,336	.62
Rent/utilities	8,524	1.54	1,162	.31
Salaries	13,074	2.37	22,386	5.96
Taxes	7,763	1.40	0	
Bank/investment fees	97	.02	73	.02
Lawyers/accountants	3,758	.68	0	
Telephone	7,046	1.27	3,192	.85
Campaign automobile	30,796	5.57	0	
Computers/office equipment	9,470	1.71	365	.10
Travel	28,463	5.15	1,845	.49
Food/meetings	2,284	.41	0	
Subtotal	**113,653**	**20.57**	**31,359**	**8.34**
Fund Raising				
Events	23,312	4.22	2,752	.73
Direct mail	5,713	1.03	2,873	.76
Telemarketing	0		0	
Subtotal	**29,025**	**5.25**	**5,625**	**1.50**
Polling	**41,300**	**7.47**	**14,280**	**3.80**
Advertising				
Electronic media	299,184	54.14	293,131	78.00
Other media	24,004	4.34	3,622	.96
Subtotal	**323,188**	**58.48**	**296,753**	**78.97**
Other Campaign Activity				
Persuasion mail/brochures	5,533	1.00	17,106	4.55
Actual campaigning	18,881	3.42	9,183	2.44
Staff/volunteers	194	.04	0	
Subtotal	**24,608**	**4.45**	**26,288**	**7.00**
Constituent Gifts/ Entertainment	**3,447**	**.62**	**0**	
Donations to				
Candidates from same state	0		0	
Candidates from other states	0		0	
Civic organizations	229	.04	15	
Ideological groups	240	.04	0	
Political parties	3,400	.62	0	
Subtotal	**3,869**	**.70**	**15**	
Unitemized Expenses	**13,530**	**2.45**	**1,464**	**.39**
Total Campaign Expenses	**$ 552,620**		**$ 375,785**	
PAC Contributions	$ 203,400		$ 0	
Individual Contributions	148,315		127,086	
Total Receipts*	379,380		378,197	

*Includes PAC and individual contributions as well as interest earned, party contributions, etc.

District 1 — OREGON

Rep. Elizabeth Furse (D)

1992 Election Results

Elizabeth Furse (D)	152,917	(52%)
Tony Meeker (R)	140,986	(48%)

Six days before the November 3 election, a poll published in the *Oregonian* gave Republican state treasurer Tony Meeker a 41 to 34 percent advantage over Democratic activist Elizabeth Furse in the race to succeed retiring Democratic Rep. Les AuCoin. The key to Furse's narrow victory was her ability to attract a sizable majority of the fence-sitters, who comprised 25 percent of the electorate.

The battle for this suburban Portland district was waged largely on the airwaves, with Furse pouring $312,976 of her broadcast budget into the fall campaign. In early October Furse began airing two introductory spots that outlined her basic campaign themes. "She's running to change the way Congress does business," began one spot that called for a 50 percent reduction in military spending and increased federal outlays for education, health care, and jobs programs. After noting that she "supports a woman's right to choose," the ad concluded with the tagline: "Elizabeth Furse for Congress. For Us."

Within days two negative spots were added to Furse's advertising mix. One slammed Meeker for failing to "tighten up procedures to reduce abuses in his office, as an independent audit told him to" and proceeded to charge that "it was Meeker who invested $20 million from the pension funds of Oregon workers in a shopping mall in London and lost every penny." The second negative ad attacked Meeker for his opposition to abortion, alluded to the London shopping mall fiasco, and pointed to news reports that questioned his fund-raising ethics. To capitalize on the electorate's anti-incumbent mood, both ads suggested that "we don't need another career politician like Tony Meeker in Congress." One final spot wrapped virtually all the positive and negative messages into one neat bundle.

Furse's political inexperience and dependence on television advertising translated into a heavy reliance on consultants. Julie Williamson of Portland collected $342,505 for creating and placing preprimary broadcast ads, placing the general election spots, and providing both polling services and general strategic advice. The Campaign Group of Philadelphia, Pa., received $72,441 for creating the five general election ads. Campaign Performance Group of San Francisco, Calif., produced one persuasion mailer for $11,810.

Having put $72,431 of his broadcast advertising budget into the Republican primary, Meeker was able to spend $222,889 on ads to counter Furse. These spots focused on the timber industry, health care, and his extensive political resume. Meeker also benefited from five independent campaigns waged on his behalf, including a $75,200 effort by the American Medical Association.

	Furse		Meeker	
Campaign Expenditures	Amount Spent	% of Total	Amount Spent	% of Total
Overhead				
Office furniture/supplies	$ 10,424	1.31	$ 8,576	1.14
Rent/utilities	12,579	1.57	3,398	.45
Salaries	92,279	11.55	119,110	15.89
Taxes	29,620	3.71	64,104	8.55
Bank/investment fees	1,235	.15	15	
Lawyers/accountants	0		400	.05
Telephone	7,915	.99	14,955	2.00
Campaign automobile	0		2,195	.29
Computers/office equipment	9,064	1.13	5,315	.71
Travel	5,356	.67	39,546	5.28
Food/meetings	148	.02	489	.07
Subtotal	**168,620**	**21.11**	**258,104**	**34.43**
Fund Raising				
Events	67,214	8.41	24,332	3.25
Direct mail	42,738	5.35	13,237	1.77
Telemarketing	0		10,495	1.40
Subtotal	**109,952**	**13.76**	**48,065**	**6.41**
Polling	**14,207**	**1.78**	**25,800**	**3.44**
Advertising				
Electronic media	393,700	49.29	295,320	39.40
Other media	2,124	.27	672	.09
Subtotal	**395,824**	**49.55**	**295,992**	**39.49**
Other Campaign Activity				
Persuasion mail/brochures	37,943	4.75	90,542	12.08
Actual campaigning	48,650	6.09	20,827	2.78
Staff/volunteers	0		33	
Subtotal	**86,593**	**10.84**	**111,402**	**14.86**
Constituent Gifts/ Entertainment	**0**		**0**	
Donations to				
Candidates from same state	0		0	
Candidates from other states	0		0	
Civic organizations	0		0	
Ideological groups	0		0	
Political parties	10		100	.01
Subtotal	**10**		**100**	**.01**
Unitemized Expenses	23,587	2.95	10,100	1.35
Total Campaign Expenses	$ 798,793		$ 749,563	
PAC Contributions	$ 186,049		$ 320,585	
Individual Contributions	588,394		387,235	
Total Receipts*	785,545		723,936	

*Includes PAC and individual contributions as well as interest earned, party contributions, etc.

OREGON — District 2

Rep. Bob Smith (R)

1992 Election Results

Bob Smith (R)	184,163	(67%)
Denzel Ferguson (D)	90,036	(33%)

First elected in 1982, Rep. Bob Smith's reelection campaigns had grown increasingly easier. He grabbed 57 percent of the votes in 1984, 60 percent in 1986, 63 percent in 1988, and 68 percent in 1990. Redistricting had done nothing to change Smith's political landscape, and he cruised to a second consecutive two-to-one win in 1992.

In 1990 Smith had invested $91,968 in advertising, despite the fact that his Democratic challenger had less than $5,000 to spend on his entire campaign. Faced with a significantly better funded challenger in 1992, Smith increased his advertising outlays to $159,475, or 40 percent of his total budget. Over the final six weeks of the campaign, he spent $67,929 to air his radio commercials. Air time on network television affiliates over the campaign's final three weeks cost $26,881. Spots on cable television added $6,329. All the ads were created and produced in-house, which allowed Smith to hold his production costs to $2,442. Although he was unopposed in the Republican primary, Smith began buying billboard space in March 1992, and over the next eight months spent $12,683 on such ads. He invested $42,821 in newspaper ads, most of which were placed through the Oregon Newspaper Advertising Corp. of Tigard.

Smith committed 12 percent of his budget to a variety of grass-roots efforts. He spent $18,606 on campaign literature, most of which was distributed by volunteers. He paid $13,240 to the state Senate Republican Campaign Committee to help cover the cost of an absentee ballot mailing. He spent $5,983 on yard signs, $1,880 on lapel stickers and balloons, $1,000 on slate mailers, and $948 on T-shirts emblazoned with the campaign's logo. To thank his volunteers, Smith spent $2,621 on various gifts.

Overhead consumed 32 percent of Smith's total budget, driven largely by the $47,503 he spent on staff salaries. As in past campaigns, Smith maintained a campaign office throughout the two-year cycle, but his total expenditures on utilities and the $165 monthly rent came to a modest $1,304. Campaign-related travel amounted to $30,634—more than three times as much as he spent on travel during the 1990 campaign. The $128,639 Smith put into overhead was 48 percent more than Democrat Denzel Ferguson spent on his long-shot challenge.

Ferguson, a retired zoology professor, said he undertook the campaign to make a statement about his environmental concerns and had few illusions about his chances. "If I ran one hundred times, I would probably not do any better," Ferguson said. "This is a very conservative and rural community."

	Smith		Ferguson	
Campaign Expenditures	Amount Spent	% of Total	Amount Spent	% of Total
Overhead				
Office furniture/supplies	$ 6,386	1.61	$ 1,214	1.40
Rent/utilities	3,810	.96	0	
Salaries	47,503	11.96	8,669	9.97
Taxes	18,568	4.67	3,391	3.90
Bank/investment fees	288	.07	5	.01
Lawyers/accountants	0		0	
Telephone	6,345	1.60	1,887	2.17
Campaign automobile	0		0	
Computers/office equipment	8,175	2.06	1,135	1.30
Travel	30,634	7.71	9,003	10.35
Food/meetings	6,930	1.74	150	.17
Subtotal	**128,639**	**32.39**	**25,452**	**29.27**
Fund Raising				
Events	22,638	5.70	923	1.06
Direct mail	24,179	6.09	17,309	19.90
Telemarketing	0		3,500	4.02
Subtotal	**46,817**	**11.79**	**21,732**	**24.99**
Polling	**5,000**	**1.26**	**0**	
Advertising				
Electronic media	103,581	26.08	18,090	20.80
Other media	55,894	14.07	0	
Subtotal	**159,475**	**40.15**	**18,090**	**20.80**
Other Campaign Activity				
Persuasion mail/brochures	19,606	4.94	1,000	1.15
Actual campaigning	24,520	6.17	15,784	18.15
Staff/volunteers	2,621	.66	0	
Subtotal	**46,747**	**11.77**	**16,784**	**19.30**
Constituent Gifts/ Entertainment	**0**		**0**	
Donations to				
Candidates from same state	1,000	.25	0	
Candidates from other states	1,000	.25	0	
Civic organizations	0		0	
Ideological groups	0		0	
Political parties	0		0	
Subtotal	**2,000**	**.50**	**0**	
Unitemized Expenses	**8,495**	**2.14**	**4,907**	**5.64**
Total Campaign Expenses	**$ 397,173**		**$ 86,964**	
PAC Contributions	$ 165,725		$ 8,550	
Individual Contributions	268,837		77,429	
Total Receipts*	462,680		87,850	

*Includes PAC and individual contributions as well as interest earned, party contributions, etc.

District 3 — OREGON

Rep. Ron Wyden (D)

1992 Election Results

Ron Wyden (D)	208,028	(77%)
Al Ritter (R)	50,235	(19%)

Although he denied it at the time, Rep. Ron Wyden's flirtation with a 1992 Senate bid had prompted him to spend $693,640 in 1990 to defeat a Republican opponent who spent just $4,354. Having opted not to fight fellow Democratic Rep. Les AuCoin for the right to challenge Republican Sen. Bob Packwood, Wyden sliced his 1992 spending to $356,057.

In preparation for a statewide race, Wyden had spent $70,923 on polling in 1990. Without that concern in 1992, he paid his pollster, Mellman & Lazarus of Washington, D.C., $16,646. Wyden had poured $154,436 into broadcast advertising in 1990, despite the fact that he had never received less than 72 percent of the vote in his solidly Democratic district and faced only token opposition. Two years later, in a year supposedly marked by widespread anti-incumbent sentiment, Wyden spent nothing on broadcast ads. He spent just $4,487 on other forms of advertising in 1992; the comparable figure for 1990 was $21,812.

As in previous campaigns, Wyden mailed copies of his annual "Oregon Report" to a list of past contributors, bringing them up to date on his work and soliciting them for additional funds. However, unlike 1990, when his senatorial flirtation prompted him to open a Washington, D.C., fund-raising office and hold events in California, Florida, Michigan, New York, Pennsylvania, and Texas, Wyden focused his modest search for individual donors on Oregon. Wyden closed his Washington office, and his political action committee (PAC) contributions dropped from $341,242 in 1990 to $123,675 in 1992. Contributions from out-of-state donors dipped from $140,771 to $6,150.

While Wyden trimmed his spending on overhead by $51,119 between 1990 and 1992, the savings did not come at the expense of his staff. After-tax salaries in 1990 totaled $93,954; in 1992 the comparable figure was $95,985. He spent $16,656 less on office supplies, $14,689 less on computers and other office equipment, and $12,264 less on travel.

Wyden gave away $38,386 of his campaign funds. He donated $21,000 to Democratic party organizations—$10,000 to the Democratic Congressional Campaign Committee, $7,500 to the Oregon House Democratic Campaign Committee, and $3,500 to the Oregon Democratic party. Donations to ideological organizations amounted to $4,355, including $2,025 to the Right to Privacy PAC and $1,700 to the Oregon National Abortion Rights Action League. In the primary, he gave District 1 House candidate Gary Conkling $962 in in-kind help, including staff-time and use of office equipment and mailing lists. When Elizabeth Furse defeated Conkling, Wyden contributed $1,000 to her general election coffers.

Campaign Expenditures	Wyden Amount Spent	Wyden % of Total	Ritter Amount Spent	Ritter % of Total
Overhead				
Office furniture/supplies	$ 7,066	1.98	$ 0	
Rent/utilities	15,500	4.35	0	
Salaries	95,985	26.96	0	
Taxes	59,809	16.80	0	
Bank/investment fees	237	.07	0	
Lawyers/accountants	0		0	
Telephone	10,157	2.85	0	
Campaign automobile	0		0	
Computers/office equipment	4,160	1.17	0	
Travel	17,839	5.01	0	
Food/meetings	1,843	.52	0	
Subtotal	**212,595**	**59.71**	**0**	
Fund Raising				
Events	15,955	4.48	0	
Direct mail	42,059	11.81	0	
Telemarketing	0		0	
Subtotal	**58,014**	**16.29**	**0**	
Polling	**16,646**	**4.68**	**0**	
Advertising				
Electronic media	0		0	
Other media	4,487	1.26	56	.93
Subtotal	**4,487**	**1.26**	**56**	**.93**
Other Campaign Activity				
Persuasion mail/brochures	1,000	.28	1,269	20.85
Actual campaigning	9,151	2.57	135	2.21
Staff/volunteers	333	.09	0	
Subtotal	**10,484**	**2.94**	**1,404**	**23.07**
Constituent Gifts/ Entertainment	**0**		**0**	
Donations to				
Candidates from same state	5,762	1.62	0	
Candidates from other states	6,000	1.69	0	
Civic organizations	1,269	.36	0	
Ideological groups	4,355	1.22	0	
Political parties	21,000	5.90	0	
Subtotal	**38,386**	**10.78**	**0**	
Unitemized Expenses	**15,444**	**4.34**	**4,625**	**76.01**
Total Campaign Expenses	**$ 356,057**		**$ 6,085**	
PAC Contributions	$ 123,675		$ 521	
Individual Contributions	66,860		2,909	
Total Receipts*	229,749		6,660	

*Includes PAC and individual contributions as well as interest earned, party contributions, etc.

OREGON   District 4

Rep. Peter A. DeFazio (D)

1992 Election Results   Peter A. DeFazio (D)   199,372   (71%)
                           Richard L. Schulz (R)   79,733   (29%)

For the third consecutive campaign, Rep. Peter A. DeFazio faced only token opposition. Retired real estate broker Richard L. Schulz actually lost the Republican primary but became the party's nominee after successfully challenging the primary results on the grounds that John D. Newkirk had not registered on time, had filed in the wrong office, and was not on an original list of candidates. While Schulz put only $5,456 into his challenge, DeFazio spent $301,047 on his reelection effort.

DeFazio spent $100,682 to maintain his campaign operation during 1991. Monthly rent on his headquarters was $275, and after-tax salaries totaled $22,316. These outlays accounted for half of the $50,772 he invested in overhead during the off-year. He spent another $20,767 on fund raising, $18,562 of which was invested in direct-mail solicitations.

DeFazio was one of the Oregon Democrats who briefly flirted during 1991 with a senatorial bid against Republican Bob Packwood, but, like Rep. Ron Wyden, DeFazio deferred to Rep. Les AuCoin. Fenn & King Communications of Washington, D.C., collected $4,500 during the off-year for advice on possible advertising themes. Johnson Research Associates, also of Washington, received $4,500 for polling advice.

Unopposed in the primary, DeFazio racked up bills totaling $200,365 during 1992, including $57,708 for overhead and $20,306 for fund raising. He paid Garin-Hart of Washington, D.C., $14,500 for polling. Despite the fact that he faced no real opposition, he opted to spend $74,189 on television and radio commercials. "Peter has never been strongly challenged, but people get apathetic," explained Curtis Robinhold, DeFazio's campaign director. "We wanted to reinforce people's identification of Peter with certain issues."

Fenn & King received $74,159 for creating and placing three positive television spots that painted DeFazio's broad philosophical positions. An ad dubbed "Peace Dividend" focused on the need to reduce military investment abroad and invest the savings in education and health care. It ended with the tagline: "It's time we took care of our own." A second spot focused on the need for affordable health care, touted the fact that DeFazio had held eleven health care forums during 1992, and proclaimed that "the time for quality health care is now." The final ad focused on DeFazio's 1989 vote against the congressional pay raise and his donation of that raise to help fund college scholarships. The campaign picked up $30 of the production costs for the ads; the remaining $4,756 was paid by the Democratic Congressional Campaign Committee.

Campaign Expenditures	DeFazio Amount Spent	DeFazio % of Total	Schulz Amount Spent	Schulz % of Total
Overhead				
Office furniture/supplies	$ 5,268	1.75	$ 0	
Rent/utilities	7,288	2.42	0	
Salaries	48,265	16.03	0	
Taxes	19,779	6.57	0	
Bank/investment fees	101	.03	0	
Lawyers/accountants	618	.21	0	
Telephone	10,429	3.46	0	
Campaign automobile	0		0	
Computers/office equipment	5,998	1.99	0	
Travel	10,737	3.57	294	5.38
Food/meetings	0		0	
Subtotal	**108,481**	**36.03**	**294**	**5.38**
Fund Raising				
Events	6,977	2.32	0	
Direct mail	34,096	11.33	0	
Telemarketing	0		0	
Subtotal	**41,073**	**13.64**	**0**	
Polling	**19,000**	**6.31**	**0**	
Advertising				
Electronic media	78,689	26.14	3,151	57.76
Other media	2,488	.83	0	
Subtotal	**81,177**	**26.96**	**3,151**	**57.76**
Other Campaign Activity				
Persuasion mail/brochures	3,157	1.05	1,471	26.96
Actual campaigning	20,640	6.86	0	
Staff/volunteers	403	.13	0	
Subtotal	**24,200**	**8.04**	**1,471**	**26.96**
Constituent Gifts/ Entertainment	**0**		**0**	
Donations to				
Candidates from same state	2,100	.70	0	
Candidates from other states	1,000	.33	0	
Civic organizations	0		0	
Ideological groups	908	.30	0	
Political parties	12,030	4.00	0	
Subtotal	**16,038**	**5.33**	**0**	
Unitemized Expenses	**11,079**	**3.68**	**539**	**9.89**
Total Campaign Expenses	**$ 301,047**		**$ 5,456**	
PAC Contributions	**$ 173,500**		**$ 500**	
Individual Contributions	**61,342**		**3,977**	
Total Receipts*	**248,887**		**6,348**	

*Includes PAC and individual contributions as well as interest earned, party contributions, etc.

District 5 — OREGON

Rep. Mike Kopetski (D)

1992 Election Results

Mike Kopetski (D)	174,443	(64%)
Jim Seagraves (R)	97,984	(36%)

After spending $859,862 to retire Republican Rep. Denny Smith in 1990, freshman Rep. Mike Kopetski never stopped running. He invested $71,405 in his off-year campaign operation. Overhead expenses amounted to $42,223 in 1991, including $4,931 for rent and utilities, $4,522 for telephone service, and $5,422 for office equipment. After-tax salary payments to his one part-time staffer totaled $12,685.

Kopetski had collected $399,283 from political action committees (PACs) in 1990, a remarkable total for a challenger, and he picked up in 1991 right where he had left off. During 1991, PACs accounted for 72 percent of the $124,662 he raised. By concentrating on the PAC community, Kopetski managed to hold his off-year fund-raising costs to $11,484.

Working on the assumption that the Republicans would mount a strong challenge to recapture the seat, Kopetski's campaign strategists began polling in August 1991. Over the next fourteen months, Public Affairs Counsel of Salem collected $38,500 for its polling services. Kopetski also paid Cooper & Secrest Associates of Alexandria, Va., $4,240 for the results of several questions added to a survey commissioned by the American Medical Association.

That strong challenge never came. Instead, Kopetski faced economist Jim Seagraves, who had just $31,667 to spend on the general election campaign after investing $5,750 to win the three-candidate Republican primary. Nevertheless, Kopetski pumped $341,889 into his reelection effort during 1992.

Public Affairs Counsel collected $65,198 for its persuasion mail efforts. An introductory mailer was sent in May to registered Democrats in Tillamook, Lincoln, and Polk counties, which Kopetski acquired through redistricting. Closer to the election, a piece profiling Kopetski's pro-choice stance on abortion was targeted to women in the three counties. The mail campaign was rounded out with endorsement letters signed by local sheriffs and other county officials.

Kopetski opted not to run any television or radio advertising, although he spent $422 to produce an ad, in case he needed one. He invested $7,903 in signs. Printed handouts, many of which were distributed by volunteers who canvassed the newly acquired portions of the district, cost $3,664. Buttons and bumper stickers cost $2,549; T-shirts for volunteers added $1,231. For providing general strategic advice, Public Affairs Counsel and the Oregon Campaign Group of Salem received $40,173 and $12,375, respectively.

Having spent more than $1.6 million to win and hold the seat over three campaigns, Kopetski announced he would not seek reelection in 1994.

Campaign Expenditures	Kopetski Amount Spent	Kopetski % of Total	Seagraves Amount Spent	Seagraves % of Total
Overhead				
Office furniture/supplies	$ 11,477	2.78	$ 1,541	4.12
Rent/utilities	13,406	3.24	248	.66
Salaries	37,334	9.03	5,614	15.00
Taxes	14,705	3.56	0	
Bank/investment fees	254	.06	76	.20
Lawyers/accountants	24,151	5.84	0	
Telephone	10,805	2.61	1,412	3.77
Campaign automobile	0		0	
Computers/office equipment	7,911	1.91	3,720	9.94
Travel	5,155	1.25	6,181	16.52
Food/meetings	847	.20	507	1.35
Subtotal	**126,045**	**30.50**	**19,299**	**51.58**
Fund Raising				
Events	33,141	8.02	729	1.95
Direct mail	17,127	4.14	1,721	4.60
Telemarketing	0		0	
Subtotal	**50,268**	**12.16**	**2,449**	**6.55**
Polling	**42,740**	**10.34**	**0**	
Advertising				
Electronic media	422	.10	9,353	25.00
Other media	2,203	.53	678	1.81
Subtotal	**2,626**	**.64**	**10,031**	**26.81**
Other Campaign Activity				
Persuasion mail/brochures	71,123	17.21	1,604	4.29
Actual campaigning	68,563	16.59	3,701	9.89
Staff/volunteers	1,354	.33	44	.12
Subtotal	**141,041**	**34.13**	**5,349**	**14.30**
Constituent Gifts/ Entertainment	**3,531**	**.85**	**0**	
Donations to				
Candidates from same state	3,600	.87	0	
Candidates from other states	11,050	2.67	0	
Civic organizations	1,086	.26	0	
Ideological groups	1,983	.48	50	.13
Political parties	10,574	2.56	239	.64
Subtotal	**28,293**	**6.85**	**289**	**.77**
Unitemized Expenses	**18,751**	**4.54**	**0**	
Total Campaign Expenses	**$ 413,294**		**$ 37,417**	
PAC Contributions	$ 306,342		$ 0	
Individual Contributions	124,168		2,850	
Total Receipts*	437,857		39,613	

*Includes PAC and individual contributions as well as interest earned, party contributions, etc.

PENNSYLVANIA — District 1

Rep. Thomas M. Foglietta (D)

1992 Election Results

Thomas M. Foglietta (D) 150,172 (81%)
Craig Snyder (R) 35,419 (19%)

Elected in 1980, Rep. Thomas M. Foglietta had never received less than 72 percent of the general election vote in five previous reelection bids. He had no overdrafts at the House bank and, while redistricting made District 1 into a majority-black district, he drew no primary opposition. His Republican opponent, Craig Snyder, had expenditures of just $44,504. Nevertheless, Foglietta spent $351,218—an increase of $116,155 over 1990.

Foglietta devoted 14 percent of his resources to electing fellow Democrats. In 1991 he gave $10,000 each to Michael DeBaradinis and Bob Barnett, old friends and former employees who made unsuccessful bids for seats on the Philadelphia City Council. He also loaned Barnett and DeBaradinis $10,000 and $5,000, respectively. Since those loans were paid back, they have not been included in Foglietta's spending totals. Foglietta tapped his campaign for two donations totaling $11,000 to Edward G. Rendell's successful mayoral campaign. In 1991 Foglietta donated $43,300 to state and local candidates, which accounted for 31 percent of his off-year spending.

During the two-year cycle, Foglietta gave $29,180 of his campaign funds to Democratic party organizations, including $10,750 to the Philadelphia Democratic party, $5,000 to the Democratic Congressional Campaign Committee, and $1,000 to IMPAC 2000, the political action committee established to assist Democrats with redistricting. Contributions to various Democratic ward organizations added $3,000.

Numerous civic and booster organizations benefited from Foglietta's generosity as well. He gave $1,000 to St. John Newman High School, $1,000 to Citizen Action, $300 to United Cerebral Palsy, and $250 to Save the Children, among others. In all, such organizations collected $10,075.

For the campaign itself, Foglietta paid the Campaign Group of Philadelphia $36,000 for creating and placing radio spots. All but $8,000 of his investment in broadcast advertising was spent prior to the April 28 primary. He spent $6,254 on newspaper ads and only $1,337 to print campaign literature. His largest single expense under "actual campaigning" was a $20,000 lump-sum payment to Barnett on December 29, 1992 for "consulting."

Overhead consumed 18 percent of Foglietta's budget, and $23,400 of that went to his nephew, Michael T. Foglietta, who served as the campaign's treasurer. In September 1992 the campaign put $1,588 down on a new car from Pacifico Lincoln in Philadelphia and began paying the monthly lease of $762.

Foglietta spent $5,580 to take long-time volunteers and local party officials to a Philadelphia Phillies baseball game. His annual Christmas parties for volunteers cost $2,357 in 1991 and $2,015 in 1992.

Campaign Expenditures	Foglietta Amount Spent	Foglietta % of Total	Snyder Amount Spent	Snyder % of Total
Overhead				
Office furniture/supplies	$ 523	.15	$ 397	.89
Rent/utilities	5,310	1.51	1,874	4.21
Salaries	12,742	3.63	6,323	14.21
Taxes	1,020	.29	0	
Bank/investment fees	0		0	
Lawyers/accountants	24,400	6.95	0	
Telephone	404	.11	871	1.96
Campaign automobile	4,687	1.33	0	
Computers/office equipment	750	.21	799	1.80
Travel	9,158	2.61	144	.32
Food/meetings	3,109	.89	0	
Subtotal	**62,102**	**17.68**	**10,408**	**23.39**
Fund Raising				
Events	66,048	18.81	3,227	7.25
Direct mail	0		0	
Telemarketing	0		0	
Subtotal	**66,048**	**18.81**	**3,227**	**7.25**
Polling	**12,800**	**3.64**	**0**	
Advertising				
Electronic media	36,000	10.25	5,125	11.52
Other media	7,729	2.20	2,950	6.63
Subtotal	**43,729**	**12.45**	**8,075**	**18.15**
Other Campaign Activity				
Persuasion mail/brochures	1,337	.38	18,306	41.13
Actual campaigning	30,896	8.80	3,805	8.55
Staff/volunteers	11,422	3.25	50	.11
Subtotal	**43,655**	**12.43**	**22,161**	**49.80**
Constituent Gifts/Entertainment	**4,571**	**1.30**	**0**	
Donations to				
Candidates from same state	42,550	12.11	0	
Candidates from other states	8,250	2.35	0	
Civic organizations	10,075	2.87	0	
Ideological groups	1,550	.44	0	
Political parties	29,180	8.31	0	
Subtotal	**91,605**	**26.08**	**0**	
Unitemized Expenses	**26,708**	**7.60**	**633**	**1.42**
Total Campaign Expenses	**$ 351,218**		**$ 44,504**	
PAC Contributions	**$ 168,450**		**$ 3,000**	
Individual Contributions	**142,776**		**20,240**	
Total Receipts*	**387,584**		**43,647**	

*Includes PAC and individual contributions as well as interest earned, party contributions, etc.

District 2 — PENNSYLVANIA

Rep. Lucien E. Blackwell (D)

1992 Election Results

Lucien E. Blackwell** (D) 164,355 (77%)
Larry Hollin (R) 47,906 (22%)

When William H. Gray III resigned in 1991 to become president of the United Negro College Fund, Philadelphia City Council member Lucien E. Blackwell, state senator Chaka Fattah, and former state secretary of public welfare John F. White, Jr., each hoped to gain the Democratic party endorsement for the special election to fill out Gray's term. In a district that had given Democratic presidential nominee Michael Dukakis 91 percent of the vote in 1988 and had routinely given Gray huge margins, that endorsement was tantamount to victory. Blackwell got the party's stamp of approval.

Undaunted, Fattah ran as the Consumer party candidate and White announced an independent campaign. Their problem was less Blackwell, who had run unsuccessfully for mayor earlier in the year, than Philadelphia's voting laws, which allowed voters to pull a single lever to cast votes for all Democratic candidates. With Harris Wofford topping the Democratic ticket in a race to fill the vacant Senate seat created by the death of Republican Sen. John Heinz, everyone knew there would be considerable straight-ticket voting.

Fattah spent $242,521, investing heavily in radio commercials. White invested $239,693, much of it on television commercials instructing voters how not to vote a straight ticket. Blackwell spent just $68,724, and $9,923 of that was invested in orange signs that urged voters to "Vote the Big Democratic Lever." Blackwell emerged with 39 percent of the vote, while Fattah and White each garnered 28 percent. Republican Nadine G. Smith-Bulford received 5 percent.

Blackwell never stopped running. Fattah opted to skip the April 28 Democratic primary and regroup for another try in 1994. Blackwell's primary opponent, C. Delores Tucker, poured $363,936 into the contest, outspending Blackwell by more than three to one. Although he could not depend on the "Big Lever" to pull him through this contest, his grass-roots organization did. While he paid Reach Communication Specialists of Philadelphia $26,975 for producing and placing radio spots, he paid several hundred supporters a total of $27,875 for making certain that voters who needed a ride to the polls or needed a babysitter to watch their children so they could vote were taken care of. This effort enabled Blackwell to pull out a 54 to 46 percent victory.

The November general election against Republican Larry Hollin was of little consequence. Between October 1 and November 23, 1992, Blackwell spent less than $45,000. Hollin invested 54 percent of his $170,933 treasury in overhead and grabbed only 22 percent of the vote.

Campaign Expenditures	Blackwell Amount Spent	Blackwell % of Total	Hollin Amount Spent	Hollin % of Total
Overhead				
Office furniture/supplies	$ 3,652	1.29	$ 6,057	3.54
Rent/utilities	4,990	1.76	5,960	3.49
Salaries	5,540	1.95	59,391	34.75
Taxes	0		12,345	7.22
Bank/investment fees	708	.25	249	.15
Lawyers/accountants	0		735	.43
Telephone	9,729	3.43	1,507	.88
Campaign automobile	1,137	.40	500	.29
Computers/office equipment	0		665	.39
Travel	16,599	5.85	5,266	3.08
Food/meetings	12,720	4.49	180	.11
Subtotal	**55,076**	**19.42**	**92,855**	**54.32**
Fund Raising				
Events	19,580	6.91	8,297	4.85
Direct mail	0		0	
Telemarketing	0		0	
Subtotal	**19,580**	**6.91**	**8,297**	**4.85**
Polling	**0**		**2,250**	**1.32**
Advertising				
Electronic media	31,927	11.26	12,559	7.35
Other media	11,015	3.88	15,636	9.15
Subtotal	**42,942**	**15.15**	**28,195**	**16.49**
Other Campaign Activity				
Persuasion mail/brochures	19,115	6.74	23,202	13.57
Actual campaigning	112,200	39.57	14,648	8.57
Staff/volunteers	1,724	.61	18	.01
Subtotal	**133,039**	**46.92**	**37,868**	**22.15**
Constituent Gifts/Entertainment	**5,754**	**2.03**	**80**	**.05**
Donations to				
Candidates from same state	3,245	1.14	0	
Candidates from other states	7,000	2.47	0	
Civic organizations	7,217	2.55	75	.04
Ideological groups	3,668	1.29	0	
Political parties	1,800	.63	85	.05
Subtotal	**22,930**	**8.09**	**160**	**.09**
Unitemized Expenses	**4,215**	**1.49**	**1,228**	**.72**
Total Campaign Expenses	**$ 283,535**		**$ 170,933**	
PAC Contributions	$ 133,010		$ 4,400	
Individual Contributions	99,748		142,107	
Total Receipts*	236,129		170,009	

*Includes PAC and individual contributions as well as interest earned, party contributions, etc.

**Totals include special election disbursements and receipts.

PENNSYLVANIA — District 3

Rep. Robert A. Borski (D)

1992 Election Results

Robert A. Borski (D)   130,828   (59%)
Charles F. Dougherty (R)   86,787   (39%)

Faced with Republican challengers who together spent less than $100,000, Rep. Robert A. Borski had not felt the need to invest in television advertising in either his 1988 or 1990 campaigns. In 1990 he had not even bothered to run radio commercials. However, with thirty-three overdrafts at the House bank and opposed in 1992 by former Rep. Charles F. Dougherty, from whom he had wrested the seat a decade earlier, Borski changed his tactics. The five-term incumbent paid the Campaign Group of Philadelphia $368,000 for creating and placing his broadcast ads.

Borski's television ad campaign opened on a positive note, touting his efforts to "attract and keep jobs here," his opposition to a trade agreement with Mexico, his support for increases in the minimum wage, and his support for health care reform. The ads did not stay positive for long. "Charlie Dougherty has run for office so often, you'd think that when he finally got elected he'd show up for work. No way," began one spot, which proceeded to note that Dougherty had missed more votes during one year in the House than Borski had missed in ten years. Other spots accused Dougherty of having voted during his previous House tenure to give tax cuts to the wealthy, while voting to slice Social Security benefits.

While Borski depended primarily on television and radio to carry his message, he spent $43,692 on campaign literature and persuasion mailings. A district-wide mailing focused on Borski's legislative accomplishments. Senior citizens were targeted with a piece attacking Dougherty's past votes on Social Security benefits.

Borski spent $1,500 for one billboard ad, which was placed along Interstate 95 and urged voters to "Reelect Congressman Borski." Ads in newspapers such as the *East Philadelphia Sun,* the *Juniata News,* the *Northeast Times,* and the *Olney Times* cost $9,123. He did not spend any money to advertise in the area's largest daily, the *Philadelphia Inquirer,* which endorsed Dougherty. Yard signs added $8,873. During the final weeks of the campaign, an in-house phonebank operation attempted to contact every registered voter over the age of 55. In all, 65 percent of Borski's budget was invested in direct appeals for votes.

While Dougherty spent $215,123 on the race, he invested only 37 percent of his campaign treasury in direct appeals for votes. Overhead consumed 49 percent of his budget. He was able to run a fairly aggressive advertising campaign only because his media adviser, Chesapeake Media of Cordova, Md., received $45,000 from the National Republican Congressional Committee and $4,000 from the National Republican Committee.

Campaign Expenditures	Borski Amount Spent	Borski % of Total	Dougherty Amount Spent	Dougherty % of Total
Overhead				
Office furniture/supplies	$ 2,131	.31	$ 4,341	2.02
Rent/utilities	19,682	2.86	11,918	5.54
Salaries	26,568	3.86	72,500	33.70
Taxes	15,082	2.19	0	
Bank/investment fees	0		78	.04
Lawyers/accountants	27,976	4.06	0	
Telephone	10,861	1.58	9,351	4.35
Campaign automobile	0		0	
Computers/office equipment	1,142	.17	2,404	1.12
Travel	3,084	.45	2,406	1.12
Food/meetings	137	.02	1,610	.75
Subtotal	106,664	15.49	104,608	48.63
Fund Raising				
Events	59,294	8.61	18,039	8.39
Direct mail	5,351	.78	0	
Telemarketing	0		0	
Subtotal	64,645	9.39	18,039	8.39
Polling	14,121	2.05	1,868	.87
Advertising				
Electronic media	368,000	53.45	25,755	11.97
Other media	13,863	2.01	4,475	2.08
Subtotal	381,863	55.46	30,230	14.05
Other Campaign Activity				
Persuasion mail/brochures	43,692	6.35	11,045	5.13
Actual campaigning	22,315	3.24	37,531	17.45
Staff/volunteers	0		876	.41
Subtotal	66,008	9.59	49,452	22.99
Constituent Gifts/ Entertainment	2,256	.33	0	
Donations to				
Candidates from same state	14,957	2.17	725	.34
Candidates from other states	2,250	.33	0	
Civic organizations	640	.09	50	.02
Ideological groups	0		300	.14
Political parties	15,025	2.18	400	.19
Subtotal	32,872	4.77	1,475	.69
Unitemized Expenses	20,120	2.92	9,450	4.39
Total Campaign Expenses	$ 688,549		$ 215,123	
PAC Contributions	$ 275,319		$ 46,154	
Individual Contributions	210,433		158,675	
Total Receipts*	512,477		215,322	

* Includes PAC and individual contributions as well as interest earned, party contributions, etc.

District 4 — PENNSYLVANIA

Rep. Ron Klink (D)

1992 Election Results

Ron Klink (D)	186,684	(79%)
Gordon R. Johnston (R)	48,484	(20%)

Rep. Joe Kolter's 56 percent showing in 1990 attracted three primary opponents in 1992, including Ron Klink, a television news anchor for KDKA-TV in Pittsburgh, and state representative Mike Veon. While Kolter spent more than $275,000 to Klink's $91,964 and Veon's $73,747, the five-term incumbent finished third, collecting only 19 percent of the vote.

Kolter proved to be his own worst enemy. In March 1992 the *Pittsburgh Press* printed excerpts from an audiotape of a Kolter campaign strategy session. Describing himself as a "political whore," Kolter noted that during the upcoming campaign he would "be going to a lot of funeral homes. Just walk in and, if I faintly remember who these people are, just walk in and shed a little tear and sign my name and take off."

With Kolter self-destructing, Klink opted to take the high road with his $30,451 preprimary advertising budget. "Our toughest decision in the primary was to lay off Kolter," recalled Dennis M. Casey, Klink's Pittsburgh-based media and fund-raising consultant. "Klink had very high name ID, but voters didn't know him as a potential policy-maker. That's where we put our money."

To that end, Klink spent $9,821 on campaign literature for the primary, most of which was invested in a thirty-nine-page booklet detailing Klink's ideas for economic growth and job creation. "We printed a ton of them," noted Casey. "We put copies of the booklet in libraries and bars in working-class sections of town where people were out of work." Response to Klink's booklet was sufficiently strong that the campaign aired commercials telling people how to obtain a copy.

Casey collected $46,793 for creating and placing most of the preprimary ads, providing general strategic and fund-raising advice, arranging a five-county helicopter tour to announce Klink's candidacy, and designing the booklet. Yard signs added $4,110.

After winning 45 percent of the Democratic primary votes, Klink had initially decided to limit his additional advertising to the $9,947 he spent on yard signs proclaiming him to be "A Citizen for Congress." However, that was before Republican Gordon R. Johnston filed a complaint with the Federal Election Commission charging that a loan Klink had made to his campaign was an illegal contribution by Klink's wife. That prompted Klink to pump $44,950 into a broadcast advertising campaign, $42,949 of which went to Casey. "He felt his wife had been attacked, and he told me, 'I want to beat this SOB and I want to beat him bad,'" Casey explained.

Campaign Expenditures	Klink Amount Spent	Klink % of Total	Johnston Amount Spent	Johnston % of Total
Overhead				
Office furniture/supplies	$ 2,411	.84	$ 338	1.78
Rent/utilities	1,800	.63	0	
Salaries	2,000	.70	2,300	12.12
Taxes	0		0	
Bank/investment fees	731	.25	0	
Lawyers/accountants	6,323	2.20	0	
Telephone	19,952	6.94	1,015	5.35
Campaign automobile	0		0	
Computers/office equipment	1,081	.38	528	2.78
Travel	24,773	8.62	4,061	21.39
Food/meetings	1,733	.60	0	
Subtotal	**60,804**	**21.17**	**8,243**	**43.43**
Fund Raising				
Events	41,897	14.58	14	.07
Direct mail	0		0	
Telemarketing	0		0	
Subtotal	**41,897**	**14.58**	**14**	**.07**
Polling	**0**		**0**	
Advertising				
Electronic media	75,401	26.25	2,743	14.45
Other media	7,327	2.55	4,224	22.26
Subtotal	**82,727**	**28.80**	**6,968**	**36.71**
Other Campaign Activity				
Persuasion mail/brochures	24,507	8.53	1,872	9.86
Actual campaigning	57,375	19.97	557	2.93
Staff/volunteers	910	.32	0	
Subtotal	**82,792**	**28.82**	**2,429**	**12.80**
Constituent Gifts/ Entertainment	297	.10	0	
Donations to				
Candidates from same state	220	.08	0	
Candidates from other states	0		0	
Civic organizations	1,068	.37	0	
Ideological groups	120	.04	0	
Political parties	730	.25	305	1.61
Subtotal	**2,138**	**.74**	**305**	**1.61**
Unitemized Expenses	**16,630**	**5.79**	**1,022**	**5.38**
Total Campaign Expenses	**$ 287,286**		**$ 18,981**	
PAC Contributions	$ 18,150		$ 0	
Individual Contributions	147,787		7,680	
Total Receipts*	264,293		14,238	

*Includes PAC and individual contributions as well as interest earned, party contributions, etc.

PENNSYLVANIA — District 5

Rep. William F. Clinger (R)

1992 Election Results William F. Clinger (R, D) 188,911 (100%)

In a year when anti-incumbent sentiment was supposedly running rampant, Rep. William F. Clinger ran unopposed for the first time in his fourteen-year House career. In four of his previous seven House campaigns, Clinger had failed to capture 60 percent of the vote. His 1990 Democratic challenger had grabbed 41 percent, despite spending just $6,767. Yet, Clinger secured the 1992 Republican nomination without a fight and even won the Democratic nomination by virtue of a primary write-in campaign.

That did not mean Clinger ran an inexpensive campaign. He spent $95,179 on his permanent campaign during the off-year, including $49,042 on overhead and $30,460 on fund raising. Overhead, fund raising, constituent entertainment, and donations to other candidates, political party organizations, and causes amounted to at least $214,496 over the two-year election cycle. Given that Clinger failed to itemize 12 percent of his expenditures, actual spending on these items was undoubtedly higher.

While rent and utilities for his permanent campaign headquarters amounted to only $5,199, Clinger paid Gerry Africa, his lone year-round campaign employee, after-tax salary payments totaling $27,073. Although many candidates did not bother to pay the required payroll taxes for their employees, Clinger not only paid the proper taxes, but he also spent $13,115 on Africa's health insurance.

Virtually all of Clinger's expenses connected with the 1992 campaign were incurred during the first four months of 1992. He spent $1,186 to air several radio spots prior to the April 28 primary but nothing on broadcast advertising for the general election. He paid Brabender Cox of Pittsburgh $3,618 for a single mailer that urged likely Democratic primary voters to write in Clinger's name. He felt no need to mail brochures prior to the general election. Per diem payments to primary election day poll watchers amounted to $2,395; they were not needed in November. In fact, between October 1 and November 26, 1992, Clinger spent just $28,367 of his campaign treasury—and $11,842 of that was simply given away to other Republican candidates and party organizations.

In October he donated $1,500 to city council candidate Jim Lynch. Shortly after the election he tapped his campaign for $1,574 to pay off several of Lynch's campaign bills, including printing, postage, and waste disposal charges. Clinger also spent $895 to pay for printing, postage, and a facilities charge incurred by state representative Lynn Herman at the State College Elks Country Club. "It's a tremendous way to party-build," noted James L. Clarke, Clinger's administrative assistant.

Campaign Expenditures	Clinger Amount Spent	% of Total
Overhead		
Office furniture/supplies	$ 5,833	2.13
Rent/utilities	5,199	1.89
Salaries	42,254	15.40
Taxes	29,291	10.67
Bank/investment fees	82	.03
Lawyers/accountants	0	
Telephone	7,065	2.57
Campaign automobile	0	
Computers/office equipment	5,167	1.88
Travel	13,330	4.86
Food/meetings	0	
Subtotal	**108,220**	**39.44**
Fund Raising		
Events	59,567	21.71
Direct mail	8,632	3.15
Telemarketing	0	
Subtotal	**68,199**	**24.85**
Polling	**0**	
Advertising		
Electronic media	1,336	.49
Other media	2,139	.78
Subtotal	**3,476**	**1.27**
Other Campaign Activity		
Persuasion mail/brochures	5,932	2.16
Actual campaigning	14,879	5.42
Staff/volunteers	1,545	.56
Subtotal	**22,356**	**8.15**
Constituent Gifts/Entertainment	**4,000**	**1.46**
Donations to		
Candidates from same state	18,542	6.76
Candidates from other states	3,850	1.40
Civic organizations	300	.11
Ideological groups	700	.26
Political parties	10,685	3.89
Subtotal	**34,077**	**12.42**
Unitemized Expenses	**34,085**	**12.42**
Total Campaign Expenses	**$ 274,413**	
PAC Contributions	$ 142,894	
Individual Contributions	130,596	
Total Receipts*	286,477	

*Includes PAC and individual contributions as well as interest earned, party contributions, etc.

District 6 — PENNSYLVANIA

Rep. Tim Holden (D)

1992 Election Results

Tim Holden (D)	108,312	(52%)
John E. Jones (R)	99,694	(48%)

In their battle to succeed retiring Rep. Gus Yatron, Democrat Tim Holden and Republican John E. Jones ultimately agreed that the key wedge issue was class. During the campaign Holden referred to Jones, a lawyer and businessman, as "the biggest crybaby I've met in my life" and labeled Jones "a little Lord Fauntleroy who is out of touch with the hard-working men and women of this community." As Trish Reilly, Holden's communications director later put it, "We made sure that people knew this was a race between a wealthy Republican and a sheriff."

After the election, Jones lamented that he unwittingly played into Holden's strategy by producing flashy persuasion mailers, dubbed "Congress Today," which were full-color knock-offs of *USA Today*, complete with the national newspaper's characteristic charts and graphs. "I think we may have out-slicked ourselves," noted Jones. "Holden's campaign looked very grass-roots and I think my mail played into people's fears that I was a fat-cat Republican."

While Jones outspent Holden by $103,545, Jones's spending in the Republican primary accounted for 84 percent of that differential. Holden spent just $31,863 through the April 28 primary and Jones spent $119,026, wiping out all but $15,481 of his advantage. That edge disappeared completely when Jones continued to outspend Holden in June. Over the last five months of the campaign, Holden actually outspent Jones by $10,498. "I spent too much money horsing around early on, when people weren't connected [to politics]," Jones said. "Holden saved all of his money until the end, while I had a full-time staff at the beginning. If I had it to do over again, I would run a very bare-bones campaign until the end."

Overall, Holden invested 61 percent of his funds in direct appeals for votes. Austin-Sheinkopf of New York collected $90,066 for creating and placing the general election broadcast ads and $3,000 for placing limited newspaper ads. While Jones opted to stick exclusively with radio, Holden added cable television to his advertising mix. Strategic Message & Design of Washington, D.C., collected $4,000 for creating persuasion mailers. "Our main message was that 'he's one of us,'" recalled Reilly. "We focused on jobs and the importance of investing in the nation's infrastructure."

Holden invested $5,636 in bus tours of the district, $8,670 in yard signs, $2,215 in an in-house phonebank, $8,095 in the state party's coordinated get-out-the-vote effort, and $6,220 in election day poll watchers. Cooper & Secrest Associates of Alexandria, Va., collected $16,799 for polling.

	Holden		Jones	
Campaign Expenditures	Amount Spent	% of Total	Amount Spent	% of Total
Overhead				
Office furniture/supplies	$ 1,883	.60	$ 4,037	.96
Rent/utilities	4,766	1.51	8,037	1.91
Salaries	17,873	5.66	30,799	7.32
Taxes	0		10,858	2.58
Bank/investment fees	0		2,292	.54
Lawyers/accountants	0		1,447	.34
Telephone	11,837	3.75	17,554	4.17
Campaign automobile	0		12,352	2.94
Computers/office equipment	3,450	1.09	6,054	1.44
Travel	2,048	.65	6,047	1.44
Food/meetings	475	.15	1,087	.26
Subtotal	**42,331**	**13.42**	**100,565**	**23.91**
Fund Raising				
Events	53,593	16.99	10,857	2.58
Direct mail	0		301	.07
Telemarketing	0		0	
Subtotal	**53,593**	**16.99**	**11,158**	**2.65**
Polling	**16,799**	**5.32**	**25,150**	**5.98**
Advertising				
Electronic media	95,689	30.33	138,054	32.82
Other media	15,391	4.88	29,111	6.92
Subtotal	**111,080**	**35.21**	**167,165**	**39.74**
Other Campaign Activity				
Persuasion mail/brochures	39,306	12.46	71,799	17.07
Actual campaigning	41,162	13.05	30,959	7.36
Staff/volunteers	2,052	.65	196	.05
Subtotal	**82,519**	**26.15**	**102,955**	**24.48**
Constituent Gifts/ Entertainment	**5,235**	**1.66**	**0**	
Donations to				
Candidates from same state	0		0	
Candidates from other states	0		0	
Civic organizations	1,405	.45	380	.09
Ideological groups	50	.02	0	
Political parties	812	.26	9,530	2.27
Subtotal	**2,267**	**.72**	**9,910**	**2.36**
Unitemized Expenses	**1,691**	**.54**	**3,704**	**.88**
Total Campaign Expenses	**$ 315,516**		**$ 420,606**	
PAC Contributions	**$ 99,400**		**$ 92,604**	
Individual Contributions	**163,715**		**305,935**	
Total Receipts*	**293,468**		**447,913**	

*Includes PAC and individual contributions as well as interest earned, party contributions, etc.

PENNSYLVANIA — District 7

Rep. Curt Weldon (R)

1992 Election Results

Curt Weldon (R)	180,648	(66%)
Frank Daly (D)	91,623	(33%)

In March 1992 three-term Rep. Curt Weldon was accused by a former director of the Partnership for Economic Development (PED), an organization founded in 1983 by Weldon, of pressuring him to use federal funds illegally to benefit Weldon's initial House bid in 1986. Potentially adding to Weldon's 1992 reelection woes were his nine overdrafts at the House bank and his 1989 vote in favor of the congressional pay raise.

None of these problems proved to be anything that a $563,283 campaign could not fix. After easily dispatching his first-ever Republican primary challenger, Weldon scored his third consecutive two-to-one general election victory. The process cost $91,119 more than Weldon's 1990 campaign—a 19 percent increase. Weldon's 1990 Democratic challenger had also tried unsuccessfully to make a campaign issue of Weldon's ties to the PED.

Weldon paid Stuart Stevens of New York $91,228 for creating and placing radio and cable television commercials. According to Douglas D. Ritter, Jr., Weldon's administrative assistant, the campaign's three television commercials consisted of interviews in which a shirt-sleeved Weldon expounded on the need for congressional reform, his constituent service efforts, and his role in fighting to hold the line on taxes and spending. The radio spots were simply the voice-overs from the television commercials. Miscellaneous production costs added $9,695. His total outlays for broadcast advertising were 16 percent higher than in 1990.

Outlays for campaign literature and persuasion mail jumped 31 percent, from $109,489 in 1990 to $143,907 in 1992. In addition to three district-wide mailings, one piece targeted likely voters in areas added by redistricting, while more tightly targeted pieces were aimed at specific towns and ethnic groups. James R. Foster & Associates of Carrollton, Texas, collected $12,000 for designing the mailings as well as four direct-mail fund-raising solicitations.

Weldon, a former volunteer fire chief, used $5,100 of his campaign funds to purchase an antique fire truck for use in various parades. He spent $4,626 on yard signs, bumper stickers, and buttons. An in-house phonebank cost $2,739. American Viewpoint of Alexandria, Va., received $24,000 for polling.

Democrat Frank Daly devoted more than $80,000 of his $180,821 budget to winning the Democratic primary. While he sent four 60,000-piece waves of preprimary persuasion mail, scarce resources limited him to printing 10,000 copies of the "Daly News," which were distributed door-to-door before the general election. He had less than $50,000 left to spend on broadcast advertising for the general election campaign.

	Weldon		Daly	
Campaign Expenditures	Amount Spent	% of Total	Amount Spent	% of Total
Overhead				
Office furniture/supplies	$ 13,536	2.40	$ 2,343	1.30
Rent/utilities	3,476	.62	8,179	4.52
Salaries	30,573	5.43	33,260	18.39
Taxes	13,784	2.45	0	
Bank/investment fees	224	.04	72	.04
Lawyers/accountants	24,000	4.26	0	
Telephone	6,403	1.14	4,863	2.69
Campaign automobile	0		0	
Computers/office equipment	7,242	1.29	3,365	1.86
Travel	7,638	1.36	580	.32
Food/meetings	9,607	1.71	0	
Subtotal	**116,482**	**20.68**	**52,662**	**29.12**
Fund Raising				
Events	67,331	11.95	4,949	2.74
Direct mail	46,911	8.33	4,686	2.59
Telemarketing	0		0	
Subtotal	**114,243**	**20.28**	**9,635**	**5.33**
Polling	**24,000**	**4.26**	**925**	**.51**
Advertising				
Electronic media	100,923	17.92	57,851	31.99
Other media	2,594	.46	1,294	.72
Subtotal	**103,517**	**18.38**	**59,145**	**32.71**
Other Campaign Activity				
Persuasion mail/brochures	143,907	25.55	44,342	24.52
Actual campaigning	18,229	3.24	9,221	5.10
Staff/volunteers	4,696	.83	0	
Subtotal	**166,831**	**29.62**	**53,563**	**29.62**
Constituent Gifts/ Entertainment	8,593	1.53	0	
Donations to				
Candidates from same state	4,500	.80	0	
Candidates from other states	500	.09	0	
Civic organizations	1,095	.19	165	.09
Ideological groups	265	.05	25	.01
Political parties	14,145	2.51	510	.28
Subtotal	**20,505**	**3.64**	**700**	**.39**
Unitemized Expenses	**9,112**	**1.62**	**4,191**	**2.32**
Total Campaign Expenses	**$ 563,283**		**$ 180,821**	
PAC Contributions	$ 185,187		$ 14,862	
Individual Contributions	257,443		137,392	
Total Receipts*	465,223		177,826	

*Includes PAC and individual contributions as well as interest earned, party contributions, etc.

District 8 — PENNSYLVANIA

Rep. James C. Greenwood (R)

1992 Election Results

James C. Greenwood (R) 129,593 (52%)
Peter H. Kostmayer (D) 114,095 (46%)

After struggling through tough reelection contests for more than a decade, Democratic Rep. Peter H. Kostmayer ran out of luck in 1992 when state senator James C. Greenwood parlayed Kostmayer's fifty overdrafts at the House bank into a 6-point victory. Outspent by $505,637, Greenwood's $722,055 budget proved sufficient to drive home his outsider message.

Given essentially a free pass in the Republican primary, Greenwood saved his entire broadcast advertising budget for the fall campaign, hitting the airwaves with introductory cable television spots in August. In September he invested about $80,000 to begin airing a commercial that encapsulated all his basic themes, which targeted Republican working women and environmentalists who had deserted Republican candidates to vote for Kostmayer in the past.

Filmed in Levittown, the spot opened with a small boy running out of his home and a mother helping her daughter get on a school bus. The spot then cut to shots of that same woman at work, having documents handed to her by her subordinates—all men. Images of the family at dinner, of the woman and her husband paying bills, and of the two kissing their daughter goodnight flashed across the screen.

As these scenes unfolded a female narrator mused, "I wonder if when Peter Kostmayer was bouncing those checks, he really thought about how the rest of us live—how we struggle to pay bills or worry about our jobs. Congressman Kostmayer even wrote a bounced check to pay his taxes. We're not voting for Pete Kostmayer this year, we're going with Jim Greenwood. Oh, they're both excellent on issues like the environment, but Jim Greenwood understands that our financial security starts with basics like a balanced budget and new job opportunities. I'm not sure Pete Kostmayer will ever get it."

Greenwood paid Welch Communications of Arlington, Va., $242,133 for creating the ad campaign, buying some of the air time, producing persuasion mailers, and supplying campaign buttons and bumper stickers. Welch also received $35,771 from the National Republican Congressional Committee to augment the persuasion mail effort. Greenwood paid Impact Media of Dallas, Texas, $16,762 for creative input to the ads, and Mentzer Media of Baltimore, Md., received $135,176 for buying time. Optima Direct of Washington, D.C., collected $42,165 for phonebanking. Public Opinion Strategies of Alexandria, Va., received $27,634 for polling.

Having spent only $46,669 of his massive budget during 1991, Kostmayer counterattacked with a $672,155 broadcast campaign. One particularly hard-hitting spot concluded, "Greenwood—A spotty record, shady money, dirty politics."

Campaign Expenditures	Greenwood Amount Spent	Greenwood % of Total	Kostmayer Amount Spent	Kostmayer % of Total
Overhead				
Office furniture/supplies	$ 4,088	.57	$ 15,642	1.27
Rent/utilities	8,447	1.17	14,102	1.15
Salaries	50,036	6.93	117,601	9.58
Taxes	26,149	3.62	50,770	4.14
Bank/investment fees	157	.02	2,002	.16
Lawyers/accountants	0		0	
Telephone	13,325	1.85	6,916	.56
Campaign automobile	0		0	
Computers/office equipment	4,734	.66	20,235	1.65
Travel	7,935	1.10	30,634	2.50
Food/meetings	776	.11	2,668	.22
Subtotal	**115,647**	**16.02**	**260,570**	**21.22**
Fund Raising				
Events	40,950	5.67	70,118	5.71
Direct mail	11,667	1.62	20,592	1.68
Telemarketing	1,000	.14	0	
Subtotal	**53,617**	**7.43**	**90,710**	**7.39**
Polling	**27,634**	**3.83**	**15,680**	**1.28**
Advertising				
Electronic media	281,258	38.95	672,155	54.75
Other media	18,228	2.52	5,121	.42
Subtotal	**299,486**	**41.48**	**677,276**	**55.17**
Other Campaign Activity				
Persuasion mail/brochures	168,016	23.27	82,565	6.73
Actual campaigning	52,590	7.28	57,472	4.68
Staff/volunteers	150	.02	2,469	.20
Subtotal	**220,756**	**30.57**	**142,506**	**11.61**
Constituent Gifts/ Entertainment	0		1,182	.10
Donations to				
Candidates from same state	0		11,293	.92
Candidates from other states	0		1,750	.14
Civic organizations	50	.01	1,137	.09
Ideological groups	0		1,237	.10
Political parties	215	.03	24,293	1.98
Subtotal	**265**	**.04**	**39,709**	**3.23**
Unitemized Expenses	4,651	.64	58	
Total Campaign Expenses	$ 722,055		$ 1,227,692	
PAC Contributions	$ 179,742		$ 530,921	
Individual Contributions	527,765		669,557	
Total Receipts*	721,654		1,239,616	

*Includes PAC and individual contributions as well as interest earned, party contributions, etc.

PENNSYLVANIA
District 9

Rep. Bud Shuster (R)

1992 Election Results   Bud Shuster (R)   182,406   (100%)

Unopposed in 1986, 1988, 1990, and again in 1992, Rep. Bud Shuster still spent $546,389 during the 1992 election cycle, an increase of $116,592 over 1990. The ten-term incumbent invested only $87,935, or 16 percent of his budget, in direct appeals for votes.

As in 1990, no one in the House could compete with Shuster when it came to dining out at campaign expense. Over the two-year cycle, Shuster spent $70,913 on meals that were unrelated to fund raising, including $25,163 in unitemized credit card bills. He spent $11,355 on meals in Washington, D.C., including $7,218 for seventeen meals at Tortilla Coast, $428 for two meals at the Willard Hotel, a $300 repast at Powerscourt Restaurant, and $289 for two dinners at Le Mistral. Across the river in suburban Virginia, Shuster spent $17,308 on meals, including $8,054 for twenty-four meals from Sutton Place Gourmet in Alexandria, $1,288 for ten meals at the Ritz Carlton Hotel in Arlington, $1,295 for five dinners at the Terrazza Restaurant in Alexandria, and $789 for four dinners at the Chart House, a restaurant overlooking the Potomac River in Alexandria. To satisfy his sweet tooth, Shuster spent $1,731 at Alexandria Pastry.

Six members of Shuster's Washington congressional staff also worked on his campaign, and $5,543 of his Washington and Virginia meal expenses were listed as "food for volunteers." His Washington staffers ate $2,462 worth of food from Tortilla Coast, $513 in chicken from Popeye's, and $845 in food from Peking Duck Gourmet. One "happy hour" visit to the Crowbar cost the campaign $226.

Shuster's dining habits were apparently more conservative when he traveled home to Pennsylvania. He billed the campaign for just $11,848 in itemized meals in the Keystone state, and none of these meals were listed as "meals for volunteers."

The lack of competition did not keep Shuster from celebrating in style. Expenses for his election night party totaled $10,001, which accounted for 20 percent of the expenses included under "actual campaigning."

Shuster spent $36,425 to charter airplanes, nearly eight times what he invested in commercial air fare. He also tapped his campaign for $4,855 to cover expenses incurred during the four-day 1992 Democratic National Convention. Nine congressional staffers collected travel reimbursements from the campaign totaling $41,329, including $19,232 paid to chief of staff Ann M. Eppard.

As in 1990, Shuster took maximum advantage of the rules requiring him to itemize only those expenditures of $200 or more. He chose not to itemize expenses totaling $92,127—17 percent of his total outlays.

Campaign Expenditures	Shuster Amount Spent	% of Total
Overhead		
Office furniture/supplies	$ 3,251	.60
Rent/utilities	0	
Salaries	7,750	1.42
Taxes	2,680	.49
Bank/investment fees	0	
Lawyers/accountants	0	
Telephone	4,377	.80
Campaign automobile	2,847	.52
Computers/office equipment	3,534	.65
Travel	102,561	18.77
Food/meetings	70,913	12.98
Subtotal	**197,914**	**36.22**
Fund Raising		
Events	125,582	22.98
Direct mail	0	
Telemarketing	0	
Subtotal	**125,582**	**22.98**
Polling	**0**	
Advertising		
Electronic media	6,886	1.26
Other media	7,642	1.40
Subtotal	**14,528**	**2.66**
Other Campaign Activity		
Persuasion mail/brochures	22,824	4.18
Actual campaigning	50,583	9.26
Staff/volunteers	0	
Subtotal	**73,407**	**13.43**
Constituent Gifts/Entertainment	**8,289**	**1.52**
Donations to		
Candidates from same state	20,147	3.69
Candidates from other states	1,000	.18
Civic organizations	1,270	.23
Ideological groups	200	.04
Political parties	11,925	2.18
Subtotal	**34,542**	**6.32**
Unitemized Expenses	**92,127**	**16.86**
Total Campaign Expenses	$ **546,389**	
PAC Contributions	$ **187,250**	
Individual Contributions	**343,403**	
Total Receipts*	**557,315**	

*Includes PAC and individual contributions as well as interest earned, party contributions, etc.

District 10 — PENNSYLVANIA

Rep. Joseph M. McDade (R)

1992 Election Results
Joseph M. McDade (R, D)   189,414   (90%)
Albert A. Smith † (I)   20,134   (10%)

Rep. Joseph M. McDade is living proof that the electorate's anti-incumbent mood in 1992 was far from universal. Even though McDade was the target of a federal investigation that led to the fifteen-term incumbent's indictment in May 1992 on bribery charges, no Democrat chose to test his popularity.

With a clear path to the Republican nomination, McDade decided to seek the Democratic nomination as well. According to William M. Dawson III, most of the $63,582 paid to his firm, Gann-Dawson of Scranton, was invested in preprimary radio spots that urged Democrats to write in McDade's name. McDade's 1,518 write-in votes were enough to capture the nomination.

For the general election, McDade spent $2,000 for the rights to a jingle originally written to commemorate the twenty-fifth anniversary of the Los Angeles Dodgers's move from Brooklyn. After the Dodgers opted not to buy the ditty, McDade decided its tagline, "miracles, memories, and you," would fit his campaign perfectly. The jingle was incorporated into a television commercial that showed footage of McDade at various points throughout his thirty years in Congress. The campaign spent $10,500 to air the ad on local network affiliates and $1,020 for cable television time. John R. Gallagher received $1,750 for placing the ads.

With no major-party opposition, McDade spent $97,000 of his campaign treasury on legal fees associated with his defense. Two Washington, D.C., law firms, Brand & Lowell and McCamish, Martin & Loeffler, received $50,000 and $10,000, respectively. Sal Cognetti, Jr., of Scranton collected $37,000.

Constituent stroking consisted primarily of year-end holiday cards that cost the campaign $7,011. McDade also paid $323 to the Lackawana County Coal Mine for statues made of anthracite coal. In addition to passing them out to visitors, McDade gave one to Hillary Clinton on the night of her husband's first State of the Union address.

The Federal Election Commission does not require full disclosure on expenditures of less than $200, and McDade made liberal use of that exemption by choosing not to list more than $42,000 in expenses. In addition, disclosure requirements are poorly defined, allowing McDade to reimburse himself $16,141 for "expenses related to campaign committee."

McDade raised $242,172 from political action committees and another $62,150 from out-of-state donors who contributed at least $200. Two-thirds of the $27,203 he spent on fund-raising events was invested in two receptions held at the Capitol Hill Club in Washington, D.C. At most, McDade raised 11 percent of his funds from in-state contributors.

Campaign Expenditures	McDade Amount Spent	% of Total
Overhead		
Office furniture/supplies	$ 1,140	.33
Rent/utilities	0	
Salaries	0	
Taxes	5,127	1.49
Bank/investment fees	0	
Lawyers/accountants	100,413	29.24
Telephone	1,711	.50
Campaign automobile	2,513	.73
Computers/office equipment	357	.10
Travel	5,143	1.50
Food/meetings	5,811	1.69
Subtotal	**122,214**	**35.59**
Fund Raising		
Events	27,203	7.92
Direct mail	9,230	2.69
Telemarketing	0	
Subtotal	**36,433**	**10.61**
Polling	**0**	
Advertising		
Electronic media	79,689	23.21
Other media	2,007	.58
Subtotal	**81,696**	**23.79**
Other Campaign Activity		
Persuasion mail/brochures	0	
Actual campaigning	14,448	4.21
Staff/volunteers	0	
Subtotal	**14,448**	**4.21**
Constituent Gifts/Entertainment	**7,698**	**2.24**
Donations to		
Candidates from same state	3,250	.95
Candidates from other states	3,000	.87
Civic organizations	3,650	1.06
Ideological groups	500	.15
Political parties	11,040	3.21
Subtotal	**21,440**	**6.24**
Unitemized Expenses	**59,468**	**17.32**
Total Campaign Expenses	$ **343,397**	
PAC Contributions	$ 242,172	
Individual Contributions	98,660	
Total Receipts*	375,429	

*Includes PAC and individual contributions as well as interest earned, party contributions, etc.

†No expenditures or receipts on file. Candidates raising or spending less than $5,000 are not required to file reports with the Federal Election Commission.

PENNSYLVANIA — District 11

Rep. Paul E. Kanjorski (D)

1992 Election Results

Paul E. Kanjorski (D)	138,875	(67%)
Michael A. Fescina (R)	68,112	(33%)

Unopposed in 1990, Rep. Paul E. Kanjorski still spent $212,630 to maintain his permanent campaign operation—an understandable precautionary move given the fact that between 1980 and Kanjorski's 1984 victory, four people had represented the district. He invested another $78,484 to keep the campaign machinery well oiled in 1991. When retired chemist Michael A. Fescina captured the Republican nomination in 1992, Kanjorski was more than ready to engage. With a $262,783 investment during 1992, Kanjorski brought his spending for the election cycle to $341,267—a 60 percent increase over 1990.

Kanjorski pumped 44 percent of his budget into broadcast advertising that focused on his constituent service and his successful efforts to bring federal dollars back to the district. Edward Mitchell Communications of Wilkes-Barre collected $146,591 for creating and placing the ads, which aired the final two weeks of the campaign. Miscellaneous production fees incurred at the Democratic Congressional Campaign Committee's Harriman Communication Center added $1,092. In September 1991 the campaign paid $1,100 to a local television station in Moosie.

Other than his broadcast advertising, Kanjorski spent almost nothing on the campaign itself. Ads in newspapers such as the *Times Leader,* the *Daily Item,* and the *Citizens Voice* cost $2,342. Payments to five local Democratic party organizations for election day get-out-the-vote efforts amounted to $3,900, including $1,200 for the April 28 primary in which he ran unopposed. He spent $2,287 to print leaflets, $215 on campaign photos, and $407 on his election night victory party at the Ramada Hotel in Wilkes-Barre.

As he had in the 1990 election cycle, Kanjorski paid monthly rent of $500 to K&K Realty of Wilkes-Barre, a company jointly owned by Kanjorski and his brother, Peter. His lone year-round employee, Susan Rinehimer, collected salary payments totaling $22,807 for maintaining the campaign's database of contributors and supporters.

Kanjorski rarely asked any of those supporters for money, relying instead on the goodwill of Washington, D.C.-based political action committees (PACs). Over the two-year cycle, PACs accounted for 79 percent of his nonparty contributions. He raised $27,552 from individuals who gave $200 or more, and $6,300 of that came from out-of-state contributors. Assuming that all of the $35,400 he raised in small donations came from in-state residents, Kanjorski collected only 19 percent of his money from Pennsylvanians.

If nothing else, Fescina's experience taught him the power of money in politics. "I'd love to run again, but I would need $300,000 before I'd even announce."

	Kanjorski		Fescina	
Campaign Expenditures	Amount Spent	% of Total	Amount Spent	% of Total
Overhead				
Office furniture/supplies	$ 3,414	1.00	$ 135	.25
Rent/utilities	12,500	3.66	600	1.10
Salaries	27,709	8.12	0	
Taxes	9,654	2.83	0	
Bank/investment fees	0		0	
Lawyers/accountants	0		0	
Telephone	5,364	1.57	458	.84
Campaign automobile	0		0	
Computers/office equipment	2,850	.84	1,500	2.74
Travel	3,099	.91	4,242	7.75
Food/meetings	3,528	1.03	242	.44
Subtotal	**68,119**	**19.96**	**7,178**	**13.12**
Fund Raising				
Events	23,667	6.94	7,573	13.84
Direct mail	0		0	
Telemarketing	0		0	
Subtotal	**23,667**	**6.94**	**7,573**	**13.84**
Polling	**18,912**	**5.54**	**0**	
Advertising				
Electronic media	148,783	43.60	34,462	62.97
Other media	2,452	.72	475	.87
Subtotal	**151,235**	**44.32**	**34,937**	**63.84**
Other Campaign Activity				
Persuasion mail/brochures	2,287	.67	2,998	5.48
Actual campaigning	4,522	1.33	1,150	2.10
Staff/volunteers	0		854	1.56
Subtotal	**6,810**	**2.00**	**5,002**	**9.14**
Constituent Gifts/ Entertainment	**12,809**	**3.75**	**0**	
Donations to				
Candidates from same state	9,735	2.85	0	
Candidates from other states	500	.15	0	
Civic organizations	9,660	2.83	0	
Ideological groups	500	.15	0	
Political parties	3,175	.93	0	
Subtotal	**23,570**	**6.91**	**0**	
Unitemized Expenses	**36,144**	**10.59**	**36**	**.07**
Total Campaign Expenses	**$ 341,267**		**$ 54,726**	
PAC Contributions	**$ 235,360**		**$ 0**	
Individual Contributions	**62,952**		**21,909**	
Total Receipts*	**311,016**		**55,029**	

*Includes PAC and individual contributions as well as interest earned, party contributions, etc.

District 12 — PENNSYLVANIA

Rep. John P. Murtha (D)

1992 Election Results John P. Murtha (D) 166,916 (100%)

Unopposed in both the primary and general elections, Rep. John P. Murtha still spent $795,101. Less than $10,000 of that total was spent on advertising and persuasion mail, while overhead expenses amounted to $364,774.

Murtha spent $377,282 to keep his campaign engine running smoothly during 1991, 46 percent of which was invested in overhead. Monthly rent on his Johnstown campaign office was $400. Salaries and payroll taxes amounted to $52,979. Fund-raising costs during the off-year amounted to $48,726.

Over the two-year cycle, Murtha spent $46,177 on his campaign automobiles. Throughout the first seventeen months of the cycle, the campaign leased a 1989 Ford Crown Victoria from Central Transportation in Ebensburg. In May 1992 Murtha used $7,000 of his campaign treasury to buy out the lease. One car was apparently not enough, and in September 1991 he began leasing a second car from Jim Dewar Olds Leasing in Johnstown. Total lease and purchase payments were $28,180. The campaign spent $8,103 to repair the cars, $5,886 to license and register them, and $4,008 to fuel them.

Murtha invested $45,395 of his treasury in constituent stroking. He spent $19,864 on gifts, including baubles from Lenox China and sweets from L&D Candies. Tickets to various sporting events cost the campaign $8,513—$3,804 for season tickets to Pittsburgh Steeler football games, $1,176 for season tickets to Washington Redskins games, $1,804 for Pittsburgh Pirates tickets, $1,080 for University of Pittsburgh at Johnstown football tickets, and $649 for tickets to the Johnstown Chiefs, a minor league baseball club. He spent $6,896 on flowers for constituents, $5,300 on year-end holiday cards, and $4,822 on constituent meals and receptions.

Contributions to other candidates, political party organizations, and causes accounted for 10 percent of Murtha's spending. He bought $11,470 worth of tickets to local party fund-raisers and gave the local parties another $3,755. He donated a total of $17,250 to a host of candidates for local and state offices and bought another $11,195 worth of tickets to their fund-raising events. Dinner tickets and donations to various charitable events amounted to $26,046.

While he had no reason to campaign, Murtha paid $93,043 to the Brier Group of Harrisburg, his general campaign strategist. Helped considerably by redistricting, Murtha still paid Donilon & Petts of Washington, D.C., $19,200 in 1991 for polling. Despite the fact that he had no opposition of any kind, Murtha spent $24,043 on poll watchers. Various get-out-the-vote efforts to benefit his Democratic colleagues cost Murtha's campaign $8,126.

Campaign Expenditures	Murtha Amount Spent	% of Total
Overhead		
Office furniture/supplies	$ 18,850	2.37
Rent/utilities	14,654	1.84
Salaries	83,672	10.52
Taxes	30,579	3.85
Bank/investment fees	1,032	.13
Lawyers/accountants	29,915	3.76
Telephone	25,943	3.26
Campaign automobile	46,177	5.81
Computers/office equipment	36,033	4.53
Travel	58,638	7.37
Food/meetings	19,281	2.43
Subtotal	**364,774**	**45.88**
Fund Raising		
Events	90,579	11.39
Direct mail	0	
Telemarketing	0	
Subtotal	**90,579**	**11.39**
Polling	**19,200**	**2.41**
Advertising		
Electronic media	80	.01
Other media	6,247	.79
Subtotal	**6,327**	**.80**
Other Campaign Activity		
Persuasion mail/brochures	3,077	.39
Actual campaigning	147,464	18.55
Staff/volunteers	808	.10
Subtotal	**151,349**	**19.04**
Constituent Gifts/Entertainment	**45,395**	**5.71**
Donations to		
Candidates from same state	32,495	4.09
Candidates from other states	3,401	.43
Civic organizations	26,046	3.28
Ideological groups	1,615	.20
Political parties	17,224	2.17
Subtotal	**80,782**	**10.16**
Unitemized Expenses	**36,694**	**4.62**
Total Campaign Expenses	$ **795,101**	
PAC Contributions	$ 540,060	
Individual Contributions	384,609	
Total Receipts*	935,459	

*Includes PAC and individual contributions as well as interest earned, party contributions, etc.

PENNSYLVANIA — District 13

Rep. Marjorie Margolies-Mezvinsky (D)

1992 Election Results

Marjorie Margolies-Mezvinsky (D)	127,685	(50%)
Jon D. Fox (R)	126,312	(50%)

When Republican Rep. Lawrence Coughlin announced he would not seek a thirteenth term, most observers assumed his replacement would come from the Republican hopefuls. No Democrat had represented the area in Congress since 1916. However, in the "Year of the Woman," Democrat Marjorie Margolies-Mezvinsky, a former television reporter, proved the pundits wrong.

Margolies-Mezvinsky's only opposition in the Democratic primary came from Bernard Tomkin, the party's 1990 nominee who had spent $16,177 on his anemic challenge to Coughlin. Tomkin was no better funded in 1992 and put just $8,361 into the primary. Margolies-Mezvinsky coasted to victory, spending $38,338 and collecting 79 percent of the vote.

In the general election Margolies-Mezvinsky faced heavily favored Montgomery County commissioner and former state representative Jon D. Fox. She paid Trippi, McMahon & Squier of Alexandria, Va., $234,050 to create and place two television commercials. While substantial, that investment was primarily channeled into air time on network affiliates, which meant she could only afford to run the spots over the final two weeks of the campaign.

Margolies-Mezvinsky came out firing with a commercial that featured a black-and-white photograph of Fox popping in and out of gopher holes marked "Tax" and "Run." Accusing Fox of voting for fourteen tax increases and running for office nine times in fourteen years, the ad proclaimed, "Most politicians tax and spend, but politician Jon Fox taxes and runs. And after Jon Fox raises your taxes, you're never sure where he'll pop up next." Included in the tax votes was one he did not make and such items as a vote for a twenty-five-cent parking meter fee. A second spot touted her endorsements by various newspapers.

At the grass-roots level, Margolies-Mezvinsky invested $31,742 in an in-house phonebank that targeted Republican women with the message that Fox favored some restrictions on abortion. Beginning with eight telephones, the phonebank expanded to nearly forty lines by election day. The campaign spent $6,729 on yard signs, $1,439 on T-shirts, and $7,150 on opposition research.

For organizing volunteers, handling the press, and helping to raise money, eight employees drew after-tax salaries totaling $140,261. Driven by payroll, which accounted for 21 percent of her total outlays, Margolies-Mezvinsky's overhead totaled $209,075.

Fox spent the bulk of his $190,644 broadcast advertising budget on radio and cable television spots, buying $72,895 worth of air time over the final two weeks. The Republican National Committee spent $25,000 to pay for air time, as well.

Campaign Expenditures	Margolies-Mezvinsky Amount Spent	% of Total	Fox Amount Spent	% of Total
Overhead				
Office furniture/supplies	$ 8,110	1.22	$ 6,573	.90
Rent/utilities	4,306	.65	17,006	2.32
Salaries	140,261	21.04	127,510	17.42
Taxes	21,803	3.27	0	
Bank/investment fees	126	.02	244	.03
Lawyers/accountants	807	.12	3,866	.53
Telephone	6,214	.93	18,680	2.55
Campaign automobile	0		0	
Computers/office equipment	12,842	1.93	11,591	1.58
Travel	12,700	1.90	3,346	.46
Food/meetings	1,908	.29	2,931	.40
Subtotal	209,075	31.36	191,748	26.20
Fund Raising				
Events	41,347	6.20	32,920	4.50
Direct mail	16,879	2.53	33,799	4.62
Telemarketing	0		0	
Subtotal	58,226	8.73	66,719	9.12
Polling	27,660	4.15	0	
Advertising				
Electronic media	234,050	35.10	190,644	26.05
Other media	2,920	.44	10,230	1.40
Subtotal	236,970	35.54	200,874	27.44
Other Campaign Activity				
Persuasion mail/brochures	44,609	6.69	176,903	24.17
Actual campaigning	49,958	7.49	74,729	10.21
Staff/volunteers	1,382	.21	4,780	.65
Subtotal	95,949	14.39	256,411	35.03
Constituent Gifts/Entertainment	1,000	.15	100	.01
Donations to				
Candidates from same state	0		400	.05
Candidates from other states	0		0	
Civic organizations	295	.04	555	.08
Ideological groups	570	.09	36	
Political parties	875	.13	1,976	.27
Subtotal	1,740	.26	2,967	.41
Unitemized Expenses	36,100	5.41	13,110	1.79
Total Campaign Expenses	$ 666,721		$ 731,929	
PAC Contributions	$ 172,273		$ 168,711	
Individual Contributions	396,415		531,712	
Total Receipts*	568,961		714,397	

*Includes PAC and individual contributions as well as interest earned, party contributions, etc.

District 14 — PENNSYLVANIA

Rep. William J. Coyne (D)

1992 Election Results

William J. Coyne (D)	165,633	(72%)
Byron W. King (R)	61,311	(27%)

Rep. William J. Coyne's five previous reelection campaigns had cost a total of $380,852. His 1992 effort cost $322,982. Coyne invested 31 percent of his treasury in broadcast advertising and only 8 percent in overhead. His Republican challenger, Byron W. King, plowed 38 percent of his $98,776 treasury into overhead and only 2 percent into broadcast ads. As he had in each of his five previous reelection campaigns, Coyne emerged with more than 70 percent of the votes.

Coyne had no campaign office, no telephone bills, and no paid staff during 1991. He spent nothing on lawyers or accountants, nothing on office equipment, and only $66 on miscellaneous supplies. Other than his $3,999 travel bill, his only other overhead expenses were $107 for meals unconnected to fund raising and $40 in bank fees. His off-year fund-raising expenses totaled just $576. By far his largest expenses for the off-year were the $9,365 he put into constituent stroking and the $25,298 he simply gave away to other candidates, Democratic party organizations, and charitable causes. Together, constituent stroking and donations accounted for 73 percent of the $47,700 he spent in 1991.

Over the two-year cycle, Coyne spent $11,247 on year-end holiday cards and $3,670 on constituent meals. Tickets to Pittsburgh Pirates baseball games cost $755. Naval Academy football tickets cost $214. He spent $288 on calendars, $270 on flowers for constituents, and $500 on miscellaneous gifts.

The Democratic primary proved to be as interesting as the general election. Al Guttman, who served as western Pennsylvania finance director for Harris Wofford's successful 1991 Senate campaign, spent $40,211 chastising Coyne for his low-key legislative approach. As Guttman's campaign literature put it, the district deserved a representative who would "do something."

Coyne opened his $600-a-month campaign office in March and paid Cooper & Secrest Associates of Alexandria, Va., $9,950 for conducting his only poll. Preprimary radio commercials produced and placed by Werner, Chepelsky & Partners of Pittsburgh cost $52,720. Campaign literature and persuasion mail added $17,499. Unimpressed by Guttman's charges, primary voters provided Coyne with a three-to-one landslide victory.

King received only $4,000 from the National Republican Congressional Committee, and that money was invested in polling. With King spending virtually nothing on advertising, Coyne had no reason to make an all-out effort. He paid Werner, Chepelsky $48,490 for producing and placing radio spots. Campaign literature and persuasion mail cost $36,648; yard signs and posters added $5,711.

Campaign Expenditures	Coyne Amount Spent	Coyne % of Total	King Amount Spent	King % of Total
Overhead				
Office furniture/supplies	$ 3,581	1.11	$ 727	.74
Rent/utilities	4,800	1.49	12,207	12.36
Salaries	8,237	2.55	20,154	20.40
Taxes	0		0	
Bank/investment fees	85	.03	0	
Lawyers/accountants	0		90	.09
Telephone	1,866	.58	1,311	1.33
Campaign automobile	0		0	
Computers/office equipment	1,450	.45	2,850	2.89
Travel	6,174	1.91	311	.31
Food/meetings	229	.07	77	.08
Subtotal	**26,423**	**8.18**	**37,727**	**38.19**
Fund Raising				
Events	23,649	7.32	5,636	5.71
Direct mail	0		2,481	2.51
Telemarketing	0		0	
Subtotal	**23,649**	**7.32**	**8,117**	**8.22**
Polling	**9,950**	**3.08**	**0**	
Advertising				
Electronic media	101,210	31.34	1,831	1.85
Other media	16,789	5.20	8,785	8.89
Subtotal	**117,999**	**36.53**	**10,617**	**10.75**
Other Campaign Activity				
Persuasion mail/brochures	57,147	17.07	22,968	23.25
Actual campaigning	14,232	4.41	12,495	12.65
Staff/volunteers	725	.22	67	.07
Subtotal	**70,104**	**21.71**	**35,530**	**35.97**
Constituent Gifts/ Entertainment	**16,944**	**5.25**	**0**	
Donations to				
Candidates from same state	12,610	3.90	0	
Candidates from other states	1,100	.34	0	
Civic organizations	22,254	6.89	45	.05
Ideological groups	2,937	.91	20	.02
Political parties	14,196	4.40	260	.26
Subtotal	**53,097**	**16.44**	**325**	**.33**
Unitemized Expenses	**4,817**	**1.49**	**6,461**	**6.54**
Total Campaign Expenses	**$ 322,982**		**$ 98,776**	
PAC Contributions	$ 172,007		$ 8,000	
Individual Contributions	78,535		46,896	
Total Receipts*	264,042		72,141	

*Includes PAC and individual contributions as well as interest earned, party contributions, etc.

PENNSYLVANIA

District 15

Rep. Paul McHale (D)

1992 Election Results

Paul McHale (D)	111,419	(52%)
Don Ritter (R)	99,520	(47%)

With $572,720 less to spend than seven-term Rep. Don Ritter, former state representative Paul McHale depended heavily on free media. "*The Morning Call* covers most of the district and gave the race extensive coverage," recalled McHale. "Debates were broadcast live, and news stories the next day would note when they would be rebroadcast. That's why I could communicate effectively against someone who outspent me by nearly three to one." Following the example of Democratic presidential nominee Bill Clinton, McHale also used the free media to respond quickly to every charge Ritter made. "We anticipated his criticisms and prepared to hold a news conference shortly after he would accuse me of something."

With his sizable cash advantage, Ritter struck first with ads attacking McHale for accepting free health care for life and other perks associated with his tenure in the state legislature. "I couldn't afford to go on the air for thirty days while he aired those ads," noted McHale, a Marine Corps veteran who served two tours in the Persian Gulf. "He ran the commercials up until election day, trying to show I was tied to the public trough, but I lost those health benefits when I resigned from the legislature to fight in the Gulf War."

Through the debates and his relatively limited advertising efforts, McHale in turn hammered Ritter for accepting $162,000 in speaking fees during his House tenure, accepting free trips to Las Vegas and Palm Springs, spending heavily on franked mail, spending more on his congressional office than any member of the state delegation, and being an ineffective legislator. On policy issues, McHale criticized Ritter's votes against the Family and Medical Leave Act and the Brady Bill. Harris & Drutt of Philadelphia collected $15,988 from McHale and $10,000 from the Democratic Congressional Campaign Committee for creating and placing cable television commercials.

McHale stuck with a positive message in his mailers, focusing on health care reform, economic development, and his record in the state legislature. The mailings were tightly targeted to reach undecided voters in precincts where McHale and his advisers felt he would be most competitive. A mailer on gun control was produced, but McHale had no money to send it.

To identify likely supporters and encourage them to turn out, McHale paid Precision Marketing of Easton $35,218 for phonebanking. Cooper & Secrest Associates of Alexandria, Va., collected $18,388 for polling. McHale's only fund-raiser, Kimberly A. Scott of Washington, D.C., received $12,464 for orchestrating political action committee (PAC) receptions, aimed primarily at Labor PACs.

Campaign Expenditures	McHale Amount Spent	McHale % of Total	Ritter Amount Spent	Ritter % of Total
Overhead				
Office furniture/supplies	$ 1,580	.51	$ 9,089	1.03
Rent/utilities	11,398	3.66	12,301	1.39
Salaries	56,409	18.13	58,651	6.64
Taxes	0		20,417	2.31
Bank/investment fees	199	.06	64	.01
Lawyers/accountants	0		3,650	.41
Telephone	10,353	3.33	11,443	1.29
Campaign automobile	0		0	
Computers/office equipment	6,096	1.96	3,804	.43
Travel	3,629	1.17	3,711	.42
Food/meetings	214	.07	0	
Subtotal	89,877	28.88	123,130	13.93
Fund Raising				
Events	27,215	8.75	86,377	9.77
Direct mail	0		12,035	1.36
Telemarketing	940	.30	0	
Subtotal	28,155	9.05	98,413	11.13
Polling	18,388	5.91	20,282	2.29
Advertising				
Electronic media	17,940	5.77	373,169	42.22
Other media	7,750	2.49	7,133	.81
Subtotal	25,690	8.26	380,302	43.03
Other Campaign Activity				
Persuasion mail/brochures	87,570	28.14	110,541	12.51
Actual campaigning	46,782	15.03	107,198	12.13
Staff/volunteers	0		142	.02
Subtotal	134,351	43.18	217,881	24.65
Constituent Gifts/Entertainment	7,922	2.55	2,396	.27
Donations to				
Candidates from same state	80	.03	5,700	.64
Candidates from other states	0		1,000	.11
Civic organizations	2,836	.91	8,986	1.02
Ideological groups	148	.05	448	.05
Political parties	485	.16	17,957	2.03
Subtotal	3,549	1.14	34,090	3.86
Unitemized Expenses	3,234	1.04	7,393	.84
Total Campaign Expenses	$ 311,166		$ 883,886	
PAC Contributions	$ 109,450		$ 500,652	
Individual Contributions	87,024		334,274	
Total Receipts*	223,578		890,459	

*Includes PAC and individual contributions as well as interest earned, party contributions, etc.

District 16 — PENNSYLVANIA

Rep. Robert S. Walker (R)

1992 Election Results

Robert S. Walker (R)   137,823   (65%)
Robert Peters (D)   74,741   (35%)

Having won his seven previous reelection bids by margins of two to one or better, Rep. Robert S. Walker had little reason to worry about Democrat Robert Peters. While the district had been significantly redrawn, the process did little to alter its overwhelmingly Republican character. Nevertheless, Walker spent $60,193 more in 1992 than he had in 1990.

Redistricting presented Walker with a constituency that was 50 percent new to him. This translated into a $30,626 increase over 1990 in expenditures for advertising and persuasion mail. Faced with an opponent who spent less than $5,000, Walker had opted in 1990 not to hire a media consultant. In 1992 he paid Brabender Cox of Pittsburgh $58,226 for designing and placing his broadcast and newspaper advertising and handling his voter contact mail. According to campaign treasurer Gregory Sahd, the theme running through all of Walker's voter outreach was, "Rep. Walker is the best friend the taxpayer ever had, fighting against pork-barrel spending."

Walker invested sparingly in traditional grass-roots campaigning. He spent only $1,964 on signs, $1,000 in support of the state party's get-out-the-vote effort, $561 on window decals, and $150 on his petition drive. Fees to send a staffer to campaign school totaled $165. Campaign photos added $605. However, unlike 1990, Walker opened a campaign office, paying rent to the Republican Committee of Lancaster County over the final six months of the campaign.

Contributions to Republican party organizations, candidates, and charitable causes increased by $7,383 over 1990. By far, the greatest beneficiary of Walker's generosity was the Republican Committee of Lancaster County, which received $28,691. Otherwise, Walker made numerous, small contributions. For example, when former Pennsylvania governor and United States Attorney General Dick Thornburgh was locked in a 1991 special election fight with Democrat Harris Wofford to fill the vacancy created by the death of Republican Sen. John Heinz, Walker sent him a check for $250. On October 2, 1992 he made $100 donations to nine Republican congressional challengers and open seat candidates in Pennsylvania.

To help pay for his modest campaign, Walker briefly hired Maxwell & Associates of Alexandria, Va. For their $3,495 fee, the fund-raising event planners helped Walker collect about one-third more from political action committees than he had in 1990, when he hired no fund-raising consultants. Anticipating that future campaigns might cost significantly more, Sahd said that Walker has continued to look for new ways to raise money, including a possible foray into direct mail.

Campaign Expenditures	Walker Amount Spent	Walker % of Total	Peters Amount Spent	Peters % of Total
Overhead				
Office furniture/supplies	$ 2,286	1.44	$ 618	5.90
Rent/utilities	4,600	2.90	250	2.38
Salaries	0		0	
Taxes	803	.51	0	
Bank/investment fees	10	.01	0	
Lawyers/accountants	0		0	
Telephone	1,178	.74	346	3.30
Campaign automobile	0		0	
Computers/office equipment	2,226	1.40	0	
Travel	9,203	5.80	0	
Food/meetings	1,937	1.22	0	
Subtotal	**22,243**	**14.03**	**1,215**	**11.58**
Fund Raising				
Events	21,784	13.74	0	
Direct mail	0		0	
Telemarketing	0		0	
Subtotal	**21,784**	**13.74**	**0**	
Polling	**0**		**0**	
Advertising				
Electronic media	23,022	14.52	3,033	28.92
Other media	5,566	3.51	0	
Subtotal	**28,588**	**18.03**	**3,033**	**28.92**
Other Campaign Activity				
Persuasion mail/brochures	33,596	21.19	2,722	25.96
Actual campaigning	4,445	2.80	1,807	17.23
Staff/volunteers	792	.50	0	
Subtotal	**38,834**	**24.49**	**4,529**	**43.18**
Constituent Gifts/ Entertainment	1,635	1.03	0	
Donations to				
Candidates from same state	3,182	2.01	0	
Candidates from other states	2,450	1.55	0	
Civic organizations	541	.34	64	.61
Ideological groups	50	.03	0	
Political parties	39,245	24.75	0	
Subtotal	**45,468**	**28.67**	**64**	**.61**
Unitemized Expenses	16	.01	1,647	15.71
Total Campaign Expenses	$ **158,569**		$ **10,488**	
PAC Contributions	$ 58,350		$ 5,305	
Individual Contributions	71,167		4,578	
Total Receipts*	134,434		10,509	

*Includes PAC and individual contributions as well as interest earned, party contributions, etc.

PENNSYLVANIA   District 17

Rep. George W. Gekas (R)   *1992 Election Results*   George W. Gekas (R)   150,158   (70%)
                                                          Bill Sturges (D)   65,881   (30%)

Republican Rep. George W. Gekas likes expensive automobiles. When it was revealed that he had been tapping his congressional office account for $883 a month to lease a car from the Pennsylvania Leasing Corp. in Harrisburg, he rationalized that "I did have a luxury car, but I have never once had a haircut that was subsidized or spent a nickel for foreign travel, never bounced a check, and every year I turn money back to the treasury from my expense account. I don't use a beeper or car phone."

Gekas also realized a public relations disaster when he saw one. In April 1992 he stopped paying for the car out of his congressional office account and started paying for it with his campaign money. When his lease expired in July, he used $3,851 of his campaign treasury for a down payment on a new car, which cost $963 each month. Over the final nine months of the election cycle, Gekas spent $8,535 on his cars.

The 1992 campaign marked the first time since 1986 that Gekas had faced Democratic opposition, and in response he increased his spending from $93,205 in 1990 to $190,890 in 1992. Even so, while he outspent Democrat Bill Sturges by a margin of three to one, Gekas's outlays were less than half as much as the typical safe incumbent spent.

Gekas did not maintain a permanent campaign office and had no paid staff during 1991. With off-year overhead and fund-raising costs of $12,944 and $13,239, respectively, Gekas managed to hold his 1991 spending to $41,385.

For the campaign itself, Hood, Light & Geise of Harrisburg handled all Gekas's advertising, collecting $77,091 for creating and placing radio, television, newspaper, and billboard ads. The ads focused on his constituent service efforts, and although they did not mention specific federal projects he had brought to the district, they pointed to the value of his legislative experience. According to Allan W. Cagnoli, Gekas's administrative assistant, the billboards and newspaper ads were targeted primarily at new constituents acquired through redistricting.

Gekas invested little in other campaign activities. He spent just $4,538 on campaign literature and persuasion mailings. Yard signs, bumper stickers, buttons, and other campaign paraphernalia cost $4,291.

Gekas tapped his campaign cash reserves for 41 percent of the money he spent during the 1992 election cycle. He paid Dan Morgan & Associates of Arlington, Va., $3,598 for designing invitations to political action committee receptions that yielded $68,435. Only $25,250 was raised from individual contributors in Pennsylvania.

	Gekas		Sturges	
Campaign Expenditures	Amount Spent	% of Total	Amount Spent	% of Total
Overhead				
Office furniture/supplies	$ 2,983	1.56	$ 393	.67
Rent/utilities	5,359	2.81	867	1.47
Salaries	0		6,663	11.29
Taxes	2,589	1.36	0	
Bank/investment fees	0		82	.14
Lawyers/accountants	16,339	8.56	4,000	6.78
Telephone	206	.11	1,446	2.45
Campaign automobile	8,535	4.47	0	
Computers/office equipment	0		0	
Travel	2,463	1.29	2,560	4.34
Food/meetings	1,825	.96	40	.07
Subtotal	**40,297**	**21.11**	**16,051**	**27.19**
Fund Raising				
Events	28,352	14.85	4,264	7.22
Direct mail	0		0	
Telemarketing	0		0	
Subtotal	**28,352**	**14.85**	**4,264**	**7.22**
Polling	**0**		**7,000**	**11.86**
Advertising				
Electronic media	56,011	29.34	0	
Other media	21,280	11.15	5,594	9.48
Subtotal	**77,291**	**40.49**	**5,594**	**9.48**
Other Campaign Activity				
Persuasion mail/brochures	4,538	2.38	24,238	41.06
Actual campaigning	7,505	3.93	725	1.23
Staff/volunteers	606	.32	0	
Subtotal	**12,649**	**6.63**	**24,963**	**42.29**
Constituent Gifts/ Entertainment	**1,616**	**.85**	**0**	
Donations to				
Candidates from same state	1,590	.83	25	.04
Candidates from other states	0		0	
Civic organizations	0		33	.06
Ideological groups	0		35	.06
Political parties	14,353	7.52	61	.10
Subtotal	**15,943**	**8.35**	**155**	**.26**
Unitemized Expenses	**14,741**	**7.72**	**1,000**	**1.69**
Total Campaign Expenses	**$ 190,890**		**$ 59,027**	
PAC Contributions	$ 68,435		$ 21,300	
Individual Contributions	26,700		20,789	
Total Receipts*	112,141		47,235	

*Includes PAC and individual contributions as well as interest earned, party contributions, etc.

District 18 — PENNSYLVANIA

Rep. Rick Santorum (R)

1992 Election Results

Rick Santorum (R)	154,024	(61%)
Frank A. Pecora (D)	96,655	(38%)

Following his 1990 upset victory over seven-term Democratic Rep. Doug Walgren, freshman Rep. Rick Santorum knew he would face a strong challenge in 1992. Democrats outnumbered Republicans by nearly two to one in the redrawn District 18, and these voters would ultimately provide Democratic presidential nominee Bill Clinton with a twenty-two-point margin over President George Bush. "He was not expected to win the first race, and in a district that's 70 percent Democratic, people said there was no way he could win again," recalled Mark D. Rodgers, Santorum's administrative assistant.

Santorum was helped considerably when the ten-candidate Democratic primary was won by Republican state senator Frank A. Pecora, who had switched parties for the race. Santorum also benefited greatly from his change in status. As a challenger in 1990, he had spent $250,877, including $80,723 on advertising and $49,954 on campaign literature and persuasion mail. In 1992 he spent $622,104, including $233,014 on advertising and $155,247 on brochures and advocacy mailings.

As a member of the so called Gang of Seven—Republican freshman who pushed House leaders to release the names of those who had overdrawn their House bank accounts—Santorum had staked claim to the outsider mantle, and he relentlessly hammered home the point. "It's time to declare war on Washington," trumpeted one Santorum mailer. Another, shaped like a boxing glove, urged voters to join the fight to "knock out career politicians." He mailed brochures detailing his plans for economic growth and providing voters with "fifty reasons to vote for Rick Santorum." Yet another piece slammed Pecora for tapping his legislative office account for $600 each month to lease a Lincoln Towncar.

Two of Santorum's three television commercials also focused on the outsider theme. An ad decrying the federal deficit depicted a group of lobbyists ordering champagne at a chic restaurant. When the waiter noted that the selection was expensive, one lobbyist instructed the waiter to send the bill to another table, where a group of children sat with nothing to eat. As Santorum noted that the lobbyist-induced deficit was being passed on to the next generation, the ad concluded with one lobbyist saying, "Oh, I'll just write a check" for the champagne—a not so thinly veiled reference to the House check scandal. Brabender Cox of Pittsburgh received $377,245 for creating and placing Santorum's broadcast advertising, producing brochures, and handling both persuasion mail and direct-mail fund-raising solicitations.

While the National Republican Congressional Committee virtually ignored Santorum's 1990 challenge, it spent $35,000 on his behalf in 1992.

Campaign Expenditures	Santorum Amount Spent	Santorum % of Total	Pecora Amount Spent	Pecora % of Total
Overhead				
Office furniture/supplies	$ 5,626	.90	$ 1,181	.39
Rent/utilities	7,481	1.20	2,464	.81
Salaries	56,626	9.10	25,600	8.46
Taxes	0		0	
Bank/investment fees	0		46	.02
Lawyers/accountants	0		0	
Telephone	10,993	1.77	4,019	1.33
Campaign automobile	0		0	
Computers/office equipment	13,341	2.14	2,130	.70
Travel	14,776	2.38	583	.19
Food/meetings	1,347	.22	2,566	.85
Subtotal	**110,190**	**17.71**	**38,589**	**12.75**
Fund Raising				
Events	47,624	7.66	33,121	10.94
Direct mail	22,646	3.64	0	
Telemarketing	0		0	
Subtotal	**70,269**	**11.30**	**33,121**	**10.94**
Polling	**5,120**	**.82**	**17,526**	**5.79**
Advertising				
Electronic media	231,516	37.22	110,772	36.58
Other media	1,498	.24	14,271	4.71
Subtotal	**233,014**	**37.46**	**125,043**	**41.30**
Other Campaign Activity				
Persuasion mail/brochures	155,247	24.96	64,161	21.19
Actual campaigning	24,585	3.95	22,434	7.41
Staff/volunteers	2,821	.45	0	
Subtotal	**182,653**	**29.36**	**86,595**	**28.60**
Constituent Gifts/ Entertainment	**5,330**	**.86**	**0**	
Donations to				
Candidates from same state	500	.08	0	
Candidates from other states	2,413	.39	0	
Civic organizations	533	.09	350	.12
Ideological groups	0		100	.03
Political parties	1,300	.21	1,100	.36
Subtotal	**4,746**	**.76**	**1,550**	**.51**
Unitemized Expenses	**10,781**	**1.73**	**354**	**.12**
Total Campaign Expenses	**$ 622,104**		**$ 302,779**	
PAC Contributions	**$ 267,454**		**$ 118,300**	
Individual Contributions	356,321		120,725	
Total Receipts*	654,854		288,862	

*Includes PAC and individual contributions as well as interest earned, party contributions, etc.

PENNSYLVANIA — District 19

Rep. Bill Goodling (R)

1992 Election Results

Bill Goodling (R)	98,599	(45%)
Paul V. Kilker (D)	74,798	(34%)
Thomas M. Humbert (I)	44,190	(20%)

Having been named one of the twenty-two worst abusers of the House bank, Rep. Bill Goodling had more than his share of problems heading into the 1992 campaign. First elected in 1974, Goodling had not seen his winning percentage drop below 70 percent in eight previous reelection campaigns. In 1990 the Democrats had not bothered to even field a candidate.

However, Goodling's 430 overdrafts at the House bank changed the political equation dramatically. A poll of district residents taken shortly after the March 1992 bank revelation found only about one-quarter of the electorate inclined to reelect Goodling. Within a month Goodling found himself facing two relatively well-funded challengers—Democratic businessman Paul V. Kilker and Thomas M. Humbert, an independent candidate who had been an aide to Housing and Urban Development Secretary Jack Kemp.

With his $121,077 budget Humbert aired television ads attacking Goodling for his overdrafts, his 1989 vote in favor of the congressional pay raise, and his votes for higher taxes. The same ads accused Kilker of being a tax-and-spend liberal.

Kilker poured $195,000 into broadcast ads designed and placed by the Campaign Group of Philadelphia. While the initial ads were positive, by October he began attacking Goodling for his overdrafts.

Goodling responded by breaking a pledge not to accept contributions of more than $300. Realizing that he would need considerably more than the $40,870 he had spent during the 1990 election cycle, Goodling formed an "Inner Circle" of $1,000 donors. That move helped him increase his individual contributions of $200 or more from $8,775 in 1990 to a still modest $90,479. Despite his considerable need for cash, Goodling did not turn to political action committees (PACs) for help. He collected only 6 percent of his money from PACs.

In early September Goodling began airing radio spots trumpeting the fact that he worked so hard in Congress and burned the midnight oil so often that he knew the cleaning people by name. He signed a pledge not to engage in negative advertising—something his opponents were obviously not about to do. Gannon, McCarthy, Mason of Washington, D.C., collected $11,250 for creating spots touting Goodling's record of delivering for the district. Multi Media Services Corp. of Alexandria, Va., received $23,960 from Goodling and a total of $51,385 from the National Republican Congressional Committee and the Republican National Committee for placing the spots.

He set up a $3,617 in-house phonebank and followed up with persuasion mailers to those identified as undecided. Additional mailers targeted senior citizens and abortion opponents.

Campaign Expenditures	Goodling Amount Spent	Goodling % of Total	Kilker Amount Spent	Kilker % of Total
Overhead				
Office furniture/supplies	$ 2,346	1.17	$ 2,696	.94
Rent/utilities	1,800	.89	800	.28
Salaries	11,726	5.83	11,350	3.98
Taxes	2,931	1.46	0	
Bank/investment fees	0		0	
Lawyers/accountants	2,086	1.04	0	
Telephone	1,842	.92	2,541	.89
Campaign automobile	0		3,000	1.05
Computers/office equipment	5,899	2.93	0	
Travel	1,659	.82	572	.20
Food/meetings	3,926	1.95	0	
Subtotal	34,217	17.01	20,958	7.34
Fund Raising				
Events	27,271	13.55	20,373	7.14
Direct mail	6,888	3.42	2,448	.86
Telemarketing	0		0	
Subtotal	34,158	16.98	22,821	7.99
Polling	4,950	2.46	12,800	4.48
Advertising				
Electronic media	36,379	18.08	195,000	68.30
Other media	7,647	3.80	0	
Subtotal	44,026	21.88	195,000	68.30
Other Campaign Activity				
Persuasion mail/brochures	32,396	16.10	17,093	5.99
Actual campaigning	37,018	18.40	14,162	4.96
Staff/volunteers	1,500	.75	0	
Subtotal	70,914	35.25	31,256	10.95
Constituent Gifts/ Entertainment	0		0	
Donations to				
Candidates from same state	0		0	
Candidates from other states	0		0	
Civic organizations	0		0	
Ideological groups	0		0	
Political parties	5,297	2.63	0	
Subtotal	5,297	2.63	0	
Unitemized Expenses	7,624	3.79	2,689	.94
Total Campaign Expenses	$ 201,187		$ 285,525	
PAC Contributions	$ 12,950		$ 58,142	
Individual Contributions	178,658		38,089	
Total Receipts*	200,014		238,418	

*Includes PAC and individual contributions as well as interest earned, party contributions, etc.

District 20 — PENNSYLVANIA

Rep. Austin J. Murphy (D)

1992 Election Results

Austin J. Murphy (D)   114,898   (51%)
Bill Townsend (R)   111,591   (49%)

Nothing seemed to faze Rep. Austin J. Murphy. Elected in 1976, he had garnered at least 70 percent of the vote in six consecutive reelection bids before slipping to a still-comfortable 63 percent in 1990. Although he had been reprimanded by the House in 1987 for allowing another member to vote for him, for keeping a phantom employee on his government payroll, and for using his official congressional resources for the benefit of his former law firm, he still managed to grab 72 percent of the general election vote in 1988. In 1990 his Democratic primary opponent, candy manufacturer William A. Nicolella, had accused Murphy of having a wife and child in the district and a live-in lover and teenage son born out of wedlock tucked away in suburban Virginia; he prevailed by 40 points in that primary and by 26 points in the general election.

However, persistent rumors that Murphy intended to retire emboldened four Democrats to enter the 1992 primary, including Washington County Commissioner Frank R. Mascara, Nicolella, and Kenneth B. Burkley, who had held Rep. John P. Murtha to 51 percent in the 1990 District 12 Democratic primary. When it was revealed that Murphy had six overdrafts at the House bank, he attracted only 36 percent of the vote and eked out a 2,643-vote victory.

Having spent $64,965 during the off-year, Murphy devoted nearly $128,000 to winning the Democratic nomination. Yet, while he was in the fight of his political life, Murphy invested just $33,907 in broadcast advertising and $12,583 in newspaper ads.

Securing the Democratic nomination in this overwhelmingly Democratic district normally assures victory in November. However, several weeks after the primary it was revealed that Murphy's congressional office records had been subpoenaed in connection with the House Post Office scandal. Although Republican nominee Bill Townsend's budget did not allow for much advertising or persuasion mail, the National Republican Congressional Committee and the Republican National Committee (RNC) sensed an upset in the making and together pumped $53,878 into the race.

With $39,391 of this cash infusion, Townsend mailed an attack piece that began: "He's been reprimanded, subpoenaed, and even taken the 5th. And now he wants to be your congressman." Townsend augmented his modest $10,528 broadcast advertising budget with $14,487 from the RNC to air radio spots hammering away with the same message.

Murphy countered with $42,827 in broadcast ads and a very limited persuasion mail effort. Inexplicably, he left more than $37,000 in his campaign treasury, despite being engaged in an all-out fight to keep his seat. He won by just 3,307 votes.

Campaign Expenditures	Murphy Amount Spent	Murphy % of Total	Townsend Amount Spent	Townsend % of Total
Overhead				
Office furniture/supplies	$ 676	.22	$ 1,653	3.29
Rent/utilities	857	.28	0	
Salaries	0		11,985	23.84
Taxes	809	.26	0	
Bank/investment fees	25	.01	0	
Lawyers/accountants	4,138	1.34	0	
Telephone	664	.21	1,426	2.84
Campaign automobile	12,886	4.16	1,095	2.18
Computers/office equipment	1,118	.36	0	
Travel	5,387	1.74	1,614	3.21
Food/meetings	10,603	3.43	0	
Subtotal	**37,163**	**12.01**	**17,773**	**35.35**
Fund Raising				
Events	20,010	6.47	2,692	5.35
Direct mail	0		1,253	2.49
Telemarketing	0		0	
Subtotal	**20,010**	**6.47**	**3,944**	**7.84**
Polling	0		0	
Advertising				
Electronic media	76,734	24.80	10,528	20.94
Other media	19,284	6.23	1,114	2.22
Subtotal	**96,017**	**31.03**	**11,643**	**23.16**
Other Campaign Activity				
Persuasion mail/brochures	25,986	8.40	4,692	9.33
Actual campaigning	20,082	6.49	4,890	9.73
Staff/volunteers	1,445	.47	0	
Subtotal	**47,513**	**15.36**	**9,581**	**19.06**
Constituent Gifts/ Entertainment	4,530	1.46	0	
Donations to				
Candidates from same state	2,300	.74	0	
Candidates from other states	0		0	
Civic organizations	40	.01	0	
Ideological groups	300	.10	0	
Political parties	6,755	2.18	0	
Subtotal	**9,395**	**3.04**	**0**	
Unitemized Expenses	**94,801**	**30.64**	**7,338**	**14.59**
Total Campaign Expenses	**$ 309,429**		**$ 50,280**	
PAC Contributions	$ 174,750		$ 7,010	
Individual Contributions	45,301		35,278	
Total Receipts*	235,296		53,209	

*Includes PAC and individual contributions as well as interest earned, party contributions, etc.

PENNSYLVANIA — District 21

Rep. Tom Ridge (R)

1992 Election Results

Tom Ridge (R)	150,729	(68%)
John C. Harkins (D)	70,802	(32%)

Unopposed in 1990, Rep. Tom Ridge had spent $361,265. Opposed in 1992 by Democrat John C. Harkins, a utility repairman with only $15,802 to spend, the five-term incumbent pumped $705,864 into his reelection effort. According to Mark R. Campbell, Ridge's administrative assistant, the increased outlays had nothing to do with Ridge's decision to run for governor, a move he announced in February 1993.

With reapportionment slicing two House seats from Pennsylvania's delegation, Ridge had reason to be concerned about redistricting. While he had no campaign office in the district during 1991, Ridge's trips to and from the district pushed his off-year travel expenses to $24,669, accounting for 19 percent of his 1991 outlays. In 1992 Ridge spent another $43,892 on travel, 87 percent of which appeared to be for trips to and from the district. During the entire 1990 cycle, Ridge had invested only $26,835 in travel.

Mapmakers ultimately extended District 21 southward, taking in most of Butler County. To reach those new voters with broadcast advertising meant buying time in the Pittsburgh media market. "We ran a fairly aggressive campaign in the southern part of the district, and it was about ten times as expensive as what we were used to," noted Campbell. Ridge's broadcast advertising budget increased more than sixfold, from $33,189 in 1990 to $239,293 in 1992. Intended or not, this massive investment in the Pittsburgh market also enabled Ridge to spread his message to a host of voters he did not represent in Congress but whom he hoped to represent as governor.

As in past campaigns, Ridge relied heavily on Brabender Cox of Pittsburgh. Over the two-year cycle, the firm collected $392,928—$238,375 for creating and placing television and radio commercials, $52,264 for producing persuasion mailers, and $102,289 for printing fund-raising invitations and direct-mail solicitations. According to Campbell, most of the broadcast budget was invested in television commercials touting Ridge's "courage, honesty, and integrity—those personal attributes he brought to Congress with him." While the mailers included additional biographical information, they also hammered home the honesty-and-integrity theme.

Engel & Tirak of Erie billed Ridge's campaign $30,700 for creating and placing program and newspaper advertising. Slightly more than half that total, $16,091, was paid during 1991. Ridge invested little in low-tech campaign paraphernalia, spending just $4,620 on yard signs, $1,314 on bumper stickers, and $2,407 on an in-house phonebank. He paid Public Opinion Strategies of Alexandria, Va., $9,000 for a benchmark poll in 1991 and $15,291 for keeping tabs on the electorate in 1992.

Campaign Expenditures	Ridge Amount Spent	Ridge % of Total	Harkins Amount Spent	Harkins % of Total
Overhead				
Office furniture/supplies	$ 7,157	1.01	$ 664	4.29
Rent/utilities	1,986	.28	0	
Salaries	24,178	3.43	0	
Taxes	13,665	1.94	0	
Bank/investment fees	0		20	.13
Lawyers/accountants	300	.04	0	
Telephone	3,815	.54	115	.74
Campaign automobile	0		0	
Computers/office equipment	6,119	.87	11	.07
Travel	68,561	9.71	75	.48
Food/meetings	0		20	.13
Subtotal	**125,782**	**17.82**	**905**	**5.85**
Fund Raising				
Events	99,465	14.09	2,339	15.11
Direct mail	62,446	8.85	0	
Telemarketing	0		0	
Subtotal	**161,911**	**22.94**	**2,339**	**15.11**
Polling	**29,231**	**4.14**	**0**	
Advertising				
Electronic media	239,293	33.90	2,388	15.43
Other media	39,486	5.59	5,824	37.63
Subtotal	**278,779**	**39.49**	**8,212**	**53.06**
Other Campaign Activity				
Persuasion mail/brochures	54,444	7.71	583	3.77
Actual campaigning	11,435	1.62	2,762	17.85
Staff/volunteers	0		0	
Subtotal	**65,878**	**9.33**	**3,345**	**21.61**
Constituent Gifts/Entertainment	**10,696**	**1.52**	**0**	
Donations to				
Candidates from same state	5,450	.77	0	
Candidates from other states	3,750	.53	0	
Civic organizations	1,760	.25	45	.29
Ideological groups	160	.02	0	
Political parties	3,525	.50	629	4.06
Subtotal	**14,645**	**2.07**	**674**	**4.35**
Unitemized Expenses	**18,942**	**2.68**	**0**	
Total Campaign Expenses	**$ 705,864**		**$ 15,476**	
PAC Contributions	$ 299,785		$ 700	
Individual Contributions	209,890		3,815	
Total Receipts*	530,372		15,801	

*Includes PAC and individual contributions as well as interest earned, party contributions, etc.

District 1 — RHODE ISLAND

Rep. Ronald K. Machtley (R)

1992 Election Results

Ronald K. Machtley (R) 135,982 (70%)
David R. Carlin, Jr. (D) 48,092 (25%)

After his upset victory over scandal-plagued Democratic Rep. Fernand J. St Germain in 1988 and an equally hard-fought triumph in 1990, Republican Rep. Ronald K. Machtley got a breather in 1992. Democratic state senator David R. Carlin, Jr., spent just $87,608 on his challenge, which was roughly 10 percent of the amount spent by St Germain in 1988 and 24 percent of the total invested by Democrat Scott Wolf in 1990.

Faced with this weaker challenge, Machtley spent $233,550 less on his 1992 campaign than he had in 1990. He sliced his advertising outlays by $173,160, a drop of 51 percent. He reduced his overhead expenses by $31,050, a 20 percent decline. He cut his fundraising costs by 24 percent, from $124,034 to $94,719. However, Machtley certainly did not ignore the campaign.

Although he had no primary opposition and only weak opposition in the fall campaign, Machtley spent $451,622 during 1992. Nearly $200,000 of that election-year investment was poured into the final month of the campaign. Determined to keep this seat in the Republican column, the Republican National Committee (RNC) and the National Republican Congressional Committee (NRCC) together spent $30,000 on Machtley's behalf.

Much of that spending was funneled through consultants. Smith & Harroff of Alexandria, Va., collected $148,504 from Machtley and $25,000 from the RNC for creating and placing four television and three radio commercials that touted his record of securing federal projects for the district and slammed Carlin's state senate voting record. Public Opinion Strategies, also of Alexandria, Va., received $8,500 from Machtley and $5,000 from the NRCC to cover the cost of polls. Machtley paid Thomas J. Cashill of Barrington $13,000 for providing general strategic advice. James R. Foster & Associates of Carrollton, Texas, collected $10,399 for coordinating the persuasion mail effort. Cherry Communications of Gainesville, Fla., received $10,000 for phonebanking.

Machtley spent $17,023 on ads in newspapers such as the *Newport Daily News, Woonsocket Call, East Providence Post, Providence Journal,* and *Pawtucket Times.* He invested $4,700 in yard signs, $4,207 in bumper stickers and other campaign paraphernalia, and $5,025 on an in-house phonebank.

Having begun the election cycle with cash reserves of only $10,355, Machtley devoted considerable attention to fund raising. He paid Dan Morgan & Associates of Arlington, Va., $16,756 for coordinating political action committee events that helped raise $223,144. A steady stream of direct mail solicitations and numerous small donor events raised $232,550 from individuals who gave less than $200.

Campaign Expenditures	Machtley Amount Spent	Machtley % of Total	Carlin Amount Spent	Carlin % of Total
Overhead				
Office furniture/supplies	$ 9,210	1.66	$ 1,580	1.80
Rent/utilities	10,306	1.86	750	.86
Salaries	51,828	9.35	5,751	6.56
Taxes	26,037	4.70	0	
Bank/investment fees	0		0	
Lawyers/accountants	0		0	
Telephone	12,546	2.26	5,805	6.63
Campaign automobile	0		0	
Computers/office equipment	11,053	1.99	749	.85
Travel	3,853	.70	1,749	2.00
Food/meetings	2,003	.36	0	
Subtotal	126,837	22.89	16,383	18.70
Fund Raising				
Events	62,331	11.25	11,730	13.39
Direct mail	32,388	5.84	1,843	2.10
Telemarketing	0		0	
Subtotal	94,719	17.09	13,573	15.49
Polling	13,200	2.38	1,000	1.14
Advertising				
Electronic media	148,980	26.88	35,666	40.71
Other media	18,818	3.40	3,168	3.62
Subtotal	167,798	30.28	38,834	44.33
Other Campaign Activity				
Persuasion mail/brochures	72,384	13.06	683	.78
Actual campaigning	39,052	7.05	9,462	10.80
Staff/volunteers	1,878	.34	0	
Subtotal	113,314	20.45	10,146	11.58
Constituent Gifts/Entertainment	12,472	2.25	0	
Donations to				
Candidates from same state	0		750	.86
Candidates from other states	0		0	
Civic organizations	706	.13	0	
Ideological groups	0		0	
Political parties	7,750	1.40	0	
Subtotal	8,456	1.53	750	.86
Unitemized Expenses	17,421	3.14	6,923	7.90
Total Campaign Expenses	$ 554,217		$ 87,608	
PAC Contributions	$ 223,144		$ 43,750	
Individual Contributions	369,501		38,051	
Total Receipts*	608,563		92,189	

*Includes PAC and individual contributions as well as interest earned, party contributions, etc.

RHODE ISLAND — District 2

Rep. Jack Reed (D)

1992 Election Results

Jack Reed (D)	144,450	(71%)
James W. Bell (R)	49,998	(24%)

Rep. Jack Reed quickly settled into the permanent campaign mode following his election to the House in 1990. While his 1992 effort cost $228,638 less than the 1990 contest, Reed increased his spending on overhead by $159,786 for the second race. Overhead accounted for 43 percent of Reed's 1992 spending.

Excluding 1990 debt repayments, Reed spent $213,068 on his permanent campaign during 1991. His off-year overhead amounted to $137,024, including $69,155 in salaries, bonuses, and benefits. Payroll taxes amounted to $24,638; interest on his outstanding loans totaled $10,190. He also spent $10,077 on computer equipment and software, $4,550 on rent and utilities, and $3,909 on office supplies. His telephone bills amounted to $7,563.

Saddled with 1990 debts totaling $219,277 and cash reserves of only $6,152, Reed invested $45,094 in fund-raising events during 1991 that helped him raise $352,601.

Reed reduced his spending for the 1992 election cycle by slashing his investment in direct appeals for votes by $363,161. While advertising, persuasion mail, and various expenditures for grass-roots organization consumed 65 percent of his $907,295 budget in 1990, such outlays accounted for only 34 percent of the $678,657 he spent during the 1992 election cycle.

For the primary contest with former state representative Spenser E. Dickinson, Reed aired two television commercials. On the positive side, one ad trumpeted the fact that Reed had no overdrafts at the House bank and had donated his congressional pay raise to start a college scholarship fund. The other ad accused Dickinson of missing 40 percent of the votes during his tenure in the state legislature, noted that Reed had been present for 99 percent of the votes during his first House term, and wrapped up by reciting the scholarships Reed's congressional pay raise had financed.

For the general election campaign against underfunded building contractor James W. Bell, ads on job creation and Reed's efforts to make college financial aid available to the middle class were added to the mix. Fenn & King Communications of Washington, D.C., collected $185,115 for creating and placing the ads. Production costs totaled $11,703.

Given the lack of strong competition, Reed invested only $9,023 in campaign literature and voter contact mailings—$110,928 less than he spent on such items in 1990. His grass-roots campaign activity cost only $22,292, or about one-third of what he spent on rallies, buttons, bumper stickers, and get-out-the-vote efforts in 1990.

Bell invested only $20,815 in direct appeals for votes and was never a threat to unseat Reed.

Campaign Expenditures	Reed Amount Spent	Reed % of Total	Bell Amount Spent	Bell % of Total
Overhead				
Office furniture/supplies	$ 4,376	.64	$ 531	1.35
Rent/utilities	10,150	1.50	1,200	3.06
Salaries	153,485	22.62	0	
Taxes	50,469	7.44	0	
Bank/investment fees	14,319	2.11	0	
Lawyers/accountants	20,220	2.98	0	
Telephone	13,223	1.95	3,810	9.71
Campaign automobile	0		0	
Computers/office equipment	18,629	2.74	282	.72
Travel	3,487	.51	0	
Food/meetings	359	.05	0	
Subtotal	**288,715**	**42.54**	**5,823**	**14.83**
Fund Raising				
Events	73,245	10.79	6,239	15.89
Direct mail	3,181	.47	0	
Telemarketing	5,156	.76	0	
Subtotal	**81,582**	**12.02**	**6,239**	**15.89**
Polling	**22,500**	**3.32**	**1,728**	**4.40**
Advertising				
Electronic media	196,818	29.00	5,363	13.66
Other media	1,541	.23	3,000	7.64
Subtotal	**198,359**	**29.23**	**8,363**	**21.30**
Other Campaign Activity				
Persuasion mail/brochures	9,023	1.33	8,207	20.90
Actual campaigning	22,292	3.28	4,245	10.81
Staff/volunteers	0		0	
Subtotal	**31,315**	**4.61**	**12,452**	**31.71**
Constituent Gifts/ Entertainment	4,304	.63	0	
Donations to				
Candidates from same state	0		0	
Candidates from other states	0		0	
Civic organizations	500	.07	0	
Ideological groups	0		0	
Political parties	0		0	
Subtotal	**500**	**.07**	**0**	
Unitemized Expenses	**51,382**	**7.57**	**4,658**	**11.86**
Total Campaign Expenses	**$ 678,657**		**$ 39,262**	
PAC Contributions	**$ 416,190**		**$ 0**	
Individual Contributions	**322,237**		**34,285**	
Total Receipts*	**816,308**		**39,695**	

*Includes PAC and individual contributions as well as interest earned, party contributions, etc.

District 1 — SOUTH CAROLINA

Rep. Arthur Ravenel, Jr. (R)

1992 Election Results

Arthur Ravenel, Jr. (R) 121,938 (66%)
Bill Oberst (D) 59,908 (33%)

Rep. Arthur Ravenel, Jr., was seeking a fourth term in 1992, but he was already running for governor in 1994. Having spent just $3,522 on fund raising during his virtually uncontested 1990 campaign, Ravenel sank $22,088 into a single event in March 1992. The dinner, held to coincide with the incumbent's sixty-fifth birthday, netted roughly $50,000. "We made a bigger effort for the birthday party in 1992 because we knew we were running for governor," noted Sharon H. Chellis, Ravenel's administrative assistant.

A big fan of the late Elvis Presley, Ravenel listed him in the birthday fund-raiser program as a member of the host committee. Ravenel paid an Elvis impersonator $250 to attend the party and spent $30 to have the entertainer's costume altered. He hired the Show Band of the South for $3,000 and paid a stage manager $212 to orchestrate the evening's events. Catering charges amounted to $14,413.

Ravenel held no events in Washington, D.C., preferring to gather his political action committee (PAC) contributions closer to home. The campaign's lone PAC reception was held in December 1991 at the Governor T. Bennett House in Charleston. For a modest investment of $3,067, plus the cost of invitations, Ravenel raised PAC contributions totaling $127,076.

In addition to a third reception in October 1992, Ravenel mailed fund-raising solicitations to a list of loyal supporters twice each year, reminding them that running for office is expensive. "It helps keep money coming in all the time," Chellis said.

These fund-raising efforts and the lack of strong opposition allowed Ravenel to increase his cash reserves from $284,458 to $430,586. On December 28, 1992, less than two months after winning reelection, Ravenel transferred those reserves into his gubernatorial campaign account.

The general election contest with Democrat Bill Oberst was uneventful. Elected in 1986, Ravenel had won reelection twice by margins of two to one, and 1992 proved no different. He invested only $31,102 in broadcast advertising. According to Chellis, the three television and three radio commercials aired over the final six weeks of the campaign, stressing Ravenel's constituent service, his efforts to save the Charleston naval shipyard, the importance of defense conversion projects to economic development, and health care. "With the trend toward Clinton, we were a little worried," explained Chellis. "Our opponent appealed to a younger, hipper audience, but he didn't have the name recognition he needed."

Lacking the resources to increase his notoriety, Oberst never mounted a serious threat.

Campaign Expenditures	Ravenel Amount Spent	Ravenel % of Total	Oberst Amount Spent	Oberst % of Total
Overhead				
Office furniture/supplies	$ 2,751	2.02	$ 1,496	2.80
Rent/utilities	7,657	5.63	2,800	5.25
Salaries	6,929	5.09	4,919	9.22
Taxes	11,737	8.62	2,581	4.84
Bank/investment fees	223	.16	0	
Lawyers/accountants	1,600	1.18	0	
Telephone	991	.73	3,344	6.26
Campaign automobile	0		0	
Computers/office equipment	5,064	3.72	3,851	7.21
Travel	5,967	4.38	1,073	2.01
Food/meetings	246	.18	0	
Subtotal	**43,165**	**31.72**	**20,064**	**37.59**
Fund Raising				
Events	33,695	24.76	3,570	6.69
Direct mail	3,722	2.73	3,942	7.38
Telemarketing	0		0	
Subtotal	**37,417**	**27.49**	**7,512**	**14.07**
Polling	**0**		**0**	
Advertising				
Electronic media	31,102	22.85	9,174	17.19
Other media	1,520	1.12	1,053	1.97
Subtotal	**32,622**	**23.97**	**10,227**	**19.16**
Other Campaign Activity				
Persuasion mail/brochures	1,103	.81	3,914	7.33
Actual campaigning	5,616	4.13	5,643	10.57
Staff/volunteers	191	.14	0	
Subtotal	**6,911**	**5.08**	**9,557**	**17.90**
Constituent Gifts/ Entertainment	23	.02	0	
Donations to				
Candidates from same state	8,000	5.88	0	
Candidates from other states	1,500	1.10	0	
Civic organizations	1,731	1.27	0	
Ideological groups	1,480	1.09	0	
Political parties	**2,990**	**2.20**	**0**	
Subtotal	**15,701**	**11.54**	**0**	
Unitemized Expenses	255	.19	6,022	11.28
Total Campaign Expenses	$ 136,095		$ 53,382	
PAC Contributions	$ 127,076		$ 0	
Individual Contributions	114,236		24,375	
Total Receipts*	282,816		56,972	

*Includes PAC and individual contributions as well as interest earned, party contributions, etc.

SOUTH CAROLINA — District 2

Rep. Floyd D. Spence (R)

1992 Election Results

Floyd D. Spence (R)	148,667	(88%)
Gebhard Sommer † (I)	20,816	(12%)

For Rep. Floyd D. Spence, the 1992 campaign was a rerun of 1990. His only opposition came from libertarian Gebhard Sommer, who had collected 11 percent of the vote in 1990. As in 1990, Sommer had less than $5,000 to spend on his token challenge. Nevertheless, Spence invested $49,366 more in his 1992 reelection effort than he had in 1990, an increase of 38 percent.

That increased spending was not incurred by his off-year permanent campaign, which cost just $20,888. He had no campaign office and no campaign car. He did not bill his campaign for off-year travel or for meals and entertainment. His payroll was a single $566 payment for secretarial services. His only donation was a $100 payment to the Greater Columbia Chamber of Commerce. He spent $500 to throw a Christmas party for local elected officials.

Spence invested 55 percent of his off-year budget in fund raising. A political action committee (PAC) reception at the Capitol Hill Club cost $6,490, including $3,677 paid to Dan Morgan & Associates of Arlington, Va., for coordinating the affair. Direct Mail Systems of St. Petersburg, Fla., received $4,432 for orchestrating a small direct mail fund-raising effort. His $11,562 fund-raising investment yielded contributions of only $47,819, with 70 percent of this coming from PACs.

This low-key approach continued through much of 1992. GamePlan, his Greenville-based general consultant, did not join the campaign until June and earned only $24,328 for its advice. Spence did not open his campaign headquarters until late September. He also waited until September to hire his only campaign employee, Andrew C. Clarkson III, who collected $3,000 during his brief stay. Spence paid Dan Morgan another $4,025 for coordinating a single PAC event. He held two in-state receptions at the Hilton Head Island Resort and regular in-home receptions but raised just $113,000 during the entire year. He spent nothing on direct-mail solicitations. "He doesn't believe in war chests and I do," noted Randy Mashburn, president of GamePlan. "We have this fight all the time."

Unlike 1990, when he spent nothing on persuasion mail and $10,342 on broadcast ads, Spence depended on free media coverage and a $59,008 persuasion mail campaign to get his message out. "We needed to beef up turnout for the Republican ticket up and down the line," explained Mashburn. "You can target voters much better with mail." Smith, Fairfield of Washington, D.C., received $10,138 for creating two mass mailings and several mailers that targeted the district's farmers.

Campaign Expenditures	Spence Amount Spent	% of Total
Overhead		
Office furniture/supplies	$ 2,786	1.55
Rent/utilities	1,710	.95
Salaries	3,566	1.99
Taxes	0	
Bank/investment fees	0	
Lawyers/accountants	7,039	3.92
Telephone	3,519	1.96
Campaign automobile	0	
Computers/office equipment	7,941	4.42
Travel	1,909	1.06
Food/meetings	0	
Subtotal	**28,471**	**15.86**
Fund Raising		
Events	40,427	22.52
Direct mail	5,072	2.83
Telemarketing	0	
Subtotal	**45,499**	**25.34**
Polling	**0**	
Advertising		
Electronic media	0	
Other media	1,126	.63
Subtotal	**1,126**	**.63**
Other Campaign Activity		
Persuasion mail/brochures	59,008	32.87
Actual campaigning	34,709	19.33
Staff/volunteers	0	
Subtotal	**93,717**	**52.20**
Constituent Gifts/Entertainment	**500**	**.28**
Donations to		
Candidates from same state	0	
Candidates from other states	2,500	1.39
Civic organizations	331	.18
Ideological groups	0	
Political parties	2,000	1.11
Subtotal	**4,831**	**2.69**
Unitemized Expenses	**5,400**	**3.01**
Total Campaign Expenses	**$ 179,544**	
PAC Contributions	**$ 108,900**	
Individual Contributions	**51,919**	
Total Receipts*	**169,036**	

*Includes PAC and individual contributions as well as interest earned, party contributions, etc.

† No expenditures or receipts on file. Candidates raising or spending less than $5,000 are not required to file reports with the Federal Election Commission.

District 3 — SOUTH CAROLINA

Rep. Butler Derrick (D)

1992 Election Results

Butler Derrick (D)	119,119	(61%)
James L. Bland (R)	75,660	(39%)

Rep. Butler Derrick cut his spending from $857,158 in 1990 to $652,239 in 1992—a 24 percent drop. Even so, Derrick spent thirty-two times as much as his Republican challenger, Aiken County Council member James L. Bland.

Derrick spent $107,266 during 1991 to maintain his permanent campaign, including $59,299 on overhead. He paid monthly rent of $300 on his campaign headquarters. After-tax salary payments to five part-time employees totaled $22,253. Payroll and income taxes added $20,886. Fund-raising expenses for the off-year amounted to $27,975.

Over the two-year election cycle, Derrick spent $17,604 on constituent stroking, $13,476 of which was spent on constituent meals. Two such meals at La Brasserie, a pricey Capitol Hill restaurant, cost the campaign $378. Other dinners at some of the Washington area's finest restaurants included a $167 repast at Prime Rib, a $271 meal at La Colline, a $282 dinner at 1789 Restaurant, and two meals totaling $475 at Red Sage. Breakfasts and lunches with constituents at the House restaurant cost $2,575. Another $3,985 was invested in gifts, including baubles from Phil Jewlers in Anderson, S.C., costing $606. Gift boxes of food from Figi's catalog came to $364.

While Bland spent $300 to air his radio ads, including a $200 buy purchased directly by a supporter, Derrick paid Fenn & King Communications of Washington, D.C., $207,022 to create and place his broadcast ads. Miscellaneous production costs added $8,106.

Derrick's initial television commercial, which began airing in early October, focused on rural health care. To distance the nine-term incumbent from his House colleagues, the spot opened with a decidedly outsider comment by Derrick that "Washington does not understand what rural people go through for their health care." The spot proceeded to tout the fact that Derrick had helped save nine rural hospitals. The second commercial, rolled out in mid-October, argued that it was time to stop spending money on Germany and Japan. "It's time for us to come back home, to worry about our country, to worry about our economic base, to worry about our jobs, and to worry about where our country is going." The final spot featured quotes from a local newspaper endorsement, pointing out that Derrick had voted against the pay raise and had never had an account at the House bank. None of the commercials mentioned Bland.

Fund-raising and Management Counsel of Atlanta, Ga., collected $50,000 for orchestrating the persuasion mail effort. Although Bland never posed a serious threat, Derrick paid Kitchens, Powell, & Kitchens of Orlando, Fla., $31,100 for polling.

	Derrick		Bland	
Campaign Expenditures	Amount Spent	% of Total	Amount Spent	% of Total
Overhead				
Office furniture/supplies	$ 3,685	.56	$ 555	2.72
Rent/utilities	12,949	1.98	0	
Salaries	64,930	9.95	1,629	7.99
Taxes	38,620	5.92	0	
Bank/investment fees	818	.13	0	
Lawyers/accountants	0		0	
Telephone	8,695	1.33	857	4.20
Campaign automobile	1,398	.21	0	
Computers/office equipment	4,324	.66	0	
Travel	25,962	3.98	1,116	5.47
Food/meetings	614	.09	0	
Subtotal	**161,994**	**24.83**	**4,157**	**20.38**
Fund Raising				
Events	84,264	12.92	950	4.66
Direct mail	2,774	.43	0	
Telemarketing	0		0	
Subtotal	**87,038**	**13.34**	**950**	**4.66**
Polling	**31,100**	**4.77**	**0**	
Advertising				
Electronic media	215,128	32.98	300	1.47
Other media	425	.07	1,007	4.94
Subtotal	**215,553**	**33.05**	**1,307**	**6.41**
Other Campaign Activity				
Persuasion mail/brochures	83,934	12.87	2,536	12.43
Actual campaigning	6,853	1.05	11,347	55.63
Staff/volunteers	0		0	
Subtotal	**90,787**	**13.92**	**13,883**	**68.06**
Constituent Gifts/ Entertainment	**17,696**	**2.71**	**0**	
Donations to				
Candidates from same state	1,500	.23	0	
Candidates from other states	6,500	1.00	0	
Civic organizations	2,824	.43	0	
Ideological groups	400	.06	0	
Political parties	17,175	2.63	0	
Subtotal	**28,399**	**4.35**	**0**	
Unitemized Expenses	**19,764**	**3.03**	**100**	**.49**
Total Campaign Expenses	**$ 652,332**		**$ 20,397**	
PAC Contributions	$ 469,870		$ 347	
Individual Contributions	173,408		12,477	
Total Receipts*	681,632		17,536	

*Includes PAC and individual contributions as well as interest earned, party contributions, etc.

SOUTH CAROLINA — District 4

Rep. Bob Inglis (R)

1992 Election Results

Bob Inglis (R)	99,879	(50%)
Liz J. Patterson (D)	94,182	(48%)

	Inglis		Patterson	
Campaign Expenditures	Amount Spent	% of Total	Amount Spent	% of Total
Overhead				
Office furniture/supplies	$ 6,654	3.10	$ 3,652	1.31
Rent/utilities	7,223	3.36	5,383	1.93
Salaries	48,689	22.66	34,802	12.50
Taxes	6,523	3.04	10,968	3.94
Bank/investment fees	134	.06	497	.18
Lawyers/accountants	304	.14	0	
Telephone	9,568	4.45	5,745	2.06
Campaign automobile	0		0	
Computers/office equipment	1,707	.79	774	.28
Travel	4,286	1.99	7,171	2.58
Food/meetings	598	.28	107	.04
Subtotal	**85,687**	**39.88**	**69,100**	**24.82**
Fund Raising				
Events	15,568	7.25	28,992	10.41
Direct mail	9,297	4.33	1,616	.58
Telemarketing	0		0	
Subtotal	**24,865**	**11.57**	**30,608**	**10.99**
Polling	**0**		**26,000**	**9.34**
Advertising				
Electronic media	12,467	5.80	93,326	33.52
Other media	33,390	15.54	9,965	3.58
Subtotal	**45,857**	**21.34**	**103,291**	**37.10**
Other Campaign Activity				
Persuasion mail/brochures	38,569	17.95	19,766	7.10
Actual campaigning	19,785	9.21	16,741	6.01
Staff/volunteers	30	.01	692	.25
Subtotal	**58,384**	**27.17**	**37,199**	**13.36**
Constituent Gifts/ Entertainment	**0**		**5,640**	**2.03**
Donations to				
Candidates from same state	0		0	
Candidates from other states	0		0	
Civic organizations	71	.03	1,929	.69
Ideological groups	0		485	.17
Political parties	0		4,175	1.50
Subtotal	**71**	**.03**	**6,589**	**2.37**
Unitemized Expenses	**0**		**0**	
Total Campaign Expenses	**$ 214,865**		**$ 278,427**	
PAC Contributions	$ 0		$ 207,910	
Individual Contributions	196,803		137,682	
Total Receipts*	226,577		351,850	

*Includes PAC and individual contributions as well as interest earned, party contributions, etc.

Few political observers believed attorney Bob Inglis stood much of a chance against Democratic incumbent Liz J. Patterson. Patterson had won three campaigns in a district held by the Republicans for eight years prior to her 1986 open seat victory. Patterson did not appear vulnerable to anti-incumbent attacks, given that she had only two overdrafts at the House bank and had voted against both the 1989 congressional pay raise and the 1990 budget summit agreement. "Most people thought we were nuts to take on an incumbent woman in the Year of the Woman," recalled Jeff Parker, Inglis's campaign manager.

Inglis, who had never sought public office, prevailed by waging an outsider campaign. "Our strategy was to run against Congress, not Patterson," Parker explained. "We said, 'here are some things you don't like about Congress, but guess what, Patterson shares some of those same characteristics.'" In contrast, Inglis portrayed himself as "a citizen statesman, not a career politician."

Lacking the resources to advertise heavily, Inglis primarily distributed his message through a network of volunteers. He spent $32,840 to produce and distribute 3,000 copies of an introductory video, which he gave to supporters with the request that they show it to at least ten friends. The video highlighted his call for term limits, his promise not to serve more than six years in the House, his call for the elimination of political action committees (PACs), and his pledge not to take PAC money. During the campaign's final week, Inglis put $12,467 into broadcast advertising, which was augmented by a $15,900 check from the National Republican Congressional Committee and a $15,000 check from the state Republican party.

Inglis opted not to mail his campaign literature. Instead, volunteers distributed a series of door-hangers, including one attack piece that was left on 75,000 doors. Emblazoned across the red card in black letters were the words, "We elected a Congress that...." Attached pull-up tabs charged that members had bounced checks, been involved in cocaine sales, and made themselves rich at the taxpayers' expense. On the back of each tab, Inglis slammed Patterson for not having done anything about the problem. Inglis spent $5,936 on yard signs that urged voters to "Reclaim Congress" and $5,004 for lapel pins and bumper stickers.

Patterson apparently never realized she was in trouble. "Inglis came from nowhere with no visible means of support," recalled Charles H. Carr, Patterson's press secretary. "Weeks before, both our polls and independent polls showed her ahead by 18 points." She lost by 5,697 votes.

District 5 — SOUTH CAROLINA

Rep. John M. Spratt, Jr. (D)

1992 Election Results

John M. Spratt, Jr. (D)	112,031	(61%)
William T. Horne (R)	70,866	(39%)

In 1990 Rep. John M. Spratt, Jr., ran unopposed and spent only $56,059. In 1992 redistricting brought him roughly 100,000 new constituents spread across three counties. That, coupled with concern over his forty-six overdrafts at the House bank, prompted Spratt to spend $381,747 to dispatch Republican William T. Horne.

Spratt paid Geddings Communications of Alexandria, Va., $184,631 to create and place five television and five radio commercials that never mentioned his overdrafts or his opponent. Instead, they touted Spratt's record of constituent service, his successful efforts to keep Shaw Air Force Base off the base closure hit list, his work on the Armed Services Committee to monitor nuclear waste disposal at the Savannah River nuclear material production plant, and his work on trade issues affecting the textile industry. The campaign directly purchased air time for $11,744. Miscellaneous production charges added $3,160.

Newspaper ads cost Spratt $37,660. A new ad was placed each week for the final five weeks of the campaign in each of the district's daily and weekly newspapers. The final ad listed hundreds of constituents who had agreed to endorse the five-term incumbent, including custodial workers as well as corporate executives. Billboard ads urging people to reelect Spratt cost $4,178. He spent $4,885 on signs and $177 for 1,000 "Vote Today" stickers, which were slapped on the signs on election eve. Bumper stickers and lapel stickers cost $840.

To introduce himself to his new constituents, Spratt mailed brochures to 40,000 households and printed an additional 20,000 brochures that were handed out by volunteers who canvassed neighborhoods and stood at factory gates in the district's three new counties. Total cost: $14,326.

Spratt largely diffused the overdraft issue by taking the offensive. Once the scandal broke, he researched his records, found that he had a problem, and began visiting newsrooms across the district with his documentation. Although Horne repeatedly asked how Spratt could expect to balance the federal budget when he could not balance his own checkbook, voters were not concerned, even though President George Bush carried the district with 45 percent of the vote. To make certain he would be prepared to put out any public relations fires that arose over the checks, Spratt paid Hickman-Brown Research of Washington, D.C., $26,000 to poll his constituents. He spent nothing on polls in 1990.

Outspent on advertising and persuasion mail by a margin of more than five to one, Horne ran 6 percentage points behind the Bush/Quayle ticket and 22 points behind Spratt.

	Spratt		Horne	
Campaign Expenditures	Amount Spent	% of Total	Amount Spent	% of Total
Overhead				
Office furniture/supplies	$ 2,090	.55	$ 315	.31
Rent/utilities	1,800	.47	800	.78
Salaries	9,880	2.59	21,619	21.09
Taxes	5,914	1.55	0	
Bank/investment fees	0		0	
Lawyers/accountants	7,200	1.89	0	
Telephone	2,822	.74	1,798	1.75
Campaign automobile	0		0	
Computers/office equipment	7,508	1.97	150	.15
Travel	2,780	.73	5,511	5.37
Food/meetings	234	.06	0	
Subtotal	**40,228**	**10.54**	**30,193**	**29.45**
Fund Raising				
Events	18,281	4.79	625	.61
Direct mail	0		0	
Telemarketing	0		0	
Subtotal	**18,281**	**4.79**	**625**	**.61**
Polling	**26,000**	**6.81**	**7,900**	**7.71**
Advertising				
Electronic media	199,535	52.27	24,476	23.87
Other media	43,252	11.33	18,818	18.35
Subtotal	**242,787**	**63.60**	**43,294**	**42.23**
Other Campaign Activity				
Persuasion mail/brochures	14,326	3.75	6,138	5.99
Actual campaigning	13,748	3.60	7,653	7.46
Staff/volunteers	0		0	
Subtotal	**28,073**	**7.35**	**13,791**	**13.45**
Constituent Gifts/Entertainment	**1,095**	**.29**	**0**	
Donations to				
Candidates from same state	1,275	.33	0	
Candidates from other states	2,200	.58	0	
Civic organizations	1,923	.50	0	
Ideological groups	2,285	.60	0	
Political parties	17,600	4.61	0	
Subtotal	**25,283**	**6.62**	**0**	
Unitemized Expenses	**0**		**6,727**	**6.56**
Total Campaign Expenses	**$ 381,747**		**$ 102,530**	
PAC Contributions	$ 146,775		$ 350	
Individual Contributions	115,586		8,445	
Total Receipts*	281,855		102,751	

*Includes PAC and individual contributions as well as interest earned, party contributions, etc.

SOUTH CAROLINA   District 6

Rep. James E. Clyburn (D)

1992 Election Results

James E. Clyburn (D)	120,647	(65%)
John R. Chase (R)	64,149	(35%)

When five-term Democratic Rep. Robin Tallon opted to retire rather than run in a redrawn majority-black district, five Democrats jumped into the fray, including South Carolina Human Affairs Commissioner James E. Clyburn, state senators Herbert U. Fielding and Frank Gilbert, and South Carolina State University professor Ken Mosely, who had twice challenged Republican Rep. Floyd D. Spence in District 2.

Clyburn spent nearly $236,000, or 59 percent of his total outlays, prior to the August 25 primary. His media adviser, Morris & Carrick of New York, collected $93,000 for creating and placing television commercials. For the primary Clyburn spent $24,045 on brochures and persuasion mail, $12,325 on billboards, $3,646 on yard signs and posters, and $1,502 on bumper stickers. For providing general strategic advice and preprimary polling services, the Feldman Group of Washington, D.C., received $8,974. Clyburn failed to report nearly $98,000 of his preprimary investment, including all the money paid to Morris & Carrick, until July 26, 1993, when he amended financial statements that had been filed with the Federal Election Commission in October 1992.

Monthly rent on Clyburn's Columbia campaign headquarters, which opened in October 1991, was $1,200. In July 1992 Clyburn began paying $300 a month to rent a second office in Florence. By the end of the primary, ten people had drawn payroll checks totaling $27,131. That did not include the $3,150 he paid election day workers to ensure that supporters who needed a ride to the polls got one. Clyburn emerged with 56 percent of the primary votes.

Clyburn could afford to relax somewhat for his general election contest with John R. Chase, a member of the Florence County Council. Morris & Carrick collected $50,000. He invested another $1,960 in signs, $2,328 in bumper stickers and other campaign paraphernalia, and $6,900 in polls conducted by the Feldman Group.

Payroll added $32,486 down the final stretch. While payroll accounted for 15 percent of his total spending, and his campaign director and press secretary collected "salary" payments for months, Clyburn paid no payroll taxes. Ordinary entrepreneurs are not permitted by federal laws to avoid paying such taxes.

Although campaign records show that Chase spent only $106,791, that significantly understates the financial resources that were committed to his failed efforts to derail Clyburn. The John R. Chase Victory Fund spent $73,584 on a supposedly independent campaign on Chase's behalf, including $32,795 for television advertising and $36,644 for persuasion mail. However, in this solidly Democratic district, these expenditures made little difference.

	Clyburn		Chase	
Campaign Expenditures	Amount Spent	% of Total	Amount Spent	% of Total
Overhead				
Office furniture/supplies	$ 3,430	.86	$ 5,173	4.84
Rent/utilities	22,090	5.56	3,843	3.60
Salaries	59,617	15.01	13,295	12.45
Taxes	0		2,391	2.24
Bank/investment fees	800	.20	275	.26
Lawyers/accountants	5,995	1.51	0	
Telephone	9,011	2.27	4,603	4.31
Campaign automobile	0		0	
Computers/office equipment	3,507	.88	1,449	1.36
Travel	7,482	1.88	330	.31
Food/meetings	408	.10	0	
Subtotal	**112,340**	**28.29**	**31,358**	**29.36**
Fund Raising				
Events	11,421	2.88	3,231	3.03
Direct mail	9,961	2.51	0	
Telemarketing	0		0	
Subtotal	**21,382**	**5.38**	**3,231**	**3.03**
Polling	**12,400**	**3.12**	**0**	
Advertising				
Electronic media	145,944	36.75	12,974	12.15
Other media	18,422	4.64	12,915	12.09
Subtotal	**164,366**	**41.39**	**25,889**	**24.24**
Other Campaign Activity				
Persuasion mail/brochures	33,563	8.45	28,851	27.02
Actual campaigning	39,607	9.97	16,069	15.05
Staff/volunteers	1,088	.27	52	.05
Subtotal	**74,258**	**18.70**	**44,972**	**42.11**
Constituent Gifts/ Entertainment	**1,100**	**.28**	**102**	**.10**
Donations to				
Candidates from same state	0		0	
Candidates from other states	0		0	
Civic organizations	0		55	.05
Ideological groups	467	.12	0	
Political parties	0		36	.03
Subtotal	**467**	**.12**	**91**	**.09**
Unitemized Expenses	**10,776**	**2.71**	**1,149**	**1.08**
Total Campaign Expenses	**$ 397,090**		**$ 106,791**	
PAC Contributions	**$ 101,210**		**$ 900**	
Individual Contributions	**155,595**		**86,005**	
Total Receipts*	**321,121**		**115,338**	

*Includes PAC and individual contributions as well as interest earned, party contributions, etc.

At Large — SOUTH DAKOTA

Rep. Tim Johnson (D)

1992 Election Results

Tim Johnson (D)	230,070	(69%)
John Timmer (R)	89,375	(27%)

Republican John Timmer had a difficult time running a negative campaign against Rep. Tim Johnson. Johnson had no overdrafts at the House bank, had voted against the congressional pay raise, and had supported a constitutional amendment requiring a balanced federal budget. "Unfortunately, he wasn't involved with the House bank, and he hasn't been a bad congressman," Timmer admitted after the campaign. "There was no way we could have won."

Having received at least 68 percent of the vote in his two previous reelection campaigns, Johnson apparently agreed with Timmer's assessment. Although he outspent Timmer by more than two to one, Johnson invested $89,123 less in his 1992 campaign than he had in his 1990 effort.

Johnson slashed his spending on broadcast advertising from $204,852 in 1990 to $111,969 in 1992 by cutting out consultants almost entirely. While Struble-Totten Communications of Washington, D.C., collected $20,000 for creating Johnson's 1990 television and radio spots, his 1992 ads were created in-house and produced at the Democratic Congressional Campaign Committee's Harriman Center. The Media Group of Columbus, Ohio, and Struble-Totten received $1,078 and $877, respectively, to cover miscellaneous 1992 production costs.

In 1992 the Johnson campaign placed its ads directly, reducing its investment in air time to $107,675 from the $150,000 it spent in 1990 using a consultant. "It was a matter of cost effectiveness," explained John Y. Deveraux, Johnson's deputy chief of staff. "In a highly competitive race where you want to be sure each ad is correctly placed to get the most for your money, we would hire a consultant."

Johnson spent $89,906 to air his television ads, which began running the first week of October. During the final week of the campaign, he invested $17,769 to air his radio spots. Both sets of ads focused on the positives of incumbency, touting his work on the Agriculture Committee and his delivery of a federal pipeline project that would bring water to homes and ranches in western South Dakota that had previously depended on wells. Several spots featured constituent testimonials. "It was very clear they weren't actors," noted Deveraux.

Much of Johnson's persuasion mail that targeted farmers and ranchers was signed by farmers and ranchers. Other mailings targeted senior citizens and owners of small businesses. Johnson's $45,044 investment in brochures and mailers was $17,091 less than he spent on such items in 1990.

Johnson spent only $191 on constituent stroking—$164 for meals and $27 for flowers.

	Johnson		Timmer	
Campaign Expenditures	Amount Spent	% of Total	Amount Spent	% of Total
Overhead				
Office furniture/supplies	$ 1,396	.37	$ 2,985	1.84
Rent/utilities	6,620	1.77	6,717	4.14
Salaries	40,033	10.69	23,517	14.51
Taxes	13,166	3.52	6,581	4.06
Bank/investment fees	562	.15	107	.07
Lawyers/accountants	0		0	
Telephone	7,844	2.09	8,538	5.27
Campaign automobile	0		0	
Computers/office equipment	6,347	1.69	2,732	1.69
Travel	21,232	5.67	14,144	8.73
Food/meetings	469	.13	107	.07
Subtotal	**97,669**	**26.08**	**65,428**	**40.36**
Fund Raising				
Events	12,576	3.36	2,975	1.84
Direct mail	22,083	5.90	8,593	5.30
Telemarketing	19,228	5.13	0	
Subtotal	**53,887**	**14.39**	**11,568**	**7.14**
Polling	**7,699**	**2.06**	**1,846**	**1.14**
Advertising				
Electronic media	111,969	29.90	35,946	22.18
Other media	10,101	2.70	14,688	9.06
Subtotal	**122,070**	**32.59**	**50,633**	**31.24**
Other Campaign Activity				
Persuasion mail/brochures	45,044	12.03	5,245	3.24
Actual campaigning	17,548	4.69	24,545	15.14
Staff/volunteers	260	.07	69	.04
Subtotal	**62,853**	**16.78**	**29,859**	**18.42**
Constituent Gifts/ Entertainment	191	.05	30	.02
Donations to				
Candidates from same state	1,000	.27	0	
Candidates from other states	0		0	
Civic organizations	225	.06	0	
Ideological groups	0		80	.05
Political parties	10,150	2.71	0	
Subtotal	**11,375**	**3.04**	**80**	**.05**
Unitemized Expenses	**18,763**	**5.01**	**2,651**	**1.64**
Total Campaign Expenses	**$ 374,505**		**$ 162,095**	
PAC Contributions	$ 221,653		$ 16,330	
Individual Contributions	205,418		99,731	
Total Receipts*	452,528		171,489	

*Includes PAC and individual contributions as well as interest earned, party contributions, etc.

TENNESSEE — District 1

Rep. James H. Quillen (R)

1992 Election Results

James H. Quillen (R)	114,797	(67%)
J. Carr "Jack" Christian † (D)	47,809	(28%)

Neither redistricting, anti-incumbent sentiment, nor realtor J. Carr "Jack" Christian's token challenge fazed Rep. James H. Quillen in 1992. While he spent $67,492 more on his 1992 reelection effort than he had in 1990, Quillen spent nothing on broadcast advertising, newspaper advertising, billboards, or persuasion mail. He invested just $3,511 in yard signs. He spent $2,132 on jackets embossed with "Quillen for Congress" and $1,747 on buttons and bumper stickers.

Overhead accounted for 69 percent of Quillen's $324,889 budget. The $222,686 he invested in his permanent campaign was $50,578 more than he spent to maintain it during the 1990 election cycle, an increase of 29 percent. "I maintain a headquarters year-round, and I've done so since I first came to Congress," explained Quillen. "It's worked for thirty-two years."

Monthly rent on Quillen's campaign headquarters tripled in 1991, from $125 to $375. His full-time office manager, Ida J. Riley, collected after-tax payroll checks totaling $88,455 before leaving the campaign in July 1992. Quillen then turned to two members of his congressional staff, who together collected $12,398 for running the office over the campaign's final two months. In all, salaries and payroll taxes amounted to $148,072, or 46 percent of Quillen's spending.

Taxes on the interest income generated by his $1.2 million cash reserves amounted to $23,633.

Relieved of the need to actively campaign, Quillen pumped $28,032 into constituent stroking. Lunches and dinners with constituents cost the campaign $12,908. He spent $10,801 of his treasury to purchase tickets to various sporting events, including $1,800 for Super Bowl tickets, $1,814 for tickets to the Kentucky Derby, $5,395 for tickets to University of Tennessee football games, and $1,792 for Washington Redskins tickets. Quillen said he attended none of these events, preferring instead to give the tickets to lucky supporters. "What I mainly do is have people from the district come in for a special dinner," Quillen explained. "I haven't been to a Redskins game in twenty-five years. The last time I went, it was a night game and I fell asleep." Quillen spent $2,163 to send flowers to express his condolences over the deaths of longtime supporters. He spent $1,120 on gifts, including $906 on liquor that he gave as "Christmas favors." Christmas cards added $1,040 to the tab.

To reward his campaign volunteers, Quillen spent $2,421 on various gifts, including $1,230 on presidential mugs from Capitol Coin and Stamp in Washington, D.C.

Campaign Expenditures	Quillen Amount Spent	% of Total
Overhead		
Office furniture/supplies	$ 3,664	1.13
Rent/utilities	10,795	3.32
Salaries	100,853	31.04
Taxes	70,852	21.81
Bank/investment fees	0	
Lawyers/accountants	5,440	1.67
Telephone	10,632	3.27
Campaign automobile	4,209	1.30
Computers/office equipment	620	.19
Travel	10,388	3.20
Food/meetings	5,234	1.61
Subtotal	**222,686**	**68.54**
Fund Raising		
Events	16,560	5.10
Direct mail	0	
Telemarketing	0	
Subtotal	**16,560**	**5.10**
Polling	**0**	
Advertising		
Electronic media	0	
Other media	0	
Subtotal	**0**	
Other Campaign Activity		
Persuasion mail/brochures	0	
Actual campaigning	7,808	2.40
Staff/volunteers	2,421	.75
Subtotal	**10,229**	**3.15**
Constituent Gifts/Entertainment	**28,032**	**8.63**
Donations to		
Candidates from same state	800	.25
Candidates from other states	0	
Civic organizations	750	.23
Ideological groups	0	
Political parties	1,120	.34
Subtotal	**2,670**	**.82**
Unitemized Expenses	**44,712**	**13.76**
Total Campaign Expenses	**$ 324,889**	
PAC Contributions	**$ 267,050**	
Individual Contributions	**80,255**	
Total Receipts*	**455,846**	

*Includes PAC and individual contributions as well as interest earned, party contributions, etc.

† No expenditures or receipts on file. Candidates raising or spending less than $5,000 are not required to file reports with the Federal Election Commission.

District 2 — TENNESSEE

Rep. John J. "Jimmy" Duncan, Jr. (R)

1992 Election Results
John J. "Jimmy" Duncan, Jr. (R)   148,377   (72%)
Troy Goodale (D)   52,887   (26%)

Rep. John J. "Jimmy" Duncan, Jr. had little reason to spend heavily on his reelection campaign. District 2 had elected a Republican to Congress every two years since the Civil War, and, as usual, the Democrats put up only token opposition in 1992. For the most part, Duncan simply carried on traditions begun by his father, who held the seat from 1964 until his death in 1988.

One such tradition was the election-year barbecue, which drew approximately 20,000 people, according to campaign treasurer Darrell Atkins. Expenses for the event totaled $29,324, including $16,864 for printing and mailing 50,000 complimentary tickets, $2,748 for meat, $1,840 for door prizes, $1,455 to rent the Knoxville Civic Auditorium, $1,358 for liability insurance, $1,068 for soft drinks, and a $600 in-kind donation to cover the cost of buses that ferried senior citizens to and from the affair. This one event accounted for 18 percent of Duncan's spending for the two-year election cycle.

Duncan also continued the practice of setting up a booth at the annual Tennessee Valley Fair where he distributed glasses of ice water. A large sign over the booth announced "Free Ice from Your Congressman—Jimmy Duncan." While it was free to constituents, the campaign spent $1,980 for the water over the two-year cycle. Cups and the booth rentals cost $895 and $593, respectively.

Lucky pennies, yet another of his father's traditions, cost the campaign $1,276.

Duncan stroked his constituents in other ways as well. He spent $10,169 of his campaign treasury on meals with constituents, including a $288 dinner at the Capitol Hill Club and a $465 repast at the House restaurant. Duncan spent a total of $3,981 at Kroger's and Sam's Wholesale for items needed for his free receptions, which Duncan and his wife held throughout the district. He spent $1,219 for sports and theater tickets, which were used for entertaining constituents. Flowers and other constituent gifts cost the campaign $2,420. Year-end holiday cards added $4,007.

Duncan did not entirely ignore the election against Democrat Troy Goodale, although his effort lasted only about three weeks. Starting in mid-October, Jim Early & Associates of Knoxville began placing newspaper ads that cost the campaign a total of $14,282. Early also collected $11,842 to cover the cost of airing the campaign's limited radio spots and a small placement fee.

Duncan raised 65 percent of his contributions the easy way, from political action committees. He held an annual fund-raiser at the Capitol Hill Club that cost $1,472 in 1991 and $1,312 in 1992.

Campaign Expenditures	Duncan Amount Spent	Duncan % of Total	Goodale Amount Spent	Goodale % of Total
Overhead				
Office furniture/supplies	$ 1,864	1.12	$ 0	
Rent/utilities	1,304	.79	0	
Salaries	9,818	5.92	0	
Taxes	219	.13	0	
Bank/investment fees	35	.02	0	
Lawyers/accountants	8,000	4.82	0	
Telephone	1,434	.86	0	
Campaign automobile	0		0	
Computers/office equipment	0		0	
Travel	4,696	2.83	0	
Food/meetings	0		0	
Subtotal	**27,371**	**16.50**	**0**	
Fund Raising				
Events	21,338	12.86	0	
Direct mail	0		0	
Telemarketing	0		0	
Subtotal	**21,338**	**12.86**	**0**	
Polling	**0**		**0**	
Advertising				
Electronic media	12,921	7.79	1,696	26.20
Other media	14,482	8.73	1,222	18.89
Subtotal	**27,403**	**16.52**	**2,918**	**45.09**
Other Campaign Activity				
Persuasion mail/brochures	0		766	11.83
Actual campaigning	43,723	26.35	0	
Staff/volunteers	0		0	
Subtotal	**43,723**	**26.35**	**766**	**11.83**
Constituent Gifts/ Entertainment	**17,815**	**10.74**	**0**	
Donations to				
Candidates from same state	0		0	
Candidates from other states	300	.18	0	
Civic organizations	4,391	2.65	0	
Ideological groups	0		0	
Political parties	4,320	2.60	0	
Subtotal	**9,011**	**5.43**	**0**	
Unitemized Expenses	**19,242**	**11.60**	**2,788**	**43.08**
Total Campaign Expenses	**$ 165,902**		**$ 6,471**	
PAC Contributions	$ 162,509		$ 0	
Individual Contributions	87,501		4,556	
Total Receipts*	258,496		6,471	

*Includes PAC and individual contributions as well as interest earned, party contributions, etc.

TENNESSEE District 3

Rep. Marilyn Lloyd (D)

1992 Election Results

Marilyn Lloyd (D)	105,693	(49%)
Zach Wamp (R)	102,763	(47%)

Rep. Marilyn Lloyd parlayed a two-to-one spending advantage into a 2,930-vote victory over Republican Zach Wamp. In the process she was forced to spend more than three times as much on her 1992 campaign as she had in 1990, despite the fact that redistricting had provided her with additional Democratic constituents. She was one of eight incumbents who won reelection despite garnering less than 50 percent of the general election votes.

Wamp ran an aggressive anti-incumbent campaign in which he called for term limits and urged voters to "Wamp Congress." One of his seven television commercials depicted a factory supervisor asking workers to raise their hands if they wanted a $35,000 pay raise; he then slammed Lloyd for voting herself such a raise. Wamp received $21,708 from the National Republican Congressional Committee to augment his $59,065 broadcast budget.

Lloyd's first television commercials were positive spots showing her with school children and senior citizens, but she quickly went on the offensive when it became clear the race had tightened. One dredged up Wamp's "criminal" past, which included writing two bad checks for a total of $20 when he was in college. "Some people felt we were digging too far into the past," admitted Sue Carlton, Lloyd's administrative assistant. "But we felt the public should know about his financial problems and arrest record." Lloyd paid William Morgan & Co. of Baton Rouge, La., $264,226 to create and place four television commercials and four companion radio spots. The Democratic Congressional Campaign Committee paid $12,306 of the production costs, while Lloyd paid $997 and an additional $900 for two small media buys.

At the outset, Lloyd's persuasion mail took the high road, touting her ability to deliver federal projects to the district. By campaign's end she was blanketing the district with negative literature similar to the television spots. Lloyd spent $9,045 on newspaper ads, $11,275 on yard signs, $5,314 on phonebanking, and $2,153 on bumper stickers and buttons. Hickman-Brown Research of Washington, D.C., collected $62,000 for polling.

Although Lloyd's receipts fell $179,940 short of her outlays, her fund-raising operation was reasonably efficient. She paid Assets Consulting Services of Falls Church, Va., $22,004 for its help in raising $272,250 from political action committees. Lloyd collected more than $9 for every dollar invested in fund raising. Interest on her cash reserves amounted to $22,894.

Lloyd spent $9,491 on constituent stroking, including $4,684 on year-end holiday cards, $1,744 on meals with constituents, and $1,547 on flowers.

Campaign Expenditures	Lloyd Amount Spent	Lloyd % of Total	Wamp Amount Spent	Wamp % of Total
Overhead				
Office furniture/supplies	$ 4,691	.73	$ 5,556	2.17
Rent/utilities	8,790	1.37	4,100	1.60
Salaries	53,586	8.33	30,521	11.90
Taxes	18,783	2.92	8,879	3.46
Bank/investment fees	21		108	.04
Lawyers/accountants	17,438	2.71	0	
Telephone	3,330	.52	7,914	3.08
Campaign automobile	0		0	
Computers/office equipment	3,600	.56	5,610	2.19
Travel	18,095	2.81	12,547	4.89
Food/meetings	3,057	.47	0	
Subtotal	**131,391**	**20.42**	**75,235**	**29.32**
Fund Raising				
Events	51,393	7.99	6,912	2.69
Direct mail	0		9,528	3.71
Telemarketing	0		0	
Subtotal	**51,393**	**7.99**	**16,440**	**6.41**
Polling	**62,000**	**9.63**	**15,258**	**5.95**
Advertising				
Electronic media	266,123	41.35	59,065	23.02
Other media	9,525	1.48	19,305	7.52
Subtotal	**275,648**	**42.83**	**78,370**	**30.54**
Other Campaign Activity				
Persuasion mail/brochures	50,261	7.81	45,138	17.59
Actual campaigning	20,776	3.23	15,494	6.04
Staff/volunteers	0		0	
Subtotal	**71,037**	**11.04**	**60,632**	**23.63**
Constituent Gifts/ Entertainment	9,491	1.47	802	.31
Donations to				
Candidates from same state	0		0	
Candidates from other states	0		0	
Civic organizations	4,025	.63	0	
Ideological groups	600	.09	0	
Political parties	12,550	1.95	1,335	.52
Subtotal	**17,175**	**2.67**	**1,335**	**.52**
Unitemized Expenses	**25,448**	**3.95**	**8,508**	**3.32**
Total Campaign Expenses	**$ 643,583**		**$ 256,579**	
PAC Contributions	$ 272,250		$ 125	
Individual Contributions	153,677		256,230	
Total Receipts*	463,643		275,655	

*Includes PAC and individual contributions as well as interest earned, party contributions, etc.

District 4 — TENNESSEE

Rep. Jim Cooper (D)

1992 Election Results

Jim Cooper (D)	98,984	(64%)
Dale Johnson † (R)	50,340	(33%)

In 1990 Rep. Jim Cooper spent $52,926 to defeat Republican businessman Claiborne Sanders, who put $12,639 into the race. In 1992 Cooper increased his outlays to $180,534, even though redistricting did little to change District 4 and he faced an opponent with less than $5,000.

Cooper's off-year campaign was virtually nonexistent. He had no campaign office or staff, and he held no fund-raisers. New computer equipment and supplies accounted for $8,439 of the $26,001 he spent. He gave $5,000 to the Democratic Congressional Campaign Committee and $1,000 to the Tennessee Democratic party. Tickets to the state party's annual Jackson Day Dinner cost $3,450. The $3,640 he spent on Christmas cards in 1991 was more than he invested in off-year campaign travel, accounting fees, meals, and office supples combined.

Little changed for the first six months of 1992. He raised only $9,767, with $3,718 of that coming from interest earned on his cash reserves. Cooper's largest single expense during this six-month period was the $2,913 he paid to Potomac Color Printers in Potomac, Md., for Christmas cards. He did not hire a campaign manager until the end of June, and his total outlays amounted to only $10,928.

Cooper invested 49 percent of his spending for the entire two-year cycle during the five weeks leading up to the August 6 Democratic primary. Unlike 1990, he opened a campaign office. To help raise his name recognition among new constituents, Cooper paid the Denson Agency of Nashville $55,156 for creating and placing television, radio, and newspaper ads. In 1990 his advertising expenditures totaled just $83. Denson collected another $2,042 for supplying the campaign's signs, buttons, and bumper stickers. Hickman-Brown Research of Washington, D.C., received $17,000 for polling, another expense Cooper had avoided in 1990. Cooper paid the state party $4,000 for its coordinated get-out-the-vote efforts. In all, Cooper spent more than $89,000 during this preprimary push and collected 85 percent of the vote.

For the general election contest with Republican Dale Johnson, Cooper all but shut down his campaign. Although he kept his headquarters open and continued to employ a campaign manager, Cooper spent nothing on advertising, persuasion mail, yard signs, or get-out-the-vote efforts. Between the August primary and the November 3 election, Cooper reported expenses of only $34,484, including two contributions totaling $10,000 to the Democratic National Committee Victory Fund.

Cooper closed out the cycle by spending another $4,337 on Christmas cards.

Campaign Expenditures	Cooper Amount Spent	% of Total
Overhead		
Office furniture/supplies	$ 1,285	.71
Rent/utilities	3,000	1.66
Salaries	14,192	7.86
Taxes	6,789	3.76
Bank/investment fees	0	
Lawyers/accountants	600	.33
Telephone	1,210	.67
Campaign automobile	0	
Computers/office equipment	16,722	9.26
Travel	9,926	5.50
Food/meetings	948	.53
Subtotal	**54,672**	**30.28**
Fund Raising		
Events	7,549	4.18
Direct mail	3,052	1.69
Telemarketing	0	
Subtotal	**10,601**	**5.87**
Polling	**17,000**	**9.42**
Advertising		
Electronic media	42,181	23.36
Other media	14,208	7.87
Subtotal	**56,388**	**31.23**
Other Campaign Activity		
Persuasion mail/brochures	0	
Actual campaigning	6,347	3.52
Staff/volunteers	0	
Subtotal	**6,347**	**3.52**
Constituent Gifts/Entertainment	**10,890**	**6.03**
Donations to		
Candidates from same state	1,000	.55
Candidates from other states	0	
Civic organizations	0	
Ideological groups	0	
Political parties	20,575	11.40
Subtotal	**21,575**	**11.95**
Unitemized Expenses	**3,062**	**1.70**
Total Campaign Expenses	**$ 180,534**	
PAC Contributions	**$ 2,500**	
Individual Contributions	**128,420**	
Total Receipts*	**164,092**	

*Includes PAC and individual contributions as well as interest earned, party contributions, etc.

† No expenditures or receipts on file. Candidates raising or spending less than $5,000 are not required to file reports with the Federal Election Commission.

TENNESSEE — District 5

Rep. Bob Clement (D)

1992 Election Results

Bob Clement (D)	125,233	(67%)
Tom Stone (R)	49,417	(26%)

Rep. Bob Clement knew he had nothing to fear from Tom Stone, his underfunded Republican opponent. Running as an independent, Stone had attracted only 18 percent of the vote in 1990, and with only $10,590 to spend in 1992, there was no chance of an upset.

Seriously considering a 1994 gubernatorial bid, Clement asked his media adviser, Morgan/Fletcher & Co. of Nashville, to develop a two-minute biographical television commercial. The spot highlighted the Clement family's political history, pointing to his father's three terms as governor and his aunt's service in the state senate. Morgan/Fletcher produced several hundred copies of an eight-minute video that were given to key supporters.

However, when Chip Forrester entered the Democratic primary, Clement's attention focused on the race at hand. Forrester, a former aide to Sen. Al Gore, attacked Clement for his one House bank overdraft and for being a captive of special interests. Forrester placed ads in restaurant restrooms encouraging people to "relieve yourself" of Clement.

Clement responded to Forrester's $93,909 challenge with television and radio commercials accusing Forrester of having betrayed Gore's trust by running. "While working for Sen. Gore, Chip was using his employment with our senator to secretly organize a campaign," Clement said in one ad. Morgan/Fletcher collected $123,722 for creating and placing the preprimary broadcast ads and producing the video.

The Tyson Organization of Fort Worth, Texas, was paid $36,560 for phonebanking and persuasion mail. "The mailers dealt with whatever the caller identified as their issue—everything from abortion to zoology," noted Barton Herbison, Clement's press secretary. Kitchens, Powell & Kitchens of Orlando, Fla., collected $16,500 for preprimary polling. Yard signs cost $6,929. Buttons and bumper stickers added $3,417. In all, Clement spent $495,758 prior to the August 6 primary, including the $147,441 he invested in his permanent campaign during the off-year. His total outlays for the two-year cycle represented a 102 percent increase over 1990.

To help him raise the money needed to pay for his increased outlays, Clement depended heavily on Creative Campaign Consultant of Washington, D.C., which received $21,292 for organizing political action committee receptions in Washington. The "Nashville Bash" held at the L'Enfant Plaza Hotel featured singers Johnny Cash and the Carter family. "The event had the dual purpose of raising money and achieving name recognition among his colleagues in Washington," explained Herbison. Excluding Creative Campaign's fee, the event cost $25,142.

Campaign Expenditures	Clement Amount Spent	Clement % of Total	Stone Amount Spent	Stone % of Total
Overhead				
Office furniture/supplies	$ 7,836	1.30	$ 14	.14
Rent/utilities	9,294	1.55	0	
Salaries	69,521	11.56	0	
Taxes	15,856	2.64	0	
Bank/investment fees	0		14	.13
Lawyers/accountants	0		0	
Telephone	6,830	1.14	273	2.58
Campaign automobile	7,076	1.18	0	
Computers/office equipment	8,451	1.41	116	1.09
Travel	28,758	4.78	0	
Food/meetings	1,553	.26	43	.41
Subtotal	**155,175**	**25.81**	**461**	**4.35**
Fund Raising				
Events	113,357	18.86	0	
Direct mail	19,493	3.24	0	
Telemarketing	0		0	
Subtotal	**132,850**	**22.10**	**0**	
Polling	**16,500**	**2.74**	**0**	
Advertising				
Electronic media	126,032	20.97	8,280	78.19
Other media	8,752	1.46	0	
Subtotal	**134,784**	**22.42**	**8,280**	**78.19**
Other Campaign Activity				
Persuasion mail/brochures	45,935	7.64	1,554	14.67
Actual campaigning	43,064	7.16	0	
Staff/volunteers	1,986	.33	0	
Subtotal	**90,985**	**15.14**	**1,554**	**14.67**
Constituent Gifts/ Entertainment	**9,440**	**1.57**	**0**	
Donations to				
Candidates from same state	2,450	.41	0	
Candidates from other states	1,100	.18	0	
Civic organizations	8,554	1.42	0	
Ideological groups	885	.15	0	
Political parties	11,170	1.86	0	
Subtotal	**24,159**	**4.02**	**0**	
Unitemized Expenses	**37,248**	**6.20**	**296**	**2.79**
Total Campaign Expenses	**$ 601,141**		**$ 10,590**	
PAC Contributions	$ 288,762		$ 0	
Individual Contributions	247,971		5,286	
Total Receipts*	557,480		11,372	

*Includes PAC and individual contributions as well as interest earned, party contributions, etc.

District 6 — TENNESSEE

Rep. Bart Gordon (D)

1992 Election Results
Bart Gordon (D) 120,177 (57%)
Marsha Blackburn (R) 86,289 (41%)

For the first time in eight years, Rep. Bart Gordon faced serious opposition. Gordon attracted two Democratic primary challengers, including abortion foe Don Schneller, who ran television commercials showing bloody fetuses. In the fall campaign, fashion consultant Marsha Blackburn ran ads attacking Gordon for his 1989 vote in favor of a congressional pay raise, his 1990 vote in favor of the budget summit compromise, and his heavy reliance on political action committee contributions. In response, Gordon increased his spending from $346,595 in 1990 to $988,377 in 1992.

Feeling he could not let the abortion spots go unanswered, Gordon pumped $138,832 into preprimary broadcast advertising, $59,071 more than he spent on such ads during the entire 1990 campaign. His media consultant, Morgan/Fletcher & Co. of Nashville, collected $39,100 for creating the spots. Television and radio air time cost $95,000 and $4,732, respectively.

To sew up the nomination, Gordon spent $35,387 to produce and distribute a twelve-page tabloid that focused on such issues as crime, health care reform, and balancing the federal budget. Morgan/Fletcher received $5,000 for designing the tabloid, which was inserted in newspapers, handed out at campaign events, and mailed. The campaign spent another $13,624 on newspaper ads and $11,662 on yard signs. Gordon captured 83 percent of the primary votes.

Against Blackburn, Gordon spent $138,128 on television air time. When one of Blackburn's mailers incorrectly purported to show pictures of Gordon's home in a swank Murfreesboro neighborhood, Gordon responded with a television commercial showing his real home—a condominium. When Blackburn ran ads claiming that Gordon had voted against a proposed constitutional amendment requiring a balanced federal budget, he shot back with a spot pointing out that he had, in fact, voted for the amendment. Gordon paid Morgan/Fletcher $6,604 for their efforts in the general election. He spent $29,877 to print additional copies of the tabloid, $12,292 on newspaper ads, and $11,816 to air his radio spots.

Gordon invested 16 percent of his funds in raising money. Gordon paid TDM Research & Communications of Birmingham, Ala., $20,055 for telemarketing. The campaign produced nearly fifty direct-mail fundraising solicitations and mailed out $45,876 worth of T-shirts to prospective donors. Fraioli/Jost of Washington, D.C., received $12,043 for maintaining the direct-mail contributor lists. These efforts yielded $146,606 in small, individual donations.

Gordon spent $9,610 to send year-end letters that brought constituents up to date on what Gordon and his staff had been doing. The letters also contained recipes from his mother.

Campaign Expenditures	Gordon Amount Spent	Gordon % of Total	Blackburn Amount Spent	Blackburn % of Total
Overhead				
Office furniture/supplies	$ 13,258	1.34	$ 2,270	1.30
Rent/utilities	17,385	1.76	4,610	2.64
Salaries	71,333	7.22	17,002	9.73
Taxes	23,103	2.34	0	
Bank/investment fees	0		81	.05
Lawyers/accountants	0		4,900	2.81
Telephone	5,031	.51	6,004	3.44
Campaign automobile	0		0	
Computers/office equipment	15,471	1.57	1,587	.91
Travel	24,147	2.44	5,101	2.92
Food/meetings	0		252	.14
Subtotal	169,728	17.17	41,808	23.94
Fund Raising				
Events	23,315	2.36	9,852	5.64
Direct mail	108,661	10.99	13,076	7.49
Telemarketing	21,393	2.16	0	
Subtotal	153,369	15.52	22,927	13.13
Polling	20,000	2.02	0	
Advertising				
Electronic media	296,118	29.96	43,937	25.16
Other media	34,901	3.53	3,566	2.04
Subtotal	331,019	33.49	47,504	27.20
Other Campaign Activity				
Persuasion mail/brochures	132,720	13.43	39,364	22.54
Actual campaigning	99,582	10.08	22,565	12.92
Staff/volunteers	397	.04	0	
Subtotal	232,700	23.54	61,929	35.46
Constituent Gifts/Entertainment	9,610	.97	0	
Donations to				
Candidates from same state	0		0	
Candidates from other states	0		0	
Civic organizations	0		225	.13
Ideological groups	0		0	
Political parties	7,700	.78	0	
Subtotal	7,700	.78	225	.13
Unitemized Expenses	64,252	6.50	267	.15
Total Campaign Expenses	$ 988,377		$ 174,660	
PAC Contributions	$ 388,590		$ 18,226	
Individual Contributions	160,456		155,357	
Total Receipts*	662,234		184,657	

*Includes PAC and individual contributions as well as interest earned, party contributions, etc.

TENNESSEE — District 7

Rep. Don Sundquist (R)

1992 Election Results

Don Sundquist (R)	125,101	(62%)
David R. Davis (D)	72,062	(36%)

Rep. Don Sundquist spent $995,922 during the 1992 election cycle—more than twice what he spent on his 1990 reelection effort. In part that massively increased spending was the result of a redistricting plan that increased Democratic strength in District 7. It also reflected the fact that Sundquist's 1990 Democratic opponent had put less than $5,000 into his token challenge, while his 1992 Democratic challenger, retired minister David R. Davis, had $93,582 to spend. However, much of the increased spending related more to Sundquist's plans to run for governor in 1994 than to his 1992 reelection effort.

Unopposed in the August 8 primary, Sundquist nevertheless began airing television and radio commercials in July. In July and August he spent $17,090 for air time on Memphis television stations, $18,319 for radio spots, and $3,252 for time on local cable television outlets. With an eye toward the 1994 gubernatorial campaign, he also spent $27,914 to buy time on Nashville television, which reached only a small proportion of District 7 voters but large numbers of voters crucial to any statewide bid. Testimonial ads featuring former senator Howard Baker and former governor Lamar Alexander focused on Sundquist's integrity and his commitment to Tennessee, not simply the parochial interests of his district.

As the House campaign heated up, Sundquist concentrated more on the election at hand. Although he lacked Sundquist's resources, Davis managed to air several radio and television commercials, including one radio spot Davis said urged viewers to "honk if you're ready for change." The ad slammed congressional leadership, the franking privilege, and the power of political action committees. Another spot charged Sundquist with siphoning money out of his congressional office and campaign accounts to enhance his personal lifestyle.

When polls showed that Davis's attacks were having an impact, Sundquist unleashed a $134,408 barrage of broadcast advertising. Television air time on network affiliates in Memphis and Nashville cost $59,857 and $34,850, respectively. He invested another $26,827 in radio spots and $3,896 on cable television ads. Penczner Productions of Memphis collected $50,358 for creating the broadcast ads; Robert McDowell, also of Memphis, billed the campaign $27,667 for placing them. Sundquist spent $84,155 on newspaper ads, $12,174 to produce and distribute copies of a campaign video, and $9,726 on billboards.

Sundquist also doubled his outlays for constituent stroking, from $23,304 in 1990 to $46,871 in 1992. He spent $19,110 on year-end holiday cards, $15,385 on gifts, and $12,376 on constituent entertainment.

	Sundquist		Davis	
Campaign Expenditures	Amount Spent	% of Total	Amount Spent	% of Total
Overhead				
Office furniture/supplies	$ 10,635	1.07	$ 356	.38
Rent/utilities	11,892	1.19	794	.85
Salaries	74,965	7.53	0	
Taxes	36,346	3.65	0	
Bank/investment fees	276	.03	401	.43
Lawyers/accountants	0		70	.07
Telephone	5,060	.51	3,566	3.81
Campaign automobile	22,211	2.23	0	
Computers/office equipment	24,580	2.47	0	
Travel	88,576	8.89	3,128	3.34
Food/meetings	4,147	.42	16	.02
Subtotal	278,688	27.98	8,332	8.90
Fund Raising				
Events	52,159	5.24	2,533	2.71
Direct mail	41,982	4.22	668	.71
Telemarketing	0		576	.62
Subtotal	94,141	9.45	3,776	4.04
Polling	20,500	2.06	0	
Advertising				
Electronic media	290,149	29.13	49,533	52.93
Other media	107,696	10.81	296	.32
Subtotal	397,845	39.95	49,829	53.25
Other Campaign Activity				
Persuasion mail/brochures	27,629	2.77	16,824	17.98
Actual campaigning	87,568	8.79	5,660	6.05
Staff/volunteers	2,353	.24	0	
Subtotal	117,550	11.80	22,484	24.03
Constituent Gifts/ Entertainment	46,871	4.71	0	
Donations to				
Candidates from same state	1,000	.10	0	
Candidates from other states	1,500	.15	0	
Civic organizations	6,748	.68	0	
Ideological groups	1,050	.11	0	
Political parties	6,800	.68	0	
Subtotal	17,098	1.72	0	
Unitemized Expenses	23,230	2.33	9,160	9.79
Total Campaign Expenses	$ 995,922		$ 93,582	
PAC Contributions	$ 359,884		$ 35,900	
Individual Contributions	387,958		47,600	
Total Receipts*	819,006		106,633	

*Includes PAC and individual contributions as well as interest earned, party contributions, etc.

District 8   TENNESSEE

Rep. John Tanner (D)

1992 Election Results

John Tanner (D)	136,852	(84%)
Lawrence J. Barnes † (I)	9,605	(6%)

Rep. John Tanner would appear to be safely ensconced in this House seat. Elected with 62 percent of the votes in 1988, Tanner ran unopposed in 1990. In 1992 Tanner's only challenge came from four underfunded independent candidates, none of whom garnered more than 6 percent of the vote. Even so, Tanner increased his spending from $125,535 in 1990 to $164,672 in 1992.

Tanner donated 19 percent of his money to other candidates, Democratic party organizations, charities, and booster groups over the two-year cycle. He wrote three checks totaling $10,000 to the Democratic Congressional Campaign Committee. He gave $9,500 to the Tennessee Democratic party and donated $1,000 to both the Democratic Leadership Council and the Conservative Democratic Political Action Committee. Fellow Democratic Reps. Eliot L. Engel (N.Y.), Les Aspin (Wis.), Marty Russo (Ill.), and Albert G. Bustamante (Texas) each received $1,000 of Tanner's campaign funds. When David R. Davis decided to challenge Tennessee Republican Rep. Don Sundquist in District 7, Tanner sent the long-shot challenger $1,000.

Tanner kept a small campaign office open throughout the two-year cycle. During the first half of 1991, he paid Union City Insurance $50 a month for office space. In July he began leasing space from his former law partner for $200 a month. Tanner had no paid staff in 1990, but in 1991 he paid two people a total of $1,725 to enter his contributor lists into the campaign's computer. While he spent less than $1,000 on meals unrelated to fund raising or constituent entertainment in 1990, the tab for such meals during the 1992 election cycle was $6,553. The campaign picked up the $2,919 tab for Tanner's stay in New York for the 1992 Democratic National Convention, helping to drive his travel expense to $19,412—a 32 percent increase over 1990.

Despite his easy victories in 1988 and 1990, Tanner paid Hickman-Brown Research of Washington, D.C., $30,000 to track the mood of the electorate. "Everything was real high, both name ID and the favorability ratings, so we decided broadcast ads weren't necessary," recalled Joe H. Hill, Tanner's district director. Instead, Tanner spent $5,095 to place quarter-page ads in each of the district's four daily and twenty-four weekly newspapers. The November Group of Washington, D.C., collected $10,703 for coordinating a small persuasion mail effort targeted at the 25,000 new constituents acquired through redistricting.

Tanner spent only $1,766 on constituent stroking, including $648 on U.S. Historical Society calendars and $457 on the congressional art contest. Christmas gifts for his volunteers cost $866.

Campaign Expenditures	Tanner Amount Spent	% of Total
Overhead		
Office furniture/supplies	$ 6,239	3.79
Rent/utilities	4,082	2.48
Salaries	1,725	1.05
Taxes	3,916	2.38
Bank/investment fees	169	.10
Lawyers/accountants	1,600	.97
Telephone	512	.31
Campaign automobile	0	
Computers/office equipment	0	
Travel	19,412	11.79
Food/meetings	6,553	3.98
Subtotal	**44,208**	**26.85**
Fund Raising		
Events	14,170	8.60
Direct mail	1,078	.65
Telemarketing	0	
Subtotal	**15,247**	**9.26**
Polling	**30,000**	**18.22**
Advertising		
Electronic media	0	
Other media	5,119	3.11
Subtotal	**5,119**	**3.11**
Other Campaign Activity		
Persuasion mail/brochures	14,570	8.85
Actual campaigning	7,371	4.48
Staff/volunteers	866	.53
Subtotal	**22,807**	**13.85**
Constituent Gifts/Entertainment	**1,766**	**1.07**
Donations to		
Candidates from same state	1,000	.61
Candidates from other states	4,000	2.43
Civic organizations	4,550	2.76
Ideological groups	200	.12
Political parties	22,300	13.54
Subtotal	**32,050**	**19.46**
Unitemized Expenses	13,476	8.18
Total Campaign Expenses	$ 164,672	
PAC Contributions	$ 164,739	
Individual Contributions	61,407	
Total Receipts*	258,798	

* Includes PAC and individual contributions as well as interest earned, party contributions, etc.

† No expenditures or receipts on file. Candidates raising or spending less than $5,000 are not required to file reports with the Federal Election Commission.

TENNESSEE
District 9

Rep. Harold E. Ford (D)

1992 Election Results

Harold E. Ford (D)	123,276	(58%)
Charles L. Black † (R)	60,606	(28%)
Richard Lipstock † (I)	14,075	(7%)

Rep. Harold E. Ford had more than his share of problems going into the 1992 campaign. He was facing a second trial on federal bank fraud charges, and between January 1, 1987 and December 31, 1991 he had diverted $393,976 from his campaign treasury to pay legal bills associated with his defense. He had 388 overdrafts at the House bank and had a redrawn district in which the black majority had dropped from 64 percent to 59 percent.

However, in the end none of that mattered to his constituents. Ford prevailed in the four-candidate Democratic primary with 65 percent of the vote and in the five-candidate general election with 58 percent. His Republican opponent in November, Charles L. Black, spent less than $5,000 on his effort to oust the nine-term incumbent.

Ford spent $105,663 less on his 1992 campaign than he had in 1990, primarily because he established a separate committee to raise money for his legal defense. That move allowed him to reduce campaign outlays for his defense from $172,000 in 1990 to $51,413 in 1992.

Unlike 1990, Ford felt the need to broadcast a limited number of preprimary ads. The campaign spent $800 to air television commercials and $2,400 on radio spots, which Ford wrote. Press secretary Calvin Burns said the ads focused on Ford's constituent outreach through regular town-hall meetings and conferences. He spent $1,272 on newspaper ads.

According to Burns, Ford's voter contact mail consisted entirely of invitations to his town meetings. He spent $10,000 for campaign stickers, $4,076 for yard signs and posters, $2,205 on a bus to ferry senior citizens to the polls for the August 6 primary, and $800 for soft drinks that were served during a voter registration drive in March 1991.

With one brother in the state senate and another on the Memphis City Council, Ford economized by running his operation from their campaign office for the primary and the Democratic headquarters for the fall campaign. His campaign salary payments included $2,600 to his son, Harold Ford, Jr. His expenses for meetings and meals unrelated to fund raising or constituent entertainment included $1,691 to the Washington Hilton for a Congressional Black Caucus meeting, $500 to the Brownstone Hotel in Memphis for a "Mayor's reception," and $625 for meetings at the International Club in Washington. Dues to the Racquet Club in Memphis added $1,260.

Ford gave little of his money away. He contributed $500 to his brother John's state senate campaign and $4,900 to a Christmas fund drive. He purchased $250 in tickets to the Myron Lowery Prayer Breakfast, and $350 in tickets to a function at the Mt. Zion A.M.E. Church.

Campaign Expenditures	Ford Amount Spent	% of Total
Overhead		
Office furniture/supplies	$ 4,811	2.52
Rent/utilities	0	
Salaries	22,674	11.88
Taxes	362	.19
Bank/investment fees	0	
Lawyers/accountants	60,213	31.55
Telephone	4,766	2.50
Campaign automobile	0	
Computers/office equipment	1,789	.94
Travel	23,896	12.52
Food/meetings	6,703	3.51
Subtotal	125,213	65.61
Fund Raising		
Events	19,636	10.29
Direct mail	0	
Telemarketing	0	
Subtotal	19,636	10.29
Polling	0	
Advertising		
Electronic media	4,675	2.45
Other media	1,522	.80
Subtotal	6,197	3.25
Other Campaign Activity		
Persuasion mail/brochures	5,521	2.89
Actual campaigning	17,481	9.16
Staff/volunteers	0	
Subtotal	23,002	12.05
Constituent Gifts/Entertainment	1,553	.81
Donations to		
Candidates from same state	500	.26
Candidates from other states	0	
Civic organizations	5,990	3.14
Ideological groups	0	
Political parties	0	
Subtotal	6,490	3.40
Unitemized Expenses	8,785	4.61
Total Campaign Expenses	$ 190,876	
PAC Contributions	$ 118,450	
Individual Contributions	79,753	
Total Receipts*	202,187	

*Includes PAC and individual contributions as well as interest earned, party contributions, etc.

† No expenditures or receipts on file. Candidates raising or spending less than $5,000 are not required to file reports with the Federal Election Commission.

District 1 — TEXAS

Rep. Jim Chapman (D)

1992 Election Results   Jim Chapman (D)   152,209   (100%)

With no primary or general election opposition, Rep. Jim Chapman devoted much of his time to running "East Texas '92," a coordinated effort to boost the fortunes of Democrats in District 1, as well as in the districts of fellow Texas Reps. Charles Wilson and Ralph M. Hall. The coordinated effort conducted phonebanks, mailed thousands of absentee ballots, and conducted a get-out-the-vote effort on election day.

He also devoted considerable energy to raising money, more than doubling his campaign cash reserves over the two-year election cycle from $126,440 to $286,303. He paid Creative Campaign Consultant of Washington, D.C., $24,404 to organize events both in Washington and back home in Texas. Political action committees responded with donations totaling $212,577, which accounted for two-thirds of Chapman's total contributions. Most of Chapman's district events were small-donor affairs, with contributions of less than $200 representing 22 percent of his total donations.

Chapman's permanent campaign headquarters in Sulphur Springs was conveniently located in a building he owns, and as the landlord he collected $175 each month. The campaign also paid monthly rent of $150 to the Ruth A. Sterling Estate.

While Chapman spent $2,679 on broadcast advertising, $2,007 of that total was for expenses incurred during the 1990 campaign for ads produced by the Campaign Group of Philadelphia, Pa. Since it had not been listed as a campaign debt and counted in his 1990 spending, it was included in his 1992 totals.

Prior to the Democratic primary, Chapman spent $455 to produce a radio spot at the Harriman Communications Center in Washington, D.C. This was twice what he spent to air the ad.

Chapman also spent $1,775 to place preprimary ads in the *Texarkana Gazette* and $728 for ads in the *Bowie County Citizen Tribune*. Ads in two other newspapers cost a total of $446. In each case the ads simply urged people to vote Democratic.

One of every seven dollars Chapman spent was simply given away to party organizations, candidates, and causes. His donations to party organizations included $6,000 to the Democratic Congressional Campaign Committee, $5,000 to the Texas Democratic party, and $1,000 to the Democratic Leadership Council. Fellow Texas Reps. Ronald D. Coleman and Bill Sarpalius received $2,000 and $1,000, respectively. Democratic Reps. Les Aspin (Wis.) and Jimmy Hayes (La.) each collected $1,000. Tony Center, who unsuccessfully challenged Minority Whip Newt Gingrich (R-Ga.), also received $1,000.

In the final month of the campaign, Chapman spent just $17,497.

Campaign Expenditures	Chapman Amount Spent	% of Total
Overhead		
Office furniture/supplies	$ 4,357	2.88
Rent/utilities	10,298	6.80
Salaries	7,735	5.11
Taxes	2,592	1.71
Bank/investment fees	30	.02
Lawyers/accountants	3,999	2.64
Telephone	1,848	1.22
Campaign automobile	0	
Computers/office equipment	2,243	1.48
Travel	35,343	23.34
Food/meetings	1,962	1.30
Subtotal	**70,407**	**46.50**
Fund Raising		
Events	42,568	28.11
Direct mail	0	
Telemarketing	0	
Subtotal	**42,568**	**28.11**
Polling	0	
Advertising		
Electronic media	2,679	1.77
Other media	3,514	2.32
Subtotal	**6,193**	**4.09**
Other Campaign Activity		
Persuasion mail/brochures	0	
Actual campaigning	5,084	3.36
Staff/volunteers	550	.36
Subtotal	**5,634**	**3.72**
Constituent Gifts/Entertainment	759	.50
Donations to		
Candidates from same state	4,000	2.64
Candidates from other states	3,500	2.31
Civic organizations	1,440	.95
Ideological groups	1,000	.66
Political parties	12,775	8.44
Subtotal	**22,715**	**15.00**
Unitemized Expenses	3,133	2.07
Total Campaign Expenses	$ 151,408	
PAC Contributions	$ 212,577	
Individual Contributions	108,656	
Total Receipts*	342,246	

*Includes PAC and individual contributions as well as interest earned, party contributions, etc.

TEXAS
District 2

Rep. Charles Wilson (D)

1992 Election Results

Charles Wilson (D)	118,625	(56%)
Donna Peterson (R)	92,176	(44%)

In past campaigns, Rep. Charles Wilson held down his overhead by running his reelection effort from his Lufkin home. However, facing extensive negative publicity about his eighty-one overdrafts at the House bank and the redoubled efforts of 1990 challenger Donna Peterson, Wilson decided it was time to rent campaign office space in 1992.

In addition to rent payments totaling $5,060, Wilson spent $1,520 on utilities; $11,088 on a new computer, software, and other supplies; $3,954 on furniture; $2,371 on other office equipment; and $2,058 on insurance.

Wilson also invested in a mobile office—a bus equipped with tables and benches—to transport him to town meetings and other campaign appearances. The total cost of $6,062 included $3,000 for the bus rental, $1,383 for gasoline, $797 for repairs, $495 for new tires, and $80 for cleaning.

Peterson was able to funnel $112,096 more into advertising in 1992 than she had in 1990, so Wilson countered by increasing his 1992 advertising budget by $167,666. He paid McKinnon Media of Austin $140,422 to create his broadcast campaign. Bonner & Tate of Austin received $10,078 for producing the ads, and Shafto & Barton of Houston collected $299,000 to cover the cost of air time and their fees for placing the ads. With more than $1.2 million at his disposal, Wilson also spent $66,857 on newspaper advertising and $32,955 on billboards.

For the first time in years, Wilson developed several formal campaign brochures. Press secretary Elaine Lang noted that mailings targeted senior citizens, women, and National Rifle Association members, among others. Gold Communications Co. of Austin and Willmon Advertising & Marketing of Lufkin collected $44,749 and $41,086, respectively, for their work on the persuasion mail.

On the more traditional, grass-roots level, Wilson invested $23,683 in yard signs and posters and $9,223 in bumper stickers and buttons. He spent $21,562 for Texas highway maps adorned with a sticker reminding people to vote for him and $19,603 for nail files, potholders, and matchbooks carrying a similar reminder.

While 65 percent of Wilson's spending was devoted to various direct appeals to voters, there was still plenty of room in his budget for constituent entertainment. His annual dominoes tournament, which drew about 400 people in 1986, attracted approximately 1,600 people in both 1991 and 1992. The combined cost of these two events was $54,681, including $37,323 for the dominoes, $2,967 to engrave them with "Vote for Charles Wilson," $1,135 for trophies, and $9,166 for fried chicken and biscuits.

	Wilson		Peterson	
Campaign Expenditures	Amount Spent	% of Total	Amount Spent	% of Total
Overhead				
Office furniture/supplies	$ 23,128	1.87	$ 13,781	4.04
Rent/utilities	12,642	1.02	1,854	.54
Salaries	81,284	6.56	29,041	8.52
Taxes	0		0	
Bank/investment fees	1,919	.15	54	.02
Lawyers/accountants	18,606	1.50	0	
Telephone	10,602	.86	20,894	6.13
Campaign automobile	0		2,911	.85
Computers/office equipment	13,653	1.10	252	.07
Travel	66,709	5.38	18,199	5.34
Food/meetings	14,293	1.15	125	.04
Subtotal	**242,837**	**19.60**	**87,110**	**25.57**
Fund Raising				
Events	51,297	4.14	5,083	1.49
Direct mail	0		6,345	1.86
Telemarketing	0		0	
Subtotal	**51,297**	**4.14**	**11,427**	**3.35**
Polling	**27,000**	**2.18**	**19,261**	**5.65**
Advertising				
Electronic media	450,496	36.35	140,052	41.10
Other media	111,351	8.99	34,025	9.99
Subtotal	**561,846**	**45.34**	**174,076**	**51.09**
Other Campaign Activity				
Persuasion mail/brochures	106,708	8.61	6,248	1.83
Actual campaigning	111,281	8.98	37,509	11.01
Staff/volunteers	31,613	2.55	64	.02
Subtotal	**249,602**	**20.14**	**43,820**	**12.86**
Constituent Gifts/ Entertainment	**86,226**	**6.96**	**1,181**	**.35**
Donations to				
Candidates from same state	0		1,000	.29
Candidates from other states	1,000	.08	0	
Civic organizations	6,422	.52	130	.04
Ideological groups	1,280	.10	376	.11
Political parties	5,875	.47	1,663	.49
Subtotal	**14,577**	**1.18**	**3,169**	**.93**
Unitemized Expenses	**5,818**	**.47**	**689**	**.20**
Total Campaign Expenses	**$ 1,239,205**		**$ 340,735**	
PAC Contributions	$ 638,825		$ 118,550	
Individual Contributions	514,357		217,803	
Total Receipts*	1,217,912		344,053	

*Includes PAC and individual contributions as well as interest earned, party contributions, etc.

District 3 — TEXAS

Rep. Sam Johnson (R)

1992 Election Results

Sam Johnson** (R)	201,569	(86%)
Noel Kopala † (I)	32,570	(14%)

When Rep. Steve Bartlett resigned from Congress in March 1991 to successfully run for mayor of Dallas, state representative Sam Johnson and eleven others jumped into the open primary for Bartlett's seat. As the second leading vote-getter in the primary, Johnson then faced fellow Republican Tom Pauken in the May special election.

To see him through the abbreviated campaign, Johnson quickly assembled a team of six consultants. Arthur J. Finkelstein & Associates of New York was paid $55,769 for conducting polls, developing television and radio commercials, and for providing general strategic advice. Spaeth Communications of Dallas received $29,750 for day-to-day campaign management, writing speeches, and assisting with ad development. Multi Media Services Corp. of Alexandria, Va., received $23,951 for placing some of the ads. James R. Foster & Associates of Carrollton collected $72,307 for handling the persuasion mail effort. Fund-raisers Carol Reed Associates and Pat Cotton Associates, both of Dallas, were paid $35,325 and $8,291, respectively. In all, Johnson spent $364,561 on the two-month campaign.

According to Lisette McSoud of Spaeth Communications, the campaign aired two television commercials during the special election campaign. The first ad focused on his opposition to proposed changes in the state income tax as a way of establishing Johnson as the antitax candidate. The second, which reviewed his record in the state legislature, was aimed at increasing Johnson's name recognition in those parts of the district where he was not well known.

Two was also the magic number for persuasion mailers. Ben Key, vice president of Foster & Associates, said the campaign hit those parts of the district represented by Johnson in the state house with a mailer "affirming what a great American he was." Other sections of the district received an introductory piece that included various endorsements.

While his fund-raising efforts were extensive, receipts did not keep pace with expenditures during this period, and Johnson ended the special election campaign with debts of $77,867. By the end of 1991, he had reduced that total to $47,118.

Eight months after winning the seat, Johnson was back campaigning for reelection. He reassembled the same team of consultants, with the exception of Spaeth. Johnson spent $284,626 in garnering 83 percent of the vote in his Republican primary contest with accountant David Corley. In the fall campaign, Johnson faced no Democratic opponent and did no advertising and little campaigning of any kind against libertarian Noel Kopala, who spent less than $5,000.

Campaign Expenditures	Johnson Amount Spent	% of Total
Overhead		
Office furniture/supplies	$ 10,824	1.41
Rent/utilities	16,393	2.14
Salaries	34,248	4.47
Taxes	0	
Bank/investment fees	6	.00
Lawyers/accountants	14,302	1.87
Telephone	7,604	.99
Campaign automobile	0	
Computers/office equipment	2,397	.31
Travel	41,840	5.46
Food/meetings	90	.01
Subtotal	**127,704**	**16.68**
Fund Raising		
Events	158,451	20.69
Direct mail	68,344	8.92
Telemarketing	0	
Subtotal	**226,796**	**29.61**
Polling	**40,741**	**5.32**
Advertising		
Electronic media	108,723	14.20
Other media	3,551	.46
Subtotal	**112,274**	**14.66**
Other Campaign Activity		
Persuasion mail/brochures	127,657	16.67
Actual campaigning	97,916	12.79
Staff/volunteers	403	.05
Subtotal	**225,976**	**29.51**
Constituent Gifts/Entertainment	**7,000**	**.91**
Donations to		
Candidates from same state	3,750	.49
Candidates from other states	1,500	.20
Civic organizations	350	.05
Ideological groups	0	
Political parties	700	.09
Subtotal	**6,300**	**.82**
Unitemized Expenses	**19,031**	**2.49**
Total Campaign Expenses	**$ 765,820**	
PAC Contributions	**$ 213,475**	
Individual Contributions	**232,885**	
Total Receipts*	**466,977**	

* *Includes PAC and individual contributions as well as interest earned, party contributions, etc.*

** *Totals include special election disbursements and receipts.*

† *No expenditures or receipts on file. Candidates raising or spending less than $5,000 are not required to file reports with the Federal Election Commission.*

TEXAS   District 4

Rep. Ralph M. Hall (D)

1992 Election Results
Ralph M. Hall (D)   128,008   (58%)
David L. Bridges (R)   83,875   (38%)

	Hall		Bridges	
Campaign Expenditures	Amount Spent	% of Total	Amount Spent	% of Total
Overhead				
Office furniture/supplies	$ 14,225	1.98	$ 1,132	3.99
Rent/utilities	24,676	3.44	1,200	4.22
Salaries	120,321	16.78	0	
Taxes	36,014	5.02	0	
Bank/investment fees	289	.04	0	
Lawyers/accountants	2,000	.28	0	
Telephone	18,691	2.61	3,094	10.89
Campaign automobile	11,368	1.59	0	
Computers/office equipment	5,653	.79	0	
Travel	21,663	3.02	2,914	10.26
Food/meetings	3,061	.43	95	.33
Subtotal	**257,962**	**35.97**	**8,435**	**29.69**
Fund Raising				
Events	32,273	4.50	300	1.06
Direct mail	0		0	
Telemarketing	0		0	
Subtotal	**32,273**	**4.50**	**300**	**1.06**
Polling	**0**		**0**	
Advertising				
Electronic media	70,891	9.88	0	
Other media	131,344	18.31	6,101	21.48
Subtotal	**202,235**	**28.20**	**6,101**	**21.48**
Other Campaign Activity				
Persuasion mail/brochures	93,522	13.04	4,565	16.07
Actual campaigning	106,172	14.80	7,130	25.10
Staff/volunteers	2,827	.39	44	.16
Subtotal	**202,521**	**28.24**	**11,740**	**41.33**
Constituent Gifts/ Entertainment	**12,628**	**1.76**	**0**	
Donations to				
Candidates from same state	100	.01	0	
Candidates from other states	500	.07	0	
Civic organizations	2,445	.34	45	.16
Ideological groups	160	.02	0	
Political parties	6,360	.89	25	.09
Subtotal	**9,565**	**1.33**	**70**	**.25**
Unitemized Expenses	**0**		**1,762**	**6.20**
Total Campaign Expenses	**$ 717,185**		**$ 28,409**	
PAC Contributions	**$ 349,840**		**$ 1,825**	
Individual Contributions	**140,756**		**28,542**	
Total Receipts*	**520,216**		**35,797**	

*Includes PAC and individual contributions as well as interest earned, party contributions, etc.

As Rep. Ralph M. Hall likes to tell it, Secretary of State James A. Baker III was about to leave for Geneva one day when he realized he did not have any of Hall's signature lucky pennies with him, so he dispatched his driver to pick some up. "Jim Baker won't go to any important meeting without one in his pocket," boasted Hall.

The silver-dyed pennies stamped with "Hall for Congress" have been a standard promotional item in Hall's campaigns since 1963. Hall glued thousands of the pennies onto his 1992 persuasion mailers. The pennies themselves cost $9,060; shipping added $901. He then paid Motor Sports Printing $3,732 for "gluing pennies—inserting and labeling envelopes." Nineteen gallons of glue cost $174.

However, pennies were not the driving force behind Hall's decision to spend more than $717,000. Nor was it his permanent campaign, which cost him only $99,327 during 1991. More than anything else, Hall's spending was driven by the fact that for the first time in a decade he faced a challenge in the Democratic primary. "I had a real tough primary opponent," noted Hall. "He had some money, and I couldn't take any chances with him."

While Hall may have overstated attorney Roger Sanders's strength, as Hall won the primary with 66 percent of the vote, the six-term incumbent obviously kicked his campaign into overdrive. Sanders declared his candidacy in January 1992 and by February Hall had expanded his campaign staff from two to nine, retained Emory, Young & Associates of Austin as his general consultant; produced brochures; purchased yard signs; and begun airing radio and television ads.

In the weeks leading up to the March 10 primary, Hall committed more than $372,000 to defeating Sanders. He spent $64,570 on newspaper ads, $41,868 to air his television commercials, and another $13,273 on radio ads. "Thank-you" newspaper ads cost $5,413.

One of Hall's largest preprimary expenditures was the $52,480 he paid Emory, Young for phonebanking. "I don't know if I will ever use it again because it was so expensive," lamented Hall. "But it was necessary."

For the general election contest with attorney David L. Bridges, Hall spent $50,472 on newspaper ads, $8,207 on radio, and $5,771 to air limited television spots. Following the election he spent another $6,381 on thank-you newspaper ads.

Hall's only permanent employee was daughter-in-law Jody Hall, who collected $39,644 in salary, including year-end bonuses of $1,430 in 1991 and $1,847 in 1992. The permanent campaign office was located in a building owned by Hall's sons.

District 5 — TEXAS

Rep. John Bryant (D)

1992 Election Results

John Bryant (D)	98,567	(59%)
Richard Stokley (R)	62,419	(37%)

Unopposed in the primary, Rep. John Bryant nevertheless sank $90,559 into a massive preprimary phonebank. According to press secretary Carlton Carl, Bryant decided to undertake the twenty-line, in-house operation because roughly 40 percent of the voters in his redrawn district were new to him.

While Carl said the main purpose of the phonebank was to identify Democrats and provide voters with information on Bryant, the phones were occasionally used for fund raising, as well. "We got more bang for the buck that way," Carl added.

In the fall campaign against Republican Richard Stokley, Bryant cut back considerably on the phonebanking effort, but it still consumed another $53,144 of the budget. "In-house phonebanking gives us more control," noted Carl. "We determine when and how much we need to do, and we've done it at a very small fraction of what a consultant would charge."

That do-it-yourself philosophy permeated the campaign. While he spent nearly $795,000 on his fifth reelection bid, Bryant retained only two consultants and paid them a total of just $26,005. John Pouland of Dallas received $1,500 for providing general strategic advice. Rindy Media of Austin was paid $24,505 for producing and placing several radio commercials prior to the November general election.

Using the phonebank to help target their messages to receptive audiences, the campaign also did all its persuasion mail. Only one mass mailing was sent out prior to November 3.

Bryant spent $219,546 to maintain his permanent campaign during 1991, including $120,765 on overhead and $46,755 on fund raising. Monthly rent on his Dallas campaign headquarters was $750. He had a permanent three-person staff—one to run the phonebank, one to build and maintain the campaign's various databases, and one who was responsible for raising money.

Overhead amounted to $171,524 in 1992, with travel accounting for $31,529 of that total. Bryant spent $5,753 of his campaign treasury while in New York for the Democratic National Convention, including $2,907 for a reception at Planet Hollywood.

To pay for his robust campaign effort, Bryant held four major fund-raising receptions each year—one each in Dallas, Austin, Houston, and Washington, D.C. There were also numerous smaller events in both Texas and Washington. Political action committees accounted for 59 percent of his donations. Contributions of $200 or more amounted to $162,416, and small donations added $86,237. Even after raising more than $600,000, Bryant still had to tap his cash reserves from past campaigns for $172,750.

Campaign Expenditures	Bryant Amount Spent	Bryant % of Total	Stokley Amount Spent	Stokley % of Total
Overhead				
Office furniture/supplies	$ 9,616	1.21	$ 2,933	5.37
Rent/utilities	20,825	2.62	2,840	5.20
Salaries	163,639	20.58	7,866	14.41
Taxes	22,277	2.80	315	.58
Bank/investment fees	0		1,118	2.05
Lawyers/accountants	3,746	.47	0	
Telephone	15,131	1.90	2,532	4.64
Campaign automobile	0		0	
Computers/office equipment	5,941	.75	129	.24
Travel	48,809	6.14	3,605	6.61
Food/meetings	2,306	.29	343	.63
Subtotal	**292,289**	**36.77**	**21,680**	**39.73**
Fund Raising				
Events	58,356	7.34	832	1.52
Direct mail	24,956	3.14	0	
Telemarketing	0		0	
Subtotal	**83,312**	**10.48**	**832**	**1.52**
Polling	0		0	
Advertising				
Electronic media	26,974	3.39	0	
Other media	18,621	2.34	4,687	8.59
Subtotal	**45,595**	**5.74**	**4,687**	**8.59**
Other Campaign Activity				
Persuasion mail/brochures	120,830	15.20	7,500	13.74
Actual campaigning	162,610	20.46	4,989	9.14
Staff/volunteers	2,197	.28	522	.96
Subtotal	**285,638**	**35.93**	**13,011**	**23.84**
Constituent Gifts/ Entertainment	7,882	.99	0	
Donations to				
Candidates from same state	13,000	1.64	0	
Candidates from other states	22,000	2.77	0	
Civic organizations	935	.12	150	.27
Ideological groups	300	.04	0	
Political parties	17,360	2.18	1,430	2.62
Subtotal	**53,595**	**6.74**	**1,580**	**2.90**
Unitemized Expenses	26,654	3.35	12,782	23.42
Total Campaign Expenses	$ 794,964		$ 54,572	
PAC Contributions	$ 353,633		$ 10,850	
Individual Contributions	248,653		22,726	
Total Receipts*	622,709		44,585	

*Includes PAC and individual contributions as well as interest earned, party contributions, etc.

TEXAS   District 6

Rep. Joe L. Barton (R)   *1992 Election Results*   Joe L. Barton (R)   189,140   (72%)
                                                                     John E. Dietrich (D) 73,933   (28%)

Rep. Joe L. Barton's campaign was the epitome of excess. To maintain his permanent campaign, Barton spent $217,796 during 1991, including $141,802 on overhead and $56,517 on fund raising. Over the course of the two-year election cycle he invested more than twenty-eight times as much in overhead as Democrat John E. Dietrich spent on his entire campaign. Overall, he outspent Dietrich by nearly seventy-eight to one.

Barton's redrawn district contained only about 20 percent of the voters he had represented in 1990, but the good news was that most of the new folks were Republicans. Republicans comprised about half of the registered voters in Barton's old district; his new district was three-quarters Republican.

As he had in previous campaigns, Barton invested heavily in phonebanking. For the primary against accountant Mike McGinn, the phonebank was strictly aimed at those people who were already known to support the incumbent. "No voter identification, just turnout efforts," noted press secretary Craig L. Murphy. Barton took 79 percent of the very light primary turnout. For the general election, Murphy said the phonebank heavily targeted "swing voters" who had not expressed an opinion about President George Bush. "We assumed we already had the Bush people," Murphy added. In all, the campaign paid National Market Share of Austin $32,008 for the phonebanks.

Preprimary polls showed Barton with relatively low name recognition in the district. To correct that, Barton hired Media Southwest of Austin to develop several television and radio spots. Although Barton ran television commercials in the primary, he stuck exclusively with radio for the general election. Media Southwest collected $97,000 for its work during the primary and another $43,821 for the fall campaign.

Barton paid Austin-based Karl Rove & Co. a total of $137,396 to handle both fund-raising and voter contact mail. Despite the fact that this was his fifth House campaign, Barton's persuasion mail took great pains to distance him from his colleagues in Washington. One mailer stressed that "he's fighting hard for the changes we want" and went on to argue that "he's helping to clean up the mess in Washington."

More than $12,000 of Barton's direct mail expenditures had nothing to do with his own reelection campaign but was instead intended to help elect others. For example, he spent $5,708 on mail promoting the candidacy of Joe Grubbs, the Republican candidate for county attorney.

Barton also spent $17,980 to purchase, insure, and maintain his new campaign car.

	Barton		Dietrich	
Campaign Expenditures	Amount Spent	% of Total	Amount Spent	% of Total
Overhead				
Office furniture/supplies	$ 28,740	2.69	$ 105	.76
Rent/utilities	8,229	.77	0	
Salaries	114,739	10.74	0	
Taxes	61,568	5.76	0	
Bank/investment fees	134	.01	275	2.00
Lawyers/accountants	56,322	5.27	0	
Telephone	44,984	4.21	0	
Campaign automobile	17,980	1.68	0	
Computers/office equipment	22,016	2.06	0	
Travel	26,205	2.45	0	
Food/meetings	7,221	.68	0	
Subtotal	**388,139**	**36.33**	**380**	**2.76**
Fund Raising				
Events	76,840	7.19	0	
Direct mail	69,543	6.51	0	
Telemarketing	0		0	
Subtotal	**146,383**	**13.70**	**0**	
Polling	**16,480**	**1.54**	**0**	
Advertising				
Electronic media	147,962	13.85	3,955	28.76
Other media	12,183	1.14	0	
Subtotal	**160,145**	**14.99**	**3,955**	**28.76**
Other Campaign Activity				
Persuasion mail/brochures	156,768	14.67	5,896	42.87
Actual campaigning	66,930	6.27	3,523	25.61
Staff/volunteers	1,562	.15	0	
Subtotal	**225,259**	**21.09**	**9,419**	**68.48**
Constituent Gifts/ Entertainment	**12,327**	**1.15**	**0**	
Donations to				
Candidates from same state	26,555	2.49	0	
Candidates from other states	19,000	1.78	0	
Civic organizations	4,290	.40	0	
Ideological groups	320	.03	0	
Political parties	65,774	6.16	0	
Subtotal	**115,939**	**10.85**	**0**	
Unitemized Expenses	**3,619**	**.34**	**0**	
Total Campaign Expenses	**$ 1,068,290**		**$ 13,754**	
PAC Contributions	$ 374,046		$ 0	
Individual Contributions	515,094		2,350	
Total Receipts*	1,018,595		13,803	

*Includes PAC and individual contributions as well as interest earned, party contributions, etc.

District 7 — TEXAS

Rep. Bill Archer (R)

1992 Election Results   Bill Archer (R)   169,407   (100%)

Running unopposed, Rep. Bill Archer made his volunteers his top priority. First elected in 1970, Archer had paid a campaign manager in only four of his previous eleven House campaigns, and he had no reason to hire one in 1992. "A few of our volunteers have been with us for more than twenty years," boasted congressional chief of staff Donald Carlson.

That loyalty was rewarded with small gifts, such as coffee mugs, glasses, and key chains inscribed with Archer's name. The most active volunteers also had their gifts individualized. Such gifts cost Archer's campaign $1,611 over the two-year cycle. Archer also threw a $1,729 Christmas party for the volunteers in 1992.

One of the volunteers' chief tasks was the maintenance of Archer's voter lists, which Carlson described as "the most up-to-date record of Republicans in the district." Archer's single biggest campaign expense was the $26,051 he paid to connect volunteers' personal computers to that list and other campaign records stored on a large mainframe maintained by BT North America in Newark, N.J.

Archer used his voter list to mail family photo Christmas cards with end-of-the-year newsletters. The newsletters, written by Archer's wife Sharon, brought supporters up to date on marriages, births, and career moves in the Archer family. Constituents learned not only what Archer had been doing in the House, but also about the projects he had undertaken around his home, such as installing new shutters. His Christmas mailings cost $16,152.

Carlson said Archer received at least ten requests for money each week from churches and charities in the district. He responded by sending gifts engraved with the House seal that could be sold at fund-raising auctions. Total cost of the gifts was $2,584.

Several times each year, Archer hosted dinners with local and state politicians and Republican organization leaders. One such affair was his annual dinner for the district's twenty precinct chairmen at the Palm Restaurant in Houston. Including the $395 for commemorative photos, the 1991 event cost the campaign $2,061; a scaled-down version of the dinner cost $1,005 in 1992. Among the other items listed as political meals on his campaign financial statements were seven dinners at the Capitol Hill Club that ranged in price from $34 to $654.

Archer held few fund-raisers during the 1992 election cycle, as evidenced by the fact that he raised only $48,942. Interest earned on his campaign cash reserves amounted to $72,769, and he took no political action committee donations.

Campaign Expenditures	Archer Amount Spent	% of Total
Overhead		
Office furniture/supplies	$ 2,135	1.75
Rent/utilities	0	
Salaries	0	
Taxes	13,951	11.46
Bank/investment fees	0	
Lawyers/accountants	3,600	2.96
Telephone	44	.04
Campaign automobile	0	
Computers/office equipment	26,051	21.40
Travel	12,252	10.06
Food/meetings	13,067	10.73
Subtotal	**71,100**	**58.40**
Fund Raising		
Events	2,996	2.46
Direct mail	0	
Telemarketing	0	
Subtotal	**2,996**	**2.46**
Polling	0	
Advertising		
Electronic media	0	
Other media	584	.48
Subtotal	**584**	**.48**
Other Campaign Activity		
Persuasion mail/brochures	6,634	5.45
Actual campaigning	4,677	3.84
Staff/volunteers	3,340	2.74
Subtotal	**14,650**	**12.03**
Constituent Gifts/Entertainment	**16,390**	**13.46**
Donations to		
Candidates from same state	0	
Candidates from other states	0	
Civic organizations	2,584	2.12
Ideological groups	0	
Political parties	3,820	3.14
Subtotal	**6,404**	**5.26**
Unitemized Expenses	**9,632**	**7.91**
Total Campaign Expenses	**$ 121,756**	
PAC Contributions	$ 0	
Individual Contributions	48,942	
Total Receipts*	121,947	

*Includes PAC and individual contributions as well as interest earned, party contributions, etc.

TEXAS   District 8

Rep. Jack Fields (R)

1992 Election Results

Jack Fields (R)	179,349	(77%)
Charles E. Robinson † (D)	53,473	(23%)

Unopposed in both 1988 and 1990, Rep. Jack Fields finally attracted Democratic opposition in 1992, but it was opposition in name only. Rancher Charles E. Robinson spent less than $5,000 on his token campaign.

Nevertheless, in the face of this weak challenge, Fields increased his spending from $420,293 in 1990 to more than $744,000 in 1992. He upped his already hefty investments in overhead by more than $81,000. Fund-raising expenses, which had totaled just $27,582 in 1990, increased nearly five-fold to $131,262 in 1992.

As in past cycles, Fields rented his permanent campaign office from the funeral home owned by his family. He also paid monthly rent of $435 on an office that opened in July 1992. Staff salaries accounted for 18 percent of the total budget. Fields spent $9,156 for a new computer, software, supplies, and service. He paid $1,112 for a new mobile telephone and $8,961 for its use, which together amounted to 39 percent of his total telephone bill. Outlays for new office equipment totaled $8,121, including $4,788 for a photocopier and $2,013 for a fax machine. Fields's membership in Continental Airlines's President's Club added $1,110 to the cost of his travel.

Fields's decision to venture into the low-yield world of direct mail contributed greatly to the dramatic increase in his fund-raising costs. Karl Rove & Associates of Austin received $19,839 for soliciting its own donor lists as well as the campaign's list of 10,000 previous contributors.

According to campaign manager Kathryn "Toy" Wood, the most successful fund-raising event of the cycle was a $500-a-ticket dinner held at the Westin Oaks Galleria in Houston several days before the Republican National Convention. The event, which featured Secretary of Labor Lynn Martin, drew approximately 500 supporters and raised more than $200,000.

In the wake of redistricting, which added four new counties to his district, Fields put more money into actual campaigning. Mailings to constituents jumped from $10,907 in the 1990 election cycle to $77,446 in 1992, with Karl Rove collecting $56,955 for handling the persuasion mail effort. Fields put $12,246 into get-out-the-vote efforts; he spent $10,938 on yard signs and posters.

Advertising increased from $21,000 in 1990 to $106,799 in 1992. Fields spent nothing on broadcast advertising in 1990, but in 1992 he paid Austin-based Media Southwest $74,814 for producing and placing several television commercials. Newspaper ads cost $19,144 and billboards added $9,897.

Tarrance & Associates of Alexandria, Va., received $12,900 for conducting polls.

Campaign Expenditures	Fields Amount Spent	% of Total
Overhead		
Office furniture/supplies	$ 26,411	3.55
Rent/utilities	15,447	2.08
Salaries	134,718	18.11
Taxes	51,004	6.85
Bank/investment fees	252	.03
Lawyers/accountants	5,000	.67
Telephone	25,655	3.45
Campaign automobile	0	
Computers/office equipment	17,277	2.32
Travel	21,494	2.89
Food/meetings	3,497	.47
Subtotal	300,754	40.42
Fund Raising		
Events	99,584	13.38
Direct mail	31,679	4.26
Telemarketing	0	
Subtotal	131,262	17.64
Polling	12,900	1.73
Advertising		
Electronic media	74,964	10.07
Other media	31,835	4.28
Subtotal	106,799	14.35
Other Campaign Activity		
Persuasion mail/brochures	77,446	10.41
Actual campaigning	50,975	6.85
Staff/volunteers	6,290	.85
Subtotal	134,711	18.10
Constituent Gifts/Entertainment	7,118	.96
Donations to		
Candidates from same state	10,500	1.41
Candidates from other states	3,000	.40
Civic organizations	680	.09
Ideological groups	0	
Political parties	10,619	1.43
Subtotal	24,799	3.33
Unitemized Expenses	25,721	3.46
Total Campaign Expenses	$ 744,065	
PAC Contributions	$ 453,076	
Individual Contributions	292,679	
Total Receipts*	757,980	

*Includes PAC and individual contributions as well as interest earned, party contributions, etc.

† No expenditures or receipts on file. Candidates raising or spending less than $5,000 are not required to file reports with the Federal Election Commission.

District 9 — TEXAS

Rep. Jack Brooks (D)

1992 Election Results

Jack Brooks (D)	118,690	(54%)
Steve Stockman (R)	96,270	(43%)

Having served forty years in the House, Rep. Jack Brooks knew how to raise huge sums of money with minimal effort. During the 1992 election cycle, Brooks spent just $32,583 to raise $558,788, a return of more than $17 for every $1 invested. Political action committees (PACs) accounted for 82 percent of Brooks's total contributions, and out-of-state donors who gave $200 or more accounted for another 10 percent.

Brooks held three fund-raising events each year—one in Washington, D.C., one in Houston, and one in Beaumont, Texas. The Washington and Houston events were traditional receptions, while the annual Beaumont soiree was the "Jack Brooks Appreciation Dinner" where approximately 1,000 people gathered to honor Brooks with modest $100 donations. However, even this dinner attracted mostly PAC representatives, as evidenced by the fact that individual Texans gave a total of only $44,155 to his campaign.

Brooks did not run a permanent campaign. He waited until September 1992 to open his headquarters and had no campaign employees during 1991, no telephone bills, no office equipment, no campaign car, and travel expenses of only $1,206. While his off-year spending amounted to $66,293, roughly one-third of that total, or $22,825, was given away to other candidates, party organizations, and causes. "He didn't want to spend much money this time," noted Dan McClung of Campaign Strategies, the Houston-based firm that managed Brooks's campaign.

Still, Brooks spent $467,026 on the campaign, while accountant Steve Stockman spent just 21 percent of that total. Brooks donated $20,000 to the Democratic Congressional Campaign Committee, $5,000 each to the Texas Democratic party and the Galveston County Democratic party committee, and $4,000 to the Jefferson County Democratic party.

For all practical purposes, Campaign Strategies was the Brooks reelection effort. The firm collected $223,655—$89,461 for producing and sending the campaign's persuasion mail, $73,806 for phonebanking, $33,549 for basic day-to-day campaign management, $15,656 for renting billboard space, and $11,183 for yard signs and posters.

According to McClung, both the billboards and the persuasion mail hit the theme "made in America makes sense to Jack Brooks." The mailers also called attention to Brooks's ability to consistently deliver federal projects, such as a new prison near Beaumont, funds for the Johnson Space Center, and flood-control dollars for Galveston.

Stockman could not compete financially. To get free publicity, he spent $442 to purchase an original World War II document concerning the Japanese surrender, which he presented to a local library.

Campaign Expenditures	Brooks Amount Spent	Brooks % of Total	Stockman Amount Spent	Stockman % of Total
Overhead				
Office furniture/supplies	$ 2,421	.52	$ 8,357	8.57
Rent/utilities	1,391	.30	3,337	3.42
Salaries	10,368	2.22	10,061	10.32
Taxes	10,581	2.27	0	
Bank/investment fees	0		132	.14
Lawyers/accountants	10,160	2.18	0	
Telephone	1,556	.33	8,090	8.30
Campaign automobile	0		0	
Computers/office equipment	1,616	.35	3,132	3.21
Travel	28,354	6.07	1,637	1.68
Food/meetings	1,335	.29	164	.17
Subtotal	**67,782**	**14.51**	**34,910**	**35.81**
Fund Raising				
Events	32,583	6.98	17,266	17.71
Direct mail	0		0	
Telemarketing	0		0	
Subtotal	**32,583**	**6.98**	**17,266**	**17.71**
Polling	**7,200**	**1.54**	**0**	
Advertising				
Electronic media	300	.06	9,915	10.17
Other media	30,004	6.42	7,139	7.32
Subtotal	**30,304**	**6.49**	**17,054**	**17.49**
Other Campaign Activity				
Persuasion mail/brochures	90,768	19.44	19,707	20.22
Actual campaigning	149,156	31.94	7,939	8.14
Staff/volunteers	0		388	.40
Subtotal	**239,924**	**51.37**	**28,035**	**28.76**
Constituent Gifts/ Entertainment	**783**	**.17**	**0**	
Donations to				
Candidates from same state	20,370	4.36	50	.05
Candidates from other states	12,500	2.68	0	
Civic organizations	4,150	.89	20	.02
Ideological groups	2,310	.49	40	.04
Political parties	38,400	8.22	0	
Subtotal	**77,730**	**16.64**	**110**	**.11**
Unitemized Expenses	**10,721**	**2.30**	**111**	**.11**
Total Campaign Expenses	**$ 467,026**		**$ 97,485**	
PAC Contributions	**$ 456,357**		**$ 17,535**	
Individual Contributions	**102,431**		**58,885**	
Total Receipts*	**606,190**		**99,616**	

*Includes PAC and individual contributions as well as interest earned, party contributions, etc.

TEXAS   District 10

Rep. J. J. Pickle (D)   *1992 Election Results*   J. J. Pickle (D)   177,233   (68%)
                                                                        Herbert Spiro (R)   68,646   (26%)

Rep. J. J. Pickle had received better than 70 percent of the vote in eleven of his fourteen reelection campaigns, but that zone of comfort had not made him complacent. "He understands you have to run a campaign, that you can't just sit on the sidelines," noted media adviser Doc Sweitzer of the Philadelphia-based Campaign Group. "But his campaign floats, based on the need."

The need in 1992 was moderately low. Retired professor Herbert Spiro had less than half the financial resources leveled at Pickle by 1990 challenger David Beilharz, so Pickle brought the level of his own spending down by 35 percent. Pickle cut his combined outlays for advertising and voter contact mail by 49 percent.

According to Sweitzer, the Campaign Group produced only two television commercials for Pickle's 1992 effort, both aimed at portraying the incumbent as someone "too valuable to lose." With little opposition, Sweitzer said the campaign was free to "take the opportunity to tell people what he was working on at the time."

One ad focused on Pickle's efforts to strengthen the federal agency that backs up private pension plans and his 1992 fight to clamp down on price-gouging practices of medical equipment suppliers. The other focused on his efforts to increase research and development on flood control and other issues of specific importance to central Texas. "We had to show that he was part of the solution, not the problem," explained Sweitzer. The Campaign Group collected $95,000 for producing and placing the ads, which both closed with the tagline: "Jake Pickle. Unique. Ours."

D. Helfert & Associates of Austin was paid $10,000 for placing ads during the final weeks of the fall campaign. The firm also received $8,558 for placing radio spots before the March Democratic primary contest against real estate agent John Longsworth, which Pickle won with 82 percent of the vote.

Pickle did not run anything resembling a permanent campaign operation, waiting until July 1992 to open his headquarters. His off-year spending totaled just $35,884, more than one-quarter of which was given away to party organizations, civic groups, and ideological organizations.

Pickle's most original campaign hand-outs remained his pickle pins. Purchased from a Texas manufacturer for $1,610, thousands of the green, pickle-shaped pins bearing the name "Jake" were assembled at the Mary Lee Work Center for $350. Another $2,090 was invested in full-sized plastic pickles that squeak when squeezed. "When you have all the small kids squeaking the pickles, you know he's been there," said campaign manager Kathy Lowry.

Campaign Expenditures	Pickle Amount Spent	Pickle % of Total	Spiro Amount Spent	Spiro % of Total
Overhead				
Office furniture/supplies	$ 12,219	3.36	$ 4,828	4.09
Rent/utilities	4,713	1.30	9,668	8.20
Salaries	61,697	16.97	19,731	16.73
Taxes	22,909	6.30	6,960	5.90
Bank/investment fees	116	.03	140	.12
Lawyers/accountants	2,719	.75	0	
Telephone	7,600	2.09	4,244	3.60
Campaign automobile	0		0	
Computers/office equipment	7,638	2.10	3,298	2.80
Travel	12,603	3.47	1,464	1.24
Food/meetings	7,756	2.13	0	
Subtotal	**139,970**	**38.50**	**50,334**	**42.68**
Fund Raising				
Events	25,957	7.14	3,313	2.81
Direct mail	0		0	
Telemarketing	0		0	
Subtotal	**25,957**	**7.14**	**3,313**	**2.81**
Polling	**11,000**	**3.03**	**0**	
Advertising				
Electronic media	113,738	31.28	56,614	48.00
Other media	8,034	2.21	1,315	1.11
Subtotal	**121,771**	**33.49**	**57,929**	**49.12**
Other Campaign Activity				
Persuasion mail/brochures	775	.21	1,498	1.27
Actual campaigning	30,586	8.41	4,392	3.72
Staff/volunteers	292	.08	183	.16
Subtotal	**31,653**	**8.71**	**6,072**	**5.15**
Constituent Gifts/ Entertainment	**220**	**.06**	**0**	
Donations to				
Candidates from same state	2,165	.60	0	
Candidates from other states	1,800	.50	0	
Civic organizations	1,869	.51	0	
Ideological groups	5,425	1.49	0	
Political parties	20,456	5.63	0	
Subtotal	**31,715**	**8.72**	**0**	
Unitemized Expenses	**1,280**	**.35**	**291**	**.25**
Total Campaign Expenses	**$ 363,566**		**$ 117,939**	
PAC Contributions	**$ 263,432**		**$ 350**	
Individual Contributions	**145,903**		**17,346**	
Total Receipts*	**421,708**		**119,690**	

*Includes PAC and individual contributions as well as interest earned, party contributions, etc.

District 11 — TEXAS

Rep. Chet Edwards (D)

1992 Election Results

Chet Edwards (D)	119,999	(67%)
James W. Broyles (R)	58,033	(33%)

What a difference two years can make. In 1990 Rep. Chet Edwards spent more than $730,000 to defeat Republican Hugh D. Shine, who invested nearly $859,000 in the bitterly contested battle for the open seat created by the retirement of Rep. Marvin Leath. By 1992 the best the district's Republicans could do was to field a candidate with only about $17,000 to spend. Edwards coasted to victory, spending $357,418.

Like most incumbents, Edwards chose to keep a campaign office open during the off-year. In 1991 Edwards spent $61,348 on his campaign overhead, including $3,213 for rent and utilities, $32,685 for staff salaries, $4,734 for supplies, $5,876 for telephone service, and $3,200 for office equipment.

Edwards's total off-year spending of $149,106 also included $57,764 for fund raising. A birthday celebration in Waco featured Democratic Gov. Ann Richards and attracted approximately 2,500 supporters who paid $10 each to dine on barbecue, Mexican food, and a huge chocolate cake. With costs totaling $22,825, the event barely broke even. Edwards also held one major off-year event aimed at political action committees, which accounted for $168,660 of the $258,792 he raised in 1991.

Unopposed in the primary, Edwards spent about $67,000 during the first six months of 1992. He invested approximately $140,000 to defeat underfunded fire department captain James W. Broyles in the November general election, half of which was spent on advertising.

Edwards ran three television commercials. According to press secretary Vance Gore, the first ad detailed Edwards's efforts to help secure federal money for construction of a dam in Mound, Texas, where the river was periodically overflowing its banks and threatening homes in the area. In the second ad, Edwards expounded on his desire to force drug companies to lower their prices. The final spot focused on his involvement in "the gang of six," six freshman Democrats pushing a constitutional amendment requiring a balanced federal budget. For developing these ads and three radio commercials, Joe Slade White & Co. of New York received $23,442. Shafto & Barton of Houston billed the campaign $39,958 to cover the costs of air time and placement fees.

Newspaper ads cost Edwards another $7,594, including $2,400 paid to Campaign Performance Group of San Francisco for design and layout. Campaign Performance also collected $8,056 as a retainer in case he needed to develop persuasion mail.

Broyles was able to spend nearly $12,000 on radio advertising and voter contact mail only after loaning his campaign $13,253.

Campaign Expenditures	Edwards Amount Spent	Edwards % of Total	Broyles Amount Spent	Broyles % of Total
Overhead				
Office furniture/supplies	$ 8,793	2.46	$ 36	.21
Rent/utilities	6,238	1.75	620	3.61
Salaries	63,905	17.88	0	
Taxes	1,740	.49	0	
Bank/investment fees	0		86	.50
Lawyers/accountants	7,562	2.12	0	
Telephone	9,453	2.64	0	
Campaign automobile	0		0	
Computers/office equipment	4,133	1.16	1,050	6.12
Travel	10,146	2.84	0	
Food/meetings	1,278	.36	0	
Subtotal	**113,249**	**31.69**	**1,791**	**10.44**
Fund Raising				
Events	94,196	26.35	0	
Direct mail	0		0	
Telemarketing	0		0	
Subtotal	**94,196**	**26.35**	**0**	
Polling	**22,095**	**6.18**	**0**	
Advertising				
Electronic media	63,610	17.80	7,895	46.03
Other media	8,149	2.28	0	
Subtotal	**71,759**	**20.08**	**7,895**	**46.03**
Other Campaign Activity				
Persuasion mail/brochures	11,025	3.08	4,030	23.50
Actual campaigning	9,412	2.63	3,376	19.68
Staff/volunteers	1,076	.30	0	
Subtotal	**21,513**	**6.02**	**7,406**	**43.18**
Constituent Gifts/Entertainment	**1,175**	**.33**	**0**	
Donations to				
Candidates from same state	2,000	.56	0	
Candidates from other states	1,846	.52	0	
Civic organizations	1,737	.49	0	
Ideological groups	175	.05	0	
Political parties	14,400	4.03	0	
Subtotal	**20,158**	**5.64**	**0**	
Unitemized Expenses	**13,273**	**3.71**	**60**	**.35**
Total Campaign Expenses	**$ 357,418**		**$ 17,152**	
PAC Contributions	$ 321,575		$ 400	
Individual Contributions	139,862		4,412	
Total Receipts*	465,342		18,415	

*Includes PAC and individual contributions as well as interest earned, party contributions, etc.

TEXAS District 12

Rep. Pete Geren (D)

1992 Election Results

Pete Geren (D)	125,492	(63%)
David Hobbs (R)	74,432	(37%)

Rep. Pete Geren had good reason to raise money in 1991. His campaign still owed him $418,645 from the personal loans he made to his 1989 special election effort, and he had finished the 1990 election cycle with campaign cash reserves of only $18,000.

Spurred by those strong incentives, Geren devoted one-third of his $100,375 off-year spending to raising money. He paid Fundraising Management Group of Washington, D.C., $15,973 to coordinate events in Washington. His largest off-year district event, held in November at Fort Worth's Worthington Hotel, cost $8,484 to stage and drew more than 500 contributors. In all, Geren's 1991 efforts yielded $144,077 from political action committees and $171,378 from individual donors. By the end of 1991 Geren had increased his cash-on-hand total to $226,886.

Unopposed in the Democratic primary, Geren was able to focus his attention entirely on Republican David Hobbs. During 1992 Geren outspent Hobbs $645,381 to $378,783, and 70 percent of that difference was pumped into advertising.

Branded by Hobbs as one of the most liberal members of Congress, Geren's advertising highlighted his record as a fiscal conservative. He touted the favorable ratings of his voting record by the Chamber of Commerce and other conservative business groups.

Strother-Duffy-Strother of Washington, D.C., received $23,155 for creating both radio and television commercials. Media Strategies & Research of Washington, D.C., billed the campaign $164,284 to cover the cost of air time and their fees for placing the ads. Additional production costs associated with the radio spots and several direct purchases of radio time by the campaign added $4,776 to the total broadcast media budget. Geren also spent $16,899 on companion newspaper ads, including the $3,965 he paid to the Todd Co. of Arlington for design and placement fees.

Administrative assistant Scott A. Sudduth said most of the $80,232 Geren spent on persuasion mail was targeted at rural Johnson and Parker counties, which he picked up in redistricting. The Todd Co. collected $8,278 for production work on the mailings.

To turn out his supporters, Geren spent $86,985 on various get-out-the-vote efforts. The Tyson Organization received $84,565 for organizing Geren's main phonebank, and fellow Democratic Rep. Martin Frost received $1,600 to help defray the costs of a joint phonebanking effort.

Hobbs sank 42 percent of his funds into persuasion mail designed by his general consultant, the Eccles Group of Houston. The National Republican Congressional Committee's coordinated campaign effort spent $32,413 on Hobbs's behalf, 86 percent of which went for voter contact mail.

Campaign Expenditures	Geren Amount Spent	Geren % of Total	Hobbs Amount Spent	Hobbs % of Total
Overhead				
Office furniture/supplies	$ 20,635	2.77	$ 20,919	5.45
Rent/utilities	20,351	2.73	6,471	1.69
Salaries	34,701	4.65	32,017	8.34
Taxes	13,997	1.88	10,816	2.82
Bank/investment fees	1,509	.20	0	
Lawyers/accountants	7,016	.94	366	.10
Telephone	24,038	3.22	13,227	3.44
Campaign automobile	0		0	
Computers/office equipment	43,028	5.77	6,906	1.80
Travel	13,137	1.76	2,271	.59
Food/meetings	4,636	.62	21	.01
Subtotal	**183,046**	**24.55**	**93,013**	**24.23**
Fund Raising				
Events	84,488	11.33	14,239	3.71
Direct mail	0		18,543	4.83
Telemarketing	0		0	
Subtotal	**84,488**	**11.33**	**32,782**	**8.54**
Polling	**14,700**	**1.97**	**8,700**	**2.27**
Advertising				
Electronic media	192,215	25.77	18,595	4.84
Other media	17,975	2.41	5,548	1.45
Subtotal	**210,189**	**28.18**	**24,143**	**6.29**
Other Campaign Activity				
Persuasion mail/brochures	80,232	10.76	160,186	41.72
Actual campaigning	127,182	17.05	58,176	15.15
Staff/volunteers	2,186	.29	0	
Subtotal	**209,600**	**28.11**	**218,362**	**56.87**
Constituent Gifts/Entertainment	**8,479**	**1.14**	**0**	
Donations to				
Candidates from same state	0		0	
Candidates from other states	0		0	
Civic organizations	3,121	.42	0	
Ideological groups	250	.03	0	
Political parties	6,280	.84	0	
Subtotal	**9,651**	**1.29**	**0**	
Unitemized Expenses	**25,605**	**3.43**	**6,947**	**1.81**
Total Campaign Expenses	**$ 745,757**		**$ 383,946**	
PAC Contributions	$ 356,168		$ 36,318	
Individual Contributions	433,695		309,372	
Total Receipts*	809,664		386,959	

*Includes PAC and individual contributions as well as interest earned, party contributions, etc.

District 13 — TEXAS

Rep. Bill Sarpalius (D)

1992 Election Results

Bill Sarpalius (D)   117,892   (60%)
Beau Boulter (R)   77,514   (40%)

While Rep. Bill Sarpalius outspent former Rep. Beau Boulter by nearly $115,000, that fact obscures more than it reveals about the dynamics of this contest.

Faced with serious opposition in the March Republican primary, Boulter was forced to invest $105,253 of his resources to secure the nomination. Once he got it, he continued to spend heavily to pump up his name recognition. Between April 1 and September 30 Boulter spent another $137,956, which left him with cash reserves of only $22,183 going into the final month of the campaign.

Sarpalius invested $122,668 to maintain his permanent, off-year campaign, including $58,631 on overhead. Because he began the election cycle with debts of $63,972, Sarpalius spent $44,871 to raise money. However, unopposed in the Democratic primary, he spent only $39,006 during the first three months of 1992. With no need to worry about name recognition, Sarpalius invested $97,316 between April 1 and the end of September and entered the final month with cash reserves of $132,204.

As a result, from October 1 through election day, Sarpalius was able to spend $191,485, 75 percent of which he put into his broadcast media effort. Boulter was able to counter with $109,853, of which $47,242 went into broadcast advertising. That $96,706 gap in eleventh-hour media was the decisive blow to Boulter's hopes of restarting his congressional career.

Sarpalius's commercials focused heavily on Boulter's poor attendance record during his four-year tenure in the House. "He was running against someone who only made 15 percent of the votes between 1985 and 1988," said chief of staff Phil C. Duncan. "We hammered at [Sarpalius's] effectiveness and high attendance record in Congress." Joe Slade White & Co. of New York received $48,201 for producing the radio and television spots. Cargill & Roush received $121,219 for placing them.

To pay off his old campaign debts and fuel his 1992 effort, Sarpalius depended heavily on political action committees (PACs). A former agricultural consultant and a member of the Agriculture Committee, Sarpalius collected $97,225 from PACs with interests in agricultural policy. In all, PAC donations accounted for 64 percent of his total contributions.

For helping to fill Sarpalius's campaign coffers, Springer Associates of Falls Church, Va., received 16 payments totaling $46,605. Dottie Mavromatis of Washington, D.C., was paid $5,500 at the end of the campaign for additional fund-raising assistance.

Sarpalius personally handed out much of his campaign literature. "He's more comfortable meeting people when he has something he can hand them," noted Duncan.

Campaign Expenditures	Sarpalius Amount Spent	Sarpalius % of Total	Boulter Amount Spent	Boulter % of Total
Overhead				
Office furniture/supplies	$ 11,587	2.44	$ 6,871	1.91
Rent/utilities	7,834	1.65	4,296	1.19
Salaries	52,332	11.02	51,621	14.34
Taxes	14,751	3.11	9,601	2.67
Bank/investment fees	8,029	1.69	105	.03
Lawyers/accountants	0		0	
Telephone	9,762	2.05	17,120	4.75
Campaign automobile	0		0	
Computers/office equipment	6,269	1.32	5,004	1.39
Travel	31,659	6.66	15,035	4.18
Food/meetings	2,826	.59	71	.02
Subtotal	**145,048**	**30.53**	**109,726**	**30.47**
Fund Raising				
Events	83,993	17.68	55,194	15.33
Direct mail	0		0	
Telemarketing	0		11,125	3.09
Subtotal	**83,993**	**17.68**	**66,318**	**18.42**
Polling	**13,750**	**2.89**	**0**	
Advertising				
Electronic media	174,693	36.77	108,099	30.02
Other media	1,138	.24	332	.09
Subtotal	**175,831**	**37.01**	**108,431**	**30.11**
Other Campaign Activity				
Persuasion mail/brochures	6,643	1.40	23,780	6.60
Actual campaigning	29,931	6.30	48,229	13.39
Staff/volunteers	6,958	1.46	526	.15
Subtotal	**43,532**	**9.16**	**72,535**	**20.14**
Constituent Gifts/ Entertainment	**1,027**	**.22**	**0**	
Donations to				
Candidates from same state	1,100	.23	0	
Candidates from other states	0		0	
Civic organizations	556	.12	140	.04
Ideological groups	0		50	.01
Political parties	300	.06	90	.02
Subtotal	**1,956**	**.41**	**280**	**.08**
Unitemized Expenses	**9,913**	**2.09**	**2,799**	**.78**
Total Campaign Expenses	**$ 475,048**		**$ 360,089**	
PAC Contributions	$ 320,769		$ 17,158	
Individual Contributions	170,511		316,368	
Total Receipts*	521,447		370,708	

*Includes PAC and individual contributions as well as interest earned, party contributions, etc.

TEXAS District 14

Rep. Greg Laughlin (D)

1992 Election Results

Greg Laughlin (D)	135,930	(68%)
Humberto J. Garza (R)	54,412	(27%)
Vic Vreeland † (I)	9,329	(5%)

Compared with 1990, the 1992 campaign was a breeze for Rep. Greg Laughlin. Instead of an opponent with nearly $480,000 to spend, Laughlin faced Republican Humberto J. Garza, who spent only $13,553. Lacking any credible opposition, Laughlin reduced his own spending from $753,476 in 1990 to $449,063 in 1992. This 40 percent cut in spending still left Laughlin with a spending advantage of thirty-three to one.

One-third of Laughlin's spending went to Maverick Communications of Austin, a consulting firm founded in 1989 by Laughlin's former congressional district director, Ken Bryan. For $153,225, Bryan designed and placed the campaign's radio and television commercials, designed and placed newspaper advertising, ran a large phonebanking operation, handled direct-mail fund raising, and conducted polls. For all practical purposes, Maverick Communications was the campaign.

Three months before the November general election, he paid an $18,250 retainer to Maverick Communications to get the ball rolling. In addition to payments for the phonebank, over the next several months the company received $14,843 to pay for television and radio air time, $20,860 to cover the cost of two rounds of newspaper ads and newspaper inserts, and a $16,000 commission for placing the ads.

Bryan said the main thrust of the campaign was to "focus on Greg's independence," rather than attack Garza. One ad, fittingly dubbed "Maverick," took pains to distance Laughlin from what Bryan described as "the rest of the Democratic delegation and the East Coast liberal establishment."

Following the election, Bryan received a $25,000 "winner's bonus" for coordinating the media and phonebanking efforts. Fundraising Management Group of Washington, D.C., received a $2,000 winner's bonus on top of the $44,345 it was paid for helping Laughlin raise $602,187.

Laughlin also devoted considerable resources to helping other Democrats in the district, including the Clinton-Gore presidential ticket. "We were more active in cooperative campaign efforts, so we stepped up our phonebanking," understated Bryan. The phonebanking effort was increased from $4,039 in 1990 to $33,665 in 1992, a rise of 733 percent.

The weakness of Garza's challenge was also evident in Laughlin's donations, which increased from $1,275 in 1990 to $29,300 in 1992. During the final month of the campaign, Laughlin made $1,000 contributions to sixteen fellow House Democrats, including Reps. Charles Wilson (Texas), Ben Erdreich (Ala.), Jerry Huckaby (La.), Sam Gejdenson (Conn.), and Dan Glickman (Kan.).

	Laughlin		Garza	
Campaign Expenditures	Amount Spent	% of Total	Amount Spent	% of Total
Overhead				
Office furniture/supplies	$ 14,022	3.12	$ 835	6.16
Rent/utilities	10,762	2.40	0	
Salaries	61,518	13.70	0	
Taxes	13,836	3.08	0	
Bank/investment fees	566	.13	108	.79
Lawyers/accountants	177	.04	0	
Telephone	9,852	2.19	1,762	13.00
Campaign automobile	0		0	
Computers/office equipment	6,852	1.53	371	2.74
Travel	24,215	5.39	2,178	16.07
Food/meetings	410	.09	166	1.23
Subtotal	**142,211**	**31.67**	**5,419**	**39.99**
Fund Raising				
Events	60,203	13.41	994	7.34
Direct mail	12,156	2.71	0	
Telemarketing	0		0	
Subtotal	**72,360**	**16.11**	**994**	**7.34**
Polling	**10,813**	**2.41**	**0**	
Advertising				
Electronic media	55,354	12.33	0	
Other media	46,611	10.38	704	5.19
Subtotal	**101,964**	**22.71**	**704**	**5.19**
Other Campaign Activity				
Persuasion mail/brochures	5,001	1.11	0	
Actual campaigning	80,600	17.95	6,253	46.14
Staff/volunteers	15	.00	173	1.27
Subtotal	**85,616**	**19.07**	**6,426**	**47.41**
Constituent Gifts/ Entertainment	**5,083**	**1.13**	**0**	
Donations to				
Candidates from same state	6,000	1.34	0	
Candidates from other states	13,500	3.01	0	
Civic organizations	300	.07	10	.07
Ideological groups	2,200	.49	0	
Political parties	7,500	1.67	0	
Subtotal	**29,500**	**6.57**	**10**	**.07**
Unitemized Expenses	**1,517**	**.34**	**0**	
Total Campaign Expenses	**$ 449,063**		**$ 13,553**	
PAC Contributions	$ 353,940		$ 974	
Individual Contributions	248,247		3,940	
Total Receipts*	618,011		13,589	

*Includes PAC and individual contributions as well as interest earned, party contributions, etc.

† No expenditures or receipts on file. Candidates raising or spending less than $5,000 are not required to file reports with the Federal Election Commission.

District 15 — TEXAS

Rep. E. "Kika" de la Garza (D)

1992 Election Results

E. "Kika" de la Garza (D)	86,351	(60%)
Tom Haughey (R)	56,549	(40%)

As chairman of the Agriculture Committee, Rep. E. "Kika" de la Garza did not need to spend much money to raise money. Those with an interest in agricultural policy came looking for him.

De la Garza held three Washington, D.C., events aimed at attracting political action committee (PAC) donations during the 1992 election cycle. He opted not to hire a consultant to organize the events, and his most expensive affair, held at the restaurant La Fonda, cost $5,906. The combined outlays for all three events totaled $10,199, including the cost of invitations and postage.

Over the two-year cycle, PACs responded with donations totaling $184,825, or 75 percent of his contributions. PACs representing companies with an interest in legislation framed by the Agriculture Committee contributed $130,759, or 53 percent of his total contributions. In contrast, de la Garza collected only $49,692 from fellow Texans. His lone district fundraiser cost the campaign $435.

Unopposed in 1990, de le Garza had invested $122,550 in his campaign. Opposed in 1992 by pastor Tom Haughey, who had less than $13,500 to spend, de la Garza more than doubled his spending to $266,103. In this staunchly Democratic district that has produced Republican opposition for de la Garza in only five of his fourteen reelection bids, the incumbent was in all likelihood more concerned with the potential impact of his 284 overdrafts at the House bank than he was with Haughey.

To inoculate against the possibility of an upset, de la Garza invested $61,396 in a broadcast advertising campaign designed by Rodd & Associates of McAllen. In addition to the $60,750 Rodd collected for designing and placing the ads, the campaign directly purchased $560 of radio air time. Rodd also received $20,250 for billboard ads and yard signs. An in-kind contribution of $86 for the use of production facilities at the Harriman Communications Center in Washington, D.C., rounded out his advertising expenses. Various get-out-the-vote efforts cost $19,658.

As in 1990, not all of the travel paid for by de la Garza's campaign was related to his reelection effort. The campaign paid the $697 air fare for a trip to Mexico to meet with President Carlos Salinas. De la Garza also billed the campaign for expenses incurred on trips to Canada, Switzerland, and Saudi Arabia. When he was given a "man of the year" award in Austin, the campaign paid for that trip, as well.

De la Garza spent $2,907 on a luncheon for the Agriculture Committee. He threw annual Christmas parties for his Washington congressional staff that cost the campaign a total of $2,017. He spent $13,860 to lease, license, and fuel his campaign car.

Campaign Expenditures	de la Garza Amount Spent	de la Garza % of Total	Haughey Amount Spent	Haughey % of Total
Overhead				
Office furniture/supplies	$ 3,126	1.17	$ 459	3.42
Rent/utilities	500	.19	0	
Salaries	1,200	.45	0	
Taxes	0		0	
Bank/investment fees	0		86	.64
Lawyers/accountants	4,000	1.50	0	
Telephone	3,248	1.22	316	2.35
Campaign automobile	13,860	5.21	0	
Computers/office equipment	758	.28	0	
Travel	27,712	10.41	536	3.98
Food/meetings	4,614	1.73	0	
Subtotal	**59,017**	**22.18**	**1,398**	**10.39**
Fund Raising				
Events	12,927	4.86	0	
Direct mail	0		0	
Telemarketing	0		0	
Subtotal	**12,927**	**4.86**	**0**	
Polling	**0**		**0**	
Advertising				
Electronic media	61,396	23.07	5,774	42.92
Other media	16,327	6.14	1,212	9.01
Subtotal	**77,724**	**29.21**	**6,987**	**51.93**
Other Campaign Activity				
Persuasion mail/brochures	0		706	5.24
Actual campaigning	45,528	17.11	4,353	32.36
Staff/volunteers	2,097	.79	0	
Subtotal	**47,625**	**17.90**	**5,059**	**37.60**
Constituent Gifts/ Entertainment	2,018	.76	0	
Donations to				
Candidates from same state	1,500	.56	0	
Candidates from other states	1,500	.56	0	
Civic organizations	5,315	2.00	10	.07
Ideological groups	437	.16	0	
Political parties	13,600	5.11	0	
Subtotal	**22,352**	**8.40**	**10**	**.07**
Unitemized Expenses	**44,439**	**16.70**	**0**	
Total Campaign Expenses	**$ 266,103**		**$ 13,453**	
PAC Contributions	$ 184,825		$ 0	
Individual Contributions	61,582		10,651	
Total Receipts*	248,430		13,695	

*Includes PAC and individual contributions as well as interest earned, party contributions, etc.

TEXAS — District 16

Rep. Ronald D. Coleman (D)

1992 Election Results

Ronald D. Coleman (D)	66,731	(52%)
Chip Taberski (R)	61,870	(48%)

Rep. Ronald D. Coleman expected a difficult primary fight. His redrawn district was 70 percent Hispanic, and his primary opponent was Hispanic businessman Charles Ponzio, Jr., a former Chamber of Commerce president.

While Coleman had no off-year campaign office or staff, he still managed to spend $154,188. Legal and accounting fees totaled $22,485, and travel costs added $18,128. A benchmark survey of his new district cost $15,000. Although fund raising consumed 42 percent of the off-year budget, he raised roughly $16,000 less than he spent.

Over the first three months of 1992, Coleman committed approximately $265,000 to defeating Ponzio in the March 10 primary. Nearly $103,000 was invested in broadcast advertising. The design, printing, and postage charges for his persuasion mail effort totaled almost $54,000. He paid forty-eight temporary employees a total of $10,581 to work the campaign's twenty-line phonebank. "Precinct organization" cost $10,000. Production and placement of yard signs amounted to $12,345.

Ponzio spent only $33,540 on his challenge. Coleman emerged with 64 percent of the primary vote.

Had it not been for his 673 overdrafts at the House bank, Coleman would probably have breezed to victory in November. He had not had Republican opposition since 1986, and the district looked more Democratic in 1992 than it had been prior to redistricting. Instead, Coleman was forced to spend $66,872 more than he raised to pull out a 4,861-vote victory over former sportscaster Chip Taberski.

With $61,693 from his own campaign treasury and a $45,000 boost from the National Republican Campaign Committee's coordinated campaign, Taberski hit the airwaves in early October. His radio and television commercials asked why federal prosecutor Malcolm Wilkey had not yet cleared Coleman of criminal wrongdoing in the House bank scandal.

Coleman's ads responded by attacking Taberski for opposing increases in the minimum wage and for his opposition to the Americans with Disabilities Act. Coleman's general election broadcast advertising investment of approximately $110,000 was augmented by a $15,730 coordinated expenditure by the Democratic Congressional Campaign Committee.

For their work in designing and placing both the primary and general election ad campaigns, Coleman paid Rindy Media of Austin $211,994. Doug Zabel & Associates of Austin and Campaign Performance Group of San Francisco, Calif., received $18,220 and $2,044, respectively, for designing persuasion mailers. Pollsters Garin-Hart of Washington, D.C., and Opinion Analysts of Austin collected $30,000 and $9,253, respectively.

	Coleman		Taberski	
Campaign Expenditures	Amount Spent	% of Total	Amount Spent	% of Total
Overhead				
Office furniture/supplies	$ 10,608	1.30	$ 8,446	4.00
Rent/utilities	10,213	1.26	6,672	3.16
Salaries	25,377	3.12	10,586	5.02
Taxes	262	.03	5,474	2.59
Bank/investment fees	3,266	.40	13	.01
Lawyers/accountants	78,753	9.68	4,512	2.14
Telephone	16,052	1.97	5,867	2.78
Campaign automobile	0		0	
Computers/office equipment	3,171	.39	390	.18
Travel	46,737	5.74	5,906	2.80
Food/meetings	1,827	.22	483	.23
Subtotal	196,265	24.12	48,349	22.91
Fund Raising				
Events	156,664	19.25	7,165	3.39
Direct mail	11,165	1.37	7,391	3.50
Telemarketing	0		0	
Subtotal	167,829	20.62	14,556	6.90
Polling	39,253	4.82	0	
Advertising				
Electronic media	213,203	26.20	61,693	29.23
Other media	3,865	.48	15,970	7.57
Subtotal	217,068	26.68	77,663	36.79
Other Campaign Activity				
Persuasion mail/brochures	108,449	13.33	16,570	7.85
Actual campaigning	65,299	8.02	49,329	23.37
Staff/volunteers	1,047	.13	150	.07
Subtotal	174,796	21.48	66,049	31.29
Constituent Gifts/ Entertainment	478	.06	118	.06
Donations to				
Candidates from same state	4,050	.50	0	
Candidates from other states	1,000	.12	0	
Civic organizations	6,077	.75	2,297	1.09
Ideological groups	805	.10	80	.04
Political parties	4,125	.51	1,010	.48
Subtotal	16,057	1.97	3,387	1.60
Unitemized Expenses	1,977	.24	951	.45
Total Campaign Expenses	$ 813,723		$ 211,073	
PAC Contributions	$ 486,544		$ 16,355	
Individual Contributions	203,873		185,668	
Total Receipts*	777,219		212,848	

*Includes PAC and individual contributions as well as interest earned, party contributions, etc.

District 17 — TEXAS

Rep. Charles W. Stenholm (D)

1992 Election Results

Charles W. Stenholm (D) 136,213 (66%)
Jeannie Sadowski (R) 69,958 (34%)

For the first time since his initial House race in 1978, Rep. Charles W. Stenholm faced Republican opposition, and he responded by spending 26 percent more than he had in 1990, much of it on direct appeals to voters. The percentage of his campaign expenditures accounted for by overhead, fund raising, and donations dropped from 75 percent in 1990 to 54 percent in 1992. While he invested only $103,125 of his 1992 budget in direct appeals to voters, that represented a $65,374 increase over 1990.

During 1991 Stenholm spent $118,540 on his permanent campaign, including nearly $41,619 on fund-raising events, $36,795 on overhead, and $13,520 on donations to various Democratic party organizations. His off-year spending was nearly seven times more than businesswoman Jeannie Sadowski was able to invest in her entire campaign.

Despite the fact that he had no primary opposition, Stenholm spent $61,144 during the first three months of 1992. The ADCRAFT Agency of Jacksboro was paid $21,331 for polling district residents, $1,183 for supplying 5,000 bumper stickers, and $3,748 for buying billboard space. He passed out a $5,000 contribution to the Democratic Congressional Campaign Committee and $1,000 donations to the Democratic Leadership Conference and the College Democrats of America.

Although Sadowski raised only $17,222 and presented no real threat, Stenholm had eighty-six overdrafts at the House bank, so he decided not to take any chances. Between July 1 and October 14 he spent $127,976, including $9,399 for a "whistle-stop" bus tour of the district. The campaign invested $3,387 in key chains and $680 in pens that were handed out at various campaign events.

ADCRAFT was paid $22,875 for a persuasion mailer sent to new constituents, $16,929 for other brochures and palm cards, $9,248 for purchasing additional billboard space, $3,478 for yard signs, $2,552 for printing campaign stationery, $1,428 for printing nametags and other material for the bus tour, $992 for additional bumper stickers, and $2,699 for other design and printing work.

Stenholm's Funday celebrations, held annually since 1979, accounted for nearly $64,000 of his spending during the two-year cycle. As always, Stenholm ran newspaper and radio ads to announce the events, which constituents paid $10 to attend. He used campaign funds to fly in other members of Congress and their spouses for a Friday evening reception at the Parker Ranch and a Saturday barbecue held behind the Ericksdahl Lutheran church.

Stenholm spent $4,759 on year-end holiday cards and $1,453 on letters of congratulation that were mailed to every graduating high school senior.

Campaign Expenditures	Stenholm Amount Spent	Stenholm % of Total	Sadowski Amount Spent	Sadowski % of Total
Overhead				
Office furniture/supplies	$ 7,285	1.92	$ 506	2.88
Rent/utilities	1,800	.47	300	1.71
Salaries	34,169	9.02	1,380	7.85
Taxes	9,396	2.48	0	
Bank/investment fees	50	.01	0	
Lawyers/accountants	3,400	.90	0	
Telephone	449	.12	3,525	20.05
Campaign automobile	0		0	
Computers/office equipment	13,993	3.69	0	
Travel	18,010	4.75	4,698	26.72
Food/meetings	2,167	.57	506	2.88
Subtotal	**90,719**	**23.94**	**10,916**	**62.09**
Fund Raising				
Events	83,227	21.96	0	
Direct mail	0		0	
Telemarketing	0		0	
Subtotal	**83,227**	**21.96**	**0**	
Polling	**21,703**	**5.73**	**0**	
Advertising				
Electronic media	0		0	
Other media	16,318	4.31	709	4.03
Subtotal	**16,318**	**4.31**	**709**	**4.03**
Other Campaign Activity				
Persuasion mail/brochures	42,921	11.33	0	
Actual campaigning	43,461	11.47	225	1.28
Staff/volunteers	425	.11	0	
Subtotal	**86,807**	**22.91**	**225**	**1.28**
Constituent Gifts/Entertainment	**8,169**	**2.16**	**0**	
Donations to				
Candidates from same state	2,250	.59	0	
Candidates from other states	4,850	1.28	0	
Civic organizations	299	.08	0	
Ideological groups	0		0	
Political parties	23,820	6.29	0	
Subtotal	**31,219**	**8.24**	**0**	
Unitemized Expenses	**40,792**	**10.76**	**5,732**	**32.60**
Total Campaign Expenses	**$ 378,954**		**$ 17,582**	
PAC Contributions	$ 274,726		$ 0	
Individual Contributions	127,686		9,767	
Total Receipts*	412,834		17,222	

*Includes PAC and individual contributions as well as interest earned, party contributions, etc.

TEXAS — District 18

Rep. Craig Washington (D)

1992 Election Results

Craig Washington (D)	111,422	(65%)
Edward Blum (R)	56,080	(33%)

On August 31, 1989, when Rep. Craig Washington announced his candidacy in the special election to fill the seat previously held by the late Rep. Mickey Leland, he made what he now views as a "naive" promise to spend no more than $50,000 on his campaign. Ultimately, he spent more than $600,000 to win that contest, but he swore it would never happen again. "This job isn't worth $600,000," he said.

It certainly did not happen in 1992. Unchallenged in the primary, Washington invested $157,837 to secure his second full term and in the process was outspent by investment banker Edward Blum by nearly $52,000.

Washington continued his practice of using consultants sparingly. Campaign Strategies of Houston, his only paid consultant, received $13,424 for designing a small persuasion mail effort. "I decide my own methods, come up with my own slogans," he explained. "I want to get me across, not some image of me."

Washington's campaign office was located in a Houston building that he owns, but he did not pay any rent to himself. He retained one part-time campaign staffer, Helen Mason. His monthly telephone bills averaged $73. Travel totaled $6,912, including $2,677 for expenses incurred in conjunction with the Democratic National Convention.

Three of Washington's congressional staffers also pulled double duty on the campaign. Former law partner and now district administrator Sidney J. Braquet received $16,600 for reviewing financial documents filed with the Federal Election Commission and for organizing fund-raisers. Office administrator Roslyn Garcia was paid $1,450 for bookkeeping, and district caseworker Greg X. White collected $300. "I make sure any work they do on my behalf occurs outside the normal workday, in the evenings and on weekends," Washington stressed.

Relying on political action committees for 70 percent of his contributions, Washington did not have to devote much energy or resources to raising money from individual supporters. Donations of $200 or more amounted to $42,300. Small contributions added $9,449.

Typical of his fund-raisers was one held to coincide with his fiftieth birthday in October 1991. Expenses for the small celebration at Cody's restaurant in Houston included $342 for beverages and $400 for "supplies and goods." The party netted between $4,000 and $5,000.

Among Washington's more unusual expenses was a $3,000 fine stemming from the campaign's failure to report all last-minute contributions to his 1989 special election effort within the prescribed forty-eight-hour timeframe.

Campaign Expenditures	Washington Amount Spent	Washington % of Total	Blum Amount Spent	Blum % of Total
Overhead				
Office furniture/supplies	$ 6,924	4.39	$ 7,772	3.71
Rent/utilities	0		1,460	.70
Salaries	36,879	23.37	25,418	12.14
Taxes	8,209	5.20	0	
Bank/investment fees	2,998	1.90	59	.03
Lawyers/accountants	6,058	3.84	0	
Telephone	1,746	1.11	4,326	2.07
Campaign automobile	0		0	
Computers/office equipment	2,002	1.27	1,084	.52
Travel	6,912	4.38	240	.11
Food/meetings	800	.51	5	.00
Subtotal	**72,529**	**45.95**	**40,364**	**19.27**
Fund Raising				
Events	8,185	5.19	2,953	1.41
Direct mail	0		40,786	19.47
Telemarketing	0		0	
Subtotal	**8,185**	**5.19**	**43,739**	**20.88**
Polling	**0**		**6,300**	**3.01**
Advertising				
Electronic media	0		19,868	9.49
Other media	5,077	3.22	3,378	1.61
Subtotal	**5,077**	**3.22**	**23,246**	**11.10**
Other Campaign Activity				
Persuasion mail/brochures	16,044	10.16	67,375	32.17
Actual campaigning	29,824	18.90	19,822	9.46
Staff/volunteers	0		797	.38
Subtotal	**45,868**	**29.06**	**87,993**	**42.01**
Constituent Gifts/Entertainment	**3,933**	**2.49**	**0**	
Donations to				
Candidates from same state	0		0	
Candidates from other states	1,000	.63	0	
Civic organizations	894	.57	0	
Ideological groups	350	.22	0	
Political parties	0		0	
Subtotal	**2,244**	**1.42**	**0**	
Unitemized Expenses	**20,002**	**12.67**	**7,814**	**3.73**
Total Campaign Expenses	**$ 157,837**		**$ 209,457**	
PAC Contributions	$ 121,250		$ 8,400	
Individual Contributions	51,749		132,348	
Total Receipts*	185,635		211,586	

*Includes PAC and individual contributions as well as interest earned, party contributions, etc.

District 19 — TEXAS

Rep. Larry Combest (R)

1992 Election Results

Larry Combest (R)	162,057	(77%)
Terry Lee Moser (D)	47,325	(23%)

Elected in 1984 with 58 percent of the vote, Republican Rep. Larry Combest received better than 60 percent of the vote in his first two re-election bids before running unopposed in 1990. Redistricting strengthened the Republican hold on this district, which provided President George Bush with 60 percent of the vote in 1992. There was never any question who would win this contest.

Still, Combest invested $69,743 in an advertising campaign designed both to introduce himself to his new constituents and to convince his old constituents that he was not the typical House member so many of them had come to distrust. The task of designing and placing that advertising campaign was turned over to Phil Price Advertising of Lubbock, which collected $60,659 for its efforts.

Price funneled $27,017 of Combest's campaign treasury into newspaper advertising, $5,700 into billboards, $19,982 into television commercials, and $5,400 into radio spots, including the firm's placement fees. The balance of the payments to Price covered production fees and the cost of distributing the ads to stations across the district. TPFV Corporate Productions of Austin received $6,916 for television production. Ogletree Productions in Lubbock collected $375 for video production.

According to DeAnn Salsky, the account supervisor at Price who handled the Combest account, the campaign aired three television commercials highlighting the incumbent's efforts in Congress to help the district. One of the ads featured Combest talking into the camera about his "clean record," which included no overdrafts at the House bank. Salsky said the radio commercials were similar, both in number and in content. The newspaper ads were a compilation of positive editorial comments from local newspapers and constituent testimonials.

For helping to plan general campaign strategy against Democrat Terry Lee Moser, Sentinel Corp. of Austin was paid $12,756. Posters and yard signs cost $3,764, and bumper stickers added $921.

Largely as a result of relatively high staff costs, overhead consumed more than one-third of Combest's budget. Those staff costs were driven primarily by payments to Jimmy Clark, a district representative on Combest's congressional staff. While Clark drew a taxpayer-funded salary that totaled $81,888 over the two-year cycle, he was able to moonlight with the campaign and pick up an additional $13,122 in 1991 and $11,451 in 1992.

Prior to the election, Combest spent $1,200 of his campaign treasury to purchase tickets to the presidential inaugural ball on the assumption that George Bush would be reelected. When things did not work out as he had hoped, Combest gave them away.

Campaign Expenditures	Combest Amount Spent	Combest % of Total	Moser Amount Spent	Moser % of Total
Overhead				
Office furniture/supplies	$ 4,790	2.45	$ 0	
Rent/utilities	0		0	
Salaries	37,365	19.14	0	
Taxes	9,759	5.00	0	
Bank/investment fees	0		0	
Lawyers/accountants	276	.14	0	
Telephone	625	.32	0	
Campaign automobile	0		0	
Computers/office equipment	1,042	.53	0	
Travel	15,279	7.83	2,698	51.91
Food/meetings	2,026	1.04	0	
Subtotal	**71,162**	**36.45**	**2,698**	**51.91**
Fund Raising				
Events	18,148	9.29	0	
Direct mail	0		0	
Telemarketing	0		0	
Subtotal	**18,148**	**9.29**	**0**	
Polling	**0**		**0**	
Advertising				
Electronic media	35,233	18.05	0	
Other media	34,510	17.68	0	
Subtotal	**69,743**	**35.72**	**0**	
Other Campaign Activity				
Persuasion mail/brochures	0		0	
Actual campaigning	22,188	11.36	2,500	48.09
Staff/volunteers	665	.34	0	
Subtotal	**22,853**	**11.70**	**2,500**	**48.09**
Constituent Gifts/ Entertainment	**7,121**	**3.65**	**0**	
Donations to				
Candidates from same state	0		0	
Candidates from other states	0		0	
Civic organizations	1,350	.69	0	
Ideological groups	0		0	
Political parties	0		0	
Subtotal	**1,350**	**.69**	**0**	
Unitemized Expenses	**4,871**	**2.49**	**0**	
Total Campaign Expenses	**$ 195,247**		**$ 5,198**	
PAC Contributions	$ 125,675		$ 0	
Individual Contributions	97,366		3,889	
Total Receipts*	241,559		4,389	

*Includes PAC and individual contributions as well as interest earned, party contributions, etc.

TEXAS

District 20

Rep. Henry B. Gonzalez (D)

1992 Election Results Henry B. Gonzalez (D) 103,755 (100%)

For the ninth time in sixteen reelection contests, Rep. Henry B. Gonzalez ran unopposed. His winning percentage had dropped below 80 percent only twice since his special election victory in 1961. Seemingly assured of this seat for as long as he wants it, Gonzalez's spending has begun to approach the level of extreme frugality consistently achieved by Reps. William H. Natcher (D-Ky.) and Andrew Jacobs, Jr. (D-Ind.).

Gonzalez spent 64 percent less on his 1992 campaign than he had in 1990, largely because he eliminated all his fund-raising expenses, which totaled $37,516 in 1990. That was accomplished simply by making the decision not to hold his traditional "Chairman's Dinner," a testimonial to Gonzalez that had cost the campaign more than $36,000 in 1990. "He has been doing less and less fund raising," noted Banking Committee staff director Kelsay R. Meek.

While Gonzalez has never held a fund-raiser in Washington, D.C., and does not actively solicit political action committee (PAC) donations, he attracts some PAC money simply by virtue of the fact that he is the ninth most senior member of the House and chairs the Banking, Finance and Urban Affairs Committee. The $11,525 he received from PACs during the 1992 election cycle was $69,275 less than he collected from PACs in 1990.

Various forms of constituent stroking constituted 38 percent of Gonzalez's spending. Year-end holiday cards cost the campaign $2,875. Another $11,873 was invested in commemorative certificates and letters sent to high school graduates and newly naturalized citizens. Constituent meals totaled only $500.

While he opted not to do any broadcast advertising, per se, Gonzalez did spend $11,000 at the House recording studio to produce five-minute reports that were broadcast weekly on local television and radio stations back home. According to Meek, Gonzalez has been broadcasting these reports in both Spanish and English for the past thirty years. His other advertising costs included a $50 ad with the San Antonio Firefighters Association, a $100 ad with the San Antonio Building Trades Council, and a $50 ad with the Alamo Silver Wings.

Other than the required $2,500 filing fee, Gonzalez's only real campaign expense was the $2,119 he paid for promotional ballpoint pens. Engraved with "Thanks a Million, Henry B. Gonzalez," the pens were given to constituents who dropped by the congressional office, to school children, and to those Gonzalez happened to encounter on his district visits.

Gonzalez's only donation during the two-year cycle was to a memorial fund established in the name of Rhobia Taylor, a longtime friend.

Campaign Expenditures	Gonzalez Amount Spent	% of Total
Overhead		
Office furniture/supplies	$ 352	.88
Rent/utilities	340	.85
Salaries	4,914	12.27
Taxes	0	
Bank/investment fees	0	
Lawyers/accountants	0	
Telephone	1,784	4.46
Campaign automobile	0	
Computers/office equipment	0	
Travel	0	
Food/meetings	972	2.43
Subtotal	8,363	20.88
Fund Raising		
Events	0	
Direct mail	0	
Telemarketing	0	
Subtotal	**0**	
Polling	**0**	
Advertising		
Electronic media	11,000	27.47
Other media	275	.69
Subtotal	**11,275**	**28.15**
Other Campaign Activity		
Persuasion mail/brochures	0	
Actual campaigning	4,619	11.53
Staff/volunteers	0	
Subtotal	**4,619**	**11.53**
Constituent Gifts/Entertainment	**15,247**	**38.07**
Donations to		
Candidates from same state	0	
Candidates from other states	0	
Civic organizations	500	1.25
Ideological groups	0	
Political parties	0	
Subtotal	**500**	**1.25**
Unitemized Expenses	**46**	**.12**
Total Campaign Expenses	$ **40,050**	
PAC Contributions	$ **11,525**	
Individual Contributions	**31,515**	
Total Receipts*	**45,040**	

*Includes PAC and individual contributions as well as interest earned, party contributions, etc.

District 21 — TEXAS

Rep. Lamar Smith (R)

1992 Election Results

Lamar Smith (R)	190,979	(72%)
James M. Gaddy (D)	62,827	(24%)

While redistricting altered the boundaries of Rep. Lamar Smith's district, it did nothing to change its political character. Having won his 1988 and 1990 House reelection contests with 93 percent and 75 percent of the vote, respectively, Smith exceeded the 70 percent threshold again in 1992.

However, the easy victories have done nothing to curb Smith's high-octane permanent campaign. In 1990 Smith spent $398,245 to defeat a hapless Democratic challenger who could muster only $15,157. Against professor James. M. Gaddy, who had only $6,236, Smith's 1992 outlays swelled to $476,202.

One-third of Smith's total spending was dedicated to the maintenance of his permanent campaign during 1991. He had a year-round campaign office staffed by one full-time employee, who collected salary payments in 1991 totaling $38,317. Two part-time employees cost the campaign another $5,816, which helped push overhead during the off-year to $72,982. Fund-raising expenses amounted to $64,946.

Over the two-year election cycle, combined expenditures for overhead and fund raising accounted for 59 percent of Smith's total spending. Salary payments alone consumed nearly one of every five dollars the campaign spent.

Smith's permanent campaign office was located on the bottom floor of a condominium he owns. During the first thirteen months of the election cycle, he charged his campaign monthly rent of $857; in February 1992 he raised the campaign's rent to $926. The campaign also paid for upkeep on the property, including $314 to Orkin Pest Control, $221 for the repair of an air conditioning unit, $194 to repair an alarm system for the building, $169 for service on a heat pump, $50 for a furnace checkup, and $203 for unspecified office repairs.

Year-end holiday cards cost the campaign $10,313. Smith spent $636 on the congressional art competition, an annual contest open to high school students in each congressional district. Winning entries are hung in the basement of the Cannon Office Building in Washington, D.C.

Smith spent slightly less than one-third of his money on direct appeals to voters. Gossen & Associates of San Antonio received $21,346 to place radio commercials. Dozens of ads in newspapers such as the *Bandera Bulletin*, the *Comfort News*, and the *Round Rock Leader* cost $19,616. Karl Rove & Co. of Austin received $58,219 for designing and mailing two brochures that touted his efforts to cut the federal government's "wasteful spending." Smith outspent his opponent by more than seventy-six to one, yet one of his mailers opened with the statement: "Even his mother calls him a penny-pincher."

Campaign Expenditures	Smith Amount Spent	Smith % of Total	Gaddy Amount Spent	Gaddy % of Total
Overhead				
Office furniture/supplies	$ 14,553	3.06	$ 475	7.62
Rent/utilities	21,509	4.52	600	9.62
Salaries	90,964	19.10	700	11.23
Taxes	0		0	
Bank/investment fees	20	.00	0	
Lawyers/accountants	0		0	
Telephone	7,684	1.61	1,237	19.84
Campaign automobile	0		0	
Computers/office equipment	3,154	.66	419	6.72
Travel	28,286	5.94	93	1.49
Food/meetings	2,543	.53	0	
Subtotal	**168,712**	**35.43**	**3,524**	**56.52**
Fund Raising				
Events	113,646	23.87	1,161	18.62
Direct mail	0		0	
Telemarketing	0		0	
Subtotal	**113,646**	**23.87**	**1,161**	**18.62**
Polling	0		0	
Advertising				
Electronic media	23,231	4.88	0	
Other media	20,153	4.23	0	
Subtotal	**43,384**	**9.11**	**0**	
Other Campaign Activity				
Persuasion mail/brochures	90,711	19.05	0	
Actual campaigning	8,654	1.82	654	10.49
Staff/volunteers	3,308	.69	0	
Subtotal	**102,672**	**21.56**	**654**	**10.49**
Constituent Gifts/Entertainment	**11,152**	**2.34**	**0**	
Donations to				
Candidates from same state	9,180	1.93	0	
Candidates from other states	4,750	1.00	0	
Civic organizations	0		0	
Ideological groups	5,000	1.05	0	
Political parties	3,513	.74	0	
Subtotal	**22,443**	**4.71**	**0**	
Unitemized Expenses	**14,193**	**2.98**	**896**	**14.37**
Total Campaign Expenses	**$ 476,202**		**$ 6,236**	
PAC Contributions	$ 134,839		$ 0	
Individual Contributions	342,340		5,421	
Total Receipts*	544,187		6,916	

*Includes PAC and individual contributions as well as interest earned, party contributions, etc.

TEXAS   District 22

Rep. Tom DeLay (R)

1992 Election Results
Tom DeLay (R)   150,221   (69%)
Richard Konrad (D)   67,812   (31%)

Rep. Tom DeLay invested nearly half of his $367,305 campaign budget in overhead. Monthly rent on his permanent campaign headquarters was $370, and he paid another $89 each month to rent storage space. Office manager Mona Stevens collected $53,024 for her efforts, and the $22,925 she collected during 1991 accounted for one-quarter of DeLay's off-year spending. The campaign bent over backwards to pick up any travel that might be construed as campaign-related, rather than charging it to DeLay's congressional travel account. As a result, travel costs totaled $44,106, or 12 percent of his budget.

DeLay's fund raising proved more efficient in 1992 than it had been in past years. Although he raised $21,903 more in 1992 than in 1990, his fund-raising costs dropped by $23,965, or 39 percent.

Rather than staging a few large, sit-down dinners, the campaign shifted primarily to small in-home receptions that tended to draw about fifty supporters. The largest receptions attracted roughly one hundred people, requiring a shift of venue to country clubs throughout the district. Administrative assistant Kenneth Carroll estimated that the campaign held an average of two small events each month. "In the past, we tried to do big events, but the return on our investment was never as high as we would have liked," explained Carroll.

At least as important as the shift away from more formal events was DeLay's increased reliance on political action committees (PACs). While he held only one Washington, D.C., event, DeLay collected $57,703 more from PACs in 1992 than in 1990. This 34 percent increase in PAC contributions was accompanied by a 25 percent decrease in individual donations. The proportion of his contributions accounted for by PACs rose from 54 percent in 1990 to 67 percent in 1992. Maxwell & Associates of Alexandria, Va., received $10,759 for coordinating the lone Washington, D.C., event.

Of the $72,902 DeLay spent between October 15 and November 23, 1992, 26 percent was simply given away. Ten Republicans seeking House seats received $1,000 contributions during this five-week stretch.

With a district bordering the expensive Houston media market and no significant opposition from Democrat Richard Konrad, DeLay bypassed broadcast advertising in favor of a limited persuasion mail campaign. Calabrese & Associates of Houston billed the campaign $32,627 for work on the brochures.

Among DeLay's largest expenditures for actual campaigning was the $5,798 he spent to host a hospitality suite for delegates and party activists attending the state Republican convention. "You sort of do it because it's expected," said Carroll.

Campaign Expenditures	DeLay Amount Spent	DeLay % of Total	Konrad Amount Spent	Konrad % of Total
Overhead				
Office furniture/supplies	$ 18,355	5.00	$ 2,811	7.06
Rent/utilities	8,880	2.42	2,000	5.03
Salaries	59,398	16.17	4,250	10.68
Taxes	16,314	4.44	0	
Bank/investment fees	0		0	
Lawyers/accountants	1,100	.30	500	1.26
Telephone	14,233	3.88	1,343	3.37
Campaign automobile	0		0	
Computers/office equipment	6,094	1.66	2,892	7.27
Travel	44,106	12.01	2,661	6.69
Food/meetings	5,998	1.63	378	.95
Subtotal	**174,478**	**47.50**	**16,834**	**42.30**
Fund Raising				
Events	32,234	8.78	4,822	12.12
Direct mail	4,315	1.17	0	
Telemarketing	1,542	.42	0	
Subtotal	**38,090**	**10.37**	**4,822**	**12.12**
Polling	**19,203**	**5.23**	**0**	
Advertising				
Electronic media	0		3,432	8.62
Other media	7,934	2.16	210	.53
Subtotal	**7,934**	**2.16**	**3,642**	**9.15**
Other Campaign Activity				
Persuasion mail/brochures	62,837	17.11	5,347	13.44
Actual campaigning	30,265	8.24	3,283	8.25
Staff/volunteers	1,496	.41	0	
Subtotal	**94,598**	**25.75**	**8,630**	**21.68**
Constituent Gifts/ Entertainment	**2,562**	**.70**	**0**	
Donations to				
Candidates from same state	7,500	2.04	0	
Candidates from other states	14,000	3.81	0	
Civic organizations	6,469	1.76	0	
Ideological groups	225	.06	0	
Political parties	2,245	.61	0	
Subtotal	**30,439**	**8.29**	**0**	
Unitemized Expenses	**0**		**5,869**	**14.75**
Total Campaign Expenses	**$ 367,305**		**$ 39,796**	
PAC Contributions	**$ 226,178**		**$ 630**	
Individual Contributions	**109,788**		**36,562**	
Total Receipts*	**341,516**		**40,621**	

*Includes PAC and individual contributions as well as interest earned, party contributions, etc.

District 23 — TEXAS

Rep. Henry Bonilla (R)

1992 Election Results

Henry Bonilla (R)	98,259	(59%)
Albert G. Bustamante (D)	63,797	(38%)

Under almost any circumstances it would have to be termed an upset when a Democratic incumbent from a heavily Democratic district outspent his Republican challenger by more than $250,000 and still lost. In Rep. Albert G. Bustamante's case, it was no upset.

Under the cloud of a grand jury investigation that would ultimately lead to his indictment and conviction on federal bribery and racketeering charges, Bustamante also was the object of voter ire for his thirty House bank overdrafts, his vote for the congressional pay raise, and his penchant for congressional fact-finding junkets. In a district where the median household income was $40,654 and the median value of homes was slightly more than $75,000, Bustamante had purchased a new home valued at well over $600,000. Finally, Bustamante had willingly accepted twenty-one new counties in the redistricting process, with much of his old political base moving into Rep. Henry B. Gonzalez's new District 20.

Presented with this panoply of negatives, television executive Henry Bonilla had more than enough resources to make his case. He invested less than $88,000 to win the Republican primary. Cavasos Associates of San Antonio was paid $3,222 for providing strategic advice. Kathy Nena Advertising of San Antonio received $44,113, including $29,497 for placement of ten-second television commercials, $4,381 for design and placement of newspaper advertising, and $10,195 for design and printing of one persuasion mailer. The campaign also directly purchased television air time totaling $6,950.

To mold his general election campaign, Bonilla assembled a team of three Texas consultants and a Washington insider. Cutting Edge Communications of San Antonio received $65,822 for providing day-to-day campaign management services. Groves, Cheney & Associates of San Antonio collected $156,630 for placing both his broadcast and newspaper advertising, as well as printing T-shirts and other promotional material. Bonilla paid Strategic Campaign Network of Dallas $4,650 for fund raising. Pollster Tarrance & Associates of Alexandria, Va., received $22,350.

According to Frank Guerra of Cutting Edge, one of Bonilla's most effective weapons was a television commercial dubbed the "good guy" ad. This testimonial featured small business owners, farmers, and ranchers describing Bonilla as "a good guy for agriculture, a good guy for energy, a good guy for Texas," Guerra said. "It was a consistent message that he was the good guy and implied that Bustamante was the bad guy."

The campaign paid a local artist $1,142 for a series of cartoons depicting Bustamante's foibles, which were used in fliers and newspaper ads.

	Bonilla		Bustamante	
Campaign Expenditures	Amount Spent	% of Total	Amount Spent	% of Total
Overhead				
Office furniture/supplies	$ 6,400	1.18	$ 3,906	.49
Rent/utilities	2,436	.45	6,460	.81
Salaries	40,505	7.44	5,150	.65
Taxes	0		4,911	.62
Bank/investment fees	845	.16	1,225	.15
Lawyers/accountants	4,481	.82	50,947	6.39
Telephone	11,051	2.03	158	.02
Campaign automobile	0		0	
Computers/office equipment	4,511	.83	1,427	.18
Travel	26,211	4.81	89,884	11.28
Food/meetings	1,252	.23	14,686	1.84
Subtotal	**97,692**	**17.94**	**178,755**	**22.42**
Fund Raising				
Events	48,398	8.89	63,496	7.97
Direct mail	4,650	.85	0	
Telemarketing	0		0	
Subtotal	**53,049**	**9.74**	**63,496**	**7.97**
Polling	**22,350**	**4.11**	**19,700**	**2.47**
Advertising				
Electronic media	192,860	35.43	232,283	29.14
Other media	17,354	3.19	9,508	1.19
Subtotal	**210,214**	**38.61**	**241,791**	**30.33**
Other Campaign Activity				
Persuasion mail/brochures	36,639	6.73	2,261	.28
Actual campaigning	109,683	20.15	216,194	27.12
Staff/volunteers	200	.04	4,009	.50
Subtotal	**146,522**	**26.91**	**222,463**	**27.91**
Constituent Gifts/ Entertainment	1,767	.32	6,669	.84
Donations to				
Candidates from same state	0		5,000	.63
Candidates from other states	0		7,000	.88
Civic organizations	150	.03	18,336	2.30
Ideological groups	0		6,843	.86
Political parties	150	.03	6,800	.85
Subtotal	**300**	**.06**	**43,979**	**5.52**
Unitemized Expenses	**12,514**	**2.30**	**20,287**	**2.54**
Total Campaign Expenses	**$ 544,407**		**$ 797,140**	
PAC Contributions	$ 109,888		$ 263,986	
Individual Contributions	370,588		143,076	
Total Receipts*	588,673		466,029	

*Includes PAC and individual contributions as well as interest earned, party contributions, etc.

TEXAS — District 24

Rep. Martin Frost (D)

1992 Election Results

Martin Frost (D)	104,174	(60%)
Steve Masterson (R)	70,042	(40%)

Rep. Martin Frost had to overcome two challenges in 1992—a redrawn district that was 60 percent new to him and his first Republican opposition since 1986. His $1.4 million spending advantage made both tasks easily surmountable.

While Dallas trust administrator Steve Masterson spent just $757 to produce broadcast advertising he never aired, Frost hired Mandate: Campaign Media of Alexandria, Va., and paid them $229,879 for developing, producing, and placing his radio and television commercials. The campaign aired two television commercials on network affiliates, three on local cable systems, and two on Spanish-language channels. According to Frost, his most effective television commercial was a constituent service spot that told the story of how he helped a woman collect benefits following the death of her firefighter husband.

While Masterson spent $24,045 on persuasion mail and newspaper advertising, Frost paid Pavlik & Associates of Fort Worth $158,061 for persuasion mail, $19,300 for newspaper ads, and $15,905 for billboard advertising. Frost said the focal point of this voter contact effort was constituent service and jobs.

In seven previous House campaigns, Frost had never felt the need to shoulder the expense of a phonebank operation, but redistricting changed his thinking. The Tyson Organization collected $101,045 for making the campaign's telephone calls, and Pavlik received $19,179 for helping to coordinate the effort.

Frost also spent a staggering $489,578 on overhead. He maintained a permanent campaign office in the NCNB Bank Tower in Dallas. In November 1991 he opened a second office in Fort Worth. In August 1992 he opened additional offices in Arlington and Duncanville. Three of Frost's congressional staffers drew salary payments from the campaign totaling $28,189, which helped push his campaign payroll to $154,438. Three Washington, D.C., law firms collected a total of $56,290 for various legal and accounting work.

Frost paid Scott Gale of the Fundraising Management Group of Washington, D.C., $49,752 for ferreting out political action committee donations and for targeting the Jewish community with fund-raising mail. Dolly Angle, an administrative assistant on Frost's congressional staff before quitting to start her own firm, received $11,110 for coordinating district fund-raisers. In all, Frost estimated that he held between fifteen and twenty events during the two-year election cycle.

For conducting the polls needed to develop his media and mail campaigns, Frost paid Kitchens, Powell & Kitchens of Orlando, Fla., $44,500. Professor Allan J. Lichtman of American University in Washington, D.C., received $14,800 for redistricting advice.

	Frost		Masterson	
Campaign Expenditures	Amount Spent	% of Total	Amount Spent	% of Total
Overhead				
Office furniture/supplies	$ 21,709	1.40	$ 6,423	4.35
Rent/utilities	46,261	2.99	6,757	4.58
Salaries	154,438	9.99	62,245	42.15
Taxes	61,608	3.98	0	
Bank/investment fees	271	.02	494	.33
Lawyers/accountants	56,563	3.66	1,120	.76
Telephone	28,728	1.86	4,525	3.06
Campaign automobile	8,537	.55	0	
Computers/office equipment	25,679	1.66	4,459	3.02
Travel	73,541	4.76	3,940	2.67
Food/meetings	12,243	.79	673	.46
Subtotal	**489,578**	**31.66**	**90,637**	**61.37**
Fund Raising				
Events	182,942	11.83	6,795	4.60
Direct mail	22,749	1.47	0	
Telemarketing	0		0	
Subtotal	**205,691**	**13.30**	**6,795**	**4.60**
Polling	**44,500**	**2.88**	**0**	
Advertising				
Electronic media	229,879	14.86	757	.51
Other media	41,340	2.67	6,796	4.60
Subtotal	**271,218**	**17.54**	**7,553**	**5.11**
Other Campaign Activity				
Persuasion mail/brochures	270,691	17.50	17,249	11.68
Actual campaigning	186,907	12.09	9,814	6.65
Staff/volunteers	941	.06	29	.02
Subtotal	**458,539**	**29.65**	**27,092**	**18.34**
Constituent Gifts/ Entertainment	**6,749**	**.44**	**0**	
Donations to				
Candidates from same state	1,850	.12	0	
Candidates from other states	1,000	.06	0	
Civic organizations	9,921	.64	997	.68
Ideological groups	2,190	.14	0	
Political parties	23,350	1.51	90	.06
Subtotal	**38,311**	**2.48**	**1,087**	**.74**
Unitemized Expenses	**31,976**	**2.07**	**14,523**	**9.83**
Total Campaign Expenses	**$ 1,546,561**		**$ 147,687**	
PAC Contributions	$ 667,804		$ 15,370	
Individual Contributions	532,235		79,987	
Total Receipts*	1,241,725		109,317	

*Includes PAC and individual contributions as well as interest earned, party contributions, etc.

District 25 — TEXAS

Rep. Michael A. Andrews (D)

1992 Election Results

Michael A. Andrews (D)	98,975	(56%)
Dolly Madison McKenna (R)	73,192	(41%)

Rep. Michael A. Andrews could not have scripted a worse scenario for his fifth reelection campaign. In a year marked by a rising tide of anti-incumbent sentiment, he had 121 overdrafts at the House bank and had voted for the congressional pay raise. In the political "Year of the Woman," he faced Dolly Madison McKenna, a well financed, pro-choice Republican. As a result, he spent $1.4 million during the 1992 election cycle—only $122,090 less than he had invested in his six previous House races combined.

Fortunately for Andrews, he began 1991 with $811,150 in his treasury and by the end of 1991 had increased those cash reserves to more than $1 million. Political action committees donated $189,350 of the $312,440 he raised during the off-year.

Overhead accounted for two-thirds of the $141,963 Andrews spent during 1991. Five part-time employees, including three of his congressional staffers, received salary payments totaling $20,477. Travel expenses amounted to $33,696. Over the last eight months of 1991, he paid $300 a month to rent space from the Harris County Democratic party.

Once he realized his electoral predicament, Andrews dramatically increased his spending. Just prior to the March 10 primary, he hired Gold Communications Co. of Austin and over the next nine months paid them $149,388 for developing persuasion mail. In early April he retained Washington, D.C.-based consultants Doak, Shrum & Associates to produce broadcast advertising, Garin-Hart for polling, and N/K Associates to provide opposition research. Over the course of the campaign, these three consultants collected $72,276, $53,000 and $21,125, respectively.

Andrews launched his broadcast campaign in mid-September. The Media Co. of Washington, D.C., collected $84,500 to buy air time in September, another $120,459 the first week of October, and $249,957 over the final three weeks of the campaign.

Andrews also received a considerable push from the American Medical Association (AMA), which paid Fenn & King Communications of Washington, D.C., $103,385 to produce and place radio commercials on his behalf. The ads never mentioned health care, but instead trumpeted Andrews's support for a middle-class income tax cut, his support for troop reductions in Europe, and his record as a crime fighter. The AMA also spent $15,600 on polls conducted by Mellman & Lazarus of Washington, D.C.

McKenna received only $19,996 in coordinated advertising assistance from the National Republican Congressional Committee to augment her heavily negative advertising campaign, and it was not enough to compete with Andrews's media blitz.

	Andrews		McKenna	
Campaign Expenditures	Amount Spent	% of Total	Amount Spent	% of Total
Overhead				
Office furniture/supplies	$ 31,871	2.28	$ 12,076	2.02
Rent/utilities	13,859	.99	16,371	2.74
Salaries	110,303	7.91	79,646	13.32
Taxes	65,046	4.66	6,517	1.09
Bank/investment fees	1,684	.12	579	.10
Lawyers/accountants	6,164	.44	808	.14
Telephone	20,815	1.49	10,783	1.80
Campaign automobile	0		0	
Computers/office equipment	21,638	1.55	14,736	2.46
Travel	71,912	5.15	10,415	1.74
Food/meetings	4,936	.35	553	.09
Subtotal	**348,230**	**24.96**	**152,484**	**25.49**
Fund Raising				
Events	50,380	3.61	48,078	8.04
Direct mail	3,076	.22	5,985	1.00
Telemarketing	0		0	
Subtotal	**53,456**	**3.83**	**54,063**	**9.04**
Polling	**53,000**	**3.80**	**24,000**	**4.01**
Advertising				
Electronic media	527,192	37.79	231,794	38.75
Other media	7,079	.51	2,459	.41
Subtotal	**534,271**	**38.30**	**234,254**	**39.17**
Other Campaign Activity				
Persuasion mail/brochures	237,054	16.99	66,047	11.04
Actual campaigning	105,668	7.57	64,621	10.80
Staff/volunteers	1,964	.14	256	.04
Subtotal	**344,687**	**24.71**	**130,924**	**21.89**
Constituent Gifts/ Entertainment	**2,262**	**.16**	**0**	
Donations to				
Candidates from same state	5,700	.41	128	.02
Candidates from other states	7,500	.54	0	
Civic organizations	15,813	1.13	103	.02
Ideological groups	2,695	.19	0	
Political parties	13,197	.95	0	
Subtotal	**44,904**	**3.22**	**231**	**.04**
Unitemized Expenses	**14,244**	**1.02**	**2,155**	**.36**
Total Campaign Expenses	**$ 1,395,054**		**$ 598,110**	
PAC Contributions	$ 527,931		$ 0	
Individual Contributions	319,053		358,206	
Total Receipts*	974,838		587,399	

*Includes PAC and individual contributions as well as interest earned, party contributions, etc.

TEXAS — District 26

Rep. Dick Armey (R)

1992 Election Results

Dick Armey (R)	150,209	(73%)
John Wayne Caton (D)	55,237	(27%)

Rep. Dick Armey spent $277,198 more on his 1992 campaign than he had in 1990, but Democrat John Wayne Caton had nothing to do with it. The 1992 contest Armey worried most about was his successful fight to wrest the chairmanship of the Republican Conference away from California Rep. Jerry Lewis.

To win that fight, Armey liberally distributed his campaign funds to a host of fellow Republicans. He made $1,000 donations to twenty-three candidates, $950 contributions to thirty-four candidates, and $500 donations to fourteen others. Most of his $1,000 gifts went to incumbents in tight races, such as Minority Whip Newt Gingrich of Georgia, Wayne T. Gilchrest of Maryland, Frank Riggs of California, Ron Marlenee of Montana, and Iowans Jim Nussle and Jim Ross Lightfoot. His largest donation, $1,450, went to Michael D. Crapo of Idaho, who won the District 2 seat vacated by Rep. Richard Stallings. He gave $900 to Texan David Hobbs, who lost to Rep. Pete Geren, and contributed $450 each to three others.

Armey also sent "issue mailers" valued at $25 each to 159 challengers and open seat contestants. These unsolicited mailings dispensed helpful hints on how to frame issues to successfully campaign against their Democratic opponents. Armey spent a total of $816 on travel related to campaign appearances he made on behalf of four challengers and open seat candidates: Richard W. Pombo (Calif.), Bryan Day (Colo.), Doug Wead (Ariz.), and Jay Dickey (Ark.).

Unrelated to his House leadership battle, Armey donated $4,000 to his son Scott's campaign for county commissioner. On the redistricting front, he also gave $5,000 to Texans Against Gerrymandering.

The boundaries of Armey's political domain were significantly altered by redistricting, which in turn mandated a much more aggressive voter contact effort than would normally be required to dispatch an opponent with less than $10,000 to spend. According to administrative assistant Brian Gunderson, "About half of the voters were voting for Armey for the first time."

Armey began reaching out to his new constituents as early as December 1991, paying his fund-raising consultant, Dan Morgan & Associates of Arlington, Va., $7,070 to step out of character and design a persuasion mailer. Closer to the general election, James R. Foster & Associates of Carrollton received $32,824 for designing five persuasion mailers. He also paid Multi Media Services Corp. of Alexandria, Va., $67,155 to buy broadcast time. Gunderson said the central theme behind all this communication was that Armey favored congressional reform and opposed excessive campaign spending.

Campaign Expenditures	Armey Amount Spent	Armey % of Total	Caton Amount Spent	Caton % of Total
Overhead				
Office furniture/supplies	$ 4,545	.96	$ 450	4.67
Rent/utilities	3,472	.73	0	
Salaries	33,338	7.01	0	
Taxes	9,949	2.09	0	
Bank/investment fees	0		357	3.70
Lawyers/accountants	3,477	.73	0	
Telephone	3,104	.65	110	1.14
Campaign automobile	0		0	
Computers/office equipment	3,108	.65	0	
Travel	14,263	3.00	2,224	23.09
Food/meetings	992	.21	0	
Subtotal	**76,247**	**16.03**	**3,141**	**32.61**
Fund Raising				
Events	42,857	9.01	0	
Direct mail	46,467	9.77	0	
Telemarketing	0		0	
Subtotal	**89,324**	**18.77**	**0**	
Polling	**12,091**	**2.54**	**0**	
Advertising				
Electronic media	75,779	15.93	0	
Other media	1,300	.27	2,127	22.08
Subtotal	**77,079**	**16.20**	**2,127**	**22.08**
Other Campaign Activity				
Persuasion mail/brochures	110,112	23.14	1,001	10.39
Actual campaigning	15,157	3.19	3,003	31.19
Staff/volunteers	0		0	
Subtotal	**125,270**	**26.33**	**4,004**	**41.58**
Constituent Gifts/ Entertainment	**5,778**	**1.21**	**0**	
Donations to				
Candidates from same state	8,275	1.74	0	
Candidates from other states	66,866	14.05	0	
Civic organizations	300	.06	0	
Ideological groups	1,000	.21	25	.26
Political parties	7,010	1.47	185	1.92
Subtotal	**83,451**	**17.54**	**210**	**2.18**
Unitemized Expenses	**6,521**	**1.37**	**148**	**1.54**
Total Campaign Expenses	**$ 475,761**		**$ 9,630**	
PAC Contributions	$ 195,110		$ 9,000	
Individual Contributions	222,030		795	
Total Receipts*	482,973		10,091	

*Includes PAC and individual contributions as well as interest earned, party contributions, etc.

District 27 — TEXAS

Rep. Solomon P. Ortiz (D)

1992 Election Results

Solomon P. Ortiz (D)	87,022	(55%)
Jay Kimbrough (R)	66,853	(43%)

First elected in 1982, Rep. Solomon P. Ortiz had run without opposition in his three previous re-election campaigns. Combined with redistricting and the fear of an anti-incumbent backlash, the mild opposition offered by attorney Jay Kimbrough prompted Ortiz to spend $207,760 more than he had in 1990.

John Nugent of Corpus Christi collected $10,000 for developing Ortiz's television commercials, and Creative Communication of Smithfield, N.C., received $62,500 for placing them. Ortiz also spent $8,734 on radio spots, including $4,797 to air commercials on KUNO, a local Spanish-language station.

Since voter turnout actually mattered this time, Ortiz invested $1,077 to purchase voter lists needed for his in-house phonebank. He spent $5,826 on campaign T-shirts and hats, $3,907 to stage campaign rallies, $3,378 on yard signs, and $3,248 on bumper stickers. In 1990 his combined spending on such items was less than $2,500.

However, no threat was sufficient to reduce Ortiz's spending on constituent entertainment. During the 1990 election cycle, he invested $21,247 in constituent meals, gifts, and year-end holiday cards. Yet when faced with his first opposition since 1984, Ortiz not only continued to wine-and-dine his friends, but actually increased his spending on such activities by $17,857.

Over the course of the 1992 election cycle, Ortiz spent $18,601 on meals described in his campaign financial disclosure forms as "meals for supporters." Ortiz paid $7,033 for such meals at restaurants in Washington, D.C., including a $612 dinner at Mr. K's and a $153 dinner at Le Rivage. Back home, Ortiz spent $7,406 to dine with constituents, including a $14 repast at Whataburger and a $15 meal at a local Denny's restaurant. Ortiz did not limit himself to restaurants in the United States, as he consumed dinners totaling $1,028 with constituents in Matamoros, Mexico. The campaign reimbursed Ortiz for another $2,372 in constituent meals at unspecified locations.

"He tries to see constituents outside the office," press secretary Cathy A. Travis explained. "There are too many distractions in the office—phone calls, staff people wanting to see him. It's better if they leave."

Expenses associated with his annual Christmas party for constituents and volunteers totaled $9,530. Year-end holiday cards added $4,686. The campaign gave $1,000 to help pay for the funeral of a constituent killed in Operation Desert Storm. Continental Airlines was paid $2,500 to ferry the Robstown, Texas, High School band to and from Washington. Flowers and other gifts cost $1,506, and another $1,281 was invested in the congressional art contest for high school students.

	Ortiz		Kimbrough	
Campaign Expenditures	Amount Spent	% of Total	Amount Spent	% of Total
Overhead				
Office furniture/supplies	$ 9,547	2.78	$ 1,219	1.52
Rent/utilities	3,991	1.16	400	.50
Salaries	9,449	2.76	17,735	22.10
Taxes	2,990	.87	0	
Bank/investment fees	242	.07	0	
Lawyers/accountants	0		0	
Telephone	8,387	2.45	2,046	2.55
Campaign automobile	2,323	.68	0	
Computers/office equipment	6,535	1.91	0	
Travel	26,344	7.68	1,051	1.31
Food/meetings	2,079	.61	0	
Subtotal	**71,889**	**20.96**	**22,451**	**27.98**
Fund Raising				
Events	61,094	17.82	5,158	6.43
Direct mail	0		0	
Telemarketing	0		0	
Subtotal	**61,094**	**17.82**	**5,158**	**6.43**
Polling	0		0	
Advertising				
Electronic media	81,234	23.69	23,481	29.27
Other media	570	.17	571	.71
Subtotal	**81,804**	**23.86**	**24,052**	**29.98**
Other Campaign Activity				
Persuasion mail/brochures	12,101	3.53	12,806	15.96
Actual campaigning	24,883	7.26	3,059	3.81
Staff/volunteers	306	.09	0	
Subtotal	**37,290**	**10.87**	**15,865**	**19.77**
Constituent Gifts/ Entertainment	**39,104**	**11.40**	**0**	
Donations to				
Candidates from same state	1,200	.35	0	
Candidates from other states	7,250	2.11	0	
Civic organizations	400	.12	0	
Ideological groups	0		0	
Political parties	5,700	1.66	500	.62
Subtotal	**14,550**	**4.24**	**500**	**.62**
Unitemized Expenses	**37,180**	**10.84**	**12,211**	**15.22**
Total Campaign Expenses	**$ 342,910**		**$ 80,237**	
PAC Contributions	$ 99,518		$ 1,950	
Individual Contributions	145,868		56,678	
Total Receipts*	274,610		64,628	

*Includes PAC and individual contributions as well as interest earned, party contributions, etc.

TEXAS   District 28

Rep. Frank Tejeda (D)

1992 Election Results

Frank Tejeda (D)	122,457	(87%)
David C. Slatter (I)	18,128	(13%)

State senator Frank Tejeda spent months preparing for what he assumed would be a hotly contested race in this new Hispanic-majority district. As a member of the state senate's redistricting committee, he had a hand in how the district lines would be drawn. He opened his campaign office in September 1991 and raised more than $100,000 by the end of the year.

As it turned out, no other Democratic or Republican candidates bothered to enter the race. While libertarian David C. Slatter did mount a token challenge, Tejeda was essentially elected before any votes had been cast. He was the only freshman elected to a new district who did not face major-party opposition, and yet he chose to run a $352,000 campaign. "I'd never been on the ballot in twelve of the thirteen counties in the district," he explained.

To increase his name recognition across that unfamiliar territory, Tejeda estimated that his campaign printed approximately 36,000 biographical sketches and thousands of palm cards, which were mailed and handed out at campaign events. He paid $19,117 to print the material and another $8,645 on mailing lists and postage.

With little opposition, Tejeda chose not to spend money on radio or television advertising. Instead, he invested $6,885 in newspaper advertising and $3,443 in billboards. He also spent $18,535 on signs, which he scattered across the 250-mile-long district.

For designing and placing his newspaper ads and billboards, Tejeda paid the Davis Group of Fort Worth $4,743. Pollster Shipley & Associates of Austin received $28,490. Rose Garcia of San Antonio was paid $19,641 for fund raising.

Overhead accounted for 44 percent of Tejeda's spending. Monthly rent on his San Antonio office was $850. Periodic salary payments to the eight people who worked for the campaign during the primary and to the five people who worked on the fall campaign totaled $72,631. Health insurance premiums for campaign manager Frances Ruiz amounted to $1,140. Tejeda paid $4,089 to lease a 1989 Jeep Cherokee and spent another $6,300 on gasoline, insurance, registration, and license plates.

Having served ten years in the state house and another six years in the state senate, Tejeda knew the political importance of well-placed charitable contributions. He donated $1,300 to the NAACP, $1,250 to the El Carmen Catholic Church, and $850 to the New Light Baptist Church, among others.

After all those campaigns, Tejeda also understood the importance of constituent stroking. He spent $1,532 on Easter cards and another $2,461 on Christmas cards.

	Tejeda		Slatter	
Campaign Expenditures	Amount Spent	% of Total	Amount Spent	% of Total
Overhead				
Office furniture/supplies	$ 7,373	2.09	$ 97	6.93
Rent/utilities	14,293	4.06	0	
Salaries	73,771	20.96	0	
Taxes	20,738	5.89	0	
Bank/investment fees	0		0	
Lawyers/accountants	0		0	
Telephone	15,736	4.47	22	1.58
Campaign automobile	10,389	2.95	0	
Computers/office equipment	5,459	1.55	0	
Travel	6,399	1.82	126	8.98
Food/meetings	1,936	.55	0	
Subtotal	**156,094**	**44.35**	**245**	**17.49**
Fund Raising				
Events	64,160	18.23	0	
Direct mail	0		0	
Telemarketing	0		0	
Subtotal	**64,160**	**18.23**	**0**	
Polling	**28,490**	**8.09**	**0**	
Advertising				
Electronic media	0		0	
Other media	11,678	3.32	0	
Subtotal	**11,678**	**3.32**	**0**	
Other Campaign Activity				
Persuasion mail/brochures	27,762	7.89	458	32.67
Actual campaigning	31,164	8.85	0	
Staff/volunteers	2,901	.82	0	
Subtotal	**61,827**	**17.57**	**458**	**32.67**
Constituent Gifts/ Entertainment	4,926	1.40	0	
Donations to				
Candidates from same state	0		0	
Candidates from other states	0		0	
Civic organizations	10,091	2.87	0	
Ideological groups	1,300	.37	0	
Political parties	0		0	
Subtotal	**11,391**	**3.24**	**0**	
Unitemized Expenses	**13,395**	**3.81**	**699**	**49.84**
Total Campaign Expenses	**$ 351,961**		**$ 1,402**	
PAC Contributions	$ 131,725		$ 0	
Individual Contributions	157,572		90	
Total Receipts*	305,673		1,567	

*Includes PAC and individual contributions as well as interest earned, party contributions, etc.

District 29 — TEXAS

Rep. Gene Green (D)

1992 Election Results
Gene Green (D)   64,064   (65%)
Clark Kent Ervin (R)   34,609   (35%)

While the general election contest between Democratic state senator Gene Green and Houston attorney Clark Kent Ervin was relatively uneventful, the Democratic primary produced more than its share of fireworks. Despite redistricting that sought to maximize the chances of electing a new Hispanic member, Green, who is white, emerged with his party's nomination after three rounds of acrimonious campaigning.

After finishing second to Houston City Council member Ben Reyes in the five-candidate primary, Green appeared to win the runoff by a mere 180 votes. However, when it was discovered that several hundred people who had voted in the Republican primary illegally crossed over to vote in the Democratic runoff, the results were overturned by a state district judge. That launched the third mud-slinging primary campaign, which Green won by 1,132 votes.

Green prevailed largely by making Reyes the issue in a series of biting attacks. Television commercials produced by McKinnon Media of Austin reminded voters that Reyes had declared personal bankruptcy, had been delinquent in paying his personal property taxes, had been arrested for driving under the influence of alcohol, and had been placed on probation after pleading no contest to misdemeanor charges of theft and of violating campaign finance laws. For producing and placing ads during the two runoff campaigns, McKinnon collected $87,113. Shafto & Barton of Houston also collected $37,008 for placing the ads. The campaign directly purchased $320 of radio air time during this period.

Gold Communications Co. of Austin was brought in to design a companion set of negative mailers. Under the headline "Time and time again, Ben Reyes has shown he thinks he's above the law," newspaper headlines listing each of Reyes's legal and financial problems were reproduced, including an investigation by the local district attorney into allegations that Reyes had ties to a local drug-smuggling ring. The total cost of Green's mail campaign for the three primary elections was $298,572, including $73,216 paid to Gold Communications and $169,433 paid to Campaign Strategies of Houston.

Green received considerable assistance from the National Rifle Association (NRA), which invested $157,926 in an independent campaign on his behalf. The NRA spent $41,411 on radio commercials and $11,647 on "endorsement phonebanks." Letters mailed by the NRA cited Reyes's problems with the district attorney and his personal bankruptcy.

Reyes was so angered by the attacks that he endorsed Ervin in the general election, but in this overwhelmingly Democratic district the endorsement was little help.

Campaign Expenditures	Green Amount Spent	Green % of Total	Ervin Amount Spent	Ervin % of Total
Overhead				
Office furniture/supplies	$ 5,172	.70	$ 17,081	3.10
Rent/utilities	5,860	.79	17,802	3.24
Salaries	41,799	5.63	61,093	11.10
Taxes	0		15,771	2.87
Bank/investment fees	33	.00	0	
Lawyers/accountants	81,054	10.92	0	
Telephone	7,609	1.02	14,777	2.69
Campaign automobile	0		11,461	2.08
Computers/office equipment	5,948	.80	2,037	.37
Travel	5,045	.68	58,088	10.56
Food/meetings	390	.05	0	
Subtotal	**152,910**	**20.60**	**198,110**	**36.00**
Fund Raising				
Events	47,105	6.35	14,902	2.71
Direct mail	0		42,917	7.80
Telemarketing	2,100	.28	0	
Subtotal	**49,205**	**6.63**	**57,819**	**10.51**
Polling	**0**		**9,300**	**1.69**
Advertising				
Electronic media	139,822	18.83	13,235	2.41
Other media	5,019	.68	5,063	.92
Subtotal	**144,841**	**19.51**	**18,298**	**3.33**
Other Campaign Activity				
Persuasion mail/brochures	354,008	47.69	118,157	21.47
Actual campaigning	32,913	4.43	127,629	23.19
Staff/volunteers	2,609	.35	9,068	1.65
Subtotal	**389,530**	**52.47**	**254,854**	**46.32**
Constituent Gifts/ Entertainment	**2,561**	**.34**	**0**	
Donations to				
Candidates from same state	0		0	
Candidates from other states	0		0	
Civic organizations	3,206	.43	560	.10
Ideological groups	0		0	
Political parties	125	.02	0	
Subtotal	**3,331**	**.45**	**560**	**.10**
Unitemized Expenses	**0**		**11,316**	**2.06**
Total Campaign Expenses	**$ 742,377**		**$ 550,257**	
PAC Contributions	**$ 402,350**		**$ 59,252**	
Individual Contributions	226,831		431,718	
Total Receipts*	702,330		514,229	

*Includes PAC and individual contributions as well as interest earned, party contributions, etc.

TEXAS — District 30

Rep. Eddie Bernice Johnson (D)

1992 Election Results

Eddie Bernice Johnson (D)	107,831	(72%)
Lucy Cain (R)	37,853	(25%)

As chair of the state senate's congressional redistricting committee, state senator Eddie Bernice Johnson's biggest battle in winning this seat was with Democratic Rep. Martin Frost over where the district's boundary lines would fall. Once she succeeded in carving most of the black and Hispanic voters out of Frost's old district and combined them with voters wrested from Democratic Rep. John Bryant, Johnson coasted to victory. She garnered 92 percent of the Democratic primary votes before walloping Republican Lucy Cain in November.

Johnson introduced herself to her future constituents largely through a persuasion mail campaign designed by Gold Communications Co. of Austin. For the primary, this effort cost Johnson $31,007, including $11,370 paid to Gold Communications. For the fall campaign against the underfunded Cain, Johnson spent another $72,428 on mail and brochures, including payments to Gold Communications totaling $40,050.

To turn out the vote for the primary, Johnson paid three consultants a total of $18,671 for phonebanking. Martin Wieser of Dallas received $12,000, Campaign Systems of Irving collected $3,776, and Charles Timms of Dallas was paid $2,895.

Other direct appeals to voters were much more limited in scope. Given the expense of advertising in the Dallas media market, Johnson's broadcast advertising was restricted to radio—$2,957 for the primary and another $4,500 for the general election campaign. Of the $3,475 she spent on newspaper advertising in such papers as the *Minority Opportunity News, El Extra,* and the *Jewish Post,* all but $400 was invested in the primary. She also placed program and journal ads totaling $1,494 with the AFL-CIO, Planned Parenthood, the Oak Cliff Chamber of Commerce, and the Oak Cliff Lions Club. Another $13,296 was spent on signs and posters.

Johnson raised 45 percent of the money she needed to wage her campaign from fellow Texans. Donations from in-state contributors who gave at least $200 amounted to $61,200. A series of fund-raisers with ticket prices starting at $25 helped her raise $65,551 from those who could not afford to make large contributions. "Her followers are not always the folk that make $40,000 a year," explained campaign treasurer Eric Moye.

In July Johnson made the pilgrimage to Washington, D.C., in search of political action committee (PAC) donations. A reception at the National Democratic Club cost the campaign $2,000, but it helped push her PAC contributions to $114,176, or 40 percent of her total receipts.

Cain threw in the towel long before election day, spending nothing after June 30.

Campaign Expenditures	Johnson Amount Spent	Johnson % of Total	Cain Amount Spent	Cain % of Total
Overhead				
Office furniture/supplies	$ 5,851	2.10	$ 0	
Rent/utilities	9,468	3.39	0	
Salaries	14,427	5.17	200	4.25
Taxes	0		0	
Bank/investment fees	86	.03	0	
Lawyers/accountants	188	.07	0	
Telephone	10,113	3.62	0	
Campaign automobile	0		0	
Computers/office equipment	514	.18	300	6.37
Travel	34,024	12.18	660	14.02
Food/meetings	547	.20	0	
Subtotal	**75,217**	**26.94**	**1,160**	**24.65**
Fund Raising				
Events	25,467	9.12	0	
Direct mail	0		1,923	40.85
Telemarketing	0		0	
Subtotal	**25,467**	**9.12**	**1,923**	**40.85**
Polling	**0**		**0**	
Advertising				
Electronic media	7,457	2.67	0	
Other media	4,969	1.78	0	
Subtotal	**12,426**	**4.45**	**0**	
Other Campaign Activity				
Persuasion mail/brochures	103,435	37.04	0	
Actual campaigning	48,711	17.44	1,302	27.65
Staff/volunteers	168	.06	0	
Subtotal	**152,313**	**54.55**	**1,302**	**27.65**
Constituent Gifts/Entertainment	**0**		**0**	
Donations to				
Candidates from same state	0		0	
Candidates from other states	100	.04	0	
Civic organizations	2,453	.88	0	
Ideological groups	105	.04	0	
Political parties	215	.08	0	
Subtotal	**2,873**	**1.03**	**0**	
Unitemized Expenses	**10,946**	**3.92**	**322**	**6.85**
Total Campaign Expenses	**$ 279,241**		**$ 4,707**	
PAC Contributions	$ 114,176		$ 1,000	
Individual Contributions	149,761		0	
Total Receipts*	283,350		2,100	

*Includes PAC and individual contributions as well as interest earned, party contributions, etc.

District 1 — UTAH

Rep. James V. Hansen (R)

1992 Election Results

James V. Hansen (R)	160,037	(65%)
Ron Holt (D)	68,712	(28%)
William J. Lawrence † (I)	16,505	(7%)

Despite collecting just 52 percent of the vote in 1990, Republican Rep. James V. Hansen did not embark on a spending spree to shore up his support. His off-year spending amounted to $40,845, and while he began the election cycle with cash reserves of only $41,944, he raised $8,575 less than he spent in 1991. His total outlays for the 1992 election cycle exceeded his 1990 spending by $20,211, a modest 9 percent increase. Challenged in 1992 by Democrat Ron Holt, an underfunded Weber State University anthropology professor, Hansen had little reason for concern.

Holt purchased and recycled the mailing lists, poll results, and campaign signs used by Kenley Brunsdale, who challenged Hansen in 1990. "We were so poor, we had to take old signs and repaint them," Holt lamented. Having initially consulted with John Ember Communications of Seattle, Wash., to glean ideas for radio and television commercials, Holt discovered he lacked the funds to execute any of those ideas. He invested $3,924 on billboard ads and $257 on newspaper ads.

Faced with this weak opposition and running in a district virtually unaltered by redistricting, Hansen opted to invest $73,122 to produce and air one television commercial and a companion radio spot that touted his record of fiscal conservatism. He invested $12,402 in billboards that conveyed the simple message: "Jim Hansen for Congress." Yard signs emblazoned with the same slogan cost $3,349. He spent nothing on persuasion mail.

Under Utah election law, candidates must receive 70 percent of the votes cast at the party nominating conventions or face their adversaries in a primary. To prepare for this, Hansen invested $17,412 in banners, signs, and campaign literature for the twelve Republican county conventions and the state nominating convention. He garnered 81 percent of the state conventioneer's ballots.

Capitol Ideas of Salt Lake City collected $98,489 for creating and placing the broadcast ads, placing the billboard ads, and providing most of the material for the state nominating convention. When Hansen was considering a gubernatorial bid in 1991, he paid Mike Murphy Media of Washington, D.C., $2,000 for consulting on an ad campaign. Dan Jones & Associates of Salt Lake City collected $13,500 for a 1991 poll to test the waters.

After-tax salaries accounted for 9 percent of his total outlays, and much of that went to Hansen's children. His son Paul collected $6,476 for running the campaign. Joseph J. Hansen received $2,216 for helping his father work the county convention delegates. Hansen's daughter Jennifer collected $1,113 for working in the campaign office.

	Hansen		Holt	
Campaign Expenditures	Amount Spent	% of Total	Amount Spent	% of Total
Overhead				
Office furniture/supplies	$ 3,991	1.66	$ 421	.56
Rent/utilities	13,018	5.41	915	1.21
Salaries	21,080	8.77	28,703	38.09
Taxes	9,013	3.75	0	
Bank/investment fees	0		0	
Lawyers/accountants	3,023	1.26	0	
Telephone	4,496	1.87	3,593	4.77
Campaign automobile	2,720	1.13	0	
Computers/office equipment	4,642	1.93	1,200	1.59
Travel	7,990	3.32	7,196	9.55
Food/meetings	2,877	1.20	0	
Subtotal	**72,850**	**30.29**	**42,027**	**55.77**
Fund Raising				
Events	30,255	12.58	452	.60
Direct mail	9,120	3.79	1,917	2.54
Telemarketing	0		0	
Subtotal	**39,375**	**16.37**	**2,369**	**3.14**
Polling	**13,500**	**5.61**	**1,000**	**1.33**
Advertising				
Electronic media	73,122	30.41	1,700	2.26
Other media	12,414	5.16	4,181	5.55
Subtotal	**85,536**	**35.57**	**5,881**	**7.80**
Other Campaign Activity				
Persuasion mail/brochures	0		6,473	8.59
Actual campaigning	22,728	9.45	9,483	12.58
Staff/volunteers	214	.09	150	.20
Subtotal	**22,942**	**9.54**	**16,106**	**21.37**
Constituent Gifts/Entertainment	**4,439**	**1.85**	**0**	
Donations to				
Candidates from same state	1,000	.42	0	
Candidates from other states	700	.29	0	
Civic organizations	0		0	
Ideological groups	0		0	
Political parties	0		350	.46
Subtotal	**1,700**	**.71**	**350**	**.46**
Unitemized Expenses	**131**	**.05**	**7,630**	**10.12**
Total Campaign Expenses	**$ 240,474**		**$ 75,363**	
PAC Contributions	$ 147,351		$ 30,550	
Individual Contributions	68,511		20,525	
Total Receipts*	221,781		64,884	

*Includes PAC and individual contributions as well as interest earned, party contributions, etc.

† No expenditures or receipts on file. Candidates raising or spending less than $5,000 are not required to file reports with the Federal Election Commission.

UTAH — District 2

Rep. Karen Shepherd (D)

1992 Election Results

Karen Shepherd (D)	127,738	(51%)
Enid Greene (R)	118,307	(47%)

Democratic state senator Karen Shepherd had several major advantages in her open seat contest with Republican Enid Greene. She outspent Greene by $128,600. While Shepherd secured her place on the November ballot at the June 27 Democratic nominating convention, Greene was forced into a costly primary. That increased Shepherd's monetary advantage in their head-to-head contest to more than $172,000.

Shepherd depended almost exclusively on television advertising to deliver her message. In late August she hit the airwaves with a sixty-second commercial that sought to establish her outsider credentials.

"When they say we need someone new to shake up Washington, they could be speaking about her," the ad began. The outsider theme was hammered home moments later when she noted, "We need change in this country and I'm very comfortable functioning as an outsider." An announcer then pointed to her support for congressional term limits and her desire to reform Congress.

To let voters know that she was one of them, the ad pointed out that Shepherd had been born and raised in Utah and had attended college, taught school, raised a family, and started a business in the state. That "family values" theme was underscored when Shepherd added, "The strength of this country can be measured by the strength of its families."

The commercial also noted that Shepherd supported a constitutional amendment requiring a balanced budget, favored cuts in foreign aid and increased spending on education, and would work to make health care more affordable. Over the next two months, five additional spots repeated these themes.

Shepherd aired two attack ads during the campaign's final weeks. The first charged that Greene's budget reduction plan was copied "from an eastern think tank" and would severely damage Utah's economy. When Greene responded to that attack with a television spot comparing Shepherd to Pinocchio, whose nose was growing with each lie, Shepherd came back with a spot that accused Greene "of insulting us with this silly negative commercial" because "she didn't do her homework." The Campaign Group of Philadelphia, Pa., received $311,424 for creating and placing the ads.

Cooper & Secrest Associates of Alexandria, Va., collected $27,220 from Shepherd and $10,000 from the Democratic Congressional Campaign Committee for polling. John Becker Public Relations of Salt Lake City received $14,064 for persuasion mailers.

Greene was outspent on broadcast advertising by more than two to one, largely because she opted to invest far more heavily than Shepherd in billboards and persuasion mail.

Campaign Expenditures	Shepherd Amount Spent	Shepherd % of Total	Greene Amount Spent	Greene % of Total
Overhead				
Office furniture/supplies	$ 9,370	1.54	$ 8,669	1.80
Rent/utilities	7,866	1.29	4,500	.93
Salaries	44,923	7.37	60,194	12.51
Taxes	14,403	2.36	84	.02
Bank/investment fees	94	.02	212	.04
Lawyers/accountants	475	.08	161	.03
Telephone	3,510	.58	3,696	.77
Campaign automobile	0		0	
Computers/office equipment	8,912	1.46	6,690	1.39
Travel	12,778	2.10	487	.10
Food/meetings	340	.06	705	.15
Subtotal	**102,671**	**16.83**	**85,397**	**17.74**
Fund Raising				
Events	33,004	5.41	8,384	1.74
Direct mail	34,328	5.63	4,809	1.00
Telemarketing	0		0	
Subtotal	**67,332**	**11.04**	**13,193**	**2.74**
Polling	**28,620**	**4.69**	**24,668**	**5.13**
Advertising				
Electronic media	311,424	51.06	151,632	31.50
Other media	8,994	1.47	40,489	8.41
Subtotal	**320,418**	**52.53**	**192,121**	**39.92**
Other Campaign Activity				
Persuasion mail/brochures	38,660	6.34	127,872	26.57
Actual campaigning	24,991	4.10	33,522	6.96
Staff/volunteers	1,547	.25	1,320	.27
Subtotal	**65,197**	**10.69**	**162,715**	**33.81**
Constituent Gifts/ Entertainment	**1,556**	**.26**	**36**	**.01**
Donations to				
Candidates from same state	500	.08	0	
Candidates from other states	0		0	
Civic organizations	0		50	.01
Ideological groups	0		90	.02
Political parties	0		32	.01
Subtotal	**500**	**.08**	**172**	**.04**
Unitemized Expenses	**23,620**	**3.87**	**3,012**	**.63**
Total Campaign Expenses	**$ 609,914**		**$ 481,314**	
PAC Contributions	$ 201,601		$ 123,150	
Individual Contributions	424,860		169,219	
Total Receipts*	640,031		471,058	

*Includes PAC and individual contributions as well as interest earned, party contributions, etc.

District 3 — UTAH

Rep. Bill Orton (D)

1992 Election Results

Bill Orton (D)   135,029   (59%)
Richard R. Harrington (R)   84,019   (37%)

Rep. Bill Orton seemed destined to have a difficult reelection campaign, even though redistricting had given him some new Democratic constituents. In its brief four-term history, District 3 had never provided the Democratic party's nominee with more than one-third of the vote until Orton grabbed the seat in 1990. By 1991 one would-be Republican challenger had already begun ridiculing Orton as "single and socialist." However, as in 1990, district Republicans self-destructed, and Orton easily won reelection.

Orton put 59 percent of his $187,934 budget into direct voter appeals. Fenn & King Communications of Washington, D.C., received $50,349 for creating and placing three television commercials, all of which were positive. Given the district's past electoral response to Democrats, Orton's first spot portrayed him as more of an independent than a Democrat. "If you have to be a political ideologue, if you have to be a member of one party or the other and vote that party line, then you want somebody else because I won't do it," Orton proclaimed. "I'll vote for the people of Utah." Striking a similar theme, Orton noted in his second spot that "there's nothing like going out and knocking on doors, introducing yourself to the person who comes to the door, and asking them how their life is going. Only in his final ad did Orton address a specific issue—his introduction of a constitutional amendment requiring a balanced federal budget.

In response to an eleventh-hour radio commercial aired by his Republican opponent, Richard R. Harrington, who received $10,002 from the National Republican Congressional Committee and $15,000 from the Utah Republican party to augment his advertising budget, Orton spent $20,666 to air a radio spot denying the charge that he favored repealing the state's right-to-work laws.

Orton spent $6,871 on campaign literature that was distributed by precinct canvassers, $5,128 on newspaper ads, and $2,829 on signs. The final weekend of the campaign, postcards touting Orton's support for social security were mailed to 35,000 households.

In February 1992 Orton hired Kristal Miller of Washington, D.C., to coordinate his political action committee (PAC) receptions. While Miller received $20,046 for her efforts over the next eleven months, it proved to be money well spent. During the off-year, the campaign had collected $70,345 from PACs without the benefit of professional help. In 1992 PACs donated $120,650 to Orton's coffer's. At most, Orton raised $37,258 from individual Utah contributors. "It's very difficult for a Democrat to raise money in this state," noted Sheldon Kinsel, Orton's field director.

Campaign Expenditures	Orton Amount Spent	Orton % of Total	Harrington Amount Spent	Harrington % of Total
Overhead				
Office furniture/supplies	$ 3,198	1.70	$ 2,625	2.99
Rent/utilities	1,232	.66	800	.91
Salaries	11,165	5.94	29,583	33.73
Taxes	5,394	2.87	6,152	7.01
Bank/investment fees	0		117	.13
Lawyers/accountants	0		0	
Telephone	3,856	2.05	1,462	1.67
Campaign automobile	0		0	
Computers/office equipment	1,193	.63	220	.25
Travel	3,497	1.86	1,280	1.46
Food/meetings	968	.51	0	
Subtotal	30,503	16.23	42,239	48.16
Fund Raising				
Events	42,809	22.78	4,574	5.21
Direct mail	797	.42	0	
Telemarketing	0		0	
Subtotal	43,606	23.20	4,574	5.21
Polling	600	.32	0	
Advertising				
Electronic media	74,439	39.61	8,592	9.80
Other media	7,723	4.11	5,207	5.94
Subtotal	82,162	43.72	13,799	15.73
Other Campaign Activity				
Persuasion mail/brochures	12,591	6.70	12,595	14.36
Actual campaigning	15,221	8.10	11,021	12.57
Staff/volunteers	168	.09	0	
Subtotal	27,980	14.89	23,616	26.93
Constituent Gifts/ Entertainment	2,000	1.06	1,562	1.78
Donations to				
Candidates from same state	0		0	
Candidates from other states	0		0	
Civic organizations	560	.30	0	
Ideological groups	0		0	
Political parties	0		0	
Subtotal	560	.30	0	
Unitemized Expenses	524	.28	1,919	2.19
Total Campaign Expenses	$ 187,934		$ 87,708	
PAC Contributions	$ 190,995		$ 24,800	
Individual Contributions	48,308		46,281	
Total Receipts*	257,559		71,306	

*Includes PAC and individual contributions as well as interest earned, party contributions, etc.

VERMONT — At Large

Rep. Bernard Sanders (I)

1992 Election Results

Bernard Sanders (I)	162,724	(58%)
Tim Philbin (R)	86,901	(31%)
Lewis E. Young † (I)	22,279	(8%)

Rep. Bernard Sanders ran a do-it-youself, grassroots campaign that stressed cooperative efforts and employed no consultants. His radio and television ads were produced by a team of five that included Sanders and his wife Jane. "You get a better sense than some consultant would of what you're trying to convey about the candidate," explained Jane Sanders, who also helps other local candidates with their media. "We also design our own polls, not just to get information about how people will vote, but also to find out how well they understand the issues," she added. Volunteers produced all of Sanders's yard signs using a silk-screening machine owned by the campaign.

While Sanders was undoubtedly able to do more with less, this do-it-yourself approach did not produce an inexpensive campaign. Hundreds of volunteers needed somewhere to work, so the campaign opened five offices across the district. Rent totaled $12,961. To make certain that volunteer efforts were coordinated, Sanders paid Carolyn Kazdin, special projects director on his congressional staff, and Jim Schumacher, his congressional staff director, after-tax campaign salaries of $35,100 and $11,725, respectively. Other part-time staffers collected checks totaling $41,881. Payroll taxes added $19,817. While there were no media consulting fees, advertising production costs totaled $22,720. He spent $103,223 to air his ads, which focused on health care reform and the importance of saving family farms. He spent $22,392 on his in-house phonebank effort, $18,454 on newspaper ads and inserts, $5,919 on bus signs, and $5,839 on bumper stickers.

To fund his campaign, Sanders relied heavily on a nationwide direct-mail fund-raising operation. Like everything else, the effort was handled entirely in-house. "Bernie has been associated with certain issues since he was mayor [of Burlington]—labor, education, and women's issues—and that's how people around the country have gotten to know him," noted Sanders's wife. "We have one of the best mailing lists in the country, and we got at least one contribution from every state." To keep track of his valuable mailing lists, Sanders spent $7,280 on computer hardware, software, and supplies. Other office equipment added $8,430.

Republican Tim Philbin, an insurance underwriter and a stalwart of the party's more conservative wing, could not match either Sanders's organization or campaign treasury. He produced and aired one television commercial and three radio spots for the primary, but he had no money to run them during the general election campaign. To get his message out, Philbin depended largely on a whistle-stop tour of the district in an old school bus.

Campaign Expenditures	Sanders Amount Spent	Sanders % of Total	Philbin Amount Spent	Philbin % of Total
Overhead				
Office furniture/supplies	$ 18,284	3.32	$ 2,991	3.75
Rent/utilities	12,961	2.35	1,050	1.32
Salaries	88,706	16.12	3,691	4.63
Taxes	19,817	3.60	1,439	1.80
Bank/investment fees	2,916	.53	185	.23
Lawyers/accountants	12,356	2.24	0	
Telephone	7,695	1.40	5,198	6.52
Campaign automobile	0		0	
Computers/office equipment	15,710	2.85	2,751	3.45
Travel	33,533	6.09	6,068	7.61
Food/meetings	474	.09	8	.01
Subtotal	212,453	38.60	23,381	29.31
Fund Raising				
Events	5,023	.91	1,567	1.96
Direct mail	119,596	21.73	7,556	9.47
Telemarketing	0		1,481	1.86
Subtotal	124,619	22.64	10,604	13.29
Polling	4,933	.90	0	
Advertising				
Electronic media	125,943	22.88	24,507	30.73
Other media	25,214	4.58	2,743	3.44
Subtotal	151,157	27.46	27,250	34.17
Other Campaign Activity				
Persuasion mail/brochures	13,184	2.40	5,993	7.51
Actual campaigning	37,669	6.84	8,109	10.17
Staff/volunteers	2,430	.44	40	.05
Subtotal	53,283	9.68	14,142	17.73
Constituent Gifts/ Entertainment	382	.07	0	
Donations to				
Candidates from same state	3,200	.58	0	
Candidates from other states	0		0	
Civic organizations	0		0	
Ideological groups	350	.06	0	
Political parties	0		285	.36
Subtotal	3,550	.65	285	.36
Unitemized Expenses	0		4,097	5.14
Total Campaign Expenses	$ 550,377		$ 79,759	
PAC Contributions	$ 147,057		$ 0	
Individual Contributions	427,938		71,064	
Total Receipts*	591,543		78,382	

*Includes PAC and individual contributions as well as interest earned, party contributions, etc.

† No expenditures or receipts on file. Candidates raising or spending less than $5,000 are not required to file reports with the Federal Election Commission.

District 1 — VIRGINIA

Rep. Herbert H. Bateman (R)

1992 Election Results

Herbert H. Bateman (R) 133,537 (58%)
Andy Fox (D) 89,814 (39%)

Rep. Herbert H. Bateman had survived his 1990 reelection bid by fewer than 3,000 votes, despite outspending former television reporter Andy Fox by nearly $450,000. For his second attempt in 1992, Fox spent nearly four times as much as he had in 1990, collected nearly 8,000 votes more than the Democratic presidential ticket, and still lost by 43,723 votes.

Redistricting had substantially helped Bateman by removing large numbers of black Democratic voters from District 1 and replacing them with white Republican constituents. He also significantly increased his spending. Having invested $548,393 in the 1990 campaign, Bateman poured $727,280 into his 1992 effort, opening up a $332,981 spending advantage over Fox.

Bateman paid the Farwell Group of New Orleans, La., $184,365 for creating and placing television and radio commercials. Initially, Bateman's ads were positive, touting his efforts to keep district military bases off the base-closure list and his leadership role "in the battle to build the new aircraft carrier at Newport News."

However, the same week Bateman began airing his positive spot, Fox began running an ad attacking him for voting against a law requiring large businesses to give workers sixty days notice of layoffs or plant closings, for voting "to slash Medicare" and "to freeze cost-of-living adjustments for people on Social Security," and for voting in favor of the congressional pay raise. Fox paid Shorr Associates of Philadelphia $108,563 for creating and placing his ads. Campaign Performance Group of San Francisco, Calif., collected $33,700 from Fox and $23,714 from the Democratic party of Virginia for two persuasion mailers that echoed several of the same themes.

Bateman responded with an ad claiming that all the votes mentioned in Fox's commercial were taken out of context and explaining why he had taken the pay raise. Another spot slammed Fox for shifting from his 1990 stance in favor of the Brady Bill to a 1992 position that prompted the National Rifle Association to support him. "Fox got pounded in the newspapers about it for days," recalled Dan Scandling, Bateman's administrative assistant.

Charles Lihn Associates of Washington, D.C., created two persuasion mailers for Bateman—one targeted at voters in defense-dependent areas and a broader piece aimed at suburban Washington, D.C., voters. Lihn also handled direct-mail fund-raising chores and collected a total of $63,229.

To identify his supporters and encourage them to turn out, Bateman paid Hanover Associates of Mechanicsville $23,563 for phonebanking. He spent $22,740 on the state party's coordinated get-out-the-vote efforts.

Campaign Expenditures	Bateman Amount Spent	Bateman % of Total	Fox Amount Spent	Fox % of Total
Overhead				
Office furniture/supplies	$ 7,702	1.06	$ 2,872	.73
Rent/utilities	13,042	1.79	2,098	.53
Salaries	111,553	15.34	50,467	12.80
Taxes	41,099	5.65	0	
Bank/investment fees	1,116	.15	1,778	.45
Lawyers/accountants	0		0	
Telephone	17,308	2.38	7,409	1.88
Campaign automobile	0		0	
Computers/office equipment	8,787	1.21	4,418	1.12
Travel	18,016	2.48	10,811	2.74
Food/meetings	2,251	.31	495	.13
Subtotal	220,874	30.37	80,348	20.38
Fund Raising				
Events	73,749	10.14	32,652	8.28
Direct mail	71,971	9.90	7,524	1.91
Telemarketing	0		0	
Subtotal	145,720	20.04	40,176	10.19
Polling	10,375	1.43	21,270	5.39
Advertising				
Electronic media	190,073	26.13	132,173	33.52
Other media	17,057	2.35	5,507	1.40
Subtotal	207,130	28.48	137,680	34.92
Other Campaign Activity				
Persuasion mail/brochures	61,803	8.50	69,021	17.50
Actual campaigning	58,373	8.03	30,594	7.76
Staff/volunteers	2,589	.36	0	
Subtotal	122,765	16.88	99,615	25.26
Constituent Gifts/ Entertainment	5,162	.71	0	
Donations to				
Candidates from same state	0		0	
Candidates from other states	0		0	
Civic organizations	512	.07	1,067	.27
Ideological groups	0		224	.06
Political parties	698	.10	785	.20
Subtotal	1,211	.17	2,076	.53
Unitemized Expenses	14,045	1.93	13,134	3.33
Total Campaign Expenses	$ 727,280		$ 394,299	
PAC Contributions	$ 294,121		$ 241,283	
Individual Contributions	448,510		122,034	
Total Receipts*	766,895		419,287	

*Includes PAC and individual contributions as well as interest earned, party contributions, etc.

VIRGINIA — District 2

Rep. Owen B. Pickett (D)

1992 Election Results

Owen B. Pickett (D)	99,253	(56%)
J. L. "Jim" Chapman IV (R)	77,797	(44%)

In creating the new majority-black District 3, Virginia's mapmakers shifted substantial numbers of black Democratic voters out of District 2. As a result, three-term Democratic Rep. Owen B. Pickett found himself running for reelection in territory that was more Republican than he might have liked.

However, unlike many other incumbents in similar circumstances, Pickett did not feel the need to spend vast sums to hold onto the seat. While he spent more than four times as much as the $82,833 he spent in 1990, when he ran unopposed, Pickett spent about $40,000 less than he had in his contested 1988 race.

Pickett managed to hold his spending down by limiting his outlays for overhead and fund raising, which together accounted for only 18 percent of his expenses. Even during the off-year, overhead and fundraising costs represented only 36 percent of his spending. He invested just $2,922 in constituent stroking, including $2,411 for year-end holiday cards. Donations to other candidates, political party organizations, and causes amounted to $5,175. Instead of putting his money into the usual trappings of the permanent campaign, Pickett poured 75 percent of his budget into direct appeals for votes.

In April 1992 Pickett hired Fenn & King Communications of Washington, D.C., and over the final eight months of the election cycle paid the firm $192,361 for creating and placing broadcast ads. Jan Crawford Communications of Paris, Va., collected $20,433 for helping to target and place the commercials. Although the planning began in April, Pickett held off running his television commercials until the second week of October.

A television ad dubbed "Navy" focused on his efforts to "make sure Washington doesn't forget" that the navy is vital to the district's economy. To distance himself from his colleagues on Capitol Hill, Pickett noted in another ad that "my best source of information is not in Washington. It's right here in the district with people like you, the people that elected me."

Over the final two weeks of the campaign, Pickett aired one commercial pointing out that while Republican J. L. "Jim" Chapman IV had attacked him for opposing a constitutional amendment requiring a balanced federal budget and for voting in favor of the congressional pay raise, he had in fact authored his own balanced budget amendment and voted against the raise. His only negative spot slammed Chapman for opposing "$43 million in Norfolk navy projects."

While Chapman invested 51 percent of his $202,102 budget in direct voter appeals, only 20 percent was put into broadcast advertising.

Pickett captured 56 percent of the vote, even though the district went Republican in the presidential race.

Campaign Expenditures	Pickett Amount Spent	Pickett % of Total	Chapman Amount Spent	Chapman % of Total
Overhead				
Office furniture/supplies	$ 2,588	.69	$ 3,708	1.83
Rent/utilities	2,375	.64	5,600	2.77
Salaries	8,756	2.35	39,711	19.65
Taxes	3,947	1.06	7,569	3.75
Bank/investment fees	0		10	
Lawyers/accountants	2,355	.63	0	
Telephone	2,319	.62	5,795	2.87
Campaign automobile	0		0	
Computers/office equipment	4,218	1.13	1,774	.88
Travel	3,801	1.02	3,288	1.63
Food/meetings	805	.22	410	.20
Subtotal	**31,163**	**8.35**	**67,866**	**33.58**
Fund Raising				
Events	33,918	9.09	13,023	6.44
Direct mail	1,720	.46	12,900	6.38
Telemarketing	0		0	
Subtotal	**35,639**	**9.55**	**25,922**	**12.83**
Polling	**18,950**	**5.08**	**0**	
Advertising				
Electronic media	218,458	58.56	40,262	19.92
Other media	8,254	2.21	7,124	3.53
Subtotal	**226,712**	**60.77**	**47,387**	**23.45**
Other Campaign Activity				
Persuasion mail/brochures	31,053	8.32	20,252	10.02
Actual campaigning	21,053	5.64	36,060	17.84
Staff/volunteers	170	.05	0	
Subtotal	**52,276**	**14.01**	**56,312**	**27.86**
Constituent Gifts/Entertainment	2,922	.78	0	
Donations to				
Candidates from same state	100	.03	0	
Candidates from other states	1,800	.48	0	
Civic organizations	360	.10	190	.09
Ideological groups	1,585	.42	0	
Political parties	1,330	.36	140	.07
Subtotal	**5,175**	**1.39**	**330**	**.16**
Unitemized Expenses	**216**	**.06**	**4,285**	**2.12**
Total Campaign Expenses	**$ 373,053**		**$ 202,102**	
PAC Contributions	**$ 128,450**		**$ 11,185**	
Individual Contributions	**132,185**		**169,879**	
Total Receipts*	**281,279**		**192,337**	

*Includes PAC and individual contributions as well as interest earned, party contributions, etc.

District 3 — VIRGINIA

Rep. Robert C. Scott (D)

1992 Election Results
Robert C. Scott (D)   132,432   (79%)
Daniel Jenkins (R)   35,780   (21%)

When Virginia's legislature added a new black-majority district around Richmond, state senator Robert C. Scott, state representative Jean Wooden Cunningham, and Virginia State Retirement System chairman Jacqueline G. Epps jumped into the Democratic primary. Together, the three spent $722,444 on their primary battle.

With fourteen years of experience in the state legislature and a proven electoral track record that included a 44 percent showing against Republican Rep. Herbert H. Bateman in 1986, Scott managed to raise $216,180 for the primary. With a $67,157 infusion from his personal bank account and $72,629 in deficit spending, he pumped $344,909 into the primary campaign.

Fenn & King Communications of Washington, D.C., billed Scott $84,388 for creating and placing one preprimary television commercial. "Some talk of change. Others cause it. Senator Bobby Scott," the spot began. It touted his efforts to speed up prosecutions in drug cases, restrict the use of armor-piercing bullets, increase the state's minimum wage, and foster new child health programs.

For the primary Scott spent $34,514 on brochures and persuasion mail and $6,005 on newspaper ads. Bumper stickers and signs added $3,367 and $1,352, respectively. Scott paid his precinct canvassers $7,575 to distribute his bumper stickers and literature. Per diem payments to his poll watchers and other election day workers totaled $17,858. Computer equipment and software to drive his preprimary direct-mail fund-raising solicitations and his persuasion mail effort cost $14,276. Pollster Ron Lester & Co. of Washington, D.C., collected $12,110.

To offset this splurge, Scott paid Erickson & Co. of Washington, D.C., $12,110 to arrange political action committee (PAC) receptions and large-donor events. Those efforts yielded PAC contributions of $90,800. Donations of $200 or more amounted to $66,609.

Scott picked up 67 percent of the primary votes. With only 15 percent of the voters bothering to cast their ballots, Scott spent $14.75 for each of the 23,381 votes he collected. For her $225,883 investment, Cunningham received 22 percent of the vote, which amounted to an average expenditure of $30.04 for each of her 7,520 votes.

In November Scott cruised to victory against Republican Daniel Jenkins. While Scott spent nearly $200,000 over the final six months of the election cycle, he invested nothing in broadcast ads, $28,393 in campaign literature and persuasion mail, and only $1,248 in newspaper ads.

Although Jenkins reported spending $16,318, his reports to the Federal Election Commission were illegible and could not be included in our analysis.

Campaign Expenditures	Scott Amount Spent	% of Total
Overhead		
Office furniture/supplies	$ 6,652	1.23
Rent/utilities	9,756	1.80
Salaries	112,618	20.79
Taxes	8,220	1.52
Bank/investment fees	0	
Lawyers/accountants	600	.11
Telephone	14,742	2.72
Campaign automobile	6,509	1.20
Computers/office equipment	28,055	5.18
Travel	13,376	2.47
Food/meetings	2,902	.54
Subtotal	**203,430**	**37.55**
Fund Raising		
Events	51,827	9.57
Direct mail	20,142	3.72
Telemarketing	0	
Subtotal	**71,969**	**13.28**
Polling	**17,110**	**3.16**
Advertising		
Electronic media	84,688	15.63
Other media	8,003	1.48
Subtotal	**92,692**	**17.11**
Other Campaign Activity		
Persuasion mail/brochures	62,907	11.61
Actual campaigning	69,582	12.84
Staff/volunteers	1,807	.33
Subtotal	**134,296**	**24.79**
Constituent Gifts/Entertainment	**28**	**.01**
Donations to		
Candidates from same state	440	.08
Candidates from other states	100	.02
Civic organizations	1,242	.23
Ideological groups	645	.12
Political parties	550	.10
Subtotal	**2,977**	**.55**
Unitemized Expenses	**19,245**	**3.55**
Total Campaign Expenses	**$ 541,747**	
PAC Contributions	**$ 185,250**	
Individual Contributions	**262,044**	
Total Receipts*	**519,276**	

*Includes PAC and individual contributions as well as interest earned, party contributions, etc.

VIRGINIA — District 4

Rep. Norman Sisisky (D)

1992 Election Results

Norman Sisisky (D)	147,649	(68%)
A. J. "Tony" Zevgolis (R)	68,286	(32%)

Rep. Norman Sisisky had adopted a relaxed campaign style, with good reason. Narrowly elected in 1982, Sisisky had not faced a Republican challenge in any of his four reelection bids. With no opposition of any kind in 1984, 1986, and 1988, Sisisky had spent a total of just $252,343. When two independent candidates stepped forward in 1990, Sisisky increased his outlays to a relatively modest $274,790.

Sisisky began the 1992 cycle very frugally. He spent just $34,622 to maintain his campaign in 1991, including a $8,053 payment to Take One Production in Morrisville, N.C., for 1990 media production costs that were not billed until 1991.

However, the District 4 that emerged from the redistricting process had voted for George Bush in 1988 and would again in 1992. When local Republicans managed to draft Hopewell City Council member A. J. "Tony" Zevgolis, Sisisky countered Zevgolis's anemic $82,069 budget with a $431,393 election-year burst.

In January 1992 Sisisky hired Fenn & King Communications of Washington, D.C., and over the next twelve months paid the firm $263,450 for creating and placing broadcast advertising. Miscellaneous production costs added $8,256. Outlays for broadcast advertising accounted for 63 percent of Sisisky's election-year spending.

In the first of his three television spots, Sisisky noted that "the greatest satisfaction to me is helping people, whether its finding a Social Security check that's lost, or getting someone in a veteran's hospital, or just breaking down the bureaucratic mess that we have in Washington." To distance himself from his colleagues on Capitol Hill, Sisisky continued with an outsider message. "I didn't come to Congress for free banking or for $10 haircuts or anything else that they got. I came here to do a job for people."

To distance himself from the Democratic leadership, which some of his constituents would find too liberal, another Sisisky spot proclaimed, "I voted with the president without any hesitation on the Persian Gulf War. When the president's right, I'll vote with him. When he's wrong, I'll vote against him. And the same holds true with my party leaders or anyone else." Sisisky's final spot focused on his commitment to vote against the "Mexican Free Trade Agreement," if he felt it would cost American jobs. None of the ads mentioned Zevgolis.

To fuel this advertising effort and generally keep tabs on the mood of the electorate, Sisisky hired pollster Hamilton & Staff of Washington, D.C., in February 1992. Over the balance of the campaign, Hamilton collected $30,000 for its efforts.

Campaign Expenditures	Sisisky Amount Spent	Sisisky % of Total	Zevgolis Amount Spent	Zevgolis % of Total
Overhead				
Office furniture/supplies	$ 5,456	1.17	$ 1,225	1.49
Rent/utilities	4,598	.99	1,420	1.73
Salaries	42,721	9.17	13,683	16.67
Taxes	6,421	1.38	0	
Bank/investment fees	0		0	
Lawyers/accountants	0		0	
Telephone	5,720	1.23	1,447	1.76
Campaign automobile	0		0	
Computers/office equipment	3,328	.71	0	
Travel	4,620	.99	650	.79
Food/meetings	488	.10	0	
Subtotal	**73,351**	**15.74**	**18,424**	**22.45**
Fund Raising				
Events	34,547	7.41	1,289	1.57
Direct mail	0		5,039	6.14
Telemarketing	0		0	
Subtotal	**34,547**	**7.41**	**6,327**	**7.71**
Polling	**30,000**	**6.44**	**0**	
Advertising				
Electronic media	279,759	60.03	24,047	29.30
Other media	274	.06	228	.28
Subtotal	**280,033**	**60.09**	**24,275**	**29.58**
Other Campaign Activity				
Persuasion mail/brochures	6,265	1.34	12,986	15.82
Actual campaigning	12,445	2.67	4,802	5.85
Staff/volunteers	0		0	
Subtotal	**18,710**	**4.01**	**17,788**	**21.67**
Constituent Gifts/Entertainment	**2,679**	**.57**	**0**	
Donations to				
Candidates from same state	1,000	.21	0	
Candidates from other states	1,000	.21	0	
Civic organizations	1,050	.23	0	
Ideological groups	833	.18	0	
Political parties	18,808	4.04	0	
Subtotal	**22,691**	**4.87**	**0**	
Unitemized Expenses	**4,004**	**.86**	**15,255**	**18.59**
Total Campaign Expenses	**$ 466,015**		**$ 82,069**	
PAC Contributions	**$ 160,750**		**$ 3,413**	
Individual Contributions	**71,558**		**36,039**	
Total Receipts*	**257,047**		**82,161**	

*Includes PAC and individual contributions as well as interest earned, party contributions, etc.

District 5 — VIRGINIA

Rep. Lewis F. Payne, Jr. (D)

1992 Election Results

Lewis F. Payne, Jr. (D)   133,031   (69%)
W. A. "Bill" Hulburt (R)   60,030   (31%)

Rep. Lewis F. Payne, Jr., spent $393,664 on his 1992 campaign. Nearly one-quarter of this was paid directly to Payne or to his wife's business, Payne, Ross Associates Advertising of Charlottesville.

For his initial House race in 1988, Payne had loaned his campaign $275,000. Although he had assets valued at between $1.9 million and $3 million, Payne attached a 10 percent interest rate to the loan. With an outstanding balance of $105,000 at the beginning of 1991, Payne's campaign paid him interest income totaling $56,179 during the 1992 election cycle. The campaign repaid only $20,000 of the principal, allowing Payne to continue accruing large sums in interest during the 1994 election cycle. Since the loan was used to pay for 1988 expenses, the repaid principal has not been included in our spending analysis.

Payne, Ross collected $38,822 from Payne's campaign for printing Christmas cards, fund-raising invitations, signs, brochures, and bumper stickers. Payments to the firm also included $1,872 for the use of a cellular telephone, $447 for balloons, $312 for "victory party supplies," and $1,024 for miscellaneous expenses.

To introduce himself to the more than 30,000 voters he acquired through redistricting, Payne paid Fenn & King Communications of Washington, D.C., $101,650 for creating and placing broadcast advertising. Three television spots touted his legislative efforts to punish oversees companies who falsely label their products "Made in the U.S.A." and his efforts to improve rural health care.

This investment was aimed at the future as much as it was directed at Republican W. A. "Bill" Hulburt. "We had the money to buy Richmond TV, and we wanted to let everyone know that if they were considering a race against us, they would have to be willing to spend money on Richmond TV," explained Ellis Woodward, Payne's communications director.

To pay for his campaign, Payne held more than forty events, with ticket prices ranging from $100 to $1,000. "We tried to do at least one event in each city in the district," Woodward noted. Mary-Margaret Cash of Lynchburg and Susan Swecker of Lexington received $9,713 and $6,704, respectively, for coordinating district events. To tap political action committee (PAC) money, Payne paid Terry C. Hoye of Alexandria $17,637. However, once Payne was certain that he would have a seat on the Ways and Means Committee, he turned over the organization of his PAC events to Alexandria-based Fiorello Consulting, which also handled that chore for Ways and Means Chairman Dan Rostenkowsi (D-Ill.). "It paid off nicely," noted Woodward.

Campaign Expenditures	Payne Amount Spent	Payne % of Total	Hulburt Amount Spent	Hulburt % of Total
Overhead				
Office furniture/supplies	$ 2,025	.51	$ 1,180	1.92
Rent/utilities	3,400	.86	5,590	9.10
Salaries	8,677	2.20	12,813	20.85
Taxes	140	.04	0	
Bank/investment fees	56,228	14.28	50	.08
Lawyers/accountants	27,288	6.93	2,613	4.25
Telephone	5,562	1.41	2,036	3.31
Campaign automobile	0		0	
Computers/office equipment	3,050	.77	3,455	5.62
Travel	3,881	.99	8,771	14.27
Food/meetings	430	.11	547	.89
Subtotal	**110,681**	**28.12**	**37,055**	**60.29**
Fund Raising				
Events	88,242	22.42	2,786	4.53
Direct mail	11,560	2.94	0	
Telemarketing	0		0	
Subtotal	**99,802**	**25.35**	**2,786**	**4.53**
Polling	**11,440**	**2.91**	**0**	
Advertising				
Electronic media	101,788	25.86	997	1.62
Other media	1,248	.32	1,972	3.21
Subtotal	**103,036**	**26.17**	**2,969**	**4.83**
Other Campaign Activity				
Persuasion mail/brochures	632	.16	2,339	3.81
Actual campaigning	45,975	11.68	15,901	25.87
Staff/volunteers	0		124	.20
Subtotal	**46,607**	**11.84**	**18,364**	**29.88**
Constituent Gifts/Entertainment	**4,098**	**1.04**	**0**	
Donations to				
Candidates from same state	916	.23	0	
Candidates from other states	0		0	
Civic organizations	0		100	.16
Ideological groups	0		0	
Political parties	12,750	3.24	135	.22
Subtotal	**13,666**	**3.47**	**235**	**.38**
Unitemized Expenses	**4,336**	**1.10**	**50**	**.08**
Total Campaign Expenses	**$ 393,664**		**$ 61,459**	
PAC Contributions	$ 219,044		$ 2,971	
Individual Contributions	198,375		27,199	
Total Receipts*	418,643		56,215	

*Includes PAC and individual contributions as well as interest earned, party contributions, etc.

VIRGINIA — District 6

Rep. Robert W. Goodlatte (R)

1992 Election Results
Robert W. Goodlatte (R) 127,309 (60%)
Stephen Alan Musselwhite (D) 84,618 (40%)

When Democratic Rep. Jim Olin decided to retire rather than seek a sixth term, district Republicans seized the opportunity. Intraparty differences between religious fundamentalists and more moderate Republicans were set aside, allowing attorney Robert W. Goodlatte to move through the nominating convention unscathed. Goodlatte spent only $51,636 to secure the nomination.

The Democrats were not as fortunate. Insurance executive Stephen Alan Musselwhite had Olin's endorsement, but that did not stop Roanoke attorneys John Edwards and John Fishwick from jumping into the race. The June 9 convention failed to produce a nominee until the fifth ballot, when Musselwhite emerged with an eleven-vote victory. Musselwhite's efforts to woo convention delegates cost $248,809.

Musselwhite paid Ambrosino & Muir of San Francisco, Calif., $30,366 for producing brochures for the convention. He paid Struble-Totten Communications of Washington, D.C., $26,829 to produce a biographical video and spent $14,248 to distribute it to convention delegates. The Tyson Organization of Fort Worth, Texas, collected $26,100 for a phonebank operation that monitored the delegate count. The Research Group of Chicago, Ill., received $11,200 for opposition research. Struble-Totten collected another $16,145 to begin planning the media campaign.

In their head-to-head confrontation, Goodlatte outspent Musselwhite by $59,186. Goodlatte paid Richard Leggett of Germantown, Md., and the Robert Goodman Agency of Baltimore, Md., $7,588 and $17,701, respectively, for writing and producing his broadcast ads. The ads slammed Musselwhite for not repaying a loan from a failed bank and for writing a letter requesting leniency for two white-collar felons. Another spot juxtaposed Goodlatte's support for term limits, a line-item veto, and federal right-to-work legislation with Musselwhite's opposition to all three. Positive commercials featuring Goodlatte with his family focused on his desire to reduce taxes and spending. Mentzer Media Service of Baltimore collected $133,356 for placing radio and television commercials over the final weeks of the campaign.

While Goodlatte invested only $24,700 in campaign literature and persuasion mail, a $49,895 infusion from the National Republican Congressional Committee allowed him to blanket the district with mailers. "The mail kept reminding people that they were tired of taxes, tired of budget deficits, sick of check bouncing, and tired of guys who think they're above the law," noted Tim Phillips, Goodlatte's administrative assistant.

Phillips and Randy Hinaman of Alexandria collected $47,253 and $22,085, respectively, for providing general strategic advice.

Campaign Expenditures	Goodlatte Amount Spent	Goodlatte % of Total	Musselwhite Amount Spent	Musselwhite % of Total
Overhead				
Office furniture/supplies	$ 4,824	1.07	$ 10,898	1.85
Rent/utilities	4,011	.89	9,120	1.55
Salaries	41,724	9.27	118,373	20.13
Taxes	8,161	1.81	47,286	8.04
Bank/investment fees	521	.12	4,017	.68
Lawyers/accountants	0		6,334	1.08
Telephone	8,863	1.97	11,582	1.97
Campaign automobile	0		0	
Computers/office equipment	5,946	1.32	1,411	.24
Travel	28,981	6.44	9,693	1.65
Food/meetings	181	.04	93	.02
Subtotal	**103,212**	**22.94**	**218,807**	**37.22**
Fund Raising				
Events	10,747	2.39	9,266	1.58
Direct mail	24,300	5.40	6,955	1.18
Telemarketing	0		7,418	1.26
Subtotal	**35,047**	**7.79**	**23,639**	**4.02**
Polling	**19,800**	**4.40**	**17,950**	**3.05**
Advertising				
Electronic media	169,066	37.58	175,095	29.78
Other media	1,573	.35	481	.08
Subtotal	**170,639**	**37.93**	**175,576**	**29.87**
Other Campaign Activity				
Persuasion mail/brochures	24,700	5.49	6,620	1.13
Actual campaigning	95,448	21.21	137,254	23.35
Staff/volunteers	0		512	.09
Subtotal	**120,148**	**26.70**	**144,385**	**24.56**
Constituent Gifts/ Entertainment	**40**	**.01**	**0**	
Donations to				
Candidates from same state	0		0	
Candidates from other states	0		0	
Civic organizations	0		0	
Ideological groups	0		0	
Political parties	0		780	.13
Subtotal	**0**		**780**	**.13**
Unitemized Expenses	**1,024**	**.23**	**6,758**	**1.15**
Total Campaign Expenses	**$ 449,909**		**$ 587,896**	
PAC Contributions	**$ 120,492**		**$ 97,890**	
Individual Contributions	**271,146**		**223,406**	
Total Receipts*	**464,535**		**597,405**	

*Includes PAC and individual contributions as well as interest earned, party contributions, etc.

District 7 — VIRGINIA

Rep. Thomas J. Bliley, Jr. (R)

1992 Election Results

Thomas J. Bliley, Jr. (R)	211,618	(83%)
Gerald E. Berg † (I)	43,267	(17%)

Rep. Thomas J. Bliley, Jr., had not received less than 60 percent of the vote since 1982, and no Democrat bothered to contest the seat in 1992. While the district's boundaries were altered substantially by redistricting, it remained solidly Republican. Nevertheless, Bliley spent $698,970 on his campaign, including $215,763 during the off-year.

Bliley's off-year spending was understandable. The state's redistricting plan was not approved until February 1992, and an early version of the plan called for Bliley's old District 3 to be merged with fellow Republican Rep. Herbert H. Bateman's District 1. "We wanted the upper hand if we were going to have to face another incumbent," noted Boyd Marcus, Bliley's campaign strategist. Bliley gave $10,000 to Virginia FAIR, an organization established to assist the state's Republicans with redistricting.

The final redistricting plan merged much of Bliley's old district with fellow Republican George F. Allen's District 7. Allen had won a 1991 special election to fill the seat vacated by Rep. D. French Slaughter, Jr., but agreed to step aside, leaving the path clear for Bliley. Bliley continued to pour money into his campaign for other reasons. "The stronger the turnout, the better for the ticket," explained Marcus.

Bliley turned day-to-day campaign management over to Marcus, his former administrative assistant who left the congressional staff to form his own consulting firm, MBM Consulting of Richmond. The campaign paid MBM $84,544 for office rent, use of computers and other office equipment, direct-mail fund-raising solicitations, miscellaneous expenses, and one staffer whose time was devoted primarily to fund raising. Direct payments to Marcus, which have been listed under actual campaigning, added $83,022.

To keep his campaign running smoothly and organize the newly acquired portions of the district, Bliley invested heavily in staff. During 1991, six part-time staffers, including four members of his congressional staff, collected payroll checks totaling $62,963. Two additional part-time employees joined the campaign in 1992, driving Bliley's election-year payroll to $90,008. Over the two-year cycle, salaries and payroll taxes accounted for 35 percent of Bliley's outlays.

Bliley's only opposition was independent candidate Gerald E. Berg, who spent less than $5,000. Relieved of the need to actively campaign, Bliley opted to forego television advertising entirely. He paid Colonial Communications of Richmond $48,671 to place radio spots, which were aimed primarily at his new constituents. He invested $23,262 in campaign literature and persuasion mail that targeted Republican primary voters and those identified as likely supporters by a $4,612 phonebanking effort. Pollster Fabrizio, McLaughlin & Associates received $10,950.

	Bliley	
Campaign Expenditures	Amount Spent	% of Total
Overhead		
Office furniture/supplies	$ 5,824	.83
Rent/utilities	19,700	2.82
Salaries	152,971	21.89
Taxes	91,757	13.13
Bank/investment fees	183	.03
Lawyers/accountants	0	
Telephone	12,460	1.78
Campaign automobile	0	
Computers/office equipment	18,706	2.68
Travel	9,021	1.29
Food/meetings	6,985	1.00
Subtotal	317,607	45.44
Fund Raising		
Events	116,524	16.67
Direct mail	48,872	6.99
Telemarketing	0	
Subtotal	165,396	23.66
Polling	10,950	1.57
Advertising		
Electronic media	48,691	6.97
Other media	3,380	.48
Subtotal	52,070	7.45
Other Campaign Activity		
Persuasion mail/brochures	23,262	3.33
Actual campaigning	101,371	14.50
Staff/volunteers	1,568	.22
Subtotal	126,202	18.06
Constituent Gifts/Entertainment	3,800	.54
Donations to		
Candidates from same state	5,000	.72
Candidates from other states	3,500	.50
Civic organizations	719	.10
Ideological groups	0	
Political parties	10,000	1.43
Subtotal	19,219	2.75
Unitemized Expenses	3,726	.53
Total Campaign Expenses	$ 698,970	
PAC Contributions	$ 441,292	
Individual Contributions	276,666	
Total Receipts*	721,526	

*Includes PAC and individual contributions as well as interest earned, party contributions, etc.

† No expenditures or receipts on file. Candidates raising or spending less than $5,000 are not required to file reports with the Federal Election Commission.

VIRGINIA   District 8

Rep. James P. Moran, Jr. (D)   *1992 Election Results*   James P. Moran, Jr. (D)   138,542   (56%)
                                                                    Kyle E. McSlarrow (R)   102,717   (42%)

While redistricting dramatically strengthened freshman Rep. James P. Moran, Jr.'s electoral position, his first reelection campaign proved nearly as bitter as his 1990 upset victory over Republican Rep. Stan Parris, who Moran referred to during the campaign as "a deceitful, fatuous jerk." In 1992 the nicest thing Moran called Republican attorney Kyle E. McSlarrow was "an anti-environmental attorney." Moran dredged up McSlarrow's teenage drug use, labeled him a right-wing extremist, and attacked him for spreading "slanderous lies."

Not to be outdone, McSlarrow called Moran a crook and accused him of lying to the public. McSlarrow added that he would be happy to match his record as a teenager to Moran's as an adult—a not-so-thinly veiled reference to a 1984 plea bargaining agreement in which Moran had agreed to plead no contest to a misdemeanor conflict of interest charge and resign his position as vice mayor of Alexandria, Va.

However, while Parris had marginally outspent Moran in 1990, Moran's new incumbent status enabled him to outspend McSlarrow by $477,228. More importantly, while McSlarrow spent $68,779 on broadcast media, Moran was able to invest $293,772.

McSlarrow struck first with a television commercial accusing Moran of attempting to derail an investigation into a bank whose directors had contributed heavily to his campaign. The ad accused Moran of seeking to cut Social Security. A radio spot attacked Moran's use of franked mail to address "puff issues."

Moran countered the latter charge with a radio spot that featured a female narrator chastising McSlarrow. "Puff issues like breast cancer? Hey, Mr. McSlarrow, take a powder." Moran's advisers also retooled a television spot used to attack Parris's anti-abortion stance in 1990. The spot showed the Statue of Liberty behind bars and warned that McSlarrow wanted to make abortion illegal. Another spot touted Moran's successful battle to keep Jack Kent Cook, owner of the Washington Redskins, from building a new football stadium in Alexandria. Trippi, McMahon, & Squier of Alexandria collected $290,634 for creating and placing the ads.

Moran invested $11,029 in bus signs proclaiming, "Jim Moran—Our choice for Congress." He spent $31,155 on two persuasion mailers and campaign leaflets—less than half what he spent on campaign literature as a challenger. Moran spent $13,974 on T-shirts, buttons, bumper stickers, and balloons; $9,624 on three rounds of phonebanking to identify and turn out his supporters; $9,145 on yard signs and posters; $2,762 on parade expenses; and $1,976 on promotional key chains.

Campaign Expenditures	Moran Amount Spent	Moran % of Total	McSlarrow Amount Spent	McSlarrow % of Total
Overhead				
Office furniture/supplies	$ 12,435	1.38	$ 12,660	2.98
Rent/utilities	17,000	1.88	12,760	3.00
Salaries	129,638	14.37	64,815	15.25
Taxes	17,428	1.93	3,137	.74
Bank/investment fees	861	.10	850	.20
Lawyers/accountants	11,500	1.27	0	
Telephone	11,950	1.32	10,827	2.55
Campaign automobile	0		0	
Computers/office equipment	14,061	1.56	23,544	5.54
Travel	15,615	1.73	1,156	.27
Food/meetings	3,637	.40	309	.07
Subtotal	234,125	25.95	130,057	30.61
Fund Raising				
Events	159,773	17.71	32,456	7.64
Direct mail	55,375	6.14	53,828	12.67
Telemarketing	0		0	
Subtotal	215,148	23.85	86,284	20.31
Polling	21,344	2.37	6,103	1.44
Advertising				
Electronic media	293,772	32.56	68,779	16.19
Other media	13,256	1.47	299	.07
Subtotal	307,028	34.03	69,078	16.26
Other Campaign Activity				
Persuasion mail/brochures	31,155	3.45	72,173	16.99
Actual campaigning	53,033	5.88	44,968	10.58
Staff/volunteers	787	.09	391	.09
Subtotal	84,975	9.42	117,532	27.66
Constituent Gifts/Entertainment	9,385	1.04	270	.06
Donations to				
Candidates from same state	1,600	.18	0	
Candidates from other states	250	.03	0	
Civic organizations	3,205	.36	20	
Ideological groups	1,350	.15	0	
Political parties	5,025	.56	50	.01
Subtotal	11,430	1.27	70	.02
Unitemized Expenses	18,705	2.07	15,519	3.65
Total Campaign Expenses	$ 902,140		$ 424,912	
PAC Contributions	$ 436,121		$ 86,389	
Individual Contributions	467,272		300,720	
Total Receipts*	925,436		426,951	

*Includes PAC and individual contributions as well as interest earned, party contributions, etc.

District 9 — VIRGINIA

Rep. Rick Boucher (D)

1992 Election Results

Rick Boucher (D)	133,284	(63%)
L. Garrett Weddle (R)	77,985	(37%)

Unopposed in 1990, Democratic Rep. Rick Boucher had spent $252,818. Faced with a $100,000 challenge in 1992 by Republican L. Garrett Weddle, Boucher spent $659,106.

Although he entered 1991 with campaign cash reserves of $401,839, Boucher invested 39,072—38 percent of his expenditures for the year—in his off-year fund-raising efforts. He paid Creative Campaign Consultant $13,461 for coordinating political action committee (PAC) events that helped push his PAC receipts for the year to $190,608. PACs accounted for 95 percent of the $199,858 Boucher raised during 1991. By January 1, 1992, Boucher's cash reserves had grown to $525,255.

PACs continued to supply the majority of Boucher's money in 1992. Creative Campaign Consultant received $16,623 for coordinating PAC fund-raising efforts, which yielded contributions totaling $213,971. Election-year donations from individual contributors amounted to $146,800.

In May 1992 Boucher paid Cooper & Secrest Associates of Alexandria, Va., $14,650 for a benchmark poll of the district. He paid them another $8,785 for a poll in October to make sure his support was holding steady. This $23,435 investment in surveys was $13,685 more than he spent on polls in 1990.

Even though he had no opposition in 1990, Boucher had invested $73,274 in advertising to let his constituents know he was interested in their votes. While Weddle lacked the money for a major advertising push, his presence on the ballot prompted Boucher to increase his advertising outlays to $200,819. He paid Fred Woods Productions of Watertown, Mass., $35,098 to produce television commercials. Air time on various network affiliates cost $148,717. The campaign spent $5,907 for air time on local cable television systems. Newspaper ads cost the campaign $9,826. None of the ads mentioned Weddle.

In 1990 Boucher had put $8,846 into campaign literature; in 1992 he increased outlays for brochures and persuasion mail to $95,215. He spent $5,257 on yard signs and posters and $4,735 on buttons, bumper stickers, and other campaign paraphernalia.

Boucher simply gave away $41,940, including $22,000 to fellow Virginians. The chief beneficiary of Boucher's generosity was state senator Jack Kennedy, who collected checks totaling $13,000 for his unsuccessful reelection bid. He gave $10,000 to the Democratic Congressional Campaign Committee.

Despite assistance from Patrick Buchanan, Sen. John Warner (R-Va.), and former Lt. Col. Oliver North, Weddle's fund-raising efforts proved unspectacular. While Boucher could afford to spend $154,624 on television air time, Weddle could counter with cable television buys totaling only $10,853.

Campaign Expenditures	Boucher Amount Spent	Boucher % of Total	Weddle Amount Spent	Weddle % of Total
Overhead				
Office furniture/supplies	$ 8,922	1.35	$ 6,445	6.21
Rent/utilities	3,450	.52	2,624	2.53
Salaries	84,689	12.85	22,073	21.26
Taxes	22,062	3.35	66	.06
Bank/investment fees	32		540	.52
Lawyers/accountants	308	.05	0	
Telephone	8,424	1.28	5,455	5.25
Campaign automobile	5,601	.85	0	
Computers/office equipment	20,691	3.14	1,246	1.20
Travel	20,693	3.14	3,868	3.72
Food/meetings	275	.04	97	.09
Subtotal	**175,146**	**26.57**	**42,414**	**40.85**
Fund Raising				
Events	77,008	11.68	8,837	8.51
Direct mail	25,196	3.82	1,044	1.01
Telemarketing	0		0	
Subtotal	**102,204**	**15.51**	**9,881**	**9.52**
Polling	**23,435**	**3.56**	**0**	
Advertising				
Electronic media	190,235	28.86	15,587	15.01
Other media	10,584	1.61	1,870	1.80
Subtotal	**200,819**	**30.47**	**17,457**	**16.81**
Other Campaign Activity				
Persuasion mail/brochures	95,215	14.45	6,050	5.83
Actual campaigning	15,839	2.40	25,249	24.32
Staff/volunteers	2,174	.33	0	
Subtotal	**113,228**	**17.18**	**31,299**	**30.14**
Constituent Gifts/ Entertainment	**2,335**	**.35**	**0**	
Donations to				
Candidates from same state	22,000	3.34	0	
Candidates from other states	7,300	1.11	0	
Civic organizations	50	.01	32	.03
Ideological groups	0		0	
Political parties	12,590	1.91	190	.18
Subtotal	**41,940**	**6.36**	**222**	**.21**
Unitemized Expenses	**0**		**2,564**	**2.47**
Total Campaign Expenses	**$ 659,106**		**$ 103,838**	
PAC Contributions	$ 404,579		$ 5,016	
Individual Contributions	154,049		78,448	
Total Receipts*	639,537		99,174	

*Includes PAC and individual contributions as well as interest earned, party contributions, etc.

VIRGINIA — District 10

Rep. Frank R. Wolf (R)

1992 Election Results

Frank R. Wolf (R)	144,471	(64%)
Raymond E. Vickery (D)	75,775	(33%)

When elected in 1980, Republican Rep. Frank R. Wolf had promised voters he would serve no more than twelve years. In 1992 Wolf changed his mind about voluntary term limits and easily defeated Democrat Raymond E. Vickery. In the process, Wolf outspent Vickery by more than two to one.

Redistricting had carved all of Arlington County and portions of Fairfax County out of District 10 and replaced these suburban voters with more conservative Republican constituents in rural Frederick and Clarke counties. Despite the fact that Vickery had more than twice as much to spend as Wolf's 1990 challenger and billed himself as the "Choice for Change," his pro-choice stance on abortion failed to excite the conservative audience, and his campaign never took off.

The restructured district forced Wolf to depend less on television than he had in prior campaigns and more on radio and newspaper ads. "We cut way back on TV from years gone by," noted Charles E. White, Wolf's administrative assistant. "It costs so much to advertise in the Washington, D.C., market, and it only covers about one-third of the district now." While the campaign invested in two television spots touting his integrity and record for constituent service, the heaviest emphasis was put into airing six radio commercials. "Commuters are drive-time captives," White explained. "You reach so many people with so little money." The DCM Group of McLean received $92,206 for creating and placing the broadcast ads.

Essentially, DCM was the campaign. In addition to handling the broadcast ads, the firm conducted the campaign's lone poll, provided general strategic advice, placed newspaper ads costing $17,666, and sent out a fund-raising solicitation to past contributors that also asked people to volunteer their time. For its efforts, DCM collected a total of $177,321.

In October Wolf put his volunteers to work on one of five phonebanks, each consisting of between ten and twenty lines. In addition to contacting known supporters, White said considerable effort was invested in contacting undecided voters. The intensive, but short-term, operation cost only $1,153.

Although Wolf had become known for his attention to parochial constituent service during his twelve years in the House, one of his brochures proclaimed, "Some people talk about change. Congressman Frank Wolf makes it happen." When area newspapers endorsed Wolf, the campaign passed out copies of the endorsements. "There's no better handout than a newspaper endorsement," explained White. Leaflets and persuasion mail cost Wolf a modest $24,464.

Campaign Expenditures	Wolf Amount Spent	Wolf % of Total	Vickery Amount Spent	Vickery % of Total
Overhead				
Office furniture/supplies	$ 3,136	.73	$ 2,095	1.10
Rent/utilities	14,885	3.46	6,565	3.44
Salaries	56,068	13.02	43,307	22.71
Taxes	30,868	7.17	19,624	10.29
Bank/investment fees	201	.05	181	.09
Lawyers/accountants	0		0	
Telephone	9,095	2.11	4,967	2.61
Campaign automobile	0		0	
Computers/office equipment	8,696	2.02	6,915	3.63
Travel	16,515	3.83	0	
Food/meetings	1,584	.37	0	
Subtotal	**141,048**	**32.75**	**83,654**	**43.88**
Fund Raising				
Events	49,186	11.42	10,461	5.49
Direct mail	20,766	4.82	4,098	2.15
Telemarketing	0		0	
Subtotal	**69,952**	**16.24**	**14,559**	**7.64**
Polling	**7,260**	**1.69**	**14,650**	**7.68**
Advertising				
Electronic media	92,431	21.46	9,969	5.23
Other media	17,666	4.10	2,196	1.15
Subtotal	**110,097**	**25.56**	**12,164**	**6.38**
Other Campaign Activity				
Persuasion mail/brochures	24,464	5.68	43,517	22.82
Actual campaigning	58,482	13.58	19,393	10.17
Staff/volunteers	0		0	
Subtotal	**82,946**	**19.26**	**62,910**	**33.00**
Constituent Gifts/Entertainment	0		0	
Donations to				
Candidates from same state	0		0	
Candidates from other states	2,350	.55	0	
Civic organizations	25	.01	0	
Ideological groups	250	.06	0	
Political parties	8,615	2.00	0	
Subtotal	**11,240**	**2.61**	**0**	
Unitemized Expenses	**8,191**	**1.90**	**2,724**	**1.43**
Total Campaign Expenses	**$ 430,734**		**$ 190,662**	
PAC Contributions	$ 180,401		$ 13,116	
Individual Contributions	257,211		150,901	
Total Receipts*	452,307		202,243	

*Includes PAC and individual contributions as well as interest earned, party contributions, etc.

District 11 — VIRGINIA

Rep. Leslie L. Byrne (D)

1992 Election Results

Leslie L. Byrne (D)	114,172	(50%)
Henry N. Butler (R)	103,119	(45%)

The open seat contest between Democratic state representative Leslie L. Byrne and George Mason University law professor Henry N. Butler turned ugly early and slid downhill from there. So vicious were the personal attacks that Gov. L. Douglas Wilder chastised the two candidates at a post-election news conference.

Although Butler outspent Byrne by $73,540, Byrne invested a significantly larger share of her resources in television advertising and outspent Butler in this pivotal category by $147,583. "We knew the real game was television," recalled Earl Bender, Byrne's chief campaign strategist and president of Avenel Associates of Washington, D.C. "Our entire gamble was to stay on three or four points and not get blown off message. We let TV drive that message."

Byrne's message was that Butler was an economic ideologue whose relationship with the right-wing Christian Coalition placed him outside the mainstream of the northern Virginia electorate. During the early stages of the campaign, Byrne ran positive spots, including one focusing on her efforts to reduce taxes. However, during the campaign's final week, when polls showed the race even, Byrne unleashed a barrage of negative advertising. One spot attacked Butler for failing to properly register his one-man consulting business and claimed that he had been expelled from college for attempted insurance fraud, wanted to eradicate federal deposit insurance on savings accounts, and supported televangelist Pat Robertson's radical antiabortion agenda.

As with many ads, the facts took a beating. Butler favored abortion rights during the first trimester of pregnancy and had been suspended, not expelled, for falsely reporting his stereo stolen. He had, in fact, failed to pay the state fee for registering his consulting firm—$50. Struble-Totten Communications of Washington, D.C., received $67,907 for creating Byrne's broadcast advertising. Pro Media of Needham, Mass., collected $369,821 for placing the spots.

Butler opted not to take the high road, either. While his campaign opened with a spot touting him as a "dynamic new leader," he quickly turned to slamming Byrne. A spoof on television phone-order record offers suggested that viewers "send no money" because taxpayers had already paid for "Leslie Byrne's 34 Big Tax Hits," which included "Leslie's 64 Percent Pay Raise." Stretching to bolster the number of Byrne's pro-tax votes, Butler had included ten votes to allow local governments to consider new taxes. When challenged on the number of tax votes, Butler pulled the spot and replaced it with a version that did not include a specific number. Rather than maximizing his investment in broadcast advertising, Butler chose to spend $120,476 on leaflets and persuasion mail.

	Byrne		Butler	
Campaign Expenditures	Amount Spent	% of Total	Amount Spent	% of Total
Overhead				
Office furniture/supplies	$ 4,199	.52	$ 12,422	1.40
Rent/utilities	9,000	1.11	15,224	1.72
Salaries	72,366	8.91	77,104	8.71
Taxes	0		26,658	3.01
Bank/investment fees	1,891	.23	64	.01
Lawyers/accountants	0		0	
Telephone	8,655	1.07	9,488	1.07
Campaign automobile	0		0	
Computers/office equipment	2,874	.35	20,749	2.34
Travel	4,923	.61	16,357	1.85
Food/meetings	385	.05	740	.08
Subtotal	104,293	12.84	178,806	20.19
Fund Raising				
Events	37,307	4.59	57,600	6.50
Direct mail	48,610	5.99	34,641	3.91
Telemarketing	0		10,614	1.20
Subtotal	85,917	10.58	102,854	11.61
Polling	29,900	3.68	21,810	2.46
Advertising				
Electronic media	443,601	54.62	296,018	33.42
Other media	659	.08	890	.10
Subtotal	444,260	54.71	296,908	33.53
Other Campaign Activity				
Persuasion mail/brochures	48,322	5.95	120,476	13.60
Actual campaigning	69,884	8.61	141,578	15.99
Staff/volunteers	0		181	.02
Subtotal	118,206	14.56	262,236	29.61
Constituent Gifts/ Entertainment	15		0	
Donations to				
Candidates from same state	0		0	
Candidates from other states	0		0	
Civic organizations	0		525	.06
Ideological groups	100	.01	0	
Political parties	0		24	
Subtotal	100	.01	549	.06
Unitemized Expenses	29,399	3.62	22,468	2.54
Total Campaign Expenses	$ 812,090		$ 885,630	
PAC Contributions	$ 309,330		$ 279,327	
Individual Contributions	417,864		516,781	
Total Receipts*	793,566		861,761	

*Includes PAC and individual contributions as well as interest earned, party contributions, etc.

WASHINGTON District 1

Rep. Maria Cantwell (D)

1992 Election Results

Maria Cantwell (D)	148,844	(55%)
Gary Nelson (R)	113,897	(42%)

By the time Republican Rep. John Miller announced he would not seek a fifth term, Democratic state representative Maria Cantwell had already laid the groundwork for her campaign. After six years in the state legislature, Cantwell could hardly be considered a political outsider, but in the "Year of the Woman" she was able to position herself as a voice for change. "Even though Maria was a traditional politician, it was easier to make the case that she was an agent of change," explained Donald McDonough, Cantwell's general campaign strategist. "Women candidates symbolized change."

Cantwell delivered her message primarily through seven television commercials created by Campaign Media Associates of Washington, D.C., which collected $59,982 for its efforts. "We spent nothing on radio and we didn't do much mail," McDonough noted. "We put our money in television ads that focused on change, and the need for deficit reduction." However, McDonough quickly added that running on an anthem of change did not mean ignoring her legislative record. "Maria had five productive years in the state legislature, and we used her experience to show how it would help her get things done in Congress."

With no other Democrat contesting the September 15 all-party primary, in which all candidates are listed on a single ballot without their party designations, Cantwell was assured of the Democratic slot on the general election ballot. She spent just $78,196 to place preprimary introductory television spots. However, once the abbreviated general election campaign began, she overwhelmed her Republican challenger, state senator Gary Nelson, with a $190,216 television blitz. "He didn't have the money to get his message out until very late in the campaign," recalled McDonough. "When he did go on the air his buy was too small to have much of an impact."

Cantwell paid pollsters Bannon Research of Boston, Mass., $22,790 to keep her apprised of any slippage in her support. The Research Group of Chicago, Ill., collected $12,040 for providing opposition research. Evans/McDonough Co. of Seattle received $65,964 from Cantwell and $5,000 from the Democratic Congressional Campaign Committee for providing strategic advice, creating the limited persuasion mailers, conducting last-minute tracking polls, supplying buttons and bumper stickers, and printing fund-raising invitations. Cantwell paid the Katz Communications Group of Seattle $2,508 for work on the persuasion mail effort.

For helping Cantwell raise $287,103 from political action committees, Campbell, Falk & Selby of Washington, D.C., received $18,564. Tradec of Seattle received $15,451 for organizing in-state events, which yielded $113,717 in contributions of $200 or more.

Campaign Expenditures	Cantwell Amount Spent	Cantwell % of Total	Nelson Amount Spent	Nelson % of Total
Overhead				
Office furniture/supplies	$ 4,558	.67	$ 1,710	.65
Rent/utilities	8,919	1.31	5,600	2.13
Salaries	74,842	11.02	35,874	13.67
Taxes	273	.04	2,767	1.05
Bank/investment fees	513	.08	0	
Lawyers/accountants	0		394	.15
Telephone	14,863	2.19	1,192	.45
Campaign automobile	0		0	
Computers/office equipment	3,915	.58	726	.28
Travel	13,158	1.94	7,723	2.94
Food/meetings	463	.07	0	
Subtotal	**121,503**	**17.88**	**55,987**	**21.34**
Fund Raising				
Events	76,623	11.28	10,237	3.90
Direct mail	9,575	1.41	7,711	2.94
Telemarketing	0		668	.25
Subtotal	**86,198**	**12.69**	**18,616**	**7.09**
Polling	**31,241**	**4.60**	**4,150**	**1.58**
Advertising				
Electronic media	333,741	49.12	79,178	30.17
Other media	500	.07	1,087	.41
Subtotal	**334,241**	**49.20**	**80,265**	**30.59**
Other Campaign Activity				
Persuasion mail/brochures	56,347	8.29	88,235	33.63
Actual campaigning	43,321	6.38	7,858	2.99
Staff/volunteers	737	.11	0	
Subtotal	**100,404**	**14.78**	**96,093**	**36.62**
Constituent Gifts/Entertainment	**964**	**.14**	**0**	
Donations to				
Candidates from same state	0		0	
Candidates from other states	0		0	
Civic organizations	0		0	
Ideological groups	0		0	
Political parties	0		280	.11
Subtotal	**0**		**280**	**.11**
Unitemized Expenses	**4,848**	**.71**	**7,013**	**2.67**
Total Campaign Expenses	**$ 679,400**		**$ 262,404**	
PAC Contributions	$ 287,103		$ 56,727	
Individual Contributions	325,151		74,391	
Total Receipts*	625,170		138,864	

*Includes PAC and individual contributions as well as interest earned, party contributions, etc.

District 2 — WASHINGTON

Rep. Al Swift (D)

1992 Election Results

Al Swift (D)	133,207	(52%)
Jack Metcalf (R)	107,365	(42%)

After thirteen years in the House, Rep. Al Swift felt it was time to move on—almost. In October 1991 Swift announced that the 1992 campaign would be his last. It was a campaign he had no intention of losing. Having spent $464,452 to win a seventh term in 1990, Swift spent $1,060,644 in 1992—nearly five times the budget of his opponent, Republican state senator Jack Metcalf.

Swift spent $213,396 on his off-year efforts, including $99,513 on overhead and $63,654 on fundraising. By August 1991 Swift had begun consultations with both Fenn & King Communications of Washington, D.C., and Campaign Performance Group of San Francisco, Calif. Fenn & King collected $8,019 during 1991 to lay the groundwork for Swift's broadcast advertising campaign. Campaign Performance received $3,300 for preliminary work on persuasion mail. T. H. Research of Portland, Ore., collected $18,000 in September for a benchmark poll of the redrawn district. Over the final six months of 1991, Payne & Associates of Seattle received $17,488 for telemarketing fund raising.

Swift never let up. In 1992 he spent $847,248, including $380,358 during October alone. He paid Fenn & King $302,662 to create and place his broadcast advertising. Campaign Performance collected $91,578 for producing three persuasion mailers. Other campaign literature and persuasion mail expenses totaled $75,822. T. H. Research and Payne collected $31,715 and $24,354, respectively. Dan Junas of Seattle received $10,000 for opposition research.

The television campaign opened with an ad focusing on Swift's plans for reshaping Super Fund legislation to ensure increased funding for environmental clean-up and less for legal fees. Other ads touted his efforts to secure Washington's "fair share" of highway funding and his work to restore Amtrak service between Seattle and Vancouver. By modern standards, the attacks were mild. One criticized Metcalf for opposing universal health care, suggesting that "maybe he'd feel a little different if he wasn't a politician who got free health insurance from the state."

However, one of Swift's persuasion mailers was not nearly so tame. The cover featured a photo of a young boy staring at a scantily dressed mannequin. Framed in an orange strip underneath the picture was the word "Unprotected." Inside, the piece charged Metcalf with refusing "to punish perverts who try to sexually exploit children."

Metcalf put 64 percent of his money into overhead and fund raising. "We had no ability to respond—no television at all and very little radio," Metcalf lamented. "In this business, you have to respond or you are dead meat."

	Swift		Metcalf	
Campaign Expenditures	Amount Spent	% of Total	Amount Spent	% of Total
Overhead				
Office furniture/supplies	$ 13,290	1.25	$ 2,720	1.35
Rent/utilities	14,957	1.41	1,700	.85
Salaries	129,867	12.24	43,121	21.47
Taxes	48,146	4.54	0	
Bank/investment fees	46		114	.06
Lawyers/accountants	10,270	.97	500	.25
Telephone	29,566	2.79	4,418	2.20
Campaign automobile	0		0	
Computers/office equipment	11,533	1.09	924	.46
Travel	53,700	5.06	10,099	5.03
Food/meetings	5,916	.56	0	
Subtotal	**317,293**	**29.92**	**63,595**	**31.67**
Fund Raising				
Events	70,056	6.61	16,135	8.04
Direct mail	9,086	.86	42,509	21.17
Telemarketing	41,842	3.94	7,093	3.53
Subtotal	**120,984**	**11.41**	**65,737**	**32.74**
Polling	**49,715**	**4.69**	**2,774**	**1.38**
Advertising				
Electronic media	318,022	29.98	24,164	12.03
Other media	1,503	.14	7,262	3.62
Subtotal	**319,525**	**30.13**	**31,427**	**15.65**
Other Campaign Activity				
Persuasion mail/brochures	170,700	16.09	10,859	5.41
Actual campaigning	40,330	3.80	14,166	7.05
Staff/volunteers	1,683	.16	50	.02
Subtotal	**212,712**	**20.06**	**25,075**	**12.49**
Constituent Gifts/ Entertainment	**10,139**	**.96**	**0**	
Donations to				
Candidates from same state	1,662	.16	0	
Candidates from other states	2,000	.19	0	
Civic organizations	938	.09	0	
Ideological groups	2,343	.22	0	
Political parties	7,448	.70	0	
Subtotal	**14,391**	**1.36**	**0**	
Unitemized Expenses	**15,885**	**1.50**	**12,194**	**6.07**
Total Campaign Expenses	**$ 1,060,644**		**$ 200,801**	
PAC Contributions	**$ 649,844**		**$ 7,797**	
Individual Contributions	**221,897**		**163,235**	
Total Receipts*	**914,905**		**200,700**	

*Includes PAC and individual contributions as well as interest earned, party contributions, etc.

WASHINGTON — District 3

Rep. Jolene Unsoeld (D)

1992 Election Results

Jolene Unsoeld (D)	138,043	(56%)
Pat Fiske (R)	108,583	(44%)

In two previous campaigns, Rep. Jolene Unsoeld had struggled mightily. In a 1988 open seat contest, she had prevailed by 627 votes, despite outspending her Republican opponent by $330,064. In 1990 she had grabbed 54 percent of the vote, while spending $1,194,227 to her Republican challenger's $835,428. With this track record, Unsoeld never stopped running.

To replenish her treasury, which contained only $5,610 on January 1, 1991, Unsoeld spent $33,021 on off-year fund raising. By year's end she had raised $104,273 from political action committees and $62,205 from individuals. After paying off 1990 debts, which are not included in this analysis, her balance sheet showed cash reserves of $74,389 at the beginning of 1992.

Unsoeld began working with her media consultant, Fenn & King Communications of Washington, D.C., in July 1991. Over the final six months of the off-year, she paid the firm $11,138 for its advice.

Redistricting had made District 3 marginally more Republican by adding territory along the Oregon border. To reach those new constituents, Unsoeld had to advertise in the pricey Portland, Ore., market. With that in mind, she ran no broadcast ads prior to the September 15 all-party primary, in which all candidates appear on a single ballot without their party identification. Chuck O'Reilly, the only other Democrat on the primary ballot, had no money to get his message out, and it was a foregone conclusion that Unsoeld would be the top Democratic vote-getter, ensuring her a place on the November ballot. Fenn & King collected another $15,568 for preparing the general election spots.

Once Unsoeld went on the air in mid-October, there was no reason to go negative. Former Republican state representative Pat Fiske hired Cottington & Marti of Minneapolis, Minn., to develop his broadcast advertising, but Fiske ran out of money in the primary and aired no commercials during the general election.

Over the final two weeks of the campaign, Unsoeld paid Fenn & King $172,559 to place her ads. Since the incumbent already had a reputation as a tough politician, Fenn & King developed one spot consisting largely of home movies of a younger Unsoeld hiking in the mountains and playing with her small children. "We decided we needed to soften her image a bit," explained Peter Fenn. The spot also bowed to the theme of "change" running through the 1992 elections. Remarking that one of her children had once challenged her to do something about her beliefs, Unsoeld proclaimed, "I've been fighting for change ever since."

Campaign Expenditures	Unsoeld Amount Spent	Unsoeld % of Total	Fiske Amount Spent	Fiske % of Total
Overhead				
Office furniture/supplies	$ 9,089	1.56	$ 2,661	1.22
Rent/utilities	5,802	1.00	5,760	2.64
Salaries	77,599	13.33	52,489	24.09
Taxes	19,467	3.34	0	
Bank/investment fees	2,168	.37	180	.08
Lawyers/accountants	1,750	.30	0	
Telephone	12,840	2.21	11,971	5.49
Campaign automobile	0		0	
Computers/office equipment	10,740	1.84	2,305	1.06
Travel	9,768	1.68	1,608	.74
Food/meetings	365	.06	145	.07
Subtotal	**149,588**	**25.69**	**77,120**	**35.39**
Fund Raising				
Events	55,905	9.60	9,981	4.58
Direct mail	32,496	5.58	5,813	2.67
Telemarketing	0		0	
Subtotal	**88,401**	**15.18**	**15,794**	**7.25**
Polling	**28,343**	**4.87**	**5,100**	**2.34**
Advertising				
Electronic media	206,498	35.47	15,554	7.14
Other media	7,517	1.29	17,951	8.24
Subtotal	**214,015**	**36.76**	**33,506**	**15.38**
Other Campaign Activity				
Persuasion mail/brochures	43,760	7.52	20,611	9.46
Actual campaigning	30,082	5.17	32,282	14.81
Staff/volunteers	463	.08	65	.03
Subtotal	**74,305**	**12.76**	**52,958**	**24.30**
Constituent Gifts/ Entertainment	**7,306**	**1.25**	**0**	
Donations to				
Candidates from same state	1,000	.17	0	
Candidates from other states	1,000	.17	0	
Civic organizations	705	.12	45	.02
Ideological groups	525	.09	0	
Political parties	10,000	1.72	50	.02
Subtotal	**13,230**	**2.27**	**95**	**.04**
Unitemized Expenses	**7,037**	**1.21**	**33,346**	**15.30**
Total Campaign Expenses	**$ 582,224**		**$ 217,919**	
PAC Contributions	**$ 365,370**		**$ 86,822**	
Individual Contributions	**283,489**		**119,124**	
Total Receipts*	**664,308**		**218,204**	

*Includes PAC and individual contributions as well as interest earned, party contributions, etc.

District 4 — WASHINGTON

Rep. Jay Inslee (D)

1992 Election Results

Jay Inslee (D)	106,556	(51%)
Richard "Doc" Hastings (R)	103,028	(49%)

State representative Jay Inslee's House campaign got off to a bumpy start. In November 1991 he announced he was considering a bid for the open seat vacated by Republican Rep. Sid Morrison, who retired after twelve years to run unsuccessfully for governor. Two months later, Inslee said he had decided not to run. In April 1992 he abruptly switched course again, deciding to fight state senator Jim Jesernig for the Democratic nomination in what was considered a safe Republican district.

Unknown and relatively underfunded, Inslee scraped together about $90,000 for the primary, $52,000 of which he borrowed. With limited resources, much of Inslee's success depended on personal, grass-roots campaigning. Inslee stood on street corners and waved to motorists. He invested $900 in precinct walk-lists, and he and an army of volunteers knocked on doors. He invested $978 in T-shirts for his volunteers. Yard signs cost $6,583.

With the help of a small staff, Inslee wrote and taped his own preprimary radio and television commercials, which portrayed him as a fiscal conservative and a social moderate. Preprimary television and radio air time cost $23,986 and $8,616, respectively. Advertising production charges totaled just $2,408. Inslee invested $17,297 to print and mail his campaign literature. Newspaper ads added $5,933. Although Jesernig spent $230,420 on his bid to win the nomination, Inslee prevailed by 1,109 votes.

While Inslee carried this do-it-yourself approach into the six-week general election campaign against former state representative Richard "Doc" Hastings, he did shift his communication strategy, relying somewhat less on shoe leather and more on advertising. During the final weeks, Inslee spent $6,942 to produce additional broadcast ads that began with Bugs Bunny's famous line, "What's up, Doc?" and proceeded to list issues on which the two candidates differed. Inslee spent $70,587 to air the spots. Newspaper advertising cost $15,329. Given his budgetary constraints and the expense of sending mass mailings, Inslee put only $8,419 into producing and mailing additional literature. He spent $2,742 on signs and $410 on T-shirts.

The Madison Group of Bellevue received $161,773 for creating and placing Hastings's ads, designing his persuasion mail, supplying direct-mail fund-raising services, running a phonebank operation, supplying buttons and bumper stickers, and providing general strategic advice. Hastings said his ads included a basic profile piece, a spot touting his support for a constitutional amendment requiring a balanced federal budget, and an ad attacking the "tax-and-spend Congress." While he outspent Inslee by $110,336, he fell 3,528 votes short.

Campaign Expenditures	Inslee Amount Spent	Inslee % of Total	Hastings Amount Spent	Hastings % of Total
Overhead				
Office furniture/supplies	$ 2,528	1.00	$ 4,822	1.32
Rent/utilities	2,100	.83	3,492	.96
Salaries	26,406	10.41	37,102	10.19
Taxes	0		0	
Bank/investment fees	133	.05	112	.03
Lawyers/accountants	838	.33	0	
Telephone	10,184	4.01	10,495	2.88
Campaign automobile	0		0	
Computers/office equipment	1,540	.61	3,574	.98
Travel	6,659	2.62	10,664	2.93
Food/meetings	795	.31	177	.05
Subtotal	**51,182**	**20.17**	**70,439**	**19.35**
Fund Raising				
Events	4,488	1.77	14,841	4.08
Direct mail	4,724	1.86	8,338	2.29
Telemarketing	0		0	
Subtotal	**9,212**	**3.63**	**23,179**	**6.37**
Polling	**0**		**15,500**	**4.26**
Advertising				
Electronic media	112,539	44.35	142,609	39.17
Other media	23,218	9.15	7,071	1.94
Subtotal	**135,757**	**53.50**	**149,681**	**41.11**
Other Campaign Activity				
Persuasion mail/brochures	25,716	10.13	45,536	12.51
Actual campaigning	30,652	12.08	55,734	15.31
Staff/volunteers	879	.35	0	
Subtotal	**57,248**	**22.56**	**101,270**	**27.82**
Constituent Gifts/Entertainment	**0**		**0**	
Donations to				
Candidates from same state	0		0	
Candidates from other states	0		0	
Civic organizations	10		13	
Ideological groups	30	.01	0	
Political parties	45	.02	50	.01
Subtotal	**85**	**.03**	**63**	**.02**
Unitemized Expenses	**255**	**.10**	**3,946**	**1.08**
Total Campaign Expenses	**$ 253,740**		**$ 364,076**	
PAC Contributions	$ 98,886		$ 129,581	
Individual Contributions	102,019		177,630	
Total Receipts*	257,153		360,445	

*Includes PAC and individual contributions as well as interest earned, party contributions, etc.

WASHINGTON — District 5

Rep. Thomas S. Foley (D)

1992 Election Results

Thomas S. Foley (D)	135,965	(55%)
John Sonneland (R)	110,443	(45%)

Rep. Thomas S. Foley and Republican John Sonneland were well acquainted. Sonneland, a Spokane surgeon who had once served as state co-chairman of Common Cause, had held Foley to 52 percent of the vote in 1980. Encouraged by his strong showing, Sonneland had tried again in 1982, but without President Ronald Reagan at the top of the ballot Sonneland was bested by Foley by a two-to-one margin. However, with anti-incumbent sentiment running sufficiently high to force a term-limit initiative onto the ballot, Sonneland decided to try his luck again in 1992.

Sonneland invested 83 percent of his $481,182 treasury in direct appeals for votes. He spent $257,040 to deliver his anti-Foley, anti-Congress message on radio and television. He paid $10,894 for newspaper ads and $5,229 for billboards emblazoned with "Fed up with Congress? Fire the Speaker" and "22 Years Is Enough"—the same slogan Foley had used in 1964 when he ousted Republican Rep. Walt Horan. While Foley had been in the House for twenty-eight years, the voters got the point. Sonneland invested $94,385 in persuasion mail and fliers.

Faced with his first tough reelection contest since 1980, Foley responded with a $397,610 television and radio advertising barrage. Press secretary Jeffrey R. Biggs said the ads were "very locally oriented" and focused on education, jobs, and health care reform. One radio spot touted Foley's decision not to run a negative campaign. Foley paid Pierce Atkins Productions of Silver Spring, Md., $65,882 for creating six television commercials and six radio spots, although only three television and four radio spots actually ran. For placing the ads, Degerness & Associates of Spokane and New Sounds Inc. of New York received $288,439 and $37,956, respectively. Miscellaneous production costs added $5,333.

Foley paid Campaign Performance Group of San Francisco, Calif., $23,175 for producing one persuasion mailer. The positive piece dovetailed with the ad campaign, ending with the claim, "Better health care and better jobs. Tom Foley brings relief to eastern Washington families." He also paid Degerness $21,737 for placing newspaper ads.

Overhead consumed 22 percent of Foley's budget, and travel was the single largest reason. In addition to the frequent trips to and from the district, Foley spent $29,206 of his campaign budget during the four-day 1992 Democratic National Convention in New York. The campaign picked up more than $25,000 in expenses at the New York Hilton for Foley and his staff.

Foley spent $7,921 on constituent stroking and donated $57,640 to various candidates, civic organizations, ideological groups, and political party organizations.

Campaign Expenditures	Foley Amount Spent	Foley % of Total	Sonneland Amount Spent	Sonneland % of Total
Overhead				
Office furniture/supplies	$ 3,488	.38	$ 2,916	.61
Rent/utilities	2,696	.30	2,875	.60
Salaries	60,480	6.63	21,546	4.48
Taxes	11,448	1.26	1,354	.28
Bank/investment fees	0		3,419	.71
Lawyers/accountants	27,469	3.01	0	
Telephone	5,006	.55	1,768	.37
Campaign automobile	0		0	
Computers/office equipment	5,543	.61	235	.05
Travel	82,659	9.06	3,644	.76
Food/meetings	769	.08	32	.01
Subtotal	**199,559**	**21.88**	**37,789**	**7.85**
Fund Raising				
Events	28,299	3.10	435	.09
Direct mail	0		1,010	.21
Telemarketing	0		0	
Subtotal	**28,299**	**3.10**	**1,445**	**.30**
Polling	**41,729**	**4.58**	**40,915**	**8.50**
Advertising				
Electronic media	397,610	43.60	257,040	53.42
Other media	23,712	2.60	16,123	3.35
Subtotal	**421,322**	**46.20**	**273,163**	**56.77**
Other Campaign Activity				
Persuasion mail/brochures	66,824	7.33	94,385	19.62
Actual campaigning	35,895	3.94	32,228	6.70
Staff/volunteers	2,052	.22	726	.15
Subtotal	**104,770**	**11.49**	**127,339**	**26.46**
Constituent Gifts/Entertainment	**7,921**	**.87**	**0**	
Donations to				
Candidates from same state	1,125	.12	0	
Candidates from other states	1,000	.11	0	
Civic organizations	1,000	.11	69	.01
Ideological groups	5,650	.62	0	
Political parties	48,865	5.36	0	
Subtotal	**57,640**	**6.32**	**69**	**.01**
Unitemized Expenses	**50,732**	**5.56**	**462**	**.10**
Total Campaign Expenses	**$ 911,972**		**$ 481,182**	
PAC Contributions	**$ 406,490**		**$ 0**	
Individual Contributions	**84,059**		**16,495**	
Total Receipts*	**561,826**		**478,555**	

*Includes PAC and individual contributions as well as interest earned, party contributions, etc.

District 6 — WASHINGTON

Rep. Norm Dicks (D)

1992 Election Results

Norm Dicks (D)	152,993	(64%)
Lauri J. Phillips (R)	66,664	(28%)
Tom Donnelly † (I)	14,490	(6%)

In 1990 Rep. Norm Dicks outspent his challenger seventy-four to one; in 1992 he increased that margin to eighty-nine to one. In the process, he spent $53,906 more on his 1992 reelection effort than he had in 1990, a 9 percent increase. This increase had nothing to do with Republican challenger Lauri J. Phillips, who spent just $6,864 on her token challenge. It had little to do with the fact that redistricting gave Dicks 170,000 new constituents spread across four large counties. While his travel costs rose by $11,677, which may reflect the increased size of his district, his investment in advertising, campaign literature, and persuasion mail declined from $288,403 in 1990 to $258,570 in 1992, a 10 percent drop.

Dicks increased his investment in overhead from $166,981 in 1990 to $230,042 in 1992, a 38 percent rise. Largely driving this increase was his $80,009 payroll, which exceeded his 1990 payroll by $24,924. That, in turn, pushed his tax payments to $32,445 from $15,900. As in past campaigns, the staff worked primarily on grass-roots activity in targeted precincts, but according to press secretary George P. Behan, the grass-roots efforts in 1992 were not concentrated in the newly acquired counties. "We gained five times the geographic area, but it's a lot of trees," noted Behan. "We concentrated our mail in those areas because it's hard to do doorbelling in such a large, diverse geographic area."

Even so, Dicks drastically reduced his outlays for persuasion mail and for the brochures dropped off by his precinct canvassers. In 1990 Dicks spent $128,369 on such material; in 1992 he cut that investment to $89,985. He spent $11,275 on posters and yard signs, $7,194 on phonebanking, $2,847 on bumper stickers and other campaign paraphernalia, and $1,067 on research. Bannon Research of Boston, Mass., collected $25,000 for polls.

Dicks's investment in broadcast advertising remained virtually constant across the two election cycles. He paid Joe Slade White & Co. of New York $36,726 for creating radio and television ads highlighting his efforts to help the district's timber industry and to generate job retraining programs to help those displaced by that industry's downsizing. Shafto & Barton of Houston, Texas, collected $101,000 for placing the spots. George Lowe Advertising, Dicks's 1990 media adviser, received $4,464 for several consulting sessions on the advertising campaign. In areas not covered by the district's major media markets, the campaign spent $20,314 on newspaper ads.

Fund raising was handled entirely in-house, with political action committee donations accounting for 59 percent of Dicks's total receipts. Individual donations of less than $200 amounted to $64,045, or 12 percent of his receipts.

	Dicks		Phillips	
Campaign Expenditures	Amount Spent	% of Total	Amount Spent	% of Total
Overhead				
Office furniture/supplies	$ 8,274	1.34	$ 499	7.28
Rent/utilities	8,316	1.35	0	
Salaries	80,009	12.97	0	
Taxes	32,445	5.26	0	
Bank/investment fees	12		0	
Lawyers/accountants	8,146	1.32	0	
Telephone	22,130	3.59	192	2.80
Campaign automobile	1,157	.19	0	
Computers/office equipment	3,811	.62	0	
Travel	57,656	9.35	252	3.67
Food/meetings	8,086	1.31	0	
Subtotal	**230,042**	**37.29**	**943**	**13.75**
Fund Raising				
Events	29,833	4.84	543	7.92
Direct mail	7,766	1.26	0	
Telemarketing	0		0	
Subtotal	**37,599**	**6.09**	**543**	**7.92**
Polling	**25,000**	**4.05**	**0**	
Advertising				
Electronic media	143,422	23.25	975	14.21
Other media	25,162	4.08	0	
Subtotal	**168,585**	**27.32**	**975**	**14.21**
Other Campaign Activity				
Persuasion mail/brochures	89,985	14.59	888	12.93
Actual campaigning	28,307	4.59	3,325	48.45
Staff/volunteers	1,205	.20	174	2.53
Subtotal	**119,497**	**19.37**	**4,387**	**63.91**
Constituent Gifts/ Entertainment	**8,275**	**1.34**	**0**	
Donations to				
Candidates from same state	4,566	.74	0	
Candidates from other states	6,000	.97	0	
Civic organizations	6,277	1.02	0	
Ideological groups	825	.13	0	
Political parties	8,080	1.31	15	.22
Subtotal	**25,749**	**4.17**	**15**	**.22**
Unitemized Expenses	**2,215**	**.36**	**0**	
Total Campaign Expenses	**$ 616,961**		**$ 6,864**	
PAC Contributions	$ 310,818		$ 0	
Individual Contributions	212,893		4,836	
Total Receipts*	546,865		6,266	

*Includes PAC and individual contributions as well as interest earned, party contributions, etc.

† No expenditures or receipts on file. Candidates raising or spending less than $5,000 are not required to file reports with the Federal Election Commission.

WASHINGTON — District 7

Rep. Jim McDermott (D)

1992 Election Results

Jim McDermott (D)	222,604	(78%)
Glenn C. Hampson (R)	54,149	(19%)

Rep. Jim McDermott spent $16,736 more during the 1992 election cycle than he had in 1990, but this increase had nothing to do with Republican Glenn C. Hampson's $14,660 challenge. McDermott gave away thirty-seven cents of every dollar he spent. The $79,580 he gave away was more than twice the amount he donated in 1990 and considerably more than twice what he spent on direct appeals for votes in 1992.

Among the prime beneficiaries of McDermott's generosity was the Democratic Congressional Campaign Committee, which received two checks totaling $10,000. One month prior to the election, McDermott also wrote a $10,000 check to the Washington Democratic Party Victory '92 Committee. In all, he donated $29,402 to various party-affiliated committees.

McDermott donated $32,000 to Democratic candidates across the country. He sent checks for $1,000 to twenty-four Democrats seeking House seats, including Eric D. Fingerhut (Ohio), Earl Pomeroy (N.D.), Eva Clayton (N.C.), Albert R. Wynn (Md.), Elaine Baxter (Iowa), Karen L. Thurman (Fla.), and Cynthia A. McKinney (Ga.). Reps. Marty Russo (Ill.), Beryl Anthony, Jr. (Ark.), and Thomas J. Downey (N.Y.) received $1,000 each for their reelection bids, as did Reps. Richard Stallings (Idaho), Les AuCoin (Ore.), and Barbara Boxer, who relinquished their seats to seek Senate seats.

Closer to home, McDermott gave $1,000 to successful Washington gubernatorial candidate Mike Lowry, and $500 each to the Democratic nominees for lieutenant governor, attorney general, insurance commissioner, and commissioner of public lands.

One of two physicians in the House, McDermott had founded a congressional task force on the international AIDS crisis and had been instrumental in pushing through legislation authorizing $156 million in housing assistance for people with AIDS. He spent $3,696 of his campaign treasury to print materials for the international AIDS conference held in June 1992. He spent $4,000 to help defray the costs of the AIDS cartoon exhibit displayed at that same conference.

Most of his other charitable and ideological contributions ranged from as little as $15 to as much as $600. He gave $350 to the Human Rights Campaign Fund, $35 to Girls Inc. of Puget Sound, $30 to the Union Gospel Mission, and $15 to the Washington Coalition to Abolish the Death Penalty.

McDermott's largest campaign expense was the $16,754 he invested in persuasion mail. He spent nothing on broadcast ads and most of his newspaper ads commemorated events such as the Chinese New Year and Martin Luther King's birthday.

In his three House campaigns, McDermott has never received less than 72 percent of the vote.

Campaign Expenditures	McDermott Amount Spent	McDermott % of Total	Hampson Amount Spent	Hampson % of Total
Overhead				
Office furniture/supplies	$ 4,899	2.26	$ 1,414	9.65
Rent/utilities	6,446	2.97	0	
Salaries	35,672	16.43	3,478	23.72
Taxes	12,198	5.62	17	.12
Bank/investment fees	70	.03	80	.55
Lawyers/accountants	0		0	
Telephone	5,560	2.56	448	3.05
Campaign automobile	0		0	
Computers/office equipment	6,474	2.98	0	
Travel	4,167	1.92	165	1.13
Food/meetings	794	.37	78	.53
Subtotal	**76,282**	**35.13**	**5,680**	**38.75**
Fund Raising				
Events	26,643	12.27	692	4.72
Direct mail	0		0	
Telemarketing	0		0	
Subtotal	**26,643**	**12.27**	**692**	**4.72**
Polling	**0**		**0**	
Advertising				
Electronic media	0		0	
Other media	2,482	1.14	0	
Subtotal	**2,482**	**1.14**	**0**	
Other Campaign Activity				
Persuasion mail/brochures	16,754	7.72	1,429	9.75
Actual campaigning	13,639	6.28	2,190	14.94
Staff/volunteers	47	.02	32	.22
Subtotal	**30,440**	**14.02**	**3,652**	**24.91**
Constituent Gifts/Entertainment	**0**		**0**	
Donations to				
Candidates from same state	4,290	1.98	0	
Candidates from other states	32,000	14.74	0	
Civic organizations	10,560	4.86	30	.20
Ideological groups	3,327	1.53	0	
Political parties	29,402	13.54	30	.20
Subtotal	**79,580**	**36.65**	**60**	**.41**
Unitemized Expenses	**1,709**	**.79**	**4,575**	**31.21**
Total Campaign Expenses	**$ 217,135**		**$ 14,660**	
PAC Contributions	$ 169,015		$ 0	
Individual Contributions	52,706		4,475	
Total Receipts*	222,346		39,520	

*Includes PAC and individual contributions as well as interest earned, party contributions, etc.

District 8 — WASHINGTON

Rep. Jennifer Dunn (R)

1992 Election Results

Jennifer Dunn (R)	155,874	(60%)
George O. Tamblyn (D)	87,611	(34%)
Bob Adams (I)	14,686	(6%)

Having led the state Republican party for eleven years, Jennifer Dunn knew how to raise money. When Republican Rep. Rod Chandler decided to leave the House to wage an unsuccessful Senate campaign, Dunn turned her fundraising prowess to her own advantage. "We raised most of our money by Jennifer Dunn personally asking for it," explained consultant John Meyers, who collected $166,400 for creating Dunn's persuasion mail and providing strategic advice.

In the all-party primary, in which all candidates are listed on a single ballot without their party designations, Dunn had to contend with state senator Pam Roach for the Republican slot on the general election ballot. Roach, an ardent abortion foe who took umbrage with Dunn's pro-choice stance and attacked her as a suburban elitist, spent $78,239 and grabbed 29 percent of the vote.

Dunn deflected the elitist charge with a television commercial that urged voters to "give Washington a good name" and laid out the things she hoped to accomplish if elected. A spot aimed at the environmental vote featured pictures of Dunn and her son in a canoe. An early proponent of the "three-strikes-and-you're-out" anti-crime legislation, Dunn's third television commercial and a companion radio spot focused on her desire to take that philosophy to Washington. Meyers said each of the spots portrayed Dunn as a reformer. The Robert Goodman Agency of Baltimore, Md., received $123,915 for creating and placing these ads and several preprimary radio spots.

Businessman George O. Tamblyn, who had switched parties to seek the Democratic nomination, began attacking Dunn in the primary with ads tying her to the conservative state Republican party platform. Dunn responded by mailing a seventeen-page booklet outlining her platform—endorsed by Housing and Urban Development Secretary Jack Kemp—to all likely Republican voters. In keeping with her outsider theme, one of her seven preprimary mailings used a baseball metaphor to note that as incumbent politicians both Tamblyn and Roach had "struck out." The brochure cited three issues on which each of her opponents had swung and missed, arguing that they were part of the problem, not part of the solution. Other mailers included an environmental piece, a piece on crime, and a letter signed by Lt. Gov. Joel Pritchard calling on Dunn to "run, Jennifer, run." Dunn received 32 percent of the primary vote.

The general election contest with Tamblyn proved significantly easier, and Dunn paid Goodman only $80,120 over the final six weeks. Tamblyn relied almost exclusively on phonebanking to get his message out. He estimated that his volunteers made 100,000 telephone calls.

Campaign Expenditures	Dunn Amount Spent	Dunn % of Total	Tamblyn Amount Spent	Tamblyn % of Total
Overhead				
Office furniture/supplies	$ 7,767	1.11	$ 11,922	2.90
Rent/utilities	17,210	2.47	6,973	1.70
Salaries	58,294	8.35	108,499	26.43
Taxes	0		17,787	4.33
Bank/investment fees	330	.05	254	.06
Lawyers/accountants	0		1,483	.36
Telephone	5,132	.74	7,272	1.77
Campaign automobile	0		0	
Computers/office equipment	10,216	1.46	13,905	3.39
Travel	10,479	1.50	12,542	3.06
Food/meetings	272	.04	791	.19
Subtotal	**109,699**	**15.72**	**181,428**	**44.20**
Fund Raising				
Events	49,878	7.15	16,467	4.01
Direct mail	26,223	3.76	7,349	1.79
Telemarketing	3,771	.54	8,087	1.97
Subtotal	**79,872**	**11.44**	**31,902**	**7.77**
Polling	**23,629**	**3.39**	**0**	
Advertising				
Electronic media	204,175	29.25	40,488	9.86
Other media	5,723	.82	39,877	9.71
Subtotal	**209,898**	**30.07**	**80,364**	**19.58**
Other Campaign Activity				
Persuasion mail/brochures	199,453	28.57	33,082	8.06
Actual campaigning	72,982	10.46	82,470	20.09
Staff/volunteers	944	.14	168	.04
Subtotal	**273,378**	**39.16**	**115,720**	**28.19**
Constituent Gifts/ Entertainment	**1,038**	**.15**	**0**	
Donations to				
Candidates from same state	0		0	
Candidates from other states	0		0	
Civic organizations	115	.02	30	.01
Ideological groups	0		95	.02
Political parties	0		60	.01
Subtotal	**115**	**.02**	**185**	**.05**
Unitemized Expenses	**415**	**.06**	**868**	**.21**
Total Campaign Expenses	**$ 698,045**		**$ 410,467**	
PAC Contributions	$ 168,373		$ 31,150	
Individual Contributions	492,444		128,297	
Total Receipts*	709,207		410,842	

*Includes PAC and individual contributions as well as interest earned, party contributions, etc.

WASHINGTON — District 9

Rep. Mike Kreidler (D)

1992 Election Results

Mike Kreidler (D)	110,902	(52%)
Pete von Reichbauer (R)	91,910	(43%)

State senators Mike Kreidler and Peter von Reichbauer disagreed on virtually everything. Kreidler, an optometrist, supported universal health care and gun control; von Reichbauer opposed both. Kreidler took a pro-choice stance on abortion; von Reichbauer campaigned against abortion in the primary and then straddled the issue in the general election by claiming that he would "oppose any effort to take away any services currently available to women in the state of Washington."

However, before Kreidler and von Reichbauer could begin slamming each other, they first had to survive Washington's all-party primary, in which candidates appear on a single ballot without benefit of party identification. That process cost Kreidler nearly $200,000, including $71,514 paid to F.D.R. Services of Seattle, his media adviser and strategic consultant. Von Reichbauer invested nearly $219,000 and mailed more than 100,000 pieces of campaign literature to fend off fellow Republican Paul Barden, a King County Council member.

Von Reichbauer won the primary with 26 percent of the vote; Kreidler finished second with 23 percent. "The key for us was surviving the primary and staying close enough to our Republican opponent to be viewed as a credible option in the general election," recalled Bob Crane, Kreidler's administrative assistant.

In the general election campaign Kreidler spent $142,861 on broadcast advertising, including one television spot that used the proverbial "bouncing ball" to attack von Reichbauer for switching his party affiliation from Democrat to Republican and for his flip-flop on the abortion issue. When von Reichbauer labeled him a carpetbagger for owning a home outside the district and renting a second home in the district to establish residency, Kreidler fired off mailers stressing the fact that he had been born in Tacoma and graduated from a high school in Curtis. Other mailers stressed his health care background, his work on the state's health care reform legislation, and his military background.

Von Reichbauer ran ads focusing on crime, his support of the death penalty, and taxes. However, he spent $138,687 less than Kreidler on broadcast ads, sticking with persuasion mail as his primary communication tool. It was a decision von Reichbauer came to regret. "I'd definitely do more TV, if I had it to do over again," he noted. "There was so much mail from other candidates competing for people's attention." The Schrock Co. of Seattle collected $173,826 from von Reichbauer and $24,245 from the National Republican Congressional Committee for handling the broadcast ads and persuasion mail.

	Kreidler		Reichbauer	
Campaign Expenditures	Amount Spent	% of Total	Amount Spent	% of Total
Overhead				
Office furniture/supplies	$ 2,486	.54	$ 9,641	2.06
Rent/utilities	10,780	2.34	9,762	2.08
Salaries	56,659	12.32	47,216	10.07
Taxes	17,066	3.71	0	
Bank/investment fees	0		8	
Lawyers/accountants	2,666	.58	65	.01
Telephone	10,941	2.38	8,551	1.82
Campaign automobile	0		0	
Computers/office equipment	2,178	.47	5,356	1.14
Travel	3,217	.70	4,119	.88
Food/meetings	0		1,282	.27
Subtotal	**105,994**	**23.05**	**85,999**	**18.35**
Fund Raising				
Events	11,053	2.40	22,544	4.81
Direct mail	15,554	3.38	13,211	2.82
Telemarketing	0		0	
Subtotal	**26,608**	**5.79**	**35,755**	**7.63**
Polling	**8,700**	**1.89**	**10,650**	**2.27**
Advertising				
Electronic media	209,375	45.54	70,688	15.08
Other media	0		2,104	.45
Subtotal	**209,375**	**45.54**	**72,792**	**15.53**
Other Campaign Activity				
Persuasion mail/brochures	63,257	13.76	245,579	52.40
Actual campaigning	29,397	6.39	14,078	3.00
Staff/volunteers	183	.04	62	.01
Subtotal	**92,838**	**20.19**	**259,719**	**55.42**
Constituent Gifts/ Entertainment	**0**		**0**	
Donations to				
Candidates from same state	0		0	
Candidates from other states	0		0	
Civic organizations	0		235	.05
Ideological groups	0		0	
Political parties	0		110	.02
Subtotal	**0**		**345**	**.07**
Unitemized Expenses	16,241	3.53	3,409	.73
Total Campaign Expenses	$ 459,755		$ 468,669	
PAC Contributions	$ 165,387		$ 138,600	
Individual Contributions	222,688		254,006	
Total Receipts*	430,480		420,106	

*Includes PAC and individual contributions as well as interest earned, party contributions, etc.

District 1 — WEST VIRGINIA

Alan B. Mollohan (D)

1992 Election Results Alan B. Mollohan (D) 172,924 (100%)

Following a bitter redistricting battle occasioned by the state's loss of one of its four House seats, Democratic Reps. Alan B. Mollohan and Harley O. Staggers, Jr., squared off in an equally acrimonious primary. It proved to be no contest.

Following a hard-fought victory in 1990, Staggers began the election cycle with campaign debts totaling $42,297 and cash reserves of only $1,647. Mollohan had cruised through the 1990 campaign and began 1991 with a campaign treasury of $136,457 and no debts. Staggers never closed the gap. On January 1, 1992 Staggers had $8,441 in the bank and debts of $36,752, while Mollohan's cash balance stood at $136,870. During the five months leading up to the May 12 primary, Mollohan committed $482,977 to the race; Staggers managed to spend $188,237.

Mollohan's $294,740 spending advantage was further magnified by the fact that he had previously represented 80 percent of the residents in the new District 1. Staggers's only hope was to drive up Mollohan's negatives, and he wasted little time.

Staggers paid Fenn & King Communications of Washington, D.C., $73,567 for creating and placing broadcast ads, including companion television and radio spots slamming Mollohan for his twelve overdrafts at the House bank and his 1989 vote in favor of a congressional pay raise. Dubbed "Rubber Man," the spots featured a country western jingle that began, "Mollohan, the Rubber Man, he's got nothin' in common with the common man. Bouncin' checks for Uncle Sam with no interest, no penalty." As the words to the song appeared on the screen, an animated check bounced from word to word. Staggers also paid Bates & Associates of Washington, D.C, $49,621 for producing persuasion mail that hammered away at the overdrafts and pay raise.

Mollohan countered by hiring Nordlinger Associates of Washington, D.C., Staggers's media consultant during the 1990 campaign. According to press secretary Ronald M. Hudok, Nordlinger produced six television commercials and two radio spots, most of which touted Mollohan's record of delivering federal projects to the district. Only during the campaign's final week did Mollohan aggressively respond to Staggers's attacks with an ad criticizing Staggers for taking the pay raise he voted against. The spot also charged that Staggers had voted to raise his own pay on five other occasions.

With his substantial cash advantage, Mollohan was able to spend $42,010 on newspaper ads and $87,022 on brochures and persuasion mail. He won 62 percent of the primary vote. Local Republicans did not bother to field a candidate to challenge him in the general election.

Campaign Expenditures	Mollohan Amount Spent	% of Total
Overhead		
Office furniture/supplies	$ 3,316	.50
Rent/utilities	600	.09
Salaries	33,274	5.03
Taxes	1,987	.30
Bank/investment fees	499	.08
Lawyers/accountants	0	
Telephone	9,795	1.48
Campaign automobile	0	
Computers/office equipment	36,633	5.53
Travel	14,763	2.23
Food/meetings	6,364	.96
Subtotal	**107,230**	**16.20**
Fund Raising		
Events	50,928	7.69
Direct mail	3,987	.60
Telemarketing	0	
Subtotal	**54,915**	**8.30**
Polling	**35,000**	**5.29**
Advertising		
Electronic media	189,771	28.67
Other media	50,544	7.64
Subtotal	**240,314**	**36.31**
Other Campaign Activity		
Persuasion mail/brochures	87,022	13.15
Actual campaigning	33,335	5.04
Staff/volunteers	3,244	.49
Subtotal	**123,601**	**18.67**
Constituent Gifts/Entertainment	**7,540**	**1.14**
Donations to		
Candidates from same state	800	.12
Candidates from other states	2,000	.30
Civic organizations	9,577	1.45
Ideological groups	400	.06
Political parties	7,965	1.20
Subtotal	**20,742**	**3.13**
Unitemized Expenses	**72,566**	**10.96**
Total Campaign Expenses	**$ 661,908**	
PAC Contributions	$ 242,669	
Individual Contributions	201,681	
Total Receipts*	494,159	

*Includes PAC and individual contributions as well as interest earned, party contributions, etc.

WEST VIRGINIA — District 2

Rep. Bob Wise (D)

1992 Election Results

Bob Wise (D)	143,988	(71%)
Samuel A. Cravotta (R)	59,102	(29%)

Rep. Bob Wise spent much of 1991 preparing for the worst. Following reapportionment, West Virginia lost one of its four House seats, which guaranteed that two of the state's four Democratic incumbents would face each other in the May 12 primary. After thinking that he had an agreement worked out with Reps. Harley O. Staggers, Jr., and Alan B. Mollohan that left him free of such an intraparty war, Wise learned that Staggers had other ideas.

Staggers's plan, which was approved by the state house and came within one vote of passage in the state senate, pitted Wise against Mollohan. While Wise continued to work to ensure that match-up would not take place, he could not afford to assume he would succeed.

Wise had invested nothing in broadcast advertising in 1990, but as soon as Staggers backed out of the original deal in March 1991, Wise paid Nordlinger Associates of Washington, D.C., $3,800 for initial consultations on his media strategy. The Research Group of Chicago, Ill., was hired in May to provide opposition research and over the remainder of 1991 collected $12,873 for its efforts.

In October 1991 the final redistricting plan was unveiled. It divided Staggers's old constituents among Wise, Mollohan, and Rep. Nick J. Rahall II. While most observers expected Staggers to run against Mollohan, Wise worried that Staggers might take him on, since he had been ceded most of Staggers's former constituents. With eight new counties to worry about, Wise immediately hired pollsters Greenberg-Lake of Washington, D.C., and paid them $26,100 over the final three months of 1991 to keep tabs on his constituents. In all, Wise spent $94,500 during the off-year, nearly twice what he spent during the entire 1990 election cycle.

Staggers opted to square off against Mollohan, but Wise still had the problem of introducing himself to more than 100,000 new constituents. He paid Nordlinger $10,000 in January. In February he opened his $400-a-month campaign headquarters. By November Wise had five part-time employees who collected after-tax salaries and benefits totaling $49,639. Greenberg-Lake received $19,101 for polling, and Michael Plante of Charleston collected $7,000 for opposition research. He paid SAID Inc. of Falls Church, Va., $19,556 for supplying electoral histories of the newly acquired counties.

Once he realized that his Republican opposition would be weak, Wise scaled back his advertising plans, spending $29,539 to air two introductory television commercials and several radio spots in the newly acquired counties.

Campaign Expenditures	Wise Amount Spent	Wise % of Total	Cravotta Amount Spent	Cravotta % of Total
Overhead				
Office furniture/supplies	$ 2,092	.64	$ 693	1.85
Rent/utilities	4,800	1.46	0	
Salaries	49,639	15.14	970	2.59
Taxes	25,693	7.84	252	.67
Bank/investment fees	68	.02	0	
Lawyers/accountants	330	.10	3,850	10.30
Telephone	6,158	1.88	1,712	4.58
Campaign automobile	0		0	
Computers/office equipment	4,959	1.51	1,566	4.19
Travel	24,688	7.53	1,681	4.50
Food/meetings	897	.27	0	
Subtotal	**119,325**	**36.39**	**10,723**	**28.69**
Fund Raising				
Events	28,971	8.84	0	
Direct mail	0		0	
Telemarketing	0		0	
Subtotal	**28,971**	**8.84**	**0**	
Polling	**45,201**	**13.79**	**0**	
Advertising				
Electronic media	44,339	13.52	11,017	29.47
Other media	250	.08	8,536	22.83
Subtotal	**44,588**	**13.60**	**19,552**	**52.30**
Other Campaign Activity				
Persuasion mail/brochures	5,382	1.64	4,294	11.49
Actual campaigning	51,568	15.73	1,132	3.03
Staff/volunteers	0		0	
Subtotal	**56,950**	**17.37**	**5,427**	**14.52**
Constituent Gifts/Entertainment	**210**	**.06**	**0**	
Donations to				
Candidates from same state	0		0	
Candidates from other states	1,000	.30	0	
Civic organizations	250	.08	0	
Ideological groups	0		0	
Political parties	14,330	4.37	0	
Subtotal	**15,580**	**4.75**	**0**	
Unitemized Expenses	**17,054**	**5.20**	**1,680**	**4.49**
Total Campaign Expenses	**$ 327,879**		**$ 37,382**	
PAC Contributions	**$ 170,755**		**$ 0**	
Individual Contributions	**105,018**		**3,212**	
Total Receipts*	**295,894**		**38,938**	

*Includes PAC and individual contributions as well as interest earned, party contributions, etc.

District 3 — WEST VIRGINIA

Rep. Nick J. Rahall II (D)

1992 Election Results

Nick J. Rahall II (D)	122,279	(66%)
Ben Waldman (R)	64,012	(34%)

Rep. Nick J. Rahall II appeared vulnerable heading into the 1992 campaign. In 1990 former representative Ken Hechler had pounded Rahall over past allegations of gambling and drinking and had held Rahall to 57 percent of the vote in the Democratic primary. In the state's most Democratic district, Rahall had then managed to grab just 52 percent of the vote against Republican Marianne R. Brewster in the general election.

Rahall's 1992 Republican challenger, Ben Waldman, was a former White House aide to Presidents Ronald Reagan and George Bush and appeared to have the fund-raising connections necessary to make the race interesting. However, redistricting strengthened Rahall's position and, in a year supposedly marked by widespread anti-incumbent sentiment, neither his past nor the strong anti-incumbent campaign waged by Waldman could turn the electorate against him.

Rahall invested 51 percent of his campaign treasury in broadcast advertising that focused heavily on his efforts to bring federal jobs to the district. He paid Politics Inc. and National Productions, both of Washington, D.C., $5,000 and $9,275, respectively, for providing creative input to the ad campaign. To save money, the campaign directly placed its radio and television spots, putting $141,578 into air time. Miscellaneous production charges added $400.

To keep his name before the voters, Rahall invested in the political tried-and-true. He spent $2,095 on yard signs and $698 on buttons. One unique gimmick was his health history booklet, in which constituents could record visits to the doctor, prescription drugs they had taken, and other medical information. On the cover, under Rahall's name, was the phrase, "Working hard for you." Personal Choices of Pineville, W.Va., supplied the booklets for $2,120.

Rahall's campaign operation in the off-year was low-key, to say the least. His only part-time employee during 1991, congressional aide Margo Mansour, collected $46 each month. Monthly rent on his only campaign office—opened in Washington, D.C., in May 1991—was $172. This modest off-year effort and a similarly sedate effort in 1992 allowed Rahall to hold his investment in overhead to $39,695, or 13 percent of his total outlays.

Fund raising consumed 16 percent of Rahall's budget. He held an annual golf tournament in the district and an annual reception in Washington, D.C., to tap into political action committee (PAC) money. PACs and out-of-state donors accounted for 85 percent of his contributions.

Waldman sank 70 percent of his $157,437 budget into overhead and fund raising. Only $17,666 of his treasury found its way into broadcast advertising.

	Rahall		Waldman	
Campaign Expenditures	Amount Spent	% of Total	Amount Spent	% of Total
Overhead				
Office furniture/supplies	$ 3,230	1.05	$ 8,516	5.41
Rent/utilities	3,439	1.12	2,953	1.88
Salaries	1,713	.56	15,950	10.13
Taxes	9,577	3.11	0	
Bank/investment fees	70	.02	34	.02
Lawyers/accountants	782	.25	0	
Telephone	0		3,892	2.47
Campaign automobile	0		0	
Computers/office equipment	652	.21	4,380	2.78
Travel	17,144	5.57	32,781	20.82
Food/meetings	3,089	1.00	368	.23
Subtotal	**39,695**	**12.90**	**68,874**	**43.75**
Fund Raising				
Events	49,648	16.13	21,719	13.80
Direct mail	0		14,094	8.95
Telemarketing	0		5,640	3.58
Subtotal	**49,648**	**16.13**	**41,454**	**26.33**
Polling	**2,500**	**.81**	**854**	**.54**
Advertising				
Electronic media	156,253	50.78	17,666	11.22
Other media	5,792	1.88	2,538	1.61
Subtotal	**162,044**	**52.66**	**20,204**	**12.83**
Other Campaign Activity				
Persuasion mail/brochures	0		10,533	6.69
Actual campaigning	6,974	2.27	13,496	8.57
Staff/volunteers	0		0	
Subtotal	**6,974**	**2.27**	**24,029**	**15.26**
Constituent Gifts/ Entertainment	**42**	**.01**	**0**	
Donations to				
Candidates from same state	8,000	2.60	0	
Candidates from other states	6,100	1.98	0	
Civic organizations	524	.17	0	
Ideological groups	482	.16	0	
Political parties	17,425	5.66	500	.32
Subtotal	**32,531**	**10.57**	**500**	**.32**
Unitemized Expenses	**14,284**	**4.64**	**1,522**	**.97**
Total Campaign Expenses	**$ 307,718**		**$ 157,437**	
PAC Contributions	$ 247,758		$ 18,849	
Individual Contributions	126,378		129,776	
Total Receipts*	444,624		151,594	

*Includes PAC and individual contributions as well as interest earned, party contributions, etc.

WISCONSIN District 1

Rep. Les Aspin (D)

1992 Election Results

Les Aspin (D)	147,495	(58%)
Mark Neumann (R)	104,352	(41%)

Unopposed in 1990, Rep. Les Aspin still spent $796,508—a sobering fact for any would-be challenger. However, few members of Congress had stronger "insider" credentials than Aspin, and, in a year marked by high anti-incumbent sentiment, developer Mark Neumann decided to try his luck. His challenge was helped considerably by an influx of $808,452 of his own money.

Neumann poured $685,131 into direct appeals for votes. He launched his general election attacks with a poster listing "ten things you haven't seen in Wisconsin lately." The poster included pictures of the late union leader Jimmy Hoffa, pilot Amelia Earhart, Elvis Presley, the Loch Ness monster, and Aspin. "I had the silly, naive idea that if I just went out and talked to the people they would understand the need for change," Neumann said.

To that end, he spent $113,856 to produce and mail 10,000 packets containing an introductory video and a folder of his position papers. He regularly mailed newsletters to his supporters. "That was until my consultants said I was doing it all wrong, that the only way to reach people was through television ads," Neumann recalled.

Neumann's ads hammered Aspin for taking taxpayer-funded junkets, using congressional privilege to fix $1,070 in parking tickets issued in Washington, and voting for the congressional pay raise. One of Neumann's television commercials, a "Lifestyles of the Rich and Famous" parody, showed scenes of a Caribbean beach and a cardboard cutout of Aspin. "Welcome to the sunny beaches of the Caribbean, and this familiar visitor: Congressman Les Aspin," intoned the Robin Leach-style narrator. "Sure it's expensive. But Les Aspin doesn't worry, because you're paying the bill. Cha, cha, cha." The Robert Goodman Agency of Baltimore, Md., collected $82,740 for creating the commercials. Mentzer Media Service, also of Baltimore, received $426,355 for placing them.

Aspin countered by spending $611,753 on direct voter appeals—a $436,168 increase over 1990. Aspin stuck primarily with positive commercials that featured him in town-meeting settings, discussing future high-tech job growth. A constituent-service spot reminded voters of Aspin's ability to deliver federal dollars to the district. One ad responding to Neumann's charges closed with a picture of Neumann and the word "unbelievable." Aspin paid Politics Inc. of Washington, D.C., $99,359 for creating the ads. Media Strategies & Research, also of Washington, collected $332,975 for placing them.

After spending $1,342,809 to hold onto his seat, Aspin resigned in January 1993 to become secretary of defense in the Clinton administration.

Campaign Expenditures	Aspin Amount Spent	Aspin % of Total	Neumann Amount Spent	Neumann % of Total
Overhead				
Office furniture/supplies	$ 15,542	1.16	$ 8,339	.91
Rent/utilities	13,734	1.02	12,096	1.32
Salaries	152,786	11.38	117,994	12.84
Taxes	84,694	6.31	12,895	1.40
Bank/investment fees	2,808	.21	343	.04
Lawyers/accountants	14,110	1.05	0	
Telephone	27,530	2.05	16,070	1.75
Campaign automobile	0		0	
Computers/office equipment	22,447	1.67	13,720	1.49
Travel	15,978	1.19	7,290	.79
Food/meetings	4,407	.33	131	.01
Subtotal	**354,036**	**26.37**	**188,879**	**20.55**
Fund Raising				
Events	159,418	11.87	13,874	1.51
Direct mail	106,410	7.92	0	
Telemarketing	0		1,113	.12
Subtotal	**265,828**	**19.80**	**14,987**	**1.63**
Polling	**77,611**	**5.78**	**27,696**	**3.01**
Advertising				
Electronic media	447,260	33.31	519,487	56.52
Other media	526	.04	122,647	13.34
Subtotal	**447,785**	**33.35**	**642,134**	**69.86**
Other Campaign Activity				
Persuasion mail/brochures	98,047	7.30	18,725	2.04
Actual campaigning	42,726	3.18	23,314	2.54
Staff/volunteers	23,195	1.73	958	.10
Subtotal	**163,968**	**12.21**	**42,997**	**4.68**
Constituent Gifts/ Entertainment	**15,348**	**1.14**	**247**	**.03**
Donations to				
Candidates from same state	1,150	.09	0	
Candidates from other states	800	.06	0	
Civic organizations	310	.02	0	
Ideological groups	40		0	
Political parties	14,310	1.07	75	.01
Subtotal	**16,610**	**1.24**	**75**	**.01**
Unitemized Expenses	**1,622**	**.12**	**2,173**	**.24**
Total Campaign Expenses	**$ 1,342,809**		**$ 919,188**	
PAC Contributions	$ 536,425		$ 2,150	
Individual Contributions	731,894		105,553	
Total Receipts*	1,359,476		944,401	

*Includes PAC and individual contributions as well as interest earned, party contributions, etc.

District 2 — WISCONSIN

Rep. Scott L. Klug (R)

1992 Election Results

Scott L. Klug (R)	183,366	(63%)
Ada Deer (D)	108,291	(37%)

Freshman Rep. Scott L. Klug quickly embraced the monetary advantages of incumbency. In 1990 Klug had spent $184,315 in upsetting Democratic incumbent Robert W. Kastenmeier, who had put $371,914 into the race. Challenged in 1992 by a Democratic opponent who had $443,644 to spend, Klug spent $824,032.

Having argued in 1990 that Kastenmeier was an entrenched incumbent who had been in Congress too long, Klug spent $106,294 during 1991 to keep his permanent campaign operation running smoothly. By the end of 1992 Klug had spent $153,815 to raise money, or just $30,500 less than he needed to win the 1990 campaign. The $226,266 he had raised from political action committees was $41,951 more than he had spent on his 1990 effort. His overhead mushroomed from $63,739 in 1990 to $138,610 in 1992.

Klug had spent $62,584 on broadcast advertising in 1990. In 1992 he pumped $261,689 into producing and airing his commercials. His tight budget in 1990 had allowed for only $1,457 in other advertising, but in 1992 he had sufficient resources to invest $26,435 in billboards and $32,103 in newspaper advertising. John Roach Projects of Madison received $15,016 for work on the advertising campaign, although Klug wrote most of the ads himself. Kennedy Communications, also of Madison, received $289,035 for placing the broadcast, newspaper, and billboard ads.

To remind voters that he was still one of them, Klug's opening television ad showed him visiting a local butcher and playing with his children in a park. A fifteen-second spot highlighted his role in the "Gang of Seven," a group of freshman Republicans who pushed for public disclosure of those who had overdrawn their House bank accounts. Another fifteen-second commercial, paired with the first to fill a thirty-second time-slot, focused on his health care reform proposals.

Klug paid Welch Communications of Arlington, Va., $29,280 for creating persuasion mailers that targeted farmers, veterans, and undecided voters. Postage, printing, and data processing costs associated with the mailings added $39,800. He spent $10,267 to produce a door-hanger that was distributed on the campaign's final weekend. He invested $6,722 in a four-page tabloid-style piece that was distributed door-to-door. To ensure that his supporters would turn out, Klug paid $45,119 to Payco American Corp. of Brookfield, Wis., for phonebanking and $15,000 to the state party's coordinated get-out-the-vote efforts.

Democratic activist Ada Deer put 53 percent of her budget into direct voter appeals. While her slogan promised that "nobody runs like Ada Deer," her campaign never gathered momentum.

Campaign Expenditures	Klug Amount Spent	Klug % of Total	Deer Amount Spent	Deer % of Total
Overhead				
Office furniture/supplies	$ 8,188	.99	$ 19,383	4.37
Rent/utilities	6,368	.77	11,594	2.61
Salaries	58,490	7.10	34,915	7.87
Taxes	20,813	2.53	0	
Bank/investment fees	1,240	.15	986	.22
Lawyers/accountants	250	.03	900	.20
Telephone	9,648	1.17	6,893	1.55
Campaign automobile	0		0	
Computers/office equipment	8,161	.99	1,542	.35
Travel	22,979	2.79	19,456	4.39
Food/meetings	2,472	.30	397	.09
Subtotal	**138,610**	**16.82**	**96,066**	**21.65**
Fund Raising				
Events	105,115	12.76	48,699	10.98
Direct mail	48,699	5.91	51,149	11.53
Telemarketing	0		3,182	.72
Subtotal	**153,815**	**18.67**	**103,030**	**23.22**
Polling	**26,940**	**3.27**	**850**	**.19**
Advertising				
Electronic media	261,689	31.76	166,205	37.46
Other media	59,718	7.25	10,745	2.42
Subtotal	**321,406**	**39.00**	**176,951**	**39.89**
Other Campaign Activity				
Persuasion mail/brochures	86,069	10.44	21,587	4.87
Actual campaigning	85,841	10.42	37,671	8.49
Staff/volunteers	1,986	.24	304	.07
Subtotal	**173,895**	**21.10**	**59,562**	**13.43**
Constituent Gifts/Entertainment	**2,732**	**.33**	**0**	
Donations to				
Candidates from same state	0		50	.01
Candidates from other states	200	.02	100	.02
Civic organizations	290	.04	40	.01
Ideological groups	255	.03	250	.06
Political parties	40		225	.05
Subtotal	**785**	**.10**	**665**	**.15**
Unitemized Expenses	5,849	.71	6,521	1.47
Total Campaign Expenses	**$ 824,032**		**$ 443,644**	
PAC Contributions	$ 226,266		$ 0	
Individual Contributions	612,067		509,991	
Total Receipts*	879,091		525,120	

*Includes PAC and individual contributions as well as interest earned, party contributions, etc.

WISCONSIN — District 3

Rep. Steve Gunderson (R)

1992 Election Results

Steve Gunderson (R)	146,903	(56%)
Paul Sacia (D)	108,664	(42%)

As always, Rep. Steve Gunderson's campaign was a family affair. His brother Matthew joined the effort as campaign manager in April 1992 and collected $26,400. His sister, Naomi Bodway, served as the campaign's general consultant. Her firm, KaestnerBodway of Middleton collected $31,585 for advice and for supplying the campaign's yard signs, buttons, and bumper stickers.

Gunderson's annual "brat party," which featured sausage, beer, ice cream, and a local band or two, was held in his parents' back yard. Bodway said the event had no set admission price, but people were asked to contribute "something." Billed as a "thank you" for loyal contributors and volunteers, the events drew between 500 and 1,000 people each year and together cost the campaign $21,482.

Gunderson invested 32 percent of his $458,850 budget in fund raising. He spent $8,000 to fly Vice President Dan Quayle in for a reception and dinner in November 1991. That one event cost Gunderson $40,531, including $14,908 for dinner at the Radisson Hotel in LaCrosse, $4,385 to rent the LaCrosse Center, $2,886 for invitations and postage, $926 for flowers, $907 to print programs, and $895 for the Howie Sturtz Orchestra. Christopher A. Holt of Sigourney, Iowa, collected $5,864 for planning the event. The LaCrosse Area Convention and Visitors Bureau received $1,108.

Country western singer Joe Diffy, who had grown up in the district, was flown in for a Labor Day concert in 1992. Gunderson's campaign paid $25,147 to stage the event, including payments totaling $12,125 to the Beacham Agency in Nashville, Tenn.

Gunderson operated a two-tiered congressional club. For a $1,000 donation, supporters became members of the "Executive Club," which entitled them to a lapel pin; a special gift, such as a pen-and-pencil set; and invitations to the annual brat party, special receptions with national political figures, and more intimate dinners with Gunderson. Seven such dinners cost the campaign a total of $4,298. For $250, supporters received a reduced package of these same benefits.

Gunderson held four events in Washington, D.C., to attract political action committee donations. He held two cocktail receptions at the Capitol Hill Club and two Oktoberfest events at Cafe Berlin. Total cost of the four events: $13,038. He also paid Synhorst & Schraad of Russell, Kan., $9,883 for telemarketing.

With little fear of being unseated by Democrat Paul Sacia, who had just $35,438 to spend on his campaign, Gunderson invested only 21 percent of his money in direct appeals for votes. Overhead consumed 38 percent of his budget. "We haven't had a serious opponent in a long time," noted Bodway.

Campaign Expenditures	Gunderson Amount Spent	Gunderson % of Total	Sacia Amount Spent	Sacia % of Total
Overhead				
Office furniture/supplies	$ 11,174	2.44	$ 1,781	5.02
Rent/utilities	8,287	1.81	0	
Salaries	72,289	15.75	2,575	7.27
Taxes	23,504	5.12	0	
Bank/investment fees	64	.01	0	
Lawyers/accountants	3,236	.71	0	
Telephone	14,804	3.23	2,707	7.64
Campaign automobile	8,419	1.83	0	
Computers/office equipment	16,066	3.50	0	
Travel	14,379	3.13	0	
Food/meetings	1,762	.38	0	
Subtotal	**173,983**	**37.92**	**7,063**	**19.93**
Fund Raising				
Events	127,331	27.75	0	
Direct mail	9,260	2.02	0	
Telemarketing	9,914	2.16	0	
Subtotal	**146,506**	**31.93**	**0**	
Polling	**31,084**	**6.77**	**0**	
Advertising				
Electronic media	33,802	7.37	11,401	32.17
Other media	9,980	2.18	2,343	6.61
Subtotal	**43,782**	**9.54**	**13,744**	**38.78**
Other Campaign Activity				
Persuasion mail/brochures	15,142	3.30	1,674	4.72
Actual campaigning	37,118	8.09	2,605	7.35
Staff/volunteers	127	.03	0	
Subtotal	**52,388**	**11.42**	**4,280**	**12.08**
Constituent Gifts/Entertainment	**8,978**	**1.96**	**0**	
Donations to				
Candidates from same state	0		0	
Candidates from other states	1,600	.35	0	
Civic organizations	0		0	
Ideological groups	0		0	
Political parties	53	.01	0	
Subtotal	**1,653**	**.36**	**0**	
Unitemized Expenses	**476**	**.10**	**10,351**	**29.21**
Total Campaign Expenses	**$ 458,850**		**$ 35,438**	
PAC Contributions	$ 222,462		$ 7,100	
Individual Contributions	191,741		9,105	
Total Receipts*	427,112		33,559	

*Includes PAC and individual contributions as well as interest earned, party contributions, etc.

District 4 — WISCONSIN

Rep. Gerald D. Kleczka (D)

1992 Election Results

Gerald D. Kleczka (D)	173,482	(66%)
Joseph L. Cook (R)	84,872	(32%)

Rep. Gerald D. Kleczka took the House bank scandal very seriously. His problem—one 44-cent overdraft—prompted a two-page statement in which he described his "deep personal embarrassment" over a $2.40 check he had written to Bell Atlantic. The check had been submitted for payment on May 31, 1990, the day before his monthly paycheck was deposited. At the time he had only $1.96 in his account. For Kleczka, the issue died there, and he chalked up his fifth consecutive landslide victory.

While he spent substantially less than the typical incumbent, Kleczka took nothing for granted in his rematch with Republican attorney Joseph L. Cook. In June 1992 Kleczka hired pollster Cooper & Secrest Associates of Alexandria, Va., and over the next six months paid the firm $32,311. Two months later his media consultant, Shorr Associates of Philadelphia, Pa., began work on the broadcast advertising campaign, ultimately collecting $103,379 for creating and placing the ads. Miscellaneous advertising production fees amounted to $20,200.

Kleczka spent $5,791 to advertise in daily and weekly newspapers, such as the *Shopper Community News,* the *Enterprise,* and the *Waukesha Freeman.* Bates & Associates of Washington, D.C., received $29,260 for producing persuasion mailers. Postage, printing, and data processing charges associated with the mailings added $32,869. He invested $2,834 in yard signs, $2,691 in research, and $3,805 in the state Democratic party's coordinated get-out-the-vote efforts. He spent $1,016 on mugs that were given to delegates attending the state party convention. In all, Kleczka invested 63 percent of his $337,358 budget in direct appeals for votes.

Not all Kleczka's spending was devoted to the usual campaign paraphernalia. He spent $4,331 on a picnic for district residents. Constituent gifts, including calendars, commemorative plaques, and items described on his Federal Election Commission reports as "public relations items," cost $2,536. He spent $658 on year-end holiday cards, $626 on flowers, and $484 on lunches and dinners with constituents. In anticipation of Bill Clinton's inauguration, Kleczka spent $2,000 of his campaign funds to cover the deposit required by Capitol Catering for the Wisconsin inaugural reception. He tapped his campaign funds for $250 to pay for inaugural tickets. His travel charges included a $1,100 payment for membership in Northwest Airlines's system of airport World Clubs.

Cook's only radio commercials were two Polish-language spots that accused Kleczka of backing the Serbs in the Bosnian conflict. As in 1990, he was tilting at windmills.

Campaign Expenditures	Kleczka Amount Spent	Kleczka % of Total	Cook Amount Spent	Cook % of Total
Overhead				
Office furniture/supplies	$ 2,650	.79	$ 196	.47
Rent/utilities	800	.24	867	2.09
Salaries	4,600	1.36	2,778	6.69
Taxes	2,723	.81	0	
Bank/investment fees	309	.09	21	.05
Lawyers/accountants	0		0	
Telephone	885	.26	694	1.67
Campaign automobile	0		0	
Computers/office equipment	3,926	1.16	0	
Travel	6,356	1.88	2,058	4.96
Food/meetings	7,534	2.23	75	.18
Subtotal	**29,783**	**8.83**	**6,688**	**16.12**
Fund Raising				
Events	33,028	9.79	225	.54
Direct mail	0		2,311	5.57
Telemarketing	0		0	
Subtotal	**33,028**	**9.79**	**2,536**	**6.11**
Polling	**32,311**	**9.58**	**0**	
Advertising				
Electronic media	123,579	36.63	1,818	4.38
Other media	7,021	2.08	6,833	16.47
Subtotal	**130,600**	**38.71**	**8,651**	**20.85**
Other Campaign Activity				
Persuasion mail/brochures	62,129	18.42	16,917	40.77
Actual campaigning	16,585	4.92	6,611	15.93
Staff/volunteers	3,655	1.08	53	.13
Subtotal	**82,369**	**24.42**	**23,581**	**56.83**
Constituent Gifts/Entertainment	**10,885**	**3.23**	**0**	
Donations to				
Candidates from same state	3,096	.92	0	
Candidates from other states	3,000	.89	0	
Civic organizations	874	.26	0	
Ideological groups	0		0	
Political parties	9,420	2.79	35	.08
Subtotal	**16,389**	**4.86**	**35**	**.08**
Unitemized Expenses	**1,993**	**.59**	**0**	
Total Campaign Expenses	**$ 337,358**		**$ 41,491**	
PAC Contributions	$ 156,407		$ 2,000	
Individual Contributions	81,506		8,055	
Total Receipts*	260,726		67,268	

*Includes PAC and individual contributions as well as interest earned, party contributions, etc.

WISCONSIN — District 5

Rep. Thomas M. Barrett (D)

1992 Election Results

Thomas M. Barrett (D)	162,344	(69%)
Donalda Ann Hammersmith (R)	71,085	(30%)

The race to succeed Democratic Rep. Jim Moody, who resigned to wage an unsuccessful Senate campaign, was in the Democratic primary, where four candidates combined to spend $1,040,251. State senator Thomas M. Barrett spent $314,329 and emerged with 41 percent of the vote. While Milwaukee County Supervisor Terrance L. Pitts had a budget of only $84,870, he was the only black candidate in the race and received strong support from Milwaukee's black community. Pitts finished second with 23 percent. Former state representative Frederick P. Kessler spent $350,965 and finished third with 19 percent. Attorney Marc Marotta spent $290,087 in capturing 16 percent of the vote. Kessler and Marotta spent $22.41 and $21.63, respectively, for each vote received.

In this free-for-all, Marotta ran ads attacking his three opponents as career politicians while pointing to the fact that he was a first-time candidate. He sent 9,000 fliers that claimed, "In April, Tom Barrett tricked us into giving him a pay raise," and went on to charge that deceptive wording in the referendum supported by Barrett and others had led voters to approve a pay raise for state legislators. He mailed another round of fliers attacking Kessler for financing his own campaign with the help of a $96,000 state consulting contract for work on redistricting. Kessler ran television ads assailing corporations for looting their pension plans, advocating a national ban on handgun sales, and demanding stronger penalties for fathers who fail to pay child support. Pitts ran ads for only the final weekend of the campaign.

Barrett poured $167,441 into preprimary television commercials that stressed his legislative accomplishments on such issues as health care, gun control, 911 emergency service, and protective services for battered women. "We didn't spend any money on radio in the primary," recalled Barrett. "There was only one major media market, which allowed us to concentrate our resources, and we spent as much money on TV as we could."

For the primary, Barrett invested $25,736 in persuasion mail and brochures that were passed out on his frequent walks through the district. "Door knocking, that's my strong suit," Barrett noted. "I've been doing it for eleven years and I've probably knocked on 70,000 to 75,000 doors. I'm like the Energizer bunny—I just keep going and going." He also spent $3,897 on phonebanking, including $1,016 paid to Teamsters Union Local 200 in Milwaukee.

The general election contest with interior designer Donalda Ann Hammersmith was anticlimactic. Barrett spent just $72,619 between the September 8 primary and the close of the cycle.

	Barrett		Hammersmith	
Campaign Expenditures	Amount Spent	% of Total	Amount Spent	% of Total
Overhead				
Office furniture/supplies	$ 4,816	1.24	$ 2,287	2.51
Rent/utilities	3,764	.97	196	.22
Salaries	30,408	7.86	22,284	24.47
Taxes	5,520	1.43	0	
Bank/investment fees	142	.04	0	
Lawyers/accountants	0		487	.54
Telephone	3,559	.92	1,322	1.45
Campaign automobile	0		0	
Computers/office equipment	350	.09	1,355	1.49
Travel	1,480	.38	1,180	1.30
Food/meetings	0		0	
Subtotal	**50,039**	**12.93**	**29,112**	**31.96**
Fund Raising				
Events	15,777	4.08	2,660	2.92
Direct mail	30,108	7.78	7,119	7.82
Telemarketing	0		0	
Subtotal	**45,886**	**11.86**	**9,779**	**10.74**
Polling	**12,373**	**3.20**	**0**	
Advertising				
Electronic media	189,855	49.06	21,328	23.42
Other media	6,215	1.61	1,260	1.38
Subtotal	**196,070**	**50.67**	**22,588**	**24.80**
Other Campaign Activity				
Persuasion mail/brochures	49,983	12.92	11,401	12.52
Actual campaigning	24,229	6.26	7,457	8.19
Staff/volunteers	1,015	.26	0	
Subtotal	**75,227**	**19.44**	**18,858**	**20.70**
Constituent Gifts/ Entertainment	**0**		**0**	
Donations to				
Candidates from same state	250	.06	0	
Candidates from other states	0		0	
Civic organizations	0		0	
Ideological groups	0		0	
Political parties	240	.06	0	
Subtotal	**490**	**.13**	**0**	
Unitemized Expenses	**6,863**	**1.77**	**10,746**	**11.80**
Total Campaign Expenses	**$ 386,948**		**$ 91,083**	
PAC Contributions	$ 154,526		$ 2,350	
Individual Contributions	189,204		66,924	
Total Receipts*	356,052		100,092	

*Includes PAC and individual contributions as well as interest earned, party contributions, etc.

District 6 — WISCONSIN

Rep. Tom Petri (R)

1992 Election Results

Tom Petri (R)	143,875	(53%)
Peggy A. Lautenschlager (D)	128,232	(47%)

Elected in 1979 to fill the vacancy created by the death of Republican Rep. William A. Steiger, Rep. Tom Petri had what looked like a perfectly safe seat. After winning 59 percent of the vote in 1980, Petri had coasted to five victories in which he received at least 65 percent of the vote. In 1986 and 1990 no Democrat had bothered to challenge him. However, that was before the ethics committee revealed his seventy-seven overdrafts at the House bank—the most by any member of the Wisconsin delegation.

Petri's overdrafts and the sense that voters were ready for a change drew state senator Peggy A. Lautenschlager into the race. A poll conducted for Lautenschlager in June by Garin-Hart of Washington, D.C., showed her trailing Petri by only 4 points, 41 to 45 percent. More importantly, 51 percent of the voters surveyed by Garin-Hart said they thought it was time to elect someone new.

Lautenschlager focused on the economy for most of the campaign. She criticized Petri for supporting budget-busting economic policies that favored the wealthy and slammed him for being a Washington insider who had lost touch with his constituents. Surprisingly, she did not attack Petri for his overdrafts until the final weeks of the campaign, when she aired an ad showing a jail door slamming shut on Petri. By then it was too late. Axelrod & Associates of Chicago, Ill., collected $165,716 from Lautenschlager and $15,000 from the Democratic Congressional Campaign Committee for creating and placing nearly a dozen television commercials and six radio spots. Additional air time cost the campaign $17,533.

Petri spent $644,507 more on his 1992 effort than he had in 1990. He paid Cottington & Marti of Edina, Minn., $333,497 for creating and placing his broadcast ads, designing his persuasion mailers, and providing strategic advice. Tarrance & Associates of Alexandria, Va., received $40,264 for polling. Petri invested $18,289 in newspaper ads and tabloid-style inserts that touted his legislative initiatives and blasted Lautenschlager's record. Billboards added $16,326.

Cottington & Marti produced ten television commercials and a similar number of radio spots, including four ads that focused on his legislative successes. One negative ad criticized Lautenschlager's previous tenure as district attorney, saying she had plea-bargained too many cases and was absent much of the time. "We took great pains to point out that she was a professional politician with a record, not some fresh face that was going to bring change," recalled Joseph F. Flader, Petri's administrative assistant.

Campaign Expenditures	Petri Amount Spent	Petri % of Total	Lautenschlager Amount Spent	Lautenschlager % of Total
Overhead				
Office furniture/supplies	$ 8,136	1.05	$ 1,082	.34
Rent/utilities	13,442	1.73	1,871	.59
Salaries	80,560	10.39	21,048	6.65
Taxes	7,660	.99	5,780	1.83
Bank/investment fees	0		0	
Lawyers/accountants	0		0	
Telephone	7,650	.99	6,160	1.95
Campaign automobile	0		0	
Computers/office equipment	16,300	2.10	1,555	.49
Travel	18,569	2.39	4,785	1.51
Food/meetings	0		0	
Subtotal	**152,318**	**19.64**	**42,280**	**13.36**
Fund Raising				
Events	27,018	3.48	21,126	6.68
Direct mail	39,220	5.06	5,693	1.80
Telemarketing	0		3,794	1.20
Subtotal	**66,238**	**8.54**	**30,612**	**9.68**
Polling	**40,264**	**5.19**	**17,800**	**5.63**
Advertising				
Electronic media	325,069	41.91	183,249	57.92
Other media	34,815	4.49	576	.18
Subtotal	**359,884**	**46.40**	**183,825**	**58.11**
Other Campaign Activity				
Persuasion mail/brochures	92,732	11.96	18,999	6.01
Actual campaigning	36,315	4.68	13,911	4.40
Staff/volunteers	3,940	.51	66	.02
Subtotal	**132,986**	**17.15**	**32,976**	**10.42**
Constituent Gifts/Entertainment	**6,748**	**.87**	**0**	
Donations to				
Candidates from same state	0		0	
Candidates from other states	0		0	
Civic organizations	0		0	
Ideological groups	0		30	.01
Political parties	0		0	
Subtotal	**0**		**30**	**.01**
Unitemized Expenses	**17,160**	**2.21**	**8,843**	**2.80**
Total Campaign Expenses	**$ 775,598**		**$ 316,366**	
PAC Contributions	**$ 204,000**		**$ 114,711**	
Individual Contributions	174,327		147,392	
Total Receipts*	433,702		333,541	

*Includes PAC and individual contributions as well as interest earned, party contributions, etc.

WISCONSIN District 7

Rep. David R. Obey (D)

1992 Election Results

David R. Obey (D)	166,200	(64%)
Dale R. Vannes (R)	91,772	(36%)

Rep. David R. Obey had never received less than 61 percent of the vote in eleven previous reelection bids. His 1992 Republican challenger, insurance agent Dale R. Vannes, had no money to advertise and spent just $20,329. Obey countered with a $524,086 campaign and took 64 percent of the vote.

Obey spent $147,376 to maintain his permanent campaign operation during the off-year, including $52,694 on overhead and $40,912 on fund raising. He paid pollster Lauer, Lalley & Associates of Washington, D.C., $10,500. During 1991 he paid his Washington-based media consultant, Greer, Margolis, Mitchell & Associates, $17,933 for creating and placing radio commercials, $2,708 for placing newspaper ads, and $3,406 for supplying fund-raising invitations. His off-year investment alone was more than seven times as much as Vannes spent on his entire campaign.

Unopposed in the Democratic primary and facing token opposition in the general election, Obey sank $376,710 into his campaign during 1992. Lauer, Lalley received $35,746 for conducting additional polls. Greer, Margolis collected $150,798 for creating and placing broadcast ads and $772 for placing newspaper ads. Bates & Associates of Washington, D.C., received $24,413 for producing persuasion mailers. The state Democratic party received $15,341 for his share of the coordinated get-out-the-vote effort.

To cover the cost of travel by Obey's wife and other family members, Obey's campaign paid United Airlines $10,239 over the two-year cycle—$6,721 of which was spent during the off-year. Obey's family members accounted for 40 percent of his campaign travel expenses. Another $1,332 of his travel budget was spent during the four-day 1992 Democratic National Convention in New York.

Obey gave $10,000 to the Democratic Congressional Campaign Committee, including a $5,000 donation in 1991 for "candidate's share of debt reduction." During the final two weeks of the campaign, Obey tapped his campaign fund to help forty-three fellow Democrats seeking House seats. He sent Tony Center (Ga.) $1,000 for his challenge to Minority Whip Newt Gingrich. Reps. Les Aspin (Wis.) and Sam Gejdenson (Conn.) each received $500 checks, as did open seat candidate James A. Barcia (Mich.). Thirty-nine candidates collected $250 checks, including Reps. Dave Nagle (Iowa), Pat Williams (Mont.), and Thomas H. Andrews (Maine).

Political action committees (PACs) and out-of-state donors who gave $200 or more accounted for 75 percent of the money he raised. To help tap the Washington, D.C., PAC community, he paid Conroy & Co. of Washington and Mary Scheckelhoff of Arlington, Va., $6,582 and $5,896, respectively.

	Obey		Vannes	
Campaign Expenditures	Amount Spent	% of Total	Amount Spent	% of Total
Overhead				
Office furniture/supplies	$ 3,749	.72	$ 168	.83
Rent/utilities	1,050	.20	750	3.69
Salaries	50,655	9.67	360	1.77
Taxes	19,103	3.65	0	
Bank/investment fees	0		0	
Lawyers/accountants	0		0	
Telephone	7,892	1.51	3,020	14.86
Campaign automobile	2,950	.56	0	
Computers/office equipment	2,587	.49	0	
Travel	25,569	4.88	1,424	7.01
Food/meetings	302	.06	0	
Subtotal	**113,858**	**21.73**	**5,723**	**28.15**
Fund Raising				
Events	69,717	13.30	773	3.80
Direct mail	0		0	
Telemarketing	0		0	
Subtotal	**69,717**	**13.30**	**773**	**3.80**
Polling	**46,246**	**8.82**	**0**	
Advertising				
Electronic media	174,864	33.37	0	
Other media	4,167	.80	0	
Subtotal	**179,030**	**34.16**	**0**	
Other Campaign Activity				
Persuasion mail/brochures	44,612	8.51	3,132	15.40
Actual campaigning	19,849	3.79	5,900	29.02
Staff/volunteers	1,398	.27	115	.57
Subtotal	**65,859**	**12.57**	**9,147**	**44.99**
Constituent Gifts/ Entertainment	**7,536**	**1.44**	**0**	
Donations to				
Candidates from same state	1,500	.29	0	
Candidates from other states	13,500	2.58	0	
Civic organizations	555	.11	0	
Ideological groups	100	.02	0	
Political parties	10,175	1.94	0	
Subtotal	**25,830**	**4.93**	**0**	
Unitemized Expenses	**16,009**	**3.05**	**4,687**	**23.05**
Total Campaign Expenses	**$ 524,086**		**$ 20,329**	
PAC Contributions	$ 267,575		$ 0	
Individual Contributions	181,809		14,273	
Total Receipts*	497,123		20,879	

*Includes PAC and individual contributions as well as interest earned, party contributions, etc.

District 8 — WISCONSIN

Rep. Toby Roth (R)

1992 Election Results

Toby Roth (R)	191,704	(70%)
Catherine L. Helms (D)	81,792	(30%)

Although seeking his eighth term, Republican Rep. Toby Roth was virtually immune to the standard anti-incumbent attacks. He had no overdrafts at the House bank. He had voted against the congressional pay raise, against the 1990 budget compromise that included several tax increases, and for a constitutional amendment requiring a balanced federal budget.

Despite the fact that a well-funded challenger had held Roth to 54 percent of the vote in 1990, no seasoned Democrat stepped forward in 1992. In fact, the only Democrat to take up the challenge was real estate broker Catherine L. Helms, whose only political experience was chairing the Green Bay mayor's Citizen Advisory Committee on Cable TV in 1976. It was no contest.

Helms sank 70 percent of her $61,422 campaign treasury into overhead, leaving her virtually no money to get her message out. After spending $1,871 to produce several television commercials, she had only $3,668 to invest in air time. Her investment in campaign literature amounted to only $1,145.

Roth began the election cycle with $93,841 and, with a $126,650 assist from political action committees (PACs), built his cash reserves to $285,797 by the end of 1991. Over the two-year cycle, Roth's in-house fund-raising operation spent $57,147 to raise $558,008 from PACs and individual contributors, a return of $9.76 for each dollar invested. PACs accounted for $292,200, or 52 percent, of these receipts. His $35,381 investment in direct-mail solicitations helped push his small donations to $156,673, or 28 percent of his nonparty contributions.

Roth invested 45 percent of his $421,159 budget in advertising. He paid Brockmeyer/Allen & Associates of Baltimore, Md., $47,766 for creating broadcast ads. Mentzer Media Services of Baltimore billed the campaign $115,754 to cover the cost of air time and placement commissions. The campaign spent another $2,124 to place ads directly, and production costs added $8,281. During the final two weeks of the campaign, Roth spent $14,020 to run ads or place inserts in twenty-five daily and weekly newspapers, including the *De Pere Journal,* the *Kaukauna Times,* the *Ashwaubenon Press,* the *Door County Advocate,* the *Marinette Eagle Star,* and the *Forest Republican.*

To keep his name before the voters, Roth invested $7,163 in yard signs and posters. Buttons, bumper stickers, and other collateral materials cost $3,572. Brochures and persuasion mail totaled $19,596.

Roth spent $21,572 on year-end holiday cards for his longtime supporters and contributors.

Campaign Expenditures	Roth Amount Spent	Roth % of Total	Helms Amount Spent	Helms % of Total
Overhead				
Office furniture/supplies	$ 4,508	1.07	$ 77	.13
Rent/utilities	2,727	.65	1,704	2.77
Salaries	18,798	4.46	37,216	60.59
Taxes	15,152	3.60	414	.67
Bank/investment fees	303	.07	0	
Lawyers/accountants	0		0	
Telephone	2,916	.69	2,858	4.65
Campaign automobile	2,194	.52	0	
Computers/office equipment	25,174	5.98	240	.39
Travel	17,698	4.20	635	1.03
Food/meetings	743	.18	0	
Subtotal	**90,213**	**21.42**	**43,143**	**70.24**
Fund Raising				
Events	21,766	5.17	1,977	3.22
Direct mail	35,381	8.40	0	
Telemarketing	0		0	
Subtotal	**57,147**	**13.57**	**1,977**	**3.22**
Polling	**7,500**	**1.78**	**0**	
Advertising				
Electronic media	173,925	41.30	5,539	9.02
Other media	14,416	3.42	0	
Subtotal	**188,341**	**44.72**	**5,539**	**9.02**
Other Campaign Activity				
Persuasion mail/brochures	19,596	4.65	1,840	3.00
Actual campaigning	13,851	3.29	1,115	1.82
Staff/volunteers	11,886	2.82	0	
Subtotal	**45,333**	**10.76**	**2,955**	**4.81**
Constituent Gifts/Entertainment	**24,697**	**5.86**	**0**	
Donations to				
Candidates from same state	0		0	
Candidates from other states	0		0	
Civic organizations	1,581	.38	0	
Ideological groups	0		0	
Political parties	20		0	
Subtotal	**1,601**	**.38**	**0**	
Unitemized Expenses	**6,325**	**1.50**	**7,807**	**12.71**
Total Campaign Expenses	**$ 421,159**		**$ 61,422**	
PAC Contributions	$ 292,200		$ 17,300	
Individual Contributions	265,808		14,387	
Total Receipts*	589,778		41,727	

*Includes PAC and individual contributions as well as interest earned, party contributions, etc.

WISCONSIN — District 9

Rep. F. James Sensenbrenner, Jr. (R)

1992 Election Results

F. James Sensenbrenner, Jr. (R)	192,898	(70%)
Ingrid K. Buxton (D)	77,362	(28%)

In seven previous House campaigns Rep. F. James Sensenbrenner, Jr., had never received less than 61 percent of the vote and had garnered at least 73 percent in his six previous reelection bids. But in 1992 he looked to the east and saw fellow Republican Rep. Guy Vander Jagt (Mich.), another seemingly invincible incumbent, go down in the primary. To make certain he would not suffer a similar fate, Sensenbrenner spent more than four times as much money on the 1992 campaign as he had in 1990. In the process, he outspent his Democratic challenger, Ingrid K. Buxton, by more than twenty to one.

To gauge the extent of voter dissatisfaction, Sensenbrenner paid Arthur J. Finkelstein & Associates of New York $33,900 for polls. "People were buying into the national media's message about how rotten Congress is," explained Mary Phillips, Sensenbrenner's campaign manager. "Our polls showed that people were moving into the undecided category, and we needed to shore up our support."

While Sensenbrenner felt television advertising would be overkill, he spent $78,131 to produce and air radio commercials aimed at convincing voters he was part of the solution, not part of the problem. To that end, the spots touted his efforts to cut government spending, his opposition to tax increases, and the high ratings accorded that voting record by the National Taxpayers Union. None of the ads mentioned Buxton. Chris Mottola of Philadelphia, Pa., received $18,275 for creating the spots, and Multi Media Services Corp. of Alexandria, Va., collected $59,828 for placing them.

Sensenbrenner invested $141,836 in persuasion mail that echoed the radio commercials. Welch Communications of Arlington, Va., received $87,516 for producing the mailers that targeted undecided voters and new constituents acquired through redistricting. Sensenbrenner also spent $5,180 to print campaign handouts, including Green Bay Packer football schedules and Milwaukee Brewer baseball schedules that he handed out at parades and other campaign events.

In past campaigns Sensenbrenner had been content to run his own phonebanking operation to turn out the vote, but in 1992 he sought professional help. Sensenbrenner paid $15,000 to Victory '92, the state party's coordinated get-out-the-vote effort, and $6,000 to Payco American Corp. of Brookfield for phonebanking. "The congressman used to run one of the largest volunteer phonebanks around, but the sophisticated targeting provided by professionals has improved so much that we bought into Victory '92," noted Phillips.

Buxton was never a factor. She spent only $7,559 on advertising and $1,604 on campaign literature.

Campaign Expenditures	Sensenbrenner Amount Spent	Sensenbrenner % of Total	Buxton Amount Spent	Buxton % of Total
Overhead				
Office furniture/supplies	$ 1,171	.26	$ 1,039	5.05
Rent/utilities	9,810	2.15	0	
Salaries	42,292	9.25	507	2.47
Taxes	17,669	3.86	0	
Bank/investment fees	0		69	.34
Lawyers/accountants	0		0	
Telephone	1,376	.30	885	4.31
Campaign automobile	0		0	
Computers/office equipment	5,812	1.27	184	.90
Travel	6,039	1.32	20	.10
Food/meetings	1,203	.26	0	
Subtotal	**85,371**	**18.67**	**2,704**	**13.15**
Fund Raising				
Events	7,292	1.59	201	.98
Direct mail	50,870	11.12	0	
Telemarketing	0		0	
Subtotal	**58,162**	**12.72**	**201**	**.98**
Polling	**33,900**	**7.41**	**0**	
Advertising				
Electronic media	78,131	17.09	3,009	14.64
Other media	0		4,550	22.13
Subtotal	**78,131**	**17.09**	**7,559**	**36.77**
Other Campaign Activity				
Persuasion mail/brochures	147,016	32.15	1,604	7.80
Actual campaigning	30,772	6.73	8,353	40.63
Staff/volunteers	602	.13	0	
Subtotal	**178,391**	**39.01**	**9,956**	**48.43**
Constituent Gifts/Entertainment	**0**		**0**	
Donations to				
Candidates from same state	309	.07	0	
Candidates from other states	0		0	
Civic organizations	0		0	
Ideological groups	0		0	
Political parties	0		0	
Subtotal	**309**	**.07**	**0**	
Unitemized Expenses	**23,001**	**5.03**	**139**	**.68**
Total Campaign Expenses	**$ 457,265**		**$ 20,560**	
PAC Contributions	$ 75,709		$ 10,507	
Individual Contributions	166,896		13,132	
Total Receipts*	283,602		29,344	

*Includes PAC and individual contributions as well as interest earned, party contributions, etc.

At Large — WYOMING

Rep. Craig Thomas (R)

1992 Election Results

Craig Thomas (R)	113,882	(58%)
Jon Herschler (D)	77,418	(39%)

Rep. Craig Thomas wasted little of his campaign funds in 1992. While he spent $1,477 on holiday cards, he did not use campaign funds to buy his constituents dinner, gifts, or flowers. Although he gave $2,000 to the state Republican party and $885 to various charities, he gave nothing to other candidates. He did not siphon off campaign funds to pay for staff parties or bottled water for his congressional offices. He did not have a campaign car, did not spend campaign funds on an election night victory party, and spent only $60 on meals unrelated to fund raising. He did splurge on a $4,085 reception for delegates who attended the state Republican convention. "We are the original cheapskates," noted Thomas's campaign manager, Gail A. Gerenger.

Thomas invested 36 percent of his campaign funds in broadcast advertising to deliver his message to 318,063 voting-age constituents spread across 97,809 square miles. According to Gerenger, that message was "straight Republican, stressing smaller government, individual freedom and ways to increase economic opportunity." Several ads touted Thomas's work on rural health care legislation.

Thomas spent $16,683 to create and place one round of ads on these same themes that ran in virtually every daily and weekly newspaper in the state. Program ads cost $100. He invested $6,559 in yard signs and $2,243 in buttons and bumper stickers. To make certain that his supporters turned out to vote, he spent $3,283 on phonebanking. Gerenger said that while the campaign prepared one persuasion mailer, they decided not to send it based on positive poll numbers provided by Tarrance & Associates of Alexandria, Va.

Cottington & Marti of Edina, Minn., received $30,658 for creating Thomas's television ads and providing general strategic advice. Kemper-Odell & Associates of Sheridan collected $147,136 for placing both the television and newspaper ads.

To pay for his campaign, Thomas spent $97,859 on fund raising. Ziebart Associates of Washington, D.C., received $57,437 for producing seven direct mail solicitations and coordinating political action committee (PAC) receptions. Thomas collected $222,403 from PACs, $143,016 from individual contributors who gave less than $200, and $96,425 from individuals who contributed at least $200.

Thomas's Democratic opponent, eye surgeon Jon Herschler, worked diligently to co-opt the health care issue, promising a heath care plan that would be universally affordable. Herschler said his radio and television ads also touted his outsider status.

Thomas managed to spend $429,444—$196,051 more than Herschler—in this "cheap" campaign.

	Thomas		Herschler	
Campaign Expenditures	Amount Spent	% of Total	Amount Spent	% of Total
Overhead				
Office furniture/supplies	$ 5,602	1.30	$ 4,276	1.83
Rent/utilities	1,200	.28	2,240	.96
Salaries	36,295	8.45	23,348	10.00
Taxes	12,826	2.99	6,798	2.91
Bank/investment fees	851	.20	80	.03
Lawyers/accountants	4,866	1.13	0	
Telephone	3,072	.72	9,568	4.10
Campaign automobile	0		0	
Computers/office equipment	1,725	.40	4,208	1.80
Travel	21,788	5.07	11,548	4.95
Food/meetings	60	.01	191	.08
Subtotal	**88,284**	**20.56**	**62,257**	**26.67**
Fund Raising				
Events	58,460	13.61	5,928	2.54
Direct mail	39,399	9.17	0	
Telemarketing	0		0	
Subtotal	**97,859**	**22.79**	**5,928**	**2.54**
Polling	**24,425**	**5.69**	**20,050**	**8.59**
Advertising				
Electronic media	153,846	35.82	111,420	47.74
Other media	16,783	3.91	635	.27
Subtotal	**170,630**	**39.73**	**112,056**	**48.01**
Other Campaign Activity				
Persuasion mail/brochures	0		14,036	6.01
Actual campaigning	33,466	7.79	13,369	5.73
Staff/volunteers	0		0	
Subtotal	**33,466**	**7.79**	**27,405**	**11.74**
Constituent Gifts/ Entertainment	**1,477**	**.34**	**0**	
Donations to				
Candidates from same state	0		40	.02
Candidates from other states	0		0	
Civic organizations	885	.21	45	.02
Ideological groups	0		0	
Political parties	2,000	.47	0	
Subtotal	**2,885**	**.67**	**85**	**.04**
Unitemized Expenses	**10,418**	**2.43**	**5,613**	**2.40**
Total Campaign Expenses	**$ 429,444**		**$ 233,393**	
PAC Contributions	**$ 222,403**		**$ 78,200**	
Individual Contributions	**239,441**		**136,924**	
Total Receipts*	**479,523**		**344,240**	

Includes PAC and individual contributions as well as interest earned, party contributions, etc.

Index

The page numbers in **bold** indicate the main entries of general election candidates in the 1992 congressional races. The page numbers in *italics* indicate tables. Congressional district numbers are shown in parentheses.

A. B. Data, 44, 86, *87,* 96, 349, 383
Abate, Frank G., D-N.J. (12), **395**
Abercrombie, Neil, D-Hawaii (1), 46, **262**
Abrams, Robert, D-N.Y., 16, *19, 22, 30,* 59, 75, 86, 90, *95,* 96, 99, **127**
Abzug, Bella, D-N.Y. (8), 407
Ackerman, Gary L., D-N.Y. (5), 28, 86, **404,** 420
Ackerman, Hood & McQueen, 372
Adams & Associates, Pat, 122
Adams, Bob, I-Wash. (8), **565**
Adams, Brock, R-Wash., 14, 140
ADCRAFT, 529
Adell Media Enterprises, Ray, 401
Adnet Associates, 333
Advanced Communications, 94
Advertising Consultants, 282
Agee, Polly A., *87,* 133
Ailes Communications, 94
Akin, Margie, I-Calif. (40), **202**
Albanese, Sal F., D-N.Y. (13), **412**
Albright Ideas, 161
Alexander, Bill, D-Ark. (1), 49-50, 63, 65, 159, 364
Alexis Thompson & Associates, 154
Allard, Wayne, R-Colo. (4), 47, **218**
Allen, George F., R-Va., 51, 553
Allen, Roslyn A., I-Calif. (13), **175**
Almstrom, Kim R., I-Calif. (18), **180**
Alter, Susan D., D-N.Y. (10), 409
Altimira Communications, 380
Ambrosino & Muir, *89,* 168, 169, 239, 266, 269, 371, 552
America Telemarketing, 205
American Data Management, 175
American Telecom, 96
American Viewpoint, 80, *89,* 225, 240, 243, 297, 413, 447, 480
Amity Unlimited, 445
Anderson, Robert C., R-N.C. (7), **437**

Andrews, Michael A., D-Texas (25), *19, 24, 26,* 62, 80, *81,* 88, *93,* **537**
Andrews Plus, 229
Andrews, Robert E., D-N.J. (1), 86, 88, *93,* **384**
Andrews, Thomas H., D-Maine (1), 44, 59, 98, **318,** 576
Angle & Associates, Dolly, 94, 536
Annunzio, Frank, D-Ill., 4, 51
Anthony, Beryl, Jr., D-Ark. (4), 47, 79-80, *81,* 162, 465, 564
Anthony, Bob, R-Okla. (6), **468**
Anti-incumbency, 3-5, 49-60
  background of nonincumbent candidates, 55, 56
  expenditures by background of nonincumbent House candidates, 55, 58
  expenditures by background of nonincumbent Senate candidates, 59-60
  expenditures by nonincumbent candidates, *54,* 55
  fund-raising ability of nonincumbent House candidates, 55-57
  impact of, 52-53
  in incumbent versus incumbent races, 51
  incumbents' response to, 53-55
  losses misattributed to, 52
  open seat candidates adding to, 50-51
  retirements attributed to, 51
Antonelli, Robert B., I-Mass. (7), **334**
Anwiller, John F., D-Calif. (47) **209**
Applegate, Douglas, D-Ohio (18), 34, 76, **461**
Aragon, Raymond Diaz, R-Colo. (1), **215**
Aragon, Robert J., D-N.M. (1), **397**
Arbanas, Fred, D-Mo. (5), 371

Archer, Bill, R-Texas (7), *32,* **519**
Armey, Dick, R-Texas (26), *35,* 36, 156, 202, **538**
Askren, David L., R-N.Y. (8), **407**
Aspin, Les, D-Wis. (1), *19, 22, 30,* 86, *93,* 149, 420, 511, 513, **570,** 576
Assets Consulting Services, 122, 391, 506
Associated Public Affairs Professionals, 281
Atkins, Chester G., D-Mass. (5), 332
Atkinson, Katy, 217
Attention!, *91,* 278
Attitude Research Corp., 108
AuCoin, Les, D-Ore., *19, 22, 35,* 59, 80, *81,* 84, 86, 88, *95,* 99, **133,** 460, 469, 471, 472, 564
Augustin, Owen, I-N.Y. (10), **409**
Austin-Sheinkopf, *85,* 204, 230, 232, 252, 323, 325, 335, 355, 412, 416, 449, 456, 457, 479
Automobiles, 13, 27-28
  top fifteen candidate expenditures on, *28*
Avenel Associates, 557
Axelrod & Associates, *85,* 270, 289, 293, 462, 575
Axinn, Joan F., D-N.Y. (4), 403
Ayers, Whit, 114

B.A.D. Campaigns, 188
Bacchus, Jim, D-Fla. (15), *93,* 149, **242**
Bachurski Associates, 215
Bachus, Spencer, R-Ala. (6), 52, **150**
Bader, Charles W., R-Calif. (41), 203
Baesler, Scotty, D-Ky. (6), **310**
Baggiano, Faye, D-Ala. (2), 146
Bailey, Michael E., R-Ind. (9), **294**
Bailey-Lauerman & Associates, 377
Baker, Bill, R-Calif. (10), 50, 88, **172**
Baker, Bob, D-Calif. (41), **203**

Baker, Brad, R-Fla. (13), 240
Baker, Richard H., R-La. (6), *19,* 90, **316**
Ball, Raymond M., D-Ohio (4), **447**
Ballard Advertising, Perry, 343
Ballenger, Cass, R-N.C. (10), **440**
Banjanin, Tom, R-Fla. (1), 228
Bannon Research, 558, 563
Banuelos, Robert John, D-Calif. (46), **208**
Baraff/Lawrence, 408, 425
Barcia, James A., D-Mich. (5), 47, **342,** 465, 576
Barden, Paul, R-Wash. (9), 566
Barkley, Dean, I-Minn. (6), **359**
Barlow, Tom, D-Ky. (1), 23, **305**
Barnard, Doug, Jr., D-Ga., 260
Barnes, Lawrence J., I-Tenn. (8), **511**
Barnett, Bob, 94, 474
Barnhart Advertising, 74, *85*
Barrett, Bill, R-Neb. (3), 44, **379**
Barrett, Thomas M., D-Wis. (5), **574**
Barrow, Tom, D-Mich. (15), **352**
Barry, Huey, Bullock & Cook Advertising, 146
Bartlett, Roscoe G., R-Md. (6), 63, 88, **325**
Bartlett, Steve, R-Texas, 515
Bartley, Bruce R., R-Ky. (2), **306**
Barton, Joe L., R-Texas (6), *19,* 21, *25, 35,* 36, 88, **518**
Bass, Lori Ann, 266, 269, 282
Bassin Associates, Robert H., 44, 86, *87,* 174, 232, 329, 383, 384
Bateman, Herbert H., R-Va. (1), **547,** 549, 553
Bates & Associates, *89,* 247, 260, 274, 358, 411, 417, 567, 573, 576
Bates, Jim, D-Calif. (50), 212
Baxmeyer, Carl H., R-Ind. (3), **288**
Baxter, Elaine, D-Iowa (3), 69, **298,** 564

Bay Communications, *89,* 284, 391
BBA, 130
Beacher & Co., 254
Bean, Linda, R-Maine (1), 44, 59, *93,* 98, **318**
Beasley Associates, 229
Beaumont, Frank, R-Mich. (16), 9, **353**
Becerra, Xavier, D-Calif. (30), **192,** 195
Becker, Daniel, R-Ga. (9), **259**
Becker Public Relations, John, 544
Beilenson, Anthony C., D-Calif. (24), 4, *35, 37,* 53, **186**
Bell, Howard, R-Okla. (4), **466**
Bell, James W., R-R.I. (2), **496**
Bell Strategic Research, 408
Beller, Ron, D-Mo. (4), 370
Below, Tobe & Associates, 186, 192, 207
Bemis, F. Gregg, Jr., R-N.M. (3), **399**
Benchmark Research Group, 92, 184
Benford, Dorothy, R-Miss. (2), **363**
Bennett & Associates, 87
Bennett, Charles E., D-Fla., 4, 56, 231
Bennett, Paul, 123
Bennett & Petts, *89*
Bennett, Robert F., R-Utah, *19, 22, 35,* 92, *95,* **138**
Bentley, Helen Delich, R-Md. (2), *19,* 21, *22,* **321**
Bentson, Lloyd, D-Texas, 63, 110, 125
Berard Media Service, Jim, 94, 361
Bereuter, Doug, R-Neb. (1), **377**
Berg, Gerald E., I-Va. (7), **553**
Berman, Howard L., D-Calif. (26), *19,* 34, *35,* 36, *37,* 76, **188**
Bernos Media, Mike, 232
Bernstein & Associates, 96
Bessinger, Larry, D-Fla. (15), 242
Beuerman Consulting, 311
Beverly, Al, R-Ga. (7), 92, **257**
Bevill, Tom, D-Ala. (4), 13, *26,* 65, **148**
Bhagwandin, Dianand D., R-N.Y. (6), **405**
Biaggi, Mario, D-N.Y. (17), 416
Biden, Joseph R., Jr., D-Del., 110
Big Sky Consulting, 212, 269, 345
Bilbray, James, D-Nev. (1), 70, 94, **380**
Bilirakis, Michael, R-Fla. (9), *30,* 88, **236**
Binder, Allan E., R-N.Y. (5), **404**
Bishop & Associates, 150
Bishop, Sanford D., Jr., D-Ga. (2), 52, 69, **252,** 410
Black, Charles L., R-Tenn. (9), 53, **512**
Blackburn, James M., I-Fla. (20), **247**
Blackburn, Marsha, R-Tenn. (6), **509**

Blackstone, Ron, R-Ill. (2), **267**
Blackwelder Communications, 438
Blackwell, Lucien E., D-Pa. (2), **475**
Blaemier Communications, *89,* 253, 287, 310, 464
Blake, Rory, D-N.C. (9), **439**
Bland, Jim, R-S.C. (3), **499**
Bliley, Thomas J., Jr., R-Va. (7), 22, **553**
Block, Arthur, D-N.Y. (8), 407
Blum, Edward, R-Texas (18), **530**
Blute, Peter I., R-Mass. (3), **330**
Boccio, Norman G., R-Ill. (7), **272**
Bocskor, Nancy, 240, 450
Bodner Consulting, Sandy, 92
Boehlert, Sherwood, R-N.Y. (23), *30,* **422**
Boehner, John A., R-Ohio (8), 39, 47, **451**
Boesch, Doyce, *91*
Bond, Christopher S., R-Mo., *19, 22, 23, 24, 26, 30, 32, 33, 34,* 59, 62, 75, 86, 88, 90, *95, 102,* 113, **124**
Bond, Pat, 192, 195
Bonilla, Henry, R-Texas (23), **535**
Bonior, David E., D-Mich. (10), 14, *19, 24, 35,* 36, 76, 88, *93,* 101, 267, **347,** 420
Bonner, Mary Pat, *87,* 466
Bonner & Tate, 514
Bonpane, Blase, I-Calif. (30), **192**
Booker & Booker, 105
Boriss, Steven K., 368
Borski, Robert A., D-Pa. (3), **476**
Boucher, Rick, D-Va. (9), **555**
Boulter, Beau, R-Texas (13), **525**
Bourgoin, David L., D-Hawaii (2), 263
Bowen, William F., D-Ohio (1), 444
Boxer, Barbara, D-Calif., *19, 22, 26, 30,* 51, 62, 63, 65, 69, 70, 75, 84, 88, 90, *95,* 96, 99, 100, *102,* **109,** 170, 171, 194, 197, 460, 564
Boynton, Paul I., R-La. (3), **313**
Brabender Cox, *89,* 94, 166, 478, 489, 491, 494
Bradford Communications, 440
Bradley, Bill, D-N.J., 110
Bradley, Gerald, D-Ill. (15), 280
Bramlett, Will, R-Miss. (5), 366
Branford Communications, 416
Braude, Evan Anderson, D-Calif. (38), **200**
Breaux, John B., D-La., 4, 9, *19, 26, 28, 30, 32, 34, 35,* 59, *95,* **122**
Brewer, William A., D-Ala. (1), **145**
Brewster, Bill, D-Okla. (3), 43, 47, 48, **465**
Bricker, William T. S., R-Md. (3), **322**
Bridges, David L., R-Texas (4), **516**
Brier Group, *91,* 135, 485
Briggs, Walter, D-Mich. (11), **348**
Brockmeyer/Allen & Associates, 292, 298, 343, 359, 373, 379, 577
Brooks, Jack, D-Texas (9), *35,* **521**

Broomfield, William S., R-Mich., 4, 348
Browder, Glen, D-Ala. (3), 83, **147,** *89,* 125, 324, 399
Brown, Corrine, D-Fla. (3), **230**
Brown, Dennis, R-Calif. (38), 200
Brown, George E., Jr., D-Calif. (42), 14, *37,* 88, 149, **204**
Brown, Ken D., R-Ohio (9), **452**
Brown, Sherrod, D-Ohio (13), **456**
Broyles, James W., R-Texas (11), **523**
Bruce, Terry L., D-Ill., 4, 51, 96, 284
Bruner, Natalie M., D-Ind. (6), 20, **291**
Bruno, Vincent J., R-La. (1), **311**
Bruster, Susie, 342
Bryan, Jon L., I-Mass. (10), **337**
Bryant, Barbara, 105
Bryant Communications, Jay, 381
Bryant, John, D-Texas (5), *22,* **517,** 542
Bryant Seaman Voter Communications, 419
Bubba, Joseph L., R-N.J. (8), **391**
Buchanan, Pat, 294, 298, 432, 555
Budget Marketing, 119
Buechner, Jack, R-Mo., 17, 52, 367, 368
Buffa, Peter, R-Calif. (45), 207
Buford & Associates, Alescia, 194
Bullock, Thad, D-Mo. (8), **374**
Bumpers, Dale, D-Ark., 21, *24,* 27, *30, 35,* 75, 84, *95,* **108**
Bundesen, Ted, R-Calif. (16), **178**
Bunning, Jim, R-Ky. (4), 84, *93,* **308**
Burdick, Quentin, D-N.D., 36, 130
Burges & Burges, 456, 457, 459, 462
Burke & Associates., Ruth, 303
Burke, Stephen, I-N.Y. (24), 423
Burkley, Kenneth B., D-Pa. (20), 493
Burr, Richard M., R-N.C. (5), **435**
Burson, Anita, 96
Burton, Dan, R-Ind. (6), 20, *34,* **291**
Bush, George, 3, 9, 44, 52, 80, 97, 107, 145, 150, 157, 183, 222, 272, 280, 284, 293, 318, 319, 320, 323, 330, 346, 347, 360, 368, 379, 389, 413, 418, 421, 429, 430, 445, 455, 491, 501, 518, 531, 550, 569
Bustamante, Albert G., D-Texas (23), *25, 26,* 27, *34,* 52, 511, **535**
Butler, Henry N., R-Va. (11), **557**
Buxton, Ingrid K., D-Wis. (9), **578**
Buyer, Steve, R-Ind. (5), 57, **290**
Byrne, Leslie L., D-Va. (11), *93,* **557**
Byron, Beverly B., D-Md (6), 49, 63, 88, 325

C & C Advertising, 396
Cain, Lucy, R-Texas (30), **542**
Cain, Ross, I-Calif. (3), **165**
Calabrese & Associates, 534
Call, W. Douglas, D-N.Y. (27), **426**
Callahan, Sonny, R-Ala. (1), *25,* **145**

Callihan, Mike, D-Colo. (3), 80, **217**
Calvert, Ken, R-Calif. (43), *23,* 48, 90, **205**
Camp, Dave, R-Mich. (4), 65, **341**
Campaign. *See* Permanent campaign.
Campaign Compendium, 468
Campaign Design Group, 90, *91,* 389
Campaign Group, 83, *85,* 92, 149, 163, 135, 211, 212, 221, 287, 332, 345, 384, 385, 433, 435, 438, 469, 474, 476, 492, 513, 522, 544
Campaign Mail & Data, 233
Campaign Management Services, 201
Campaign Media Associates, 558
Campaign Performance Group, 83, 86, 88, *89,* 92, 150, 163, 165, 177, 181, 204, 211, 221, 223, 242, 253, 258, 259, 267, 285, 286, 289, 302, 320, 323, 325, 329, 332, 376, 378, 384, 400, 402, 469, 523, 528, 547, 559, 562
Campaign Services, 296
Campaign Services Group, *87,* 356
Campaign Strategies, *89, 91,* 96, 521, 530, 541
Campaign Support Services, 356
Campaign Systems, 542
Campaign Technology Corp., 447
Campaign Tele-Resources, *91,* 273, 379
Campaign Telecommunications, 90, *91, 132,* 208, 213, 214, 236, 256, 316
Campaigns & Elections, 90, *91,* 283
Campaigns, Research & Demographics, 277
Campbell, Ben Nighthorse, D-Colo., 51, 74, *81,* 86, *95,* **111**
Campbell, Falk & Selby, 558
Campbell, Tom, R-Calif., 65, 176
Canady, Charles T., R-Fla. (12), **239**
Cannon, Joe, R-Utah, 138
Cantwell, Maria, D-Wash. (1), 14, 72, **558**
Capitol Ideas, 543
Cardin, Benjamin L., D-Md. (3), **322**
Cargill & Roush, 525
Carl, Douglas, R-Mich. (10), 76, **347**
Carley, John, R-Mo. (4), **370**
Carlin, David R., Jr., D-R.I. (1), **495**
Carlyle Gregory Co., *91*
Carper, Thomas R., D-Del., 51, 227
Carr, Bob, D-Mich. (8), *19,* 23, 59, 88, *93,* 98, **345**
Carville & Begala, *91,* 135
Casey Co., Dennis M., 477
Cash, Mary-Margaret, 551
Cashill, Thomas J., 495
Castle, Michael N., R-Del. (AL), 14, 59, **227**
Castleberry & Co., 442
Caton, John Wayne, D-Texas (26), **538**
Cavasos Associates, 535

582 Index

Center, Tony, D-Ga. (6), **256,** 513, 576
Chandler, Ralph, 114
Chandler, Rod, R-Wash., 14, *22, 24, 63, 80, 81, 95,* **140,** 565
Chandler, Thomas R., D-Ohio (2), **445**
Chapman, J. L, "Jim" IV, R-Va. (2), **548**
Chapman, Jim, D-Texas (1), **513**
Charlton Research Co., 202
Chase, John R., R-S.C. (6), **502**
Checota, Joseph W., D-Wis., 141
Cherry Communications, *91,* 234, 243, 245, 256, 319, 356, 412, 426, 495
Cherry, John D., Jr., D-Mich. (5), 342
Chesapeake Media, 235, 476
Christian, J. Carr "Jack," D-Tenn. (1), **504**
Christmas, Barbara, D-Ga. (1), 75-76, **251**
Chrysler, Dick, R-Mich. (8), 22, 92, *93,* 98, **345**
Chun & Yonamine, 263
Cine Vision Films Co., 119
Clark & Associates, Jimmy, 317
Clark, Herman, R-Ga. (6), 256
Clark Media Services, Maggie, 365
Clary & Associates, 464
Clay, William L., D-Mo. (1), 52, 53, 100, **367**
Clayton, Eva, D-N.C. (1), **431,** 564
Clec Canvass Network, 117
Clement, Bob, D-Tenn. (5), 37-38, 90, **508**
Clinger, William F., R-Pa. (5), **478**
Clinton, Bill, 3, 23, 31, 76, 88, 97, 101, 305, 330, 353, 357, 385, 399, 413, 425, 429, 442, 466, 488, 491, 497, 526, 570, 573
Cloud, Tal L., R-Calif. (19), **181**
Clyburn, James E., D-S.C. (6), 48, **502**
CMT Advertising, 213, 214
Coats, Daniel R., R-Ind., *19,* 21, 22, *30, 32,* 59, *95,* **118,** 289
Coble, Howard, R-N.C. (6), **436**
Col-Sol, 312
Coleman & Christison, 354, 357, 358
Coleman, Ronald D., D-Texas (16), 408, 513, **528**
Coleman, Tom, R-Mo. (6), 62, 63, 65, *80,* **372**
Coleman, Tommy, 252
Coley and Associates, 351
Collings, Debbie, I-Ariz. (4), **156**
Collins, Barbara-Rose, D-Mich. (15), *30,* 45-46, 48, 100, 272, **352**
Collins, Cardiss, D-Ill. (7), *25, 30, 32,* **272**
Collins, Mac, R-Ga. (3), **253**
Collins, Virginia, R-Alaska (AL), 152
Colonial Communications, 553
Colorado Media Group, 218

Combest, Larry, R-Texas (19), **531**
Combs & Heathcott, 108
Comerford, John P., D-Fla. (16), **243**
Communications Co., 150
Communications Group, 160
Competitive Edge Research & Communication, 92, 184
Complete Pictures, 258, 302
Computer Operations, 84
Conboy, Martin D., R-Mass. (9), **336**
Condit, Gary A., D-Calif. (18), *25, 37,* 76, **180**
Conhor, Marty, R-Ala. (6), 150
Conrad, Kent, D-N.D., *24, 30,* 31, *32, 35,* 36, 75, 84, 86, 88, *95,* 129, **130,** 443
Conroy & Co., *87, 576*
Considine, Terry, R-Colo., 74, 86, *95,* **111**
Constituent entertainment and gifts, 13, 18, 31-33, 45-47
  by House freshmen, 45-47
  top fifteen candidate expenditures on holiday cards, *32*
  top twenty-five candidate expenditures on, *30*
Consultants, 20, 83-96
  campaign management, 90
    top fifteen campaign management consultants, *91*
  fund-raising, 84, 86
    telemarketers, 86
    top twenty-five direct-mail consultants, *87*
    top twenty-five event consultants, *87*
  general, 90
    top fifteen general consultants, *91*
  get-out-the-vote, 90, 92
    top fifteen get-out-the-vote consultants, *91*
  House candidates spending on, top fifty, *93*
  media, 83-84
    top fifty media consultants, *85*
  party coordinated payments to, 83, 84, 88, 90
  persuasion mail, 86, 88
    top twenty-five persuasion mail consultants, *89*
  polling, 88, 90
    top twenty-five polling consultants, *89*
  Senate candidates spending on, top fifty, *95*
  total payments to, 83
Conte, Silvio O., D-Mass., 328
Conyers, John, Jr., D-Mich. (14), 38, **351**
Cook Agency, William, 231
Cook, Joseph L., R-Wis. (4), **573**
Cookfair Associates, 421, 422, 424
Cooper, Jim, D-Tenn. (4), **507**
Cooper & Secrest Associates, 79, 88, *89,* 239, 287, 293, 299, 302, 320,

371, 428, 429, 473, 479, 487, 488, 544, 555, 573
Coordinated expenditures by national political parties, 5, 57, 74-79, 84, 88, 90, 96
  Democratic Congressional Campaign Committee, 74, 75, 76, 79, 88
  Democratic National Committee, 74, 75, 76, 88
  Democratic Senatorial Campaign Committee, 74, 75, 76, 84, 88, 90, 96
  National Republican Campaign Committee, 5, 57, 74, 75, 76
  National Republican Senatorial Committee, 74, 75, 76, 84, 88, 90, 96
  Republican National Committee, 74, 76
Copeland, Gary D., I-Calif. (45), **207**
Coppersmith, Sam, D-Ariz. (1), **153**
Cordray, Richard, D-Ohio (15), **458**
Corley, David, R-Texas (3), 515
Costello, Jerry F., D-Ill. (12), *19,* 25, 99, **277**
Cottington & Marti, *85,* 359, 379, 560, 575, 579
Cotton Associates, Pat, 515
Coughlin, Lawrence, R-Pa., 486
Coverdell, Paul, R-Ga. (22), 75, *80, 95,* 99, **114,** 190, 448
Cowart, Joseph, 146
Cox & Associates, 244
Cox, C. Christopher, R-Calif. (47), **209**
Cox, John W., Jr., D-Ill. (16), 52, **281,** 408
Coyle, McConnell & O'Brien, 84, *87,* 110
Coyne, William J., D-Pa. (14), **487**
Crabb, Juanita M., D-N.Y. (26), 69, 425
Craft & Associates, 137
Cramer, Robert E. "Budd," D-Ala. (5), *28,* 47-48, **149**
Crane, Philip M., R-Ill. (8), **273**
Cranston, Alan, D-Calif., 22, 37, 65, 75. 167, 194
Crapo, Michael D., R-Idaho (2), 36, 83, **265,** 538
Craver Matthews Smith & Co., *87,* 96, 109
Cravotta, Samuel A., R-W. Va. (2), **568**
Crawford Communications, Jan, *85,* 96, 548
Creative Campaign Consultant, *87,* 432, 434, 508, 513, 555
Creative Communication, 539
Creative Concepts, 336
Creative Marketing & Advertising, 113
Creative Media, 348
Creative Media Planning, 301

Crest Films, 92, 184
Crone, Betsy, *87,* 123
Cronin, Paul W., R-Mass. (5), **332**
CT Associates, *87*
Cunningham, Bob, R-Ga. (8), **258**
Cunningham, Jean Wooden, D-Va. (3), 549
Cunningham, Randy "Duke," R-Calif. (51), 4, *30,* 40, 212, **213,** 214
Cutting Edge Communications, *91,* 535

D'Amato, Alfonse M., R-N.Y., 9, 13, 16, 18, *19,* 20, 21, *22,* 23, *24, 25, 26,* 27, *28, 30, 32,* 33, *34, 35,* 59, 75, *84,* 88, 90, *95,* 96, 99, 100, 101, *102,* 112, **127,** 132, 430
Daggett, Diana, 397
Dahl, Demar, R-Nev., **125**
Dalrymple, Jack, R-N.D., **130**
Dalton Media Studios, 181
Daly, Daniel W., R-Mass. (10), **337**
Daly, Frank, D-Pa. (7), **480**
Dannemeyer, William E., R-Calif., 55
Danner, Pat, D-Mo. (6), 62, 63, *80,* **372**
Darden, George "Buddy," D-Ga. (7), 92, 94, **257**
Daschle, Tom, D-S.D., *19,* 21, 22, 23, *24, 26, 30, 34, 35,* 36, 59, 75, 86, *95, 102,* **137**
Davis, Andy, D-Mich. (6), **343**
Davis, David, I-Calif. (29), **191**
Davis, David R., D-Tenn. (7), 37, **510,** 511
Davis, Don, R-N.C. (2), *81,* **432**
Davis Group, 540
Davis, Magda Montiel, D-Fla. (18), **245**
Davis, Peter W., R-Ohio (3), **446**
Davis, Robert W., R-Mich., 50, 51, 338
Day, Bryan, R-Colo. (2), 5, **216,** 538
Day Research, Richard, 277
DCM Group, 556
Deal, Nathan, D-Ga. (9), **259**
Deaton, Thomas Patrick, D-Mo. (7), **373**
Decision Research Corp., 457, 462
Deddeh, Wadie P., D-Calif. (50), 212
Deer, Ada, D-Wis. (2), 39, 70, **571**
DeFazio, Peter A., D-Ore. (4), **472**
Degerness & Associates, 562
de la Garza, E. "Kika," D-Texas (15), **527**
DeLauro, Rosa, D-Conn. (3), 46-47, 84, *93,* **223**
DeLay, Tom, R-Texas (22), 27, **534**
Dellums, Ronald V., D-Calif. (9), 3, 13, 18, *19, 26, 30,* 35, 36, 37, 76, *102,* **171**
DeLoach, George L., D-Ga. (11), 261
Denson Agency, 507
Denton, Phil, D-Fla. (6), **233**

Index **583**

Derrick, Butler, D-S.C. (3), **499**
DeSisti & Associates, 294
Deutsch, Peter, D-Fla. (20), **247**
Devens, John S., D-Alaska (AL), *81,* **152**
DeWine, Mike, R-Ohio, *28,* 38, 47, *81, 84,* 90, *95,* **131**, 450
Diaz, Angel, R-N.Y. (12), **411**
Diaz-Balart, Lincoln, R-Fla. (21), **248**
Dickey, Jay, R-Ark. (4), 57, **162**, 538
Dickinson, Bill, R-Ala., 4, 146
Dickinson, Spencer E., D-R.I. (2), 496
Dicks, Norm, D-Wash. (6), *26,* **563**
Dietrich, John E., D-Texas (6), **518**
Dingell, John D., D-Mich. (16), 9, 14, *19, 25, 30, 32, 34, 35,* 88, *102,* **353**
Dinsmore, Robert S., R-Calif. (5), **167**
DioGuardi, Joseph J., R-N.Y. (18), *19,* 90, **417**
DiPerna, Paula, D-N.Y. (23), **422**
Direct Communication, 202
Direct Communications, 151
Direct Mail Specialists, 94
Direct Mail Systems, *87,* 88, *89,* 233, 234, 236, 240, 249, 265, 498
Directions by King & Associates, 83, 163
Dittman Research Corp of Alaska, 106, 138
Dixon, Alan J., D-Ill., 59, 62, 117
Dixon, Julian C., D-Calif. (32), *35,* 36, *37,* 76, **194**
Dixon, Larry, R-Ala. (2), 146
Doak, Shrum & Associates, *85,* 92, 123, 131, 135, 198, 304, 369, 442, 537
Dodd, Christopher J., D-Conn., *19, 21, 22, 26, 27, 28, 30, 32,* 33, *34, 35,* 84, 88, *95,* 99, **112**
Dole, Bob, R-Kan., *19,* 20, *26,* 27, 30, *35,* 36, 38, 69, 75, 84, 99, **120**, 136, 231, 245, 328, 430
Donaldson, Lisa A., D-Mich. (4), 65, **341**
Donations, 13, 20, 34-37, 47
  by House freshmen, 47
  top twenty-five candidate expenditures on, *35*
Donilon & Petts, 485
Donnelly, Tom, I-Wash. (6), **563**
Dooley, Calvin, D-Calif. (20), *35, 37,* 40, 47, **182**
Doolittle, John T., R-Calif. (4), 47, 48, 94, **166**, 189, 210
Dorgan, Byron L., D-N.D., 31, *35,* 51, **129**, 443
Doring & Co., W. F., 409
Dornan, Robert K., R-Calif. (46), 18, *19,* 29, *30,* 84, 90, 92, *93,* 100, 189, 207, **208**, 223
Dougherty, Charles F., R-Pa. (3), **476**

Douglas, James H., R-Vt., **139**
Downey, Michael, R-Md. (6), 325
Downey, Thomas J., D-N.Y. (2), *19, 21, 22, 23, 24, 28,* 47, 59, 88, *93,* **401**, 465, 564
Dreier, David, R-Calif. (28), 20, *35,* **190**
Dresch, Stephen P., R-Mich. (1), 338
Dresner, Sykes, Jordan & Townsend, 301
Droogsma, Timothy R., R-Minn. (1), **354**
Drye, J. Wendell, I-N.C. (8), **438**
Dudley, Jim, R-Ga. (2), 69, **252**
Duncan, John J. "Jimmy," Jr., R-Tenn. (2), **505**
Dunn, Jennifer, R-Wash. (8), 63-64, **565**
Durbin, Richard J., D-Ill. (20), 75, 86, 88, 92, *93,* **285**, 327
Duren, B. Kwaku, I-Calif. (37), **199**
DWD Software Development Corp., 432, 434
Dwyer, Bernard J., D-N.J., 51, 389
Dykes, Edward R., D-Calif. (16), 178
Dymally, Lynn, D-Calif. (37), 199
Dymally, Mervyn M., D-Calif., 199
Dyson, Michele, R-Md. (4), **323**

Early & Associates, Jim, 505
Early, Joseph D., D-Mass. (3), *28, 30, 34,* **330**
Eberle, Bruce W., 84
Eccles Group, 524
Eckart, Dennis E., D-Ohio, 4, 456
Eckman, Harold, R-N.H., 126
Edmonds Powell Media, *85,* 152, 372, 376
Edmondson, Drew, D-Okla. (2), 73, 74, *80,* 98, 464
Edwards, Chet, D-Texas (11), 44, 94, **523**
Edwards, Don, D-Calif. (16), *35,* 36, *37,* 76, **178**
Edwards, John, D-Va. (6), 552
Edwards, Mickey, R-Okla. (5), 448, 467
Eichenbaum, Henke & Associates, *85,* 141
Election year spending, 13, 18
Eldridge, Ronnie, D-N.Y. (8), 407
Elgin, Syferd, Drake, 225
Ellinger, Charles W., R-Ky. (6), **310**
Ellis-Hart Associates, 170
Ember Communications, John, 503
Emerson, Bill, R-Mo. (8), **374**
EMILY's List, 69, 140, 158, 168, 195, 211, 232, 254, 431
Emory, Young & Associates, 153, 516
Emprise Designs, 124
Engel, Eliot L., D-N.Y. (17), *25,* **416**, 511
Engel & Triak, 494
English, Glenn, D-Okla. (6), *28,* **468**

English, Karan, D-Ariz. (6), 50, **158**
Enterprise Consultants, 312
Epps, Jacqueline G., D-Va. (3), 549
Erdreich, Ben, D-Ala. (6), 52, *93,* 150, 526
Erickson & Co., *87,* 269, 549
Ervin, Clark Kent, R-Texas (29), 26, **541**
Eshoo, Anna G., D-Calif. (14), 65, 69, 170, **176**
Espy, Mike, D-Miss. (2), 20, 23-24, **363**
Evans & Associates, J. D., 299
Evans, Lane, D-Ill. (17), 86, **282**
Evans/McDonough Co., 72, 558
Event Planners, 94, 166
Everett, Terry, R-Ala. (2), *23,* 50, 57, *93,* **146**
Evets Management Services, 315
Ewing, Thomas W., R-Ill. (15), *19,* **280**

F.D.R. Services, 566
Fabrizio, McLaughlin & Associates, *89, 91,* 128, 318, 402, 419, 553
Faeth and Faeth, 308
Fairbank, Bregman & Maullin, *89,* 204, 211, 212
Faircloth, Lauch, R-N.C., *30,* 59, *80,* 90, *95,* 99, **128**
Farber, Michael, D-Calif. (48), **170**
Farmelli, Mary J., I-Mass. (5), **332**
Farrell Media, 94
Farwell Group, 251, 256, 265, 307, 468, 547
Fascell, Dante B., D-Fla., 244
Fattah, Chaka, D-Pa. (1), 475
Fawell, Harris W., R-Ill. (13), **278**
Fazio, Vic, D-Calif. (3), 14, *19, 25, 30, 35,* 36, *37, 80, 81,* 84, 88, 92, *93,* **165**, 195, 420
Feighan, Edward F., D-Ohio, 462
Feingold, Russell D., D-Wis., *19, 28, 95, 102,* **141**
Feinstein, Dianne, D-Calif., 4, *19, 22, 26, 30,* 59, 63, 65, 69, 74, 75, 86, 88, 90, *95,* **110**, 170, 171
Feldman Group, *89,* 323, 502
Fenn & King Communications, 49, 51, 57, 71, 80, *85,* 148, 253, 264, 267, 284, 297, 310, 324, 347, 359, 391, 400, 411, 417, 446, 464, 468, 472, 496, 499, 537, 545, 548, 549, 550, 551, 559, 560, 567
Ferguson, Anita Perez, D-Calif. (23), 5, 14, 52, 69, **185**
Ferguson, Denzel, D-Ore. (2), **470**
Ferraro, Geraldine A., D-N.Y., 96, 127
Fescina, Michael A., R-Pa. (11), **484**
Fielding, Ed, R-Fla. (23), **250**
Fielding, Herbert U., D-S.C. (6), 502
Fields, Cleo, D-La. (4), **314**
Fields, Jack, R-Texas (8), 9, *19, 22,* 88, **520**
Fierro, Mark, 94, 380

Filante, Bill, R-Calif. (6), *23,* **168**
Filner, Bob, D-Calif. (50), 22, *23,* 69, 92, *93,* **212**
Fingerhut, Eric D., D-Ohio (19), **462,** 564
Finkelstein & Associates, Arthur J., 88, *89,* 90, *91,* 96, 128, 213, 214, 418, 419, 461, 515, 578
Finnegan, Gerry, D-Neb. (1), **377**
Fiorello Consulting, 551
First Tuesday, 154
Fish, Hamilton, Jr., R-N.Y. (19), *23,* **418**
Fisher, Lowell, D-Neb. (3), 44, **379**
Fishwick, John, D-Va. (6), 552
Fiske, Pat, R-Wash. (3), **560**
Fitrakis, Bob, D-Ohio (12), **451**
Flake, Floyd H., D-N.Y. (6), 28, **405**
Fletcher, Roy, 314, 315, 317
Flint, Mike, 146
Flores, Joan Milke, R-Calif. (36), *22, 23,* 65, 189, **198**
Florio, James J., D-N.J., 92, 384, 390, 392
Flourney & Associates, 458
FMR Group, 94, 375
Foglietta, Thomas M., D-Pa. (1), *35,* 94, **474**
Foley, Thomas S., D-Wash. (5), 4, *26,* 27, *35,* 140, 182, 267, 399, **562**
Ford, Gerald, 119
Ford, Harold E., D-Tenn. (9), 24, *25,* 27, 53, **512**
Ford, Wendell H., D-Ky., *19,* 20, *26, 28, 30,* 33, *35,* 36, 84, *95,* **121**
Ford, William D., D-Mich. (13), *28,* 32, *102,* **350**
Forrest, Vaughn S., R-Fla. (7), *23,* 234, 235
Forrester, Chip, D-Tenn. (5), 508
Forsch, Gary, R-Calif. (26), **188**
Foster & Associates, James R., 80, *87, 89,* 185, 241, 297, 480, 495, 515, 538
Foster, Ernest N., I-N.Y. (11), 410
Fosterfilm, 366
Fowler, Tillie, R-Fla. (4), 4, 56, **231**
Fowler, Wyche, Jr., D-Ga., *19, 24, 26, 28, 30, 32, 34, 35,* 75, *81,* 84, 88, 90, *95,* 99, *102,* **114**, 448
Fox, Andy, D-Va. (1), 14, 47, 465, **547**
Fox, Jon D., R-Pa. (13), 22, 23, **486**
Fraioli/Jost, 86, *87,* 92, 181, 192, 276, 285, 288, 305, 335, 350, 353, 376, 384, 415, 509
Franco, Reuben D., R-Calif. (31), **193**
Frank, Barney, D-Mass. (4), 150, **331**
Frankel, Lois, D-Fla. (23), 250
Franks, Bob, R-N.J. (7), **390**
Franks, Donna, 24
Franks, Gary A., R-Conn. (5), 24, 27, 43, 69, 80, *81,* **225**
Franzen Multimedia, John, 50, *85,* 179, 216, 288, 358

584 Index

Frazier, William G., R-Ind. (2), **287**
Frederick/Schneiders, *89,* 96, 228, 247, 269
Freedman, Elliot Roy, D-Calif. (2), **164**
Freshmen, House, 39-48
    average expenditures in 1990, 39-40
    average expenditures in 1992, 40
    constituent entertainment, 45-47
    donations, 47
    fund raising, 40
    off-year spending, 40, 43
Friedman Associates, Cynthia, 135
Frisa, Daniel, R-N.Y. (4), 403
Frost, Martin, D-Texas (24), 18, *19, 21, 22, 25, 26, 30,* 86, 90, *93,* 94, 524, **536,** 542
Frost Productions, Jack, 106
Fundamentals, 87
Fund raising, 14, 18, 29, 31, 40, 84, 86-87
    by House freshmen, 40
    by women candidates, 63-65, 69-70
    top twenty-five candidate expenditures on, *30*
    top twenty-five direct-mail fund-raising consultants, *87*
    top twenty-five fund-raising event consultants, *87*
Fund-raising and Management Counsel, 499
Fundraising Management Group, 86, *87,* 96, 135, 524, 526, 536
Furse, Elizabeth, D-Ore. (1), 61, 69, **469,** 471

Gaddy, James M., D-Texas (21), **533**
Gaffney, Alice E., I-N.Y. (9), 61, **408**
Gaffney, Michael, I-N.Y. (11), **410**
Galanty & Company, 222
Gallagher, John R., 483
Gallegly, Elton, R-Calif. (23), 5, *19,* 52, **185,** 210
Gallo, Dean A., R-N.J. (11), 29, *30,* **394**
Galvin, Siegel, Kemper Advertising, 444
GamePlan, 498
Gann Dawson, 483
Gannon, McCarthy, Mason, 297, 492
Gantt, Harvey B., D-N.C., 9
Garamendi, Patricia, D-Calif. (11), 62, 69, **173**
Garcia, Bonifacio, D-Calif. (31), 193
Garcia, Carmen, 24, 196
Garcia, Rose, 540
Garin-Hart, 88, *89,* 92, 129, 130, 139, 141, 148, 198, 285, 306, 317, 350, 353, 402, 443, 472, 528, 537, 575
Gardner, Robert A., R-Ohio (19), **462**

Garn, Jake, R-Utah, 138
Garth Group, *85,* 134
Garza, Humberto J., R-Texas (14), **526**
Gastil, Janet M., D-Calif. (52), **214**
Gaylord & Co., Joseph, 91
Geake, R. Robert, R-Mich. (13), **350**
Geddings Communcations, 54, 501
Gejdenson, Sam, D-Conn. (2), *19,* 21, 47, 57-58, 98, **222,** 408, 465, 526, 576
Gekas, George W., R-Pa. (17), 76, **490**
Gephardt, Richard A., D-Mo. (3), 9, 14, 17-18, *19,* 21, *22, 26,* 27, *30,* 38, 52, 86, 88, 92, *93,* 267, 367, **369**
Geren, Pete, D-Texas (12), *19,* 36, 86, 90, **524,** 538
Geto & De Milly, *85,* 90, *91,* 96
Gianakos & Chalk Agency, 364
Gibbons, Sam M., D-Fla. (11), *19, 22,* **238**
Gilbert, Alice L., R-Mich. (11), 348
Gilbert, Frank, D-S.C. (6), 502
Gilbert, Rachel S., R-Idaho (1), **264**
Gilchrest, Wayne T., R-Md. (1), 23, 36, 47, 59, **320,** 538
Gilchrist, Liz, I-Miss. (4), **365**
Gillienkirk, Jeff, 96
Gillmor, Paul E., R-Ohio (5), *35,* 37, 47, 101, **448**
Gilman, Benjamin A., R-N.Y. (20), *32,* **419**
Gilmartin, James H. "Gil," D-Calif. (25), **189**
Gingrich, Newt, R-Ga. (6), 4, 18, *19, 21, 22, 26, 30,* 36, 47, 55, 90, 92, *93, 102,* 156, 166, 201, 223, 236, 245, 253, **256,** 257, 283, 448, 450, 513, 538, 576
Glenn, John, D-Ohio, *22,* 27, *30, 35,* 38, 47, 75, 84, 86, 88, *95,* **131,** 450
Glickman, Dan, D-Kan. (4), 81, *93,* **304,** 526
Golar, Simeon, D-N.Y. (6), 405
Gold Communications Co., 69, 74, 86, *87, 89,* 92, 94, 110, 122, 257, 369, 514, 537, 541, 542
Goldman Associates, 337
Gonzalez, Henry B., D-Texas (20), 52, **532,** 535
Goodale, Troy, D-Tenn. (2), **505**
Goodlatte, Robert W., R-Va. (6), **552**
Goodling, Bill, R-Pa. (19), **492**
Goodman Agency, Robert, *85,* 248, 318, 324, 552, 565, 570
Gordon & Associates, Steven H., *87,* 116
Gordon & Schwenkmeyer, 86, *91,* 110, 117
Gordon, Bart, D-Tenn. (6), 90, *102,* **509**
Gordon, John W., R-Mich. (14), **351**
Gore, Al, 508
Gorman, Jeffrey R., D-N.J. (6), 389
Gorski, Dennis T., D-N.Y. (30), **429**

Goss, Porter J., R-Fla. (14), **241**
Gossen & Associates, 533
Goudie, LaVinia "Vicky," R-N.C. (4), 68, **434**
Gould, Diane, 293
Gould, Noel, 122
Gouty Co., Robert, 190, 203
Gradison, Bill, R-Ohio (2), 300, **445**
Graham, Bob, D-Fla., *19, 30, 32,* 33, *34, 35,* 75, 84, 88, *95,* 101, **113**
Graham, Dick, R-Fla. (7), 234
Gramm, Phil, R-Texas, 225
Grams, Rod, R-Minn. (6), **359**
Grandy, Fred, R-Iowa (5), **300**
Granite Group, 166
Grant, Bill, R-Fla., **113**
Grass Roots Association, 380
Grassley, Charles E., R-Iowa, *30,* 31, *35,* 66, 86, 90, *95, 102,* **119,** 298
Gray, William H., III, D-Pa., 100, 475
Great Lakes Communications, 74, 96
Green, Bill, R-N.Y. (14), *22, 25,* 52, 63, **413**
Green, Gene, D-Texas (29), 25, 79, *80,* 94, **541**
Green, Peter, R-Calif. (45), 207
Greenberg-Lake, 74, 76, 88, *89,* 112, 277, 289, 345, 347, 353, 384, 401, 438, 568
Greene, Enid, R-Utah (2), **544**
Greene, Richard H., I-Calif. (36), **198**
Greenwood, James C., R-Pa. (8), 23, 56-57, *93,* **481**
Greer, Margolis, Mitchell & Associates, 74, 84, *85,* 109, 121, 130, 139, 223, 576
Gregg, Judd, R-N.H., **126**
Grevatt, Martha Kathryn, I-Ohio, **131**
Griffin, Robin Dornan, 24, 208
Gropper, John L., R-Vt., 139
Grossman, Nicki, D-Fla. (20), 247
Grote, Steve, I-Ohio (1), **444**
Grotta Co., John, *89,* 132
Groundswell Direct, 330
Group 53, 124
Groves, Cheney & Associates, 535
Guarini, Frank J., D-N.J., 396
Gudenas, Edmund, I-Ohio (11), **454**
Gunderson, Steve, R-Wis. (3), 24, 29, **572**
Guttierrez, Luis V., D-Ill. (4), **269**
Guttman, Al, D-Pa. (14), 487
Guzman, Robert, R-Calif. (33), **195**
GVA Productions, 432

Haar, Charlene, R-S.D., 28, 59, 62, 69, **137**
Hagglund, Carey, *87*
Hair, Mattox, D-Fla. (4), 56, **231**
Hall, Ralph M., D-Texas (4), 24, 513, **516**
Hall, Tony P., D-Ohio (3), **446**
Hamburg, Dan, D-Calif. (1), 83, **163**

Hamilton, Lee H., D-Ind. (9), **294**
Hamilton & Staff, 245, 550
Hammelman Associates, *87,* 177
Hammerschmidt, John Paul, R-Ark., 161
Hammersmith, Donalda Ann, R-Wis. (5), **574**
Hampson, Glenn C., R-Wash. (7), **564**
Hamrick, Steve, R-Ky. (1), **305**
Hancock, Mel, R-Mo. (7), **373**
Haney, Robert P., Jr., D-N.J. (13), **396**
Hanover Associates, 547
Hanover Communications, 59, *85,* 128
Hansen, Daniel M., I-Nev. (2), **381**
Hansen, James V., R-Utah (1), **543**
Hardy, Rick, R-Mo. (9), 57, **375**
Hare, Don, D-Mich. (5), 342
Harkin, Tom, D-Iowa, 84
Harkins, John C., D-Pa. (21), **494**
Harlan-Evans, 202
Harman, Jane, D-Calif. (36), *19, 22,* 65, 69, 88, *93,* 167, **198**
Harnell-Cohen Associates, 255
Harold, Paul, D-Mass. (10), 337
Harrington, Richard R., R-Utah (3), **545**
Harris, Claude, D-Ala., 51
Harris & Drutt, 488
Harrison & Goldberg, 108, 310, 328
Hartnett, Thomas F., R-S.C., **136**
Hartstone, Roger, D-Ariz. (3), **155**
Harvey, Paul, R-Miss. (5), 366
Haskins, Brad, R-Mich. (7), 344
Hastert, Dennis, R-Ill. (14), 9, 29, 53, **279**
Hastings, Alcee L., D-Fla. (23), **250**
Hastings, Richard "Doc," R-Wash. (4), **561**
Hatch, Bill, R-N.H. (2), **383**
Hatcher, Charles, D-Ga., 52, 69, 252, 410
Hattery, Thomas H., D-Md. (6), 49, 63, 88, **325**
Haughey, Tom, R-Texas (15), **527**
Havely, Robert S., 432
Hawkins, Ronald C., D-Ill. (18), **283**
Hayes, Charles A., D-Ill. (1), 266, 410
Hayes, Fredric, R-La. (7), **317**
Hayes, Jimmy, D-La. (7), 53, **317,** 513
Hayes, Terry, R-Ark. (1), **159**
Hays, John Doug, D-Ky. (5), 5, **309**
Headquarters, basic expenses, 18, 20-21
    top twenty-five candidate expenditures on, 19
Heath, Josie, D-Colo., 74, 111
Heather, Jerry, 169
Hebrock & Associates, 245, 248
Heffernan, Edward J., D-Md. (8), **327**
Hefley, Joel, R-Colo. (5), **219**

Hefner, W. G. "Bill," D-N.C. (8), 28, **438**
Heinz, John, R-Pa., 29, 67, 84, 134, 135, 475, 489
Helfert & Associates, D., 522
Helms, Catherine L., D-Wis. (8), **577**
Helms, Jesse, R-N.C., 5, 9, 59, 84, 128, 273, 439, 442
Henry, Paul B., R-Mich. (3), **340**
Henspeter, Floyd A., I-Minn. (8), 361
Herbert, Bea, D-Calif. (51), **213**
Herbolsheimer, Robert T., R-Ill. (11), **276**
Herger, Wally, R-Calif. (2), 53, **164**
Hernandez, J. "Jay," R-Calif. (34), **196**
Herschensohn, Bruce, R-Calif., *19, 22, 26, 30,* 75, 79, *80, 81,* 84, 86, *95,* 96, 99, **109**
Herschler, Jon, D-Wyo. (AL), **579**
Hertel, Dennis M., D-Mich., 349
Herwig, Phil, R-Minn. (8), **361**
Heskett, Clifford S., D-Ohio (7), 43, **450**
Hewes, Billy, R-Miss. (5), 366
Hickey, Michael C., Jr., D-Md. (2), **321**
Hickman-Brown Research, *89,* 121, 123, 366, 501, 506, 507, 511
High Plains Advertising Agency, 301
High Tech Campaign Consultants, 178
Hildt, Barbara, D-Mass. (6), 333
Hill Research Consultants, *89,* 92, 184, 217
Hill, Anita F., 3-4, 61, 62, 63, 67, 68, 69, 134, 168
Hill, Jerry, R-Okla. (2), **464**
Hilliard, Earl F., D-Ala. (7), 149, **151**
Hilton & Myers Advertising, 157
Hinaman, Randy, *91,* 552
Hinchey, Maurice D., D-N.Y. (26), 69, **425**
Hinds, Margery, I-Calif. (26) **188**
Hinkle & Scannel Advertising, 302
Hoagland, Peter, D-Neb. (2), *25,* 88, **378**
Hobbs, David, R-Texas (12), 36, **524,** 538
Hobson, David L., R-Ohio (7), 43, 47, **450**
Hochbrueckner, George J., D-N.Y. (1), **400,** 420
Hoekstra, Peter, R-Mich. (2), 50, 52, **339**
Hofeld, Albert F., D-Ill., 59, 117
Hogan, Lawrence J., Jr., R-Md. (5), **324**
Hogan, Nolan & Stites, 445
Hogan, Tom, R-Fla. (5), **232**
Hogsett, Joseph H., D-Ind., 59, 84, 86, *95,* **118**

Hoke, Martin R., R-Ohio (10), 57, 63, **453**
Holiday cards, top fifteen candidate expenditures on, *32*
Holden, Tim, D-Pa. (6), **479**
Holekamp, Malcolm L., R-Mo. (3), 17, **369**
Hollin, Larry, R-Pa. (2), **475**
Hollings, Ernest F., D-S.C., *19,* 21, *22, 24, 26, 30, 32, 34, 35,* 88, *95,* **136**
Holloway, Clyde C., R-La. (6), **316**
Holt, Christopher A., 572
Holt, Ron, D-Utah (1), **453**
Holtzman, Elizabeth, D-N.Y., 96, 127
Honigman, Dave, R-Mich. (11), 348
Hood, Light & Geise, 490
Hood, Robin, D-N.C. (6), **436**
Hoover & Associates, Don, 463
Hopcraft Communications, 83, *91,* 163
Hopkins, Larry J., R-Ky., 51, 310
Horn, Joan Kelly, D-Mo. (2), 17, 52, 63, 367, **368**
Horn, Steve, R-Calif. (38), **200**
Horne, William T., R-S.C. (5), 54, **501**
Horton, Frank, R-N.Y., 51, 426
Horvath, Janos, R-Ind. (10), 14, **295**
Hosley, Morrison J., Jr., R-N.Y. (24), *81,* **423**
Hottman Edwards Advertising, 321
Houghton, Amo, R-N.Y. (31), 16, **430**
Houston Communications, John, 413
Hoye, Terry C., 551
Hoyer, Steny H., D-Md. (5), 14, *19, 24, 30, 93,* **324**
HTH & Associates, 374
Hubbard, Carroll, Jr., D-Ky. (1), 23, 51, 101, 305
Huckabee, Mike, R-Ark., **108**
Huckaby, Jerry, D-La. (5), *30, 93, 102,* **315,** 526
Huckaby Rodriguez, *91,* 92, 164, 184, 201
Hudgens, Ralph, R-Ga. (10), **260**
Huening, Tom, R-Calif. (14), 65, **176**
Huffington, Michael, R-Calif. (22), 4, *19, 22, 25, 34,* 52, 55, 57, 65, 88, 92, *93,* 98, **184**
Hughes, Brian M., D-N.J. (4), **387**
Hughes, William J., D-N.J. (2), 92, **385**
Hulburt, W. A. "Bill," R-Va. (5), **551**
Humbert, Thomas M., I-Pa. (19) , **492**
Hunt Communications, 371
Hunt, Ed, R-Calif. (20), **182**
Hunt, Marmillion & Associates, *91*
Hunter, Duncan, R-Calif. (52), *30,* 90, **214**
Hunter, G. William, R-Calif. (9), **171**

Hunter, Susan, 262, 337
Husik & Associates, Mark, 395
Hutchinson, Barbara, I-Calif. (50), 69, **212**
Hutchinson, Tim, R-Ark. (3), **161**
Hutchison, Kay Bailey, R-Texas, 63
Hutto, Earl, D-Fla. (1), 55, 96, **228**
Hyde Co., Anne, 55, 96, 201
Hyde, Henry J., R-Ill. (6), **271**

IMPAC 2000, 34, 37
Impact Media, 481
Independent expenditures, 73-74, 79-81, 98
 by the AFL-CIO, 73, 74, *81*
 by the American Medical Association, 79, 80, *81*
 by the Auto Dealers and Drivers for Free Trade, 81
 by the California Association of Realtors, 74
 by the English Language Political Action Committee, 74
 by the National Abortion Rights Action League, 74, *81*
 by the National Association of Realtors, 74, 79, 80, *81*
 by the National Committee to Preserve Social Security and Medicare, 73
 by the National Rifle Association, 73, 79, *80,* 81, 98
 by the National Right to Life Committee, 80, *81*
 by the Small Business Coalition, 73
 top fifteen independent expenditures, by organization, 79
Information Research Associates, 279
Inglis, Bob, R-S.C. (4), 63, **500**
Inhofe, James M., R-Okla. (1), **463**
Inouye, Daniel K., D-Hawaii, 9, 13, *19,* 21, *26, 28, 30,* 33, *34, 35,* 37, *95,* 101, 112, **115,** 117
Inslee, Jay, D-Wash. (4), **561**
Intelligent Software Systems, 44, 174, 383
Investments, 20
Irvin, Wilma Knox, D-La. (2), **312**
Issues Management Group, 311
Istook, Ernest Jim, Jr., R-Okla. (5), **467**

J.A.G. Associates, 279
J.G.R. & Associates, 245
J.L. Media, 463, 468
JASA Associates, 302
Jackson, Dorothy, 410
Jacobs, Andrew, Jr., D-Ind. (10), 13-14, **295,** 532
Jacobs, Jeffrey P., R-Ohio (13), 456
Jamestown Associates, 395
Jantsch Communications, 372
Jarvis, Judy, R-Calif. (49), 62, 64, 75, **211**
Jayhawk Consulting, 303

JDS Group, 177
Jefferson Marketing, 84
Jefferson, William J., D-La. (2), 47, 48, 61, **312**
Jenkins, Daniel, R-Va. (3), **549**
Jensen, Barbara, D-N.J. (6), 389
Jesernig, Jim, D-Wash. (4), **561**
Jezer, Rhea, D-N.Y. (25), **424**
JHM & Associates, 146
John and Engel, 274
Johnson & Associates, 282, 328
Johnson & Associates, Wayne C., 164, 166, 173
Johnson, Brook, R-Conn., 84, 90, *95,* 99, **112**
Johnson, Dale, R-Tenn. (4), **507**
Johnson, Don, D-Ga. (10), **260**
Johnson, Eddie Bernice, D-Texas (30), 64, **542**
Johnson, Nancy L., R-Conn. (6), 9, 22, *24,* **226**
Johnson Research Associates, 472
Johnson, Roger C., I-La. (2), **312**
Johnson, Sam, R-Texas (3), *19, 30,* 90, **515**
Johnson Survey Research, Bill, *89,* 396, 405
Johnson, Tim, D-S.D. (AL), 54, 86, 94, **503**
Johnston, Bennett, D-Calif. (6), 168
Johnston, Gordon R., R-Pa. (4), 57, **477**
Johnston, Harry A., D-Fla. (19), **246**
Johnston, J. Bennett, D-La., 86, 168
Jones & Associates, Dan, 138, 543
Jones, Ben, D-Ga. (10), 254, 260, 365
Jones, Charles, D-La. (4), **314**
Jones, Earl, D-N.C. (12), 442
Jones, John E., R-Pa. (6), **479**
Jones, Kervin, R-Ala. (7), **151**
Jones, Shelia A., I-Ill. (9), **274**
Jones, Walter B., Jr., D-N.C. (1), 431
Jontz, Jim, D-Ind. (5), 57, **290**
Jordan, Mary E., I-Alaska, **106**
JRA Communications, 154
Jude, Tad, D-Minn. (6), 359
Junas, Dan, 559

KaestnerBodway, 24, 572
Kagel Research Associates, 138
Kahn, Doug, D-Calif. (27), **189**
Kanjorski, Paul E., D-Pa. (11), *32,* **484**
Kaplan Advertising, 122
Kaplovitz Associates, Barry, 332
Kaptur, Marcy, D-Ohio (9), 76, **452**
Kara Group, 246
Kasich, John R., R-Ohio (12), **455**
Kasten, Bob, R-Wis., 18, *19,* 21, *22, 26, 30, 32,* 80, *81,* 86, 88, *95, 102,* **117,** 141
Katz Communications Group, 558
Kaye & Associates, Michael, 125
Keating, Charles H., Jr., 131
Kelly, John, D-Mich. (14), 351

Kemp, Jack, 107, 127, 156, 184, 223, 245, 318, 492, 565
Kemper-Odell & Associates, 579
Kempthorn, Dirk, R-Idaho, *95,* **116**
Kennedy, Beverly, R-Fla. (20), 247
Kennedy, Joseph P., II, D-Mass. (8), *19,* 21, *26, 30,* 61, **335,** 336
Kennedy, Michael J., D-Ill. (10), **275**
Kennedy Communications, 571
Kennelly, Barbara B., D-Conn. (1), 34, 53, 221
Kent Industries, 380
Kerry, John, D-Mass., 84
Kessler, Frederick P., D-Wis. (5), 574
Ketchel, Terry, R-Fla. (1), 55, **228**
Keyes, Alan L., R-Md., 101, **123**
Khachaturian, Jon, I-La., 4, 9, 59, **122**
Kielhorn & Associates, Thomas, *89*
Kildee, Dale E., D-Mich. (9), *34,* **346**
Kilker, Paul V., D-Pa. (19), **492**
Killian & Co. Advertising, 274
Kim, Jay C., R-Calif. (41), *23,* 48, **203**
Kimbrough, Jay, R-Texas (27), **539**
King, Byron W., R-Pa. (14), **487**
King, James H., I-Fla. (14), **241**
King, Peter T., R-N.Y. (3), 59, **402**
Kingston, Jack, R-Ga. (1), 75-76, **251**
Kinney Productions, Paul, *85,* 140, 169, 175
Kirschbaum Corporate Marketing, 106
Kitchens, Powell & Kitchens, *89,* 94, 239, 246, 257, 468, 499, 508, 536
Kleczka, Gerald D., D-Wis. (4), **573**
Klein & Associates, Walt, 218
Klein Associates, Barbara, *87,* 96
Klein, Herbert C., D-N.J. (8), *93,* **391**
Klink, Ron, D-Pa. (4), 57, **477**
Klug, Scott L., R-Wis. (2), 39, **571**
Knapp, Cheryl Davis, D-Fla. (9), **236**
Knollenberg, Joe, R-Mich. (11), **348**
Koch, Edward, 127
Koerner Associates, Christine, 147, 287, 289
Kolbe, Jim, R-Ariz. (5), **157**
Kolbe, Tom, D-Colo. (6), **220**
Kolodziej, Gloria J., I-N.J. (8), **391**
Kolter, Joe, D-Pa. (4), 3, 52, 57, 477
Kondner, Kenneth, R-Md. (7), **326**
Konrad, Richard, D-Texas (22), **534**
Kooistra, Carol S., D-Mich. (3), **340**
Koop, C. Everett, 275
Kopala, Noel, I-Texas (3), **515**
Kopetski, Mike, D-Ore. (5), 39, **473**
Korsmo, John T., R-N.D. (AL), **443**
Kostmayer, Peter H., D-Pa. (8), 23, *24,* 56, *93,* 408, **481**
Kovaleski, Chuck, D-Fla. (8), **235**
KRC Research, *89,* 92, 270, 408
Kraft, Lorelei, D-Minn. (7), 360

Kranzler Kingsley Communications Corp., *85,* 129, 130
Kreidler, Mike, D-Wash. (9), **566**
Kucinich, Dennis, D-Ohio (19), 462
Kurtz, Bill, R-Mich. (1), 338
Kuumba, Amani S., I-Calif. (16), **178**
Kuwata Communications, 90, *91*
Kyl, Jon, R-Ariz. (4), 20, **156**
Kyrillos, Joseph M., R-N.J. (6), **389**

LaFalce, John J., D-N.Y. (29), **428**
Lagomarsino, Robert J., R-Calif. (22), 4, 5, 22, 52, 98, 184, 185, 210
Lake Productions, Sandi, 240
Lambert, Blanche, D-Ark. (1), 49-50, 63, 65, **159**
Lamm, Richard D., D-Colo., 74, 111
Lamontagne, Ovide, R-N.H. (1), 382
Lancaster, H. Martin, D-N.C. (3), 432, **433**
Lander, Joseph L., 232
Lantos, Tom, D-Calif. (12), 20, 23, 24, *25, 30, 32, 35,* 37, 44, 76, 86, **174,** 383
LaRocco, Larry, D-Idaho (1), **264**
Large, Ingrid/Studio Advertising, 419
Larkin, Patrick, R-Mass. (1), **328**
Laruccia, Janice, 192
Lauer, Lalley & Associates, 76, *89,* 299, 306, 310, 358, 576
Laughlin, Greg, D-Texas (14), 86, 94, **526**
Lautenschlager, Peggy A., D-Wis. (6), **575**
Lawlor, James J., D-Conn. (5), 43, 69, 80, **225**
Lawrence, William J., I-Utah (1), **543**
Lazio, Rick A., R-N.Y. (2), 59, **401**
Leach, Jim, R-Iowa (1), **296,** 298
Legal services, 18, 24-25
  top twenty-five House candidate expenditures on, 25
Leahey, Joseph P., D-N.Y. (31), **430**
Leahy, Patrick J., D-Vt., 16, *28, 30, 32, 34, 35,* 36, 84, 88, **139**
Lee & Associates, Silas, 312
Lee, Douglas E., R-Ill. (19), **284**
Lee, Roger & Carol Beddo Associates, *89,* 211, 212, 431
Leggett, Richard, 552
Lehman, Richard H., D-Calif. (19), *35, 37,* 86, *93,* **181,** 364
Lehman, William, D-Fla., 26, 244
Lehmann, Lucie, 123
Lent, Norman F., R-N.Y., 51, 402
Lepinske, Harry C., R-Ill. (3), **268**
Lester & Associates, Ron, 244, 261, 549
Levin, Carl, D-Mich., 86
Levin, Sander M., D-Mich. (12), *22, 24, 25, 30, 93,* **349**
Levine, Jonathan L., D-N.Y. (20), **419**

Levine, Mel, D-Calif., 69, 100, 194
Levine, Paula, 87
Levy, David A., R-N.Y. (4), **403**
Lewis, James M., I-Ala. (7), **151**
Lewis, Jerry, R-Calif. (40), 33, *34, 35,* 36, **202,** 538
Lewis, John, D-Ga. (5), 27, **255**
Lewis, Steve, D-Okla., *28, 102,* 132
Lewis, Tom, R-Fla. (16), **243**
Lichtman, Allan J., 536
Lieberman, Joseph I., D-Conn., 110
Lightfoot Advertising, Harry, 374
Lightfoot, Jim Ross, R-Iowa (3), *26,* 36, 90, **298,** 538
Lightle, Bill, D-Ga. (8), 258
Lihn Associates, Charles, 547
Like Dempictures & Post, 160
Lindblad, John Paul, I-Calif. (24), **186**
Linder, John, R-Ga. (4), 23, 50, **254**
Linn, Dave, I-Calif. (9), **171**
Lipinski, William O., D-Ill. (3), 4, **268**
Lippe, Pamela, 96
Lipstock, Richard, I-Tenn. (9), **512**
Little, Larry D., D-N.C. (12), 442
Livingston, Robert L., R-La. (1), 61, 97, **311**
Lloyd, Marilyn, D-Tenn. (3), 70, **506**
Lloyd-Jones, Jean, D-Iowa, 63, 65-66, 69, **119**
LoBiondo, Frank A., R-N.J. (2), **385**
Long, Jill L., D-Ind. (4), **289**
Long, Ronald J., R-Iowa (3), 298
Longsworth, John, D-Texas (10), 522
Loomis & Pollock, 262
Lorenz, Mindy, I-Calif. (22), **184**
Losser & Associates, *87,* 117
Love, Tom, D-Kan. (3), **303**
Lovett, Woodrow, R-Ga. (11), **261**
Lowe Advertising, George, 563
Lowe, Ted, I-Calif. (48), **210**
Lowery, Bill, R-Calif., 4, 51, 213
Lowey, Nita M., D-N.Y. (18), 25, 90, **416**
Lucas, Frank R., D-N.J. (5), **388**
Ludeman, Cal R., R-Minn. (2), **355**
Luken, Charles, D-Ohio (1), 444
Lukens Co., *87,* 300
Lukens, Donald E. "Buz," R-Ohio, 4
Lum, Albert C., D-Calif. (30), 192
Lumina, Luke, I-Mass. (4), **331**
Lunde & Burger, 402
Lunde, Paul, R-Iowa (4), **299**
Lungren & Co., *87*

Machtley, Ronald K., R-R.I. (1), 448, **495**
Mackin, Lawrence C., I-Mass. (9), **336**
MacWilliams/Cosgrove, 319, 337, 425
Macy & Associates, Tim, *87*
Maddox & Associates, John, 80, 217, 265
Madigan, Edward, R-Ill., 279, 280

Madison Group, *87, 89,* 140, 561
Mahe Jr. & Associates, Eddie, 90, *91,* 106
Maitland, Ian, R-Minn. (4), **357**
Makiaris Media Services, 226
Malberg, Patricia, D-Calif. (4), 166
Malchow & Co., *87,* 92, 112, 337
Mallan, Lloyd "Jeff," I-Hawaii (2), **263**
Maloney, Carolyn B., D-N.Y. (14), 63, **413**
Maltese, Serphin, 96
Mandate: Campaign Media, 536
Mandell, Paul, D-Minn. (3), 43, **356**
Mangopoulos, John, R-Mich. (8), 345
Mankivsky, Kathy, 279
Mann, David, D-Ohio (1), **444**
Manton, Thomas J., D-N.Y. (7), *30, 35,* **406**
Manzullo, Donald, R-Ill. (16), **281**
Margolies-Mezvinsky, Marjorie, D-Pa. (13), *22,* **486**
Margolis, Gwen, D-Fla. (22), 14, 80, 88, **249**
Market Strategies, *89,* 92
Marketing Associates, *87*
Marketing Research Institute, 281
Marketing Resource Group, *85, 89,* 345
Marketing Strategies, 278
Markey, Edward J., D-Mass. (7), 90, **334**
Marlenee, Ron, R-Mont. (AL), *19, 22, 26, 28, 30,* 36, *93,* **376,** 538
Marmen Computing, 343
Marotta, Marc, D-Wis. (5), 574
Martin Public Relations, Bill, 381
Martin, David O'B., R-N.Y., 423
Martin, Linda B., I-Hawaii, 115
Martin, Lynn, 107, 281, 520
Martinez, Matthew G., D-Calif. (31), *37,* **193**
Marttila & Kiley, 334, 335, 408
Mascara, Frank R., D-Pa. (20), 493
Mason Lundberg & Associates, *91,* 92, 184, 201, 208
Masterson, Steve, R-Texas (24), **536**
Matrixx Marketing, *91*
Matsui, Robert T., D-Calif. (5), *19, 25, 30, 32, 34, 35,* 36, *37,* 76, **167**
Mattis, Charles D., D-Ill. (15), **280**
Maverick Communications, 94, 526
Mavromatis, Dottie, 525
Mavroules, Nicholas, D-Mass. (6), 24, *25,* **333**
Maxwell & Associates, *87,* 90, *91,* 94, 155, 157, 249, 489, 534
Maynard, Richard E., D-Ill. (17), 282
Mazzoli, Romano L., D-Ky. (3), 307
MBM Consulting, *91,* 553
McCabe, Patricia, D-Calif. (45), **207**
McCain, John, R-Ariz., *19,* 24, *26, 30, 32, 35,* 36, 59, 61, 65, 66-67, 75, 85-86, *95,* 102, **107**
McCampbell, Bill, R-Calif. (17), **179**

McCandless, Al, R-Calif. (44), **206**
McCanse & Associates, Ross, 125
McCarthy, Leo T., D-Calif., 69, 170
McCarthy, Neil, D-N.Y. (19), **418**
McClanahan, Molly, D-Calif. (39), 55-56, **201**
McClintock, Tom, R-Calif. (24), 53, **186**
McCloskey, Frank, D-Ind. (8), **293**
McCollum, Bill, R-Fla. (8), 23, *24*, 234, **235**
McConkey, William, 106
McCorkle III, Pope, 432
McCormack, Tim, D-Ohio (19), 462
McCormick, Edward J., III, R-Mass. (4), **331**
McCrery, Jim, R-La. (5), 23, 24, 315, 448
McCuen, W. J. "Bill," D-Ark. (4), 79, *80*, **162**
McCullogh Advertising, 146
McCurdy, Dave, D-Okla. (4), 26, 27, *30*, 31, **466**
McDade, Joseph M., R-Pa. (10), 24, 25, *102*, **483**
McDermott, Jim, D-Wash. (7), *35*, 36, **564**
McDougall Associates, 333
McDowell, Robert, 510
McElroy, Mike, D-Mich. (1), 338
McEwen, Bob, R-Ohio (6), *26, 32, 47*, **449**
McGinn, Mike, R-Texas (6), 518
McGowan, Patrick K., D-Maine (2), **319**
McGrath, Raymond J., R-N.Y., 403
McHale, Paul, D-Pa. (15), 79, **488**
McHugh, John M., R-N.Y. (24), **423**
McHugh, Matthew F., D-N.Y., 69, 425
McInnis, Scott, R-Colo. (3), 80, *81*, **217**
McKenna, Dolly Madison, R-Texas (25), 62, **537**
McKeon & Associates, 268, 279, 280
McKeon, Howard P. "Buck," R-Calif. (25), **187**
McKinney, Cynthia A., D-Ga. (11), 14, 48, **261**, 564
McKinnon Media, 94, 161,.257, 514, 541
McManus, Gretchen S., I-N.Y. (31), **430**
McMillan, Alex, R-N.C. (9), 9, **439**
McMillan, Jack L., R-Miss. (4), **365**
McMillen, Tom, D-Md. (1), *19*, 21, 23, *24, 26, 30*, 59, 88, *93*, **320**
McNair, Chris, D-Ala., 105
McNally, Temple & Associates, 88, *89*, 92, 157, 172, 184
McNulty, Michael R., D-N.Y. (21), *35*, **420**
McSlarrow, Kyle E., R-Va. (8), 47, **554**
M. E. M. & Associates, 321

Meals, 13, 33-34
Mecham, Evan, I-Ariz., **107**
Media Co., *85*, 92, 135, 198, 304, 369, 537
Media Group, 94, 129, 136, 137, 289, 293, 462, 503
Media Placement, 222
Media Plus, *85*, 140, 392
Media Solutions, *85*, 114
Media Southwest, 518, 520
Media Strategies, 49, 159, 373
Media Strategies & Research, *85*, 161, 240, 242, 315, 322, 466, 524, 570
Media Strategy Associates, 96
Media Targeting, 231
Media Team, *85*, 94, 131, 132, 308, 386
Meehan, Martin T., D-Mass. (5), *93*, **332**
Meek, Carrie, D-Fla. (17), 149, **244**
Meeker, Tony, R-Ore. (1), **469**
Mellman & Lazarus, 74, 76, 80, 88, *89*, 92, 324, 349, 432, 471, 537
Mendenhall, Warner D., D-Ohio (16), 9, **459**
Menendez, Robert, D-N.J. (13), 48, **396**
Mentzer Media Services, *85*, 253, 292, 481, 552, 570, 577
Merrill, Bruce D., 119
Message & Media, 389, 396
Metcalf, Jack, R-Wash. (2), **559**
Metz, Larry, R-Fla. (19), **246**
Meyer Associates, 86, 96, 137, 282, 354, 360
Meyers Co., Michael D., 92
Meyers, Jan, R-Kan. (3), **303**
Meyers, John, 565
Mfume, Kweisi, D-Md. (7), *30*, 31-32, *34*, **326**
Mica, John L., R-Fla. (7), 23, 88, **234**, 235
Michaux, Mickey, D-N.C. (12), 442
Michel, Robert H., R-Ill. (18), *30, 32*, 90, 226, **283**
Mikulski, Barbara A., D-Md., *19, 24, 30, 34, 35*, 86, *95*, 101, **123**
Miles Associates, Bill, 362
Miller, Dan, R-Fla. (13), 57, 88, **240**
Miller, Clarence E., R-Ohio (6), 449
Miller, George, D-Calif. (7), *32, 35, 37*, 76, 99, **169**
Miller, John, R-Wash. (1), 558
Miller, Kristal, 545
Miller, Mark, I-Ohio (13), **456**
Miller, William E., Jr., R-N.Y. (29), **428**
Miltner, John H., D-Mich. (2), **339**
Mims, Tom, D-Fla. (12), **239**
Mineta, Norman Y., D-Calif. (15), *19, 30, 32, 35*, 36, *37*, 88, **177**
Minge, David, D-Minn. (2), **355**
Mink, Patsy T., D-Hawaii (2), **263**
Mitchell Communications, Edward, *85*, 484

Mitchell, George J., D-Maine, 97, 110, 125
Moakley, Joe, D-Mass. (9), *19, 22, 24, 25*, **336**
Moffitt, Karen, D-Fla. (10), **237**
Molina-Avila, Martha, 192
Molinari, Susan, R-N.Y. (13), **412**
Mollohan, Alan B., D-W. Va. (1), *102*, *567*, 568
Monroe Marketing, 251
Montgomery & Associates, Elizabeth, 300
Montgomery, Arthur S., R-Mo. (1), **367**
Montgomery, G. V. "Sonny," D-Miss. (3), **364**
Moody, Edward "Gomer," R-Mo. (5), **371**
Moody, Jim, D-Wis., 141, 460, 574
Moore Information, *89*, 92, 206, 210
Moorhead, Carlos J., R-Calif. (27), 55, **189**
Moorman, Jesse A., I-Calif. (27), **189**
Moppert, Bob, R-N.Y. (26), **425**
Moran, James P., Jr., D-Va. (8), *30*, 47, 48, **554**
Morella, Constance A., R-Md. (8), **327**
Morgan, Robert, R-Ohio (14), **457**
Morgan & Associates, Dan, *87*, 187, 206, 214, 220, 225, 226, 245, 249, 395, 439, 490, 495, 498, 538
Morgan & Co., William, 452, 506
Morgan/Fletcher & Co., 37-38, 261, 508, 509
Moriarty, Stephen A., R-Minn. (5), **358**
Morris & Carrick, 74, *85*, 110, 167, 353, 408, 502
Morris, Richard, *91*, 234
Morris, Rita-Louise A., D-N.Y. (5), 404
Morrison, Sid, R-Wash., 561
Morrissey, Donald J., 235
Moseley-Braun, Carol, D-Ill., *19, 22, 26, 27, 28, 30*, 59, 61, 62, 63, 65, 69, 75, 84, 86, *95*, 101, *102*, **117**
Mosely, Ken, D-S.C. (6), 502
Moser, Terry Lee, D-Texas (19), **531**
Mottola, Chris, 134, 140, 447, 578
Mourdock, Richard E., R-Ind. (8), **293**
Mrazek, Robert J., D-N.Y., 51
Mueller, Margaret R., R-Ohio (13), 448, **456**
Muir, Don, 169
Multi Media Services Corp., 84, *85*, 96, 127, 402, 406, 418, 423, 492, 515, 538, 578
Munkittrick, Cindy, I-Fla. (5), **232**
Munster, Edward W., R-Conn. (2), 57-58, **222**
Murkowski, Frank H., R-Alaska, *26, 28, 30, 32, 34, 35*, 90, *95*, **106**
Murphy, Austin J., D-Pa. (20), 76, *102*, **493**

Murphy, James E., 96
Murphy, Kathleen M., I-N.Y. (13), **412**
Murphy Media, Mike, *85*, 116, 217, 241, 290, 344, 390, 543
Murray & Associates, David J., *89*, 388
Murray, Patty, D-Wash., 4, 63, 65, 69, 75, 80, 90, *95*, *140*
Murtha, John P., D-Pa. (12), 13, *19, 26, 28, 30, 34, 35*, 101, 460, **485**, 493
Musselwhite, Stephen Alan, D-Va. (6), **552**
Muxlow, Keith, R-Mich. (5), **342**
MWM, *87*, 96
Mybeck, Walter R., D-Ariz. (4), 20, **156**
Myers, John T., R-Ind. (7), *28*, 33, **292**

Nadler, Jerrold, D-N.Y. (8), **407**
Nagle, Dave, D-Iowa (2), *22*, 23, 43, 51, *297*, 576
Nakash, Alice Harriett, I-Mass. (8), 61, **335**
Napolitan Associates, Joseph, 329
Natcher, William H., D-Ky. (2), 13, 76, 295, **306**, 532
National Call Center, 236
National Management Consultants, 314
National Market Share, 518
National Media, 80, 84, *85*, 94, 112, 131, 132, 236, 239, 240, 249, 308, 356, 372, 386, 401
National Productions, 569
National Telecommunications Services, 80, 109, 413
Neal, Richard E., D-Mass. (2), **329**
Neal, Stephen L., D-N.C. (5), 408, **435**
Needham, Pamela D., 86, *87*, 123
Neill, Ben, D-N.C. (10), **440**
Neilson & Associates, Peggy, 252
Nelson, Gary, R-Wash. (1), **558**
Nelson/Ralston/Robb Communications, 156
Nena Advertising, Kathy, 535
Nethken, Frank K., R-Md. (6), 325
Neumann, Mark, R-Wis. (1), *93*, **570**
New Sounds Inc., 370, 562
New South Research, 146
Newhouse, Richard G., I-Calif. (46), **190**
Newkirk, John D., R-Ore. (4), 472
Nichols, Dick, R-Kan. (4), 304
Nickles, Don, R-Okla., *22*, 24, *30*, *35*, 84, 88, 90, *95*, *102*, **132**
Nicolella, William A., D-Pa. (20), 493
Niebauer-Stall, Lisa, D-Minn. (5), 358
N/K Associates, 328, 537
Noble & Associates, 124
Nolte Communications, 281

Noonan, Mike, I-Calif. (41), **203**
Nordlinger Associates, *85,* 148, 218, 247, 346, 567, 568
Norman, Nancy, R-N.Y. (21), **420**
North, Oliver, 555
Norton, Eleanor Holmes, D-D.C., 61, 63, 272
November Group, 88, *89,* 92, 136, 238, 369, 392, 401, 511
Nugent, John, 539
Nussle, Jim, R-Iowa (2), 3, 36, 43, 47, 51, *93,* **297,** 538

Oakar, Mary Rose, D-Ohio (10), *25, 30,* 57, 63, *93,* 101, *102,* **453**
Oberst, Bill, Jr., D-S.C. (1), **497**
Oberstar, James L., D-Minn. (8), *35,* 36, 94, **361**
Obey, David R., D-Wis. (7), **576**
Ochoa, Gloria, D-Calif. (22), 4, 98, **184**
O'Dell, Gloria, D-Kan., 69, 75, **120**
Odell, Roper & Associates, *87,* 225, 394, 395
Off-year spending, 9, 13, 18
  top twenty-five candidate expenditures on, *19*
Olin, Jim, D-Va., 552
Olver, John W., D-Mass. (1), *19, 22,* 84, 86, 92, *93,* **328**
Omann, Bernie, R-Minn. (7), **360**
One Acorn Management, 309
O'Neil, Griffin & Associates, 126, 382
O'Neill, Megan, R-Mich. (9), **346**
Opinion Analysts, 528
Oppidan Group, 453
Optima Direct, 86, *91,* 481
Oregon Campaign Group, 473
O'Reilly, Chuck, D-Was. (3), 560
Oriez, Charles A., D-Colo. (5), **219**
Orlins, Steve A., D-N.Y. (3), 59, 88, *93,* **402**
Orman Communications, Jim, 181
Ortiz, Solomon P., D-Texas (27), *30, 32,* **539**
Orton, Bill, D-Utah (3), **545**
Owens, Major R., D-N.Y. (11), **410**
Owens, Wayne, D-Utah, 30, *95,* **138**
Oxley, Michael G., R-Ohio (4), *35,* **447**

PAC-COM, *87,* 135
P.A.C.E., 124
Pacific Communication Concepts, 195
Packard, Ron, R-Calif. (48), **210**
Packwood, Bob, R-Ore., 9, 18, *19, 22, 23, 24, 30, 35,* 59, 80, *81,* 86, 90, *95,* 99-100, *102,* 109, **133,** 471, 472
PACs. *See* Political action committees.
Padaro Group, 201
Palermo, Alfred D., R-N.J. (10), **393**
Pallone, Frank, Jr., D-N.J. (6), 22, 24, 53, **389**

Pamplin, Rick, I-Calif. (25), **187**
Panetta, Leon E., D-Calif. (17), *30, 32, 35, 37,* 76, 99, **179**
Pansino, Salvatore, R-Ohio (17), **460**
Pappageorge, John, R-Mich. (12), **349**
Parker Group, *91,* 151
Parker, Mike, D-Miss. (4), **365**
Parrish-Smith Associates, 260
Pastor, Ed, D-Ariz. (2), *19,* **154**
Patrick, Kerry, R-Kan. (3), 303
Patterson, Liz J., D-S.C. (4), 63, **500**
Pauken, Tom, R-Texas (3), 515
Pavlik & Associates, *89,* 536
Paxon, Bill, R-N.Y.(27), **426,** 428
Payco American Corp., 39, *91,* 92, 227, 240, 265, 390, 458, 571, 578
Payne & Associates, 559
Payne & Co., Daniel B., 331
Payne, Donald M., D-N.J. (10), 24, **393**
Payne, Lewis F., Jr., D-Va. (5), **551**
Payne, Ross Associates, 551
Payne, William, 24, 393
Payton & Associates, Tony, *91,* 381
Pease, Don J., D-Ohio, 456
Pecora, Frank A., D-Pa. (18), **491**
Pederson & Thompson, 153, 338, 371
Pelosi, Nancy, D-Calif. (8), 27, *35,* 36, 37, 76, **170**
PEM Management, 128
Penczner Productions, 510
Pendleton Productions, 106
Penichet, Jeff J., D-Calif. (30), 192
Penn & Schoen Associates, *89,* 96, 391, 392, 416, 438, 444
Penny, Timothy J., D-Minn. (1), **354**
Penta Corp., 280
Perkins, Carl C., D-Ky., 51
Perkins Group, *85,* 118, 291
Permanent campaign, 9, 13-14, 17-38
  automobiles, 13, 27-28
    top fifteen candidate expenditures on, *28*
  average costs of, 20
  constituent entertainment and gifts, 13, 18, 31-33
    top fifteen candidate expenditures on holiday cards, *32*
    top twenty-five candidate expenditures on, *30*
  consultants, 20
  donations, 13, 20, 34-37
    top twenty-five candidate expenditures on, *35*
  election year spending, 13, 18
  fund raising, 18, 29, 31
    top twenty-five candidate expenditures on, *30*
  headquarters basic expenses, 18, 20-21
    top twenty-five candidate expenditures on, *19*
  investments, 20

  legal services, 18, 24-25
    top twenty-five House candidate expenditures on, *25*
  meals, 13, 33-34
  off-year spending, 9, 13, 18
    top twenty-five candidate expenditures on, *19*
  role in seeking higher office, 37-38
  staff salaries, 18, 21-24
    top twenty-five candidate expenditures on, *22*
  substitute for local party organizations, 18, 38
  travel, 18, 25-27
    top twenty-five candidate expenditures on, *26*
Perot, H. Ross, 3, 44, 280, 361, 379
Persons Communications, Todd, 234
Peters, Louanner, I-Ill. (2), **267**
Peters, Robert, D-Pa. (16), **489**
Peterson, Collin C., D-Minn. (7), 40, **360**
Peterson, Donna, R-Texas (2), 62, **514**
Peterson, Pete, D-Fla. (2), **229**
Petr, Robert T., R-Md. (2), 321
Petri, Tom, R-Wis. (6), **575**
Pettyjohn, Jimmy Coy, R-Nev. (1), **380**
Phil-Jac Productions, 244
Philbin, Tim, R-Vt. (AL), **546**
Phillips, Lauri J., R-Wash. (6), **563**
Phillips, Tim, 31, 466, 552
Phone Ventures, 139
Piccirillo Productions, 202
Pickett, Owen B., D-Va. (2), **548**
Pickle, J. J., D-Texas (10), **522**
Pierce Atkins Productions, 562
Pierce, Steven D., R-Mass. (1), *81,* 328
Pierson, Charles W., R-Ind. (4), **289**
Pitts, Terrance L., D-Wis. (5), 574
Planning Experts, 266
Plante, Michael, 568
Plaxco & Associates, John L., 86, *87*
PM Consulting Corp., 107
Political action committees, 13, 14, 29, 30, 31, 34, 40, 69, 73, 84, 97-98
Political Advertising Consultants, *91*
Political Consulting & Management, *91*
Politics Inc., 160, 315, 350, 372, 569, 570
Polito, William P., R-N.Y. (28), 70, **427**
Polka, Sandi, 176
Pollack, Susan, 112
Pollard, Tommy, R-N.C. (3), **433**
Pombo, Richard W., R-Calif. (11), 62, **173,** 189, 538
Pomeroy, Earl, D-N.D. (AL), 31, **443,** 564
Ponzio, Charles J., D-Texas (16), 528
Poore, Floyd G., D-Ky. (4), **308**
Porter, John Edward, R-Ill. (10), **275**

Poshard, Glenn, D-Ill. (19), 4, 51, 96, **284**
Pouland, John, 517
Precision Marketing, *89, 91,* 134, 488
Premier, Maldonado & Associates, 414
Preston Group, 121
Preston, Bob, D-N.H. (1), **382**
Price Advertising, Phil, 531
Price, Bill, R-Okla. (5), **467**
Price, David, D-N.C. (4), 68, **434**
Price, Kamuela, R-Hawaii (2), **263**
Price, Patricia, 217
Pritchett, Jess M., D-Neb. (2), **378**
Privette, Coy C., R-N.C. (8), **438**
Pro Media, *85,* 136, 137, 427, 557
Proctor, Kenneth L., I-Mich. (7), **344**
Product Development, 86
Professional Management, 342
Profit Marketing & Communications, *85*
Progressive Communications, 153
Progressive Group, 171
Pryce, Deborah, R-Ohio (15), 448, **458**
Public Affairs Counsel, 473
Public Opinion Strategies, 80, *89,* 145, 217, 249, 265, 290, 303, 319, 320, 343, 413, 421, 424, 481, 494, 495
Public Sector, 94

Q & A Partners, 269
Quayle, Dan, 29, 119, 164, 181, 225, 289, 346, 572
Quezada, Leticia, D-Calif. (30), 192
Quillen, James H., R-Tenn. (1), *30, 32-33,* **504**
Quinn, Jack, R-N.Y. (30), **429**
Quinn/Lamb Media, 202
Quirk, Maxine B., I-Calif. (47), **209**

Rahall, Nick J., II, D-W. Va. (3), 568, **569**
Rainbow Advertising, 401, 453
Ramsey, Thomas P., III, D-Ga. (9), 259
Ramstad, Jim, R-Minn. (3), 13, *30,* 43, **356**
Rangel, Charles B., D-N.Y. (15), *19, 35, 102,* **414**
Rapp & Associates, Jerry, 283
Raritan Associates, 413
Rauh, John, D-N.H., **126**
Ravenel, Arthur, Jr., R-S.C. (1), 37, **497**
Ravenscroft, Margaret M., D-N.Y. (24), **423**
Ravosa, Anthony W., Jr., R-Mass. (2), **329**
Ray, Richard, D-Ga. (3), *28, 52, 81, 93,* **253**
Reach Communication Specialists, 475

Reagan, Ronald, 136, 440, 455, 463, 562, 569
Redder, Tom, D-Colo. (4), **218**
Redistricting, 4, 5, 9, 14, 50, 51, 52, 55, 57, 63
Reed Associates, Carol, 515
Reed, Jack, D-R.I. (2), 22, 40, **496**
Reed, Rick, R-Hawaii, 9, **115**
Reform, 97-102
  alternatives, 100-102
  House and Senate bills, 97-100
Regula, Ralph, R-Ohio (16), 5, 9, 47, 448, **459**
Reich, Jonathan Abram, D-Ill. (14), 9, **279**
Reid, Harry, D-Nev., *19, 24, 26, 30, 32, 34, 35, 95, 102,* **125**
Reid, Shirley, 268, 408
Reidelbach, Linda S., I-Ohio (15), **458**
Reilly Campaigns, Clinton, *89,* 167, 406
Reliance Consultants, 24, 363
Rendon Co., 329
Renshaw, Lisa G., R-Md. (1), 320
Research Group, 96, 347, 378, 384, 391, 552, 558, 568
Research/Strategy/Management, 341
Response Dynamics, 29, 84, *87,* 107, 208
Ress, Bill, R-Ohio (18), **461**
Reyes, Ben, D-Texas (29), 25, 79, *80,* **541**
Reynolds, Mel, D-Ill. (2), 52, 57, **267**
RHM, 90, *91*
Rhodes, John J., III, R-Ariz. (1), 90, **153**, 448
Rhodes, Virginia, D-Ohio (1), 444
Rich, Smith & Rich, 265
Richards, Leonard J., D-Minn. (8), 361
Richardson, Bill, D-N.M. (3), *26, 35,* 86, 195, **399**
Richardson, H. L. "Bill," R-Calif. (3), *30,* **165**, 189
Richman, Martin, R-N.Y. (17), **416**
Ridder/Braden, *91*
Ridge, Tom, R-Pa. (21), *26,* 27, **494**
Riggs, Frank, R-Calif.(1), *30,* 36, 40, 43, 47, 52, 83, **163**, 210, 538
Rinaldo, Matthew J., R-N.J. (3), 390
Rindy Media, 517, 528
Ringe Media, 92, 184
Ritter, Al, R-Ore. (3), **471**
Ritter, Don, R-Pa. (15), 79, *93,* **488**
RO/LO Creative, 158
Roach Projects, John, 571
Roach, Pam, R-Wash. (8), 565
Robb, Charles S., D-Va., 101
Robbins, Mark A., R-Calif. (29), **191**
Roberts, Christine, I-Calif. (11), **173**
Roberts, David, D-N.Y. (22), **421**
Roberts, Pat, R-Kan. (1), **301**, 304
Robertson, Pat, 432, 557

Robinson, Charles E., D-Texas (8), 9, **520**
Rockefeller, John D., IV, D-W.Va., 110, 140
Rodd & Associates, 527
Rodriguez-Schieman, Hildegarde, R-Ill. (4), **269**
Roe, Robert A., D-N.J., 51, 391
Roemer, Tim, D-Ind. (3), **288**
Rogers, Harold, R-Ky. (5), 5, *32,* 53-54, *93, 102,* **309**
Rohrabacher, Dana, R-Calif. (45), **207**
Roma, Patrick J., R-N.J. (9), **392**
Romaine, Edward P., R-N.Y. (1), **400**
Roosa, Chris, R-Miss. (5), 366
Roots Development, 154
Ros-Lehtinen, Ileana, R-Fla. (18), **245**
Rose, Charlie, D-N.C. (7), 28, **437**
Ross Inc., 283
Ross Communications, 176
Rostenkowski, Dan, D-Ill. (5), 3, 14, 20, 21, 24, *25,* 33, *34, 93,* 267, 268, **270**, 551
Roth, Toby, R-Wis. (8), *30, 32,* **577**
Rothman-Serot, Geri, D-Mo., 59, 62, 63, 69, *95,* **124**
Rothschild, Beryl E., R-Ohio (11), **454**
Rotterman & Associates, 435
Roukema, Marge, R-N.J. (5), **388**
Rove & Company, Karl, 86, *87,* 88, *89,* 132, 233, 316, 518, 520, 533
Rowan & Michaels, 370, 383
Rowland, J. Roy, D-Ga. (8), **258**
Rowland, Richard O., I-Hawaii, 115
Roybal, Edward R., D-Calif., 192, 195
Roybal-Allard, Lucille, D-Calif. (33), **195**
Royce, Ed, R-Calif. (39), 55-56, 189, **201**
Ruder-Finn, 265
Rudman, Warren B., R-N.H., 4, 126
Ruppe, Philip E., R-Mich. (1), **338**
Rush, Bobby L., D-Ill. (1), 266, 410
Rusk, Donald M., D-Calif. (40), **202**
Russo, Marsh & Associates, *85, 89,* 96, 127, 187, 206, 213, 280
Russo, Marty, D-Ill. (3), 4, 170, 268, 511, 564
Rutan, Dick, R-Calif. (42), 189, 190, **204**
Ryan, Judith M., R-Calif. (46), *81,* 208
Ryan & Ryan Public Relations, 403
Ryan, Timothy E., D-N.J. (3), **386**

SAID Inc., 568
Sabo, Martin Olav, D-Minn. (5), **358**
Sacia, Paul, D-Wis. (3), 572
Sadowski, Jeannie, R-Texas (17), **529**
Sage Advertising, 376
Salaries, staff, 18, 21-24

Sanders, Bernard, I-Vt. (AL), *24,* 29, **546**
Sanders, Roger, D-Texas (4), 516
Sandler-Innocenzi, 80, *85,* 162, 217, 234, 265, 309, 320, 397
Sanford, Terry, D-N.C., *19,* 21, *22, 24, 26, 28, 30, 34, 35,* 59, 84, 90, *95,* 99, **128**
Sangmeister, George E., D-Ill. (11), 276, 408
Sann Communications, 413
Santorum, Rick, R-Pa. (18), 47, 166, **491**
Sargent, Claire, D-Ariz., 4, 59, 65, 66, 69, 75, 107
Sarpalius, Bill, D-Texas (13), 513, **525**
Saunders, Carla, 455
Sautter Communications, 289, 293
Savage, Gus, D-Ill. (2), 52, 57, 267
Sawyer, Tom, D-Ohio (14), **457**
Saxton, H. James, R-N.J. (3), 94, **386**
Schaefer, Dan, R-Colo. (6), **220**
Schaffer, Jack, R-Ill. (16), 281
Scheckelhoff, Mary, 576
Schenk, Lynn, D-Calif. (49), 64, 75, *93,* **211**
Scheuer, James H., D-N.Y., 51
Schiff, Steven H., R-N.M. (1), **397**
Schiliro, Philip M., D-N.Y. (4), **403**
Schlafly, Phyllis, 298
Schloemer, Ken, R-Ill. (17), **282**
Schneller, Don, D-Tenn. (6), 509
Schnurr & Jackson, 421
Scholl, Dave, R-Calif. (7), 99, **169**
Schreurs & Associates, *85,* 119, 296, 297, 298
Schrock Company, 566
Schroeder, Patricia, D-Colo. (1), *32,* 62, **215**, 228
Schropfer, Dave, D-Conn. (4), **224**
Schulz, Richard L., R-Ore. (4), 472
Schumer, Charles E., D-N.Y. (9), *35,* 61, **408**, 428
Schwartz, Larry, 408
Schwarz, John, R-Mich. (7), 344
Scott, Dennis, R-Ark. (2), **160**
Scott, Kimberly A., *87,* 246, 247, 314, 396, 488
Scott, Robert C., D-Va. (3), **549**
Scott, Tom, R-Conn. (3), **223**
Seagraves, Jim, R-Ore. (5), **473**
Seay, Lewis E., D-Mo. (4), 370
Sellers, Richard, R-Ala., 9, 59, **105**
Selph, John, D-Okla. (1), 149, **463**
Sendelsky, Leonard R., D-N.J. (7), **390**
Senden, Brad, 289
Sennet, Fred, D-Ohio (8), **451**
Sensenbrenner, F. James, Jr., R-Wis. (9), **578**
Sentinel Corp., 531
Serafin & Associates, 270
Serrano, Jose E., D-N.Y. (16), **415**
Services for Organizational Renewal, 109

Sette, Lou, R-N.J. (5), 388
Severin/Aviles Associates, 9, 333, 406, 439
Seymour, John, R-Calif., 4, 18, *19, 21, 22, 26, 30,* 59, 63, 65, 74, 75, 81, 84, 90, *95,* **110**, 170
SFM Media, 256
Sferrazza, Pete, D-Nev. (2), 70, **381**
Shafto & Barton, 74, *85,* 111, 135, 177, 239, 298, 376, 392, 401, 514, 523, 541, 563
Shapiro & Associates, Beth, 252
Shapiro & Associates, Lynn, 394
Share Systems, 417
Sharp, Philip R., D-Ind. (2), **287**
Sharpe, Mark, R-Fla. (11), **238**
Sharpton, Al, D-N.Y., 96, 127, 414
Shaw, E. Clay, Jr., R-Fla. (22), *24,* 80, *81,* 84, 88, *93,* **249**
Shays, Christopher, R-Conn. (4), **224**
Shea, Dennis C., R-N.Y. (7), **406**
Shea, Michael P., 336
Sheehan Associates, 291, 374
Sheehan Associates, Michael, 96
Sheehan, Thomas R., I-Mass. (2), **329**
Sheehy, Knopf & Shaver, 294, 307
Shelby, Richard C., D-Ala., 9, *26,* 35, 36, 59, 84, 86, 90, 92, *95,* **105**
Shelby/Blaskeg, *87,* 458
Shepherd, Karen, D-Utah (2), 69, **544**
Shimkus, John M., R-Ill. (20), 75, **285**
Shipley & Associates, 540
Shooter, Don, R-Ariz. (2), **154**
Shorr Associates, *85,* 92, 258, 259, 260, 285, 302, 320, 402, 428, 431, 434, 547, 573
Shuster, Bud, R-Pa. (9), *19, 26,* 27, 33, *34, 102,* **482**
Signature Entertainment, 203
Sikorski, Gerry, D-Minn. (6), 88, *93,* **359**
Silby & Associates, Barbara, *87,* 466
Silver State Communication, 203
Simmons & Co., 371, 373
Simon, Paul, D-Ill. (2), 84, 86
Simons Media Techniques, 229
Simpson, Dick, D-Ill. (5), 270
Sinsheimer Group, 148, 332, 433, 438
Sipple Strategic Communications, *85,* 124, 133
Sisisky, Norman, D-Va. (4), 53, **550**
Skaggs, David E., D-Colo. (2), 5, **216**
Skeen, Joe, R-N.M. (2), **398**
Skelton Grover & Associates, 198
Skelton, Ike, D-Mo. (4), *30, 32,* **370**
Skoien, Gary, R-Ill. (8), 273
Slason, Eugene F., D-Conn. (6), 9, **226**
Slatter, David C., I-Texas (28), 48, **540**
Slattery, Jim, D-Kan. (2), **302**

Slaughter, Louise M., D-N.Y. (28), 70, 426, **427**
Sledge, Don, R-Ala. (3), **147**
Sloan, Gurney, 94
Smith & Harroff, 67, *85,* 107, 227, 298, 319, 327, 374, 377, 398, 426, 451, 458, 495
Smith-Bulford, Nadine G., R-Pa. (1), 475
Smith, Fairfield, 498
Smith, Al, I-Conn. (4), **224**
Smith, Albert A., I-Pa. (10), **483**
Smith, Bob, D-N.J. (6), 389
Smith, Bob, R-Ore. (2), **470**
Smith, Buster, D-Fla. (2), 229
Smith, Christopher H., R-N.J. (4), **387**
Smith, David, 432
Smith, Georgia, D-Calif. (44), **206**
Smith, Lamar, R-Texas (21), 21, 23, 88, **533**
Smith, Lawrence J., D-Fla., 51
Smith, Neal, D-Iowa (4), **299**
Smith, Nick, R-Mich. (7), **344**
Smith, Sheila D., D-Ill. (8), **273**
Smith, Terry R-Ala. (5), **149**
Smith, Tony, D-Alaska, 86, **106**
Snell, Rand, D-Fla. (13), **240**
Snowe, Olympia J., R-Maine (2), 76, **319**
Snyder, Craig, R-Pa. (1), **474**
Sohn, Herb, R-Ill. (9), 274
Sohn, Stephen A., R-Mass. (7), 90, **334**
Solarz, Stephen J., D-N.Y., 52, 62, 63, 408, 411, 428
Solem/Loeb & Associates, 169
Solomon, Gerald B.H., R-N.Y. (22), **421**
Solomon, Lee A., R-N.J. (1), **384**
Sommer, Gebhart, I-S.C. (2), **498**
Sonneland, John, R-Wash. (5), **562**
Sosa, Dan, Jr., D-N.M. (2), **398**
Souto, Javier D., R-Fla. (21), 248
Spaeth Communications, 515
Specialized Media Services, *85,* 92, 184
Specter, Arlen, R-Pa., 14, 18, *19,* 21, *22, 23, 24, 26, 28, 30, 32, 33, 34, 35,* 61, 65, 67-68, 69, 75, 79, 80, *95,* 99, *102,* **134**
Spector Associates, Harry, 426, 429
Spence, Floyd D., R-S.C. (2), **498, 502**
Spencer Market Research, 458
Spencer Research Associates, 247
Spencer-Roberts & Associates, 90, **91**
Spiridellis, Ona, D-N.J. (11), **394**
Spiro, Herbert, R-Texas (10), **522**
Spratt, John M., Jr., D-S.C. (5), 54, **501**
Springer Associates, *87,* 229, 346, 349, 525
Squier/Eskew/Knapp/Ochs Communications, 84, *85,* 105, 108, 112, 113, 150, 165, 182, 237, 253, 274, 328, 443
Stabler, Paul R., R-Ga. (5), **255**
Staff salaries, 18, 21-24
  top twenty-five candidate expenditures on, *22*
Staggers, Harley O., D-W.Va. (1), 461, 567, 568
Stainer & Associates, Kurt, *91*
Stallings, Richard, D-Idaho, 36, 84, 86, 88, **116,** 265, 564
Stannard, Sarah, I-Ariz. (6), **158**
Stark, Pete, D-Calif. (13), *37,* 76, 86, 99, **175**
Starr, Mike, R-Ill. (12), **277**
Starr, Seigle & McCombs, *85,* 115
Staskiewicz, Ronald L., R-Neb. (2), **378**
Staton & Hughes, 176
Stearns, Cliff, R-Fla. (6), **233**
Steele, Philip L., R-Conn. (1), 53, **221**
Stein Media, Peggy, 425
Steinberg & Associates, Arnold, *89,* 189, 201, 207
Steinberg, Cathey, D-Ga. (4), *23,* **254**
Steinem, Gloria, 65, 168
Stenholm, Charles W., D-Texas (17), **529**
Stephens, Richard "Even," I-Fla. (22), **249**
Sterling Advertising & Public Relations, 150
Stevens, John S., D-N.C. (11), **441**
Stevens, Stuart, 118, 119, 225, 430, 480
Stockman, Steve, R-Texas (9), **521**
Stockstill, Lyle, R-La., **122**
Stokes, Louis, D-Ohio (11), 25, 27, 52, 76, 100-101, 414, **454**
Stokes, Robert W., R-Okla. (3), 43, **465**
Stokes, Susan B., R-Ky. (3), **307**
Stokley, Richard, R-Texas (5), **517**
Stone, Tom, R-Tenn. (5), **508**
Stonecash, Jeff, 424
Strata-Tech, 250
Strategic Campaign Network, 535
Strategic Message & Design, 479
Strategic Planning Service, 418, 423
Strategic Telecommunications, 356
Strategy Group, 269
Strickland, Martha "Mickey," R-Ala. (4), 65, **148**
Strickland, Ted, D-Ohio (6), **449**
Strong & Associates, James, 268
Strother-Duffy-Strother, 49, 79, 159, 162, 231, 242, 245, 255, 466, 524
Strub, Sean, 337
Struble-Totten Communications, *85,* 94, 96, 129, 136, 137, 322, 349, 427, 503, 552, 557
Studds, Gerry E., D-Mass. (10), *22, 30,* 88, *93,* **337**
Stump, Bob, R-Ariz. (3), 28, **155**
Stupak, Bart, D-Mich. (1), **338**
Sturges, Bill, D-Pa. (17), 76, **490**
Suero, Jose A., I-N.Y. (15), **414**
Sugiyama, Glenn T., D-Ill. (9), 274
Sullivan, Kathleen M., R-Ill. (10), 275
Sullivan, Louis W., 245
Summit Group, 153, 154
Sundquist, Don, R-Tenn. (7), *26, 28, 30, 32,* 37, **510,** 511
Sununu, John, 156
Sutton, Warner C. Kimo, R-Hawaii (1), **262**
SWT Associates, 466
Swecker, Susan, 551
Swett, Dick, D-N.H. (2), 37, 44-45, 86, 174, 364, **383**
Swift, Al, D-Wash. (2), **559**
Swinehart Political Agency, 362
Swinney, Carl M., I-Calif. (34), **196**
Sydness, Steve, R-N.D., 84, **129**
Synar, Mike, D-Okla. (2), 73, 74, 79, 80, 90, *93,* 97, 98, *102,* **464**
Synhorst & Schraad, 86, 119, 572

T. H. Research, 559
T-Catalyst, 335
Taberski, Chip, R-Texas (16), **528**
Taborsak, Lynn H., I-Conn. (5), 43, 69, 80, **225**
Takano, Mark A., D-Calif. (43), 167, **205**
Take One Productions, 550
Talent, James M., R-Mo. (2), 63, **368**
Tallon, Robin, D-S.C., 51, 502
Tamblyn, George O., D-Wash. (8), 64, **565**
Tanner, John, D-Tenn. (8), **511**
Target Enterprises, 74, 84, *85,* 92, 109, 184
Target Inc., 80
Target Research Associates, 270
Tarrance & Associates, 80, *89,* 94, 119, 233, 356, 387, 426, 436, 458, 520, 535, 575, 579
Tauzin, W. J. "Billy," D-La. (3), 38, **313**
Taylor, Charles H., R-N.C. (11), 47, **441**
Taylor, Gene, D-Miss. (5), **366**
TDM Research & Communications, 509
Teague & Associates, John, 105
Tejeda, Frank, D-Texas (28), 48, **540**
Telemark, 90, *91,* 212, 265, 397, 398
Telemark America, *91,* 309
Telephone Contact, 92
Temple, Dennis Michael, D-Ill. (13), **278**
Tennant, Alexander T., R-Mass. (6), 333
Terris & Jaye, 80, 83, 163, 435
Terry, Randall A., I-N.Y. (23), 422
Teyler, Verne, R-Calif. (13), **175**
Tharp, Vern, I-Colo. (2), **216**
Theemling, Fred J., Jr., R-N.J. (13), **396**
Thomas, "Able" Mable, D-Ga. (5), 255
Thomas, Bill, R-Calif. (21), 9, 53, 65, **183**
Thomas, Clarence, 3, 61, 62, 69, 134, 168, 318
Thomas, Craig, R-Wyo. (AL), **579**
Thompson, Anne, R-La. (1), **311**
Thornburgh, Dick, R-Pa., *19, 26, 29, 30,* 80, 81, 84, 86, 90, *95,* **135,** 489
Thornton, Ray, D-Ark. (2), **160**
Thurman, Karen L., D-Fla. (5), 14, 149, **232,** 564
Thurmond, Michael, D-Ga. (11), 261
Timbes & Yeager, *91,* 92, 105, 145
Timmer, John, R-S.D. (AL), **503**
Timms, Charles, 542
Todd Company, 524
Toevs, Jim, D-Ariz. (5), **157**
Tolbert Inc., 231
Tolley, Bill, R-Fla. (15), **242**
Tomkin, Bernard, D-Pa. (13), 486
Tomlin, Jim, R-Calif. (12), 20, **174**
Torkildsen, Peter, R-Mass. (6), 23, 24, **333**
Torres, Esteban E., D-Calif. (34), 24, *37,* 76, **196**
Torricelli, Robert G., D-N.J. (9), **392**
Towns, Edolphus, D-N.Y. (10), *30, 34, 35,* 53, **409,** 414
Townsend, Bill, R-Pa. (20), 76, **493**
Tradec, 558
Traficant, James A., Jr., D-Ohio (17), 76, **460**
Tramutola, Larry, 175
Traxler, Bob, D-Mich., 51, 342
Trippi, McMahon & Squier, *85,* 168, 173, 227, 238, 338, 371, 373, 429, 486, 554
Truman, Nate, R-Calif. (35), **197**
Tucker & Associates, 219, 236
Tucker, C. Delores, D-Pa. (1), 475
Tucker, Walter R., III, D-Calif. (37), 48, 96, **199**
Turner, Phil, I-Calif. (44), 206
Twede-Evans Political, *85,* 138
Tyler, Ted, R-N.C. (1), **431**
Tynan & Associates, Kevin B., *89,* 270
Tyson Organization, 90, *91,* 105, 464, 508, 524, 536, 552

Udall, Morris K., D-Ariz., 154
Unger/Thomas, 123
Unistat, 275
Unsoeld, Jolene, D-Wash. (3), 3, 24, 70-71, **560**
Unsoeld, Terres, 24
Upton, Fred, R-Mich. (6), **343**
Urban Strategy, 269

Index 591

Valdez & Associates, Joyce, *87*
Valencia, Tony, R-Calif. (50), 69, **212**
Valentine, Tim, D-N.C. (2), *30,* **432**
Van Slyke, Jim, R-Kan. (2), **302**
Vander Jagt, Guy, R-Mich. (2), 3, 50, 52, 339, 578
Vannes, Dale R., R-Wis. (7), **576**
VanWinkle, John, D-Ark. (3), **161**
Velazquez, Nydia M., D-N.Y. (12), 62, 63, **411**
Vento, Bruce F., D-Minn. (4), *35,* 36, **357**
Veon, Mike, D-Pa. (4), 477
Vickery, Raymond E., D-Va. (10), **556**
Vincent, Charles C., R-Mich. (15), **352**
Visclosky, Peter J., D-Ind. (1), **286**
Volkmer, Harold L., D-Mo. (9), 57, **375**
Vollmer, Deborah A., D-Calif. (21), 9, 53, 65, **183**
von Reichbauer, Pete, R-Wash. (9), **566**
VP Film and Tape, 318
Vreeland, Vic, I-Texas (14), **526**
Vucanovich, Barbara F., R-Nev. (2), 26, 62, 70, 380, **381**
Vucich, David J., R-Ind. (1), **286**

Wachtel, Al, D-Calif. (28), 20, **190**
Wagner, Marye, 112
Wagner, Ray, R-Fla. (2), **229**
Waksberg, Morry, R-Calif. (30), **192**
Waldman, Ben, R-W. Va. (3), **569**
Walker, Eugene P., D-Ga. (11), 261
Walker, George Herbert, III, R-Mo. (2), 368
Walker, Jay, R-Ill. (1), **266**
Walker, Robert S., R-Pa. (16), *35,* 94, **489**
Wallace, George C., Jr., D-Ala. (2), 50, **146,** 149
Walsh, James T., R-N.Y. (25), **424**
Walters, Michael, R-N.Y. (16), **415**
Wamp, Zach, R-Tenn. (3), 70, **506**
Ward, Fritz R., I-Calif. (42), **204**
Warner, John, R-Va., 555
Warren & Associates, Tracy, 300
Warren, Seth L., I-Kan. (4), **304**

Warwick & Associates, Mal, *87,* 171
Washington, Barbara Gore, R-N.C. (12), **442**
Washington, Craig, D-Texas (18), 96, **530**
Washington Political Group, *91,* 146
Waters, Maxine, D-Calif. (35), *37,* 48, 71-72, 76, **197,** 199, 272
Watershed Group, 463
Watkins, Barry W., D-Ill. (6), 271
Watt, Melvin, D-N.C. (12), 48, **442**
Waxman, Henry A., D-Calif. (29), 4, 14, 26, 34, *35,* 36, 37, 52, 76, 100, 186, **191,** 403
Wayman Productions, 224
Wead, Doug, R-Ariz. (6), **158,** 538
Weber, Bob, I-Calif. (32), **194**
Weber, Vin, R-Minn., 51, 156, 355
Webster, Dan, D-Fla. (7), **234**
Weddle, L. Garrett, R-Va. (9), **555**
Wedum, Ellen E., D-Ind. (7), 62, **292**
Weidner, Don, R-Fla. (3), **230**
Weil & Associates, Gus, 316
Weiner & Weiner, 316
Weinstock-Rose, Kay, 356
Weiss, Noris, 318
Weiss, Ted, D-N.Y. (8), 407
Welch Communications, *89,* 320, 390, 394, 481, 571, 578
Weldon, Curt, R-Pa. (7), **480**
Wells, Dorothy L., I-Calif. (19), **181**
Wellstone, Paul, D-Minn., 358
Welty, Harry Robb, I-Minn. (8), **361**
Wern, Rausch, Locke Advertising, 459
Werner, Chepelsky & Partners, 487
Wesbury, Stewart A., R-Ill. (13), 278
West, Duane, D-Kan. (1), **301**
Western International Media Corp., *85,* 125, 254
Western Pacific Research, *91,* 183
Western Wats Center, *89,* 190
Weston Marketing, Merv, 383
Wheat, Alan, D-Mo. (5), **371**
Whitaker, Clyde E., R-Miss. (1), **362**
White & Co., Joe Slade, 74, *85,* 111, 177, 239, 298, 318, 376, 378, 392, 401, 523, 525, 563
White, Donna, I-Calif. (48), **210**

White, John F., Jr., D-Pa. (1), 475
White Productions, Bob, 232
Whitten, Jamie L., D-Miss. (1), **362**
Wick, Robert, R-Calif. (15), **177**
Wieser, Martin, 542
Wilkey, Malcolm, 287, 528
Williams, Alexander, Jr., D-Md. (4), 323
Williams & Associates, 333
Williams, David L., R-Ky., 20, **121**
Williams, J. Carolyn, D-Ind. (4), 289
Williams, J.D., D-Idaho (2), **265**
Williams, Laurie, D-Okla. (5), 47, 465, **467**
Williams, Michael E., R-Miss. (3), **364**
Williams, Pat, D-Mont. (AL), 22, 24, 26, 30, 59, *81, 86, 93,* **376,** 576
Williams, Wendell H., D-Calif. (10), 88, **172**
Williams, William R., I-Calif. (32), **194**
Williamson, Julie, 469
Williamson, Richard, R-Ill., 22, 30, 59, 84, 90, *95,* **117**
Willmon Advertising & Marketing, 514
Wilson, Bob, D-Ga. (4), 254
Wilson, Charles, D-Texas (2), 23, 26, 30, 31, *34,* 62, *93,* 513, **514,** 526
Wilson Communications, 205, 450
Wilson, Pete, R-Calif., 90, 110
Winner/Bragg, 197
Winning Direction, 87
Winning Strategies, 342
Winningham, Robert, 294
Winward Moody Agency, 153
Wirth, Tim, D-Colo., 4, 74, 111
Wisconsin Research, 141
Wise Associates, Jim, *87,* 109, 169, 178, 180
Wise, Bob, D-W. Va. (2), **568**
Wiseman Public Relations, 463
Wofford, Harris, D-Pa., *19, 22, 26,* 29, 31, *80, 81,* 84, 86, *95,* **135,** 475, 487, 489
Wolf, Frank R., R-Va. (10), **556**
Wolin, Marc, R-Calif. (8), **170**
Woo, S.B., D-Del. (AL), **227**
Woods, Al, I-Fla. (23), **250**
Woods Productions, Fred, 555

Woodward Co., Henry, 453
Woolsey, Lynn, D-Calif. (6), 62, 90, *102,* **168**
Worley, David, D-Ga. (3), 253
Wren, Carter, 59, 128
Wyden, Ron, D-Ore. (3), **471,** 472
Wylie, Chalmers P., R-Ohio, 51, 458
Wyman, Phillip D., R-Calif. (25), 187
Wynn, Albert R., D-Md. (4), **323,** 564

Yancy, Charles Calvin, D-Mass. (8), 335
Yates, Sidney R., D-Ill. (9), **274**
Yatron, Gus, D-Pa., 51, 479
Yeakel, Lynn, D-Pa., *19, 22, 26, 30,* 61, 62, 65, 67-68, 69, 70, 75, 79, 86, *95,* 99, **134**
Year of the Woman, 61-72
   background of nonincumbents, 63-65
   diversity among women candidates, 61-69
   fund raising, 63-65, 69-70
   incumbents, 70-72
Yellin Media Services, 331, 336
Yost, Eric R., R-Kan. (4), 81, **304**
Young & Associates, George, 189
Young, C.W. Bill, R-Fla. (10), 94, 96, **237**
Young, Don, R-Alaska (AL), *26, 30,* **152,** 448
Young, Lewis E., D-Vt. (AL), **546**
Youngs, Curtis, D-Calif. (19), 181
Yustein, Jackie, 391

Zabel & Associates, Doug, 528
Zakin Associates, Alan, 395
Zeliff, Bill, R-N.H. (1), 25, 40, 47, 48, **382**
Zenkich, Elias R. R-Ill. (5), **270**
Zerbe Political Consulting, 53, 164
Zevgolis, A. J., R-Va. (4), **550**
Ziebart Associates, *87,* 265, 376, 579
Zimmer, Dick, R-N.J. (12), *30,* 46, **395**
Zimmerman & Markman, 282
Zonneveld, Jan J., D-Iowa (1), **296**